IRENE C. FOUNTAS
GAY SU PINNELL

The FOUNTAS AND PINNELL

LEVELED BOOK LIST K-8+

Volume 2

Heinemann
Portsmouth, NH

Heinemann
361 Hanover Street
Portsmouth, NH 03801-3912
www.heinemann.com

Offices and agents throughout the world

Library of Congress Cataloging-in-Publication Data
Fountas, Irene C.
  The Fountas and Pinnell leveled book list K-8+ / Irene C. Fountas, Gay Su Pinnell. — 2013/2015 edition.
    volumes cm.
ISBN 978-0-325-04907-6 (v. 1) — ISBN 978-0-325-04908-3 (v. 2)
1. Reading (Elementary). 2. Reading (Middle school). 3. Book leveling. I. Pinnell, Gay Su. II. Title.
LB1573.F638 2013+
372.41—dc23   2013016740

Printed in the United States of America on acid-free paper
17 16 15 14 13 VP 1 2 3 4 5

We dedicate this extensive resource to our colleague

Carol Woodworth

with much fondness and deep appreciation.

CONTENTS

Access to the Fountas & Pinnell Leveled Books Website (LBW)
- Go to www.heinemann.com/products/LBW002119.aspx
- Click "Buy" to add the item to your shopping cart.
- Enter **FPLBW** as a coupon code
- Click "Apply Coupon" [The Heinemann website will then require that you login or create a new account first]
- Click on the blue "log in" link where you will be prompted to **Login** or **Create a New Account**
- When done, you will be brought back to your shopping cart
- Click "Checkout"
- Fill in the additional Customer Information
- Click "Continue"
- Click "Place Order"

Once completed, you will receive an email confirmation with a license key and link to the LBW. *The first time you log in,* you will need to click on the "New Subscribers" tab and enter your login info. After this initial login, you will just go to the main login window and log in.

Introduction to the Book List

All teachers want their students to be successful, confident readers. This process begins with sensitive and responsive reading instruction; an understanding of how books support the "learning to read" process; and access to a sufficient quantity of high-quality books at appropriate instructional levels. In our books *Guided Reading: Good First Teaching for All Children* (Heinemann 1996); *Guiding Readers and Writers: Teaching Comprehension, Genre, and Content Literacy* (Heinemann 2001); *Teaching for Comprehending and Fluency: Thinking, Talking, and Writing About Reading, K–8* (Heinemann 2006); and *Genre Study: Teaching with Fiction and Nonfiction Books* (Heinemann 2012), we describe a comprehensive language and literacy framework designed to help students develop a broad and integrated range of reading, writing, and language competencies.

Then in *Leveled Books K–8: Matching Texts to Readers for Effective Teaching* (Heinemann 2006), we focus on the texts you will need to support a rich environment for literacy teaching and learning, beginning with a description of the most effective ways to use books in the classroom. That book also describes our gradient of leveled texts and its uses. We encourage the use of leveled books for instruction in guided reading and small-group literacy intervention lessons. Our levels will help you make good choices for students at various stages of reading development. For the specific characteristics of texts at each level and the competencies students need to acquire at each level, refer to our book, *The Continuum of Literacy Learning, K–8* (Heinemann 2007).

This book—*The Fountas and Pinnell Leveled Book List, K–8*—is a reference resource of over 45,000 titles that have been through a systematic, in-depth analysis by teams of experts who are experienced in analyzing features of texts as well as in teaching guided reading. The list includes a wide variety of genres and formats, fiction and nonfiction, all leveled through this reliable process. Of course, we can't possibly level every book published. As you get to know characteristics of books at our levels, talk with colleagues about the books you have that are not yet part of this list and assign them a tentative level.

The leveling process is ongoing, including constant review and revision, as books are used by teachers in the classroom. "Leveling" is not an exact science, though it is a comprehensive analysis. A level is an approximation, not an absolute designation; not all books on a level are precisely alike. There are many variables to take into account as text difficulty is determined. A text's demands and supports cannot be reduced to a mathematical formula. The concepts of "easier" and "harder" must always be understood in relation to the complex and interrelated text factors that we describe in *Leveled Books K–8*. What's more, myriad student factors have an impact on text readability as well.

The readability of a text is influenced by the background knowledge required of the reader to understand the text, the reader's facility with word solving, the number of complex sentences embedded in the text, and so on. The specialized process of determining text difficulty is a challenge worthy of our time because the more we learn about texts, the better we understand their demands on the individual readers we teach—the first step in matching books to readers.

The most current book list can be found at *www.fountasandpinnellleveledbooks.com*. This online database version of the book list is updated constantly with hundreds of new titles as well as revisions to existing levels as they are needed. On the Leveled Books Site, you can sort by title, author, series, publisher, level, genre, short story, graphic text, and mature content with lower level text demands. Book collections continually evolve. You build your collection slowly over time as you test books with students. We hope our text gradient and this comprehensive book list will help you select texts that are "just right" for your readers.

How to Use the Book List

The list is sorted alphabetically by book title. The tabs along the page edge make it possible to quickly turn to the letter you want.

As you will see, there are six columns on each page. The contents of each column are described below.

❑ **Title:** The first column indicates the title of the book. Books are placed alphabetically by the first word of the title—unless it is a, an, or the, in which case the article follows the title. Titles beginning with a numeral are placed at the beginning of the list in order by number.

❑ **Level:** The second column indicates the level assigned to the book, from A to Z or Z+. We use the letter A to indicate the easiest books to read and the letter Z to identify the most challenging books. In addition, we have added titles recommended for high school, which are labeled Z+ and are integrated throughout the book. More detailed descriptions of the text features of each level can be found in Leveled Books K–8. Two other abbreviations are used in this column:

• *WB (Wordless Books):* Books without any words in them at all (books that tell a story only in pictures) are excellent for the development of oral language and so are included in our list. However, they are not "leveled" in the same sense that the other books in the list are leveled.

• *LB (Label Books):* These are books with only one word or a very short phrase on every page. As with Wordless Books, we find leveling these books inappropriate. We do not recommend label books for use in guided reading, although students may enjoy them for other purposes in the classroom.

❑ **Genre:** The third column indicates the type of book, or genre. Genre is a term that means type of text. We have classified each book as one genre though you will find there are some books that have elements of more than one. With the wealth and variety of children's books available today, it is sometimes difficult to make a precise designation of genre for a particular text. A text may have some features of an informational text, such as describing a series of actions, but the characters in the illustrations may be animals talking or getting dressed like people. In this case, the text would be fantasy. In this list, if the material in the text or illustrations has elements of fantasy, the book is classified as fantasy. In addition, there are many "hybrid texts" that combine elements of fiction and nonfiction; for example, a group of fictional children might visit a museum and learn a great deal about fossils. The text would be realistic fiction but would provide authentic information to the reader. Where any part of the text is fiction, we have designated it as fiction. You will want to analyze texts carefully, however, to take advantage of all the text characteristics and learning opportunities.

The following codes are used to indicate genre:

• *TL - Traditional Literature*
• *RF - Realistic Fiction*
• *HF - Historical Fiction*
• *SF - Science Fiction*
• *F - Fantasy*
• *B - Biography (includes autobiography and memoir)*
• *I - Information Book*

❑ **Words:** The fourth column provides the number of words appearing in the book. Note: "250+" indicates the book contains more than 250 words.

❑ **Author/Series:** The fifth column provides the name of the author or specific reading series.

❑ **Publisher/Distributor:** The sixth column indicates the publisher's or distributor's name. A list of addresses and phone numbers for each publisher or distributor of reading series and collections can be found in Appendix A. Trade books listed with the author's name are available from a variety of distributors.

Short Story Collection

❏ You'll notice that some books are marked with an * (asterisk). The asterisk indicates that the book is a collection of short stories. Some collections contain selections in which each story is completely independent of the others. In other collections, the stories are interrelated in some way, such as short biographies or a common character or theme. These stories can often be read out of order.

❏ Graphic Text: You will also notice a category, marked with a # (pound sign). The pound sign indicates a graphic text, or a text that is written with illustrations and speech bubbles in a sequence.

❏ Mature Content with Lower Level Text Demands: Lastly, you will also see titles marked with the ^ sign. This sign designates a text containing more sophisticated themes or mature content with lower level text demands for the reader.

The true test of any leveling system, of course, is using the texts with students over time. We have included a form on the following page, **Evaluation Response for Text Gradient,** to gather more information about the books on our list and to provide you the opportunity to suggest new books for leveling. We want teachers in many different geographic areas to test the books and provide feedback based on their use with students in guided reading. We invite you to send feedback to us at any time. As the online database and this book are revised, we will take your comments and suggestions into consideration.

Evaluation Response for Text Gradient

Directions: Since any text gradient is always in the process of construction as it is used with varying groups of children, we expect our list to change every year. We encourage you to try the levels with your students and to provide feedback based on your own experiences. Please suggest changes to existing book levels and suggest new books for the list. Please provide the information requested below.

Name: _____ Grade Level You Teach: _____

Telephone: ( ) _____ E-mail address: _____

Address (street, city, state): _____

Book Evaluated:

Book Title: _____

Level: A B C D E F G H I J K L M N O P Q R S T U V W X Y Z Z+

Author: _____

Publisher: _____

This book is:

_____ A book listed on the gradient that I have evaluated with my class.
(Complete SECTION A and make comments in SECTION C.)

_____ A book listed on the gradient that I am recommending as a benchmark for a level.
(Complete SECTION A and make comments in SECTION C.)

_____ A new book that I suggest adding to the collection.
(Complete SECTION B and make comments in SECTION C.)

SECTION A: (for an evaluation of a book currently included in the list)

Is it appropriately placed on the level (explain)? _____
To what level should the book be moved?

A B C D E F G H I J K L M N O P Q R S T U V W X Y Z Z+

Are there points of difficulty that make it harder than it seems? _____

_____

Is the text supportive in ways that might not be noticeable when examining the superficial characteristics?

_____

SECTION B: (for the recommendation of a new book) Indicate recommended level: _____

How does this book support readers at this level? _____

_____

What challenges does it offer? _____

_____

SECTION C: Please place additional comments on the back or on another sheet.

Mail or fax (603–431–7840) this form to:
Leveled Book List Suggestions
c/o Heinemann
361 Hanover Street
Portsmouth, NH 03801–3912

TITLE	LEVEL	GENRE	WORD COUNT	AUTHOR / SERIES	PUBLISHER / DISTRIBUTOR
M & M and The Bad News Babies	K	RF	250+	Ross, Pat	Penguin Group
M & M and the Big Bag	K	RF	250+	Ross, Pat	Penguin Group
M & M and the Halloween Monster	K	RF	250+	Ross, Pat	Penguin Group
M & M and the Haunted House Game	K	RF	250+	Ross, Pat	Penguin Group
M & M and the Mummy Mess	K	RF	250+	Ross, Pat	Penguin Group
M & M and the Santa Secrets	K	RF	250+	Ross, Pat	Penguin Group
M & M and the Super Child Afternoon	K	RF	250+	Ross, Pat	Penguin Group
M. C. Higgins the Great	X	RF	250+	Hamilton, Virginia	Macmillan
M1 Abrams Main Battle Tank, The	U	I	250+	Cross-Sections	Capstone Press
M109A6 Paladin, The	U	I	250+	Cross-Sections	Capstone Press
M2 Bradley Infantry Fighting Vehicle, The	U	I	250+	Cross-Sections	Capstone Press
M270 Multiple Rocket Launcher, The	U	I	250+	Cross-Sections	Capstone Press
Ma and Pa Dracula	O	F	250+	Martin, Ann M.	Scholastic
Maasai Dreamer: A Story from Kenya	R	RF	250+	Reading Expeditions	National Geographic
Mabel the Whale	I	F	250+	King, Patricia	Pearson Publishing Group
Mac & Cheese, Pleeeeze!	L	RF	250+	Math Matters	Kane Press
Mac and the Messmaker	L	RF	250+	Social Studies Connects	Kane Press
Macaroni and Rice and Bread by the Slice: What Is in the Grains Group?	N	I	525	Food Is CATegorical	Millbrook Press
Macaw	M	I	250+	A Day in the Life: Rain Forest Animals	Heinemann Library
Macaws	K	I	209	Colorful World of Animals	Capstone Press
Macbeth	X	HF	7400	Dominoes one	Oxford University Press
#Macbeth	Z	F	250+	Manga Shakespeare	Amulet Books
MacGregors and the MacDougalls, The	N	RF	250+	Bookweb	Rigby
Machines	C	I	36	Little Celebrations	Pearson Learning Group
Machines	J	I	44	Sunshine	Wright Group/McGraw Hill
Machines	E	I	44	Twig	Wright Group/McGraw Hill
Machines at Work	H	I	101	Little Red Readers	Sundance
Machines Go to Work	J	RF	218	Low, William	Henry Holt & Co.
Machines Help Us Do Work	L	I	160	Windows on Literacy	National Geographic
Machines in Construction	U	I	250+	Theme Sets	National Geographic
Machines in Health	U	I	250+	Theme Sets	National Geographic
Machines in Sports	U	I	250+	Theme Sets	National Geographic
Machines in the Home	N	I	250+	Home Connection Collection	Rigby
Machines in the Home	U	I	250+	Theme Sets	National Geographic
Machines Make Fun Rides	I	I	182	Windows on Literacy	National Geographic
Machines Make It Move	V	I	250+	Reading Expeditions	National Geographic
Machines Picture Pops	M	I	250+	Priddy, Roger	Priddy Books
Machines That Fly	I	I	111	Windows on Literacy	National Geographic
Machines That Go	A	I	32	Red Rocket Readers	Flying Start Books
Machines That Work	D	I	93	Shutterbug Books	Steck-Vaughn
Machines: Simple and Compound	S	I	250+	Reading Expeditions	National Geographic
Mack Forgot!	B	RF	56	Literacy by Design	Rigby
Mack the Cat	C	RF	59	Reading Street	Pearson
Mack's Big Day	L	RF	464	PM Plus Story Books	Rigby
Mad Love	Z+	F	250+	Selfors, Suzanne	Walker & Company
Mad Scientist, The	M	F	250+	Woodland Mysteries	Wright Group/McGraw Hill
Mad Scientist's Secret, The	P	SF	250+	Miller, Marvin	Scholastic
Madagascar	O	I	1550	A Ticket to …	Carolrhoda Books
Madagascar	P	I	1834	Country Explorers	Lerner Publishing Group
Madam C. J. Walker	T	B	3934	History Maker Bios	Lerner Publishing Group
Madam C.J. Walker	S	B	250+	Amazing Americans	Wright Group/McGraw Hill
#Madam C.J. Walker and New Cosmetics	T	B	250+	Graphic Library	Capstone Press

TITLE	LEVEL	GENRE	WORD COUNT	AUTHOR / SERIES	PUBLISHER / DISTRIBUTOR
Madam C.J. Walker: Pioneer Buisnesswoman	P	B	250+	Great African Americans	Capstone Press
Madame C. J. Walker	Q	B	494	Independent Readers Social Studies	Houghton Mifflin Harcourt
Madame Pamplemouse and Her Incredible Edibles	S	F	250+	Kingfisher, Rupert	Bloomsbury Children's Books
Madapple	Z+	RF	250+	Meldrum, Christina	Alfred A. Knopf
Made in America	U	I	250+	WorldScapes	ETA/Cuisenaire
Made of Wood	J	I	264	Rigby Flying Colors	Rigby
Made with Glass	F	I	106	Cherrington, Janelle	Scholastic
Madeline	K	F	250+	Bemelmans, Ludwig	Scholastic
Madeline's Rescue	K	F	250+	Bemelmans, Ludwig	Scholastic
Made's Birthday	L	RF	250+	Little Celebrations	Pearson Learning Group
Mae Jemison	R	B	250+	Bookshop	Mondo Publishing
^Mae Jemison	N	B	250+	Explore Space!	Capstone Press
Mae Jemison	N	B	240	First Biographies	Capstone Press
Mae Jemison: Astronaut	N	B	250+	Beginning Biographies	Pearson Learning Group
Mae Jemison: Making Dreams Come True	N	B	540	Leveled Readers	Houghton Mifflin Harcourt
Mae Jemison: Space Pioneer	P	B	250+	Great African Americans	Capstone Press
Mae-Nerd	C	F	44	Teacher's Choice Series	Pearson Learning Group
Maestro, The	Z	RF	250+	Wynne-Jones, Tim	Groundwood Books
Magellan: Ferdinand Magellan and the First Trip Around the World	U	B	250+	Exploring the World	Compass Point Books
Maggie McGee and Me at the Mint	O	RF	1579	Reading Street	Pearson
Maggie Moves Away	H	RF	327	Adventures in Reading	Pearson Learning Group
Maggie Walker: Business Leader	N	B	250+	Beginning Biographies	Pearson Learning Group
Maggie's Pets	I	RF	250+	Early Transitional, Set 1	Pioneer Valley
*Magic	Z+	RF	250+	Brown, Sarah & McNeil, Gil (Editors)	Bloomsbury Children's Books
Magic All Around	L	F	250+	Literacy 2000	Rigby
Magic Amber, The: A Korean Legend	O	TL	250+	Legends of the World	Troll Associates
Magic and Other Misdemeanors: The Sisters Grimm	U	F	250+	Buckley, Michael	Amulet Books
Magic Beans, The	E	TL	239	Fairy Tales and Folklore	Norwood House Press
Magic Boots, The	I	F	250+	Storyworlds	Heinemann
Magic Box, The	K	F	250+	Brenner, Barbara	Bantam Books
Magic by Heart	U	F	250+	Gordon, Amy	Holiday House
Magic by the Lake	T	F	250+	Eager, Edward	Harcourt
Magic Carpet, The	J	F	250+	Storyworlds	Heinemann
Magic Coat, The	J	F	250+	Storyworlds	Heinemann
Magic Desk, The	J	F	229	Dominie Readers	Pearson Learning Group
Magic Fan, The	P	TL	250+	Baker, Keith	Harcourt, Inc.
Magic Finger, The	N	F	250+	Dahl, Roald	Penguin Group
Magic Fish, The	L	TL	870	Littledale, Freya	Scholastic
Magic Fish, The	J	TL	250+	Rylant, Cynthia	Scholastic
Magic Food	C	F	26	Smart Start	Rigby
Magic Glasses Day	K	RF	718	Rigby Flying Colors	Rigby
Magic Half, The	T	F	250+	Barrows, Annie	Bloomsbury Children's Books
Magic Hat, The	J	F	566	Pawprints Teal	Pioneer Valley
Magic Hat, The	I	F	250+	Storyworlds	Heinemann
Magic Horse, The	L	TL	839	Springboard	Wright Group/McGraw Hill
Magic Jigsaw, The	K	F	250+	Rigby Star Quest	Rigby
Magic Machine, The	C	F	163	Sunshine	Wright Group/McGraw Hill

* Collection of short stories   # Graphic text
^ Mature content with lower level text demands

TITLE	LEVEL	GENRE	WORD COUNT	AUTHOR / SERIES	PUBLISHER / DISTRIBUTOR
Magic Maple Syrup	S	I	1092	Red Rocket Readers	Flying Start Books
Magic Money	L	RF	250+	Adler, David A.	Random House
Magic Money Box, The	E	I	71	Learn to Read	Creative Teaching Press
Magic Moscow, The	P	RF	250+	Pinkwater, Daniel	Aladdin
Magic Noodle Show, The	N	RF	250+	Orbit Chapter Books	Pacific Learning
Magic Nutcracker, The	G	F	250+	Easy Stories	Norwood House Press
Magic of Coyote, The	O	RF	2265	Reading Street	Pearson
Magic of Light and Sound, The	V	I	250+	Reading Expeditions	National Geographic
Magic of Movies, The	T	I	1303	Leveled Readers	Houghton Mifflin Harcourt
Magic of Movies, The	T	I	1303	Leveled Readers/CA	Houghton Mifflin Harcourt
Magic of Movies, The	T	I	1303	Leveled Readers/TX	Houghton Mifflin Harcourt
Magic of Teamwork, The	M	F	873	Leveled Readers	Houghton Mifflin Harcourt
Magic of Teamwork, The	M	F	873	Leveled Readers/CA	Houghton Mifflin Harcourt
Magic of Teamwork, The	M	F	873	Leveled Readers/TX	Houghton Mifflin Harcourt
Magic Passport, The	N	F	250+	Navigators Fiction Series	Benchmark Education
Magic Pear Tree, The	I	TL	207	Little Celebrations	Pearson Learning Group
Magic Pickle	R	F	250+	Morse, Scott	Scholastic
Magic Pickle and the Planet of the Grapes	Q	F	250+	Morse, Scott	Scholastic
Magic Pomegranate, The	N	TL	1466	On My Own Folklore	Millbrook Press
Magic Porridge Pot, The	I	TL	321	New Way Orange	Steck-Vaughn
Magic Porridge Pot, The	L	TL	497	Sunshine	Wright Group/McGraw Hill
Magic Pot, The	E	F	100	Smith, Laura	Scholastic
Magic Rabbit, The	K	F	250+	Cate, Annette LeBlanc	Candlewick Press
Magic Ride, The	M	F	170	Book Bank	Wright Group/McGraw Hill
Magic School Bus	P	F	250+	Cole, Joanna; Degen, Bruce	Scholastic
Magic School Bus and the Electric Field Trip, The	P	F	250+	Cole, Joanna; Degen, Bruce	Scholastic
Magic School Bus and the Science Fair Expedition, The	P	F	250+	Cole, Joanna & Degen, Bruce	Scholastic
Magic School Bus Answers Questions, The	P	F	250+	Cole, Joanna; Degen, Bruce	Scholastic
Magic School Bus at the Waterworks, The	P	F	250+	Cole, Joanna; Degen, Bruce	Scholastic
Magic School Bus Blows Its Top, The	P	F	250+	Cole, Joanna; Degen, Bruce	Scholastic
Magic School Bus Briefcase, The	P	F	250+	Cole, Joanna; Degen, Bruce	Scholastic
Magic School Bus Butterfly and the Bog Beast, The	P	F	250+	Cole, Joanna; Degen, Bruce	Scholastic
Magic School Bus Explores the Senses, The	P	F	250+	Cole, Joanna; Degen, Bruce	Scholastic
Magic School Bus Explores the World of Animals, The	P	F	250+	Cole, Joanna; Degen, Bruce	Scholastic
Magic School Bus Food Chain Frenzy, The	Q	F	250+	Capeci, Anne	Scholastic
Magic School Bus Gets a Bright Idea, The	P	F	250+	Cole, Joanna; Degen, Bruce	Scholastic
Magic School Bus Gets All Dried Up, The	P	F	250+	Cole, Joanna; Degen, Bruce	Scholastic
Magic School Bus Gets Ants in Its Pants, The	P	F	250+	Cole, Joanna; Degen, Bruce	Scholastic
Magic School Bus Gets Baked in a Cake, The	P	F	250+	Cole, Joanna; Degen, Bruce	Scholastic
Magic School Bus Gets Cold Feet, The	P	F	250+	Cole, Joanna; Degen, Bruce	Scholastic
Magic School Bus Gets Eaten, The	P	F	250+	Cole, Joanna; Degen, Bruce	Scholastic
Magic School Bus Gets Programmed, The	P	F	250+	Cole, Joanna; Degen, Bruce	Scholastic
Magic School Bus Goes Upstream, The	P	F	250+	Cole, Joanna; Degen, Bruce	Scholastic
Magic School Bus Going Batty, The	P	F	250+	Cole, Joanna; Degen, Bruce	Scholastic
Magic School Bus Hops Home, The	P	F	250+	Cole, Joanna; Degen, Bruce	Scholastic
Magic School Bus in a Pickle, The	P	F	250+	Cole, Joanna; Degen, Bruce	Scholastic
Magic School Bus in the Arctic, The	P	F	250+	Cole, Joanna; Degen, Bruce	Scholastic
Magic School Bus in the Haunted Museum, The	P	F	250+	Cole, Joanna; Degen, Bruce	Scholastic
Magic School Bus in the Rain Forest, The	P	F	250+	Cole, Joanna; Degen, Bruce	Scholastic
Magic School Bus in the Time of the Dinosaurs, The	P	F	250+	Cole, Joanna; Degen, Bruce	Scholastic

M

TITLE	LEVEL	GENRE	WORD COUNT	AUTHOR / SERIES	PUBLISHER / DISTRIBUTOR
Magic School Bus Inside a Beehive, The	P	F	250+	Cole, Joanna; Degen, Bruce	Scholastic
Magic School Bus Inside a Hurricane, The	P	F	250+	Cole, Joanna; Degen, Bruce	Scholastic
Magic School Bus Inside Ralphie, The	P	F	250+	Cole, Joanna; Degen, Bruce	Scholastic
Magic School Bus Inside the Earth, The	P	F	250+	Cole, Joanna; Degen, Bruce	Scholastic
Magic School Bus Inside the Human Body, The	P	F	250+	Cole, Joanna; Degen, Bruce	Scholastic
Magic School Bus Kicks Up a Storm, The	P	F	250+	Cole, Joanna; Degen, Bruce	Scholastic
Magic School Bus Liz Sorts It Out, The	P	F	250+	Cole, Joanna; Degen, Bruce	Scholastic
Magic School Bus Lost in the Solar System, The	P	F	250+	Cole, Joanna; Degen, Bruce	Scholastic
Magic School Bus Makes a Rainbow, The	P	F	250+	Cole, Joanna; Degen, Bruce	Scholastic
Magic School Bus Meets the Rot Squad, The	P	F	250+	Cole, Joanna; Degen, Bruce	Scholastic
Magic School Bus on the Ocean Floor, The	P	F	250+	Cole, Joanna; Degen, Bruce	Scholastic
Magic School Bus Out of This World, The	P	F	250+	Cole, Joanna; Degen, Bruce	Scholastic
Magic School Bus Plants Seeds, The	P	F	250+	Cole, Joanna; Degen, Bruce	Scholastic
Magic School Bus Plays Ball, The	P	F	250+	Cole, Joanna; Degen, Bruce	Scholastic
Magic School Bus Science Explorations, The	P	F	250+	Cole, Joanna; Degen, Bruce	Scholastic
Magic School Bus Search for the Missing Bones, The	P	F	250+	Cole, Joanna; Degen, Bruce	Scholastic
Magic School Bus Sees Stars, The	P	F	250+	Cole, Joanna; Degen, Bruce	Scholastic
Magic School Bus Shows and Tells, The	P	F	250+	Cole, Joanna; Degen, Bruce	Scholastic
Magic School Bus Space Explorers, The	P	F	250+	Cole, Joanna; Degen, Bruce	Scholastic
Magic School Bus Spins a Web, The	P	F	250+	Cole, Joanna; Degen, Bruce	Scholastic
Magic School Bus Takes a Dive, The	P	F	250+	Cole, Joanna; Degen, Bruce	Scholastic
Magic School Bus Taking Flight, The	P	F	250+	Cole, Joanna; Degen, Bruce	Scholastic
Magic School Bus The Truth About Bats, The	P	F	250+	Cole, Joanna; Degen, Bruce	Scholastic
Magic School Bus The Wild Whale Watch, The	P	F	250+	Cole, Joanna; Degen, Bruce	Scholastic
Magic School Bus Twister Trouble, The	P	LB	F	Cole, Joanna; Degen, Bruce	Scholastic
Magic School Bus Ups and Downs, The	P	F	250+	Cole, Joanna; Degen, Bruce	Scholastic
Magic School Bus Visits the Planets, The	P	F	250+	Cole, Joanna; Degen, Bruce	Scholastic
Magic School Bus Wet All Over, The	P	F	250+	Cole, Joanna; Degen, Bruce	Scholastic
Magic Shoes, The	M	RF	250+	Storyteller Summer Skies	Wright Group/McGraw Hill
Magic Shoes, The	I	F	250+	Storyworlds	Heinemann
Magic Show Review, The	M	RF	250+	Tristars	Richard C. Owen
Magic Show, The	B	RF	29	Sails	Rigby
Magic Squad and the Dog of Great Potential, The	P	RF	250+	Quattlebaum, Mary	Bantam Books
Magic Squares and More	Q	I	250+	WorldScapes	ETA/Cuisenaire
Magic Store, The	I	RF	203	Sunshine	Wright Group/McGraw Hill
Magic Sword, The	L	F	250+	Cambridge Reading	Pearson Learning Group
Magic Tricks	P	I	250+	Games Around the World	Compass Point Books
Magic Tricks	G	RF	156	The King School Series	Townsend Press
Magic Tricks	P	I	250+	Tristars	Richard C. Owen
Magic Trident, The	H	F	250+	Storyworlds	Heinemann
Magic Under Glass	Z	F	250+	Dolamore, Jaclyn	Bloomsbury Children's Books
Magic Village	H	RF	188	The King School Series	Townsend Press
Magic Wand, The	E	F	100	Start to Read	School Zone
Magic Wheel, The	P	I	250+	Voyages	SRA/McGraw Hill
Magic!	LB	RF	23	Twig	Wright Group/McGraw Hill
Magical Adventures of Pretty Pearl, The	W	F	250+	Hamilton, Virginia	HarperTrophy
Magical Maze, The	M	F	250+	Reading Safari	Mondo Publishing
Magical Mischief: Jokes that Shock and Amaze	O	F	1795	Make Me Laugh!	Lerner Publishing Group
Magical Monty	M	RF	250+	Hurwitz, Johanna	Candlewick Press
Magician, The: The Secrets of the Immortal Nicholas Flamel	X	F	250+	Scott, Michael	Delacorte Press

* Collection of short stories   # Graphic text
^ Mature content with lower level text demands

TITLE	LEVEL	GENRE	WORD COUNT	AUTHOR / SERIES	PUBLISHER / DISTRIBUTOR
Magician's Elephant, The	U	F	250+	DiCamillo, Kate	Candlewick Press
Magician's House, A	I	F	214	Sunshine	Wright Group/McGraw Hill
Magician's Lunch	I	F	272	Jellybeans	Rigby
Magician's Nephew, The	T	F	250+	Lewis, C. S.	HarperTrophy
Magnet Book, The	T	I	250+	Levine, Shar; Johnstone, Leslie	Sterling Publishing
Magnet Fishing Game	A	I	28	How-To Series	Benchmark Education
Magnet Time	I	I	212	Independent Readers Science	Houghton Mifflin Harcourt
Magnet, The	D	I	115	Sun Sprouts	ETA/Cuisenaire
Magnetism	Q	I	1722	Early Bird Energy	Lerner Publishing Group
Magnetism and Electricity: The Broken Toy Car	R	I	250+	iScience	Norwood House Press
Magnetism and Electromagnets	R	I	1261	Science Support Readers	Houghton Mifflin Harcourt
Magneto Versus Wolverine	L	F	250+	Marvel Super Hero Squad	Little Brown and Company
Magnets	E	I	52	Discovery Links	Newbridge
Magnets	C	I	55	Early Connections	Benchmark Education
Magnets	K	I	352	Explorations	Okapi Educational Materials
Magnets	K	I	352	Explorations	Eleanor Curtain Publishing
Magnets	G	I	113	Factivity Series	Pearson Learning Group
Magnets	F	I	77	Forces and Motion	Lerner Publishing Group
^Magnets	P	I	250+	Our Physical World	Capstone Press
Magnets	G	I	71	Phonics Readers	Compass Point Books
Magnets	S	I	250+	Reading Expeditions	National Geographic
Magnets	K	I	250+	Rigby Star Quest	Rigby
Magnets	M	I	458	Science Support Readers	Houghton Mifflin Harcourt
Magnets	B	I	28	Seedlings	Continental Press
Magnets	F	I	79	Sunshine	Wright Group/McGraw Hill
Magnets	J	I	259	Windows on Literacy	National Geographic
Magnets in Medicine	Y	I	2083	Leveled Readers Science	Houghton Mifflin Harcourt
^Magnets Push, Magnets Pull	O	I	250+	Science Starts	Capstone Press
Magnets Quiz	N	I	549	Springboard	Wright Group/McGraw Hill
Magnets: Pulling Together, Pushing Apart	M	I	250+	Amazing Science	Picture Window Books
Magnificent Masks	S	I	250+	Bookweb	Rigby
Magnificent Monarchs	L	I	281	Glaser, Linda	Millbrook Press
Magnifying Glass	C	I	32	Simple Tools	Lerner Publishing Group
Magnifying Glass, A	N	I	475	Sun Sprouts	ETA/Cuisenaire
Magnifying Glass, The	C	I	45	Foundations	Wright Group/McGraw Hill
Magpie's Baking Day	F	F	132	PM Story Books	Rigby
Magpie's Tail, The	L	TL	543	Pacific Literacy	Pacific Learning
Mahakala and Other Insect-Eating Dinosaurs	N	I	250+	Dinosaur Find	Picture Window Books
Mahatma Gandhi	Z	B	3171	Leveled Readers	Houghton Mifflin Harcourt
Mahatma Gandhi	Z	B	3171	Leveled Readers/CA	Houghton Mifflin Harcourt
Mahatma Gandhi	Z	B	3171	Leveled Readers/TX	Houghton Mifflin Harcourt
^Mahatma Gandhi: The Power of Peace	U	B	250+	Hameray Biography Series	Hameray Publishing Group
Mai Li's Surprise	F	RF	63	Books for Young Learners	Richard C. Owen
Mail Came Today, The	C	RF	35	Carousel Readers	Pearson Learning Group
Mail Carrier	D	I	27	Benchmark Rebus	Marshall Cavendish
Mail Carriers	M	I	250+	Community Helpers	Red Brick Learning
Mail Comes to Main Street, The	I	I	232	Early Explorers	Benchmark Education
Mail Harry to the Moon!	J	F	250+	Harris, Robie & Emberley, Michael	Little Brown and Company
Mail It... From Here to There	Q	I	915	Reading Street	Pearson
Mail Myself to You	E	RF	60	Little Celebrations	Pearson Learning Group
Mailbox, The	D	RF	93	Alpha kids	Sundance
Mailman Mario & His Boris-Busters	L	RF	250+	Parker, John	Pearson Learning Group
Main Street	F	I	87	Leveled Readers Social Studies	Houghton Mifflin Harcourt

* Collection of short stories   # Graphic text
^ Mature content with lower level text demands

TITLE	LEVEL	GENRE	WORD COUNT	AUTHOR / SERIES	PUBLISHER / DISTRIBUTOR
Main Street	Q	RF	250+	Martin, Ann M.	Scholastic
Main Street Mystery, The	H	RF	196	Literacy by Design	Rigby
Maine	T	I	250+	Hello U.S.A.	Lerner Publishing Group
Maine	S	I	250+	Land of Liberty	Red Brick Learning
Maine	R	I	250+	This Land Is Your Land	Compass Point Books
Maine Coon Cats	R	I	250+	All About Cats	Capstone Press
Maine Coon Cats	I	I	112	Cats	Capstone Press
Maine Coons Are the Best!	Q	I	1361	The Best Cats Ever	Lerner Publishing Group
Maine Is the Pine Tree State	O	I	211	Larkin, Bruce	Wilbooks
Maine: Facts and Symbols	O	I	250+	The States and Their Symbols	Capstone Press
Mai's Big Surprise	J	RF	250+	The Wright Skills	Wright Group/McGraw Hill
Maisie's Race	L	RF	250+	Take Two Books	Wright Group/McGraw Hill
Maisy Bakes a Cake	I	F	97	Cousins, Lucy	Candlewick Press
Maisy Goes to Preschool	I	F	227	Cousins, Lucy	Candlewick Press
Maisy Goes to the City	I	F	258	Cousins, Lucy	Candlewick Press
Maisy Goes to the Museum	I	F	204	Cousins, Lucy	Candlewick Press
Maisy's Amazing Big Book of Learning	I	F	232	Cousins, Lucy	Candlewick Press
Maisy's First Clock	F	F	64	Cousins, Lucy	Candlewick Press
Maisy's Wonderful Weather Book	J	F	164	Cousins, Lucy	Candlewick Press
Major Jump	B	F	21	Sunshine	Wright Group/McGraw Hill
Makah, The: Whaling Tribe of the Northwest	S	I	250+	Explore More	Wright Group/McGraw Hill
Make a "Talking" Card	H	I	165	Sunshine	Wright Group/McGraw Hill
Make a Bird Feeder	D	I	62	How-To Series	Benchmark Education
Make a Boat That Floats	I	I	126	Book Bank	Wright Group/McGraw Hill
Make a Bottle Garden	L	I	250+	Lighthouse	Rigby
Make a Bottle Orchestra	J	I	250+	Sunshine	Wright Group/McGraw Hill
Make a Cloud, Measure the Wind	M	I	250+	Take Two Books	Wright Group/McGraw Hill
Make a Dinosaur	H	I	208	Sun Sprouts	ETA/Cuisenaire
Make a Drum	C	I	29	Early Connections	Benchmark Education
Make a Face: Verbs in Action	L	I	250+	Bookworms	Marshall Cavendish
Make a Fruit Salad	D	I	102	Springboard	Wright Group/McGraw Hill
Make a Funny Face	C	I	41	InfoTrek	ETA/Cuisenaire
Make a Glider	G	I	57	Storyteller-Setting Sun	Wright Group/McGraw Hill
Make a Guitar	J	I	540	Sunshine	Wright Group/McGraw Hill
Make a House	F	I	41	iOpeners	Pearson Learning Group
Make a Kite	F	I	49	Story Steps	Rigby
Make a Kite	A	I	20	Vocabulary Readers	Houghton Mifflin Harcourt
Make a Kite	A	I	20	Vocabulary Readers/CA	Houghton Mifflin Harcourt
Make a Lei	F	I	39	Pacific Literacy	Pacific Learning
Make a Marionette	K	I	349	How-To Series	Benchmark Education
Make a Monster	E	I	31	Windows on Literacy	National Geographic
Make a Music Shaker	E	RF	113	InfoTrek	ETA/Cuisenaire
Make a Necklace	E	I	106	How-To Series	Benchmark Education
Make a Paper Airplane	J	I	158	How-To Series	Benchmark Education
Make a Pinata	C	I	16	Little Celebrations	Pearson Learning Group
Make a Pinata	I	I	152	Windows on Literacy	National Geographic
Make a Plan of Your Classroom	E	I	94	How-To Series	Benchmark Education
Make a Raft	F	I	186	Take Two Books	Wright Group/McGraw Hill
Make a Rainbow Fish	G	I	139	Sun Sprouts	ETA/Cuisenaire
Make a Safety Puppet	E	I	107	How-To Series	Benchmark Education
Make a Salad	A	I	32	Red Rocket Readers	Flying Start Books
Make a Salad Face	F	I	82	Voyages	SRA/McGraw Hill
Make a Shake and a Bakeless Cake	L	I	250+	Take Two Books	Wright Group/McGraw Hill
Make a Sundial	K	I	250+	How-To Series	Benchmark Education

* Collection of short stories   # Graphic text
^ Mature content with lower level text demands

TITLE	LEVEL	GENRE	WORD COUNT	AUTHOR / SERIES	PUBLISHER / DISTRIBUTOR
Make a Tune	J	I	246	Kratky, Lada	Hampton Brown
Make a Turkey	C	I	14	Bebop Books	Lee & Low Books Inc.
Make a Valentine	D	RF	33	Bookshop	Mondo Publishing
Make a Wish, Molly	O	RF	250+	Cohen, Barbara	Bantam Books
Make a Worm Farm	E	I	98	Sun Sprouts	ETA/Cuisenaire
Make an Animal Mobile	H	I	116	How-to Series	Benchmark Education
Make an Island	J	I	199	How-To Series	Benchmark Education
Make Dinosaur Eggs	I	I	188	Sunshine	Wright Group/McGraw Hill
Make It Go	L	I	250+	InfoTrek Plus	ETA/Cuisenaire
Make It Go	S	I	250+	PM Extensions	Rigby
Make It Move	N	I	250+	InfoTrek	ETA/Cuisenaire
Make It Move!	E	I	29	Canizares, Susan; Chessen, Betsey	Scholastic
Make It Move!	N	I	215	Yellow Umbrella Books	Capstone Press
Make It Spin	D	I	18	Pacific Literacy	Pacific Learning
Make It!	A	RF	21	Phonics and Friends	Hampton Brown
Make It! Ship It!	K	I	250+	Spyglass Books	Compass Point Books
Make It, Wear It	P	I	250+	iOpeners	Pearson Learning Group
Make Lemonade	Z	RF	250+	Wolff, Virginia Euwer	Scholastic
Make Like a Tree and Leave	U	RF	250+	Danziger, Paula	PaperStar
Make Masks for a Play	J	I	540	Sunshine	Wright Group/McGraw Hill
Make Mini Movies	I	I	309	Sunshine	Wright Group/McGraw Hill
Make Music	A	I	32	Red Rocket Readers	Flying Start Books
Make My Name	E	F	63	Reading Safari	Mondo Publishing
Make Prints and Patterns	K	I	454	Sunshine	Wright Group/McGraw Hill
*Make Room For Elisa	N	RF	250+	Hurwitz, Johanna	Penguin Group
Make Sense of Your Senses	J	I	250+	InfoTrek	ETA/Cuisenaire
Make Sense!	F	RF	115	Silly Millies	Millbrook Press
Make Things That Move	O	I	250+	Sunshine	Wright Group/McGraw Hill
Make Way for Ducklings	L	RF	250+	McCloskey, Robert	Puffin Books
Make Way for Sam Houston	X	B	250+	Fritz, Jean	G.P. Putnam's Sons Books for Young Readers
Make Way for Tooth Decay	K	F	250+	Katz, Bobbi	Scholastic
Make Your Own Crystals	N	I	395	In Step Readers	Rigby
Make Your Own Monster	I	I	239	Rigby Star Quest	Rigby
Make Your Own Music	K	I	250+	InfoTrek Plus	ETA/Cuisenaire
Make Your Own Party	I	I	314	Sunshine	Wright Group/McGraw Hill
Make Your Own Terrarium	P	I	1380	Leveled Readers Science	Houghton Mifflin Harcourt
Maker of Machines: A Story about Eli Whitney	S	B	8690	Creative Minds Biographies	Lerner Publishing Group
Maker of Things	O	B	250+	Meet The Author	Richard C. Owen
Making a Bird	B	I	32	PM Plus Nonfiction	Rigby
Making a Book	H	I	174	Red Rocket Readers	Flying Start Books
Making a Book	L	I	401	Rigby Flying Colors	Rigby
Making a Bug Habitat	K	I	250+	How-To Series	Benchmark Education
Making a Butterfly	C	I	71	PM Math Readers	Rigby
Making a Cake	G	I	125	Little Red Readers	Sundance
Making a Castle	H	I	184	PM Math Readers	Rigby
Making a Cat and a Mouse	D	I	121	PM Plus Nonfiction	Rigby
Making a Caterpillar	E	I	115	PM Plus Nonfiction	Rigby
Making a Clock Cake	J	RF	389	PM Math Readers	Rigby
Making a Community Work	K	RF	250+	InfoTrek	ETA/Cuisenaire
Making a Difference	N	RF	1648	Gear Up!	Wright Group/McGraw Hill
Making a Difference	V	B	250+	Literacy By Design	Rigby
Making a Difference in the World	O	B	250+	Meet the Author	Richard C. Owen

TITLE	LEVEL	GENRE	WORD COUNT	AUTHOR / SERIES	PUBLISHER / DISTRIBUTOR
Making a Dinosaur	B	I	32	PM Plus Nonfiction	Rigby
Making a Friend	B	F	30	Bonnell, Kris	Reading Reading Books
Making a Garden	A	RF	28	Foundations	Wright Group/McGraw Hill
Making a Go-Cart	T	I	250+	Sunshine	Wright Group/McGraw Hill
Making a Hat	C	I	24	Windows on Literacy	National Geographic
Making a Home	D	I	102	Leveled Readers	Houghton Mifflin Harcourt
Making a Home	D	I	102	Leveled Readers/CA	Houghton Mifflin Harcourt
Making a Home	D	I	102	Leveled Readers/TX	Houghton Mifflin Harcourt
Making a House	C	I	89	Early Connections	Benchmark Education
Making a Magazine	O	I	496	Vocabulary Readers	Houghton Mifflin Harcourt
Making a Magnet	I	I	185	Sun Sprouts	ETA/Cuisenaire
Making a Map	L	I	293	Rigby Focus	Rigby
Making a Memory	D	I	53	Ballinger, Margaret	Scholastic
Making a Movie	L	I	460	Red Rocket Readers	Flying Start Books
Making a Mud Pie	C	RF	105	Leveled Readers	Houghton Mifflin Harcourt
Making a Mud Pie	C	RF	105	Leveled Readers/CA	Houghton Mifflin Harcourt
Making a Mural	H	I	128	Vocabulary Readers	Houghton Mifflin Harcourt
Making a Newspaper	M	I	317	Leveled Readers	Houghton Mifflin Harcourt
Making a Newspaper	M	I	317	Leveled Readers/CA	Houghton Mifflin Harcourt
Making a Newspaper	M	I	317	Leveled Readers/TX	Houghton Mifflin Harcourt
Making a Park	F	I	168	On Our Way to English	Rigby
Making a Pizza	A	I	32	Leveled Literacy Intervention/ Orange System	Heinemann
Making a Plate	H	I	183	Ready Readers	Pearson Learning Group
Making a Rabbit	B	I	32	PM Plus Nonfiction	Rigby
Making a Rabbit with Shapes	E	I	138	Early Connections	Benchmark Education
Making a Snowman	A	I	32	Leveled Literacy Intervention/ Orange System	Heinemann
Making a Terrarium	L	I	250+	How-To Series	Benchmark Education
Making a Toy House	G	I	132	PM Plus Nonfiction	Rigby
Making a Tree House	A	F	27	Leveled Readers	Houghton Mifflin Harcourt
Making a Tree House	A	F	27	Leveled Readers/CA	Houghton Mifflin Harcourt
Making a TV Documentary	P	I	250+	Wonder World	Wright Group/McGraw Hill
Making a Weather Station	M	I	250+	How-To Series	Benchmark Education
Making Art	J	I	250+	Rosen Real Readers	Rosen Publishing Group
Making Books for Fun!	S	I	250+	For Fun! Crafts	Compass Point Books
Making Breakfast	E	I	129	Rigby Flying Colors	Rigby
Making Breakfast	F	I	59	Windows on Literacy	National Geographic
Making Brownies	E	RF	89	McAlpin, MaryAnn	Short Tales Press
Making Butter	H	I	187	Literacy by Design	Rigby
Making Caterpillars and Butterflies	I	I	162	Literacy 2000	Rigby
Making Clay	O	I	792	Leveled Readers Science	Houghton Mifflin Harcourt
Making Collages	J	I	250+	Bookshop	Mondo Publishing
Making Concrete	I	I	136	Alphakids	Sundance
Making Crafts From Around the World	O	I	250+	Navigators How-To Series	Benchmark Education
Making Flavors and Fragrances	S	I	2032	Leveled Readers Science	Houghton Mifflin Harcourt
Making Friends	J	RF	214	Foundations	Wright Group/McGraw Hill
Making Friends in Mali	T	RF	5116	Reading Street	Pearson
Making Friends on Beacon Street	M	RF	250+	Literacy 2000	Rigby
Making Gingerbread Men	M	I	806	Springboard	Wright Group/McGraw Hill
Making Granny Grasshead	K	I	362	Sun Sprouts	ETA/Cuisenaire
Making Great Greeting Cards & Gifts	Q	I	250+	Navigators How-To Series	Benchmark Education
Making Healthy Choices	U	I	250+	Reading Expeditions	National Geographic
Making Holes	E	I	134	Sails	Rigby

Organized Alphabetically by Title
Storable Database at www.fountasandpinnellleveledbooks.com

* Collection of short stories   # Graphic text
^ Mature content with lower level text demands

TITLE	LEVEL	GENRE	WORD COUNT	AUTHOR / SERIES	PUBLISHER / DISTRIBUTOR
Making Honey	I	I	220	Red Rocket Readers	Flying Start Books
Making Ice Cream	J	I	176	How-To Series	Benchmark Education
Making Ice Cream	H	I	162	Sun Sprouts	ETA/Cuisenaire
Making It Go: The Life and Work of Robert Fulton	T	B	250+	Science Readers	Teacher Created Materials
Making It Go?	F	I	106	Independent Readers Science	Houghton Mifflin Harcourt
Making Lily Laugh!	M	RF	250+	Dreyer, Ellen	Pearson Learning Group
Making Lunch	D	I	70	Rigby Flying Colors	Rigby
Making Maple Syrup	F	I	91	Nonfiction Set 5	Literacy Footprints
Making Maps	T	I	250+	Navigators Science Series	Benchmark Education
Making Milk	F	I	104	Red Rocket Readers	Flying Start Books
Making Money	H	I	129	Rosen Real Readers	Rosen Publishing Group
Making Money	I	I	234	Yellow Umbrella Books	Red Brick Learning
Making Mount Rushmore	M	I	250+	Twig	Wright Group/McGraw Hill
Making Mountains	B	I	35	Gosset, Rachel; Ballinger, Margaret	Scholastic
Making Movies	T	I	1297	Leveled Readers	Houghton Mifflin Harcourt
Making Movies	T	I	1297	Leveled Readers/CA	Houghton Mifflin Harcourt
Making Movies	T	I	1297	Leveled Readers/TX	Houghton Mifflin Harcourt
Making Movies	LB	I	43	Sunshine	Wright Group/McGraw Hill
Making Movies	Q	I	250+	Trackers	Pacific Learning
Making Moving Models	T	I	250+	High-Fliers	Pacific Learning
Making Murals	K	I	423	Leveled Readers	Houghton Mifflin Harcourt
Making Murals	K	I	423	Leveled Readers/CA	Houghton Mifflin Harcourt
Making Murals	K	I	423	Leveled Readers/TX	Houghton Mifflin Harcourt
Making Music	H	RF	71	Early Readers	Compass Point Books
Making Music	L	I	356	Rigby Flying Colors	Rigby
Making Music	K	I	174	Windows on Literacy	National Geographic
Making Music	C	I	35	Wonder World	Wright Group/McGraw Hill
Making Myths	T	I	250+	The News	Richard C. Owen
Making Oatmeal	E	I	38	Interaction	Rigby
Making of My Special Hand, The: Madison's Story	O	RF	250+	Heelan, Jamee Riggio	Peachtree
Making Pancakes	D	RF	39	Carousel Readers	Pearson Learning Group
Making Pancakes	G	I	91	Windows on Literacy	National Geographic
Making Paper	I	I	284	Little Green Readers	Sundance
Making Paper	H	I	128	Rigby Focus	Rigby
Making Party Food	I	I	221	PM Plus Nonfiction	Rigby
Making Party Hats	F	I	168	PM Math Readers	Rigby
Making Patterns	L	I	250+	Early Connections	Benchmark Education
Making Patterns	C	I	30	Twig	Wright Group/McGraw Hill
Making Pictures	B	RF	48	Foundations	Wright Group/McGraw Hill
Making Pictures	C	I	48	Gear Up!	Wright Group/McGraw Hill
Making Pictures	G	I	132	Vocabulary Readers	Houghton Mifflin Harcourt
Making Pizza	F	I	140	McAlpin, MaryAnn	Short Tales Press
Making Pizza	C	I	60	Nonfiction Set 3	Literacy Footprints
Making Pizza with Math	J	I	250+	On Our Way to English	Rigby
Making Pop-ups	N	I	250+	Bookshop	Mondo Publishing
Making Pop-ups	O	I	250+	Brian, Janeen	Mondo Publishing
Making Puppets	C	I	86	Vocabulary Readers	Houghton Mifflin Harcourt
Making Puppets	C	I	86	Vocabulary Readers/CA	Houghton Mifflin Harcourt
Making Raisins	E	I	35	Windows on Literacy	National Geographic
Making Roads	I	I	176	Sails	Rigby
Making Rules	K	I	447	Early Explorers	Benchmark Education

TITLE	LEVEL	GENRE	WORD COUNT	AUTHOR / SERIES	PUBLISHER / DISTRIBUTOR
Making Sense of Dollars and Cents	M	I	393	Reading Street	Pearson
Making Sense of Your Senses	P	I	250+	Navigators Science Series	Benchmark Education
Making Shapes	H	I	206	Early Connections	Benchmark Education
Making Shapes	S	I	250+	PM Plus Nonfiction	Rigby
Making Shapes	K	I	250+	Yellow Umbrella Books	Capstone Press
Making Snack Mix	G	I	188	In Step Readers	Rigby
Making Sound	N	I	422	Science Support Readers	Houghton Mifflin Harcourt
Making Soup	B	I	53	Leveled Literacy Intervention/ Orange System	Heinemann
Making Soup	C	RF	77	Leveled Readers Emergent	Houghton Mifflin Harcourt
Making Special Effects	P	I	250+	Windows on Literacy	National Geographic
Making the Right Moves	J	RF	250+	HSP/Harcourt Trophies	Harcourt, Inc.
Making the World a Better Place	K	I	544	Reading Street	Pearson
Making the World a Better Place: The Stories of Social Reformers	T	B	250+	Rigby Literacy	Rigby
Making Things	D	RF	64	Foundations	Wright Group/McGraw Hill
Making Tortillas	H	I	104	Windows on Literacy	National Geographic
Making Work Easy	M	I	250+	Explorations	Eleanor Curtain Publishing
Making Work Easy	M	I	250+	Explorations	Okapi Educational Materials
Making Yogurt	N	I	250+	Pacific Literacy	Pacific Learning
^Mako Shark	N	I	250+	Shark Zone	Capstone Press
Mako Shark	J	I	123	Sharks	Capstone Press
Malawi: Keeper of the Trees	D	I	250+	Little Celebrations	Pearson Learning Group
Malcolm Magpie	F	I	126	Storyteller-Setting Sun	Wright Group/McGraw Hill
Malcolm X	Z	B	250+	Just the Facts Biographies	Lerner Publishing Group
Malcolm X: By Any Means Necessary	Z	B	250+	Myers, Walter Dean	Scholastic
Malcolm X: Force for Change	S	B	250+	Great African Americans	Capstone Press
Mali: Civilizations Past to Present	S	I	250+	Reading Expeditions	National Geographic
Malinali: The Slave Who Traded Words for Freedom	T	B	250+	Bookshop	Mondo Publishing
Malka	Z	HF	250+	Pressler, Mirjam	Philomel
Mall Mystery, The	M	F	250+	Woodland Mysteries	Wright Group/McGraw Hill
Mallard Ducks	K	I	346	Pull Ahead Books	Lerner Publishing Group
Mallards	H	I	105	Wetland Animals	Capstone Press
Mallory Goes Green	O	RF	15506	Friedman, Laurie	Carolrhoda Books
Mallory in the Spotlight	O	RF	16116	Friedman, Laurie	Carolrhoda Books
Mallory on Board	O	RF	17665	Friedman, Laurie	Carolrhoda Books
Mallory on the Move	O	RF	250+	Friedman, Laurie	Lerner Publishing Group
Mallory vs. Max	O	RF	250+	Friedman, Laurie	Lerner Publishing Group
Mallory's Guide to Boys, Brothers, Dads, and Dogs	O	RF	15711	Friedman, Laurie	Darby Creek Publishing
Malted Falcon, The: A Chet Gecko Mystery	Q	F	250+	Hale, Bruce	Harcourt, Inc.
Maltese Falcon, The	Z+	RF	250+	Hammett, Dashiell	Random House
Mama	LB	F	29	Winter, Jeanette	Harcourt
Mama and Kit Go Away	D	F	84	Leveled Readers	Houghton Mifflin Harcourt
Mama and Papa Have a Store	Q	RF	250+	Carling, Amelia Lau	Dial/Penguin
Mama Cut My Hair	H	RF	134	Books for Young Learners	Richard C. Owen
Mama Do You Love Me?	L	RF	250+	Joosse, Barbara	Scholastic
Mama for Owen, A	M	RF	250+	Bauer, Marion Dane	Simon & Schuster
Mama Goes to School	D	RF	47	Visions	Wright Group/McGraw Hill
Mama Hen, Come Quick	C	F	35	Ready Readers	Pearson Learning Group
Mama Zooms	I	F	174	Cowen-Fletcher, J.	Scholastic
Mama, Let's Dance	W	RF	250+	Hermes, Patricia	Scholastic
Mama's Llamas	J	F	159	Books for Young Learners	Richard C. Owen

* Collection of short stories   # Graphic text
^ Mature content with lower level text demands

TITLE	LEVEL	GENRE	WORD COUNT	AUTHOR / SERIES	PUBLISHER / DISTRIBUTOR
Mama's Wild Child	L	F	250+	Aston, Dianna Hutts	Charlesbridge
Mamba and the Crocodile Bird	I	F	250+	Storyworlds	Heinemann
Mammal	W	I	250+	Eyewitness Books	DK Publishing
Mammals	M	I	134	Exploring the Animal Kingdom	Capstone Press
Mammals	N	I	250+	Simply Science	Compass Point Books
Mammals	P	I	950	Time for Kids	Teacher Created Materials
Mammals	H	I	134	Yellow Umbrella Books	Red Brick Learning
Mammals Around the World	N	I	979	Rigby Flying Colors	Rigby
Mammals of the Sea	Q	I	250+	Explorers	Wright Group/McGraw Hill
Mammals Who Morph: The Universe Tells Our Evolution Story	W	I	3950	Sharing Nature with Children	Dawn Publications
Mammals: Hairy, Milk-Making Animals	M	I	250+	Amazing Science	Picture Window Books
Mammoth	T	I	250+	Sails	Rigby
Mammoth Academy in Trouble, The	N	F	250+	Layton, Neal	Henry Holt & Co.
Mammoth Academy, The	N	F	250+	Layton, Neal	Henry Holt & Co.
Mammoth Hunters, The	Q	F	250+	Bookweb	Rigby
Mammoth Mammals	Q	I	250+	Explorer Books-Pathfinder	National Geographic
Mammoth Mammals	P	I	250+	Explorer Books-Pioneer	National Geographic
Mammoth Mistake, A	K	RF	250+	Rigby Literacy	Rigby
Mammoth Mistake, A	K	RF	250+	Rigby Star Plus	Rigby
Mammoths and Mastodons: Titans of the Ice Age	V	I	250+	Bardoe, Cheryl	Harry N. Abrams
Mammoths: Ice-Age Giants	Z	I	250+	Agenbroad, Dr. Larry D.; Nelson, Lisa	Lerner Publishing Group
Mamo Is Trading Again	K	TL	250+	Wheeler, Janine	Hampton Brown
Man from Mars, The	K	SF	250+	Popcorn	Sundance
Man from The Sky	S	RF	250+	Avi	Beech Tree Books
Man in the Ceiling, The	T	RF	250+	Feiffer, Jules	HarperTrophy
Man in the Iron Mask, The	V	HF	250+	WorldScapes	ETA/Cuisenaire
Man in the Moon and Other Moon Tales, The	N	RF	322	Independent Readers Science	Houghton Mifflin Harcourt
Man in the Moon, The	H	I	173	Pair-It Books	Steck-Vaughn
Man in the Moon, The	L	F	928	Pair-It Turn and Learn	Steck-Vaughn
Man in the Moon, The	I	F	248	Storyteller	Wright Group/McGraw Hill
Man on the Moon	N	I	317	Avenues	Hampton Brown
Man on the Moon: How a Photograph Made Anything Seem Possible	Y	I	250+	Captured History	Compass Point Books
Man Out at First	M	RF	250+	Christopher, Matt	Little Brown and Company
Man Who Digs Dinosaurs, The	Q	I	1278	Leveled Readers	Houghton Mifflin Harcourt
Man Who Digs Dinosaurs, The	Q	I	1278	Leveled Readers/CA	Houghton Mifflin Harcourt
Man Who Digs Dinosaurs, The	Q	I	1278	Leveled Readers/TX	Houghton Mifflin Harcourt
Man Who Enjoyed Grumbling, The	L	F	250+	Sunshine	Wright Group/McGraw Hill
Man Who Flies With Birds, The	Y	I	10352	Vogel, Carole Garbuny & Leshem, Yossi	Kar-Ben Publishing
Man Who Kept His Heart in a Bucket, The	S	TL	250+	Levitin, Sonia	Penguin Group
Man Who Made Puppets, The	E	I	106	Leveled Readers	Houghton Mifflin Harcourt
Man Who Made Puppets, The	E	I	106	Leveled Readers/CA	Houghton Mifflin Harcourt
Man Who Made Puppets, The	E	I	106	Leveled Readers/TX	Houghton Mifflin Harcourt
Man Who Measured the World, The	V	HF	250+	PM Extensions	Rigby
Man Who Named the Clouds, The	R	B	250+	Hannah, Julie and Holub, Joan	Albert Whitman & Co.
Man Who Paints Nature, The	O	B	250+	Meet The Author	Richard C. Owen
Man Who Rode the Tiger, The	L	TL	250+	PM Story Books	Rigby
Man Who Tricked a Ghost, The	N	TL	250+	Yep, Laurence	Troll Associates
Man Who Walked Between the Towers, The	Q	HF	250+	Gerstein, Mordicai	Square Fish
Man Who Was Poe, The	Y	HF	250+	Avi	Avon Books
Man, the Boy, and the Donkey, The	I	TL	234	Story Box	Wright Group/McGraw Hill

TITLE	LEVEL	GENRE	WORD COUNT	AUTHOR / SERIES	PUBLISHER / DISTRIBUTOR
Manatee Mom	F	F	172	Silly Millies	Millbrook Press
Manatee Winter	K	RF	250+	Zoehfeld, Kathleen Weidnetz	Scholastic
Manatee, The	E	I	75	Bonnell, Kris/Animals in Danger	Reading Reading Books
Manatee, The	V	I	250+	Silverstein, A.; Nunn, L.	Millbrook Press
Manatees	O	I	1589	Early Bird Nature Books	Lerner Publishing Group
Manatees	G	I	73	Pebble Books	Red Brick Learning
Manatees	H	I	124	Under the Sea	Capstone Press
Manatees	N	I	250+	World of Mammals	Capstone Press
Manatees and Dugongs	M	I	250+	Take Two Books	Wright Group/McGraw Hill
Manet	Z	B	250+	Eyewitness Books	DK Publishing
^Manga Touch	V	RF	250+	Orca Currents	Orca Books
Mango Tree, The	H	RF	272	Storyworlds	Heinemann
Mango Tree, The	E	F	163	Sun Sprouts	ETA/Cuisenaire
Mango's Revenge	R	F	250+	Bookshop	Mondo Publishing
Mango-Shaped Space, A	V	RF	250+	Mass, Wendy	Little Brown and Company
Mangrove Forest Food Chain, A: A Who-Eats-What Adventure in Asia	U	I	6964	Follow That Food Chain	Lerner Publishing Group
Mangrove Swamp	R	I	1136	Vocabulary Readers	Houghton Mifflin Harcourt
Mangrove Swamp	R	I	1136	Vocabulary Readers/CA	Houghton Mifflin Harcourt
Mangrove Swamp	R	I	1136	Vocabulary Readers/TX	Houghton Mifflin Harcourt
Manhattan Project, The: the Race to the Atomic Bomb	Y	I	2925	Leveled Readers Science	Houghton Mifflin Harcourt
Maniac Magee	W	RF	250+	Spinelli, Jerry	Scholastic
Manly Ferry Pigeon, The	K	RF	250+	Sunshine	Wright Group/McGraw Hill
Manners at a Friend's Home	L	I	250+	Manners	Capstone Press
Manners at a Friend's House	J	I	250+	Way to Be!	Picture Window Books
Manners at a Restaurant	L	I	250+	Manners	Capstone Press
Manners at the Library	L	I	250+	Manners	Capstone Press
Manners in the Classroom	L	I	250+	Manners	Capstone Press
Manners in the Lunchroom	J	I	250+	Way to Be!	Picture Window Books
#Manners Matter in the Classroom	L	I	250+	First Graphics: Manners Matter	Capstone Press
#Manners Matter in the Library	L	I	250+	First Graphics: Manners Matter	Capstone Press
#Manners Matter on a Field Trip	L	I	250+	First Graphics: Manners Matter	Capstone Press
#Manners Matter on the Playground	L	I	250+	First Graphics: Manners Matter	Capstone Press
Manners of a Pig, The	I	F	250+	Bookshop	Mondo Publishing
Manners on the Playground	L	I	250+	Manners	Capstone Press
Manners on the School Bus	J	I	250+	Way to Be!	Picture Window Books
Manners on the Telephone	L	I	250+	Manners	Capstone Press
Manners Please	C	RF	27	Pair-It Books	Steck-Vaughn
Manners with a Library Book	J	I	250+	Way to Be!	Picture Window Books
Mannings, The: Football's Famous Family	R	B	250+	High Five Reading	Capstone Press
Manny's Story	L	RF	869	Leveled Readers	Houghton Mifflin Harcourt
Manny's Story	L	RF	869	Leveled Readers/CA	Houghton Mifflin Harcourt
Manny's Story	L	RF	869	Leveled Readers/TX	Houghton Mifflin Harcourt
Manolito Four-Eyes	T	RF	250+	Lindo, Elvira	Marshall Cavendish
Manolito Four-Eyes: The 2nd Volume of the Great Encyclopedia of My Life	T	RF	250+	Lindo, Elvira	Marshall Cavendish
Manolito Four-Eyes: The 3rd Volume of the Great Encyclopedia of My Life	T	RF	250+	Lindo, Elvira	Marshall Cavendish
Mansa Musa: Leader of Mali	X	B	250+	Primary Source Readers	Teacher Created Materials
Mansion in the Mist, The	S	F	250+	Bellairs, John	Puffin Books
Mantis, The	J	I	144	Readlings/Predator Bugs	American Reading Company
Mantises	A	I	112	Readlings/Predator Bugs	American Reading Company
Mantu the Elephant	K	F	250+	Rigby Literacy	Rigby

* Collection of short stories   # Graphic text
^ Mature content with lower level text demands

TITLE	LEVEL	GENRE	WORD COUNT	AUTHOR / SERIES	PUBLISHER / DISTRIBUTOR
Manual of House Monsters, A	O	F	250+	Marijanovic, Stanislav	Mondo Publishing
Manx Are the Best!	Q	I	1011	The Best Cats Ever	Lerner Publishing Group
Manx Cats	R	I	250+	All About Cats	Capstone Press
Manx Cats	I	I	133	Cats	Capstone Press
Many Faces of George Washington, The	X	I	24580	McClafferty, Carla Killough	Carolrhoda Books
Many Feelings	G	RF	171	The King School Series	Townsend Press
Many Friends, Many Languages	D	I	98	Fiesta Series	Pearson Learning Group
Many Happy Returns: A Review of Recycling	R	I	250+	Literacy 2000	Rigby
Many Homes	B	I	48	Literacy by Design	Rigby
Many Kinds of Bats	J	I	292	Leveled Readers	Houghton Mifflin Harcourt
Many Kinds of Bats	J	I	292	Leveled Readers/CA	Houghton Mifflin Harcourt
Many Kinds of Bats	J	I	292	Leveled Readers/TX	Houghton Mifflin Harcourt
Many Kinds of Birds	I	I	290	Leveled Readers	Houghton Mifflin Harcourt
Many Kinds of Matter: A Look at Solids, Liquids and Gases	M	I	250+	Lightning Bolt Books	Lerner Publishing Group
Many People, Many Places	K	I	475	InfoTrek	ETA/Cuisenaire
Many Rides of Paul Revere, The	Z	I	250+	Giblin, James Cross	Scholastic
*Many Thousand Gone: African Americans From Slavery to Freedom	X	TL	250+	Hamilton, Virginia	Alfred A. Knopf
Many Waters	V	F	250+	L'Engle, Madeleine	Bantam Books
Many Ways to 100	I	I	250+	Yellow Umbrella Books	Red Brick Learning
Many Ways to Be a Soldier	O	HF	1486	On My Own History	Millbrook Press
Many Ways to Move: A Look at Motion	L	I	365	Lightning Bolt Books	Lerner Publishing Group
Many Ways to Work	J	I	250+	Literacy by Design	Rigby
Many Ways: How Families Practice Their Beliefs and Religions	N	I	156	Shelley Rotner's Early Childhood Library	Millbrook Press
Many-Sided Shapes	D	I	48	Bookworms	Marshall Cavendish
Maori of New Zealand, The	U	I	1168	Vocabulary Readers	Houghton Mifflin Harcourt
Maori of New Zealand, The	U	I	1168	Vocabulary Readers/CA	Houghton Mifflin Harcourt
Maori of New Zealand, The	U	I	1168	Vocabulary Readers/TX	Houghton Mifflin Harcourt
Mao's Last Dancer	Y	B	250+	Cunxin, Li	Walker & Company
Map and the Treasure, The	L	F	292	Leveled Readers	Houghton Mifflin Harcourt
Map and the Treasure, The	L	F	292	Leveled Readers/CA	Houghton Mifflin Harcourt
Map and the Treasure, The	L	F	292	Leveled Readers/TX	Houghton Mifflin Harcourt
Map Book, The	F	I	144	Sunshine	Wright Group/McGraw Hill
Map Fun	C	RF	39	Seedlings	Continental Press
Map Mania	S	I	250+	DiSpezio, Michael A.	Sterling Publishing
Map Mysteries	M	I	250+	Home Connection Collection	Rigby
Map of My House, A	B	I	75	Early Explorers	Benchmark Education
Map of Our School, A	E	I	142	Dominie Factivity Series	Pearson Learning Group
Map to Fun, A	G	RF	182	InfoTrek	ETA/Cuisenaire
Map, The	D	RF	74	Math Stories	Pearson Learning Group
Maple Syrup	I	I	250+	The Rowland Reading Program Library	Rowland Reading Foundation
Maple Thanksgiving, The	L	F	250+	Little Celebrations	Pearson Learning Group
Maple Tree	O	I	250+	Life Cycles	Creative Teaching Press
Maple Tree, The	R	I	1573	Reading Street	Pearson
Maple Trees	F	I	118	Pebble Books	Capstone Press
Mapping Earth from Space	Z	I	250+	Science Missions	Raintree
Mapping North America	M	I	148	Windows on Literacy	National Geographic
Mapping Our World	K	I	250+	Spyglass Books	Compass Point Books
Mapping the Way	H	I	179	Early Explorers	Benchmark Education
Mapping the World	Q	I	250+	InfoQuest	Rigby
Mapping the World	O	I	250+	Orbit Chapter Books	Pacific Learning

* Collection of short stories   # Graphic text
^ Mature content with lower level text demands

TITLE	LEVEL	GENRE	WORD COUNT	AUTHOR / SERIES	PUBLISHER / DISTRIBUTOR
Maps	G	I	142	Early Connections	Benchmark Education
Maps	C	I	11	Geography	Lerner Publishing Group
Maps	R	I	250+	Haslam, Andrew	World Book
Maps	G	I	99	Learn to Read	Creative Teaching Press
Maps	K	I	150	Phonics Readers	Compass Point Books
Maps	Q	I	250+	Rigby Focus	Rigby
Maps	K	I	237	Take Two Books	Wright Group/McGraw Hill
Maps	L	I	139	Windows on Literacy	National Geographic
Maps & Globes	O	I	250+	Knowlton, Jack	HarperCollins
Maps and Charts	M	I	549	Red Rocket Readers	Flying Start Books
Maps and Codes	P	I	250+	Wildcats	Wright Group/McGraw Hill
Maps and Mapping	P	I	250+	Science Kids	Kingfisher
Maps and Mapping	R	I	250+	Young Discoverers	Kingfisher
Maps and Our World	Q	I	250+	Explorers	Wright Group/McGraw Hill
Maps Are Cool: How to Read Them, Plan Them, and Create Them	U	I	250+	Bookshop	Mondo Publishing
Maps Show Us the Way	H	I	94	Rosen Real Readers	Rosen Publishing Group
Maps, Maps, Maps	E	I	47	Rosen Real Readers	Rosen Publishing Group
Maps: Earth Matters	L	I	250+	Bookworms	Marshall Cavendish
Maps: Getting From Here to There	V	I	250+	Weiss, Harvey	Houghton Mifflin Harcourt
Mara's Clouds	J	F	414	Springboard	Wright Group/McGraw Hill
*Mara's Stories: Glimmers in the Darkness	Y	HF	250+	Schmidt, Gary	Square Fish
Marathon	M	I	551	Big Cat	Pacific Learning
Marathon Race, The	L	F	250+	Reading Safari	Mondo Publishing
Marathon, The	P	RF	250+	Literacy by Design	Rigby
Marble Game, The	F	RF	250+	Reading Safari	Mondo Publishing
Marble Patch, The	J	RF	250+	PM Story Books	Rigby
Marbles	P	I	250+	Games Around the World	Compass Point Books
Marbles	L	I	475	Red Rocket Readers	Flying Start Books
Marcella	L	RF	250+	Literacy 2000	Rigby
March Along with Me	D	F	56	Literacy 2000	Rigby
March for Freedom	J	I	132	Twig	Wright Group/McGraw Hill
March of the Ankylosaurus: Dinosaur Cove	N	F	250+	Stone, Rex	Scholastic
March on Washington, The	P	I	304	Vocabulary Readers	Houghton Mifflin Harcourt
March to the Park	K	F	444	Leveled Literacy Intervention/ Blue System	Heinemann
March, March, Marching	D	RF	60	Teacher's Choice Series	Pearson Learning Group
Marching Band	LB	RF	35	Urmston, Kathleen; Evans, Karen	Kaeden Books
Marching Bands	L	I	166	Vocabulary Readers	Houghton Mifflin Harcourt
Marching Bands	L	I	166	Vocabulary Readers/CA	Houghton Mifflin Harcourt
Marching to Freedom: The Story of Martin Luther King, Jr.	P	B	250+	Milton, Joyce	Bantam Books
Marching with Aunt Susan	Q	HF	250+	Murphy, Claire Rudolf	Peachtree
Marcias's Madness: The Sisters 8	Q	F	250+	Baratz-Logsted, Lauren	Sandpiper Books
Marcie's Birthday Dig	Q	RF	250+	Leveled Readers Language Support	Houghton Mifflin Harcourt
Marco Polo: History's Great Adventurer	Y	B	250+	Twist, Clint	Candlewick Press
Marco Polo: Marco Polo and the Silk Road to China	U	B	250+	Exploring the World	Compass Point Books
Marco Saves Grandpa	I	RF	232	Foundations	Wright Group/McGraw Hill
Marco's Run	G	RF	199	Green Light Readers	Harcourt
Mardi Gras	H	I	84	Vocabulary Readers	Houghton Mifflin Harcourt
Mare for Young Wolf, A	L	HF	250+	Shefelman, Janice	Random House
Margaret Bourke-White	O	B	250+	Welch, Catherine	Carolrhoda Books
Margaret Bourke-White: A Photographer's Life	P	B	250+	Keller, Emily	Lerner Publishing Group

TITLE	LEVEL	GENRE	WORD COUNT	AUTHOR / SERIES	PUBLISHER / DISTRIBUTOR
Margaret Bourke-White: Life Through the Lens	X	B	3041	Leveled Readers	Houghton Mifflin Harcourt
Margaret E. Mooney: Essentially M	R	B	250+	Author at Work	Richard C. Owen
Margaret Mahy	L	B	250+	Sunshine	Wright Group/McGraw Hill
Margaret Wise Brown	O	B	250+	Greene, Carol	Children's Press
Margarito's Carvings	L	I	250+	Little Celebrations	Pearson Learning Group
Margo and Marky's Adventures in Reading	N	F	250+	In the Library	Picture Window Books
Margret and Hans Rey	J	I	237	Leveled Readers	Houghton Mifflin Harcourt
Margret and Hans Rey	J	I	237	Leveled Readers/CA	Houghton Mifflin Harcourt
Margret and Hans Rey	J	I	237	Leveled Readers/TX	Houghton Mifflin Harcourt
Maria	I	RF	72	City Kids	Rigby
Maria and Mr. Feathers	K	RF	250+	Kimball, Hannah	Pearson Learning Group
Maria and the Baker's Bread	K	TL	250+	Liu, Daphne	Hampton Brown
Maria Goes to School	E	RF	174	Foundations	Wright Group/McGraw Hill
Maria Mitchell	O	B	291	Independent Readers Science	Houghton Mifflin Harcourt
Maria Sanz de Sautuola	S	B	250+	Bookshop	Mondo Publishing
Maria Sharapova	P	B	250+	Amazing Athletes	Lerner Publishing Group
Maria Tallchief	E	B	48	Independent Readers Social Studies	Houghton Mifflin Harcourt
Maria Tallchief	R	B	250+	Native American Histoies	Steck-Vaughn
Maria Tallchief American Ballerina	P	B	1355	Leveled Readers/CA	Houghton Mifflin Harcourt
Maria Tallchief American Ballerina	P	B	1355	Leveled Readers/TX	Houghton Mifflin Harcourt
Maria Tallchief, American Ballerina	P	B	1355	Leveled Readers	Houghton Mifflin Harcourt
Maria Tallchief: Prima Ballerina	N	B	250+	Beginning Biographies	Pearson Learning Group
Maria von Trapp: Beyond the Sound of Music	V	B	250+	Trailblazer Biographies	Carolrhoda Books
Maria: A Christmas Story	R	RF	250+	Taylor, Theodore	Avon Books
Mariachi Band, The	A	I	32	In Step Readers	Rigby
Mariachi Kid, The	O	B	250+	WorldScapes	ETA/Cuisenaire
Marian Anderson	N	B	246	First Biographies	Capstone Press
Marian Anderson	R	B	4112	History Maker Bios	Lerner Publishing Group
Marian Anderson, American Hero	M	B	645	Leveled Readers Social Studies	Houghton Mifflin Harcourt
Marian Anderson: Singer	V	B	250+	American Women of Achievement	Chelsea House
Marian Wright Edelman: For Every Child	S	B	2406	Leveled Readers	Houghton Mifflin Harcourt
Maria's Diary	R	RF	250+	Wonder World	Wright Group/McGraw Hill
Maria's Dream	U	SF	250+	Reading Safari	Mondo Publishing
Maria's House	F	RF	138	Seedlings	Continental Press
Maria's Nonna	I	RF	467	Rigby Flying Colors	Rigby
Marie Antoinette Queen of France	T	B	250+	Queens and Princesses	Capstone Press
Marie Curie	P	B	250+	Early Biographies	Compass Point Books
Marie Curie	R	B	250+	Getting to Know the World's Greatest Inventors and Scientists	Children's Press
Marie Curie	R	B	3486	History Maker Bios	Lerner Publishing Group
Marie Curie	S	B	1924	Independent Readers Science	Houghton Mifflin Harcourt
Marie Curie	N	B	182	Pebble Books	Capstone Press
#Marie Curie and Radioactivity	T	B	250+	Inventions and Discovery	Capstone Press
Marie Curie: Mother of Modern Physics	Y	B	250+	Sterling Biographies	Sterling Publishing
Marie Curie: Pioneering Physicist	V	B	250+	Science Readers	Teacher Created Materials
Marie Mitchell	O	B	250+	Independent Readers Science	Houghton Mifflin Harcourt
Marie: Summer in the Country	Q	HF	250+	Girlhood Journeys	Aladdin
Mariel of Redwall	Z	F	250+	Jacques, Brian	Avon Books
Mariela's Camping Adventure	I	RF	338	In Step Readers	Rigby
Marie-Maud	J	I	515	Leveled Readers Language Support	Houghton Mifflin Harcourt
Marie-Maud Becomes a Citizen	L	RF	563	Leveled Readers Social Studies	Houghton Mifflin Harcourt
Marigold and Grandma on the Town	J	F	250+	Calmenson, Stephanie	HarperTrophy

TITLE	LEVEL	GENRE	WORD COUNT	AUTHOR / SERIES	PUBLISHER / DISTRIBUTOR
Marigold and the Feather of Hope, the Journey Begins: The Fairy Chronicles	Q	F	13340	Sweet, J.H.	Sourcebooks
Marigolds for Dona Remedios	M	RF	250+	Story Vines	Wright Group/McGraw Hill
Marina Silva: Conserving the Rain Forest	N	B	812	Leveled Readers Science	Houghton Mifflin Harcourt
Marine Life	S	I	2605	Reading Street	Pearson
^Marines of the U.S. Marine Corps	N	I	168	People of the U.S. Armed Forces	Capstone Press
Mario Mixwell	M	B	250+	Take Two Books	Wright Group/McGraw Hill
Mario Molina: Above the Clouds	X	B	2464	Leveled Readers Science	Houghton Mifflin Harcourt
Marion Jones: Quest for Gold	R	B	1337	Leveled Readers	Houghton Mifflin Harcourt
Mario's Mayan Journey	P	F	250+	Bookshop	Mondo Publishing
Marisol's Mystery	H	RF	245	Literacy by Design	Rigby
Marjorie Harris Carr	O	B	546	Leveled Readers Science	Houghton Mifflin Harcourt
Marjory Stoneman Douglas	N	B	294	Independent Readers Social Studies	Houghton Mifflin Harcourt
Mark McGuire, Home Run King	P	B	250+	Leveled Readers Language Support	Houghton Mifflin Harcourt
Mark McGwire	R	B	250+	Sports Heroes	Red Brick Learning
Mark McGwire: Home Run Hero	Q	B	960	Leveled Readers	Houghton Mifflin Harcourt
Mark Sanchez	P	B	2125	Amazing Athletes	Lerner Publishing Group
Mark Twain	V	B	250+	A&E Biography	Lerner Publishing Group
Mark Twain	W	B	250+	Cox, Clinton	Scholastic
Mark Twain	V	B	250+	Just the Facts Biographies	Lerner Publishing Group
Mark T-W-A-I-N: A Story About Samuel Clemens	R	B	8718	Creative Minds Biographies	Carolrhoda Books
Mark Twain: Young Writer	O	B	250+	Childhood of Famous Americans	Aladdin
Mark, The	Z	F	250+	Nadol, jen	Bloomsbury Children's Books
Marked: (House of Night)	Z+	F	250+	Cast, P. C. & Kristin	St. Martin's Griffin
Market Day for Mrs. Wordy	J	RF	177	Sunshine	Wright Group/McGraw Hill
Market, The	D	RF	48	Joy Readers	Pearson Learning Group
Market, The	A	I	15	Leveled Readers	Houghton Mifflin Harcourt
Market, The	A	I	15	Leveled Readers/CA	Houghton Mifflin Harcourt
Market, The	B	F	30	Sails	Rigby
Marketplace, The	E	RF	58	Visions	Wright Group/McGraw Hill
Markets	D	I	44	Chanko, Pamela; Berger, Samantha	Scholastic
Markets	F	I	68	Our Global Community	Heinemann Library
Markets Around the World	O	I	871	Time for Kids	Teacher Created Materials
Markie the Moonman	T	SF	2759	Reading Street	Pearson
Marks in the Sand	F	I	121	Windows on Literacy	National Geographic
Mark's Monster	I	F	250+	Reading Unlimited	Pearson Learning Group
Marla's Idea	J	RF	443	Reading Street	Pearson
Marlfox: A Novel of Redwall	Z	F	250+	Jacques, Brian	Ace Books
Marmalade's Nap	F	F	57	Wheeler, Cindy	Alfred A. Knopf
Marmalade's Snowy Day	F	F	61	Wheeler, Cindy	Alfred A. Knopf
Marrying Malcolm Murgatroyd	T	RF	250+	Farrell, Mame	Sunburst
Mars	Q	I	1821	Early Bird Astronomy	Lerner Publishing Group
Mars	J	I	139	Exploring the Galaxy	Capstone Press
Mars	S	I	250+	Our Solar System	Compass Point Books
Mars	N	I	829	Our Universe	Lerner Publishing Group
Mars	L	I	220	Rigby Focus	Rigby
Mars	Q	I	250+	The Galaxy	Capstone Press
Mars	M	I	250+	The Solar System	Capstone Press
Mars	R	I	250+	Theme Sets	National Geographic
^Mars	W	I	250+	World Mythology	Capstone Press

* Collection of short stories   # Graphic text
^ Mature content with lower level text demands

TITLE	LEVEL	GENRE	WORD COUNT	AUTHOR / SERIES	PUBLISHER / DISTRIBUTOR
Mars and Venus: Space Exploration	V	I	250+	Navigators Science Series	Benchmark Education
Mars on Earth	W	I	2610	Leveled Readers	Houghton Mifflin Harcourt
Mars on Earth	W	I	2610	Leveled Readers/CA	Houghton Mifflin Harcourt
Mars on Earth	W	I	2610	Leveled Readers/TX	Houghton Mifflin Harcourt
Mars, Our Closest Neighbor	S	I	1366	Leveled Readers Science	Houghton Mifflin Harcourt
Mars: Mysteries of the Red Planet	X	I	3297	Leveled Readers	Houghton Mifflin Harcourt
Mars: The Red Planet	L	I	250+	Rosen Real Readers	Rosen Publishing Group
Marsh Island	N	RF	250+	Orca Echoes	Orca Books
Marsh Morning	P	RF	482	Berkes, Marianne	Millbrook Press
Marsh Music	P	F	304	Berkes, Marianne	Millbrook Press
Marshall and His Green High-Tops	L	F	250+	Amy, Camille Blue	Camille Publishing
Marshfield Dreams: When I Was a Kid	S	B	250+	Fletcher, Ralph	Henry Holt & Co.
Marta and the Bicycle	K	F	250+	Zullo, Germano	Kane/Miller Book Publishers
Marta's Cupcake Problem	G	RF	168	Early Connections	Benchmark Education
Martha and Skits Out West	N	F	250+	Martha Speaks	Houghton Mifflin Harcourt
Martha Berry: A Woman of Courageous Spirit and Bold Dreams	W	B	250+	Blackburn, Joyce	Peachtree
Martha Calling	L	F	250+	Martha Speaks	Houghton Mifflin Harcourt
Martha Camps Out	K	F	250+	Martha Speaks	Houghton Mifflin Harcourt
Martha Doesn't Say Sorry!	K	F	293	Berger, Samantha	Little Brown and Company
Martha Graham, Modern Dancer	P	B	982	Leveled Readers	Houghton Mifflin Harcourt
Martha in the Middle	L	F	250+	Fearnley, Jan	Candlewick Press
Martha on the Case	N	F	250+	Martha Speaks	Houghton Mifflin Harcourt
Martha Says It with Flowers	L	RF	250+	Martha Speaks	Houghton Mifflin Harcourt
Martha Washington	M	B	229	First Ladies	Capstone Press
Martha Washington	N	B	1793	On My Own Biography	Lerner Publishing Group
Martha Washington: America's First First Lady	O	B	250+	Childhood of Famous Americans	Aladdin
Martial Arts	U	I	250+	Boldprint	Steck-Vaughn
^Martial Arts	R	I	250+	Download	Hameray Publishing Group
Martial Arts	R	I	250+	Orbit Chapter Books	Pacific Learning
Martial Arts for Fun!	S	I	250+	Activities for Fun	Compass Point Books
Martian Goo	E	F	65	Salem, Lynn; Stewart, Josie	Continental Press
Martians Are People, Too	N	F	250+	Navigators Fiction Series	Benchmark Education
Martians Don't Take Temperatures	M	F	250+	Dadey, Debbie; Jones, Marcia Thornton	Scholastic
Martin and the Teacher's Pets	K	RF	250+	Chardiet, Bernice; Maccarone, Grace	Scholastic
Martin and the Tooth Fairy	K	RF	250+	Chardiet, Bernice; Maccarone, Grace	Scholastic
Martin Luther King	T	B	250+	Bray, Rosemary L.	William Morrow
Martin Luther King	X	B	9871	Oxford Bookworms Library	Oxford University Press
Martin Luther King Day	L	I	250+	Lowery, Linda	Scholastic
Martin Luther King Jr.	S	B	250+	Amazing Americans	Wright Group/McGraw Hill
Martin Luther King Jr.	Q	B	250+	Early Biographies	Compass Point Books
Martin Luther King Jr.	S	B	3426	History Maker Bios	Lerner Publishing Group
Martin Luther King Jr.	W	B	250+	Just the Facts Biographies	Lerner Publishing Group
Martin Luther King Jr.	S	B	250+	Primary Source Readers	Teacher Created Materials
Martin Luther King Jr. Day	I	I	125	American Holidays	Lerner Publishing Group
Martin Luther King Jr. Day	Q	I	250+	Holiday Histories	Heinemann
Martin Luther King Jr. Day	O	I	1693	On My Own Holidays	Lerner Publishing Group
Martin Luther King Jr.: A Life of Determination	O	B	486	Pull Ahead Books	Lerner Publishing Group
^Martin Luther King Jr.: A Powerful Voice for Peaceful Change	S	B	250+	Hameray Biography Series	Hameray Publishing Group
#Martin Luther King Jr.: Great Civil Rights Leader	S	B	250+	Graphic Library	Capstone Press

TITLE	LEVEL	GENRE	WORD COUNT	AUTHOR / SERIES	PUBLISHER / DISTRIBUTOR
Martin Luther King, Day	M	I	274	Holidays and Festivals	Heinemann Library
Martin Luther King, Jr.	M	B	290	Famous Americans	Capstone Press
Martin Luther King, Jr.	P	B	250+	Photo-Illustrated Biographies	Red Brick Learning
Martin Luther King, Jr.	O	B	250+	Rookie Biographies	Children's Press
Martin Luther King, Jr.	J	I	110	Shutterbug Books	Steck-Vaughn
Martin Luther King, Jr.	Q	B	798	Time for Kids	Teacher Created Materials
Martin Luther King, Jr. and the March on Washington	M	I	250+	All Aboard Reading	Grosset & Dunlap
Martin Luther King, Jr. and the March Toward Freedom	R	B	250+	Hakim, Rita	Millbrook Press
Martin Luther King, Jr. Day	L	I	138	National Holidays	Capstone Press
Martin Luther King, Jr., A Man Who Changed Things	O	B	250+	Greene, Carol	Children's Press
Martin Luther King, Jr.: Preacher, Freedom Fighter, Peacemaker	M	B	250+	Biographies	Picture Window Books
Martin Luther King, Jr.: Young Man with a Dream	O	B	250+	Childhood of Famous Americans	Aladdin
Martin Luther King: Dreaming of Equality	V	B	250+	Trailblazer Biographies	Carolrhoda Books
Martin Van Buren	U	B	250+	Profiles of the Presidents	Compass Point Books
Martin Van Buren: Eighth President	R	B	250+	Getting to Know the U.S. Presidents	Children's Press
Martina the Beautiful Cockroach	P	TL	1037	Deedy, Carmen Agra	Peachtree
Martin's Mice	P	F	250+	King-Smith, Dick	Alfred A. Knopf
Martin's Mighty Hit	M	RF	390	Windmill Books	Rigby
Marty Ardvark	J	F	250+	Let's Read Together	Kane Press
Marty Solves a Mystery	M	RF	1391	In Step Readers	Rigby
Marvella and the Moon	F	F	250+	Bookshop	Mondo Publishing
Marvelous Mammals	F	I	99	Independent Readers Science	Houghton Mifflin Harcourt
Marvelous Marine Animals	S	I	1000	Leveled Readers/TX	Houghton Mifflin Harcourt
Marvelous Me	F	F	29	Literacy 2000	Rigby
Marvelous Me Helping in Discovery Peak	E	RF	96	Run to Reading	Discovery Peak
Marvelous Me Inside and Out	K	RF	250+	All About Me	Picture Window Books
Marvelous Me Taking Care of Myself	A	I	33	Run to Reading	Discovery Peak
Marvelous Menus	N	F	250+	Sails	Rigby
Marvelous Metals	U	I	1616	Independent Readers Science	Houghton Mifflin Harcourt
Marvelous Migration	Q	I	1398	Reading Street	Pearson
Marvelous Treasure, The	M	RF	481	Sunshine	Wright Group/McGraw Hill
Marvin and the Mean Words	M	RF	250+	Kline, Suzy	PaperStar
Marvin One Too Many	J	RF	250+	Paterson, Katherine	HarperCollins
Marvin Redpost (Class President)	M	RF	250+	Sachar, Louis	Random House
Marvin Redpost, Super Fast, Out of Control!	M	RF	250+	Sachar, Louis	Random House
Marvin Redpost: A Flying Birthday Cake?	M	RF	250+	Sachar, Louis	Random House
Marvin Redpost: Alone in His Teacher's House	M	RF	250+	Sachar, Louis	Random House
Marvin Redpost: Is He a Girl?	M	RF	250+	Sachar, Louis	Random House
Marvin Redpost: Kidnapped at Birth?	M	RF	250+	Sachar, Louis	Random House
Marvin Redpost: Why Pick on Me?	M	RF	250+	Sachar, Louis	Random House
Marvin, the Christmas Cat	N	F	250+	Tristars	Richard C. Owen
Marvin's Birthday	K	RF	250+	Pacific Literacy	Pacific Learning
Marvin's Egg	H	F	501	Sails	Rigby
Marvin's Manners	E	RF	32	Pair-It Books	Steck-Vaughn
Marvin's Trip to Mars	I	F	571	Appleton-Smith, Laura	Flyleaf Publishing
Marvin's Woolly Mammoth	I	F	264	Sails	Rigby
#Marwe: Into the Land of the Dead	R	TL	1780	Graphic Myths and Legends	Lerner Publishing Group
Mary and Jody in the Movies: Lucky Foot Stable Series	R	RF	41500	Dawson, JoAnn S.	Sourcebooks

* Collection of short stories   # Graphic text
^ Mature content with lower level text demands

TITLE	LEVEL	GENRE	WORD COUNT	AUTHOR / SERIES	PUBLISHER / DISTRIBUTOR
Mary Anning, Fossil Hunter	R	B	1307	Independent Readers Science	Houghton Mifflin Harcourt
Mary Anning: Fossil Hunter	O	B	1576	On My Own Biography	Lerner Publishing Group
Mary by Myself	Q	F	250+	Smith, Jane Denitz	HarperTrophy
Mary Cassatt	S	B	250+	Masterpieces: Artists and Their Works	Capstone Press
Mary Cassatt: Portrait of an American Impressionist	W	B	250+	Trailblazer Biographies	Carolrhoda Books
Mary Celeste Mystery, The	S	I	250+	Storyteller-Mountain Peaks	Wright Group/McGraw Hill
Mary Had a Little Lamb	K	TL	250+	Trapani, Iza	Charlesbridge
Mary Leakey	W	B	2174	Leveled Readers Social Studies	Houghton Mifflin Harcourt
Mary Marony and the Chocolate Surprise	M	RF	250+	Kline, Suzy	Bantam Books
Mary Marony and the Snake	M	RF	250+	Kline, Suzy	Bantam Books
Mary Marony Hides Out	M	RF	250+	Kline, Suzy	Bantam Books
Mary Marony, Mummy Girl	M	RF	250+	Kline, Suzy	Bantam Books
Mary McLeod Bethune	U	B	250+	Amazing Americans	Wright Group/McGraw Hill
Mary McLeod Bethune	U	B	250+	Cornerstones of Freedom	Children's Press
Mary McLeod Bethune	O	B	250+	Greenfield, Eloise	HarperTrophy
Mary McLeod Bethune	P	B	250+	Photo-Illustrated Biographies	Red Brick Learning
Mary McLeod Bethune - Voice of Black Hope	S	B	250+	Meltzer, Milton	Puffin Books
Mary McLeod Bethune: A Life of Resourcefulness	O	B	552	Pull Ahead Books	Lerner Publishing Group
Mary McLeod Bethune: Empowering Educator	P	B	250+	Great African Americans	Capstone Press
*Mary on Horseback	Q	RF	250+	Wells, Rosemary	Puffin Books
Mary Todd Lincoln: Girl of the Bluegrass	O	B	250+	Childhood of Famous Americans	Aladdin
Mary Walker: Civil War Surgeon and Feminist	W	B	250+	Signature Lives	Compass Point Books
Mary Wore Her Red Dress	D	F	170	Peek, Merle	Clarion
Mary, Mary	D	TL	21	Jumbled Tumbled Tales & Rhymes	Rigby
Mary, Queen of Scots	Z	HF	6540	Oxford Bookworms Library	Oxford University Press
Maryland	T	I	250+	Hello U.S.A.	Lerner Publishing Group
Maryland	S	I	250+	Land of Liberty	Red Brick Learning
Maryland	R	I	250+	This Land Is Your Land	Compass Point Books
Maryland Colony, The	R	I	250+	The American Colonies	Capstone Press
Maryland: Facts and Symbols	O	I	250+	The States and Their Symbols	Capstone Press
Mascot, The	K	RF	558	In Step Readers	Rigby
^Maserati	O	I	250+	Fast Cars	Capstone Press
Mask Book, The	L	I	217	Twig	Wright Group/McGraw Hill
Mask Makers, The	K	RF	242	Leveled Readers	Houghton Mifflin Harcourt
Mask, The	E	I	45	Pair-It Books	Steck-Vaughn
Masks	J	I	136	Gear Up!	Wright Group/McGraw Hill
Masks	M	I	250+	Literacy 2000	Rigby
Masks	C	I	41	Pebble Books	Capstone Press
Masks	F	I	125	Red Rocket Readers	Flying Start Books
Masks	D	I	109	Sails	Rigby
Masks	E	I	62	Wonder World	Wright Group/McGraw Hill
Masks and Face Painting	M	I	250+	Start with Art	Heinemann Library
Masquerade	Z	F	250+	De La Cruz, Melissa	Hyperion
Mass Production and the Model T: Building the Car for Everyone	R	I	250+	Literacy by Design	Rigby
Massachusetts	T	I	250+	Hello U.S.A.	Lerner Publishing Group
Massachusetts	S	I	250+	Land of Liberty	Red Brick Learning
Massachusetts	T	I	250+	Theme Sets	National Geographic
Massachusetts	R	I	250+	This Land Is Your Land	Compass Point Books
Massachusetts 54th, The: African American Soldiers of the Union	V	I	250+	Let Freedom Ring	Capstone Press

* Collection of short stories   # Graphic text
^ Mature content with lower level text demands

TITLE	LEVEL	GENRE	WORD COUNT	AUTHOR / SERIES	PUBLISHER / DISTRIBUTOR
Massachusetts Bay Colony, The	R	I	250+	The American Colonies	Capstone Press
Massachusetts: Facts and Symbols	O	I	250+	The States and Their Symbols	Capstone Press
Massie: The Clique Summer Collection	X	RF	250+	Harrison, Lisi	Little Brown and Company
#Master of Shadows, The: Book Three	S	F	3045	The Elsewhere Chronicles	Lerner Publishing Group
Master of the Weather	O	F	250+	The Adventures of Sam X	Stone Arch Books
Master Puppeteer, The	X	HF	250+	Paterson, Katherine	HarperCollins
Masterpiece	U	F	250+	Broach, Elise	Henry Holt & Co.
Masterpiece, The	K	F	250+	Storyteller-Lightning Bolts	Wright Group/McGraw Hill
Mastiffs Are the Best!	Q	I	1064	The Best Dogs Ever	Lerner Publishing Group
Matchbox Collection, A	K	I	250+	Stepping Stones	Nelson/Michaels Assoc.
Matchbox, The	S	HF	250+	Literacy 2000	Rigby
Matchlock Gun, The	P	HF	250+	Edmonds, Walter D.	G.P. Putnam's Sons Books for Young Readers
Material Resources	R	I	1932	Science Support Readers	Houghton Mifflin Harcourt
Materializer, The	S	SF	250+	Sails	Rigby
Materials	L	I	250+	Discovery World	Rigby
Materials Science	Z	I	7192	Cool Science	Lerner Publishing Group
Math Around the Globe	T	I	250+	Navigators Math Series	Benchmark Education
Math at the Olympics	T	I	250+	Navigators Math Series	Benchmark Education
Math at the Store	G	I	127	Amato, William	Scholastic
Math Bee, The	P	B	795	Leveled Readers	Houghton Mifflin Harcourt
Math Chat: A Glossary of Terms	M	I	250+	Twig	Wright Group/McGraw Hill
Math Counts	L	I	250+	Pluckrose, Henry	Scholastic
Math Fair Blues	K	RF	250+	Math Matters	Kane Press
Math in a Democracy	T	I	250+	Navigators Math Series	Benchmark Education
Math in the Garden	R	I	250+	Navigators Math Series	Benchmark Education
Math Is Everywhere	F	I	95	Sunshine	Wright Group/McGraw Hill
Math Master, The	N	RF	250+	Literacy by Design	Rigby
Math Master, The	N	RF	250+	On Our Way to English	Rigby
Math on the Moon	O	I	250+	Navigators Math Series	Benchmark Education
Math to Build On	U	I	250+	Navigators Math Series	Benchmark Education
Math to Munch On	T	I	250+	Navigators Math Series	Benchmark Education
Math Today and Tomorrow	T	SF	2035	Leveled Readers	Houghton Mifflin Harcourt
Math Today and Tomorrow	T	SF	2035	Leveled Readers/CA	Houghton Mifflin Harcourt
Math Today and Tomorrow	T	SF	2035	Leveled Readers/TX	Houghton Mifflin Harcourt
Math- Who Needs It?	J	I	366	In Step Readers	Rigby
Math Wiz, The	N	RF	250+	Duffey, Betsy	Penguin Group
Mathematical Thinkers	T	I	250+	Navigators Math Series	Benchmark Education
Mathew Brady: Civil War Photographer	T	B	250+	A First Book	Franklin Watts
Math-terpieces: The Art of Problem-Solving	Q	I	250+	Tang, Greg	Scholastic
Matilda	S	F	250+	Dahl, Roald	Penguin Group
Matilda Bone	X	HF	250+	Cushman, Karen	Clarion
Matilda's Plans	O	F	250+	Sails	Rigby
Matisse	S	B	250+	Masterpieces: Artists and Their Works	Capstone Press
Matsumura's Ice Sculpture	I	I	94	iOpeners	Pearson Learning Group
Matt Drives the Car	D	RF	136	Early Emergent, Set 3	Pioneer Valley
Matter	Q	I	2389	Early Bird Energy	Lerner Publishing Group
Matter	X	I	250+	Mission: Science	Compass Point Books
^Matter	P	I	250+	Our Physical World	Capstone Press
Matter and Energy: Finding the Power	Q	I	250+	iScience	Norwood House Press
Matter in Ecosystems	R	I	1861	Science Support Readers	Houghton Mifflin Harcourt
Matter of Balance, A	L	B	250+	Voyages	SRA/McGraw Hill

* Collection of short stories   # Graphic text
^ Mature content with lower level text demands

TITLE	LEVEL	GENRE	WORD COUNT	AUTHOR / SERIES	PUBLISHER / DISTRIBUTOR
Matter of Conscience, A: The Trial of Anne Hutchinson	U	HF	250+	Nichols, Joan Kane	Steck-Vaughn
Matter of Trust, A	Z	RF	250+	Schraff, Anne	Townsend Press
Matter Splatter!	T	I	250+	InfoQuest	Rigby
Matter, Matter Everywhere	W	I	250+	Reading Expeditions	National Geographic
Matter: See It, Touch It, Taste It, Smell It	N	I	250+	Amazing Science	Picture Window Books
Matthew and Emma	C	RF	49	PM Stars	Rigby
Matthew and Tilly	L	RF	250+	Jones, Rebecca C.	Penguin Group
Matthew Henson	L	B	250+	Biography	Benchmark Education
Matthew Henson	N	B	207	First Biographies	Capstone Press
Matthew Henson	S	B	3437	History Maker Bios	Lerner Publishing Group
#Matthew Henson: Arctic Adventurer	S	B	250+	Graphic Library	Capstone Press
Matthew Henson: Arctic Explorer	O	B	250+	Sunshine	Wright Group/McGraw Hill
Matthew Likes to Read	J	RF	144	Pacific Literacy	Pacific Learning
Matthew the Magician	E	RF	116	Learn to Read	Creative Teaching Press
Matthew's Meadow	V	RF	250+	Bliss, Corinne Demas	Harcourt Brace
Matthew's Story: From England to Plimouth Colony	T	HF	250+	Reading Expeditions	National Geographic
Matthew's Tantrum	J	RF	250+	Literacy 2000	Rigby
Mattimeo: A Tale from Redwall	Z	F	250+	Jacques, Brian	Avon Books
Matt's Cairo Caper	U	RF	250+	WorldScapes	ETA/Cuisenaire
Matt's Good Idea	G	RF	226	PM Stars	Rigby
Maud and Anne	W	B	2073	Leveled Readers	Houghton Mifflin Harcourt
Maud and Anne	W	B	2073	Leveled Readers/CA	Houghton Mifflin Harcourt
Maud and Anne	W	B	2073	Leveled Readers/TX	Houghton Mifflin Harcourt
Maui and the Sun	M	TL	359	Pacific Literacy	Pacific Learning
Maui and the Sun	I	TL	267	Story Box	Wright Group/McGraw Hill
Maui and the Wind	N	TL	799	Springboard	Wright Group/McGraw Hill
Maura's Angel	X	F	250+	Banks, Lynne Reid	Avon Books
Maurice Sendak	L	B	201	First Biographies	Red Brick Learning
Max	M	F	250+	Graham, Bob	Candlewick Press
Max	J	RF	234	Isadora, Rachel	Macmillan
Max & Mo Go Apple Picking	I	F	250+	Lakin, Patricia	Aladdin
Max & Mo Make a Snowman	I	F	284	Lakin, Patricia	Aladdin
Max and Jake	G	RF	212	PM Plus Story Books	Rigby
Max and Maddy and the Bursting Balloons Mystery	O	RF	250+	Smith, Alexander McCall	Bloomsbury Children's Books
Max and Maddy and the Chocolate Money Mystery	O	RF	250+	Smith, Alexander McCall	Bloomsbury Children's Books
Max and Maddy and the Chocolate Money Mystery	O	RF	250+	Smith, Alexander McCall	Bloomsbury Children's Books
Max and Me and the Time Machine	T	SF	250+	Greer, Gery; Ruddick, Bob	HarperTrophy
Max and Mintie	K	F	250+	Home Connection Collection	Rigby
Max and the Alpaca	L	F	828	Sun Sprouts	ETA/Cuisenaire
Max and the Apples	E	F	189	Storyworlds	Heinemann
Max and the Birdhouse	G	RF	190	PM Plus Story Books	Rigby
Max and the Cat	E	F	154	Storyworlds	Heinemann
Max and the Clouds	E	F	211	Sun Sprouts	ETA/Cuisenaire
Max and the Drum	E	F	171	Storyworlds	Heinemann
Max and the Little Plant	E	RF	134	PM Plus Story Books	Rigby
Max and the Storm	I	F	475	Sun Sprouts	ETA/Cuisenaire
Max at the Fair	H	F	245	Sun Sprouts	ETA/Cuisenaire
Max Celebrates Ramadan	I	RF	196	Read-it! Readers	Picture Window Books
Max Comes Home	A	RF	24	First Stories	Pacific Learning
Max Gets Ready	C	RF	48	Rigby Literacy	Rigby

TITLE	LEVEL	GENRE	WORD COUNT	AUTHOR / SERIES	PUBLISHER / DISTRIBUTOR
Max Gets Ready	C	RF	48	Rigby Star	Rigby
Max Goes Fishing	E	RF	147	PM Plus Story Books	Rigby
Max Goes Shopping	E	RF	103	Read-It! Readers	Picture Window Books
Max Goes to the Farmers' Market	E	RF	140	Read-it! Readers	Picture Window Books
Max Goes to the Fire Station	F	RF	191	Read-it! Readers	Picture Window Books
Max Goes to the Nature Center	E	RF	197	Read-it! Readers	Picture Window Books
Max Goes to the Recycling Center	F	RF	163	Read-it! Readers	Picture Window Books
Max in a Tree	D	F	86	Sun Sprouts	ETA/Cuisenaire
Max Is a Star!	F	RF	160	Leveled Readers Language Support	Houghton Mifflin Harcourt
Max Jumps	B	F	37	Sun Sprouts	ETA/Cuisenaire
Max Malone and the Great Cereal Rip-off	N	RF	250+	Herman, Charlotte	Henry Holt & Co.
Max Malone Makes a Million	N	RF	250+	Herman, Charlotte	Henry Holt & Co.
Max Malone the Magnificent	N	RF	250+	Herman, Charlotte	Scholastic
Max Malone, Superstar	N	RF	250+	Herman, Charlotte	Scholastic
Max Monkey	C	F	57	Red Rocket Readers	Flying Start Books
Max on a Hill	E	F	80	Sun Sprouts	ETA/Cuisenaire
Max on Ice	E	F	219	Sun Sprouts	ETA/Cuisenaire
Max Planck: Revolutionary Physicist	Y	B	250+	Mission: Science	Compass Point Books
Max Planck: Uncovering the World of Matter	W	B	250+	Science Readers	Teacher Created Materials
Max Rides His Bike	E	RF	143	PM Plus Story Books	Rigby
Max Saves a Frog	G	RF	208	PM Stars	Rigby
Max the Man Mountain	Q	RF	250+	McFarlane, Peter	HarperCollins
Max the Mighty	W	RF	250+	Philbrick, Rodman	Scholastic
Max the Mouse and the Moon	Q	F	250+	Reading Safari	Mondo Publishing
Max the Pet Show Star	G	RF	175	Leveled Readers	Houghton Mifflin Harcourt
Max Visits London	K	RF	250+	Leveled Readers Language Support	Houghton Mifflin Harcourt
Max Wants to Fly	E	F	159	Storyworlds	Heinemann
Max, Honey and Hay	J	F	496	Sun Sprouts	ETA/Cuisenaire
Max, Our School Dog	D	I	51	Kaleidoscope Collection	Hameray Publishing Group
Max: A Maximum Ride Novel	X	SF	250+	Patterson, James	Little Brown and Company
Maxie, Rosie, and Earl - Partners in Grime	O	RF	250+	Park, Barbara	Random House
Maximum Ride: Saving the World and Other Extreme Sports	X	SF	250+	Patterson, James	Little Brown and Company
Maximum Ride: School's Out-Forever	X	SF	250+	Patterson, James	Little Brown and Company
Maximum Ride: The Angel Experiment	X	SF	250+	Patterson, James	Little Brown and Company
Maximum Ride: The Final Warning	X	SF	250+	Patterson, James	Little Brown and Company
Max's ABC	K	F	250+	Wells, Rosemary	Penguin Group
Max's Box	B	RF	43	Little Celebrations	Pearson Learning Group
Max's Glasses	L	RF	250+	Navigators Fiction Series	Benchmark Education
Max's Job	G	RF	170	Early Explorers	Benchmark Education
Max's New Friend	K	F	250+	Rigby Rocket	Rigby
Maxwell Moose's Mountain Monster	J	F	642	Animal Antics A to Z	Kane Press
Maxwell's Moutain	L	F	250+	Becker, Shari	Charlesbridge
May Chinn: The Best Medicine	U	B	250+	Butts, Ellen; Schwartz, Joyce	W. H. Freeman & Co.
May I Please Have a Cookie?	F	F	199	Morris, Jennifer E.	Scholastic
May I Stay Home Today?	E	RF	73	Tadpoles	Rigby
May Search	F	I	164	Shutterbug Books	Steck-Vaughn
Maya Angelou	Z	B	250+	Just the Facts Biographies	Lerner Publishing Group
Maya Angelou	W	B	250+	Spain, Valerie	Random House
Maya Angelou: Greeting the Morning	W	B	250+	King, Sarah E.	Millbrook Press
Maya Angelou: Journey of the Heart	W	B	250+	Pettit, Jayne	Puffin Books
Maya Angelou: Poet, Performer, Activist	Z	B	250+	Signature Lives	Compass Point Books

* Collection of short stories   # Graphic text
^ Mature content with lower level text demands

TITLE	LEVEL	GENRE	WORD COUNT	AUTHOR / SERIES	PUBLISHER / DISTRIBUTOR
Maya in the Past and Present, The	T	I	250+	Reading Expeditions	National Geographic
Maya Lin: Architect	N	B	250+	Beginning Biographies	Pearson Learning Group
Maya Moore	P	B	1884	Amazing Athletes	Lerner Publishing Group
Maya the Adventureless	P	F	250+	Scooters	ETA/Cuisenaire
Maya, The	P	I	250+	A New True Book	Children's Press
Maya, The	R	I	250+	First Reports	Compass Point Books
Maya, The	S	I	250+	Journey Into Civilization	Chelsea House
Maya, The	U	I	250+	Navigators Social Studies Series	Benchmark Education
^Mayan Writing in Mesoamerica	U	I	250+	On Deck	Rigby
Mayas Incas and Aztecs	X	I	250+	Primary Source Readers	Teacher Created Materials
Maya's Storm	P	RF	250+	In Step Readers	Rigby
Maybe I'll Be	D	F	49	Carousel Readers	Pearson Learning Group
Maybe Later	N	F	250+	Orca Echoes	Orca Books
Maybe Yes, Maybe No, Maybe Maybe	M	RF	250+	Patron, Susan	Bantam Books
Maybelle Goes to Tea	L	F	250+	Speck, Katie	Square Fish
Maybelle in the Soup	L	F	250+	Speck, Katie	Square Fish
Mayflower Compact, The	W	I	250+	Reading Expeditions	National Geographic
Mayflower, The	R	I	250+	The Library of the Pilgrims	Rosen Publishing Group
Mayor Mom	K	RF	315	Reading Street	Pearson
Mayors	L	I	250+	Community Workers	Compass Point Books
Mayors	M	I	630	Pull Ahead Books	Lerner Publishing Group
Maze Craze, The	N	I	250+	Pacific Literacy	Pacific Learning
Maze of Bones, The (The 39 Clues)	U	F	250+	Riordan, Rick	Scholastic
Maze Race, The	J	F	442	Springboard	Wright Group/McGraw Hill
Maze Runner, The	X	SF	250+	Dashner, James	Delacorte Press
Maze, The	V	RF	250+	Hobbs, Will	Morrow Junior Books
Mazes Are Amazing!	K	I	220	Vocabulary Readers	Houghton Mifflin Harcourt
*McBroom's Wonderful One-Acre Farm	O	F	250+	Fleischman, Sid	Beech Tree Books
McBungle's African Safari	I	F	336	Traditional Tales & More	Rigby
McFig & McFly	P	F	250+	Drescher, Henrik	Candlewick Press
McGinty's Friend	L	F	250+	Sails	Rigby
McMurdo Station	P	I	860	Leveled Readers	Houghton Mifflin Harcourt
McMurdo Station	P	I	860	Leveled Readers/CA	Houghton Mifflin Harcourt
McMurdo Station	P	I	860	Leveled Readers/TX	Houghton Mifflin Harcourt
Me	LB	RF	15	Handprints A	Educators Publishing Service
Me	A	I	24	PM Starters	Rigby
Me	C	RF	41	Reading Corners	Pearson Learning Group
Me (boy)	C	I	34	Tonon, Terry	Kaeden Books
Me (girl)	C	I	34	Tonon, Terry	Kaeden Books
Me and My Animal Friends	K	F	250+	Covert, Ralph	Henry Holt & Co.
Me and My Brother	C	RF	36	Ohi, Ruth	Annick Press
Me and My Dog	B	RF	55	Lighthouse	Ginn & Co.
Me and My Dog	F	RF	115	Sunshine	Wright Group/McGraw Hill
Me and My Little Brain	T	RF	250+	Fitzgerald, John D.	Dell
Me and My Newt	N	F	250+	High-Fliers	Pacific Learning
Me and My Pup	C	RF	34	Leveled Readers Language Support	Houghton Mifflin Harcourt
Me and My Shadow	H	F	247	Momentum Literacy Program	Troll Associates
Me and My Sister	C	RF	33	Ohi, Ruth	Annick Press
Me and Rupert Goody	Q	RF	250+	O'Connor, Barbara	Scholastic
Me Hungry	I	F	51	Tankard, Jeremy	Candlewick Press
Me Oh Maya	P	F	250+	Scieszka, Jon	Penguin Group
Me on the Map	I	I	250+	Sweeney, Joan	Dragonfly Books

TITLE	LEVEL	GENRE	WORD COUNT	AUTHOR / SERIES	PUBLISHER / DISTRIBUTOR
Me Too	K	RF	136	Mayer, Mercer	Donovan
Me Too!	G	F	200	Bookshop	Mondo Publishing
Me Too!	D	F	70	Sunshine	Wright Group/McGraw Hill
Me!	B	RF	19	Reading Street	Pearson
Me!: Healthy Body, Healthy Mind	Y	I	250+	Boldprint	Steck-Vaughn
Me, Frida	R	B	250+	Novesky, Amy	Harry N. Abrams
Me, Mop, and the Moondance Kid	S	RF	250+	Myers, Walter Dean	Bantam Books
Me, Penelope	Z+	RF	250+	Jahn-Clough, Lisa	Houghton Mifflin Harcourt
Mealworms	P	I	250+	Life Cycles	Capstone Press
Mealworms	K	I	136	Watch It Grow	Capstone Press
Mean Behind the Screen: What You Need To Know About Cyberbullying	Y	I	250+	What's the Issue?	Compass Point Books
Mean Dream Wonder Machine, The	O	F	250+	High-Fliers	Pacific Learning
Mean Giant, The	C	F	69	Sun Sprouts	ETA/Cuisenaire
Mean Machines: A Spot-it Challenge	J	I	250+	Spot It	Capstone Press
Mean 'Ole Crankfender	L	F	1397	Auto-B-Good	Rising Star Studios
Meanest Thing to Say, The	K	RF	250+	Cosby, Bill	Scholastic
Meanies	F	F	158	Story Box	Wright Group/McGraw Hill
Meanies Came to School, The	E	F	135	Story Basket	Wright Group/McGraw Hill
Meanies in the House	H	F	152	The Joy Cowley Collection	Hameray Publishing Group
Meanies' Night Out	I	F	271	The Joy Cowley Collection	Hameray Publishing Group
Meanie's Party, A	I	F	250+	The Story Basket	Wright Group/McGraw Hill
Meanies' Trick, The	E	F	93	Story Box	Wright Group/McGraw Hill
Measure	L	I	229	Spyglass Books	Compass Point Books
Measure and Compare	M	I	354	Early Explorers	Benchmark Education
Measure and Cook	I	I	408	Shutterbug Books	Steck-Vaughn
Measure for Measure	U	I	250+	PM Plus	Rigby
Measure It	H	I	122	Dominie Factivity Series	Pearson Publishing Group
Measure It	C	I	56	Twig	Wright Group/McGraw Hill
Measure Me	E	I	112	InfoTrek	ETA/Cuisenaire
Measure the Motion	H	I	146	Leveled Readers Science	Houghton Mifflin Harcourt
Measure Up!	K	I	303	Early Connections	Benchmark Education
Measurement	J	I	132	Windows on Literacy	National Geographic
Measurement Action	M	I	250+	Yellow Umbrella Books	Red Brick Learning
Measurement and Data	J	I	51	Windows on Literacy	National Geographic
Measurement Mysteries	G	I	124	Learn to Read	Creative Teaching Press
Measurement Tools	I	I	131	Windows on Literacy	National Geographic
Measurement: The Measured Mystery	Q	I	250+	iScience	Norwood House Press
Measuring Cup	C	I	29	Simple Tools	Lerner Publishing Group
Measuring Day	J	RF	607	InfoTrek	ETA/Cuisenaire
Measuring in the Garden	F	I	131	Math Around Us	Heinemann Library
Measuring Matter	S	I	250+	Navigators Science Series	Benchmark Education
Measuring Motion	H	I	113	Leveled Readers Science	Houghton Mifflin Harcourt
Measuring the Weather	R	I	250+	Gaynor, Bill	Pacific Learning
Measuring the Weather	L	I	401	Reading Street	Pearson
Measuring Time	E	I	217	Early Connections	Benchmark Education
Measuring Tools	M	I	250+	Early Connections	Benchmark Education
Measuring Up	R	I	250+	Orbit Chapter Books	Pacific Learning
Measuring Weather	E	I	99	Independent Readers Science	Houghton Mifflin Harcourt
Meat and Protein	I	I	170	Healthy Eating	Heinemann Library
Meat and Protein Group, The	H	I	117	The Food Guide Pyramid	Capstone Press
Meat Eaters, Plant Eaters	K	I	156	Planet Earth	Rigby
Meat Pies	D	I	21	Bebop Books	Lee & Low Books Inc.

* Collection of short stories   # Graphic text
^ Mature content with lower level text demands

TITLE	LEVEL	GENRE	WORD COUNT	AUTHOR / SERIES	PUBLISHER / DISTRIBUTOR
^Meat-Eating Plants and Other Extreme Plant Life	T	I	250+	Extreme Life	Capstone Press
Meat-Eating Plants Next Door, The	Q	RF	250+	Pair-It Books	Steck-Vaughn
Meats and Proteins	F	I	103	Food Groups	Lerner Publishing Group
Medal for Icky, A	E	RF	101	The Rowland Reading Program Library	Rowland Reading Foundation
Medal for Molly, A	N	RF	250+	PM Collection	Rigby
Medal for Nickie, A	K	RF	262	Sunshine	Wright Group/McGraw Hill
Medical Alert	Z	I	250+	Boldprint	Steck-Vaughn
Medical Pioneers	P	B	250+	Navigators Biography Series	Benchmark Education
Medical Zone, The	O	F	250+	The Funny Zone	Norwood House Press
^Medieval Arms and Armor	Q	I	250+	The Middle Ages	Capstone Press
^Medieval Castles	Q	I	250+	The Middle Ages	Capstone Press
Medieval Days	S	I	250+	InfoQuest	Rigby
Medieval Feast, A	Q	I	250+	Aliki	HarperCollins
Medieval Knights	S	I	250+	Fierce Fighters	Raintree
^Medieval Knights	Q	I	250+	The Middle Ages	Capstone Press
Medieval Life	X	I	250+	Eyewitness Books	DK Publishing
^Medieval Plague, The	S	I	250+	The Middle Ages	Capstone Press
Medieval Times	T	I	250+	Boldprint	Steck-Vaughn
Medieval Town	R	I	250+	Worldwise	Franklin Watts
Medieval Warfare	Z	I	250+	Boldprint	Steck-Vaughn
Medio Pollito: A Spanish Tale	O	F	250+	Kimmel, Eric A.	Marshall Cavendish
^Medusa	W	I	250+	World Mythology	Capstone Press
Meerkat	L	I	250+	A Day in the Life: Desert Animals	Heinemann Library
Meerkat Chat	L	I	250+	Story Steps	Rigby
Meerkats	I	I	125	African Animals	Capstone Press
Meerkats	O	I	250+	Weaver, Robyn	Red Brick Learning
Meet a Community Helper	D	RF	41	Independent Readers Social Studies	Houghton Mifflin Harcourt
Meet Abraham Lincoln	O	B	250+	Cary, Barbara	Step-Up Books
Meet Addy	Q	HF	250+	The American Girls Collection	Pleasant Company
Meet an Author: Laura Kvasnosky	E	B	54	Sunshine	Wright Group/McGraw Hill
Meet Benjamin Franklin	O	B	250+	Scarf, Maggi	Step-Up Books
Meet Calliope Day	R	F	250+	Haddad, Charles	Random House
Meet Dino Sue!	L	I	394	Vocabulary Readers	Houghton Mifflin Harcourt
Meet Dino Sue!	L	I	394	Vocabulary Readers/CA	Houghton Mifflin Harcourt
Meet Dino Sue!	L	I	394	Vocabulary Readers/TX	Houghton Mifflin Harcourt
Meet Erdene	P	I	250+	iOpeners	Pearson Learning Group
Meet Farm Animals	LB	I	23	Reach	National Geographic
Meet Felicity	Q	HF	250+	The American Girls Collection	Pleasant Company
Meet Firefighter Jen	I	I	250+	Rosen Real Readers	Rosen Publishing Group
Meet George Washington	O	B	250+	Heilbroner, Joan	Random House
Meet Hillary Rodham Clinton	Q	B	250+	Spain, Valerie	Random House
Meet Jane Goodall	N	B	250+	Windows on Literacy	National Geographic
Meet Jane Mt. Pleasant	H	B	183	Leveled Readers Science	Houghton Mifflin Harcourt
Meet John F. Kennedy	Q	B	250+	White, Nancy Bean	Random House
Meet Johnny Appleseed	D	B	32	Independent Readers Social Studies	Houghton Mifflin Harcourt
Meet Josefina	Q	HF	250+	The American Girls Collection	Pleasant Company
Meet Kirsten	Q	HF	250+	The American Girls Collection	Pleasant Company
Meet Lottie	F	RF	163	Larkin's Little Readers	Wilbooks
Meet M & M	K	RF	250+	Ross, Pat	Penguin Group
Meet Mammoth (Ogg and Bob)	L	F	250+	Fraser, Ian	Marshall Cavendish

TITLE	LEVEL	GENRE	WORD COUNT	AUTHOR / SERIES	PUBLISHER / DISTRIBUTOR
Meet Martha	F	F	196	Martha Speaks	Houghton Mifflin Harcourt
Meet Martin Luther King, Jr.	R	B	250+	DeKay, James T.	Random House
Meet Me at the Water Hole	H	I	144	Storyteller-Night Crickets	Wright Group/McGraw Hill
Meet Messy Fred	I	F	250+	Popcorn	Sundance
Meet Molly	Q	HF	250+	The American Girls Collection	Pleasant Company
*Meet Monster: Six Stories about the World's Friendliest Monster	J	F	250+	Blance, Ellen & Cook, Ann	Marshall Cavendish
*Meet Mr. and Mrs. Green	L	F	250+	Baker, Keith	Harcourt, Inc.
Meet Mr. Cricket	E	F	86	Carousel Readers	Pearson Learning Group
Meet Mr. Hydeous	Q	F	250+	Extreme Monsters	Penny Candy Press
Meet My Family	C	RF	71	Early Connections	Benchmark Education
Meet My Mouse	H	RF	135	Little Celebrations	Pearson Learning Group
Meet Officer Jerry	H	I	173	Rosen Real Readers	Rosen Publishing Group
Meet Our Families	D	RF	108	InfoTrek	ETA/Cuisenaire
Meet Samantha	Q	HF	250+	The American Girls Collection	Pleasant Company
Meet Samuel Adams	P	B	447	Vocabulary Readers	Houghton Mifflin Harcourt
Meet Some Tricksters!	J	I	301	Vocabulary Readers	Houghton Mifflin Harcourt
Meet the Astros	O	I	1050	Smart About Sports	Norwood House Press
Meet the Austins	W	RF	250+	L'Engle, Madeleine	Laurel-Leaf Books
Meet the Boys	C	RF	37	McAlpin, MaryAnn	Short Tales Press
Meet the Bugs!	L	I	250+	Scooters	ETA/Cuisenaire
Meet the Cardinals	O	I	939	Smart About Sports	Norwood House Press
Meet the Cubs	O	I	1066	Smart About Sports	Norwood House Press
Meet the Dodgers	O	I	1221	Smart About Sports	Norwood House Press
Meet the Dogs of Bedlam Farm	M	I	250+	Katz, Jon	Henry Holt & Co.
Meet the Easter Bunny (Hop)	J	F	250+	Paul, Cinco & Daurio, Ken	Little Brown and Company
Meet the Feet	J	I	189	Leveled Readers	Houghton Mifflin Harcourt
Meet the Johnson Family	G	RF	52	Windows on Literacy	National Geographic
Meet the Lincoln Lions Band	L	RF	250+	Giff, Patricia Reilly	Bantam Books
Meet the Manatee	M	I	841	Vocabulary Readers	Houghton Mifflin Harcourt
Meet the Manatee	M	I	841	Vocabulary Readers/CA	Houghton Mifflin Harcourt
Meet the Maya	V	I	1783	Reading Street	Pearson
Meet the Meerkats	L	I	250+	World Quest Adventures	World Quest Learning
*Meet the Molesons	L	F	250+	Bos, Burny	North-South Books
Meet the Octopus	K	I	250+	Bookshop	Mondo Publishing
Meet the Ojibwa	R	I	1383	Vocabulary Readers	Houghton Mifflin Harcourt
Meet the Ojibwa	R	I	1383	Vocabulary Readers/CA	Houghton Mifflin Harcourt
Meet the Ojibwa	R	I	1383	Vocabulary Readers/TX	Houghton Mifflin Harcourt
Meet the Planets	O	F	724	McGranaghan, John	Sylvan Dell Publishing
Meet the Rays	O	I	972	Smart About Sports	Norwood House Press
Meet the Red Sox	O	I	1084	Smart About Sports	Norwood House Press
Meet the United States Government	S	I	1173	Reading Street	Pearson
Meet the Villains of Villainville	L	F	250+	Marvel Super Hero Squad	Little Brown and Company
Meet the Villarreals	M	B	387	Kratky, Lada Josefa	Hampton Brown
Meet the Yankees	O	I	1112	Smart About Sports	Norwood House Press
Meet Thomas Jefferson	O	B	250+	Barrett, Marvin	Step-Up Books
Meet Tom Paxton	I	B	229	Little Celebrations	Pearson Learning Group
Meet William Joyce	I	B	207	Little Celebrations	Pearson Learning Group
Meet Yo-Yo Ma	R	B	1406	Leveled Readers	Houghton Mifflin Harcourt
Meeting Amelia Earhart	O	HF	969	Reading Street	Pearson
Meeting Miss 405	O	RF	250+	Orca Young Readers	Orca Books
Meeting Pickles	I	RF	308	PM Stars Bridge Books	Rigby
Meeting Sqauwky	N	I	250+	Books for Young Learners	Richard C. Owen
#Meeting, The	M	F	250+	Mr. Badger and Mrs. Fox	Graphic Universe

* Collection of short stories   # Graphic text
^ Mature content with lower level text demands

TITLE	LEVEL	GENRE	WORD COUNT	AUTHOR / SERIES	PUBLISHER / DISTRIBUTOR
Meg and Jim's Sled Trip	I	RF	264	Appleton-Smith, Laura	Flyleaf Publishing
Meg and Mog	J	F	236	Nicoll, Helen	Viking/Penguin
Meg and the Lost Pencil Case	F	RF	226	Parasmo, Greg	Scholastic
Meg Goes to Bed	B	RF	48	PM Photo Stories	Rigby
Meg in the Middle	J	RF	250+	The Rowland Reading Program Library	Rowland Reading Foundation
Meg Mackintosh and The Case of the Curious Whale Watch	O	RF	250+	Landon, Lucinda	Secret Passage Press
Meg Mackintosh and The Case of the Missing Babe Ruth Baseball	O	RF	250+	Landon, Lucinda	Secret Passage Press
Meg Mackintosh and The Mystery at Camp Creepy	O	RF	250+	Landon, Lucinda	Secret Passage Press
Meg Mackintosh and The Mystery at the Medieval Castle	O	RF	250+	Landon, Lucinda	Secret Passage Press
Meg Mackintosh and The Mystery at the Soccer Match	O	RF	250+	Landon, Lucinda	Secret Passage Press
Meg Mackintosh and The Mystery in the Locked Library	O	RF	250+	Landon, Lucinda	Secret Passage Press
Megacites	S	I	250+	Connectors	Pacific Learning
Megalosaurus	J	I	131	Dinosaurs and Prehistoric Animals	Capstone Press
^Megamouth Shark	N	I	250+	Shark Zone	Capstone Press
Megamouth Shark	J	I	142	Sharks	Capstone Press
Megamouths and Hammerheads	I	I	403	Sails	Rigby
Megan in Ancient Greece	Q	F	250+	Korman, Susan	Magic Attic
Megan's Balancing Act	Q	RF	250+	Korman, Susan	Magic Attic
Megan's Island	R	RF	250+	Roberts, Willo Davis	Aladdin
Meg's Cat	F	RF	117	Lighthouse	Rigby
Meg's Dearest Wish	Q	HF	250+	The Little Women Journals	Avon Books
Meg's Eggs	C	F	38	New Way Red	Steck-Vaughn
Meg's Mad Magnet	H	F	145	Supersonics	Rigby
Meg's Messy Room	C	RF	52	PM Photo Stories	Rigby
Meg's Tiny Red Teddy	C	RF	64	PM Photo Stories	Rigby
Meg's Warm Clothes	B	RF	34	Gear Up!	Wright Group/McGraw Hill
Mei Fuh: Memories From China	P	B	250+	Schaeffer, Edith	Houghton Mifflin Harcourt
Mel Spells	M	RF	822	Leveled Readers	Houghton Mifflin Harcourt
Mel Spells	M	RF	822	Leveled Readers/CA	Houghton Mifflin Harcourt
Melancholy of Haruhi Suzumiya, The	Z	F	250+	Tanigawa, Nagaru	Little Brown and Company
Meli at School	G	I	207	Leveled Literacy Intervention/Blue System	Heinemann
Meli at the Pet Shop	E	I	148	Leveled Literacy Intervention/Blue System	Heinemann
Meli at the Vet	E	I	141	Leveled Literacy Intervention/Blue System	Heinemann
Meli on the Stairs	C	I	91	Leveled Literacy Intervention/Green System	Heinemann
Melissa's Colorful World	F	RF	83	Larkin's Little Readers	Wilbooks
Melleron's Magic	Q	F	250+	High-Fliers	Pacific Learning
Melleron's Monsters	Q	F	250+	High-Fliers	Pacific Learning
Melonhead	S	RF	250+	Kelly, Katy	Delacorte Press
Melrose and Croc: An Adventure to Remember	J	F	250+	Clark, Emma Chichester	Walker & Company
Melt It, Shape It: Glass	F	I	250+	Nelson, May	Scholastic
Melting	F	I	69	Bookshop	Mondo Publishing
Melting Away	R	I	250+	Explorer Books-Pathfinder	National Geographic
Melting Away	P	I	250+	Explorer Books-Pioneer	National Geographic
Melting Ice Cubes	C	I	50	Rigby Flying Colors	Rigby

TITLE	LEVEL	GENRE	WORD COUNT	AUTHOR / SERIES	PUBLISHER / DISTRIBUTOR
*Melting Snow Sculptures and Other Cases, The	O	RF	250+	Simon, Seymour	Avon Books
Melting Stones	Y	F	250+	Pierce, Tamora	Scholastic
Melvin and the Boy	I	RF	250+	Castillo, Lauren	Henry Holt & Co.
Member of the Wedding	W	RF	250+	McCullers, Carson	New Directions
Memoirs of a Bookbat	Z	RF	250+	Lasky, Kathryn	Harcourt, Inc.
Memoirs of a Teenage Amnesiac	Z+	RF	250+	Zevin, Gabrielle	Square Fish
Memorial Day	I	I	96	American Holidays	Lerner Publishing Group
Memorial Day	Q	I	250+	Holiday Histories	Heinemann
Memorial Day	M	I	232	Holidays and Festivals	Heinemann Library
Memorial Day	L	I	250+	National Holidays	Red Brick Learning
Memories	Q	RF	250+	Reading Safari	Mondo Publishing
Memories for Mom	P	RF	1517	Leveled Readers	Houghton Mifflin Harcourt
Memories of Anne Frank	X	B	250+	Gold, Alison Leslie	Scholastic
Memories of Vietnam: War in the First Person	Z	HF	250+	Weiss, Ellen	Scholastic
Memory Boy	Z	F	250+	Weaver, Will	HarperCollins
Memphis Grizzlies, The	S	I	4034	Team Spirit	Norwood House Press
Men in Baseball	N	I	611	Reading Street	Pearson
Meow, What Now?	G	F	186	Seedlings	Continental Press
Merchant of Death, The: Pendragon	X	F	250+	MacHale, D.J.	Aladdin
Merchant of Venice, The	Z+	HF	250+	Hinds, Gareth	Candlewick Press
Mercury	Q	I	250+	A True Book	Children's Press
Mercury	Q	I	1763	Early Bird Astronomy	Lerner Publishing Group
Mercury	J	I	126	Exploring the Galaxy	Capstone Press
Mercury	S	I	250+	Our Solar System	Compass Point Books
Mercury	N	I	705	Our Universe	Lerner Publishing Group
Mercury	Q	I	250+	The Galaxy	Capstone Press
Mercury	M	I	250+	The Solar System	Capstone Press
Mercury	R	I	250+	Theme Sets	National Geographic
Mercy on These Teenage Chimps	U	RF	250+	Soto, Gary	Harcourt, Inc.
Mercy Otis Warren: A Woman of the Revolution	X	B	2210	Leveled Readers	Houghton Mifflin Harcourt
Mercy Watson Fights Crime	K	F	250+	DiCamillo, Kate	Candlewick Press
Mercy Watson Goes for a Ride	K	F	250+	DiCamillo, Kate	Candlewick Press
Mercy Watson Thinks Like a Pig	K	F	250+	Di Camillo, Kate	Candlewick Press
Mercy Watson to the Rescue	K	F	250+	DiCamillo, Kate	Candlewick Press
Mercy Watson: Something Wonky This Way Comes	K	F	250+	DiCamillo, Kate	Candlewick Press
Merlin and the Dragons	U	TL	250+	Yolen, Jane	Penguin Group
Merlin: The Young Merlin Trilogy	V	TL	250+	Yolen, Jane	Scholastic
Mermaid and the Octopus	F	F	139	Big Cat	Pacific Learning
Mermaid in the Bathtub	O	F	11700	Peetom, Laura	Fitzhenry & Whiteside
Mermaid Island	L	F	250+	Frith, Margaret	Grosset & Dunlap
Mermaid Sister	L	F	250+	Fraser, Mary Ann	Walker & Company
Mermaids	Q	I	250+	Mythical Creatures	Raintree
Mermaids and Mermen	U	I	3787	Fantasy Chronicles	Lerner Publishing Group
Mermaids Don't Run Track	M	F	250+	Dadey, Debbie; Jones, Marcia Thornton	Scholastic
Merry Christmas, Amelia Bedelia	L	F	250+	Parish, Peggy	William Morrow
Merry Christmas, Dear Dragon	F	F	312	Dear Dragon	Norwood House Press
Merry Christmas, Geronimo!	O	F	250+	Stilton, Geronimo	Scholastic
Merry-Go-Round	C	RF	66	Teacher's Choice Series	Pearson Learning Group
Merry-Go-Round	A	RF	36	The King School Series	Townsend Press
Merry-Go-Round, The	C	RF	84	PM Story Books	Rigby
Merry-Go-Round, The	C	RF	45	Ready Readers	Pearson Learning Group
Merry-Go-Round, The	C	RF	62	Sunshine	Wright Group/McGraw Hill

* Collection of short stories   # Graphic text
^ Mature content with lower level text demands

TITLE	LEVEL	GENRE	WORD COUNT	AUTHOR / SERIES	PUBLISHER / DISTRIBUTOR
Mesopotamia	W	I	250+	Navigators Social Studies Series	Benchmark Education
Mesopotamia	X	I	250+	Primary Source Readers	Teacher Created Materials
Mess Monster	G	F	179	Literacy 2000	Rigby
Mess, A	D	F	34	Ready Readers	Pearson Learning Group
Mess, The	D	RF	55	My First Reader	Grolier
Mess, The	B	RF	40	Sun Sprouts	ETA/Cuisenaire
Message by Balloon	I	RF	404	Red Rocket Readers	Flying Start Books
Message from Camp	I	RF	307	Red Rocket Readers	Flying Start Books
Message from Danny Bell, A	I	RF	587	Rigby Flying Colors	Rigby
Message in a Bottle	M	RF	250+	PM Plus Chapter Books	Rigby
Message to the World, A	S	I	813	Vocabulary Readers	Houghton Mifflin Harcourt
Message, The	R	F	250+	Applegate, K. A.	Scholastic
Messages from Mars	S	SF	250+	Leedy, Loreen & Schuerger, Andrew	Holiday House
Messages Without Words	Q	I	250+	Sunshine	Wright Group/McGraw Hill
Messenger	Y	F	250+	Lowry, Lois	Houghton Mifflin Harcourt
Messiest Room on the Planet, The	L	F	250+	Social Studies Connects	Kane Press
Messy Bessey	I	RF	63	Rookie Readers	Children's Press
Messy Bessey's Closet	K	RF	92	Rookie Readers	Children's Press
Messy Bessey's Family Reunion	J	RF	190	McKissack, Patricia & Fredrick	Scholastic
Messy Bessey's Garden	I	RF	60	Rookie Readers	Children's Press
Messy Bessey's School Desk	J	RF	104	Rookie Readers	Children's Press
Messy Desks	O	I	250+	Infotrek Plus	ETA/Cuisenaire
Messy Mark	F	RF	180	First Start	Troll Associates
Messy Meals	J	F	87	Franco, Betsy	Scholastic
Messy Monsters, The	G	F	167	Carousel Readers	Pearson Learning Group
Messy Moose	C	F	45	Little Books	Sadlier-Oxford
Messy Room, A	F	RF	152	The King School Series	Townsend Press
Messy Rooms, The	F	F	103	Lester the Lion Series	Pioneer Valley
Metal	G	I	129	Materials	Lerner Publishing Group
Metal Detector Detective	K	RF	377	Reading Street	Pearson
Metamorphic Rocks	S	I	250+	Let's Rock	Heinemann Library
^Metamorphic Rocks	Q	I	250+	On Deck	Rigby
#Metamorphosis, The	Z+	F	250+	Edge	Hampton Brown
#Metamorphosis, The	Z+	F	250+	Kafka, Franz	Hampton Brown
Meteorite!: The Last Days of the Dinosaurs	W	I	250+	Norris, Richard	Steck-Vaughn
Meteorologists	M	I	250+	Community Helpers	Red Brick Learning
Meteors and Comets	Q	I	1783	Early Bird Astronomy	Lerner Publishing Group
Meteors and Meteorites	Q	I	250+	The Galaxy	Red Brick Learning
Meteors, Comets, and Asteroids	X	I	3166	Leveled Readers	Houghton Mifflin Harcourt
Meteors, Comets, and Asteroids	X	I	3166	Leveled Readers/CA	Houghton Mifflin Harcourt
Meteors, Comets, and Asteroids	X	I	3166	Leveled Readers/TX	Houghton Mifflin Harcourt
Meteors: The Truth Behind Shooting Stars	T	I	250+	Aronson, Billy	Franklin Watts
Metric Math	T	I	250+	Navigators Math Series	Benchmark Education
Metropolitan Cow	N	F	250+	Egan, Tim	Houghton Mifflin Harcourt
Mexican Community, A	J	I	606	Vocabulary Readers	Houghton Mifflin Harcourt
Mexican Community, A	J	I	606	Vocabulary Readers/CA	Houghton Mifflin Harcourt
Mexican Feast, A: The Foods and Recipes of Mexico	P	I	250+	Rosen Real Readers	Rosen Publishing Group
Mexican Festival, A	J	RF	267	Leveled Readers	Houghton Mifflin Harcourt
Mexican Festival, A	J	RF	267	Leveled Readers/CA	Houghton Mifflin Harcourt
Mexican Festival, A	J	RF	267	Leveled Readers/TX	Houghton Mifflin Harcourt
Mexican Holiday, A	C	I	24	The Candid Collection	Pearson Learning Group

TITLE	LEVEL	GENRE	WORD COUNT	AUTHOR / SERIES	PUBLISHER / DISTRIBUTOR
^Mexican Immigrants in America: An Interactive History Adventure	V	HF	250+	You Choose Books	Capstone Press
Mexican Immigration	V	I	250+	Theme Sets	National Geographic
Mexican War, 1846-1848, The	V	I	250+	Let Freedom Ring	Capstone Press
^Mexican-American War, The	R	I	250+	On Deck	Rigby
Mexico	LB	I	22	Canizares, Susan; Chanko, Pamela	Scholastic
Mexico	O	I	250+	Countries of the World	Red Brick Learning
Mexico	Q	I	250+	First Reports: Countries	Compass Point Books
Mexico	P	I	250+	Many Cultures, One World	Capstone Press
Mexico	LB	I	14	Readlings	American Reading Company
Mexico	R	I	250+	Theme Sets	National Geographic
Mexico	M	I	340	Time for Kids	Teacher Created Materials
Mexico ABCs: A Book About the People and Places of Mexico	Q	I	250+	Country ABCs	Picture Window Books
Mexico City Is Muy Grande	M	I	250+	Twig	Wright Group/McGraw Hill
Mexico in Colors	N	I	250+	World of Colors	Capstone Press
Mexico: A Question and Answer Book	P	I	250+	Questions and Answers: Countries	Capstone Press
Mexico: Civilizations Past to Present	S	I	250+	Reading Expeditions	National Geographic
Mexico: Everyday Kids Now and Then	S	HF	250+	Reading Expeditions	National Geographic
Mexico's Smoking Mountains	W	I	1955	Leveled Readers	Houghton Mifflin Harcourt
Mia and Nomar	K	B	464	Vocabulary Readers	Houghton Mifflin Harcourt
Mia and Nomar	K	B	464	Vocabulary Readers/CA	Houghton Mifflin Harcourt
Mia and Nomar	K	B	464	Vocabulary Readers/TX	Houghton Mifflin Harcourt
Mia Hamm	R	B	250+	Sports Heroes	Red Brick Learning
Mia Hamm, Journey of a Soccer Champion	S	B	1730	Leveled Readers	Houghton Mifflin Harcourt
Mia Hamm, Soccer Star	J	B	390	Vocabulary Readers	Houghton Mifflin Harcourt
Mia Hamm, Soccer Star	J	B	390	Vocabulary Readers/CA	Houghton Mifflin Harcourt
Mia Hamm: Soccer Star	Q	B	250+	Leveled Readers Language Support	Houghton Mifflin Harcourt
Mia the Bridesmaid Fairy: Rainbow Magic	L	F	250+	Meadows, Daisy	Scholastic
Miami Dolphins, The	S	I	250+	Team Spirit	Norwood House Press
Miami Gets It Straight	M	RF	250+	McKissack, Fredrick & Patricia	Random House
Miami Heat, The	S	I	4014	Team Spirit	Norwood House Press
Mia's Sun Hat	E	RF	32	Start to Read	School Zone
Micawber	Q	F	250+	Lithgow, John	Simon & Schuster
Mice	O	I	250+	Holmes, Kevin J.	Red Brick Learning
Mice	H	I	143	Literacy 2000	Rigby
Mice	J	I	250+	PM Animal Facts: Orange	Rigby
Mice and Beans	N	F	250+	Ryan, Pam Munoz	Scholastic
Mice and Max	G	F	169	Carousel Readers	Pearson Learning Group
Mice at Bat	I	F	250+	Oechsli, Kelly	HarperTrophy
Mice Have a Meeting, The	I	TL	250+	PM Plus Story Books	Rigby
Mice on Ice	H	F	51	Easy Phonics Readers	Teacher Created Materials
Mice on Ice	C	F	34	KinderReaders	Rigby
Mice on Ice	I	F	211	Sunshine	Wright Group/McGraw Hill
Mice, The	B	F	30	Sails	Rigby
Michael and the Chicks	G	RF	210	Developing Set 4	Pioneer Valley
Michael and the Eggs	G	RF	154	Oxford Reading Tree	Oxford University Press
Michael in the Hospital	E	RF	91	Oxford Reading Tree	Oxford University Press
Michael Jackson: Ultimate Music Legend	X	B	6328	Gateway Biographies	Lerner Publishing Group
Michael Jordan	T	B	250+	Christopher, Matt	Little Brown and Company
Michael Jordan	M	B	250+	Edwards, Nick	Scholastic
Michael Jordan	Q	B	250+	Lovitt, Chip	Scholastic

* Collection of short stories   # Graphic text
^ Mature content with lower level text demands

TITLE	LEVEL	GENRE	WORD COUNT	AUTHOR / SERIES	PUBLISHER / DISTRIBUTOR
Michael Jordan: The Best Ever	T	B	250+	High Five Reading	Red Brick Learning
Michael Phelps	P	B	1848	Amazing Athletes	Lerner Publishing Group
Michael Phelps: Revised Edition	P	B	1830	Amazing Athletes	Lerner Publishing Group
Michael Rosen's Sad Book	T	RF	250+	Rosen, Michael	Candlewick Press
Michael Vick	P	B	250+	Amazing Athletes	Lerner Publishing Group
Michael Vick: Revised Edition	Q	B	1826	Amazing Athletes	Lerner Publishing Group
Michael's Picture	C	RF	33	Little Celebrations	Pearson Learning Group
Michelangelo	S	B	250+	Masterpieces: Artists and Their Works	Red Brick Learning
Michelangelo and the Italian Renaissance	U	B	2119	Reading Street	Pearson
Michelangelo: His Life and Art	R	B	250+	Rosen Real Readers	Rosen Publishing Group
Michelle Kwan	N	B	250+	Biography	Benchmark Education
Michelle Kwan	R	B	250+	Sports Heroes	Red Brick Learning
Michelle Kwan	U	B	250+	Sports Heroes and Legends	Lerner Publishing Group
Michelle Kwan, Champion	M	B	499	Leveled Readers	Houghton Mifflin Harcourt
Michelle Kwan, Champion	M	B	499	Leveled Readers/CA	Houghton Mifflin Harcourt
Michelle Kwan, Champion	M	B	499	Leveled Readers/TX	Houghton Mifflin Harcourt
Michelle Obama	M	B	229	First Ladies	Capstone Press
Michelle Obama	T	B	5777	Gateway Biographies	Lerner Publishing Group
Michelle Wie	F	I	153	Leveled Readers	Houghton Mifflin Harcourt
Michelle Wie	F	I	153	Leveled Readers/CA	Houghton Mifflin Harcourt
Michelle Wie	F	I	153	Leveled Readers/TX	Houghton Mifflin Harcourt
Michelle Wie: She's Got the Power!	Q	B	250+	High Five Reading	Red Brick Learning
Michigan	T	I	250+	Hello U.S.A.	Lerner Publishing Group
Michigan	S	I	250+	Land of Liberty	Red Brick Learning
Michigan	Q	I	250+	One Nation	Capstone Press
Michigan	R	I	250+	This Land Is Your Land	Compass Point Books
Michigan Outdoor Photos	A	I	28	Larkin, Bruce	Books for a Cause, Inc.
Michigan Wolverines, The	S	I	4197	Team Spirit	Norwood House Press
Michigan: Facts and Symbols	O	I	250+	The States and Their Symbols	Capstone Press
Mick and Max	G	RF	169	Carousel Readers	Pearson Learning Group
Mickel and the Blacksmith	M	F	250+	Sun Sprouts	ETA/Cuisenaire
Mickey & Me	T	F	250+	Gutman, Dan	HarperTrophy
Mickey Maloney	I	RF	371	Sails	Rigby
Mickey Maloney - Spy	N	RF	250+	Sails	Rigby
Mickey Maloney's Mail	M	RF	250+	Sails	Rigby
Mickey Maloney's Missing Bag	G	RF	230	Sails	Rigby
Mickey Mantle	U	B	250+	Sports Heroes and Legends	Lerner Publishing Group
Mickey's Secret	K	RF	250+	Rigby Literacy	Rigby
Micro Monsters	U	I	250+	DK Readers	DK Publishing
Micro Monsters: Extreme Encounters with Invisible Armies	Y	I	250+	Kingdom	Kingfisher
Microscope	C	I	40	Simple Tools	Lerner Publishing Group
Microscope	C	I	46	Story Box	Wright Group/McGraw Hill
Midday Meals Around the World	M	I	250+	Meals Around the World	Picture Window Books
Middle Ages, The	R	I	250+	Journey Through History	Barron's Educational
Middle Ages, The	Y	I	250+	Reading Expeditions	National Geographic
^Middle Ages, The: An Interactive History Adventure	W	HF	250+	You Choose Books	Capstone Press
Middle East, The	W	I	250+	Kingfisher Knowledge	Kingfisher
Middle Moffat, The	T	RF	250+	Estes, Eleanor	Language for Learning Assoc.
Middle of Nowhere, The	K	RF	250+	Rigby Literacy	Rigby

TITLE	LEVEL	GENRE	WORD COUNT	AUTHOR / SERIES	PUBLISHER / DISTRIBUTOR
Middle School, The Worst Years of My Life	T	RF	250+	Patterson, James & Tebbetts, Chris	Little Brown and Company
Midge in the Hospital	E	RF	91	Oxford Reading Tree	Oxford University Press
Midnight Bakery	R	I	250+	Bookweb	Rigby
Midnight Charter, The	Y	F	250+	Whitley, David	Roaring Brook Press
Midnight Circus, The	WB	F	0	Collington, Peter	Alfred A. Knopf
Midnight for Charlie Bone	U	F	250+	Nimmo, Jenny	Orchard Books
Midnight Fox, The	R	RF	250+	Byars, Betsy	Scholastic
Midnight Horse, The	V	F	250+	Fleischman, Sid	Bantam Books
Midnight in the Tunnel	M	RF	250+	PM Extensions	Rigby
Midnight Journeys: Travels in the Mysterious World of Sleep	S	I	250+	Literacy by Design	Rigby
Midnight Journeys: Travels in the Mysterious World of Sleep	S	I	250+	Rigby Literacy	Rigby
Midnight Kid, The	L	RF	1756	Science Solves It!	Kane Press
Midnight Lady: The Horses of Half Moon Ranch	S	RF	20000	Oldfield, Jenny	Sourcebooks
Midnight Library, The	S	F	250+	Graves, Damien	Scholastic
Midnight Lightning	P	RF	250+	Bookweb	Rigby
Midnight Magic	U	F	250+	Avi	Scholastic
Midnight Menace, The	Q	RF	250+	Reading Expeditions	National Geographic
Midnight on the Moon	M	F	250+	Osborne, Mary Pope	Random House
Midnight Palace, The	W	F	250+	Zafon, Carlos Ruiz	Little Brown and Company
Midnight Pig, The	M	F	250+	Action Packs	Rigby
Midnight Rescue	N	RF	250+	Literacy Tree	Rigby
Midnight Ride of Sybil Ludington, The	P	B	250+	Literacy by Design	Rigby
Midnight Ride of Sybil Ludington, The	P	B	250+	On Our Way to English	Rigby
Midnight Ride, The	M	I	400	Avenues	Hampton Brown
Midnight: Warriors, The New Prophecy	U	F	250+	Hunter, Erin	HarperCollins
#Midsummer Night's Dream, A	Z	F	250+	Manga Shakespeare	Amulet Books
Midway Monkey Madness	L	F	250+	DC Super-Pets	Picture Window Books
Midwest States, The	R	I	250+	Navigators Social Studies Series	Benchmark Education
Midwest Today, The	S	I	250+	Reading Expeditions	National Geographic
Midwest, The	T	I	250+	Reading Expeditions	National Geographic
Midwest, The: Its History and People	S	I	250+	Reading Expeditions	National Geographic
Midwife's Apprentice, The	X	HF	250+	Cushman, Karen	HarperTrophy
Midwinter Nightingale	X	F	250+	Aiken, Joan	Yearling Books
Mieko and the Fifth Treasure	O	HF	250+	Coerr, Eleanor	Bantam Books
*Mighty 12, The: Superheroes of Greek Myth	U	TL	250+	Smith, Charles R.	Little Brown and Company
Mighty Animal Cells	Z	I	250+	Microquests	Lerner Publishing Group
Mighty Bison	K	I	297	Pull Ahead Books	Lerner Publishing Group
Mighty Forces	S	I	250+	Orbit Collections	Pacific Learning
Mighty Hippopotamus, The	T	I	250+	Bookshop	Mondo Publishing
Mighty Hurricane, The	L	I	250+	Gear Up!	Wright Group/McGraw Hill
Mighty Ironclads and Other Amazements	U	I	2454	Independent Readers Social Studies	Houghton Mifflin Harcourt
Mighty Lever, The	P	I	250+	InfoTrek	ETA/Cuisenaire
Mighty Machines	I	I	127	Windows on Literacy	National Geographic
Mighty Machines Picture Puzzles	M	I	157	Look, Look Again	Capstone Press
Mighty Mammals	Q	I	250+	Explorers	Wright Group/McGraw Hill
Mighty Maya, The	U	I	250+	Leveled Readers Language Support	Houghton Mifflin Harcourt
Mighty Mekong, The	T	I	250+	WorldScapes	ETA/Cuisenaire
Mighty Minibeasts	N	I	250+	Sun Sprouts	ETA/Cuisenaire
Mighty Miss Malone, The	U	HF	250+	Curtis, Christopher Paul	Wendy Lamb Books
Mighty Monty	M	RF	250+	Hurwitz, Johanna	Candlewick Press

* Collection of short stories   # Graphic text
^ Mature content with lower level text demands

TITLE	LEVEL	GENRE	WORD COUNT	AUTHOR / SERIES	PUBLISHER / DISTRIBUTOR
Mighty Mountains	K	I	246	Explorations	Okapi Educational Materials
Mighty Mountains	K	I	246	Explorations	Eleanor Curtain Publishing
Mighty Movers, Mighty Diggers	K	I	250+	Scooters	ETA/Cuisenaire
Mighty Mssissippi, The	K	I	250+	On Our Way to English	Rigby
Mighty Mystery	M	RF	796	Red Rocket Readers	Flying Start Books
Mighty Rome!	S	I	250+	InfoQuest	Rigby
Mighty, Mighty Daffodils, The	Q	RF	1373	Leveled Readers/TX	Houghton Mifflin Harcourt
Mighty, Mighty Daffodils, The	Q	RF	1373	Leveled Readers	Houghton Mifflin Harcourt
Mighty, Mighty Daffodils, The	Q	RF	1373	Leveled Readers/CA	Houghton Mifflin Harcourt
Mighty, The	V	RF	250+	Philbrick, Rodman	Scholastic
Migrant Mother: How a Photograph Defined the Great Depression	Y	I	250+	Captured History	Compass Point Books
Migrant Music, A	W	I	2170	Reading Street	Pearson
Migration	H	I	142	Discovering Nature's Cycles	Lerner Publishing Group
Migration, The	D	I	45	Wonder World	Wright Group/McGraw Hill
Migty Casey	K	RF	250+	Preller, James	Feiwel and Friends
Miguel Hidalgo	O	B	1042	Leveled Readers Language Support	Houghton Mifflin Harcourt
Miguel Hidalgo, Father of Mexican Independence	Q	B	1145	Leveled Readers Social Studies	Houghton Mifflin Harcourt
Mike and Tony: Best Friends	G	RF	171	Ziefert, Harriet	Penguin Group
Mike Fink	N	TL	2003	On My Own Folklore	Lerner Publishing Group
Mike Ghost's Delicious Rainbow	F	F	157	TOTTS	Tott Publications
Mike Swan, Sink or Swim	J	RF	250+	Heiligman, Deborah	Bantam Books
Mike's Bike	E	RF	82	Dominie Phonics Readers	Pearson Learning Group
Mike's Bike	J	RF	250+	Supersonics	Rigby
Mike's First Haircut	G	RF	136	First Start	Troll Associates
Mike's New Bike	F	RF	183	First Start	Troll Associates
Mile High, A	K	F	331	Book Bank	Wright Group/McGraw Hill
Mile-a-Minute Vine, The	K	F	511	Reading Street	Pearson
Miles on the Mississippi	M	I	337	Independent Readers Social Studies	Houghton Mifflin Harcourt
Miles Standish: Colonial Leader	U	B	250+	Let Freedom Ring	Red Brick Learning
Miley Ray Cyrus	S	B	250+	Star Biographies	Capstone Press
Military and Government Technology	Y	I	250+	From Fail to Win! Learning from Bad Ideas	Raintree
Military Helicopters	H	I	106	Mighty Machines	Capstone Press
Milk and Cheese	I	I	180	Healthy Eating	Heinemann Library
Milk from a Cow	G	I	129	Rigby Flying Colors	Rigby
Milking	F	RF	67	Wonder World	Wright Group/McGraw Hill
Milkshake Man, The	L	F	250+	Take Two Books	Wright Group/McGraw Hill
Milkweed	Y	HF	250+	Spinelli, Jerry	Random House
Milkweed Bugs	K	I	144	Watch It Grow	Capstone Press
Milky Way, The	Q	I	1711	Early Bird Astronomy	Lerner Publishing Group
Milky Way, The	K	I	336	Red Rocket Readers	Flying Start Books
Milky Way, The	M	I	250+	The Solar System	Capstone Press
Mill Girls	S	I	884	Vocabulary Readers	Houghton Mifflin Harcourt
Mill Girls	S	I	884	Vocabulary Readers/CA	Houghton Mifflin Harcourt
Mill Girls	S	I	884	Vocabulary Readers/TX	Houghton Mifflin Harcourt
Mill on the Hill, The	I	F	187	Supersonics	Rigby
Millard Fillmore	U	B	250+	Profiles of the Presidents	Compass Point Books
Millard Fillmore: Thirteenth President	R	B	250+	Getting to Know the U.S. Presidents	Children's Press
Millennium Prophecies	Z	I	250+	Unsolved Mysteries	Steck-Vaughn
Miller Who Tried to Please Everyone, The	K	TL	250+	Aesop's Fables	Pearson Learning Group

TITLE	LEVEL	GENRE	WORD COUNT	AUTHOR / SERIES	PUBLISHER / DISTRIBUTOR
Millicent Min, Girl Genius	X	RF	250+	Yee, Lisa	Scholastic
Millie in the Snow	L	F	250+	Steffensmeier, Alexander	Walker & Company
Millie Monster	I	F	315	Springboard	Wright Group/McGraw Hill
Millie's Adventure	J	RF	250+	Scooters	ETA/Cuisenaire
Millie's Marvellous Hat	K	F	565	Kitamura, Satoshi	Andersen Press USA
Million Dollar Putt, The	S	RF	250+	Gutman, Dan	Hyperion
Million Dollar Shot, The	S	RF	250+	Gutman, Dan	Hyperion
Million Dollar Strike, The	S	RF	250+	Gutman, Dan	Hyperion
Million Dots, A	P	I	250+	Clements, Andrew	Simon & Schuster
Million Miles from Boston, A	T	RF	250+	Day, Karen	Wendy Lamb Books
Million-Dollar Throw	V	RF	250+	Lupica, Mike	Philomel
Millions	U	RF	250+	Boyce, Frank Cottrell	HarperTrophy
Millions of Cats	K	F	250+	Ga'g, Wanda	Scholastic
Milo and the Fire Engine Parade	J	RF	250+	Bookshop	Mondo Publishing
Milo and the Greatest Trick Ever!	J	RF	250+	Bookshop	Mondo Publishing
Milo's Great Invention	M	RF	250+	Pair-It Books	Steck-Vaughn
Milton Hershey	R	B	3529	History Maker Bios	Lerner Publishing Group
Milton Hershey: Chocolate King Town Builder	P	B	250+	Simon, Charnan	Children's Press
Milton the Early Riser	J	F	148	Kraus, Robert	Aladdin
Milwaukee Brewers, The	S	I	250+	Team Spirit	Norwood House Press
Milwaukee Brewers, The (Revised Edition)	S	I	250+	Team Spirit	Norwood House Press
Milwaukee Bucks, The	S	I	250+	Team Spirit	Norwood House Press
Milwaukee Cows	E	F	79	Story Box	Wright Group/McGraw Hill
Mimi	J	F	250+	Baicker-McKee, Carol	Bloomsbury Children's Books
Mimosa and the River of Wisdom: The Fairy Chronicles	Q	F	11700	Sweet, J.H.	Sourcebooks
Mina's Day	J	I	292	Reading Street	Pearson
Mina's Spring of Colors	S	RF	250+	Gilmore, Rachna	Fitzhenry & Whiteside
^Mind Games	X	SF	250+	The Extraordinary Files	Hameray Publishing Group
Mind Games: Zac Power	O	F	250+	Larry, H. I.	Feiwel and Friends
Mind Readers: Science Examines ESP	W	I	250+	24/7 Science Behind the Scenes	Scholastic
Mindblind	X	RF	250+	Roy, Jennifer	Marshall Cavendish
Minerals	R	I	1713	Early Bird Earth Systems	Lerner Publishing Group
Minerals	Q	I	250+	Exploring the Earth	Capstone Press
^Minerals	Q	I	250+	On Deck	Rigby
Minerals: A Resource Our World Depends On	V	I	250+	Managing Our Resources	Heinemann
Minerva's Dream	M	F	250+	Pair-It Books	Steck-Vaughn
Mine's the Best	G	RF	104	Bonsall, Crosby	HarperCollins
Ming Lo Moves the Mountain	J	F	250+	Lobel, Arnold	Scholastic
Ming on Mars	O	F	250+	In Step Readers	Rigby
Ming the Mesenger	F	RF	91	Reading Street	Pearson
Minh's New Life	L	RF	250+	PM Plus Story Books	Rigby
Mini Mammals	R	I	250+	Explorers	Wright Group/McGraw Hill
Mini Markets or Mega Stores?	R	I	250+	WorldScapes	ETA/Cuisenaire
Miniature Schnauzers Are the Best!	Q	I	1394	The Best Dogs Ever	Lerner Publishing Group
Minibeasts	LB	I	12	Big Cat	Pacific Learning
Minibeasts	LB	I	15	Rigby Rocket	Rigby
Minibeasts	Q	I	250+	The News	Richard C. Owen
Minister's Daughter, The	Z+	F	250+	Hearn, Julie	Simon Pulse
Mink, a Fink, a Skating Rink, A: What is a Noun?	O	I	335	Words Are CATegorical	Millbrook Press
Minnesota	T	I	250+	Hello U.S.A.	Lerner Publishing Group
Minnesota	R	I	250+	This Land Is Your Land	Compass Point Books

* Collection of short stories   # Graphic text
^ Mature content with lower level text demands

TITLE	LEVEL	GENRE	WORD COUNT	AUTHOR / SERIES	PUBLISHER / DISTRIBUTOR
Minnesota Timberwolves, The	S	I	4046	Team Spirit	Norwood House Press
Minnesota Twins, The	S	I	250+	Team Spirit	Norwood House Press
Minnesota Twins, The (Revised Edition)	S	I	250+	Team Spirit	Norwood House Press
Minnesota Vikings, The	S	I	250+	Team Spirit	Norwood House Press
Minnesota: Facts and Symbols	O	I	250+	The States and Their Symbols	Capstone Press
Minnie and Moo Go to Paris	J	F	250+	Cazet, Denys	DK Publishing
Minnie and Moo The Attack of the Easter Bunnies	J	F	250+	Cazet, Denys	HarperCollins
Minnie and Moo Will You Be My Valentine?	J	F	250+	Cazet, Denys	HarperCollins
Minpins, The	P	F	250+	Dahl, Roald	Penguin Group
Min's Plane Ride	B	RF	49	Bookshop	Mondo Publishing
Min-Yo and the Moon Dragon	N	TL	250+	Hillman, Elizabeth	Harcourt Brace
Miracle at the Plate	P	RF	250+	Christopher, Matt	Little Brown and Company
Miracle Girls, The	X	RF	250+	Dayton, Anne & Vanderbilt, May	FaithWords
Miracle Material, A	V	I	250+	Navigators Science Series	Benchmark Education
Miracle on 49th Street	X	RF	250+	Lupica Mike	Puffin Books
Miracle Wimp	Z+	RF	250+	Kraft, Erik P.	Little Brown and Company
Miracle Worker, The	Z	B	250+	Gibson, William	Bantam Books
Miracle's Boys	Z	RF	250+	Edge	Hampton Brown
Miracle's Boys	Z	RF	250+	Woodson, Jacqueline	Penguin Group
Miracles on Maple Hill	R	RF	250+	Sorensen, Virginia	Scholastic
Miraculous Journey of Edward Tulane, The	U	F	250+	DiCamillo, Kate	Candlewick Press
Miranda and the Movies	U	HF	250+	Kendall, Jane	Harcourt Brace
Miranda Cosgrove	S	B	250+	Star Biographies	Capstone Press
Mirandy and Brother Wind	R	F	250+	McKissack, Patricia	Alfred A. Knopf
Miriam Colon: Actor and Theater Founder	N	B	250+	Beginning Biographies	Pearson Learning Group
Miriam Dives Into a Good Book	N	F	653	Leveled Readers	Houghton Mifflin Harcourt
Mirounga's Pup	L	RF	250+	Books for Young Learners	Richard C. Owen
Mirror	WB	I	0	Baker, Jeannie	Candlewick Press
^Mirror Image	W	RF	250+	Orca Currents	Orca Books
Mirror Image, A	G	I	198	Shutterbug Books	Steck-Vaughn
Mirror Image: How Guys See Themselves	Y	I	250+	What's the Issue?	Compass Point Books
Mirror Magic	C	RF	20	Harry's Math Books	Outside the Box
Mirror, The	D	RF	112	Story Box	Wright Group/McGraw Hill
Mirrorscape	V	F	250+	Wilks, Mike	Egmont USA
Misa Learns to Ride	I	RF	342	Rigby Flying Colors	Rigby
Mischief	M	RF	250+	Pacific Literacy	Pacific Learning
*Mischief and Mayhem	P	F	250+	Storyteller Chapter Books	Wright Group/McGraw Hill
^Miserable Life of Medieval Peasants, The	R	I	250+	The Middle Ages	Capstone Press
Miserable Mill, The	V	F	250+	Snicket, Lemony	Scholastic
Misfits, The	W	RF	250+	Howe, James	Aladdin
Misfortune Cookie, The	N	F	250+	The Zack Files	Grosset & Dunlap
Misha Disappears	K	RF	250+	Literacy 2000	Rigby
Mishi-Na	I	F	217	Sunshine	Wright Group/McGraw Hill
Mishmash	N	RF	250+	Cone, Molly	Pocket Books
Mishmash and the Substitute Teacher	O	RF	250+	Cone, Molly	Houghton Mifflin Harcourt
Miss Daisy Is Crazy!	O	RF	250+	Gutman, Dan	HarperTrophy
Miss Flutter Remembers	K	F	2100	Sims, Henrietta Barbara	Kaeden Books
Miss Fuzzy	H	F	219	Handprints D	Educators Publishing Service
Miss Geeta's Hair	D	F	44	Joy Readers	Pearson Learning Group
Miss Geneva's Lantern	P	RF	250+	Bookshop	Mondo Publishing
Miss Grimble	I	RF	265	Sails	Rigby
Miss Hen's Feast	I	F	434	Leveled Readers	Houghton Mifflin Harcourt

TITLE	LEVEL	GENRE	WORD COUNT	AUTHOR / SERIES	PUBLISHER / DISTRIBUTOR
Miss Holly Is Too Jolly!	O	RF	250+	Gutman, Dan	HarperTrophy
Miss Keen Needs Help	I	RF	305	Early Explorers	Benchmark Education
Miss Laney Is Zany!	O	RF	250+	Gutman, Dan	HarperTrophy
Miss Lazar Is Bizarre!	O	RF	250+	Gutman, Dan	HarperTrophy
Miss Mary Mack	J	F	250+	Hoberman, Mary Ann	Little Brown and Company
Miss McKenzie Had a Farm	J	F	515	Pair-It Books	Steck-Vaughn
Miss Messier's Mess	J	RF	596	InfoTrek	ETA/Cuisenaire
Miss Mingo and the Fire Drill	L	F	250+	Harper, Jamie	Candlewick Press
Miss Mouse Gets Married	K	TL	250+	Folk Tales	Wright Group/McGraw Hill
Miss Muffett and the Spider	I	F	270	Ready Readers	Pearson Learning Group
Miss Nelson Has a Field Day	L	RF	250+	Allard, Harry	Scholastic
Miss Nelson Is Back	L	RF	250+	Allard, Harry	Houghton Mifflin Harcourt
Miss Nelson Is Missing	L	RF	598	Allard, Harry	Houghton Mifflin Harcourt
Miss Piggy's Night Out	J	F	250+	Hunter, Sandra H.	Puffin Books
Miss Popple's Pets	A	RF	28	Literacy 2000	Rigby
Miss Rumphius	M	RF	250+	Cooney, Barbara	Penguin Group
Miss Small Is Off the Wall!	O	RF	250+	Gutman, Dan	HarperTrophy
Miss Smith's Incredible Storybook	M	F	250+	Garland, Michael	Scholastic
Miss Suki Is Kooky!	O	RF	250+	Gutman, Dan	HarperTrophy
Miss Thackery and the Bee	M	RF	250+	PM Plus Chapter Books	Rigby
Miss Tutu's Star	L	RF	250+	Newman, Leslea	Harry N. Abrams
Miss Wire's Christmas Surprise	K	F	250+	I Am Reading	Kingfisher
#Missile Mouse and the Star Crusher	U	SF	250+	Parker, Jake	Scholastic
Missiles and Rockets	V	I	4341	Military Hardware in Action	Lerner Publishing Group
^Missing	S	RF	250+	Spirn, M. Sobel	Stone Arch Books
Missing Cat, The	I	RF	414	Leveled Literacy Intervention/ Green System	Heinemann
Missing Coconut	K	RF	250+	The Rowland Reading Program Libary	Rowland Reading Foundation
Missing Earrings, The	D	F	98	Georgie Giraffe	Literacy Footprints
^Missing Fang, The	T	F	250+	Dragonblood	Stone Arch Books
Missing Fossil Mystery, The	L	RF	250+	Herman, Emily	Hyperion
Missing 'Gator of Gumbo Limbo, The	S	RF	250+	George, Jean Craighead	HarperTrophy
Missing Glasses, The	D	RF	99	Emergent Set 4	Pioneer Valley
Missing Glove, The	F	RF	212	Leveled Readers	Houghton Mifflin Harcourt
Missing Glove, The	F	RF	212	Leveled Readers/CA	Houghton Mifflin Harcourt
Missing Glove, The	F	RF	212	Leveled Readers/TX	Houghton Mifflin Harcourt
Missing Keys, The	K	RF	819	Rigby Flying Colors	Rigby
Missing Lighthouse, The	Q	RF	250+	Reading Expeditions	National Geographic
Missing May	W	RF	250+	Rylant, Cynthia	Bantam Books
Missing Necklace, The	H	F	231	Reading Unlimited	Pearson Learning Group
Missing on Superstition Mountain	S	RF	250+	Broach, Elise	Henry Holt & Co.
Missing Osprey Nest, The	Q	RF	250+	Ragged Island Mysteries	Wright Group/McGraw Hill
Missing Parrot, The	J	RF	491	Early Connections	Benchmark Education
Missing Pet Mystery, The	H	RF	174	Instant Readers	Harcourt School Publishers
Missing Pet, The	K	RF	618	Pair-It Books	Steck-Vaughn
Missing Pieces	Q	RF	250+	Power Up!	Steck-Vaughn
Missing Puppy Spots, The	F	RF	168	In Step Readers	Rigby
Missing Puppy, The	C	F	67	Bella and Rosie Series	Literacy Footprints
Missing Sisters	X	HF	250+	Maguire, Gregory	HarperCollins
Missing Suit, The	H	F	250+	Phonics and Friends	Hampton Brown
Missing Tooth, The	J	RF	250+	Cole, Joanna	Random House
Missing Will, The	M	RF	250+	Woodland Mysteries	Wright Group/McGraw Hill
Missing!	Q	HF	250+	Capeci, Anne	Peachtree

* Collection of short stories   # Graphic text
^ Mature content with lower level text demands

TITLE	LEVEL	GENRE	WORD COUNT	AUTHOR / SERIES	PUBLISHER / DISTRIBUTOR
Missing!	L	RF	699	Rigby Flying Colors	Rigby
Mission Addition	L	F	250+	Leedy, Loreen	Holiday House
^Mission Control	N	I	250+	Explore Space!	Red Brick Learning
Mission of Addition, The	N	I	358	Math Is CATegorical	Millbrook Press
Mission to Mars	Y	I	250+	Science Missions	Raintree
Mission: Steel	P	I	250+	Rigby Focus	Rigby
Missions and Ranchos	W	I	250+	Reading Expeditions	National Geographic
Missions in Space: 1955- Present	T	I	250+	Reading Expeditions	National Geographic
Mississippi	T	I	250+	Hello U.S.A.	Lerner Publishing Group
Mississippi	R	I	250+	This Land Is Your Land	Compass Point Books
Mississippi Bridge	S	HF	250+	Taylor, Mildred	Bantam Books
Mississippi Marvis Barnes	P	TL	1000	Leveled Readers/TX	Houghton Mifflin Harcourt
Mississippi River, The	M	I	250+	Rookie Read-About Geography	Children's Press
Mississippi Trial, 1955	Z+	HF	250+	Crowe, Chris	Penguin Group
Mississippi: Facts and Symbols	O	I	250+	The States and Their Symbols	Capstone Press
Missoula, Montana	Q	I	250+	Theme Sets	National Geographic
Missouri	T	I	250+	Hello U.S.A.	Lerner Publishing Group
Missouri	R	I	250+	This Land Is Your Land	Compass Point Books
Missouri: Facts and Symbols	O	I	250+	The States and Their Symbols	Capstone Press
Mistakes That Worked	T	I	250+	Jones, Charlotte Foltz	Bantam Books
Mister Mole's Stove	J	F	604	Appleton-Smith, Laura	Flyleaf Publishing
Mister Wolf's Plan	E	F	84	Rigby Rocket	Rigby
Misty Gordon and the Mystery of the Ghost Pirates	S	F	250+	Kennedy, Kim	Harry N. Abrams
Misty Gordon and the Mystery of the Ghost Pirates	S	F	250+	Kennedy, Kim	Amulet Books
Misty of Chincoteague	R	RF	250+	Henry, Marguerite	Aladdin
Misty Sleeps	E	RF	56	Books for Young Learners	Richard C. Owen
Misty's Mischief	H	F	61	Campbell, Rod	Viking/Penguin
Misty's Twilight	R	RF	250+	Henry, Marguerite	Aladdin
Mitch and Amy	O	RF	250+	Cleary, Beverly	HarperCollins
Mitch to the Rescue	I	RF	302	PM Story Books-Orange	Rigby
Mitchell Is Moving	J	F	250+	Sharmat, Marjorie Weinman	Simon & Schuster
Mitchell's Readathon	J	RF	665	InfoTrek	ETA/Cuisenaire
Mitt for Me, A	B	RF	34	First Stories	Pacific Learning
Mitten, The	M	TL	250+	Brett, Jan	Scholastic
Mitten, The	D	TL	212	Leveled Literacy Intervention/ Blue System	Heinemann
Mittens	G	RF	165	Schaefer, Lola M.	HarperTrophy
Mitzi's World	N	I	250+	Raffin, Deborah	Harry N. Abrams
Mix It Up	C	I	35	Twig	Wright Group/McGraw Hill
Mix It Up!	C	I	44	Leveled Readers Science	Houghton Mifflin Harcourt
Mix It Up!	D	I	52	Rigby Focus	Rigby
Mix, Make, and Munch	J	I	245	Home Connection Collection	Rigby
#Mixed Signals	S	SF	250+	Recon Academy	Stone Arch Books
Mixed-Up Chameleon, The	K	F	250+	Carle, Eric	HarperTrophy
Mixed-Up Max	Q	F	250+	King-Smith, Dick	Troll Associates
Mixed-Up Mystery, A	T	I	1541	Independent Readers Science	Houghton Mifflin Harcourt
Mixed-Up Shoes, The	C	RF	55	Bonnell, Kris	Reading Reading Books
Mixed-Up Vegetables	U	I	1591	Reading Street	Pearson
Mixed-Up Wigs, The	I	F	199	Leveled Readers	Houghton Mifflin Harcourt
Mixed-Up Wishing Well, The	N	F	250+	Rigby Rocket	Rigby
Mixing	C	I	28	Changing Matter	Lerner Publishing Group
Mixing Colors	B	I	15	Rigby Literacy	Rigby

* Collection of short stories   # Graphic text
^ Mature content with lower level text demands

Organized Alphabetically by Title   **507**

TITLE	LEVEL	GENRE	WORD COUNT	AUTHOR / SERIES	PUBLISHER / DISTRIBUTOR
Mixing Paints	C	F	120	Red Rocket Readers	Flying Start Books
Mixing Things	C	I	51	Leveled Readers Science	Houghton Mifflin Harcourt
Mixing, Kneading, and Baking: The Baker's Art	P	I	2248	Reading Street	Pearson
Miyu and the Cranes for Peace	Q	RF	949	Leveled Readers	Houghton Mifflin Harcourt
MM Mouse at the Movies	J	RF	318	Sails	Rigby
Mmm . . . Very Nice	E	F	91	Home Connection Collection	Rigby
Mmm Apples	E	F	92	Bonnell, Kris	Reading Reading Books
Mmm Milk	D	I	46	Little Celebrations	Pearson Learning Group
#Mo and Jo: Fighting Together Forever	N	F	250+	Haspiel, Dean & Lynch, Jay	Toon Books
Moana Makana	R	RF	250+	WorldScapes	ETA/Cuisenaire
Moana's Island	J	RF	450	Sunshine	Wright Group/McGraw Hill
Mobile Days	U	I	250+	PM Extensions	Rigby
Moccasin Trail	W	RF	250+	McGraw, Eloise	Scholastic
Moccasins	LB	I	20	Twig	Wright Group/McGraw Hill
Mocking Jay	Z	F	250+	Collins, Suzanne	Scholastic
Mockingbird	W	RF	250+	Erskine, Kathryn	Puffin Books
Model, The	B	I	18	Smart Start	Rigby
Models	G	I	231	Yellow Umbrella Books	Red Brick Learning
Modern Dance	S	I	250+	Dance	Capstone Press
Modern Middle East	V	I	250+	Primary Source Readers	Teacher Created Materials
Modern Times	R	I	250+	Journey Through History	Barron's Educational
Mog at the Zoo	L	F	250+	Nicoll, Helen	Penguin Group
Moggy the Mouser	J	F	250+	Voyages	SRA/McGraw Hill
Mog's Mumps	L	F	250+	Nicoll, Helen	Penguin Group
Mohandas Gandhi	U	B	1298	Time for Kids	Teacher Created Materials
Mohandas Gandhi: A Life of Integrity	P	B	584	Pull Ahead Books	Lerner Publishing Group
Mojo and Weeza and the Funny Thing	G	F	147	Big Cat	Pacific Learning
Mojo and Weeza and the New Hat	F	F	146	Big Cat	Pacific Learning
Moki	Q	HF	250+	Penny, Grace Jackson	Penguin Group
Molds. Mushrooms & Other Fungi	Y	I	250+	Kingdom Classification	Compass Point Books
Moldy Mystery, A	M	RF	250+	Science Solves It!	Kane/Miller Book Publishers
Mole Sisters and the Blue Egg, The	G	F	84	Schwartz, Roslyn	Annick Press
Mole Sisters and the Busy Bees, The	I	F	115	Schwartz, Roslyn	Annick Press
Mole Sisters and the Cool Breeze, The	I	F	121	Schwartz, Roslyn	Annick Press
Mole Sisters and the Fairy Ring, The	H	F	83	Schwartz, Roslyn	Annick Press
Mole Sisters and the Moonlit Night, The	I	F	111	Schwartz, Roslyn	Annick Press
Mole Sisters and the Piece of Moss, The	I	F	111	Schwartz, Roslyn	Annick Press
Mole Sisters and the Question, The	I	F	105	Schwartz, Roslyn	Annick Press
Mole Sisters and the Rainy Day, The	G	F	91	Schwartz, Roslyn	Annick Press
Mole Sisters and the Wavy Wheat, The	I	F	110	Schwartz, Roslyn	Annick Press
Mole Sisters and the Way Home, The	H	F	85	Schwartz, Roslyn	Annick Press
Mole's in Love	L	F	250+	Bedford, David	Tiger Tales
*Mollie Whuppie	K	TL	250+	New Way Orange	Steck-Vaughn
Molly and Harry	H	F	328	Sails	Rigby
Molly in the Middle	K	RF	1413	Real Kids Readers	Millbrook Press
Molly Learns a Lesson	Q	HF	250+	The American Girls Collection	Pleasant Company
Molly Makes a Graph	G	RF	110	Seedlings	Continental Press
Molly Monster's Party	C	F	86	Springboard	Wright Group/McGraw Hill
Molly Pitcher	N	B	208	First Biographies	Capstone Press
Molly Pitcher	S	B	2173	People to Remember Series	January Books
Molly Pitcher: Young Patriot	O	B	250+	Childhood of Famous Americans	Aladdin
Molly Saves the Day	Q	HF	250+	The American Girls Collection	Pleasant Company
Molly the Brave and Me	K	RF	250+	O'Connor, Jane	Random House
Molly the Goldfish Fairy: Rainbow Magic	L	F	250+	Meadows, Daisy	Scholastic

* Collection of short stories   # Graphic text
^ Mature content with lower level text demands

TITLE	LEVEL	GENRE	WORD COUNT	AUTHOR / SERIES	PUBLISHER / DISTRIBUTOR
Molly's Bracelet	I	RF	250+	Voyages	SRA/McGraw Hill
Molly's Broccoli	I	RF	233	Ready Readers	Pearson Learning Group
Molly's Hard Bargain	I	RF	180	Instant Readers	Harcourt School Publishers
Molly's Mailbox	F	RF	122	Teacher's Choice Series	Pearson Learning Group
Molly's New Team	F	RF	161	Leveled Readers	Houghton Mifflin Harcourt
Molly's New Team	F	RF	161	Leveled Readers/CA	Houghton Mifflin Harcourt
Molly's New Team	F	RF	161	Leveled Readers/TX	Houghton Mifflin Harcourt
Molly's Pilgrim	M	RF	250+	Cohen, Barbara	Bantam Books
Molly's Surprise	Q	HF	250+	The American Girls Collection	Pleasant Company
Molly's Trampoline	J	F	407	Sails	Rigby
Mom	B	I	32	InfoTrek	ETA/Cuisenaire
Mom	A	RF	25	Leveled Literacy Intervention/Orange System	Heinemann
Mom	A	I	24	PM Starters	Rigby
Mom and Dad Are Palindromes: A Dilemma for Words . . . and Backwards	L	F	250+	Schulman, Mark	Chronicle Books
Mom and Kayla	B	RF	69	Leveled Literacy Intervention/Green System	Heinemann
Mom at the Football Game	J	F	381	Sails	Rigby
Mom at the Market	J	RF	301	Sails	Rigby
Mom at Work	B	I	56	Rigby Flying Colors	Rigby
Mom Can Fix Anything	D	RF	74	Learn to Read	Creative Teaching Press
Mom Dresses Up	A	RF	46	Mom and Dad Series	Pioneer Valley
Mom Goes Shopping	A	RF	34	Mom and Dad Series	Pioneer Valley
Mom Is a Painter	B	I	34	Bebop Books	Lee & Low Books Inc.
Mom Is Busy	B	RF	33	Handprints A	Educators Publishing Service
Mom Likes Hats	A	RF	40	Mom and Dad Series	Pioneer Valley
Mom Named Dad, A	L	RF	250+	Rigby Literacy	Rigby
Mom Paints the House	H	RF	220	Foundations	Wright Group/McGraw Hill
Mom, You're Fired!	O	RF	250+	Robinson, Nancy K.	Scholastic
Momentous Decision, A	X	I	3354	Leveled Readers	Houghton Mifflin Harcourt
Momentous Decision, A	X	I	3354	Leveled Readers/CA	Houghton Mifflin Harcourt
Mommy Book, The	H	I	148	Parr, Todd	Little Brown and Company
Mommy Do You Love Me?	K	F	250+	Willis, Jeanne	Candlewick Press
Mommy Is a Soft, Warm Kiss	L	RF	279	Greene, Rhonda Gowler	Walker & Company
Mommy, Carry Me Please!	I	F	134	Cabrera, Jane	Holiday House
Mommy, Where Are You?	B	RF	64	Ziefert, Harriet; Boon, Emilie	Puffin Books
Momotaro	M	F	631	Sunshine	Wright Group/McGraw Hill
Moms	B	RF	34	Handprints B	Educators Publishing Service
Moms	A	I	31	Tiny Treasures	Pioneer Valley
Moms and Dads	A	I	36	PM Starters	Rigby
Mom's Bad Hair Day	E	RF	89	Bonnell, Kris	Reading Reading Books
Mom's Bag	I	RF	404	Sails	Rigby
Mom's Birthday	I	RF	229	Sunshine	Wright Group/McGraw Hill
Mom's Birthday	E	RF	103	The King School Series	Townsend Press
Mom's Diet	I	RF	228	Sunshine	Wright Group/McGraw Hill
Mom's Getting Married	K	RF	376	Sunshine	Wright Group/McGraw Hill
Mom's Haircut	H	RF	99	Literacy 2000	Rigby
Mom's Hat	C	RF	39	Joy Readers	Pearson Learning Group
Mom's Hat	C	RF	114	Sails	Rigby
Mom's New Car	D	RF	116	Foundations	Wright Group/McGraw Hill
Mom's New Car	D	RF	119	Springboard	Wright Group/McGraw Hill
Mom's Salsa Garden	F	RF	196	On Our Way to English	Rigby

TITLE	LEVEL	GENRE	WORD COUNT	AUTHOR / SERIES	PUBLISHER / DISTRIBUTOR
Mom's Secret	H	RF	143	Costain, Meredith	Scholastic
Mom's Shoes	E	RF	133	Handprints C, Set 2	Educators Publishing Service
Mom's Shoes	J	RF	298	Sails	Rigby
Mom's Stories	D	RF	32	Vocabulary Readers	Houghton Mifflin Harcourt
Mon Hung and Mon Lung	I	RF	250+	On Our Way to English	Rigby
Mona Mousa, Code, The	O	F	250+	Stilton, Geronimo	Scholastic
Monarch Butterflies	G	I	56	Pebble Books	Capstone Press
Monarch Butterflies	K	I	414	Pull Ahead Books	Lerner Publishing Group
Monarch Butterflies	R	I	250+	Theme Sets	National Geographic
Monarch Butterfly	I	I	28	Book Bank	Wright Group/McGraw Hill
Monarch Butterfly	N	I	250+	Gibbons, Gail	Holiday House
Monarch Butterfly	N	I	250+	Life Cycles	Creative Teaching Press
Monarch Butterfly, The	I	I	152	Foundations	Wright Group/McGraw Hill
Monarch Mystery	E	I	117	Literacy by Design	Rigby
Monarchs on the Move	N	I	629	Leveled Readers	Houghton Mifflin Harcourt
Monarchs on the Move	N	I	629	Leveled Readers/CA	Houghton Mifflin Harcourt
Monarchs on the Move	N	I	629	Leveled Readers/TX	Houghton Mifflin Harcourt
Monday Came	K	RF	250+	Voyages	SRA/McGraw Hill
Mondo and Gordo Weather the Storm	L	F	759	Early Connections	Benchmark Education
Monet	X	B	250+	Eyewitness Books	DK Publishing
Monet	S	B	250+	Masterpieces: Artists and Their Works	Red Brick Learning
Monet	R	B	250+	Venezia, Mike	Children's Press
Money	M	I	250+	Early Connections	Benchmark Education
Money	C	I	35	Early Math	Lerner Publishing Group
Money	U	I	250+	News Extra	Richard C. Owen
Money	T	I	250+	Richardson, Adele	Creative Education
Money	M	I	250+	Spyglass Books	Compass Point Books
Money	J	I	250+	Twig	Wright Group/McGraw Hill
Money and You	O	I	250+	Reading Expeditions	National Geographic
Money Boot, The	N	RF	250+	Russell, Ginny	Fitzhenry & Whiteside
Money Hungry	V	RF	250+	Flake, Sharon G.	Scholastic
Money in My Pocket	G	I	133	Twig	Wright Group/McGraw Hill
Money Math	H	I	247	Yellow Umbrella Books	Red Brick Learning
Money Riddles That Count	K	I	250+	Pair-It Books	Steck-Vaughn
Money Saving and Spending	I	I	174	Rosen Real Readers	Rosen Publishing Group
Money, Money, Money	R	I	1242	Vocabulary Readers	Houghton Mifflin Harcourt
Money, Money, Money	R	I	1242	Vocabulary Readers/CA	Houghton Mifflin Harcourt
Money, Money, Money!	O	I	250+	Bookweb	Rigby
Mongols, The	S	I	250+	Journey Into Civilization	Chelsea House
Monica and the Summer Party	M	RF	250+	Sunflower	Intercultural Center for Research in Education
Monica Goes to the Zoo	M	RF	250+	Sunflower	Intercultural Center for Research in Education
Monique's Moon Log	M	I	644	In Step Readers	Rigby
Monkey	A	I	32	Leveled Literacy Intervention/ Green System	Heinemann
Monkey and Fire	J	TL	372	Literacy 2000	Rigby
Monkey and Gorilla	E	F	150	Sails	Rigby
Monkey and the Crocodile, The	L	TL	486	Pawprints Teal	Pioneer Valley
Monkey and the Mummy	C	F	34	Brand New Readers	Candlewick Press
Monkey Baby Grows Up, A	K	I	363	Baby Animals	Lerner Publishing Group
Monkey Bridge, The	D	F	66	Sunshine	Wright Group/McGraw Hill
Monkey Buisness	L	I	250+	Storyteller-Shooting Stars	Wright Group/McGraw Hill

* Collection of short stories   # Graphic text
^ Mature content with lower level text demands

TITLE	LEVEL	GENRE	WORD COUNT	AUTHOR / SERIES	PUBLISHER / DISTRIBUTOR
Monkey Eats Worms	B	F	39	Brand New Readers	Candlewick Press
Monkey Flies Away	B	F	37	Brand New Readers	Candlewick Press
Monkey Hop, The	C	F	26	Joy Readers	Pearson Learning Group
Monkey Island	V	RF	250+	Fox, Paula	Orchard Books
Monkey Monkey Monkey	L	F	250+	MacLennan, Cathy	Sterling Publishing
Monkey Moves	B	I	16	Pair-It Books	Steck-Vaughn
Monkey on the Roof	D	RF	92	PM Plus Story Books	Rigby
Monkey Paint	F	F	157	Gear Up!	Wright Group/McGraw Hill
Monkey Play	G	F	148	Step into Reading	Random House
Monkey Pudding and Other Dessert Recipes	S	I	250+	Fun Food for Cool Cooks	Capstone Press
Monkey See, Monkey Do	E	F	89	Gave, Marc	Scholastic
Monkey the Mummy	E	F	34	Brand New Readers	Candlewick Press
Monkey Tricks	E	F	81	Joy Readers	Pearson Learning Group
Monkey Tricks	H	RF	328	PM Collection	Rigby
Monkey Trouble	O	RF	250+	WorldScapes	ETA/Cuisenaire
Monkey Watch	I	F	262	Sails	Rigby
Monkey with a Toolbelt	N	F	642	Monroe, Chris	Carolrhoda Books
Monkey with a Toolbelt and the Noisy Problem	N	F	881	Monroe, Chris	Carolrhoda Books
Monkey, The	A	I	32	On Our Way to English	Rigby
Monkey, Watch Out!	B	F	26	Brand New Readers	Candlewick Press
Monkey, Where Are You?	C	F	37	Brand New Readers	Candlewick Press
Monkey-Monkey's Trick	I	F	250+	McKissack, Patricia	Houghton Mifflin Harcourt
Monkeys	B	I	27	Canizares, Susan; Chanko, Pamela	Scholastic
Monkeys	G	I	27	Reading Unlimited	Pearson Learning Group
Monkeys	A	F	18	Sails	Rigby
Monkeys & Apes	K	I	250+	PM Animal Facts: Turquoise	Rigby
Monkeys and the Universe	L	F	250+	Banks, Kate	Farrar, Straus, & Giroux
Monkey's Friends	C	F	36	Literacy 2000	Rigby
Monkey's Loose Tooth	C	F	31	Brand New Readers	Candlewick Press
Monkey's Ride	I	F	350	Sails	Rigby
Monkey's Tail	B	F	76	Sails	Rigby
Monkeys, Diverse Animals	U	I	250+	Sails	Rigby
Monsieur Armand	M	F	250+	Book Blazers	ETA/Cuisenaire
Monsoon Afternoon	N	RF	250+	Sheth, Kashmira	Peachtree
Monsoon Civilizations	V	I	2591	Independent Readers Social Studies	Houghton Mifflin Harcourt
Monsoon Makers, The	U	RF	250+	WorldScapes	ETA/Cuisenaire
Monsoons of India	W	I	2070	Leveled Readers	Houghton Mifflin Harcourt
Monsoons of India	W	I	2070	Leveled Readers/CA	Houghton Mifflin Harcourt
Monsoons of India	W	I	2070	Leveled Readers/TX	Houghton Mifflin Harcourt
Monster	Z	RF	250+	Edge	Hampton Brown
Monster	Z	RF	250+	inZone Books	Hampton Brown
Monster	Z	RF	250+	Myers, Walter Dean	HarperCollins
Monster	I	F	201	Read Alongs	Rigby
Monster and the Baby	D	F	48	Mueller, Virginia	Puffin Books
Monster at the Beach, The	E	RF	82	Storyteller-Moon Rising	Wright Group/McGraw Hill
Monster Bait	M	RF	250+	Scooters	ETA/Cuisenaire
Monster Bones, The Story of a Dinosaur Fossil	Q	I	250+	Science Works	Picture Window Books
Monster Bug	L	RF	1042	Science Solves It!	Kane Press
Monster Bus	F	F	103	The Monster Bus Series	Pearson Learning Group
Monster Bus Goes on a Hot Air Balloon Trip	I	F	254	The Monster Bus Series	Pearson Learning Group
Monster Bus Goes to the Races	H	F	158	The Monster Bus Series	Pearson Learning Group

TITLE	LEVEL	GENRE	WORD COUNT	AUTHOR / SERIES	PUBLISHER / DISTRIBUTOR
Monster Bus Goes to Yellowstone Park	I	F	259	The Monster Bus Series	Pearson Learning Group
Monster Can't Sleep	D	F	52	Mueller, Virginia	Puffin Books
Monster Cookbook, A	N	I	250+	First Cookbooks	Capstone Press
Monster Fish Frenzy	Q	F	250+	Wiley & Grampa's Creature Features	Little Brown and Company
Monster for Hire	M	F	250+	Wilson, Trevor	Mondo Publishing
Monster for Miss Owen, A	H	RF	185	Storyworlds	Heinemann
Monster from Mercury, The	L	F	250+	Popcorn	Sundance
Monster from the Sea, The	K	TL	250+	Bank Street	Bantam Books
Monster Health Book, The : A Guide to Eating Healthy, Being Active & Feeling Great for Monsters & Kids!	S	I	250+	Miller, Edward	Holiday House
Monster House, A	LB	F	12	Sails	Rigby
Monster in the Attic, The	F	RF	151	Literacy by Design	Rigby
Monster in the Backpack, The	K	F	250+	Moser, Lisa	Candlewick Press
Monster in the Cave, The	J	F	250+	Lighthouse	Ginn & Co.
Monster in the Maze: The Story of the Minotaur	M	TL	250+	All Aboard Reading	Grosset & Dunlap
Monster in the Wardrobe, The	O	F	250+	High-Fliers	Pacific Learning
Monster Is Coming!, The	K	F	250+	Rigby Star	Rigby
Monster Is Coming, The	K	F	250+	Rigby Literacy	Rigby
Monster Lunch	O	F	250+	Orca Echoes	Orca Books
Monster Machines	V	I	250+	Boldprint	Steck-Vaughn
Monster Machines	M	I	250+	Explorations	Okapi Educational Materials
Monster Machines	M	I	250+	Explorations	Eleanor Curtain Publishing
Monster Manners	J	F	250+	Cole, Joanna	Scholastic
Monster Math	G	F	158	Maccarone, Grace	Scholastic
Monster Math Picnic	G	F	98	Maccarone, Grace	Scholastic
Monster Math School Time	G	F	120	Maccarone, Grace	Scholastic
Monster Mayhem: Jokes to Scare You Silly!	O	F	1641	Make Me Laugh!	Lerner Publishing Group
Monster Meal	C	F	47	Rigby Star	Rigby
Monster Meals	C	F	33	Literacy 2000	Rigby
Monster Mess	A	F	18	Big Cat	Pacific Learning
Monster Money	H	F	130	Maccarone, Grace	Scholastic
Monster Money Book, The	N	F	1035	Avenues	Hampton Brown
Monster Mop	LB	F	8	Ready Readers	Pearson Learning Group
Monster Movie	K	F	250+	Cole, Joanna	Scholastic
Monster of Mirror Mountain, The	K	F	250+	Literacy 2000	Rigby
Monster of the Year	S	F	250+	Coville, Bruce	Pocket Books
Monster Party	A	F	29	Bookshop	Mondo Publishing
Monster Party	A	F	20	Literacy 2000	Rigby
Monster Party	A	F	20	Smart Start	Rigby
^Monster Planet	T	SF	250+	Orme, David	Stone Arch Books
Monster Rabbit Runs Amuck!	M	RF	250+	Giff, Patricia Reilly	Bantam Books
Monster Sandwich, A	C	F	36	Story Box	Wright Group/McGraw Hill
Monster Sleepover!	J	F	139	Beck, Scott	Harry N. Abrams
Monster Songs	I	RF	527	Real Kids Readers	Millbrook Press
Monster Soup	LB	F	33	Rigby Literacy	Rigby
Monster Stew	F	F	61	Dominie Readers	Pearson Learning Group
Monster Stew	F	F	117	Learn to Read	Creative Teaching Press
Monster Town, The	A	F	24	Sails	Rigby
Monster Trucks	M	I	250+	Horsepower	Capstone Press
Monster Trucks	H	I	133	Mighty Machines	Capstone Press
Monster Trucks	L	I	137	On Deck	Rigby
Monster Trucks	L	I	354	Pull Ahead Books	Lerner Publishing Group

* Collection of short stories   # Graphic text
^ Mature content with lower level text demands

TITLE	LEVEL	GENRE	WORD COUNT	AUTHOR / SERIES	PUBLISHER / DISTRIBUTOR
Monster Trucks	Q	I	250+	Wild Rides!	Red Brick Learning
Monster Trucks on the Move	K	I	365	Lightning Bolt Books	Lerner Publishing Group
Monster Under My Bed, The	H	F	198	Gruber, Suzanne	Troll Associates
Monster Under The Bed, The	K	F	250+	Ready Readers	Pearson Learning Group
Monster Who Ate Darkness, The	L	F	250+	Dunbar, Joyce	Candlewick Press
Monster Who Ate My Peas, The	O	F	250+	Schnitzlein, Danny	Peachtree
Monster Who Did My Math, The	O	F	1256	Schnitzlein, Danny	Peachtree
Monster, Monster	C	F	38	Reading Corners	Pearson Learning Group
Monster, The	D	RF	29	Harry's Math Books	Outside the Box
Monster, The	C	RF	83	Sun Sprouts	ETA/Cuisenaire
Monsterology: The Complete Book of Monstrous Beasts	X	I	250+	Steer, Dugald	Candlewick Press
Monsters	Z	I	7201	The Unexplained	Lerner Publishing Group
Monsters	C	F	30	TOTTS	Tott Publications
Monsters Always Welcome!	L	F	250+	Scooters	ETA/Cuisenaire
Monster's Clothes, The	LB	F	12	Sails	Rigby
Monsters Don't Scuba Dive	M	F	250+	Dadey, Debbie; Jones, Marcia Thornton	Scholastic
Monster's New Friend, The	K	F	250+	Rigby Literacy	Rigby
Monsters Next Door, The	L	RF	250+	Dadey, Debbie; Jones, Marcia Thornton	Scholastic
Monsters of Burwood, The	O	F	250+	Sails	Rigby
Monsters of Morley Manor, The	S	F	250+	Coville, Bruce	Harcourt, Inc.
Monsters of the Deep	L	I	250+	Marine Life For Young Readers	Pearson Learning Group
^Monsters of the Deep: Deep Sea Adaptation	T	I	250+	Extreme Life	Capstone Press
Monsters of the Myth	T	I	522	Vocabulary Readers	Houghton Mifflin Harcourt
Monster's Party, The	C	F	92	Story Box	Wright Group/McGraw Hill
Monster's Ring, The	R	F	250+	Coville, Bruce	Pocket Books
Monsters' Tea Party, The	E	F	129	Learn to Read	Creative Teaching Press
Monsters' Test, The	O	F	570	Heinz, Brian J.	Millbrook Press
Monsters!	S	I	250+	Boldprint	Steck-Vaughn
Monsters!	D	F	45	My First Reader	Grolier
Montana	T	I	250+	Hello U.S.A.	Lerner Publishing Group
Montana	R	I	250+	This Land Is Your Land	Compass Point Books
Montana Bed and Breakfast	K	RF	119	Larkin's Little Readers	Wilbooks
Montana: Facts and Symbols	O	I	250+	The States and Their Symbols	Capstone Press
Monterey Bay Area Missions	V	I	6236	Exploring California Missions	Lerner Publishing Group
Montezuma and the Aztecs	X	I	2755	Leveled Readers	Houghton Mifflin Harcourt
Montezuma and the Aztecs	X	I	2755	Leveled Readers/CA	Houghton Mifflin Harcourt
Montezuma and the Aztecs	X	I	2755	Leveled Readers/TX	Houghton Mifflin Harcourt
Montezuma: Aztec Ruler	X	B	250+	Primary Source Readers	Teacher Created Materials
Montgomery Bus Boycott, The	T	I	1432	Leveled Readers	Houghton Mifflin Harcourt
Montgomery Bus Boycott, The	T	I	1432	Leveled Readers/CA	Houghton Mifflin Harcourt
Montgomery Bus Boycott, The	T	I	1432	Leveled Readers/TX	Houghton Mifflin Harcourt
Months	F	I	93	Calendars	Lerner Publishing Group
Months	H	I	135	The Calendar	Capstone Press
Months of the Year	I	I	187	Measuring Time	Heinemann Library
Monticello	V	I	250+	Cornerstones of Freedom	Children's Press
Monticello	T	I	250+	We The People	Compass Point Books
Monty and the Ghost Train	C	F	48	Storyworlds	Heinemann
Monty at McBurgers	D	F	40	Storyworlds	Heinemann
Monty at the Party	C	F	46	Storyworlds	Heinemann
Monty at the Seaside	C	F	38	Storyworlds	Heinemann
Monty, the Missing Cat	E	RF	100	Developing Books	Pioneer Valley

TITLE	LEVEL	GENRE	WORD COUNT	AUTHOR / SERIES	PUBLISHER / DISTRIBUTOR
Monuments and Mummies	T	I	250+	InfoQuest	Rigby
Moog-Moog, Space Barber	N	F	250+	Teague, Mark	Scholastic
Moominland Winter	S	F	250+	Jansson, Tove	Farrar, Straus, & Giroux
Moominpappa at Sea	S	F	250+	Jansson, Tove	Farrar, Straus, & Giroux
Moominsummer Madness	S	F	250+	Jansson, Tove	Farrar, Straus, & Giroux
Moominvalley in November	S	F	250+	Jansson, Tove	Farrar, Straus, & Giroux
Moon	F	RF	38	Books for Young Learners	Richard C. Owen
Moon	S	I	250+	Our Solar System	Compass Point Books
Moon	H	I	108	Space	Lerner Publishing Group
Moon and Beyond, The	U	I	250+	Power Up!	Steck-Vaughn
Moon and the Mirror, The	M	TL	250+	Literacy 2000	Rigby
Moon Book, The	P	I	250+	Gibbons, Gail	Holiday House
Moon Boy	J	F	250+	Bank Street	Bantam Books
Moon Bridge, The	W	HF	250+	Savin, Marcia	Scholastic
Moon Cake, The	E	RF	127	Joy Readers	Pearson Learning Group
Moon Car Race, The	D	F	107	Springboard	Wright Group/McGraw Hill
Moon Festival, The	G	RF	202	Reading Street	Pearson
Moon Journal	L	RF	250+	Rigby Literacy	Rigby
Moon Kids	T	SF	5379	Reading Street	Pearson
Moon Lady and Her Festival, The	M	F	635	Reading Street	Pearson
Moon Landing	V	I	250+	Platt, Richard	Candlewick Press
Moon Landing, The	G	RF	189	Springboard	Wright Group/McGraw Hill
Moon Over High Street, The	T	RF	250+	Babbitt, Natalie	Scholastic
Moon Over Manifest	U	HF	250+	Vanderpool, Clare	Delacorte Press
Moon Over Tennessee: A Boy's Civil War Journal	W	B	250+	Crist-Evans, Craig	Houghton Mifflin Harcourt
Moon Rope: Un Lazo a la Luna	K	TL	250+	Ehlert, Lois	Harcourt
Moon Shadow	W	RF	250+	Platt, Chris	Peachtree
Moon Stories	J	F	250+	Ready Readers	Pearson Learning Group
Moon Story	E	RF	157	Sunshine	Wright Group/McGraw Hill
Moon, The	U	I	250+	A First Book	Franklin Watts
Moon, The	J	I	204	Dominie Factivity Series	Pearson Learning Group
Moon, The	Q	I	1735	Early Bird Astronomy	Lerner Publishing Group
Moon, The	I	I	165	Exploring the Galaxy	Capstone Press
Moon, The	Q	I	250+	Eye on the Universe	Crabtree
Moon, The	L	I	295	Gear Up!	Wright Group/McGraw Hill
Moon, The	D	F	139	Joy Readers	Pearson Learning Group
Moon, The	N	I	250+	Literacy 2000	Rigby
Moon, The	N	I	754	Our Universe	Lerner Publishing Group
Moon, The	K	I	126	Out In Space	Red Brick Learning
Moon, The	S	I	1601	Reading Street	Pearson
Moon, The	D	I	51	Rigby Focus	Rigby
Moon, The	A	F	30	Sails	Rigby
Moon, The	M	I	250+	The Solar System	Capstone Press
Moon, The	L	I	139	Twig	Wright Group/McGraw Hill
Moonbeam Cow	K	TL	228	Books for Young Learners	Richard C. Owen
Moonflower, The	O	I	250+	Loewer, Peter & Jean	Peachtree
Moonhorse	M	F	250+	Osborne, Mary Pope	Alfred A. Knopf
Moonlight	D	RF	48	Literacy 2000	Rigby
Moonlight Man, The	U	F	250+	Wright, Betty Ren	Scholastic
Moonlight on the River	R	RF	250+	Kovacs, Deborah	Penguin Group
Moonlit Owl, You	I	RF	225	Cambridge Reading	Pearson Learning Group
Moonrise: Warriors, The New Prophecy	U	F	250+	Hunter, Erin	HarperCollins
Moonwalk: The First Trip to the Moon	O	I	250+	Donnelly, Judy	Random House
Moorchild, The	W	F	250+	McGraw, Eloise	Scholastic

* Collection of short stories # Graphic text
^ Mature content with lower level text demands

TITLE	LEVEL	GENRE	WORD COUNT	AUTHOR / SERIES	PUBLISHER / DISTRIBUTOR
Moose	O	I	1633	Early Bird Nature Books	Lerner Publishing Group
Moose	E	I	100	Vocabulary Readers	Houghton Mifflin Harcourt
Moose	E	I	100	Vocabulary Readers/CA	Houghton Mifflin Harcourt
Moose	B	I	34	Zoozoo-Animal World	Cavallo Publishing
Moose and Magpie	N	F	1646	Restrepo, Bettina	Sylvan Dell Publishing
Moose and Mouse	J	F	250+	I Am Reading	Kingfisher
Moose Crossing (Moose and Hildy)	L	F	250+	Greene, Stephanie	Marshall Cavendish
Moose Is Loose, A	F	F	120	Little Readers	Houghton Mifflin Harcourt
*Moose Tales	J	F	250+	Van Laan, Nancy	Houghton Mifflin Harcourt
Moose, The	R	I	250+	Wildlife of North America	Red Brick Learning
Moose's Big Idea (Moose and Hildy)	L	F	250+	Greene, Stephanie	Marshall Cavendish
Moose's Loose Tooth	G	F	142	Spinelle, Nancy Louise	Kaeden Books
Moosling in Winter	K	F	429	Leveled Literacy Intervention/ Blue System	Heinemann
Moosling the Baby Sitter	G	F	230	Leveled Literacy Intervention/ Blue System	Heinemann
Moosling the Hero	L	F	374	Leveled Literacy Intervention/ Blue System	Heinemann
Mop	C	RF	74	Leveled Literacy Intervention/ Orange System	Heinemann
Moppet on the Run	J	RF	250+	PM Story Books	Rigby
Moray Eels and Cleaner Shrimp Work Together	K	I	250+	Animals Working Together	Capstone Press
More About Boy: Roald Dahl's Tales from Childhood	V	B	250+	Dahl, Roald	Farrar, Straus, & Giroux
More About Paddington	Q	F	250+	Bond, Michael	Houghton Mifflin Harcourt
More Adventures of the Great Brain	T	RF	250+	Fitzgerald, John D.	Yearling Books
More and More Clowns	D	F	249	Van Allen, Roach	SRA/McGraw Hill
More Food for the Big Cat	E	RF	82	Bonnell, Kris	Reading Reading Books
More Marine Mammals	K	I	324	Larkin's Little Readers	Wilbooks
More Monsters in School	N	RF	250+	Godfrey, M.	Fitzhenry & Whiteside
"More More More," Said the Baby	I	RF	250+	Williams, Vera B.	Scholastic
More or Less Fish Story	E	F	68	Wylie, Joanne & David	Children's Press
More or Less: A Rain Forest Counting Book	I	I	139	Counting Books	Capstone Press
More Pepper for Carl	D	RF	87	Bonnell, Kris	Reading Reading Books
More Perfect than the Moon	R	HF	250+	MacLachlan, Patricia	HarperCollins
More Perfect Union, A: The Story of Our Constitution	S	I	250+	Maestro, Betsy & Giulio	William Morrow
More Places to Visit	L	I	238	Windows on Literacy	National Geographic
More Science of You	Q	I	250+	Reading Expeditions	National Geographic
More Spaghetti I Say	G	F	340	Gelman, Rita	Scholastic
More Spaghetti!	I	RF	250+	PM Plus Story Books	Rigby
*More Stories from Grandma's Attic	O	RF	250+	Richardson, Arleta	Chariot Victor Publishing
*More Stories Huey Tells	O	RF	250+	Cameron, Ann	Alfred A. Knopf
*More Stories Julian Tells	O	RF	250+	Cameron, Ann	Random House
*More Tales of Amanda Pig	L	F	1939	Van Leeuwen, Jean	Penguin Group
*More Tales of Oliver Pig	L	F	250+	Van Leeuwen, Jean	Puffin Books
More Than a Meal	H	RF	172	Avenues	Hampton Brown
More Than Anything Else	R	HF	250+	Bradby, Marie	Scholastic
More Than One	I	F	238	Sunshine	Wright Group/McGraw Hill
More Than the Blues	Z	I	250+	What's the Issue?	Compass Point Books
More Trouble	H	F	264	Bella and Rosie Series	Literacy Footprints
More Water, Please! Animals in Dry Places	M	I	250+	Literacy by Design	Rigby
*More! More! More!	M	TL	250+	Story Box	Wright Group/McGraw Hill
More, The Merrier, The	Q	RF	250+	Mazer, Anne	Scholastic
Morgan Horses Are My Favorite!	O	I	250+	My Favorite Horses	Lerner Publishing Group

* Collection of short stories   # Graphic text
^ Mature content with lower level text demands

TITLE	LEVEL	GENRE	WORD COUNT	AUTHOR / SERIES	PUBLISHER / DISTRIBUTOR
Morgan's Zoo	Q	F	250+	Howe, James	Aladdin
Morgy Coast to Coast	P	RF	250+	Lewis, Maggie	Houghton Mifflin Harcourt
Morgy Makes His Move	O	RF	250+	Lewis, Maggie	Houghton Mifflin Harcourt
^Mormon Pioneer Trail, The	Q	I	250+	On Deck	Rigby
Morning and Night	C	I	112	Vocabulary Readers	Houghton Mifflin Harcourt
Morning and Night	C	I	112	Vocabulary Readers/CA	Houghton Mifflin Harcourt
Morning Bath	J	F	250+	Sunshine	Wright Group/McGraw Hill
Morning Dance, The	K	RF	268	Jellybeans	Rigby
Morning Girl	S	HF	250+	Dorris, Michael	Hyperion
Morning Meals Around the World	M	I	250+	Meals Around the World	Picture Window Books
Morning Queen, The	J	F	250+	Sunshine	Wright Group/McGraw Hill
Morning Star	J	F	250+	Literacy 2000	Rigby
Morning, Noon, and Night	LB	I	4	Reach	National Geographic
Morocco	P	I	1956	Country Explorers	Lerner Publishing Group
Morphing Monster, The	T	F	250+	Reading Safari	Mondo Publishing
Morris and Boris at the Circus	J	F	250+	Wiseman, Bernard	HarperTrophy
Morris Goes to School	J	F	250+	Wiseman, Bernard	HarperTrophy
Morris Plays Hide and Seek	I	F	304	Big Cat	Pacific Learning
Morris the Moose	H	F	250+	Wiseman, Bernard	HarperTrophy
Morse and the Telegraph	N	B	524	Leveled Readers Science	Houghton Mifflin Harcourt
Morte D' Arthur, Le	Z+	TL	250+	Malory, Sir Thomas	Hyperion
Moses	V	B	250+	Weatherford, Carole Boston	Hyperion
Mosquito	C	I	46	Book Bank	Wright Group/McGraw Hill
Mosquito Bite	T	I	250+	Siy, Alexandra	Charlesbridge
Mosquito Buzzed, A	E	F	133	Little Readers	Houghton Mifflin Harcourt
^Mosquito King, The	T	F	250+	Welvaert, Scott R.	Stone Arch Books
Mosquitoes	P	I	2297	Early Bird Nature Books	Lerner Publishing Group
Mosquitoes	E	I	39	Pebble Books	Grolier
Mosquitoes	I	I	193	Sails	Rigby
Mosquitoes: Tiny Insect Troublemakers	T	I	3101	Insect World	Lerner Publishing Group
Mossflower	Z	F	250+	Jacques, Brian	Ace Books
Most Beautiful Child, The	M	TL	250+	Cambridge Reading	Pearson Learning Group
Most Beautiful Place in the World, The	O	RF	250+	Cameron, Ann	Alfred A. Knopf
Most Dangerous Animals, The	K	I	250+	EXtreme Animals	Capstone Press
Most Excellent Community Service Project, The	R	RF	250+	Reading Street	Pearson
Most Perfect Spot, The	K	F	250+	Goode, Diane	HarperCollins
Most Scary Ghost	H	F	355	Jellybeans	Rigby
Most Terrible Creature in the World, The	M	F	340	Pacific Literacy	Pacific Learning
Most Unusual Pet, The	J	RF	250+	Scooters	ETA/Cuisenaire
Most Wonderful Doll in the World, The	O	RF	250+	McGinley, Phyllis	Scholastic
Mostly Michael	Q	RF	250+	Smith, Robert Kimmel	Bantam Books
Mostly Monty	M	RF	250+	Hurwitz, Johanna	Candlewick Press
Mostly True Adventures of Homer P. Figg, The	X	HF	250+	Philbrick, Rodman	Scholastic
Mother and Me	B	RF	48	Spinelle, Nancy Louise	Kaeden Books
Mother Animals	B	I	45	Bonnell, Kris	Reading Reading Books
Mother Bear's Scarf	E	F	152	PM Stars	Rigby
Mother Bird	C	RF	75	PM Plus Story Books	Rigby
Mother Dog and Her Puppies, A	L	I	250+	All About Dogs	Literacy Footprints
Mother Duck's Walk	F	F	288	On Our Way to English	Rigby
Mother Giant's Book Review	N	F	250+	Springboard	Wright Group/McGraw Hill
Mother Goose Caper, The	K	F	799	Georgie Giraffe	Literacy Footprints
Mother Hen	G	F	205	Book Bank	Wright Group/McGraw Hill
Mother Hippopotamus	LB	F	7	Foundations	Wright Group/McGraw Hill
Mother Hippopotamus Gets Wet	J	F	421	Foundations	Wright Group/McGraw Hill

* Collection of short stories   # Graphic text
^ Mature content with lower level text demands

TITLE	LEVEL	GENRE	WORD COUNT	AUTHOR / SERIES	PUBLISHER / DISTRIBUTOR
Mother Hippopotamus Goes Canoeing	L	F	250+	Foundations	Wright Group/McGraw Hill
Mother Hippopotamus Goes Shopping	C	F	79	Foundations	Wright Group/McGraw Hill
Mother Hippopotamus's Dry Skin	I	F	201	Foundations	Wright Group/McGraw Hill
Mother Hippopotamus's Hiccups	I	F	162	Foundations	Wright Group/McGraw Hill
#Mother Jones: Labor Leader	T	B	250+	Graphic Library	Capstone Press
Mother Nature Goes Nuts! Amazing Natural Disasters	W	I	250+	Klutz	Scholastic
Mother Octopus	J	RF	119	Books for Young Learners	Richard C. Owen
Mother Osprey: Nursery Rhymes for Buoys & Gulls	Q	TL	250+	Nolan, Euey	Sylvan Dell Publishing
Mother Sea Turtle	K	I	240	Foundations	Wright Group/McGraw Hill
Mother Sea Turtle	F	I	155	Leveled Literacy Intervention/ Blue System	Heinemann
Mother Sun's Rest Day	H	F	250+	Momentum Literacy Program	Troll Associates
Mother Teresa	M	B	250+	First Biographies	Red Brick Learning
Mother Teresa	S	B	3716	History Maker Bios	Lerner Publishing Group
Mother Teresa	O	B	1672	On My Own Biography	Lerner Publishing Group
Mother Teresa of Calcutta	Q	B	250+	WorldScapes	ETA/Cuisenaire
Mother Teresa: A Life of Caring	O	B	454	Pull Ahead Books	Lerner Publishing Group
^Mother Teresa: Mother to the Poor	T	B	250+	Hameray Biography Series	Hameray Publishing Group
Mother Tiger and Her Cubs	G	F	212	PM Plus Story Books	Rigby
Mothers	F	I	49	Families	Capstone Press
Mothers	B	I	26	Pebble Books	Capstone Press
Mothers and Babies	F	I	163	PM Science Readers	Rigby
Mother's Day	F	I	128	Fiesta Holiday Series	Pearson Learning Group
Mother's Day	E	RF	118	PM Plus Story Books	Rigby
Mother's Day Surprises	K	F	250+	Krensky, Stephen	Marshall Cavendish
Mother's Helpers	K	RF	250+	Ready Readers	Pearson Learning Group
Mother's Journey, A	O	RF	1660	Markle, Sandra	Charlesbridge
^Mothman: The Unsolved Mystery	R	I	250+	Mysteries of Science	Capstone Press
Moths	I	I	102	Bugs, Bugs, Bugs	Capstone Press
Moths	I	I	65	Pebble Books	Red Brick Learning
Mothstorm: The Horror from Beyond Uranus Georgium Sidus!	Y	F	250+	Reeve, Philip	Bloomsbury Children's Books
Motion	I	I	155	Instant Readers	Harcourt School Publishers
^Motion	P	I	250+	Our Physical World	Capstone Press
Motion	Q	I	250+	Simply Science	Compass Point Books
Motion: Push and Pull, Fast and Slow	N	I	250+	Amazing Science	Picture Window Books
^Motocross	R	I	250+	Download	Hameray Publishing Group
Motocross Cycles	Q	I	250+	Wild Rides!	Capstone Press
Motocross Double-Cross	Q	RF	250+	Maddox, Jake	Stone Arch Books
Motorbike Race, The	C	RF	48	Joy Readers	Pearson Learning Group
Motorbike Racer	O	B	250+	Wonder World	Wright Group/McGraw Hill
Motorbikes	Y	I	250+	Boldprint	Steck-Vaughn
Motorcross Freestyle	M	I	250+	Horsepower	Capstone Press
Motorcycle Photo, The	J	RF	250+	PM Plus Story Books	Rigby
Motorcycle Police	S	I	250+	Law Enforcement	Capstone Press
Motorcycle Road Racing	W	I	4756	Motor Mania	Lerner Publishing Group
^Motorcycles	T	I	250+	Download	Hameray Publishing Group
Motorcycles	H	I	112	Mighty Machines	Capstone Press
Motorcycles	N	I	367	Pull Ahead Books	Lerner Publishing Group
^Motorcycles of the Past	M	I	250+	On Deck	Rigby
Motorcycles on the Move	K	I	367	Lightning Bolt Books	Lerner Publishing Group
Motorcycles: The Ins and Outs of Superbikes, Choppers, and Other Motorcycles	V	I	250+	Velocity-RPM	Capstone Press

TITLE	LEVEL	GENRE	WORD COUNT	AUTHOR / SERIES	PUBLISHER / DISTRIBUTOR
Mound Builders, The	P	I	426	Independent Readers Social Studies	Houghton Mifflin Harcourt
Mound of the Dead: The City of Mohenjo-Daro	X	I	2018	Independent Readers Social Studies	Houghton Mifflin Harcourt
Mount Rushmore	O	I	250+	American Symbols	Picture Window Books
Mount Rushmore	Q	I	250+	Let's See	Compass Point Books
Mount Rushmore	D	I	36	Leveled Readers Language Support	Houghton Mifflin Harcourt
Mount Rushmore	N	I	381	Lightning Bolt Books	Lerner Publishing Group
Mount Rushmore	P	I	653	Pull Ahead Books	Lerner Publishing Group
Mount St. Helens	O	I	250+	Early Connections	Benchmark Education
Mount St. Helen's	P	I	782	Reading Street	Pearson
Mount St. Helen's: A Mountain Explodes	O	I	250+	Literacy by Design	Rigby
Mount Vernon	V	I	250+	Cornerstones of Freedom	Children's Press
Mountain Adventure	R	RF	250+	Reading Expeditions	National Geographic
Mountain Animals	D	I	48	Benchmark Rebus	Marshall Cavendish
Mountain Bike Challenge, The	Q	I	250+	Orbit Chapter Books	Pacific Learning
Mountain Bike Mania	O	RF	250+	Action Packs	Rigby
Mountain Bikes	Q	I	250+	Wild Rides!	Capstone Press
Mountain Biking	M	I	250+	To the Extreme	Capstone Press
Mountain Food Chains	T	I	250+	Protecting Food Chains	Heinemann Library
Mountain Gorillas	O	I	2986	Early Bird Nature Books	Lerner Publishing Group
Mountain Gorillas	O	I	250+	Wonder World	Wright Group/McGraw Hill
Mountain Gorillas in Danger	N	I	250+	Soar To Success	Houghton Mifflin Harcourt
Mountain Hike, The	F	RF	176	Developing Books, Set 2	Pioneer Valley
Mountain Lion, The	O	I	250+	Crewe, Sabrina	Steck-Vaughn
Mountain Lions	S	I	2323	Animal Predators	Lerner Publishing Group
Mountain Man and the President, The	Q	B	250+	First Reports	Compass Point Books
Mountain Manor Mystery	S	RF	250+	Bookshop	Mondo Publishing
Mountain Men of the West	S	I	250+	The Library of the Westward Expansion	Rosen Publishing Group
Mountain Mona	L	F	820	Big Cat	Pacific Learning
Mountain of Blintzes, A	N	RF	250+	Goldin, Barbara Diamond	Marshall Cavendish
Mountain Rescue	I	I	209	Sails	Rigby
Mountain, The	J	F	348	Leveled Readers	Houghton Mifflin Harcourt
Mountain, The	J	F	348	Leveled Readers/CA	Houghton Mifflin Harcourt
Mountain, The	J	F	348	Leveled Readers/TX	Houghton Mifflin Harcourt
Mountains	L	I	250+	Early Connections	Benchmark Education
Mountains	Q	I	250+	First Reports	Compass Point Books
Mountains	J	I	293	Landforms	Lerner Publishing Group
Mountains	P	I	250+	Science Kids	Kingfisher
Mountains	R	I	250+	The Wonders of Our World	Crabtree
Mountains	S	I	250+	Weitzman, David	Steck-Vaughn
Mountains and Highlands	W	I	250+	Biomes Atlases	Raintree
Mountains of Fire	M	I	153	Windows on Literacy	National Geographic
Mountains of Quilt, The	N	F	250+	Willard, Nancy	Harcourt Brace
Mountains, Earthquakes and Volcanoes	U	I	2583	Science Support Readers	Houghton Mifflin Harcourt
Mountains, Hills, and Cliffs	M	I	250+	PM Plus Nonfiction	Rigby
Mountains: The Land Around Us	S	I	250+	Reading Expeditions	National Geographic
Mounted Police	S	I	250+	Law Enforcement	Capstone Press
Mounted Police	I	I	200	On Deck	Rigby
Mouse	C	F	78	Leveled Literacy Intervention/ Orange System	Heinemann
Mouse	C	F	40	Story Box	Wright Group/McGraw Hill
Mouse and Bear	A	F	26	Leveled Readers	Houghton Mifflin Harcourt

* Collection of short stories   # Graphic text
^ Mature content with lower level text demands

TITLE	LEVEL	GENRE	WORD COUNT	AUTHOR / SERIES	PUBLISHER / DISTRIBUTOR
Mouse and Bear	A	F	26	Leveled Readers/CA	Houghton Mifflin Harcourt
Mouse and Bear Are Friends	A	F	35	Leveled Readers	Houghton Mifflin Harcourt
Mouse and Bear Are Friends	A	F	35	Leveled Readers/CA	Houghton Mifflin Harcourt
Mouse and Crocodile	L	TL	573	Leveled Readers	Houghton Mifflin Harcourt
Mouse and Crocodile	L	TL	573	Leveled Readers/CA	Houghton Mifflin Harcourt
Mouse and Crocodile	L	TL	573	Leveled Readers/TX	Houghton Mifflin Harcourt
Mouse and Mole: A Winter Wonderland	L	F	250+	Yee, Wong Herbert	Houghton Mifflin Harcourt
Mouse and Mole: Fine Feathered Friends	L	F	250+	Yee, Wong Herbert	Houghton Mifflin Harcourt
Mouse and Moose	LB	I	7	Reading Street	Pearson
Mouse and Owl	I	RF	250+	Start to Read	School Zone
Mouse and the Elephant, The	J	TL	250+	Little Readers	Houghton Mifflin Harcourt
Mouse and the Elephant, The	I	TL	250+	The Rowland Reading Program Libary	Rowland Reading Foundation
Mouse and the Motorcycle, The	O	F	250+	Cleary, Beverly	Avon Books
Mouse Around	WB	F	0	Collington, Peter	Alfred A. Knopf
Mouse Called Wolf, A	O	F	250+	King-Smith, Dick	Alfred A. Knopf
Mouse Deer and the Crocodiles	J	TL	250+	The Rowland Reading Program Libary	Rowland Reading Foundation
Mouse Deer and the Crocodiles, The	J	TL	250+	PM Plus Story Books	Rigby
Mouse Deer Escapes, The	J	TL	250+	PM Plus Story Books	Rigby
Mouse Family's Misadventure, The	K	F	250+	InfoTrek	ETA/Cuisenaire
Mouse Finds a House	D	F	72	Start to Read	School Zone
Mouse Hunt	C	RF	40	Brand New Readers	Candlewick Press
Mouse in the Forest, The	I	I	211	Leveled Readers	Houghton Mifflin Harcourt
Mouse in the House, A	G	RF	228	Jasper the Cat	Pioneer Valley
Mouse Island Marathon, The	O	F	250+	Stilton, Geronimo	Scholastic
Mouse Magic	O	RF	250+	Baglio, Ben M.	Scholastic
Mouse Manual	M	F	250+	Sails	Rigby
Mouse Mapper, The	I	F	273	Take Two Books	Wright Group/McGraw Hill
Mouse Monster	J	F	302	Jellybeans	Rigby
Mouse of Amherst, The	Q	F	250+	Spires, Elizabeth	Farrar, Straus, & Giroux
Mouse on the Moon, A	D	F	55	Dominie Readers	Pearson Learning Group
Mouse Party!	M	F	250+	Little Celebrations	Pearson Learning Group
Mouse Rap, The	W	RF	250+	Myers, Walter Dean	HarperTrophy
*Mouse Soup	J	F	1350	Lobel, Arnold	HarperCollins
Mouse Stone, The	K	F	250+	Lighthouse	Ginn & Co.
*Mouse Tales	J	F	1519	Lobel, Arnold	HarperCollins
Mouse Train	B	F	48	Story Box	Wright Group/McGraw Hill
Mouse Views	D	RF	29	McMillan, Bruce	Holiday House
Mouse Who Wanted to Marry, The	J	F	250+	Bank Street	Bantam Books
Mouse, The	C	F	26	Pacific Literacy	Pacific Learning
Mouse-Deer Must Be Quick!	K	TL	250+	Foland, Constance	Hampton Brown
Mousehunter, The	T	F	250+	Milway, Alex	Little Brown and Company
Mouse's Baby Blanket	D	F	68	Brown, Beverly Swerdlow	Continental Press
Mouse's House	D	F	70	New Way Red	Steck-Vaughn
Mouse's Meadow	C	I	62	Independent Readers Science	Houghton Mifflin Harcourt
Mousetrap	G	RF	49	Snowball, Diane	Scholastic
Mousie Love	L	F	250+	Chaconas, Dori	Bloomsbury Children's Books
Moustachio's Best Magic Trick	M	RF	250+	Tristars	Richard C. Owen
Moutaineering Adventures	S	I	250+	Dangerous Adventures	Red Brick Learning
Mouths	B	I	33	Animal Traits	Lerner Publishing Group
Mouths And Noses	M	I	250+	Voyages	SRA/McGraw Hill
Move Along: Verbs in Action	K	I	250+	Bookworms	Marshall Cavendish

* Collection of short stories   # Graphic text
^ Mature content with lower level text demands

TITLE	LEVEL	GENRE	WORD COUNT	AUTHOR / SERIES	PUBLISHER / DISTRIBUTOR
Move It	E	I	58	Wonder World	Wright Group/McGraw Hill
Move It!	O	I	281	Early Explorers	Benchmark Education
Move It!	R	I	250+	Orbit Chapter Books	Pacific Learning
Move It!	L	I	268	Spyglass Books	Compass Point Books
Move It! Work It! A Song About Simple Machines	N	I	250+	Science Songs	Picture Window Books
Move It!: The Story of Animation	P	I	250+	Rigby Literacy	Rigby
Move Like Us!	H	RF	250+	Home Connection Collection	Rigby
Move Over!	E	F	118	Story Basket	Wright Group/McGraw Hill
Move to the Beat	L	I	250+	InfoTrek Plus	ETA/Cuisenaire
Moves Make the Man, The	Z	RF	250+	Brooks, Bruce	HarperTrophy
Movie FX	U	I	250+	Boldprint	Steck-Vaughn
Movie Magic	T	I	250+	Sunshine	Wright Group/McGraw Hill
Movin' On In	M	RF	250+	Social Studies Connects	Kane Press
Movin' On!: Dreams, Careers, Success	W	I	250+	Boldprint	Steck-Vaughn
Moving	J	I	250+	Growing Up	Heinemann Library
Moving	B	I	56	Little Red Readers	Sundance
Moving	R	RF	2569	Reading Street	Pearson
Moving	G	I	156	Vocabulary Readers	Houghton Mifflin Harcourt
Moving	G	I	156	Vocabulary Readers/CA	Houghton Mifflin Harcourt
Moving	G	I	156	Vocabulary Readers/TX	Houghton Mifflin Harcourt
Moving and Shaking	Q	I	250+	Bookweb	Rigby
Moving Away	F	RF	140	InfoTrek	ETA/Cuisenaire
Moving Day	D	RF	90	Foundations	Wright Group/McGraw Hill
Moving Day	F	F	206	Kalan, Robert	Greenwillow Books
Moving Day	G	RF	215	Momentum Literacy Program	Troll Associates
Moving Day	K	F	379	Reading Street	Pearson
Moving Day	H	RF	315	Rigby Flying Colors	Rigby
Moving Day	LB	RF	28	Rigby Literacy	Rigby
Moving Day	C	RF	35	Rigby Star	Rigby
Moving Day	D	RF	64	Rookie Readers	Children's Press
Moving Day	F	RF	55	Shuter, Jane and Reynoldson, Fiona	Rigby
Moving Day	E	RF	110	Sunshine	Wright Group/McGraw Hill
Moving Day Surprise	H	RF	209	Bebop Books	Lee & Low Books Inc.
Moving From Place to Place	E	I	86	Shutterbug Books	Steck-Vaughn
Moving Home	M	I	250+	Explorations	Okapi Educational Materials
Moving Home	M	I	250+	Explorations	Eleanor Curtain Publishing
Moving In	E	RF	82	Foundations	Wright Group/McGraw Hill
Moving Mama to Town	X	RF	250+	Young, Ronder Thomas	Bantam Books
Moving on Sand and Snow	E	I	156	Sails	Rigby
Moving Things	M	I	250+	Sunshine	Wright Group/McGraw Hill
Moving to America	E	RF	81	Carousel Readers	Pearson Learning Group
Moving to America: My Travel Scrapbook	K	I	308	Dominie Factivity Series	Pearson Learning Group
Moving with Machines	N	I	272	Early Explorers	Benchmark Education
Moving Without Legs	O	I	250+	Sails	Rigby
Moving World, A	W	I	250+	PM Extensions	Rigby
Mozart	N	RF	250+	PM Extensions	Rigby
Mozart Question, The	W	RF	250+	Morpurgo, Michael	Candlewick Press
Mozart Season, The	X	RF	250+	Wolff, Virginia Euwer	Henry Holt & Co.
Mr. and Mrs. Murphy and Bernard	K	F	250+	Little Celebrations	Pearson Learning Group
Mr. and Mrs. Portly and Their Little Dog, Snack	M	RF	250+	Jordan, Sandra	Farrar, Straus, & Giroux
Mr. Ape	O	F	250+	King-Smith, Dick	Alfred A. Knopf
Mr. Beekman's Deli	H	F	96	Story Basket	Wright Group/McGraw Hill

* Collection of short stories   # Graphic text
^ Mature content with lower level text demands

TITLE	LEVEL	GENRE	WORD COUNT	AUTHOR / SERIES	PUBLISHER / DISTRIBUTOR
Mr. Beep	M	F	250+	Read Alongs	Rigby
Mr. Big Goes on Holiday	G	F	177	Storyworlds	Heinemann
Mr. Big Goes to the Park	F	F	186	Storyworlds	Heinemann
Mr. Big Has a Party	G	F	177	Storyworlds	Heinemann
Mr. Big Is a Big Help	G	F	212	Storyworlds	Heinemann
Mr. Bitter's Butter	H	F	231	Story Basket	Wright Group/McGraw Hill
Mr. Brown	C	RF	20	KinderReaders	Rigby
Mr. Bumbleticker	B	F	28	Foundations	Wright Group/McGraw Hill
Mr. Bumbleticker Goes Shopping	J	F	391	Foundations	Wright Group/McGraw Hill
Mr. Bumbleticker Goes to the Zoo	L	RF	250+	Foundations	Wright Group/McGraw Hill
Mr. Bumbleticker Likes to Cook	I	F	196	Foundations	Wright Group/McGraw Hill
Mr. Bumbleticker Likes to Fix Machines	I	F	142	Foundations	Wright Group/McGraw Hill
Mr. Bumbleticker's Apples	I	F	338	Foundations	Wright Group/McGraw Hill
Mr. Bumbleticker's Birthday	E	F	110	Foundations	Wright Group/McGraw Hill
Mr. Bun's Stew	F	RF	73	Joy Starters	Pearson Learning Group
Mr. Burger Is a Farmer	H	I	106	InfoTrek	ETA/Cuisenaire
Mr. Clutterbus	H	F	250+	Voyages	SRA/McGraw Hill
Mr. Cool	K	F	250+	I Am Reading	Kingfisher
Mr. Crawford	E	RF	119	Foundations	Wright Group/McGraw Hill
Mr. Cricket Finds a Friend	G	F	134	Carousel Readers	Pearson Learning Group
Mr. Cricket Takes a Vacation	E	F	165	Carousel Readers	Pearson Learning Group
Mr. Cricket's New Home	F	F	121	Carousel Readers	Pearson Learning Group
Mr. Croc Rocks	K	F	250+	Read-it! Chapter Books	Picture Window Books
Mr. Davis Is a Security Officer	F	I	101	InfoTrek	ETA/Cuisenaire
Mr. Docker Is Off His Rocker!	O	RF	250+	Gutman, Dan	HarperTrophy
Mr. Dugas Is a Carpenter	F	I	84	InfoTrek	ETA/Cuisenaire
Mr. Egg	E	F	22	Pair-It Books	Steck-Vaughn
Mr. Fahrenheit and Mr. Celsius	T	I	1330	Leveled Readers Science	Houghton Mifflin Harcourt
Mr. Fin's Trip	E	F	130	Ready Readers	Pearson Learning Group
Mr. Fixit	H	RF	196	Sunshine	Wright Group/McGraw Hill
Mr. Fizzle, the Man Who Went "Boo!"	I	F	250+	Home Connection Collection	Rigby
Mr. Florentine's Violin	M	RF	250+	Bookweb	Rigby
Mr. Fluff at Laura's House	F	RF	134	Developing Books Set 4	Pioneer Valley
Mr. Granite Is from Another Planet!	O	RF	250+	Gutman, Dan	HarperTrophy
Mr. Greg's Garden	E	RF	118	Windows on Literacy	National Geographic
Mr. Grim and the Goose That Laid Golden Eggs	O	TL	1723	Reading Street	Pearson
Mr. Grump	D	F	73	Sunshine	Wright Group/McGraw Hill
Mr. Gumpy's Motor Car	L	RF	250+	Burningham, John	HarperCollins
Mr. Gumpy's Outing	L	RF	283	Burningham, John	Henry Holt & Co.
Mr. Hoot's Room	J	F	250+	The Wright Skills	Wright Group/McGraw Hill
Mr. Hynde Is Out of His Mind!	O	RF	250+	Gutman, Dan	HarperTrophy
Mr. Jay's Bad Day	G	RF	72	Windows on Literacy	National Geographic
Mr. Kean's Garden	M	RF	250+	Literacy by Design	Rigby
Mr. Kean's Garden	M	RF	250+	On Our Way to English	Rigby
Mr. Klutz Is Nuts!	O	RF	250+	Gutman, Dan	HarperTrophy
Mr. Lee's Worm Farm	L	RF	250+	Scooters	ETA/Cuisenaire
Mr. Lincoln's Drummer	W	HF	250+	Wisler, G. Clifton	Penguin Group
Mr. Louie Is Screwy!	O	RF	250+	Gutman, Dan	HarperTrophy
Mr. Macky Is Wacky!	O	RF	250+	Gutman, Dan	HarperTrophy
Mr. Magee's Goats	I	F	354	Sails	Rigby
Mr. Mancini's Rats	K	F	250+	Popcorn	Sundance
Mr. Marvel and the Cake	D	F	119	Storyworlds	Heinemann
Mr. Marvel and the Car	D	F	118	Storyworlds	Heinemann
Mr. Marvel and the Lemonade	D	F	100	Storyworlds	Heinemann

TITLE	LEVEL	GENRE	WORD COUNT	AUTHOR / SERIES	PUBLISHER / DISTRIBUTOR
Mr. Marvel and the Washing	D	F	100	Storyworlds	Heinemann
Mr. McCready's Cleaning Day	H	F	119	Shilling, Tracy	Scholastic
Mr. McGillicuddy's Clocks	M	RF	250+	Voyages	SRA/McGraw Hill
Mr. McGrah's New Car	H	F	119	Book Bank	Wright Group/McGraw Hill
Mr. Merton's Vacation	K	RF	250+	Sails	Rigby
Mr. Miller's Old Car	F	RF	108	Seedlings	Continental Press
Mr. Mulch's Magic Mixtures	L	F	250+	Cambridge Reading	Pearson Learning Group
Mr. Mysterious & Company	R	F	250+	Fleischman, Sid	Beech Tree Books
Mr. Nobody	J	RF	499	Red Rocket Readers	Flying Start Books
Mr. Noisy	D	F	90	Learn to Read	Creative Teaching Press
Mr. Noisy Builds a House	D	F	35	Learn to Read	Creative Teaching Press
Mr. Noisy Paints His House	E	F	159	Learn to Read	Creative Teaching Press
Mr. Noisy's Book of Patterns	G	F	47	Learn to Read	Creative Teaching Press
Mr. Noisy's Helpers	F	F	81	Learn to Read	Creative Teaching Press
Mr. Pappas Is a Waiter	F	I	106	InfoTrek	ETA/Cuisenaire
Mr. Pepperpot's Pet	K	F	250+	Literacy 2000	Rigby
Mr. Popper's Penguins	Q	F	250+	Atwater, Richard & Florence	Little Brown and Company
Mr. Post's Class	O	RF	1606	Reading Street	Pearson
Mr. Potter's Pet	N	F	250+	King-Smith, Dick	Hyperion
Mr. President Goes to School	N	F	250+	Walton, Rick	Peachtree
*Mr. President: A Book of U.S. Presidents	S	B	250+	Sullivan, George	Scholastic
Mr. Putter & Tabby Catch the Cold	J	RF	250+	Rylant, Cynthia	Harcourt, Inc.
Mr. Putter & Tabby Feed the Fish	J	RF	250+	Rylant, Cynthia	Harcourt, Inc.
Mr. Putter & Tabby Paint the Porch	J	RF	250+	Rylant, Cynthia	Harcourt, Inc.
Mr. Putter & Tabby Row the Boat	J	RF	250+	Rylant, Cynthia	Harcourt Trade
Mr. Putter & Tabby Run the Race	J	RF	250+	Rylant, Cynthia	Harcourt, Inc.
Mr. Putter & Tabby See the Stars	J	RF	250+	Rylant, Cynthia	Harcourt
Mr. Putter & Tabby Spill the Beans	J	RF	250+	Rylant, Cynthia	Harcourt, Inc.
Mr. Putter & Tabby Spin the Yarn	J	RF	250+	Rylant, Cynthia	Harcourt, Inc.
Mr. Putter & Tabby Take the Train	J	RF	250+	Rylant, Cynthia	Harcourt Trade
Mr. Putter & Tabby Toot the Horn	J	RF	250+	Rylant, Cynthia	Harcourt Trade
Mr. Putter & Tabby Write the Book	J	RF	250+	Rylant, Cynthia	Harcourt, Inc.
Mr. Putter and Tabby Bake the Cake	J	RF	250+	Rylant, Cynthia	Harcourt Trade
Mr. Putter and Tabby Clear the Decks	J	RF	250+	Rylant, Cynthia	Sandpiper Books
Mr. Putter and Tabby Fly the Plane	J	RF	250+	Rylant, Cynthia	Harcourt Trade
Mr. Putter and Tabby Pick the Pears	J	RF	250+	Rylant, Cynthia	Harcourt Trade
Mr. Putter and Tabby Pour the Tea	J	RF	250+	Rylant, Cynthia	Harcourt Trade
Mr. Putter and Tabby Walk the Dog	J	RF	250+	Rylant, Cynthia	Harcourt Trade
Mr. Rabbit and the Moon	F	F	137	New Way Red	Steck-Vaughn
Mr. Revere and I	U	F	250+	Lawson, Robert	Little Brown and Company
Mr. Rice Is a Salesperson	F	I	93	InfoTrek	ETA/Cuisenaire
Mr. Rover Takes Over	G	F	203	Maccarone, Grace	Scholastic
Mr. Sanchez and the Kick Ball Champ	I	RF	529	Appleton-Smith, Laura	Flyleaf Publishing
Mr. Sharp's Shapes	J	F	374	InfoTrek	ETA/Cuisenaire
Mr. Smarty Loves to Party	F	F	101	Storyteller-Moon Rising	Wright Group/McGraw Hill
Mr. Strike Out	P	RF	4361	Maddox, Jake	Stone Arch Books
Mr. Sun and Mr. Sea	I	TL	202	Little Celebrations	Pearson Learning Group
Mr. Sun and Mr. Sea	L	TL	506	Sunshine	Wright Group/McGraw Hill
Mr. Sunny Is Funny!	O	RF	250+	Gutman, Dan	HarperTrophy
Mr. Tucket	U	HF	250+	Paulsen, Gary	Bantam Books
Mr. Turner Is an Actor	F	I	99	InfoTrek	ETA/Cuisenaire
Mr. Verdi's New Path	I	F	250+	Home Connection Collection	Rigby
Mr. Whisper	H	F	325	Sunshine	Wright Group/McGraw Hill

* Collection of short stories   # Graphic text
^ Mature content with lower level text demands

TITLE	LEVEL	GENRE	WORD COUNT	AUTHOR / SERIES	PUBLISHER / DISTRIBUTOR
Mr. Whisper and Miss Candy	I	RF	221	The Joy Cowley Collection	Hameray Publishing Group
Mr. Whisper and the Big Noise	I	RF	316	The Joy Cowley Collection	Hameray Publishing Group
Mr. Whisper's Sore Ear	I	RF	294	The Joy Cowley Collection	Hameray Publishing Group
Mr. Wind	F	F	37	Literacy 2000	Rigby
Mr. Wink	E	F	86	Ready Readers	Pearson Learning Group
Mr. Wolf	D	F	48	Joy Readers	Pearson Learning Group
Mr. Wolf Leaves Town	H	TL	208	Alphakids	Sundance
Mr. Wolf Tries Again	H	TL	218	Alphakids	Sundance
Mr. Wumple's Travels	I	F	259	Read Alongs	Rigby
Mr. Wu's Shop of Curiosities	R	F	250+	Literacy by Design	Rigby
Mrs. Always Goes Shopping	M	RF	423	Sunshine	Wright Group/McGraw Hill
Mrs. Armitage: Queen of the Road	M	F	250+	Blake, Quentin	Peachtree
Mrs. Barnett's Birthday	I	RF	135	Sunshine	Wright Group/McGraw Hill
Mrs. Bean	I	RF	250+	Rigby Rocket	Rigby
Mrs. Bold	F	RF	94	Literacy 2000	Rigby
Mrs. Brice's Mice	I	F	250+	Hoff, Syd	HarperTrophy
Mrs. Bubble's Baby	M	F	250+	Pacific Literacy	Pacific Learning
Mrs. Cheng's Surprise	G	RF	186	Leveled Readers	Houghton Mifflin Harcourt
Mrs. Cole Is a Bus Driver	F	I	105	InfoTrek	ETA/Cuisenaire
Mrs. Cook's Hats	LB	RF	31	Mader, Jan	Kaeden Books
Mrs. Coonely Is Loony!	O	RF	250+	Gutman, Dan	HarperTrophy
Mrs. Dole Is Out of Control!	O	RF	250+	Gutman, Dan	HarperTrophy
Mrs. Frisby and the Rats of NIMH	V	F	250+	O'Brien, Robert C.	Aladdin
Mrs. Grindy's Shoes	I	F	211	Sunshine	Wright Group/McGraw Hill
Mrs. Hippo's Pizza Parlor	J	F	250+	I Am Reading	Kingfisher
Mrs. Honey's List	J	RF	250+	Voyages	SRA/McGraw Hill
Mrs. Huggins and Her Hen Hannah	K	F	250+	Dabcovich, Lydia	Dutton Children's Books
Mrs. Jafee Is Daffy!	O	RF	250+	Gutman, Dan	HarperTrophy
Mrs. Jeepers' Batty Vacation	L	RF	250+	Dadey, Debbie; Jones, Marcia Thornton	Scholastic
Mrs. Jeepers in Outer Space	M	RF	250+	Dadey, Debbie; Jones, Marcia Thornton	Scholastic
Mrs. Kangaroo's Trip	F	F	120	Early Connections	Benchmark Education
Mrs. Keen	G	RF	88	City Stories	Rigby
Mrs. Kormel Is Not Normal!	O	RF	250+	Gutman, Dan	HarperTrophy
Mrs. Lunch	LB	F	17	Joy Readers	Pearson Learning Group
Mrs. Marigold's Menagerie	Q	RF	250+	Sails	Rigby
Mrs. McGee's Coconut	M	F	250+	Nolan, Allia Zobel	Tiger Tales
Mrs. McNosh Hangs Up Her Wash	H	F	166	Little Celebrations	Pearson Learning Group
Mrs. Mog's Cats	F	F	124	Rigby Literacy	Rigby
Mrs. Mog's Cats	F	F	126	Rigby Star	Rigby
Mrs. Muddle's Mud-Puddle	I	F	181	Sunshine	Wright Group/McGraw Hill
Mrs. Murphy's Bears	I	RF	188	Little Readers	Houghton Mifflin Harcourt
Mrs. Murphy's Crows	H	RF	120	Books for Young Learners	Richard C. Owen
Mrs. Noodlekugel	J	F	250+	Pinkwater, Daniel	Candlewick Press
Mrs. Patches and Her Fudge	J	F	250+	The Wright Skills	Wright Group/McGraw Hill
Mrs. Patty Is Batty!	O	RF	250+	Gutman, Dan	HarperTrophy
*Mrs. Piggle-Wiggle	O	F	250+	MacDonald, Betty	Scholastic
*Mrs. Piggle-Wiggle's Farm	O	F	250+	MacDonald, Betty	Scholastic
*Mrs. Piggle-Wiggle's Magic	O	F	250+	MacDonald, Betty	Scholastic
Mrs. Pomelili's Wet Week	G	F	215	Book Bank	Wright Group/McGraw Hill
Mrs. Popinpop's Ghost	G	RF	186	Springboard	Wright Group/McGraw Hill
Mrs. Popinpop's New Novel	N	RF	250+	Springboard	Wright Group/McGraw Hill

TITLE	LEVEL	GENRE	WORD COUNT	AUTHOR / SERIES	PUBLISHER / DISTRIBUTOR
"Mrs. Riley Bought Five Itchy Aardvarks" and Other Painless Tricks for Memorizing Science Facts	T	I	3465	Cleary, Brian P.	Millbrook Press
Mrs. Roopy Is Loopy!	O	RF	250+	Gutman, Dan	HarperTrophy
Mrs. Sato's Hens	D	F	51	Little Celebrations	Pearson Learning Group
Mrs. Sato's Hens	D	F	51	Little Readers	Houghton Mifflin Harcourt
Mrs. Sheep's Garden	K	F	953	Kratky, Lada	Hampton Brown
Mrs. Snip Snap	G	F	183	Red Rocket Readers	Flying Start Books
Mrs. Spider's Beautiful Web	H	F	250+	PM Story Books	Rigby
Mrs. Tuck's Little Tune	F	RF	195	Ready Readers	Pearson Learning Group
Mrs. West Is a Daycare Worker	F	I	102	InfoTrek	ETA/Cuisenaire
Mrs. Wishy-Washy	E	F	102	Story Box	Wright Group/McGraw Hill
Mrs. Wishy-Washy and the Big Farm Fair	I	F	173	The Joy Cowley Collection	Hameray Publishing Group
Mrs. Wishy-Washy and the Big Tub	I	F	160	The Joy Cowley Collection	Hameray Publishing Group
Mrs. Wishy-Washy and the Big Wash	I	F	227	The Joy Cowley Collection	Hameray Publishing Group
Mrs. Wishy-Washy on TV	G	F	192	The Joy Cowley Collection	Hameray Publishing Group
Mrs. Wishy-Washy's Birthday	I	F	200	The Joy Cowley Collection	Hameray Publishing Group
Mrs. Wishy-Washy's Tub	B	F	38	Story Box	Wright Group/McGraw Hill
Mrs. Yee Is a Teacher	H	I	102	InfoTrek	ETA/Cuisenaire
Mrs. Yonkers Is Bonkers!	O	RF	250+	Gutman, Dan	HarperTrophy
Ms. Coco Is Loco!	O	RF	250+	Gutman, Dan	HarperTrophy
Ms. F Goes Back to School	O	RF	1114	Leveled Readers	Houghton Mifflin Harcourt
Ms. F Goes Back to School	O	RF	1114	Leveled Readers/CA	Houghton Mifflin Harcourt
Ms. F Goes Back to School	O	RF	1114	Leveled Readers/TX	Houghton Mifflin Harcourt
Ms. Hakeem Is a Food Bank Volunteer	H	I	90	InfoTrek	ETA/Cuisenaire
Ms. Hannah Is Bananas!	O	RF	250+	Gutman, Dan	HarperTrophy
Ms. Hawkins and the Bake Sale	K	RF	643	Leveled Readers	Houghton Mifflin Harcourt
Ms. Hawkins and the Bake Sale	K	RF	643	Leveled Readers/CA	Houghton Mifflin Harcourt
Ms. Hawkins and the Bake Sale	K	RF	643	Leveled Readers/TX	Houghton Mifflin Harcourt
Ms. Hill Is a Nurse	F	I	97	InfoTrek	ETA/Cuisenaire
Ms. Kim Is a Web Designer	H	I	107	InfoTrek	ETA/Cuisenaire
Ms. Krup Cracks Me Up!	O	RF	250+	Gutman, Dan	HarperTrophy
Ms. LaGrange Is Strange!	O	RF	250+	Gutman, Dan	HarperTrophy
Ms. Pinkerville, You're Our Star!	M	RF	717	Leveled Readers	Houghton Mifflin Harcourt
Ms. Pinkerville, You're Our Star!	M	RF	717	Leveled Readers/CA	Houghton Mifflin Harcourt
Ms. Pinkerville, You're Our Star!	M	RF	717	Leveled Readers/TX	Houghton Mifflin Harcourt
Ms. Todd Is Odd!	O	RF	250+	Gutman, Dan	HarperTrophy
Mt. St. Helens	S	I	1492	Independent Readers Science	Houghton Mifflin Harcourt
Much Ado About Aldo	O	RF	250+	Hurwitz, Johanna	Penguin Group
#Much Ado About Nothing	Z	RF	250+	Manga Shakespeare	Amulet Books
Mud	D	RF	68	Lewison, Wendy Cheyette	Random House
Mud	B	RF	30	Science	Outside the Box
Mud Fairy, The	M	F	250+	Young, Amy	Bloomsbury Children's Books
Mud Girl	Z+	RF	250+	Acheson, Alison	Fitzhenry & Whiteside
Mud Mess	D	F	106	Stone Arch Readers	Stone Arch Books
Mud Pie	C	RF	14	Literacy 2000	Rigby
Mud Pies	E	RF	143	Start to Read	School Zone
Mud Pies	C	RF	56	TOTTS	Tott Publications
Mud Pony, The	M	TL	250+	Reading Rainbow	Scholastic
Mud Pony, The	L	TL	764	Sunshine	Wright Group/McGraw Hill
Mud Puddles	C	RF	24	TOTTS	Tott Publications
Mud Soup	J	RF	250+	Step into Reading	Random House
Mud Tortillas	I	RF	250+	Bebop Books	Lee & Low Books Inc.

* Collection of short stories   # Graphic text
^ Mature content with lower level text demands

TITLE	LEVEL	GENRE	WORD COUNT	AUTHOR / SERIES	PUBLISHER / DISTRIBUTOR
Mud Walk	E	F	183	Story Box	Wright Group/McGraw Hill
Mud!	D	RF	68	Lewison, Wendy Cheyette	Scholastic
Mud!	E	RF	94	Real Kids Readers	Millbrook Press
Mud, Mud, Mud	G	I	83	Windows on Literacy	National Geographic
Muddle Farm	C	F	44	Rigby Star	Rigby
Muddledy Fuddledy Mixed-Up Day, The	M	F	250+	Redhead, Janet Slater	Steck-Vaughn
Muddy Car, The	D	RF	74	Bonnell, Kris	Reading Reading Books
Muddy Mess, The	F	RF	147	Leveled Literacy Intervention/ Blue System	Heinemann
Mudflows and Landslides	W	I	250+	Disasters Up Close	Lerner Publishing Group
Mudshark	T	F	250+	Paulsen, Gary	Scholastic
Mudskipper	G	I	132	Twig	Wright Group/McGraw Hill
Mudskipper and the Water	D	F	57	Bonnell, Kris	Reading Reading Books
Mudskipper, The	A	F	30	Bonnell, Kris	Reading Reading Books
Mudskippers	D	I	58	Bonnell, Kris/About	Reading Reading Books
Mufaro's Beautiful Daughters: An African Tale	N	TL	250+	Steptoe, John	Scholastic
Muffin Goes to Sea	F	F	250+	Classroom Library Set A	Options Publishing Inc.
Muffin Is Trapped	J	RF	250+	PM Story Books	Rigby
Muffy and Fluffy	F	RF	155	First Start	Troll Associates
Muffy's Secret Admirer	M	RF	250+	Brown, Marc	Little Brown and Company
Muggie Maggie	O	RF	250+	Cleary, Beverly	Avon Books
Muhammad Ali	T	B	250+	Amazing Americans	Wright Group/McGraw Hill
Muhammad Ali	U	B	250+	Christopher, Matt	Little Brown and Company
Muhammad Ali	X	B	250+	Just the Facts Biographies	Lerner Publishing Group
Muhammad Ali	U	B	250+	Sports Heroes and Legends	Lerner Publishing Group
#Muhammad Ali: American Champion	S	B	250+	Graphic Library	Capstone Press
^Muhammad Ali: Heavyweight Champion of the World	T	B	250+	Hameray Biography Series	Hameray Publishing Group
Muhammed Ali: The Greatest	P	B	250+	Great African Americans	Capstone Press
Mukatar and the Camels	P	RF	250+	Graber, Janet	Henry Holt & Co.
Mule's Hat, The	G	F	204	Dominie Readers	Pearson Learning Group
Multiple Choice	U	RF	250+	Tashjian, Janet	Square Fish
Multiply on the Fly	N	I	276	Slade, Suzanne	Sylvan Dell Publishing
Multi-Tasker, The	V	RF	3226	Leveled Readers	Houghton Mifflin Harcourt
Mumbo Jumbo's Shoes	I	F	130	Book Bus	Creative Edge
Mummies	M	I	250+	All Aboard Reading	Grosset & Dunlap
^Mummies	S	I	250+	Ancient Egypt	Capstone Press
Mummies	Q	I	250+	Trail Blazers	Ransom Publishing
Mummies and Their Mysteries	X	I	250+	Wilcox, Charlotte	Carolrhoda Books
Mummies Don't Coach Softball	M	F	250+	Dadey, Debbie; Jones, Marcia Thornton	Scholastic
Mummies in the Morning	M	F	250+	Osborne, Mary Pope	Random House
Mummies Made in Egypt	T	I	250+	Aliki	HarperCollins
Mummies, Pyramids, and Pharaohs: A Book About Ancient Egypt	S	I	250+	Gibbons, Gail	Scholastic
Mummies, Tombs, and the Afterlife	T	I	250+	High-Fliers	Pacific Learning
Mummy	Y	I	250+	Eyewitness Books	DK Publishing
*Mummy and Other Adventures of Sam & Alice, The	J	F	250+	Gutierrez, Akemi	Houghton Mifflin Harcourt
Mummy Mania	N	RF	250+	Girlz Rock!	Mondo Publishing
Mummy Math: An Adventure in Geometry	P	F	250+	Neuschwander, Cindy	Square Fish
Mummy with No Name, The	O	F	250+	Stilton, Geronimo	Scholastic
Mummy, The	X	I	4728	Monster Chronicles	Lerner Publishing Group
Mummy's Curse, The	O	F	250+	Supa Doopers	Sundance
Mummy's Gold, The	L	F	250+	McMullan, Kate	Grosset & Dunlap

TITLE	LEVEL	GENRE	WORD COUNT	AUTHOR / SERIES	PUBLISHER / DISTRIBUTOR
Mumps	D	RF	108	Carousel Readers	Pearson Learning Group
Mumps	D	RF	112	PM Story Books	Rigby
Munch Together	B	F	33	Reading Street	Pearson
Munch! Munch!	D	RF	109	Rigby Flying Colors	Rigby
Munching Mark	G	RF	88	Tadpoles	Rigby
Munching Monster	I	F	261	Storyteller-Moon Rising	Wright Group/McGraw Hill
Munching, Crunching, Sniffing, and Snooping	L	I	250+	DK Readers	DK Publishing
Munga, the Lonely Monster	K	F	566	Springboard	Wright Group/McGraw Hill
Mural, The	O	RF	801	Leveled Readers	Houghton Mifflin Harcourt
Mural, The	F	I	262	Visions	Wright Group/McGraw Hill
Murals for Joy	N	RF	745	Leveled Readers	Houghton Mifflin Harcourt
Murder Afloat	V	HF	250+	Conly, Jane Leslie	Hyperion
Murder, My Tweet: A Chet Gecko Mystery	R	F	250+	Hale, Bruce	Harcourt, Inc.
Murders in the Rue Morgue, The	Y	HF	6995	Oxford Bookworms Library	Oxford University Press
Murphy and Mousetrap	O	RF	250+	Orca Young Readers	Orca Books
Muscle Cars	W	I	6462	Motor Mania	Lerner Publishing Group
^Muscle Cars	N	I	201	Rev It Up!	Capstone Press
Muscles	T	I	250+	Theme Sets	National Geographic
Muscles: Our Muscular System	S	I	250+	Simon, Seymour	HarperTrophy
Muscular System, The	P	I	1929	Early Bird Body Systems	Lerner Publishing Group
Muscular System, The	K	I	131	Human Body Systems	Red Brick Learning
Museum 1 2 3	K	I	80	The Metropolitan Museum of Art	Little Brown and Company
Museum Book: A Guide to Strange and Wonderful Collections, The	T	I	250+	Mark, Jan	Candlewick Press
Museum Trip	WB	F	0	Lehman, Barbara	Houghton Mifflin Harcourt
Museum, The	D	RF	41	Sunshine	Wright Group/McGraw Hill
Mush, Mush!	O	I	250+	WorldScapes	ETA/Cuisenaire
Mushroom in the Rain	K	F	250+	Ginsburg, Mirra	Aladdin
Mushrooms and Other Fungi	P	I	250+	Sunshine	Wright Group/McGraw Hill
Mushrooms and Toadstools	K	I	250+	Explorations	Eleanor Curtain Publishing
Mushrooms and Toadstools	K	I	250+	Explorations	Okapi Educational Materials
Mushrooms for Dinner	G	F	177	PM Story Books	Rigby
Music	Z	I	250+	Eyewitness Books	DK Publishing
Music	A	I	45	Vocabulary Readers	Houghton Mifflin Harcourt
Music	A	I	45	Vocabulary Readers/CA	Houghton Mifflin Harcourt
Music	A	I	45	Vocabulary Readers/TX	Houghton Mifflin Harcourt
Music - Magic and Imagination	U	I	250+	Connectors	Pacific Learning
Music Counts	P	I	250+	Navigators Math Series	Benchmark Education
Music Gets the Blues	V	I	2463	Reading Street	Pearson
Music Machine, The	G	F	231	Sunshine	Wright Group/McGraw Hill
Music Madness: Questioning Music and Music Videos	U	I	250+	Media Literacy	Capstone Press
Music Makers	V	I	250+	High-Fliers	Pacific Learning
Music of Dolphins, The	V	RF	250+	Hesse, Karen	Scholastic
Music of Tito Puente, The	J	B	127	Vocabulary Readers	Houghton Mifflin Harcourt
Music Students	E	RF	83	Dominie Phonics Reader	Pearson Learning Group
Music Technology	R	I	250+	PM Plus Nonfiction	Rigby
Music, Music, Music!	T	I	250+	InfoQuest	Rigby
Music: From the Voice to Electronica	U	I	250+	Timeline History	Heinemann Library
Musical Adventure, A	D	RF	78	Reading Street	Pearson
Musical Chairs	G	RF	206	Red Rocket Readers	Flying Start Books
Musical Genius, A Story About Wolfgang Amadeus Mozart	T	B	8784	Creative Minds Biographies	Carolrhoda Books
*Musicians and Their Music	S	B	250+	Pair-It Books	Steck-Vaughn

* Collection of short stories   # Graphic text
^ Mature content with lower level text demands

TITLE	LEVEL	GENRE	WORD COUNT	AUTHOR / SERIES	PUBLISHER / DISTRIBUTOR
Musician's Daughter, The	Z+	HF	250+	Dunlap, Susanne	Bloomsbury Children's Books
Musk Oxen	S	I	250+	Animal Prey	Lerner Publishing Group
Muskrats	H	I	114	Wetland Animals	Capstone Press
Mustangs	U	I	250+	Gillespie, Lorraine	Red Brick Learning
Mutiny on the Bounty	Y	HF	5825	Oxford Bookworms Library	Oxford University Press
Mutt and the Lifeguards	M	RF	754	Sunshine	Wright Group/McGraw Hill
Mutts	R	I	250+	All About Dogs	Capstone Press
Mutts	I	I	131	Dogs	Capstone Press
My 13th Season	T	RF	250+	Roberts, Kristi	Henry Holt & Co.
My Accident	C	RF	46	PM Starters	Rigby
My Airplane Trip	K	RF	684	Rigby Flying Colors	Rigby
My Alien	LB	F	12	Sails	Rigby
My Apartment	LB	RF	20	Visions	Wright Group/McGraw Hill
My Apple Tree	D	I	48	Yellow Umbrella Books	Red Brick Learning
My Babies	D	RF	65	Potato Chip Books	American Reading Company
My Baby	D	F	64	Storyteller-First Snow	Wright Group/McGraw Hill
My Baby Brother	C	RF	60	The King School Series	Townsend Press
My Baby Sister	A	RF	32	Leveled Literacy Intervention/ Orange System	Heinemann
My Backpack	A	RF	32	Early Connections	Benchmark Education
My Backpack	B	I	72	First Stories	Pacific Learning
My Backpack	A	F	21	Leveled Readers	Houghton Mifflin Harcourt
My Backpack	A	F	21	Leveled Readers/CA	Houghton Mifflin Harcourt
My Backpack	H	I	134	Windows on Literacy	National Geographic
My Backyard	LB	I	14	Little Books for Early Readers	University of Maine
My Backyard	A	RF	33	McAlpin, MaryAnn	Short Tales Press
My Balloon Man	C	I	56	First Stories	Pacific Learning
My Balloon Ride	O	I	250+	Windows on Literacy	National Geographic
My Baseball Book	M	I	250+	Gibbons, Gail	Scholastic
My Bath	A	RF	32	Leveled Literacy Intervention/ Green System	Heinemann
My Beach Bag	E	I	102	Early Explorers	Benchmark Education
My Bean Plant	H	I	146	Windows on Literacy	National Geographic
My Bear	A	RF	48	Leveled Literacy Intervention/ Orange System	Heinemann
My Bed	E	RF	65	Book Bus	Creative Edge
My Bed Is Soft	B	I	42	Windows on Literacy	National Geographic
My Best Friend	C	RF	63	Carousel Readers	Pearson Learning Group
My Best Friend	I	RF	147	Hutchins, Pat	Greenwillow Books
My Best Friend	C	RF	28	Little Celebrations	Pearson Learning Group
My Best Sandwich	D	RF	25	Hartley, Susan; Armstrong, Shane	Scholastic
My Big Bear	B	I	75	Leveled Literacy Intervention/ Orange System	Heinemann
My Big Box	D	RF	94	Voyages	SRA/McGraw Hill
My Big Brother	B	RF	64	Leveled Literacy Intervention/ Orange System	Heinemann
My Big Brother	C	RF	49	On Our Way to English	Rigby
My Big Brother	E	I	103	PM Nonfiction-Yellow	Rigby
My Big Brother Ned	B	RF	38	Leveled Readers	Houghton Mifflin Harcourt
My Big Brother Ned	B	RF	38	Leveled Readers/CA	Houghton Mifflin Harcourt
My Big Car	C	RF	62	Handprints B	Educators Publishing Service
My Big Dinosaur World	T	I	250+	Mugford, Simon	Priddy Books
My Big Family	B	I	34	Time for Kids	Teacher Created Materials

TITLE	LEVEL	GENRE	WORD COUNT	AUTHOR / SERIES	PUBLISHER / DISTRIBUTOR
My Big Pig	A	RF	32	Literacy by Design	Rigby
My Big Rock	B	RF	42	Bebop Books	Lee & Low Books Inc.
My Big Sister	E	RF	107	Kaleidoscope Collection	Hameray Publishing Group
My Big Surprise	H	F	139	Instant Readers	Harcourt School Publishers
My Big Tree	D	I	120	PM Science Readers	Rigby
My Big Wheel	C	RF	38	Visions	Wright Group/McGraw Hill
My Big, Big Kick	J	F	351	Red Rocket Readers	Flying Start Books
My Bike	F	I	108	Pacific Literacy	Pacific Learning
My Bike	D	I	38	Storyteller-First Snow	Wright Group/McGraw Hill
My Bike	A	I	19	Vocabulary Readers	Houghton Mifflin Harcourt
My Bike	A	I	19	Vocabulary Readers/CA	Houghton Mifflin Harcourt
My Bike Ride	C	RF	30	Big Cat	Pacific Learning
My Bird Journal	N	I	250+	Literacy by Design	Rigby
My Birthday	F	RF	131	Rigby Flying Colors	Rigby
My Birthday Party	LB	RF	16	Little Readers	Houghton Mifflin Harcourt
My Birthday Party	C	RF	38	Visions	Wright Group/McGraw Hill
My Birthday Surprise	G	RF	153	Foundations	Wright Group/McGraw Hill
My Black Cat	C	RF	52	Early Emergent	Pioneer Valley
My Boat	G	RF	133	Sunshine	Wright Group/McGraw Hill
My Body	C	I	47	Discovery World	Rigby
My Body	M	I	250+	Early Connections	Benchmark Education
My Body	B	I	28	On Our Way to English	Rigby
My Body	D	I	250+	Sun Sprouts	ETA/Cuisenaire
My Body Head to Toe	K	RF	250+	All About Me	Picture Window Books
My Body Works	E	I	131	Twig	Wright Group/McGraw Hill
My Bones	I	I	148	My Body	Capstone Press
My Bones and Muscles: What's Inside Me?	N	I	250+	Bookworms	Marshall Cavendish
My Book	A	I	32	Early Connections	Benchmark Education
My Book	A	RF	17	Maris, Ron	Viking/Penguin
My Book	C	RF	63	PM Plus Story Books	Rigby
My Book	C	RF	32	Sunshine	Wright Group/McGraw Hill
My Book of the Seasons	H	I	271	PM Science Readers	Rigby
My Box	D	RF	94	Books for Young Learners	Richard C. Owen
My Box	WB	RF	0	Instant Readers	Harcourt School Publishers
My Box	A	RF	94	Smart Start	Rigby
My Brain	J	I	152	My Body	Capstone Press
My Brain: What's Inside Me?	O	I	250+	Bookworms	Marshall Cavendish
My Breakfast	D	RF	54	Lighthouse	Rigby
My Breakfast	G	RF	167	Rigby Flying Colors	Rigby
My Brother	B	RF	48	Leveled Readers	Houghton Mifflin Harcourt
My Brother	B	RF	48	Leveled Readers/CA	Houghton Mifflin Harcourt
My Brother	D	RF	51	Rise & Shine	Hampton Brown
My Brother Bert	K	F	216	Hughes, Ted	Farrar, Straus, & Giroux
My Brother Is a Superhero	S	RF	250+	Sheldon, Dyan	Candlewick Press
My Brother Is a Visitor From Another Planet	S	RF	250+	Sheldon, Dyan	Candlewick Press
*My Brother Louis Measures Worms and Other Louis Stories	T	RF	250+	Robinson, Barbara	HarperTrophy
My Brother Sam Is Dead	Y	HF	250+	Collier, James & Christopher	Scholastic
My Brother Wants to Be Like Me	D	RF	62	Mader, Jan	Kaeden Books
My Brother, Ant	J	RF	250+	Byars, Betsy	Viking/Penguin
My Brother, My Sister, and I	V	HF	250+	Watkins, Yoko Kawashima	Aladdin
My Brother, Owen	I	RF	150	Book Bank	Wright Group/McGraw Hill
My Brother, the Brat	E	RF	62	Hall, Kirsten	Scholastic
My Brother, the Bridesmaid	M	RF	250+	Lighthouse	Ginn & Co.

* Collection of short stories   # Graphic text
^ Mature content with lower level text demands

TITLE	LEVEL	GENRE	WORD COUNT	AUTHOR / SERIES	PUBLISHER / DISTRIBUTOR
My Brother, the Knight	M	RF	250+	Social Studies Connects	Kane Press
My Brother, the Pest	I	RF	459	Real Kids Readers	Millbrook Press
My Brother, the Spy	N	RF	250+	Supa Doopers	Sundance
#My Brother's a Keeper	S	RF	3162	Hardcastle, Michael	Stone Arch Books
My Brother's Hero	W	RF	250+	Fogelin, Adrian	Peachtree
My Brother's Motorcycle	D	RF	45	Visions	Wright Group/McGraw Hill
My Brown Bear Barney	H	RF	82	Butler, Dorothy	Morrow
My Brown Cow	D	I	62	Story Box	Wright Group/McGraw Hill
My Buddy	B	RF	80	Adams, Lorraine & Bruvold, Lynn	Eaglecrest Books
My Buddy	B	RF	32	First Stories	Pacific Learning
My Buddy, My Friend	D	RF	33	Visions	Wright Group/McGraw Hill
My Bug Box	E	RF	99	Books for Young Learners	Richard C. Owen
My Busy Day	B	RF	41	Early Emergent	Pioneer Valley
My Busy Week	H	RF	122	InfoTrek	ETA/Cuisenaire
My Busy Week	I	I	178	Windows on Literacy	National Geographic
My Calculator Book	E	RF	50	Gosset, Rachel; Ballinger, Margaret	Scholastic
My Camera	D	RF	67	Gear Up!	Wright Group/McGraw Hill
My Camera	C	RF	41	Rigby Literacy	Rigby
My Camera	C	RF	41	Rigby Star	Rigby
My Camp-Out	E	RF	81	Real Kids Readers	Millbrook Press
My Car	A	RF	40	On Our Way to English	Rigby
My Cat	A	I	37	Early Connections	Benchmark Education
My Cat	A	RF	47	First Stories	Pacific Learning
My Cat	A	RF	28	Leveled Readers	Houghton Mifflin Harcourt
My Cat	A	RF	25	Leveled Readers	Houghton Mifflin Harcourt
My Cat	A	RF	28	Leveled Readers Science	Houghton Mifflin Harcourt
My Cat	A	RF	25	Leveled Readers/CA	Houghton Mifflin Harcourt
My Cat	B	RF	47	Lighthouse	Rigby
My Cat	F	RF	42	My World	Steck-Vaughn
My Cat	D	RF	40	Ready Readers	Pearson Learning Group
My Cat	D	I	42	Sunshine	Wright Group/McGraw Hill
My Cat	H	I	79	Taylor, Judy	Macmillan
My Cat and I	B	I	31	Windows on Literacy	National Geographic
My Cat Muffin	C	RF	35	Gardner, Marjory	Scholastic
My Cat Sam	H	F	147	Supersonics	Rigby
My Caterpillar Report	E	I	94	Rigby Flying Colors	Rigby
My Cats	B	RF	42	Gear Up!	Wright Group/McGraw Hill
My Cats	A	RF	41	Robinson, Eileen	Scholastic
*My Cat's Surprise	D	RF	71	New Way Blue	Steck-Vaughn
My Chair	B	RF	24	Pacific Literacy	Pacific Learning
My Cheese	B	F	35	Sails	Rigby
My Chinese New Year	D	I	56	Rigby Star Quest	Rigby
My Circus Family	C	F	42	Bookshop	Mondo Publishing
My Circus Friend	C	F	42	Lake, Mary Dixon	Mondo Publishing
My City	C	I	99	Rigby Literacy	Rigby
My Class	LB	I	14	Stewart, Josie; Salem, Lynn	Continental Press
My Classroom	A	I	31	At School Series	Pioneer Valley
My Clock is Sick	D	F	45	Ready Readers	Pearson Learning Group
My Clothes	LB	RF	16	Carousel Earlybirds	Pearson Learning Group
My Clothes	C	RF	86	Foundations	Wright Group/McGraw Hill
My Clothes	A	I	35	On Our Way to English	Rigby
My Clothes	B	RF	36	PM Plus Starters	Rigby

TITLE	LEVEL	GENRE	WORD COUNT	AUTHOR / SERIES	PUBLISHER / DISTRIBUTOR
My Clothes	LB	F	12	Sails	Rigby
My Clothes	LB	I	12	Vocabulary Readers	Houghton Mifflin Harcourt
My Color	B	I	22	Mann, Rachel	Scholastic
My Colors	C	RF	58	McAlpin, MaryAnn	Short Tales Press
My Computer	F	I	76	Wonder World	Wright Group/McGraw Hill
My Continent	I	I	117	My World	Capstone Press
My Cousin Jake	H	RF	123	City Stories	Rigby
My Cousin, the Alien: Alien Agent	T	SF	19335	Service, Pamela F.	Carolrhoda Books
My Cushion!	B	RF	20	Rigby Rocket	Rigby
My Dad	E	RF	103	McAlpin, MaryAnn	Short Tales Press
My Dad	E	I	114	PM Nonfiction-Yellow	Rigby
My Dad	F	I	79	Talk About Books	Pearson Learning Group
My Dad and I	B	RF	52	Handprints B	Educators Publishing Service
My Dad Cooks	C	RF	29	Carousel Readers	Pearson Learning Group
My Dad Has Asthma	I	I	138	Wonder World	Wright Group/McGraw Hill
My Dad Is a Chef	H	I	169	Dominie Factivity Series	Pearson Learning Group
My Dad Is a Drummer	L	RF	250+	InfoTrek	ETA/Cuisenaire
My Dad Lost His Job	E	RF	76	Carousel Readers	Pearson Learning Group
My Dad the Dragon	Q	F	8874	French, Jackie	Stone Arch Books
My Dad, the Rock-and-Roll Penguin	L	F	250+	Reading Safari	Mondo Publishing
My Dadima Wears a Sari	M	RF	250+	Sheth, Kashmira	Peachtree
My Dad's a Birdman	S	RF	250+	Almond, David	Candlewick Press
My Dad's Truck	E	I	57	Costain, Merideth	Scholastic
My Daniel	T	HF	250+	Conrad, Pam	HarperTrophy
My Darling Kitten	WB	RF	0	Collington, Peter	Alfred A. Knopf
My Darling, My Hamburger	Z+	RF	250+	Zindel, Paul	Bantam Books
My Day	C	RF	51	Barney, Mike	Kaeden Books
My Day	D	RF	80	InfoTrek	ETA/Cuisenaire
My Day	C	RF	44	Rise & Shine	Hampton Brown
My Day	B	RF	24	Sunshine	Wright Group/McGraw Hill
My Day	LB	RF	29	We Both Read	Treasure Bay
My Day: Morning, Noon, and Night	J	RF	250+	All About Me	Picture Window Books
My Desperate Love Diary	Z+	RF	250+	Rettig, Liz	Holiday House
My Dog	C	RF	79	Early Emergent	Pioneer Valley
My Dog	A	RF	72	Instant Readers	Harcourt School Publishers
My Dog	A	RF	22	Leveled Readers	Houghton Mifflin Harcourt
My Dog	A	RF	22	Leveled Readers/CA	Houghton Mifflin Harcourt
My Dog	G	RF	79	My World	Steck-Vaughn
My Dog	A	I	32	Rigby Flying Colors	Rigby
My Dog	D	I	51	Sunshine	Wright Group/McGraw Hill
My Dog	G	I	72	Taylor, Judy	Macmillan
My Dog	D	RF	38	Visions	Wright Group/McGraw Hill
My Dog	C	I	46	Vocabulary Readers	Houghton Mifflin Harcourt
My Dog and I	B	RF	55	Lighthouse	Rigby
*My Dog and Other Stories	I	RF	250+	Story Steps	Rigby
My Dog Ben	C	RF	19	Voyages	SRA/McGraw Hill
My Dog Fluffy	A	I	27	Cherrington, Janelle	Scholastic
My Dog Fuzzy	B	RF	27	Books for Young Learners	Richard C. Owen
My Dog Kam	E	RF	73	InfoTrek	ETA/Cuisenaire
My Dog Rusty	G	RF	75	City Stories	Rigby
My Dog Talks	E	RF	250+	Herman, Gail	Scholastic
My Dog the Dinosaur	Q	F	8918	French, Jackie	Stone Arch Books
My Dog Willy	C	RF	71	Little Readers	Houghton Mifflin Harcourt

* Collection of short stories   # Graphic text
^ Mature content with lower level text demands

TITLE	LEVEL	GENRE	WORD COUNT	AUTHOR / SERIES	PUBLISHER / DISTRIBUTOR
My Dog, Miffy	D	RF	38	Visions	Wright Group/McGraw Hill
My Dog, My Cat, My Mama, and Me	H	RF	164	Gray, Nigel	Candlewick Press
My Dog's A Scaredy Cat: A Halloween Tail	R	RF	250+	Winkler, Henry and Oliver, Lin	Grosset & Dunlap
My Dog's the Best	F	RF	175	Calmenson, Stephanie	Scholastic
My Doll	A	F	32	Sun Sprouts	ETA/Cuisenaire
My Doll	E	RF	86	Yukish, Joe	Kaeden Books
My Dream	C	RF	34	Wildsmith, Brian	Oxford University Press
My Dream of Martin Luther King	R	I	250+	Ringgold, Faith	Crown Publishers
My Elephant My Friend	O	I	250+	WorldScapes	ETA/Cuisenaire
My Even Day	M	F	250+	Fisher, Doris & Sneed, Dani	Sylvan Dell Publishing
My Face to the Wind	W	HF	250+	Dear America	Scholastic
My Faces	E	RF	62	Rhythm 'N' Rhyme Readers	Pearson Learning Group
My Fair Godmother	Y	F	250+	Rallison, Janette	Walker & Company
My Family	B	RF	55	Adams, Lorraine & Bruvold, Lynn	Eaglecrest Books
My Family	B	RF	31	Bebop Books	Lee & Low Books Inc.
My Family	B	RF	87	Carousel Earlybirds	Pearson Learning Group
My Family	B	RF	46	First Stories	Pacific Learning
My Family	N	I	250+	Kinkade, Sheila	Charlesbridge
My Family	B	F	69	Leveled Literacy Intervention/ Orange System	Heinemann
My Family	D	I	88	Leveled Readers	Houghton Mifflin Harcourt
My Family	A	I	25	Leveled Readers	Houghton Mifflin Harcourt
My Family	A	RF	28	Leveled Readers Social Studies	Houghton Mifflin Harcourt
My Family	A	I	25	Leveled Readers/CA	Houghton Mifflin Harcourt
My Family	B	I	46	Reach	National Geographic
My Family	LB	F	12	Sails	Rigby
My Family	A	RF	28	Sunshine	Wright Group/McGraw Hill
My Family	LB	I	12	Vocabulary Readers	Houghton Mifflin Harcourt
My Family & the Wasps	N	F	250+	Parker, John	Pearson Learning Group
My Family Band	C	RF	50	Instant Readers	Harcourt School Publishers
My Family Has Fun	A	RF	28	Leveled Readers Emergent	Houghton Mifflin Harcourt
My Family Has Jobs	I	I	214	Early Explorers	Benchmark Education
My Family History (Fancy Nancy)	J	RF	250+	O'Connor, Jane	HarperCollins
My Family Keeps Fit	G	RF	98	Windows on Literacy	National Geographic
My Family Love and Care, Give and Share	K	RF	250+	All About Me	Picture Window Books
My Family Pictures	A	I	20	Leveled Readers	Houghton Mifflin Harcourt
My Family Pictures	A	I	20	Leveled Readers/CA	Houghton Mifflin Harcourt
My Family Split Up	H	RF	85	City Kids	Rigby
My Family Tree	O	RF	250+	Book Blazers	ETA/Cuisenaire
My Family Tree	J	RF	250+	InfoTrek	ETA/Cuisenaire
My Family Tree	D	I	107	Story Steps	Rigby
My Family Tree	I	I	229	Windows on Literacy	National Geographic
My Farm	N	RF	250+	Lester, Alison	Houghton Mifflin Harcourt
My Father	J	RF	194	Mayer, Laura	Scholastic
My Father the Dog	M	RF	193	Bluemle, Elizabeth	Candlewick Press
My Father the Mad Professor	P	F	250+	Action Packs	Rigby
My Father, the Angel of Death	U	RF	250+	Villareal, Ray	Pinata Publishing
My Father, the Clown	Y	RF	3497	Leveled Readers	Houghton Mifflin Harcourt
My Father, the Clown	Y	RF	3497	Leveled Readers/CA	Houghton Mifflin Harcourt
My Father, the Clown	Y	RF	3497	Leveled Readers/TX	Houghton Mifflin Harcourt
My Father's Dragon	N	F	250+	Gannett, Ruth Stiles	Random House
My Father's Shop	L	RF	250+	Ichikawa, Satomi	Kane/Miller Book Publishers
My Favorite Bear	J	I	146	Books for Young Learners	Richard C. Owen
My Favorite Bear	F	F	70	Gabriel, Andrea	Charlesbridge

TITLE	LEVEL	GENRE	WORD COUNT	AUTHOR / SERIES	PUBLISHER / DISTRIBUTOR
My Favorite Days	J	I	250+	Rigby Literacy	Rigby
My Favorite Foods	I	RF	100	Early Readers	Compass Point Books
My Favorite Foods	D	I	107	Vocabulary Readers	Houghton Mifflin Harcourt
My Favorite Foods	D	I	107	Vocabulary Readers/CA	Houghton Mifflin Harcourt
My Favorite Foods	D	I	107	Vocabulary Readers/TX	Houghton Mifflin Harcourt
My Favorite Fruit	B	I	35	Bonnell, Kris	Reading Reading Books
My Favorite Michael	K	RF	250+	Heiman, Laura	Tiger Tales
My Favorite Place	J	RF	464	Books for Young Learners	Richard C. Owen
My Favorite School Helper	E	I	61	Little Celebrations	Pearson Learning Group
My Feet	B	RF	35	Reed, Janet	Scholastic
My Feet	B	I	25	Twig	Wright Group/McGraw Hill
My Feet Are Just Right	I	I	220	Sunshine	Wright Group/McGraw Hill
My First Book About the Internet	M	I	250+	Cromwell, Sharon	Troll Associates
My First Book of Arabic Words	LB	I	144	My First Book	Capstone Press
*My First Book of Biographies: Great Men and Women Every Child Should Know	P	B	250+	Marzollo, Jean	Scholastic
My First Book of French Words	LB	I	143	My First Book	Capstone Press
My First Book of German Words	LB	I	143	My First Book	Capstone Press
My First Book of Greek Words	LB	I	144	My First Book	Capstone Press
My First Book of Hindi Words	LB	I	144	My First Book	Capstone Press
My First Book of Italian Words	LB	I	144	My First Book	Capstone Press
My First Book of Korean Words	LB	I	144	My First Book	Capstone Press
My First Book of Mandarin Chinese Words	LB	I	143	My First Book	Capstone Press
My First Book of Polish Words	LB	I	144	My First Book	Capstone Press
My First Book of Portuguese Words	LB	I	144	My First Book	Capstone Press
My First Book of Spanish Words	LB	I	143	My First Book	Capstone Press
My First Book of Vietnamese Words	LB	I	144	My First Book	Capstone Press
My First Business: Lemonade Stand	K	RF	548	Leveled Readers Social Studies	Houghton Mifflin Harcourt
My first Day at a New School	J	I	250+	Growing Up	Heinemann Library
My First Hike	F	RF	70	Woolf, Catherine Maria	Dawn Publications
My First Sleepover	J	I	250+	Growing Up	Heinemann Library
My First Snow	F	I	127	Independent Readers Science	Houghton Mifflin Harcourt
My First Trip on an Airplane	J	I	250+	Growing Up	Heinemann Library
My Fish	A	RF	24	Phonics and Friends	Hampton Brown
My Fish Are Fine with Me	G	RF	78	City Stories	Rigby
My Fish Bowl	B	I	29	Foundations	Wright Group/McGraw Hill
My Fish Does Not Chirp	E	I	77	Ready Readers	Pearson Learning Group
My Fish Tank	J	I	238	Windows on Literacy	National Geographic
My Five Senses	F	I	142	Early Connections	Benchmark Education
My Five Senses	C	I	36	Independent Readers Science	Houghton Mifflin Harcourt
My Five Senses	D	I	127	Leveled Literacy Intervention/ Green System	Heinemann
My Five Senses	F	I	42	Rosen Real Readers	Rosen Publishing Group
My Five Senses	LB	I	5	Windows on Literacy	National Geographic
My Flower Garden	A	I	19	Leveled Readers	Houghton Mifflin Harcourt
My Flower Garden	A	I	19	Leveled Readers/CA	Houghton Mifflin Harcourt
My Fly	C	F	115	Bonnell, Kris	Reading Reading Books
My Food Pyramid	J	I	206	Healthy Eating	Heinemann Library
My Fort	LB	I	17	Little Books for Early Readers	University of Maine
*My Fort, Four Friends Go Camping	J	RF	221	Easy-for-Me Reading	Child 1st Publications
My Friend	E	RF	95	Foundations	Wright Group/McGraw Hill
My Friend	B	I	64	Leveled Literacy Intervention/ Green System	Heinemann
My Friend	B	RF	41	Sunshine	Wright Group/McGraw Hill

* Collection of short stories   # Graphic text
^ Mature content with lower level text demands

TITLE	LEVEL	GENRE	WORD COUNT	AUTHOR / SERIES	PUBLISHER / DISTRIBUTOR
My Friend Alan	D	RF	65	Carousel Readers	Pearson Learning Group
My Friend and I	C	RF	78	Windows on Literacy	National Geographic
My Friend at School	C	RF	30	Visions	Wright Group/McGraw Hill
My Friend Goes Left	F	RF	72	Start to Read	School Zone
My Friend Gorilla	G	RF	125	Morozumi, Atsuko	Farrar, Straus, & Giroux
My Friend Jess	H	RF	124	Wonder World	Wright Group/McGraw Hill
My Friend Maya Loves to Dance	L	RF	231	Hudson, Cheryl Willis	Harry N. Abrams
My Friend Meg	U	RF	250+	Book Blazers	ETA/Cuisenaire
My Friend Rabbit	F	F	81	Rohmann, Eric	Square Fish
My Friend the Monster	N	F	250+	Bulla, Clyde Robert	Harper & Row
My Friend the Monster	J	F	250+	Taylor, Eleanor	Bloomsbury Children's Books
My Friend Trent	H	RF	186	Foundations	Wright Group/McGraw Hill
My Friend, Mandela	R	B	250+	High-Fliers	Pacific Learning
My Friends	G	F	152	Gomi, Taro	Scholastic
My Friends	D	RF	58	Little Celebrations	Pearson Learning Group
My Friends at School	G	I	248	Dominie Factivity Series	Pearson Learning Group
My Friends at School	C	I	84	Vocabulary Readers	Houghton Mifflin Harcourt
My Friends at School	C	I	84	Vocabulary Readers/CA	Houghton Mifflin Harcourt
My Friends the Flowers	L	F	322	Lach, William	Harry N. Abrams
My Frisbee	B	RF	31	Rigby Literacy	Rigby
My Frog Log	N	RF	250+	On Our Way to English	Rigby
My Garden	B	I	37	Ostrow, Jesse S.	Scholastic
My Garden	C	I	33	Rosen Real Readers	Rosen Publishing Group
My Garden	B	F	40	Sails	Rigby
My Global Address	G	I	84	Learn to Read	Creative Teaching Press
My Go-Cart	K	I	467	Sun Sprouts	ETA/Cuisenaire
My Goldfish	G	I	239	Walker, Pamela	Scholastic
My Goose Betsy	L	F	250+	Braun, Trudi	Candlewick Press
My Grandfather's Face	B	RF	27	Literacy 2000	Rigby
My Grandma	A	RF	24	Adams, Lorraine & Bruvold, Lynn	Eaglecrest Books
My Grandma	E	RF	67	Early Connections	Benchmark Education
My Grandma and Grandpa	E	I	130	PM Nonfiction	Rigby
My Grandma, the Rock Star	L	RF	250+	Rigby Literacy	Rigby
My Grandpa	B	RF	58	Adams, Lorraine & Bruvold, Lynn	Eaglecrest Books
My Grandpa	F	I	75	Bookshop	Mondo Publishing
My Great Big Brother	F	RF	65	Book Bank	Wright Group/McGraw Hill
My Great-Aunt Arizona	N	RF	250+	Houston, Gloria	HarperCollins
My Green Thumb	K	F	351	Leveled Readers	Houghton Mifflin Harcourt
My G-r-r-r-reat Uncle Tiger	L	F	250+	Riordan, James	Peachtree
My Gymnastics Class	F	I	33	iOpeners	Pearson Learning Group
My Hair	F	RF	124	Bookshop	Mondo Publishing
My Half Day	N	F	347	Fisher, Doris and Sneed, Dani	Sylvan Dell Publishing
My Hamburger	E	RF	108	Rigby Flying Colors	Rigby
My Hamster, Van	E	RF	73	Ready Readers	Pearson Learning Group
My Hands	B	RF	48	Red Rocket Readers	Flying Start Books
My Hands Sing the Blues	O	HF	250+	Harvey, Jeanne Walker	Marshall Cavendish
My Hard-Boiled Egg	F	I	94	Windmill Books	Rigby
My Hat	A	RF	30	Sails	Rigby
My Heart	J	I	125	My Body	Capstone Press
My Heart and Blood: What's Inside Me?	N	I	250+	Bookworms	Marshall Cavendish
My Heart Is on the Ground	W	HF	250+	Dear America	Scholastic
My Heartbeat	Z+	RF	250+	Freymann-Weyr, Garret	Houghton Mifflin Harcourt
My Helicopter Ride	C	F	42	Foundations	Wright Group/McGraw Hill

TITLE	LEVEL	GENRE	WORD COUNT	AUTHOR / SERIES	PUBLISHER / DISTRIBUTOR
My Hero	P	I	250+	Infotrek Plus	ETA/Cuisenaire
My Hero	J	I	250+	Literacy by Design	Rigby
My Hero!	B	I	37	Shutterbug Books	Steck-Vaughn
My Hiroshima	T	HF	250+	Morimoto, Junko	Penguin Group
My Hobby	H	I	155	Rigby Focus	Rigby
My Holiday Diary	F	RF	95	Stepping Stones	Nelson/Michaels Assoc.
My Home	B	I	67	On Our Way to English	Rigby
My Home	K	F	250+	Rhyme and Analogy	Oxford University Press
My Home	B	I	49	Science	Outside the Box
My Home	A	F	56	Smart Start	Rigby
My Home	C	F	46	Story Box	Wright Group/McGraw Hill
My Home	C	RF	56	Sunshine	Wright Group/McGraw Hill
My Home Is High	B	F	23	Literacy 2000	Rigby
My Home Is Just Right for Me	G	F	250+	Momentum Literacy Program	Troll Associates
My Home Walls, Floors, Ceilings, and Doors	L	RF	250+	All About Me	Picture Window Books
My Horse	B	I	22	Bebop Books	Lee & Low Books Inc.
My House	G	RF	43	Book Bunny Series	Creative Edge
My House	A	RF	40	Carousel Earlybirds	Pearson Learning Group
My House	F	RF	52	Cat on the Mat	Oxford University Press
My House	B	I	74	Leveled Readers	Houghton Mifflin Harcourt
My House	B	I	74	Leveled Readers/CA	Houghton Mifflin Harcourt
My House	F	RF	126	Literacy 2000	Rigby
My House	E	F	79	My First Reader	Grolier
My House	A	I	27	Peters, Catherine	Scholastic
My House	B	I	25	Voyages	SRA/McGraw Hill
My Invisible Sister	Q	F	250+	Colin, Beatrice & Pinto, Sara	Bloomsbury Children's Books
My Island Reef	T	RF	250+	Reading Safari	Mondo Publishing
My Jobs	C	RF	58	InfoTrek	ETA/Cuisenaire
My Kitchen	F	I	80	Rockwell, Harlow	Morrow
My Kite	C	RF	37	Williams, Deborah	Kaeden Books
My Last Best Friend	O	RF	250+	Bowe, Julie	Houghton Mifflin Harcourt
My Left Hand	K	RF	828	Rigby Flying Colors	Rigby
My Letter	C	RF	51	Wonder World	Wright Group/McGraw Hill
My Life	K	RF	250+	Pistone, Paul	Scholastic
My Life and Death by Alexandra Canarsie	Y	RF	250+	O'Keefe, Susan Heyboer	Peachtree
My Life as a Book	S	RF	250+	Tashjian, Janet	Henry Holt & Co.
My Life as a Fifth-Grade Comedian	T	RF	250+	Levy, Elizabeth	HarperTrophy
My Life in a Town	C	I	24	Rosen Real Readers	Rosen Publishing Group
My Life in Dog Years	S	B	250+	Paulsen, Gary	Bantam Books
My Life in Pink & Green	T	RF	250+	Greenwald, Lisa	Amulet Books
My Life in the Mountains	D	I	59	Rosen Real Readers	Rosen Publishing Group
My Life on an Island	C	I	43	Rosen Real Readers	Rosen Publishing Group
My Life with Birds	O	RF	250+	Sails	Rigby
My Life with the Lincolns	Z	HF	250+	Brandeis, Gayle	Henry Holt & Co.
My Little Brother	C	RF	38	Gear Up!	Wright Group/McGraw Hill
My Little Brother	C	RF	59	Windmill Books	Rigby
My Little Brother Ben	D	RF	35	Books for Young Learners	Richard C. Owen
My Little Cat	B	RF	57	PM Plus Starters	Rigby
My Little Dog	C	F	90	PM Starters	Rigby
My Little Fish	B	RF	49	Rigby Flying Colors	Rigby
My Little House	D	RF	67	InfoTrek	ETA/Cuisenaire
My Little Kitten	D	RF	64	Windows on Literacy	National Geographic
My Little Mouse	C	I	32	Book Bank	Wright Group/McGraw Hill

* Collection of short stories   # Graphic text
^ Mature content with lower level text demands

TITLE	LEVEL	GENRE	WORD COUNT	AUTHOR / SERIES	PUBLISHER / DISTRIBUTOR
My Little Sister	C	RF	36	First Stories	Pacific Learning
My Little Sister	D	RF	44	Joy Readers	Pearson Learning Group
My Little Sister	E	I	120	PM Nonfiction-Yellow	Rigby
My Little Sister	G	RF	143	Story Box	Wright Group/McGraw Hill
My Lizard	G	RF	246	Handprints D	Educators Publishing Service
My Loose Tooth	C	RF	62	Kaleidoscope Collection	Hameray Publishing Group
My Lost Top	E	RF	70	Ready Readers	Pearson Learning Group
My Louisiana Sky	T	RF	250+	Holt, Kimberly Willis	Random House
My Lucky Hat	J	F	250+	Bookshop	Mondo Publishing
My Lunch	C	RF	70	Early Emergent	Pioneer Valley
My Lunch	A	I	32	Leveled Literacy Intervention/ Orange System	Heinemann
My Lunch	A	I	35	On Our Way to English	Rigby
My Lunch	A	I	32	Rigby Flying Colors	Rigby
My Lungs	I	I	130	My Body	Capstone Press
My Lungs: What's Inside Me?	N	I	250+	Bookworms	Marshall Cavendish
My Magic Bike	G	F	121	Worthington, Lisa & Moon, Susan	Kaeden Books
My Magnet	F	I	112	Windows on Literacy	National Geographic
My Mama	C	RF	25	Visions	Wright Group/McGraw Hill
My Mama Had a Dancing Heart	O	RF	250+	Gray, Libba Moore	Scholastic
My Map Book	LB	I	42	Fanelli, Sara	HarperCollins
My Mei Mei	O	RF	250+	Young, Ed	Philomel
My Messy Room	D	RF	82	Packard, Mary	Scholastic
My Models	E	RF	143	Early Connections	Benchmark Education
My Mom	B	I	40	Little Books for Early Readers	University of Maine
My Mom	F	I	91	Talk About Books	Pearson Learning Group
My Mom and Dad	D	RF	86	Story Box	Wright Group/McGraw Hill
My Mom and Dad Take Care of Me	B	I	44	Windows on Literacy	National Geographic
My Mom and I	A	RF	42	Little Books for Early Readers	University of Maine
My Mom Is a TV News Anchor	J	I	216	Dominie Factivity Series	Pearson Learning Group
My Mom Is the Mayor	K	RF	160	Larkin's Little Readers	Wilbooks
My Mom the Mayor	N	RF	250+	Windows on Literacy	National Geographic
My Mom the Pirate	Q	F	9067	French, Jackie	Stone Arch Books
My Mom's Apron	I	RF	216	Books for Young Learners	Richard C. Owen
My Monster and Me	B	F	37	Ready Readers	Pearson Learning Group
My Monster Friends	F	F	94	Literacy 2000	Rigby
My Monster Mama Loves Me So	J	F	250+	Leuck, Laura	Scholastic
My Most Excellent Year: A Novel of Love, Mary Poppins & Fenway Park	Z	RF	250+	Kulger, Steve	Speak
My Mother Got Married (And Other Disasters)	P	RF	250+	Park, Barbara	Random House
My Mother Talks to Trees	M	RF	250+	Gove, Doris	Peachtree
My Mummy Couldn't Read	M	RF	638	Rigby-Wilcox, Carey	C Unique Creations Inc.
My Muscles	I	I	101	My Body	Capstone Press
My Mysterious World	O	B	250+	Meet The Author	Richard C. Owen
My Name Is America	Z	HF	250+	White, Ellen Emerson	Scholastic
My Name Is Buddy Biscuit (But You Can Call Me Buddy)	B	F	34	McGougan, Kathy	Buddy Books Publishing
My Name Is Erica Montoya de la Cruz	K	RF	804	Books for Young Learners	Richard C. Owen
My Name Is Maria Isabel	N	RF	250+	Ada, Alma Flor	Aladdin
My Name Is Not Angelica	V	HF	250+	O'Dell, Scott	Bantam Books
My Name Is Not Easy	X	HF	250+	Edwardson, Debby Dahl	Marshall Cavendish
My Name Is Stilton, Geronimo Stilton	O	F	250+	Stilton, Geronimo	Scholastic
My Name Is Yoon	M	RF	250+	Recorvits, Helen	Farrar, Straus, & Giroux

TITLE	LEVEL	GENRE	WORD COUNT	AUTHOR / SERIES	PUBLISHER / DISTRIBUTOR
My Name Is Yun Jim	N	RF	250+	Sunshine	Wright Group/McGraw Hill
My Native American School	F	RF	86	Gould, Carol	Kaeden Books
My Neighborhood	K	I	250+	Early Connections	Benchmark Education
My Neighborhood	J	RF	391	Leveled Readers	Houghton Mifflin Harcourt
My Neighborhood	E	RF	71	Reading Street	Pearson
My Neighborhood Places and Faces	K	RF	250+	All About Me	Picture Window Books
My Nest	C	I	42	Little Celebrations	Pearson Learning Group
My Nest Is Best	D	RF	92	Foundations	Wright Group/McGraw Hill
My New Bed	F	RF	109	McAlpin, MaryAnn	Short Tales Press
My New Best Friend	O	RF	250+	Bowe, Julie	Sandpiper Books
My New Boy	F	F	102	Step into Reading	Random House
My New Friend	B	RF	30	Windows on Literacy	National Geographic
My New House	C	RF	26	Reading Corners	Pearson Learning Group
My New Mom	K	RF	282	Sunshine	Wright Group/McGraw Hill
My New Pet	A	RF	32	Literacy by Design	Rigby
My New Pet	F	RF	105	Little Readers	Houghton Mifflin Harcourt
My New Pet	E	I	151	Sun Sprouts	ETA/Cuisenaire
My New Quilt	H	I	170	Rigby Focus	Rigby
My New Rocket	D	F	128	Bookshop	Mondo Publishing
My New Room	D	I	108	PM Science Readers	Rigby
My New School	E	RF	68	Hall, Kirsten/My First Reader	Children's Press
My New School	A	I	40	Leveled Literacy Intervention/ Green System	Heinemann
My New School	A	I	32	On Our Way to English	Rigby
My New Shoes	C	RF	60	The King School Series	Townsend Press
My New Truck	C	I	71	First Stories	Pacific Learning
My Noodle Necklace	C	I	75	Rigby Flying Colors	Rigby
My Old Cat	E	RF	110	Foundations	Wright Group/McGraw Hill
My Old Cat and the Computer	F	RF	81	Foundations	Wright Group/McGraw Hill
My Old Gold Boat	G	F	51	Easy Phonics Readers	Teacher Created Materials
My One Hundred Adventures	X	RF	250+	Horvath, Polly	Schwartz & Wade Books
My Own Place	J	RF	250+	Voyages	SRA/McGraw Hill
My Own Two Feet	W	B	250+	Cleary, Beverly	Avon Books
My Painting	B	RF	31	First Stories	Pacific Learning
My Pal Al	E	RF	81	Real Kids Readers	Millbrook Press
My Party	WB	I	0	Big Cat	Pacific Learning
My Party	C	I	35	The Candid Collection	Pearson Learning Group
My Pen Pal	K	RF	250+	Twig	Wright Group/McGraw Hill
My Pen Pal, Pat	K	RF	1298	Real Kids Readers	Millbrook Press
My Penguin Osbert	M	F	250+	Kimmel, Elizabeth Cody	Candlewick Press
My Pet	C	I	18	KinderReaders	Rigby
My Pet	A	I	25	Leveled Readers	Houghton Mifflin Harcourt
My Pet	A	I	25	Leveled Readers/CA	Houghton Mifflin Harcourt
My Pet	D	RF	65	Salem, Lynn; Stewart, Josie	Continental Press
My Pet Bobby	E	F	150	Little Readers	Houghton Mifflin Harcourt
My Pet Cat	A	RF	32	Leveled Readers	Houghton Mifflin Harcourt
My Pet Cat	A	RF	32	Leveled Readers/CA	Houghton Mifflin Harcourt
My Pet Ferrets	P	I	5911	All About Pets	Lerner Publishing Group
My Pet Fish	P	I	7027	All About Pets	Lerner Publishing Group
My Pet Lizards	P	I	5591	All About Pets	Lerner Publishing Group
My Pet Rabbit	P	I	6188	All About Pets	Lerner Publishing Group
My Pet Rat	P	I	5934	All About Pets	Lerner Publishing Group
My Pet Zoo	E	F	58	Dominie Readers	Pearson Learning Group
My Photo Journal	I	I	242	Shutterbug Books	Steck-Vaughn

* Collection of short stories   # Graphic text
^ Mature content with lower level text demands

TITLE	LEVEL	GENRE	WORD COUNT	AUTHOR / SERIES	PUBLISHER / DISTRIBUTOR
My Picture	C	RF	37	Carousel Readers	Pearson Learning Group
My Picture	A	RF	23	Story Box	Wright Group/McGraw Hill
My Pigs	F	I	123	Miller, Heather	Scholastic
My Place	A	RF	28	Foundations	Wright Group/McGraw Hill
My Place	Q	I	250+	Orbit Collections	Pacific Learning
My Place	A	RF	34	Story Steps	Rigby
My Planet	A	I	28	Smart Start	Rigby
My Plant	D	I	96	Rigby Literacy	Rigby
My Play House	B	RF	71	Leveled Readers	Houghton Mifflin Harcourt
My Play House	B	RF	71	Leveled Readers/CA	Houghton Mifflin Harcourt
My Pony	C	RF	49	Rise & Shine	Hampton Brown
My Pony Minnie	E	RF	59	Sunshine	Wright Group/McGraw Hill
My Prairie Summer	M	RF	250+	Pair-It Books	Steck-Vaughn
My Pumpkin	C	I	52	Teacher's Choice Series	Pearson Learning Group
My Pup	D	RF	65	Leveled Readers	Houghton Mifflin Harcourt
My Puppy	B	RF	29	Gear Up!	Wright Group/McGraw Hill
My Puppy	A	RF	39	Leveled Literacy Intervention/ Green System	Heinemann
My Puppy	B	I	72	Literacy by Design	Rigby
My Puppy	C	RF	33	Little Celebrations	Pearson Learning Group
My Puppy	B	RF	14	Sunshine	Wright Group/McGraw Hill
My Puppy	B	RF	24	Windows on Literacy	National Geographic
My Red Rowboat	E	RF	89	Early Readers	Compass Point Books
My Red Scarf	F	I	120	Rigby Focus	Rigby
My Ride	C	RF	56	Foundations	Wright Group/McGraw Hill
My River	F	F	53	Halpern, Shari	Scholastic
My Robot	B	F	38	Joy Starters	Pearson Learning Group
My Rocket	A	F	28	KinderReaders	Rigby
My Rocks	C	RF	43	Early Connections	Benchmark Education
My Room	A	RF	28	Carousel Earlybirds	Pearson Learning Group
My Room	A	I	32	Leveled Literacy Intervention/ Orange System	Heinemann
My Room	A	RF	15	Leveled Readers Emergent	Houghton Mifflin Harcourt
My Room	LB	RF	14	Ready Readers	Pearson Learning Group
My Room	A	RF	15	Twig	Wright Group/McGraw Hill
My Sand Castle	C	RF	44	PM Plus Starters	Rigby
My Sand Pie	B	I	33	Rigby Flying Colors	Rigby
My School	A	I	34	At School Series	Pioneer Valley
My School	LB	I	22	Emberley, Rebecca	Little Brown and Company
My School	A	RF	32	Handprints A	Educators Publishing Service
My School	B	I	34	Little Readers	Houghton Mifflin Harcourt
My School	C	RF	40	TOTTS	Tott Publications
My School	A	I	20	Vocabulary Readers	Houghton Mifflin Harcourt
My School	A	I	20	Vocabulary Readers/CA	Houghton Mifflin Harcourt
My School Day	LB	I	6	Windows on Literacy	National Geographic
My School Lunch	C	I	54	Bonnell, Kris	Reading Reading Books
My School, Your School	F	I	72	Take Two Books	Wright Group/McGraw Hill
My Science Project	M	RF	250+	On Our Way To English	Rigby
My Scrapbook	K	I	312	Storyteller Nonfiction	Wright Group/McGraw Hill
My Search for Fossils	S	I	250+	Literacy by Design	Rigby
My Search for My Father	X	RF	2402	Leveled Readers	Houghton Mifflin Harcourt
My Search for My Father	X	RF	2402	Leveled Readers/CA	Houghton Mifflin Harcourt
My Search for My Father	X	RF	2402	Leveled Readers/TX	Houghton Mifflin Harcourt

TITLE	LEVEL	GENRE	WORD COUNT	AUTHOR / SERIES	PUBLISHER / DISTRIBUTOR
My Secret Hiding Place	G	RF	155	First Start	Troll Associates
My Secret Life as a Ping-Pong Wizard	R	RF	250+	Winkler, Henry and Oliver, Lin	Grosset & Dunlap
My Secret Place	G	RF	121	Wonder World	Wright Group/McGraw Hill
My Secret War Diary	Z	HF	250+	Albright, Flossie	Candlewick Press
My Senator and Me: A Dog's-Eye View of Washington, D.C.	N	F	250+	Kennedy, Edward M.	Scholastic
My Shadow	A	RF	29	Book Bank	Wright Group/McGraw Hill
My Shadow	C	RF	42	Foundations	Wright Group/McGraw Hill
My Shadow	E	I	46	Pacific Literacy	Pacific Learning
My Shadow	F	RF	116	Ready Readers	Pearson Learning Group
My Shadow	C	RF	35	Sunshine	Wright Group/McGraw Hill
My Shadow Clock	H	I	180	Sun Sprouts	ETA/Cuisenaire
My Shapes	E	I	74	Joy Starters	Pearson Learning Group
My Shoes	B	RF	25	Rise & Shine	Hampton Brown
My Side of the Mountain	U	RF	250+	George, Jean Craighead	Penguin Group
My Sister Annie	S	RF	250+	Dodds, Bill	Boyds Mills Press
My Sister Is My Friend	B	RF	32	Instant Readers	Harcourt School Publishers
My Sister Jess	I	RF	120	Supersonics	Rigby
My Sister June	H	RF	182	Ready Readers	Pearson Learning Group
My Sister the Witch	R	RF	250+	Conford, Ellen	Troll Associates
My Sister's Getting Married	K	RF	300	Foundations	Wright Group/McGraw Hill
My Sister's Surprise	T	RF	2298	Leveled Readers	Houghton Mifflin Harcourt
My Sister's Surprise	T	RF	2298	Leveled Readers/CA	Houghton Mifflin Harcourt
My Sister's Surprise	T	RF	2298	Leveled Readers/TX	Houghton Mifflin Harcourt
My Skateboard	LB	I	11	Big Cat	Pacific Learning
My Skateboard	D	RF	89	Carousel Readers	Pearson Learning Group
My Skateboard	I	RF	81	City Kids	Rigby
My Skateboard	G	I	81	Sun Sprouts	ETA/Cuisenaire
My Skin	D	I	64	Wonder World	Wright Group/McGraw Hill
My Skin Looks After Me	G	I	82	Pacific Literacy	Pacific Learning
My Skin: What's Inside Me?	N	I	250+	Bookworms	Marshall Cavendish
My Sloppy Tiger	I	F	211	Sunshine	Wright Group/McGraw Hill
My Sloppy Tiger Goes to School	J	F	217	Sunshine	Wright Group/McGraw Hill
My Snowman	B	I	66	First Stories	Pacific Learning
My Snowman	D	I	113	PM Science Readers	Rigby
My Son, the Time Traveler	N	F	250+	The Zack Files	Grosset & Dunlap
My Special Book	B	I	45	Storyteller	Wright Group/McGraw Hill
My Special Job	E	RF	110	Pacific Literacy	Pacific Learning
My Special Place	E	RF	33	Home Connection Collection	Rigby
My Special Place	E	RF	116	Teacher's Choice Series	Pearson Learning Group
My Special Wish	G	RF	178	Domine Readers	Pearson Publishing Group
My Stepmother	I	RF	121	City Stories	Rigby
My Steps	K	RF	250+	Bebop Books	Lee & Low Books Inc.
My Stomach	J	I	144	My Body	Capstone Press
My Stomach: What's Inside Me?	N	I	250+	Bookworms	Marshall Cavendish
My Story	A	RF	17	Wonder World	Wright Group/McGraw Hill
My Stuffed Animals	C	RF	50	Handprints B	Educators Publishing Service
My Suitcase	LB	RF	16	Handprints A	Educators Publishing Service
My Summer Without Baseball and Other Disasters	N	RF	3491	In Step Readers	Rigby
My Summertime Camping Trip	J	RF	585	Appleton-Smith, Laura	Flyleaf Publishing
My Take-Away Day	E	RF	115	InfoTrek	ETA/Cuisenaire

* Collection of short stories   # Graphic text
^ Mature content with lower level text demands

TITLE	LEVEL	GENRE	WORD COUNT	AUTHOR / SERIES	PUBLISHER / DISTRIBUTOR
My Teacher	A	I	32	At School Series	Pioneer Valley
My Teacher Flunked the Planet	S	F	250+	Coville, Bruce	Pocket Books
My Teacher Fried My Brains	S	F	250+	Coville, Bruce	Pocket Books
My Teacher Glows in the Dark	S	F	250+	Coville, Bruce	Pocket Books
My Teacher Helps Me	C	RF	37	Visions	Wright Group/McGraw Hill
My Teacher Is an Alien	S	F	250+	Coville, Bruce	Pocket Books
My Teacher Turns into a Tyrannosaurus	O	F	250+	Supa Doopers	Sundance
My Teacher, My Dad	J	RF	296	Leveled Readers	Houghton Mifflin Harcourt
My Teacher, My Dad	J	RF	296	Leveled Readers/CA	Houghton Mifflin Harcourt
My Teacher, My Dad	J	RF	296	Leveled Readers/TX	Houghton Mifflin Harcourt
My Teacher's Leaving	I	RF	154	City Kids	Rigby
My Things	LB	F	12	Sails	Rigby
My Three-Wheeler	C	RF	38	Visions	Wright Group/McGraw Hill
My Tiger Cat	E	F	76	Frankford, Marilyn	Kaeden Books
^My Time as Caz Hazard	Z+	RF	250+	Orca Soundings	Orca Books
My Time Box	I	RF	225	Early Connections	Benchmark Education
My Tooth Is About to Fall Out	I	RF	173	Maccarone, Grace	Scholastic
My Tooth Is Loose!	H	RF	250+	Silverman, Martin	Puffin Books
My Tower	C	RF	61	PM Plus Story Books	Rigby
My Tower	A	RF	15	Windmill Books	Wright Group/McGraw Hill
My Town	A	I	33	Early Connections	Benchmark Education
My Town at Work	M	I	250+	Windows on Literacy	National Geographic
My Town Used To Be Small	G	I	79	Windows on Literacy	National Geographic
My Toy Box Is Heavy	D	RF	99	Windows on Literacy	National Geographic
My Toys	A	I	25	Explorations	Eleanor Curtain Publishing
My Toys	A	I	25	Explorations	Okapi Educational Materials
My Toys	A	RF	28	Little Books for Early Readers	University of Maine
My Treasure Garden	J	RF	134	Book Bank	Wright Group/McGraw Hill
My Trip	A	F	30	Sails	Rigby
My Truck	C	RF	32	Windows on Literacy	National Geographic
My Turn Your Turn	D	RF	78	Book Bus	Creative Edge
My Twin!	C	RF	40	Ready Readers	Pearson Learning Group
My Two Families	K	RF	250+	PM Story Books-Silver	Rigby
My Two Grandmas	I	RF	235	Sun Sprouts	ETA/Cuisenaire
My Two Homes	E	RF	69	Carousel Readers	Pearson Learning Group
My Uncle Martin's Words for America	R	I	250+	Watkins, Angela Farris	Harry N. Abrams
My Uncle the Werewolf	Q	F	9674	French, Jackie	Stone Arch Books
My Uncle's Truck	C	RF	24	Visions	Wright Group/McGraw Hill
My Undersea World	Q	I	250+	Literacy by Design	Rigby
My Unwilling Witch Gets a Makeover	Q	F	250+	Oram, Hiawyn	Little Brown and Company
My Unwilling Witch Goes to Ballet School	Q	F	250+	Oram, Hiawyn	Walker & Company
My Unwilling Witch Sleep Over	Q	F	250+	Oram, Hiawyn	Little Brown and Company
My Unwilling Witch Starts a Girl Band	Q	F	250+	Oram, Hiawyn	Little Brown and Company
My Vacation	C	RF	56	McAlpin, MaryAnn	Short Tales Press
My Vacation	D	RF	60	Rigby Literacy	Rigby
My Very Hungry Pet	F	RF	334	Reading Corners	Pearson Learning Group
My Very Own Room	L	RF	250+	Perez, Amada Irma	Children's Book Press
My Vicksburg	W	HF	250+	Rinaldi, Ann	Houghton Mifflin Harcourt
My Vivid Town	I	RF	332	Appleton-Smith, Laura	Flyleaf Publishing
My Walk	WB	I	0	Windows on Literacy	National Geographic
My Walk Home	F	RF	71	Windows on Literacy	National Geographic
My Wartime Summers	V	HF	250+	Cutler, Jane	HarperCollins
My Weather Station	G	I	313	Leveled Readers Science	Houghton Mifflin Harcourt
My Week	D	RF	137	Early Connections	Benchmark Education

* Collection of short stories   # Graphic text
^ Mature content with lower level text demands

TITLE	LEVEL	GENRE	WORD COUNT	AUTHOR / SERIES	PUBLISHER / DISTRIBUTOR
My Weekly Chores	C	RF	44	Visions	Wright Group/McGraw Hill
My Weird Mother	M	RF	250+	Supa Doopers	Sundance
My Wild Woolly	F	F	87	Instant Readers	Harcourt Trade
My Wild Woolly	E	F	91	Rigby Rocket	Rigby
My Wonderful Aunt, Story Five	M	F	493	Sunshine	Wright Group/McGraw Hill
My Wonderful Aunt, Story Four	M	F	436	Sunshine	Wright Group/McGraw Hill
My Wonderful Aunt, Story One	M	F	193	Sunshine	Wright Group/McGraw Hill
My Wonderful Aunt, Story Six	M	F	432	Sunshine	Wright Group/McGraw Hill
My Wonderful Aunt, Story Three	M	F	392	Sunshine	Wright Group/McGraw Hill
My Wonderful Aunt, Story Two	M	F	199	Sunshine	Wright Group/McGraw Hill
My Wonderful Chair	F	F	109	Windmill Books	Wright Group/McGraw Hill
My Worst Best Friend	Y	RF	250+	Sheldon, Dyan	Candlewick Press
My Writing Day	O	B	250+	Meet The Author	Richard C. Owen
My Yard	A	I	19	Leveled Readers	Houghton Mifflin Harcourt
My Yard	A	I	19	Leveled Readers/CA	Houghton Mifflin Harcourt
My Zoo Album	F	I	168	PM Science Readers	Rigby
Mysteries from Long Ago	P	I	936	Leveled Readers	Houghton Mifflin Harcourt
Mysteries from Long Ago	P	I	936	Leveled Readers/CA	Houghton Mifflin Harcourt
Mysteries from Long Ago	P	I	936	Leveled Readers/TX	Houghton Mifflin Harcourt
Mysteries of Chaco Canyon, The	V	I	250+	Explore More	Wright Group/McGraw Hill
Mysteries of Pompeii	X	I	3180	Vocabulary Readers	Houghton Mifflin Harcourt
Mysteries of Pompeii	X	I	3180	Vocabulary Readers/CA	Houghton Mifflin Harcourt
Mysteries of Sherlock Holmes	S	I	250+	Edge	Hampton Brown
Mysteries of the Ancients	Z	I	250+	Unsolved Mysteries	Steck-Vaughn
Mysteries of the Bermuda Triangle	Z	I	2348	Leveled Readers	Houghton Mifflin Harcourt
Mysteries of the Deep	R	I	531	Vocabulary Readers	Houghton Mifflin Harcourt
Mysteries of the Mummy Kids	Y	I	250+	Halls, Kelly Milner	Darby Creek Publishing
Mysteries of the Phoenicians	Z	I	2041	Leveled Readers	Houghton Mifflin Harcourt
Mysteries of the Phoenicians	Z	I	2041	Leveled Readers/CA	Houghton Mifflin Harcourt
Mysteries of the Phoenicians	Z	I	2041	Leveled Readers/TX	Houghton Mifflin Harcourt
Mysteries of UFOs, The	Z	I	250+	Unsolved Mysteries	Steck-Vaughn
Mysteries Unwrapped: Lost Civilizations	X	I	250+	Linnea, Sharon	Sterling Publishing
Mysterious Animal Tracks, The	K	RF	250+	Literacy by Design	Rigby
Mysterious Bali	P	RF	250+	Reading Safari	Mondo Publishing
Mysterious Benedict Society and the Perilous Journey, The	V	SF	250+	Stewart, Trenton Lee	Little Brown and Company
Mysterious Benedict Society and the Prisoner's Dilema, The	V	SF	250+	Stewart, Trenton Lee	Little Brown and Company
Mysterious Benedict Society, The	V	SF	250+	Stewart, Trenton Lee	Little Brown and Company
Mysterious Bone, The	L	B	320	Leveled Readers	Houghton Mifflin Harcourt
Mysterious Bone, The	L	B	320	Leveled Readers/CA	Houghton Mifflin Harcourt
Mysterious Bone, The	L	B	320	Leveled Readers/TX	Houghton Mifflin Harcourt
Mysterious Cheese Thief, The	O	F	250+	Stilton, Geronimo	Scholastic
Mysterious Edge of the Heroic World, The	Z	RF	250+	Konigsburg, E. L.	Atheneum Books
Mysterious Giant Squid, The	Z	I	2415	Leveled Readers	Houghton Mifflin Harcourt
*Mysterious Green Swimmer and Other Cases, The	O	RF	250+	Simon, Seymour	Avon Books
Mysterious Healing	Z	I	250+	Unsolved Mysteries	Steck-Vaughn
Mysterious Howling, The (The Incorrigible Children of Ashton Place)	V	F	250+	Wood, Mayrose	HarperCollins
Mysterious I.O.U., The	M	RF	250+	Woodland Mysteries	Wright Group/McGraw Hill
Mysterious Island, The: The Secrets of Droon	O	F	250+	Abbott, Tony	Scholastic
Mysterious Mask, The	O	RF	250+	Klooz	Stone Arch Books
Mysterious Ms. Martin, The	N	RF	250+	On Our Way To English	Rigby

* Collection of short stories   # Graphic text
^ Mature content with lower level text demands

TITLE	LEVEL	GENRE	WORD COUNT	AUTHOR / SERIES	PUBLISHER / DISTRIBUTOR
Mysterious Neighbor, The	L	RF	1014	In Step Readers	Rigby
Mysterious Neighbor, The	L	RF	250+	Literacy By Design	Rigby
Mysterious Ocean Highway: Benjamin Franklin and the Gulf Stream	T	B	250+	Heiligman, Deborah	Steck-Vaughn
Mysterious Places	T	I	250+	Boldprint	Steck-Vaughn
Mysterious Spinners	Q	TL	250+	Bookshop	Mondo Publishing
Mysterious Superhero, The	L	F	1104	Leveled Readers	Houghton Mifflin Harcourt
Mysterious Superhero, The	L	F	1104	Leveled Readers/CA	Houghton Mifflin Harcourt
Mysterious Superhero, The	L	F	1104	Leveled Readers/TX	Houghton Mifflin Harcourt
*Mysterious Tracks and Other Cases, The	O	RF	250+	Simon, Seymour	Avon Books
Mystery Ancestor	Q	I	250+	Rigby Focus	Rigby
Mystery at Area 51, The	Q	RF	250+	Marsh, Carol	Gallopade International
Mystery at Hollywood, The	Q	RF	250+	Marsh, Carol	Gallopade International
Mystery at Kickingbird Lake, The: Ghost Twins	P	F	250+	Regan, Dian Curtis	Scholastic
Mystery at Motown, The	Q	RF	250+	Marsh, Carol	Gallopade International
Mystery at Summer Camp	Q	RF	250+	Reading Expeditions	National Geographic
Mystery at the Club Sandwich	O	F	250+	Cushman, Doug	Clarion Books
Mystery at the White House	R	F	250+	Pair-It Books	Steck-Vaughn
Mystery at the Zoo	T	RF	1733	Leveled Readers	Houghton Mifflin Harcourt
Mystery Bay	P	RF	250+	Action Packs	Rigby
Mystery Box, The	I	RF	326	New Way Orange	Steck-Vaughn
Mystery Coin	J	RF	379	Independent Readers Social Studies	Houghton Mifflin Harcourt
Mystery Fish: Secrets of the Coelacanth	O	I	1678	On My Own Science	Lerner Publishing Group
Mystery Food	E	RF	62	Leveled Readers Science	Houghton Mifflin Harcourt
Mystery for Mickey Maloney, A	J	RF	383	Sails	Rigby
Mystery Fruit	K	I	364	Vocabulary Readers	Houghton Mifflin Harcourt
Mystery Fruit	K	I	364	Vocabulary Readers/CA	Houghton Mifflin Harcourt
Mystery in the Arctic	V	I	250+	PM Collection	Rigby
Mystery in the Attic, The	L	RF	250+	Leveled Readers Language Support	Houghton Mifflin Harcourt
Mystery in the Night Woods	M	F	250+	Peterson, John	Scholastic
Mystery in the Twin Cities, The	Q	RF	250+	Marsh, Carol	Gallopade International
Mystery Man, The	K	RF	250+	Rigby Literacy	Rigby
Mystery Mask, The	N	RF	250+	Literacy by Design	Rigby
Mystery of Allegra, The	W	F	6115	Oxford Bookworms Library	Oxford University Press
Mystery of Campion Cave, The	P	RF	1950	Take Two Books	Wright Group/McGraw Hill
Mystery of Hermit Dan, The	N	RF	250+	Parish, Peggy	Yearling Books
Mystery of Lighthouse Cave, The	P	RF	250+	Leveled Readers Language Support	Houghton Mifflin Harcourt
Mystery of Magnets, The	P	I	250+	iOpeners	Pearson Learning Group
Mystery of Magnets, The	V	I	250+	Reading Expeditions	National Geographic
Mystery of Mazes, The	O	I	250+	Wonder World	Wright Group/McGraw Hill
Mystery of Moody Manor, The	Q	F	250+	Ragged Island Mysteries	Wright Group/McGraw Hill
Mystery of Mr. Nice, The: A Chet Gecko Mystery	Q	F	250+	Hale, Bruce	Harcourt, Inc.
Mystery of Mrs. Kim, The	M	RF	250+	Rigby Literacy	Rigby
Mystery of Mrs. Kim, The	M	RF	250+	Rigby Star Plus	Rigby
Mystery of Pony Hollow, The	N	F	250+	Hall, Lynn	Random House
Mystery of Sarah Beth, The	L	RF	250+	Putnam, Polly	Pearson Learning Group
Mystery of the Bay Monster	J	RF	250+	Literacy by Design	Rigby
Mystery of the Blue Box, The	N	I	841	Independent Readers Science	Houghton Mifflin Harcourt
Mystery of the Blue Ring, The	L	RF	250+	Giff, Patricia Reilly	Bantam Books
Mystery of the Clever Cat, The	J	RF	250+	Literacy by Design	Rigby
Mystery of the Clever Cat, The	J	RF	250+	On Our Way to English	Rigby

* Collection of short stories   # Graphic text
^ Mature content with lower level text demands

TITLE	LEVEL	GENRE	WORD COUNT	AUTHOR / SERIES	PUBLISHER / DISTRIBUTOR
Mystery of the Clock Tower, The	Q	RF	250+	Reading Safari	Mondo Publishing
Mystery of the Cocos Gold	Q	HF	250+	High-Fliers	Pacific Learning
Mystery of the Cupboard	R	F	250+	Banks, Lynne Reid	Avon Books
Mystery of the Dark Old House, The	M	F	250+	Woodland Mysteries	Wright Group/McGraw Hill
Mystery of the Fire in the Sky	Q	RF	250+	Mystery Solvers	Troll Associates
Mystery of the Flattened Flowers, The	J	RF	454	Springboard	Wright Group/McGraw Hill
Mystery of the Fool & the Vanisher, The	W	F	250+	Ellwand, David & Ruth	Candlewick Press
Mystery of the Jubilee Emerald, The	R	RF	250+	Bookshop	Mondo Publishing
Mystery of the Missing Berries, The	J	RF	250+	Literacy by Design	Rigby
Mystery of the Missing Cookies, The	K	RF	445	Early Explorers	Benchmark Education
Mystery of the Missing Dog, The	J	F	250+	Levy, Elizabeth	Scholastic
Mystery of the Missing Dog, The	M	RF	250+	Woodland Mysteries	Wright Group/McGraw Hill
Mystery of the Missing Garden Gnome, The	R	RF	250+	Book Blazers	ETA/Cuisenaire
Mystery of the Missing Leopard, The	Q	F	250+	Leonhardt, Alice	Steck-Vaughn
Mystery of the Missing Malamute, The	M	RF	250+	Sunshine	Wright Group/McGraw Hill
Mystery of the Missing Mystery, The	M	RF	250+	Rigby Rocket	Rigby
Mystery of the Missing Red Mitten, The	H	RF	246	Little Readers	Houghton Mifflin Harcourt
Mystery of the Mona Lisa, The	P	SF	250+	Secret Agent Jack Stalwart	Weinstein Books
Mystery of the Noises in the Attic, The	N	RF	606	Leveled Readers	Houghton Mifflin Harcourt
Mystery of the Phantom Pony, The	N	RF	250+	Hall, Lynn	Random House
Mystery of the Pirate Ghost, The	L	F	250+	Hayes, Geoffrey	Random House
#Mystery of the Roanoke Colony, The	R	I	250+	Graphic Library	Capstone Press
Mystery of the Sea Jellies, The	N	RF	1350	Gear Up!	Wright Group/McGraw Hill
Mystery of the Silver Spoons, The	Q	RF	250+	Book Blazers	ETA/Cuisenaire
Mystery of the Stolen Bike, The	M	F	250+	Brown, Marc	Little Brown and Company
Mystery of the Talking Tail, The	M	F	250+	Supa Doopers	Sundance
Mystery of the Three Keys, The	M	RF	250+	Woodland Mysteries	Wright Group/McGraw Hill
Mystery of the Tooth Gremlin, The	L	RF	250+	Graves, Bonnie	Hyperion
Mystery of the Trembling Earth, The	T	F	250+	Reading Safari	Mondo Publishing
Mystery on Maple Street, The	Q	RF	1153	Leveled Readers	Houghton Mifflin Harcourt
Mystery on Maple Street, The	Q	RF	1153	Leveled Readers/CA	Houghton Mifflin Harcourt
Mystery on Maple Street, The	Q	RF	1153	Leveled Readers/TX	Houghton Mifflin Harcourt
Mystery on October Road	O	RF	250+	Herzig, A. C.; Mali, Jane	Scholastic
Mystery on Penn Street	G	RF	214	On Our Way to English	Rigby
Mystery Seed, The	I	RF	250+	Windows on Literacy	National Geographic
Mystery Seeds	L	RF	250+	Reading Unlimited	Pearson Learning Group
Mystery Stamps, The	N	RF	250+	Windows on Literacy	National Geographic
*Mystery Stories	R	RF	250+	Higgins, James	Houghton Mifflin Harcourt
Mystery to Me, A	Q	I	250+	Orbit Collections	Pacific Learning
Mystery Trip, The	L	RF	525	Rigby Flying Colors	Rigby
Mystery Valley	P	SF	250+	Bookweb	Rigby
Mystic Phyles, The: Beasts	T	F	10462	Brockway, Stephanie	Charlesbridge
Myth or Mystery?	Q	F	250+	Literacy Tree	Rigby
Mythical Beasts	T	F	250+	Wildcats	Wright Group/McGraw Hill
Mythical Horse, The	T	I	250+	Sunshine	Wright Group/McGraw Hill
Mythmakers	S	I	250+	Wildcats	Wright Group/McGraw Hill
Mythology	Y	I	250+	Eyewitness Books	DK Publishing
*Myths	S	TL	250+	Goodman, Ronald; Pierce, Robert; Wagner, Betty Jane	Houghton Mifflin Harcourt
Myths and Legends	S	TL	250+	Boldprint	Steck-Vaughn
Myths and Legends	T	I	250+	Kids Discover Reading	Wright Group/McGraw Hill
Myths of a Different Feather	U	TL	250+	Literacy By Design	Rigby

* Collection of short stories   # Graphic text
^ Mature content with lower level text demands

TITLE	LEVEL	GENRE	WORD COUNT	AUTHOR / SERIES	PUBLISHER / DISTRIBUTOR
N	LB	I	14	Readlings	American Reading Company
Nabeel's New Pants: An Eid Tale	K	RF	250+	Gilani-Williams, Fawzia	Marshall Cavendish
Nadia Comaneci	M	B	250+	Take Two Books	Wright Group/McGraw Hill
Nailed	Z+	RF	250+	Jones, Patrick	Walker & Company
Naked Mole-Rat Letters, The	T	RF	250+	Amato, Mary	Holiday House
Naked Mole-Rat, The	J	I	134	Weird Animals	Capstone Press
Name for a Dog, A	I	RF	258	Windmill Books	Rigby
Name for Rabbit, A	H	F	94	Pacific Literacy	Pacific Learning
Name Garden, A	F	I	125	Sunshine	Wright Group/McGraw Hill
Name Is the Same, The	G	RF	115	Ready Readers	Pearson Learning Group
Name Jar, The	N	RF	250+	Choi, Yangsook	Dell
Name of Honor, A	T	HF	250+	Bookshop	Mondo Publishing
Name of the Game Was Murder, The	Y	RF	250+	Nixon, Joan Lowery	Laurel-Leaf Books
Name of This Book Is Secret, The	U	F	250+	Bosch, Pseudonymous	Little Brown and Company
Name That Plant	I	I	383	Shutterbug Books	Steck-Vaughn
Name That Style: All About Isms in Art	Y	I	3863	Raczka, Bob	Millbrook Press
Name, The	H	RF	159	Voyages	SRA/McGraw Hill
Named, The	Z	F	250+	Curly, Marianne	Bloomsbury Children's Books
Names and Games	H	I	115	Literacy Tree	Rigby
Naming of Tishkin Silk, The	P	RF	250+	Millard, Glenda	Farrar, Straus, & Giroux
Naming the Cat	L	RF	250+	Soar To Success	Houghton Mifflin Harcourt
Nan the Red Hen!	C	RF	43	Reading Street	Pearson
Nana Rescue, The	J	RF	250+	Voyages	SRA/McGraw Hill
Nana's House	D	RF	133	Leveled Readers	Houghton Mifflin Harcourt
Nana's House	D	RF	133	Leveled Readers/CA	Houghton Mifflin Harcourt
Nana's House	D	RF	133	Leveled Readers/TX	Houghton Mifflin Harcourt
Nana's in the Plum Tree	M	RF	250+	Pacific Literacy	Pacific Learning
Nana's Kitchen	J	RF	250+	Walton, Darwin McBeth	Steck-Vaughn
Nana's Orchard	F	RF	92	Gould, Carol	Kaeden Books
Nana's Place	I	RF	211	Gibson, Akimi; Meyer, K.	Scholastic
Nana's Sweet Potato Pie	E	RF	233	Visions	Wright Group/McGraw Hill
Nana's Tomatoes	M	RF	587	Leveled Readers Science	Houghton Mifflin Harcourt
Nancy and Plum	S	RF	250+	MacDonald, Betty	Alfred A. Knopf
Nannies for Hire	M	RF	250+	Hest, Amy	William Morrow
Nanny Goat's Nap	C	F	96	Ready Readers	Pearson Learning Group
Nanotechnology	Z	I	6581	Cool Science	Lerner Publishing Group
Nanotechnology	Z	I	2839	Leveled Readers	Houghton Mifflin Harcourt
Nanotechnology	Z	I	2839	Leveled Readers/CA	Houghton Mifflin Harcourt
Nanotechnology	Z	I	2839	Leveled Readers/TX	Houghton Mifflin Harcourt
Nap Time	C	RF	24	KinderReaders	Rigby
Nap Time for Gilbert	D	F	83	Gilbert the Pig	Pioneer Valley
Nap Time for Lily	D	RF	79	Emergent Set 4	Pioneer Valley
Napping House, The	I	F	268	Wood, Don & Audrey	Harcourt Trade
Narrative of the Life of Frederick Douglass, An American Slave	Z+	B	250+	Edge	Hampton Brown
Narwhal	L	I	250+	A Day in the Life: Polar Animals	Heinemann Library
Narwhal Whales Up Close	M	I	250+	First Facts-Whales and Dolphins Up Close	Capstone Press
NASA	M	I	250+	The Solar System	Capstone Press
NASCAR at the Track	U	I	4409	The Science of NASCAR	Lerner Publishing Group
NASCAR Behind the Scenes	U	I	4568	The Science of NASCAR	Lerner Publishing Group

TITLE	LEVEL	GENRE	WORD COUNT	AUTHOR / SERIES	PUBLISHER / DISTRIBUTOR
NASCAR Designed to Win	U	I	4465	The Science of NASCAR	Lerner Publishing Group
NASCAR in the Driver's Seat	U	I	4425	The Science of NASCAR	Lerner Publishing Group
NASCAR in the Pits	U	I	4973	The Science of NASCAR	Lerner Publishing Group
NASCAR Safety on the Track	U	I	4635	The Science of NASCAR	Lerner Publishing Group
NASCAR's Greatest Moments	S	I	250+	NASCAR Racing	Capstone Press
Nasty, Stinky Sneakers	R	RF	250+	Bunting, Eve	HarperTrophy
Nat and Harry Meet a Dinosaur	I	RF	416	Rigby Flying Colors	Rigby
Nat and Harry Play Soccer	G	RF	201	Rigby Flying Colors	Rigby
Nat Love	S	B	3919	History Maker Bios	Lerner Publishing Group
Nat Turner: Rebellious Slave	U	B	250+	Let Freedom Ring	Capstone Press
Nat, Nan, and Pam	C	RF	30	Leveled Readers	Houghton Mifflin Harcourt
Natalia and Her Grandma	N	RF	250+	Sunflower	Intercultural Center for Research in Education
Natalie & Naughtily	L	F	250+	Kirsch, Vincent X.	Bloomsbury Children's Books
Natalie Du Toit	O	B	250+	Lighthouse	Ginn & Co.
Natchez Under the Hill	T	HF	250+	Applegate, Stan	Peachtree
Nate the Great	K	RF	250+	Sharmat, Marjorie Weinman	Bantam Books
Nate the Great and Me	K	RF	250+	Sharmat, Marjorie Weinman	Random House
Nate the Great and the Boring Beach Bag	K	RF	250+	Sharmat, Marjorie Weinman	Bantam Books
Nate the Great and the Crunchy Christmas	K	RF	250+	Sharmat, Marjorie Weinman	Bantam Books
Nate the Great and the Fishy Prize	K	RF	250+	Sharmat, Marjorie Weinman	Bantam Books
Nate the Great and the Halloween Hunt	K	RF	250+	Sharmat, Marjorie Weinman	Bantam Books
Nate the Great and the Lost List	K	RF	250+	Sharmat, Marjorie Weinman	Bantam Books
Nate the Great and the Missing Key	K	RF	250+	Sharmat, Marjorie Weinman	Bantam Books
Nate the Great and the Mushy Valentine	K	RF	250+	Sharmat, Marjorie Weinman	Bantam Books
Nate the Great and the Musical Note	K	RF	250+	Sharmat, Marjorie Weinman	Bantam Books
Nate the Great and the Phony Clue	K	RF	250+	Sharmat, Marjorie Weinman	Bantam Books
Nate the Great and the Pillowcase	K	RF	250+	Sharmat, Marjorie Weinman	Bantam Books
Nate the Great and the Snowy Trail	K	RF	250+	Sharmat, Marjorie Weinman	Bantam Books
Nate the Great and the Sticky Case	K	RF	250+	Sharmat, Marjorie Weinman	Bantam Books
Nate the Great and the Stolen Base	K	RF	250+	Sharmat, Marjorie Weinman	Bantam Books
Nate the Great and the Tardy Tortoise	K	RF	250+	Sharmat, Marjorie Weinman	Bantam Books
Nate the Great Goes Down in the Dumps	K	RF	250+	Sharmat, Marjorie Weinman	Bantam Books
Nate the Great Goes Undercover	K	RF	250+	Sharmat, Marjorie Weinman	Bantam Books
Nate the Great Saves the King of Sweden	K	RF	250+	Sharmat, Marjorie Weinman	Bantam Books
Nate the Great Stalks Stupidweed	K	RF	250+	Sharmat, Marjorie Weinman	Bantam Books
Nathan and Nicholas Alexander	K	F	250+	Delacre, Lulu	Scholastic
Nathan Fox: Dangerous Times	Y	HF	250+	Brittney, L.	Feiwel and Friends
Nathan Hale	S	B	2931	People to Remember Series	January Books
Nathan Hale Patriot Spy	P	B	1923	On My Own Biography	Lerner Publishing Group
#Nathan Hale: Revolutionary Spy	T	B	250+	Graphic Library	Capstone Press
Nathaniel Comes to Town	S	RF	4072	Reading Street	Pearson
Nation	X	F	250+	Pratchett, Terry	HarperCollins
Nation at War: Soldiers, Saints, and Spies	Y	I	250+	The Civil War	Carus Publishing Company
Nation of Immigrants, A	M	I	528	Avenues	Hampton Brown
Nation of Immigrants, A	Q	I	1479	Leveled Readers Language Support	Houghton Mifflin Harcourt
Nation of Many Colors, A	T	I	2498	Reading Street	Pearson
Nation of Nations, A	S	HF	1931	Leveled Readers Social Studies	Houghton Mifflin Harcourt
Nation of Parks, A	O	I	250+	Literacy By Design	Rigby
^Nation Torn Apart, A: The Battle of Gettysburg	X	I	250+	Bloodiest Battles	Capstone Press
National Anthem, The	S	I	250+	A True Book	Children's Press
National Guard, The: Modern Minutemen	T	I	1809	Reading Street	Pearson

* Collection of short stories   # Graphic text
^ Mature content with lower level text demands

TITLE	LEVEL	GENRE	WORD COUNT	AUTHOR / SERIES	PUBLISHER / DISTRIBUTOR
National Holiday, A	N	I	491	Leveled Readers Language Support	Houghton Mifflin Harcourt
National Parks	S	I	250+	iOpeners	Pearson Learning Group
National Parks	M	I	250+	Yellow Umbrella Books	Red Brick Learning
National Parks America's Best Idea	U	I	250+	Rigby Literacy	Rigby
^National Security Agency, The: Cracking Secret Codes	S	I	250+	Line of Duty	Capstone Press
National Velvet	X	RF	250+	Bagnold, Enid	Avon Books
Native American Art	O	I	250+	Motil, Rebecca	Scholastic
Native American Art from the Pueblos	P	I	250+	Rosen Real Readers	Rosen Publishing Group
Native American Baskets	L	I	195	Phonics Readers	Compass Point Books
Native American Book of Change, The	W	I	250+	Native People Native Ways	Beyond Words
Native American Book of Knowledge, The	W	I	250+	Native People Native Ways	Beyond Words
Native American Book of Life, The	W	I	250+	Native People Native Ways	Beyond Words
Native American Book of Wisdom, The	W	I	250+	Native People Native Ways	Beyond Words
Native American Folktales	J	I	288	Vocabulary Readers	Houghton Mifflin Harcourt
Native American Folktales	J	I	288	Vocabulary Readers/CA	Houghton Mifflin Harcourt
Native American Folktales	J	I	288	Vocabulary Readers/TX	Houghton Mifflin Harcourt
Native American Foods and Recipes	O	I	250+	Rosen Real Readers	Rosen Publishing Group
Native American Homes	M	I	250+	Pair-It Turn and Learn	Steck-Vaughn
*Native American Stories	Q	TL	250+	Bruchac, Joseph	Fulcrum Publishing
Native Americans	P	I	250+	Explorers	Wright Group/McGraw Hill
Native Americans	O	I	250+	Navigators Social Studies Series	Benchmark Education
Native Americans at the Time of the Explorers	S	I	250+	Navigators Social Studies Series	Benchmark Education
Native Americans of the Eastern Woodlands	R	I	250+	Navigators Social Studies Series	Benchmark Education
Native Americans of the Plains	R	I	250+	Navigators Social Studies Series	Benchmark Education
Native Americans of the Southwest	R	I	250+	Navigators Social Studies Series	Benchmark Education
Native Peoples	R	I	250+	Navigators Social Studies Series	Benchmark Education
Nat's New Soccer Ball	G	RF	214	Rigby Flying Colors	Rigby
Natural and Human-Made	I	I	107	Nature Basics	Capstone Press
Natural Disasters	U	I	250+	Boldprint	Steck-Vaughn
^Natural Disasters	R	I	250+	Download	Hameray Publishing Group
Natural History Museum, The	K	I	250+	Stepping Stones	Nelson/Michaels Assoc.
Natural Landmarks	L	I	249	Early Explorers	Benchmark Education
Natural Resources	O	I	1296	Leveled Readers Language Support	Houghton Mifflin Harcourt
Natural Writer: A Story About Marjorie Kinnan Rawlings	R	B	7847	Creative Minds Biographies	Carolrhoda Books
Nature Club, The	O	RF	755	Leveled Readers	Houghton Mifflin Harcourt
Nature Girl	Z+	RF	250+	Hiaasen, Carl	Grand Central Publishing
Nature Hike	C	HF	32	Twig	Wright Group/McGraw Hill
Nature in Focus	T	I	250+	Navigators Science Series	Benchmark Education
Nature of Cats and Dogs, The	X	I	3193	Vocabulary Readers	Houghton Mifflin Harcourt
Nature of Cats and Dogs, The	X	I	3193	Vocabulary Readers/CA	Houghton Mifflin Harcourt
Nature Reserves	N	I	720	Leveled Readers	Houghton Mifflin Harcourt
Nature Reserves	N	I	720	Leveled Readers/CA	Houghton Mifflin Harcourt
Nature Scales: Weighing Environmental Issues	U	I	250+	Rigby Literacy	Rigby
Nature Trail	B	RF	39	Rigby Star	Rigby
Nature Walk, The	A	RF	40	Handprints A	Educators Publishing Service
Nature! Wild and Wonderful	O	B	250+	Meet The Author	Richard C. Owen
Nature's Amazing Partners	J	I	288	Extreme Readers	School Specialty Publishing
Nature's Celebration	M	I	250+	Literacy 2000	Rigby
Nature's Extremes - Wild Weather	U	I	250+	Connectors	Pacific Learning
Nature's Fireworks: A Book About Lightning	M	I	250+	Amazing Science	Picture Window Books

* Collection of short stories   # Graphic text
^ Mature content with lower level text demands

TITLE	LEVEL	GENRE	WORD COUNT	AUTHOR / SERIES	PUBLISHER / DISTRIBUTOR
Nature's Green Umbrella: Tropical Rain Forests	Q	I	250+	Gibbons, Gail	HarperCollins
Nature's Power	Q	I	250+	Pair-It Books	Steck-Vaughn
Nature's Sculptures	M	I	250+	Literacy by Design	Rigby
Nature's Wonders	V	I	250+	News Extra	Richard C. Owen
Naughty Ann, The	G	F	159	PM Story Books	Rigby
Naughty Goldilocks	A	TL	32	Red Rocket Readers	Flying Start Books
Naughty Hamster, The	G	RF	195	Storyworlds	Heinemann
Naughty Happy Monkey	C	F	33	Joy Readers	Pearson Learning Group
Naughty Joe	C	RF	34	Storyworlds	Heinemann
Naughty Kitten!	LB	RF	18	Smart Start	Rigby
Naughty Monkey	B	F	30	Sails	Rigby
Naughty Nancy Goes to School	WB	F	0	Goodall, John S.	Andre Deutsch
Naughty Patch	D	RF	74	Foundations	Wright Group/McGraw Hill
Navajo Code Talkers, The	U	I	2549	Independent Readers Social Studies	Houghton Mifflin Harcourt
Navajo Longwalk	S	HF	250+	Armstrong, Nancy M.	Scholastic
Navajo, The	U	I	250+	The Heinle Reading Library	Thomson Learning
Navajo, The	P	I	830	Vocabulary Readers	Houghton Mifflin Harcourt
Navajo, The	P	I	830	Vocabulary Readers/CA	Houghton Mifflin Harcourt
Navajos, The	T	I	3668	Native American Histoies	Lerner Publishing Group
^Navy Seals, The	T	I	250+	Elite Military Forces	Capstone Press
Near and Far	E	I	93	Early Explorers	Benchmark Education
Near And Far	C	I	29	Location	Lerner Publishing Group
Near and Far	I	I	238	Where Words	Capstone Press
^Near Death Experiences	X	I	250+	The Unexplained	Capstone Press
^Near Death Experiences: The Unsolved Mystery	S	I	250+	Mysteries of Science	Capstone Press
Near One Cattail	P	I	946	Sharing Nature with Children	Dawn Publications
Nebraska	T	I	250+	Hello U.S.A.	Lerner Publishing Group
Nebraska	R	I	250+	This Land Is Your Land	Compass Point Books
Nebraska: Facts and Symbols	O	I	250+	The States and Their Symbols	Capstone Press
*Necessary Noise	Z+	RF	250+	Cart, Michael	HarperCollins
Necessary Roughness	Y	RF	250+	Edge	Hampton Brown
*Necklace of Raindrops and Other Stories, A	S	TL	250+	Aiken, Joan	Random House
Necklace, The	D	RF	82	Dominie Math Stories	Pearson Learning Group
Necklaces	B	RF	34	Phonics and Friends	Hampton Brown
Necks Out for Adventure	O	F	250+	Ering, Timothy Basil	Candlewick Press
Ned	C	RF	30	Leveled Readers Language Support	Houghton Mifflin Harcourt
Ned Kelly	X	B	5775	Oxford Bookworms Library	Oxford University Press
Ned Rides for the Pony Express	T	HF	2910	Leveled Readers	Houghton Mifflin Harcourt
Ned Rides for the Pony Express	T	HF	2910	Leveled Readers/CA	Houghton Mifflin Harcourt
Ned Rides for the Pony Express	T	HF	2910	Leveled Readers/TX	Houghton Mifflin Harcourt
Ned's Noise Machine	C	F	36	Rigby Literacy	Rigby
Ned's Noise Machine	C	F	32	Rigby Star	Rigby
Need	Z+	F	250+	Jones, Carrie	Bloomsbury Children's Books
Need for Speed, The	T	I	250+	Story Surfers	ETA/Cuisenaire
Needing a Friend	O	RF	250+	PM Plus Chapter Books	Rigby
Needs and Wants	C	I	43	Early Connections	Benchmark Education
Needs and Wants	H	I	154	Pebble Books	Capstone Press
Needs and Wants	D	I	107	Yellow Umbrella Books	Red Brick Learning
Neeny Coming, Neeny Going	Q	RF	250+	English, Karen	Bridge Water Paperback
Nefertiti of Egypt	T	B	250+	Queens and Princesses	Capstone Press
Negro Leagues of Baseball, The	V	I	3319	Leveled Readers Social Studies	Houghton Mifflin Harcourt

N

* Collection of short stories   # Graphic text
^ Mature content with lower level text demands

TITLE	LEVEL	GENRE	WORD COUNT	AUTHOR / SERIES	PUBLISHER / DISTRIBUTOR
Neighbor From Outer Space, The	N	F	250+	George, Maureen	Scholastic
Neighborhood Clubhouse, The	J	RF	474	Visions	Wright Group/McGraw Hill
Neighborhood Event, The	I	RF	309	Leveled Readers	Houghton Mifflin Harcourt
Neighborhood Nonsense	S	RF	250+	Sails	Rigby
Neighborhood Party, The	P	RF	250+	Leveled Readers Language Support	Houghton Mifflin Harcourt
Neighborhood Party, The	C	RF	60	Pair-It Books	Steck-Vaughn
Neighborhood Picnic, The	G	I	157	Visions	Wright Group/McGraw Hill
Neighborhood Soup: A Play	J	RF	250+	Windows on Literacy	National Geographic
Neighborhoods	F	I	91	Reading Street	Pearson
Neighborhoods of Los Angeles	Y	I	2583	Vocabulary Readers	Houghton Mifflin Harcourt
Neighborhoods of Los Angeles	Y	I	2583	Vocabulary Readers/CA	Houghton Mifflin Harcourt
Neighbors	I	I	244	Leveled Readers	Houghton Mifflin Harcourt
Neighbors	I	I	244	Leveled Readers/CA	Houghton Mifflin Harcourt
Neighbors	I	I	244	Leveled Readers/TX	Houghton Mifflin Harcourt
Neighbors at Work	F	I	125	Early Connections	Benchmark Education
Neil Armstrong	R	B	250+	Amazing Americans	Wright Group/McGraw Hill
^Neil Armstrong	N	B	250+	Explore Space!	Capstone Press
Neil Armstrong	S	B	3498	History Maker Bios	Lerner Publishing Group
Neil Armstrong Is My Uncle & Other Lies Muscle Man McGinty Told Me	T	HF	250+	Marino, Nan	Roaring Brook Press
Neil Armstrong: Young Flyer	O	B	250+	Childhood of Famous Americans	Aladdin
Nellie Bly	R	B	3270	History Maker Bios	Lerner Publishing Group
Nellie Bly	J	B	270	Leveled Readers Social Studies	Houghton Mifflin Harcourt
Nellie McClung	X	B	250+	The Canadians	Fitzhenry & Whiteside
Nelson Gets a Fright	K	RF	387	PM Story Books	Rigby
Nelson Is Kidnapped	M	RF	250+	PM Story Books-Silver	Rigby
Nelson Mandela	Q	B	250+	First Biographies	Steck-Vaughn
Nelson Mandela	T	B	3253	History Maker Bios	Lerner Publishing Group
Nelson Mandela	X	B	250+	Just the Facts Biographies	Lerner Publishing Group
Nelson Mandela	O	B	250+	Rookie Biographies	Children's Press
Nelson Mandela: "No Easy Walk to Freedom"	X	B	250+	Denenberg, Barry	Scholastic
Nelson Mandela: A Life of Persistence	P	B	516	Pull Ahead Books	Lerner Publishing Group
^Nelson Mandela: Freedom Fighter for His Country	T	B	250+	Hameray Biography Series	Hameray Publishing Group
Nelson Mandela: Freedom for South Africa	T	B	250+	Dell, Pamela	Children's Press
Nelson Mandela: Long Walk to Freedom	T	B	250+	Van Wyk, Chris (Abridged)	Roaring Brook Press
Nelson Mandela: South Africa's Silent Voice of Protest	X	B	250+	Hargrove, Jim	Children's Press
Nelson Mandela: The Fight for Freedom	T	B	250+	Orbit Chapter Books	Pacific Learning
Nelson the Baby Elephant	J	RF	350	PM Collection	Rigby
Nelson's Adventurous Day	M	F	250+	Sun Sprouts	ETA/Cuisenaire
Nemo and the Ship of Gold	O	I	250+	Leveled Readers Language Support	Houghton Mifflin Harcourt
Neo Leo: The Ageless Ideas of Leonardo da Vinci	S	I	250+	Barretta, Gene	Henry Holt & Co.
Neptune	Q	I	250+	A True Book	Children's Press
Neptune	Q	I	1730	Early Bird Astronomy	Lerner Publishing Group
Neptune	J	I	125	Exploring the Galaxy	Capstone Press
Neptune	S	I	250+	Our Solar System	Compass Point Books
Neptune	N	I	713	Our Universe	Lerner Publishing Group
Neptune	Q	I	250+	The Galaxy	Capstone Press
Neptune	M	I	250+	The Solar System	Capstone Press
Neptune's Children	Z+	F	250+	Dobkin, Bonnie	Walker & Company

* Collection of short stories   # Graphic text
^ Mature content with lower level text demands

TITLE	LEVEL	GENRE	WORD COUNT	AUTHOR / SERIES	PUBLISHER / DISTRIBUTOR
NERDS: National Espionage, Rescue, and Defense Society	V	RF	250+	Buckley, Michael	Amulet Books
Nero Hawley's Fight for Freedom	Q	B	545	Vocabulary Readers	Houghton Mifflin Harcourt
^Nervous	R	F	250+	Norman, Tony	Stone Arch Books
Nervous System, The	S	I	250+	A True Book	Children's Press
Nervous System, The	P	I	1917	Early Bird Body Systems	Lerner Publishing Group
Nervous System, The	M	I	213	Human Body Systems	Red Brick Learning
Nest for Celeste, A	U	F	250+	Cole, Henry	HarperCollins
Nest Full of Eggs, A	B	I	25	Pair-It Books	Steck-Vaughn
Nest of Grass, A	H	I	359	Sails	Rigby
Nest on the Beach, The	H	RF	243	PM Plus Story Books	Rigby
Nest, The	C	F	32	Story Box	Wright Group/McGraw Hill
Nest, The	B	I	21	Storyteller	Wright Group/McGraw Hill
Nest, The	C	F	34	Sunshine	Wright Group/McGraw Hill
Nesting Place, The	K	HF	356	PM Collection	Rigby
Nesting Places	B	I	36	Sails	Rigby
Nestor	K	F	250+	Bookshop	Mondo Publishing
Nests	D	I	58	Literacy 2000	Rigby
Nests	L	I	656	Rigby Flying Colors	Rigby
Nests	B	I	54	Sails	Rigby
Nests	M	I	222	Vocabulary Readers	Houghton Mifflin Harcourt
Nests	C	I	35	Wonder World	Wright Group/McGraw Hill
Nests, Nests, Nests	C	I	42	Canizares, Susan; Reid, Mary	Scholastic
Netherlands	Q	I	250+	First Reports: Countries	Compass Point Books
Netherlands, The	O	I	250+	Countries of the World	Red Brick Learning
Nettie's Journey	T	HF	250+	From Many Peoples	Fitzhenry & Whiteside
Nettie's Trip South	T	HF	250+	Turner, Ann	Scholastic
Nevada	T	I	250+	Hello U.S.A.	Lerner Publishing Group
Nevada	R	I	250+	This Land Is Your Land	Compass Point Books
Nevada Is the Silver State	O	I	212	Larkin, Bruce	Wilbooks
Nevada: Facts and Symbols	O	I	250+	The States and Their Symbols	Capstone Press
Never Be	D	RF	73	Salem, Lynn; Stewart, Josie	Continental Press
Never Bored on Boards	O	I	250+	Literacy 2000	Rigby
Never Bring a Little Piggy Home	I	F	121	Domine Readers	Pearson Publishing Group
Never Cry Wolf	Z	B	250+	Mowat, Farley	Bantam Books
Never Hit a Ghost with a Baseball Bat	O	RF	250+	Clifford, Eth	Scholastic
Never Hitch a Ride With a Martian!	N	SF	250+	Orbit Chapter Books	Pacific Learning
Never Say Never	G	F	225	Ready Readers	Pearson Learning Group
Never Say Quit	T	RF	250+	Wallace, Bill	Pocket Books
Never Snap at a Bubble	G	F	89	Giant Step Reader	Educational Insights
Never So Green	Z+	RF	250+	Johnston, Tim	Farrar, Straus, & Giroux
Never Trust a Cat Who Wears Earrings	N	F	250+	The Zack Files	Grosset & Dunlap
Never Turn Back: Father Serra's Mission	S	B	250+	Rawls, Jim	Steck-Vaughn
Never War, The: Pendragon	X	F	250+	MacHale, D.J.	Aladdin
Never Wash Your Hair!	O	F	250+	High-Fliers	Pacific Learning
Never-Told Story, The	H	RF	138	Literacy Tree	Rigby
New Americans, The: Colonial Times 1620-1689	S	I	250+	Maestro, Betsy	HarperCollins
New and Old	B	I	46	Windows on Literacy	National Geographic
New at the Zoo	E	F	84	New Reader Series	Bungalo Books
New Baby	WB	RF	0	McCullu, Emily Arnold	Harper & Row
New Baby Calf, The	H	RF	240	Chase, Edith; Reid, Barbara	Scholastic
New Baby, A	J	F	636	McAlpin, MaryAnn	Short Tales Press
New Baby, The	E	RF	133	PM Story Books	Rigby
New Babysitter, The	E	RF	156	Rigby Rocket	Rigby

TITLE	LEVEL	GENRE	WORD COUNT	AUTHOR / SERIES	PUBLISHER / DISTRIBUTOR
New Balloon, A	E	RF	36	Pacific Literacy	Pacific Learning
New Bear at School, The	L	F	250+	Weston, Carrie	Scholastic
New Beds	F	RF	173	Rigby Flying Colors	Rigby
New Beginnings	J	RF	277	Books for Young Learners	Richard C. Owen
New Bike, The	F	RF	96	Start to Read	School Zone
New Bike, The	J	RF	526	Sunshine	Wright Group/McGraw Hill
New Boots	E	RF	127	PM Plus Story Books	Rigby
New Boy	Z	HF	250+	Houston, Julian	Houghton Mifflin Harcourt
New Boy, The	I	RF	250+	Storyworlds	Heinemann
New Brother or Sister, A	J	I	250+	Growing Up	Heinemann Library
New Building, The	H	RF	78	Sunshine	Wright Group/McGraw Hill
New Butterfly, The	D	I	55	Sun Sprouts	ETA/Cuisenaire
New Car, The	K	RF	250+	Sunshine	Wright Group/McGraw Hill
New Cat, The	B	F	29	Pacific Literacy	Pacific Learning
New Chicks, The	K	F	680	Arctic Adventures	Pioneer Valley
New Children, The	H	RF	161	Storyworlds	Heinemann
New Citizens	L	I	250+	Twig	Wright Group/McGraw Hill
New Class Pet, The	J	RF	250+	On Our Way to English	Rigby
New Clothes	F	RF	107	Windows on Literacy	National Geographic
New Club, The	I	RF	267	Leveled Readers	Houghton Mifflin Harcourt
New Clubhouse, The	K	RF	553	Springboard	Wright Group/McGraw Hill
New Clues About Dinosaurs	O	I	250+	Rigby Literacy	Rigby
New Coach Blues	Q	RF	250+	Power Up!	Steck-Vaughn
New Coat for Anna, A	M	HF	250+	Ziefert, Harriet	Scholastic
New Cougars, The	V	I	2790	Vocabulary Readers	Houghton Mifflin Harcourt
New Cougars, The	V	I	2790	Vocabulary Readers/CA	Houghton Mifflin Harcourt
New Cougars, The	V	I	2790	Vocabulary Readers/TX	Houghton Mifflin Harcourt
New Dog in Town	L	RF	250+	Social Studies Connects	Kane Press
New Dog, A	D	RF	52	Oxford Reading Tree	Oxford University Press
New Energy	M	I	549	Red Rocket Readers	Flying Start Books
New England Patriots, The	S	I	5023	Team Spirit	Norwood House Press
New England's Whales	Q	I	856	Independent Readers Social Studies	Houghton Mifflin Harcourt
New Field, The	M	RF	945	Leveled Readers	Houghton Mifflin Harcourt
New Field, The	M	RF	945	Leveled Readers/CA	Houghton Mifflin Harcourt
New Field, The	M	RF	945	Leveled Readers/TX	Houghton Mifflin Harcourt
New Forest, The	J	RF	250+	Talking Points Series	Pearson Learning Group
New Found Land	Z+	HF	250+	Wolf, Allan	Candlewick Press
New France	S	I	250+	Orbit Chapter books	Pacific Learning
New Friend at the Beach, A	G	F	372	Bella and Rosie Series	Literacy Footprints
New Friend, A	G	RF	224	Literacy by Design	Rigby
New Friends	E	RF	159	InfoTrek	ETA/Cuisenaire
New Friends	E	RF	89	Leveled Readers Language Support	Houghton Mifflin Harcourt
New Friends in a New Land: A Thanksgiving Story	N	I	250+	Stamper, Judith Bauer	Steck-Vaughn
New Generation of Warriors, A: The History of Mixed Martial Arts	T	I	250+	The World of Mixed Martial Arts	Capstone Press
New Girl in Class, A	S	RF	1942	Reading Street	Pearson
New Girl, The	L	RF	250+	Go Girl!	Feiwel and Friends
New Girl, The	I	RF	234	On Our Way to English	Rigby
New Girl, The	K	RF	250+	Pacific Literacy	Pacific Learning
New Glasses for Max	H	RF	239	PM Plus Story Books	Rigby
New Gym Shoes	F	RF	175	Yukish, Joe	Kaeden Books

TITLE	LEVEL	GENRE	WORD COUNT	AUTHOR / SERIES	PUBLISHER / DISTRIBUTOR
New Hampshire	T	I	250+	Hello U.S.A.	Lerner Publishing Group
New Hampshire	R	I	250+	This Land Is Your Land	Compass Point Books
New Hampshire Colony, The	R	I	250+	The American Colonies	Capstone Press
New Hampshire: Facts and Symbols	O	I	250+	The States and Their Symbols	Capstone Press
New Hat, The	C	RF	37	Rigby Literacy	Rigby
New Hat, The	C	RF	57	Rigby Star	Rigby
New Highway, The	C	I	67	Foundations	Wright Group/McGraw Hill
New Home for Fish, A	D	I	63	Coulton, Mia	Maryruth Books
New Home, A	D	F	45	Green Light Readers	Harcourt
New Horizons	S	I	250+	Orbit Collections	Pacific Learning
New House for Mole and Mouse, A	G	F	223	Ziefert, Harriet	Penguin Group
New House, A	F	F	118	Fried, Mary	Keep Books
New House, The	D	F	112	Bookshop	Mondo Publishing
New House, The	I	F	451	Pickles the Dog Series	Pioneer Valley
New House, The	B	F	31	Sails	Rigby
New House, The	LB	F	15	Sunshine	Wright Group/McGraw Hill
New House, The	I	RF	371	Take Two Books	Wright Group/McGraw Hill
New Ice-Cream Machine, A	G	RF	350	Sails	Rigby
New Jersey	T	I	250+	Hello U.S.A.	Lerner Publishing Group
New Jersey	Q	I	250+	One Nation	Red Brick Learning
New Jersey	R	I	250+	This Land Is Your Land	Compass Point Books
New Jersey Colony, The	R	I	250+	The American Colonies	Capstone Press
New Jersey Nets, The	S	I	4543	Team Spirit	Norwood House Press
New Jersey: Facts and Symbols	O	I	250+	The States and Their Symbols	Capstone Press
New Kid at School, The	T	I	2615	Reading Street	Pearson
New Kid in Town	N	RF	250+	Kroll, Stephen	Avon Books
New Kid on the Court	N	RF	776	Leveled Readers	Houghton Mifflin Harcourt
New Kid on the Court	N	RF	776	Leveled Readers/CA	Houghton Mifflin Harcourt
New Kid on the Court	N	RF	776	Leveled Readers/TX	Houghton Mifflin Harcourt
New Kid, The	J	RF	278	Reading Street	Pearson
New Kid, The	F	RF	124	Real Kids Readers	Millbrook Press
*New Kids in Town	Y	B	250+	Bode, Janet	Scholastic
New Kind of Art, A	T	I	527	Vocabulary Readers	Houghton Mifflin Harcourt
New Kind of Magic, The	P	F	250+	Szymanski, Lois	Avon Books
New Kite, The	E	RF	78	Big Cat	Pacific Learning
New Land, The: A First Year on the Prairie	M	HF	250+	Reynolds, Marilynn	Orca Books
New Language, New Friends	Q	I	250+	iOpeners	Pearson Learning Group
New Life in the Big City, A	T	HF	2761	Reading Street	Pearson
New Light for the Lodge, A	L	F	250+	Take Two Books	Wright Group/McGraw Hill
New Look, The	F	RF	187	Dominie Math Stories	Pearson Learning Group
New Mexico	T	I	250+	Hello U.S.A.	Lerner Publishing Group
New Mexico	R	I	250+	This Land Is Your Land	Compass Point Books
New Mexico	S	I	250+	Thompson, Kathleen	Steck-Vaughn
New Mexico: Facts and Symbols	O	I	250+	The States and Their Symbols	Capstone Press
New Moon	Z+	F	250+	Meyer, Stephanie	Little Brown and Company
New Name for Lois, A	R	HF	1382	Leveled Readers	Houghton Mifflin Harcourt
New Name for Lois, A	R	HF	1382	Leveled Readers/CA	Houghton Mifflin Harcourt
New Name for Lois, A	R	HF	1382	Leveled Readers/TX	Houghton Mifflin Harcourt
New Neighbors, The	J	RF	386	PM Stars Bridge Books	Rigby
New Nest, A	LB	I	14	Pair-It Books	Steck-Vaughn
New Nest, The	F	RF	207	Foundations	Wright Group/McGraw Hill
New Orleans Hornets, The	S	I	4758	Team Spirit	Norwood House Press
New Orleans Saints, The	S	I	250+	Team Spirit	Norwood House Press
New Pants	B	F	20	Story Box	Wright Group/McGraw Hill

* Collection of short stories   # Graphic text
^ Mature content with lower level text demands

TITLE	LEVEL	GENRE	WORD COUNT	AUTHOR / SERIES	PUBLISHER / DISTRIBUTOR
New Paper, Everyone!	G	I	53	Pacific Literacy	Pacific Learning
New Park, The	H	RF	256	Reading Street	Pearson
New Pen, The	L	F	250+	On Our Way to English	Rigby
New Pen, The	I	F	277	The Joy Cowley Collection	Hameray Publishing Group
New Pet, The	LB	RF	14	Rigby Star	Rigby
New Pig in Town (Fitch & Chip)	I	F	250+	Wheeler, Lisa	Aladdin
New Place to Live, A	E	F	144	Springboard	Wright Group/McGraw Hill
New Place, The	I	I	280	Sails	Rigby
New Places, New Faces	R	I	250+	WorldScapes	ETA/Cuisenaire
New Plants: Seeds in the Soil Patch	O	I	1200	iScience	Norwood House Press
New Playground, The	D	RF	80	Gear Up!	Wright Group/McGraw Hill
New Policeman, The	Y	F	250+	Thompson, Kate	Greenwillow Books
New Puppy, A	G	I	250+	Momentum Literacy Program	Troll Associates
New Puppy, The	A	I	40	Leveled Literacy Intervention/ Green System	Heinemann
New Red Bed, The	G	F	92	We Both Read	Treasure Bay
New Road, The	D	I	49	Joy Readers	Pearson Learning Group
New Roof, The	G	RF	237	Leveled Literacy Intervention/ Blue System	Heinemann
New School for Megan, A	J	RF	250+	PM Story Books	Rigby
New School, A	B	RF	24	Vocabulary Readers	Houghton Mifflin Harcourt
New School, A	G	RF	137	Windows on Literacy	National Geographic
New School, The	J	RF	210	City Kids	Rigby
New Schoolmates	J	RF	464	Springboard	Wright Group/McGraw Hill
New Scooter, The	G	RF	175	Gear Up!	Wright Group/McGraw Hill
New Shoes	C	RF	29	Wonder World	Wright Group/McGraw Hill
New Skin, A	D	I	71	Sails	Rigby
New Sled, The	E	RF	85	Leveled Readers	Houghton Mifflin Harcourt
New Slippers	E	RF	132	Adams, Lorraine & Bruvold, Lynn	Eaglecrest Books
New Sneakers	F	RF	34	Oxford Reading Tree	Oxford University Press
New Soccer Nets	G	RF	123	Early Connections	Benchmark Education
New Tricks	I	RF	250+	Voyages	SRA/McGraw Hill
New Way, A	T	RF	250+	Reading Safari	Mondo Publishing
New Ways	M	RF	250+	PM Plus Chapter Books	Rigby
New Wheels, The	I	RF	266	Sails	Rigby
New World Record, A	L	RF	250+	Scooters	ETA/Cuisenaire
New Year Called Tet, A	K	I	250+	On Our Way to English	Rigby
New Year's Around the World	O	I	250+	Trumbore, Cindy	Pearson Learning Group
New Year's Day	Q	I	250+	Holiday Histories	Heinemann
New Year's Day	J	I	109	Holidays and Celebrations	Capstone Press
New York	T	I	250+	Hello U.S.A.	Lerner Publishing Group
New York	S	I	250+	Land of Liberty	Red Brick Learning
New York	Q	I	250+	One Nation	Capstone Press
New York	T	I	4640	Oxford Bookworms Library	Oxford University Press
New York	R	I	250+	This Land Is Your Land	Compass Point Books
New York	S	I	250+	Thompson, Kathleen	Steck-Vaughn
New York City	T	I	250+	Kent, Deborah	Children's Press
New York City Buildings	F	I	59	Books for Young Learners	Richard C. Owen
New York Colony, The	R	I	250+	The American Colonies	Capstone Press
New York Giants, The	S	I	250+	Team Spirit	Norwood House Press
New York Jets, The	S	I	4560	Team Spirit	Norwood House Press
New York Knicks, The	S	I	250+	Team Spirit	Norwood House Press
New York Mets, The	S	I	250+	Team Spirit	Norwood House Press
New York Mets, The (Revised Edition)	S	I	250+	Team Spirit	Norwood House Press

N

TITLE	LEVEL	GENRE	WORD COUNT	AUTHOR / SERIES	PUBLISHER / DISTRIBUTOR
New York Rangers, The	S	I	4931	Team Spirit	Norwood House Press
New York Yankees, The	S	I	250+	Team Spirit	Norwood House Press
New York Yankees, The (Revised Edition)	S	I	250+	Team Spirit	Norwood House Press
New York Yankees, The: The Most Successful Team in Major League History	T	I	250+	Christopher, Matt	Little Brown and Company
New York: Facts and Symbols	O	I	250+	The States and Their Symbols	Capstone Press
*New Yorkers	X	RF	5895	Oxford Bookworms Library	Oxford University Press
New Zealand	P	I	1837	Country Explorers	Lerner Publishing Group
New Zealand ABCs: A Book About the People and Places of New Zealand	Q	I	250+	Country ABCs	Picture Window Books
*Newbery Christmas, A: Fourteen Stories of Christmas by Newbery Award-Winning Authors	W	RF	250+	Greenberg, Martin H.; Waugh, Charles G.	Delacorte Press
*Newbery Halloween, A: A Dozen Scary Stories by Newbery Award-Winning Authors	W	F	250+	Greenberg, Martin H.; Waugh, Charles G.	Delacorte Press
Newborn Animals	J	I	250+	Momentum Literacy Program	Troll Associates
Newf	N	TL	250+	Killilea, Marie	G.P. Putnam's Sons Books for Young Readers
Newfoundlands	Q	I	250+	All About Dogs	Capstone Press
Newfoundlands Are the Best!	Q	I	941	The Best Dogs Ever	Lerner Publishing Group
News	C	I	40	Joy Starters	Pearson Learning Group
News and Views	P	I	250+	Sails	Rigby
News Flash!	R	I	250+	Hill, Sharon	Pacific Learning
News on Shoes	J	I	153	Storyteller	Wright Group/McGraw Hill
News Rules	W	I	3219	Vocabulary Readers	Houghton Mifflin Harcourt
News Rules	W	I	3219	Vocabulary Readers/CA	Houghton Mifflin Harcourt
Newspaper Carriers	M	I	250+	Community Helpers	Red Brick Learning
Newspaper for Dad, A	G	RF	192	New Way Green	Steck-Vaughn
Newspaper Kids, The	Q	RF	250+	Phillips, Juanita	HarperCollins
Newspaper Scoop	N	RF	250+	Girlz Rock!	Mondo Publishing
Newspaper, The	G	RF	132	Twig	Wright Group/McGraw Hill
Newt	J	F	250+	Novak, Matt	HarperTrophy
Newton and Gravity	W	I	2603	Vocabulary Readers	Houghton Mifflin Harcourt
Newton and Gravity	W	I	2603	Vocabulary Readers/CA	Houghton Mifflin Harcourt
Newton and Gravity	W	I	2603	Vocabulary Readers/TX	Houghton Mifflin Harcourt
Newton and Me	M	RF	495	Mayer, Lynne	Sylvan Dell Publishing
Newton's Laws	Z	I	2853	Leveled Readers Science	Houghton Mifflin Harcourt
Newton's Laws	W	I	250+	Reading Expeditions	National Geographic
Nexi Robot, The	U	I	4961	A Great Idea	Norwood House Press
Next Door	A	F	31	Rigby Literacy	Rigby
Next Door Neighbour, The	I	RF	250+	Storyworlds	Heinemann
Next Door Pets	B	F	31	Rigby Star	Rigby
Next Spring an Oriole	N	HF	250+	Whelan, Gloria	Random House
Next Stop!	I	RF	250+	Ellis, Sarah	Fitzhenry & Whiteside
Next Stop, New York City!	O	RF	250+	Giff, Patricia Reilly	Bantam Books
Next Time I Will	K	RF	250+	Bank Street	Bantam Books
Next to Mexico	T	RF	250+	Nails, Jennifer	Houghton Mifflin Harcourt
Nez Perce Tribe, The	P	I	250+	Native Peoples	Red Brick Learning
Nez Perce, The	R	I	250+	First Reports	Compass Point Books
Nez Perce, The: People of the Northwest	S	I	250+	Theme Sets	National Geographic
Niagara Falls Or Does It?	R	RF	250+	Winkler, Henry and Oliver, Lin	Grosset & Dunlap
Niagra Falls	L	I	184	Rosen Real Readers	Rosen Publishing Group
Niagra Falls, The Power of Water	T	I	1840	Independent Readers Science	Houghton Mifflin Harcourt
Nibble, Nibble, Jenny Archer	M	RF	250+	Conford, Ellen	Little Brown and Company
Nibbles	J	RF	250+	Cambridge Reading	Pearson Learning Group
Nibbly Mouse	E	F	116	Voyages	SRA/McGraw Hill

* Collection of short stories   # Graphic text
^ Mature content with lower level text demands

TITLE	LEVEL	GENRE	WORD COUNT	AUTHOR / SERIES	PUBLISHER / DISTRIBUTOR
Nicaragua	O	I	250+	Countries of the World	Red Brick Learning
Nice and Polite	H	RF	187	The King School Series	Townsend Press
Nice Hit!: You Can Play Baseball	M	I	250+	Game Day	Picture Window Books
Nice Mice in the Rice, The	J	F	165	Sounds Like Reading	Lerner Publishing Group
Nice New Neighbors	K	RF	250+	Brandenberg, Franz	Scholastic
Nicest Day, The	L	RF	400	Leveled Readers	Houghton Mifflin Harcourt
Nick Goes Fishing	I	RF	123	Yukish, Joe	Kaeden Books
Nick the Fix-It Man	D	RF	40	Reading Street	Pearson
Nick Wants a Puppy	J	F	250+	Scooters	ETA/Cuisenaire
Nickels and Pennies	E	I	53	Williams, Deborah	Kaeden Books
Nicketty-Nacketty Noo-Noo-Noo	K	F	250+	Cowley, Joy	Mondo Publishing
Nickey's Meadow	N	RF	1745	Reading Street	Pearson
Nick's Glasses	D	RF	51	Pacific Literacy	Pacific Learning
Nick's Pet	E	F	119	Teacher's Choice Series	Pearson Learning Group
Nicky Upstairs and Downstairs	G	F	179	Ziefert, Harriet	Penguin Group
Nicolaus Copernicus: The Earth Is a Planet	S	B	250+	Bookshop	Mondo Publishing
Nicole Digs a Hole	G	RF	138	Start to Read	School Zone
Nicole Helps Grandma	B	I	35	Little Books for Early Readers	University of Maine
Nigeria	O	I	250+	Countries of the World	Red Brick Learning
Night	Z	B	250+	Wiesel, Elie	Bantam Books
Night and Day	E	I	112	Ready Readers	Pearson Learning Group
Night Animals	D	RF	56	Ready Readers	Pearson Learning Group
Night Animals	F	I	168	Rigby Rocket	Rigby
Night at the Beach, A	S	I	250+	Literacy By Design	Rigby
Night at the Beach, A	S	I	250+	Rigby Literacy	Rigby
Night Attack Gunships: The AC-130H Spectres	V	I	250+	War Planes	Capstone Press
Night Bird, The	Q	TL	1172	Leveled Readers/TX	Houghton Mifflin Harcourt
Night Birds on Nantucket	V	HF	250+	Aiken, Joan	Houghton Mifflin Harcourt
Night Boat to Freedom	S	HF	250+	Raven, Margot Thesis	Square Fish
Night Cat	L	I	250+	World Quest Adventures	World Quest Learning
Night Crossing, The	O	HF	250+	Ackerman, Karen	Alfred A. Knopf
Night Crossing, The	P	SF	250+	Bookweb	Rigby
Night Diving	H	I	101	Twig	Wright Group/McGraw Hill
Night Dragon, The	J	F	494	Sun Sprouts	ETA/Cuisenaire
Night Fairy, The	R	F	250+	Schlitz, Laura Amy	Candlewick Press
Night Fishing	S	RF	250+	PM Plus Chapter Books	Rigby
Night Fliers: Moths in Your Backyard	M	I	250+	Backyard Bugs	Picture Window Books
Night Flyers, The	W	HF	250+	Jones, Elizabeth McDavid	Pleasant Company
Night Games	H	F	158	Fried, Mary	Keep Books
Night I Disappeared, The	Z+	RF	250+	Deaver, Julie Reece	Simon & Schuster
Night I Flunked My Field Trip, The	R	RF	250+	Winkler, Henry and Oliver, Lin	Grosset & Dunlap
Night in the Desert	D	I	69	Carousel Readers	Pearson Learning Group
Night in the Kingdom, A	X	RF	3375	Leveled Readers	Houghton Mifflin Harcourt
Night in the Kingdom, A	X	RF	3375	Leveled Readers/CA	Houghton Mifflin Harcourt
Night in the Kingdom, A	X	RF	3375	Leveled Readers/TX	Houghton Mifflin Harcourt
Night Journey, The	T	HF	250+	Lasky, Kathryn	Puffin Books
Night Journeys	U	HF	250+	Avi	Avon Books
Night Light, The	K	RF	554	Leveled Readers	Houghton Mifflin Harcourt
Night Light, The	J	F	250+	Smith, Susan Mathias	Pearson Learning Group
Night Lights	I	I	130	Gear Up!	Wright Group/McGraw Hill
Night Lights	H	I	172	Independent Readers Science	Houghton Mifflin Harcourt
Night Lights, A Cruise Around the Solar System	R	I	250+	Hill, David	Pacific Learning
Night Music	P	HF	250+	Voyages in Time	Wright Group/McGraw Hill
Night Noises	M	RF	250+	Fox, Mem	Harcourt, Inc.

TITLE	LEVEL	GENRE	WORD COUNT	AUTHOR / SERIES	PUBLISHER / DISTRIBUTOR
Night Noises	G	RF	97	Storyteller-Moon Rising	Wright Group/McGraw Hill
Night Noises	G	RF	104	Sunshine	Wright Group/McGraw Hill
Night of the Blue Heads, The	O	RF	250+	Klooz	Stone Arch Books
Night of the Chupacabras	Y	RF	250+	Lee, Marie G.	Avon Books
Night of the Gargoyles	Q	F	250+	Bunting, Eve	Clarion Books
Night of the Hurricane's Fury, The	M	HF	1562	On My Own History	Millbrook Press
Night of the Killer Waves	V	HF	3001	Leveled Readers	Houghton Mifflin Harcourt
Night of the Killer Waves	V	HF	3001	Leveled Readers/CA	Houghton Mifflin Harcourt
Night of the Killer Waves	V	HF	3001	Leveled Readers/TX	Houghton Mifflin Harcourt
Night of the Living Eggnog	Q	F	250+	Wiley & Grampa's Creature Features	Little Brown and Company
Night of the Ninjas	M	F	250+	Osborne, Mary Pope	Random House
Night of the Pumpkins, The	K	RF	250+	On Our Way to English	Rigby
Night of the Spadefoot Toads	T	RF	250+	Harley, Bill	Peachtree
Night of the Ticklers, The	N	SF	250+	High-Fliers	Pacific Learning
Night of the Twisters	U	RF	250+	Ruckman, Ivy	HarperTrophy
Night Out, The	M	RF	250+	Sails	Rigby
Night Owls, The	M	I	368	Wonder World	Wright Group/McGraw Hill
Night Queen's Blue Velvet Dress, The	Q	F	250+	Pair-It Books	Steck-Vaughn
Night Rabbits	O	RF	250+	Posey, Lee	Peachtree
Night Runner	Z	F	250+	Turner, Max	St. Martin's Griffin
Night Shift	Q	I	250+	Explorer Books-Pathfinder	National Geographic
Night Shift	P	I	250+	Explorer Books-Pioneer	National Geographic
Night Shift	B	I	47	Ryan, Josh	Scholastic
Night Sky	LB	I	15	Twig	Wright Group/McGraw Hill
Night Sky, The	H	I	146	Discovering Nature's Cycles	Lerner Publishing Group
Night Sky, The	G	RF	226	Ready Readers	Pearson Learning Group
Night Sky, The	G	I	120	Windows on Literacy	National Geographic
Night Swimmers, The	S	RF	250+	Byars, Betsy	Dell
*Night Terrors, Stories of Shadow and Substance	Z	F	250+	Duncan, Lois	Aladdin
Night the Chimneys Fell, The	M	HF	1812	On My Own History	Millbrook Press
Night the Heads Came, The	Y	SF	250+	Sleator, William	Puffin Books
Night the Lights Went Out, The	H	RF	155	Little Readers	Houghton Mifflin Harcourt
Night the White Deer Died, The	Z	HF	250+	Paulsen, Gary	Dell
Night to Remember, A	U	HF	2377	Leveled Readers	Houghton Mifflin Harcourt
Night to Remember, A	U	HF	2377	Leveled Readers/CA	Houghton Mifflin Harcourt
Night to Remember, A	U	HF	2377	Leveled Readers/TX	Houghton Mifflin Harcourt
Night to Remember, A	Z+	HF	250+	Lord, Walter	Bantam Books
Night Train, The	E	F	65	Story Box	Wright Group/McGraw Hill
Night Walk	F	RF	51	Books for Young Learners	Richard C. Owen
Night Walk	E	RF	47	Prokopchak, Ann	Kaeden Books
Night Walk, The	G	RF	91	Instant Readers	Harcourt School Publishers
Night Walk, The	K	RF	667	PM Story Books-Gold	Rigby
Night Walker, The	P	RF	1189	Thompson, Richard	Fitzhenry & Whiteside
Night Without Stars, A	S	RF	250+	Howe, James	Aladdin
Night Work	I	I	193	Sails	Rigby
Night Workers	D	I	120	Leveled Literacy Intervention/Blue System	Heinemann
Night You Were Born, The	L	RF	250+	McCormick, Wendy	Peachtree
Nightingale, The	N	TL	250+	PM Plus Chapter Books	Rigby
Nightingale, The	J	TL	563	Tales from Hans Andersen	Wright Group/McGraw Hill
Nightjohn	Z	HF	250+	Paulsen, Gary	Bantam Books
Nightmare	M	RF	250+	Action Packs	Rigby

* Collection of short stories   # Graphic text
^ Mature content with lower level text demands

TITLE	LEVEL	GENRE	WORD COUNT	AUTHOR / SERIES	PUBLISHER / DISTRIBUTOR
Nightmare Hill	F	RF	129	Developing Books, Set 1	Pioneer Valley
*Nightmare Hour: Time for Terror	W	F	250+	Stine, R. L.	HarperCollins
Nightmare Mountain	X	RF	250+	Kehret, Peg	Puffin Books
#Nightmare on Zombie Island	U	F	10122	Twisted Journeys	Graphic Universe
Night's Nice	K	I	250+	Emberley, Barbara & Ed	Little Brown and Company
Nighttime	C	RF	25	Science	Outside the Box
Nighttime	C	RF	44	Story Box	Wright Group/McGraw Hill
Nighttime: Too Dark to See	O	F	250+	Strasser, Todd	Scholastic
Nighty Night!	L	F	250+	Wild, Margaret	Peachtree
Nighty-Nightmare	R	F	250+	Howe, James	Avon Books
Niki's Walk	WB	RF	0	Tanner, Jane	Curriculum Press
Nikki & Deja	N	RF	250+	English, Karen	Clarion Books
Nikki & Deja: Birthday Blues	N	RF	250+	English, Karen	Clarion Books
Nikki & Deja: Election Madness	N	RF	250+	English, Karen	Clarion Books
Nikki & Deja: The Newsy News Newsletter	N	SF	250+	English, Karen	Clarion Books
Nikki & Deja: Wedding Drama	N	RF	250+	English, Karen	Clarion Books
Nikki Giovanni	T	B	1729	Leveled Readers	Houghton Mifflin Harcourt
Nikki Giovanni: A Special Poet	O	B	605	Leveled Readers	Houghton Mifflin Harcourt
Nikola Tesla: Physicist, Inventor, Electrical Engineer	W	B	250+	Signature Lives	Compass Point Books
Nile Crocodiles	A	I	56	Readlings/Animals of Africa	American Reading Company
Nile River Food Chain, A: A Who-Eats-What Adventure	U	I	7490	Follow That Food Chain	Lerner Publishing Group
Niles Likes to Smile	F	RF	80	Little Books	Sadlier-Oxford
Nina and Nolan Build a Nonsense Poem	N	RF	1100	Poetry Builders	Norwood House Press
Nina Bonita	L	F	250+	Machado, Ana Maria	Kane/Miller Book Publishers
#Nina in That Makes Me Mad	M	RF	250+	Knight Hilary	Toon Books
Nina Nandu's Nervous Noggin	J	F	584	Animal Antics A to Z	Kane Press
Nina Wows KWOW	N	RF	1200	Leveled Readers/TX	Houghton Mifflin Harcourt
Nina, the Pinta, and the Vanishing Treasure, The	P	RF	250+	Santopolo, Jill	Orchard Books
Nina's Shells	E	RF	111	Gear Up!	Wright Group/McGraw Hill
Nine Children at the Pool	F	I	157	PM Math Readers	Rigby
Nine Days of Camping, The	E	RF	254	Twig	Wright Group/McGraw Hill
Nine Ducks Nine	I	F	250+	Hayes, Sarah	Candlewick Press
Nine Lives of Adventure Cat, The	L	F	250+	Clymer, Susan	Scholastic
Nine Man Tree	Z	RF	250+	Peck, Robert Newton	Random House
Nine Men Chase a Hen	G	F	74	Start to Read	School Zone
*Nine True Dolphin Stories	M	I	250+	Davidson, Margaret	Scholastic
Ninja	S	I	250+	Fierce Fighters	Raintree
Ninja	T	I	250+	Warriors of History	Capstone Press
Ninjas Don't Bake Pumpkin Pies	M	RF	250+	Dadey, Debbie; Jones, Marcia Thornton	Scholastic
Ninjas, Piranhas, and Galileo	V	RF	250+	Smith, Greg Leitich	Little Brown and Company
Ninth Ward	U	RF	250+	Rhodes, Jewell Parker	Little Brown and Company
Nishal's Box	I	F	250+	Cambridge Reading	Pearson Learning Group
Nissa's Place	Y	RF	250+	LaFaye, A.	Simon & Schuster
No and Me	Z+	RF	250+	De Vigan, Delphine	Bloomsbury Children's Books
No Arm in Left Field	Q	RF	250+	Christopher, Matt	Little Brown and Company
No Babysitters Allowed	J	F	250+	Stewart, Amber	Bloomsbury Children's Books
No Ball Games	I	F	250+	Rigby Literacy	Rigby
No Ball Games Here	H	RF	128	Ziefert, Harriet	Penguin Group
No Biting Puma!	J	F	401	Be Nice at School	Carolrhoda Books

TITLE	LEVEL	GENRE	WORD COUNT	AUTHOR / SERIES	PUBLISHER / DISTRIBUTOR
No Bows!	LB	RF	48	Duke, Shirley Smith	Peachtree
No Bridge	D	F	117	Red Rocket Readers	Flying Start Books
No Buzz for the Bees	G	F	245	Sails	Rigby
No Cookies Before Dinner	D	RF	138	Developing Books, Set 1	Pioneer Valley
No Copycats Allowed!	L	RF	250+	Graves, Bonnie	Hyperion
No Dinner for Black Cat!	I	F	253	Sails	Rigby
No Dinner for Sally	J	RF	340	Literacy 2000	Rigby
No Dogs Allowed	F	RF	73	Books for Young Learners	Richard C. Owen
*No Dogs Allowed	O	RF	250+	Cutler, Jane	Farrar, Straus, & Giroux
No Eggs for Eddie	C	F	33	Brand New Readers	Candlewick Press
No Extras	F	RF	90	Literacy 2000	Rigby
No Fair!	Q	I	250+	Kids Talk	Picture Window Books
No Fair!	P	RF	250+	On Our Way to English	Rigby
No Fighting, No Biting!	K	RF	250+	Minarik, Else Holmelund	HarperTrophy
No Flying in the House	P	F	250+	Brock, Betty	HarperCollins
No Good in Art	I	RF	250+	Cohen, Miriam	Bantam Books
No Jumping On The Bed!	L	F	250+	Arnold, Tedd	Scholastic
No Jumping!	C	RF	102	Sails	Rigby
No Laughing Matter	R	RF	250+	Power Up!	Steck-Vaughn
No Laughing Matter	Q	RF	250+	Ragged Island Mysteries	Wright Group/McGraw Hill
No Luck	F	RF	120	Stewart, Josie; Salem, Lynn	Continental Press
No Mail for Mitchell	H	F	250+	Siracusa, Catherine	Random House
No Matter How You Play It	J	I	129	Instant Readers	Harcourt School Publishers
No Money? No Problem!	L	RF	250+	Social Studies Connects	Kane Press
No Monsters Here	J	F	432	Jennings, Sharon	Fitzhenry & Whiteside
No More Bread!	K	RF	876	Rigby Gigglers	Rigby
No More Cotton Blues	X	HF	3559	Leveled Readers	Houghton Mifflin Harcourt
No More Cotton Blues	X	HF	3559	Leveled Readers/CA	Houghton Mifflin Harcourt
No More Cotton Blues	X	HF	3559	Leveled Readers/TX	Houghton Mifflin Harcourt
No More Lost and Found	J	I	137	Vocabulary Readers	Houghton Mifflin Harcourt
No More Magic	R	SF	250+	Avi	Alfred A. Knopf
No More Monsters for Me!	J	F	250+	Parish, Peggy	HarperTrophy
^No More Pranks	Z+	RF	250+	Orca Soundings	Orca Books
No More Pumpkins (2nd-Grade Friends)	L	RF	250+	Catalanotto, Peter & Schembri, Pamela	Henry Holt & Co.
No More Teasing: Katie Woo	J	RF	250+	Manushkin, Fran	Picture Window Books
No Need for Words	S	I	250+	InfoQuest	Rigby
No New Pants!	E	RF	110	Real Kids Readers	Millbrook Press
No One But You	M	RF	250+	Wood, Douglas	Candlewick Press
No One Else Like Me	D	I	129	Early Connections	Benchmark Education
No One Home	C	F	37	Schaefer, Carole Lexa/Brand New Readers	Candlewick Press
No One Is Going to Nashville	O	RF	250+	Jukes, Mavis	Alfred A. Knopf
No One Likes Me	D	F	71	Sun Sprouts	ETA/Cuisenaire
No One Saw: Ordinary Things Through the Eyes of an Artist	P	I	129	Raczka, Bob	Lerner Publishing Group
No One Should Have Six Cats!	J	RF	250+	Smith, Susan Mathias	Pearson Learning Group
No Ordinary Day	W	RF	250+	Ellis, Deborah	Groundwood Books
No Passengers Beyond This Point	U	F	250+	Choldenko, Gennifer	Dial/Penguin
No Pay? No Way!	T	RF	250+	Power Up!	Steck-Vaughn
No Peas, Please!	I	RF	247	Athey, Victoria	Kaeden Books
No Place for a Pig	K	F	250+	Use Your Imagination	Steck-Vaughn
No Place for Magic	U	F	250+	Baker, E. D.	Bloomsbury Children's Books

* Collection of short stories   # Graphic text
^ Mature content with lower level text demands

TITLE	LEVEL	GENRE	WORD COUNT	AUTHOR / SERIES	PUBLISHER / DISTRIBUTOR
No Place Like Home	N	F	879	Leveled Readers	Houghton Mifflin Harcourt
No Place Like Home	N	F	879	Leveled Readers/CA	Houghton Mifflin Harcourt
No Place Like Home	N	F	879	Leveled Readers/TX	Houghton Mifflin Harcourt
No Place to Turn	Z	I	2820	Vocabulary Readers	Houghton Mifflin Harcourt
No Place to Turn	Z	I	2820	Vocabulary Readers/CA	Houghton Mifflin Harcourt
No Pretty Pictures: A Child of War	Z	B	250+	Lobel, Anita	Greenwillow Books
^No Problem	Z+	RF	250+	Orca Soundings	Orca Books
No Problem!	M	RF	250+	Rigby Gigglers	Rigby
No Promises in the Wind	Z	HF	250+	Hunt, Irene	Berkley Books
No Room for a Dog	N	RF	250+	Nichols, Joan Kane	Hearst
No Roses for Harry!	J	F	250+	Zion, Gene	HarperTrophy
No Rules	D	RF	83	Kaleidoscope Collection	Hameray Publishing Group
No Rules for Rex!	L	RF	250+	Social Studies Connects	Kane Press
No Running!	H	RF	183	Lighthouse	Rigby
No Safe Place	P	SF	250+	Orbit Double Takes	Pacific Learning
No Singing Today	H	RF	250+	Bookshop	Mondo Publishing
No Snacks, Jack!	E	RF	248	Reed, Janet	Scholastic
No Snow Toys	F	RF	155	Bonnell, Kris	Reading Reading Books
No Snow!	D	F	94	Leveled Readers	Houghton Mifflin Harcourt
No Snow!	D	F	94	Leveled Readers/CA	Houghton Mifflin Harcourt
No Space to Waste	K	RF	250+	Storyteller-Lightning Bolts	Wright Group/McGraw Hill
No Space to Waste	Q	I	250+	WorldScapes	ETA/Cuisenaire
No Sword Fighting in the House	K	RF	250+	Hill, Susanna Leonard	Holiday House
No Talking	R	RF	250+	Clements, Andrew	Scholastic
No Time to Lose	S	HF	250+	Power Up!	Steck-Vaughn
No Tooth, No Quarter!	K	F	250+	Buller, Jon	Random House
No Trouble at All	J	RF	559	InfoTrek	ETA/Cuisenaire
No Trouble at All!	M	RF	250+	Literacy Tree	Rigby
No TV	I	RF	299	Sails	Rigby
No Valentines for Katie: Katie Woo	J	RF	250+	Manushkin, Fran	Picture Window Books
No Way Back	T	F	250+	Story Surfers	ETA/Cuisenaire
No Way, Tooth Decay!	T	F	1186	Leveled Readers	Houghton Mifflin Harcourt
No Way, Winky Blue!	N	RF	4053	Jane, Pamela	Mondo Publishing
No!	WB	TL	0	McPhail, David	Roaring Brook Press
No, Bo!	D	RF	109	Handprints C, Set 1	Educators Publishing Service
No, Buddy!	C	RF	46	McGougan, Kathy	Buddy Books Publishing
No, I Won't	E	F	174	Seedlings	Continental Press
No, No	D	F	91	Story Box	Wright Group/McGraw Hill
No, Tim!	C	RF	68	Early Explorers	Benchmark Education
No, You Can't	D	RF	52	Sunshine	Wright Group/McGraw Hill
Noah's Ark	T	I	250+	Cambridge Reading	Pearson Learning Group
Noah's Ark	WB	F	0	Spier, Peter	Doubleday Books
Noah's Bark	L	F	501	Krensky, Stephen	Carolrhoda Books
No-Bark Dog, The	J	RF	250+	Williamson, Stan	Pearson Publishing Group
*Nobel Prize Winners	T	B	250+	Hacker, Carlotta	Crabtree
Noble Boy and the Brick Maker, The	U	HF	3380	Reading Street	Pearson
Noble French Patriot, A	X	B	2958	Leveled Readers	Houghton Mifflin Harcourt
Noble French Patriot, A	X	B	2958	Leveled Readers/CA	Houghton Mifflin Harcourt
Noble French Patriot, A	X	B	2958	Leveled Readers/TX	Houghton Mifflin Harcourt
Nobody Does It Better: Gossip Girl	Z+	RF	250+	von Ziegesar, Cecily	Little Brown and Company
*Nobody Gonna Turn Me 'Round: Stories and Songs of the Civil Rights Movement	V	I	250+	Rappaport, Doreen	Candlewick Press
Nobody Knew My Name	I	RF	276	Foundations	Wright Group/McGraw Hill

TITLE	LEVEL	GENRE	WORD COUNT	AUTHOR / SERIES	PUBLISHER / DISTRIBUTOR
Nobody Listens to Andrew	I	F	250+	Little Readers	Houghton Mifflin Harcourt
Nobody Owns the Sky: The Story of "Brave Bessie" Coleman	M	B	250+	Lindbergh, Reeve	Candlewick Press
Nobody's Family Is Going to Change	U	RF	250+	Fitzhugh, Louise	Farrar, Straus, & Giroux
Nocturnal Animals	N	I	725	Springboard	Wright Group/McGraw Hill
Noel	M	F	390	Johnston, Tony	Carolrhoda Books
Noggin and Bobbin By the Sea	I	F	204	Little Celebrations	Pearson Learning Group
Noggin and Bobbin in the Garden	E	F	57	Little Celebrations	Pearson Learning Group
No-Good Dog, A	N	RF	250+	Sails	Rigby
Noise	G	RF	138	Sunshine	Wright Group/McGraw Hill
Noise Festival, The	J	RF	250+	Sunshine	Wright Group/McGraw Hill
Noise in the Night	I	F	250+	Start to Read	School Zone
Noises	E	I	49	Literacy 2000	Rigby
Noises in the Night	K	RF	250+	Literacy by Design	Rigby
Noises in the Night	K	RF	250+	On Our Way to English	Rigby
Noises!!!	C	RF	98	Teacher's Choice Series	Pearson Learning Group
Noisy and Quiet	A	I	26	Vocabulary Readers	Houghton Mifflin Harcourt
Noisy Animals	A	I	32	Red Rocket Readers	Flying Start Books
Noisy Barn	F	I	106	Bright Baby	Priddy Books
Noisy Breakfast	D	F	32	Blonder, Ellen	Scholastic
Noisy Neighbors	M	F	250+	I Am Reading	Kingfisher
Noisy Nora	I	F	204	Wells, Rosemary	Scholastic
Noisy Toys	E	RF	77	Home Connection Collection	Rigby
Nomads - A Wandering People	S	I	250+	Connectors	Pacific Learning
Noodle Race, The	G	RF	199	PM Photo Stories	Rigby
Noodle Up Your Nose, A	L	RF	250+	Orca Echoes	Orca Books
Nooks, Crannies, and Hiding Places	Q	RF	5282	Take Two Books	Wright Group/McGraw Hill
Noonday Friends, The	R	RF	250+	Stolz, Mary	Scholastic
Nora Plays All Day	B	RF	42	Little Books	Sadlier-Oxford
Nora's Money	H	RF	254	On Our Way to English	Rigby
Norma Jean, Jumping Bean	J	F	250+	Cole, Joanna	Random House
Norman Newman and the Werewolf of Walnut Street	Q	F	250+	Conford, Ellen	Troll Associates
Norman Rockwell	T	B	250+	Cohen, Joel H.	Grolier
North America	N	I	250+	Continents	Capstone Press
North America	Q	I	250+	Petersen, David	Grolier
North America	L	I	494	Pull Ahead Books	Lerner Publishing Group
North America: Geography and Environments	W	I	250+	Reading Expeditions	National Geographic
North America: People and Places	X	I	250+	Reading Expeditions	National Geographic
North American Explorers	R	I	250+	World Discovery History Readers	Scholastic
North American Indian	V	I	250+	Eyewitness Books	DK Publishing
North by Night: A Story of the Underground Railroad	X	HF	250+	Ares, Katherine	Yearling Books
North Carolina	T	I	250+	Fradin, Dennis Brindell	Children's Press
North Carolina	T	I	250+	Hello U.S.A.	Lerner Publishing Group
North Carolina	S	I	250+	Portrait of America	Steck-Vaughn
North Carolina	R	I	250+	This Land Is Your Land	Compass Point Books
North Carolina Colony, The	R	I	250+	The American Colonies	Capstone Press
North Carolina: Facts and Symbols	O	I	250+	The States and Their Symbols	Capstone Press
North Dakota	T	I	250+	Hello U.S.A.	Lerner Publishing Group
North Dakota	R	I	250+	This Land Is Your Land	Compass Point Books
North Dakota: Facts and Symbols	O	I	250+	The States and Their Symbols	Capstone Press
North of Beautiful	Z	RF	250+	Headley, Justina Chen	Little Brown and Company
North Pole Walk	R	I	250+	Orbit Double Takes	Pacific Learning

* Collection of short stories   # Graphic text
^ Mature content with lower level text demands

TITLE	LEVEL	GENRE	WORD COUNT	AUTHOR / SERIES	PUBLISHER / DISTRIBUTOR
North Star to Freedom	U	I	250+	Gorrell, Gena K.	Random House
Northeast Indians, The: Daily Life in the 1500s	O	I	250+	Native American Life	Capstone Press
Northeast Today, The	S	I	250+	Reading Expeditions	National Geographic
Northeast, The	R	I	250+	Navigators Social Studies Series	Benchmark Education
Northeast, The	T	I	250+	Reading Expeditions	National Geographic
Northeast, The: Its History and People	S	I	250+	Reading Expeditions	National Geographic
Northern Lights	M	I	578	Pull Ahead Books	Lerner Publishing Group
Northwest Indians, The: Daily Life in the 1700s	O	I	250+	Native American Life	Capstone Press
Norway	O	I	1459	A Ticket to …	Carolrhoda Books
Norway	P	I	1783	Country Explorers	Lerner Publishing Group
Nory Ryan's Song	T	HF	250+	Giff, Patricia Reilly	Delacorte Press
Nose Book	E	I	111	Perkins, Al	Random House
Nose for Trouble, A	P	RF	250+	Wilson, Nancy Hope	Avon Books
Nose Horns, The	M	I	371	Sails	Rigby
Nose Knows, The	L	RF	1107	Science Solves It!	Kane Press
Noses	B	I	33	Animal Traits	Lerner Publishing Group
Noses	E	I	56	Literacy 2000	Rigby
Noses	C	RF	46	Science	Outside the Box
^Nostradamus	X	B	250+	The Unexplained	Capstone Press
Nosy Spider, The	G	F	199	Springboard	Wright Group/McGraw Hill
Not Enough Cupcakes	I	F	292	Talking Point Series	Pearson Learning Group
Not Enough Water	D	RF	84	Armstrong, Shane; Hartley, Susan	Scholastic
*Not Guilty	X	B	250+	Sullivan, George	Scholastic
Not I, Not I	E	TL	254	Fairy Tales and Folklore	Norwood House Press
Not in a Thousand Years	R	RF	250+	PM Chapter Books	Rigby
Not It!	E	RF	177	Handprints C	Educators Publishing Service
Not Just Any Boy	H	F	221	Reading Street	Pearson
Not Just Second Place	Q	RF	1200	Leveled Readers/TX	Houghton Mifflin Harcourt
Not Last Night But the Night Before	K	F	250+	McNaughton, Colin	Candlewick Press
Not Me, Said the Monkey	G	F	118	West, Colin	Harper & Row
Not Much Room on the Mushroom	J	F	310	Take Two Books	Wright Group/McGraw Hill
Not Norman: A Goldfish Story	L	F	250+	Bennett, Kelly	Candlewick Press
Not Now! Said the Cow	J	TL	250+	Bank Street	Bantam Books
Not Now, Sam	F	RF	159	Early Connections	Benchmark Education
Not That I Care	V	RF	250+	Vail, Rachel	Scholastic
Not Too Many	G	RF	193	Sun Sprouts	ETA/Cuisenaire
Not Too Small at All	H	RF	250+	Salem, Lynn	Continental Press
Not Too Small at All	I	F	251	Seedlings	Continental Press
*Not Too Young and Other Stories	L	RF	250+	New Way Literature	Steck-Vaughn
Not Very Messy, Unless …	F	F	94	Seedlings	Continental Press
Not What It Seems	P	RF	250+	Wildcats	Wright Group/McGraw Hill
Not When It's Hot	D	F	79	Phonics and Friends	Hampton Brown
Not With Our Blood	Y	HF	250+	Massie, Elizabeth	Tom Doherty
Not Worms!	K	RF	888	Rigby Gigglers	Rigby
Not Yet!	D	RF	64	Reading Links	Steck-Vaughn
Not Yet, Nathan	G	RF	127	Cambridge Reading	Pearson Learning Group
Not Your Usual Goat	K	F	656	Leveled Readers	Houghton Mifflin Harcourt
Notes From a Liar and Her Dog	T	RF	250+	Choldenko, Gennifer	Puffin Books
Notes from Mom	F	RF	99	Salem, Lynn; Stewart, Josie	Continental Press
Notes to Dad	F	RF	114	Stewart, Josie; Salem, Lynn	Continental Press
Nothin' But Net	R	RF	250+	Christopher, Matt	Little Brown and Company
Nothing but Air	Q	RF	250+	Story Surfers	ETA/Cuisenaire
Nothing But The Truth	U	RF	250+	Avi	Hearst

* Collection of short stories   # Graphic text
^ Mature content with lower level text demands

Organized Alphabetically by Title   **559**
Storable Database at www.fountasandpinnellleveledbooks.com

TITLE	LEVEL	GENRE	WORD COUNT	AUTHOR / SERIES	PUBLISHER / DISTRIBUTOR
Nothing but the Truth	M	I	250+	Trackers	Pacific Learning
Nothing But the Truth (and a Few White Lies)	Y	RF	250+	Headley, Justina Chen	Little Brown and Company
Nothing But Trouble, Trouble, Trouble	Q	RF	250+	Hermes, Patricia	Scholastic
Nothing Can Keep Us Together: Gossip Girl	Z+	RF	250+	von Ziegesar, Cecily	Little Brown and Company
Nothing Ever Happens	F	F	49	City Stories	Rigby
Nothing Ever Happens on 90th Street	Q	RF	250+	Schotter, Roni	Scholastic
Nothing in the Mailbox	F	RF	73	Books for Young Learners	Richard C. Owen
Nothing Stays the Same	E	RF	86	Reading Street	Pearson
Nothing to Be Scared About	K	RF	343	Sunshine	Wright Group/McGraw Hill
Nothing to Fear	W	HF	250+	Koller, Jackie French	Harcourt, Inc.
Nothing's Fair in Fifth Grade	R	RF	250+	DeClements, Barthe	Scholastic
Not-Just-Anybody Family, The	R	RF	250+	Byars, Betsy	Holiday House
Not-Quite-So-Easy Origami	R	I	250+	Origami	Capstone Press
*Not-So-Dead Fish and Other Cases, The	O	RF	250+	Simon, Seymour	Avon Books
Not-So-Jolly Roger, The	P	F	250+	Scieszka, Jon	Penguin Group
Not-So-Perfect Rosie	N	RF	250+	Giff, Patricia Reilly	Penguin Group
Not-So-Scary-Scarecrow, The	I	RF	166	Ready Readers	Pearson Learning Group
Not-So-Weird Emma	O	RF	250+	Warner, Sally	Puffin Books
Nouns and Verbs Have a Field Day	O	F	250+	Pulver, Robin	Holiday House
Noura Comes to Cleveland	L	RF	717	Leveled Readers Social Studies	Houghton Mifflin Harcourt
Novio Boy	X	RF	250+	Edge	Hampton Brown
Novio Boy	X	RF	250+	Soto, Gary	Harcourt Trade
Now and Ben: The Modern Inventions of Benjamin Franklin	O	B	250+	Barretta, Gene	Henry Holt & Co.
Now and Long Ago	L	I	189	Phonics Readers	Compass Point Books
Now and Then	Q	I	250+	Literacy by Design	Rigby
Now and Then	D	I	78	Windows on Literacy	National Geographic
Now Hiring: White House Dog	M	F	250+	Bazer, Gina & Lehner, Renanah	Walker & Company
Now I Am Eight	K	I	250+	Explorations	Eleanor Curtain Publishing
Now I Am Eight	K	I	250+	Explorations	Okapi Educational Materials
Now I Am Five	I	RF	582	Sunshine	Wright Group/McGraw Hill
Now I Feel Better	F	RF	155	The King School Series	Townsend Press
Now I Know: Animals at Night	I	I	207	Berger, Melvin & Gilda	Scholastic
Now I Know: Bears	I	I	218	Berger, Melvin & Gilda	Scholastic
Now I Know: Butterflies	I	I	159	Berger, Melvin & Gilda	Scholastic
Now I Know: Dolphins and Porpoises	I	I	201	Berger, Melvin & Gilda	Scholastic
Now I Ride	D	I	63	Carousel Readers	Pearson Learning Group
Now Is Now	M	RF	250+	PM Plus Chapter Books	Rigby
Now Is Your Time! The African-American Struggle	Y	I	250+	Myers, Walter Dean	HarperCollins
Now It's Hot	C	I	49	Rigby Focus	Rigby
Now Listen, Stanley	K	F	250+	Literacy 2000	Rigby
Now Showing in Your Living Room	P	I	885	Leveled Readers	Houghton Mifflin Harcourt
Now Showing in Your Living Room	P	I	885	Leveled Readers/CA	Houghton Mifflin Harcourt
Now Showing in Your Living Room	P	I	885	Leveled Readers/TX	Houghton Mifflin Harcourt
Now We Can Go	C	RF	25	Jonas, Ann	Greenwillow Books
Now You See It, Now You Don't	M	I	204	Independent Readers Science	Houghton Mifflin Harcourt
Now You See Me . . . Now You Don't	N	F	250+	The Zack Files	Grosset & Dunlap
Nowhere and Nothing	I	RF	143	Sunshine	Wright Group/McGraw Hill
Nubs: The True Story of a Mutt, a Marine & a Miracle	Q	I	250+	Dennis, Brian, Larson, Kirby, & Nethery, Mary	Little Brown and Company
Nuclear Power	X	I	250+	Energy at Work	Capstone Press
Nugget on the Flight Deck	T	I	250+	Newman, Patricia	Walker & Company
Number Cruncher, The	L	F	250+	Sunshine	Wright Group/McGraw Hill

* Collection of short stories   # Graphic text
^ Mature content with lower level text demands

TITLE	LEVEL	GENRE	WORD COUNT	AUTHOR / SERIES	PUBLISHER / DISTRIBUTOR
Number Games	M	I	540	Red Rocket Readers	Flying Start Books
Number Games Around the World	S	I	250+	Navigators Math Series	Benchmark Education
Number Know-How	T	I	250+	Reading Expeditions	National Geographic
Number One	J	F	170	Pacific Literacy	Pacific Learning
Number the Stars	U	HF	250+	Lowry, Lois	Bantam Books
Numbering All the Bones	Y	HF	250+	Rinaldi, Ann	Hyperion
Numbers	B	I	86	Canizares, Susan; Moreton, Daniel	Scholastic
Numbers All Around	LB	I	12	Canizares, Susan; Chessen, Betsey	Scholastic
Numbers All Around	B	I	40	Yellow Umbrella Books	Red Brick Learning
Numbers All around Me	G	F	140	Learn to Read	Creative Teaching Press
Numbers and You	O	I	250+	Windows on Literacy	National Geographic
Numbers Are Everywhere	E	I	125	Early Connections	Benchmark Education
Numbers Are Everywhere	E	I	131	Twig	Wright Group/McGraw Hill
Numbers at Work	K	I	276	Red Rocket Readers	Flying Start Books
Numbers Big and Small	K	I	476	Early Explorers	Benchmark Education
Numbers Count	Q	I	250+	Trackers	Pacific Learning
Numbers in Our World	B	I	72	Windows on Literacy	National Geographic
Numbers We Know	J	I	139	Spyglass Books	Compass Point Books
Numbers: Counting It Up	L	I	250+	Exploring Math	Capstone Press
Nurse	E	I	24	Work People Do	Lerner Publishing Group
Nurse Nan and Her Tools	A	I	32	Run to Reading	Discovery Peak
Nurse Shark	J	I	148	Sharks	Capstone Press
Nurses	M	I	250+	Community Helpers	Red Brick Learning
Nurses	M	I	250+	Community Workers	Compass Point Books
Nurses	M	I	509	Pull Ahead Books	Lerner Publishing Group
Nurses: Then and Now	O	I	250+	Primary Source Readers	Teacher Created Materials
Nut Pie for Jud, A	D	I	46	Ready Readers	Pearson Learning Group
Nutcracker, The	J	F	250+	Rigby Rocket	Rigby
Nuts	T	RF	250+	Cook, Kacy	Marshall Cavendish

TITLE	LEVEL	GENRE	WORD COUNT	AUTHOR / SERIES	PUBLISHER / DISTRIBUTOR
Oak Tree, An	I	I	141	Book Bus	Creative Edge
Oak Street Party, The	C	RF	57	Peters, Catherine	Scholastic
Oak Tree and Fir Tree	G	F	102	New Way Red	Steck-Vaughn
Oak Tree Controversy	N	RF	250+	Bookweb	Rigby
Oak Tree, The	C	I	34	Big Cat	Pacific Learning
Oak Trees	F	I	91	Life Cycles	Lerner Publishing Group
Oak Trees	F	I	132	Pebble Books	Capstone Press
Oak Trees	J	I	375	Reading Street	Pearson
Oak Tree's Life, An	F	I	153	Watch It Grow	Heinemann Library
Oakland A's, The	S	I	250+	Team Spirit	Norwood House Press
Oakland Athletics, The (Revised Edition)	S	I	250+	Team Spirit	Norwood House Press
Oakland Fire, The	V	HF	250+	Reading Expeditions	National Geographic
Oakland Raiders, The	S	I	4637	Team Spirit	Norwood House Press
Oatmeal	F	I	96	Wonder World	Wright Group/McGraw Hill
Obadiah	G	TL	105	Story Box	Wright Group/McGraw Hill
Obadiah the Bold	N	RF	250+	Turkle, Brinton	Penguin Group
Obama: Only in America	T	B	250+	Weatherford, Carole Boston	Marshall Cavendish
Obee & Mungedeech	T	RF	250+	Martin, Trude	Aladdin
Obesity	K	I	250+	Health Matters	Capstone Press
Obey, Don't Stray: Obedience	K	F	1288	Salerno, Tony Character Classics	Character Building Company
Objection! Have You Got What It Takes to Be a Lawyer?	W	I	250+	On the Job	Compass Point Books
Objects in Motion	N	I	450	Science Support Readers	Houghton Mifflin Harcourt
Observations of Emma Boyle, The	U	RF	2623	Leveled Readers	Houghton Mifflin Harcourt
Obstacle Course, The	H	RF	211	Foundations	Wright Group/McGraw Hill
Obstacle Course, The	K	RF	531	Springboard	Wright Group/McGraw Hill
Obstacles in Our Way	L	RF	250+	Home Connection Collection	Rigby
Ocean	F	I	119	Habitats	Lerner Publishing Group
Ocean Alphabet Book, The	M	I	250+	Pallotta, Jerry	Charlesbridge
Ocean Animals	D	I	24	Benchmark Rebus	Marshall Cavendish
Ocean Animals	J	I	204	Early Connections	Benchmark Education
Ocean Animals	P	I	250+	Theme Sets	National Geographic
Ocean by the Lake, The	N	I	250+	Little Celebrations	Pearson Learning Group
Ocean Detectives: Solving Mysteries of the Sea	W	I	250+	Cerullo, Mary	Steck-Vaughn
Ocean Divers	O	I	250+	Landform Adventurers	Raintree
Ocean Exploration	P	I	250+	Reading Expeditions	National Geographic
Ocean Explorers	Q	I	250+	InfoQuest	Rigby
Ocean Facts	D	I	40	Rosen Real Readers	Rosen Publishing Group
Ocean Flight Adventure	O	HF	250+	Tristars	Richard C. Owen
Ocean Food Chains	T	I	250+	Protecting Food Chains	Heinemann Library
Ocean Food Webs	Q	I	2172	Early Bird Food Webs	Lerner Publishing Group
Ocean Hide and Seek	N	I	326	Kramer, Jennifer Evans	Sylvan Dell Publishing
Ocean Life	Q	I	250+	Explorers	Wright Group/McGraw Hill
Ocean Life Encyclopedia	V	I	250+	Bookshop	Mondo Publishing
Ocean Life: Tide Pool Creatures	Q	I	250+	Leonhardt, Alice	Steck-Vaughn
Ocean Oddities	S	I	250+	Underwater Encounters	Hameray Publishing Group
Ocean of Blood (The Saga of Larten Crepsley)	X	F	250+	Shan, Darren	Little Brown and Company
*Ocean of Story, The: Fairy Tales From India	U	TL	250+	Ness, Caroline	Lothrop, Lee & Shepard
Ocean Picture Pops	M	I	250+	Priddy, Roger	Priddy Books
Ocean Plants	N	I	250+	Life in the World's Biomes	Capstone Press
Ocean Seasons	N	I	386	Hirschi, Ron	Sylvan Dell Publishing
Ocean Tide Pool	N	I	250+	Habitats	Children's Press
Ocean Tides	M	I	250+	Rosen Real Readers	Rosen Publishing Group

* Collection of short stories   # Graphic text
^ Mature content with lower level text demands

TITLE	LEVEL	GENRE	WORD COUNT	AUTHOR / SERIES	PUBLISHER / DISTRIBUTOR
Ocean Waves	B	I	21	Twig	Wright Group/McGraw Hill
Ocean, The	H	F	362	Bella and Rosie Series	Literacy Footprints
Ocean, The	H	I	139	Yellow Umbrella Books	Red Brick Learning
Oceana and Antartica: Geography and Environments	W	I	250+	Reading Expeditions	National Geographic
Oceania and Antarctica: People and Places	X	I	250+	Reading Expeditions	National Geographic
Oceanography	Q	I	2127	Independent Readers Social Studies	Houghton Mifflin Harcourt
Oceans	Q	I	250+	Ecosystems	Red Brick Learning
Oceans	Q	I	250+	First Reports	Compass Point Books
Oceans	R	I	250+	The Wonders of Our World	Crabtree
Oceans and Beaches	W	I	250+	Biomes Atlases	Raintree
Oceans Around Us, The	T	I	250+	Reading Expeditions	National Geographic
Oceans of Grass: The Prairie	O	I	707	Leveled Readers Social Studies	Houghton Mifflin Harcourt
Oceans of Resources	U	I	1962	Reading Street	Pearson
Oceans of the World	R	I	250+	InfoQuest	Rigby
Oceans, Seas, and Coasts	M	I	250+	PM Plus Nonfiction	Rigby
Oceans: Earth Matters	L	I	250+	Bookworms	Marshall Cavendish
Ocicats	R	I	250+	All About Cats	Capstone Press
Octavia and Her Purple Ink Cloud	L	F	463	Rathmell, Donna & Doreen	Sylvan Dell Publishing
Octavia Boone's Big Questions About Life, the Universe and Everything	T	RF	250+	Rupp, Rebecca	Candlewick Press
October Days	A	I	24	Leveled Readers	Houghton Mifflin Harcourt
October Days	A	I	24	Leveled Readers/CA	Houghton Mifflin Harcourt
Octopus	L	I	250+	A Day in the Life: Sea Animals	Heinemann Library
Octopus for Dinner!	F	F	147	Sails	Rigby
Octopus Goes to School	C	F	42	Bordelon, Carolyn	Continental Press
Octopus Soup	WB	F	0	Mayer, Mercer	Marshall Cavendish
Octopus, Cuttlefish, and Squid	O	I	250+	Sun Sprouts	ETA/Cuisenaire
Octopus, The	E	I	119	Sails	Rigby
Octopuses	T	I	250+	Animal Prey	Lerner Publishing Group
Octopuses	O	I	1350	Early Bird Nature Books	Lerner Publishing Group
Octopuses	G	I	47	Ocean Life	Capstone Press
Octopuses	J	I	94	Under the Sea	Capstone Press
Octopuses and Squids	O	I	328	Wonder World	Wright Group/McGraw Hill
Octopuses, Squid & Cuttlefish	L	I	231	Marine Life For Young Readers	Pearson Learning Group
Octupus, The	I	I	106	Readlings/Marine Life	American Reading Company
Odd and Even Numbers	I	I	250+	Yellow Umbrella Books	Red Brick Learning
Odd Comics, The	D	RF	51	The Rowland Reading Program Library	Rowland Reading Foundation
Odd Jobs	U	I	250+	Boldprint	Steck-Vaughn
Odd Jobs: The Wackiest Jobs You've Never Heard Of!	T	I	250+	Weiss, Ellen	Aladdin
Odd One Out	H	I	255	Red Rocket Readers	Flying Start Books
Odd or Not? - Transportation with a Difference	U	I	250+	Connectors	Pacific Learning
Odd Picnic, The	H	RF	150	The Rowland Reading Program Library	Rowland Reading Foundation
Odd Socks	G	RF	83	Literacy 2000	Rigby
*Oddballs	X	B	250+	Sleator, William	Puffin Books
*Odder Than Ever	Z	F	250+	Coville, Bruce	Harcourt Trade
*Oddest of All	U	F	250+	Coville, Bruce	Harcourt, Inc.
*Oddly Enough	Z	F	250+	Coville, Bruce	Pocket Books
*Odds Are Good	Z	F	250+	Coville, Bruce	Harcourt, Inc.
Odds on Oliver	P	RF	250+	Greene, Carol	Puffin Books
Odin's Wisdom	Z	TL	2644	Leveled Readers	Houghton Mifflin Harcourt

TITLE	LEVEL	GENRE	WORD COUNT	AUTHOR / SERIES	PUBLISHER / DISTRIBUTOR
#Odysseus: Escaping Poseidon's Curse	V	TL	4044	Graphic Myths and Legends	Graphic Universe
Odyssey: A Greek Play for Students, The	W	TL	250+	Bookshop	Mondo Publishing
Of Beetles & Angels: A Boy's Remarkable Journey from a Refugee Camp to Harvard	Y	B	250+	Asgedom, Mawl	Little Brown and Company
Of Colors and Things	WB	I	0	Hoban, Tana	Scholastic
Of Heroes and Villians	Z	RF	250+	Misfits Inc.	Peachtree
Of Mice and Men	Z	RF	250+	Steinbeck, John	Penguin Group
Of Nightingales That Weep	U	HF	250+	Paterson, Katherine	HarperCollins
Of Sound Mind	W	RF	250+	Edge	Hampton Brown
Off and Running	S	RF	250+	Soto, Gary	Dell
Off Like the Wind!: The First Ride of the Pony Express	T	HF	250+	Spradlin, Michael P.	Walker & Company
Off Season, The	Z+	RF	250+	Murdock, Catherine Gilbert	Houghton Mifflin Harcourt
Off the Map: The Journals of Lewis and Clark	U	I	250+	Roop, Peter & Connie	Walker & Company
Off the Rim	Q	RF	250+	Bowen, Fred	Peachtree
Off to Africa	S	B	250+	WorldScapes	ETA/Cuisenaire
Off to Grandma's House	D	RF	80	Little Celebrations	Pearson Learning Group
Off to School	D	I	125	Red Rocket Readers	Flying Start Books
Off to School	C	RF	45	Story Steps	Rigby
Off to Sea: An Inside Look at a Research Cruise	T	I	250+	Kovacs, Deborah	Steck-Vaughn
Off to Squintum's/The Four Musicians	N	TL	1268	Collins, Gillian	Mondo Publishing
Off to the City	B	F	43	Davidson, Avelyn	Scholastic
Off to the Library	C	RF	46	Seedlings	Continental Press
Off to the Shop	H	F	323	Storyteller-Night Crickets	Wright Group/McGraw Hill
Off to Work	B	RF	41	Literacy 2000	Rigby
Off We Go!	LB	RF	16	Pacific Literacy	Pacific Learning
Officer Buckle and Gloria	L	F	250+	Rathman, Peggy	Scholastic
Officer Gonzalez and Cindy	G	I	128	Dominie Factivity Series	Pearson Learning Group
Officer Spence Makes No Sense!	O	RF	250+	Gutman, Dan	HarperTrophy
Officially Interesting	Q	RF	1460	Leveled Readers	Houghton Mifflin Harcourt
Off-Road Truck Racing	S	I	250+	Motor Sports	Red Brick Learning
Ogden Nash: Playing with Words	U	B	1770	Leveled Readers	Houghton Mifflin Harcourt
Oggie Cooder	Q	RF	250+	Weeks, Sarah	Scholastic
Ogs Discover Fire and Other Stuff, The	N	F	250+	Navigators Drama Series	Benchmark Education
Oh a Hunting We Will Go	E	TL	346	Langstaff, John	Macmillan
Oh Boy, Boston!	O	RF	250+	Giff, Patricia Reilly	Bantam Books
Oh Dear	F	F	109	Campbell, Rod	Macmillan
Oh My! It Must Be the Sky!	K	F	1097	Appleton-Smith, Laura	Flyleaf Publishing
Oh No Otis!	E	F	45	Rookie Readers	Children's Press
Oh No!	E	RF	118	Bookshop	Mondo Publishing
Oh No!	E	F	118	Sun Sprouts	ETA/Cuisenaire
Oh No!	D	RF	80	The King School Series	Townsend Press
Oh No!	F	RF	122	Traditional Tales & More	Rigby
Oh No, It's Robert	M	RF	250+	Seuling, Barbara	Scholastic
Oh No, No Shorts!	C	F	47	Brand New Readers	Candlewick Press
Oh Say, I Can't See	P	F	250+	Scieszka, Jon	Penguin Group
Oh, Baby!	E	RF	87	Joy Starters	Pearson Learning Group
Oh, Baby!	G	I	121	Literacy by Design	Rigby
Oh, Brother	P	RF	250+	Wilson, Johnniece M.	Scholastic
Oh, Cats!	E	RF	93	Buck, Nola	HarperTrophy
Oh, Columbus!	K	F	250+	Literacy 2000	Rigby
Oh, Jump in a Sack	E	F	130	Story Box	Wright Group/McGraw Hill
Oh, No!	C	F	53	Joy Readers	Pearson Learning Group

* Collection of short stories   # Graphic text
^ Mature content with lower level text demands

TITLE	LEVEL	GENRE	WORD COUNT	AUTHOR / SERIES	PUBLISHER / DISTRIBUTOR
Oh, No!	A	F	46	Leveled Literacy Intervention/ Green System	Heinemann
Oh, No!	G	RF	128	Little Celebrations	Pearson Learning Group
Oh, No! Ladybug Go!	D	I	69	Bonnell, Kris	Reading Reading Books
Oh, No, Sherman	E	RF	66	Erickson, Betty	Continental Press
Oh, the Places He Went: A Story About Dr. Seuss	R	B	8621	Creative Minds Biographies	Carolrhoda Books
Oh, What a Daughter!	L	F	250+	Literacy 2000	Rigby
Oh, Zebra!	B	F	32	Zoozoo-Into the Wild	Cavallo Publishing
Ohio	T	I	250+	Hello U.S.A.	Lerner Publishing Group
Ohio	S	I	250+	Land of Liberty	Red Brick Learning
Ohio	Q	I	250+	One Nation	Capstone Press
Ohio	T	I	250+	Theme Sets	National Geographic
Ohio	R	I	250+	This Land Is Your Land	Compass Point Books
Ohio	S	I	250+	Thompson, Kathleen	Steck-Vaughn
Ohio State Buckeyes, The	S	I	5637	Team Spirit	Norwood House Press
Ohio: Facts and Symbols	O	I	250+	The States and Their Symbols	Capstone Press
Oil on Water	P	I	250+	Sails	Rigby
Oil Spill!	L	I	250+	Soar To Success	Houghton Mifflin Harcourt
Oil Spills	P	I	250+	Rigby Focus	Rigby
Oil!	P	I	450	Independent Readers Social Studies	Houghton Mifflin Harcourt
Oils (Just a Bit) to Keep Your Body Fit: What Are Oils?	N	I	325	Food Is CATegorical	Millbrook Press
Oink Oink	LB	F	15	Geisert, Arthur	Houghton Mifflin Harcourt
Ojibwa Animal Stories	U	I	3204	Vocabulary Readers	Houghton Mifflin Harcourt
Ojibwa Animal Stories	U	I	3204	Vocabulary Readers/CA	Houghton Mifflin Harcourt
Ojibwa Animal Stories	U	I	3204	Vocabulary Readers/TX	Houghton Mifflin Harcourt
Ojibwa Indians, The	P	I	250+	Native Peoples	Red Brick Learning
Ojibwa, The: Wild Rice Gatherers	R	I	250+	America's First Peoples	Capstone Press
Ojibwe, The	T	I	4405	Native American Histoies	Lerner Publishing Group
Okay for Now	Y	HF	250+	Schmidt, Gary D.	Clarion Books
Oklahoma	T	I	250+	Hello U.S.A.	Lerner Publishing Group
Oklahoma	R	I	250+	This Land Is Your Land	Compass Point Books
Oklahoma City Thunder, The	S	I	4276	Team Spirit	Norwood House Press
Oklahoma: Facts and Symbols	O	I	250+	The States and Their Symbols	Capstone Press
Ol' Bloo's Boogie Woogie Band and Blues Ensemble	Q	F	250+	Huling, Jan	Peachtree
Ola Shakes It Up	T	RF	250+	Hyppolite, Joanne	Random House
Ola's Wake	R	RF	250+	Stone, B. J.	Henry Holt & Co.
Old and New	B	I	54	Early Connections	Benchmark Education
Old and New	C	I	50	Interaction	Rigby
Old and New	G	I	54	Sun Sprouts	ETA/Cuisenaire
Old Bark's Cure	X	HF	3382	Leveled Readers	Houghton Mifflin Harcourt
Old Bark's Cure	X	HF	3382	Leveled Readers/CA	Houghton Mifflin Harcourt
Old Bark's Cure	X	HF	3382	Leveled Readers/TX	Houghton Mifflin Harcourt
Old Blue Pickup Truck, The	K	RF	250+	Ransom, Candice F.	Walker & Company
Old Bones	M	RF	848	Sunshine	Wright Group/McGraw Hill
Old Bumpy Alligator	E	F	69	Books for Young Learners	Richard C. Owen
Old Cans and Cars	I	I	224	Explorations	Eleanor Curtain Publishing
Old Cans and Cars	I	I	224	Explorations	Okapi Educational Materials
Old Car, The	F	RF	135	Voyages	SRA/McGraw Hill
Old Cat, New Cat	G	RF	169	Wonder World	Wright Group/McGraw Hill
Old Cat, The	I	RF	302	Sails	Rigby
Old Chisholm Trail, The	N	HF	250+	Schanzer, Rosalyn	National Geographic

TITLE	LEVEL	GENRE	WORD COUNT	AUTHOR / SERIES	PUBLISHER / DISTRIBUTOR
Old Devil Wind	J	F	250+	Martin, Jr., Bill	Harcourt Trade
Old Enough for Magic	L	F	250+	Pickett, A.	HarperTrophy
Old Family Recipe, An	K	RF	378	Avenues	Hampton Brown
Old Friend, An	J	RF	250+	Sunshine	Wright Group/McGraw Hill
Old Friends	M	RF	345	Literacy 2000	Rigby
Old Friends, Near Friends	J	I	250+	Rigby Literacy	Rigby
Old Glory	P	I	250+	Windows on Literacy	National Geographic
Old Gold: Gold in the Ancient World	X	I	1197	Reading Street	Pearson
Old Grizzly	H	F	185	Sunshine	Wright Group/McGraw Hill
Old Hat, New Hat	H	F	115	Berenstain, Stan & Jan	Random House
Old House, The	J	RF	375	Story Box	Wright Group/McGraw Hill
Old Jacket, New Jacket	I	RF	375	Leveled Literacy Intervention/ Blue System	Heinemann
*Old Key, The	T	TL	250+	Literacy 2000	Rigby
Old King Cole	E	TL	33	Jumbled Tumbled Tales & Rhymes	Rigby
Old King Cole	C	F	29	Seedlings	Continental Press
Old MacDonald Had a Farm	D	TL	103	Jones, Carol	Houghton Mifflin Harcourt
Old MacDonald Had a Farm	F	TL	250+	PM Readalongs	Rigby
Old MacDonald Had a Farm	D	TL	118	Rounds, Glen	Holiday House
Old MacDonald Had a Farm	J	TL	250+	Traditional Songs	Picture Window Books
Old MacDonald's Fun Time Farm	B	F	34	Instant Readers	Harcourt School Publishers
Old Magic	Z+	SF	250+	Curley, Marianne	Simon & Schuster
Old Malolo Had a Farm	H	F	250+	Sunshine	Wright Group/McGraw Hill
Old Man and His Door, The	M	RF	250+	Soto, Gary	PaperStar
Old Man and the Bear, The	M	RF	250+	Hanel, Wolfram	North-South Books
Old Man and the Sea, The	Z+	RF	250+	Hemingway, Ernest	Scribner
Old Man's Mitten, The	I	TL	378	Bookshop	Mondo Publishing
Old Meadow, The	S	F	250+	Selden, George	Farrar, Straus, & Giroux
Old Mother Hubbard	H	F	117	Literacy 2000	Rigby
Old New York City	S	I	250+	Leveled Readers	Houghton Mifflin Harcourt
Old Oak Tree, The	F	F	108	Little Celebrations	Pearson Learning Group
Old Recipe Book, The	L	F	250+	Take Two Books	Wright Group/McGraw Hill
Old Red Rocking Chair, The	M	RF	250+	Root, Phyllis	Scholastic
Old School, New School	E	I	120	Early Connections	Benchmark Education
^Old Spanish Trail, The	Q	I	250+	On Deck	Rigby
Old Steam Train, The	F	RF	43	Literacy 2000	Rigby
Old Store, New Store	C	I	56	Leveled Readers Social Studies	Houghton Mifflin Harcourt
Old Teddy	I	F	302	Sun Sprouts	ETA/Cuisenaire
Old Teeth, New Teeth	F	I	53	Wonder World	Wright Group/McGraw Hill
Old Toad, The	E	F	189	Phonics and Friends	Hampton Brown
Old Tom and the Rogue	P	HF	250+	Wilson, Trevor	Pearson Learning Group
Old Tom, Man of Mystery	K	F	250+	Hobbs, Leigh	Peachtree
Old Tom's Holiday	L	F	250+	Hobbs, Leigh	Peachtree
Old Train, The	F	RF	68	Books for Young Learners	Richard C. Owen
Old Tree, The	M	F	250+	Brown, Ruth	Candlewick Press
Old Tree, The	T	RF	2667	Leveled Readers	Houghton Mifflin Harcourt
Old Tree, The	T	RF	2667	Leveled Readers/CA	Houghton Mifflin Harcourt
Old Tree, The	T	RF	2667	Leveled Readers/TX	Houghton Mifflin Harcourt
Old Tuatara	C	F	33	Pacific Literacy	Pacific Learning
Old Willis Place, The	U	F	250+	Hahn, Mary Downing	Clarion Books
Old Woman and Her Pig, The: An Old English Tale	K	TL	250+	Litzinger, Rosanne	Harcourt Brace
Old Woman and the Hen, The	C	TL	48	Storyworlds	Heinemann

* Collection of short stories   # Graphic text
^ Mature content with lower level text demands

TITLE	LEVEL	GENRE	WORD COUNT	AUTHOR / SERIES	PUBLISHER / DISTRIBUTOR
Old Woman and the Pig, The	D	RF	68	Tiger Cub	Peguis
Old Woman in a Shoe, The	E	TL	38	Jumbled Tumbled Tales & Rhymes	Rigby
Old Woman Who Lived in a Shoe, The	D	F	56	Seedlings	Continental Press
Old Woman Who Lived in a Vinegar Bottle	M	TL	1161	Douglas, Ann	Mondo Publishing
Old Woman Who Lived in a Vinegar Bottle	I	TL	250+	Storyworlds	Heinemann
Old Woman, The	H	F	69	Sunshine	Wright Group/McGraw Hill
Old Woman's Nose, The	K	F	250+	Sunshine	Wright Group/McGraw Hill
Old Yeller	V	RF	250+	Gipson, Fred	Scholastic
Old, Tired Giving Tree, The	J	F	169	Dominie Readers	Pearson Learning Group
Old-Timers	T	RF	2884	Reading Street	Pearson
Olga's New Mobile	D	RF	100	In Step Readers	Rigby
Olga's New Mobile	D	RF	100	Literacy by Design	Rigby
Olive and Snowflake	I	RF	250+	Lyon, Tammie	Marshall Cavendish
*Oliver and Amanda's Halloween	L	F	250+	Van Leeuwen, Jean	Puffin Books
Oliver and the Balloons	A	I	29	Tiny Treasures	Pioneer Valley
Oliver and the Bird Feeder	L	F	679	Pawprints Teal	Pioneer Valley
Oliver Goes Camping	B	RF	40	Tiny Treasures	Pioneer Valley
Oliver Otter's Own Office	K	F	672	Animal Antics A to Z	Kane Press
*Oliver Pig at School	L	F	250+	Van Leeuwen, Jean	Puffin Books
Oliver the Musician	K	F	406	Pawprints Teal	Pioneer Valley
Oliver Trades Places	L	F	250+	Scooters	ETA/Cuisenaire
*Oliver, Amanda, and Grandmother Pig	L	F	250+	Van Leeuwen, Jean	Puffin Books
Olive's Ocean	V	RF	250+	Henkes, Kevin	HarperCollins
Olivia Agnew's Wild Imagination	M	F	250+	Wonder World	Wright Group/McGraw Hill
Olivia Kidney Stops for No One	T	F	250+	Potter, Ellen	Puffin Books
Olivia the Orchid Fairy: Rainbow Magic	L	F	250+	Meadows, Daisy	Scholastic
Olly the Octopus	H	F	250+	Storyworlds	Heinemann
Olympic Champions	N	RF	250+	Boyz Rule!	Mondo Publishing
Olympic Champions	S	I	250+	iOpeners	Pearson Learning Group
Olympic Dreams	O	RF	250+	Navigators Fiction Series	Benchmark Education
Olympic Softball Stars	R	I	577	Vocabulary Readers	Houghton Mifflin Harcourt
Olympics and the Mini Olympics, The	N	I	250+	Take Two Books	Wright Group/McGraw Hill
Olympics, The	U	I	250+	Christopher, Matt	Little Brown and Company
Olympics, The	Q	I	250+	Gear Up!	Wright Group/McGraw Hill
Olympics, The	L	I	250+	Trackers	Pacific Learning
Olympics, The	O	I	250+	Windows on Literacy	National Geographic
Omar on Board	K	F	615	Kovalski, Maryann	Fitzhenry & Whiteside
Omar on Ice	K	F	575	Kovalski, Maryann	Fitzhenry & Whiteside
Omar's Halloween	K	F	250+	Kovalski, Maryann	Fitzhenry & Whiteside
Omar's Surprise	E	RF	144	On Our Way to English	Rigby
*Omega Files, The	W	F	5830	Oxford Bookworms Library	Oxford University Press
^Omen and the Ghost, The	T	F	250+	Townsend, John	Stone Arch Books
On a Boat	B	RF	20	Novek, Minda	Scholastic
On a Chair	C	F	30	Story Box	Wright Group/McGraw Hill
On a Cold, Cold Day	C	F	33	Tadpoles	Rigby
On a Coral Reef	B	I	68	Early Explorers	Benchmark Education
On a Dark and Scary Night	F	F	50	Shared Reading	Rigby
On a Farm	D	I	43	Benchmark Rebus	Marshall Cavendish
On a Hill	D	RF	53	Start to Read	School Zone
On a Log	A	I	42	On Our Way to English	Rigby
On a Map	D	I	60	Windows on Literacy	National Geographic
On a Ranch	Q	I	1676	Reading Street	Pearson
On a Reef	B	I	75	In Step Readers	Rigby

TITLE	LEVEL	GENRE	WORD COUNT	AUTHOR / SERIES	PUBLISHER / DISTRIBUTOR
On a Treasure Hunt	J	I	245	Windows on Literacy	National Geographic
On a Tropical Island	T	I	250+	WorldScapes	ETA/Cuisenaire
On a Walk	A	RF	5	Ready Readers	Pearson Learning Group
On a Windy Night	M	F	250+	Day, Nancy Raines	Harry N. Abrams
On All Kinds of Days	C	I	50	Yellow Umbrella Books	Red Brick Learning
On and Off	B	I	60	PM Plus Nonfiction	Rigby
On and Off the Road	C	I	58	Bonnell, Kris	Reading Reading Books
On and Off the Road	M	I	250+	Wildcats	Wright Group/McGraw Hill
On Board the Santa Maria	T	I	2391	Independent Readers Social Studies	Houghton Mifflin Harcourt
On Board the Titanic	T	I	250+	Tanaka, Shelley	Hyperion/Madison Press
On Board with Captain Cook	Q	B	250+	WorldScapes	ETA/Cuisenaire
On Christmas Eve	WB	RF	0	Collington, Peter	Alfred A. Knopf
On Course	S	RF	2360	Leveled Readers	Houghton Mifflin Harcourt
On Course	S	RF	2360	Leveled Readers/CA	Houghton Mifflin Harcourt
On Earth	B	I	35	Leveled Readers Social Studies	Houghton Mifflin Harcourt
On Fortune's Wheel	Z	F	250+	Voigt, Cynthia	Aladdin
On Friday the Giant	K	F	240	The Giant	Wright Group/McGraw Hill
^On Guard	P	RF	250+	Maddox, Jake,	Stone Arch Books
On Guard	R	RF	250+	Napoli, Donna Jo	Puffin Books
On Location: Secrets of My Hollywood Life	Y	RF	250+	Calonita, Jen	Little Brown and Company
On Monday the Giant	K	F	250+	The Giant	Wright Group/McGraw Hill
On My Honor	S	RF	250+	Bauer, Marion Dane	Bantam Books
On My Journey Now: Looking at African-American History Through the Spirituals	X	I	250+	Giovanni, Nikki	Candlewick Press
On My Street	H	I	292	Visions	Wright Group/McGraw Hill
On My Way	N	B	250+	DePaola, Tomie	Penguin Group
On My Way to Buy Eggs	K	RF	250+	Chen, Chih-Yuan	Scholastic
On One Flower: Butterflies, Ticks and a Few More Icks	O	RF	990	Sharing Nature with Children	Dawn Publications
On Our Farm	A	I	14	Bebop Books	Lee & Low Books Inc.
On Our Street	C	RF	52	Little Red Readers	Sundance
On Our Way Home	I	F	113	Braun, Sebatien	Sterling Publishing
On Safari	J	I	250+	Rigby Rocket	Rigby
On Safari	A	I	28	Smart Start	Rigby
On Safari	N	I	250+	Windows on Literacy	National Geographic
On Saturday	C	RF	44	Handprints B	Educators Publishing Service
On Saturday	C	I	28	Little Red Readers	Sundance
On Site	S	I	250+	Pollock, John	Mondo Publishing
On Stage	E	I	94	Early Connections	Benchmark Education
On Stage	U	I	250+	Where's the Science Here?	Lerner Publishing Group
On Sunday the Giant	K	F	250+	The Giant	Wright Group/McGraw Hill
On the Air	L	I	250+	Rigby Literacy	Rigby
On the Air	S	I	250+	Wonder World	Wright Group/McGraw Hill
On the Ball	N	I	250+	Pacific Literacy	Pacific Learning
On the Banks of Plum Creek	Q	HF	250+	Wilder, Laura Ingalls	HarperCollins
On the Banks of the Bayou	Q	HF	250+	MacBride, Roger Lea	HarperCollins
On the Beach	J	I	258	Leveled Readers	Houghton Mifflin Harcourt
On the Beach	B	RF	28	Smart Start	Rigby
On the Beams	N	I	328	Independent Readers Social Studies	Houghton Mifflin Harcourt
On the Blue Comet	U	F	250+	Wells, Rosemary	Candlewick Press
On the Bridge at Avignon	F	TL	250+	PM Readalongs	Rigby

* Collection of short stories   # Graphic text
^ Mature content with lower level text demands

TITLE	LEVEL	GENRE	WORD COUNT	AUTHOR / SERIES	PUBLISHER / DISTRIBUTOR
On the Computer	D	I	67	Twig	Wright Group/McGraw Hill
On the Course With... Tiger Woods	T	B	250+	Christopher, Matt	Little Brown and Company
On the Court With... Kobe Bryant	T	B	250+	Christopher, Matt	Little Brown and Company
On the Court With... Shaquille O'Neal	T	B	250+	Christopher, Matt	Little Brown and Company
On the Court With...Dwight Howard	T	B	250+	Christopher, Matt	Little Brown and Company
On the Court With...LeBron James	T	B	250+	Christopher, Matt	Little Brown and Company
On the Devil's Court	Z	RF	250+	Deuker, Carl	Little Brown and Company
On the Edge	S	I	250+	Action Packs	Rigby
On the Edge	S	I	250+	Orbit Collections	Pacific Learning
On the Far Side Of The Mountain	V	RF	250+	George, Jean Craighead	Puffin Books
On the Farm	N	RF	250+	Boyz Rule!	Mondo Publishing
On the Farm	N	I	141	Elliott, David	Candlewick Press
On the Farm	N	I	250+	iOpeners	Pearson Learning Group
On the Farm	C	I	18	Literacy 2000	Rigby
On the Farm	I	RF	250+	Literacy by Design	Rigby
On the Farm	A	I	35	On Our Way to English	Rigby
On the Farm	D	RF	18	Sun Sprouts	ETA/Cuisenaire
On the Farm	A	I	21	Vocabulary Readers	Houghton Mifflin Harcourt
On the Farm	A	I	24	Vocabulary Readers	Houghton Mifflin Harcourt
On the Farm	A	I	21	Vocabulary Readers/CA	Houghton Mifflin Harcourt
On the Farm	B	I	62	Windows on Literacy	National Geographic
On the Field With... Alex Rodrigez	T	B	250+	Christopher, Matt	Little Brown and Company
On the Field With... Derek Jeter	T	B	250+	Christopher, Matt	Little Brown and Company
On the Field with...Peyton and Eli Manning	T	B	250+	Christopher, Matt	Little Brown and Company
On the Field With... Albert Pujols	T	B	250+	Christopher, Matt	Little Brown and Company
On the Go	G	I	69	Big Shiny Machines	Kingfisher
On the Go	C	RF	43	Learn to Read	Creative Teaching Press
On the Go	C	I	39	Time for Kids	Teacher Created Materials
On the Go	G	I	250+	Yellow Umbrella Books	Red Brick Learning
On the Ground	LB	I	11	Animal Homes	Lerner Publishing Group
On the Ground	C	I	40	Sunshine	Wright Group/McGraw Hill
On the Halfpipe With... Tony Hawk	T	B	250+	Christopher, Matt	Little Brown and Company
On the High Seas	E	RF	104	Reading Street	Pearson Learning Group
On the Job	W	I	250+	Boldprint	Steck-Vaughn
On the Job	F	RF	79	City Stories	Rigby
On the Job	Q	I	250+	Orbit Collections	Pacific Learning
On the Launch Pad: A Counting Book About Rockets	J	I	71	Know Your Numbers	Picture Window Books
On the Limit	W	RF	250+	Redline Racing Series	Fitzhenry & Whiteside
On the Line	Q	RF	250+	Bowen, Fred	Peachtree
On the Line	P	RF	4726	Maddox, Jake	Stone Arch Books
On the Line	B	RF	35	Teacher's Choice Series	Pearson Learning Group
On the List	N	F	250+	Sails	Rigby
On the Long Drive	T	HF	2505	Leveled Readers	Houghton Mifflin Harcourt
On the Long Drive	T	HF	2505	Leveled Readers/CA	Houghton Mifflin Harcourt
On the Long Drive	T	HF	2505	Leveled Readers/TX	Houghton Mifflin Harcourt
On the Map	J	I	280	Pair-It Turn and Learn	Steck-Vaughn
On the Menu	R	I	250+	Explorer Books-Pathfinder	National Geographic
On the Menu	P	I	250+	Explorer Books-Pioneer	National Geographic
On the Menu	N	F	250+	Sails	Rigby
On the Moon	H	I	77	Windows on Literacy	National Geographic
On the Move	S	I	250+	Sunshine	Wright Group/McGraw Hill
On the Move	U	I	250+	The News	Richard C. Owen
On the Move	B	I	28	Windows on Literacy	National Geographic

TITLE	LEVEL	GENRE	WORD COUNT	AUTHOR / SERIES	PUBLISHER / DISTRIBUTOR
On the Move	D	I	26	Wonder World	Wright Group/McGraw Hill
On the Night You Were Born	M	F	250+	Tillman, Nancy	Feiwel and Friends
On the Open Plains	J	I	250+	Momentum Literacy Program	Troll Associates
On the Playground	B	I	47	Early Connections	Benchmark Education
On the Playground	E	I	127	Explorations	Eleanor Curtain Publishing
On the Playground	E	I	127	Explorations	Okapi Educational Materials
On the Right Track	N	I	250+	Home Connection Collection	Rigby
On the Road	C	I	47	Teacher's Choice Series	Pearson Learning Group
On the Road: Down Girl and Sit	M	F	250+	Nolan, Lucy	Marshall Cavendish
On the Rocks	A	I	42	Windows on Literacy	National Geographic
On the Roof of the World	M	I	250+	The Rowland Reading Program Library	Rowland Reading Foundation
^On the Run	P	RF	3897	Townson, H	Stone Arch Books
On the Run: Verbs in Action	K	I	250+	Bookworms	Marshall Cavendish
On the Scale, a Weighty Tale	O	I	353	Cleary, Brian P.	Millbrook Press
On the School Bus	F	RF	62	Little Readers	Houghton Mifflin Harcourt
On the Seashore	A	I	24	Sails	Rigby
On the Silk Road: Ancient Baghdad	V	I	250+	Leveled Readers Language Support	Houghton Mifflin Harcourt
On the Slant: Jane Yolen	T	B	250+	Author at Work	Richard C. Owen
On the Track With... Jeff Gordon	T	B	250+	Christopher, Matt	Little Brown and Company
On the Trail of the Bushman	Q	RF	250+	Orca Young Readers	Orca Books
On the Way Home	S	HF	250+	Wilder, Laura Ingalls	HarperCollins
On the Way to School	D	I	143	Dominie Factivity Series	Pearson Learning Group
On the Way to School	A	I	32	Leveled Literacy Intervention/ Orange System	Heinemann
On the Way to the Moon	O	I	250+	Gold, Becky	Pearson Learning Group
On the Weekend	H	I	349	Explorations	Okapi Educational Materials
On the Weekend	H	I	349	Explorations	Eleanor Curtain Publishing
On the Weekend	WB	I	0	Windows on Literacy	National Geographic
On the Wild Frontier	L	I	250+	HSP/Harcourt Trophies	Harcourt, Inc.
On the Wild Side	Q	B	250+	InfoQuest	Rigby
On Thin Ice	O	I	250+	WorldScapes	ETA/Cuisenaire
On This Earth	D	I	71	Rise & Shine	Hampton Brown
On Thursday the Giant	K	F	250+	The Giant	Wright Group/McGraw Hill
On Top of Concord Hill	Q	HF	250+	Wilkes, Maria D.	HarperCollins
On Top of Spaghetti	G	F	105	Little Celebrations	Pearson Learning Group
On Top of the World	Q	I	588	Vocabulary Readers	Houghton Mifflin Harcourt
On Top of the World	T	B	250+	WorldScapes	ETA/Cuisenaire
On Tuesday the Giant	K	F	250+	The Giant	Wright Group/McGraw Hill
On Uncle John's Farm	P	RF	536	Fitz-Gibbon, Sally	Fitzhenry & Whiteside
On Vacation	D	I	88	Little Red Readers	Sundance
On Wednesday the Giant	K	F	250+	The Giant	Wright Group/McGraw Hill
On Wings of a Dragon	Y	F	250+	Taylor, Cora	Fitzhenry & Whiteside
On With the Show!	M	I	250+	Pair-It Books	Steck-Vaughn
On With the Show!	K	RF	1438	Real Kids Readers	Millbrook Press
Once	Y	HF	250+	Gleitzman, Morris	Henry Holt & Co.
Once a Mouseà	L	TL	250+	Brown, Marcia	Aladdin
Once and Future King, The	Z+	TL	250+	White, T.H.	Ace Books
Once I Was a Plum Tree	Q	RF	250+	Hurwitz, Johanna	Beech Tree Books
*Once in a Wood: Ten Tales from Aesop	M	TL	250+	Rice, Eve (Retold)	Houghton Mifflin Harcourt
Once on This Island	S	HF	250+	Whelan, Gloria	HarperTrophy
Once Upon a Crime: The Sisters Grimm	U	F	250+	Buckley, Michael	Amulet Books
Once Upon a Marigold	W	F	250+	Ferris, Jean	Harcourt Trade

* Collection of short stories   # Graphic text
^ Mature content with lower level text demands

TITLE	LEVEL	GENRE	WORD COUNT	AUTHOR / SERIES	PUBLISHER / DISTRIBUTOR
Once upon a Rhyme	M	F	250+	Pacific Literacy	Pacific Learning
Once Upon a Story	M	I	227	Vocabulary Readers	Houghton Mifflin Harcourt
Once Upon a Time	G	TL	154	Joy Starters	Pearson Learning Group
Once Upon a Time	T	I	250+	Literacy 2000	Rigby
Once Upon a Time	O	B	250+	Meet The Author	Richard C. Owen
Once Upon a Time	H	F	243	Ready Readers	Pearson Learning Group
Once Upon a Time	G	RF	154	Red Rocket Readers	Flying Start Books
Once Upon a Time in Junior High	U	RF	250+	Norment, Lisa	Scholastic
Once When I Was Shipwrecked	L	F	250+	Literacy 2000	Rigby
One	LB	I	17	Count on It!	Marshall Cavendish
One Blue Hen	F	F	108	Cambridge Reading	Pearson Learning Group
One Afternoon	H	RF	154	Avenues	Hampton Brown
One and Only Special Me, The	E	RF	73	Learn to Read	Creative Teaching Press
One and Only Stuey Lewis, The	M	RF	250+	Schoenberg, Jane	Farrar, Straus, & Giroux
One and Only You, The	W	I	250+	Rigby Literacy	Rigby
One Bad Thing About Father, The	M	RF	250+	Monjo, F. N.	HarperTrophy
One Bear All Alone	H	F	107	Bucknall, Caroline	Dial/Penguin
One Bee Got on the Bus	C	F	43	Ready Readers	Pearson Learning Group
One Big Building: A Counting Book About Construction	J	I	88	Know Your Numbers	Picture Window Books
One Bird	Y	RF	250+	Mori, Kyoko	Ballantine Books
One Bird Sat on the Fence	C	I	40	Wonder World	Wright Group/McGraw Hill
One Birthday, Two Traditions	D	RF	56	Independent Readers Social Studies	Houghton Mifflin Harcourt
One Checkered Flag: A Counting Book About Racing	J	I	69	Know Your Numbers	Picture Window Books
One Chick, One Egg	D	F	64	Step-By-Step Series	Pearson Learning Group
One Chili Pepper	L	RF	722	Reading Street	Pearson
One Clean House	H	RF	250+	Literacy by Design	Rigby
One Cold, Wet Night	D	F	134	Story Box	Wright Group/McGraw Hill
One Crazy Summer	W	HF	250+	Williams-Garcia, Rita	HarperCollins
One Day	C	RF	48	Teacher's Choice Series	Pearson Learning Group
One Day Everything Went Wrong	K	RF	250+	Vreeken, Elizabeth	Pearson Learning Group
One Day in May	N	F	710	Leveled Readers	Houghton Mifflin Harcourt
One Day in the Alpine Tundra	P	I	250+	George, Jean Craighead	HarperCollins
One Day in the Desert	P	I	250+	George, Jean Craighead	HarperCollins
One Day in the Tropical Rain Forest	P	I	250+	George, Jean Craighead	HarperTrophy
One Day in the Woods	P	I	250+	George, Jean Craighead	HarperTrophy
One Day, Two Stars	N	RF	250+	Leveled Readers Language Support	Houghton Mifflin Harcourt
One Drop of Water and a Million More	K	I	156	Book Bank	Wright Group/McGraw Hill
One Duck Stuck	L	F	250+	Root, Phyllis	Candlewick Press
One- Eyed Jake	M	F	547	Hutchins, Pat	Morrow
One False Note (The 39 Clues)	U	F	250+	Korman, Gordon	Scholastic
One Fat Frog	C	I	65	Vocabulary Readers	Houghton Mifflin Harcourt
One Fat Frog	C	I	65	Vocabulary Readers/CA	Houghton Mifflin Harcourt
One Fat Summer	Y	RF	250+	Lipsyte, Robert	HarperCollins
One for You and One for Me	C	RF	27	Blaxland, Wendy	Scholastic
One for You and One for Me	I	I	354	Early Connections	Benchmark Education
One Frog, One Fly	C	F	26	Blaxland, Wendy	Scholastic
One Giant Leap	S	I	250+	Fraser, Mary Ann	Henry Holt & Co.
One Giant Splash: A Counting Book About The Ocean	L	I	105	Know Your Numbers	Picture Window Books
One Giant Step	T	I	2570	Reading Street	Pearson
One Green Apple	O	RF	250+	Bunting, Eve	Clarion Books

O

* Collection of short stories   # Graphic text
^ Mature content with lower level text demands

TITLE	LEVEL	GENRE	WORD COUNT	AUTHOR / SERIES	PUBLISHER / DISTRIBUTOR
One Green Frog	H	I	215	Yellow Umbrella Books	Red Brick Learning
One Happy Classroom	D	RF	49	Rookie Readers	Children's Press
One Hot Summer Night	I	RF	126	Bookshop	Mondo Publishing
One Hundred Books	I	I	217	Story Box	Wright Group/McGraw Hill
One Hundred Hungry Ants	K	F	250+	Pinczes, Elinor	Houghton Mifflin Harcourt
One Hundredth Thing about Caroline, The	R	RF	250+	Lowry, Lois	Bantam Books
One Hungry Monster	K	F	239	O'Keefe, Susan Heyboer	Little Brown and Company
One Hunter	LB	F	15	Hutchins, Pat	Greenwillow Books
One in the Middle Is the Green Kangaroo, The	M	RF	250+	Blume, Judy	Bantam Books
One Is a Snail, Ten Is a Crab	I	I	134	Sayre, April Pulley & Sayre, Jeff	Candlewick Press
One Is Enough	I	F	187	Dominie Math Stories	Pearson Learning Group
One Little Chicken: A Counting Book	K	F	144	Elliot, David	Holiday House
One Little Elephant	H	F	174	Sunshine	Wright Group/McGraw Hill
One Little Slip	C	F	33	Instant Readers	Harcourt School Publishers
One Little, Two Little, Three Little Pilgrims	J	HF	147	Hennessy, B. G.	Scholastic
One Lucky Summer	O	RF	250+	Kvasnosky, Laura McGee	Penguin Group
One Man Show	O	B	250+	Meet The Author	Richard C. Owen
^One Million Lost: The Battle of the Somme	X	I	250+	Bloodiest Battles	Capstone Press
One Million Men and Me	L	RF	534	Lyons, Kelly Starling	Just Us Books
One Monday Morning	G	F	180	Shulevitz, Uri	Scribner
One More Child	D	RF	28	Harry's Math Books	Outside the Box
One More Frog	F	RF	266	PM Math Readers	Rigby
One More River	V	HF	250+	Banks, Lynne Reid	Avon Books
*One More River to Cross	X	B	250+	Haskins, Jim	Scholastic
One More Sheep	M	F	250+	Kelly, Mij & Ayto, Russell	Peachtree
^One More Step	Z	RF	250+	Orca Soundings	Orca Books
One More Time	C	RF	45	Instant Readers	Harcourt School Publishers
One Night	I	RF	92	Carter, Jackie	Scholastic
One Night	Z+	RF	250+	Qualey, Marsha	Penguin Group
One Night in the Coral Sea	R	I	250+	Collard III, Sneed B.	Charlesbridge
One O'Clock Is Time for One Nap	D	RF	56	Harry's Math Books	Outside the Box
One Odd Day	M	F	260	Fisher, Doris & Sneed, Dani	Sylvan Dell Publishing
One of Each	L	F	250+	Hoberman, Mary Ann	Little Brown and Company
One Picture	B	I	58	PM Math Readers	Rigby
One Piece at a Time	T	RF	250+	Power Up!	Steck-Vaughn
One Piece Missing	K	SF	250+	Rigby Literacy	Rigby
*One Potato, Tu: Seven Stories	T	RF	250+	Pearson, Gayle	Scholastic
One Quiet Afternoon	I	F	155	Instant Readers	Harcourt School Publishers
One Quiet Night	C	RF	42	Red Rocket Readers	Flying Start Books
One Racer	F	I	106	Leveled Readers Science	Houghton Mifflin Harcourt
One Room Schools	I	I	250+	Vocabulary Readers/TX	Houghton Mifflin Harcourt
One Smart Chick	G	F	250+	Rigby Literacy	Rigby
One Smart Cookie	K	F	250+	Nez, John	Albert Whitman & Co.
One Smart Goose	L	F	250+	Church, Caroline Jayne	Scholastic
One Soccer Game	C	RF	29	Harry's Math Books	Outside the Box
One Sock, Two Socks	H	RF	179	Reading Corners	Pearson Learning Group
One Special Dog	Q	RF	250+	Pair-It Books	Steck-Vaughn
One Step, Two Steps	D	I	98	Explorations	Eleanor Curtain Publishing
One Step, Two Steps	D	I	98	Explorations	Okapi Educational Materials
One Stormy Night	F	RF	165	Story Basket	Wright Group/McGraw Hill
One Sun in the Sky	E	RF	120	Windmill Books	Wright Group/McGraw Hill
One Ted Falls Out of Bed	J	F	162	Donaldson, Julia	Henry Holt & Co.
One Thing I'm Good At	R	RF	250+	Williams, Karen Lynn	William Morrow
One Thousand Currant Buns	H	F	213	Sunshine	Wright Group/McGraw Hill

* Collection of short stories   # Graphic text
^ Mature content with lower level text demands

TITLE	LEVEL	GENRE	WORD COUNT	AUTHOR / SERIES	PUBLISHER / DISTRIBUTOR
One Tiny Turtle	N	RF	250+	Read and Wonder	Candlewick Press
One True Bear	K	F	250+	Dewan, Ted	Walker & Company
*One Voice Please	T	TL	250+	McBratney, Sam	Candlewick Press
One Who Came Back, The	X	RF	250+	Mazzio, Joann	Houghton Mifflin Harcourt
One Wolf Howls	N	I	350	Cohn, Scotti	Sylvan Dell Publishing
One, One Is the Sun	B	RF	42	Story Box	Wright Group/McGraw Hill
One, Two, Buckle My Shoe	D	TL	27	Instant Readers	Harcourt School Publishers
One, Two, Three, Four	LB	F	21	KinderReaders	Rigby
One, Two, Three, Four	D	F	89	Rise & Shine	Hampton Brown
One, Two, Three, Four, Five!	D	RF	44	Reading Street	Pearson
One-Dog Canoe	K	F	250+	Casanova, Mary	Square Fish
One-Eyed Cat	S	RF	250+	Fox, Paula	Bantam Books
One-Handed Catch	W	HF	250+	Auch, MJ	Square Fish
Oneidas, The	S	I	1428	Leveled Readers	Houghton Mifflin Harcourt
Oneidas, the	S	I	1428	Leveled Readers/CA	Houghton Mifflin Harcourt
Oneidas, The	S	I	1428	Leveled Readers/TX	Houghton Mifflin Harcourt
One-Man Band	H	RF	144	Leveled Readers Science	Houghton Mifflin Harcourt
One-Minute Muffin	H	RF	250+	Reading Safari	Mondo Publishing
One-of-a-Kind Stamps and Crafts	P	I	3828	Ross, Kathy	Millbrook Press
*One-Way Ticket	V	RF	5520	Oxford Bookworms Library	Oxford University Press
Oni Wa Soto	M	TL	250+	Story Vines	Wright Group/McGraw Hill
Onion John	U	HF	250+	Krumgold, Joseph	Harper & Row
Onion Sundaes	L	RF	250+	Adler, David A.	Random House
Onion Tears	Q	RF	250+	Kidd, Diana	William Morrow
*On-Line Spaceman and Other Cases, The	O	RF	250+	Simon, Seymour	Avon Books
Only a Witch Can Fly	M	F	250+	McGhee, Alison	Feiwel and Friends
Only an Octopus	H	RF	236	Literacy 2000	Rigby
Only Earth and Sky Last Forever	Y	HF	250+	Benchley, Nathaniel	HarperCollins
Only in Australia	P	I	250+	WorldScapes	ETA/Cuisenaire
Only in Dreams	M	F	197	Use Your Imagination	Steck-Vaughn
Only in Your Dreams: Gossip Girl	Z+	RF	250+	von Ziegesar, Cecily	Little Brown and Company
Only One	J	I	185	Harshman, Marc	Dutton Children's Books
Only the Names Remain: The Cherokees and the Trail of Tears	S	I	250+	Bealer, Alex W.	Little Brown and Company
Ontario	T	I	250+	Hello Canada	Fitzhenry & Whiteside
On-the-Go Schwarmas and Other Middle-Eastern Dishes	R	I	250+	Kids Dish	Picture Window Books
Oodle Doodles Tuna Noodle and Other Salad Recipes	S	I	250+	Fun Food for Cool Cooks	Capstone Press
Oodles of Noodles	K	I	403	Red Rocket Readers	Flying Start Books
Oogly Gum Chasing Game, The	K	F	250+	Literacy 2000	Rigby
Ooh La La, Lottie	K	F	250+	I Am Reading	Kingfisher
Oops!	D	F	62	Mayer, Mercer	Penguin Group
Oops! Why Did I Do That?	K	RF	416	Early Connections	Benchmark Education
Oops, Mr. Wishy-Washy	I	F	223	The Joy Cowley Collection	Hameray Publishing Group
Open Door Club, The	L	RF	570	Leveled Readers	Houghton Mifflin Harcourt
Open It!	D	I	27	Pacific Literacy	Pacific Learning
Open Wide	G	I	189	Home Connection Collection	Rigby
Open Wide	C	F	56	Mitchell, Robin	Scholastic
Open Wide!	O	I	250+	Tristars	Richard C. Owen
Open Your Eyes, Sidney Miffet	H	RF	107	Seedlings	Continental Press
Open Your Mouth	F	F	201	Sunshine	Wright Group/McGraw Hill
Opening Night	X	I	2265	Leveled Readers	Houghton Mifflin Harcourt
Opening Night	M	RF	250+	Navigators Fiction Series	Benchmark Education

Organized Alphabetically by Title
Storable Database at www.fountasandpinnellleveledbooks.com

TITLE	LEVEL	GENRE	WORD COUNT	AUTHOR / SERIES	PUBLISHER / DISTRIBUTOR
Operation Communication	V	I	250+	WorldScapes	ETA/Cuisenaire
Operation Elephant Foot	G	RF	149	Springboard	Wright Group/McGraw Hill
Operation Migration	S	B	250+	WorldScapes	ETA/Cuisenaire
Operation Redwood	U	RF	250+	French, S. Terrell	Amulet Books
Operation Typhoon Shore	X	F	250+	Mowll, Joshua	Candlewick Press
Ophelia	Z	HF	250+	Klein, Lisa	Bloomsbury Children's Books
Opossums	O	I	1853	Early Bird Nature Books	Lerner Publishing Group
Opossums	J	I	179	Nocturnal Animals	Capstone Press
Opposite of Pig, The	K	F	250+	Little Celebrations	Pearson Learning Group
Opposite, The	L	F	250+	MacRae, Tom	Peachtree
Opposites	A	I	53	Red Rocket Readers	Flying Start Books
Oprah Winfrey, A Voice for the People	U	B	250+	Brooks, Philip	Grolier
Oprah: The Little Speaker	Q	B	250+	Weatherford, Carole Boston	Marshall Cavendish
Optimus Prime's Friends and Foes	M	SF	250+	Transformers: Dark of the Moon	Little Brown and Company
Optometrist	O	I	250+	Bookweb	Rigby
Optometrist, The	G	I	191	PM Nonfiction-Blue	Rigby
Orange	B	I	63	Bookworms	Marshall Cavendish
Orange	B	I	26	Colors	Lerner Publishing Group
Orange All Around	B	I	92	Color My World	American Reading Company
Orange Cheeks	M	RF	250+	O'Callahan, Jay	Peachtree
Orange Everywhere	K	I	306	Lightning Bolt Books	Lerner Publishing Group
Orange Floats, An	K	I	331	Reading Street	Pearson
Orange Peel's Pocket	M	RF	250+	Lewis, Rose	Harry N. Abrams
Orange: Seeing Orange All Around Us	K	I	250+	Colors	Capstone Press
Oranges for Orange Juice	F	I	25	Learn to Read	Creative Teaching Press
Orangutan	L	I	250+	A Day in the Life: Rain Forest Animals	Heinemann Library
Orangutan	A	I	52	Readlings/Animals of Asia	American Reading Company
Orangutan	C	I	36	Zoozoo-Into the Wild	Cavallo Publishing
Orangutans	I	I	208	Sails	Rigby
Orbiting Eyes: The Science of Artificial Satellites	X	I	250+	Headline Science	Compass Point Books
Orbiting the Sun	W	I	2326	Reading Street	Pearson
Orca Song	K	RF	250+	Armour	Scholastic
Orca Whales	H	I	85	Salem, Lynn	Continental Press
Orca Whales	F	I	85	Seedlings	Continental Press
*Orca's Family and More Northwest Coast Stories	P	TL	250+	Challenger, James Robert	Heritage House
Orchestra, The	C	F	33	Foundations	Wright Group/McGraw Hill
Ordinal Numbers	D	I	49	Early Math	Lerner Publishing Group
Ordinary Genius, The Story of Albert Einstein	U	B	250+	McPherson, Stephanie S.	Lerner Publishing Group
Ordinary Miracles	Y	RF	250+	Tolan, Stephanie S.	Morrow
Oregon	T	I	250+	Hello U.S.A.	Lerner Publishing Group
Oregon	T	I	250+	Theme Sets	National Geographic
Oregon	R	I	250+	This Land Is Your Land	Compass Point Books
Oregon Trail, The	S	I	250+	A True Book	Children's Press
Oregon Trail, The	V	I	250+	Cornerstones of Freedom	Children's Press
Oregon Trail, The	V	I	250+	Let Freedom Ring	Red Brick Learning
^Oregon Trail, The	Q	I	250+	On Deck	Rigby
Oregon Trail, The	T	I	250+	The Heinle Reading Library	Thomson Learning
Oregon Trail, The	S	I	250+	The Library of the Westward Expansion	Rosen Publishing Group
Oregon Trail, The	S	I	1424	Vocabulary Readers	Houghton Mifflin Harcourt

* Collection of short stories   # Graphic text
^ Mature content with lower level text demands

TITLE	LEVEL	GENRE	WORD COUNT	AUTHOR / SERIES	PUBLISHER / DISTRIBUTOR
Oregon Trail, The	S	I	1424	Vocabulary Readers/CA	Houghton Mifflin Harcourt
Oregon Trail, The	T	I	250+	We The People	Compass Point Books
Oregon: Facts and Symbols	O	I	250+	The States and Their Symbols	Capstone Press
Organisms of Long Ago	R	I	1012	Science Support Readers	Houghton Mifflin Harcourt
Oriental Cats	Q	I	250+	All About Cats	Capstone Press
Oriental Cats	I	I	107	Cats	Capstone Press
Origami	L	I	250+	How-To Series	Benchmark Education
Origami for Fun!	S	I	250+	For Fun! Crafts	Compass Point Books
Origami: The Fun and Funky Art of Paper Folding	Q	I	250+	Crafts	Capstone Press
Original Adventures of Hank the Cowdog, The	Q	F	250+	Erickson, John R.	Gulf
Orlando Magic, The	S	I	4288	Team Spirit	Norwood House Press
Orphan of Ellis Island, The	S	HF	250+	Woodruff, Elvira	Scholastic
Orphan Train	K	HF	250+	The Wright Skills	Wright Group/McGraw Hill
Orphan Train Adventures: Caught in the Act	W	HF	250+	Nixon, Joan Lowery	Bantam Books
Orphan Train Adventures: Circle of Love	W	HF	250+	Nixon, Joan Lowery	Bantam Books
Orphan Train Adventures: Dangerous Promise, A	W	HF	250+	Nixon, Joan Lowery	Dell
Orphan Train Adventures: Family Apart, A	W	HF	250+	Nixon, Joan Lowery	Dell
Orphan Train Adventures: In the Face of Danger	W	HF	250+	Nixon, Joan Lowery	Dell
Orphan Train Adventures: Keeping Secrets	W	HF	250+	Nixon, Joan Lowery	Dell
Orphan Train Adventures: Place to Belong, A	W	HF	250+	Nixon, Joan Lowery	Dell
Orphan Train Children: Aggie's Home	Q	HF	250+	Nixon, Joan Lowery	Yearling Books
Orphan Train Journey	S	HF	1247	Leveled Readers	Houghton Mifflin Harcourt
Orphan Train Rider: One Boy's True Story	V	I	250+	Warren, Andrea	Scholastic
Orson Welles and The War of the Worlds	V	I	1917	Leveled Readers	Houghton Mifflin Harcourt
Orson's Tummy Ache	B	F	51	Leveled Literacy Intervention/ Green System	Heinemann
Orwell's Luck	V	F	250+	Jennings, Richard	Houghton Mifflin Harcourt
Osama Bin Laden	Y	B	250+	A&E Biography	Lerner Publishing Group
Oscar & Tatiana	N	RF	250+	Literacy 2000	Rigby
Oscar and the Bat: A Book About Sound	M	F	250+	Start with Science	Candlewick Press
Oscar and the Bird: A Book About Electricity	N	F	250+	Start with Science	Candlewick Press
Oscar and the Cricket: A Book About Moving and Rolling	M	F	250+	Start With Science	Candlewick Press
Oscar and the Frog: A Book About Growing	M	F	250+	Start with Science	Candlewick Press
Oscar and the Moth: A Book About Light and Dark	M	F	250+	Start With Science	Candlewick Press
Oscar and the Snail: A Book About Things We Use	M	F	250+	Start with Science	Candlewick Press
Oscar De La Hoya: The Golden Boy	P	B	250+	Great Hispanics	Capstone Press
Oscar Did It!	E	RF	160	The Joy Cowley Collection	Hameray Publishing Group
Oscar Otter	J	F	250+	Benchley, Nathaniel	HarperTrophy
Oscar's Day	J	I	154	iOpeners	Pearson Learning Group
Osceola: Patriot and Warrior	T	B	250+	Jumper, Moses; Sonder, Ben	Steck-Vaughn
Osprey	M	I	250+	Cambridge Reading	Pearson Learning Group
Ostrich	L	I	250+	A Day in the Life: Grassland Animals	Heinemann Library
Ostriches	O	I	1323	Early Bird Nature Books	Lerner Publishing Group
Ostriches	M	I	250+	Sails	Rigby
Oswald	WB	RF	0	The Rowland Reading Program Library	Rowland Reading Foundation
Oswald Adds	B	RF	24	The Rowland Reading Program Library	Rowland Reading Foundation

O

TITLE	LEVEL	GENRE	WORD COUNT	AUTHOR / SERIES	PUBLISHER / DISTRIBUTOR
Oswald and Ben	D	RF	158	The Rowland Reading Program Library	Rowland Reading Foundation
#Othello	Z	F	250+	Manga Shakespeare	Amulet Books
Othello: A Novel	Z	HF	250+	Edge	Hampton Brown
Other Side of Blue, The	Z+	RF	250+	Patterson, Valerie O.	Graphia
Other Side of Dark, The	Z+	RF	250+	Nixon, Joan Lowery	Random House
Other Side of the Lake, The	L	F	250+	Little Celebrations	Pearson Learning Group
Other Side of the Sky, The	Y	B	250+	Edge	Hampton Brown
Other Side of the World, The	J	F	206	Dominie Readers	Pearson Learning Group
Other Side, The	G	F	182	Sun Sprouts	ETA/Cuisenaire
Other Side, The	Q	RF	250+	Woodson, Jaqueline	G.P. Putnam's Sons
*Other Victims, The: First-Person Stories of Non-Jews Persecuted by the Nazis	Z+	I	250+	Friedman, Ina R.	Houghton Mifflin Harcourt
Others See Us	Z	F	250+	Sleator, William	Puffin Books
Otherwise Known As Sheila the Great	R	RF	250+	Blume, Judy	Bantam Books
Otis & Sydney and the Best Birthday Ever	K	F	250+	Numeroff, Laura	Harry N. Abrams
Otis Spofford	O	RF	250+	Cleary, Beverly	Avon Books
Otter Goes Swimming	C	F	40	Brand New Readers	Candlewick Press
Otter Makes Bubbles	D	F	36	Brand New Readers	Candlewick Press
Otter Rescue	L	I	641	Gear Up!	Wright Group/McGraw Hill
Otter, Otter	C	I	39	Phonics and Friends	Hampton Brown
Otters	H	I	437	Sails	Rigby
Otter's Apples	C	F	28	Brand New Readers	Candlewick Press
Otter's Picnic	C	F	34	Brand New Readers	Candlewick Press
Otto the Cat	I	F	250+	Herman, Gail	Grosset & Dunlap
Otto: The Boy Who Loved Cars	K	F	250+	LaReau, Kara	Roaring Brook Press
Ottoline and the Yellow Cat	P	F	250+	Riddell, Chris	HarperCollins
Otto's Lunchbox	I	F	250+	Rigby Rocket	Rigby
#Otto's Orange Day	M	F	250+	Cammuso, Frank & Lynch, Jay	Toon Books
Ouch!	LB	RF	40	Literacy 2000	Rigby
Ouch!	L	RF	250+	Noonan, Diana	Pearson Learning Group
Ouch!	B	I	40	Science	Outside the Box
Ouch!: What Happens When a Bone Breaks or a Muscle Tears	P	I	250+	On Our Way to English	Rigby
Our "Current" World	T	I	250+	Navigators Social Studies Series	Benchmark Education
Our Adobe House	L	I	250+	Greetings	Rigby
Our America	S	I	250+	Literacy By Design	Rigby
Our American Flag	O	I	250+	Sunshine	Wright Group/McGraw Hill
Our Baby	G	RF	164	Breakthrough	Longman
Our Baby	J	RF	128	Foundations	Wright Group/McGraw Hill
Our Baby	B	RF	14	Literacy 2000	Rigby
Our Baby	E	I	90	PM Nonfiction-Yellow	Rigby
Our Baby	D	RF	70	Voyages	SRA/McGraw Hill
Our Bakery	H	RF	230	Leveled Readers	Houghton Mifflin Harcourt
Our Bakery	H	RF	230	Leveled Readers/CA	Houghton Mifflin Harcourt
Our Bakery	H	RF	230	Leveled Readers/TX	Houghton Mifflin Harcourt
Our Bodies	J	I	250+	PM Plus Nonfiction	Rigby
Our Book of Maps	N	I	250+	Discovery World	Rigby
Our Busy Bodies	K	I	144	Home Connection Collection	Rigby
Our Butterflies	D	I	99	Rigby Flying Colors	Rigby
Our Camping Trip	E	RF	120	Lighthouse	Rigby
Our Car	G	I	94	Bookshop	Mondo Publishing
Our Car	C	RF	32	Sunshine	Wright Group/McGraw Hill

* Collection of short stories   # Graphic text
^ Mature content with lower level text demands

TITLE	LEVEL	GENRE	WORD COUNT	AUTHOR / SERIES	PUBLISHER / DISTRIBUTOR
Our Cat	E	RF	99	Foundations	Wright Group/McGraw Hill
Our Changing Earth	R	I	250+	Belcher, Angie	Pacific Learning
Our Changing Earth: An Encyclopedia of Landforms	O	I	250+	Literacy by Design	Rigby
Our Changing Earth: An Encyclopedia of Landforms	O	I	250+	On Our Way to English	Rigby
Our Changing Planet	P	I	250+	InfoQuest	Rigby
Our Children Can Soar: A Celebration of Rosa, Barack, and the Pioneers of Change	M	I	76	Cook, Michelle	Bloomsbury Children's Books
Our Chore Chart	D	I	65	Storyteller-First Snow	Wright Group/McGraw Hill
Our Class	E	I	200	Leveled Readers	Houghton Mifflin Harcourt
Our Class	E	I	200	Leveled Readers/CA	Houghton Mifflin Harcourt
Our Class	E	I	200	Leveled Readers/TX	Houghton Mifflin Harcourt
Our Class and the Very Big Rabbit!	K	F	927	Big Cat	Pacific Learning
Our Class Band	A	RF	30	Leveled Readers	Houghton Mifflin Harcourt
Our Class Band	A	RF	30	Leveled Readers/CA	Houghton Mifflin Harcourt
Our Class Survey	F	I	128	Early Connections	Benchmark Education
Our Classroom	E	RF	53	Leveled Readers Social Studies	Houghton Mifflin Harcourt
Our Classroom	A	I	20	Vocabulary Readers	Houghton Mifflin Harcourt
Our Classroom	A	I	20	Vocabulary Readers/CA	Houghton Mifflin Harcourt
Our Clothes	J	I	250+	PM Plus Nonfiction	Rigby
Our Clubhouse	WB	I	0	Windows on Literacy	National Geographic
#Our Crazy Class Election: Comic Guy	N	RF	250+	Roland, Timothy	Scholastic
Our Dad	C	RF	41	Little Books for Early Readers	University of Maine
Our Dairy Farm	L	I	562	Rigby Flying Colors	Rigby
Our Day	B	F	30	Sails	Rigby
Our Day at Nana's House	D	RF	137	Leveled Readers	Houghton Mifflin Harcourt
Our Day at Nana's House	D	RF	137	Leveled Readers/CA	Houghton Mifflin Harcourt
Our Day at Nana's House	D	RF	137	Leveled Readers/TX	Houghton Mifflin Harcourt
Our Day at the Bakery	H	RF	274	Leveled Readers	Houghton Mifflin Harcourt
Our Day at the Bakery	H	RF	274	Leveled Readers/CA	Houghton Mifflin Harcourt
Our Day at the Bakery	H	RF	274	Leveled Readers/TX	Houghton Mifflin Harcourt
Our Disappearing Rain Forest	Q	I	1467	Reading Street	Pearson
Our Dog	D	I	113	PM Science Readers	Rigby
Our Dog Sam	B	RF	56	Literacy 2000	Rigby
Our Earth	D	I	33	Discovery Links	Newbridge
Our Earth	F	I	53	Rosen Real Readers	Rosen Publishing Group
Our Earth	M	I	604	Time for Kids	Teacher Created Materials
Our Elections	V	I	250+	I Know America	Millbrook Press
Our Endangered Planet (Oceans)	W	I	250+	Hoff, Mary; Rodgers, Mary	Lerner Publishing Group
Our Eyes	I	I	869	Sunshine	Wright Group/McGraw Hill
Our Families	B	I	52	Leveled Readers Social Studies	Houghton Mifflin Harcourt
Our Families	B	I	26	Rigby Literacy	Rigby
Our Families Help	D	I	82	Early Connections	Benchmark Education
Our Family Band	F	RF	129	Red Rocket Readers	Flying Start Books
Our Family Reunion	B	RF	32	Seedlings	Continental Press
Our Family Vacation	A	F	29	Leveled Readers	Houghton Mifflin Harcourt
Our Family Vacation	A	F	29	Leveled Readers/CA	Houghton Mifflin Harcourt
Our Farm	C	I	37	Rosen Real Readers	Rosen Publishing Group
Our Favorite Food	D	I	121	Explorations	Okapi Educational Materials
Our Favorite Food	D	I	121	Explorations	Eleanor Curtain Publishing
Our Favorite Things To Do	F	I	241	Yellow Umbrella Books	Capstone Press
Our Favorites	G	I	217	Learn to Read	Creative Teaching Press
Our Feelings	L	I	250+	Rigby Star Quest	Rigby

TITLE	LEVEL	GENRE	WORD COUNT	AUTHOR / SERIES	PUBLISHER / DISTRIBUTOR
Our Fish	F	I	161	PM Science Readers	Rigby
Our Five Senses	G	I	100	Gear Up!	Wright Group/McGraw Hill
Our Five Senses	B	I	23	Rigby Star Quest	Rigby
Our Five Senses	E	I	99	Yellow Umbrella Books	Red Brick Learning
Our Five Senses on the Farm	B	I	40	Bonnell, Kris/About	Reading Reading Books
Our Flag	U	I	250+	I Know America	Millbrook Press
Our Flag	C	I	21	Leveled Readers Social Studies	Houghton Mifflin Harcourt
Our Flag	D	I	62	On Our Way to English	Rigby
Our Flag	I	I	93	Phonics Readers	Compass Point Books
Our Flag	M	HF	250+	Rothman, Cynthia	Scholastic
Our Four Walls	L	RF	422	Leveled Readers	Houghton Mifflin Harcourt
Our Garage	F	RF	80	Urmston, Kathleen; Evans, Karen	Kaeden Books
Our Garden	B	RF	54	Leveled Literacy Intervention/ Green System	Heinemann
Our Garden	B	I	16	Literacy 2000	Rigby
Our Garden	M	I	250+	On Our Way to English	Rigby
Our Garden	L	RF	1032	Reading Street	Pearson
Our Garden	E	RF	96	The King School Series	Townsend Press
Our Gift to the Beach	D	I	83	In Step Readers	Rigby
Our Gift to the Beach	D	I	83	Literacy by Design	Rigby
Our Goat	D	RF	27	Costain, Meredith	Scholastic
Our Government	Q	I	250+	Navigators Social Studies Series	Benchmark Education
Our Government	M	I	250+	People, Spaces & Places	Rand McNally
Our Government	N	I	155	Windows on Literacy	National Geographic
Our Grandad	C	RF	30	Sunshine	Wright Group/McGraw Hill
Our Granny	C	RF	41	Sunshine	Wright Group/McGraw Hill
Our Heritage	S	I	250+	WorldScapes	ETA/Cuisenaire
Our Home Is the Pond	E	I	52	Independent Readers Science	Houghton Mifflin Harcourt
Our Homes	C	I	50	Dominie Factivity Series	Pearson Learning Group
Our Homes	G	RF	277	InfoTrek	ETA/Cuisenaire
Our House Had a Mouse	E	F	102	Worthington, Denise	Continental Press
Our House Is a Safe House	G	I	163	PM Plus Nonfiction	Rigby
Our Inside Story	W	I	250+	InfoQuest	Rigby
Our Jobs	A	I	15	Vocabulary Readers	Houghton Mifflin Harcourt
Our Jobs	A	I	15	Vocabulary Readers/CA	Houghton Mifflin Harcourt
Our Journey	P	I	250+	On Our Way to English	Rigby
Our Journey West	W	I	250+	Reading Expeditions	National Geographic
Our Leaders	J	I	110	Government	Lerner Publishing Group
Our Liberty Bell	T	I	250+	Magaziner, Henry Jonas	Holiday House
Our Libraries	U	I	250+	I Know America	Millbrook Press
Our Library	I	RF	320	Leveled Readers	Houghton Mifflin Harcourt
Our Library	I	RF	320	Leveled Readers/CA	Houghton Mifflin Harcourt
Our Library	I	RF	320	Leveled Readers/TX	Houghton Mifflin Harcourt
Our Lucky Day	O	HF	250+	Windows on Literacy	National Geographic
Our Lunch Boxes	E	I	142	Rigby Flying Colors	Rigby
Our Magazine Article	P	I	250+	Rigby Focus	Rigby
Our Market	F	I	147	Explorations	Eleanor Curtain Publishing
Our Market	F	I	147	Explorations	Okapi Educational Materials
Our Mom	E	I	107	PM Nonfiction-Yellow	Rigby
Our Money	J	I	255	Early Connections	Benchmark Education
Our Money	U	I	250+	I Know America	Millbrook Press
Our Money	E	I	74	Leveled Readers Social Studies	Houghton Mifflin Harcourt
Our Moon	H	I	161	Early Connections	Benchmark Education
Our Moon	N	I	832	Pair-It Turn and Learn	Steck-Vaughn

* Collection of short stories   # Graphic text
^ Mature content with lower level text demands

TITLE	LEVEL	GENRE	WORD COUNT	AUTHOR / SERIES	PUBLISHER / DISTRIBUTOR
Our Moon	N	I	250+	Yellow Umbrella Books	Red Brick Learning
Our Mysterious Universe	Y	I	250+	iOpeners	Pearson Learning Group
Our National Holidays	Q	I	250+	Let's See	Compass Point Books
Our National Park System	M	I	642	Gear Up!	Wright Group/McGraw Hill
Our National Parks	Q	I	250+	Let's See	Compass Point Books
Our National Symbols	U	I	250+	I Know America	Millbrook Press
Our National Treasures	O	I	250+	Bookshop	Mondo Publishing
Our Natural Resources	M	I	1234	Leveled Readers Social Studies	Houghton Mifflin Harcourt
Our Nature Chart	C	I	82	Early Connections	Benchmark Education
Our Neighborhood	B	I	72	Red Rocket Readers	Flying Start Books
Our New Baby	F	RF	59	City Stories	Rigby
Our New House	G	RF	68	PM Plus Nonfiction	Rigby
Our New House	G	RF	167	Windows on Literacy	National Geographic
Our New Life in America	U	I	250+	Reading Expeditions	National Geographic
Our New Principal	K	RF	149	City Kids	Rigby
Our New Puppy	C	RF	29	Windows on Literacy	National Geographic
Our Old Friend, Bear	J	RF	250+	PM Story Books-Silver	Rigby
Our Only May Amelia	R	HF	250+	Holm, Jennifer	HarperCollins
Our Painted Village	P	I	250+	WorldScapes	ETA/Cuisenaire
Our Parents	G	I	142	PM Nonfiction-Blue	Rigby
Our Party	B	RF	40	Leveled Readers Social Studies	Houghton Mifflin Harcourt
Our Pet Rabbit	B	I	35	Gear Up!	Wright Group/McGraw Hill
Our Pets	B	I	67	Early Connections	Benchmark Education
Our Pets	C	I	109	Leveled Literacy Intervention/ Orange System	Heinemann
Our Pets	F	I	163	PM Science Readers	Rigby
Our Place in Space	N	I	164	Windows on Literacy	National Geographic
Our Place, Their Place	Q	I	250+	WorldScapes	ETA/Cuisenaire
Our Planet	R	I	250+	Worldwise	Franklin Watts
Our Playhouse	D	RF	46	Voyages	SRA/McGraw Hill
Our Polliwogs	I	RF	91	Books for Young Learners	Richard C. Owen
Our Pumpkin	B	I	29	Learn to Read	Creative Teaching Press
Our Puppy	M	I	873	Rigby Flying Colors	Rigby
Our Rocket	B	I	28	Pacific Literacy	Pacific Learning
Our Room	A	RF	22	Leveled Readers	Houghton Mifflin Harcourt
Our Room	A	RF	22	Leveled Readers/CA	Houghton Mifflin Harcourt
Our Sand Castle	H	RF	229	Rigby Flying Colors	Rigby
Our School	H	RF	98	City Kids	Rigby
Our School	A	F	22	Leveled Readers	Houghton Mifflin Harcourt
Our School	F	RF	182	Leveled Readers	Houghton Mifflin Harcourt
Our School	A	F	22	Leveled Readers/CA	Houghton Mifflin Harcourt
Our School	F	RF	182	Leveled Readers/CA	Houghton Mifflin Harcourt
Our School	F	RF	182	Leveled Readers/TX	Houghton Mifflin Harcourt
Our School	C	I	46	Twig	Wright Group/McGraw Hill
Our School	H	RF	46	Well-Being Series	Pearson Learning Group
Our School Community	C	I	83	Early Explorers	Benchmark Education
Our Seasons	O	I	250+	Lin, Grace & McKneally, Ranida T.	Charlesbridge
Our Seasons	WB	I	0	Reach	National Geographic
Our Senses	F	I	182	Discovery Links	Newbridge
Our Senses	F	I	77	Nonfiction Set 5	Literacy Footprints
Our Senses	D	I	39	Rise & Shine	Hampton Brown
Our Senses	K	I	179	Spyglass Books	Compass Point Books
Our Skeleton	I	I	105	Sunshine	Wright Group/McGraw Hill

TITLE	LEVEL	GENRE	WORD COUNT	AUTHOR / SERIES	PUBLISHER / DISTRIBUTOR
Our Soccer Team	G	RF	139	Literacy Tree	Rigby
Our Solar System	T	I	250+	Navigators Science Series	Benchmark Education
Our Solar System	Q	I	250+	Reading Expeditions	National Geographic
Our Solar System	O	I	1502	Science Support Readers	Houghton Mifflin Harcourt
Our Solar System: Earth	P	I	250+	Navigators Science Series	Benchmark Education
Our Solar System: The Moon	P	I	250+	Navigators Science Series	Benchmark Education
Our Solar System: The Sun	Q	I	250+	Navigators Science Series	Benchmark Education
Our Star, the Sun	N	I	599	Leveled Readers Science	Houghton Mifflin Harcourt
Our Statue of Liberty	N	I	250+	Nason, Thelma	Pearson Learning Group
*Our Stories, Our Songs African Children Talk About AIDS	Y	I	28897	Ellis, Deborah	Fitzhenry & Whiteside
Our Street	E	I	97	Leveled Readers Language Support	Houghton Mifflin Harcourt
Our Street	C	RF	40	Sunshine	Wright Group/McGraw Hill
Our Sun	J	I	166	Early Connections	Benchmark Education
Our Sun	K	I	229	Pair-It Turn and Learn	Steck-Vaughn
Our Sun	I	I	189	Rosen Real Readers	Rosen Publishing Group
Our Supreme Court	W	I	250+	I Know America	Millbrook Press
Our Teacher	G	RF	168	Windows on Literacy	National Geographic
Our Teacher, Miss Pool	D	F	62	Pacific Literacy	Pacific Learning
Our Thanksgiving	H	RF	70	Weinberger, Kimberly	Scholastic
Our Town	C	I	103	Leveled Readers	Houghton Mifflin Harcourt
Our Town	C	I	103	Leveled Readers/CA	Houghton Mifflin Harcourt
Our Town	C	I	103	Leveled Readers/TX	Houghton Mifflin Harcourt
Our Town	I	I	189	Literacy by Design	Rigby
Our Town	B	RF	37	Little Red Readers	Sundance
Our Town	N	I	250+	Rigby Focus	Rigby
Our Town	G	RF	129	Well-Being Series	Pearson Learning Group
Our Town	Y	F	250+	Wilder, Thorton	HarperPerennial
Our Town	H	I	129	Windows on Literacy	National Geographic
Our Town Mural	M	RF	660	Leveled Readers	Houghton Mifflin Harcourt
Our Toy Box	A	I	29	Red Rocket Readers	Flying Start Books
Our Transportation Systems	T	I	250+	I Know America	Millbrook Press
Our Tree	E	RF	53	Joy Starters	Pearson Learning Group
Our Tree House	F	F	88	Red Rocket Readers	Flying Start Books
Our Tree House	E	RF	144	Twig	Wright Group/McGraw Hill
Our Vegetable Garden	I	I	344	Rigby Flying Colors	Rigby
Our Week	C	RF	37	Storyteller-First Snow	Wright Group/McGraw Hill
Our White House: Looking in, Looking Out	Y	I	250+	National Children's Book and Literacy Alliance	Candlewick Press
Our World Is Big	B	I	28	Windows on Literacy	National Geographic
Our World of Mysteries: Fascinating Facts About the Planet Earth	X	I	250+	Lord, Suzanne	Scholastic
Our World of Water: Children and Water Around the World	Q	I	250+	Hollyer, Beatrice	Henry Holt & Co.
Our World of Wonders	Q	I	250+	Canetti, Yanitzia	Steck-Vaughn
Our Yard	D	I	120	PM Science Readers	Rigby
Out After Dark	H	RF	114	Book Bank	Wright Group/McGraw Hill
Out and About	Q	I	250+	Explorers	Wright Group/McGraw Hill
Out and About at the Apple Orchard	M	I	250+	Field Trips	Picture Window Books
Out and About at the Aquarium	M	I	250+	Field Trips	Picture Window Books
Out and About at the Bakery	M	I	250+	Field Trips	Picture Window Books
Out and About at the Dairy Farm	M	I	250+	Field Trips	Picture Window Books
Out and About at the Fire Station	M	I	250+	Field Trips	Picture Window Books
Out and About at the Orchestra	M	I	250+	Field Trips	Picture Window Books

* Collection of short stories   # Graphic text
^ Mature content with lower level text demands

TITLE	LEVEL	GENRE	WORD COUNT	AUTHOR / SERIES	PUBLISHER / DISTRIBUTOR
Out and About at the Planetarium	M	I	250+	Field Trips	Picture Window Books
Out and About at the Post Office	M	I	250+	Field Trips	Picture Window Books
Out and About at the Science Center	M	I	250+	Field Trips	Picture Window Books
Out and About at the Supermarket	M	I	250+	Field Trips	Picture Window Books
Out and About at the Vet Clinic	M	I	250+	Field Trips	Picture Window Books
Out and About at the Zoo	M	I	250+	Field Trips	Picture Window Books
Out for Lunch	F	RF	235	Leveled Literacy Intervention/ Green System	Heinemann
Out in Space	A	I	32	Red Rocket Readers	Flying Start Books
Out in Space	L	I	224	Spyglass Books	Compass Point Books
Out in the Big Wild World	K	F	430	Jellybeans	Rigby
Out in the Snow	H	I	163	Red Rocket Readers	Flying Start Books
Out in the Weather	B	I	56	PM Starters	Rigby
Out of an Egg	I	I	103	Gear Up!	Wright Group/McGraw Hill
Out of Bounds	Z	HF	250+	Naidoo, Beverly	HarperCollins
Out of Bounds	M	RF	250+	PM Plus Chapter Books	Rigby
Out of Control	T	I	250+	Orbit Collections	Pacific Learning
Out of Control: The Science of Wildfires	X	I	250+	Headline Science	Compass Point Books
Out of Darkness: The Story of Louis Braille	S	B	250+	Freedman, Russell	Houghton Mifflin Harcourt
Out of His League	Z+	RF	250+	Flynn, Pat	Walker & Company
Out of My Mind	S	RF	250+	Draper, Sharon M.	Atheneum Books
Out of Order	T	RF	250+	Hicks, Betty	Square Fish
Out of Reach	G	RF	86	Literacy Tree	Rigby
Out of Sight	C	I	52	Rigby Literacy	Rigby
Out of Sight, Out of Mind	Q	RF	250+	Mazer, Anne	Scholastic
Out of the Blue	Z+	RF	250+	Rottman, S. L.	Peachtree
Out of the Dark: Nikki Grimes	W	B	250+	Author at Work	Richard C. Owen
Out of the Dust	X	HF	250+	Hesse, Karen	Scholastic
Out of the Egg	E	I	118	Sails	Rigby
Out of the Ocean	M	RF	432	Frasier, Debra	Harcourt
Out of This World	T	I	250+	Story Surfers	ETA/Cuisenaire
Out of This World	L	I	250+	Trackers	Pacific Learning
*Out of War	Z	B	250+	Edge	Hampton Brown
Out the Door	E	RF	150	Rookie Readers	Children's Press
Out the Window	D	I	79	Vocabulary Readers	Houghton Mifflin Harcourt
Out the Window	D	I	79	Vocabulary Readers/CA	Houghton Mifflin Harcourt
Out There - Travel	U	I	250+	Boldprint	Steck-Vaughn
Out to Play	C	F	69	Leveled Literacy Intervention/ Orange System	Heinemann
Outback Adventure	R	RF	250+	Reading Expeditions	National Geographic
Outback Adventure, The	O	RF	250+	WorldScapes	ETA/Cuisenaire
Outback School	G	RF	131	Take Two Books	Wright Group/McGraw Hill
Outcast of Redwall, The	Z	F	250+	Jacques, Brian	Ace Books
Outcast, The: Guardians of Ga'Hoole	V	F	250+	Lasky, Kathryn	Scholastic
Outcast: Warriors, Power of Three	U	F	250+	Hunter, Erin	HarperCollins
Outcasts of 19 Schuyler Place, The	W	RF	250+	Konigsburg, E. L.	Aladdin
Outdoor Adventures	W	I	250+	iOpeners	Pearson Learning Group
Outer Banks, The	R	I	1353	Leveled Readers	Houghton Mifflin Harcourt
Outer Banks, The	R	I	1353	Leveled Readers/CA	Houghton Mifflin Harcourt
Outer Banks, The	R	I	1353	Leveled Readers/TX	Houghton Mifflin Harcourt
Outer Space	O	I	622	Time for Kids	Teacher Created Materials
Outing, An	E	RF	68	Sunshine	Wright Group/McGraw Hill
Outrageously Alice	Y	RF	250+	Naylor, Phyllis Reynolds	Aladdin
Outside	F	RF	211	McAlpin, MaryAnn	Short Tales Press

TITLE	LEVEL	GENRE	WORD COUNT	AUTHOR / SERIES	PUBLISHER / DISTRIBUTOR
Outside and Inside	C	I	43	Twig	Wright Group/McGraw Hill
Outside and Inside Bats	Q	I	250+	Markle, Sandra	Simon & Schuster
Outside and Inside Kangaroos	Q	I	250+	Markle, Sandra	Atheneum Books
Outside and Inside Sharks	Q	I	250+	Markle, Sandra	Simon & Schuster
Outside and Inside Snakes	Q	I	250+	Markle, Sandra	Simon & Schuster
Outside and Inside Spiders	Q	I	250+	Markle, Sandra	Simon & Schuster
Outside Art	L	I	250+	Trackers	Pacific Learning
Outside Dog, The	K	RF	250+	Pomerantz, Charlotte	HarperTrophy
Outside Games	H	I	230	Springboard	Wright Group/McGraw Hill
Outside the Window	B	I	31	Vocabulary Readers	Houghton Mifflin Harcourt
Outside, Inside	D	RF	97	Teacher's Choice Series	Pearson Learning Group
Outsiders, The	Z	RF	250+	Edge	Hampton Brown
Outsiders, The	Z	RF	250+	Hinton, S. E.	Penguin Group
Outwitting the Tiger	L	TL	250+	Voyages	SRA/McGraw Hill
Oval	C	I	34	Shapes	Lerner Publishing Group
Ovals	D	I	30	Bookworms	Marshall Cavendish
Ovals Around Town	J	I	275	Shapes Around Town	Capstone Press
Ovals: Seeing Ovals All Around Us	K	I	214	Shapes	Capstone Press
Over and Over	D	RF	39	Ray's Readers	Outside the Box
Over And Under	C	I	41	Location	Lerner Publishing Group
Over in Australia: Amazing Animals Down Under	M	F	250+	Connecting Children and Nature	Dawn Publications
Over in the Arctic	M	F	462	Sharing Nature with Children	Dawn Publications
Over in the Jungle, A Rainforest Rhyme	M	F	427	Sharing Nature with Children	Dawn Publications
Over in the Meadow	F	TL	228	Cambridge Reading	Pearson Learning Group
Over in the Meadow	G	TL	242	Little Readers	Houghton Mifflin Harcourt
Over in the Meadow	F	TL	250+	PM Readalongs	Rigby
Over in the Ocean, In a Coral Reef	M	F	431	Sharing Nature with Children	Dawn Publications
Over My Dead Body: 43 Old Cemetery Road: Book Two	U	F	250+	Klise, Kate	Sandpiper Books
Over Sea, Under Stone	X	F	250+	Cooper, Susan	Simon & Schuster
Over the Bridge	B	I	50	Little Red Readers	Sundance
Over the Marble Mountain	E	RF	92	Voyages	SRA/McGraw Hill
Over the Oregon Trail	D	I	131	Twig	Wright Group/McGraw Hill
Over the Rainbow	T	B	250+	High-Fliers	Pacific Learning
Over the River	B	F	72	Leveled Literacy Intervention/ Orange System	Heinemann
Over the Wall	Y	RF	250+	Ritter, John H.	Puffin Books
Over Under in the Garden	WB	I	0	Schories, Pat	Farrar, Straus, & Giroux
Over, Under, In, And Ouch!	I	F	287	Silly Millies	Millbrook Press
Overcoming Challenges: The Life of Charles F. Bolden, Jr.	Q	B	250+	Walton, Darwin McBeth	Steck-Vaughn
^Overdrive	X	RF	250+	Orca Soundings	Orca Books
Overground, Underground	S	I	250+	WorldScapes	ETA/Cuisenaire
^Overland Trail, The	Q	I	250+	On Deck	Rigby
Overnight	Y	RF	250+	Griffin, Adele	Speak
Over-Under	E	RF	29	Rookie Readers	Children's Press
Owen & Mzee: The True Story of a Remarkable Friendship	R	I	250+	Hatkoff, Isabella & Craig & Kahumbu, Dr. Paula	Scholastic
Owl	J	I	250+	See How They Grow	DK Publishing
Owl	B	I	47	Zoozoo-Animal World	Cavallo Publishing
Owl and Mouse in the House	J	F	383	Sails	Rigby
Owl and the Pussy Cat	L	TL	215	Lear, Edward	Scholastic
*Owl at Home	J	F	1488	Lobel, Arnold	HarperCollins
Owl Babies	K	F	250+	Waddell, Martin	Candlewick Press

* Collection of short stories   # Graphic text
^ Mature content with lower level text demands

TITLE	LEVEL	GENRE	WORD COUNT	AUTHOR / SERIES	PUBLISHER / DISTRIBUTOR
Owl in the Office	Q	RF	250+	Baglio, Ben M.	Scholastic
Owl Moon	O	B	250+	Yolen, Jane	Scholastic
Owl Rescue	G	RF	157	Gear Up!	Wright Group/McGraw Hill
Owl Vs. Mouse	L	I	250+	Predator Vs. Prey	Raintree
Owl, That's Who!, An	E	I	31	Rosen Real Readers	Rosen Publishing Group
Owlbert	K	RF	250+	Soar To Success	Houghton Mifflin Harcourt
Owliver	H	F	106	Kraus, Robert	Simon & Schuster
Owls	P	I	1749	Animal Predators	Lerner Publishing Group
Owls	N	I	250+	Gibbons, Gail	Holiday House
Owls	O	I	250+	Holmes, Kevin J.	Red Brick Learning
Owls	R	I	250+	Kalman, Bobbie	Crabtree
Owls	I	I	250+	Pebble Books	Red Brick Learning
Owls	M	I	250+	PM Animal Facts: Gold	Rigby
Owls in the Family	P	F	250+	Mowat, Farley	Bantam Books
Owls in the Garden	L	RF	670	PM Collection	Rigby
Owls in the Snow	J	I	422	Sails	Rigby
Owls Live in Trees	E	I	73	Berger, Melvin & Gilda	Scholastic
Owls: The Silent Hunters	T	I	250+	Animals in Order	Franklin Watts
*Owning It	Z+	RF	250+	Gallo, Donald R.	Candlewick Press
Ox-Bow Incident, The	Z+	HF	250+	Clark, Walter Van Tilburg	Random House
Oxcart Day	N	RF	250+	WorldScapes	ETA/Cuisenaire
Ox-Cart Man	K	HF	250+	Hall, Donald	Scholastic
Ozlo's Beard	J	F	250+	Lighthouse	Ginn & Co.

TITLE	LEVEL	GENRE	WORD COUNT	AUTHOR / SERIES	PUBLISHER / DISTRIBUTOR
P	LB	I	14	Readlings	American Reading Company
^P Is for Pom Pom!: A Cheerleading Alphabet	N	I	250+	Alphabet Fun	Capstone Press
P. J. Funnybunny Camps Out	I	F	250+	Sadler, Marilyn	Random House
P. W. Cracker Sees the World	Q	F	250+	Yoshizawa, Linda	Steck-Vaughn
P.S. I Loathe You	X	RF	250+	Harrison, Lisi	Little Brown and Company
P.S. Longer Letter Later	U	RF	250+	Danziger, Paula; Martin, Ann M.	Scholastic
Pablo Picasso	P	B	250+	Lowery, Linda	Lerner Publishing Group
Pablo Picasso	S	B	250+	Scott Foresman Reading	Pearson Publishing Group
Pablo's Fiesta	E	RF	91	On Our Way to English	Rigby
Pacal: A Maya King	R	B	250+	High-Fliers	Pacific Learning
Pacific Crossing	T	RF	250+	Soto, Gary	Harcourt, Inc.
Pacific Island Scrapbook	N	I	591	Big Cat	Pacific Learning
Pacific Northwest, The	R	I	250+	Navigators Social Studies Series	Benchmark Education
Pacific Ocean, The	N	I	250+	Oceans	Capstone Press
Pacific Passage	T	RF	250+	Reading Safari	Mondo Publishing
Pack 109	J	F	164	Thaler, Mike	Scholastic
Pack a Picnic	E	F	140	Learn to Read	Creative Teaching Press
Pack of Lies, A	Z+	F	250+	McCaughrean, Geraldine	Marshall Cavendish
Package, The	E	RF	35	Bauer, Roger	Kaeden Books
Packed with Poison! Deadly Animal Defenses	O	I	1793	On My Own Science	Lerner Publishing Group
Packing	B	RF	37	Foundations	Wright Group/McGraw Hill
Packing My Bag	A	I	32	Leveled Literacy Intervention/ Orange System	Heinemann
Packing My Bag	B	RF	52	PM Starters	Rigby
Paco's Garden	G	RF	118	Books for Young Learners	Richard C. Owen
Paco's Snowman	L	RF	330	Leveled Readers	Houghton Mifflin Harcourt
Paco's Snowman	L	RF	330	Leveled Readers/CA	Houghton Mifflin Harcourt
Paco's Snowman	L	RF	330	Leveled Readers/TX	Houghton Mifflin Harcourt
Pact of the Wolves, The	Z+	F	250+	Blazon, Nina	Annick Press
Paddington Abroad	Q	F	250+	Bond, Michael	Houghton Mifflin Harcourt
Paddington at Large	Q	F	250+	Bond, Michael	Houghton Mifflin Harcourt
Paddington at Work	Q	F	250+	Bond, Michael	Houghton Mifflin Harcourt
Paddington Goes to Town	Q	F	250+	Bond, Michael	Houghton Mifflin Harcourt
Paddington Helps Out	Q	F	250+	Bond, Michael	Houghton Mifflin Harcourt
Paddington Marches On	Q	F	250+	Bond, Michael	Houghton Mifflin Harcourt
Paddington on Screen	Q	F	250+	Bond, Michael	Houghton Mifflin Harcourt
Paddington on Stage	Q	F	250+	Bond, Michael	Houghton Mifflin Harcourt
Paddington on Top	Q	F	250+	Bond, Michael	Houghton Mifflin Harcourt
Paddington Takes the Air	Q	F	250+	Bond, Michael	Houghton Mifflin Harcourt
Paddington Takes the Test	Q	F	250+	Bond, Michael	Houghton Mifflin Harcourt
Paddington Takes to TV	Q	F	250+	Bond, Michael	Houghton Mifflin Harcourt
Paddington's Storybook	Q	F	250+	Bond, Michael	Houghton Mifflin Harcourt
Pagan's Crusade	Y	HF	250+	Jinks, Catherine	Candlewick Press
Pagan's Vows	Z+	HF	250+	Jinks, Catherine	Candlewick Press
Pagemaster, The	P	F	250+	Horowitz, Jordan	Scholastic
Pain and the Great One, The	M	RF	250+	Blume, Judy	Yearling Books
Paint a Picture	A	F	24	Red Rocket Readers	Flying Start Books
Paint Brush Kid, The	M	RF	250+	Bulla, Clyde Robert	Random House
Paint the Sky	LB	F	14	Sunshine	Wright Group/McGraw Hill
Paintball	Q	I	250+	X-Sports	Capstone Press
^Paintball Blast	Q	RF	4301	Maddox, Jake	Stone Arch Books
^Paintball Invasion	Q	RF	250+	Maddox, Jake	Stone Arch Books
Painted Earth Temple: The Buffalo Woman Trilogy, Book Two	Z	HF	250+	Merrifield, Heyoka	Atria Books

* Collection of short stories   # Graphic text
^ Mature content with lower level text demands

TITLE	LEVEL	GENRE	WORD COUNT	AUTHOR / SERIES	PUBLISHER / DISTRIBUTOR
Painted Lady Butterflies	K	I	162	Watch It Grow	Capstone Press
Painter, The	A	F	39	Leveled Literacy Intervention/ Green System	Heinemann
Painter, The	C	RF	31	Ray's Readers	Outside the Box
Painters	A	I	23	Twig	Wright Group/McGraw Hill
Painting	A	RF	40	Leveled Literacy Intervention/ Orange System	Heinemann
Painting	E	RF	135	Scott, Janine	Scholastic
Painting	M	I	250+	Start with Art	Heinemann Library
Painting	C	RF	24	Story Box	Wright Group/McGraw Hill
Painting Day, The	H	RF	250+	Voyages	SRA/McGraw Hill
Painting from Caves to Computers	O	I	578	Vocabulary Readers	Houghton Mifflin Harcourt
Painting From Caves to Computers	O	I	578	Vocabulary Readers/CA	Houghton Mifflin Harcourt
Painting From Caves to Computers	O	I	578	Vocabulary Readers/TX	Houghton Mifflin Harcourt
Painting History	J	RF	242	On Our Way to English	Rigby
Painting Lesson, The	K	F	250+	Pacific Literacy	Pacific Learning
Painting Patterns	A	RF	31	InfoTrek	ETA/Cuisenaire
Painting Shapes	F	I	148	Early Connections	Benchmark Education
Painting the Ocean	M	RF	885	Leveled Readers	Houghton Mifflin Harcourt
Painting the Ocean	M	RF	885	Leveled Readers/CA	Houghton Mifflin Harcourt
Painting the Ocean	M	RF	885	Leveled Readers/TX	Houghton Mifflin Harcourt
Pair of Babies, A	D	I	70	Early Connections	Benchmark Education
Pair of Socks, A	I	F	123	Murphy, Stuart J.	Scholastic
Paiute Princess: The Story of Sarah Winnemucca	X	B	250+	Ray, Deborah Kogan	Farrar, Straus, & Giroux
Pajama Party	M	RF	250+	Hest, Amy	William Morrow
Pajama Party, The	D	F	46	Sunshine	Wright Group/McGraw Hill
Pakistan	W	I	250+	Countries and Cultures	Capstone Press
Pakistan	P	I	1759	Country Explorers	Lerner Publishing Group
Pal the Pony	G	RF	224	Herman, R. A.	Grosset & Dunlap
Palapalooza	L	RF	250+	Social Studies Connects	Kane Press
Paleontology: Digging for Dinosaurs and More	U	I	1597	Reading Street	Pearson
Palm Trees	H	I	123	Pebble Books	Capstone Press
Paloma's Party	L	I	250+	Little Celebrations	Pearson Learning Group
Palomino Horses	I	I	150	Horses	Capstone Press
Pam	D	F	41	Reading Street	Pearson
Pam & Sam at the Park	C	F	108	Carousel Earlybirds	Pearson Learning Group
Pam & Sam at the Zoo	C	F	84	Carousel Earlybirds	Pearson Learning Group
Pam & Sam Fly Over the City	C	F	80	Carousel Earlybirds	Pearson Learning Group
Pam & Sam on the Beach	C	F	94	Carousel Earlybirds	Pearson Learning Group
Pam, Pam	F	F	231	Springboard	Wright Group/McGraw Hill
Pamphleteers of the Revolution	V	I	2717	Leveled Readers	Houghton Mifflin Harcourt
Pamphleteers of the Revolution	V	I	2717	Leveled Readers/CA	Houghton Mifflin Harcourt
Pamphleteers of the Revolution	V	I	2717	Leveled Readers/TX	Houghton Mifflin Harcourt
Pam's Runners	M	RF	250+	Reading Safari	Mondo Publishing
Pan Woman	P	RF	1145	Leveled Readers	Houghton Mifflin Harcourt
Panama Canal, The	W	I	250+	Cornerstones of Freedom	Children's Press
Pancake, The	K	TL	250+	Lobel, Anita	Bantam Books
Pancakes	G	RF	181	Foundations	Wright Group/McGraw Hill
Pancakes	W	SF	3080	Leveled Readers	Houghton Mifflin Harcourt
Pancakes	W	SF	3080	Leveled Readers/CA	Houghton Mifflin Harcourt
Pancakes	W	SF	3080	Leveled Readers/TX	Houghton Mifflin Harcourt
Pancakes	WB	RF	0	Rigby Literacy	Rigby
Pancakes	G	RF	294	Sails	Rigby

* Collection of short stories   # Graphic text
^ Mature content with lower level text demands

Organized Alphabetically by Title   **585**
Storable Database at www.fountasandpinnellleveledbooks.com

TITLE	LEVEL	GENRE	WORD COUNT	AUTHOR / SERIES	PUBLISHER / DISTRIBUTOR
Pancakes	L	I	700	Springboard	Wright Group/McGraw Hill
Pancakes for Breakfast	H	F	99	Books for Young Learners	Richard C. Owen
Pancakes for Breakfast	WB	F	0	DePaola, Tomie	Doubleday Books
Pancakes for Breakfast	C	RF	108	Emergent	Pioneer Valley
Pancakes for Supper	O	F	250+	Isaacs, Anne	Scholastic
Pancakes for Supper	H	RF	96	Literacy 2000	Rigby
Pancakes!	F	F	106	Ready Readers	Pearson Learning Group
Pancakes, Crackers, and Pizza	C	RF	63	Rookie Readers	Children's Press
Panda Babies	C	I	31	Little Celebrations	Pearson Learning Group
Panda Bear, The	D	I	28	Rosen Real Readers	Rosen Publishing Group
Panda Bears	J	I	120	Larkin's Little Readers	Wilbooks
Panda Math: Learning About Subtraction from Hua Mei and Mei Sheng	Q	I	250+	Nagda, Ann Whitehead	Henry Holt & Co.
Panda Puzzle, The	N	RF	250+	A to Z Mysteries	Random House
Panda, The	L	I	250+	Sunshine	Wright Group/McGraw Hill
Pandas	K	I	243	Nonfiction Set 8	Literacy Footprints
Pandas	E	I	75	Time for Kids	Teacher Created Materials
Pandas Are Coming!	O	I	250+	On Our Way to English	Rigby
Panda's Birthday Surprise	F	F	141	Seedlings	Continental Press
Pandas' Earthquake Escape	M	RF	830	Perry, Phyllis J.	Sylvan Dell Publishing
Pandas Have Cubs	M	I	250+	Animals and Their Young	Compass Point Books
Pandas in the Mountains	M	F	735	PM Collection	Rigby
Pandas Nap	B	F	28	Reading Street	Pearson
Panda's Surprise	H	F	242	Little Readers	Houghton Mifflin Harcourt
Pandora Gets Angry	U	F	250+	Hennesy, Carolyn	Bloomsbury Children's Books
Pandora Gets Heart	U	F	250+	Hennesy, Carolyn	Bloomsbury Children's Books
Pandora Gets Jealous	U	F	250+	Hennesy, Carolyn	Bloomsbury Children's Books
Pandora Gets Lazy	U	F	250+	Hennesy, Carolyn	Bloomsbury Children's Books
Pandora Gets Vain	U	F	250+	Hennesy, Carolyn	Bloomsbury Children's Books
Pandora's Box	Q	RF	250+	Literacy 2000	Rigby
Pandora's Box: A Greek Myth	L	TL	250+	Storyteller Chapter Books	Wright Group/McGraw Hill
Pangaea	X	I	3186	Leveled Readers Science	Houghton Mifflin Harcourt
Panning for Gold	O	RF	825	Leveled Readers Science	Houghton Mifflin Harcourt
Pansies for Mom	G	I	56	Windows on Literacy	National Geographic
Papa Penguin's Surprise	F	RF	136	Seedlings	Continental Press
Papa's Birthday	G	RF	249	Leveled Literacy Intervention/Green System	Heinemann
Papagayo the Mischief Maker	N	TL	250+	McDermott, Gerald	Harcourt Trade
Paparazzi Princess: Secrets of My Hollywood Life	Y	RF	250+	Calonita, Jen	Little Brown and Company
Papa's Latkes	O	RF	250+	Edwards, Michelle	Candlewick Press
Papa's Spaghetti	G	F	248	Literacy 2000	Rigby
Papa's Wild Child	L	F	250+	Aston, Dianna Hutts	Charlesbridge
Paper Art	C	I	29	Little Celebrations	Pearson Learning Group
Paper Bag Trail	E	RF	67	Schreiber, Anne; Doughty, A.	Scholastic
Paper Bag, The	D	RF	82	Books for Young Learners	Richard C. Owen
Paper Birds, The	K	RF	363	Foundations	Wright Group/McGraw Hill
Paper Capers	Q	I	250+	Storyteller-Raging Rivers	Wright Group/McGraw Hill
Paper Chains	I	I	364	Red Rocket Readers	Flying Start Books
Paper Chains to Ten	E	RF	139	InfoTrek	ETA/Cuisenaire

* Collection of short stories   # Graphic text
^ Mature content with lower level text demands

TITLE	LEVEL	GENRE	WORD COUNT	AUTHOR / SERIES	PUBLISHER / DISTRIBUTOR
Paper Crane, The	M	F	250+	Soar To Success	Houghton Mifflin Harcourt
Paper Crunch	K	I	250+	Rigby Literacy	Rigby
Paper Daughter	W	RF	250+	Ingold, Jeanette	Harcourt, Inc.
Paper from Wood: Dollhouse Decisions	O	I	1125	iScience	Norwood House Press
Paper Games	I	F	240	The Joy Cowley Collection	Hameray Publishing Group
Paper Lanterns	N	RF	250+	Czernecki, Stefan	Charlesbridge
Paper Patchwork	F	I	54	Pacific Literacy	Pacific Learning
Paper Pictures	H	I	196	Sun Sprouts	ETA/Cuisenaire
Paper Route, The	K	RF	314	New Way Green	Steck-Vaughn
Paper Shapes	N	I	250+	Voyages	SRA/McGraw Hill
Paper Theater	Q	I	1275	Vocabulary Readers	Houghton Mifflin Harcourt
Paper Theater	Q	I	1275	Vocabulary Readers/CA	Houghton Mifflin Harcourt
Paper Trail, The	I	RF	297	Red Rocket Readers	Flying Start Books
Paper Trail, The	I	RF	253	Windmill Books	Rigby
Paper Wagon, The	M	TL	250+	Orca Echoes	Orca Books
Paperboy, The	N	RF	373	Pilkey, Dav	Orchard Books
Parachute Adventure	O	F	1868	Take Two Books	Wright Group/McGraw Hill
Parachutes	J	RF	145	Storyteller-Moon Rising	Wright Group/McGraw Hill
Parachuting Hamsters and Andy Russell	N	RF	250+	Adler, David A.	Harcourt, Inc.
Parade in Valencia	K	RF	214	Leveled Readers Language Support	Houghton Mifflin Harcourt
Parade, The	A	RF	32	Leveled Literacy Intervention/Orange System	Heinemann
Parade, The	B	I	56	Leveled Readers Emergent	Houghton Mifflin Harcourt
Parade, The	B	RF	67	PM Plus Starters	Rigby
Parades!	C	I	24	Pair-It Books	Steck-Vaughn
Parakeet Girl, The	J	F	250+	Sadler, Marilyn	Random House
Parakeets	J	I	250+	PM Animal Facts: Orange	Rigby
Parallel Universe of Liars, The	Z+	RF	250+	Johnson, Kathleen Jeffrie	Millbrook Press
Paralympic Games	M	I	518	Red Rocket Readers	Flying Start Books
Paramedics to the Rescue: When Every Second Counts	U	I	250+	High Five Reading	Red Brick Learning
^Paranormal, The	S	I	250+	Download	Hameray Publishing Group
Parasites: Nature's Stowaways	S	I	250+	Orbit Chapter Books	Pacific Learning
Pardon? Said the Giraffe	F	F	123	West, Colin	Harper & Row
Parents	G	I	157	Families	Heinemann Library
Parents	C	I	60	Pebble Books	Capstone Press
Parents	F	I	82	People	Capstone Press
Parents' Night Fright	K	RF	250+	Levy, Elizabeth	Scholastic
Park for Everyone, A	L	I	668	Gear Up!	Wright Group/McGraw Hill
Park Rangers	M	I	250+	Community Helpers	Red Brick Learning
Park Ranger's Day, A	H	I	195	Rosen Real Readers	Rosen Publishing Group
Park Soccer	N	RF	250+	Boyz Rule!	Mondo Publishing
Park Train, The	D	RF	88	Springboard	Wright Group/McGraw Hill
Park, The	A	RF	40	Leveled Literacy Intervention/Orange System	Heinemann
Park, The	A	I	32	Rigby Flying Colors	Rigby
Park, The	G	RF	155	Windows on Literacy	National Geographic
Parker's Problem	P	RF	850	Leveled Readers	Houghton Mifflin Harcourt
Parker's Problem	P	RF	850	Leveled Readers/CA	Houghton Mifflin Harcourt
Parker's Problem	P	RF	850	Leveled Readers/TX	Houghton Mifflin Harcourt
Park's Quest	U	RF	250+	Paterson, Katherine	Puffin Books
Parliament of Blood, The	Z	F	250+	Richards, Justin	Bloomsbury Children's Books
Parrot in the Bat's Cave	E	F	152	Sails	Rigby

* Collection of short stories   # Graphic text
^ Mature content with lower level text demands

Organized Alphabetically by Title   **587**
Storable Database at www.fountasandpinnellleveledbooks.com

TITLE	LEVEL	GENRE	WORD COUNT	AUTHOR / SERIES	PUBLISHER / DISTRIBUTOR
Parrot in the Oven: Mi Vida	Z	RF	250+	Edge	Hampton Brown
Parrot Pandemonium: The Pet Sitter	O	F	250+	Sykes, Julie	Kingfisher
Parrot Talk	K	RF	250+	Cambridge Reading	Pearson Learning Group
Parrotfish	G	I	51	Ocean Life	Capstone Press
Parrots	J	I	94	Pebble Books	Red Brick Learning
Parrots	I	I	181	Sails	Rigby
Parrots: Colorful Birds	M	I	250+	The Wild World of Animals	Capstone Press
Part of Me	W	RF	250+	Holt, Kimberly Willis	Square Fish
Part of the Sky, A	Z	HF	250+	Peck, Robert Newton	Random House
Part of the Team	I	RF	288	InfoTrek	ETA/Cuisenaire
Particular Cow, A	J	F	111	Fox, Mem	Harcourt, Inc.
Partners	L	I	159	Home Connection Collection	Rigby
Parts Make Up a Whole	J	I	219	Early Connections	Benchmark Education
Parts of a Plant	J	I	136	Larkin, Bruce	Wilbooks
Parts of a Plant	K	I	164	Phonics Readers	Compass Point Books
Parts of a Whole	G	I	161	Early Connections	Benchmark Education
Parts of a Whole	M	I	250+	Yellow Umbrella Books	Capstone Press
Parts of Ecosystems	R	I	1504	Science Support Readers	Houghton Mifflin Harcourt
Party Clothes	E	RF	132	Jasper the Cat	Pioneer Valley
Party Clown, The	F	RF	182	PM Photo Stories	Rigby
Party Food	A	I	25	Rigby Focus	Rigby
Party for a Rabbit, A	C	F	70	Early Connections	Benchmark Education
Party for Bear, A	B	F	27	Gear Up!	Wright Group/McGraw Hill
Party for Brown Mouse, A	E	F	149	PM Plus Story Books	Rigby
Party for Buddy, A	F	F	187	McGougan, Kathy	Buddy Books Publishing
Party for Panda, A	G	I	162	Leveled Literacy Intervention/ Blue System	Heinemann
Party for Pedro, A	F	RF	87	Reading Street	Pearson
Party Game, The	G	RF	115	Home Connection Collection	Rigby
Party Games	J	RF	399	Foundations	Wright Group/McGraw Hill
Party Girl	Z+	RF	250+	Ewing, Lynne	Random House
Party Hats	B	RF	72	PM Plus Starters	Rigby
Party Is Here, The	A	RF	32	Literacy by Design	Rigby
Party on Mars	P	F	250+	Reading Safari	Mondo Publishing
Party Time	J	I	250+	Rigby Literacy	Rigby
Party Time at the Milky Way	I	F	160	Sunshine	Wright Group/McGraw Hill
Party, A	A	RF	28	Leveled Readers Emergent	Houghton Mifflin Harcourt
Party, A	LB	RF	14	Story Box	Wright Group/McGraw Hill
Party, The	A	F	24	Bonnell, Kris	Reading Reading Books
Party, The	F	RF	56	Book Bus	Creative Edge
Party, The	B	RF	93	First Stories	Pacific Learning
Party, The	D	RF	26	Ready Readers	Pearson Learning Group
Party, The	A	F	24	Sails	Rigby
Party, The: Goodness	K	RF	1484	Salerno, Tony Character Classics	Character Building Company
Paru Has a Bath	J	RF	242	Pacific Literacy	Pacific Learning
Parvana's Journey	W	RF	250+	Ellis, Deborah	Douglas & McIntyre
Parzival: The Quest of the Grail Knight	T	TL	250+	Paterson, Katherine	Puffin Books
Pasquale's Gift	J	RF	250+	Voyages	SRA/McGraw Hill
Pass It On	I	RF	299	Red Rocket Readers	Flying Start Books
Pass the Energy, Please!	P	I	1617	Sharing Nature with Children	Dawn Publications
Pass the Pasta, Please	D	I	63	Storyteller-Setting Sun	Wright Group/McGraw Hill
Pass the Pasta, Please!	C	I	45	Johns, Linda	Scholastic
Pass the Present	C	F	86	Storyteller-First Snow	Wright Group/McGraw Hill

* Collection of short stories   # Graphic text
^ Mature content with lower level text demands

PQ

TITLE	LEVEL	GENRE	WORD COUNT	AUTHOR / SERIES	PUBLISHER / DISTRIBUTOR
Passage to Freedom: The Sugihara Story	U	B	250+	Mochizuki, Ken	Lee & Low Books Inc.
Passage, The	Z	HF	250+	Killgore, James	Peachtree
Passager: The Young Merlin Trilogy	V	F	250+	Yolen, Jane	Scholastic
Passing Poetry	R	RF	785	Leveled Readers	Houghton Mifflin Harcourt
Passover	K	I	152	Holidays and Celebrations	Capstone Press
Passover	O	I	250+	Holidays and Festivals	Compass Point Books
Passover	O	I	1579	On My Own Holidays	Lerner Publishing Group
Passover: Jewish Celebration of Freedom	M	I	250+	Holidays and Culture	Capstone Press
Passport to Earth	P	I	250+	Sails	Rigby
Past Work, Future Work	S	I	250+	PM Extensions	Rigby
Pasta	N	I	250+	Little Celebrations	Pearson Learning Group
Pasta	I	I	125	Rigby Rocket	Rigby
Pastry School in Paris: An Adventure in Capacity	M	RF	250+	Neuschwander, Cindy	Henry Holt & Co.
Pat and Nat	A	RF	21	Rigby Star	Rigby
Pat and Pea Soup	J	RF	187	Books for Young Learners	Richard C. Owen
Pat and Pig	B	F	34	Leveled Readers	Houghton Mifflin Harcourt
Pat Mora, the Storyteller	L	B	278	Vocabulary Readers	Houghton Mifflin Harcourt
Pat Mora: Two Languages, One Poet	P	B	769	Leveled Readers	Houghton Mifflin Harcourt
Pat the Penguin	C	F	23	Reading Street	Pearson
Pat, Pat, Pat	B	RF	37	Book Bank	Wright Group/McGraw Hill
Patch, The	L	RF	250+	Heddley, Justina Chen	Charlesbridge
Patches	M	RF	250+	Szymanski, Lois	Avon Books
Patching Up the Past	W	I	250+	WorldScapes	ETA/Cuisenaire
Patchwork Cat, The	L	F	250+	Mayne, William	Penguin Group
Patchwork Path, The	R	HF	250+	Stroud, Bettye	Candlewick Press
Patchwork Patterns	G	RF	64	Little Celebrations	Pearson Learning Group
Patchwork Quilt, The	O	RF	250+	Flournoy, Valerie	Scholastic
Patent Process, The	U	I	2067	Reading Street	Pearson
Path to Frog's New Home, The	E	RF	118	Reading Street	Pearson
Pathfinder: Mission to Mars	P	I	250+	Rigby Literacy	Rigby
Paths to Freedom	S	I	250+	Reading Expeditions	National Geographic
Patience	M	I	250+	Everyday Character Education	Capstone Press
Patiently Alice	Z+	RF	250+	Naylor, Phyllis Reynolds	Simon Pulse
Patrick	O	F	250+	Book Blazers	ETA/Cuisenaire
Patrick and the Leprechaun	L	TL	677	PM Collection	Rigby
Patrick Doyle is Full of Blarney	O	HF	250+	Armstrong, Jennifer	Random House
Patrick Henry	S	B	250+	Amazing Americans	Wright Group/McGraw Hill
Patrick Henry	S	B	3990	History Maker Bios	Lerner Publishing Group
#Patrick Henry: Liberty or Death	T	B	250+	Graphic Library	Capstone Press
#Patrick in a Teddy Bear's Picnic and Other Stories	M	F	250+	Hayes, Geoffrey	Toon Books
Patriotic Citizens	K	I	222	Early Explorers	Benchmark Education
Patron Saint of Butterflies, The	Z	RF	250+	Galante, Cecilia	Bloomsbury Children's Books
Pat's New Puppy	E	RF	88	Reading Unlimited	Pearson Learning Group
Pat's Perfect Pizza	C	RF	37	Ready Readers	Pearson Learning Group
Pat's Picture	G	RF	243	Take Two Books	Wright Group/McGraw Hill
Pat's Train	D	RF	22	KinderReaders	Rigby
Patsy Mink	W	B	2489	Leveled Readers	Houghton Mifflin Harcourt
Patsy Mink	W	B	2489	Leveled Readers/CA	Houghton Mifflin Harcourt
Patsy Mink	W	B	2489	Leveled Readers/TX	Houghton Mifflin Harcourt
Patsy Mink and Title IX	W	I	2170	Leveled Readers	Houghton Mifflin Harcourt
Patsy Mink and Title IX	W	I	2170	Leveled Readers/CA	Houghton Mifflin Harcourt

PQ

TITLE	LEVEL	GENRE	WORD COUNT	AUTHOR / SERIES	PUBLISHER / DISTRIBUTOR
Patsy Mink and Title IX	W	I	2170	Leveled Readers/TX	Houghton Mifflin Harcourt
Pattern Bugs	K	F	369	Harris, Trudy	Millbrook Press
Pattern Fish	K	F	395	Harris, Trudy	Millbrook Press
Pattern Parade, The	F	RF	96	InfoTrek	ETA/Cuisenaire
Pattern Performers, The	J	RF	624	InfoTrek	ETA/Cuisenaire
Pattern Walk, A	C	I	79	InfoTrek	ETA/Cuisenaire
Patterns	C	I	32	Berger, Samantha; Moreton, Daniel	Scholastic
Patterns	C	I	35	Discovery Links	Newbridge
Patterns	C	I	35	Early Math	Lerner Publishing Group
Patterns	A	I	24	In Step Readers	Rigby
Patterns	E	I	57	Literacy 2000	Rigby
Patterns	I	I	195	Red Rocket Readers	Flying Start Books
Patterns	J	I	122	Spyglass Books	Compass Point Books
Patterns	C	I	57	Story Steps	Rigby
Patterns	K	I	307	Yellow Umbrella Books	Red Brick Learning
Patterns All Around	B	I	55	Early Connections	Benchmark Education
Patterns All Around	E	I	36	Shutterbug Books	Steck-Vaughn
Patterns All Around Me	E	I	181	Learn to Read	Creative Teaching Press
Patterns and Textures: Who Took the Pets?	R	I	250+	iScience	Norwood House Press
Patterns Are Fun!	C	I	35	Story Steps	Rigby
Patterns Around the World	G	I	76	Windows on Literacy	National Geographic
Patterns at the Beach	E	I	95	Early Connections	Benchmark Education
Patterns at the Museum	F	I	125	Math Around Us	Heinemann Library
Patterns, Shapes, and Symmetry	J	I	81	Windows on Literacy	National Geographic
Patterns: What Comes Next?	L	I	250+	Exploring Math	Capstone Press
Patty and Pop's Picnic	C	RF	57	Little Books	Sadlier-Oxford
Patty Cat	J	F	288	Let's Read Together	Kane Press
Paul	F	I	54	Pacific Literacy	Pacific Learning
Paul and Lucy	J	RF	250+	Stepping Stones	Nelson/Michaels Assoc.
Paul Bunyan	J	TL	250+	Jumbled Tumbled Tales & Rhymes	Rigby
Paul Bunyan	I	TL	319	My 1st Classic Story	Picture Window Books
Paul Bunyan	N	TL	1831	On My Own Folklore	Lerner Publishing Group
Paul Bunyan	N	TL	250+	Tall Tales	Compass Point Books
Paul Bunyan and the Love-Struck Ox	K	TL	250+	The Rowland Reading Program Libary	Rowland Reading Foundation
Paul Cezanne	R	B	250+	Venezia, Mike	Children's Press
Paul Gauguin	R	B	250+	Venezia, Mike	Children's Press
*Paul Harvey's the Rest of the Story	Z	I	250+	Harvey, Jr., Paul	Bantam Books
Paul Klee	R	B	250+	Venezia, Mike	Children's Press
Paul Laurence Dunbar, Poet	S	B	542	Vocabulary Readers	Houghton Mifflin Harcourt
Paul Revere	V	B	250+	Cornerstones of Freedom	Children's Press
Paul Revere	N	B	237	First Biographies	Capstone Press
Paul Revere	S	B	3318	History Maker Bios	Lerner Publishing Group
Paul Revere	N	B	265	Rookie Biographies	Children's Press
Paul Revere and the American Revolution	T	I	2218	Reading Street	Pearson
Paul Revere, Hero on Horseback	T	B	1292	Vocabulary Readers/CA	Houghton Mifflin Harcourt
Paul Revere, Hero on Horseback	T	B	1292	Vocabulary Readers/TX	Houghton Mifflin Harcourt
Paul Revere, Rider of the Revolution	T	B	1292	Vocabulary Readers	Houghton Mifflin Harcourt
Paul Revere's Midnight Ride	S	I	1177	Reading Street	Pearson
#Paul Revere's Ride	T	B	250+	Graphic Library	Capstone Press
Paul Revere's Ride	S	HF	250+	Literacy 2000	Rigby
Paul Revere's Ride	N	I	250+	Our American Story	Picture Window Books

* Collection of short stories   # Graphic text
^ Mature content with lower level text demands

PQ

TITLE	LEVEL	GENRE	WORD COUNT	AUTHOR / SERIES	PUBLISHER / DISTRIBUTOR
Paul Revere's Ride	T	B	250+	We The People	Compass Point Books
Paul Robeson	U	B	250+	Amazing Americans	Wright Group/McGraw Hill
Paul Sereno: Digging for Dinosaurs	T	I	250+	Reading Expeditions	National Geographic
Paul the Artist	P	RF	1356	Leveled Readers	Houghton Mifflin Harcourt
Paul the Pitcher	D	RF	86	Rookie Readers	Children's Press
Paula Bunyan	N	TL	250+	Root, Phyllis	Farrar, Straus, & Giroux
Paula's Pickle Picnic	K	RF	688	Underwood, Barbara J.	Kaeden Books
Paulo the Pilot	C	RF	62	Reading Safari	Mondo Publishing
Paulo the Pilot	I	RF	273	Red Rocket Readers	Flying Start Books
Paulo the Pilot	F	F	131	Windmill Books	Rigby
Paul's Day at School	B	I	38	Little Books for Early Readers	University of Maine
Pawnee Nation, The	P	I	250+	Native Peoples	Red Brick Learning
Pawpaw Patch	F	TL	174	PM Readalongs	Rigby
*Paws and Claws and Other Stories	D	F	120	Story Steps	Rigby
Paws and Claws: Learn About Animal Tracks	L	I	465	Reading Street	Pearson
Paws Off, Cheddarface!	O	F	250+	Stilton, Geronimo	Scholastic
Paws, Claws, Hands, and Feet	L	F	96	Hutmacher, Kimberly	Sylvan Dell Publishing
Pay Attention!	K	RF	458	Leveled Readers	Houghton Mifflin Harcourt
Pay Attention!	K	RF	458	Leveled Readers/CA	Houghton Mifflin Harcourt
Pay Attention!	K	RF	458	Leveled Readers/TX	Houghton Mifflin Harcourt
Payback Time	Y	RF	250+	Deuker, Carl	Houghton Mifflin Harcourt
Pea Blossom, The	L	TL	250+	Pooole, Amy Lowry	Holiday House
Pea or the Flea?, The	F	RF	66	Start to Read	School Zone
Peace Book, The	I	I	194	Parr, Todd	Little Brown and Company
Peace Makers	V	B	250+	InfoQuest	Rigby
Peace Ring, The	L	F	250+	Cambridge Reading	Pearson Learning Group
Peaceful Piggy Yoga	M	F	111	MacLean, Kerry Lee	Albert Whitman & Co.
Peaceful Protest	U	I	1710	Vocabulary Readers	Houghton Mifflin Harcourt
Peaceful Protest	U	I	1710	Vocabulary Readers/CA	Houghton Mifflin Harcourt
Peacefulness	L	I	250+	Character Education	Red Brick Learning
Peacefulness	N	I	250+	Everyday Character Education	Capstone Press
Peaches	Z+	RF	250+	Anderson, Jodi Lynn	HarperTrophy
Peaches All the Time	J	I	149	Early Connections	Benchmark Education
Peaches on the Beaches, The	J	F	189	Sounds Like Reading	Lerner Publishing Group
Peaches the Pig	E	F	120	Little Readers	Houghton Mifflin Harcourt
Peacocks	K	I	207	Colorful World of Animals	Capstone Press
Peacocks	O	I	1681	Early Bird Nature Books	Lerner Publishing Group
Peacock's Tail	L	TL	344	Leveled Readers	Houghton Mifflin Harcourt
Peacock's Tail	L	TL	344	Leveled Readers/CA	Houghton Mifflin Harcourt
Peacock's Tail	L	TL	344	Leveled Readers/TX	Houghton Mifflin Harcourt
Peak	T	RF	250+	Smith, Roland	Harcourt, Inc.
Peanut	L	F	250+	Lucas, David	Candlewick Press
Peanut	Q	I	250+	Selsam, Millicent	William Morrow
Peanut Butter	E	RF	60	Little Celebrations	Pearson Learning Group
Peanut Butter and Jelly	E	RF	164	Little Readers	Houghton Mifflin Harcourt
Peanut Butter and Jelly	H	I	136	Shutterbug Books	Steck-Vaughn
Peanut Butter and Jelly	G	F	156	Wescott, Nadine B.	Penguin Group
Peanut Butter Gang, The	K	F	250+	Siracusa, Catherine	Hyperion
Peanut for the Little Chipmunk, A	E	RF	97	Coulton, Mia	Maryruth Books
Peanut-Free Cafe, The	L	RF	250+	Koster, Gloria	Albert Whitman & Co.
Peanuts	E	RF	123	Dominie Readers	Pearson Learning Group
Peanuts	K	I	250+	Rigby Literacy	Rigby
Peanuts	K	I	250+	Rigby Star Quest	Rigby
Peanuts	J	F	250+	Sunshine	Wright Group/McGraw Hill

* Collection of short stories   # Graphic text
^ Mature content with lower level text demands

TITLE	LEVEL	GENRE	WORD COUNT	AUTHOR / SERIES	PUBLISHER / DISTRIBUTOR
Peanuts	J	I	149	Windows on Literacy	National Geographic
Pearl Learns A Lesson	L	F	1291	Appleton-Smith, Laura	Flyleaf Publishing
Pearl of the Soul of the World, The	Y	F	250+	Pierce, Meredith Ann	Little Brown and Company
Pearl the Cloud Fairy: Rainbow Magic	L	F	250+	Meadows, Daisy	Scholastic
Pearl Verses the World	P	RF	250+	Murphy, Sally	Candlewick Press
Pearl, The	Z	RF	250+	Steinbeck, John	Penguin Group
Peas	E	I	93	Bonnell, Kris/About	Reading Reading Books
Peas and Potatoes: 1, 2, 3	B	RF	44	Pair-It Books	Steck-Vaughn
Peas Are Good	D	RF	109	Bonnell, Kris	Reading Reading Books
Peas in a Pod	F	F	173	Cambridge Reading	Pearson Learning Group
Pebble First Guide to Horses, The	N	I	250+	Pebble First Guides	Capstone Press
Pebble First Guide to Lizards, The	N	I	250+	Pebble First Guides	Capstone Press
Pebble First Guide to Nocturnal Animals, The	N	I	250+	Pebble First Guides	Capstone Press
Pebble First Guide to Rocks and Minerals, The	N	I	250+	Pebble First Guides	Capstone Press
Pebble First Guide to Spiders, The	N	I	250+	Pebble First Guides	Capstone Press
Pebble First Guide to Texas Symbols, The	N	I	250+	Pebble First Guides	Capstone Press
Pebble First Guide to the Solar System, The	N	I	250+	Pebble First Guides	Capstone Press
Pebble First Guide to Whales, The	N	I	250+	Pebble First Guides	Capstone Press
Pebble First Guide to Wildcats, The	N	I	250+	Pebble First Guides	Capstone Press
Pebble First Guides to Butterflies, The	N	I	250+	Pebble First Guides	Capstone Press
Pebble First Guides to Penguins, The	N	I	250+	Pebble First Guides	Capstone Press
Pebble First Guides to Snakes, The	N	I	250+	Pebble First Guides	Capstone Press
Pebble First Guides to Songbirds, The	N	I	250+	Pebble First Guides	Capstone Press
Pebbles	C	RF	30	Science	Outside the Box
Pebbles, Sand, and Silt: The Neighbor's Garden	O	I	1200	iScience	Norwood House Press
Pecos Bill	Q	TL	250+	Kellogg, Steven	HarperCollins
Pecos Bill	N	TL	1965	On My Own Folklore	Lerner Publishing Group
Pecos Bill	N	TL	250+	Tall Tales	Compass Point Books
#Pecos Bill: Colossal Cowboy	O	TL	250+	Graphic Spin	Stone Arch Books
Pedal Power	C	I	22	Pacific Literacy	Pacific Learning
Pedal Power	J	I	226	Rigby Literacy	Rigby
Pedal Power	J	I	226	Rigby Star Quest	Rigby
Peddler's Caps, The	J	TL	250+	PM Story Books-Purple	Rigby
#Pedro & Me: Friendship, Loss, & What I Learned	Z+	B	250+	Winick, Judd	Henry Holt & Co.
Pedro's Gift	T	RF	250+	Reading Street	Pearson
Pedro's Journal	Q	HF	250+	Conrad, Pam	Scholastic
Pee Wee & Plush	O	F	250+	Hurwitz, Johanna	Chronicle Books
Pee Wee Scouts	L	RF	250+	Delton, Judy	Yearling Books
Pee Wee Scouts on First	L	RF	250+	Delton, Judy	Bantam Books
Pee Wee Scouts on Parade	L	RF	250+	Delton, Judy	Bantam Books
Pee Wee Scouts on Skis	L	RF	250+	Delton, Judy	Bantam Books
Pee Wee Scouts: A Big Box of Memories	L	RF	250+	Delton, Judy	Bantam Books
Pee Wee Scouts: A Pee Wee Christmas	L	RF	250+	Delton, Judy	Bantam Books
Pee Wee Scouts: Bad, Bad Bunnies	L	RF	250+	Delton, Judy	Bantam Books
Pee Wee Scouts: Blue Skies, French Fries	L	RF	250+	Delton, Judy	Bantam Books
Pee Wee Scouts: Bookworm Buddies	L	RF	250+	Delton, Judy	Bantam Books
Pee Wee Scouts: Camp Ghost Away	L	RF	250+	Delton, Judy	Bantam Books
Pee Wee Scouts: Computer Clues	L	RF	250+	Delton, Judy	Bantam Books
Pee Wee Scouts: Cookies and Crutches	L	RF	250+	Delton, Judy	Bantam Books
Pee Wee Scouts: Eggs with Legs	L	RF	250+	Delton, Judy	Bantam Books
Pee Wee Scouts: Fishy Wishes	L	RF	250+	Delton, Judy	Bantam Books
Pee Wee Scouts: Greedy Groundhogs	L	RF	250+	Delton, Judy	Bantam Books
Pee Wee Scouts: Grumpy Pumpkins	L	RF	250+	Delton, Judy	Bantam Books

PQ

* Collection of short stories   # Graphic text
^ Mature content with lower level text demands

TITLE	LEVEL	GENRE	WORD COUNT	AUTHOR / SERIES	PUBLISHER / DISTRIBUTOR
Pee Wee Scouts: Halloween Helpers	L	RF	250+	Delton, Judy	Bantam Books
Pee Wee Scouts: Lights, Action, Land-Ho!	L	RF	250+	Delton, Judy	Bantam Books
Pee Wee Scouts: Lucky Dog Days	L	RF	250+	Delton, Judy	Bantam Books
Pee Wee Scouts: Moans and Groans and Dinosaur Bones	L	RF	250+	Delton, Judy	Bantam Books
Pee Wee Scouts: Molly for Mayor	L	RF	250+	Delton, Judy	Bantam Books
Pee Wee Scouts: Peanut-Butter Pilgrims	L	RF	250+	Delton, Judy	Bantam Books
Pee Wee Scouts: Pedal Power	L	RF	250+	Delton, Judy	Bantam Books
Pee Wee Scouts: Pee Wee Pool Party	L	RF	250+	Delton, Judy	Bantam Books
Pee Wee Scouts: Piles of Pets	L	RF	250+	Delton, Judy	Bantam Books
Pee Wee Scouts: Planet Pee Wee	L	RF	250+	Delton, Judy	Bantam Books
Pee Wee Scouts: Rosy Noses, Freezing Toes	L	RF	250+	Delton, Judy	Bantam Books
Pee Wee Scouts: Send in the Clowns	L	RF	250+	Delton, Judy	Bantam Books
Pee Wee Scouts: Sky Babies	L	RF	250+	Delton, Judy	Bantam Books
Pee Wee Scouts: Sonny's Secret	L	RF	250+	Delton, Judy	Bantam Books
Pee Wee Scouts: Spring Sprouts	L	RF	250+	Delton, Judy	Bantam Books
Pee Wee Scouts: Stage Frightened	L	RF	250+	Delton, Judy	Bantam Books
Pee Wee Scouts: Super Duper Pee Wee!	L	RF	250+	Delton, Judy	Bantam Books
Pee Wee Scouts: Teeny Weeny Zucchinis	L	RF	250+	Delton, Judy	Bantam Books
Pee Wee Scouts: That Mushy Stuff	L	RF	250+	Delton, Judy	Bantam Books
Pee Wee Scouts: The Pee Wee Jubilee	L	RF	250+	Delton, Judy	Bantam Books
Pee Wee Scouts: The Pooped Troop	L	RF	250+	Delton, Judy	Bantam Books
Pee Wee Scouts: Trash Bash	L	RF	250+	Delton, Judy	Bantam Books
Pee Wee Scouts: Tricks and Treats	L	RF	250+	Delton, Judy	Bantam Books
Pee Wee Scouts: Wild, Wild West	L	RF	250+	Delton, Judy	Bantam Books
Peek-a-boo	F	F	131	Storyworlds	Heinemann
Peek-a-boo at the Zoo	E	F	49	New Reader Series	Bungalo Books
Peekaboo School Is Cool	J	F	158	Dominie Readers	Pearson Learning Group
Peeking Prairie Dogs	K	I	372	Pull Ahead Books	Lerner Publishing Group
Peeled	T	RF	250+	Bauer, Joan	Speak
Peep!	E	RF	97	Luthardt, Kevin	Peachtree
Peep!: A Little Book About Taking a Leap	I	F	108	Van Lieshout, Maria	Feiwel and Friends
Peepers	N	RF	250+	Bunting, Eve	Harcourt, Inc.
Peering into Darkness	S	I	250+	Reading Expeditions	National Geographic
Pee-Wee's Tale	O	F	250+	Hurwitz, Johanna	Chronicle Books
Pegasus	M	RF	250+	PM Extensions	Rigby
Peggy's Letters	O	HF	250+	Orca Young Readers	Orca Books
Peggy's Pickles	I	RF	269	Windows on Literacy	National Geographic
Peg-leg Pete Gets the Blues	L	F	250+	The Rowland Reading Program Libary	Rowland Reading Foundation
Pele	H	B	36	Canizares, Susan; Berger, Samantha	Scholastic
Pelicans, Cormorants, and Their Kin	T	I	250+	Animals in Order	Franklin Watts
Pemba's Song: A Ghost Story	Y	F	250+	Nelson, Marilyn & Hegamin, Tonya C.	Scholastic
Pen and a Painting, A	S	TL	1444	Leveled Readers	Houghton Mifflin Harcourt
Pen and a Painting, A	S	TL	1444	Leveled Readers/CA	Houghton Mifflin Harcourt
Pen and a Painting, A	S	TL	1444	Leveled Readers/TX	Houghton Mifflin Harcourt
Pen is Mightier Than the Sword, The	Q	RF	250+	Mazer, Anne	Scholastic
Pen Pals	D	RF	92	Bookshop	Mondo Publishing
Pen Pals	K	RF	589	Leveled Literacy Intervention/ Blue System	Heinemann
Pen Pals	J	RF	250+	On Our Way to English	Rigby
Penalty, The	Z+	F	250+	Peet, Mal	Candlewick Press
Pencil, The	N	F	250+	Ahlberg, Allan	Candlewick Press

* Collection of short stories   # Graphic text
^ Mature content with lower level text demands

Organized Alphabetically by Title   **593**
Storable Database at www.fountasandpinnellleveledbooks.com

TITLE	LEVEL	GENRE	WORD COUNT	AUTHOR / SERIES	PUBLISHER / DISTRIBUTOR
Pencil, The	B	I	97	PM Starters	Rigby
Penderwicks at Point Mouette, The	T	RF	250+	Birdsall, Jeanne	Alfred A. Knopf
Penderwicks, The: A Summer Tale of Four Sisters, Two Rabbits, and a Very Interesting Boy	T	RF	250+	Birdsall, Jane	Yearling Books
Penelope and Pip Build a Prose Poem	N	RF	1100	Poetry Builders	Norwood House Press
Penguin and the Pea, The	M	TL	250+	Perlman, Janet	Scholastic
Penguin Chick Grows Up, A	K	I	744	Baby Animals	Carolrhoda Books
Penguin Chick, The	I	I	105	Windows on Literacy	National Geographic
Penguin Family, The	J	I	301	Leveled Readers	Houghton Mifflin Harcourt
Penguin Lady, The	K	F	443	Cole, Carol A.	Sylvan Dell Publishing
Penguin Parents	P	I	250+	Explorer Books-Pathfinder	National Geographic
Penguin Parents	P	I	250+	Explorer Books-Pioneer	National Geographic
Penguin Pete	L	F	250+	Pfister, Marcus	North-South Books
Penguin Rescue	L	RF	250+	PM Story Books	Rigby
Penguin, The	O	I	250+	Crewe, Sabrina	Steck-Vaughn
Penguins	F	I	123	Bonnell, Kris/About	Reading Reading Books
Penguins	O	I	1696	Early Bird Nature Books	Lerner Publishing Group
Penguins	O	I	250+	First Reports	Compass Point Books
Penguins	O	I	250+	Holmes, Kevin J.	Red Brick Learning
Penguins	J	I	311	Leveled Readers	Houghton Mifflin Harcourt
Penguins	J	I	311	Leveled Readers/CA	Houghton Mifflin Harcourt
Penguins	J	I	311	Leveled Readers/TX	Houghton Mifflin Harcourt
Penguins	H	I	106	Polar Animals	Capstone Press
Penguins	L	I	250+	Reed, Janet	Scholastic
Penguins	D	I	250+	Rosen Real Readers	Rosen Publishing Group
Penguins	K	I	265	Take Two Books	Wright Group/McGraw Hill
Penguins	H	I	109	Under the Sea	Capstone Press
Penguins	O	I	250+	Woolley, M.; Pigdon, K.	Mondo Publishing
Penguins Are Waterbirds	K	I	250+	Bookshop	Mondo Publishing
Penguin's Chicks	D	I	38	Pacific Literacy	Pacific Learning
Penguin's Chicks	E	I	38	Pacific Literacy	Pacific Learning
Penguin's Life, A	F	I	130	Watch It Grow	Heinemann Library
Penguins of the Galápagos	P	I	250+	Young Readers' Series	Barron's Educational
Penguins on Parade	O	F	250+	Little Celebrations	Pearson Learning Group
Penguins On Parade	P	I	1593	Reading Street	Pearson
Penguins on the Go	D	I	24	Shutterbug Books	Steck-Vaughn
Penguins!	N	I	250+	Gibbons, Gail	Holiday House
Penina Levine Is a Potato Pancake	Q	RF	250+	O'Connell, Rebecca	Roaring Brook Press
Peninsulas	N	I	250+	Earthforms	Capstone Press
Pennies in a Jar	O	HF	250+	Chaconas, Dori	Peachtree
Pennsylvania	T	I	250+	Hello U.S.A.	Lerner Publishing Group
Pennsylvania	Q	I	250+	One Nation	Capstone Press
Pennsylvania	T	I	250+	Theme Sets	National Geographic
Pennsylvania	R	I	250+	This Land Is Your Land	Compass Point Books
Pennsylvania Colony, The	R	I	250+	The American Colonies	Capstone Press
Pennsylvania State Symbols	M	I	105	Larkin, Bruce	Wilbooks
Pennsylvania: Facts and Symbols	O	I	250+	The States and Their Symbols	Capstone Press
Penny and the Punctuation Bee	N	F	250+	Donohue, Moira Rose	Albert Whitman & Co.
Penny Candy	K	I	250+	Early Connections	Benchmark Education
Penny Changes the Day, A	J	RF	250+	Pair-It Books	Steck-Vaughn
Penny from Heaven	T	HF	250+	Holm, Jennifer L.	Yearling Books
Penny Hen	J	F	359	Let's Read Together	Kane Press
Penny Pulls the Plug	J	F	407	Rigby Gigglers	Rigby
Penny the Pony Fairy: Rainbow Magic	L	F	250+	Meadows, Daisy	Scholastic

* Collection of short stories   # Graphic text
^ Mature content with lower level text demands

TITLE	LEVEL	GENRE	WORD COUNT	AUTHOR / SERIES	PUBLISHER / DISTRIBUTOR
Penny's Plane	B	RF	30	Gear Up!	Wright Group/McGraw Hill
Pentagon	C	I	33	Shapes	Lerner Publishing Group
People and Pets	L	I	250+	Trackers	Pacific Learning
People and Places	R	I	250+	Rigby Focus	Rigby
People and Places	H	I	240	Yellow Umbrella Books	Red Brick Learning
People and the Environment	I	I	214	Ecology	Lerner Publishing Group
People and the Sea	Q	I	250+	Go Facts Science	Newbridge
People Are Living Things	K	I	250+	Home Connection Collection	Rigby
People Are Working	E	I	71	Pacific Literacy	Pacific Learning
People at Work	J	I	250+	Momentum Literacy Program	Troll Associates
People Build Dams	F	I	46	Windows on Literacy	National Geographic
People Can Build	E	I	46	Sunshine	Wright Group/McGraw Hill
People Change the Land	H	I	222	Yellow Umbrella Books	Red Brick Learning
*People Could Fly, American Black Folktales	X	TL	250+	Hamilton, Virginia	Alfred A. Knopf
People Dance	E	I	46	Wonder World	Wright Group/McGraw Hill
People Do Silly Things	F	RF	119	Worthington, Lisa & Moon, Susan	Kaeden Books
People from the Past	R	I	250+	Explorers	Wright Group/McGraw Hill
People Go Up	A	I	18	Windows on Literacy	National Geographic
People in Fall	F	I	86	All About Fall	Capstone Press
People in My Town	A	I	36	Rosen Real Readers	Rosen Publishing Group
People in Stories	G	RF	114	Breakthrough	Longman Group UK
People in the Rain Forest	O	I	250+	Pirotta, Saviour	Steck-Vaughn
People in the Town	D	I	91	Vocabulary Readers	Houghton Mifflin Harcourt
People in the Town	D	I	91	Vocabulary Readers/CA	Houghton Mifflin Harcourt
People in the Town	D	I	91	Vocabulary Readers/TX	Houghton Mifflin Harcourt
People in Winter	H	I	96	All About Winter	Capstone Press
People Live Here	F	I	42	Windows on Literacy	National Geographic
People Live in the Desert	J	I	163	Windows on Literacy	National Geographic
People Movers: Machines That Move People	G	I	138	Factivity Series	Pearson Learning Group
*People of Action	Q	I	250+	Literacy by Design	Rigby
People of the Amazon Rain Forest	V	I	2381	Reading Street	Pearson
People of the Amazon Rain Forest, The	W	I	250+	Explore More	Wright Group/McGraw Hill
People of the American Revolution	T	B	250+	Navigators Social Studies Series	Benchmark Education
People of the Breaking Day	T	I	250+	Sewall, Marcia	Aladdin Paperbacks
People of the Ice Age	K	I	286	Rigby Focus	Rigby
People of the Pacific Rim	S	I	250+	InfoQuest	Rigby
People of the Past	Q	I	250+	Explorer Books-Pathfinder	National Geographic
People of the Past	P	I	250+	Explorer Books-Pioneer	National Geographic
People of the Past	W	I	250+	InfoQuest	Rigby
People on the Beach	F	RF	87	Carousel Readers	Pearson Learning Group
People on the Move	Q	I	250+	iOpeners	Pearson Learning Group
People Parts	B	I	42	Independent Readers Science	Houghton Mifflin Harcourt
People Patterns	K	I	348	Finding Patterns	Capstone Press
People Planet, The	V	I	250+	Orbit Chapter Books	Pacific Learning
People Power: Buying and Selling in the United States	U	I	250+	In Step Readers	Rigby
People Power: Buying and Selling in the United States	U	I	250+	Literacy By Design	Rigby
People Say Hello	C	I	37	Learn to Read	Creative Teaching Press
People Use Tools	A	I	24	Early Connections	Benchmark Education
People Who Help Us	D	I	62	Foundations	Wright Group/McGraw Hill
People Who Keep You Safe	C	I	84	Careers Series	Benchmark Education
People Who Lead Us	I	I	155	Windows on Literacy	National Geographic

* Collection of short stories   # Graphic text
^ Mature content with lower level text demands

Organized Alphabetically by Title   **595**
Storable Database at www.fountasandpinnellleveledbooks.com

TITLE	LEVEL	GENRE	WORD COUNT	AUTHOR / SERIES	PUBLISHER / DISTRIBUTOR
People Who Save Animals	E	I	143	Careers Series	Benchmark Education
People Who Traveled with Lewis and Clark, The	N	B	555	Leveled Readers Social Studies	Houghton Mifflin Harcourt
People Who Use Magnets at Work	H	I	148	Early Connections	Benchmark Education
People Work	G	I	232	Yellow Umbrella Books	Red Brick Learning
People Work at the Supermarket	E	I	77	Windows on Literacy	National Geographic
People Work in Our Community	I	I	190	Early Explorers	Benchmark Education
People, Plants, and Animals	H	I	154	InfoTrek	ETA/Cuisenaire
People's President, The	R	B	1372	Leveled Readers	Houghton Mifflin Harcourt
People's President, The	R	B	1372	Leveled Readers/CA	Houghton Mifflin Harcourt
People's President, The	R	B	1372	Leveled Readers/TX	Houghton Mifflin Harcourt
Pepins and Their Problems, The	V	F	250+	Horvath, Polly	Square Fish
Pepita Talks Twice	L	RF	250+	Lachtman, Ofelia Dumas	Pinata Publishing
Pepper Goes to School	H	RF	125	Foundations	Wright Group/McGraw Hill
Pepper Sees Me	A	I	28	Little Books for Early Readers	University of Maine
Pepperland	Z	RF	250+	Delaney, Mark	Peachtree
Peppers	D	I	32	Rise & Shine	Hampton Brown
Pepper's Adventure	H	RF	250+	PM Story Books	Rigby
Perchance to Dream	Z	F	250+	Mantchev, Lisa	Feiwel and Friends
Percival	I	RF	303	Literacy 2000	Rigby
Percy Gets Upset	L	F	314	I See I Learn	Charlesbridge
Percy Lavon Julian: Pioneering Chemist	W	B	250+	Signature Lives	Compass Point Books
Percy Plays It Safe	K	F	209	I See I Learn	Charlesbridge
Perfect	G	RF	225	The Rowland Reading Program Library	Rowland Reading Foundation
Perfect Cat-Sitter, The	N	RF	250+	Nagda, Ann Whitehead	Holiday House
Perfect Chemistry	Z+	RF	250+	Elkeles, Simone	Walker & Company
Perfect Dog, A	J	F	594	Pickles the Dog Series	Pioneer Valley
Perfect Instrument, The	O	RF	786	Leveled Readers	Houghton Mifflin Harcourt
Perfect Kite Weather	C	I	56	Vocabulary Readers	Houghton Mifflin Harcourt
Perfect Monster, The	L	F	250+	I Am Reading	Kingfisher
Perfect Paper	K	I	250+	Rigby Literacy	Rigby
Perfect Paper Planes	K	RF	250+	PM Plus Story Books	Rigby
Perfect Patterns	P	I	250+	WorldScapes	ETA/Cuisenaire
Perfect Person, The	Q	SF	250+	Bookweb	Rigby
Perfect Pet, The	Q	F	250+	Bookweb	Rigby
Perfect Pet, The	C	RF	30	Instant Readers	Harcourt School Publishers
Perfect Pet, The	C	RF	29	Rigby Rocket	Rigby
Perfect Pets	H	I	218	Red Rocket Readers	Flying Start Books
Perfect Picnic, The	G	F	271	Leveled Literacy Intervention/ Blue System	Heinemann
Perfect Pirate's Present, The	M	F	250+	Tristars	Richard C. Owen
Perfect Pizza, The	I	RF	250+	Rigby Star	Rigby
Perfect Pizza, The	G	RF	167	Windows on Literacy	National Geographic
Perfect Place to Paint, The	K	I	383	Leveled Readers	Houghton Mifflin Harcourt
Perfect Place to Paint, The	K	I	383	Leveled Readers/CA	Houghton Mifflin Harcourt
Perfect Place, The	H	RF	157	Pair-It Turn and Learn	Steck-Vaughn
Perfect Pony, A	O	RF	250+	Szymanski, Lois	Avon Books
Perfect Present, The	L	RF	250+	Lighthouse	Ginn & Co.
Perfect Pretzels	L	I	232	Twig	Wright Group/McGraw Hill
Perfect Thanksgiving, The	K	RF	250+	Spinelli, Eileen	Square Fish
Perfect the Pig	L	F	250+	Jeschke, Susan	Scholastic
Perfectly Arugula	L	F	250+	Dillard, Sarah	Sterling Publishing
Peril in the Bessledorf Parachute Factory	U	RF	250+	Naylor, Phyllis Reynolds	Atheneum Books
Peril on the Sea	W	HF	250+	Cadnum, Michael	Farrar, Straus, & Giroux

* Collection of short stories   # Graphic text
^ Mature content with lower level text demands

TITLE	LEVEL	GENRE	WORD COUNT	AUTHOR / SERIES	PUBLISHER / DISTRIBUTOR
Perilous Passage	S	HF	1273	Leveled Readers	Houghton Mifflin Harcourt
Perilous Passage	S	HF	1273	Leveled Readers/CA	Houghton Mifflin Harcourt
Perilous Passage	S	HF	1273	Leveled Readers/TX	Houghton Mifflin Harcourt
Perilous Road, The	U	HF	250+	Steele, William	Scholastic
*Period Pieces: Stories for Girls	Z+	RF	250+	Deak, Erzsi & Litchman, Kristin Embry	HarperCollins
Periwinkle and the Cave of Courage: The Fairy Chronicles	Q	F	12100	Sweet, J.H.	Sourcebooks
Perks of Being a Wallflower, The	Z+	RF	250+	Chbosky, Jan	Simon & Schuster
Perky Otter	J	F	430	Let's Read Together	Kane Press
Perla's Family	H	RF	207	Reading Safari	Mondo Publishing
Perlitas	I	RF	98	Books for Young Learners	Richard C. Owen
Perri Plays Possum	M	F	1276	Leveled Readers	Houghton Mifflin Harcourt
Perri Plays Possum	M	F	1276	Leveled Readers/CA	Houghton Mifflin Harcourt
Perri Plays Possum	M	F	1276	Leveled Readers/TX	Houghton Mifflin Harcourt
Perseus and Medusa	V	TL	250+	Leveled Readers Language Support	Houghton Mifflin Harcourt
#Perseus: The Hunt for Medusa's Head	W	TL	3133	Graphic Myths and Legends	Lerner Publishing Group
Persian Cats	R	I	250+	All About Cats	Capstone Press
Persian Cats	I	I	122	Cats	Capstone Press
Persians Are the Best!	Q	I	1460	The Best Cats Ever	Lerner Publishing Group
Person from Planet X, The	H	F	250+	Sunshine	Wright Group/McGraw Hill
Personality Potion, The	O	RF	250+	High-Fliers	Pacific Learning
Perspective: Discover the Theory and Techniques of Perspective, From the Renaissance to Pop Art	Z	I	250+	Eyewitness Books	DK Publishing
Peru	O	I	250+	Countries of the World	Red Brick Learning
Peru	P	I	250+	Country Explorers	Lerner Publishing Group
Peru: Civilizations Past to Present	S	I	250+	Reading Expeditions	National Geographic
Peru's Mountains	Q	I	250+	Theme Sets	National Geographic
Pesky Fly, The	A	F	35	Springboard	Wright Group/McGraw Hill
Pesky Paua, The	H	F	267	Book Bank	Wright Group/McGraw Hill
Pests and Plagues	U	I	250+	Story Surfers	ETA/Cuisenaire
Pet Care	E	I	35	Chessen, Betsey	Scholastic
Pet Costume Party	G	RF	283	Stone Arch Readers	Stone Arch Books
Pet Day	F	RF	92	Home Connection Collection	Rigby
Pet Day	G	RF	175	Instant Readers	Harcourt School Publishers
Pet Day	E	F	70	Sun Sprouts	ETA/Cuisenaire
Pet Day at School	I	RF	198	City Kids	Rigby
Pet Day at School	E	I	103	Story Steps	Rigby
Pet Dogs and Working Dogs	E	I	99	Springboard	Wright Group/McGraw Hill
Pet Dreams	K	F	410	Leveled Readers	Houghton Mifflin Harcourt
Pet Fish	F	I	98	Classroom Pets	Lerner Publishing Group
Pet for Me, A	E	RF	152	Alphakids	Sundance
Pet for Me, A	C	RF	73	Early Emergent	Pioneer Valley
Pet for Pat, A	D	RF	45	Rookie Readers	Children's Press
Pet for Sol, A	N	RF	619	Leveled Readers	Houghton Mifflin Harcourt
Pet for You, A	K	I	531	Pair-It Books	Steck-Vaughn
Pet Frog	F	I	99	Classroom Pets	Lerner Publishing Group
Pet Guinea Pig	F	I	96	Classroom Pets	Lerner Publishing Group
Pet Hamster	F	I	93	Classroom Pets	Lerner Publishing Group
Pet Hermit Crab	F	I	112	Classroom Pets	Lerner Publishing Group
Pet Heroes	N	I	250+	Corse, Nicole	Scholastic
Pet Hospital, The	E	RF	121	The Rowland Reading Program Library	Rowland Reading Foundation

Pet Parade	O	RF	250+	Giff, Patricia Reilly	Bantam Books
Pet Parade	C	F	33	Literacy 2000	Rigby
Pet Peeves	M	RF	250+	Social Studies Connects	Kane Press
Pet Perspectives	U	I	250+	Sails	Rigby
Pet Pictures	J	I	181	Vocabulary Readers	Houghton Mifflin Harcourt
Pet Rabbits	I	I	365	Vocabulary Readers/TX	Houghton Mifflin Harcourt
Pet Riddles and Jokes	I	F	154	Instant Readers	Harcourt School Publishers
Pet Shop	D	F	167	Story Box	Wright Group/McGraw Hill
Pet Shop Problem, A	M	F	250+	Tristars	Richard C. Owen
Pet Shop, The	C	RF	32	Oxford Reading Tree	Oxford University Press
Pet Show!	K	RF	250+	Keats, Ezra Jack	Aladdin
Pet Show, The	I	RF	263	Dominie Math Series	Pearson Publishing Group
Pet Show, The	A	I	25	Leveled Readers	Houghton Mifflin Harcourt
Pet Show, The	A	I	25	Leveled Readers/CA	Houghton Mifflin Harcourt
Pet Sitters Plus Five	L	RF	250+	Springstubb, Tricia	Scholastic
Pet Store, The	A	I	49	Bookshop	Mondo Publishing
Pet Store, The	A	I	32	Leveled Literacy Intervention/ Orange System	Heinemann
Pet Store, The	A	RF	32	On Our Way to English	Rigby
Pet Tarantula, The	I	I	208	Storyteller Nonfiction	Wright Group/McGraw Hill
Pet That Fits, A	M	RF	404	Leveled Readers/TX	Houghton Mifflin Harcourt
Pet That I Want, The	E	F	57	Packard, Mary	Scholastic
Pet Tricks	G	RF	208	In Step Readers	Rigby
Pet Vet	N	I	250+	Pacific Literacy	Pacific Learning
Pet Vet, The	E	RF	101	Real Kids Readers	Millbrook Press
Pet Your Pet	H	F	93	Early Readers	Compass Point Books
Petal's Problems: The Sisters 8	Q	F	250+	Baratz-Logsted, Lauren	Sandpiper Books
Petalwink Learns to Fly	L	F	1013	Larsen, Angela Sage	Three Trees, Inc.
*Pete and the Brownies, Looking for Pete, Pete's Hideout	K	RF	459	Easy-for-Me Reading	Child 1st Publications
Pete Discovers Gravity	M	RF	947	Early Connections	Benchmark Education
Pete for President	M	RF	250+	Social Studies Connects	Kane Press
Pete Little	G	F	222	PM Story Books	Rigby
Pete Paints a Picture	C	RF	87	Story Steps	Rigby
Pete Penguin and the Bullies	L	F	837	Arctic Adventures	Pioneer Valley
Pete the Parakeet	F	F	133	First Start	Troll Associates
Peter and Polly Make a Healthy Sandwich	D	F	63	Joy Starters	Pearson Learning Group
Peter and Polly Make Bookmarks	E	F	80	Joy Starters	Pearson Learning Group
Peter and Polly Make Faces	D	F	66	Joy Starters	Pearson Learning Group
Peter and the North Wind	L	TL	250+	Littledale, Freya	Scholastic
Peter and the Pennytree	G	F	119	First Start	Troll Associates
Peter and the Starcatchers	X	F	250+	Barry, Dave & Pearson, Ridley	Hyperion
Peter and the Wolf	J	TL	871	Big Cat	Pacific Learning
Peter and the Wolf	J	TL	250+	PM Plus Story Books	Rigby
Peter Pan	X	F	250+	Barrie, J. M.	Aladdin
Peter Peter Picks a Pumpkin House	K	F	250+	Graham, Christine	Henry Holt & Co.
Peter Pig's House	E	F	67	Joy Starters	Pearson Learning Group
Peter Piper	E	TL	32	Jumbled Tumbled Tales & Rhymes	Rigby
Peter Salem: Hero of the Revolution	T	B	1096	Independent Readers Social Studies	Houghton Mifflin Harcourt
Peter Stuyvesant: New Amsterdam and the Origins of New York	W	B	250+	The Library of American Lives and Times	Rosen Publishing Group
Peter Tchaikovsky	R	B	250+	Venezia, Mike	Children's Press
Peter the Pumpkin-Eater	M	RF	250+	Action Packs	Rigby

* Collection of short stories   # Graphic text
^ Mature content with lower level text demands

PQ

TITLE	LEVEL	GENRE	WORD COUNT	AUTHOR / SERIES	PUBLISHER / DISTRIBUTOR
Peter's Chair	J	RF	250+	Keats, Ezra Jack	HarperTrophy
Peter's Dream	I	F	186	Start to Read	School Zone
Peter's Harvest	Q	RF	1085	Leveled Readers	Houghton Mifflin Harcourt
Peter's Move	H	RF	224	Little Readers	Houghton Mifflin Harcourt
Peter's Painting	F	F	147	Bookshop	Mondo Publishing
Peter's Treasure Hunt	I	RF	280	Springboard	Wright Group/McGraw Hill
Pete's a Pizza	K	RF	248	Steig, William	Scholastic
Pete's Bad Day	G	RF	164	Ready Readers	Pearson Learning Group
Pete's New Shoes	G	RF	91	Literacy 2000	Rigby
Pete's Peacock	F	RF	89	Dominie Phonics Reader	Pearson Learning Group
Pete's Secret Plan	J	F	342	Take Two Books	Wright Group/McGraw Hill
Pete's Story	L	F	250+	Literacy 2000	Rigby
Pete's Tickets	D	RF	65	Seedlings	Continental Press
Petey	O	SF	250+	High-Fliers	Pacific Learning
Pets	P	I	250+	Animals Are Amazing	Carus Publishing Company
Pets	D	I	64	Explorations	Eleanor Curtain Publishing
Pets	D	I	64	Explorations	Okapi Educational Materials
Pets	L	I	250+	I Wonder Why	Kingfisher
Pets	C	RF	88	Leveled Literacy Intervention/ Green System	Heinemann
Pets	F	RF	56	Literacy 2000	Rigby
Pets	B	I	66	Little Readers	Houghton Mifflin Harcourt
Pets	J	I	196	Nonfiction Set 7	Literacy Footprints
Pets	J	F	90	Pacific Literacy	Pacific Learning
Pets	E	I	63	Phonetic Connections	Benchmark Education
Pets	A	I	33	PM Starters	Rigby
Pets	B	I	31	Vocabulary Readers	Houghton Mifflin Harcourt
Pets at School	A	I	33	Leveled Readers	Houghton Mifflin Harcourt
Pets at School	A	I	33	Leveled Readers/CA	Houghton Mifflin Harcourt
Pet's Best Pal, A	G	I	162	The Rowland Reading Program Library	Rowland Reading Foundation
Pets for the Twins	E	RF	101	Leveled Readers	Houghton Mifflin Harcourt
Pets for Us	D	I	69	Bonnell, Kris	Reading Reading Books
Pets from the Rain Forest	S	I	250+	Explore More	Wright Group/McGraw Hill
Pets in a Jar: Collecting and Caring for Small Wild Animals	W	I	250+	Simon, Seymour	Penguin Group
Pets Lost-and-Found	L	I	250+	Rigby Literacy	Rigby
Pets Need People	M	I	250+	Literacy 2000	Rigby
Pets, The	C	RF	28	Learn to Read	Creative Teaching Press
Pets, The	A	RF	24	Sails	Rigby
Petting Farm, The	E	I	67	Bonnell, Kris	Reading Reading Books
Petting Gilbert	H	F	218	Gilbert the Pig	Pioneer Valley
*Petty Crimes	W	RF	250+	Soto, Gary	Harcourt, Inc.
Peyton Manning	P	B	1570	Amazing Athletes	Lerner Publishing Group
Peyton Manning	U	B	250+	Sports Heroes and Legends	Lerner Publishing Group
Phan's Diary	N	RF	250+	PM Collection	Rigby
Phantom Isles, The	W	F	250+	Alter, Stephen	Bloomsbury Children's Books
Phantom of the Opera	W	F	6230	Oxford Bookworms Library	Oxford University Press
Phantom of the Water Park	Q	F	250+	Wiley & Grampa's Creature Features	Little Brown and Company
Phantom Robber Mystery, The	M	RF	792	Springboard	Wright Group/McGraw Hill
^Phantom Striker, The	S	F	250+	Zucker, Jonny	Stone Arch Books
Phantom Subway, The	O	F	250+	Stilton, Geronimo	Scholastic
Phantom Tollbooth, The	W	F	250+	Juster, Norton	Bantam Books

PQ

TITLE	LEVEL	GENRE	WORD COUNT	AUTHOR / SERIES	PUBLISHER / DISTRIBUTOR
Phantoms Don't Drive Sports Cars	M	F	250+	Dadey, Debbie; Jones, Marcia Thornton	Scholastic
Pharaoh: Life and Afterlife of a God	W	I	250+	Kennett, David	Walker & Company
Pharoh's Secret, The	W	F	250+	Moss, Marissa	Amulet Books
Phases of the Moon	J	I	164	Patterns in Nature	Capstone Press
Pheasant and Kingfisher	L	TL	250+	Bookshop	Mondo Publishing
Pheasant Hunting	S	I	250+	The Great Outdoors	Red Brick Learning
Phenomena: Secrets of the Senses	Z	I	250+	Jackson, Donna M.	Little Brown and Company
Pheonix Suns, The	S	I	4872	Team Spirit	Norwood House Press
Philadelphia 76ers, The	S	I	250+	Team Spirit	Norwood House Press
Philadelphia Phillies, The	S	I	250+	Team Spirit	Norwood House Press
Philadelphia Phillies, The (Revised Edition)	S	I	250+	Team Spirit	Norwood House Press
Philadelphia, 1756	M	I	273	Vocabulary Readers	Houghton Mifflin Harcourt
Philadelphia, 1756	M	I	273	Vocabulary Readers/CA	Houghton Mifflin Harcourt
Philadelphia, 1756	M	I	273	Vocabulary Readers/TX	Houghton Mifflin Harcourt
Philadephia Eagles, The	S	I	5055	Team Spirit	Norwood House Press
Philip Hall Likes Me. I Reckon Maybe.	Y	RF	250+	Greene, Bette	Puffin Books
Philippa and the Dragon	G	F	137	Literacy 2000	Rigby
Philippa Fisher's Fairy Godsister	S	F	250+	Kessler, Liz	Candlewick Press
Philippines	O	I	1482	A Ticket to …	Carolrhoda Books
Philippines	P	I	2013	Country Explorers	Lerner Publishing Group
Philippines, The	O	I	250+	Countries of the World	Red Brick Learning
Phillis Wheatley	S	B	250+	Amazing Americans	Wright Group/McGraw Hill
Phillis Wheatley	U	B	250+	Let Freedom Ring	Red Brick Learning
Phillis Wheatley	T	B	2200	Leveled Readers	Houghton Mifflin Harcourt
Phillis Wheatley	T	B	2200	Leveled Readers/CA	Houghton Mifflin Harcourt
Phillis Wheatley	T	B	2200	Leveled Readers/TX	Houghton Mifflin Harcourt
Phillis Wheatley	Q	B	250+	Primary Source Readers	Teacher Created Materials
Phillis Wheatly: Poet	N	B	250+	Beginning Biographies	Pearson Learning Group
#Philo Farnsworth and the Television	U	B	250+	Inventions and Discovery	Capstone Press
Phineas Gage: A Gruesome but True Story About Brain Science	X	B	250+	Fleischman, John	Houghton Mifflin Harcourt
Phoebe The Spy	R	HF	250+	Griffin, Judith Berry	Scholastic
Phoenix Rising	W	RF	250+	Hesse, Karen	Penguin Group
Photo	Y	I	250+	Boldprint	Steck-Vaughn
Photo Album, The	J	RF	249	In Step Readers	Rigby
Photo Book, The	C	RF	50	PM Story Books	Rigby
Photo Contest, The	O	RF	250+	Leveled Readers Language Support	Houghton Mifflin Harcourt
Photo Time	C	RF	59	PM Plus Story Books	Rigby
Photograph, The	I	F	250+	Popcorn	Sundance
Photographic Memory	O	RF	250+	PM Collection	Rigby
Photographs	M	I	250+	Start with Art	Heinemann Library
Photograpy	R	I	250+	Tristars	Richard C. Owen
Photos Can Fool You!	W	I	250+	Rigby Literacy	Rigby
Photos, Photos	N	I	250+	Wildcats	Wright Group/McGraw Hill
Photosynthesis	W	I	250+	The Heinle Reading Library	Thomson Learning
Phyllis Wheatley: First African-American Poet	N	B	250+	Rookie Biographies	Children's Press
Physics of Flying, The	Z	I	1692	Leveled Readers Science	Houghton Mifflin Harcourt
Physics: Why Matter Matters!	Z	I	250+	Green, Dan	Kingfisher
Piano Recital, The	K	RF	250+	Rigby Literacy	Rigby
Piano, The	V	RF	6070	Oxford Bookworms Library	Oxford University Press
Picasso	S	B	250+	Masterpieces: Artists and Their Works	Red Brick Learning

* Collection of short stories   # Graphic text
^ Mature content with lower level text demands

PQ

TITLE	LEVEL	GENRE	WORD COUNT	AUTHOR / SERIES	PUBLISHER / DISTRIBUTOR
Picasso	R	B	250+	Venezia, Mike	Children's Press
Picasso and Minou	Q	HF	250+	Maltbie, P. I.	Charlesbridge
Pick a Pet	C	RF	40	Little Celebrations	Pearson Learning Group
Pick a Plant!	WB	I	0	Reach	National Geographic
Pick a Pumpkin	I	F	250+	Leveled Readers Language Support	Houghton Mifflin Harcourt
Pick a Pumpkin Mrs. Millie!	L	F	250+	Cox, Judy	Marshall Cavendish
Pick Me	J	F	518	Sun Sprouts	ETA/Cuisenaire
Pick Out a Person	N	I	250+	Trackers	Pacific Learning
Pick Up Nick!	H	RF	219	Ready Readers	Pearson Learning Group
Picked for the Team	L	RF	709	PM Collection	Rigby
Picking a Pet	I	I	224	Sunshine	Wright Group/McGraw Hill
Picking a Pumpkin	D	RF	49	Bonnell, Kris	Reading Reading Books
Picking Apples	E	RF	128	Developing Books	Pioneer Valley
Picking Apples	F	I	53	Pebble Books	Capstone Press
Picking Apples and Pumpkins	L	I	250+	Hutchings, Amy & Richard	Scholastic
Picking Blackberries	G	RF	171	Adams, Lorraine & Bruvold, Lynn	Eaglecrest Books
Picking Flowers	A	I	35	Adams, Lorraine & Bruvold, Lynn	Eaglecrest Books
Picking Up Papers	K	RF	161	City Kids	Rigby
Pickle Puss	L	RF	250+	Giff, Patricia Reilly	Bantam Books
Pickles and the Hole	I	F	517	Pickles the Dog Series	Pioneer Valley
Pickles and the Very Large Fly	J	RF	504	PM Stars Bridge Books	Rigby
Pickles Are Great	B	RF	25	Bonnell, Kris	Reading Reading Books
Pickles Gets Lost	G	RF	154	Pickles the Dog Series	Pioneer Valley
Pickles Goes to School	E	RF	90	Pickles the Dog Series	Pioneer Valley
Pickles Helps Out	F	RF	160	Pickles the Dog Series	Pioneer Valley
Pickles in My Soup	F	F	88	Rookie Reader	Children's Press
Pickup Trucks	D	I	60	Bonnell, Kris/About	Reading Reading Books
Pickup Trucks	W	I	7224	Motor Mania	Lerner Publishing Group
Pickup Trucks	L	I	392	Pull Ahead Books	Lerner Publishing Group
Pickup Trucks on the Move	K	I	294	Lightning Bolt Books	Lerner Publishing Group
Picky Eater, The	R	RF	1238	Leveled Readers	Houghton Mifflin Harcourt
Picky Eater, The	R	RF	1238	Leveled Readers/CA	Houghton Mifflin Harcourt
Picky Eater, The	R	RF	1238	Leveled Readers/TX	Houghton Mifflin Harcourt
Picky Peggy	L	RF	1416	Science Solves It!	Kane Press
Picky Prince, The	J	F	250+	Rigby Literacy	Rigby
Picnic	C	F	28	Brand New Readers	Candlewick Press
Picnic	WB	RF	0	McCully, Emily Arnold	Harper & Row
Picnic at Camp Shalom	L	RF	250+	Jules, Jacqueline	Kar-Ben Publishing
Picnic Boat, The	G	RF	210	PM Plus Story Books	Rigby
Picnic for Two, A	C	I	71	PM Math Readers	Rigby
Picnic in October, A	P	RF	250+	Bunting, Eve	Harcourt, Inc.
Picnic in the Rain, A	D	F	158	Leveled Literacy Intervention/Blue System	Heinemann
Picnic in the Sand, A	LB	RF	14	Ready Readers	Pearson Learning Group
Picnic in the Sky, The	D	F	80	Foundations	Wright Group/McGraw Hill
Picnic Lunch, A	F	F	120	Little Dinosaur	Literacy Footprints
Picnic on the Sidewalk	F	RF	108	Seedlings	Continental Press
Picnic Plans	E	RF	144	InfoTrek	ETA/Cuisenaire
Picnic Tea	I	RF	224	Stepping Stones	Nelson/Michaels Assoc.
Picnic Tree, The	H	RF	201	PM Photo Stories	Rigby
Picnic Weather	J	RF	282	Gear Up!	Wright Group/McGraw Hill
Picnic, The	E	RF	89	Adams, Lorraine & Bruvold, Lynn	Eaglecrest Books
Picnic, The	LB	I	14	Avenues	Hampton Brown

* Collection of short stories   # Graphic text
^ Mature content with lower level text demands

TITLE	LEVEL	GENRE	WORD COUNT	AUTHOR / SERIES	PUBLISHER / DISTRIBUTOR
Picnic, The	LB	RF	18	Book Bank	Wright Group/McGraw Hill
Picnic, The	LB	RF	48	First Stories	Pacific Learning
Picnic, The	B	F	38	Gear Up!	Wright Group/McGraw Hill
Picnic, The	D	RF	96	Handprints C, Set 1	Educators Publishing Service
Picnic, The	G	RF	151	Home Connection Collection	Rigby
Picnic, The	A	F	32	Leveled Literacy Intervention/ Green System	Heinemann
Picnic, The	C	RF	48	Teacher's Choice Series	Pearson Learning Group
Picnic, The	F	RF	122	Wonder World	Wright Group/McGraw Hill
Pictographs	K	I	250+	Making Graphs	Capstone Press
Picture Book of Abraham Lincoln, A	M	B	250+	Adler, David A.	Holiday House
Picture Book of Amelia Earhart, A	M	B	250+	Adler, David A.	Holiday House
Picture Book of Anne Frank, A	R	B	250+	Adler, David A.	Holiday House
Picture Book of Benjamin Franklin, A	M	B	250+	Adler, David A.	Holiday House
Picture Book of Christopher Columbus, A	M	B	250+	Adler, David A.	Holiday House
Picture Book of Davy Crockett, A	M	B	250+	Adler, David A.	Holiday House
Picture Book of Eleanor Roosevelt, A	N	B	250+	Adler, David A.	Holiday House
Picture Book of Florence Nightingale, A	M	B	250+	Adler, David A.	Holiday House
Picture Book of Frederick Douglass, A	N	B	250+	Adler, David A.	Holiday House
Picture Book of George Washington Carver, A	O	B	250+	Adler, David A.	Holiday House
Picture Book of George Washington, A	N	B	250+	Adler, David A.	Holiday House
Picture Book of Harriet Tubman, A	P	B	250+	Adler, David A.	Holiday House
Picture Book of Helen Keller, A	M	B	250+	Adler, David A.	Holiday House
Picture Book of Jackie Robinson, A	M	B	250+	Adler, David A.	Holiday House
Picture Book of Jesse Owens, A	N	B	250+	Adler, David A.	Holiday House
Picture Book of John F. Kennedy, A	N	B	250+	Adler, David A.	Holiday House
Picture Book of John Hancock, A	Q	B	250+	Adler, David A. & Adler, Michael S.	Holiday House
Picture Book of Louis Braille, A	M	B	250+	Adler, David A.	Holiday House
Picture Book of Martin Luther King, Jr., A	M	B	250+	Adler, David A.	Holiday House
Picture Book of Patrick Henry, A	N	B	250+	Adler, David A.	Holiday House
Picture Book of Paul Revere, A	M	B	250+	Adler, David A.	Holiday House
Picture Book of Robert E. Lee, A	N	B	250+	Adler, David A.	Holiday House
Picture Book of Rosa Parks, A	P	B	250+	Adler, David A.	Holiday House
Picture Book of Sacagawea, A	P	B	250+	Adler, David A.	Holiday House
Picture Book of Samuel Adams, A	Q	B	250+	Adler, David A. & Adler, Michael S.	Holiday House
Picture Book of Simon Bolivar, A	Q	B	250+	Adler, David A.	Bantam Books
Picture Book of Sitting Bull, A	M	B	250+	Adler, David A.	Holiday House
Picture Book of Sojourner Truth, A	N	B	250+	Adler, David A.	Holiday House
Picture Book of Thomas Alva Edison, A	M	B	250+	Adler, David A.	Holiday House
Picture Book of Thomas Alva Edison, A	M	B	1302	Avenues	Hampton Brown
Picture Book of Thomas Jefferson, A	N	B	250+	Adler, David A.	Holiday House
Picture Book of Thurgood Marshall, A	N	B	250+	Adler, David A.	Holiday House
Picture Bride	Z+	HF	250+	Edge	Hampton Brown
Picture for Harold's Room, A	H	F	550	Johnson, Crockett	HarperCollins
Picture for Marc, A	N	HF	250+	Kimmel, Eric A.	Random House
Picture Numbers	V	I	250+	WorldScapes	ETA/Cuisenaire
Picture of Dorian Gray, The	Y	F	10245	Oxford Bookworms Library	Oxford University Press
Picture of Freedom, A	T	HF	250+	McKissack, Patricia C.	Scholastic
Picture Perfect	Z	RF	250+	Alphin, Elaine Marie	Carolrhoda Books
Picture Perfect Word Book	LB	I	250+	Avenues	Hampton Brown
Picture the Dead	Z	HF	250+	Griffin, Adele & Brown, Lisa	Sourcebooks

* Collection of short stories   # Graphic text
^ Mature content with lower level text demands

TITLE	LEVEL	GENRE	WORD COUNT	AUTHOR / SERIES	PUBLISHER / DISTRIBUTOR
Picture This!	U	I	250+	Bookweb	Rigby
Picture Tricks	I	I	250+	Phonics Readers Plus	Steck-Vaughn
Picture, A	C	I	58	Storyteller-First Snow	Wright Group/McGraw Hill
Picture-Perfect Pattern, A	L	RF	830	InfoTrek	ETA/Cuisenaire
Pictures	E	RF	76	Teacher's Choice Series	Pearson Learning Group
Pictures in the Sky	P	I	648	Reading Street	Pearson
Pictures of Hollis Woods	V	RF	250+	Giff, Patricia Reilly	Scholastic
Pictures of Hugs	F	RF	230	Leveled Literacy Intervention/ Green System	Heinemann
Pictures of My Family	D	I	49	Gear Up!	Wright Group/McGraw Hill
Pictures to Words: The Origins of Writing	V	I	2032	Independent Readers Social Studies	Houghton Mifflin Harcourt
Pie	Q	HF	250+	Weeks, Sarah	Scholastic
Pie Day	H	F	250+	Phonics and Friends	Hampton Brown
Pie Graphs	K	I	411	Making Graphs	Capstone Press
Pie Magic	N	F	250+	Cornell, Laura	Beech Tree Books
Pie Thief, A: a play	J	F	250+	Story Box	Wright Group/McGraw Hill
Pie, The	F	RF	117	Developing Books, Set 1	Pioneer Valley
Piece of Cake	I	I	250+	Home Connection Collection	Rigby
Pieces of Another World	M	RF	1128	Rockliff, Mara	Sylvan Dell Publishing
Pied Piper	L	TL	250+	Hunia, Fran	Ladybird Books
Pied Piper of Hamelin, The	K	TL	250+	Hautzig, Deborah	Random House
Pied Piper of Hamelin, The	L	TL	250+	Storybook Classics	Picture Window Books
Pied Piper, The	I	TL	250+	Storyworlds	Heinemann
Pied Piper, The	M	TL	585	Sunshine	Wright Group/McGraw Hill
Pierre	K	RF	490	Sendak, Maurice	Scholastic
Pierre August Renoir	R	B	250+	Venezia, Mike	Children's Press
Pig	B	I	34	Zoozoo-Animal World	Cavallo Publishing
Pig in a Wig, The	L	F	250+	MacDonald, Alan	Peachtree
Pig in the Spigot, The	N	F	250+	Wilbur, Richard	Harcourt, Inc.
Pig on the Swing	G	F	242	Reading Safari	Mondo Publishing
Pig Pickin' (Moose and Hildy)	L	F	250+	Greene, Stephanie	Marshall Cavendish
Pig Scrolls, The	X	F	250+	Shipton, Paul	Candlewick Press
Pig That Learned to Jig, The	I	F	140	Wonder World	Wright Group/McGraw Hill
Pig Who Saved the World, The	X	F	250+	Shipton, Paul	Candlewick Press
Pig William's Midnight Walk	H	F	354	Book Bank	Wright Group/McGraw Hill
Pig's New House	E	F	222	Leveled Literacy Intervention/ Blue System	Heinemann
^Pigboy	T	RF	250+	Orca Currents	Orca Books
Pig-Boy: A Trickster Tale from Hawai'i	N	TL	250+	McDermott, Gerald	Houghton Mifflin Harcourt
Pigeon Feathers	L	TL	250+	Books for Young Learners	Richard C. Owen
Pigeon Has Feelings, Too!, The	G	F	85	Willems, Mo	Scholastic
Pigeon Hero!	K	HF	250+	Redmond, Shirley Raye	Aladdin
Pigeon Princess, The	P	F	250+	Storyteller-Autumn Leaves	Wright Group/McGraw Hill
Piggies in the Pumpkin Patch	J	F	82	Peterson, Mary, & Rofe, Jennifer	Charlesbridge
Piggle	K	F	250+	Bonsall, Crosby	HarperCollins
Piggy's Bath	B	F	29	Brand New Readers	Candlewick Press
Piggy's Bedtime	C	F	32	Brand New Readers	Candlewick Press
Piggy's Pictures	B	F	30	Brand New Readers	Candlewick Press
Piggy's Sandwich	C	F	36	Brand New Readers	Candlewick Press
Piglet and Granny	K	F	250+	Wild, Margaret	Harry N. Abrams
Piglet and Papa	K	F	250+	Wild, Margaret	Harry N. Abrams
Piglet in a Playpen	Q	RF	250+	Baglio, Ben M.	Scholastic
Piglet in a Playpen	P	RF	250+	Daniels, Lucy	Barron's Educational

* Collection of short stories   # Graphic text
^ Mature content with lower level text demands

TITLE	LEVEL	GENRE	WORD COUNT	AUTHOR / SERIES	PUBLISHER / DISTRIBUTOR
#Pigling: A Cinderella Story	R	TL	2527	Graphic Myths and Legends	Lerner Publishing Group
Pigman & Me, The	Z	B	250+	Zindel, Paul	Dell
Pigman's Legacy, The	Z	RF	250+	Zindel, Paul	Harper & Row
Pignic	M	F	152	Miranda, Anne	Boyds Mills Press
Pignocchio	L	F	250+	Pair-It Books	Steck-Vaughn
Pigpen Party, The	I	F	186	Literacy Tree	Rigby
Pigs	G	I	104	Farm Animals	Lerner Publishing Group
Pigs	C	F	29	Learn to Read	Creative Teaching Press
Pigs	L	I	250+	PM Animal Facts: Purple	Rigby
Pigs	D	I	54	Vocabulary Readers	Houghton Mifflin Harcourt
Pigs and Piglets	B	I	33	Animal Families	Lerner Publishing Group
Pigs at Odds	L	F	250+	Axelrod, Amy	Aladdin
Pigs Have Piglets	M	I	250+	Animals and Their Young	Compass Point Books
Pig's Life, A	D	I	98	Reading Street	Pearson
Pigs Might Fly	R	F	250+	King-Smith, Dick	Scholastic
Pigs on the Farm	G	I	72	Pebble Books	Capstone Press
Pigs Peek	C	F	28	Books for Young Learners	Richard C. Owen
Pig's Tall Hat	E	F	81	Leveled Readers Language Support	Houghton Mifflin Harcourt
Pigs, The	B	TL	83	Leveled Readers	Houghton Mifflin Harcourt
Pigs, The	B	TL	83	Leveled Readers/CA	Houghton Mifflin Harcourt
Pigs, The	B	TL	83	Leveled Readers/TX	Houghton Mifflin Harcourt
Pigsty	K	F	250+	Teague, Mark	Scholastic
Pike River Phantom, The	R	F	250+	Wright, Betty	Scholastic
Pilar Speaks Up	T	RF	1354	Leveled Readers	Houghton Mifflin Harcourt
Pile in Pete's Room, The	K	RF	745	Sunshine	Wright Group/McGraw Hill
Pilgrams' First Thanksgiving, The	M	I	250+	Thanksgiving	Picture Window Books
Pilgrim Children Had Many Chores	F	I	47	Learn to Read	Creative Teaching Press
Pilgrim Voices: Our First Year in the New World	T	HF	250+	Roop, Connie & Peter	Walker & Company
#Pilgrims and the First Thanksgiving, The	R	I	250+	Graphic Library	Capstone Press
Pilgrims' First Year, The	O	I	919	Reading Street	Pearson
Pilgrims of Plimouth, The	T	I	250+	Sewall, Marcia	Simon & Schuster
Pilgrims of Plymouth	K	I	257	Goodman, Susan E.	National Geographic
Pilgrims of Rayne, The: Pendragon	X	F	250+	MacHale, D.J.	Aladdin
Pilgrims, The	V	I	250+	Cornerstones of Freedom	Children's Press
Pilgrims, The	R	I	250+	The Heinle Reading Library	Thomson Learning
Pill Bug's Life, A	K	I	303	Nature Upclose	Children's Press
Pillbugs	K	I	161	Watch It Grow	Capstone Press
Pillow Sale, The	B	F	26	KinderReaders	Rigby
Pilots	M	I	250+	Community Workers	Compass Point Books
Pilots	J	I	219	On Deck	Rigby
Pin It! Fix It!	E	F	76	Phonics and Friends	Hampton Brown
Pin the Tail on the Donkey	J	RF	459	Red Rocket Readers	Flying Start Books
Pinata Party	C	RF	31	Bebop Books	Lee & Low Books Inc.
Pinata Time	D	RF	71	Teacher's Choice Series	Pearson Learning Group
Pinballs, The	S	RF	250+	Byars, Betsy	HarperTrophy
Pincher Martin	Z+	RF	250+	Golding, William	Harcourt Trade
Pinduli	O	F	250+	Cannon, Janell	Scholastic
Pine Hollow: Changing Leads	W	RF	250+	Bryant, Bonnie	Bantam Books
Pine Hollow: Conformation Faults	W	RF	250+	Bryant, Bonnie	Bantam Books
Pine Hollow: Reining In	W	RF	250+	Bryant, Bonnie	Bantam Books
Pine Hollow: The Long Ride	W	RF	250+	Bryant, Bonnie	Bantam Books
Pine Hollow: The Trail Home	W	RF	250+	Bryant, Bonnie	Bantam Books
Pine Trees	H	I	138	Pebble Books	Capstone Press

* Collection of short stories   # Graphic text
^ Mature content with lower level text demands

PQ

TITLE	LEVEL	GENRE	WORD COUNT	AUTHOR / SERIES	PUBLISHER / DISTRIBUTOR
Ping-Pong	D	I	78	Nonfiction Set 3	Literacy Footprints
Ping-Pong	D	RF	89	Rigby Star	Rigby
Pink Book, The	A	I	108	Readlings/ Color My World	American Reading Company
Pink Everywhere	K	I	308	Lightning Bolt Books	Lerner Publishing Group
Pink Pig	B	RF	23	Ready Readers	Pearson Learning Group
Pink Snow and Other Weird Weather	K	I	250+	All Aboard Reading	Grosset & Dunlap
Pink: Seeing Pink All around Us	L	I	250+	Colors	Capstone Press
Pinkeye	K	I	250+	Health Matters	Capstone Press
Pinky and Rex	L	RF	250+	Howe, James	Simon & Schuster
Pinky and Rex and the Bully	L	RF	250+	Howe, James	Simon & Schuster
Pinky and Rex and the Double-Dad Weekend	L	RF	250+	Howe, James	Simon & Schuster
Pinky and Rex and the Mean Old Witch	L	RF	250+	Howe, James	Simon & Schuster
Pinky and Rex and the New Baby	L	RF	250+	Howe, James	Simon & Schuster
Pinky and Rex and the New Neighbors	L	RF	250+	Howe, James	Simon & Schuster
Pinky and Rex and the Perfect Pumpkin	L	RF	250+	Howe, James	Simon & Schuster
Pinky and Rex and the School Play	L	RF	250+	Howe, James	Simon & Schuster
Pinky and Rex and the Spelling Bee	L	RF	250+	Howe, James	Simon & Schuster
Pinky and Rex Get Married	L	RF	250+	Howe, James	Simon & Schuster
Pinky and Rex Go to Camp	L	RF	250+	Howe, James	Aladdin
Pinky Dinky Doo Shrinky Pinky!	K	F	250+	Step into Reading	Random House
Pinky the Pig	C	RF	77	Leveled Literacy Intervention/ Blue System	Heinemann
Pinocchio	F	TL	357	Fairy Tales and Folklore	Norwood House Press
Pinocchio	J	TL	250+	Jumbled Tumbled Tales & Rhymes	Rigby
Pins in the Map	L	RF	566	Reading Street	Pearson
Pioneer Bear	L	F	250+	Sandin, Joan	Random House
Pioneer Cat	N	HF	250+	Hooks, William H.	Random House
Pioneer Families	L	I	250+	Rosen Real Readers	Rosen Publishing Group
Pioneer Girl, The Story of Laura Ingalls Wilder	R	B	250+	Anderson, William	HarperCollins
Pioneer Trails	V	I	250+	Primary Source Readers	Teacher Created Materials
Pioneer Way, The	Q	I	250+	Kummer, Patricia K.	Steck-Vaughn
Pioneering Ecologists	R	B	250+	Science Readers	Teacher Created Materials
Pioneers	T	I	250+	Sandler, Martin W.	HarperTrophy
Pioneers in Cell Biology	V	B	250+	Science Readers	Teacher Created Materials
Pioneers in Medicine	U	B	250+	Navigators Biography Series	Benchmark Education
Pioneers of Earth Science	T	B	250+	Science Readers	Teacher Created Materials
Pioneers of Light and Sound	W	B	250+	Science Readers	Teacher Created Materials
^Pioneers: Life as a Homesteader	Q	I	250+	On Deck	Rigby
Pip and the Little Monkey	F	RF	112	Oxford Reading Tree	Oxford University Press
Pip at the Zoo	F	RF	70	Oxford Reading Tree	Oxford University Press
Piper Reed Gets a Job	N	RF	250+	Holt, Kimberly Willis	Henry Holt & Co.
Piper Reed: Navy Brat	N	RF	250+	Willis Holt, Kimberly	Square Fish
Piper Reed: The Great Gypsy	N	RF	250+	Willis Holt, Kimberly	Square Fish
Pippa the Poppy Fairy: Rainbow Magic	L	F	250+	Meadows, Daisy	Scholastic
Pippa's Pet Pest	D	RF	35	Home Connection Collection	Rigby
Pippi Goes on Board	O	F	250+	Lindgren, Astrid	Puffin Books
Pippi in the South Seas	O	F	250+	Lindgren, Astrid	Puffin Books
Pippi Longstocking	O	F	250+	Lindgren, Astrid	Penguin Group
Piranha	L	I	250+	A Day in the Life: Rain Forest Animals	Heinemann Library
Piranhas	O	I	1327	Early Bird Nature Books	Lerner Publishing Group
Piranhas	I	I	213	Sails	Rigby
Pirate	X	I	250+	Eyewitness Books	DK Publishing

PQ

TITLE	LEVEL	GENRE	WORD COUNT	AUTHOR / SERIES	PUBLISHER / DISTRIBUTOR
Pirate Attack	N	RF	250+	Boyz Rule!	Mondo Publishing
Pirate Bob	N	F	250+	Lasky, Kathryn	Charlesbridge
Pirate Code, The: Life of a Pirate	T	I	250+	The Real World of Pirates	Capstone Press
Pirate Cookbook, A	N	I	250+	First Cookbooks	Capstone Press
Pirate Feast, The	H	F	172	Story Basket	Wright Group/McGraw Hill
Pirate Fish	E	F	62	Coulton, Mia	Maryruth Books
Pirate Gear: Cannons, Swords, and the Jolly Roger	T	I	250+	The Real World of Pirates	Capstone Press
Pirate Hideouts: Secret Spots and Shelters	T	I	250+	The Real World of Pirates	Capstone Press
Pirate Island Adventure	N	RF	250+	Parish, Peggy	Yearling Books
Pirate Party	L	F	884	Big Cat	Pacific Learning
Pirate Pete	P	F	250+	Kennedy, Kim	Harry N. Abrams
Pirate Pete and the Monster	E	F	144	Storyworlds	Heinemann
Pirate Pete and the Treasure Island	E	F	145	Storyworlds	Heinemann
Pirate Pete Keeps Fit	E	F	139	Storyworlds	Heinemann
Pirate Pete Loses His Hat	E	F	139	Storyworlds	Heinemann
Pirate Pete's Giant Adventure	P	F	250+	Kennedy, Kim	Harry N. Abrams
Pirate Pete's Talk Like A Pirate	P	F	250+	Kennedy, Kim	Harry N. Abrams
Pirate Pie	M	F	250+	Orbit Chapter Books	Pacific Learning
Pirate Ships: Sailing the High Seas	T	I	250+	The Real World of Pirates	Capstone Press
Pirate Traps	K	F	370	Story Box	Wright Group/McGraw Hill
Pirate Treasure	H	F	168	Gear Up!	Wright Group/McGraw Hill
Pirate Treasure: Stolen Riches	T	I	250+	The Real World of Pirates	Capstone Press
^Pirate, Big Fist, and Me, The	S	RF	10615	Gosson, M.J.	Stone Arch Books
Pirateology Handbook, The	X	HF	250+	Lubber, Captain William	Candlewick Press
Pirates	B	F	43	Big Cat	Pacific Learning
Pirates	R	I	250+	Take Two Books	Wright Group/McGraw Hill
Pirates	Q	I	250+	Trackers	Pacific Learning
Pirates & Smugglers	X	I	250+	Kingfisher Knowledge	Kingfisher
*Pirate's Blood and Other Case Files, The: Saxby Smart, Private Detective	S	RF	250+	Cheshire, Simon	Roaring Brook Press
Pirates Don't Wear Pink Sunglasses	M	F	250+	Dadey, Debbie; Jones, Marcia Thornton	Scholastic
Pirates Drive Buses	N	F	250+	Morgan, Christopher & Curtis, Neil	Roaring Brook Press
Pirates Eat Porridge	N	F	250+	Morgan, Christopher & Curtis, Neil	Roaring Brook Press
Pirates of Pompeii, The: The Roman Mysteries	U	HF	250+	Lawrence, Caroline	Puffin Books
Pirates Past Noon	M	F	250+	Osborne, Mary Pope	Scholastic
Pirate's Promise	N	RF	250+	Bulla, Clyde Robert	HarperTrophy
Pirate's Treasure, The	E	F	63	Joy Readers	Pearson Learning Group
Pirates!	Z+	HF	250+	Rees, Celia	Bloomsbury Children's Books
Pirates, The	L	RF	621	Leveled Literacy Intervention/ Blue System	Heinemann
Pirates: Raiders of the High Seas	V	HF	250+	DK Readers	DK Publishing
Pi-Shu, the Little Panda	N	F	250+	Butler, John	Peachtree
Pit and the Pendulum, The	W	RF	6000	Oxford Bookworms Library	Oxford University Press
Pit Bulls Are the Best!	Q	I	1229	The Best Dogs Ever	Lerner Publishing Group
Pita's Birthday	H	F	250+	Ready to Read	Pacific Learning
Pitch and Throw, Grasp and Know: What is a Synonym?	O	I	246	Words Are CATegorical	Millbrook Press
Pitching Trouble	N	RF	250+	Kroll, Stephen	Avon Books
Pitt Street Pirates	O	F	5117	Dreary, Terry	Stone Arch Books
Pittsburgh Penguins, The	S	I	5094	Team Spirit	Norwood House Press

* Collection of short stories   # Graphic text
^ Mature content with lower level text demands

TITLE	LEVEL	GENRE	WORD COUNT	AUTHOR / SERIES	PUBLISHER / DISTRIBUTOR
Pittsburgh Pirates, The	S	I	250+	Team Spirit	Norwood House Press
Pittsburgh Pirates, The (Revised Edition)	S	I	250+	Team Spirit	Norwood House Press
Pittsburgh Steelers, The	S	I	250+	Team Spirit	Norwood House Press
Pitty Pitty Pat	C	F	45	Little Celebrations	Pearson Learning Group
Pizza	D	I	42	Benchmark Rebus	Marshall Cavendish
Pizza	C	F	24	Brand New Readers	Candlewick Press
Pizza Day	G	I	156	Springboard	Wright Group/McGraw Hill
Pizza for Carl	D	RF	66	Bonnell, Kris	Reading Reading Books
Pizza for Dinner	H	RF	164	Literacy 2000	Rigby
Pizza for Everyone	K	I	251	Pair-It Books	Steck-Vaughn
Pizza for Me	G	RF	225	In Step Readers	Rigby
Pizza Maker, The	D	RF	57	Harry's Math Books	Outside the Box
Pizza Monster, The (Olivia Sharp)	L	RF	250+	Sharmat, Marjorie Weinman	Yearling Books
Pizza Parts	O	I	250+	Early Connections	Benchmark Education
Pizza Party!	F	RF	79	Maccarone, Grace	Scholastic
Pizza Pat	I	TL	274	Step into Reading	Random House
Pizza Pokey	I	F	280	Pair-It Books	Steck-Vaughn
Pizza That We Made	H	RF	249	Holub, Joan	Puffin Books
Pizza with a Twist	N	F	1684	Reading Street	Pearson
Pizza, The	D	RF	100	Foundations	Wright Group/McGraw Hill
Place Called Heartbreak, A: A Story of Vietnam	U	I	250+	Myers, Walter Dean	Steck-Vaughn
Place for a Bed, A	E	I	130	Sails	Rigby
Place For Birds, A	P	I	250+	Stewart, Melissa	Peachtree
Place for Butterflies, A	P	I	250+	Stewart, Melissa	Peachtree
Place For Fish, A	P	I	250+	Stewart, Melissa	Peachtree
Place for Frogs, A	P	I	250+	Stewart, Melissa	Peachtree
Place for Nicholas, A	E	RF	82	Instant Readers	Harcourt Trade
Place in My Town, A	H	I	184	Vocabulary Readers	Houghton Mifflin Harcourt
Place in My Town, A	H	I	184	Vocabulary Readers/CA	Houghton Mifflin Harcourt
Place in the Sun, A	U	HF	250+	Rubalcaba, Jill	Puffin Books
#Place to Call Home, A	L	F	250+	Deacon, Alexis	Candlewick Press
Place to Call Home, A	Y	RF	250+	Koller, Jackie French	Aladdin
*Place to Hide, A	Y	B	250+	Petit, Jayne	Scholastic
Place to Live, A	O	I	250+	Orbit Chapter Books	Pacific Learning
Place to Paint, A	K	I	335	Leveled Readers	Houghton Mifflin Harcourt
Place to Paint, A	K	I	335	Leveled Readers/CA	Houghton Mifflin Harcourt
Place to Sleep, A	B	F	25	Sails	Rigby
Place Value	N	I	324	Yellow Umbrella Books	Red Brick Learning
Places	C	I	88	Little Red Readers	Sundance
Places Around the World	K	I	287	Time for Kids	Teacher Created Materials
Places Around Town	WB	I	0	Reach	National Geographic
Places I Like	B	I	49	Little Red Readers	Sundance
Places in My Community	F	I	64	Windows on Literacy	National Geographic
Places in Our Town, The	D	I	108	Leveled Readers	Houghton Mifflin Harcourt
Places in Our Town, The	D	I	108	Leveled Readers/CA	Houghton Mifflin Harcourt
Places in Our Town, The	D	I	108	Leveled Readers/TX	Houghton Mifflin Harcourt
Places in the United States	J	I	200	Leveled Readers	Houghton Mifflin Harcourt
Places on Earth	F	I	32	Windows on Literacy	National Geographic
Places to Go	B	I	42	Time for Kids	Teacher Created Materials
Places to Visit	L	I	202	Windows on Literacy	National Geographic
Places We Live	L	I	383	Yellow Umbrella Books	Red Brick Learning
Places We See	B	RF	24	Windows on Literacy	National Geographic
Places Where People Live	H	I	189	Springboard	Wright Group/McGraw Hill
^Plague, The	T	F	250+	Harlen, Jonathan	Stone Arch Books

TITLE	LEVEL	GENRE	WORD COUNT	AUTHOR / SERIES	PUBLISHER / DISTRIBUTOR
Plain and Fancy	WB	I	0	Vocabulary Readers	Houghton Mifflin Harcourt
Plain Girl	Q	RF	250+	Sorensen, Virginia	Harcourt Trade
Plains	J	I	262	Landforms	Lerner Publishing Group
Plains Animals	D	I	49	Benchmark Rebus	Marshall Cavendish
Plains: The Land Around Us	S	I	250+	Reading Expeditions	National Geographic
Plan a Party	E	I	47	Vocabulary Readers	Houghton Mifflin Harcourt
Plane Ride, The	F	I	68	Little Red Readers	Sundance
Plane Rides	G	I	160	Walker, Pamela	Scholastic
Planes and How They Work	Q	I	892	Time for Kids	Teacher Created Materials
^Planes of the Past	M	I	238	On Deck	Rigby
Planes, Rockets, and Other Flying Machines	W	I	250+	Graham, Ian	Franklin Watts
Planes, Trains, and More	E	I	43	iOpeners	Pearson Learning Group
Planet Boring	P	F	250+	Cook, Nathan	Pacific Learning
Planet Earth	W	I	250+	Navigators	Kingfisher
Planet Earth	L	I	197	Rigby Focus	Rigby
Planet Earth	P	I	250+	Science Kids	Kingfisher
Planet Earth Fact File	P	I	250+	Rigby Focus	Rigby
Planet of Junior Brown, The	Z	RF	250+	Hamilton, Virginia	Aladdin
Planet Patrol	V	I	250+	News Extra	Richard C. Owen
Planet Patrol: A Kid's Action Guide to Earth Care	R	I	250+	Lorbiecki, Marybeth	Two-Can Publishing
Planet Race, The	G	F	160	Take Two Books	Wright Group/McGraw Hill
Planet Watch	P	I	250+	Literacy by Design	Rigby
Planet X	L	SF	250+	Popcorn	Sundance
Planet Zogo	L	F	663	Leveled Readers	Houghton Mifflin Harcourt
Planet Zogo	L	F	663	Leveled Readers/CA	Houghton Mifflin Harcourt
Planet Zogo	L	F	663	Leveled Readers/TX	Houghton Mifflin Harcourt
Planets Around the Sun	L	I	250+	Simon, Seymour	SeaStar Books
Planets Around the Sun	L	I	250+	Simon, Seymour	Chronicle Books
Planets in Our Solar System	N	I	250+	Windows on Literacy	National Geographic
Planets of Our Solar System	M	I	250+	Rigby Focus	Rigby
Planets, The	Q	I	101	Explorers	Wright Group/McGraw Hill
Planets, The	M	I	250+	Gibbons, Gail	Holiday House
Planets, The	K	I	142	Out In Space	Red Brick Learning
Planets, The	L	I	95	Take Two Books	Wright Group/McGraw Hill
Planets, The	J	I	101	Wonder World	Wright Group/McGraw Hill
Planning a Birthday Party	N	I	250+	Bookshop	Mondo Publishing
Planning Dinner	H	RF	250+	Urmston, Kathleen; Evans, Karen	Kaeden Books
Plant	W	I	250+	Eyewitness Books	DK Publishing
Plant a Plant	A	I	32	Red Rocket Readers	Flying Start Books
Plant and Animal Partners	M	I	587	Early Connections	Benchmark Education
Plant Atlas	T	I	250+	Navigators Science Series	Benchmark Education
Plant Blossoms	M	I	250+	Look Once Look Again	Creative Teaching Press
Plant Discoveries	P	I	250+	Literacy by Design	Rigby
Plant Fruits and Seeds	M	I	250+	Look Once Look Again	Creative Teaching Press
Plant Genetics	U	I	250+	Navigators Science Series	Benchmark Education
Plant Has Needs, A	A	I	28	Early Explorers	Benchmark Education
Plant Has Parts, A	E	I	77	Early Explorers	Benchmark Education
Plant Kingdom, The	Q	I	250+	Explorers	Wright Group/McGraw Hill
Plant Leaves	N	I	250+	Look Once Look Again	Creative Teaching Press
Plant Life	J	I	122	Windows on Literacy	National Geographic
Plant Life Cycles	L	I	670	Science Support Readers	Houghton Mifflin Harcourt
Plant Packages: A Book About Seeds	M	I	250+	Growing Things	Picture Window Books

* Collection of short stories   # Graphic text
^ Mature content with lower level text demands

PQ

TITLE	LEVEL	GENRE	WORD COUNT	AUTHOR / SERIES	PUBLISHER / DISTRIBUTOR
Plant Parts	LB	I	14	Reach	National Geographic
Plant Patterns	K	I	286	Finding Patterns	Capstone Press
Plant Picture, A	B	RF	20	Windows on Literacy	National Geographic
Plant Plumbing: A Book About Roots and Stems	M	I	250+	Growing Things	Picture Window Books
Plant Power	U	I	250+	Reading Expeditions	National Geographic
Plant Products	S	I	250+	The Life of Plants	Heinemann
Plant Stems and Roots	N	I	250+	Look Once Look Again	Creative Teaching Press
Plant Systems	U	I	1177	Science Support Readers	Houghton Mifflin Harcourt
Plant That Ate Dirty Socks Goes Up in Space	S	F	250+	McArthur, Nancy	Avon Books
Plant, The	A	I	32	Sun Sprouts	ETA/Cuisenaire
Planting a Garden	D	I	48	Leveled Readers Language Support	Houghton Mifflin Harcourt
Planting a Garden	E	I	62	Ready Readers	Pearson Learning Group
Planting and Growing	E	I	100	On Our Way to English	Rigby
Planting Beans and Beets	E	I	53	Leveled Readers	Houghton Mifflin Harcourt
Plants	J	I	162	Early Connections	Benchmark Education
Plants	B	I	51	Leveled Readers Science	Houghton Mifflin Harcourt
Plants	I	I	250+	Momentum Literacy Program	Troll Associates
Plants	O	I	250+	Rigby Focus	Rigby
Plants	I	I	325	Science Support Readers	Houghton Mifflin Harcourt
Plants	P	I	250+	Simply Science	Compass Point Books
Plants	G	I	28	Windows on Literacy	National Geographic
Plants and Animals in Antarctica	R	I	1161	Reading Street	Pearson
Plants and Animals in Different Seasons	K	I	447	Early Explorers	Benchmark Education
Plants and Animals Live Here	F	I	54	Windows on Literacy	National Geographic
Plants and Flowers	M	I	250+	It's Science!	Children's Press
Plants and Seeds	I	I	148	Sunshine	Wright Group/McGraw Hill
Plants and Soil - A Great Partnership	P	I	250+	InfoTrek	ETA/Cuisenaire
Plants and the Environment	I	I	239	Ecology	Lerner Publishing Group
Plants Eat Meat, Too	I	I	215	Sails	Rigby
Plants Grow From Seeds	I	I	109	Phonics Readers	Compass Point Books
Plants in the Park	B	I	35	Windows on Literacy	National Geographic
Plants of My Aunt	J	F	429	Jellybeans	Rigby
Plants of the Coral Reef	W	I	1832	Leveled Readers Science	Houghton Mifflin Harcourt
Plants of the Redwood Forest	O	I	913	Leveled Readers	Houghton Mifflin Harcourt
Plants of the Redwood Forest	O	I	913	Leveled Readers/CA	Houghton Mifflin Harcourt
Plants of the Redwood Forest	O	I	913	Leveled Readers/TX	Houghton Mifflin Harcourt
Plants on a Farm	E	I	112	World of Farming	Heinemann Library
Plants on My Plate	G	I	101	Windows on Literacy	National Geographic
Plants that Eat Animals	L	I	250+	Read-About Science	Children's Press
Plants That Eat Bugs	H	I	150	Leveled Literacy Intervention/ Blue System	Heinemann
Plants That Never Ever Bloom	N	I	250+	Heller, Ruth	Scholastic
Plants We Use	R	I	250+	Navigators Science Series	Benchmark Education
Plants We Use	K	I	250+	On Our Way to English	Rigby
Plastic	G	I	93	Materials	Lerner Publishing Group
Plastic	F	I	132	Materials	Heinemann Library
Plastic Bottle's Journey, A	M	I	250+	Follow-It!	Picture Window Books
Plate Tectonics	X	I	250+	Mission Science	Compass Point Books
Plateaus	J	I	267	Landforms	Lerner Publishing Group
Platypus	P	I	1098	Short, Joan.; Green, J.; Bird, Bettina	Mondo Publishing
Platypus	P	I	1984	Take Two Books	Wright Group/McGraw Hill
Platypuses	K	I	178	Australian Animals	Capstone Press

PQ

TITLE	LEVEL	GENRE	WORD COUNT	AUTHOR / SERIES	PUBLISHER / DISTRIBUTOR
Play and Ride	C	RF	88	Leveled Literacy Intervention/ Orange System	Heinemann
Play Ball	LB	I	7	Bookshop	Mondo Publishing
Play Ball	F	RF	250+	Let's Play	Norwood House Press
*Play Ball Like the Hall of Famers: The Inside Scoop from 19 Baseball Greats	R	I	250+	Krasner, Steven	Peachtree
*Play Ball Like the Pros: Tips for Kids from 20 Big League Stars	R	I	250+	Krasner, Steven	Peachtree
Play Ball!	R	I	250+	Boldprint	Steck-Vaughn
Play Ball!	D	RF	30	Books for Young Learners	Richard C. Owen
Play Ball!	B	F	26	Brand New Readers	Candlewick Press
Play Ball!	R	I	250+	Explorer Books-Pathfinder	National Geographic
Play Ball!	P	I	250+	Explorer Books-Pioneer	National Geographic
Play Ball!	R	I	250+	Explorers	Wright Group/McGraw Hill
Play Ball!	F	RF	49	Instant Readers	Harcourt School Publishers
Play Ball!	C	I	80	Leveled Literacy Intervention/ Green System	Heinemann
Play Ball!	C	I	97	Literacy by Design	Rigby
Play Ball!	LB	I	14	Twig	Wright Group/McGraw Hill
Play Ball, Amelia Bedelia	L	F	250+	Parish, Peggy	Harper & Row
Play Ball, Kate	D	RF	39	Giant First Step	Troll Associates
Play Ball, Sherman	F	RF	88	Erickson, Betty	Continental Press
Play Ball: Verbs in Action	K	I	250+	Bookworms	Marshall Cavendish
Play by the Rules	I	I	188	Early Explorers	Benchmark Education
Play Date	K	RF	250+	Math Matters	Kane Press
Play Date, The	G	RF	258	Leveled Literacy InterventionBlue System	Heinemann
Play Dough	C	RF	63	Foundations	Wright Group/McGraw Hill
Play It Again Sam	I	RF	139	Literacy 2000	Rigby
Play It Safe!	G	I	92	Phonics Readers	Compass Point Books
Play Money for Polly and Peter	D	F	49	Joy Starters	Pearson Learning Group
Play of the Day	S	RF	1485	Leveled Readers	Houghton Mifflin Harcourt
Play of the Day	S	RF	1485	Leveled Readers/CA	Houghton Mifflin Harcourt
Play of the Day	S	RF	1485	Leveled Readers/TX	Houghton Mifflin Harcourt
Play the Game	R	I	250+	Orbit Collections	Pacific Learning
Play Together	B	F	25	Reading Street	Pearson
Play with Max Monkey	H	F	353	Red Rocket Readers	Flying Start Books
Play with Me	E	F	118	Bella and Rosie Series	Literacy Footprints
Play with Me	D	F	67	Bonnell, Kris	Reading Reading Books
Play, Bear	G	F	219	Sun Sprouts	ETA/Cuisenaire
Play, Louis, Play!	O	F	250+	Weinstein, Muriel Harris	Bloomsbury Children's Books
Play, Play, Play, Dear Dragon	E	F	254	Dear Dragon	Norwood House Press
Play, The	B	RF	33	First Stories	Pacific Learning
Play, The	A	I	32	Leveled Literacy Intervention/ Orange System	Heinemann
Play, The	L	RF	588	Leveled Readers	Houghton Mifflin Harcourt
Play, The	B	RF	52	PM Plus Starters	Rigby
Play, The	D	RF	61	Reading Street	Pearson
Play, The	C	RF	23	Rigby Literacy	Rigby
Play, The	C	RF	22	Rigby Star	Rigby
Playful Platypus, The	C	F	35	Learn to Read	Creative Teaching Press
Playground Fun	D	I	127	Early Connections	Benchmark Education
Playground Games	G	I	133	Red Rocket Readers	Flying Start Books
Playground in the Yard, The	G	RF	261	Springboard	Wright Group/McGraw Hill

* Collection of short stories   # Graphic text
^ Mature content with lower level text demands

TITLE	LEVEL	GENRE	WORD COUNT	AUTHOR / SERIES	PUBLISHER / DISTRIBUTOR
Playground Opposites	B	I	21	Pair-It Books	Steck-Vaughn
Playground Play	B	RF	39	Handprints B	Educators Publishing Service
Playground Problem Solvers	G	F	199	Learn to Read	Creative Teaching Press
Playground Science	R	I	250+	iOpeners	Pearson Learning Group
Playground, The	C	RF	108	Early Emergent	Pioneer Valley
Playground, The	A	I	16	Twig	Wright Group/McGraw Hill
Playhouse for Monster	C	F	34	Mueller, Virginia	Whitman
Playhouse, The	K	RF	197	Pacific Literacy	Pacific Learning
Playhouse, The	C	RF	34	Rigby Literacy	Rigby
Playhouse, The	F	RF	158	Springboard	Wright Group/McGraw Hill
Playing	A	RF	24	Davidson, Avelyn	Scholastic
Playing	B	RF	55	First Stories	Pacific Learning
Playing	A	I	39	PM Starters	Rigby
Playing	B	RF	37	Tiny Treasures	Pioneer Valley
Playing at Home	B	RF	72	Rigby Flying Colors	Rigby
Playing at Lily's House	H	I	212	On Our Way to English	Rigby
Playing Ball	E	RF	170	Handprints C, Set 2	Educators Publishing Service
Playing Dress Up	A	RF	40	Leveled Literacy Intervention/ Orange System	Heinemann
Playing Favorites	N	RF	250+	Kroll, Steven	Avon Books
^Playing Forward	P	RF	250+	Maddox, Jake,	Stone Arch Books
Playing Games	F	RF	89	Phonics Readers	Pearson Learning Group
Playing in the Cold	K	I	172	Larkin, Bruce	Wilbooks
Playing in the Snow	C	RF	61	Early Emergent	Pioneer Valley
Playing It Safe	F	I	135	Early Connections	Benchmark Education
Playing Outside	A	I	36	Explorations	Eleanor Curtain Publishing
Playing Outside	A	I	36	Explorations	Okapi Educational Materials
Playing Outside	C	RF	56	PM Plus Starters	Rigby
Playing Safely	L	I	579	Pull Ahead Books	Lerner Publishing Group
Playing Soccer	I	RF	123	Foundations	Wright Group/McGraw Hill
Playing Sports	B	I	24	Early Connections	Benchmark Education
Playing to Win: The Story of Althea Gibson	Q	B	250+	Deans, Karen	Holiday House
Playing Together	B	I	56	Leveled Literacy Intervention/ Orange System	Heinemann
Playing Together	D	I	110	Vocabulary Readers	Houghton Mifflin Harcourt
Playing Together	D	I	110	Vocabulary Readers/CA	Houghton Mifflin Harcourt
Playing with Blocks	C	RF	82	Leveled Literacy Intervention/ Orange System	Heinemann
Playing with Dad	F	RF	146	Foundations	Wright Group/McGraw Hill
Playing With Dough	D	I	94	PM Plus Nonfiction	Rigby
Playing with Milly	F	RF	151	PM Stars	Rigby
Playing with My Cat	C	RF	83	Early Emergent	Pioneer Valley
Playing with Shapes	C	I	57	InfoTrek	ETA/Cuisenaire
Playing with Words	S	I	250+	Action Packs	Rigby
Playing with Words	O	B	250+	Meet The Author	Richard C. Owen
Playmate for Jack, A	F	F	194	Jack and Daisy	Pioneer Valley
Playoff Dreams	P	RF	250+	Bowen, Fred	Peachtree
Play's the Thing, The: A Story About William Shakespeare	T	B	6778	Creative Minds Biographies	Carolrhoda Books
Playtime	C	RF	49	Bonnell, Kris	Reading Reading Books
Playtime	C	F	66	Voyages	SRA/McGraw Hill
Please Don't Be Mine, Julie Valentine!	R	RF	250+	Strasser, Todd	Scholastic
Please Don't Sneeze!	I	TL	404	Storyteller	Wright Group/McGraw Hill

* Collection of short stories   # Graphic text
^ Mature content with lower level text demands

TITLE	LEVEL	GENRE	WORD COUNT	AUTHOR / SERIES	PUBLISHER / DISTRIBUTOR
Please Don't Wake the Animals: A Book About Sleep	P	I	250+	Batten, Mary	Peachtree
Please Read to Me	E	RF	98	Developing Set 4	Pioneer Valley
Please Stop Barking!	K	RF	250+	Tristars	Richard C. Owen
Please Wait to Be Seated	I	RF	537	Dominie Math Series	Pearson Publishing Group
Please Write in This Book	Q	RF	250+	Amato, Mary	Holiday House
Please, Do Not Drop Your Jelly Beans	I	RF	180	Storyteller-Night Crickets	Wright Group/McGraw Hill
Please, Miss	H	RF	90	Cambridge Reading	Pearson Learning Group
Please, Mom!	D	RF	92	Lighthouse	Rigby
Pleased to Eat You	G	F	144	Silly Millies	Millbrook Press
Pleasing the Ghost	V	F	250+	Creech, Sharon	HarperCollins
Pledge of Allegiance in Translation, The: What It Really Means	V	I	250+	Kids' Translations	Capstone Press
Pledge of Allegiance, The	N	I	250+	American Symbols	Capstone Press
Pledge of Allegiance, The	S	I	250+	Symbols of America	Marshall Cavendish
Plenty of Pets	F	RF	173	Instant Readers	Harcourt School Publishers
Plenty of Plants	E	I	89	Gear Up!	Wright Group/McGraw Hill
Plop and the Frog Tower	H	F	247	Rigby Flying Colors	Rigby
Plop!	G	F	176	Rigby Flying Colors	Rigby
Plop!	C	F	30	Story Box	Wright Group/McGraw Hill
Plop, the Water Monster	H	F	365	Rigby Flying Colors	Rigby
Plumbers	M	I	250+	Community Helpers	Red Brick Learning
Pluto	Q	I	250+	A First Book	Franklin Watts
Pluto	Q	I	250+	A True Book	Children's Press
Pluto	S	I	250+	Our Solar System	Compass Point Books
Pluto	N	I	760	Our Universe	Lerner Publishing Group
Pluto	Q	I	250+	The Galaxy	Capstone Press
Pluto: A Dwarf Planet	Q	I	1562	Early Bird Astronomy	Lerner Publishing Group
Pluto: A Dwarf Planet	J	I	157	Exploring the Galaxy	Capstone Press
Pluto: A Dwarf Planet	M	I	250+	The Solar System	Capstone Press
Plymouth Colony, The	U	I	250+	Let Freedom Ring	Red Brick Learning
Plymouth Colony, The	T	I	250+	We The People	Compass Point Books
Plymouth Partnership, A: Pilgrims and Native Americans	R	I	250+	The Library of the Pilgrims	Rosen Publishing Group
Plymouth: Surviving the First Winter	R	I	250+	The Library of the Pilgrims	Rosen Publishing Group
Poachers in the Pingos	Q	RF	250+	Orca Young Readers	Orca Books
Pocahontas	R	B	250+	Amazing Americans	Wright Group/McGraw Hill
Pocahontas	Q	B	250+	Early Biographies	Compass Point Books
Pocahontas	M	B	250+	First Biographies	Red Brick Learning
Pocahontas	Q	B	838	Independent Readers Social Studies	Houghton Mifflin Harcourt
Pocahontas	O	B	2137	On My Own Biography	Lerner Publishing Group
Pocahontas	T	B	5320	Oxford Bookworms Library	Oxford University Press
Pocahontas	Q	B	250+	Primary Source Readers	Teacher Created Materials
Pocahontas and the Strangers	R	HF	250+	Bulla, Clyde Robert	Scholastic
Pocahontas: 1595-1617	S	B	250+	American Indian Biographies	Capstone Press
Pocahontas: Daughter of a Chief	N	B	250+	Rookie Biographies	Children's Press
Pocahontas: Peacemaker and Friend to the Colonists	M	B	250+	Biographies	Picture Window Books
Pocahontas: The Life of an Indian Princess	M	B	250+	Rosen Real Readers	Rosen Publishing Group
Pocket for Corduroy, A	K	F	250+	Freeman, Don	Scholastic
Pocket Full of Acorns, A	L	RF	250+	Beames, Michael	Pearson Learning Group
Pocket Full of Seeds, A	V	HF	250+	Sachs, Marilyn	Scholastic
Pocket Money	K	RF	835	Rigby Flying Colors	Rigby
Pocket Pal	E	F	78	Kaleidoscope Collection	Hameray Publishing Group

* Collection of short stories   # Graphic text
^ Mature content with lower level text demands

TITLE	LEVEL	GENRE	WORD COUNT	AUTHOR / SERIES	PUBLISHER / DISTRIBUTOR
Pocketful of Goobers, A: Story of George Washington Carver	Q	B	250+	Mitchell, Barbara	Carolrhoda Books
Pockets	D	RF	98	Red Rocket Readers	Flying Start Books
Pockets	D	RF	32	Visions	Wright Group/McGraw Hill
Pod of Killer Whales, A	U	I	250+	Jean-Michel Cousteau Presents	London Town Press
Poem for Grandma, A	M	RF	250+	Leveled Readers Language Support	Houghton Mifflin Harcourt
Poet from the Plains, A	N	B	353	Vocabulary Readers	Houghton Mifflin Harcourt
Poetry of Basketball, The	P	RF	250+	Leveled Readers Language Support	Houghton Mifflin Harcourt
Poggy Frog	F	F	151	Gear Up!	Wright Group/McGraw Hill
Poggy Frog and the Cows	I	F	229	Gear Up!	Wright Group/McGraw Hill
Poggy Frog and the Flies	G	F	204	Gear Up!	Wright Group/McGraw Hill
Poggy Frog's Contest	I	F	314	Gear Up!	Wright Group/McGraw Hill
Poggy Frog's Song	H	F	201	Gear Up!	Wright Group/McGraw Hill
Point Blank	Z	SF	250+	Horowitz, Anthony	Scholastic
^#Point-Blank Paintball	S	RF	250+	Sports Illustrated Kids	Stone Arch Books
Poison Apples, The	X	RF	250+	Archer, Lily	Square Fish
Poison Dart Frog	L	I	250+	A Day in the Life: Rain Forest Animals	Heinemann Library
Poison Dart Frogs	K	I	208	Colorful World of Animals	Capstone Press
Poison Dart Frogs	R	I	250+	Theme Sets	National Geographic
^Poison Evidence	Z	I	250+	Forensic Crime Solvers	Capstone Press
Poison Island: Zac Power	O	F	250+	Larry, H. I.	Feiwel and Friends
Poison Ivy	W	RF	250+	Koss, Amy Goldman	Square Fish
Poison Ivy Expert (Fancy Nancy)	J	RF	250+	O'Connor, Jane	HarperCollins
^Poison Pages	T	F	711	Dahl, Michael	Stone Arch Books
Poison Pen	R	RF	250+	Sunshine	Wright Group/McGraw Hill
^Poison Plate	U	RF	250+	Spirn, M. Sobel	Stone Arch Books
^Poisoned Planet: Pollution in Our World	O	I	250+	On Deck	Rigby
Poisonous Animals	F	I	147	Sails	Rigby
Poland	O	I	1959	A Ticket to …	Carolrhoda Books
Poland	P	I	1916	Country Explorers	Lerner Publishing Group
Polar Babies	F	I	115	Susan Ring	Random House
Polar Bear	B	I	40	Zoozoo-Animal World	Cavallo Publishing
Polar Bear Math: Learning About Fractions from Klondike and Snow	S	I	250+	Nagda, Ann Whitehead & Bickel, Cindy	Henry Holt & Co.
Polar Bear Pete	H	F	273	Leveled Readers	Houghton Mifflin Harcourt
Polar Bear Pete	H	F	273	Leveled Readers/CA	Houghton Mifflin Harcourt
Polar Bear Pete	H	F	273	Leveled Readers/TX	Houghton Mifflin Harcourt
Polar Bear Vs. Seal	L	I	250+	Predator Vs. Prey	Raintree
Polar Bear, The	E	I	100	Bonnell, Kris/Animals in Danger	Reading Reading Books
Polar Bear, The	R	I	250+	Wildlife of North America	Red Brick Learning
Polar Bears	L	I	250+	A Day in the Life: Polar Animals	Heinemann Library
Polar Bears	P	I	1807	Animal Predators	Lerner Publishing Group
Polar Bears	K	I	250+	Bears	Capstone Press
Polar Bears	O	I	1683	Early Bird Nature Books	Lerner Publishing Group
Polar Bears	F	I	50	Gear Up!	Wright Group/McGraw Hill
Polar Bears	M	I	678	Nonfiction Indigo	Pioneer Valley
Polar Bears	F	I	77	Pebble Books	Capstone Press
Polar Bears	N	I	250+	PM Animal Facts: Silver	Rigby
Polar Bears	H	I	106	Polar Animals	Capstone Press
Polar Bears	K	I	412	Pull Ahead Books	Lerner Publishing Group
Polar Bears	F	I	77	Story Steps	Rigby
Polar Bears	E	I	78	Vocabulary Readers	Houghton Mifflin Harcourt

PQ

TITLE	LEVEL	GENRE	WORD COUNT	AUTHOR / SERIES	PUBLISHER / DISTRIBUTOR
Polar Bears	G	I	67	Windows on Literacy	National Geographic
Polar Bears	K	I	276	Wonder World	Wright Group/McGraw Hill
Polar Bears	N	I	250+	World of Mammals	Capstone Press
Polar Bears Past Bedtime	M	F	250+	Osborne, Mary Pope	Random House
Polar Bears: In Living Color	L	I	250+	Rigby Literacy	Rigby
Polar Climate	R	I	250+	Theme Sets	National Geographic
Polar Exploration Adventures	S	I	250+	Dangerous Adventures	Red Brick Learning
Polar Habitats	M	I	821	Early Explorers	Benchmark Education
Polar Opposites	J	F	131	Brooks, Erik	Marshall Cavendish
Polar Plants	N	I	250+	Life in the World's Biomes	Capstone Press
Polar Regions	N	I	250+	Habitats of the World	Pearson Learning Group
Polar Sun	M	F	250+	Grindley, Sally	Peachtree
Poles Apart	J	F	250+	Rigby Literacy	Rigby
Poles Apart	J	F	250+	Rigby Star	Rigby
Poles Apart	Q	I	978	Vocabulary Readers	Houghton Mifflin Harcourt
Poles Apart	Q	I	978	Vocabulary Readers/CA	Houghton Mifflin Harcourt
Poles, The	M	I	675	Vocabulary Readers/CA	Houghton Mifflin Harcourt
Police	I	RF	195	Board Buddies	Marshall Cavendish
Police Car	B	I	72	Leveled Literacy Intervention/ Blue System	Heinemann
Police Cars	I	I	177	Community Vehicles	Capstone Press
Police Cars	G	I	125	Mighty Machines	Capstone Press
Police Cars	L	I	466	Pull Ahead Books	Lerner Publishing Group
Police Cars	M	I	250+	Transportation	Compass Point Books
Police Cars in Action	L	I	250+	Transportation Zone	Capstone Press
Police Files	N	RF	250+	Sails	Rigby
Police in the Community	I	I	225	Vocabulary Readers	Houghton Mifflin Harcourt
Police in the Community	I	I	225	Vocabulary Readers/CA	Houghton Mifflin Harcourt
Police in the Community	I	I	225	Vocabulary Readers/TX	Houghton Mifflin Harcourt
Police Officer	D	I	38	Benchmark Rebus	Marshall Cavendish
Police Officer	C	I	24	Work People Do	Lerner Publishing Group
Police Officer Mom	E	RF	125	Joy Starters	Pearson Learning Group
Police Officers	M	I	250+	Community Helpers	Red Brick Learning
Police Officers	L	I	250+	Community Workers	Compass Point Books
Police Officers	K	I	399	Pull Ahead Books	Lerner Publishing Group
Police on the Go, The	B	I	44	Bonnell, Kris/About	Reading Reading Books
Police Station	D	I	33	Community Buildings	Lerner Publishing Group
Police Work	O	I	250+	Sails	Rigby
Police: Then and Now	P	I	250+	Primary Source Readers	Teacher Created Materials
Politeness	M	I	250+	Character Education	Red Brick Learning
Political Activism: How You Can Make a Difference	T	I	250+	Take Action	Capstone Press
#Political Elections	V	I	250+	Cartoon Nation	Capstone Press
#Political Parties	V	I	250+	Cartoon Nation	Capstone Press
Polka Dots!	F	I	102	Little Celebrations	Pearson Learning Group
Pollution	F	I	46	Wonder World	Wright Group/McGraw Hill
Pollution Solution?	S	I	250+	WorldScapes	ETA/Cuisenaire
Polly	A	RF	32	Leveled Literacy Intervention/ Orange System	Heinemann
Polly and Peter Make Hats	D	F	52	Joy Starters	Pearson Learning Group
Polly and Peter Make Masks	D	F	74	Joy Starters	Pearson Learning Group
Polly and Peter Make Place Mats	C	F	36	Joy Starters	Pearson Learning Group
Polly and Peter Share Lemonade	E	F	98	Joy Starters	Pearson Learning Group
Polly Perkins's Pictures	I	RF	377	Springboard	Wright Group/McGraw Hill

* Collection of short stories   # Graphic text
^ Mature content with lower level text demands

TITLE	LEVEL	GENRE	WORD COUNT	AUTHOR / SERIES	PUBLISHER / DISTRIBUTOR
Polly Porcupine's Painting Prizes	K	F	752	Animal Antics A to Z	Kane Press
Polly's Pet Polar Bear	G	F	279	Leveled Readers	Houghton Mifflin Harcourt
Polly's Pet Polar Bear	G	F	279	Leveled Readers/CA	Houghton Mifflin Harcourt
Polly's Pet Polar Bear	G	F	279	Leveled Readers/TX	Houghton Mifflin Harcourt
Polly's Shop	E	RF	130	Ready Readers	Pearson Learning Group
Polo and Lily	WB	F	0	Faller, Regis	Roaring Brook Press
Polo and the Dragon	WB	F	0	Faller, Regis	Roaring Brook Press
Polo and the Magic Flute	WB	F	0	Faller, Regis	Roaring Brook Press
Polo and the Magician	WB	F	0	Faller, Regis	Roaring Brook Press
Polonium's Treasure	S	RF	250+	Tristars	Richard C. Owen
Pomeranians Are the Best!	Q	I	1314	The Best Dogs Ever	Lerner Publishing Group
Pompeii . . . Buried Alive!	N	I	250+	Kunhardt, Edith	Random House
Pompeii, The Lost City	V	I	2090	Reading Street	Pearson
Ponce de Leon: Juan Ponce de Leon Searches for the Fountain of Youth	U	B	250+	Exploring the World	Compass Point Books
Pond for Tim, A	D	RF	62	Counters & Seekers	Steck-Vaughn
Pond Hockey Challenge, The	K	RF	250+	Yevchak, Kathryn	Kaeden Books
Pond Party	D	F	33	Little Celebrations	Pearson Learning Group
Pond Walk	M	F	250+	Wallace, Nancy Elizabeth	Marshall Cavendish
Pond Where Harriet Lives, The	H	TL	151	Storyteller	Wright Group/McGraw Hill
Pond, A	LB	I	14	Discovery Links	Newbridge
Pond, The	B	I	34	Big Cat	Pacific Learning
Pond, The	A	I	37	Bonnell, Kris	Reading Reading Books
Pond, The	C	I	25	Books for Young Learners	Richard C. Owen
Pond, The	C	F	54	Joy Readers	Pearson Learning Group
Ponds	F	I	117	Early Explorers	Benchmark Education
Pong Song, The	E	F	46	Rigby Star	Rigby
Ponies at the Point	Q	RF	250+	Baglio, Ben M.	Scholastic
Pony Club, The	H	RF	228	PM Photo Stories	Rigby
Pony Crazy	J	RF	250+	Hapka, Catherine	HarperCollins
Pony Express Dreams	S	HF	250+	In Step Readers	Rigby
Pony Express to the Rescue	N	HF	250+	HSP/Harcourt Trophies	Harcourt, Inc.
Pony Express, The	V	I	250+	Cornerstones of Freedom	Children's Press
Pony Express, The	I	I	128	Independent Readers Social Studies	Houghton Mifflin Harcourt
Pony Express, The	U	I	250+	We The People	Compass Point Books
Pony For Jeremiah, A	R	HF	250+	Miller, Robert H.	Silver Burdett Press
Pony Island	P	HF	250+	Ransom, Candice F.	Walker & Company
Pony Named Shawney, A	P	RF	3075	Small, Mary	Mondo Publishing
Pony on the Porch	Q	RF	250+	Baglio, Ben M.	Scholastic
Pony Pals: A Pony for Keeps	O	RF	250+	Betancourt, Jeanne	Scholastic
Pony Pals: A Pony in Trouble	O	RF	250+	Betancourt, Jeanne	Scholastic
Pony Pals: Detective Pony	O	RF	250+	Betancourt, Jeanne	Scholastic
Pony Pals: Don't Hurt My Pony	O	RF	250+	Betancourt, Jeanne	Scholastic
Pony Pals: Give Me Back My Pony	O	RF	250+	Betancourt, Jeanne	Scholastic
Pony Pals: Good-bye Pony	O	RF	250+	Betancourt, Jeanne	Scholastic
Pony Pals: I Want a Pony	O	RF	250+	Betancourt, Jeanne	Scholastic
Pony Pals: Keep Out, Pony!	O	RF	250+	Betancourt, Jeanne	Scholastic
Pony Pals: Pony to the Rescue	O	RF	250+	Betancourt, Jeanne	Scholastic
Pony Pals: Pony-Sitters	O	RF	250+	Betancourt, Jeanne	Scholastic
Pony Pals: Runaway Pony	O	RF	250+	Betancourt, Jeanne	Scholastic
Pony Pals: The Blind Pony	O	RF	250+	Betancourt, Jeanne	Scholastic
Pony Pals: The Ghost Pony	O	RF	250+	Betancourt, Jeanne	Scholastic
Pony Pals: The Girl Who Hated Ponies	O	RF	250+	Betancourt, Jeanne	Scholastic

PQ

* Collection of short stories   # Graphic text
^ Mature content with lower level text demands

TITLE	LEVEL	GENRE	WORD COUNT	AUTHOR / SERIES	PUBLISHER / DISTRIBUTOR
Pony Pals: The Lonely Pony	O	RF	250+	Betancourt, Jeanne	Scholastic
Pony Pals: The Wild Pony	O	RF	250+	Betancourt, Jeanne	Scholastic
Pony Pals: Too Many Ponies	O	RF	250+	Betancourt, Jeanne	Scholastic
Pony Parade	O	RF	250+	Baglio, Ben M.	Scholastic
Pony Tails: Jasmine and the Jumping Pony	P	RF	250+	Bryant, Bonnie	Bantam Books
Pony Tails: Jasmine's Christmas Ride	P	RF	250+	Bryant, Bonnie	Bantam Books
Pony Tails: May Takes the Lead	P	RF	250+	Bryant, Bonnie	Bantam Books
Pony Trouble	L	RF	250+	Gasque, Dale Blackwell	Hyperion
Poochie the Poodle	F	RF	155	Gear Up!	Wright Group/McGraw Hill
Poodles	R	I	250+	All About Dogs	Capstone Press
Poodles	I	I	115	Dogs	Capstone Press
Poodles Are the Best!	Q	I	2072	The Best Dogs Ever	Lerner Publishing Group
Pookie and Joe	K	F	250+	Literacy 2000	Rigby
Pool Boy	Y	RF	250+	Simmons, Michael	Roaring Brook Press
Pool of Fire, The	V	F	250+	Christopher, John	Aladdin
Pool Pals	N	RF	250+	Girlz Rock!	Mondo Publishing
Pool Party	L	RF	250+	Martha Speaks	Houghton Mifflin Harcourt
Pool, The	D	RF	129	Handprints C, Set 1	Educators Publishing Service
Pool, The	D	F	141	Leveled Literacy Intervention/ Green System	Heinemann
Poop Happened! A History of the World from the Bottom Up	X	I	250+	Albee, Sarah	Walker & Company
^Poop-Eaters: Dung Beetles in the Food Chain	T	I	250+	Extreme Life	Capstone Press
Poopsie Pomerantz Pick Up Your Feet	P	RF	250+	Giff, Patricia Reilly	Dell
Poor Carl	J	F	265	Carlson, Nancy	Carolrhoda Books
Poor Girl, Rich Girl	T	RF	250+	Wilson, Johnniece Marshall	Language for Learning Assoc.
Poor Little Kittens	P	RF	1173	Leveled Readers	Houghton Mifflin Harcourt
Poor Miss Dee!	I	RF	247	Story Box	Wright Group/McGraw Hill
Poor Old Polly	F	F	111	Story Box	Wright Group/McGraw Hill
Poor Panda	WB	F	0	Rigby Literacy	Rigby
Poor Polly Pig	F	F	57	Start to Read	School Zone
Poor Puppy!	B	RF	52	First Stories	Pacific Learning
Poor Sore Hungry Giant	H	F	231	The Joy Cowley Collection	Hameray Publishing Group
Poor Sore Paw, The	I	F	244	Sunshine	Wright Group/McGraw Hill
Pop . . . Pop . . . Popcorn	C	I	40	Home Connection Collection	Rigby
Pop and Robby	I	F	328	Sails	Rigby
Pop Pop and Grandpa	I	RF	194	Bebop Books	Lee & Low Books Inc.
Pop Pop Pop Pop Pop	B	F	36	Brand New Readers	Candlewick Press
Pop Pop Popcorn!	F	RF	207	Leveled Literacy Intervention/ Blue System	Heinemann
POP Pops the Popcorn	E	RF	60	Ready Readers	Pearson Learning Group
Pop- Up Farm IQ	M	I	250+	Priddy, Roger	Priddy Books
Pop! A Play	D	F	105	Rigby Star	Rigby
Pop! Pop! Pop!	D	RF	84	Reading Street	Pearson
Popcorn	D	F	75	Green Light Readers	Harcourt
Popcorn	LB	RF	16	Handprints A	Educators Publishing Service
Popcorn and Candy	I	I	161	Windows on Literacy	National Geographic
Popcorn Book, The	N	I	250+	DePaola, Tomie	Holiday House
Popcorn Book, The	K	I	208	Reading Unlimited	Pearson Learning Group
Popcorn Days & Buttermilk Nights	U	RF	250+	Paulsen, Gary	Penguin Group
Popcorn Fun	H	RF	217	PM Plus Story Books	Rigby
Popcorn Plants	Q	I	1852	Early Bird Nature Books	Lerner Publishing Group

* Collection of short stories   # Graphic text
^ Mature content with lower level text demands

Popcorn Shop, The	J	RF	250+	Low, Alice	Scholastic
Pope John Paul II	X	B	250+	A&E Biography	Lerner Publishing Group
*Poppleton	J	F	250+	Rylant, Cynthia	Scholastic
*Poppleton and Friends	J	F	250+	Rylant, Cynthia	Blue Sky Press
*Poppleton Everyday	J	F	250+	Rylant, Cynthia	Scholastic
*Poppleton Forever	J	F	250+	Rylant, Cynthia	Scholastic
*Poppleton Has Fun	J	F	250+	Rylant, Cynthia	Scholastic
*Poppleton in Fall	J	F	250+	Rylant, Cynthia	Scholastic
*Poppleton in Spring	J	F	250+	Rylant, Cynthia	Scholastic
Poppy	S	F	250+	Avi	Avon Books
Poppy and Rye	S	F	250+	Avi	Avon Books
Poppy, Josh, and the Hurricane	H	RF	225	Gear Up!	Wright Group/McGraw Hill
Poppy, The	K	I	152	Pacific Literacy	Pacific Learning
Poppy's Return	S	F	250+	Avi	HarperTrophy
Poppy's Timeline	U	RF	1759	Leveled Readers	Houghton Mifflin Harcourt
Pop's Truck	K	RF	250+	Voyages	SRA/McGraw Hill
Popular Pets	N	I	250+	Tristars	Richard C. Owen
Populations	Y	I	2006	Science Support Readers	Houghton Mifflin Harcourt
Pop-Up Dino IQ	M	I	250+	Priddy, Roger	Priddy Books
Porc in New York, A	P	F	250+	Stock, Catherine	Holiday House
Porcupine, A	D	I	49	Wonder World	Wright Group/McGraw Hill
Porcupines	R	I	250+	Animal Prey	Lerner Publishing Group
Porcupines	J	I	190	Nocturnal Animals	Capstone Press
Porcupine's Boo-Boo	D	F	52	Tiny Treasures	Pioneer Valley
Porcupine's First Day at School	L	F	606	Pawprints Teal	Pioneer Valley
Porcupine's Kite	J	F	372	Pawprints Teal	Pioneer Valley
Porcupine's Pajama Party	J	F	250+	Harshman, Terry Webb	HarperTrophy
Porridge That Was Too Hot, The	F	TL	286	Rigby Flying Colors	Rigby
^Porsche	O	I	250+	Fast Cars	Capstone Press
Port, The	L	I	250+	Explorations	Okapi Educational Materials
Port, The	L	I	250+	Explorations	Eleanor Curtain Publishing
Portia and the Math Problems	N	B	250+	Leveled Readers Language Support	Houghton Mifflin Harcourt
Portland Trail Blazers, The	S	I	250+	Team Spirit	Norwood House Press
Portraits in Greatness	U	B	250+	Navigators Biography Series	Benchmark Education
Portraits of African-American Heroes	V	B	250+	Bolden, Tonya	Scholastic
^Portuguese Colonies in the Americas	S	I	250+	On Deck	Rigby
Portuguese Water Dogs Are the Best!	Q	I	1529	The Best Dogs Ever	Lerner Publishing Group
Poseur	Z+	RF	250+	Maude, Rachel	Little Brown and Company
Poseur: The Good, the Fab and the Ugly	Z+	RF	250+	Maude, Rachel	Little Brown and Company
Possibilities of Sainthood, The	Z	RF	250+	Freitas, Donna	Farrar, Straus, & Giroux
Possum Always Rings Twice, The: A Chet Gecko Mystery	R	F	250+	Hale, Bruce	Harcourt, Inc.
Possum Babies, The	H	F	252	Sails	Rigby
Possum's Bare Tail	N	TL	770	Leveled Readers	Houghton Mifflin Harcourt
Possum's Three Fine Friends	K	F	250+	Bannister, Barbara	Kaeden Books
Postal Carrier	C	I	29	Work People Do	Lerner Publishing Group
Postal Workers	M	I	720	Pull Ahead Books	Lerner Publishing Group
Postal Workers: Then and Now	P	I	250+	Primary Source Readers	Teacher Created Materials
Postcard Pest, The	M	RF	250+	Giff, Patricia Reilly	Bantam Books
Postcard, The	X	RF	250+	Abbott, Tony	Little Brown and Company
Postcards From France	N	I	250+	Arnold, Helen	Steck-Vaughn
Postcards From Kenya	N	I	250+	Arnold, Helen	Steck-Vaughn

PQ

TITLE	LEVEL	GENRE	WORD COUNT	AUTHOR / SERIES	PUBLISHER / DISTRIBUTOR
Postcards from Pluto: A Tour of the Solar System	N	F	250+	Leedy, Loreen	Scholastic
Postcards from Pop	H	RF	122	Literacy Tree	Rigby
Postcards From South Africa	N	I	250+	Dawson, Zoe	Steck-Vaughn
Postcards From Vietnam	N	I	250+	Allard, Denise	Steck-Vaughn
Postcards to Paul	G	RF	147	Windows on Literacy	National Geographic
Postman Pete	J	RF	250+	Bookshop	Mondo Publishing
*Pot of Gold, A/Clever Farmer, The	L	TL	250+	Pacific Literacy	Pacific Learning
Pot of Gold, The	J	TL	655	Big Cat	Pacific Learning
Pot of Gold, The	I	TL	266	Reading Unlimited	Pearson Learning Group
Pot of Stone Soup, A	L	TL	250+	Ready Readers	Pearson Learning Group
Potato	N	RF	250+	Peirce, Robin	Wright Group/McGraw Hill
Potato Chips	I	RF	101	City Kids	Rigby
Potato Harvest Time	A	I	33	Little Books for Early Readers	University of Maine
Potato Pride	P	RF	1000	Leveled Readers	Houghton Mifflin Harcourt
Potato Printing	G	I	174	Sun Sprouts	ETA/Cuisenaire
Potato: A Tale From the Great Depression	L	HF	250+	Soar To Success	Houghton Mifflin Harcourt
Potatoes	F	I	92	Life Cycles	Lerner Publishing Group
Potatoes	I	I	78	Windows on Literacy	National Geographic
Potatoes on Tuesday	C	F	28	Little Celebrations	Pearson Learning Group
Potatoes, Potatoes	H	I	91	Wonder World	Wright Group/McGraw Hill
Potter in Fiji, A	N	I	453	Wonder World	Wright Group/McGraw Hill
Pouch!	G	F	150	Stein, David Ezra	G.P. Putnam's Sons
Pouncing Bobcats	K	I	411	Pull Ahead Books	Lerner Publishing Group
Pourquoi Tales	N	TL	523	Vocabulary Readers	Houghton Mifflin Harcourt
Powder Monkey, The	Q	HF	250+	High-Fliers	Pacific Learning
Powder Puff Puzzle, The	L	RF	250+	Giff, Patricia Reilly	Bantam Books
Power Machines	N	I	250+	Robbins, Ken	Henry Holt & Co.
Power of Corn, The	P	I	1092	Leveled Readers/TX	Houghton Mifflin Harcourt
Power of Energy, The	K	I	187	Physical Science	Capstone Press
Power of Gandhi, The	U	B	250+	Power Up!	Steck-Vaughn
*Power of Light, The	V	TL	250+	Singer, Isaac Bashevis	Farrar, Straus, & Giroux
Power of Nature, The	K	I	274	Early Connections	Benchmark Education
Power of Our People, The	U	I	1529	Reading Street	Pearson
Power of the Wind, The	L	I	250+	Literacy by Design	Rigby
Power of Un, The	T	SF	250+	Etchemendy, Nancy	Scholastic
Power of Water, The	N	I	250+	Home Connection Collection	Rigby
Power of Wind, The	V	I	1653	Leveled Readers	Houghton Mifflin Harcourt
Power of Wind, The	T	I	1983	Leveled Readers Science	Houghton Mifflin Harcourt
Power of Wind, The	V	I	1653	Leveled Readers/CA	Houghton Mifflin Harcourt
Power Out!	J	RF	167	Avenues	Hampton Brown
Power Partners	T	I	250+	Literacy by Design	Rigby
Power to Vote, The	J	I	193	Early Explorers	Benchmark Education
Powerboats	L	I	110	On Deck	Rigby
Powerboats	N	I	464	Pull Ahead Books	Lerner Publishing Group
Powerful People	L	I	211	Pair-It Turn and Learn	Steck-Vaughn
Powerful Plant Cells	Z	I	250+	Microquests	Lerner Publishing Group
#Powerful World of Energy with Max Axiom Super Scientist, The	W	I	250+	Graphic Library	Capstone Press
Powerhouse, Inside a Nuclear Power Plant	Z	I	250+	Wilcox, Charlotte	Carolrhoda Books
Power-Packed Plants	O	I	250+	InfoQuest	Rigby
Powers	Z+	F	250+	Jacobs, Deborah Lynn	Square Fish
Powers of Congress, The	W	I	250+	Cornerstones of Freedom	Children's Press
Powers of the Mind	Z	I	250+	Unsolved Mysteries	Steck-Vaughn

* Collection of short stories   # Graphic text
^ Mature content with lower level text demands

TITLE	LEVEL	GENRE	WORD COUNT	AUTHOR / SERIES	PUBLISHER / DISTRIBUTOR
Powhatan, The: A Confederacy of Native American Tribes	S	I	250+	American Indian Nations	Capstone Press
Powwow	F	I	29	Books for Young Learners	Richard C. Owen
Powwow	Q	I	250+	WorldScapes	ETA/Cuisenaire
Powwow Summer: A Family Celebrates the Circle of Life	S	I	250+	Rendon, Marcie R.	Carolrhoda Books
Powwow, The	I	RF	328	Adams, Lorraine & Bruvold, Lynn	Eaglecrest Books
Practice Makes Perfect	K	RF	250+	On Our Way to English	Rigby
Practice Makes Perfect	D	RF	111	Teacher's Choice Series	Pearson Learning Group
Praire Storms	O	RF	445	Pattinson, Darcy	Sylvan Dell Publishing
Prairie Danger	T	HF	1722	Leveled Readers	Houghton Mifflin Harcourt
Prairie Dogs	Q	I	250+	Animal Prey	Lerner Publishing Group
Prairie Dogs	L	I	212	Twig	Wright Group/McGraw Hill
Prairie Dogs - Social Animals	S	I	250+	Sails	Rigby
Prairie Dogs and Their Burrows	J	I	130	Animal Homes	Capstone Press
Prairie Dog's Burrow	L	I	250+	Prairie Adventures	Smithsonian
Prairie Plants	N	I	250+	Life in the World's Biomes	Capstone Press
Prairie School	Q	I	505	Vocabulary Readers	Houghton Mifflin Harcourt
Prairie Songs	Q	HF	250+	Conrad, Pam	HarperTrophy
Prairie Town	F	I	62	Seedlings	Continental Press
Prairie Winter	T	HF	250+	Geisert, Bonnie	Houghton Mifflin Harcourt
Praying Mantis	H	I	112	Readlings/ Bugs	American Reading Company
Praying Mantis, The	D	I	46	Pacific Literacy	Pacific Learning
Praying Mantises	H	I	96	Bugs, Bugs, Bugs!	Red Brick Learning
Praying Mantises	U	I	250+	Insect World: Hungry Insect Heroes	Lerner Publishing Group
Praying Mantises	I	I	78	Insects	Red Brick Learning
Preacher's Boy	T	RF	250+	Paterson, Katherine	Houghton Mifflin Harcourt
Precious Stones	T	I	1331	Leveled Readers Science	Houghton Mifflin Harcourt
Precise Patterns	U	I	250+	WorldScapes	ETA/Cuisenaire
^Predators	Q	I	250+	Download	Hameray Publishing Group
Predators	N	I	803	Springboard	Wright Group/McGraw Hill
Predators in the Rain Forest	O	I	250+	Pirotta, Saviour	Steck-Vaughn
Predators!	U	I	250+	Boldprint	Steck-Vaughn
Predicting the Weather	I	I	202	Early Explorers	Benchmark Education
Predicting the Weather	P	I	857	Vocabulary Readers	Houghton Mifflin Harcourt
Predicting the Weather	P	I	857	Vocabulary Readers/CA	Houghton Mifflin Harcourt
Predictions	T	RF	250+	Halliday, John	Margaret K. McElderry Books
Prehistoric Life	L	I	105	Windows on Literacy	National Geographic
Prehistoric Record Breakers	N	I	250+	Discovery World	Rigby
Prehistory to Egypt	R	I	250+	Journey Through History	Barron's Educational
Preparing for Lift-Off	Q	I	453	Vocabulary Readers	Houghton Mifflin Harcourt
Presence, The	Y	F	250+	Bunting, Eve	Graphia
Present for Karl, A	C	RF	81	PM Photo Stories	Rigby
Present for LaNita, A	L	RF	835	Leveled Readers Social Studies	Houghton Mifflin Harcourt
Present for Our Teacher, A	H	I	189	Explorations	Eleanor Curtain Publishing
Present for Our Teacher, A	H	I	189	Explorations	Okapi Educational Materials
Present for Santa Claus, A	L	F	250+	Wood, David	Candlewick Press
Present From Aunt Skidoo, The	M	RF	250+	Literacy 2000	Rigby
Present, The	B	I	36	First Stories	Pacific Learning
Present, The	E	F	30	Literacy 2000	Rigby
Presentation, The	S	RF	2568	Leveled Readers	Houghton Mifflin Harcourt
Presentation, The	S	RF	2568	Leveled Readers/CA	Houghton Mifflin Harcourt

PQ

TITLE	LEVEL	GENRE	WORD COUNT	AUTHOR / SERIES	PUBLISHER / DISTRIBUTOR
Presentation, The	S	RF	2568	Leveled Readers/TX	Houghton Mifflin Harcourt
Presents	D	F	43	Storyteller-First Snow	Wright Group/McGraw Hill
Presents	H	RF	211	Storyworlds	Heinemann
Presents for Grace	H	RF	283	Red Rocket Readers	Flying Start Books
Presents for Jack and Billy	D	RF	105	PM Stars	Rigby
Presents for Mom	A	RF	18	Bonnell, Kris	Reading Reading Books
Presents, The	B	F	30	Sails	Rigby
Presidency of the United States, The	V	I	250+	American Civics	Red Brick Learning
Presidency, The	S	I	250+	A True Book	Children's Press
Presidency, The	Q	I	250+	Let's See	Compass Point Books
President Barack Obama	L	B	353	Marks, Jennifer L.	Capstone Press
President for the People, A	R	B	1317	Leveled Readers	Houghton Mifflin Harcourt
President for the People, A	R	B	1317	Leveled Readers/CA	Houghton Mifflin Harcourt
President for the People, A	R	B	1317	Leveled Readers/TX	Houghton Mifflin Harcourt
President George Washington	N	B	250+	Our American Story	Picture Window Books
President Lincoln, Willie Kettles, and the Telegraph Machine	S	HF	3699	History Speaks	Millbrook Press
President Obama	U	I	250+	Time for Kids	Capstone Press
President of the Underground Railroad: A Story about Levi Coffin	S	B	7965	Creative Minds Biographies	Lerner Publishing Group
President of the United States, The	T	I	250+	Pair-It Books	Steck-Vaughn
President of the Whole Fifth Grade	S	RF	250+	Winston, Sherri	Little Brown and Company
President, Vice President, and Cabinet, The: A Look at the Executive Branch	R	I	1058	Searchlight Books	Lerner Publishing Group
Presidential Elections	W	I	250+	Cornerstones of Freedom	Children's Press
President's Daughter, The	Z+	RF	250+	White, Ellen Emerson	Feiwel and Friends
Presidents' Day	J	I	103	American Holidays	Lerner Publishing Group
Presidents' Day	Q	I	250+	Holiday Histories	Heinemann
Presidents' Day	J	I	184	Holidays and Festivals	Heinemann Library
Presidents' Day	L	I	250+	National Holidays	Red Brick Learning
Presidents' Day	N	I	250+	Rookie Read-About Holidays	Children's Press
President's Murderer, The	Y	RF	5270	Oxford Bookworms Library	Oxford University Press
Press a Button	E	I	43	Windows on Literacy	National Geographic
Presto Pizza	J	I	216	Red Rocket Readers	Flying Start Books
Presto's New Pet	K	F	250+	Rigby Rocket	Rigby
Pretend You Love Me	Z+	RF	250+	Peters, Julie Anne	Little Brown and Company
Pretty Cat	D	RF	54	Potato Chip Books	American Reading Company
Pretty Committee Strikes Back, The: The Clique	Y	RF	250+	Harrison, Lisi	Little Brown and Company
Pretty Cool, for a Cat	Q	RF	1707	Leveled Readers	Houghton Mifflin Harcourt
Pretty Face, A	W	RF	2615	Dominoes starter	Oxford University Press
Pretty Good Magic	J	RF	250+	Dubowski, Cathy East & Mark	Random House
Pretty in Print: Questioning Magazines	S	I	250+	Media Literacy	Capstone Press
Pretty Like Us	W	RF	250+	Williams, Carol Lynch	Peachtree
Previously	N	F	250+	Ahlberg, Allan	Candlewick Press
Price of a Pipeline, The	U	I	2608	Reading Street	Pearson
Prickles the Porcupine	K	RF	430	PM Plus Story Books	Rigby
Prickly Porcupines	K	I	339	Pull Ahead Books	Lerner Publishing Group
Pride of Lions, A	H	I	95	Windows on Literacy	National Geographic
Pride of Puerto Rico: The Life of Roberto Clemente	W	B	250+	Walker, Paul Robert	Harcourt Trade
Pride of the Rockets	N	RF	250+	Kroll, Stephen	Avon Books
Primavera	X	HF	250+	Beaufrand, Mary Jane	Little Brown and Company
Prince Among Donkeys, A	K	RF	250+	Rigby Literacy	Rigby
Prince Among Killers, A: Oathbreaker Part 2	Z	F	250+	Vaught, S R & Redmond, J B	Bloomsbury Children's Books

Organized Alphabetically by Title
Storable Database at www.fountasandpinnellleveledbooks.com

* Collection of short stories   # Graphic text
^ Mature content with lower level text demands

Prince Amos	R	RF	250+	Paulsen, Gary	Bantam Books
Prince of Fenway Park, The	U	F	250+	Baggott, Julianna	HarperCollins
Prince of the Mist, The	V	F	250+	Zafon, Carlos Ruiz	Little Brown and Company
Prince William	Q	B	250+	Rand, Gloria	Henry Holt & Co.
Prince's Carpet, The	L	TL	669	In Step Readers	Rigby
Princess Academy	V	F	250+	Hale, Shannon	Bloomsbury Children's Books
Princess and the Castle, The	J	F	250+	Leonhardt, Alice	Steck-Vaughn
Princess and the Dragon, The	C	F	20	Rigby Rocket	Rigby
Princess and the Manatee, The	O	F	1000	Leveled Readers/TX	Houghton Mifflin Harcourt
Princess and the Pea	K	TL	480	Traditional Tales	Pioneer Valley
Princess and the Pea, The	J	TL	250+	Literacy by Design	Rigby
Princess and the Pea, The	I	TL	250+	Storyworlds	Heinemann
Princess and the Pea, The	I	TL	304	Traditional Tales	Pearson Learning Group
Princess and the Peas, The	K	TL	250+	Enrichment	Wright Group/McGraw Hill
Princess and the Pets, The	K	F	250+	I Am Reading	Kingfisher
Princess and the Wise Woman, The	K	TL	250+	Ready Readers	Pearson Learning Group
Princess Bride, The	Z+	TL	250+	Goldman, William	Ballantine Books
Princess Cookbook, A	N	I	250+	First Cookbooks	Capstone Press
^Princess Diana: The People's Princess	S	B	250+	Hameray Biography Series	Hameray Publishing Group
Princess Diaries, The	Z	RF	250+	Cabot, Meg	HarperTrophy
Princess Euphorbia	N	RF	250+	Supa Doopers	Sundance
Princess for a Week	Q	F	250+	Wright, Betty Ren	Holiday House
Princess Grace of Monaco	S	B	250+	Queens and Princesses	Capstone Press
Princess in Love	Z	RF	250+	Cabot, Meg	HarperTrophy
Princess Josie's Pets	L	RF	250+	Macdonald, Maryann	Hyperion
Princess Kiko of Japan	S	B	250+	Queens and Princesses	Capstone Press
Princess of Glass	X	F	250+	George, Jessica Day	Bloomsbury Children's Books
Princess of the Fillmore Street School, The (Olivia Sharp)	L	RF	250+	Sharmat, Marjorie Weinman	Yearling Books
Princess of the Midnight Ball	X	F	250+	George, Jessica Day	Bloomsbury Children's Books
Princess Pig and the Pink Purse	L	F	760	Pawprints Teal	Pioneer Valley
Princess Posey and the First Grade Parade	K	RF	250+	Greene, Stephanie	G.P. Putnam's Sons
Princess Rosa's Winter	L	F	250+	I Am Reading	Kingfisher
Princess Rosa's Winter	L	F	250+	Storyteller-Shooting Stars	Wright Group/McGraw Hill
Princess Who Couldn't Cry, The	G	TL	300	Ready Readers	Pearson Learning Group
Princess Who Loved to Cook, The	M	F	250+	Cartwright, Pauline	Pearson Learning Group
Princess Who Wanted the Moon, The	M	F	250+	Lane, Sheila; Kemp, Marion	Wood Lock Educational
Princess, The	I	RF	252	The Rowland Reading Program Library	Rowland Reading Foundation
Princess, the Mud Pies, and the Dragon, The	I	TL	250+	Little Readers	Houghton Mifflin Harcourt
Princesses Are Not Perfect	L	F	250+	Lum, Kate	Bloomsbury Children's Books
Princesses Don't Wear Jeans	M	RF	250+	Bookshop	Mondo Publishing
Principal Fred Won't Go to Bed	L	F	250+	Crimi, Carolyn	Marshall Cavendish
Principal from the Black Lagoon, The	K	F	250+	Thaler, Mike	Scholastic
Principals	J	I	546	Pull Ahead Books	Lerner Publishing Group
Print It!	R	I	1209	Vocabulary Readers	Houghton Mifflin Harcourt
Print It!	R	I	1209	Vocabulary Readers/CA	Houghton Mifflin Harcourt
Print It!	R	I	1209	Vocabulary Readers/TX	Houghton Mifflin Harcourt
Printed Words of the Revolution	V	I	2645	Leveled Readers	Houghton Mifflin Harcourt
Printed Words of the Revolution	V	I	2645	Leveled Readers/CA	Houghton Mifflin Harcourt
Printed Words of the Revolution	V	I	2645	Leveled Readers/TX	Houghton Mifflin Harcourt

PQ

* Collection of short stories   # Graphic text
^ Mature content with lower level text demands

TITLE	LEVEL	GENRE	WORD COUNT	AUTHOR / SERIES	PUBLISHER / DISTRIBUTOR
Printer, The	O	HF	250+	Uhlberg, Myron	Peachtree
Printing Machine, The	G	F	102	Literacy 2000	Rigby
^Printing Press, The: An Information Revolution	R	I	250+	On Deck	Rigby
Prints	M	I	250+	Start with Art	Heinemann Library
Priscilla and the Dinosaurs	K	RF	340	Sunshine	Wright Group/McGraw Hill
Priscilla and the Great Santa Search	N	F	250+	Hobbie, Nathaniel	Little Brown and Company
Priscilla and the Pink Planet	N	F	250+	Hobbie, Nathaniel	Little Brown and Company
Priscilla and the Pixie Princess	N	F	250+	Hobbie, Nathaniel	Little Brown and Company
Priscilla and the Splish-Splash Surprise	N	F	250+	Hobbie, Nathaniel	Little Brown and Company
Priscilla Superstar!	N	RF	250+	Hobbie, Nathaniel	Little Brown and Company
Prisoner for Liberty	O	B	1465	On My Own History	Millbrook Press
Prisoner of Dieppe: World War II	W	HF	250+	I Am Canada	Scholastic
Prisoner of Zenda, The	W	RF	10710	Oxford Bookworms Library	Oxford University Press
#Prison-Ship Adventure of James Forten, Revolutionary War Captive, The	R	HF	916	History's Kid Heros	Graphic Universe
Private Captain: A Story of Gettysburg	W	HF	250+	Crisp, Marty	Philomel
Private Joel and the Sewell Mountain Seder	R	HF	2537	Fireside, Bryna J.	Kar-Ben Publishing
Private Notebook of Katie Roberts, Age 11, The	P	RF	250+	Hest, Amy	Candlewick Press
Private Thoughts of Amelia E. Rye, The	W	HF	250+	Shimko, Bonnie	Farrar, Straus, & Giroux
Prize for Purry, A	K	RF	250+	Literacy 2000	Rigby
Prize Goat	J	F	533	Sun Sprouts	ETA/Cuisenaire
Pro Sports: How Did They Begin?	S	I	250+	Wulffson, Don L.	Mondo Publishing
Pro Stock Car Racing	S	I	250+	Motor Sports	Red Brick Learning
Pro Stock Cars	Q	I	250+	Wild Rides!	Red Brick Learning
Pro Stock Trucks	T	I	250+	The World's Fastest	Red Brick Learning
Probability	P	I	250+	Early Connections	Benchmark Education
Problem Child, The: The Sisters Grimm	U	F	250+	Buckley, Michael	Amulet Books
Problem with Meli, The	J	I	333	Leveled Literacy Intervention/ Blue System	Heinemann
Problems with My Pudding	N	I	950	Leveled Readers Science	Houghton Mifflin Harcourt
Proboscis Monkey, the	J	I	147	Weird Animals	Capstone Press
Processed Food	F	I	54	Wonder World	Wright Group/McGraw Hill
Producing Goods	N	I	213	Windows on Literacy	National Geographic
Professor Gylden Lox's Hair School	S	F	4800	Take Two Books	Wright Group/McGraw Hill
Professor Science and the Salamander Stumper	Q	RF	2579	Reading Street	Pearson
Profiles in Sports Courage	U	B	250+	Rappaport, Ken	Peachtree
Progressives, The	V	I	250+	Reading Expeditions	National Geographic
Prohibition	X	I	2560	Independent Readers Social Studies	Houghton Mifflin Harcourt
Project Apollo	Q	I	250+	A True Book	Children's Press
Project Bug	V	RF	3641	Leveled Readers	Houghton Mifflin Harcourt
Project Bug	V	RF	3641	Leveled Readers/CA	Houghton Mifflin Harcourt
Project Bug	V	RF	3641	Leveled Readers/TX	Houghton Mifflin Harcourt
Project Gemini	Q	I	250+	A True Book	Children's Press
Project Mercury	Q	I	250+	A True Book	Children's Press
Project Mulberry	T	RF	250+	Park, Linda Sue	Houghton Mifflin Harcourt
Project Seahorse	V	I	250+	Scientists in the Field	Houghton Mifflin Harcourt
Promise Me the Moon	V	RF	250+	Barnes, Joyce Annette	Penguin Group
Promises to the Dead	Y	HF	250+	Hahn, Mary Downing	Sandpiper Books
Proof of Magic	Q	F	250+	Ragged Island Mysteries	Wright Group/McGraw Hill
Properties of Matter	S	I	1748	Science Support Readers	Houghton Mifflin Harcourt
Prophecy of the Sisters	Y	F	250+	Zink, Michelle	Little Brown and Company
Prophecy of the Stones, The	Z	F	250+	Bujor, Flavia	Hyperion
Protecting Earth's Air Quality	X	I	11018	Saving Our Living Earth	Lerner Publishing Group

* Collection of short stories   # Graphic text
^ Mature content with lower level text demands

TITLE	LEVEL	GENRE	WORD COUNT	AUTHOR / SERIES	PUBLISHER / DISTRIBUTOR
Protecting Earth's Land	X	I	10697	Saving Our Living Earth	Lerner Publishing Group
Protecting Earth's Rain Forests	X	I	11411	Saving Our Living Earth	Lerner Publishing Group
Protecting Earth's Water Supply	X	I	10317	Saving Our Living Earth	Lerner Publishing Group
Protecting Endangered Animals	T	I	1928	Vocabulary Readers	Houghton Mifflin Harcourt
Protecting Endangered Animals	T	I	1928	Vocabulary Readers/CA	Houghton Mifflin Harcourt
Protecting Our Oceans	U	I	250+	Navigators Science Series	Benchmark Education
Protecting Sea Turtles	R	I	250+	Leveled Readers Language Support	Houghton Mifflin Harcourt
Protecting Sea Turtles	M	I	250+	Windows on Literacy	National Geographic
Protecting the Past	W	I	250+	WorldScapes	ETA/Cuisenaire
Protecting the Planet	U	I	250+	Reading Expeditions	National Geographic
Protecting the Planet: Environmental Activism	T	I	250+	Green Generation	Compass Point Books
Protecting Your Home: A Book About Firefighters	H	I	89	Community Workers	Picture Window Books
Protectors, The	Y	RF	3223	Leveled Readers	Houghton Mifflin Harcourt
Protester's Song, The	Z	RF	250+	Misfits Inc.	Peachtree
Protozoans, Algea, & Other Protists	Z	I	250+	Kingdom Classification	Compass Point Books
Proud Achilles	V	TL	2386	Leveled Readers	Houghton Mifflin Harcourt
Proud Achilles	V	TL	2386	Leveled Readers/CA	Houghton Mifflin Harcourt
Proud Achilles	V	TL	2386	Leveled Readers/TX	Houghton Mifflin Harcourt
Proud Taste for Scarlet and Miniver	W	F	250+	Konigsburg, E. L.	Dell
Providing Goods	K	I	122	Windows on Literacy	National Geographic
Prowling the Seas: Exploring the Hidden World of Ocean Predators	U	I	250+	Turner, Pamela S.	Walker & Company
Prudence	N	I	250+	Character Education	Red Brick Learning
PS Brothers, The	O	RF	250+	Boelts, Maribeth	Houghton Mifflin Harcourt
PS, I Love You Gramps	O	RF	250+	Literacy Tree	Rigby
#Psyche & Eros: The Lady and the Monster	W	TL	2679	Graphic Myths and Legends	Lerner Publishing Group
Psychic Detective	R	F	2645	Khoury, George	January Books
^Psychic Powers: The Unsolved Mystery	P	I	250+	Mysteries of Science	Capstone Press
^Psychics	X	I	250+	The Unexplained	Capstone Press
PT Boats	T	I	250+	Land and Sea	Capstone Press
Pterodactyl at the Airport	K	F	185	Wesley & the Dinosaurs	Wright Group/McGraw Hill
Pterosaur's Long Flight	I	HF	301	PM Story Books-Orange	Rigby
PT's Terrible Problem	P	F	1240	Leveled Readers	Houghton Mifflin Harcourt
PT's Terrible Problem	P	F	1240	Leveled Readers/CA	Houghton Mifflin Harcourt
PT's Terrible Problem	P	F	1240	Leveled Readers/TX	Houghton Mifflin Harcourt
Public Library, The	K	I	250+	Stepping Stones	Nelson/Michaels Assoc.
Pudding Problems	N	RF	921	Leveled Readers Science	Houghton Mifflin Harcourt
Puddle Play	K	F	460	Leveled Literacy Intervention/ Blue System	Heinemann
Puddle, The	I	F	325	McPhail, David	Farrar, Straus, & Giroux
Puddles	B	F	38	Brand New Readers	Candlewick Press
Puddles	E	RF	73	Kaleidoscope Collection	Hameray Publishing Group
Puddles	D	I	114	PM Science Readers	Rigby
Pueblo	K	I	114	Leveled Readers Social Studies	Houghton Mifflin Harcourt
Pueblo Indians, The	P	I	250+	Native Peoples	Red Brick Learning
Pueblo Ruins	Q	I	250+	Rigby Literacy	Rigby
Pueblo, The	R	I	250+	First Reports	Compass Point Books
Pueblo, The: Southwestern Potters	R	I	250+	America's First Peoples	Capstone Press
Pueblos, The: People of the Southwest	S	I	250+	Theme Sets	National Geographic
Puerto Rico	O	I	1906	A Ticket to …	Carolrhoda Books
Puerto Rico	P	I	1827	Country Explorers	Lerner Publishing Group
Puerto Rico	T	I	250+	Hello U.S.A.	Lerner Publishing Group

* Collection of short stories   # Graphic text
^ Mature content with lower level text demands

Organized Alphabetically by Title   **623**
Storable Database at www.fountasandpinnellleveledbooks.com

TITLE	LEVEL	GENRE	WORD COUNT	AUTHOR / SERIES	PUBLISHER / DISTRIBUTOR
Puerto Rico	K	I	175	Nonfiction Set 6	Literacy Footprints
Puerto Rico	R	I	250+	This Land Is Your Land	Compass Point Books
Puerto Rico: Facts and Symbols	O	I	250+	The States and Their Symbols	Capstone Press
Puffer Fish	I	I	121	Under the Sea	Capstone Press
Puffin	B	I	34	Zoozoo-Animal World	Cavallo Publishing
Puffins	E	I	87	Bonnell, Kris/About	Reading Reading Books
Puffins	U	I	5713	Nature Watch	Lerner Publishing Group
Puffins	H	I	121	Polar Animals	Capstone Press
Puffins	S	I	250+	Quinlan, Susan E.	Carolrhoda Books
Puffins	H	I	104	Seedlings	Continental Press
Puffling	K	F	250+	Wild, Margaret	Feiwel and Friends
Puffy Popovers and Other Get-Out-of-Bed Breakfasts	R	I	250+	Kids Dish	Picture Window Books
Pug and Chug	I	F	250+	Supersonics	Rigby
Pug in a Truck	L	F	250+	Coffelt, Nancy	Houghton Mifflin Harcourt
Pugs	R	I	250+	All About Dogs	Capstone Press
Pugs	I	I	128	Dogs	Capstone Press
Pugs Are the Best!	Q	I	1387	The Best Dogs Ever	Lerner Publishing Group
Pug's Walk	E	RF	84	Joy Starters	Pearson Learning Group
Pukeko Morning	G	I	148	Pacific Literacy	Pacific Learning
Pukey Book of Vomit, The	S	I	250+	The Amazingly Gross Human Body	Capstone Press
Pulleys	Q	I	1643	Early Bird Energy Physics Books	Lerner Publishing Group
Pulleys to the Rescue	O	I	250+	Simple Machine to the Rescue	Capstone Press
Pulling Down the Walls: The Struggle of African American Performers	U	I	2697	Reading Street	Pearson
Pullman Strike, The	V	I	1541	Leveled Readers Social Studies	Houghton Mifflin Harcourt
Pulls	G	I	171	How Things Move	Heinemann Library
Pumpkin Farm, The	D	RF	106	McAlpin, MaryAnn	Short Tales Press
Pumpkin Grows, A	E	I	176	Bookshop	Mondo Publishing
Pumpkin Grows, The	B	I	24	On Our Way to English	Rigby
Pumpkin Harvest	F	I	92	All About Fall	Capstone Press
Pumpkin Hill	M	F	250+	Spurr, Elizabeth	Holiday House
Pumpkin House, The	J	F	250+	Literacy 2000	Rigby
Pumpkin Seeds, The	I	I	217	Storyteller	Wright Group/McGraw Hill
Pumpkin That Kim Carved, The	H	RF	149	Little Readers	Houghton Mifflin Harcourt
Pumpkin, The	E	I	56	Story Box	Wright Group/McGraw Hill
Pumpkins	F	I	76	Bonnell, Kris/About	Reading Reading Books
Pumpkins	F	I	100	Plant Life Cycles	Lerner Publishing Group
Pumpkins	M	I	250+	Ray, Mary Lyn	Harcourt Trade
Pumpkins	L	I	250+	Robbins, Ken	Square Fish
Pumpkins and Apples	I	F	311	Reading Street	Pearson
Pumpkins in Fall	D	I	41	Shutterbug Books	Steck-Vaughn
Punched Paper	I	I	250+	Bebop Books	Lee & Low Books Inc.
Punchinello	F	TL	250+	PM Readalongs	Rigby
Punctuation Celebration	M	I	250+	Bruno, Elisa Knight	Scholastic
Punctuation Station, The	M	F	299	Cleary, Brian P.	Millbrook Press
Punished!	Q	F	9988	Lubar, David	Darby Creek Publishing
Punny Places: Jokes to Make You Mappy!	O	F	1703	Make Me Laugh!	Lerner Publishing Group
Punxsutawney Phyllis	K	F	250+	Hill, Susanna Leonard	Holiday House
Pup Camps Out	G	F	115	Reading Street	Pearson
^Puppet Master, The	T	F	250+	The Extraordinary Files	Hameray Publishing Group
Puppet Pals	C	I	35	Little Celebrations	Pearson Learning Group

* Collection of short stories   # Graphic text
^ Mature content with lower level text demands

TITLE	LEVEL	GENRE	WORD COUNT	AUTHOR / SERIES	PUBLISHER / DISTRIBUTOR
Puppet Play, A	C	I	54	Storyteller-First Snow	Wright Group/McGraw Hill
Puppet Show	F	RF	105	First Start	Troll Associates
Puppet Show, The	A	RF	67	InfoTrek	ETA/Cuisenaire
Puppet Show, The	A	RF	35	Leveled Literacy Intervention/ Orange System	Heinemann
Puppet Show, The	E	I	25	Literacy 2000	Rigby
Puppet Show, The	B	RF	25	Phonics and Friends	Hampton Brown
Puppet Show, The	O	I	250+	PM Extensions	Rigby
Puppet, The	A	I	24	On Our Way to English	Rigby
Puppeteer's Apprentice, The	Z	HF	250+	Love, D. Anne	Simon & Schuster
Puppets	G	I	47	Canizares, Susan; Berger, Samantha	Scholastic
Puppets	P	I	250+	Literacy Tree	Rigby
Puppets	J	I	250+	Little Celebrations	Pearson Learning Group
Puppets	K	I	380	Rigby Flying Colors	Rigby
Puppets	J	I	297	The Rowland Reading Program Library	Rowland Reading Foundation
Puppets for a Play	D	I	45	Home Connection Collection	Rigby
Puppets, Puppets, Puppets	K	I	537	Vocabulary Readers	Houghton Mifflin Harcourt
Puppets, Puppets, Puppets	K	I	537	Vocabulary Readers/CA	Houghton Mifflin Harcourt
Puppets, Puppets, Puppets	K	I	537	Vocabulary Readers/TX	Houghton Mifflin Harcourt
Puppets, The	C	F	91	Leveled Literacy Intervention/ Green System	Heinemann
Puppies Can Play	B	I	42	Bonnell, Kris	Reading Reading Books
Puppies in the Pantry	Q	RF	250+	Baglio, Ben M.	Scholastic
Puppies! Puppies! Puppies!	J	RF	250+	Meyers, Susan	Scholastic
Puppies, Dogs, and Blue Northers	S	I	250+	Paulsen, Gary	Delacorte Press
Puppy at the Door	J	RF	250+	PM Plus Story Books	Rigby
Puppy Chase, The	I	RF	250+	Cambridge Reading	Pearson Learning Group
Puppy Danny	E	RF	136	Coulton, Mia	Maryruth Books
Puppy Love	N	RF	250+	Duffey, Betsy	Puffin Books
Puppy Mudge Finds a Friend	E	RF	76	Rylant, Cynthia	Aladdin
Puppy Mudge Has a Snack	D	RF	97	Rylant, Cynthia	Aladdin
Puppy Mudge Loves His Blanket	D	RF	88	Rylant, Cynthia	Aladdin
Puppy Mudge Takes a Bath	E	RF	103	Rylant, Cynthia	Aladdin
Puppy Mudge Wants to Play	E	RF	98	Rylant, Cynthia	Aladdin
Puppy Named Boss, A	J	F	374	Jack and Daisy	Pioneer Valley
Puppy Play	D	RF	67	Emergent Books	Pioneer Valley
Puppy Puzzle	O	RF	250+	Baglio, Ben M.	Scholastic
Puppy Raiser, A	J	I	437	Reading Street	Pearson
Puppy School	G	I	155	Red Rocket Readers	Flying Start Books
Puppy Trouble	G	F	168	Bella and Rosie Series	Literacy Footprints
Puppy Who Wanted a Boy, The	L	F	250+	Thayer, Jane	Scholastic
Puppy, The	B	RF	37	First Stories	Pacific Learning
Puppy, The	H	RF	176	The King School Series	Townsend Press
Puppy, The	A	I	15	Vocabulary Readers	Houghton Mifflin Harcourt
Puppy, The	A	I	15	Vocabulary Readers/CA	Houghton Mifflin Harcourt
Pup's Tale, A	N	F	250+	Martha Speaks	Houghton Mifflin Harcourt
Pure Dead Wicked	W	F	250+	Gliori, Debi	Random House
Purple	B	I	54	Bookworms	Marshall Cavendish
Purple	B	I	26	Colors	Lerner Publishing Group
Purple All Around	B	I	84	Color My World	American Reading Company
Purple Climbing Days	M	RF	250+	Giff, Patricia Reilly	Bantam Books

* Collection of short stories   # Graphic text
^ Mature content with lower level text demands

TITLE	LEVEL	GENRE	WORD COUNT	AUTHOR / SERIES	PUBLISHER / DISTRIBUTOR
Purple Everywhere	K	I	322	Lightning Bolt Books	Lerner Publishing Group
Purple Is Part of a Rainbow	E	RF	131	Rookie Readers	Children's Press
Purple Pussycat, The	F	F	281	Easy Stories	Norwood House Press
Purple Sluggy Worry Warts, The: Quentin Quirk's Magic Works	P	F	250+	Kain, Matt	Kingfisher
Purple Snerd, The	H	F	216	Green Light Readers	Harcourt
Purple Walrus and Other Perfect Pets	O	RF	250+	Wildcats	Wright Group/McGraw Hill
Purple: Seeing Purple All Around Us	K	I	250+	Colors	Capstone Press
Purr-fect Pete	K	F	250+	I Am Reading	Kingfisher
Pursuit of the Ivory Poachers, The	P	SF	250+	Secret Agent Jack Stalwart	Weinstein Books
Push and Pull	I	I	91	Forces and Motion	Lerner Publishing Group
Push and Pull	G	I	49	iOpeners	Pearson Learning Group
Push and Pull	E	I	36	The Way Things Move	Capstone Press
Push and Pull	H	I	184	Yellow Umbrella Books	Red Brick Learning
Push It or Pull It?	F	RF	162	Instant Readers	Harcourt School Publishers
Push or Pull	L	I	316	Independent Readers Science	Houghton Mifflin Harcourt
Push or Pull	H	I	159	Red Rocket Readers	Flying Start Books
Push or Pull?	LB	I	7	Discovery Links	Newbridge
Push or Pull?	J	I	154	Phonics Readers	Compass Point Books
Push or Pull?	C	I	73	Windows on Literacy	National Geographic
Push!	D	RF	21	Oxford Reading Tree	Oxford University Press
Push, Pull, Lift!	K	I	247	Early Explorers	Benchmark Education
Pushcart War, The	Y	F	250+	Merrill, Jean	Bantam Books
Pushing and Pulling	A	I	18	Big Cat	Pacific Learning
Pushing and Pulling	J	I	250+	Explorations	Eleanor Curtain Publishing
Pushing and Pulling	J	I	250+	Explorations	Okapi Educational Materials
Pushing the Limits	T	I	250+	Connectors	Pacific Learning
Puss in Boots	I	TL	258	My 1st Classic Story	Picture Window Books
Puss in Boots	N	TL	250+	Perrault, Charles	Farrar, Straus, & Giroux
Puss-in-Boots	K	TL	250+	PM Tales and Plays-Purple	Rigby
Puss'n Boots	M	TL	687	Pawprints Teal	Pioneer Valley
Pussy Cat	F	TL	143	Literacy 2000	Rigby
Pussy Cat, Pussy Cat	D	F	44	Seedlings	Continental Press
Put Inclined Planes to the Test	Q	I	1234	Searchlight Books	Lerner Publishing Group
Put Levers to the Test	Q	I	1647	Searchlight Books	Lerner Publishing Group
Put Me in the Zoo	H	B	250+	Lopshire, Robert	Random House
Put Pulleys to the Test	Q	I	1567	Searchlight Books	Lerner Publishing Group
Put Screws to the Test	Q	I	1352	Searchlight Books	Lerner Publishing Group
Put Wedges to the Test	Q	I	1436	Searchlight Books	Lerner Publishing Group
Put Wheels and Axles to the Test	Q	I	1608	Searchlight Books	Lerner Publishing Group
Putting Frosting on the Cake	D	F	120	Leveled Readers	Houghton Mifflin Harcourt
Putting Frosting on the Cake	D	F	120	Leveled Readers/CA	Houghton Mifflin Harcourt
Putting Frosting on the Cake	D	F	120	Leveled Readers/TX	Houghton Mifflin Harcourt
Putting on a Concert and The Television News	L	RF	250+	Voyages	SRA/McGraw Hill
Putting on a Play	Q	I	424	Vocabulary Readers	Houghton Mifflin Harcourt
Putting Up the Tent	F	RF	119	Reading Street	Pearson
Putt-Putt Golf	G	RF	267	The Rowland Reading Program Library	Rowland Reading Foundation
Puzzle of the Missing Panda, The	P	SF	250+	Secret Agent Jack Stalwart	Weinstein Books
Puzzle Power Drain, The	O	RF	250+	Klooz	Stone Arch Books
Puzzle, The	B	RF	32	Smart Start	Rigby
Puzzle, The	A	I	32	Sun Sprouts	ETA/Cuisenaire
Puzzle,The	B	I	28	Storyteller Nonfiction	Wright Group/McGraw Hill
Puzzling Out Patterns	W	I	250+	Reading Expeditions	National Geographic

* Collection of short stories   # Graphic text
^ Mature content with lower level text demands

TITLE	LEVEL	GENRE	WORD COUNT	AUTHOR / SERIES	PUBLISHER / DISTRIBUTOR
Pyjama Party, The	K	RF	250+	Cambridge Reading	Pearson Learning Group
Pyramid	L	I	143	Bookworms	Marshall Cavendish
Pyramid	X	I	250+	Eyewitness Books	DK Publishing
Pyramid	X	I	250+	Macaulay, David	Scholastic
Pyramid	C	I	32	Solid Shapes	Lerner Publishing Group
Pyramids	K	I	239	3-D Shapes	Capstone Press
^Pyramids	S	I	250+	Ancient Egypt	Capstone Press
Pyramids & Mummies	R	I	250+	Simon, Seymour	Chronicle Books
Pyramids in the Bush: A Book about Mallee Fowl	T	I	250+	Sunshine	Wright Group/McGraw Hill
Pyramids of Ancient Egypt, The	V	I	250+	Leveled Readers Language Support	Houghton Mifflin Harcourt
Pyramids of Egypt, The	S	I	250+	Rosen Real Readers	Rosen Publishing Group
Pyramids of Giza, The	W	I	1718	Leveled Readers	Houghton Mifflin Harcourt
Python Caught the Eagle, The	C	F	60	Voyages	SRA/McGraw Hill
Pythons	I	I	139	African Animals	Capstone Press
Qillak	M	RF	250+	Take Two Books	Wright Group/McGraw Hill
Quack and the Petting Zoo	L	F	699	Pawprints Teal	Pioneer Valley
Quack!	E	F	48	Ready Readers	Pearson Learning Group
Quack, Quack, Quack	D	F	97	Carousel Readers	Pearson Learning Group
Quack, Quack, Quack!	I	F	219	Sunshine	Wright Group/McGraw Hill
Quack, Said the Billy Goat	H	F	88	Causley, Charles	Harper & Row
Quackenstein Hatches a Family	O	F	250+	Bardhan-Quallen, Sudipta	Harry N. Abrams
Quackers, the Troublesome Duck	M	F	250+	Ellen, Leslie	Pearson Learning Group
Quail Club, The	P	RF	250+	Marsden, Carolyn	Candlewick Press
Quake!	T	RF	250+	Cottonwood, Joe	Language for Learning Assoc.
Quake!: Disaster in San Francisco, 1906	T	HF	250+	Karwoski, Gail Langer	Peachtree
Quanah Parker	S	B	3563	History Maker Bios	Lerner Publishing Group
Quarter Story, The	E	I	99	Williams, Deborah	Kaeden Books
Quarterback Sneak	P	RF	250+	Maddox, Jake	Stone Arch Books
Quarters for Everyone	S	RF	1798	Leveled Readers	Houghton Mifflin Harcourt
Quarters Toss, The	P	RF	250+	Leveled Readers Language Support	Houghton Mifflin Harcourt
Queen and the Dragon, The	I	F	243	New Way Green	Steck-Vaughn
Queen Bee Needs to be Free	K	F	738	Appleton-Smith, Laura	Flyleaf Publishing
Queen Christina of Sweden	T	B	250+	Queens and Princesses	Capstone Press
Queen Cleopatra	Z	B	250+	Just the Facts Biographies	Lerner Publishing Group
Queen Eleanor: Independent Spirit in the Medieval World	X	B	250+	Brooks, Polly Schoyer	Houghton Mifflin Harcourt
Queen Elizabeth I of England	T	B	250+	Queens and Princesses	Capstone Press
Queen for a Day	L	F	1367	Auto-B-Good	Rising Star Studios
Queen Isabella's Feast	K	F	900	InfoTrek	ETA/Cuisenaire
Queen Jelly Bean	J	F	250+	The Wright Skills	Wright Group/McGraw Hill
Queen Made a Quilt	D	RF	46	Ray's Readers	Outside the Box
Queen of Egypt	V	B	250+	WorldScapes	ETA/Cuisenaire
Queen of Everything, The	Z+	RF	250+	Caletti, Deb	Simon & Schuster
Queen of Hearts	Z	HF	250+	Brooks, Martha	Farrar, Straus, & Giroux
Queen of Hearts, The	E	TL	26	Jumbled Tumbled Tales & Rhymes	Rigby
Queen of Secrets	Z+	RF	250+	Meyerhoff, Jenny	Farrar, Straus, & Giroux
Queen of the Bean	N	RF	250+	Action Packs	Rigby
Queen of the Falls	R	B	250+	Van Allsburg, Chris	Houghton Mifflin Harcourt
Queen of the Pool	N	RF	250+	PM Collection	Rigby
^Queen of the Toilet Bowl	S	RF	250+	Orca Currents	Orca Books

PQ

* Collection of short stories   # Graphic text
^ Mature content with lower level text demands

TITLE	LEVEL	GENRE	WORD COUNT	AUTHOR / SERIES	PUBLISHER / DISTRIBUTOR
Queen on a Quilt	C	F	26	Ready Readers	Pearson Learning Group
Queen Rania of Jordan	S	B	250+	Queens and Princesses	Capstone Press
Queen's Daughter, The	Z+	HF	250+	Coventry, Susan	Henry Holt & Co.
Queen's New Seat, The	H	F	230	Springboard	Wright Group/McGraw Hill
Queens of Ancient Egypt	Y	I	3160	Vocabulary Readers/CA	Houghton Mifflin Harcourt
Queens of Ancient Eqypt	Y	I	3160	Vocabulary Readers	Houghton Mifflin Harcourt
Queen's Parrot, The: A Play	J	TL	365	Literacy 2000	Rigby
Quentin Quokka's Quick Questions	M	F	712	Animal Antics A to Z	Kane Press
Quest for California's Gold, The	S	I	250+	The Library of the Westward Expansion	Rosen Publishing Group
#Quest for Dragon Mountain, The	U	F	250+	Twisted Journeys	Graphic Universe
Quest For Medusa's Head, The	W	TL	1385	Leveled Readers	Houghton Mifflin Harcourt
Quest for the Golden Seesaw, The	O	F	250+	High-Fliers	Pacific Learning
Quest for the Moon	X	I	3419	Vocabulary Readers	Houghton Mifflin Harcourt
Quest for the Moon	X	I	3419	Vocabulary Readers/CA	Houghton Mifflin Harcourt
Quest to Digest, The	S	I	250+	Corcoran, Mary K.	Charlesbridge
Queste: Septimus Heap #4	X	F	250+	Sage, Angie	HarperCollins
Questions and Answers About Forest Animals	P	I	250+	Chinery, Michael	Kingfisher
Questions and Answers About Freshwater Animals	P	I	250+	Chinery, Michael	Kingfisher
Questions, Questions, Questions	F	RF	190	Visions	Wright Group/McGraw Hill
Quests for Gold	X	I	2050	Reading Street	Pearson
Quick and Quiet	B	F	38	Phonics and Friends	Hampton Brown
Quick Baby Zebra, The	H	RF	97	Seedlings	Continental Press
Quick Chick	J	F	250+	Hoban, Julia	Puffin Books
Quick Duck, The	H	F	165	Phonics Readers	Scholastic
Quick Picnic, A	B	RF	42	Red Rocket Readers	Flying Start Books
Quick Thinking	L	RF	549	In Step Readers	Rigby
Quick, Go Peek!	E	F	83	Little Celebrations	Pearson Learning Group
Quicksand: HIV/AIDS in Our Lives	W	I	250+	Anonymous	Candlewick Press
Quiet Bunny	L	F	250+	McCue, Lisa	Sterling Publishing
Quiet in the Library	E	RF	102	Rigby Rocket	Rigby
Quiet in the Library!	H	F	113	Sunshine	Wright Group/McGraw Hill
Quiet Morning for Mom, A	H	RF	169	Lighthouse	Rigby
Quiet Owls	K	I	385	Pull Ahead Books	Lerner Publishing Group
Quiet TV Lunch, A	L	F	250+	Popcorn	Sundance
Quiet World, The	K	RF	250+	Voyages	SRA/McGraw Hill
Quillan Games, The: Pendragon	X	F	250+	MacHale, D.J.	Aladdin
Quilt for Kiri, A	K	RF	367	Pacific Literacy	Pacific Learning
Quilt for Kristy, A	J	RF	250+	The Wright Skills	Wright Group/McGraw Hill
Quilt Story, The	L	HF	250+	Johnston, Tony; DePaola, Tomie	Scholastic
Quilt with a Difference, A	N	I	250+	Pacific Literacy	Pacific Learning
Quilt, The	I	RF	165	Jonas, Ann	Morrow
Quilting for Fun!	S	I	250+	For Fun! Crafts	Compass Point Books
Quilting in America	I	I	152	Vocabulary Readers	Houghton Mifflin Harcourt
Quilting Memories	L	I	471	Reading Street	Pearson
Quilts	C	RF	35	Foundations	Wright Group/McGraw Hill
Quilts	E	I	131	Twig	Wright Group/McGraw Hill
Quirky Times At Quagmire Castle	Q	F	9190	Wallace, Karen	Stone Arch Books
Quite Contrary Man, The: A True American Tale	P	TL	250+	Hyatt, Paricia Rusch	Harry N. Abrams
Quiz Show	N	RF	250+	On Our Way To English	Rigby
Quiz Whiz	P	I	250+	Jackson, Tom & Callery, Sean	Kingfisher
Quork Attack	L	F	250+	Rigby Literacy	Rigby
Quork Attack	L	F	250+	Rigby Star Plus	Rigby

* Collection of short stories   # Graphic text
^ Mature content with lower level text demands

TITLE	LEVEL	GENRE	WORD COUNT	AUTHOR / SERIES	PUBLISHER / DISTRIBUTOR
R	LB	I	14	Readlings	American Reading Company
R is for Radish!	J	F	250+	Coxe, Molly	Random House
R.S.P.C.A.	O	I	250+	Tristars	Richard C. Owen
R2-D2 and Friends	N	SF	250+	Star Wars	DK Publishing
Rabbi and the Twenty-nine Witches, The	O	TL	250+	Hirsh, Marilyn	Marshall Cavendish
Rabbit and Coyote	J	TL	522	Rigby Flying Colors	Rigby
Rabbit and Fox	D	F	87	Sails	Rigby
Rabbit and the Coyote, The	Q	F	979	Leveled Readers	Houghton Mifflin Harcourt
Rabbit and Turtle Go To School	E	F	84	Green Light Readers	Harcourt
Rabbit and Turtle Go to School	E	F	67	Instant Readers	Harcourt Trade
Rabbit Catches the Sun	M	TL	621	Sunshine	Wright Group/McGraw Hill
Rabbit Dance, The	L	TL	563	Gear Up!	Wright Group/McGraw Hill
Rabbit for You, A: Caring for Your Rabbit	M	I	250+	Pet Care	Picture Window Books
Rabbit in the Garden, The	E	RF	90	Benchmark Rebus	Marshall Cavendish
Rabbit Makes Toast	K	F	250+	Popcorn	Sundance
Rabbit Race	O	RF	250+	Baglio, Ben M.	Scholastic
Rabbit Rescue	L	RF	427	Gear Up!	Wright Group/McGraw Hill
Rabbit Stew	L	F	250+	Literacy 2000	Rigby
Rabbit, The	H	RF	59	Burningham, John	Crowell
Rabbits	D	I	37	All About Pets	Red Brick Learning
Rabbits	E	I	76	Bonnell, Kris/About	Reading Reading Books
Rabbits	F	I	96	Life Cycles	Lerner Publishing Group
Rabbits	N	I	250+	Literacy 2000	Rigby
Rabbits & Raindrops	I	F	185	Arnosky, Jim	Scholastic
Rabbits and Their Burrows	J	I	136	Animal Homes	Capstone Press
Rabbit's Birthday Kite	J	F	250+	Bank Street	Bantam Books
Rabbits' Ears	F	RF	179	PM Plus Story Books	Rigby
Rabbit's Feelings	C	F	53	Gear Up!	Wright Group/McGraw Hill
Rabbit's Garden	B	F	42	Gear Up!	Wright Group/McGraw Hill
Rabbit's Garden	L	F	661	Leveled Readers	Houghton Mifflin Harcourt
Rabbit's Garden	L	F	661	Leveled Readers/CA	Houghton Mifflin Harcourt
Rabbit's Garden	L	F	661	Leveled Readers/TX	Houghton Mifflin Harcourt
Rabbit's Garden Troubles	L	F	652	Leveled Readers	Houghton Mifflin Harcourt
Rabbit's Garden Troubles	L	F	652	Leveled Readers/CA	Houghton Mifflin Harcourt
Rabbit's Garden Troubles	L	F	652	Leveled Readers/TX	Houghton Mifflin Harcourt
Rabbits Have Bunnies	M	I	250+	Animals and Their Young	Compass Point Books
Rabbits in Space	J	F	216	Talking Point Series	Pearson Learning Group
Rabbit's Legend	L	TL	704	Red Rocket Readers	Flying Start Books
Rabbits on the Farm	I	I	103	Pebble Books	Red Brick Learning
Rabbit's Party	G	F	351	Bunting, Eve; Sloan-Childers, E.	Scholastic
Rabbit's Pumpkin	B	F	29	Gear Up!	Wright Group/McGraw Hill
Rabbit's Real Birthday	J	F	250+	Rigby Literacy	Rigby
Rabbit's Robber	L	F	250+	Popcorn	Sundance
Rabbit's Skating Party	D	F	89	Handprints B	Educators Publishing Service
Rabbit's Surprise Birthday	J	F	250+	Rigby Star	Rigby
Rabbit's Tail	K	TL	250+	Cambridge Reading	Pearson Learning Group
Rabbit's Tricks	I	F	250+	Story Box	Wright Group/McGraw Hill
Rabble Starkey	T	RF	250+	Lowry, Lois	Bantam Books
Raccoon Cookies	H	F	136	Gear Up!	Wright Group/McGraw Hill
Raccoon on the Moon	I	RF	250+	Start to Read	School Zone
Raccoon Wakes Up	C	RF	66	PM Stars	Rigby
Raccoons	O	I	2107	Early Bird Nature Books	Lerner Publishing Group
Raccoons	J	I	195	Nocturnal Animals	Capstone Press

R

* Collection of short stories   # Graphic text
^ Mature content with lower level text demands

TITLE	LEVEL	GENRE	WORD COUNT	AUTHOR / SERIES	PUBLISHER / DISTRIBUTOR
Raccoons	M	I	250+	PM Animal Facts: Gold	Rigby
Race Across Alaska, The	M	I	250+	HSP/Harcourt Trophies	Harcourt, Inc.
Race Across America, The	O	F	250+	Stilton, Geronimo	Scholastic
Race Against Time	Q	I	250+	Bookweb	Rigby
Race Against Time	U	I	250+	High-Fliers	Pacific Learning
Race Car Dreamers	N	RF	250+	Boyz Rule!	Mondo Publishing
Race Car, The	B	F	30	Sails	Rigby
Race Cars	I	I	417	Sails	Rigby
Race Cars	M	I	250+	Transportation	Compass Point Books
Race Day	D	F	58	Reading Street	Pearson
Race Day	K	RF	597	Red Rocket Readers	Flying Start Books
Race Day	O	I	250+	Windows on Literacy	National Geographic
Race Is On, The	D	F	45	New Way Red	Steck-Vaughn
^Race of a Lifetime, The	N	RF	1837	Norman, Tony	Stone Arch Books
Race of the River Runner	P	HF	540	Leveled Readers	Houghton Mifflin Harcourt
Race to Green End, The	J	F	506	PM Collection	Rigby
Race to the Moon	J	I	441	Red Rocket Readers	Flying Start Books
Race to the Mountain, The	H	TL	174	Leveled Readers Language Support	Houghton Mifflin Harcourt
Race to the North Pole	Q	B	250+	WorldScapes	ETA/Cuisenaire
Race to the Pole	R	I	250+	Windows on Literacy	National Geographic
Race to the South Pole	R	I	250+	Discovery Links	Newbridge
Race to the South Pole	S	I	1367	Vocabulary Readers	Houghton Mifflin Harcourt
Race to the South Pole	S	I	1367	Vocabulary Readers/CA	Houghton Mifflin Harcourt
Race to the South Pole, The	W	I	2859	Reading Street	Pearson
Race, The	B	RF	78	Leveled Readers Emergent	Houghton Mifflin Harcourt
Race, The	E	F	30	Little Celebrations	Pearson Learning Group
Race, The	F	RF	145	Little Readers	Houghton Mifflin Harcourt
Race, The	I	F	451	New Way Green	Steck-Vaughn
Race, The	C	RF	25	Sunshine	Wright Group/McGraw Hill
Race, The	B	RF	34	Windmill Books	Wright Group/McGraw Hill
Racecar Bob in Panama	Q	RF	1021	Leveled Readers	Houghton Mifflin Harcourt
Racecar Bob in Panama	Q	RF	1021	Leveled Readers/CA	Houghton Mifflin Harcourt
Racecar Bob in Panama	Q	RF	1021	Leveled Readers/TX	Houghton Mifflin Harcourt
Racecars: The Ins and Outs of Stock Cars, Dragsters, and Open-Wheelers	V	I	250+	Velocity-RPM	Capstone Press
Rachel Carson	J	B	279	Leveled Readers	Houghton Mifflin Harcourt
Rachel Carson, Scientist and Writer	N	B	370	Independent Readers Social Studies	Houghton Mifflin Harcourt
Rachel Carson: A Life of Responsibility	N	B	324	Pull Ahead Books	Lerner Publishing Group
Rachel Carson: Friend of Nature	N	B	250+	Rookie Biographies	Children's Press
Rachel Carson: Nature's Guardian	S	B	250+	Science Readers	Teacher Created Materials
Rachel Carson: Renowned Marine Biologist and Environmentalist	U	B	250+	Mission: Science	Compass Point Books
Rachel Carson: Writer and Scientist	N	B	250+	Beginning Biographies	Pearson Learning Group
Rachel to the Rescue	O	RF	250+	Supa Doopers	Sundance
Racing Along	G	I	76	Big Shiny Machines	Kingfisher
Racing Cars, The	C	RF	68	Rigby Flying Colors	Rigby
Racing Danger	Q	I	737	Leveled Readers	Houghton Mifflin Harcourt
Racing Floods	T	I	250+	Awesome Forces of Nature	Heinemann Library
Racing for Diamonds	Q	RF	250+	Orca Young Readers	Orca Books
Racing the Past	Y	RF	250+	Deans, Sis	Puffin Books
Racing with the Sun	Q	I	250+	Orbit Double Takes	Pacific Learning
Radar and Grandpa	C	RF	71	Kaleidoscope Collection	Hameray Publishing Group

* Collection of short stories   # Graphic text
^ Mature content with lower level text demands

TITLE	LEVEL	GENRE	WORD COUNT	AUTHOR / SERIES	PUBLISHER / DISTRIBUTOR
Radar Jammers: The EA-6B Prowlers	U	I	250+	War Planes	Capstone Press
Radio	O	I	250+	Let's See	Compass Point Books
Radio	S	I	250+	Theme Sets	National Geographic
Radio Scare	T	I	250+	Leveled Readers Language Support	Houghton Mifflin Harcourt
Radio, The	Q	I	250+	Great Inventions	Red Brick Learning
^Radio, The: The World Tunes In	R	I	250+	On Deck	Rigby
Raewyn's Got the Writing Bug Again	N	B	250+	Voyages	SRA/McGraw Hill
*Rafi and Rosi	K	F	250+	Delacre, Lulu	HarperCollins
Raft, The	O	RF	250+	LaMarche, Jim	HarperTrophy
Rag Coat, The	Q	HF	250+	Mills, Lauren	Little Brown and Company
Ragbag	G	F	41	Supersonics	Rigby
Ragdoll Cats	Q	I	250+	All About Cats	Capstone Press
Ragdoll Cats	I	I	118	Cats	Capstone Press
Ragdolls Are the Best!	Q	I	1565	The Best Cats Ever	Lerner Publishing Group
Raggin': A Story about Scott Joplin	S	B	6409	Creative Minds Biographies	Lerner Publishing Group
Raging Dragon, The (Will to Conquer Series: Book 2)	Z	F	250+	Lamensdorf, Len	SeaScape Press
Ragweed	U	F	250+	Avi	Avon Books
Railroad John and the Red Rock Run	R	F	250+	Crunk, Tony	Peachtree
Railroad Revolution	R	I	618	Vocabulary Readers	Houghton Mifflin Harcourt
Railroad Toad	K	F	178	Schade, Susan	Random House
Railroad, The	R	I	250+	Theme Sets	National Geographic
Railway Children, The	T	RF	9295	Oxford Bookworms Library	Oxford University Press
Rain	A	I	59	Getting Around	American Reading Company
Rain	LB	I	56	Kalan, Robert	Greenwillow Books
Rain	C	RF	34	Learn to Read	Creative Teaching Press
Rain	B	I	87	Leveled Literacy Intervention/ Orange System	Heinemann
Rain	G	RF	68	Literacy 2000	Rigby
Rain	D	I	44	Little Celebrations	Pearson Learning Group
Rain	B	RF	52	Reading Corners	Pearson Learning Group
Rain	D	RF	45	Step-By-Step Series	Pearson Learning Group
Rain	J	F	250+	Stojic, Manya	Dragonfly Books
Rain	J	I	250+	Voyages	SRA/McGraw Hill
Rain	K	I	263	Weather	Capstone Press
Rain and the Sun, The	E	I	45	Wonder World	Wright Group/McGraw Hill
Rain Came Down, The	J	RF	250+	Shannon, David	Scholastic
Rain Forest	N	F	250+	Cowcher, Helen	Scholastic
Rain Forest	R	I	250+	Worldwise	Franklin Watts
Rain Forest Adventure	L	F	482	Pair-It Books	Steck-Vaughn
Rain Forest Adventure	S	RF	250+	Reading Expeditions	National Geographic
Rain Forest Alert!	T	I	250+	Literacy by Design	Rigby
Rain Forest Animals	D	I	42	Benchmark Rebus	Marshall Cavendish
Rain Forest Animals	J	I	151	Phonics Readers	Compass Point Books
Rain Forest Animals	P	I	250+	Theme Sets	National Geographic
Rain Forest Discovery	K	RF	250+	Windows on Literacy	National Geographic
Rain Forest Encyclopedia	N	I	250+	Literacy by Design	Rigby
Rain Forest Food	E	I	125	Early Connections	Benchmark Education
Rain Forest Food Chain, A	U	I	8835	Follow That Food Chain	Lerner Publishing Group
Rain Forest Food Chains	T	I	250+	Protecting Food Chains	Heinemann Library
Rain Forest Plants	I	I	151	Alphakids	Sundance
Rain Forest Plants	N	I	250+	Life in the World's Biomes	Capstone Press
Rain Forest Plants	M	I	580	Lundberg, Linda	Harcourt School Publishers

TITLE	LEVEL	GENRE	WORD COUNT	AUTHOR / SERIES	PUBLISHER / DISTRIBUTOR
Rain Forest Secrets	P	I	250+	Dorros, Arthur	Scholastic
Rain Forest Tree, A	Q	I	250+	Kite, Lorien	Crabtree
Rain Forest Vacation	P	I	250+	Literacy by Design	Rigby
Rain Forest, A	LB	I	18	Rigby Focus	Rigby
Rain Forest, The	Q	I	191	Action Packs	Rigby
Rain Forest, The	N	I	191	Windows on Literacy	National Geographic
Rain Forests	Q	I	250+	Ecosystems	Red Brick Learning
Rain Forests	Q	I	250+	First Reports	Compass Point Books
Rain Forests	S	I	250+	The Heinle Reading Library	Thomson Learning
Rain Forests: Facts vs. Fiction	T	I	250+	Explore More	Wright Group/McGraw Hill
Rain Ghost, The	X	F	250+	Kilworth, Garry	Scholastic
Rain in the Hills	D	RF	41	Book Bank	Wright Group/McGraw Hill
Rain Is Not My Indian Name	Z	RF	250+	Smith, Cynthia Leitich	HarperCollins
Rain Is Water	E	I	82	PM Plus Nonfiction	Rigby
Rain or Shine	Q	I	250+	Explorers	Wright Group/McGraw Hill
Rain or Shine?	C	I	21	Twig	Wright Group/McGraw Hill
Rain Play	H	RF	115	Cotton, Cynthia	Henry Holt & Co.
Rain Puddle	J	RF	250+	Holl, Adelaide	Morrow
Rain Rain Rivers	N	RF	172	Shulevitz, Uri	Farrar, Straus, & Giroux
Rain Today	A	I	25	Leveled Readers	Houghton Mifflin Harcourt
Rain Today	A	I	25	Leveled Readers/CA	Houghton Mifflin Harcourt
Rain! Rain!	D	RF	29	Rookie Readers	Children's Press
Rain, Rain	E	RF	58	Pacific Literacy	Pacific Learning
Rain, Rain, and More Rain	H	RF	250+	Momentum Literacy Program	Troll Associates
Rain, Rain, Rain	C	F	36	Sails	Rigby
Rain, Rivers, and Rain Again	M	I	250+	Sunshine	Wright Group/McGraw Hill
Rain, Snow, and Hail	J	I	250+	Discovery World	Rigby
Rain, The	G	RF	171	Foundations	Wright Group/McGraw Hill
Rain, The	C	RF	76	Leveled Readers Emergent	Houghton Mifflin Harcourt
Rainbow Balloons	D	F	99	Red Rocket Readers	Flying Start Books
Rainbow Bird, A	LB	I	18	Pair-It Books	Steck-Vaughn
Rainbow Clown, The	C	RF	55	Reading Safari	Mondo Publishing
Rainbow Clubhouse, The	I	RF	483	Rigby Flying Colors	Rigby
Rainbow Fish, The	M	F	250+	Pfister, Marcus	North-South Books
Rainbow Glider, The	O	RF	250+	Reading Safari	Mondo Publishing
Rainbow Mystery, The	K	RF	1185	Science Solves It!	Kane Press
Rainbow of My Own	J	F	52	Freeman, Don	Penguin Group
Rainbow of Parrots, A	B	I	60	Springboard	Wright Group/McGraw Hill
Rainbow Parrot	I	TL	174	Literacy Tree	Rigby
Rainbow Party, The	J	RF	558	Red Rocket Readers	Flying Start Books
*Rainbow People, The	V	F	250+	Yep, Lawrence	HarperTrophy
Rainbow Solution, The	N	RF	250+	Literacy 2000	Rigby
Rainbow Somewhere, A	G	RF	201	Ready Readers	Pearson Learning Group
Rainbow Town	B	RF	30	Sails	Rigby
Rainbow Wings	M	F	250+	Sunshine	Wright Group/McGraw Hill
Rainbow, A	B	I	29	Rigby Focus	Rigby
Rainbow, The	C	I	59	Rigby Flying Colors	Rigby
Rainbows	L	I	250+	Rigby Literacy	Rigby
Rainbows All Around	M	RF	250+	Hardin, Suzanne	Pacific Learning
Rainbows and Moonbeams	I	RF	238	Sunshine	Wright Group/McGraw Hill
Rainbows of the Sea	L	I	250+	Thomas, Meredith	Mondo Publishing
Rainbows: Wonders of Nature	L	I	250+	Bookworms	Marshall Cavendish
Raindrop, A	C	RF	41	Teacher's Choice Series	Pearson Learning Group
Raindrops	B	I	34	Bookshop	Mondo Publishing

* Collection of short stories   # Graphic text
^ Mature content with lower level text demands

TITLE	LEVEL	GENRE	WORD COUNT	AUTHOR / SERIES	PUBLISHER / DISTRIBUTOR
Raindrops	C	RF	66	Gay, Sandy	Scholastic
Raindrops	I	I	70	Rookie Readers	Children's Press
Raindrop's Journey, A	M	I	250+	Follow-It!	Picture Window Books
Rainforest Grew All Around, The	M	F	565	Mitchell, Susan K.	Sylvan Dell Publishing
Rainforest Math	O	I	250+	WorldScapes	ETA/Cuisenaire
Rainforest Romp	L	F	212	Amazing Animals	Kingfisher
Rainforest, The	K	I	252	Red Rocket Readers	Flying Start Books
Rainforests	U	I	6480	Oxford Bookworms Library	Oxford University Press
Rainy	T	RF	250+	Deans, Sis	Henry Holt & Co.
Rainy	B	I	23	Weather	Lerner Publishing Group
Rainy Day	E	I	85	Early Explorers	Benchmark Education
Rainy Day	A	I	20	Leveled Readers	Houghton Mifflin Harcourt
Rainy Day	A	I	20	Leveled Readers/CA	Houghton Mifflin Harcourt
Rainy Day Adventure, The	M	F	250+	On Our Way to English	Rigby
Rainy Day Alphabet Book	E	RF	82	Posner, Jackie; Wiener, Sara	Scholastic
Rainy Day Counting	B	I	30	Twig	Wright Group/McGraw Hill
Rainy Day Dream	WB	F	0	Chesworth, Michael	Farrar, Straus, & Giroux
Rainy Day for Sammy, A	H	RF	249	Urmston, Kathleen; Urmston, Graig	Kaeden Books
Rainy Day Fun	F	RF	193	Palazzo, Janet	Troll Associates
Rainy Day Grump, The	H	RF	394	Real Kids Readers	Millbrook Press
Rainy Day Solution, A	K	I	161	Vocabulary Readers	Houghton Mifflin Harcourt
Rainy Day Story	K	RF	749	InfoTrek	ETA/Cuisenaire
Rainy Day, A	D	RF	72	Evans, Lynette	Scholastic
Rainy Day, A	B	RF	61	Leveled Literacy Intervention/ Green System	Heinemann
Rainy Day, A	A	RF	32	Literacy by Design	Rigby
Rainy Day, A	D	RF	105	New Way Blue	Steck-Vaughn
Rainy Day, A	E	I	52	Pebble Books	Capstone Press
Rainy Day, A	C	RF	27	Reading Street	Pearson
Rainy Day, A	E	I	90	Weather	Lerner Publishing Group
Rainy Day, Sunny Day	E	F	135	Early Connections	Benchmark Education
Rainy Days at School	H	RF	118	City Kids	Rigby
Rairarubia	S	F	250+	Adams, W. Royce	Lost Coast Press
Raisin in the Sun, A	Z	HF	250+	Edge	Hampton Brown
Raisin in the Sun, A	Z	HF	250+	Hansberry, Lorraine	Vintage Books
Raising Funds	J	I	250+	Vocabulary Readers	Houghton Mifflin Harcourt
Raising Funds	J	I	250+	Vocabulary Readers/CA	Houghton Mifflin Harcourt
Raising Funds	J	I	250+	Vocabulary Readers/TX	Houghton Mifflin Harcourt
Raising the Flag: How a Photograph Gave a Nation Hope in Wartime	Y	I	250+	Captured History	Compass Point Books
^Raising the Flag: The Battle of Iwo Jima	X	I	250+	Bloodiest Battles	Capstone Press
Raj the Bookstore Tiger	L	F	250+	Pelley, Kathleen T.	Charlesbridge
Rally Car Race	J	RF	250+	PM Plus Story Books	Rigby
Rally Cars	M	I	250+	Horsepower	Capstone Press
Rally Cars	W	I	6760	Motor Mania	Lerner Publishing Group
Ralph Fletcher: Reflections	T	B	250+	Author at Work	Richard C. Owen
Ralph S. Mouse	O	F	250+	Cleary, Beverly	HarperTrophy
Ramadan	O	I	1632	On My Own Holidays	Lerner Publishing Group
Ramadan and Id-ul-Fitr	K	I	137	Holidays and Festivals	Heinemann Library
Ramona and Her Father	O	RF	250+	Cleary, Beverly	Avon Books
Ramona and Her Mother	O	RF	250+	Cleary, Beverly	Avon Books
Ramona Forever	O	RF	250+	Cleary, Beverly	Hearst

R

TITLE	LEVEL	GENRE	WORD COUNT	AUTHOR / SERIES	PUBLISHER / DISTRIBUTOR
Ramona Quimby, Age 8	O	RF	250+	Cleary, Beverly	Hearst
Ramona the Brave	O	RF	250+	Cleary, Beverly	Hearst
Ramona the Pest	O	RF	250+	Cleary, Beverly	Avon Books
#Ramp Rats: A Graphic Guide Adventure	T	RF	250+	O'Donnell, Liam	Orca Books
Ranch Life	J	HF	395	Reading Street	Pearson
Rand and the Fox, The	H	TL	93	Cambridge Reading	Pearson Learning Group
Randy Moss	Y	B	250+	Sports Heroes	Red Brick Learning
^Randy Orton	T	B	250+	Stars of Pro Wrestling	Capstone Press
Randy's Room	C	RF	32	Harry's Math Books	Outside the Box
Ranger Rose Helps the Animals	A	I	32	Run to Reading	Discovery Peak
Ranger's Apprentice: The Ruins of Gorlan	U	F	250+	Flanagan, John	Scholastic
Rani Comes to Stay	E	RF	156	PM Photo Stories	Rigby
Ransom	Z	RF	250+	Duncan, Lois	Laurel-Leaf Books
Rap a Tap Tap Here's Bojangles- Think of That!	J	B	199	Dillon, Leo & Diane	Scholastic
Rap Party, The	H	RF	300	Foundations	Wright Group/McGraw Hill
Rapid Changes on Earth	Q	I	1135	Science Support Readers	Houghton Mifflin Harcourt
Rapid Robert Roadrunner	H	F	125	Reese, Bob	Children's Press
Raptors: Hunters in the Sky	R	I	250+	Sunshine.	Wright Group/McGraw Hill
Rapunzel	L	TL	250+	Literacy 2000	Rigby
Rapunzel	I	TL	258	My 1st Classic Story	Picture Window Books
#Rapunzel's Revenge	U	TL	250+	Hale, Shanon and Dean	Bloomsbury Children's Books
Rascal	V	HF	250+	North, Sterling	Scholastic
Rascal	G	RF	108	Rigby Literacy	Rigby
Rascal: The Puppy Place	N	RF	250+	Miles, Ellen	Scholastic
Rash	X	SF	250+	Hautman, Pete	Simon Pulse
Rashee and the Seven Elephants	M	RF	250+	Little Celebrations	Pearson Learning Group
Rat	Z+	RF	250+	Cheripko, Jan	Boyds Mills Press
Rat Brain Fiasco, The (Splurch Academy)	Q	F	250+	Berry, Julie & Gardner, Sally	Grosset & Dunlap
Rat Princess, The	M	TL	250+	Rigby Rocket	Rigby
Rat Squad	P	SF	250+	High-Fliers	Pacific Learning
Rat-a-tat-tat	E	F	98	Big Cat	Pacific Learning
Rat-a-tat-tat	E	F	107	Literacy 2000	Rigby
Rats	O	I	1406	Early Bird Nature Books	Lerner Publishing Group
Rats	S	I	250+	Keeping Unusual Pets	Heinemann Library
Rats	I	I	193	Sails	Rigby
Rat's Funny Story	C	F	39	Story Box	Wright Group/McGraw Hill
*Rats on the Range and Other Stories	O	F	250+	Marshall, James	Penguin Group
*Rats on the Roof and Other Stories	O	F	250+	Marshall, James	Penguin Group
Rat's Tale, A	T	F	250+	Seidler, Tor	HarperTrophy
*Rats!	O	RF	250+	Cutler, Jane	Farrar, Straus, & Giroux
Rats, Bats, and Black Puddings	K	TL	714	Pacific Literacy	Pacific Learning
Rattlesnake Looks for Food, The	E	RF	105	Foundations	Wright Group/McGraw Hill
Rattlesnakes	T	I	2442	Animal Predators	Lerner Publishing Group
Rattlesnakes	H	I	96	Desert Animals	Capstone Press
Rattlesnakes	M	I	250+	Snakes	Capstone Press
Rattletrap Car	L	F	250+	Root, Phyllis	Candlewick Press
Ratty Tatty	H	F	181	Sunshine	Wright Group/McGraw Hill
Rave Reviews	P	RF	250+	Sails	Rigby
Raven and the Fox, The	L	TL	250+	Storybook Classics	Picture Window Books
Raven Necklace, The	E	RF	83	Adams, Lorraine & Bruvold, Lynn	Eaglecrest Books
Raven Rise: Pendragon	X	F	250+	MacHale, D.J.	Aladdin
Raven, The	C	I	129	Adams, Lorraine & Bruvold, Lynn	Eaglecrest Books
Ravenmaster's Secret, The	U	HF	250+	Woodruff, Elvira	Scholastic

* Collection of short stories   # Graphic text
^ Mature content with lower level text demands

TITLE	LEVEL	GENRE	WORD COUNT	AUTHOR / SERIES	PUBLISHER / DISTRIBUTOR
*Raven's Call and More Northwest Coast Stories	P	TL	250+	Challenger, James Robert	Heritage House
Raven's Gift	L	F	160	Books For Young Learners	Richard C. Owen
#Raven's Revenge	T	F	3689	Masters, Anthony	Stone Arch Books
Raving about Rainforests	V	I	250+	News Extra	Richard C. Owen
Ray & Me	T	F	250+	Gutman, Dan	HarperCollins
Ray Charles	P	B	250+	Mathis, Sharon Bell	Lee & Low Books Inc.
Ray Ran	C	RF	34	Ray's Readers	Outside the Box
Raymond and Nelda	K	F	250+	Bottner, Barbara	Peachtree
Rays	I	I	48	Pebble Books	Red Brick Learning
Rays	I	I	117	Under the Sea	Capstone Press
Reach for the Stars	Y	I	250+	High-Fliers	Pacific Learning
Reach for the Stars	Q	RF	250+	Mazer, Anne	Scholastic
Reach for Your Dreams	F	RF	115	Reading Street	Pearson
Reach Out	V	I	250+	WorldScapes	ETA/Cuisenaire
Reaching for Sun	U	RF	250+	Zimmer, Tracie Vaughn	Bloomsbury Children's Books
Reaching for the Sky	T	I	250+	In Step Readers	Rigby
Reaching for the Sky	T	I	250+	Literacy by Design	Rigby
Reaching New Heights	T	I	250+	WorldScapes	ETA/Cuisenaire
Reaching the Sky	C	RF	46	Sunshine	Wright Group/McGraw Hill
Reaction We Need, The	U	I	2708	Leveled Readers Science	Houghton Mifflin Harcourt
^Reactor, The	R	SF	1854	Powell, J.	Stone Arch Books
Read a Zillion Books	O	B	250+	Meet The Author	Richard C. Owen
Read All About It!	T	RF	1609	Leveled Readers	Houghton Mifflin Harcourt
Read All About It!	T	RF	1609	Leveled Readers/CA	Houghton Mifflin Harcourt
Read All About It!	T	RF	1609	Leveled Readers/TX	Houghton Mifflin Harcourt
Read All About It!	S	HF	250+	On Our Way to English	Rigby
Read Anything Good Lately?	M	RF	140	Allen, Susan & Lindaman, Jane	Millbrook Press
Read the Signs	I	F	250+	Literacy by Design	Rigby
Read to Your Bunny	F	F	38	Wells, Rosemary	Scholastic
Readcoats in America	T	I	1299	Vocabulary Readers	Houghton Mifflin Harcourt
Reading	B	I	60	Vocabulary Readers	Houghton Mifflin Harcourt
Reading	B	I	60	Vocabulary Readers/CA	Houghton Mifflin Harcourt
Reading	B	I	60	Vocabulary Readers/TX	Houghton Mifflin Harcourt
Reading a Graph	F	I	251	Early Connections	Benchmark Education
Reading a Map	M	I	250+	Rosen Real Readers	Rosen Publishing Group
Reading Buddies	B	F	34	Galaxy Girl	Literacy Footprints
Reading Contest, The	H	RF	230	The King School Series	Townsend Press
Reading Is Everywhere	D	RF	53	Sunshine	Wright Group/McGraw Hill
Reading Lesson, The	F	RF	78	Teacher's Choice Series	Pearson Learning Group
Reading Makes You Feel Good	I	I	259	Parr, Todd	Little Brown and Company
Reading Partners	A	I	48	At School Series	Pioneer Valley
Reading Robot, The	H	F	224	Sunshine	Wright Group/McGraw Hill
Reading Room, The	G	RF	231	In Step Readers	Rigby
Reading Signs	D	I	37	Shutterbug Books	Steck-Vaughn
Reading Signs With Ranger Rosa	E	RF	59	Run to Reading	Discovery Peak
Reading Together	A	I	46	Vocabulary Readers	Houghton Mifflin Harcourt
Reading Together	A	I	46	Vocabulary Readers/CA	Houghton Mifflin Harcourt
Reading Together	A	I	46	Vocabulary Readers/TX	Houghton Mifflin Harcourt
Reading Under the Covers	D	RF	25	Visions	Wright Group/McGraw Hill
Reading with Eva and Pogo	I	RF	328	Gear Up!	Wright Group/McGraw Hill
Ready for Fall	G	F	204	Early Explorers	Benchmark Education
Ready for Lift Off	C	RF	45	Red Rocket Readers	Flying Start Books
Ready for Liftoff	L	I	294	Vocabulary Readers	Houghton Mifflin Harcourt

TITLE	LEVEL	GENRE	WORD COUNT	AUTHOR / SERIES	PUBLISHER / DISTRIBUTOR
Ready for Liftoff	L	I	294	Vocabulary Readers/CA	Houghton Mifflin Harcourt
Ready for Liftoff	L	I	294	Vocabulary Readers/TX	Houghton Mifflin Harcourt
Ready for School	C	RF	41	Teacher's Choice Series	Pearson Learning Group
Ready for School	E	RF	77	Windmill Books	Rigby
Ready for Second Grade	L	RF	295	Leveled Readers	Houghton Mifflin Harcourt
Ready for Second Grade	L	RF	295	Leveled Readers/CA	Houghton Mifflin Harcourt
Ready for Second Grade	L	RF	295	Leveled Readers/TX	Houghton Mifflin Harcourt
Ready for Take-Off!	O	I	250+	Bookweb	Rigby
Ready for Winter	K	I	185	Larkin, Bruce	Wilbooks
Ready Steady Jump	D	I	25	Pacific Literacy	Pacific Learning
Ready to Dream	N	RF	250+	Napoli, Donna Jo & Furrow, Elena	Bloomsbury Children's Books
Ready, Get Set, Go!	G	RF	137	First Start	Troll Associates
Ready, Set, Go	H	F	250+	Stadler, John	HarperTrophy
Ready, Set, Go!	D	I	26	Canizares, Susan; Chanko, Pamela	Scholastic
Ready, Set, Go!	K	RF	250+	Pacific Literacy	Pacific Learning
Ready, Set, Go!	B	RF	40	Windows on Literacy	National Geographic
Ready, Set, Jump!	M	I	250+	Rigby Literacy	Rigby
Ready, Set, Oops!	L	RF	250+	Science Solves It!	Kane Press
Ready, Set, Pedal!	F	RF	165	On Our Way to English	Rigby
Ready, Set . . . WAIT!: What Animals Do Before a Hurricane	M	I	376	Zelch, Patti R.	Sylvan Dell Publishing
Ready, Steady, Rhyme!	J	RF	250+	Rigby Literacy	Rigby
Real Band, A	G	RF	183	Leveled Readers	Houghton Mifflin Harcourt
Real Band, A	G	RF	183	Leveled Readers/CA	Houghton Mifflin Harcourt
Real Band, A	G	RF	183	Leveled Readers/TX	Houghton Mifflin Harcourt
Real Classy: Silly School Jokes	O	F	1880	Make Me Laugh!	Lerner Publishing Group
Real Facts About Rivers	I	I	159	Rosen Real Readers	Rosen Publishing Group
Real Heroes Don't Wear Capes	L	RF	250+	Social Studies Connects	Kane Press
Real Hoops	Q	RF	250+	Bowen, Fred	Peachtree
Real Horses	J	RF	250+	The Rowland Reading Program Library	Rowland Reading Foundation
Real McCoy, The: The Life of an African-American Inventor	T	B	250+	Towle, Wendy	Scholastic
Real Me, The	L	RF	250+	Social Studies Connects	Kane Press
Real or Not?- Art Fakes and Fakers	U	I	250+	Connectors	Pacific Learning
Real Princess, The	I	TL	193	Jumbled Tumbled Tales & Rhymes	Rigby
Real Question, The	Z+	RF	250+	Fogelin, Adrian	Fitzhenry & Whiteside
Real Spy's Guide to Becoming a Spy, The	V	I	250+	Earnest, Peter & Harper, Suzanne	Harry N. Abrams
Real Team Soccer	R	RF	1207	Leveled Readers	Houghton Mifflin Harcourt
Real Thief, The	U	F	250+	Steig, William	Farrar, Straus, & Giroux
Reality Bug, The: Pendragon	X	F	250+	MacHale, D.J.	Aladdin
Real-Life Dragons	S	I	250+	Dragons	Capstone Press
Really Funny Riddles	K	I	243	Joke Books	Capstone Press
Really Rabbits	K	F	533	Kroll, Virginia	Charlesbridge
Really Truly Bingo	K	F	250+	Kvasnosky, Laura McGee	Candlewick Press
Really, Really Big Questions About Life, the Universe and Everything	W	I	250+	Kingfisher Knowledge	Kingfisher
Really, Really Cold!	O	I	781	Vocabulary Readers	Houghton Mifflin Harcourt
Really, Really Cold!	O	I	781	Vocabulary Readers/CA	Houghton Mifflin Harcourt
Really, Really Cold!	O	I	781	Vocabulary Readers/TX	Houghton Mifflin Harcourt
Really?	L	RF	1506	Real Kids Readers	Millbrook Press
Real-Skin Rubber Monster Mask, The	H	F	104	Cohen, Miriam	Bantam Books

* Collection of short stories   # Graphic text
^ Mature content with lower level text demands

TITLE	LEVEL	GENRE	WORD COUNT	AUTHOR / SERIES	PUBLISHER / DISTRIBUTOR
Reaper, The	R	I	250+	Theme Sets	National Geographic
Reason for a Flower, The	N	I	250+	Heller, Ruth	Scholastic
Reason to Run, A	Q	RF	250+	Leveled Readers Language Support	Houghton Mifflin Harcourt
Reasons for Seasons, The	M	I	250+	Gibbons, Gail	Holiday House
Rebecca and the Concert	I	RF	374	PM Story Books	Rigby
Rebecca at the Fun Fair	E	RF	87	Big Cat	Pacific Learning
Rebecca's Rashness: The Sisters 8	Q	F	250+	Baratz-Logsted, Lauren	Sandpiper Books
Rebecca's Story	L	HF	250+	The Rowland Reading Program Library	Rowland Reading Foundation
Rebecca's Story: An Ellis Island Adventure	O	HF	250+	HSP/Harcourt Trophies	Harcourt, Inc.
^Rebel Glory	U	RF	250+	Orca Sports	Orca Books
Rebels and Revolutions	X	I	250+	InfoQuest	Rigby
^Rebel's Tag	V	RF	250+	Orca Currents	Orca Books
Rebound	V	RF	250+	Krech, Bob	Marshall Cavendish
Rebuilding a Nation: Picking up the Pieces	Y	I	250+	The Civil War	Carus Publishing Company
Rebus Bears, The	I	F	250+	Reit, Seymour	Bantam Books
Recess	A	I	27	At School Series	Pioneer Valley
Recess	B	RF	26	Teacher's Choice Series	Pearson Learning Group
Recess Time	D	RF	59	Kaleidoscope Collection	Hameray Publishing Group
Recipe for Learning	M	RF	879	Leveled Readers	Houghton Mifflin Harcourt
Recipe for Learning	M	RF	879	Leveled Readers/CA	Houghton Mifflin Harcourt
Recipe for Learning	M	RF	879	Leveled Readers/TX	Houghton Mifflin Harcourt
Recipe for Rebellion	T	F	250+	Hopkins, Cathy	Kingfisher
Reconstruction: Rebuilding after the Civil War	V	I	250+	Let Freedom Ring	Capstone Press
Rectangle	B	I	32	Shapes	Lerner Publishing Group
Rectangles	D	I	36	Bookworms	Marshall Cavendish
Rectangles Around Town	J	I	309	Shapes Around Town	Capstone Press
Rectangles: Seeing Rectangles All Around Us	K	I	199	Shapes	Capstone Press
Rectangular Prism	L	I	43	Solid Shapes	Lerner Publishing Group
Recycle	C	I	16	Conservation	Lerner Publishing Group
Recycle It!	G	I	118	Discovery Links	Newbridge
Recycle Michael	F	RF	134	Storyteller	Wright Group/McGraw Hill
Recycle!	M	I	250+	Gibbons, Gail	Little Brown and Company
Recycle!	B	I	33	Leveled Readers Science	Houghton Mifflin Harcourt
Recycle, Reuse, and Reduce!	K	I	445	Vocabulary Readers	Houghton Mifflin Harcourt
Recycle, Reuse, and Reduce!	K	I	445	Vocabulary Readers/CA	Houghton Mifflin Harcourt
Recycle, Reuse, and Reduce!	K	I	445	Vocabulary Readers/TX	Houghton Mifflin Harcourt
Recycled Tires	U	I	250+	A Great Idea	Norwood House Press
Re-Cycles	M	I	750	Cycles	Lerner Publishing Group
Re-Cycles	L	I	250+	Cycles	Millbrook Press
Recycling a Can	M	I	250+	Rosen Real Readers	Rosen Publishing Group
Recycling Contest, The	K	RF	604	Leveled Readers	Houghton Mifflin Harcourt
Recycling Contest, The	K	RF	604	Leveled Readers/CA	Houghton Mifflin Harcourt
Recycling Contest, The	K	RF	604	Leveled Readers/TX	Houghton Mifflin Harcourt
Recycling Dump	D	I	48	Little Celebrations	Pearson Learning Group
Recycling Plastic	V	I	250+	Sauklis, Anthony	Houghton Mifflin Harcourt
Recycling Plastic	O	I	250+	Sun Sprouts	ETA/Cuisenaire
Red	B	I	63	Bookworms	Marshall Cavendish
Red	B	I	26	Colors	Lerner Publishing Group
Red	E	F	71	Instant Readers	Harcourt School Publishers
Red Adair: The Story of an Oil Well Fighter	U	B	250+	High-Fliers	Pacific Learning
Red All Around	A	I	52	Color My World	American Reading Company
Red and Blue and Yellow	D	I	100	PM Nonfiction-Red	Rigby

R

TITLE	LEVEL	GENRE	WORD COUNT	AUTHOR / SERIES	PUBLISHER / DISTRIBUTOR
Red and Blue Mittens	M	RF	250+	Reading Unlimited	Pearson Learning Group
Red and I Visit the Vet	F	RF	196	Ready Readers	Pearson Learning Group
Red and the Big Bad Wolf	W	F	1357	Leveled Readers	Houghton Mifflin Harcourt
Red Apples for Me	D	RF	69	Bonnell, Kris	Reading Reading Books
Red Balloon, The	C	RF	34	Joy Readers	Pearson Learning Group
Red Balloons, The	B	RF	55	Literacy by Design	Rigby
Red Balloons, The	B	RF	55	On Our Way to English	Rigby
Red Bird, The	D	RF	64	Reading Street	Pearson
Red Bird's Nest	E	F	149	Sails	Rigby
Red Block, Blue Block	D	I	108	PM Math Readers	Rigby
Red Box, The	H	RF	250+	Phonics Readers Plus	Steck-Vaughn
Red Boy's New Game	I	RF	332	PM Stars Bridge Books	Rigby
Red Butterfly : How a Princess Smuggled the Secret of Silk Out of China	P	TL	250+	Noyes, Deborah	Candlewick Press
Red Cap	W	HF	250+	Wisler, G. Clifton	Penguin Group
Red Cowgirl Boots	F	RF	279	Rigby Flying Colors	Rigby
Red Cross, The	O	I	606	Early Explorers	Benchmark Education
Red Dog	U	RF	250+	Wallace, Bill	Simon & Schuster
*Red Doll and Other Stories, The	H	F	250+	New Way Literature	Steck-Vaughn
Red Egg and Ginger	M	RF	250+	Greetings	Rigby
Red Everywhere	J	I	320	Lightning Bolt Books	Lerner Publishing Group
Red Flyer, The	K	RF	552	Springboard	Wright Group/McGraw Hill
Red Foxes	J	I	215	Nocturnal Animals	Capstone Press
Red Foxes	K	I	318	Pull Ahead Books	Lerner Publishing Group
Red Ghost, The	M	F	250+	Bauer, Marion Dane	Random House
Red Hot Pet, A	L	F	250+	Rigby Gigglers	Rigby
Red Is Best	I	RF	309	Stinson, Kathy	Annick Press
Red Kangaroo	L	I	250+	A Day in the Life: Desert Animals	Heinemann Library
Red Lantern Festival, The: A Play Based on a Chinese Folktale	M	TL	250+	Windows on Literacy	National Geographic
Red Magic Marker, The	K	F	243	Dominie Readers	Pearson Learning Group
Red Means Good Fortune: A Story of San Francisco's Chinatown	S	I	250+	Goldin, Barbara Diamond	Penguin Group
Red Midnight	Y	HF	250+	Mikaelsen, Ben	HarperTrophy
Red Necklace, The: A Story of the French Revolution	Z	HF	250+	Gardner, Sally	Speak
Red Nose Frost: A Traditional Tale From Russia	L	TL	250+	Rigby Literacy	Rigby
Red or Blue?	LB	RF	13	Ready Readers	Pearson Learning Group
Red Pajamas, The	D	F	98	Leveled Literacy Intervention/ Blue System	Heinemann
Red Pizzas for a Blue Count	O	F	250+	Stilton, Geronimo	Scholastic
Red Planet, The	O	I	765	Leveled Readers	Houghton Mifflin Harcourt
Red Planet, The	O	I	765	Leveled Readers/CA	Houghton Mifflin Harcourt
Red Planet, The	O	I	765	Leveled Readers/TX	Houghton Mifflin Harcourt
Red Planet, The	S	I	250+	Orbit Double Takes	Pacific Learning
Red Puppy	C	RF	85	PM Plus Story Books	Rigby
Red Ribbon Rosie	M	RF	250+	Marzollo, Jean	Random House
Red Riding Hood	M	TL	250+	Marshall, James	Puffin Books
Red Riding Hood	A	TL	32	Red Rocket Readers	Flying Start Books
*Red Riding Hood and the Flower in the Woods	L	TL	250+	New Way Literature	Steck-Vaughn
Red River Girl	U	HF	250+	Sommerdorf, Norma	Holiday House
Red Rose, The	E	F	127	Story Box	Wright Group/McGraw Hill
Red Scare, The	Z	I	3314	Vocabulary Readers	Houghton Mifflin Harcourt
Red Scare, The	Z	I	3314	Vocabulary Readers/CA	Houghton Mifflin Harcourt

* Collection of short stories   # Graphic text
^ Mature content with lower level text demands

TITLE	LEVEL	GENRE	WORD COUNT	AUTHOR / SERIES	PUBLISHER / DISTRIBUTOR
Red Scarf Girl: Memoir of the Cultural Revolution	Z	B	250+	Jiang, Ji Li	HarperTrophy
#Red Sea Sharks, The	X	F	250+	The Adventures of Tintin	Little Brown and Company
Red Shoes, The	L	RF	250+	Sails	Rigby
Red Socks and Yellow Socks	G	F	155	Sunshine	Wright Group/McGraw Hill
Red Sox and the World Series, The	O	I	460	Vocabulary Readers	Houghton Mifflin Harcourt
Red Squirrel Hides Some Nuts	E	RF	128	PM Plus Story Books	Rigby
Red Squirrel's Adventure	H	RF	223	PM Plus Story Books	Rigby
Red Ted and the Lost Things	L	F	250+	Rosen, Michael	Candlewick Press
Red Ted at the Beach	E	F	163	Storyworlds	Heinemann
Red Ted Goes to School	E	RF	183	Storyworlds	Heinemann
Red Thread, The: An Adoption Fairy Tale	L	TL	250+	Lin, Grace	Albert Whitman & Co.
Red Wolf Country	Q	RF	250+	London, Jonathan	Scholastic
Red, White & True Blue Mallory	O	RF	15286	Friedman, Laurie	Lerner Publishing Group
Red, White and Blue and Katie Woo	J	RF	250+	Manushkin, Fran	Picture Window Books
Red, White, and Blue	LB	I	21	Canizares, Susan; Chessen, Betsey	Scholastic
Red: Seeing Red All Around Us	L	I	250+	Colors	Capstone Press
Redcoats and Petticoats	R	HF	1867	Avenues	Hampton Brown
Redcoats in America	T	I	1299	Vocabulary Readers/CA	Houghton Mifflin Harcourt
Redcoats in America	T	I	1299	Vocabulary Readers/TX	Houghton Mifflin Harcourt
Red-Eyed Tree Frogs	O	I	2636	Early Bird Nature Books	Lerner Publishing Group
Reds and Blues	B	RF	57	Reading Street	Pearson
Red-Tailed Hawk, The	L	RF	197	Books For Young Learners	Richard C. Owen
Red-Tails Take Manhattan: The Story of Pale Male	T	I	250+	Literacy By Design	Rigby
Reduce	D	I	28	Conservation	Lerner Publishing Group
Reduce, Reuse, and Recycle	K	I	326	Early Connections	Benchmark Education
Reducing Garbage	M	I	250+	Making a Difference	Sea-to-Sea Publications
Redwall	Z	F	250+	Jacques, Brian	Avon Books
Redwood Forests, The	M	I	456	Lightning Bolt Books	Lerner Publishing Group
Redwoods, Hemlocks & Other Cone-Bearing Plants	Y	I	250+	Kingdom Classification	Compass Point Books
Redy to Ride	F	RF	103	City Stories	Rigby
Reef	Y	I	250+	Scubazoo	DK Publishing
Reefs	R	I	250+	Early Bird Earth Science	Lerner Publishing Group
Reefs	T	I	250+	iOpeners	Pearson Learning Group
Reel Heroes	X	I	250+	Boldprint	Steck-Vaughn
Reflections	I	F	110	Jonas, Ann	Morrow
Reflections of Me: Girls and Body Image	Y	I	250+	What's the Issue?	Compass Point Books
#Refreshing Look at Renewable Energy with Max Axiom, Super Scientist, A	T	I	250+	Graphic Library	Capstone Press
^Refuge Cove	W	RF	250+	Orca Soundings	Orca Books
Refugees, The	S	RF	250+	Orbit Chapter Books	Pacific Learning
Regarding the Fountain: A Tale, in Letter, of Liars and Leaks	U	RF	250+	Klise, Kate	Avon Books
Regarding the Trees: A Splintered Saga Rooted in Secrets	V	RF	250+	Klise, Kate	Sandpiper Books
Regina's Ride	P	RF	1017	Leveled Readers	Houghton Mifflin Harcourt
Regions from Coast to Coast	O	I	250+	Literacy by Design	Rigby
Reindeer	L	I	250+	A Day in the Life: Polar Animals	Heinemann Library
Reindeer Crunch and Other Christmas Recipes	S	I	250+	Fun Food for Cool Cooks	Capstone Press
Relationships of Living Things	R	I	250+	Atwater, Mary et al.	Macmillan/McGraw Hill
Relay Race, The	H	RF	234	PM Stars	Rigby
Rella's Wish	R	TL	1207	Leveled Readers	Houghton Mifflin Harcourt

* Collection of short stories   # Graphic text
^ Mature content with lower level text demands

R

TITLE	LEVEL	GENRE	WORD COUNT	AUTHOR / SERIES	PUBLISHER / DISTRIBUTOR
REM World	U	F	250+	Philbrick, Rodman	Scholastic
Remainder of One, A	L	F	250+	Pinczes, Elinor J.	Houghton Mifflin Harcourt
Remarkable Journey of Prince Jen, The	V	F	250+	Alexander, Lloyd	Bantam Books
Remarkable Pencils, The	S	F	4606	Take Two Books	Wright Group/McGraw Hill
Remarkable Robots	P	I	994	Vocabulary Readers	Houghton Mifflin Harcourt
Remarkable Robots	P	I	994	Vocabulary Readers/CA	Houghton Mifflin Harcourt
Remarkable Robots	P	I	994	Vocabulary Readers/TX	Houghton Mifflin Harcourt
Remarkable Romans, The	Y	I	2053	Leveled Readers	Houghton Mifflin Harcourt
Remarkable Romans, The	Y	I	2053	Leveled Readers/CA	Houghton Mifflin Harcourt
Remarkable Romans, The	Y	I	2053	Leveled Readers/TX	Houghton Mifflin Harcourt
Rembrandt	S	B	250+	Masterpieces: Artists and Their Works	Capstone Press
Remember Miranda	X	RF	5060	Oxford Bookworms Library	Oxford University Press
Remember Not To Forget: A Memory of the Holocaust	V	I	250+	Finkelstein, Norman H.	William Morrow
Remember the Ladies: A Story About Abigail Adams	R	B	8915	Creative Minds Biographies	Carolrhoda Books
Remember the Ladies: The First Women's Rights Convention	U	I	250+	Johnston, Norma	Scholastic
Remember the Rules!	E	RF	118	Early Explorers	Benchmark Education
Remembering Mrs. Rossi	P	RF	250+	Hest, Amy	Candlewick Press
Remembering the Big Quake	R	I	250+	Orbit Chapter Books	Pacific Learning
Remnants	W	SF	250+	Applegate, K. A.	Scholastic
Rena and Rio Build a Rhyme	N	RF	1100	Poetry Builders	Norwood House Press
Renaissance	Z	I	250+	Eyewitness Books	DK Publishing
Renaissance and Reformation	Y	I	250+	Reading Expeditions	National Geographic
Renaissance, The	W	I	250+	Orbit Chapter Books	Pacific Learning
Rent a Third Grader	O	RF	250+	Hiller, B. B.	Scholastic
Replay	T	RF	250+	Creech, Sharon	HarperCollins
Report Card, The	R	RF	250+	Clements, Andrew	Aladdin
Report to the Principal's Office	U	RF	250+	Spinelli, Jerry	Scholastic
Reptile	V	I	250+	Eyewitness Books	DK Publishing
Reptile Farm, The	I	I	228	Sun Sprouts	ETA/Cuisenaire
Reptile Park, The	N	I	963	Rigby Flying Colors	Rigby
Reptiles	S	I	250+	Boldprint	Steck-Vaughn
Reptiles	M	I	250+	Exploring the Animal Kingdom	Capstone Press
Reptiles	M	I	569	Red Rocket Readers	Flying Start Books
Reptiles	P	I	250+	Science Kids	Kingfisher
Reptiles and Amphibians	R	I	250+	Explorers	Wright Group/McGraw Hill
Reptiles and Amphibians	L	I	250+	Rosen Real Readers	Rosen Publishing Group
Reptiles and Amphibians	P	I	944	Time for Kids	Teacher Created Materials
Reptiles as Pets	O	I	1109	Vocabulary Readers	Houghton Mifflin Harcourt
Reptiles as Pets	O	I	1109	Vocabulary Readers/CA	Houghton Mifflin Harcourt
Reptiles as Pets	O	I	1109	Vocabulary Readers/TX	Houghton Mifflin Harcourt
Reptiles: Scaly-Skinnned Animals	M	I	250+	Amazing Science	Picture Window Books
Rescue	O	I	250+	Infotrek Plus	ETA/Cuisenaire
#Rescue Adventure of Stenny Green, Hindenburg Crash Eyewitness, The	R	HF	1204	History's Kid Heros	Graphic Universe
Rescue at Red Rock	U	RF	250+	WorldScapes	ETA/Cuisenaire
Rescue at Sea	J	RF	250+	Storyworlds	Heinemann
Rescue Boats	G	I	124	Mighty Machines	Capstone Press
Rescue Dogs	V	I	2617	Vocabulary Readers	Houghton Mifflin Harcourt
Rescue Dogs	V	I	2617	Vocabulary Readers/CA	Houghton Mifflin Harcourt
Rescue Dogs	V	I	2617	Vocabulary Readers/TX	Houghton Mifflin Harcourt
Rescue Helicopters in Action	M	I	250+	Transportation Zone	Capstone Press

* Collection of short stories   # Graphic text
^ Mature content with lower level text demands

TITLE	LEVEL	GENRE	WORD COUNT	AUTHOR / SERIES	PUBLISHER / DISTRIBUTOR
#Rescue in Antarctica: An Isabel Soto Geography Adventure	S	F	250+	Graphic Expeditions	Capstone Press
Rescue on Ruapehu	M	RF	250+	Rigby Literacy	Rigby
Rescue on the Outer Banks	N	HF	1724	On My Own History	Lerner Publishing Group
Rescue Pup	N	RF	280	Orca Young Readers	Orca Books
Rescue!	J	RF	250+	Lighthouse	Rigby
Rescue!	J	RF	250+	Sunshine	Wright Group/McGraw Hill
Rescue!	O	RF	250+	Wildcats	Wright Group/McGraw Hill
Rescue, The	L	RF	176	Pacific Literacy	Pacific Learning
Rescue, The	H	RF	155	PM Extensions-Green	Rigby
Rescue, The	A	F	35	Springboard	Wright Group/McGraw Hill
Rescue, The: Guardians of Ga'Hoole	V	F	250+	Lasky, Kathryn	Scholastic
Rescuers, The	S	F	250+	Sharp, Margery	Dell
Rescuing Mr. Black	I	RF	452	Rigby Flying Colors	Rigby
Rescuing Nelson	J	F	369	PM Collection	Rigby
Rescuing Stranded Whales	L	I	554	Reading Street	Pearson
Rescuing the Whooping Crane	S	I	1143	Leveled Readers	Houghton Mifflin Harcourt
Rescuing the Whooping Crane	S	I	1143	Leveled Readers/CA	Houghton Mifflin Harcourt
Rescuing the Whooping Crane	S	I	1143	Leveled Readers/TX	Houghton Mifflin Harcourt
Research for the Social Improvement and General Betterment of Lydia Goldblatt & Julie Graham-Chang	T	RF	250+	Ignatow, Amy	Amulet Books
^Resistance	U	HF	250+	Jungman, Ann	Stone Arch Books
Resistance, The	Z+	SF	250+	Malley, Gemma	Bloomsbury Children's Books
Respect	L	I	250+	Character Education	Red Brick Learning
Respect	L	I	250+	Everyday Character Education	Capstone Press
Respect	G	RF	163	Well-Being Series	Pearson Learning Group
Respect the Winds	M	TL	250+	Take Two Books	Wright Group/McGraw Hill
Respecting Others	F	I	68	Citizenship	Lerner Publishing Group
Respiration and Circulation	X	I	250+	Reading Expeditions	National Geographic
Respiratory System, The	P	I	2445	Early Bird Body Systems	Lerner Publishing Group
Respiratory System, The	M	I	212	Human Body Systems	Red Brick Learning
Responsibility	L	I	250+	Character Education	Red Brick Learning
Responsibility	L	I	250+	Everyday Character Education	Capstone Press
^Responsible	Z+	RF	250+	Orca Soundings	Orca Books
Restless Humanity	V	I	1436	Reading Street	Pearson
Restless Spirit	Z	B	250+	Partridge, Elizabeth	Penguin Group
Return of Rinaldo, the Sly Fox	M	TL	250+	Scheffler, Ursel	North-South Books
Return of the Great Brain, The	T	RF	250+	Fitzgerald, John D.	Dell
Return of the Home Run Kid	Q	RF	250+	Christopher, Matt	Scholastic
Return of the Third-Grade Ghosthunters, The	M	RF	250+	Maccarone, Grace	Scholastic
Return of the Wolf, The	S	RF	250+	Literacy By Design	Rigby
Return of the Yellowstone Grizzly, The	S	I	2122	Leveled Readers	Houghton Mifflin Harcourt
Return of the Yellowstone Grizzly, The	S	I	2122	Leveled Readers/CA	Houghton Mifflin Harcourt
Return of the Yellowstone Grizzly, The	S	I	2122	Leveled Readers/TX	Houghton Mifflin Harcourt
Return of Wild Whoopers, The	X	I	3122	Leveled Readers	Houghton Mifflin Harcourt
Return to Gill Park	S	RF	250+	Gordon, Amy	Holiday House
Return to Howliday Inn	P	F	250+	Howe, James	Avon Books
Return to Lost City (Dinotopia)	T	F	250+	Ciencin, Scott	Random House
Return to Titanic	Q	I	250+	Explorer Books-Pathfinder	National Geographic
Return to Titanic	P	I	250+	Explorer Books-Pioneer	National Geographic
Returnable Girl	Z+	RF	250+	Lowell, Pamela	Marshall Cavendish
Reunion in the Sky	Y	RF	3313	Leveled Readers	Houghton Mifflin Harcourt

TITLE	LEVEL	GENRE	WORD COUNT	AUTHOR / SERIES	PUBLISHER / DISTRIBUTOR
Reunion in the Sky	Y	RF	3313	Leveled Readers/CA	Houghton Mifflin Harcourt
Reunion in the Sky	Y	RF	3313	Leveled Readers/TX	Houghton Mifflin Harcourt
Reunion, The	O	HF	250+	Orca Young Readers	Orca Books
Reuse	D	I	27	Conservation	Lerner Publishing Group
Reuse and Recycle	I	I	118	Instant Readers	Harcourt School Publishers
Reuse and Recycle	M	I	725	Nonfiction Indigo	Pioneer Valley
Revenge of Captain Blood, The	O	F	250+	High-Fliers	Pacific Learning
Revenge of the McNasty Brothers, The (Melvin Beederman, Superhero)	N	F	250+	Trine, Greg	Henry Holt & Co.
Revenge of the Mummy	P	RF	250+	Parker, A. E.	Scholastic
Revenge of the Tribes	Y	I	250+	History for Young Canadians	Fitzhenry & Whiteside
Revenge of the Wannabes	X	RF	250+	Harrison, Lisi	Little Brown and Company
Revolution	V	I	12260	Dominoes three	Oxford University Press
Revolution Is Not a Dinner Party	W	HF	250+	Compestine, Ying Chang	Henry Holt & Co.
Revolution News	W	I	250+	The History News	Candlewick Press
Revolution of Sabine, The	X	HF	250+	Ain, Beth Levine	Candlewick Press
Revolution!	X	I	250+	Boldprint	Steck-Vaughn
Revolution!	V	HF	3239	Leveled Readers	Houghton Mifflin Harcourt
Revolutionary Poet: A Story About Phillis Wheatley	S	B	250+	Weidt, Maryann N.	Carolrhoda Books
Revolutionary War on Wednesday	M	F	250+	Osborne, Mary Pope	Random House
Revolutionary War, The	V	I	250+	America Goes to War	Red Brick Learning
^Revolutionary War, The: An Interactive History Adventure	T	HF	250+	You Choose Books	Capstone Press
Revolutions That Shaped America	V	I	250+	Explore More	Wright Group/McGraw Hill
Revolver	Z	HF	250+	Sedgwick, Marcus	Roaring Brook Press
Reward for Work Well Done, The: Jonas Salk	Q	B	250+	High-Fliers	Pacific Learning
Rex	A	F	32	Leveled Literacy Intervention/ Orange System	Heinemann
Rex Loves the Rain	B	RF	33	Windows on Literacy	National Geographic
Rex Plays Fetch	J	RF	250+	PM Plus Story Books	Rigby
Rex Runs Away	G	RF	225	On Our Way to English	Rigby
Rex to the Rescue	G	F	159	Sunshine	Wright Group/McGraw Hill
Rex's Box	D	RF	49	Reading Street	Pearson
Rex's Dance	E	F	103	Little Readers	Houghton Mifflin Harcourt
Rhinos	O	I	250+	Holmes, Kevin J.	Red Brick Learning
Rhode Island	T	I	250+	Hello U.S.A.	Lerner Publishing Group
Rhode Island	R	I	250+	This Land Is Your Land	Compass Point Books
Rhode Island Colony, The	R	I	250+	The American Colonies	Capstone Press
Rhode Island: Facts and Symbols	O	I	250+	The States and Their Symbols	Capstone Press
Rhombus	L	I	29	Shapes	Lerner Publishing Group
Rhyme Game, The	G	RF	159	Storyteller-Setting Sun	Wright Group/McGraw Hill
Rhymes	A	I	9	Ready Readers	Pearson Learning Group
Rhymes with Witches	Z+	RF	250+	Myracle, Lauren	Amulet Books
Rhyming Princess	J	F	480	Storyteller	Wright Group/McGraw Hill
Rhyming Riddles	H	I	240	Cambridge Reading	Pearson Learning Group
Rhythm and Shoes	N	I	250+	Pacific Literacy	Pacific Learning
Rhythm Is Everywhere	N	I	532	Vocabulary Readers	Houghton Mifflin Harcourt
Rhythm Is Everywhere	N	I	532	Vocabulary Readers/CA	Houghton Mifflin Harcourt
Ribbit!	A	I	7	Little Celebrations	Pearson Learning Group
Ribbon, The	C	I	46	Rise & Shine	Hampton Brown
Ribsy	O	RF	250+	Cleary, Beverly	Hearst
Ric and Rin Run!	B	F	24	Reading Street	Pearson
Ricardo's Way	I	RF	339	Ancona, George	Scholastic

R

* Collection of short stories   # Graphic text
^ Mature content with lower level text demands

TITLE	LEVEL	GENRE	WORD COUNT	AUTHOR / SERIES	PUBLISHER / DISTRIBUTOR
Rice	L	I	132	Literacy Tree	Rigby
Rice	O	I	250+	Windows on Literacy	National Geographic
Rice - From Paddy Field to Plate	N	I	740	Springboard	Wright Group/McGraw Hill
Rice Cakes	H	F	332	Literacy 2000	Rigby
Rice Is Nice	K	I	405	Red Rocket Readers	Flying Start Books
Rich and Famous Body and the Empty Checkbook, The	N	RF	250+	Wonder World	Wright Group/McGraw Hill
Rich or Poor?	W	I	250+	WorldScapes	ETA/Cuisenaire
Richard M. Nixon	U	B	250+	Profiles of the Presidents	Compass Point Books
Richard M. Nixon: Thirty-seventh President	R	B	250+	Getting to Know the U.S. Presidents	Children's Press
Richard Nixon	T	B	3812	History Maker Bios	Lerner Publishing Group
Richard Petty	Q	B	250+	NASCAR Racing	Capstone Press
Riches from Earth	S	I	250+	Navigators Science Series	Benchmark Education
Riches from Nature	K	I	382	Early Connections	Benchmark Education
Riches from the Earth	V	I	1352	Reading Street	Pearson
Richie the Greedy Mouse	I	F	179	Sunshine	Wright Group/McGraw Hill
Rick and Rosie	B	RF	28	Phonics and Friends	Hampton Brown
Rick Is Sick	D	F	53	Green Light Readers	Harcourt
Rick's Dream Adventure	K	F	250+	World Quest Adventures	World Quest Learning
Ricky Ricotta's Mighty Robot vs. The Mecha-Monkeys From Mars	L	SF	250+	Pilkey, Dav	Scholastic
Ricky Ricotta's Mighty Robot vs. The Uranium Unicorns From Uranus	L	F	250+	Pilkey, Dav	Scholastic
Ricky's Rat Gang	K	F	250+	I Am Reading	Kingfisher
Riddle Book	F	F	189	Reading Unlimited	Pearson Learning Group
Riddle of Redstone Castle, The	P	HF	250+	Tristars	Richard C. Owen
Riddle of Redstone Ruins, The	P	RF	250+	Tristars	Richard C. Owen
Riddle of the Anasazi, The	Z	I	1637	Leveled Readers	Houghton Mifflin Harcourt
Riddle of The Red Purse, The	L	RF	250+	Giff, Patricia Reilly	Bantam Books
Riddle of the Rosetta Stone, The	V	I	250+	Giblin, James Cross	HarperTrophy
Riddle of the Seaplanes, The	R	RF	250+	Storyteller-Mountain Peaks	Wright Group/McGraw Hill
Riddle-Me-Ree, What Can It Be?	I	RF	86	Book Bus	HarperCollins
Riddles	E	I	51	Literacy 2000	Rigby
Riddles and Jokes	K	F	250+	Gilbreath, Alice Thompson	Pearson Learning Group
Riddles of the Universe	S	I	250+	Orbit Chapter Books	Pacific Learning
Ride in the Country, A	D	RF	83	Carousel Readers	Pearson Learning Group
Ride On: Bikes and Riders Who Rule	W	I	250+	Boldprint	Steck-Vaughn
Ride Right: Bicycle Safety	J	I	250+	How to Be Safe	Picture Window Books
^ Ride That Really Was Haunted, The	Q	RF	250+	Brezenoff, Steve/Field Trip Mysteries	Stone Arch Books
Ride The Wild River	P	I	250+	Rigby Literacy	Rigby
Ride to the Top: Tony Hawk and Andy MacDonald	P	B	250+	All Aboard Reading	Grosset & Dunlap
Ride, A	LB	F	12	Sails	Rigby
Ride, Roll, and Run	F	RF	157	Windows on Literacy	National Geographic
Ride, The	A	F	24	Avenues	Hampton Brown
Rides	Y	I	250+	Boldprint	Steck-Vaughn
Rides Are Fun	WB	I	0	Windows on Literacy	National Geographic
Rides, The	B	RF	42	Sails	Rigby
Riding	G	I	87	Benchmark Rebus	Marshall Cavendish
Riding	C	RF	67	Foundations	Wright Group/McGraw Hill
Riding	B	I	35	On Our Way to English	Rigby
Riding	H	I	210	Wonder World	Wright Group/McGraw Hill
Riding a Wave	V	I	250+	WorldScapes	ETA/Cuisenaire

TITLE	LEVEL	GENRE	WORD COUNT	AUTHOR / SERIES	PUBLISHER / DISTRIBUTOR
Riding Bicycles	H	I	150	Nonfiction Set 8	Literacy Footprints
Riding Freedom	P	HF	250+	Ryan, Pam Munoz	Scholastic
Riding High	U	RF	250+	King, Donna	Kingfisher
Riding High	K	RF	529	PM Story Books	Rigby
Riding My New Bike	E	I	132	Vocabulary Readers	Houghton Mifflin Harcourt
Riding My New Bike	E	I	132	Vocabulary Readers/CA	Houghton Mifflin Harcourt
Riding on Roller Coasters	R	I	250+	On Our Way to English	Rigby
Riding Out the Quake	U	RF	6171	Reading Street	Pearson
Riding Out the Storm	S	RF	1426	Leveled Readers	Houghton Mifflin Harcourt
Riding the Bubbly Seas	O	RF	250+	Sails	Rigby
Riding the Skateboard Ramps	K	RF	250+	PM Plus Story Books	Rigby
Riding the Steam Train	L	I	250+	Pacific Literacy	Pacific Learning
Riding to Craggy Rock	J	RF	386	PM Collection	Rigby
Riding to School	B	I	35	Leveled Readers	Houghton Mifflin Harcourt
Riding to School	B	I	35	Leveled Readers/CA	Houghton Mifflin Harcourt
Riding with the Camel Corps	W	HF	3451	Leveled Readers	Houghton Mifflin Harcourt
Riding with the Camel Corps	W	HF	3451	Leveled Readers/CA	Houghton Mifflin Harcourt
Riding with the Camel Corps	W	HF	3451	Leveled Readers/TX	Houghton Mifflin Harcourt
Riding with the Pony Express	T	HF	2776	Leveled Readers	Houghton Mifflin Harcourt
Riding with the Pony Express	T	HF	2776	Leveled Readers/CA	Houghton Mifflin Harcourt
Riding with the Pony Express	T	HF	2776	Leveled Readers/TX	Houghton Mifflin Harcourt
Riding with the Vaqueros	T	HF	1790	Leveled Readers	Houghton Mifflin Harcourt
Rifle, The	T	HF	250+	Paulsen, Gary	Dell
Right at Home	K	I	250+	Spyglass Books	Compass Point Books
Right Behind You	Z+	RF	250+	Giles, Gail	Little Brown and Company
Right Fly, The	U	RF	1878	Leveled Readers	Houghton Mifflin Harcourt
Right Match, The	E	RF	113	Dominie Math Stories	Pearson Learning Group
Right or Wrong?	O	RF	250+	Wildcats	Wright Group/McGraw Hill
Right Outside My Window	H	RF	121	Bookshop	Mondo Publishing
Right Pet, The	D	F	66	Leveled Readers	Houghton Mifflin Harcourt
Right Place for Jupiter, The	K	RF	250+	PM Story Books-Silver	Rigby
Right Place, Right Time	L	I	629	Gear Up!	Wright Group/McGraw Hill
Right Place, The	F	RF	165	In Step Readers	Rigby
Right to Rule, The	W	I	250+	WorldScapes	ETA/Cuisenaire
Right to Survive, The	T	I	250+	Connectors	Pacific Learning
Righteous Revenge of Artemis Bonner, The	U	RF	250+	Myers, Walter Dean	HarperTrophy
Riley's Cake	H	RF	279	Rigby Flying Colors	Rigby
Rinaldo the Sly Fox	M	TL	250+	Scheffler, Ursel	North-South Books
Ring of Endless Light, A	W	F	250+	L'Engle, Madeleine	Dell
Ring of Fire, The	V	I	2580	Leveled Readers Social Studies	Houghton Mifflin Harcourt
Ringo's Assignment	N	F	250+	Springboard	Wright Group/McGraw Hill
Ring-Tailed Lemurs	O	I	1791	Early Bird Nature Books	Lerner Publishing Group
*Rio Grande Stories	W	RF	250+	Meyer, Carolyn	Harcourt, Inc.
Riot	Y	HF	250+	Myers, Walter Dean	Egmont USA
Rip Current Rescue	T	RF	250+	Reading Street	Pearson
#Rip Van Winkle & The Legend of Sleepy Hollow	T	F	1950	Dominoes starter	Oxford University Press
Ripe Red Tomatoes	I	RF	191	Gear Up!	Wright Group/McGraw Hill
Ripeka's Carving	J	RF	250+	Literacy 2000	Rigby
*Rip-Roaring Russell	M	RF	250+	Hurwitz, Johanna	Penguin Group
Rip's Secret Spot	E	RF	116	Green Light Readers	Harcourt
Riptide	O	RF	250+	Weller, Frances Ward	G.P. Putnam's Sons Books for Young Readers
Rise and Fall of the Incas, The	S	I	250+	Orbit Chapter Books	Pacific Learning

* Collection of short stories   # Graphic text
^ Mature content with lower level text demands

TITLE	LEVEL	GENRE	WORD COUNT	AUTHOR / SERIES	PUBLISHER / DISTRIBUTOR
Rise and Shine, Mariko-chan	K	RF	250+	Tomioka, Chiyoko	Scholastic
Rise of Scourge: Warriors Manga	U	F	250+	Hunter, Erin	HarperCollins
Rise of the Heroes: Hero.com	W	F	250+	Briggs, Andy	Walker & Company
Rising River, The	T	HF	2648	Leveled Readers	Houghton Mifflin Harcourt
Rising River, The	T	HF	2648	Leveled Readers/CA	Houghton Mifflin Harcourt
Rising River, The	T	HF	2648	Leveled Readers/TX	Houghton Mifflin Harcourt
Rising Stars of the NBA	P	B	250+	Layden, Joe	Scholastic
Rising Storm: Warriors, Book 4	U	F	250+	Hunter, Erin	HarperCollins
Rising Up, Falling Down	L	I	205	Spyglass Books	Compass Point Books
Rita at the Fair	C	F	32	Brand New Readers	Candlewick Press
Rita Blows Bubbles	C	F	25	Brand New Readers	Candlewick Press
Rita Moreno	K	B	250+	Leveled Readers Language Support	Houghton Mifflin Harcourt
Rita Moreno: Shining Star	M	B	593	Leveled Readers	Houghton Mifflin Harcourt
Rita Rolls	C	RF	36	Little Celebrations	Pearson Learning Group
River Apart, A	X	HF	250+	Sutherland, Robert	Fitzhenry & Whiteside
River as a Road, The	T	I	250+	Explore More	Wright Group/McGraw Hill
River Beds:Sleeping in the World's Rivers	O	RF	250+	Karwoski, Gail Langer	Sylvan Dell Publishing
River Between Us, The	X	HF	250+	Peck, Richard	Puffin Books
River Food Chains	T	I	250+	Protecting Food Chains	Heinemann Library
River Grows, The	E	I	70	Ready Readers	Pearson Learning Group
River Kept Rising, The	T	HF	2707	Leveled Readers	Houghton Mifflin Harcourt
River Kept Rising, The	T	HF	2707	Leveled Readers/CA	Houghton Mifflin Harcourt
River Kept Rising, The	T	HF	2707	Leveled Readers/TX	Houghton Mifflin Harcourt
River Life	N	I	250+	Windows on Literacy	National Geographic
River of No Return	T	RF	1845	Leveled Readers	Houghton Mifflin Harcourt
River of Wind, The: Guardians of Ga'Hoole	V	F	250+	Lasky, Kathryn	Scholastic
River Otter	I	I	208	Independent Readers Science	Houghton Mifflin Harcourt
River Patrol Boats	T	I	250+	Land and Sea	Capstone Press
River Race	N	HF	250+	Leveled Readers Language Support	Houghton Mifflin Harcourt
River Rafting Fun	J	RF	250+	PM Plus Story Books	Rigby
River Ran Wild, A	Q	I	250+	Cherry, Lynne	Hampton Brown
River Rapids Ride, The	J	RF	283	Sunshine	Wright Group/McGraw Hill
River Rats	O	RF	250+	Belcher, Angie	Pacific Learning
River Rescue	L	RF	250+	Reading Safari	Mondo Publishing
River Runners	M	RF	250+	Literacy Tree	Rigby
River Secrets	X	F	250+	Hale, Shannon	Bloomsbury Children's Books
River Through the Ages	U	I	250+	Steele, Philip	Troll Associates
River Travel	R	I	1263	Vocabulary Readers	Houghton Mifflin Harcourt
River Travel	R	I	1263	Vocabulary Readers/CA	Houghton Mifflin Harcourt
River Travel	S	I	1200	Vocabulary Readers/TX	Houghton Mifflin Harcourt
River, The	Z+	RF	250+	Beaufrand, Mary Jane	Little Brown and Company
River, The	J	I	222	Explorations	Eleanor Curtain Publishing
River, The	J	I	222	Explorations	Okapi Educational Materials
River, The	D	I	42	Foundations	Wright Group/McGraw Hill
River, The	R	RF	250+	Paulsen, Gary	Dell
River, The	C	I	40	Science	Outside the Box
River, The	J	I	280	Sun Sprouts	ETA/Cuisenaire
Riverboat Bill	H	F	250+	Take Two Books	Wright Group/McGraw Hill
Rivers	K	I	220	Take Two Books	Wright Group/McGraw Hill
Rivers & Lakes	R	I	250+	The Wonders of Our World	Crabtree
Rivers and Lakes: The Land Around Us	S	I	250+	Reading Expeditions	National Geographic

R

* Collection of short stories   # Graphic text
^ Mature content with lower level text demands

TITLE	LEVEL	GENRE	WORD COUNT	AUTHOR / SERIES	PUBLISHER / DISTRIBUTOR
Rivers in the Rain Forest	O	I	250+	Pirotta, Saviour	Steck-Vaughn
River's Journey, A	G	I	116	Rigby Focus	Rigby
River's Journey, The	N	I	221	Windows on Literacy	National Geographic
Rivers of Dance	S	I	250+	Harcourt Trophies	Harcourt, Inc.
Rivers of Fire	U	F	250+	Carman, Patrick	Little Brown and Company
Rivers of Zadaa, The: Pendragon	X	F	250+	MacHale, D.J.	Aladdin
Rivers, Lakes, Streams, and Ponds	W	I	250+	Biomes Atlases	Raintree
Rivers, Streams, and Lakes	M	I	250+	PM Plus Nonfiction	Rigby
Roach on the Fridge, A	N	RF	250+	Sails	Rigby
Road Builders	I	F	185	Leveled Literacy Intervention/ Blue System	Heinemann
Road Goes By, A	J	I	250+	Momentum Literacy Program	Troll Associates
Road Robber	I	F	250+	Sunshine	Wright Group/McGraw Hill
Road Rules	F	I	153	Red Rocket Readers	Flying Start Books
Road Through the Ages	U	I	250+	Steele, Philip	Troll Associates
Road to Freedom, A	V	HF	250+	Reading Expeditions	National Geographic
Road to Memphis, The	X	HF	250+	Taylor, Mildred D.	Penguin Group
Road to Nevermore, The (Billy Bones)	U	F	250+	Lincoln, Christopher	Little Brown and Company
Road to Paris, The	T	RF	250+	Grimes, Nikki	Puffin Books
Road to Revolution	T	I	250+	Reading Expeditions	National Geographic
Road to Revolution	W	I	2850	Vocabulary Readers	Houghton Mifflin Harcourt
Road to Revolution	W	I	2850	Vocabulary Readers/CA	Houghton Mifflin Harcourt
Road to Revolution	W	I	2850	Vocabulary Readers/TX	Houghton Mifflin Harcourt
#Road to Revolution!	U	I	250+	The Cartoon Chronicles of America	Bloomsbury Children's Books
Road to Riches	X	I	250+	Boldprint	Steck-Vaughn
Road to Seneca Falls, The	R	B	250+	Swain, Gwenyth	Carolrhoda Books
Road Trip	S	RF	250+	Orca Young Readers	Orca Books
Road Trip, The	R	RF	250+	In Step Readers	Rigby
Road Work Ahead	I	RF	207	Little Readers	Houghton Mifflin Harcourt
Road Works	R	I	881	Red Rocket Readers	Flying Start Books
Roadrunner	L	I	250+	A Day in the Life: Desert Animals	Heinemann Library
Roadrunner	J	I	353	Vocabulary Readers	Houghton Mifflin Harcourt
Roadrunner	J	I	353	Vocabulary Readers/CA	Houghton Mifflin Harcourt
Roadrunners, The	M	I	441	Leveled Literacy Intervention/ Blue System	Heinemann
Roads and Bridges	I	RF	253	Alphakids	Sundance
Roadwork	K	RF	250+	Sutton, Sally	Candlewick Press
Roald Dahl: A Life of Imagination	N	B	558	Pull Ahead-Biographies	Lerner Publishing Group
Roald Dahl's Revolting Rhymes	R	F	250+	Dahl, Roald	Puffin Books
Roanoke Colony, The	S	I	1090	Leveled Readers Language Support	Houghton Mifflin Harcourt
Roanoke: The Lost Colony	T	I	250+	The Library of the Thirteen Colonies and The Lost Colony	Rosen Publishing Group
Roar Like a Tiger	E	RF	148	PM Plus Story Books	Rigby
Roaring '20s, The	W	I	250+	Reading Expeditions	National Geographic
Roaring Down the Rapids	O	RF	634	Leveled Readers	Houghton Mifflin Harcourt
Rob, Mom, and Socks	D	RF	44	Reading Street	Pearson
Robber Flies	A	I	56	Readlings/ Predator Bugs	American Reading Company
Robber Pig and the Ginger Bear	M	F	403	Read Alongs	Rigby
Robber Pig and the Green Eggs	M	F	250+	Read Alongs	Rigby
Robber, The	B	RF	25	Smart Start	Rigby
Robber, The	M	RF	1255	Sunshine	Wright Group/McGraw Hill
Robber's Mask, The	S	RF	250+	Sails	Rigby
Robbers, The	I	RF	275	Sails	Rigby

* Collection of short stories   # Graphic text
^ Mature content with lower level text demands

TITLE	LEVEL	GENRE	WORD COUNT	AUTHOR / SERIES	PUBLISHER / DISTRIBUTOR
Robbie Hood, Hurricane Hunter	S	B	1150	Independent Readers Science	Houghton Mifflin Harcourt
Robbie Woods and His Merry Men	N	RF	250+	High-Fliers	Pacific Learning
Robby in the River	I	RF	250+	Lighthouse	Rigby
Robe of Skulls, The	S	F	250+	French, Vivian	Candlewick Press
Robert and the Rocket	H	F	146	Waldron, Leesa	Scholastic
Robert Ballard: Discovering Underwater Treasures	T	I	250+	Reading Expeditions	National Geographic
Robert E. Lee	U	B	250+	Amazing Americans	Wright Group/McGraw Hill
Robert E. Lee	S	B	4141	History Maker Bios	Lerner Publishing Group
Robert E. Lee	U	B	250+	Let Freedom Ring	Red Brick Learning
Robert E. Lee	T	B	1940	Leveled Readers Social Studies	Houghton Mifflin Harcourt
Robert E. Lee	S	B	2538	People to Remember Series	January Books
Robert E. Lee	S	B	250+	Primary Source Readers	Teacher Created Materials
Robert E. Lee: Duty and Honor	Y	B	250+	The Civil War	Carus Publishing Company
#Robert E. Lee: The Story of the Great Confederate General	V	B	250+	Graphic Library	Capstone Press
Robert Frost: New England Poet	R	B	250+	Leveled Readers Language Support	Houghton Mifflin Harcourt
Robert Frost: The Journey of a Poet	U	B	963	Leveled Readers	Houghton Mifflin Harcourt
Robert Fulton	L	B	222	Famous People in Transportation	Red Brick Learning
Robert Fulton: A Life of Innovation	P	B	408	Pull Ahead Books	Lerner Publishing Group
Robert Goddard	L	B	203	Famous People in Transportation	Red Brick Learning
Robert Makes a Graph	H	I	160	Coulton, Mia	Kaeden Books
Robert Pattinson	S	B	250+	Star Biographies	Capstone Press
Robert Smalls Sails to Freedom	P	B	1861	On My Own History	Lerner Publishing Group
Robert the Rose Horse	I	F	250+	Heilbroner, Joan	Random House
Roberto Clemente	P	B	250+	DK Readers	DK Publishing
Roberto Clemente	P	B	250+	On Our Way to English	Rigby
Roberto Clemente	M	B	250+	Rookie Biographies	Children's Press
Roberto Clemente	U	B	250+	Sports Heroes and Legends	Lerner Publishing Group
Roberto Clemente	S	B	250+	Time for Kids	Teacher Created Materials
Roberto Clemente, Baseball Superstar	V	B	1776	Leveled Readers	Houghton Mifflin Harcourt
Roberto Clemente: A Life of Generosity	N	B	590	Pull Ahead-Biographies	Lerner Publishing Group
Roberto Clemente: Athlete and Hero	N	B	250+	Beginning Biographies	Pearson Learning Group
Roberto Clemente: Baseball Superstar	N	B	250+	Rookie Biographies	Children's Press
Roberto Clemente: Baseball's Humanitarian Hero	Y	B	250+	Trailblazer Biographies	Carolrhoda Books
Roberto's Smile	C	RF	43	Story Box	Wright Group/McGraw Hill
#Robin Hood	U	TL	2241	Shepard, Aaron & Watson, Anne (Retold)	Stone Arch Books
Robin Hood and the Silver Trophy	L	TL	250+	PM Tales and Plays-Silver	Rigby
Robin Hood and the Tricky Butcher	L	TL	250+	Read it! Readers	Picture Window Books
Robin Hood Meets Little John	L	TL	250+	PM Story Books	Rigby
#Robin Hood: Outlaw of Sherwood Forest	V	TL	3946	Graphic Myths and Legends	Graphic Universe
Robin Hood: The Tale of the Great Outlaw Hero	T	TL	250+	DK Readers	DK Publishing
Robin in the Tree, The	E	I	81	Benchmark Rebus	Marshall Cavendish
Robins	F	I	101	Animal Life Cycles	Lerner Publishing Group
^Robin's First Flight: Batman	P	F	250+	DC Superheroes	Stone Arch Books
Robins in the Spring	D	I	48	Bonnell, Kris	Reading Reading Books
Robins: Songbirds of Spring	K	I	331	Posada, Mia	Carolrhoda Books
Robinson Crusoe	P	TL	250+	Dolch, E. W.; Marguerite, P.	Scholastic
Robinson Crusoe	T	HF	250+	High-Fliers	Pacific Learning
Robinson Crusoe	T	HF	6830	Oxford Bookworms Library	Oxford University Press
Robocat	K	F	295	Leveled Readers	Houghton Mifflin Harcourt

TITLE	LEVEL	GENRE	WORD COUNT	AUTHOR / SERIES	PUBLISHER / DISTRIBUTOR
Robocat Stops Crime!	J	F	323	Leveled Readers Language Support	Houghton Mifflin Harcourt
Robot at the Zoo	E	F	126	Red Rocket Readers	Flying Start Books
Robot Batteries	E	F	81	Joy Starters	Pearson Learning Group
Robot Bedtime	E	F	121	Joy Starters	Pearson Learning Group
Robot Crash	H	F	185	Storyteller	Wright Group/McGraw Hill
Robot Rescue	R	SF	1566	Leveled Readers	Houghton Mifflin Harcourt
Robot Rescue	R	SF	1566	Leveled Readers/CA	Houghton Mifflin Harcourt
Robot Rescue	R	SF	1566	Leveled Readers/TX	Houghton Mifflin Harcourt
Robot Trouble	O	F	250+	On Our Way to English	Rigby
Robot Went Shopping	E	F	121	Joy Starters	Pearson Learning Group
Robot, The	B	F	49	Big Cat	Pacific Learning
Robot, The	B	F	30	Sails	Rigby
Robot, The	A	F	18	Smart Start	Rigby
Robot-a-Cise	K	F	250+	Sunshine	Wright Group/McGraw Hill
Robotics	X	I	7390	Cool Science	Lerner Publishing Group
Robots	G	I	106	Big Cat	Pacific Learning
Robots	P	I	250+	Explorations	Okapi Educational Materials
Robots	P	I	250+	Explorations	Eleanor Curtain Publishing
Robots	K	I	157	Gear Up!	Wright Group/McGraw Hill
Robots	S	I	250+	iOpeners	Pearson Learning Group
Robots	K	I	520	Red Rocket Readers	Flying Start Books
Robots	I	I	184	Sails	Rigby
Robots' Car, The	C	F	127	Sails	Rigby
Robots, The	C	RF	96	Storyworlds	Heinemann
Rock	M	I	250+	Materials	Capstone Press
Rock	E	I	104	Materials	Heinemann Library
^Rock Art Rebel	S	RF	10559	Cosson, M. J.	Stone Arch Books
Rock Band, The	O	RF	1797	Take Two Books	Wright Group/McGraw Hill
Rock Basics	J	I	118	Nature Basics	Capstone Press
Rock Boss, The	G	F	257	Sails	Rigby
^Rock Climbing	S	I	250+	Download	Hameray Publishing Group
Rock Climbing	Q	I	250+	Extreme Sports	Red Brick Learning
Rock Climbing	O	I	250+	Sunshine	Wright Group/McGraw Hill
Rock Climbing at Yosemite National Park	T	I	250+	Explore More	Wright Group/McGraw Hill
Rock Climbing: Making It to the Top	S	I	250+	High Five Reading	Red Brick Learning
Rock Collectors	G	I	158	Dominie Factivity Series	Pearson Learning Group
Rock Garden, The	H	RF	139	Windmill Books	Rigby
Rock Hunters	Q	I	250+	InfoQuest	Rigby
Rock in the Road, The	J	F	457	Pacific Literacy	Pacific Learning
Rock Kit, The	M	I	424	Reading Street	Pearson
Rock 'n' Roll	X	I	250+	Boldprint	Steck-Vaughn
Rock Pools	I	I	250+	Momentum Literacy Program	Troll Associates
Rock Pools	G	I	266	Rigby Flying Colors	Rigby
Rock Pools, The	B	I	49	PM Starters	Rigby
Rock Records	Y	I	250+	iOpeners	Pearson Learning Group
Rock Records	Q	I	250+	Reading Expeditions	National Geographic
Rock Star	N	RF	250+	Boyz Rule!	Mondo Publishing
Rock Stars	P	I	250+	Trackers	Pacific Learning
Rock, Brock, and the Savings Shock	M	RF	250+	Bair, Sheila	Albert Whitman & Co.
Rock-a-Bye Moon	H	F	107	Pair-It Books	Steck-Vaughn
^Rocket into Space	X	SF	250+	The Extraordinary Files	Hameray Publishing Group
Rocket Man: The Mercury Adventure of John Glenn	T	B	250+	Ashby, Ruth	Peachtree

TITLE	LEVEL	GENRE	WORD COUNT	AUTHOR / SERIES	PUBLISHER / DISTRIBUTOR
Rocket Man: The Story of Robert Goddard	W	B	250+	Trailblazer Biographies	Carolrhoda Books
Rocket Ship, The	I	RF	250+	PM Plus Story Books	Rigby
Rocket Surpise, A	L	RF	250+	Sunshine	Wright Group/McGraw Hill
Rocket to the Moon	I	F	156	Korda, Lerryn	Candlewick Press
Rocket, The	F	RF	41	City Stories	Rigby
Rockets	N	I	250+	Explore Space!	Red Brick Learning
Rockets	C	I	49	Little Celebrations	Pearson Learning Group
Rockets	H	I	167	The Rowland Reading Program Library	Rowland Reading Foundation
Rockets	P	I	250+	Wonder World	Wright Group/McGraw Hill
Rockhound Hannah	J	RF	353	Pair-It Turn and Learn	Steck-Vaughn
Rockies, The	N	I	250+	Early Social Studies	Newbridge
Rockin' Reptiles	L	F	250+	Calmenson, Stephanie & Cole	Beech Tree Books
Rocking and Rolling Along	I	RF	73	Evangeline Nicholas Collection	Wright Group/McGraw Hill
Rockity Rock	C	RF	36	KinderReaders	Rigby
Rocks	F	I	112	Discovery Links	Newbridge
Rocks	R	I	2389	Early Bird Earth Systems	Lerner Publishing Group
Rocks	L	I	157	Early Connections	Benchmark Education
Rocks	Q	I	250+	Exploring the Earth	Capstone Press
Rocks	B	I	33	Leveled Readers Science	Houghton Mifflin Harcourt
Rocks	E	I	59	Science	Harcourt School Publishers
Rocks	N	I	250+	Simply Science	Compass Point Books
Rocks	N	I	250+	Sun Sprouts	ETA/Cuisenaire
Rocks	D	I	49	Voyages	SRA/McGraw Hill
Rocks	F	I	85	What Earth Is Made Of	Lerner Publishing Group
Rocks	G	I	101	Windows on Literacy	National Geographic
Rocks & Fossils	W	I	250+	Kingfisher Knowledge	Kingfisher
Rocks & Minerals	R	I	250+	The Wonders of Our World	Crabtree
Rocks and Earth	G	I	196	PM Science Readers	Rigby
Rocks and Fossils	M	I	250+	Rosen Real Readers	Rosen Publishing Group
Rocks and Minerals	T	I	250+	Mission: Science	Compass Point Books
Rocks and Minerals	T	I	250+	Reading Expeditions	National Geographic
Rocks and Minerals	Q	I	1238	Science Support Readers	Houghton Mifflin Harcourt
Rocks and Minerals: A Gem of a Book!	W	I	250+	Green, Dan	Kingfisher
Rocks and Minerals: The World Beneath Our Feet	T	I	250+	Pair-It Books	Steck-Vaughn
Rocks From Space	M	I	250+	Rigby Focus	Rigby
Rocks in His Head	O	HF	250+	Hurst, Carol Otis	Greenwillow Books
Rocks Rocks Rocks	E	I	76	Independent Readers Science	Houghton Mifflin Harcourt
Rocks, Sand, and Soil	K	I	138	Larkin, Bruce	Wilbooks
Rocks, Soils and Fossils	M	I	618	Science Support Readers	Houghton Mifflin Harcourt
Rocks: Hard, Soft, Smooth, and Rough	N	I	250+	Amazing Science	Picture Window Books
Rocky Mountain Fur Trade, The	S	I	250+	The Library of the Westward Expansion	Rosen Publishing Group
Rocky Mountain National Park	N	I	389	Nonfiction Set 9	Literacy Footprints
Rocky Mountains, The	N	I	591	Lightning Bolt Books	Lerner Publishing Group
Rocky Recess	L	RF	250+	Read it! Readers	Picture Window Books
Rocky Shore Report, The	L	RF	614	Red Rocket Readers	Flying Start Books
Rocky Vacation, A	P	RF	250+	Windows on Literacy	National Geographic
Rocky's Road Home	L	F	629	Leveled Readers	Houghton Mifflin Harcourt
Rocky's Road Home	L	F	629	Leveled Readers/CA	Houghton Mifflin Harcourt
Rocky's Road Home	L	F	629	Leveled Readers/TX	Houghton Mifflin Harcourt
Rodeo Boy	M	F	250+	Too Cool	Pacific Learning

R

TITLE	LEVEL	GENRE	WORD COUNT	AUTHOR / SERIES	PUBLISHER / DISTRIBUTOR
Rodeo Contest	M	I	1216	Leveled Readers Language Support	Houghton Mifflin Harcourt
Rodeo Rocky: The Horses of Half Moon Ranch	S	RF	28600	Oldfield, Jenny	Sourcebooks
Rodeo Under the Sea	I	F	250+	Literacy by Design	Rigby
Rodeo Under the Sea	I	F	250+	On Our Way to English	Rigby
Rodeo!	R	I	1107	Leveled Readers	Houghton Mifflin Harcourt
Rodeo!	N	I	1186	Leveled Readers Social Studies	Houghton Mifflin Harcourt
Rodeo!	R	I	1107	Leveled Readers/CA	Houghton Mifflin Harcourt
Rodeo!	R	I	1107	Leveled Readers/TX	Houghton Mifflin Harcourt
Rodney, the Surfing Duck	N	F	250+	Supa Doopers	Sundance
Rodzina	Y	HF	250+	Cushman, Karen	Clarion
Roger Federer	P	B	1715	Amazing Athetes	Lerner Publishing Group
Rogue Elephant	R	RF	250+	Story Surfers	ETA/Cuisenaire
Rogue Robot	P	F	250+	Bookweb	Rigby
Role Models	G	I	145	Families	Heinemann Library
Roles of Living Things	U	I	1856	Science Support Readers	Houghton Mifflin Harcourt
Roll of Thunder, Hear My Cry	W	HF	250+	Taylor, Mildred D.	Penguin Group
Roll On, Columbia	R	I	826	Independent Readers Social Studies	Houghton Mifflin Harcourt
Roll Out the Red Rug	E	F	68	Ready Readers	Pearson Learning Group
Roll Over	F	F	220	Gerstein, Mordicai	Crown Publishers
Roll Over!	C	F	201	Peek, Merle	Clarion
Roller Blades, The	F	RF	137	Foundations	Wright Group/McGraw Hill
Roller Coaster	C	RF	45	Joy Readers	Pearson Learning Group
^Roller Coaster	T	F	250+	Powell, J.	Stone Arch Books
Roller Coaster Ride	K	RF	484	PM Plus Story Books	Rigby
Roller Coaster Ride, The	G	RF	106	Carousel Readers	Pearson Learning Group
Roller Coaster, The	D	RF	115	Handprints C, Set 1	Educators Publishing Service
Roller Coaster, The	B	F	34	KinderReaders	Rigby
Roller Coaster, The	I	RF	194	Sunshine	Wright Group/McGraw Hill
Roller Coaster, The	H	RF	206	The King School Series	Townsend Press
Roller Coasters	Q	I	250+	Wild Rides!	Capstone Press
Roller Skates!	J	RF	250+	Calmenson, Stephanie	Scholastic
Rollerama	N	RF	250+	Supa Doopers	Sundance
Rollercoaster	K	RF	250+	Rigby Literacy	Rigby
Rollercoaster	K	RF	250+	Rigby Star	Rigby
Rollercoaster Science	N	I	250+	Rigby Literacy	Rigby
Rollers and Blades	I	I	204	Take Two Books	Wright Group/McGraw Hill
Rolling	F	I	72	Benchmark Rebus	Marshall Cavendish
Rolling	C	I	46	Sun Sprouts	ETA/Cuisenaire
Rolling Along: The Story of Taylor and His Wheelchair	L	RF	250+	Heelan, Jamee Riggio	Peachtree
Rolling Right Along	S	I	250+	PM Extensions	Rigby
Rollo and Tweedy and the Ghost at Dougal Castle	K	F	250+	Allen, Laura Jean	HarperTrophy
*Roly-Poly	I	F	1227	Story Box	Wright Group/McGraw Hill
Roly-Poly Ravioli and Other Italian Dishes	R	I	250+	Kids Dish	Picture Window Books
Roma Roller Skater	I	RF	238	Take Two Books	Wright Group/McGraw Hill
Roman Diary: The Journal of Iliona of Mytilini, Who Was Captured and Sold as a Slave in Rome, AD107	W	HF	250+	Platt, Richard	Candlewick Press
Roman News, The	W	I	250+	The History News	Candlewick Press
Roman Oracle, The	U	HF	250+	Sails	Rigby
Romana Acosta Banuelos	K	B	218	Leveled Readers Social Studies	Houghton Mifflin Harcourt

* Collection of short stories   # Graphic text
^ Mature content with lower level text demands

TITLE	LEVEL	GENRE	WORD COUNT	AUTHOR / SERIES	PUBLISHER / DISTRIBUTOR
Romans, The	T	I	250+	Tristars	Richard C. Owen
Romans, The: Life in Ancient Rome	V	I	2261	Ancient Civilizations	Millbrook Press
Romare Bearden	R	I	1005	Vocabulary Readers	Houghton Mifflin Harcourt
Romare Bearden	R	I	1005	Vocabulary Readers/CA	Houghton Mifflin Harcourt
Romare Bearden	R	I	1005	Vocabulary Readers/TX	Houghton Mifflin Harcourt
Rome	W	I	250+	Primary Source Readers	Teacher Created Materials
Rome	V	I	250+	Theme Sets	National Geographic
Rome Is Burning	Y	I	1214	Leveled Readers	Houghton Mifflin Harcourt
Rome Is Burning	Y	I	1214	Leveled Readers/CA	Houghton Mifflin Harcourt
Rome Is Burning	Y	I	1214	Leveled Readers/TX	Houghton Mifflin Harcourt
Rome: Civilizations Past to Present	S	I	250+	Reading Expeditions	National Geographic
Rome: Everyday Kids Now and Then	S	HF	250+	Reading Expeditions	National Geographic
#Romeo and Juliet	Z	HF	250+	Manga Shakespeare	Amulet Books
Romiette and Julio	Z	RF	250+	Edge	Hampton Brown
Ronald Reagan	T	B	3587	History Maker Bios	Lerner Publishing Group
^Ronald Reagan: Actor, Politician World Leader	T	B	250+	Hameray Biography Series	Hameray Publishing Group
Ronald Reagan: Fortieth President	R	B	250+	Getting to Know the U.S. Presidents	Children's Press
Ronald W. Reagan	U	B	250+	Profiles of the Presidents	Compass Point Books
Ronny Rat, Racing Driver	F	F	132	Joy Starters	Pearson Learning Group
Roof and a Door, A	D	I	93	PM Nonfiction-Red	Rigby
#Rooftop Adventure of Minnie and Tessa, Factory Fire Survivors, The	Q	HF	606	History's Kid Heroes	Lerner Publishing Group
Rookie of the Year	Y	RF	250+	Tunis, John R.	Harcourt
Room Decorating: Make Your Space Unique	Q	I	250+	Crafts	Capstone Press
Room for One More	G	RF	132	City Stories	Rigby
Room for Pip	E	F	175	Bookshop	Mondo Publishing
Room for the Animals?: How Urban Growth Affects Wildlife	V	I	250+	Literacy By Design	Rigby
Room on Lorelei Street, A	Z+	RF	250+	Pearson, Mary E.	Henry Holt & Co.
Room One	S	RF	250+	Clements, Andrew	Aladdin
Rooney 'Roo	J	F	445	Let's Read Together	Kane Press
Rooster and the Fox, The	Q	TL	594	Ward, Helen	Carolrhoda Books
Rooster and the Weather Vane, The	H	F	235	First Start	Troll Associates
Rooster Trouble	H	F	279	Sails	Rigby
Rooster's Gift, The	M	F	250+	Conrad, Pam	HarperCollins
Root Cellar, The	V	HF	250+	Lunn, Janet	Penguin Group
Roots	E	I	31	Parts of Plants	Lerner Publishing Group
Roots	H	I	121	Plant Parts	Capstone Press
Roots of the Blues	V	I	1293	Reading Street	Pearson
Roots: Uncertain Journeys, New Beginnings	Y	I	250+	Boldprint	Steck-Vaughn
Rope Sports	O	I	250+	Extreme Sports	Raintree
Rope Swing, The	E	RF	77	Oxford Reading Tree	Oxford University Press
^Ropes of Revolution: The Tale of the Boston Tea Party	T	HF	250+	Gunderson, J.	Stone Arch Books
Rory and Tina Go Skiiing	E	F	118	Springboard	Wright Group/McGraw Hill
Rory's Big Chance	L	RF	971	PM Plus Story Books	Rigby
Rosa and Fredo	M	F	250+	Supa Doopers	Sundance
Rosa at the Beach	C	RF	35	Brand New Readers	Candlewick Press
Rosa at the Farm	B	RF	20	Brand New Readers	Candlewick Press
Rosa at the Zoo	H	RF	135	Pacific Literacy	Pacific Learning
Rosa Catches a Fish	C	F	42	Brand New Readers	Candlewick Press
Rosa Loves to Walk	C	RF	57	Brand New Readers	Candlewick Press
Rosa Parks	Q	B	250+	Early Biographies	Compass Point Books

R

TITLE	LEVEL	GENRE	WORD COUNT	AUTHOR / SERIES	PUBLISHER / DISTRIBUTOR
Rosa Parks	N	B	248	First Biographies	Red Brick Learning
Rosa Parks	P	B	250+	Greenfield, Eloise	HarperTrophy
Rosa Parks	S	B	3433	History Maker Bios	Lerner Publishing Group
Rosa Parks	O	B	250+	In Step Readers	Rigby
Rosa Parks	Q	B	250+	Photo-Illustrated Biographies	Red Brick Learning
#Rosa Parks and the Montgomery Bus Boycott	S	B	250+	Graphic Library	Capstone Press
Rosa Parks: A Life of Courage	P	B	583	Pull Ahead Books	Lerner Publishing Group
Rosa Parks: Hero of Our Time	N	B	250+	Beginning Biographies	Pearson Learning Group
Rosa Parks: My Story	U	B	250+	Parks, Rosa	Scholastic
Rosa Plants a Tree	C	RF	29	Brand New Readers	Candlewick Press
Rosa the Painter	J	RF	394	Leveled Readers	Houghton Mifflin Harcourt
Rosa the Painter	J	RF	394	Leveled Readers/CA	Houghton Mifflin Harcourt
Rosa the Painter	J	RF	394	Leveled Readers/TX	Houghton Mifflin Harcourt
Rosalyn Yalow	W	B	2138	Leveled Readers Science	Houghton Mifflin Harcourt
Rosa's Adventure	S	TL	1403	Leveled Readers	Houghton Mifflin Harcourt
Rosa's Adventure	S	TL	1403	Leveled Readers/CA	Houghton Mifflin Harcourt
Rosa's Adventure	S	TL	1403	Leveled Readers/TX	Houghton Mifflin Harcourt
Rosa's Rebozo	M	TL	250+	On Our Way To English	Rigby
Rosa's Room	K	RF	250+	Bottner, Barbara	Peachtree
Rosa's Sandwich	C	RF	31	Brand New Readers	Candlewick Press
Rosa's Tonsils	K	RF	337	Foundations	Wright Group/McGraw Hill
Rose	F	F	82	Wheeler, Cindy	Alfred A. Knopf
Rose Avenue Street Sale, The	L	RF	890	InfoTrek	ETA/Cuisenaire
Rose in My Garden, The	P	TL	250+	Lobel, Arnold	Scholastic
Rose on the River, A	T	HF	250+	Storyteller -Mounatin Peaks	Wright Group/McGraw Hill
Rose Rest Home, The	K	RF	304	Sunshine	Wright Group/McGraw Hill
Rose Street Twins, The	Q	RF	250+	Reading Safari	Mondo Publishing
Roses for Anna	K	RF	250+	Rigby Literacy	Rigby
Roses for Renee	J	RF	395	Evangeline Nicholas Collection	Wright Group/McGraw Hill
Rosetta Stone, The	U	I	1089	Reading Street	Pearson
Rosie and Fred	D	RF	105	Rigby Flying Colors	Rigby
Rosie and the Audition	K	RF	763	PM Stars Bridge Books	Rigby
Rosie and the Bug Jar	D	RF	112	Leveled Readers	Houghton Mifflin Harcourt
Rosie and the Bug Jar	D	RF	112	Leveled Readers/CA	Houghton Mifflin Harcourt
Rosie at the Zoo	H	RF	135	Pacific Literacy	Pacific Learning
Rosie Demands the Bill	K	RF	841	PM Stars Bridge Books	Rigby
Rosie Goes Home	K	RF	983	PM Stars Bridge Books	Rigby
Rosie Is Cold	E	F	129	Bella and Rosie Series	Literacy Footprints
Rosie Moves In	K	RF	711	PM Stars Bridge Books	Rigby
Rosie Raccoon's Rock and Roll Raft	K	F	700	Animal Antics A to Z	Kane Press
Rosie the Riveter	Z	I	250+	Colman, Penny	Crown Publishers
Rosie, the Nosy Goat	D	RF	56	Sunshine	Wright Group/McGraw Hill
Rosie: A Visiting Dog's Story	N	I	250+	Soar To Success	Houghton Mifflin Harcourt
Rosie's Bear	C	F	62	Tiny Treasures	Pioneer Valley
Rosie's Big City Ballet	N	RF	250+	Giff, Patricia Reilly	Penguin Group
Rosie's Button Box	G	RF	233	Stepping Stones	Nelson/Michaels Assoc.
Rosie's House	K	RF	250+	Literacy 2000	Rigby
Rosie's Nutcracker Dreams	N	RF	250+	Giff, Patricia Reilly	Penguin Group
Rosie's Party	E	F	111	Little Readers	Houghton Mifflin Harcourt
Rosie's Pool	G	F	130	Little Readers	Houghton Mifflin Harcourt
Rosie's Story	L	RF	250+	Bookshop	Mondo Publishing
Rosie's Walk	F	F	32	Hutchins, Pat	Macmillan
*Rotating Rollerblades and Other Cases, The	O	RF	250+	Simon, Seymour	Avon Books

* Collection of short stories   # Graphic text
^ Mature content with lower level text demands

TITLE	LEVEL	GENRE	WORD COUNT	AUTHOR / SERIES	PUBLISHER / DISTRIBUTOR
Rotten Egg, The	H	RF	211	The Rowland Reading Program Library	Rowland Reading Foundation
Rotten Reggie	G	RF	232	TOTTS	Tott Publications
Rotten School Day	N	RF	250+	Boyz Rule!	Mondo Publishing
Rottweilers	R	I	250+	All About Dogs	Capstone Press
Rottweilers Are the Best!	Q	I	1322	The Best Dogs Ever	Lerner Publishing Group
Rough and Smooth	H	I	172	Explorations	Okapi Educational Materials
Rough and Smooth	H	I	172	Explorations	Eleanor Curtain Publishing
Rough Riders, The	W	B	250+	Cornerstones of Freedom	Children's Press
Rough Waters	Y	RF	250+	Rottman, S. L.	Peachtree
Rough-Face Girl, The	S	TL	250+	Martin, Rafe; Shannon, David	Scholastic
Round	C	I	40	Windmill Books	Rigby
Round and Round	B	I	51	Red Rocket Readers	Flying Start Books
Round and Round	C	RF	38	Story Box	Wright Group/McGraw Hill
Round and Round the Seasons Go	E	I	43	Learn to Read	Creative Teaching Press
Round and Round: The Story of Wheels	N	I	250+	Home Connection Collection	Rigby
Round Around Us	C	I	65	Bonnell, Kris	Reading Reading Books
Round Like a Circle	B	I	60	Windows on Literacy	National Geographic
Round the World	T	B	250+	High-Fliers	Pacific Learning
Route 66	O	I	696	Vocabulary Readers	Houghton Mifflin Harcourt
Route 66	O	I	696	Vocabulary Readers/CA	Houghton Mifflin Harcourt
Route 66	O	I	696	Vocabulary Readers/TX	Houghton Mifflin Harcourt
Route 66: Main Street of America	X	I	250+	Bookshop	Mondo Publishing
Row Row Row Your Boat	K	TL	160	Trapani, Iza	Charlesbridge
Row Your Boat	C	F	18	Literacy 2000	Rigby
Row Your Boat	C	F	18	Literacy Tree	Rigby
Row, Row, Row Your Boat	J	RF	250+	Bank Street	Bantam Books
Roxy	WB	F	0	Ready to Read	Pacific Learning
Roy and the Parakeet	E	F	74	Oxford Reading Tree	Oxford University Press
Roy at the Fun Park	G	RF	111	Oxford Reading Tree	Oxford University Press
Roy G. Biv	D	F	68	Story Box	Wright Group/McGraw Hill
Roy Halladay	P	B	250+	Amazing Athletes	Lerner Publishing Group
Royal Baby-Sitters, The	J	RF	435	Sunshine	Wright Group/McGraw Hill
Royal Dinner, The	H	F	250+	Literacy Tree	Rigby
Royal Drum, The	L	TL	250+	Bookshop	Mondo Publishing
Royal Family, The	LB	F	17	Stewart, Josie; Salem, Lynn	Continental Press
Royal Goose, The	H	F	198	Ready Readers	Pearson Learning Group
Royal Mummies: Remains From Ancient Egypt, The	W	I	250+	Mummies	Capstone Press
Royal Road, The	S	RF	2407	Leveled Readers	Houghton Mifflin Harcourt
Royal Road, The	S	RF	2407	Leveled Readers/CA	Houghton Mifflin Harcourt
Royal Road, The	S	RF	2407	Leveled Readers/TX	Houghton Mifflin Harcourt
Royal Rodent Rescue	L	F	250+	DC Super-Pets	Picture Window Books
Royal Zookeeper, The	K	F	431	Early Connections	Benchmark Education
Roy's First Day	C	RF	125	InfoTrek	ETA/Cuisenaire
Rubber	M	I	250+	Materials	Capstone Press
Rubber	O	I	250+	Rigby Focus	Rigby
Rubber Duck	I	F	170	Early Readers	Compass Point Books
Rubber Inventor: The Story of Charles Goodyear	S	B	912	Independent Readers Science	Houghton Mifflin Harcourt
Rubbery Arms and Baggy Bodies	O	I	250+	Sails	Rigby
Rubbish and Recycling	T	I	250+	The News	Richard C. Owen
Rube Goldberg's Silly Machines	R	B	438	Independent Readers Science	Houghton Mifflin Harcourt
Ruby and the Ocean	J	RF	406	Gear Up!	Wright Group/McGraw Hill

TITLE	LEVEL	GENRE	WORD COUNT	AUTHOR / SERIES	PUBLISHER / DISTRIBUTOR
Ruby and the Smoke, The	Y	F	250+	Pullman, Phillip	Laurel-Leaf Books
Ruby Bridges	R	B	2687	History Maker Bios	Lerner Publishing Group
Ruby Bridges Goes to School: My True Story	K	B	250+	Bridges, Ruby	Scholastic
Ruby Holler	V	RF	250+	Creech, Sharon	HarperCollins
Ruby Red and Sky Blue	E	RF	157	Rigby Rocket	Rigby
Ruby the Copycat	K	RF	250+	Rathman, Peggy	Scholastic
Ruby the Red Fairy: Rainbow Magic	L	F	250+	Meadows, Daisy	Scholastic
Ruby Valentine Saves the Day	K	F	619	Friedman, Laurie	Carolrhoda Books
Ruff and Me	C	RF	30	First Stories	Pacific Learning
Ruffles Needs Help!	L	RF	903	InfoTrek	ETA/Cuisenaire
Rug Weavers	J	RF	182	Leveled Readers Language Support	Houghton Mifflin Harcourt
Ruined	Z	F	250+	Morris, Paula	Scholastic
Rule of Won, The	Z+	RF	250+	Petrucha, Stefan	Walker & Company
Ruler	C	I	32	Simple Tools	Lerner Publishing Group
Rulers of Persia	Y	I	2401	Leveled Readers	Houghton Mifflin Harcourt
Rulers of Persia	Y	I	2401	Leveled Readers/CA	Houghton Mifflin Harcourt
Rulers of Persia	Y	I	2401	Leveled Readers/TX	Houghton Mifflin Harcourt
Rules	J	I	265	Early Connections	Benchmark Education
Rules	R	RF	250+	Lord, Cynthia	Scholastic
Rules and Laws	J	I	111	Government	Lerner Publishing Group
Rules Are Cool	H	RF	173	InfoTrek	ETA/Cuisenaire
Rules at School	E	I	101	Early Explorers	Benchmark Education
Rules for Pets	C	F	54	Joy Readers	Pearson Learning Group
Rules Have Changed, The	P	F	250+	Reading Safari	Mondo Publishing
Rules Help	C	I	69	Windows on Literacy	National Geographic
Rules of Attraction	Z+	RF	250+	Elkeles, Simone	Walker & Company
Rules of the Net	M	RF	250+	Read-it! Readers	Picture Window Books
Rules of the Ride	P	RF	1023	Leveled Readers	Houghton Mifflin Harcourt
Rules of the Universe by Austin W. Itale	U	SF	250+	Vaupel, Robin	Holiday House
Rumble & Spew: Gross Stuff in Your Stomach and Intestines	U	I	4751	Gross Body Science	Millbrook Press
Rumble, Rumble, Boom!	D	I	26	Pacific Literacy	Pacific Learning
Rummage Sale, The	E	RF	81	Oxford Reading Tree	Oxford University Press
Rumpelstiltskin	J	TL	250+	Bookshop	Mondo Publishing
Rumpelstiltskin	J	TL	250+	Jumbled Tumbled Tales & Rhymes	Rigby
Rumpelstiltskin	M	TL	250+	Once Upon a Time	Wright Group/McGraw Hill
Rumpelstiltskin	K	TL	250+	PM Tales and Plays-Gold	Rigby
Rumpelstiltskin	J	TL	940	Traditional Tales	Pearson Learning Group
Rumpelstiltskin	N	TL	250+	Zelinsky, Paul O.	Scholastic
Rum-Tum-Tum	E	F	62	Story Box	Wright Group/McGraw Hill
Run and Hike, Play and Bike: What Is Physical Activity?	N	I	304	Food Is CATegorical	Millbrook Press
Run Away Home…And Be Free.	R	HF	250+	McKissack, Patricia	Scholastic
Run Fast	D	I	96	Sails	Rigby
Run for It!	D	F	64	Rigby Literacy	Rigby
Run!	B	F	28	Sunshine	Wright Group/McGraw Hill
Run! Run!	C	F	64	Bookshop	Mondo Publishing
Run, Haley, Run!	D	RF	64	Kaleidoscope Collection	Hameray Publishing Group
Run, Rabbit!	A	RF	14	Landman, Yael	Scholastic
Run, Rabbit, Run!	D	RF	96	PM Plus Story Books	Rigby
Run, Roadrunner	L	I	250+	Prairie Adventures	Smithsonian
Run, Run, Run	B	RF	19	Joy Readers	Pearson Learning Group

* Collection of short stories   # Graphic text
^ Mature content with lower level text demands

TITLE	LEVEL	GENRE	WORD COUNT	AUTHOR / SERIES	PUBLISHER / DISTRIBUTOR
Runaround Rowdy	L	RF	250+	PM Story Books	Rigby
Runaway Ball, The	K	RF	250+	Rigby Literacy	Rigby
Runaway Becky Citra	O	RF	250+	Orca Young Readers	Orca Books
Runaway Dinner, The	N	F	250+	Ahlberg, Allan	Candlewick Press
Runaway Dragon, The	U	F	250+	Coombs, Kate	Farrar, Straus, & Giroux
Runaway Dreidel!	M	F	250+	Newman, Leslea	Square Fish
Runaway Hank	J	RF	250+	The Wright Skills	Wright Group/McGraw Hill
Runaway Monkey	B	F	39	Stewart, Josie; Salem, Lynn	Continental Press
Runaway Ralph	O	F	250+	Cleary, Beverly	Hearst
Runaway Rascal	O	RF	250+	Baglio, Ben M.	Scholastic
Runaway Sandy	E	RF	97	Leveled Readers	Houghton Mifflin Harcourt
Runaway to Freedom: A Story of the Underground Railway	T	I	250+	Smucker, Barbara	HarperTrophy
Runaway Wheel, The	G	RF	204	Reading Safari	Mondo Publishing
Runaway Wheels, The	B	F	32	Pair-It Books	Steck-Vaughn
Runner	Z	RF	250+	Deuker, Carl	Graphia
Running	C	RF	39	Foundations	Wright Group/McGraw Hill
Running	A	RF	31	Sun Sprouts	ETA/Cuisenaire
Running	F	RF	185	Visions	Wright Group/McGraw Hill
Running Bear	H	F	122	Alborough, Jez	Alfred A. Knopf
Running Dream, The	X	RF	250+	Draanen, Wendelin Van	Random House
Running for President	S	I	1167	Vocabulary Readers	Houghton Mifflin Harcourt
Running for President	S	I	1167	Vocabulary Readers/CA	Houghton Mifflin Harcourt
Running for President	S	I	1167	Vocabulary Readers/TX	Houghton Mifflin Harcourt
Running for the Bus	S	RF	250+	Literacy by Design	Rigby
Running Free: The Jami Goldman Story	P	B	250+	Literacy by Design	Rigby
Running on the Cracks	Y	RF	250+	Donaldson, Julia	Henry Holt & Co.
Running Out of Time	W	SF	250+	Haddix, Margaret Peterson	Simon & Schuster
^Running Rivals	P	RF	250+	Maddox, Jake	Stone Arch Books
Running Shoes, The	K	RF	519	PM Plus Story Books	Rigby
Runt	Q	F	250+	Bauer, Marion Dane	Clarion Books
Rupert and the Griffin	Q	F	250+	Literacy 2000	Rigby
Rupert Goes to School	K	RF	250+	Storyteller-Lightning Bolts	Wright Group/McGraw Hill
Rupert Likes to Play	C	I	51	Kaleidoscope Collection	Hameray Publishing Group
Rupert's Ice Cream Shop	G	RF	273	Sails	Rigby
Rupert's Rainbow Ice Cream	I	RF	335	Sails	Rigby
Rural Communities	K	I	191	Early Explorers	Benchmark Education
Rural Veterinarian, A	R	I	1390	Leveled Readers	Houghton Mifflin Harcourt
Rural Veterinarian, A	R	I	1390	Leveled Readers/CA	Houghton Mifflin Harcourt
Rural Veterinarian, A	R	I	1390	Leveled Readers/TX	Houghton Mifflin Harcourt
Rush Hour	D	RF	111	Rigby Star	Rigby
Rush, Rush, Rush	E	RF	52	Ready Readers	Pearson Learning Group
Rushing for Gold	N	I	713	Leveled Readers	Houghton Mifflin Harcourt
Rushing for Gold	N	I	713	Leveled Readers/CA	Houghton Mifflin Harcourt
Rushing for Gold	N	I	713	Leveled Readers/TX	Houghton Mifflin Harcourt
*Russell and Elisa	M	RF	250+	Hurwitz, Johanna	Penguin Group
*Russell Rides Again	M	RF	250+	Hurwitz, Johanna	Penguin Group
*Russell Sprouts	M	RF	250+	Hurwitz, Johanna	Penguin Group
Russia	O	I	250+	Countries of the World	Red Brick Learning
Russia	P	I	2014	Country Explorers	Lerner Publishing Group
Russia	Y	I	250+	Eyewitness Books	DK Publishing
Russia	Q	I	250+	First Reports: Countries	Compass Point Books
Russia ABCs: A Book About the People and Places of Russia	Q	I	250+	Country ABCs	Picture Window Books

* Collection of short stories   # Graphic text
^ Mature content with lower level text demands

TITLE	LEVEL	GENRE	WORD COUNT	AUTHOR / SERIES	PUBLISHER / DISTRIBUTOR
Russia in Colors	N	I	250+	World of Colors	Capstone Press
Russia: A Question and Answer Book	P	I	250+	Questions and Answers: Countries	Capstone Press
^Russian Colonies in the Americas	S	I	250+	On Deck	Rigby
Rusty the Rascal	L	RF	250+	Windows on Literacy	National Geographic
Ruth and the Green Book	R	HF	1492	Ramsey, Calvin Alexander	Carolrhoda Books
Rutherford B. Hayes	U	B	250+	Profiles of the Presidents	Compass Point Books
Rutherford B. Hayes: Nineteenth President	R	B	250+	Getting to Know the U.S. Presidents	Children's Press
Ruthie's Perfect Poem	N	RF	744	Leveled Readers	Houghton Mifflin Harcourt
Ryan Howard	P	B	250+	Amazing Athletes	Lerner Publishing Group
Ryan Howard: Revised Edition	P	B	1908	Amazing Athletes	Lerner Publishing Group
Ryan Respects	L	RF	250+	The Way I Act	Albert Whitman & Co.
Ryan's Dog Ringo	P	RF	250+	Literacy 2000	Rigby

R

* Collection of short stories   # Graphic text
^ Mature content with lower level text demands

TITLE	LEVEL	GENRE	WORD COUNT	AUTHOR / SERIES	PUBLISHER / DISTRIBUTOR
S	LB	I	14	Readlings	American Reading Company
S.O.S.! Save Our Swamp!	I	RF	276	Pair-It Turn and Learn	Steck-Vaughn
Sabertooth Cat	I	I	120	Dinosaur and Prehistoric Animals	Capstone Press
^Sabertooth Cat	N	I	250+	Extinct Monsters	Capstone Press
Saber-Toothed Cats	N	I	1520	On My Own History	Lerner Publishing Group
Sabino Canyon Animals	F	I	65	Larkin's Little Readers	Wilbooks
Sable	O	RF	250+	Hesse, Karen	Henry Holt & Co.
Sacagawea	U	B	250+	Amazing Americans	Wright Group/McGraw Hill
Sacagawea	S	B	3627	History Maker Bios	Lerner Publishing Group
Sacagawea	N	B	242	Leveled Readers	Houghton Mifflin Harcourt
Sacagawea	P	B	250+	Photo-Illustrated Biographies	Red Brick Learning
Sacagawea: 1788-1812	S	B	250+	American Indian Biographies	Capstone Press
^Sacagawea: A Journey of Discovery	R	B	250+	Hameray Biography Series	Hameray Publishing Group
#Sacagawea: Journey Into the West	R	B	250+	Graphic Library	Capstone Press
Sacagawea's Journey	M	B	250+	Leveled Readers Language Support	Houghton Mifflin Harcourt
Sacajawea	N	B	250+	Biography	Benchmark Education
Sacajawea	Y	B	250+	Bruchac, Joseph	Harcourt Trade
Sacajawea	T	B	2775	People to Remember Series	January Books
Sacajawea: Her True Story	N	B	250+	Milton, Joyce	Scholastic
Sack Race, A	E	RF	106	New Way Blue	Steck-Vaughn
Sacks of Gold	I	F	263	Sunshine	Wright Group/McGraw Hill
Sacramento Kings, The	S	I	4860	Team Spirit	Norwood House Press
Sacred Leaf	W	RF	250+	Ellis, Deborah	Groundwood Books
Sad	D	I	18	Feelings	Lerner Publishing Group
Sad Monster	E	F	160	Handprints D, Set 1	Educators Publishing Service
Sadako and the Thousand Cranes	R	B	250+	Springboard	Wright Group/McGraw Hill
Sadako and the Thousand Paper Cranes	R	HF	250+	Coerr, Eleanor	Bantam Books
Saddest Dog, The	M	RF	250+	PM Plus Chapter Books	Rigby
Sadie and the Snowman	L	RF	250+	Morgan, Allen	Scholastic
Sadie, Remember	L	HF	250+	Kline, Carol	Sundance
Safari	P	I	250+	Bateman, Robert	Little Brown and Company
Safe at Home	S	RF	250+	Lupica, Mike	Puffin Books
Safe at Work	D	I	99	Early Connections	Benchmark Education
Safe Harbor, A	K	I	167	Windows on Literacy	National Geographic
Safe Haven, A	U	I	2439	Reading Street	Pearson
Safe Homes	F	I	117	Reading Street	Pearson
Safe Place for Tigers, A	I	I	124	Gear Up!	Wright Group/McGraw Hill
Safe Place, The	H	TL	147	Pacific Literacy	Pacific Learning
Safe Return	Q	RF	250+	Dexter, Catherine	Candlewick Press
^Safecrackers	Q	F	250+	Zucker, Jonny	Stone Arch Books
Safety	C	I	35	Interaction	Rigby
Safety at the Playground	E	I	42	Rosen Real Readers	Rosen Publishing Group
Safety Counts	C	F	52	Learn to Read	Creative Teaching Press
Safety First	F	I	195	Dominie Factivity Series	Pearson Learning Group
Safety First	C	I	131	Twig	Wright Group/McGraw Hill
Safety in Numbers	J	I	250+	Evans, Lynette	Scholastic
Safety on the School Bus	E	I	38	Rosen Real Readers	Rosen Publishing Group
Safety Signs	G	I	112	Early Connections	Benchmark Education
Sagebrush and Paintbrush: The Story of Charlie Russell, the Cowboy Artist	W	B	250+	Bookshop	Mondo Publishing
Saguaro	E	I	44	Books for Young Learners	Richard C. Owen
Saguaro Cactus	Q	I	1513	Early Bird Nature Books	Lerner Publishing Group

S

TITLE	LEVEL	GENRE	WORD COUNT	AUTHOR / SERIES	PUBLISHER / DISTRIBUTOR
Saguaro Cactus	N	I	250+	Habitats	Children's Press
Saguaro National Park	O	I	250+	A True Book	Children's Press
Saguaro National Park Birds	G	I	78	Larkin's Little Readers	Wilbooks
Sahara Desert, The	S	I	1909	Leveled Readers Language Support	Houghton Mifflin Harcourt
Sahara Special	S	RF	250+	Codell, Esme Raji	Hyperion
Sahara, The	N	I	250+	Leveled Readers	Houghton Mifflin Harcourt
Sahwira: An African Friendship	V	HF	250+	Marsden, Carolyn & Matzigkeit, Philip	Candlewick Press
Sail Away	J	I	115	Crews, Donald	HarperTrophy
Sail Away, Little Boat	K	F	383	Buell, Janet	Carolrhoda Books
Sailboat Race, The	J	F	330	Leveled Readers	Houghton Mifflin Harcourt
Sailboat Race, The	J	F	330	Leveled Readers/CA	Houghton Mifflin Harcourt
Sailboat Race, The	J	F	330	Leveled Readers/TX	Houghton Mifflin Harcourt
Sailing Adventures	S	I	250+	Dangerous Adventures	Red Brick Learning
Sailing the Stars	T	I	2187	Reading Street	Pearson
Sailing to a New Land	K	HF	250+	PM Plus Story Books	Rigby
Sailing to Safety	N	HF	1005	Leveled Readers	Houghton Mifflin Harcourt
Sailing to Safety	N	HF	1005	Leveled Readers/CA	Houghton Mifflin Harcourt
Sailing to Safety	N	HF	1005	Leveled Readers/TX	Houghton Mifflin Harcourt
Sailing with Sam	I	RF	250+	Windows on Literacy	National Geographic
Sailor Sam	I	RF	241	Sails	Rigby
Sailor Sam and the Balloons	I	RF	254	Sails	Rigby
Sailor Sam and the Birds	F	RF	148	Sails	Rigby
Sailor Sam and the Boots	F	RF	227	Sails	Rigby
Sailor Sam and the Captain	I	F	341	Sails	Rigby
Sailor Sam and the Coconuts	H	F	248	Sails	Rigby
Sailor Sam and the Goat	J	RF	319	Sails	Rigby
Sailor Sam Gets Lost	I	F	423	Sails	Rigby
Sailor Sam in Trouble	F	RF	186	Sails	Rigby
Sailor Sam Up the Mast	I	RF	298	Sails	Rigby
Sailors	A	RF	18	Sails	Rigby
^Sailors of the U.S. Navy	N	I	165	People of the U.S. Armed Forces	Capstone Press
Saint Bernards Are the Best!	Q	I	1073	The Best Dogs Ever	Lerner Publishing Group
Salad	A	F	36	Carousel Earlybirds	Pearson Learning Group
Salad Feast, A	D	RF	57	Little Readers	Houghton Mifflin Harcourt
Salad Vegetables	LB	I	15	Foundations	Wright Group/McGraw Hill
Salad Vegetables	A	I	27	Story Box	Wright Group/McGraw Hill
Salamandastron	Z	F	250+	Jacques, Brian	Ace Books
Salamander Spell, The	U	F	250+	Baker, E. D.	Bloomsbury Children's Books
Salamanders	F	I	89	Animal Life Cycles	Lerner Publishing Group
Salamanders and Alligators	M	I	710	Leveled Readers Science	Houghton Mifflin Harcourt
#Salem Brownstone	Y	F	250+	Dunning, John Harris	Candlewick Press
Salem Days: Life in a Colonial Seaport	T	I	250+	Adventures in Colonial America	Troll Associates
#Salem Witch Trials, The	U	I	250+	Graphic Library	Capstone Press
Salem Witch Trials, The	V	I	250+	Let Freedom Ring	Capstone Press
Salem Witch Trials, The	U	I	1093	Leveled Readers Social Studies	Houghton Mifflin Harcourt
Sally and the Daisy	C	RF	60	PM Story Books	Rigby
Sally and the Elephant	C	RF	50	PM Stars	Rigby
Sally and the Elephant	C	I	45	Wonder World	Wright Group/McGraw Hill
Sally and the Leaves	C	RF	55	PM Stars	Rigby
Sally and the Sparrows	E	RF	151	PM Extensions-Yellow	Rigby
Sally and the Wild Puppy	I	RF	270	Reading Street	Pearson

* Collection of short stories   # Graphic text
^ Mature content with lower level text demands

TITLE	LEVEL	GENRE	WORD COUNT	AUTHOR / SERIES	PUBLISHER / DISTRIBUTOR
Sally Gets a Job	J	F	250+	Huneck. Susan	Harry N. Abrams
Sally Goes to the Beach	I	F	193	Huneck, Stephen	Harry N. Abrams
Sally Goes to the Farm	I	F	152	Huneck, Stephen	Harry N. Abrams
Sally Ride	H	B	77	Leveled Readers Social Studies	Houghton Mifflin Harcourt
Sally Ride in Space	L	B	235	Vocabulary Readers	Houghton Mifflin Harcourt
Sally Ride: Astronaut, Scientist, Teacher	M	B	250+	Biographies	Picture Window Books
Sally Snip Snap's Party	H	TL	326	Red Rocket Readers	Flying Start Books
Sally Spider's Accident	I	F	250+	Reading Safari	Mondo Publishing
Sally Spinner Finds a Home	K	F	250+	Reading Safari	Mondo Publishing
Sally the Great	H	RF	250+	Home Connection Collection	Rigby
Sally's Beans	D	RF	123	PM Story Books	Rigby
Sally's Big Save	M	RF	250+	Social Studies Connects	Kane/Miller Book Publishers
Sally's Friends	F	RF	128	PM Story Books	Rigby
Sally's Great Balloon Adventure	K	F	330	Huneck, Stephen	Harry N. Abrams
Sally's New Shoes	B	RF	58	PM Starters	Rigby
Sally's Picture	G	RF	125	Literacy 2000	Rigby
Sally's Red Bucket	E	RF	127	PM Story Books	Rigby
Sally's Snow Adventure	J	F	250+	Huneck. Susan	Harry N. Abrams
Sally's Snowman	C	RF	57	PM Stars	Rigby
Sally's Spaceship	E	RF	86	Ready Readers	Pearson Learning Group
Sally's Surprise	M	RF	1918	Take Two Books	Wright Group/McGraw Hill
Sally's Surprise Garden	H	RF	148	Literacy Tree	Rigby
Salmon	N	I	250+	Bookshop	Mondo Publishing
Salmon Forest	M	I	250+	Suzuki, David & Ellis, Sarah	Greystone Books
Salmon Forest, The	Q	RF	250+	WorldScapes	ETA/Cuisenaire
Salmon Story, A	G	I	132	Twig	Wright Group/McGraw Hill
Salmon Stream	M	I	586	Sharing Nature with Children	Dawn Publications
*Salmon's Journey and More Northwest Coast Stories	P	TL	250+	Challenger, James Robert	Heritage House
Sal's Closet	D	RF	144	The Rowland Reading Program Library	Rowland Reading Foundation
Salt	J	I	247	Rigby Focus	Rigby
Salt	U	I	250+	Theme Sets	National Geographic
Salt Caravan, The	S	I	250+	WorldScapes	ETA/Cuisenaire
Salt in His Shoes	O	B	250+	Jordan, Deloris & Jordan, Roslyn M.	Aladdin
Salt Lick Boom Town	J	F	577	Reading Street	Pearson
Salton Sea, The	V	I	3036	Leveled Readers	Houghton Mifflin Harcourt
Salton Sea, The	V	I	3036	Leveled Readers/CA	Houghton Mifflin Harcourt
Salton Sea, The	V	I	3036	Leveled Readers/TX	Houghton Mifflin Harcourt
Saltwater Fishing	S	I	250+	The Great Outdoors	Capstone Press
Salty Dog	L	RF	250+	Rand, Gloria	Henry Holt & Co.
Salty Tale, A	O	TL	793	Gear Up!	Wright Group/McGraw Hill
Sam	D	RF	87	Early Connections	Benchmark Education
Sam	C	RF	17	KinderReaders	Rigby
Sam and Bingo	C	RF	53	PM Plus Story Books	Rigby
Sam and Dasher	G	RF	53	Rookie Readers	Children's Press
*Sam and Jack: Three Stories	C	F	65	Green Light Readers	Harcourt
Sam and Kim	O	I	250+	Pacific Literacy	Pacific Learning
Sam and Mac	H	F	146	Pair-It Turn and Learn	Steck-Vaughn
Sam and Nate	L	RF	250+	Orca Echoes	Orca Books
Sam and Papa	B	RF	65	Leveled Literacy Intervention/ Green System	Heinemann
Sam and the Bag	B	F	31	Green Light Readers	Harcourt

TITLE	LEVEL	GENRE	WORD COUNT	AUTHOR / SERIES	PUBLISHER / DISTRIBUTOR
Sam and the Firefly	J	F	250+	Eastman, Philip D.	Random House
Sam and the Lucky Money	N	RF	250+	Soar To Success	Houghton Mifflin Harcourt
Sam and the Waves	D	RF	122	PM Plus Story Books	Rigby
Sam Bennett's New Shoes	L	RF	1339	Thermes, Jennifer	Carolrhoda Books
Sam Collier and the Founding of Jamestown	O	HF	1996	On My Own History	Lerner Publishing Group
Sam Finds the Party	K	RF	714	Leveled Readers	Houghton Mifflin Harcourt
Sam Finds the Party	K	RF	714	Leveled Readers/CA	Houghton Mifflin Harcourt
Sam Finds the Party	K	RF	714	Leveled Readers/TX	Houghton Mifflin Harcourt
Sam Finds the Way	H	F	219	Early Explorers	Benchmark Education
Sam Goes Riding	F	RF	121	Gear Up!	Wright Group/McGraw Hill
Sam Goes to School	E	RF	131	PM Plus Story Books	Rigby
Sam Hides Red Ted	E	RF	170	Storyworlds	Heinemann
Sam Houston	N	B	248	Pebble Books	Capstone Press
Sam Houston: Soldier and Statesman	V	B	250+	Let Freedom Ring	Capstone Press
Sam King and Little Bull	L	RF	250+	Wilson, Trevor	Pearson Learning Group
Sam Picks Glasses	D	RF	120	Connolly, Fran	Kim.FIG.Fern
Sam Plays Paddle Ball	F	F	161	PM Plus Story Books	Rigby
Sam Samurai	P	F	250+	Scieszka, Jon	Penguin Group
Sam the Big, Bad Cat	E	F	86	Big Cat	Pacific Learning
Sam the Duck	C	RF	28	Reading Street	Pearson
Sam the Garbage Hound	G	F	53	Rookie Readers	Children's Press
Sam the Minuteman	J	HF	250+	Benchley, Nathaniel	HarperTrophy
Sam the Scarecrow	F	F	143	First Start	Troll Associates
Sam Who Never Forgets	K	F	281	Rice, Eve	Morrow
Sam Writes	D	RF	62	Book Bank	Wright Group/McGraw Hill
*Sam, Sam, and Other Stories	F	F	250+	Story Steps	Rigby
Samantha Hansen Has Rocks in Her Head	S	RF	250+	Viau, Nancy	Amulet Books
Samantha Saves the Day	Q	HF	250+	The American Girls Collection	Pleasant Company
Samantha Saves the Stream	L	RF	790	Early Explorers	Benchmark Education
Samantha the Swimming Fairy: Rainbow Magic	L	F	250+	Meadows, Daisy	Scholastic
Samantha's Brother	L	RF	700	Rigby Flying Colors	Rigby
Samantha's Sea	R	I	250+	Storyteller-Whispering Pines	Wright Group/McGraw Hill
Samantha's Solar Spin	L	F	250+	Reading Safari	Mondo Publishing
Samantha's Surprise	Q	HF	250+	The American Girls Collection	Pleasant Company
Same and Different	E	RF	106	McAlpin, MaryAnn	Short Tales Press
Same but Different	I	RF	184	Sunshine	Wright Group/McGraw Hill
Same Idea, Different Year	M	RF	250+	Bookweb	Rigby
Same Stuff as Stars, The	V	RF	250+	Paterson, Katherine	Clarion
Same Sun Here	W	RF	250+	House, Silas & Vaswani, Neela	Candlewick Press
Same Team	C	I	44	The Candid Collection	Pearson Learning Group
Same, but Different	I	I	210	Sails	Rigby
Same, But Different, The	Q	RF	1205	Leveled Readers	Houghton Mifflin Harcourt
Samir and Yonatan	Z	RF	250+	Carmi, Daniella	Scholastic
Sammy	B	RF	32	Urmston, Kathleen	Kaeden Books
Sammy at the Farm	C	RF	83	Urmston, Kathleen; Evans, Karen	Kaeden Books
Sammy Gets a Bath	C	RF	33	Evans, Karen	Kaeden Books
Sammy Gets a Ride	F	RF	91	Evans, Karen; Urmston, Kathleen	Kaeden Books
Sammy Keyes and the Art of Deception	T	RF	250+	Van Draanen, Wendelin	Random House
Sammy Keyes and the Curse of Moustache Mary	T	RF	250+	Van Draanen, Wendelin	Random House
Sammy Keyes and the Dead Giveaway	T	RF	250+	Van Draanen, Wendelin	Yearling Books
Sammy Keyes and the Hotel Thief	T	RF	250+	Van Draanen, Wendelin	Random House
Sammy Keyes and the Runaway Elf	T	RF	250+	Van Draanen, Wendelin	Random House
Sammy Keyes and the Sisters of Mercy	T	RF	250+	Van Draanen, Wendelin	Random House
Sammy Keyes and the Skeleton Man	T	RF	250+	Van Draanen, Wendelin	Random House

S

* Collection of short stories   # Graphic text
^ Mature content with lower level text demands

TITLE	LEVEL	GENRE	WORD COUNT	AUTHOR / SERIES	PUBLISHER / DISTRIBUTOR
Sammy Loves to Run	C	RF	32	Evans, Karen	Kaeden Books
Sammy Skunk's Super Sniffer	K	F	747	Animal Antics A to Z	Kane Press
Sammy Sosa	P	B	1705	Amazing Athletes	Lerner Publishing Group
Sammy Sosa	R	B	250+	Sports Heroes	Red Brick Learning
Sammy the Seal	H	F	250+	Hoff, Syd	HarperTrophy
Sammy: Classroom Guinea Pig, The	L	RF	250+	Berenzy, Alix	Square Fish
Sammy's Hamburger Caper	I	F	250+	Urmston, Kathleen	Kaeden Books
Sammy's Moving	F	F	166	Evans, Karen; Urmston, Kathleen	Kaeden Books
Sammy's Slippery Day	H	RF	263	Urmston, Kathleen; Urmston, Graig	Kaeden Books
Sammy's Sneeze	D	RF	69	Home Connection Collection	Rigby
Sammy's Special Day	D	RF	41	Urmston, Kathleen	Kaeden Books
Sammy's Supper	I	RF	293	Reading Unlimited	Pearson Learning Group
Samoan Song, A	O	I	250+	WorldScapes	ETA/Cuisenaire
Sam's Ball	D	RF	64	Lindgren, Barbro	Morrow
Sam's Balloon	C	RF	54	PM Plus Story Books	Rigby
Sam's Big Clean-up	K	RF	287	Windmill Books	Rigby
Sam's Big Day	H	RF	74	Cat on the Mat	Oxford University Press
Sam's Birthday	F	RF	116	Kaleidoscope Collection	Hameray Publishing Group
Sam's Cap	E	RF	78	Dominie Phonics Reader	Pearson Learning Group
Sam's Cookie	D	RF	52	Lindgren, Barbro	Morrow
Sam's Dad	L	RF	250+	Storyteller Chapter Books	Wright Group/McGraw Hill
Sam's Dinosaur Bone	I	RF	238	Sun Sprouts	ETA/Cuisenaire
Sam's Dog	D	RF	52	Sun Sprouts	ETA/Cuisenaire
Sam's Glasses	M	RF	250+	Literacy 2000	Rigby
#Sam's Goal	O	RF	2378	Hardcastle, Michael	Stone Arch Books
Sam's Haircut	H	RF	226	PM Plus Story Books	Rigby
Sam's Magic Moment	M	RF	250+	Rigby Literacy	Rigby
Sam's Mask	E	RF	36	Pacific Literacy	Pacific Learning
Sam's Painting	F	RF	181	PM Plus Story Books	Rigby
Sam's Pet	G	F	78	Rookie Readers	Children's Press
Sam's Picnic	D	RF	104	PM Plus Story Books	Rigby
Sam's Race	C	RF	64	PM Plus Story Books	Rigby
Sam's Ride	N	RF	250+	Orca Echoes	Orca Books
Sam's Seasons	E	RF	143	Pair-It Books	Steck-Vaughn
Sam's Snacks	I	F	250+	Cambridge Reading	Pearson Learning Group
Sam's Sneaker Squares	M	RF	250+	Math Matters	Kane Press
Sam's Solution	K	RF	250+	Literacy 2000	Rigby
Sam's Teddy Bear	D	RF	60	Lindgren, Barbro	Morrow
Sam's Wagon	D	RF	83	Lindgren, Barbro	Morrow
#Samuel Adams: Patriot and Statesman	T	B	250+	Graphic Library	Capstone Press
Samuel de Champlain	S	B	1752	Leveled Readers Language Support	Houghton Mifflin Harcourt
Samuel de Champlain in Canada	V	B	3002	Leveled Readers	Houghton Mifflin Harcourt
Samuel de Champlain: Commander of New France	U	B	1694	Leveled Readers Social Studies	Houghton Mifflin Harcourt
Samuel Eaton's Day: A Day in the Life of a Pilgrim Boy	Q	I	250+	Waters, Kate	Scholastic
#Samuel Morse and the Telegraph	V	B	250+	Graphic Library	Capstone Press
Samuel's Choice	S	HF	250+	Berleth, Richard	Scholastic
Samuel's Sprout	F	RF	194	Little Celebrations	Pearson Learning Group
Samurai	S	I	250+	Fierce Fighters	Raintree
Samurai	T	I	250+	Warriors of History	Capstone Press
Samurai and His Daughter, The	S	TL	250+	Ciddor, Anna	Scholastic

S

TITLE	LEVEL	GENRE	WORD COUNT	AUTHOR / SERIES	PUBLISHER / DISTRIBUTOR
Samurai's Daughter, The	Q	TL	250+	San Souci, Robert D.	Penguin Group
San Antonio Spurs, The	S	I	4588	Team Spirit	Norwood House Press
San Antonio: The River City	P	I	250+	On Our Way to English	Rigby
San Diego Chargers, The	S	I	250+	Team Spirit	Norwood House Press
San Diego Padres, The	S	I	250+	Team Spirit	Norwood House Press
San Diego Padres, The (Revised Edition)	S	I	250+	Team Spirit	Norwood House Press
San Domingo	R	I	250+	Henry, Marguerite	Scholastic
San Francisco 49ers, The	S	I	250+	Team Spirit	Norwood House Press
San Francisco Bay Area Missions	X	I	4846	Exploring California Missions	Lerner Publishing Group
San Francisco Earthquake, The	U	HF	250+	Reading Expeditions	National Geographic
San Francisco Earthquake, The	Q	I	618	Vocabulary Readers	Houghton Mifflin Harcourt
San Francisco Exploratorium, The	O	I	250+	Little Celebrations	Pearson Learning Group
San Francisco Giants, The	S	I	250+	Team Spirit	Norwood House Press
San Francisco Giants, The (Revised Edition)	S	I	250+	Team Spirit	Norwood House Press
San Francisco Shakes	U	I	2116	Independent Readers Science	Houghton Mifflin Harcourt
San Francisco: Then and Now	P	I	476	Independent Readers Social Studies	Houghton Mifflin Harcourt
Sand	E	RF	78	Giant Step Readers	Educational Insights
Sand	H	I	49	iOpeners	Pearson Learning Group
Sand	B	I	32	Voyages	SRA/McGraw Hill
Sand	M	I	250+	Windows on Literacy	National Geographic
Sand Castle Contest	N	RF	949	Leveled Readers	Houghton Mifflin Harcourt
Sand Castle Contest	N	RF	949	Leveled Readers/CA	Houghton Mifflin Harcourt
Sand Castle Contest	N	RF	949	Leveled Readers/TX	Houghton Mifflin Harcourt
Sand Castle Contest, The	E	RF	173	Pair-It Books	Steck-Vaughn
Sand Castle, The	G	F	257	Bella and Rosie Series	Literacy Footprints
Sand Castle, The	K	F	388	Leveled Readers	Houghton Mifflin Harcourt
Sand Castle, The	K	F	388	Leveled Readers/CA	Houghton Mifflin Harcourt
Sand Castle, The	K	F	388	Leveled Readers/TX	Houghton Mifflin Harcourt
Sand Castles	G	RF	80	Wonder World	Wright Group/McGraw Hill
Sand Castles and Guitars	J	RF	250+	Literacy by Design	Rigby
Sand on The Move: The Story of Dunes	U	I	250+	A First Book	Franklin Watts
Sand Picnic, The	E	RF	123	New Way White	Steck-Vaughn
Sandcastle, The	A	I	32	First Stories	Pacific Learning
Sandcastle, The	C	I	31	Sun Sprouts	ETA/Cuisenaire
Sandcastles	J	I	419	Leveled Readers Science	Houghton Mifflin Harcourt
Sandhill Cranes	O	I	1420	Early Bird Nature Books	Lerner Publishing Group
Sandman to the Rescue	T	RF	1758	Leveled Readers	Houghton Mifflin Harcourt
Sandra Day O'Connor	R	B	250+	Amazing Americans	Wright Group/McGraw Hill
Sandra Day O'Connor	O	B	318	Independent Readers Social Studies	Houghton Mifflin Harcourt
Sandwich Brigade, The	S	RF	3675	Reading Street	Pearson
Sandwich Hero, The	K	RF	250+	Literacy 2000	Rigby
Sandwich Person, A	G	I	63	Wonder World	Wright Group/McGraw Hill
Sandwich, The	C	RF	68	Carousel Earlybirds	Pearson Learning Group
Sandwich, The	J	RF	250+	Story Box	Wright Group/McGraw Hill
Sandwich, The	F	RF	135	The King School Series	Townsend Press
Sandwiches	D	RF	64	New Way	Steck-Vaughn
Sandwiches, Sandwiches	D	RF	54	Pair-It Books	Steck-Vaughn
Sandy	C	F	32	Ready Readers	Pearson Learning Group
Sandy Gets a Leash	D	RF	120	PM Stars	Rigby
Sandy Goes to the Vet	G	RF	187	PM Stars	Rigby
Sandy Koufax	U	B	250+	Sports Heroes and Legends	Lerner Publishing Group

S

* Collection of short stories   # Graphic text
^ Mature content with lower level text demands

TITLE	LEVEL	GENRE	WORD COUNT	AUTHOR / SERIES	PUBLISHER / DISTRIBUTOR
Sandy Runs Away	E	RF	102	Leveled Readers Language Support	Houghton Mifflin Harcourt
Sandy's Suitcase	K	RF	250+	Edwards, Elsy	SRA/McGraw Hill
Sanitation Workers	M	I	703	Pull Ahead Books	Lerner Publishing Group
Sanitation Workers: Then and Now	O	I	250+	Primary Source Readers	Teacher Created Materials
Santa Claus Doesn't Mop Floors	M	F	250+	Dadey, Debbie; Jones, Marcia Thornton	Scholastic
Santa Fe Trail, The	V	I	250+	Cornerstones of Freedom	Children's Press
^Santa Fe Trail, The	Q	I	250+	On Deck	Rigby
Santa Fe Trail, The	T	I	250+	We The People	Compass Point Books
Santa Fe, Then and Now	U	I	1393	Vocabulary Readers	Houghton Mifflin Harcourt
Santa Secret, The	K	RF	250+	Wallace, Carol	Holiday House
Santana	D	I	84	Springboard	Wright Group/McGraw Hill
Santa's Book of Names	L	F	250+	McPhail, David	Little Brown and Company
Santa's Eleven Months Off	L	F	672	Reiss, Mike	Peachtree
Santa's Last Present	L	F	250+	Murail, Marie-Aude & Elvire	Peachtree
Santa's Secrets Revealed	P	F	1897	Solheim, James	Carolrhoda Books
Santa's Suit	E	F	154	Little Elf	Literacy Footprints
Santasaurus	K	F	250+	Sharkey, Niamh	Candlewick Press
Sante Fe, Then and Now	U	I	1393	Vocabulary Readers/CA	Houghton Mifflin Harcourt
Sante Fe, Then and Now	U	I	1393	Vocabulary Readers/TX	Houghton Mifflin Harcourt
Santo and I	E	RF	135	Windows on Literacy	National Geographic
Sara Crewe	O	HF	250+	Burnett, Frances Hodgson	Scholastic
Sara Steps Over	U	F	250+	Reading Safari	Mondo Publishing
Sarah	Z+	RF	250+	Steinbeck, John	Penguin Group
Sarah and the Barking Dog	I	RF	328	PM Story Books-Orange	Rigby
Sarah and Will	H	RF	251	Alphakids	Sundance
Sarah Bishop	X	HF	250+	O'Dell, Scott	Scholastic
Sarah Emma Edmonds Was a Great Pretender	T	B	1197	Jones, Carrie	Carolrhoda Books
Sarah Morton's Day: Day in the Life of a Pilgrim Girl, A	Q	I	250+	Waters, Kate	Scholastic
Sarah Simpson's Rules for Living	T	RF	250+	Rupp, Rebecca	Candlewick Press
Sarah Snail	E	RF	55	Voyages	SRA/McGraw Hill
Sarah Sparrow Likes Rain	F	F	77	Reading Safari	Mondo Publishing
Sarah, Plain and Tall	R	HF	250+	MacLachlan, Patricia	HarperTrophy
Sarah's Choice	K	RF	371	Reading Street	Pearson
Sarah's Pet	J	RF	250+	Storyteller-Shooting Stars	Wright Group/McGraw Hill
Sarah's Seed	E	RF	107	Literacy Tree	Rigby
Sara's Lovely Songs	I	RF	250+	Ready Readers	Pearson Learning Group
Sarny: A Life Remembered	W	HF	250+	Paulsen, Gary	Delacorte Press
Sasha Cohen	U	B	250+	Sports Heroes and Legends	Lerner Publishing Group
Sasha's Mission	Y	HF	3229	Leveled Readers	Houghton Mifflin Harcourt
Sasha's Mission	Y	HF	3229	Leveled Readers/CA	Houghton Mifflin Harcourt
Sasha's Mission	Y	HF	3229	Leveled Readers/TX	Houghton Mifflin Harcourt
Sasquatch	U	F	250+	Smith, Roland	Hyperion
Satchel Paige	R	B	250+	Cline-Ransome, Lesa	Aladdin Paperbacks
#Satchel Paige: Striking out Jim Crow	X	HF	250+	Sturm, James	Hyperion
Satellites	Y	I	250+	Cool Science	Lerner Publishing Group
Satellites	O	I	250+	Let's See	Compass Point Books
Satellites Are Everywhere!	O	I	250+	Literacy by Design	Rigby
Saturday Adventure, The	J	RF	250+	Rigby Literacy	Rigby
Saturday Adventure, The	J	RF	250+	Rigby Rocket	Rigby
Saturday Cat, The	F	RF	167	Literacy by Design	Rigby
Saturday Club, The	K	RF	250+	Melton, Holly	Hampton Brown

S

* Collection of short stories   # Graphic text
^ Mature content with lower level text demands

TITLE	LEVEL	GENRE	WORD COUNT	AUTHOR / SERIES	PUBLISHER / DISTRIBUTOR
Saturday Morning	G	RF	180	Pacific Literacy	Pacific Learning
Saturday Morning Breakfast	E	RF	65	Teacher's Choice Series	Pearson Learning Group
Saturday Morning Soccer	H	RF	332	PM Stars	Rigby
Saturday Morning Treasure Hunt, The	R	RF	250+	Storyteller-Raging Rivers	Wright Group/McGraw Hill
Saturday Mornings	D	RF	63	Bookshop	Mondo Publishing
Saturday Night at the Dinosaur Stomp	N	F	250+	Shields, Carol Diggory	Candlewick Press
Saturday Night Dirt	X	RF	250+	Weaver, Will	Square Fish
Saturday Sandwiches	I	RF	154	Evangeline Nicholas Collection	Wright Group/McGraw Hill
Saturdays and Teacakes	P	RF	250+	Laminack, Lester L.	Peachtree
Saturdays with Pop	O	RF	250+	Literacy by Design	Rigby
Saturdays with Sam	V	RF	2900	Leveled Readers/CA	Houghton Mifflin Harcourt
Saturdays with Sam	V	RF	2900	Leveled Readers/TX	Houghton Mifflin Harcourt
Saturday's with Sam	V	RF	2900	Leveled Readers	Houghton Mifflin Harcourt
Saturdays, The	V	RF	250+	Enright, Elizabeth	Henry Holt & Co.
Saturn	N	I	250+	A First Book	Franklin Watts
Saturn	Q	I	250+	A True Book	Children's Press
Saturn	Q	I	1562	Early Bird Astronomy	Lerner Publishing Group
Saturn	P	I	250+	Explorer Books-Pioneer	National Geographic
Saturn	J	I	136	Exploring the Galaxy	Capstone Press
Saturn	S	I	250+	Our Solar System	Compass Point Books
Saturn	N	I	702	Our Universe	Lerner Publishing Group
Saturn	Q	I	250+	The Galaxy	Capstone Press
Saturn	M	I	250+	The Solar System	Capstone Press
Saturn	R	I	250+	Theme Sets	National Geographic
Saturn for My Birthday	M	RF	250+	McGranaghan, John	Sylvan Dell Publishing
Saturn: The Ring World	Q	I	250+	Explorer Books-Pathfinder	National Geographic
Saturnalia	W	HF	250+	Fleischman, Paul	HarperCollins
Saudi Arabia	O	I	1558	A Ticket to …	Carolrhoda Books
Saudi Arabia	P	I	1488	Country Explorers	Lerner Publishing Group
Sauk and Fox, The	R	I	1329	Reading Street	Pearson
Saul's Special Pet	J	F	250+	Leveled Readers Language Support	Houghton Mifflin Harcourt
Saurophaganax and Other Meat-Eating Dinosaurs	N	I	250+	Dinosaur Find	Picture Window Books
Sausage Spy, The	G	RF	297	Sails	Rigby
Savage, The	Z+	RF	250+	Almond, David	Candlewick Press
Savanna Food Chain, A	U	I	7493	Follow That Food Chain	Lerner Publishing Group
Savannah's Concert	K	F	250+	Literacy by Design	Rigby
Savannas of Africa, The	K	I	323	Early Explorers	Benchmark Education
Save Our Earth	S	I	250+	iOpeners	Pearson Learning Group
Save Our Sea Turtles	M	I	801	Leveled Readers	Houghton Mifflin Harcourt
Save Our Sea Turtles	M	I	801	Leveled Readers/CA	Houghton Mifflin Harcourt
Save Our Sea Turtles	R	I	1000	Vocabulary Readers/TX	Houghton Mifflin Harcourt
Save our Tree	D	I	56	Leveled Readers Social Studies	Houghton Mifflin Harcourt
Save Queen of Sheba	V	HF	250+	Moeri, Louise	Puffin Books
Save Stan's Tree	G	F	201	Literacy by Design	Rigby
Save That Trash!	G	I	181	Ready Readers	Pearson Learning Group
Save the Birds	M	RF	250+	On Our Way To English	Rigby
Save the Everglades	R	I	250+	Stamper, Judith Bauer	Steck-Vaughn
Save the Manatee	N	I	250+	Friesinger, Alison	Random House
Save the Rain Forests	L	I	250+	Fowler, Allan	Scholastic
Save the Rain Forests	L	I	250+	Read-About Science	Children's Press
Save the River!	M	SF	250+	Pair-It Books	Steck-Vaughn
Save the Sea Turtles!	M	I	250+	Leonhardt, Alice	Steck-Vaughn

* Collection of short stories   # Graphic text
^ Mature content with lower level text demands

TITLE	LEVEL	GENRE	WORD COUNT	AUTHOR / SERIES	PUBLISHER / DISTRIBUTOR
Save the Sharks	S	I	1034	Leveled Readers	Houghton Mifflin Harcourt
Save the Sharks!	S	I	1034	Leveled Readers/CA	Houghton Mifflin Harcourt
Saved from the Sea	S	I	1376	Vocabulary Readers	Houghton Mifflin Harcourt
Saved from the Sea	S	I	1376	Vocabulary Readers/CA	Houghton Mifflin Harcourt
Saved from the Sea	S	I	1376	Vocabulary Readers/TX	Houghton Mifflin Harcourt
Saving Audie: A Pit Bull Puppy Gets a Second Chance	Q	I	250+	Patent, Dorothy Hinshaw	Walker & Company
Saving a Humpback Whale	S	RF	250+	Reading Expeditions	National Geographic
Saving America's Wild Horses	Q	I	494	Vocabulary Readers	Houghton Mifflin Harcourt
Saving an American Symbol	V	I	1870	Reading Street	Pearson
Saving Endangered Species	T	I	2193	Reading Street	Pearson
Saving Energy at Home	Q	I	250+	Rigby Focus	Rigby
Saving Frogs	Q	I	250+	Scooters	ETA/Cuisenaire
^Saving Grace	Z+	RF	250+	Orca Soundings	Orca Books
Saving Greedy Guts	L	RF	862	Rigby Gigglers	Rigby
Saving Hoppo	I	RF	250+	PM Plus Story Books	Rigby
Saving Jessica	Y	RF	250+	McDaniel, Lurlene	Laurel-Leaf Books
Saving Juliet	Z	F	250+	Selfors, Suzanne	Walker & Company
Saving Money	T	I	250+	How Economics Works	Lerner Publishing Group
Saving Money	M	I	250+	Learning About Money	Capstone Press
Saving Money	O	I	250+	Let's See	Compass Point Books
Saving Money	E	I	123	Money	Lerner Publishing Group
Saving Our Planet	G	I	317	Factivity Series	Pearson Learning Group
Saving Planet Earth	S	SF	1603	Leveled Readers	Houghton Mifflin Harcourt
Saving Planet Earth	S	SF	1603	Leveled Readers/CA	Houghton Mifflin Harcourt
Saving Planet Earth	S	SF	1603	Leveled Readers/TX	Houghton Mifflin Harcourt
Saving Scruffy	I	RF	212	Literacy by Design	Rigby
Saving Sea Turtles	S	I	1483	Leveled Readers	Houghton Mifflin Harcourt
Saving Shadow	K	RF	250+	Read-it! Readers	Picture Window Books
Saving the Egret	W	I	2663	Vocabulary Readers	Houghton Mifflin Harcourt
Saving the Egret	W	I	2663	Vocabulary Readers/CA	Houghton Mifflin Harcourt
Saving the Egret	W	I	2663	Vocabulary Readers/TX	Houghton Mifflin Harcourt
Saving the Family Farm	U	RF	250+	Reading Expeditions	National Geographic
Saving the General	T	RF	2740	Leveled Readers	Houghton Mifflin Harcourt
Saving the General	T	RF	2740	Leveled Readers/CA	Houghton Mifflin Harcourt
Saving the General	T	RF	2740	Leveled Readers/TX	Houghton Mifflin Harcourt
Saving the Griffin	S	F	250+	Nitz, Kristin Wolden	Peachtree
Saving the Liberty Bell	O	HF	1806	On My Own History	Lerner Publishing Group
Saving the Mexican Wolves	V	I	3004	Leveled Readers	Houghton Mifflin Harcourt
Saving the Mexican Wolves	V	I	3004	Leveled Readers/CA	Houghton Mifflin Harcourt
Saving the Mexican Wolves	V	I	3004	Leveled Readers/TX	Houghton Mifflin Harcourt
Saving the Oceans	N	I	250+	Explorations	Okapi Educational Materials
Saving the Oceans	N	I	250+	Explorations	Eleanor Curtain Publishing
Saving the Panda	J	I	269	Red Rocket Readers	Flying Start Books
Saving the Park	K	RF	872	InfoTrek	ETA/Cuisenaire
Saving the Park	N	RF	250+	Orbit Chapter Books	Pacific Learning
Saving the Rainforests	L	I	250+	Explorations	Okapi Educational Materials
Saving the Rainforests	L	I	250+	Explorations	Eleanor Curtain Publishing
Saving the Sarus Crane	T	I	250+	WorldScapes	ETA/Cuisenaire
Saving the Stegosaurus: Dinosaur Cove	N	F	250+	Stone, Rex	Scholastic
Saving the Yellow Eye	P	I	250+	Darby, John	Pacific Learning
Saving the Zog	S	SF	250+	Power Up!	Steck-Vaughn
Saving Tigers	K	I	430	Red Rocket Readers	Flying Start Books
Saving Tigers	K	I	347	Springboard	Wright Group/McGraw Hill

TITLE	LEVEL	GENRE	WORD COUNT	AUTHOR / SERIES	PUBLISHER / DISTRIBUTOR
Saving Up	G	I	189	Explorations	Okapi Educational Materials
Saving Up	G	I	189	Explorations	Eleanor Curtain Publishing
Saving Water and Energy	L	I	790	Rigby Flying Colors	Rigby
Saving Wild One	V	RF	2109	Leveled Readers	Houghton Mifflin Harcourt
Savvy	U	F	250+	Law, Ingrid	Puffin Books
*Saxby Smart: Private Detective	S	RF	250+	Cheshire, Simon	Roaring Brook Press
Say "Cheese"	L	RF	250+	Giff, Patricia Reilly	Bantam Books
Say "Hi" Up High	F	F	61	Early Readers	Compass Point Books
Say Cheese	J	I	169	Rigby Focus	Rigby
Say Cheese!	F	RF	128	Storyteller-Moon Rising	Wright Group/McGraw Hill
Say Good Night	G	F	59	Start to Read	School Zone
Say Good Night	G	RF	155	Ziefert, Harriet	Puffin Books
Say Hello	G	RF	77	Foreman, Jack & Michael	Candlewick Press
Say Hello	G	RF	77	Foreman, Jack & Michael	Candlewick Press
Say Hello!	A	RF	15	Avenues	Hampton Brown
Say Hello!	A	RF	15	Rise & Shine	Hampton Brown
Say Hola, Sarah	N	RF	250+	Giff, Patricia Reilly	Bantam Books
Say in San Juan, A	M	I	621	Vocabulary Readers	Houghton Mifflin Harcourt
Say It with Music: A Story about Irving Berlin	S	B	8710	Creative Minds Biographies	Lerner Publishing Group
Say It, Sign It	G	RF	169	Epstein, Elaine	Scholastic
Say Please!	H	F	83	Ross, Tony	Kane/Miller Book Publishers
Say the Word	Z+	RF	250+	Garsee, Jeannine	Bloomsbury Children's Books
Say Yes	W	RF	250+	Couloumbis, Audrey	G.P. Putnam's Sons Books for Young Readers
Say-Hey and the Babe: Two Mostly True Baseball Stories	T	HF	250+	Waldman, Neil	Holiday House
Saying Goodbye to Lulu	L	RF	250+	Demas, Corinne	Little Brown and Company
Scale	C	I	29	Simple Tools	Lerner Publishing Group
Scales	E	I	86	Body Coverings	Lerner Publishing Group
^Scaly Blood Squirters and Other Extreme Reptiles	T	I	250+	Extreme Life	Capstone Press
Scaly Things	Q	I	250+	Explorers	Wright Group/McGraw Hill
Scamp	M	RF	250+	PM Plus Chapter Books	Rigby
Scams: Schemes, Cons, and Hoaxes	T	I	250+	Connectors	Pacific Learning
Scare and Dare	H	RF	284	Alphakids	Sundance
Scare for Bear, A	F	F	182	Sun Sprouts	ETA/Cuisenaire
Scare in the City, A	N	RF	863	Avenues	Hampton Brown
Scare in the City, A	N	RF	250+	Chanek, Sherilin	Hampton Brown
Scarecrow	J	RF	600	Red Rocket Readers	Flying Start Books
Scarecrow	R	F	386	Rylant, Cynthia	Harcourt Brace
Scarecrow, A	F	F	85	Larkin's Little Readers	Wilbooks
Scarecrow, The	C	F	31	Literacy 2000	Rigby
Scarecrow, The	D	RF	97	Little Red Readers	Sundance
Scarecrow, The	L	RF	250+	Pacific Literacy	Pacific Learning
Scarecrows	F	I	85	All About Fall	Capstone Press
Scarecrows	D	I	39	Pebble Books	Capstone Press
Scarecrow's Friends	C	F	56	Start to Read	School Zone
Scarecrow's Hair	D	F	142	Sails	Rigby
Scarecrow's Hat, The	J	F	250+	Brown, Ken	Peachtree
Scared	D	RF	59	Twig	Wright Group/McGraw Hill
Scared at Night	H	RF	250+	Early Transitional, Set 2	Pioneer Valley
Scared Bear, The	D	F	146	InfoTrek	ETA/Cuisenaire
Scared Stiff	V	F	250+	Malcolm, Jahnna N.	Scholastic

* Collection of short stories   # Graphic text
^ Mature content with lower level text demands

TITLE	LEVEL	GENRE	WORD COUNT	AUTHOR / SERIES	PUBLISHER / DISTRIBUTOR
Scaredy Bears	K	F	250+	Sunshine	Wright Group/McGraw Hill
Scaredy Cat	C	F	85	Learn to Read	Creative Teaching Press
Scaredy Cat	A	RF	29	Rigby Literacy	Rigby
Scaredy Cat	A	RF	29	Rigby Star	Rigby
Scaredy Cat Runs Away	D	F	57	Learn to Read	Creative Teaching Press
Scaredy Dog	K	RF	250+	Thomas, Jane Resh	Hyperion
Scaredy Dog!	L	F	250+	I Am Reading	Kingfisher
Scaredy Kat: Suddenly Supernatural	R	F	250+	Kimmel, Elizabeth Cody	Little Brown and Company
Scaredy-Cat Catcher	N	RF	250+	Hicks, Betty	Roaring Brook Press
Scare-Kid	K	F	250+	Literacy 2000	Rigby
Scarlet Macaws	L	I	113	Seedlings	Continental Press
Scarlett the Garnet Fairy: Rainbow Magic	L	F	250+	Meadows, Daisy	Scholastic
Scary Day, The	N	RF	250+	Bennett, Jean	Pacific Learning
Scary Hair	H	F	242	Big Cat	Pacific Learning
Scary Larry	G	F	62	Rookie Readers	Children's Press
Scary Masks, The	F	RF	147	PM Photo Stories	Rigby
Scary Monster	C	F	19	Eifrig, Kate	Kaeden Books
Scary Noises	G	F	125	Fried, Mary	Keep Books
Scary Sharks	O	I	250+	Fearsome, Scary, and Creepy Animals	Enslow Publishers, Inc.
Scary Spiders!	J	RF	198	Sunshine	Wright Group/McGraw Hill
Scary Stories 3: More Tales to Chill Your Bones	V	TL	250+	Schwartz, Alvin	Scholastic
Scat	W	RF	250+	Hiaasen, Carl	Alfred A. Knopf
Scat! Said the Cat	D	F	33	Sunshine	Wright Group/McGraw Hill
Scatterbrain	T	RF	250+	Reading Street	Pearson
Scavenger Hunt, The	J	F	790	Little Dinosaur	Literacy Footprints
Scavengers and Junk Eaters	O	I	2039	Take Two Books	Wright Group/McGraw Hill
Scene of the Crime	V	I	250+	Rose, Malcolm	Kingfisher
Scepter of the Ancients	Y	F	250+	Landy, Derek	HarperCollins
Schernoff Discoveries, The	T	RF	250+	Paulsen, Gary	Dell
School	D	I	50	Berger, Samantha; Chanko, Pamela	Scholastic
School	D	I	32	Community Buildings	Lerner Publishing Group
School Bus	LB	RF	51	Crews, Donald	Morrow
School Bus Drivers	M	I	250+	Community Helpers	Red Brick Learning
School Bus Drivers	K	I	506	Pull Ahead Books	Lerner Publishing Group
School Bus Ride, The	G	RF	160	Little Red Readers	Sundance
School Bus, The	E	RF	60	Sunshine	Wright Group/McGraw Hill
#School Children's Blizzard, The	S	I	250+	Disasters in History	Capstone Press
School Concert, The	K	RF	250+	Rigby Star Plus	Rigby
School Day!	A	RF	16	Cervantes, Jesus	Scholastic
School Days	U	I	250+	Literacy 2000	Rigby
School Days	WB	I	0	Reach	National Geographic
School Days in 1700	Q	I	975	Independent Readers Social Studies	Houghton Mifflin Harcourt
School Days Long Ago and Today	A	I	32	Leveled Readers Social Studies	Houghton Mifflin Harcourt
School Days, Cool Days!	J	RF	250+	Storyteller-Shooting Stars	Wright Group/McGraw Hill
School Fair, The	J	RF	250+	PM Plus Story Books	Rigby
School Fair, The	I	RF	250+	Storyworlds	Heinemann
School in a Garden	N	I	888	Leveled Readers/TX	Houghton Mifflin Harcourt
School in Colonial America	K	I	148	Welcome Books	Children's Press
School in Many Cultures	I	I	113	Life Around the World	Capstone Press
School in the Outback	O	I	250+	WorldScapes	ETA/Cuisenaire
School Is Closed	H	F	250+	Phonics Readers Plus	Steck-Vaughn

TITLE	LEVEL	GENRE	WORD COUNT	AUTHOR / SERIES	PUBLISHER / DISTRIBUTOR
*School Journal Part 1: Numbers 1-5	N	RF	250+	Learning Media	Richard C. Owen
*School Journal Part 2: Numbers 1-4	O	RF	250+	Learning Media	Richard C. Owen
*School Journal Part 3: Numbers 1-3	O	RF	250+	Learning Media	Richard C. Owen
School Long Ago	M	I	430	Leveled Readers/TX	Houghton Mifflin Harcourt
School Lunch	LB	RF	14	Ready Readers	Pearson Learning Group
School Mouse, The	P	F	250+	King-Smith, Dick	Hyperion
School Mural, The	L	RF	250+	Pair-It Books	Steck-Vaughn
School Newspaper	F	I	84	On Deck	Rigby
School Newspaper, The	O	I	250+	Sunshine	Wright Group/McGraw Hill
#School of Evil	U	F	10860	Twisted Journeys	Graphic Universe
School of Fear	V	RF	250+	Daneshvari, Gitty	Little Brown and Company
School on Stilts	U	I	250+	WorldScapes	ETA/Cuisenaire
School Places	A	I	22	Reach	National Geographic
School Play Stars	N	RF	250+	Girlz Rock!	Mondo Publishing
School Play, The	G	RF	103	City Stories	Rigby
School Principals	M	I	250+	Community Helpers	Red Brick Learning
School Recyclers	L	RF	380	Leveled Readers Science	Houghton Mifflin Harcourt
School Rules	I	F	365	Reading Street	Pearson
School Safety	F	I	41	Safety	Lerner Publishing Group
School Secretaries	M	I	250+	Community Helpers	Red Brick Learning
School Spirit: Suddenly Supernatural	R	F	250+	Kimmel, Elizabeth Cody	Little Brown and Company
School Story, The	R	RF	250+	Clements, Andrew	Aladdin Paperbacks
School Then and Now	I	I	106	Then and Now	Lerner Publishing Group
School Times: A Spot-It Challenge	J	I	250+	Spot It	Capstone Press
School Today and Long Ago	H	I	110	Windows on Literacy	National Geographic
School Tools	LB	I	14	Reach	National Geographic
School Trip Estimation	J	I	231	Early Explorers	Benchmark Education
School Vacation	J	RF	113	City Kids	Rigby
School, A	LB	RF	14	Avenues	Hampton Brown
School, The	E	RF	27	Burningham, John	Crowell
School: Then and Now	L	I	310	Reading Street	Pearson
Schoolchildren's Blizzard, The	L	HF	1555	On My Own History	Lerner Publishing Group
Schooled	V	RF	250+	Korman, Gordon	Hyperion
Schools	C	I	31	We Are Alike and Different	Lerner Publishing Group
Schools Around the World	E	I	78	Pair-It Books	Steck-Vaughn
Schools Around the World	O	I	1065	Vocabulary Readers	Houghton Mifflin Harcourt
Schools Around the World	O	I	1065	Vocabulary Readers/CA	Houghton Mifflin Harcourt
School's Out	N	RF	250+	Hurwitz, Johanna	Scholastic
Schools Then and Now	C	I	37	Early Explorers	Benchmark Education
Schools Then and Now	N	I	622	Vocabulary Readers	Houghton Mifflin Harcourt
Schools Then and Now	N	I	622	Vocabulary Readers/CA	Houghton Mifflin Harcourt
Schools Then and Now	N	I	622	Vocabulary Readers/TX	Houghton Mifflin Harcourt
Schoolyard Mystery, The	L	RF	250+	Levy, Elizabeth	Scholastic
Schoolyard Snickers: Classy Jokes That Make the Grade	O	F	2222	Make Me Laugh!	Lerner Publishing Group
Schwa Was Here, The	Y	RF	250+	Shusterman, Neal	Dutton Children's Books
Science - Just Add Salt	L	I	250+	Markle, Sandra	Scholastic
Science All Around	R	I	250+	Literacy by Design	Rigby
Science and Your Health	M	I	189	Health and Your Body	Capstone Press
Science Around the House	Q	I	250+	Reading Expeditions	National Geographic
Science at the Airport	P	I	250+	Reading Expeditions	National Geographic
Science at the Aquarium	P	I	250+	Reading Expeditions	National Geographic
Science at the Grocery	P	I	250+	Reading Expeditions	National Geographic
Science at the Mall	Q	I	250+	Reading Expeditions	National Geographic

* Collection of short stories   # Graphic text
^ Mature content with lower level text demands

TITLE	LEVEL	GENRE	WORD COUNT	AUTHOR / SERIES	PUBLISHER / DISTRIBUTOR
Science at the Park	P	I	250+	Reading Expeditions	National Geographic
Science at the Sandy Shore	P	I	250+	Reading Expeditions	National Geographic
Science at the Zoo	P	I	250+	Reading Expeditions	National Geographic
Science Experiments That Explode and Implode	R	I	250+	Kitchen Science	Capstone Press
Science Experiments That Fizz and Bubble	R	I	250+	Kitchen Science	Capstone Press
Science Experiments That Fly and Move	R	I	250+	Kitchen Science	Capstone Press
Science Experiments That Surprise and Delight	R	I	250+	Kitchen Science	Capstone Press
Science Fair Surprise, The	Q	RF	250+	Burke, Melissa Blackwell	Steck-Vaughn
Science Fair, The	I	RF	135	Reading Street	Pearson
Science Fiction Pioneer: A Story About Jules Verne	T	B	8148	Creative Minds Biographies	Carolrhoda Books
Science of Cooking, The	T	I	250+	PM Plus	Rigby
Science of You, The	Q	I	250+	Reading Expeditions	National Geographic
Science Outside	I	I	33	Canizares, Susan; Chessen, Betsey	Scholastic
Science Tools	E	I	52	Canizares, Susan; Chessen, Betsey	Scholastic
Science Zone, The	O	F	250+	The Funny Zone	Norwood House Press
Scientific Discovery in the Renaissance	W	I	250+	Navigators Social Studies Series	Benchmark Education
Scientist of Old, A	J	B	155	Dominie Factivity Series	Pearson Learning Group
Scientist, The	G	I	195	Adventures in Reading	Pearson Learning Group
Scientists	I	I	56	Chanko, Pamela; Berger, Samantha	Scholastic
Scientists at Work	M	I	250+	Yellow Umbrella Books	Red Brick Learning
Scientists in Space	U	I	3502	Leveled Readers Science	Houghton Mifflin Harcourt
Scissors	D	I	51	Storyteller-Setting Sun	Wright Group/McGraw Hill
Scit, Scat, Scaredy Cat!	F	F	59	Sunshine	Wright Group/McGraw Hill
Scooter's Busy Monday	I	RF	312	Rigby Flying Colors	Rigby
Scooter's School Trip	I	RF	562	Rigby Flying Colors	Rigby
Score!: You Can Play Soccer	M	I	250+	Game Day	Picture Window Books
Score: The Action and Artistry of Hockey's Magnificent Moment	U	I	250+	Stewart, Mark & Kennedy, Mike	Millbrook Press
Scoring Points	P	RF	250+	Leveled Readers Language Support	Houghton Mifflin Harcourt
Scorpion	L	I	250+	A Day in the Life: Desert Animals	Heinemann Library
Scorpions	Z	RF	250+	Myers, Walter Dean	HarperTrophy
Scotland: A Question and Answer Book	P	I	250+	Questions & Answers: Countries	Capstone Press
Scots Pine, The	M	I	250+	Cambridge Reading	Pearson Learning Group
Scottish Fold Cats	I	I	119	Cats	Capstone Press
Scout and the River	C	F	81	Handprints B	Educators Publishing Service
Scrambled States of America Talent Show, The	N	F	250+	Keller, Laurie	Henry Holt & Co.
Scrambled States of America, The	N	F	250+	Keller, Laurie	Henry Holt & Co.
Scrapbooking: Keep Your Special Memories	Q	I	250+	Crafts	Capstone Press
Scraping the Sky	T	I	250+	Rigby Literacy	Rigby
Scrapman	N	F	250+	High-Fliers	Pacific Learning
Scrapman and Scrapcat	N	F	250+	High-Fliers	Pacific Learning
Scrapman and the Incredible Flying Machine	N	F	250+	High-Fliers	Pacific Learning
Scrappers No Easy Out	Q	RF	250+	Hughes, Dean	Aladdin
Scrappers No Fear	Q	RF	250+	Hughes, Dean	Aladdin
Scraps of Time 1928: A Song for Harlem	Q	HF	250+	McKissack, Patricia C.	Puffin Books
#Scratch and Sniff in the Odd Math Lesson	J	F	234	The Rowland Reading Program Library	Rowland Reading Foundation
#Scratch and Sniff in Tummy Trouble	L	F	250+	The Rowland Reading Program Libary	Rowland Reading Foundation
Scratch My Back	D	F	66	Foundations	Wright Group/McGraw Hill

* Collection of short stories   # Graphic text
^ Mature content with lower level text demands

TITLE	LEVEL	GENRE	WORD COUNT	AUTHOR / SERIES	PUBLISHER / DISTRIBUTOR
Scratching's Catching!	L	F	250+	I Am Reading	Kingfisher
Scream, The	K	RF	509	Leveled Literacy Intervention/ Blue System	Heinemann
Screech!	D	RF	43	Literacy 2000	Rigby
^Screw Loose	O	F	3211	Prince, A.	Stone Arch Books
Screws	Q	I	1505	Early Bird Energy Physics Books	Lerner Publishing Group
Screws to the Rescue	O	I	250+	Simple Machine to the Rescue	Capstone Press
Scribbler of Dreams	Z+	RF	250+	Bro, Margueritte Harmon	Fitzhenry & Whiteside
Scribbles	H	F	195	The Rowland Reading Program Library	Rowland Reading Foundation
Scribe of Ancient China, A	W	HF	2134	Leveled Readers	Houghton Mifflin Harcourt
Scritch-Scratch Noise, The	J	F	337	Springboard	Wright Group/McGraw Hill
Scrubbing Machine, The	F	F	148	Story Box	Wright Group/McGraw Hill
Scrubbly-Bubbly Car Wash, The	K	RF	179	O'Garden, Irene	HarperCollins
Scruff	I	RF	250+	Rigby Rocket	Rigby
Scruffy	I	RF	250+	Leveled Readers	Houghton Mifflin Harcourt
Scruffy	K	RF	250+	Parish, Peggy	HarperTrophy
Scruffy Messed It Up	G	RF	105	Literacy 2000	Rigby
Scruffy Runs Away	F	RF	187	PM Photo Stories	Rigby
Scrumptious Sundae	B	RF	18	Literacy 2000	Rigby
Scruncher Goes Wandering	M	RF	250+	Krailing, Tessa	Barron's Educational
Scuba Diving	P	I	250+	Trackers	Pacific Learning
Scuba Kid	N	RF	250+	PM Extensions	Rigby
Scuba School	S	I	250+	Underwater Encounters	Hameray Publishing Group
Sculpture	L	I	250+	Little Celebrations	Pearson Learning Group
Sculpture	K	I	272	Storyteller	Wright Group/McGraw Hill
Sculptures	M	I	250+	Start with Art	Heinemann Library
Se±or Armadillo and Friends	E	F	155	Joy Starters	Pearson Learning Group
Se±or Armadillo Makes an Airplane	E	F	51	Joy Starters	Pearson Learning Group
Se±or Armadillo's Cold	E	F	80	Joy Starters	Pearson Learning Group
Se±or Armadillo's Skis	E	F	73	Joy Starters	Pearson Learning Group
Se±or Armadillo's Very Fine Truck	E	F	145	Joy Starters	Pearson Learning Group
Sea and Land Animals	J	I	250+	Windows on Literacy	National Geographic
Sea Anemones	G	I	58	Ocean Life	Capstone Press
Sea Animals	K	I	250+	Little Red Readers	Sundance
Sea Animals	B	I	46	Vocabulary Readers	Houghton Mifflin Harcourt
Sea Battle, A	S	I	978	Leveled Readers Language Support	Houghton Mifflin Harcourt
Sea Cave	T	RF	250+	Reading Safari	Mondo Publishing
Sea Creatures	K	I	332	Gear Up!	Wright Group/McGraw Hill
Sea Creatures You Can Draw	R	I	1680	Ready, Set, Draw!	Millbrook Press
Sea Giants of Dinosaur Time	P	I	1235	Meet the Dinosaurs	Lerner Publishing Group
Sea Habitats	L	I	597	Rigby Flying Colors	Rigby
Sea Horses	O	I	2252	Early Bird Nature Books	Lerner Publishing Group
Sea Horses	F	I	67	Ocean Life	Capstone Press
Sea Horses	J	I	178	Oceans Alive	Bellwether Media
Sea Horses	J	I	90	Under the Sea	Capstone Press
Sea Jellies	Q	I	1317	Gear Up!	Wright Group/McGraw Hill
Sea Life	A	I	32	Red Rocket Readers	Flying Start Books
Sea Life	I	I	143	Time for Kids	Teacher Created Materials
Sea Lights	L	I	128	Books for Young Learners	Richard C. Owen
Sea Lions	O	I	2933	Early Bird Nature Books	Lerner Publishing Group
Sea Lions	J	I	316	Vocabulary Readers	Houghton Mifflin Harcourt
Sea Lions	M	I	618	Vocabulary Readers	Houghton Mifflin Harcourt

* Collection of short stories   # Graphic text
^ Mature content with lower level text demands

TITLE	LEVEL	GENRE	WORD COUNT	AUTHOR / SERIES	PUBLISHER / DISTRIBUTOR
Sea Lions	J	I	316	Vocabulary Readers/CA	Houghton Mifflin Harcourt
Sea Lions	M	I	618	Vocabulary Readers/CA	Houghton Mifflin Harcourt
Sea Lions	M	I	618	Vocabulary Readers/TX	Houghton Mifflin Harcourt
Sea Monkeys	M	RF	250+	Scooters	ETA/Cuisenaire
Sea Monsters	R	I	250+	Explorer Books-Pathfinder	National Geographic
Sea Monsters	P	I	250+	Explorer Books-Pioneer	National Geographic
Sea Monsters Don't Ride Motorcycles	M	RF	250+	Dadey, Debbie; Jones, Marcia Thornton	Scholastic
Sea of Animals, A	K	I	213	Spyglass Books	Compass Point Books
Sea of Dreams	WB	F	0	Nolan, Dennis	Roaring Brook Press
Sea of Trolls, The	X	F	250+	Farmer, Nancy	Simon Pulse
Sea Otter	H	I	106	Under the Sea	Capstone Press
Sea Otter Goes Hunting	J	RF	250+	PM Plus Story Books	Rigby
Sea Otter Inlet	O	I	250+	Godkin, Celia	Fitzhenry & Whiteside
Sea Otter Rescue: The Aftermath of an Oil Spill	W	I	250+	Smith, Roland	Scholastic
Sea Otters	N	I	588	Springboard	Wright Group/McGraw Hill
Sea Otters	L	I	406	Storyteller Nonfiction	Wright Group/McGraw Hill
Sea Snakes	I	I	66	Pebble Books	Red Brick Learning
Sea Snakes	H	I	105	Under the Sea	Capstone Press
Sea Star	R	RF	250+	Henry, Marguerite	Aladdin
Sea Star, A	E	I	82	Ready Readers	Pearson Learning Group
Sea Stars	F	I	130	Bonnell, Kris/About	Reading Reading Books
Sea Stars	E	I	63	Ocean Life	Capstone Press
Sea Stars	K	I	289	Sun Sprouts	ETA/Cuisenaire
Sea Stars	H	I	131	Under the Sea	Capstone Press
Sea Turtle	K	I	250+	A Day in the Life: Sea Animals	Heinemann Library
Sea Turtle Family, The	T	SF	1926	Leveled Readers	Houghton Mifflin Harcourt
Sea Turtle Family, The	T	SF	2580	Leveled Readers/CA	Houghton Mifflin Harcourt
Sea Turtle Family, The	T	SF	2580	Leveled Readers/TX	Houghton Mifflin Harcourt
Sea Turtle Night	I	I	200	Ready Readers	Pearson Learning Group
Sea Turtles	O	I	1704	Early Bird Nature Books	Lerner Publishing Group
Sea Turtles	K	I	238	Gear Up!	Wright Group/McGraw Hill
Sea Turtles	L	I	553	Leveled Readers	Houghton Mifflin Harcourt
Sea Turtles	L	I	296	Marine Life For Young Readers	Pearson Learning Group
Sea Turtles	G	I	50	Pebble Books	Red Brick Learning
Sea Turtles	L	I	489	Springboard	Wright Group/McGraw Hill
Sea Turtles	J	I	118	Under the Sea	Capstone Press
Sea Turtles	S	I	250+	Underwater Encounters	Hameray Publishing Group
Sea Turtles At Risk	N	I	791	Reading Street	Pearson
Sea Turtles in Danger	O	I	250+	Literacy by Design	Rigby
Sea Turtles in the Sand	E	I	107	Bonnell, Kris	Reading Reading Books
Sea Turtles: Ocean Nomads	U	I	250+	Cerullo, Mary M.	Dutton Children's Books
Sea Urchins	G	I	51	Ocean Life	Capstone Press
Sea Urchins	H	I	113	Under the Sea	Capstone Press
Sea Wall, The	K	I	251	Foundations	Wright Group/McGraw Hill
Sea Where I Swim, The	F	I	134	Voyages	SRA/McGraw Hill
Sea Wind	R	RF	250+	PM Chapter Books	Rigby
Sea, The	C	I	63	Leveled Literacy Intervention/ Blue System	Heinemann
Sea, The	A	I	20	Leveled Readers	Houghton Mifflin Harcourt
Sea, The	A	I	20	Leveled Readers/CA	Houghton Mifflin Harcourt
Seabirds	S	I	250+	A First Book	Franklin Watts
Seafaring Life, The	R	I	1558	Reading Street	Pearson
Seagull Is Clever	E	RF	98	PM Story Books	Rigby

TITLE	LEVEL	GENRE	WORD COUNT	AUTHOR / SERIES	PUBLISHER / DISTRIBUTOR
Seagull, The	C	F	78	Story Steps	Rigby
Seahaven Squids and the Amazing Pet Wash, The	R	RF	1569	Reading Street	Pearson
Seahorses	M	I	250+	Bookshop	Mondo Publishing
Seahorses, Pipefishes, and Their Kin	T	I	250+	Animals in Order	Franklin Watts
Seal	L	I	250+	A Day in the Life: Sea Animals	Heinemann Library
Seal	M	I	250+	Cambridge Reading	Pearson Learning Group
Seal Who Wanted to Live, The	O	F	1000	Leveled Readers/TX	Houghton Mifflin Harcourt
Sealed with a Diss: The Clique	X	RF	250+	Harrison, Lisi	Little Brown and Company
Seals	G	I	42	Pebble Books	Red Brick Learning
Seals	H	I	79	Polar Animals	Capstone Press
Seals	F	I	123	Readlings/ Marine Animals	American Reading Company
Seals	I	I	103	Under the Sea	Red Brick Learning
Seals & Sea Lions	L	I	273	Marine Life for Young Readers	Pearson Learning Group
Seals and Sea Lions	N	I	250+	Take Two Books	Wright Group/McGraw Hill
Seals of the World	J	I	251	Vocabulary Readers	Houghton Mifflin Harcourt
^Seals That Wouldn't Swim, The	Q	RF	250+	Brezenoff, Steve/Field Trip Mysteries	Stone Arch Books
Seaman: The Dog Who Explored the West with Lewis & Clark	U	HF	250+	Karwoski, Gail Langer	Peachtree
Search and Discover	O	I	250+	Discovery Links	Newbridge
Search for Delicious, The	U	F	250+	Babbitt, Natalie	Farrar, Straus, & Giroux
Search for Gold, The	Q	I	250+	In Step Readers	Rigby
Search for New Lands, The	S	I	250+	Literacy by Design	Rigby
Search for Oil	V	I	3343	Leveled Readers Science	Houghton Mifflin Harcourt
Search for Sidney's Smile, The	I	RF	108	Kornblatt, Marc	Simon & Schuster
Search for Sunken Treasure, The	O	F	250+	Stilton, Geronimo	Scholastic
Search for the Lost Cave, The	M	F	250+	Woodland Mysteries	Wright Group/McGraw Hill
Search for the Sunken Treasure, The	P	SF	250+	Secret Agent Jack Stalwart	Weinstein Books
#Search, The	Y	HF	250+	Heuvel, Eric	Farrar, Straus, & Giroux
Searcher and Old Tree, The	M	F	259	McPhail, David	Charlesbridge
Searching for Arctic Oil	V	I	250+	Science Missions	Raintree
Searching for Dinosaurs	U	I	2309	Reading Street	Pearson
Searching for My Father	X	RF	2703	Leveled Readers	Houghton Mifflin Harcourt
Searching for My Father	X	RF	2703	Leveled Readers/CA	Houghton Mifflin Harcourt
Searching for My Father	X	RF	2703	Leveled Readers/TX	Houghton Mifflin Harcourt
Searching for Sea Lions	P	I	250+	Orbit Chapter Books	Pacific Learning
Searching for Sunken Treasure	R	RF	250+	Reading Expeditions	National Geographic
Seashells	L	I	186	Marine Life For Young Readers	Pearson Learning Group
Seashells by the Seashore	L	RF	441	Sharing Nature with Children	Dawn Publications
Season of Secrets	T	F	250+	Nicholls, Sally	Scholastic
Season Search: A Spot-It Challenge	J	I	354	Spot-It	Capstone Press
Season to Season	I	RF	322	InfoTrek	ETA/Cuisenaire
Season to Season	F	I	113	Pair-It Books	Steck-Vaughn
Seasons	O	I	250+	A True Book	Children's Press
Seasons	H	I	99	Discovering Nature's Cycles	Lerner Publishing Group
Seasons	C	I	28	Discovery World	Rigby
Seasons	B	I	24	InfoTrek	ETA/Cuisenaire
Seasons	H	I	119	Instant Readers	Harcourt School Publishers
Seasons	L	I	251	Leveled Readers	Houghton Mifflin Harcourt
Seasons	A	I	28	Leveled Readers Science	Houghton Mifflin Harcourt
Seasons	L	I	251	Leveled Readers/CA	Houghton Mifflin Harcourt
Seasons	L	I	251	Leveled Readers/TX	Houghton Mifflin Harcourt
Seasons	K	I	266	Nonfiction Set 8	Literacy Footprints

S

* Collection of short stories   # Graphic text
^ Mature content with lower level text demands

TITLE	LEVEL	GENRE	WORD COUNT	AUTHOR / SERIES	PUBLISHER / DISTRIBUTOR
Seasons	H	I	354	Science Support Readers	Houghton Mifflin Harcourt
Seasons	N	I	250+	Simply Science	Compass Point Books
Seasons	F	I	95	Spinelle, Nancy Louise	Kaeden Books
Seasons	A	I	29	Vocabulary Readers	Houghton Mifflin Harcourt
Seasons	H	I	250+	Yellow Umbrella Books	Red Brick Learning
Seasons and Weather	M	I	250+	PM Plus Nonfiction	Rigby
Seasons Around the World	K	I	353	Leveled Readers	Houghton Mifflin Harcourt
Seasons Around the World	K	I	353	Leveled Readers/CA	Houghton Mifflin Harcourt
Seasons Around the World	K	I	353	Leveled Readers/TX	Houghton Mifflin Harcourt
Seasons Change	F	I	80	Reading Street	Pearson
Seasons Come and Go	J	RF	282	InfoTrek	ETA/Cuisenaire
Seasons Go 'Round	V	I	250+	Literacy By Design	Rigby
Seasons of the Year	G	I	180	Measuring Time	Heinemann Library
Seasons of the Year	J	I	176	Patterns in Nature	Capstone Press
Seasons of the Year, The	L	I	332	Leveled Readers	Houghton Mifflin Harcourt
Seasons of the Year, The	L	I	332	Leveled Readers/CA	Houghton Mifflin Harcourt
Seasons of the Year, The	L	I	332	Leveled Readers/TX	Houghton Mifflin Harcourt
Seasons on a Farm	F	I	112	World of Farming	Heinemann Library
Seasons Project	H	I	218	Sun Sprouts	ETA/Cuisenaire
Seasons, The	D	I	84	Early Connections	Benchmark Education
Seasons, The	J	I	193	Phonics Readers	Compass Point Books
Seasons, The	C	RF	84	Rigby Focus	Rigby
Seat Belt for Joey, A	D	F	94	On Our Way to English	Rigby
Seat Belt Song, The	K	RF	505	PM Collection	Rigby
Seattle Mariners, The	S	I	250+	Team Spirit	Norwood House Press
Seattle Mariners, The (Revised Edition)	S	I	250+	Team Spirit	Norwood House Press
Seattle Seahawks, The	S	I	250+	Team Spirit	Norwood House Press
Seawall	O	RF	250+	PM Collection	Rigby
Seaward	X	F	250+	Cooper, Susan	Simon & Schuster
Seb & Sasha	U	RF	250+	Book Blazers	ETA/Cuisenaire
Sebastian	G	F	162	Alphakids	Sundance
Sebastian's Roller Skates	M	RF	250+	de DTu Prats, Joan	Kane/Miller Book Publishers
Secession: The Southern States Leave the Union	V	I	250+	Let Freedom Ring	Red Brick Learning
Second Birthday, A	L	I	250+	Greetings	Rigby
Second Chance	N	RF	250+	Kroll, Stephen	Avon Books
Second Chance, A	M	RF	250+	Rigby Flying Colors	Rigby
Second Grade - Friends Again!	M	RF	250+	Cohen, Miriam	Scholastic
Second Mrs. Giaconda, The	T	HF	250+	Konigsburg, E. L.	Language for Learning Assoc.
Second Story Sally	N	RF	250+	Supa Doopers	Sundance
Second Summer of the Sisterhood, The	Z+	RF	250+	Pearson, Mary E	Harcourt Trade
Second-Grade Friends	M	RF	250+	Cohen, Miriam	Scholastic
Second-Grade Star	N	RF	250+	Alberts, Nancy	Scholastic
Secondhand Sneakers, The	M	F	250+	Literacy by Design	Rigby
Secondhand Star	L	RF	250+	Macdonald, Maryann	Hyperion
Secret	G	RF	114	Instant Readers	Harcourt School Publishers
Secret Agent Dog	N	F	250+	Martha Speaks	Houghton Mifflin Harcourt
Secret Agent Heroes	N	RF	250+	Boyz Rule!	Mondo Publishing
Secret Agent, The	Z	RF	12501	Dominoes three	Oxford University Press
^Secret American History: From Witch Trials to Internment Camps	Y	I	250+	Secret America	Capstone Press
^Secret American People: From Secret Societies to Secret Agents	Y	I	250+	Secret America	Capstone Press

TITLE	LEVEL	GENRE	WORD COUNT	AUTHOR / SERIES	PUBLISHER / DISTRIBUTOR
^Secret American Places: From UFO Crash Sites to Government Hideouts	T	I	250+	Secret America	Capstone Press
^Secret American Treasures: From Hidden Vaults to Sunken Riches	T	I	250+	Secret America	Capstone Press
Secret at the Polk Street School, The	M	RF	250+	Giff, Patricia Reilly	Bantam Books
Secret Camera, A	Q	RF	250+	Tristars	Richard C. Owen
Secret Cave, The	I	RF	250+	PM Plus Story Books	Rigby
Secret Circus, The	I	F	111	Wright, Johanna	Roaring Brook Press
Secret Club, The	L	RF	250+	Go Girl!	Feiwel and Friends
Secret Code, The	G	RF	69	Rookie Readers	Children's Press
Secret Cupbaord, The	O	F	250+	Tristars	Richard C. Owen
Secret Fishing Gear, The	K	RF	508	Springboard	Wright Group/McGraw Hill
Secret Friend, The	E	RF	196	Little Celebrations	Pearson Learning Group
Secret Friend, The	E	RF	189	Little Readers	Houghton Mifflin Harcourt
Secret Garden, The	U	RF	250+	Burnett, Frances H.	Scholastic
Secret Garden, The	U	RF	10715	Oxford Bookworms Library	Oxford University Press
Secret Garden, The (Abridged)	S	RF	12000	Hear It Read It	Sourcebooks
#Secret Ghost, The: A Mystery with Distance and Measurement	P	RF	2597	Manga Math Mysteries	Graphic Universe
Secret Hideaway, The	K	RF	618	PM Collection	Rigby
Secret History of Giants or the Codex Giganticum, The	Y	F	250+	Berk, Ari	Candlewick Press
Secret Inside the Log, The	J	RF	361	Leveled Readers	Houghton Mifflin Harcourt
Secret Inside the Log, The	J	RF	361	Leveled Readers/CA	Houghton Mifflin Harcourt
Secret Land of the Past	N	F	250+	Schlein, Miriam	Scholastic
Secret Language of Girls, The	V	RF	250+	Dowell, Frances O'Roark	Aladdin Paperbacks
Secret Life of Amanda K. Woods, The	T	RF	250+	Cameron, Ann	Scholastic
Secret Life of Trees, The	M	I	250+	DK Readers	DK Publishing
Secret Lives of Mr. and Mrs. Smith, The	K	F	395	Sunshine	Wright Group/McGraw Hill
Secret Lunch Special, The (2nd-Grade Friends)	L	RF	250+	Catalanotto, Peter & Schembri, Pamela	Henry Holt & Co.
Secret Message, The	E	RF	68	Literacy Tree	Rigby
Secret Message, The	J	RF	427	PM Math Readers	Rigby
Secret Missions	U	I	250+	Connectors	Pacific Learning
Secret Notes	G	RF	214	Sun Sprouts	ETA/Cuisenaire
Secret of Bunratty Castle, The	Q	F	250+	Action Packs	Rigby
Secret of Cacklefur Castle, The	O	F	250+	Stilton, Geronimo	Scholastic
Secret of Foghorn Island, The	L	F	250+	Step into Reading	Random House
Secret of Iguando, The	V	F	250+	Bookshop	Mondo Publishing
Secret of Kiribu Tapu Lagoon, The	S	I	250+	Literacy 2000	Rigby
Secret of NIMH, The	V	F	250+	O'Brien, Robert C.	Scholastic
Secret of Robber's Cave, The	Q	RF	250+	Gregory, Kristiana	Scholastic
Secret of Sarah Revere, The	X	HF	250+	Rinaldi, Ann	Harcourt
Secret of Silk, The	K	I	234	Rigby Focus	Rigby
Secret of Spooky House, The	J	F	352	Sunshine	Wright Group/McGraw Hill
Secret of the Circle-K Cave, The	L	RF	1444	Science Solves It!	Kane Press
Secret of the Flying Cows, The	O	RF	250+	Klooz	Stone Arch Books
Secret of the Monster Book, The	M	F	250+	Woodland Mysteries	Wright Group/McGraw Hill
Secret of the Old Oak Trunk, The	M	F	250+	Woodland Mysteries	Wright Group/McGraw Hill
Secret of the Sacred Temple, The	P	SF	250+	Secret Agent Jack Stalwart	Weinstein Books
Secret of the Seal, The	P	RF	250+	Davis, Deborah	Alfred A. Knopf
Secret of the Silver Shoes, The	Q	F	250+	Massie, Elizabeth	Steck-Vaughn
Secret of the Song, The	M	F	250+	Woodland Mysteries	Wright Group/McGraw Hill
Secret of the Stone House, The	T	F	250+	From Many Peoples	Fitzhenry & Whiteside

* Collection of short stories   # Graphic text
^ Mature content with lower level text demands

TITLE	LEVEL	GENRE	WORD COUNT	AUTHOR / SERIES	PUBLISHER / DISTRIBUTOR
Secret of the Three Treasures	Q	RF	250+	Simner, Janni Lee	Holiday House
#Secret of the Unicorn, The	U	F	250+	The Adventures of Tintin	Little Brown and Company
Secret of Zoom, The	U	F	250+	Jonell, Lynne	Henry Holt & Co.
Secret Olivia Told Me, The	J	RF	257	Joy, N.	Just Us Books
Secret on the Wall, The	S	HF	250+	Power Up!	Steck-Vaughn
Secret Recipe	I	I	182	Sun Sprouts	ETA/Cuisenaire
^Secret Room, The	T	F	250+	Townson, H.	Stone Arch Books
Secret Scars	Z	I	250+	What's the Issue?	Compass Point Books
Secret School, The	T	HF	250+	Avi	Harcourt, Inc.
#Secret Science Alliance and the Copycat Crook, The	U	RF	250+	Davis, Eleanor	Bloomsbury Children's Books
#Secret Scooter	K	RF	292	My 1st Graphic Novel	Stone Arch Books
Secret Secret Passage, The	P	RF	250+	Parker, A. E.	Scholastic
Secret Signs	O	RF	250+	Orca Young Readers	Orca Books
Secret Silver Lining, A	Q	RF	250+	Ragged Island Mysteries	Wright Group/McGraw Hill
Secret So Special, A	N	RF	250+	Sails	Rigby
Secret Soccer Ball Maker, The	G	RF	191	Take Two Books	Wright Group/McGraw Hill
Secret Soldier, The	R	TL	250+	WorldScapes	ETA/Cuisenaire
Secret Soldier, The: The Story of Deborah Sampson	O	B	250+	McGovern, Ann	Scholastic
Secret Soup	E	RF	51	Literacy 2000	Rigby
Secret Under the Tree, The (The Adventures of Benny and Watch)	J	RF	250+	Warner, Gertrude Chandler	Albert Whitman & Co.
Secret Valentine	G	F	223	First Start	Troll Associates
Secret Valley, The	O	HF	250+	Bulla, Clyde Robert	Scholastic
Secret Water, The	L	TL	250+	Liu, Daphne	Hampton Brown
Secret World of Spies, The	R	I	250+	Scooters	ETA/Cuisenaire
Secret World of Walter Anderson, The	S	B	250+	Bass, Hester	Candlewick Press
Secret, The	N	RF	250+	PM Collection	Rigby
Secret, The	K	TL	250+	Rigby Star Plus	Rigby
Secret, The: A Traditional Tale From Wales	K	TL	250+	Rigby Literacy	Rigby
^Secrets and Lies	W	SF	250+	The Extraordinary Files	Hameray Publishing Group
Secrets in the Fire	Z	HF	250+	Mankell, Henning	Annick Press
Secrets in the Sea	O	I	798	Vocabulary Readers	Houghton Mifflin Harcourt
Secrets in the Sea	O	I	798	Vocabulary Readers/CA	Houghton Mifflin Harcourt
Secrets in the Shadows	Z+	RF	250+	Brashares, Ann	Random House
Secrets of Coral Reefs, The	U	I	250+	Jean-Michel Cousteau Presents	London Town Press
Secrets of Dripping Fang Book One: The Onts	S	F	250+	Greenburg, Dan	Harcourt, Inc.
Secrets of Greymoor	S	HF	250+	Clark, Clara Gillow	Candlewick Press
Secrets of Kelp Forests, The	U	I	250+	Jean-Michel Cousteau Presents	London Town Press
Secrets of My Hollywood Life	Y	RF	250+	Calonita, Jen	Little Brown and Company
Secrets of Rapa Nui, The	Z	I	2362	Leveled Readers	Houghton Mifflin Harcourt
Secrets of the Cicada Summer	T	RF	250+	Beaty, Andrea	Amulet Books
Secrets of the Clan: Warriors	U	F	250+	Hunter, Erin	HarperCollins
Secrets of the Desert	Q	I	250+	Literacy 2000	Rigby
Secrets of the Fun Park	O	I	250+	Home Connection Collection	Rigby
Secrets of the Mummies	W	I	250+	DK Readers	DK Publishing
Secrets of the Rain Forest	O	I	250+	Myers, Edward	Pearson Learning Group
Secrets of the Seahorse	H	I	228	In Step Readers	Rigby
Secrets of the Shipwreck, The	Q	RF	250+	Reading Safari	Mondo Publishing
Secrets of the Sirens	W	F	250+	Golding, Julia	Marshall Cavendish
Secrets of the Sky	U	I	250+	InfoQuest	Rigby
Secrets of Tidepools, The	U	I	250+	Jean-Michel Cousteau Presents	London Town Press
Secrets of Tropical Rainforests, The	U	I	250+	Wild Life Series	London Town Press

S

TITLE	LEVEL	GENRE	WORD COUNT	AUTHOR / SERIES	PUBLISHER / DISTRIBUTOR
Secrets, Lies, Gizmos, and Spies: A History of Spies and Espionage	Z	I	250+	Coleman, Janet Wyman	Harry N. Abrams
Sector 7	WB	F	0	Wiesner, David	Clarion
Security Guards	M	I	250+	Community Helpers	Red Brick Learning
^Sedimentary Rocks	Q	I	250+	On Deck	Rigby
See a Tiger	C	F	34	Zoozoo-Into the Wild	Cavallo Publishing
See for Your Self	O	B	250+	Meet the Author	Richard C. Owen
See How It Grows	C	I	34	Learn to Read	Creative Teaching Press
See How They Run: Campaign Dreams, Election Schemes, and the Race to the White House	U	I	250+	Goodman, Susan E.	Bloomsbury Children's Books
See Me	WB	I	0	Vocabulary Readers	Houghton Mifflin Harcourt
See Me Play	D	F	79	Black, Laura	Harcourt
See Me Reading	D	RF	35	Ray's Readers	Outside the Box
See Me Ride	B	F	56	Red Rocket Readers	Flying Start Books
See Me Work	B	I	71	Literacy by Design	Rigby
See No Evil	Z+	RF	250+	Gavin, Jamila	Farrar, Straus, & Giroux
^See No Evil	Y	RF	250+	Orca Currents	Orca Books
See Our Show	C	RF	38	Rigby Focus	Rigby
See the Animals	A	I	24	Animals	American Reading Company
See the Boats Go!	D	RF	42	Windows on Literacy	National Geographic
See the Firefighter	A	I	23	Avenues	Hampton Brown
See the Horse	A	I	27	Animals	American Reading Company
See the Ocean	B	RF	26	Science	Outside the Box
See the Seasons	B	I	16	Instant Readers	Harcourt School Publishers
See the Shapes	B	I	37	Rigby Focus	Rigby
See the Trees	D	I	108	Vocabulary Readers	Houghton Mifflin Harcourt
See the Trees	D	I	108	Vocabulary Readers/CA	Houghton Mifflin Harcourt
See the U.S.A.	M	I	250+	Windows on Literacy	National Geographic
See the Wind Blow	E	I	105	Early Connections	Benchmark Education
See the Yak Yak	J	F	88	Step into Reading	Random House
See You in Second Grade	J	RF	250+	Cohen, Miriam	Bantam Books
See You in Spring	H	F	293	Early Explorers	Benchmark Education
See You Later, Gladiator	P	F	250+	Scieszka, Jon	Penguin Group
See You Tomorrow, Charles	J	RF	250+	Cohen, Miriam	Bantam Books
Seed for Sid, A	E	F	131	Leveled Readers	Houghton Mifflin Harcourt
Seed for Sid, A	E	F	131	Leveled Readers/CA	Houghton Mifflin Harcourt
Seed for Sid, A	E	F	131	Leveled Readers/TX	Houghton Mifflin Harcourt
Seed is a Promise, A	O	I	250+	Merrill, Claire	Scholastic
Seed Needs Help, A	G	I	140	Early Explorers	Benchmark Education
Seed Song, The	E	I	41	Learn to Read	Creative Teaching Press
Seed Surprise	E	RF	67	Seedlings	Continental Press
Seed Vault, The	U	I	5895	A Great Idea	Norwood House Press
#Seed, Sprout, Fruit: An Apple Tree Life Cycle	N	I	250+	First Graphics	Capstone Press
Seed, The	D	I	51	Sunshine	Wright Group/McGraw Hill
Seed, The	LB	I	14	Wonder World	Wright Group/McGraw Hill
*Seedfolks	W	RF	250+	Fleischman, Paul	HarperTrophy
Seeds	B	I	30	Avenues	Hampton Brown
Seeds	E	I	30	Parts of Plants	Lerner Publishing Group
Seeds	J	I	210	Pebble Books	Capstone Press
Seeds	H	I	124	Plant Parts	Capstone Press
Seeds	I	I	351	Rigby Flying Colors	Rigby
Seeds	B	I	30	Rise & Shine	Hampton Brown
Seeds	K	I	250+	Sunshine	Wright Group/McGraw Hill

* Collection of short stories   # Graphic text
^ Mature content with lower level text demands

S

TITLE	LEVEL	GENRE	WORD COUNT	AUTHOR / SERIES	PUBLISHER / DISTRIBUTOR
Seeds and Plants	H	I	173	Dominie Factivity Series	Pearson Learning Group
Seeds Go, Seeds Grow	L	I	250+	Science Starts	Capstone Press
Seeds Grow	I	I	90	Sunshine	Wright Group/McGraw Hill
Seeds Grow Into Plants	G	I	78	Windows on Literacy	National Geographic
Seeds On the Move	H	I	113	Explorations	Okapi Educational Materials
Seeds On the Move	H	I	113	Explorations	Eleanor Curtain Publishing
Seeds We Eat	B	I	26	Bonnell, Kris/About	Reading Reading Books
Seeds, Seeds, Seeds	E	I	96	Sunshine	Wright Group/McGraw Hill
Seeing	K	I	149	Pebble Books	Capstone Press
Seeing	E	I	79	Senses	Lerner Publishing Group
Seeing	M	I	250+	The Senses	Capstone Press
Seeing and Hearing Well	M	I	674	Pull Ahead Books	Lerner Publishing Group
Seeing Earth from Space	Y	I	250+	Lauber, Patricia	Scholastic
Seeing Eye to Eye	U	I	250+	Power Up!	Steck-Vaughn
Seeing Is Believing	K	I	320	Yellow Umbrella Books	Red Brick Learning
Seeing Is Not Believing	U	I	250+	iOpeners	Pearson Learning Group
Seeing Sayings	N	RF	866	Leveled Readers	Houghton Mifflin Harcourt
Seeing Sayings	N	RF	866	Leveled Readers/CA	Houghton Mifflin Harcourt
Seeing Sayings	N	RF	866	Leveled Readers/TX	Houghton Mifflin Harcourt
Seeing Stars	L	RF	801	Leveled Readers	Houghton Mifflin Harcourt
Seeing Stars	L	RF	801	Leveled Readers/CA	Houghton Mifflin Harcourt
Seeing Stone, The	Y	F	250+	Crossley-Holland, Kevin	Scholastic
Seeing the Circle	O	B	250+	Meet The Author	Richard C. Owen
Seeing the School Doctor	K	RF	167	City Kids	Rigby
Seeing the Sky	M	RF	250+	Windows on Literacy	National Geographic
Seeing Things Up Close	F	I	72	Windows on Literacy	National Geographic
Seeing with Heat	R	I	436	Independent Readers Science	Houghton Mifflin Harcourt
Seekers of Truth	U	B	250+	Real Lives	Troll Associates
Seeking Freedom	Y	I	2207	Leveled Readers	Houghton Mifflin Harcourt
Seeking Freedom	Y	I	2207	Leveled Readers/CA	Houghton Mifflin Harcourt
Seeking Freedom	Y	I	2207	Leveled Readers/TX	Houghton Mifflin Harcourt
Seems, The: The Glitch in Sleep	V	F	250+	Hulme, John & Wexler, Michael	Bloomsbury Children's Books
Sees Behind Trees	T	HF	250+	Dorris, Michael	Language for Learning Assoc.
Seesaw, The	C	RF	100	Emergent	Pioneer Valley
Seesaw, The	C	F	46	Voyages	SRA/McGraw Hill
See-saw, The	A	F	24	Big Cat	Pacific Learning
See-Saw, The	D	RF	87	Storyworlds	Heinemann
Seiko the Watchdog	M	F	250+	Storyteller Summer Skies	Wright Group/McGraw Hill
Selchie's Seed, The	W	F	250+	Oppenheim, Shulamith Levey	Harcourt Brace
Selena Who Speaks in Silence	J	RF	311	Evangeline Nicholas Collection	Wright Group/McGraw Hill
Self Portrait	O	B	250+	Meet the Author	Richard C. Owen
Self-Control: Self-Control	K	RF	2582	Salerno, Tony Character Classics	Character Building Company
Self-Discipline	N	I	250+	Character Education	Red Brick Learning
Self-Discipline	M	I	250+	Everyday Character Education	Capstone Press
Selfish Dog, The	D	F	109	Storyworlds	Heinemann
Selfish Giant, The	L	F	250+	Literacy 2000	Rigby
Selfish, Giant, The	L	TL	250+	Storybook Classics	Picture Window Books
^Self-Propelled Howitzers: The M109A6 Paladins	T	I	250+	War Machines	Capstone Press
Self-Respect	M	I	250+	Character Education	Red Brick Learning
Selling Things	A	I	20	Leveled Readers	Houghton Mifflin Harcourt
Selling Things	A	I	20	Leveled Readers/CA	Houghton Mifflin Harcourt

S

TITLE	LEVEL	GENRE	WORD COUNT	AUTHOR / SERIES	PUBLISHER / DISTRIBUTOR
Selma Burke: Artist	N	B	250+	Beginning Biographies	Pearson Learning Group
Selu and Kana Ti	K	TL	250+	Folk Tales	Mondo Publishing
Seminole Indians, The	P	I	250+	Native Peoples	Red Brick Learning
Seminole, The	R	I	250+	First Reports	Compass Point Books
Seminole, The: Patchworkers of the Everglades	R	I	250+	America's First Peoples	Capstone Press
Seminoles, The	T	I	4470	Native American Histoies	Lerner Publishing Group
Semitrucks	M	I	250+	Horsepower	Capstone Press
Semitrucks	H	I	114	Mighty Machines	Capstone Press
Semitrucks in Actions	M	I	250+	Transportation Zone	Capstone Press
Send a Message	L	I	236	Discovery Links	Newbridge
Send Me a Message	J	I	173	Dominie Factivity Series	Pearson Learning Group
Send Me Down a Miracle	X	RF	250+	Nolan, Han	Harcourt, Inc.
Sending Messages	B	I	49	Wonder World	Wright Group/McGraw Hill
Sending of Dragons, A	X	F	250+	Yolen, Jane	Harcourt, Inc.
Sending Signals	H	I	163	Literacy Tree	Rigby
Seneca Chief, Army General: A Story about Ely Parker	S	B	8687	Creative Minds Biographies	Lerner Publishing Group
Senor Armadillo Goes to Town	F	F	116	Joy Starters	Pearson Learning Group
Senor Armadillo's Car	F	F	113	Joy Starters	Pearson Learning Group
Senor Armadillo's Letter	E	F	156	Joy Starters	Pearson Learning Group
Senor Armadillo's Shoes	F	F	188	Joy Starters	Pearson Learning Group
Senor Felipe's Alphabet Adventure: El Alfabeto Espanol	L	F	250+	Vargo, Sharon Hawkins	Millbrook Press
Sensational Seasons	Q	I	705	Reading Street	Pearson
Sensational!	O	I	250+	Bookweb	Rigby
Sense of Place, A	Q	I	250+	Orbit Collections	Pacific Learning
Sense of Taste, The	O	I	250+	A True Book	Children's Press
Senses	E	I	66	Voyages	SRA/McGraw Hill
Senses at the Seashore	I	I	123	Shelley Rotner's Early Childhood Library	Millbrook Press
Senses in the City	I	I	152	Shelley Rotner's Early Childhood Library	Millbrook Press
Senses on the Farm	I	I	178	Shelley Rotner's Early Childhood Library	Millbrook Press
Senses, The	F	I	24	Windows on Literacy	National Geographic
Separate Ways	L	RF	833	PM Plus Story Books	Rigby
Separate Worlds	Q	I	858	Vocabulary Readers	Houghton Mifflin Harcourt
Separate Worlds	Q	I	858	Vocabulary Readers/CA	Houghton Mifflin Harcourt
Separate Worlds	Q	I	858	Vocabulary Readers/TX	Houghton Mifflin Harcourt
September 11, 2001	U	I	250+	Cornerstones of Freedom	Children's Press
September 11, 2001 Attack on New York City	Z	I	250+	Hampton, Wilborn	Candlewick Press
September 11, 2001: Attack on New York City	Z	I	250+	Edge	Hampton Brown
September Sisters, The	Z	RF	250+	Cantor, Jillian	HarperCollins
Sequoyah	S	B	3594	History Maker Bios	Lerner Publishing Group
Sequoyah	O	B	865	Leveled Readers Social Studies	Houghton Mifflin Harcourt
Sequoyah	Q	B	1340	Vocabulary Readers	Houghton Mifflin Harcourt
Sequoyah	Q	B	1340	Vocabulary Readers/CA	Houghton Mifflin Harcourt
Sequoyah, Cherokee Leader	N	B	826	Leveled Readers Language Support	Houghton Mifflin Harcourt
Serena and Venus Williams	T	B	250+	Sports Heroes	Red Brick Learning
Sergio Makes a Splash!	J	F	250+	Rodriguez, Edel	Little Brown and Company
Sergio Saves the Game!	J	F	250+	Rodriguez, Edel	Little Brown and Company
Serpent on My Skin	O	F	250+	The Adventures of Sam X	Stone Arch Books
Serpent's Children, The	W	HF	250+	Yep, Laurence	HarperTrophy

S

* Collection of short stories   # Graphic text
^ Mature content with lower level text demands

TITLE	LEVEL	GENRE	WORD COUNT	AUTHOR / SERIES	PUBLISHER / DISTRIBUTOR
Servant and the Water Princess, The: A Story of Ancient India	O	HF	250+	Historical Tales	Picture Window Books
Server	E	I	28	Work People Do	Lerner Publishing Group
Serves Two Hundred	S	RF	2585	Leveled Readers	Houghton Mifflin Harcourt
Serves Two Hundred	S	RF	2585	Leveled Readers/CA	Houghton Mifflin Harcourt
Serves Two Hundred	S	RF	2585	Leveled Readers/TX	Houghton Mifflin Harcourt
Serving the Community	K	I	250+	Windows on Literacy	National Geographic
Set in Stone	L	I	250+	Yellow Umbrella Books	Red Brick Learning
Sets in Nature	F	I	132	Red Rocket Readers	Flying Start Books
Sets of Picture Cards	J	RF	260	PM Math Readers	Rigby
Sets: Sorting into Groups	L	I	250+	Exploring Math	Capstone Press
Setting the Table	A	I	32	Leveled Literacy Intervention/ Orange System	Heinemann
Seven	H	RF	131	Early Connections	Benchmark Education
Seven Big Bubbles	F	RF	94	Gear Up!	Wright Group/McGraw Hill
Seven Blind Mice	K	TL	250+	Young, Ed	Puffin Books
Seven Chinese Brothers, The	P	TL	250+	Mahy, Margaret	Scholastic
Seven Continents	L	I	202	Windows on Literacy	National Geographic
Seven Continents, The	M	I	250+	Rigby Star Quest	Rigby
Seven Cool Cats	F	F	97	Seedlings	Continental Press
*Seven Fables, Seven Truths	R	TL	250+	Pair-It Books	Steck-Vaughn
Seven Fat Cats	G	F	152	The Story Basket	Wright Group/McGraw Hill
Seven Fathers	P	TL	250+	Ramsden, Ashley	Roaring Brook Press
Seven Foolish Fishermen	K	TL	250+	PM Tales and Plays-Gold	Rigby
Seven in a Line	F	I	138	PM Math Readers	Rigby
Seven Is a Lucky Number	H	RF	194	Dominie Factivity Series	Pearson Publishing Group
Seven Kisses in a Row	O	RF	250+	MacLachlan, Patricia	HarperCollins
Seven Little Bunnies	I	F	255	Stiegemeyer, Julie	Marshall Cavendish
Seven Little Ducks	F	TL	190	PM Readalongs	Rigby
Seven Little Kids, The	G	TL	363	Folk Tales	Pioneer Valley
Seven Little Monsters	H	F	55	Sendak, Maurice	HarperCollins
Seven Natural Wonders of Africa	U	I	9306	Seven Wonders	Lerner Publishing Group
Seven Natural Wonders of Asia and the Middle East	U	I	250+	Seven Wonders	Lerner Publishing Group
Seven Natural Wonders of Australia and Oceania	V	I	12126	Seven Wonders	Lerner Publishing Group
Seven Natural Wonders of Central and South America	V	I	9103	Seven Wonders	Lerner Publishing Group
Seven Natural Wonders of Europe	U	I	9658	Seven Wonders	Lerner Publishing Group
Seven Natural Wonders of North America	V	I	10171	Seven Wonders	Lerner Publishing Group
Seven Natural Wonders of the Arctic, Antarctica, and the Oceans	V	I	10035	Seven Wonders	Lerner Publishing Group
Seven Natural Wonders of the World	S	I	250+	Literacy by Design	Rigby
Seven Natural Wonders, The	Q	I	250+	Navigators Social Studies Series	Benchmark Education
Seven Serpents Trilogy, The	Y	HF	130000	O'Dell, Scott	Sourcebooks
Seven Spools of Thread: A Kwanzaa Story	N	TL	250+	Medearis, Angela Shelf	Scholastic
Seven Stones of Sligo	O	TL	250+	PM Collection	Rigby
*Seven Strange and Ghostly Tales	Y	F	250+	Jacques, Brian	Penguin Group
Seven Treasure Hunts, The	M	RF	250+	Byars, Betsy	HarperTrophy
Seventh Grade Weirdo	S	RF	250+	Wardlaw, Lee	Scholastic
Seventh Tower, The: The Fall	W	F	250+	Nix, Garth	Scholastic
^Sewer Rats	V	RF	250+	Orca Currents	Orca Books
Sewers and the Rats That Love Them: The Disgusting Story Behind Where It All Goes	S	I	250+	Sanitation Investigation	Capstone Press
Sewing Machine, The	Q	I	250+	Great Inventions	Capstone Press

S

TITLE	LEVEL	GENRE	WORD COUNT	AUTHOR / SERIES	PUBLISHER / DISTRIBUTOR
Sex Smarts: You and Your Sexuality	Z+	I	250+	What's the Issue?	Compass Point Books
Shabanu: Daughter of the Wind	Z	RF	250+	Staples, Suzanne Fisher	Random House
Shackleton Expedition, The	S	I	250+	Fine, Jil	Children's Press
Shades of Gray	W	HF	250+	Reeder, Carolyn	Avon Books
Shadow Dance	D	RF	66	Little Celebrations	Pearson Learning Group
#Shadow Door, The: Book One	S	F	3789	The Elsewhere Chronicles	Lerner Publishing Group
Shadow in the Dark, The	W	F	250+	Dark Man	Ransom Publishing
Shadow of a Bull	U	RF	250+	Wojciechowska, Maia	Simon & Schuster
Shadow of a Doubt	Z	RF	250+	Rottman, S.L.	Peachtree
Shadow of Malabrow, The: The Perilous Realm	X	F	250+	Wharton, Thomas	Candlewick Press
Shadow of the Wolf	N	I	250+	Whelan, Gloria	Random House
Shadow Over Second	M	RF	250+	Christopher, Matt	Little Brown and Company
Shadow Play	WB	I	0	Windows on Literacy	National Geographic
Shadow Puppets	H	I	163	Alphakids	Sundance
Shadow Puppets	K	I	236	Rigby Focus	Rigby
#Shadow Spies, The: Book Two	S	F	2666	The Elsewhere Chronicles	Lerner Publishing Group
Shadow Thieves, The	X	F	250+	Ursu, Anne	Aladdin Paperbacks
Shadow, The	WB	F	0	Diamond, Donna	Candlewick Press
Shadow: The Puppy Place	N	RF	250+	Miles, Ellen	Scholastic
Shadows	A	I	52	Getting Around	American Reading Company
Shadows	F	I	110	Independent Readers Science	Houghton Mifflin Harcourt
Shadows	G	F	95	Joy Starters	Pearson Learning Group
Shadows	D	RF	35	Literacy 2000	Rigby
Shadows	J	I	250+	Otto, Carolyn B.	Scholastic
Shadows	E	RF	190	Visions	Wright Group/McGraw Hill
Shadows	F	I	130	Wonder World	Wright Group/McGraw Hill
*Shadows & Moonshine	V	TL	250+	Aiken, Joan	David R. Godine
Shadows and Shade	J	I	250+	Explorations	Eleanor Curtain Publishing
Shadows and Shade	J	I	250+	Explorations	Okapi Educational Materials
Shadows on the Wall	G	I	183	Red Rocket Readers	Flying Start Books
Shadows, The (The Books of Elsewhere)	T	F	250+	West, Jacqueline	Dial/Penguin
*Shady Deal, The: Tales of Cleverness and Cunning	Q	TL	250+	Literacy 2000	Rigby
Shag Goes Fishing, The	E	RF	51	Ready to Read	Pacific Learning
Shaggy	C	RF	23	Windows on Literacy	National Geographic
Shaggy Sheep, The	J	RF	301	Wonders	Hampton Brown
Shaggy the Sheep	I	RF	407	Red Rocket Readers	Flying Start Books
Shaji in New York	T	RF	1906	Leveled Readers	Houghton Mifflin Harcourt
Shake Rattle and Roll	U	I	250+	Rigby Literacy	Rigby
Shake, Rumble, and Roll	Q	I	250+	InfoQuest	Rigby
Shakespeare Makes the Playoffs	W	RF	250+	Koertge, Ron	Candlewick Press
Shakespeare Stealer, The	X	HF	250+	Blackwood, Gary	Scholastic
Shakespeare's Secret	T	RF	250+	Broach, Elise	Henry Holt & Co.
Shall I Knit You a Hat?	L	F	250+	Klise, Kate	Square Fish
Shall We Dance?	L	I	250+	The Rowland Reading Program Library	Rowland Reading Foundation
Shamus	J	F	386	Sails	Rigby
Shane	V	HF	250+	Schaefer, Jack	Random House
Shane and Ned	E	F	52	Windmill Books	Rigby
Shanghai Shadows	Z	HF	250+	Ruby, Lois	Holiday House
Shannon and the World's Tallest Leprechaun	M	F	250+	Callahan, Sean	Albert Whitman & Co.
Shannon the Ocean Fairy: Rainbow Magic	L	F	250+	Meadows, Daisy	Scholastic
Shante Keys and the New Year's Peas	L	RF	250+	Piernas-Davenport, Gail	Albert Whitman & Co.
Shape Explorers, The	P	RF	250+	In Step Readers	Rigby

S

Organized Alphabetically by Title
Storable Database at www.fountasandpinnellleveledbooks.com

* Collection of short stories   # Graphic text
^ Mature content with lower level text demands

TITLE	LEVEL	GENRE	WORD COUNT	AUTHOR / SERIES	PUBLISHER / DISTRIBUTOR
Shape in the Dark, The: A Story of Hadrian's Wall	Z	HF	2603	Leveled Readers	Houghton Mifflin Harcourt
Shape Maker, The	A	RF	24	Harry's Math Books	Outside the Box
Shape of Things, The	I	I	140	Dodds, Dayle Ann	Candlewick Press
Shape of Things, The	K	I	124	Spyglass Books	Compass Point Books
Shape Parade	B	F	23	Gear Up!	Wright Group/McGraw Hill
Shape Search	H	I	260	InfoTrek	ETA/Cuisenaire
Shape Story, A	D	RF	56	Seedlings	Continental Press
Shape Walk	C	RF	25	Little Celebrations	Pearson Learning Group
Shapes	J	I	196	Beginning to Learn About	Steck-Vaughn
Shapes	LB	I	12	Big Cat	Pacific Learning
Shapes	D	I	98	Carousel Readers	Pearson Learning Group
Shapes	B	I	19	Discovery World	Rigby
Shapes	B	I	40	Early Connections	Benchmark Education
Shapes	B	I	64	On Our Way to English	Rigby
Shapes	C	I	30	Rise & Shine	Hampton Brown
Shapes	B	I	29	Shutterbug Books	Steck-Vaughn
Shapes	A	I	16	Time for Kids	Teacher Created Materials
Shapes	A	I	24	Urmston, Kathleen; Evans, Karen	Kaeden Books
Shapes	C	I	31	Visions	Wright Group/McGraw Hill
Shapes	G	I	42	Windows on Literacy	National Geographic
Shapes and Solids	K	I	237	Early Explorers	Benchmark Education
Shapes and Solids Outdoors	N	I	348	Early Explorers	Benchmark Education
Shapes Around the World	M	I	250+	On Our Way to English	Rigby
Shapes at My House	H	I	203	Early Explorers	Benchmark Education
Shapes at the Beach	D	I	46	Rosen Real Readers	Rosen Publishing Group
Shapes at the Mall	B	I	41	InfoTrek	ETA/Cuisenaire
Shapes Everywhere	E	I	82	Early Connections	Benchmark Education
Shapes in Music	H	I	154	Spot the Shape	Heinemann Library
Shapes in My World	D	I	47	Visions	Wright Group/McGraw Hill
Shapes in Sports	H	I	132	Spot the Shape	Heinemann Library
Shapes in the City	K	I	191	Twig	Wright Group/McGraw Hill
Shapes in the Kitchen	F	I	117	Math Around Us	Heinemann Library
Shapes in the Sky: A Book About Clouds	M	I	250+	Amazing Science	Picture Window Books
Shapes of Water, The: Stories About Patterns and Shapes	N	I	250+	Orbit Chapter Books	Pacific Learning
Shapes on the Seashore	B	I	30	Big Cat	Pacific Learning
Shapes with a Rope	F	I	153	PM Math Readers	Rigby
Shapes, Shapes, All Over the Place	E	I	127	Dominie Readers	Pearson Learning Group
Shapes: Discovering Flats and Solids	L	I	250+	Exploring Math	Capstone Press
Shaping Earth's Surface	R	I	1811	Science Support Readers	Houghton Mifflin Harcourt
Shaping of the Continents, The	V	I	2960	Reading Street	Pearson
Shaping the Constitution	T	I	250+	Navigators Social Studies Series	Benchmark Education
Shaping the Earth	L	I	233	Rigby Focus	Rigby
Shaquille O'Neal: Revised Edition	P	B	1854	Amazing Atheles	Lerner Publishing Group
Shar	D	RF	113	Sails	Rigby
Share and Take Turns	K	I	263	Learning to Get Along	Free Spirit Publishing
Share Bear	D	F	96	Sun Sprouts	ETA/Cuisenaire
Sharing	C	RF	33	Harry's Math Books	Outside the Box
Sharing	C	I	107	Leveled Readers	Houghton Mifflin Harcourt
Sharing	C	I	107	Leveled Readers/CA	Houghton Mifflin Harcourt
Sharing	C	I	107	Leveled Readers/TX	Houghton Mifflin Harcourt
Sharing	C	RF	24	Literacy 2000	Rigby
Sharing a Dream	O	B	913	Leveled Readers	Houghton Mifflin Harcourt

S

* Collection of short stories   # Graphic text
^ Mature content with lower level text demands

TITLE	LEVEL	GENRE	WORD COUNT	AUTHOR / SERIES	PUBLISHER / DISTRIBUTOR
Sharing a Dream	O	B	913	Leveled Readers/CA	Houghton Mifflin Harcourt
Sharing a Dream	O	B	913	Leveled Readers/TX	Houghton Mifflin Harcourt
Sharing a Pizza	H	I	94	Windows on Literacy	National Geographic
Sharing a Room	K	RF	425	Gear Up!	Wright Group/McGraw Hill
Sharing Danny's Dad	G	RF	89	Little Celebrations	Pearson Learning Group
Sharing Homes	D	I	41	Hiris, Monica	Kaeden Books
Sharing Our Stories	J	I	474	Early Explorers	Benchmark Education
Sharing Snowy	M	RF	250+	Orca Echoes	Orca Books
Sharing Time	D	RF	113	Carousel Readers	Pearson Learning Group
Shark	L	I	250+	A Day in the Life: Sea Animals	Heinemann Library
Shark	W	I	250+	Eyewitness Books	DK Publishing
Shark	B	I	69	Vocabulary Readers	Houghton Mifflin Harcourt
Shark	B	I	69	Vocabulary Readers/CA	Houghton Mifflin Harcourt
Shark	B	I	69	Vocabulary Readers/TX	Houghton Mifflin Harcourt
Shark and Crab	H	TL	238	Red Rocket Readers	Flying Start Books
Shark Attack!	K	I	301	Explorations	Okapi Educational Materials
Shark Attack!	K	I	301	Explorations	Eleanor Curtain Publishing
Shark Attack!: Bethany Hamilton's Story of Survival	S	I	250+	True Tales of Survival	Capstone Press
Shark Girl	O	I	250+	Infotrek Plus	ETA/Cuisenaire
Shark in a Sack	C	F	65	Sunshine	Wright Group/McGraw Hill
Shark in School	N	RF	250+	Giff, Patricia Reilly	Bantam Books
Shark in the Dark	L	F	250+	Bently, Peter	Walker & Company
Shark Lady: The Adventures of Eugenie Clark	O	B	250+	McGovern, Ann	Scholastic
Shark Park	Q	RF	250+	Story Surfers	ETA/Cuisenaire
Shark Tales	R	I	250+	Explorer Books-Pathfinder	National Geographic
Shark Tales	P	I	250+	Explorer Books-Pioneer	National Geographic
Shark Watch	M	I	250+	Michaels, Joel	Worthington Press
Shark with No Teeth, The	J	F	250+	Storyworlds	Heinemann
Shark!	L	I	479	Leveled Readers Science	Houghton Mifflin Harcourt
Shark!: The Truth Behind the Terror	T	I	250+	High Five Reading	Red Brick Learning
Sharks	M	I	1050	Avenues	Hampton Brown
Sharks	N	I	250+	Bookshop	Mondo Publishing
Sharks	O	I	250+	First Reports	Compass Point Books
Sharks	M	I	250+	Gibbons, Gail	Holiday House
Sharks	L	I	250+	Guiberson, Brenda Z.	Scholastic
Sharks	O	I	250+	Holmes, Kevin J.	Red Brick Learning
Sharks	W	I	250+	Kingfisher Knowledge	Kingfisher
Sharks	R	I	1102	Leveled Readers	Houghton Mifflin Harcourt
Sharks	R	I	1102	Leveled Readers/CA	Houghton Mifflin Harcourt
Sharks	R	I	1102	Leveled Readers/TX	Houghton Mifflin Harcourt
Sharks	U	I	3087	Nature Watch	Lerner Publishing Group
Sharks	N	I	519	Pawprints Teal	Pioneer Valley
Sharks	G	I	42	Pebble Books	Red Brick Learning
Sharks	E	I	126	Readlings/ Marine Animals	American Reading Company
Sharks	H	I	155	Ready Readers	Pearson Learning Group
Sharks	M	I	250+	Rigby Rocket	Rigby
Sharks	T	I	250+	Simon, Seymour	HarperTrophy
Sharks	S	I	250+	Story Surfers	ETA/Cuisenaire
Sharks	P	I	250+	Tristars	Richard C. Owen
Sharks	I	I	84	Under the Sea	Capstone Press
Sharks	N	I	250+	Windows on Literacy	National Geographic
Sharks	L	I	238	Wonder World	Wright Group/McGraw Hill
Sharks and Other Dangers of the Deep	N	I	250+	Smart Kids	Priddy Books

* Collection of short stories   # Graphic text
^ Mature content with lower level text demands

S

TITLE	LEVEL	GENRE	WORD COUNT	AUTHOR / SERIES	PUBLISHER / DISTRIBUTOR
Sharks and Rays	Q	I	250+	Explorers	Wright Group/McGraw Hill
Sharks and Rays	L	I	250+	Marine Life For Young Readers	Pearson Learning Group
Sharks Under Attack	S	I	1055	Leveled Readers	Houghton Mifflin Harcourt
Sharks Under Attack	S	I	1055	Leveled Readers/CA	Houghton Mifflin Harcourt
Sharon the Shark	I	F	266	Supersonics	Rigby
Sharon's Shapes	D	RF	35	Windows on Literacy	National Geographic
Shattered Bones: True Survival Stories	Y	I	2825	Powerful Medicine	Lerner Publishing Group
Shattered!: Tragedy and Triumph	Z	I	250+	Boldprint	Steck-Vaughn
Shattering Earthquakes	T	I	250+	Awesome Forces of Nature	Heinemann Library
Shattering, The: Guardians of Ga'Hoole	V	F	250+	Lasky, Kathryn	Scholastic
Shaun White	P	B	1931	Amazing Athletes	Lerner Publishing Group
Shaun White: Revised Edition	P	B	1846	Amazing Athletes	Lerner Publishing Group
Shawl, The	R	RF	250+	Book Blazers	ETA/Cuisenaire
Shawnee, The	R	I	250+	First Reports	Compass Point Books
She Loves You, She Loves You Notà	Z+	RF	250+	Peters, Julie Anne	Little Brown and Company
She Said	C	RF	35	Ready Readers	Pearson Learning Group
She Touched the World:Laura Bridgeman, Deaf Blind Pioneer	W	B	250+	Alexander, Sally Hobart & Robert	Clarion Books
She, The	Z+	RF	250+	Plum-Ucci, Carol	Harcourt, Inc.
Sheeba	L	F	250+	Noonan, Diana	Pearson Learning Group
Sheep	F	I	100	Farm Animals	Lerner Publishing Group
Sheep	R	F	250+	Hobbs, Valerie	Square Fish
Sheep	L	I	250+	PM Animal Facts: Purple	Rigby
Sheep	B	I	34	Zoozoo-Animal World	Cavallo Publishing
Sheep Blast Off!	H	F	149	Shaw, Nancy	Houghton Mifflin Harcourt
Sheep Have Lambs	M	I	250+	Animals and Their Young	Compass Point Books
Sheep in a Jeep	G	F	83	Shaw, Nancy	Houghton Mifflin Harcourt
Sheep on a Ship	G	F	118	Shaw, Nancy	Houghton Mifflin Harcourt
Sheep on the Farm	G	I	66	Pebble Books	Capstone Press
Sheep Out to Eat	H	F	144	Shaw, Nancy	Houghton Mifflin Harcourt
Sheep Sheep Sheep	J	TL	250+	Redhead, Janet Slater	Steck-Vaughn
Sheep Take a Hike	H	F	160	Shaw, Nancy	Houghton Mifflin Harcourt
Sheep Trick or Treat	I	F	210	Shaw, Nancy	Houghton Mifflin Harcourt
Sheepdog in the Snow	Q	RF	250+	Baglio, Ben M.	Scholastic
Sheepdog Max	F	F	171	Sun Sprouts	ETA/Cuisenaire
Sheep's Bell	C	RF	37	Ready Readers	Pearson Learning Group
Sheila Rae, the Brave	K	F	250+	Henkes, Kevin	Scholastic
*Shelf Life	Y	RF	250+	Paulsen, Gary	Simon & Schuster
Shell	W	I	250+	Eyewitness Books	DK Publishing
She'll Be Comin' 'Round the Mountain	M	TL	250+	Sturges, Philemon	Little Brown and Company
She'll Be Coming Around the Mountain	J	TL	250+	Bank Street	Bantam Books
She'll Be Coming Around the Mountain	E	TL	250+	Learn to Read	Creative Teaching Press
She'll Be Coming Around the Mountain	J	TL	250+	Traditional Songs	Picture Window Books
Shell Homes	I	I	163	Sails	Rigby
Shell Shopping	F	RF	145	Ready Readers	Pearson Learning Group
Shell-Flower	S	I	1761	Leveled Readers	Houghton Mifflin Harcourt
Shell-Flower and the Strangers	R	I	250+	Leveled Readers	Houghton Mifflin Harcourt
Shells	E	I	93	Body Coverings	Lerner Publishing Group
Shells	F	I	246	Rigby Flying Colors	Rigby
Shells	A	I	34	Rigby Literacy	Rigby
Shells	E	I	133	Sails	Rigby
Shells	B	I	39	Seedlings	Continental Press
Shelter	I	I	60	Canizares, Susan; Moreton, Daniel	Scholastic

S

TITLE	LEVEL	GENRE	WORD COUNT	AUTHOR / SERIES	PUBLISHER / DISTRIBUTOR
Shelter Dog Blues	N	F	250+	Martha Speaks	Houghton Mifflin Harcourt
Shelter Dogs: Amazing Stories of Adopted Strays	P	I	250+	Kehret, Peg	Albert Whitman & Co.
Shelter from The Wind	Z	RF	250+	Bauer, Marion Dane	Marshall Cavendish
Shep the Sheep of Caladeen	K	F	829	Appleton-Smith, Laura	Flyleaf Publishing
Sheriffs and Deputy Sheriffs	S	I	250+	Law Enforcement	Capstone Press
Sherlock Holmes and the Baker Street Irregulars: The Fall of the Amazing Zalindas	V	HF	250+	Mack, Tracy & Citrin, Michael	Orchard Books
*Sherlock Holmes Short Stories	W	RF	6280	Oxford Bookworms Library	Oxford University Press
Sherlock Holmes: The Case of the Blue Diamond	T	RF	5823	Dominoes one	Oxford University Press
Sherlock Hounds: Our Heroic Search and Rescue Dogs	S	I	250+	Bookshop	Mondo Publishing
Sherman	C	RF	48	Seedlings	Continental Press
Sherman in the Talent Show	H	RF	310	Seedlings	Continental Press
Sherman Shoots . . .	B	RF	16	Ray's Readers	Outside the Box
Sherman's Happy Walk	E	RF	69	Seedlings	Continental Press
Sherman's Lost and Found	G	RF	188	Seedlings	Continental Press
Sherman's Shenanigans	E	RF	52	Seedlings	Continental Press
Sherpa Guide, A	N	I	610	Vocabulary Readers	Houghton Mifflin Harcourt
Sherpa Guide, A	N	I	610	Vocabulary Readers/CA	Houghton Mifflin Harcourt
Sherpa Guide, A	N	I	610	Vocabulary Readers/TX	Houghton Mifflin Harcourt
Sheryl Swoopes	R	B	250+	Sports Heroes	Red Brick Learning
She's Got Game!	U	I	250+	Boldprint	Steck-Vaughn
Shetland Ponies	I	I	134	Horses	Capstone Press
Shetland Ponies Are My Favorite!	O	I	250+	My Favorite Horses	Lerner Publishing Group
Shetland Pony, The	R	I	250+	Horses	Capstone Press
Shh!	C	RF	61	Bonnell, Kris	Reading Reading Books
Shh! We're Writing the Constitution	T	I	250+	Fritz, Jean	G.P. Putnam's Sons
SHHH	F	RF	66	Henkes, Kevin	Greenwillow Books
Shhhh!	G	F	68	Kline, Suzy	Whitman
Shifter Karts: High-Speed Go-Karts	M	I	250+	Horsepower	Capstone Press
Shifting Ground	S	HF	250+	Power Up!	Steck-Vaughn
Shifting Perspectives	V	I	250+	InfoQuest	Rigby
Shifting Sands	R	I	250+	InfoQuest	Rigby
Shifting Society, A	V	I	2439	Reading Street	Pearson
Shifty Shark, The	P	F	250+	Tristars	Richard C. Owen
Shih Tzus	R	I	250+	All About Dogs	Capstone Press
Shih Tzus	I	I	162	Dogs	Capstone Press
Shih Tzus Are the Best!	Q	I	1451	The Best Dogs Ever	Lerner Publishing Group
Shiloh	R	RF	250+	Naylor, Phyllis Reynolds	Bantam Books
Shimmer of Butterflies, A	U	I	250+	Wild Life Series	London Town Press
Shine	Z+	RF	250+	Myracle, Lauren	Amulet Books
Shine Sun	F	RF	115	Rookie Readers	Children's Press
Shingo's Grandfather	K	RF	370	Sunshine	Wright Group/McGraw Hill
Shingu, Japan: Communities Around the World	S	I	250+	Reading Expeditions	National Geographic
*Shining Blue Planet and Other Cases, The	O	RF	250+	Simon, Seymour	Avon Books
Shintaro's Umbrellas	I	RF	95	Books for Young Learners	Richard C. Owen
Shiny Baby Penguin, The	G	RF	108	Seedlings	Continental Press
Ship Breaker	Y	SF	250+	Bacigalupi, Paolo	Little Brown and Company
Ship in a Bottle, The	Q	RF	250+	Ragged Island Mysteries	Wright Group/McGraw Hill
Ship is Coming!, A	M	RF	250+	On Our Way to English	Rigby
Ships	T	I	250+	Crowther, Robert	Candlewick Press
Ships	L	I	275	Wonder World	Wright Group/McGraw Hill

TITLE	LEVEL	GENRE	WORD COUNT	AUTHOR / SERIES	PUBLISHER / DISTRIBUTOR
Ships at Sea	K	I	250+	PM Plus	Rigby
Shipwreck at the Bottom of the World	Y	I	250+	Armstrong, Jennifer	Crown Publishers
Shipwreck in the South China Sea	R	I	250+	On Our Way to English	Rigby
Shipwreck on the Pirate Islands	O	F	250+	Stilton, Geronimo	Scholastic
Shipwreck Saturday	K	RF	250+	Cosby, Bill	Scholastic
Shipwreck Search: Discovery of the H.L. Hunley	N	I	1809	On My Own History	Lerner Publishing Group
Shipwreck! Debbie Kiley's Story of Survival	S	I	250+	True Tales of Survival	Capstone Press
#Shipwrecked on Mad Island	U	F	11720	Twisted Journeys	Graphic Universe
Shipwrecked!	Q	F	250+	Bookweb	Rigby
Shirley Chisholm	S	B	1396	Leveled Readers	Houghton Mifflin Harcourt
Shirley Chisholm	S	B	1396	Leveled Readers/CA	Houghton Mifflin Harcourt
Shirley Chisholm	S	B	1396	Leveled Readers/TX	Houghton Mifflin Harcourt
Shirley Chisholm: Congresswoman	N	B	250+	Beginning Biographies	Pearson Learning Group
Shiva's Fire	Y	F	250+	Staples, Suzanne Fisher	HarperTrophy
Shiver Me Letters: A Pirate ABC	L	F	250+	Sobel, June	Houghton Mifflin Harcourt
Shivers	R	I	250+	Boldprint	Steck-Vaughn
Shivers in the Fridge, The	L	F	250+	Manushkin. Fran	Dutton Children's Books
#Shocking World of Electricity with Max Axiom, Super Scientist; The	V	I	250+	Graphic Library	Capstone Press
Shoe	K	RF	250+	Literacy by Design	Rigby
Shoe	K	RF	250+	Rigby Literacy	Rigby
Shoe Grabber, The	I	F	260	Read Alongs	Rigby
Shoe Town	G	F	134	Green Light Readers	Harcourt
Shoe, A	A	F	24	Sails	Rigby
Shoebag	P	F	250+	James, Mary	Scholastic
Shoeless Joe & Me	T	F	250+	Gutman, Dan	HarperTrophy
Shoemaker and the Elves, The	J	TL	250+	Sunshine	Wright Group/McGraw Hill
Shoemaker and the Elves, The	I	TL	436	Traditional Tales	Pioneer Valley
Shoes	D	F	79	Book Bank	Wright Group/McGraw Hill
Shoes	A	RF	16	Little Celebrations	Pearson Learning Group
Shoes	B	RF	40	Little Readers	Houghton Mifflin Harcourt
Shoes	D	RF	150	Sun Sprouts	ETA/Cuisenaire
Shoes	F	I	73	Talk About Books	Pearson Learning Group
Shoes	D	I	150	Winthrop, Elizabeth	HarperTrophy
Shoes by Twos	H	RF	211	Dominie Math Series	Pearson Publishing Group
Shoes for Everyone: A Story About Jan Matzeliger	R	B	250+	Mitchell, Barbara	Carolrhoda Books
Shoes Through the Ages	Q	I	250+	Brill, Marlene Targ	Steck-Vaughn
Shoes, Shoes, Shoes	H	RF	274	Real Kids Readers	Millbrook Press
Shoeshine Girl	N	RF	250+	Bulla, Clyde Robert	HarperTrophy
Shoeshine Girl	S	HF	1731	Leveled Readers	Houghton Mifflin Harcourt
Shoeshine Girl	S	HF	1731	Leveled Readers/CA	Houghton Mifflin Harcourt
Shoeshine Girl	S	HF	1731	Leveled Readers/TX	Houghton Mifflin Harcourt
Shonto Begay: His Life and Work	Y	B	2196	Leveled Readers	Houghton Mifflin Harcourt
Shoo Fly	D	RF	76	Sun Sprouts	ETA/Cuisenaire
Shoo!	E	RF	191	Rigby Rocket	Rigby
Shoo!	C	F	37	Sunshine	Wright Group/McGraw Hill
Shoo, Crow! Shoo!	F	F	41	Early Readers	Compass Point Books
Shoo, Fly	B	F	31	Science	Outside the Box
Shoo, Fly	J	RF	336	Storyteller	Wright Group/McGraw Hill
Shoo, Fly Guy!	I	F	250+	Arnold, Tedd	Scholastic
Shoo, Fly!	B	RF	24	Story Box	Wright Group/McGraw Hill
*Shoo, Shoo, Shoo! and Other Stories	H	F	239	Story Steps	Rigby

TITLE	LEVEL	GENRE	WORD COUNT	AUTHOR / SERIES	PUBLISHER / DISTRIBUTOR
Shoo, Spider!	I	RF	250+	Scooters	ETA/Cuisenaire
Shoot of Corn, A	L	RF	250+	Cambridge Reading	Pearson Learning Group
Shooting Star, The	M	RF	661	PM Collection	Rigby
Shooting Stars	R	RF	250+	Costello, Emily	Dell
Shooting the Moon	T	HF	250+	Dowell, Frances O'Roark	Atheneum Books
Shooting the Sun: A Chinese Myth	L	TL	509	Springboard	Wright Group/McGraw Hill
Shopping	E	RF	170	Handprints C, Set 2	Educators Publishing Service
Shopping	C	I	41	Interaction	Rigby
Shopping	J	I	254	Leveled Readers	Houghton Mifflin Harcourt
Shopping	D	RF	26	Literacy 2000	Rigby
Shopping	C	I	78	Little Red Readers	Sundance
Shopping	E	I	45	Read-More Books	Pearson Learning Group
Shopping	B	RF	31	Rigby Star	Rigby
Shopping	A	F	25	Sails	Rigby
Shopping	E	RF	101	Storyteller-Setting Sun	Wright Group/McGraw Hill
Shopping	LB	RF	15	Sunshine	Wright Group/McGraw Hill
Shopping	J	RF	250+	Sunshine	Wright Group/McGraw Hill
Shopping	D	RF	44	Sunshine	Wright Group/McGraw Hill
Shopping at the Mall	G	RF	145	Urmston, Kathleen; Evans, Karen	Kaeden Books
Shopping at the Supermarket	B	I	46	Foundations	Wright Group/McGraw Hill
Shopping Cart, The	B	RF	48	Bonnell, Kris	Reading Reading Books
Shopping Day	D	I	44	Vocabulary Readers	Houghton Mifflin Harcourt
Shopping for School	C	RF	33	Visions	Wright Group/McGraw Hill
Shopping in Many Cultures	I	I	92	Life Around the World	Capstone Press
Shopping List, The	F	RF	153	Rigby Flying Colors	Rigby
Shopping List, The	I	F	284	Storyteller	Wright Group/McGraw Hill
Shopping List, The	D	RF	80	The King School Series	Townsend Press
Shopping List, The	G	I	120	Windows on Literacy	National Geographic
Shopping Mall, The	B	I	44	PM Starters	Rigby
Shopping Trip, A	D	RF	84	InfoTrek	ETA/Cuisenaire
Shopping with a Crocodile	L	F	250+	Pacific Literacy	Pacific Learning
Shopping with Dad	G	I	212	Factivity Series	Pearson Learning Group
Shopping with Dad	C	RF	43	Home Connection Collection	Rigby
Shopping with Dad	C	RF	72	Windows on Literacy	National Geographic
Shopping with Grandma	F	RF	162	PM Photo Stories	Rigby
Shopping with the Meanies	H	F	225	The Story Basket	Wright Group/McGraw Hill
Shopping with the Nicholas Family	I	RF	276	Early Explorers	Benchmark Education
Shores of Freedom	S	I	250+	InfoQuest	Rigby
Short and Tall: An Animal Opposites Book	J	I	250+	Animal Opposites	Capstone Press
Short Second Life of Bree Tanner, The	Z+	F	250+	Meyer, Stephanie	Little Brown and Company
Short: Walking Tall When You're Not Tall at All	Y	I	250+	Schwartz, John	Roaring Brook Press
Shortcut	O	F	250+	Macaulay, David	Houghton Mifflin Harcourt
Shortest Kid in the World	K	RF	250+	Bliss, Corinne Demas	Random House
Shortstop from Tokyo	P	RF	250+	Christopher, Matt	Little Brown and Company
Shorty	M	RF	250+	Literacy 2000	Rigby
Shoshones, The	T	I	3888	Native American Histoies	Lerner Publishing Group
Shosun's Mistake	N	SF	250+	Sails	Rigby
Shots	I	RF	90	City Kids	Rigby
Should I Share My Ice Cream?	H	F	242	Willems, Mo	Hyperion
Should Kids Play Video Games?	T	I	250+	Bookshop	Mondo Publishing

S

* Collection of short stories   # Graphic text
^ Mature content with lower level text demands

TITLE	LEVEL	GENRE	WORD COUNT	AUTHOR / SERIES	PUBLISHER / DISTRIBUTOR
Should There Be Presidential Term Limits? (Flipsides)	V	I	250+	Bookshop	Mondo Publishing
Should There Be Space Exploration?	U	I	250+	Bookshop	Mondo Publishing
Should There Be Zoos?: A Persuasive Text	S	I	250+	Bookshop	Mondo Publishing
Should This Have Happened?	Q	I	250+	Sails	Rigby
Should We Drill for Oil in Protected Areas? (Flipsides)	W	I	250+	Bookshop	Mondo Publishing
Should We Have Pets?: A Persuasive Text	N	I	250+	Bookshop	Mondo Publishing
Should You Ever?	I	F	69	Tiger Cub	Peguis
Shoveling Snow	F	RF	109	Cummings, Pat	Scholastic
Show and Tell	E	RF	214	Alphakids	Sundance
Show and Tell	K	RF	201	City Kids	Rigby
Show and Tell	G	RF	190	First Start	Troll Associates
Show and Tell	G	RF	207	HSP/Harcourt Trophies	Harcourt, Inc.
Show and Tell	B	F	20	Leveled Readers	Houghton Mifflin Harcourt
Show and Tell	A	F	20	Leveled Readers/CA	Houghton Mifflin Harcourt
Show and Tell	A	RF	32	Little Books	Sadlier-Oxford
Show and Tell	I	RF	201	Little Celebrations	Pearson Learning Group
Show and Tell	F	RF	111	Little Red Readers	Sundance
Show and Tell	H	RF	407	Real Kids Readers	Millbrook Press
Show Me a Shape	B	RF	52	Red Rocket Readers	Flying Start Books
Show Me a Snake Hole	L	RF	250+	Frederick, Shirley	Hampton Brown
Show Must Go On!, The	L	RF	586	Leveled Readers	Houghton Mifflin Harcourt
Show of Hands, A	L	I	250+	Rigby Literacy	Rigby
Show Time at the Polk Street School	M	RF	250+	Giff, Patricia Reilly	Bantam Books
Show Us Your Wings	G	I	132	Yellow Umbrella Books	Red Brick Learning
Show What You Can Do	R	RF	250+	In Step Readers	Rigby
Show, The	A	RF	40	Leveled Literacy Intervention/ Orange System	Heinemann
Show, The	A	RF	25	Leveled Readers	Houghton Mifflin Harcourt
Show, The	A	RF	25	Leveled Readers/CA	Houghton Mifflin Harcourt
Show, The	A	F	24	Sails	Rigby
Show-and-Tell	H	RF	205	Cambridge Reading	Pearson Learning Group
Show-and-Tell	J	RF	220	Foundations	Wright Group/McGraw Hill
Show-and-Tell Frog, The	J	RF	250+	Oppenheim, Joanna	Bantam Books
Show-and-Tell Sam	F	F	92	Rookie Readers	Children's Press
Show-and-Tell War, The	N	RF	250+	Smith, Janice Lee	HarperTrophy
Show-Off Frog	L	F	907	Pair-It Turn and Learn	Steck-Vaughn
Show-Off, The	K	RF	928	PM Stars Bridge Books	Rigby
Show-Off, The (Moose and Hildy)	L	F	250+	Greene, Stephanie	Marshall Cavendish
Shredderman: Attack of the Tigger	R	RF	250+	Van Draanen, Wendelin	Scholastic
Shredderman: Secret Identity	R	RF	250+	Van Draanen, Wendelin	Scholastic
Shrewbettina Goes to Work	WB	F	0	Goodall, John	McElderry
Shrimp	H	I	95	Under the Sea	Capstone Press
Shrublands	W	I	250+	Biomes Atlases	Raintree
Shugg's Pet Octopus	M	F	250+	Rigby Gigglers	Rigby
Shush!	D	RF	29	Pacific Literacy	Pacific Learning
Shut the Door	D	RF	46	Visions	Wright Group/McGraw Hill
Shy Ana	I	RF	196	Reading Street	Pearson
Shy Charles	L	F	250+	Wells, Rosemary	Puffin Books
Shy Creatures, The	M	F	250+	Mack, David	Feiwel and Friends
Shy People's Picnic, The	M	F	250+	Little Celebrations	Pearson Learning Group
Si Won's Victory	M	RF	250+	Little Celebrations	Pearson Learning Group
Siamese Are the Best!	Q	I	1388	The Best Cats Ever	Lerner Publishing Group

S

* Collection of short stories   # Graphic text
^ Mature content with lower level text demands

Storable Database at www.fountasandpinnellleveledbooks.com

TITLE	LEVEL	GENRE	WORD COUNT	AUTHOR / SERIES	PUBLISHER / DISTRIBUTOR
Siamese Cats	R	I	250+	All About Cats	Capstone Press
Siamese Cats	I	I	117	Cats	Capstone Press
Siberian Huskies	I	I	134	Dogs	Capstone Press
Siberian Survivor	R	I	250+	Explorer Books-Pathfinder	National Geographic
Siberian Survivor	P	I	250+	Explorer Books-Pioneer	National Geographic
Sick Bear, The	D	RF	61	Joy Readers	Pearson Learning Group
Sick Day, A	I	RF	331	InfoTrek	ETA/Cuisenaire
Sick in Bed	F	RF	109	Little Red Readers	Sundance
Sick Rooster, The	I	F	265	Sails	Rigby
Sick, Nasty Medical Practices	T	I	250+	Horrible Things	Capstone Press
Sid and Sam	E	RF	120	Buck, Nola	HarperTrophy
Siddhartha Gautama: The Buddha	X	B	250+	Primary Source Readers	Teacher Created Materials
Side by Side	M	I	250+	Explorations	Eleanor Curtain Publishing
Side by Side	M	I	250+	Explorations	Okapi Educational Materials
Side Effects	X	RF	250+	Koss, Amy Goldman	Roaring Brook Press
Sidekick, The	L	F	1309	Reading Street	Pearson
Sidetrack Sam	K	RF	250+	Literacy 2000	Rigby
Sidewalk Story	N	RF	250+	Mathis, Sharon Bell	Penguin Group
Sidewalk, The	A	RF	32	Leveled Literacy Intervention/ Orange System	Heinemann
Sideways Arithmetic from Wayside School	S	I	250+	Sachar, Louis	Scholastic
*Sideways Stories from Wayside School	P	F	250+	Sachar, Louis	Hearst
Sidney Crosby	P	B	2067	Amazing Athetes	Lerner Publishing Group
Siege, The	K	F	250+	Book Blazers	ETA/Cuisenaire
Siege, The: Guardians of Ga'Hoole	V	F	250+	Lasky, Kathryn	Scholastic
Sierra	Q	I	250+	Siebert, Diane	HarperCollins
Sieur de La Salle	Q	B	250+	Biographies-Great Explorers	Capstone Press
Sight, The	Z	F	250+	Clement-Davies, David	Penguin Group
Sight, The: Warriors, Power of Three	U	F	250+	Hunter, Erin	HarperCollins
Sights and Sounds of New York City's Chinatown, The	M	I	507	Reading Street	Pearson
Sigmond Slitherforth	O	F	250+	Wonder World	Wright Group/McGraw Hill
Sign of the Beaver	T	HF	250+	Speare, Elizabeth George	Bantam Books
Sign of the Chrysanthemum, The	U	RF	250+	Paterson, Katherine	HarperTrophy
Signer for Independence, A: John Hancock	T	B	250+	We the People	Compass Point Books
Signs	G	RF	127	Breakthrough	Longman
Signs	F	I	40	Canizares, Susan; Chanko, Pamela	Scholastic
Signs	C	I	40	Carousel Earlybirds	Pearson Learning Group
Signs	B	I	24	Literacy 2000	Rigby
Signs	C	I	35	Little Celebrations	Pearson Learning Group
Signs	E	I	131	Twig	Wright Group/McGraw Hill
Signs	LB	I	21	Yellow Umbrella Books	Red Brick Learning
Signs Ahead	N	RF	250+	Infotrek Plus	ETA/Cuisenaire
Signs All Around	E	RF	90	InfoTrek	ETA/Cuisenaire
Signs All Around Us	G	I	165	Gear Up!	Wright Group/McGraw Hill
Signs All Around Us	M	I	900	Vocabulary Readers	Houghton Mifflin Harcourt
Signs All Around Us	M	I	900	Vocabulary Readers/CA	Houghton Mifflin Harcourt
Signs Are Everywhere	J	I	276	Vocabulary Readers	Houghton Mifflin Harcourt
Signs Are Everywhere	J	I	276	Vocabulary Readers/CA	Houghton Mifflin Harcourt
Signs Are Everywhere	J	I	276	Vocabulary Readers/TX	Houghton Mifflin Harcourt
Signs in Our Neighborhood	I	RF	191	InfoTrek	ETA/Cuisenaire
Signs of Spring	H	F	250+	Bookshop	Mondo Publishing
Signs on the Way	F	I	106	Windows on Literacy	National Geographic

Organized Alphabetically by Title
Storable Database at www.fountasandpinnellleveledbooks.com

* Collection of short stories   # Graphic text
^ Mature content with lower level text demands

S

TITLE	LEVEL	GENRE	WORD COUNT	AUTHOR / SERIES	PUBLISHER / DISTRIBUTOR
Signs, Songs, and Symbols of America	S	I	1278	Reading Street	Pearson
Silent Boy, The	Y	RF	250+	Lowry, Lois	Houghton Mifflin Harcourt
Silent Hero, The	O	I	250+	Shea, George	Random House
Silent Sam	G	RF	146	Bebop Books	Lee & Low Books Inc.
Silent to the Bone	V	RF	250+	Konigsburg, E. L.	Atheneum Books
Silent World, A	L	RF	250+	Literacy 2000	Rigby
Silhouetted by the Blue	Y	RF	250+	Jones, Traci L.	Farrar, Straus, & Giroux
Silk	U	I	250+	Theme Sets	National Geographic
Silk & Venom: Searching for a Dangerous Spider	X	I	250+	Lasky, Kathryn	Candlewick Press
Silk Road, The	V	I	1594	Leveled Readers	Houghton Mifflin Harcourt
Silk Road, The	V	I	1594	Leveled Readers/CA	Houghton Mifflin Harcourt
Silk Road, The	V	I	1594	Leveled Readers/TX	Houghton Mifflin Harcourt
Silk Route, The	U	HF	250+	Major, John S.	HarperCollins
Silk Umbrellas	S	RF	250+	Marsden, Carolyn	Candlewick Press
Silkworm Moths	P	I	1375	Early Bird Nature Books	Lerner Publishing Group
Silkworms	L	I	328	Explorations	Okapi Educational Materials
Silkworms	L	I	328	Explorations	Eleanor Curtain Publishing
Silkworms	P	I	250+	Life Cycles	Capstone Press
Silkworms	N	I	250+	Take Two Books	Wright Group/McGraw Hill
Silkworms	K	I	160	Watch It Grow	Capstone Press
Silly Aunt Tilly	H	F	176	Instant Readers	Harcourt School Publishers
Silly Billy	L	RF	250+	Browne, Anthony	Candlewick Press
Silly Billys	H	F	250+	Sunshine	Wright Group/McGraw Hill
Silly Cat	C	F	48	Sails	Rigby
Silly Cat Tricks	D	F	83	Teacher's Choice Series	Pearson Learning Group
Silly Clown	B	RF	35	Sails	Rigby
Silly Day	F	RF	71	Kaleidoscope Collection	Hameray Publishing Group
#Silly Lilly and the Four Seasons	J	RF	166	Rosenstiehl, Agnes	Toon Books
#Silly Lilly in What Will I Be Today?	J	RF	227	Rosenstiehl, Agnes	Toon Books
Silly Old Possum	C	RF	41	Story Box	Wright Group/McGraw Hill
Silly Sally	C	RF	24	Rookie Readers	Children's Press
Silly Story of Goldie Locks and the Three Squares, The	K	TL	250+	Maccarone, Grace	Scholastic
Silly Supper, The	J	RF	250+	The Wright Skills	Wright Group/McGraw Hill
Silly Suzy Goose	I	F	92	Horacek, Petr	Candlewick Press
Silly Tilly's Thanksgiving Dinner	K	F	250+	Hoban, Lillian	HarperCollins
Silly Tilly's Valentine	K	F	250+	Hoban, Lillian	HarperTrophy
Silly Times with Two Silly Trolls	I	F	250+	Jewell, Nancy	HarperTrophy
Silly Tricks	B	F	30	Sails	Rigby
Silly Willy	M	RF	250+	Bookshop	Mondo Publishing
Silly Willy and Silly Billy	J	F	221	Foundations	Wright Group/McGraw Hill
Silver	N	RF	250+	Whelan, Gloria	Random House
Silver and Gold Everywhere	J	I	329	Lightning Bolt Books	Lerner Publishing Group
Silver and Prince	L	RF	250+	PM Story Books-Silver	Rigby
Silver and Stripes	K	F	1187	Reading Street	Pearson
Silver Balloon, The	P	F	250+	Bonners, Susan	Farrar, Straus, & Giroux
Silver Donkey	V	HF	250+	Hartnett, Sonya	Candlewick Press
Silver Horn, The	S	F	250+	Bookshop	Mondo Publishing
Silver Pony, The	WB	F	0	Ward, Lynd	Houghton Mifflin Harcourt
# Silverfin: A James Bond Adventure	W	RF	250+	Higson, Charlie	Hyperion
Silverfin: A James Bond Adventure	W	F	250+	Higson, Charlie	Hyperion
Silverwing: How One Small Bat Became a Noble Hero	U	F	250+	Oppel, Kenneth	Simon & Schuster

S

TITLE	LEVEL	GENRE	WORD COUNT	AUTHOR / SERIES	PUBLISHER / DISTRIBUTOR
Silvia Hops Home	E	RF	163	On Our Way to English	Rigby
Silvia's Soccer Game	F	RF	138	Ready Readers	Pearson Learning Group
Simon and the Aliens	N	SF	250+	Supa Doopers	Sundance
Simon Bolivar	W	B	1858	Leveled Readers Social Studies	Houghton Mifflin Harcourt
Simone's Travels	L	RF	1297	Reading Street	Pearson
Simon's Big Challenge	Q	RF	250+	Pair-It Books	Steck-Vaughn
Simon's Scoop	N	RF	250+	Literacy by Design	Rigby
Simon's Sea Monster	I	RF	250+	Reading Safari	Mondo Publishing
Simple Machines	L	I	250+	Early Connections	Benchmark Education
Simple Machines	Q	I	250+	Rosen Real Readers	Rosen Publishing Group
Simple Machines	O	I	250+	Windows on Literacy	National Geographic
Simple Machines at Work	L	I	399	Reading Street	Pearson
Simple Machines in Compound Machines	P	I	856	Reading Street	Pearson
Simple Solution	I	RF	250+	Literacy Tree	Rigby
Simple System, A	V	I	250+	WorldScapes	ETA/Cuisenaire
Simple Technology	J	I	196	Red Rocket Readers	Flying Start Books
Simply Alice	Z	RF	250+	Naylor, Phyllis Reynolds	Simon & Schuster
Simply Sam	E	RF	69	Voyages	SRA/McGraw Hill
#Sinbad	T	F	2350	Dominoes starter	Oxford University Press
#Sinbad: Sailing into Peril	V	TL	3314	Graphic Myths and Legends	Graphic Universe
Sing a Song	E	F	154	Story Box	Wright Group/McGraw Hill
Sing a Song of People	I	RF	151	Avenues	Hampton Brown
Sing Down the Moon	T	HF	250+	O'Dell, Scott	Language for Learning Assoc.
Sing for Your Father, Su Phan	W	HF	250+	Pevsner, Stella; Tang, Fay	Bantam Books
Sing for Your Supper	P	HF	250+	High-Fliers	Pacific Learning
*Sing to the Moon	K	F	2448	Story Box	Wright Group/McGraw Hill
Singer and the First Lady, The	T	I	1488	Vocabulary Readers	Houghton Mifflin Harcourt
Singer and the First Lady, The	T	I	1488	Vocabulary Readers/CA	Houghton Mifflin Harcourt
Singer and the First Lady, The	T	I	1488	Vocabulary Readers/TX	Houghton Mifflin Harcourt
Singing Crickets	M	RF	250+	Glaser, Linda	Millbrook Press
*Singing Drum, The	T	TL	250+	Literacy 2000	Rigby
Singing Duck, The	I	F	391	Leveled Literacy Intervention/ Blue System	Heinemann
*Singing for Mrs. Pettigrew: Stories and Essays from a Writing Life	W	F	250+	Morpurgo, Michael	Candlewick Press
Singing Giant, The	H	F	250+	Rigby Star	Rigby
Singing Giant, The: A Play	H	F	250+	Rigby Star	Rigby
Singing Giant, The: A Play	H	F	250+	Rigby Literacy	Rigby
Singing Giant, The: A Story	H	F	250+	Rigby Literacy	Rigby
Singing Princess, The	K	F	250+	Literacy by Design	Rigby
Singing Princess, The	K	F	250+	Rigby Literacy	Rigby
Singing Robins	K	I	397	Pull Ahead Books	Lerner Publishing Group
Singing Sensation	O	F	250+	Stilton, Geronimo	Scholastic
Single Parent Families	I	I	89	My Family	Capstone Press
Single Shard, A	U	HF	250+	Park, Linda Sue	Clarion
Sing-Song Tree, The	L	I	250+	Sunshine	Wright Group/McGraw Hill
Sink or Float	F	I	91	Instant Readers	Harcourt School Publishers
Sink or Float?	C	I	36	Independent Readers Science	Houghton Mifflin Harcourt
Sink or Float?	E	I	112	Learn to Read	Creative Teaching Press
Sink or Float?	E	I	159	Vocabulary Readers	Houghton Mifflin Harcourt
Sink or Float?	E	I	159	Vocabulary Readers/CA	Houghton Mifflin Harcourt
Sink or Float?	E	I	159	Vocabulary Readers/TX	Houghton Mifflin Harcourt
#Sinking of the Titanic, The	T	I	250+	Graphic Library	Capstone Press

* Collection of short stories   # Graphic text
^ Mature content with lower level text demands

TITLE	LEVEL	GENRE	WORD COUNT	AUTHOR / SERIES	PUBLISHER / DISTRIBUTOR
Sione Went Fishing	I	RF	225	Sunshine	Wright Group/McGraw Hill
Sione's Talo	H	TL	164	Nelisi, Lino	Scholastic
Sioux Indians, The	P	I	250+	Native Peoples	Red Brick Learning
Sioux, The	R	I	250+	First Reports	Compass Point Books
Sioux, The	T	I	4485	Native American Histoies	Lerner Publishing Group
Sioux, The: Nomadic Buffalo Hunters	R	I	250+	America's First Peoples	Capstone Press
Sir Arthur	P	B	250+	Apte, Sunita	Scholastic
Sir Cumference and the Dragon of Pi	Q	HF	250+	Neuschwander, Cindy	Charlesbridge
Sir Cumference and the First Round Table	Q	HF	250+	Neuschwander, Cindy	Charlesbridge
Sir Cumference and the Great Knight of Angleland	Q	HF	250+	Neuschwander, Cindy	Charlesbridge
Sir Cumference and the Isle of Immeter	Q	HF	250+	Neuschwander, Cindy	Charlesbridge
Sir Cumference and the Sword in the Cone	Q	HF	250+	Neuschwander, Cindy	Scholastic
Sir Down, Dog	G	RF	192	Sun Sprouts	ETA/Cuisenaire
Sir Edmund Hillary	R	I	1437	Vocabulary Readers	Houghton Mifflin Harcourt
Sir Edmund Hillary	R	B	1437	Vocabulary Readers/CA	Houghton Mifflin Harcourt
Sir Hans Sloane	O	B	766	Leveled Readers	Houghton Mifflin Harcourt
Sir Hans Sloane	O	B	766	Leveled Readers/CA	Houghton Mifflin Harcourt
Sir Hans Sloane	O	B	766	Leveled Readers/TX	Houghton Mifflin Harcourt
Sir Ryan's Quest	L	F	250+	Deeble, Jason	Roaring Brook Press
Sir Small and the Dragonfly	G	F	250+	Step into Reading	Random House
Sir Tom	T	HF	1617	Reading Street	Pearson
Sir Walter Raleigh	S	B	3532	History Maker Bios	Lerner Publishing Group
Sister	W	RF	250+	Greenfield, Eloise	HarperCollins
Sister Anne's Hands	R	HF	250+	Lorbiecki, Marybeth	Puffin Books
Sister Bear: A Norse Tale	O	TL	250+	Yolen Jane	Marshall Cavendish
Sister Ella	Q	HF	250+	High-Fliers	Pacific Learning
*Sister Love and Other Crime Stories	Y	RF	5565	Oxford Bookworms Library	Oxford University Press
Sister Mischief	Z+	RF	250+	Goode, Laura	Candlewick Press
Sister Spider Knows	W	RF	250+	Fogelin, Adrian	Peachtree
Sister Spirit	L	RF	250+	Go Girl!	Feiwel and Friends
Sister Tricksters	S	TL	250+	San Souci, Robert D.	August House Publishers
Sisterhood of the Traveling Pants, The	Z+	RF	250+	Schraff, Anne	Townsend Press
Sisters	F	I	63	Families	Capstone Press
Sisters	B	I	28	Pebble Books	Capstone Press
Sisters	E	I	77	Talk About Books	Pearson Learning Group
Sisters & Brothers: Sibling Relationships in the Animal World	R	I	250+	Jenkins, Steve & Page, Robin	Houghton Mifflin Harcourt
Sisters Against Slavery: A Story about Sarah and Angelina Grimke	S	B	8509	Creative Minds Biographies	Lerner Publishing Group
Sisters and Brothers	A	I	15	Vocabulary Readers	Houghton Mifflin Harcourt
Sisters and Brothers	A	I	15	Vocabulary Readers/CA	Houghton Mifflin Harcourt
Sisters Club, The	P	RF	250+	McDonald, Megan	Pleasant Company Publications
Sisters Club, The: Rule of Three	Q	RF	250+	McDonald, Megan	Candlewick Press
Sisters Play Soccer	R	RF	1426	Leveled Readers	Houghton Mifflin Harcourt
Sisters Play Soccer	R	RF	1426	Leveled Readers/CA	Houghton Mifflin Harcourt
Sisters Play Soccer	R	RF	1426	Leveled Readers/TX	Houghton Mifflin Harcourt
Sisters Red	Y	F	250+	Pearce, Jackson	Little Brown and Company
Sistrsic92 (Meg)	Z+	RF	250+	Dellasega, Cheryl	Marshall Cavendish
Sit Still!	K	RF	315	Carlson, Nancy	Carolrhoda Books
Sit, Ned!	D	RF	67	Leveled Readers	Houghton Mifflin Harcourt
Sit, Pig!	A	RF	20	Vocabulary Readers	Houghton Mifflin Harcourt
Sit, Sam	F	RF	165	Early Connections	Benchmark Education

S

TITLE	LEVEL	GENRE	WORD COUNT	AUTHOR / SERIES	PUBLISHER / DISTRIBUTOR
Sit-In: How Four Friends Stood Up by Sitting Down	S	HF	250+	Pinkney, Andrea Davis	Little Brown and Company
Sitting	E	F	46	Literacy 2000	Rigby
Sitting Bull	S	B	250+	History Maker Bios	Lerner Publishing Group
Sitting Bull	N	B	217	Pebble Books	Capstone Press
Sitting Bull	R	B	250+	Primary Source Readers	Teacher Created Materials
Sitting Bull	N	B	250+	Rookie Biographies	Children's Press
Sitting in My Box	F	F	169	Lillegard, Dee	Marshall Cavendish
Sitting Pretty	L	RF	533	Gear Up!	Wright Group/McGraw Hill
Six Cats	C	RF	50	Joy Readers	Pearson Learning Group
Six Empty Pockets	F	RF	85	Rookie Readers	Children's Press
Six Fat Cubs	D	F	52	Reading Street	Pearson
Six Fine Fish	F	F	252	Ready Readers	Pearson Learning Group
Six Fish in a Mix	D	I	79	Phonics and Friends	Hampton Brown
Six Foolish Fishermen	L	TL	715	Elkin, Benjamin	Children's Press
Six Go By	C	F	24	Ready Readers	Pearson Learning Group
Six Innings: A Game in the Life	T	RF	250+	Preller, James	Feiwel and Friends
Six Legs	B	I	34	Harry's Math Books	Outside the Box
Six Little Chicks	F	F	227	Sun Sprouts	ETA/Cuisenaire
Six Pieces of Cake	C	RF	40	Harry's Math Books	Outside the Box
Six Sheep Sip Thick Shakes	L	F	270	Cleary, Brian P.	Millbrook Press
Six Silly Brothers	K	TL	616	Sun Sprouts	ETA/Cuisenaire
Six Silly Foxes	G	F	147	Green Light Readers	Harcourt
Six Things to Make	L	I	250+	Bookshop	Mondo Publishing
Six Under the Sea	E	I	158	PM Math Readers	Rigby
Six Voyages of Pleasant Fieldmouse, The	R	F	250+	Wahl, Jan	Tom Doherty
Six Wet Pets	B	F	31	Leveled Readers Language Support	Houghton Mifflin Harcourt
Six-Dinner Sid	L	F	250+	Moore, Inga	Scholastic
Sixteen Runaway Pumpkins	J	F	250+	Ochiltree, Dianne	Margaret K. McElderry Books
*Sixteen Short Stories by Outstanding Writers	Z	RF	250+	Gallo, Donald R.	Dell
Sixth Grade Can Really Kill You	S	RF	250+	DeClements, Barthe	Scholastic
Sixth Grade Secrets	S	RF	250+	Sachar, Louis	Scholastic
Sixth-Grade Sleepover	R	RF	250+	Bunting, Eve	Scholastic
Sixty-Eight Rooms, The	U	F	250+	Malone, Marianne	Random House
Size: Many Ways to Measure	L	I	250+	Exploring Math	Capstone Press
Sizes	C	I	32	Discovery World	Rigby
Sizewise	S	I	250+	The News	Richard C. Owen
Sizing Up Shapes	T	I	250+	Reading Expeditions	National Geographic
Skate Jam, The	P	RF	250+	Orbit Double Takes	Pacific Learning
Skateboard Bill	J	RF	79	Voyages	SRA/McGraw Hill
Skateboard City	Q	RF	250+	Power Up!	Steck-Vaughn
Skateboard for Alex, A	I	F	229	Javernick, Ellen	Kaeden Books
^Skateboard Power	P	RF	1298	Zucker, Jonny	Stone Arch Books
#Skateboard Sonar	Q	RF	250+	Sports Illustrated Kids	Stone Arch Books
Skateboard Standout	M	F	250+	Too Cool	Pacific Learning
Skateboard Tough	Q	RF	250+	Christopher, Matt	Little Brown and Company
Skateboarder, The	I	I	175	Sun Sprouts	ETA/Cuisenaire
Skateboarder's Club, The	O	RF	250+	On Our Way to English	Rigby
Skateboarding	F	RF	147	Developing Books, Set 1	Pioneer Valley
^Skateboarding	R	I	250+	Download	Hameray Publishing Group
Skateboarding	N	I	463	Gear Up!	Wright Group/McGraw Hill

* Collection of short stories   # Graphic text
^ Mature content with lower level text demands

S

TITLE	LEVEL	GENRE	WORD COUNT	AUTHOR / SERIES	PUBLISHER / DISTRIBUTOR
Skateboarding	M	I	250+	Horsepower	Capstone Press
Skateboarding	C	RF	35	Lowe, Diane	Kaeden Books
Skateboarding	H	I	106	Nonfiction Set 6	Literacy Footprints
Skateboarding	O	I	250+	PM Nonfiction-Emerald	Rigby
Skateboarding	J	I	330	Red Rocket Readers	Flying Start Books
Skateboarding	Q	I	250+	X-Sports	Capstone Press
Skateboarding Greats: Champs of the Ramps	Q	I	250+	Skateboarding	Red Brick Learning
Skateboarding History: From the Backyard to the Big Time	Q	I	250+	Skateboarding	Red Brick Learning
Skateboards	N	I	250+	Windows on Literacy	National Geographic
Skateboards: Designs and Equipment	Q	I	250+	Skateboarding	Red Brick Learning
Skate Park Challenge	P	RF	4116	Maddox, Jake	Stone Arch Books
Skateparks: Grab Your Skateboard	Q	I	250+	Skateboarding	Red Brick Learning
Skater Chicks	N	RF	250+	Girlz Rock!	Mondo Publishing
Skates for Luke	I	RF	346	PM Story Books-Orange	Rigby
Skates of Uncle Richard, The	P	RF	250+	Fenner, Carol	Random House
Skateway to Freedom	V	HF	250+	Alma, Ann	Orca Books
Skating	B	F	35	Foundations	Wright Group/McGraw Hill
Skating	C	F	52	Story Box	Wright Group/McGraw Hill
Skating at Rainbow Lake	J	RF	250+	PM Story Books-Silver	Rigby
Skating on Thin Ice	G	F	130	First Start	Troll Associates
Skating to Fame	Q	I	524	Vocabulary Readers	Houghton Mifflin Harcourt
Skating Trail, The	I	RF	250+	PM Plus Story Books	Rigby
Skating Whiz	E	RF	40	Visions	Wright Group/McGraw Hill
Skeeter	N	RF	250+	PM Chapter Books	Rigby
Skeletal System, The	P	I	2167	Early Bird Body Systems	Lerner Publishing Group
Skeletal System, The	K	I	166	Human Body Systems	Red Brick Learning
Skeleton and Muscles, The	P	I	690	Time for Kids	Teacher Created Materials
Skeleton Clues	L	I	250+	Trackers	Pacific Learning
Skeleton in the Smithsonian, The	N	RF	250+	Roy, Ron	Random House
Skeleton Key	X	SF	250+	Horowitz, Anthony	Speak
Skeleton Man	V	F	250+	Bruchac, Joseph	Scholastic
Skeleton On The Bus, The	J	F	250+	Literacy 2000	Rigby
Skeletons	I	I	98	Storyteller	Wright Group/McGraw Hill
Skeletons Don't Play Tubas	M	F	250+	Dadey, Debbie; Jones, Marcia Thornton	Scholastic
Skeletons Inside and Out	S	I	250+	iOpeners	Pearson Learning Group
Ski Lesson, The	H	I	155	Storyteller-Moon Rising	Wright Group/McGraw Hill
Ski Race, The	F	RF	155	Springboard	Wright Group/McGraw Hill
Ski School	LB	RF	34	Little Books for Early Readers	University of Maine
Skier, The	B	RF	48	PM Starters	Rigby
Skimper-Scamper	G	F	208	Instant Readers	Harcourt Trade
Skin	E	I	105	Body Coverings	Lerner Publishing Group
Skin	F	I	97	Literacy 2000	Rigby
Skin	T	I	250+	Theme Sets	National Geographic
Skin I'm In, The	W	RF	250+	Flake, Sharon G.	Hyperion
Skin Like Milk, Hair of Silk: What Are Similies and Metaphors?	O	I	287	Words Are CATegorial	Millbrook Press
Skin, Skin	E	I	44	Wonder World	Wright Group/McGraw Hill
Skinny	Z+	RF	250+	Kaslik, Ibi	Walker & Company
Skinny-Bones	P	RF	250+	Park, Barbara	Random House
Skip Count Song, The	F	I	84	Learn to Read	Creative Teaching Press
Skip Counting	D	I	34	Early Math	Lerner Publishing Group

S

TITLE	LEVEL	GENRE	WORD COUNT	AUTHOR / SERIES	PUBLISHER / DISTRIBUTOR
Skip Through the Seasons	K	I	216	Blackstone, Stella	Barefoot Books
Skipper to the Rescue: Butterfly Meadow	M	F	250+	Moss, Olivia	Scholastic
Skipper's Balloon	E	RF	62	Oxford Reading Tree	Oxford University Press
Skipper's Birthday	E	RF	64	Oxford Reading Tree	Oxford University Press
Skipper's Idea	E	RF	81	Oxford Reading Tree	Oxford University Press
Skipper's Laces	E	RF	66	Oxford Reading Tree	Oxford University Press
Skippy's New Friends	J	F	250+	The Rowland Reading Program Library	Rowland Reading Foundation
Skirt, The	N	RF	250+	Soto, Gary	Bantam Books
Skittles and Skullbones	J	F	250+	Supersonics	Rigby
Skull of Truth, The	T	F	250+	Coville, Bruce	Harcourt
Skunk Cooks Soup	G	F	299	Leveled Readers	Houghton Mifflin Harcourt
Skunk Cooks Soup	G	F	299	Leveled Readers/CA	Houghton Mifflin Harcourt
Skunk Cooks Soup	G	F	299	Leveled Readers/TX	Houghton Mifflin Harcourt
Skunk Girl	Y	RF	250+	Karim, Sheba	Farrar, Straus, & Giroux
Skunk on the Bus, The	H	F	250+	The Rowland Reading Program Library	Rowland Reading Foundation
Skunk Wants to Play	D	F	95	Math Stories	Pearson Learning Group
Skunk with No Stripes, The	H	F	333	Leveled Literacy Intervention/ Green System	Heinemann
Skunks	R	I	250+	Animal Prey	Lerner Publishing Group
Skunks	M	I	250+	PM Animal Facts: Gold	Rigby
Skunks	H	I	111	Seedlings	Continental Press
Sky	N	RF	506	Leveled Readers	Houghton Mifflin Harcourt
^Sky Bikers	P	F	250+	Norman, Tony	Stone Arch Books
Sky Boys: How They Built the Empire State Building	Q	HF	250+	Hopkinson, Deborah & Ransome, James E.	Schwartz & Wade Books
Sky Changes	M	I	250+	PM Plus Nonfiction	Rigby
Sky Colors	G	I	147	Shutterbug Books	Steck-Vaughn
Sky Dogs	U	RF	250+	Yolen, Jane	Harcourt Brace
Sky High	L	F	619	Pair-It Books	Steck-Vaughn
Sky Is Falling Down, The	D	TL	101	Joy Readers	Pearson Learning Group
Sky Is Falling, The	F	TL	186	Folk Tales	Pioneer Valley
Sky Is Falling, The	I	F	181	Storyteller-Setting Sun	Wright Group/McGraw Hill
Sky Is Falling, The	E	TL	186	Traditional Tales	Pioneer Valley
Sky Is the Limit, The	N	I	250+	Trackers	Pacific Learning
Sky Rider	O	RF	250+	Belcher, Angie	Pacific Learning
Sky the Blue Fairy: Rainbow Magic	L	F	250+	Meadows, Daisy	Scholastic
Sky Time	F	F	366	Phonics and Friends	Hampton Brown
Sky Watch	Q	I	250+	Explorers	Wright Group/McGraw Hill
Sky Watchers	G	RF	172	Windows on Literacy	National Geographic
Sky, The	LB	I	16	Handprints A	Educators Publishing Service
Sky, The	A	I	40	Leveled Literacy Intervention/ Green System	Heinemann
^Skydiving	S	I	250+	Download	Hameray Publishing Group
Skydiving	N	I	250+	Sun Sprouts	ETA/Cuisenaire
SkyFire	J	F	250+	Asch, Frank	Scholastic
*Skygazers: From Hypatia to Faber	T	B	250+	Mission: Science	Compass Point Books
Sky-High Dreams	Q	HF	1123	Leveled Readers	Houghton Mifflin Harcourt
Sky-High Dreams	Q	HF	1123	Leveled Readers/CA	Houghton Mifflin Harcourt
Sky-High Dreams	Q	HF	1123	Leveled Readers/TX	Houghton Mifflin Harcourt
Skyjack!	Z	RF	8685	Oxford Bookworms Library	Oxford University Press
Skylark	R	HF	250+	MacLachlan, Patricia	HarperTrophy
Sky's the Limit, The	P	I	250+	Orbit Chapter Books	Pacific Learning

* Collection of short stories   # Graphic text
^ Mature content with lower level text demands

TITLE	LEVEL	GENRE	WORD COUNT	AUTHOR / SERIES	PUBLISHER / DISTRIBUTOR
Sky's the Limit, The	Q	RF	250+	Wildcats	Wright Group/McGraw Hill
Sky's the Limit, The: Naturally Funny Jokes	O	F	1731	Make Me Laugh!	Lerner Publishing Group
Skyscraper	L	I	164	Bookworms	Marshall Cavendish
SkyScraper, The	K	I	252	Little Red Readers	Sundance
Skyscrapers	L	I	298	Red Rocket Readers	Flying Start Books
Skyscrapers	O	I	250+	Simon, Seymour	Chronicle Books
Slake's Limbo	Y	RF	250+	Holman, Felice	Aladdin
Slam	Z+	RF	250+	Hornby, Nick	G.P. Putnam's Sons
Slam Dunk	S	RF	250+	Christopher, Matt	Little Brown and Company
Slam Dunk Magician	M	F	250+	Too Cool	Pacific Learning
Slam Dunk Sanchez	G	RF	238	Sunshine	Wright Group/McGraw Hill
Slam Dunk Saturday	M	RF	250+	Marzollo, Jean	Random House
Slam Dunk Shoes	Q	RF	250+	Maddox, Jake	Stone Arch Books
Slam!	W	RF	250+	Myers, Walter Dean	Scholastic
Slapshot!	W	I	250+	Boldprint	Steck-Vaughn
Slave Dancer, The	Y	HF	250+	Fox, Paula	Random House
Slave Trade in Early America, The	V	I	250+	Let Freedom Ring	Capstone Press
Slavery in America	T	I	250+	Primary Source Readers	Teacher Created Materials
Slawter (The Demonata Series)	Z+	F	250+	Shan, Darren	Little Brown and Company
Sled Dog Morning, A	I	RF	310	Appleton-Smith, Laura	Flyleaf Publishing
Sled Dog, The	F	RF	180	The Rowland Reading Program Library	Rowland Reading Foundation
Sled, A	D	RF	53	The Rowland Reading Program Library	Rowland Reading Foundation
Sled, The	D	RF	84	Leveled Readers Language Support	Houghton Mifflin Harcourt
Sledding	D	F	34	Brand New Readers	Candlewick Press
Sledding	A	F	58	Leveled Readers	Houghton Mifflin Harcourt
Sledding	A	F	58	Leveled Readers/CA	Houghton Mifflin Harcourt
Sledding	A	F	58	Leveled Readers/TX	Houghton Mifflin Harcourt
Sledding Adventures, The	F	F	186	Arctic Stories	Pioneer Valley
Sleep	O	I	250+	Trackers	Pacific Learning
Sleep Out, The	J	RF	645	Red Rocket Readers	Flying Start Books
Sleep Tight	H	RF	163	Cambridge Reading	Pearson Learning Group
Sleep Tight Spaceboy	G	F	112	Spaceboy	Literacy Footprints
^Sleep Walker	X	F	250+	The Extraordinary Files	Hameray Publishing Group
Sleep, Big Bear, Sleep!	L	F	250+	Wright, Maureen	Marshall Cavendish
Sleepaway Girls	Y	RF	250+	Calonita, Jen	Little Brown and Company
Sleepers, Wake	T	SF	250+	Jacobs, Paul Samuel	Language for Learning Assoc.
Sleeping	I	RF	114	Book Bank	Wright Group/McGraw Hill
Sleeping	E	I	43	Literacy 2000	Rigby
Sleeping Animals	H	I	194	Alphakids	Sundance
Sleeping Bear Dune, The: An Ojibway Legend	M	TL	250+	Windows on Literacy	National Geographic
Sleeping Beauty	K	TL	250+	Enrichment	Wright Group/McGraw Hill
Sleeping Beauty	L	TL	250+	Storybook Classics	Picture Window Books
Sleeping Beauty	L	TL	590	Traditional Tales	Pioneer Valley
Sleeping Beauty, The	L	TL	250+	PM Tales and Plays-Silver	Rigby
Sleeping Giant of Goll, The; The Secrets of Droon	O	F	250+	Abbott, Tony	Scholastic
Sleeping Out	D	RF	49	Story Box	Wright Group/McGraw Hill
Sleeping, Dreaming	P	I	250+	Wonder World	Wright Group/McGraw Hill
Sleep-Over Mouse	D	F	63	My First Reader	Grolier
Sleepover Party, The	I	RF	330	Adams, Lorraine & Bruvold, Lynn	Eaglecrest Books

TITLE	LEVEL	GENRE	WORD COUNT	AUTHOR / SERIES	PUBLISHER / DISTRIBUTOR
Sleep-Over!	L	RF	250+	Go Girl!	Feiwel and Friends
Sleepover, The	N	RF	250+	Girlz Rock!	Mondo Publishing
Sleepover, The	H	RF	297	Leveled Readers	Houghton Mifflin Harcourt
Sleepover, The	F	RF	261	Rigby Flying Colors	Rigby
Sleepovers	V	I	250+	10 Things You Need to Know About	Capstone Press
^Sleepwalker	O	RF	1920	Powell, J.	Stone Arch Books
Sleepy Bear	E	I	153	Foundations	Wright Group/McGraw Hill
Sleepy Bear	F	I	80	Literacy 2000	Rigby
Sleepy Dog	D	F	118	Ziefert, Harriet	Random House
Sleepy Polar Bear	H	F	97	Hiris, Monica	Kaeden Books
Sleepy Tiger	B	F	41	Sails	Rigby
Sleepy Zoo	B	F	58	Sun Sprouts	ETA/Cuisenaire
Sleepyville Wakes Up	T	HF	3021	Reading Street	Pearson
Slice of Pizza, A	I	RF	175	Twig	Wright Group/McGraw Hill
Slide and Slurp, Scratch and Burp: More About Verbs	O	I	287	Words Are CATegorical	Millbrook Press
Slides	D	I	58	Pacific Literacy	Pacific Learning
Sliding into Home	T	RF	250+	Butler, Dori Hillestad	Peachtree
Slightly Invisible	N	F	250+	Child, Lauren	Candlewick Press
Slim Shorty and the Mules	L	RF	411	Reading Unlimited	Pearson Learning Group
Slime Molds and Fungi	W	I	250+	Nature Close-Up	Blackbirch Press
Slimy Book of Spit, The	S	I	250+	The Amazingly Gross Human Body	Capstone Press
Slimy Skin	B	I	37	Sails	Rigby
Slimy Story, A	L	RF	1350	Science Solves It!	Kane Press
Slinky Scaly Snakes!	K	I	250+	DK Readers	DK Publishing
Slip and Slide	I	RF	250+	Phonics and Friends	Hampton Brown
Slip and Slide	K	I	215	Spyglass Books	Compass Point Books
Slip! Slide! Skate!	I	RF	250+	Herman, Gail	Scholastic
Slippery Planet, The	L	F	250+	Cambridge Reading	Pearson Learning Group
Slippery Slope, The	V	F	250+	Snicket, Lemony	Scholastic
Slippery, Sloppery Spaghetti	H	RF	250+	Home Connection Collection	Rigby
Slipping	X	F	250+	Bell, Cathleen Davitt	Bloomsbury Children's Books
Slither and Slide	H	I	112	Gear Up!	Wright Group/McGraw Hill
Slither McCreep and His Brother, Joe	K	RF	250+	Johnston, Tony	Harcourt Brace
Slithering Snakes	L	I	316	Red Rocket Readers	Flying Start Books
Slithery Snakes and Unicorns	I	F	289	Sunshine	Wright Group/McGraw Hill
Slog's Dad	X	RF	250+	Almond, David	Candlewick Press
Sloppy Copy Slipup, The	P	RF	250+	DiSalvo, DyAnne	Holiday House
Sloppy Tiger and the Party	I	F	293	Sunshine	Wright Group/McGraw Hill
Sloppy Tiger Bedtime	I	F	320	Sunshine	Wright Group/McGraw Hill
Sloppy Tiger on the Bus	H	F	272	The Joy Cowley Collection	Hameray Publishing Group
Sloppy Tiger Washes the Floor	G	F	199	The Joy Cowley Collection	Hameray Publishing Group
Sloppy Tigers's Picnic	H	F	242	The Joy Cowley Collection	Hameray Publishing Group
Slow	G	I	144	How Things Move	Heinemann Library
Slow and Fast	B	I	31	Handprints A	Educators Publishing Service
Slow Changes on Earth	Q	I	1394	Science Support Readers	Houghton Mifflin Harcourt
Slow Changes on Earth	Q	I	250+	Windows on Literacy	National Geographic
Slow Down, Sara	L	RF	1052	Science Solves It!	Kane Press
Slow Movers	B	I	49	Red Rocket Readers	Flying Start Books
Slow Poke Snail	G	RF	117	Instant Readers	Harcourt School Publishers
Slow Race, The	I	RF	337	InfoTrek	ETA/Cuisenaire

S

* Collection of short stories   # Graphic text
^ Mature content with lower level text demands

TITLE	LEVEL	GENRE	WORD COUNT	AUTHOR / SERIES	PUBLISHER / DISTRIBUTOR
Slowest Animals, The	K	I	250+	EXtreme Animals	Capstone Press
Slowpoke	K	RF	250+	Math Matters	Kane Press
^Sludge and Slime: Oil Spills in Our World	O	I	250+	On Deck	Rigby
Sluefoot Sue's Wild Ride	T	TL	1831	Leveled Readers	Houghton Mifflin Harcourt
Slug and Bug	B	F	42	Leveled Readers Language Support	Houghton Mifflin Harcourt
Slug Is Born, A	F	I	131	Sails	Rigby
Slug Makes a House	F	F	219	Rigby Rocket	Rigby
Slug the Sea Monster	H	F	250+	Storyworlds	Heinemann
Slugs	G	I	143	Bonnell, Kris/About	Reading Reading Books
Slugs	O	I	1282	Early Bird Nature Books	Lerner Publishing Group
Slugs	N	F	466	Greenberg, David	Little Brown and Company
Slugs and Snails	N	I	250+	Bookshop	Mondo Publishing
Slugs and Snails	P	I	250+	Mini Pets	Steck-Vaughn
Slugs and Snails	H	I	132	Wonder World	Wright Group/McGraw Hill
Slumber Party Organizer, The	P	I	250+	Sunshine	Wright Group/McGraw Hill
Slump, The	N	RF	250+	Kroll, Stephen	Avon Books
Slumpbuster, The (The Super Sluggers)	Q	RF	250+	Markey, Kevin	HarperCollins
Slurp! Burp!	E	F	107	Rigby Rocket	Rigby
Sly Fox and Little Red Hen	K	TL	250+	PM Tales and Plays-Purple	Rigby
Sly Fox and Red Hen	F	TL	314	Hunia, Fran	Ladybird Books
Sly Spy, The (Olivia Sharp)	L	RF	250+	Sharmat, Marjorie Weinman	Yearling Books
Sly Squirrel's Tall Tales	L	F	1162	InfoTrek	ETA/Cuisenaire
Sly Tom	N	TL	250+	Sun Sprouts	ETA/Cuisenaire
Small Adventure of Popeye and Elvis, The	S	RF	250+	O'Connor, Barbara	Farrar, Straus, & Giroux
Small and Large	E	I	89	iOpeners	Pearson Learning Group
Small as an Elephant	U	RF	250+	Richard Jacobson, Jennifer	Candlewick Press
Small Baby Raccoon, A	G	RF	104	Ready Readers	Pearson Learning Group
Small Bad Wolf	K	F	250+	I Am Reading	Kingfisher
Small Pig	I	F	250+	Lobel, Arnold	HarperTrophy
Small Rabbit Goes Visiting	H	F	445	Book Bank	Wright Group/McGraw Hill
Small Sailboat, A	I	RF	135	Books for Young Learners	Richard C. Owen
Small Screen	S	I	250+	Boldprint	Steck-Vaughn
Small Steps	Z	RF	250+	Sachar, Louis	Delacorte Press
Small Steps: The Year I Got Polio	U	B	250+	Kehret, Peg	Albert Whitman & Co.
Small Treasures	F	RF	52	Gibson, Akimi	Scholastic
Small Trip, A	G	RF	103	Reading Street	Pearson
Small Wolf	J	HF	250+	Benchley, Nathaniel	HarperTrophy
Small World, A	H	RF	146	Sunshine	Wright Group/McGraw Hill
Smallest Cow in the World, The	K	RF	250+	Paterson, Katherine	HarperTrophy
Smallest Dinosaurs, The	P	I	1115	Meet the Dinosaurs	Lerner Publishing Group
Smallest Horses, The	J	RF	250+	PM Plus Story Books	Rigby
Smallest Tree, The	K	F	250+	Literacy 2000	Rigby
Smart Art	N	RF	250+	Literacy by Design	Rigby
Smart Dog	N	RF	2182	Reading Street	Pearson
Smart Mouse, The	K	TL	597	Leveled Readers	Houghton Mifflin Harcourt
Smart Mouse, The	K	TL	597	Leveled Readers/CA	Houghton Mifflin Harcourt
Smart Mouse, The	K	TL	597	Leveled Readers/TX	Houghton Mifflin Harcourt
Smart Pigs	H	RF	102	Stewart, Josie	Continental Press
Smarter Than Squirrels: Down Girl and Sit	M	F	250+	Nolan, Lucy	Marshall Cavendish
Smartest Bear and His Brother Oliver, The	N	F	250+	Bach, Alice	Bantam Books
Smartest Dinosaurs, The	P	I	1195	Meet the Dinosaurs	Lerner Publishing Group
*Smartest Man in Ireland, The	S	F	250+	Hunter, Mollie	Harcourt Brace
Smartest One in Class, The	H	RF	68	City Stories	Rigby

S

TITLE	LEVEL	GENRE	WORD COUNT	AUTHOR / SERIES	PUBLISHER / DISTRIBUTOR
Smarty No Pants	G	F	210	The Joy Cowley Collection	Hameray Publishing Group
Smarty Pants	E	F	116	Story Box	Wright Group/McGraw Hill
Smarty Pants and the Talent Show	F	F	139	The Joy Cowley Collection	Hameray Publishing Group
Smarty Pants at the Circus	H	F	169	The Joy Cowley Collection	Hameray Publishing Group
Smarty Sara	H	RF	250+	Step into Reading	Random House
Smasher	O	RF	250+	King-Smith, Dick	Random House
^Smashing Scroll, The	T	F	799	Dahl, Michael	Stone Arch Books
Smelling	I	I	111	Pebble Books	Red Brick Learning
Smelling	E	I	88	Senses	Lerner Publishing Group
Smelling	M	I	250+	The Senses	Capstone Press
Smelling!	H	I	146	Sails	Rigby
Smells	A	RF	40	Leveled Literacy Intervention/ Green System	Heinemann
Smells All Around Us	G	I	202	PM Science Readers	Rigby
Smells Good!	H	I	216	PM Science Readers	Rigby
Smells Like Dog	S	F	250+	Selfors, Suzanne	Little Brown and Company
Smells Like Treasure	S	F	250+	Selfors, Suzanne	Little Brown and Company
Smelly Armor	J	F	282	Story Box	Wright Group/McGraw Hill
Smelly Skunks	H	I	147	Sails	Rigby
Smile	D	F	38	Read-Alongs	Rigby
Smile a Lot!	J	F	310	Carlson, Nancy	Carolrhoda Books
Smile and Say "Cheetah"	I	RF	200	World Quest Adventures	World Quest Learning
Smile If You Like Circles	J	I	250+	Phonics Readers Plus	Steck-Vaughn
Smile! Said Dad	D	RF	66	Pacific Literacy	Pacific Learning
Smile, Baby!	F	RF	165	Little Readers	Houghton Mifflin Harcourt
Smile, The	D	RF	53	Pacific Literacy	Pacific Learning
Smile, The	K	RF	253	Read Alongs	Rigby
Smiles	F	RF	366	Visions	Wright Group/McGraw Hill
Smiling	J	I	137	Small World	Lerner Publishing Group
Smiling Salad, A	C	RF	32	Pair-It Books	Steck-Vaughn
Smiling Stan, the Pedicab Man	E	RF	121	Joy Readers	Pearson Learning Group
Smith: John Smith and the Settlement of Jamestown	U	B	250+	Exploring the World	Compass Point Books
Smiths and Their Animals, The	J	RF	468	Leveled Readers	Houghton Mifflin Harcourt
Smiths and Their Animals, The	J	RF	468	Leveled Readers/CA	Houghton Mifflin Harcourt
Smiths and Their Animals, The	J	RF	468	Leveled Readers/TX	Houghton Mifflin Harcourt
Smog, Dust, and Toads	R	I	250+	Orbit Chapter Books	Pacific Learning
Smoke	T	RF	250+	Jukes, Mavis	Farrar, Straus, & Giroux
Smoke Jumpers	I	I	199	On Deck	Rigby
Smokejumpers: Battling the Forest Flames	T	I	250+	High Five Reading	Red Brick Learning
Smokey the Dragon	M	F	250+	Bennett, Jean	Pearson Learning Group
Smokie	E	RF	47	Carousel Readers	Pearson Learning Group
#Smoking Mountain, The: The Story of Popocatepetl and Iztaccihuatl	W	TL	2393	Graphic Myths and Legends	Lerner Publishing Group
Smoky the Cow Horse	S	RF	250+	James, Will	Scholastic
Smooth and Rough	K	I	250+	Animal Opposites	Capstone Press
Smooth or Rough	G	I	130	Properties of Materials	Heinemann Library
Smooth or Rough?	D	I	49	Rigby Focus	Rigby
Smudge-Face: A Native American Cinderella Tale	M	TL	580	Leveled Readers	Houghton Mifflin Harcourt
Smugglers' Mine, The: Something Wickedly Weird	R	F	250+	Mould, Chris	Roaring Brook Press
Smushy Bus, The	L	F	744	Helakoski, Leslie	Millbrook Press
Snack Attack	O	F	250+	Scooters	ETA/Cuisenaire
Snack Attack Mystery, The	L	F	250+	Levy, Elizabeth	Scholastic

S

* Collection of short stories   # Graphic text
^ Mature content with lower level text demands

TITLE	LEVEL	GENRE	WORD COUNT	AUTHOR / SERIES	PUBLISHER / DISTRIBUTOR
Snack for Gilbert, A	B	RF	28	Gilbert the Pig	Pioneer Valley
Snack for Roberto, A	D	RF	82	Early Emergent, Set 2	Pioneer Valley
Snack Time	G	RF	59	City Kids	Rigby
Snack Time	B	RF	48	InfoTrek	ETA/Cuisenaire
Snack Time	F	RF	148	Red Rocket Readers	Flying Start Books
Snack Time	A	I	19	Vocabulary Readers	Houghton Mifflin Harcourt
Snack Time	A	I	19	Vocabulary Readers/CA	Houghton Mifflin Harcourt
Snack Time Around the World	M	I	250+	Meals Around the World	Picture Window Books
Snacks	D	RF	19	Joy Readers	Pearson Learning Group
Snacks for Healthy Teeth	H	I	136	Healthy Teeth	Capstone Press
Snaggle Doodles	M	RF	250+	Giff, Patricia Reilly	Bantam Books
Snail Girl	H	RF	250+	Momentum Literacy Program	Troll Associates
Snail Hits the Trail	K	F	1107	Appleton-Smith, Laura	Flyleaf Publishing
Snail Race, The	H	F	223	Springboard	Wright Group/McGraw Hill
Snail Saves the Day	G	F	76	Stadler, John	HarperCollins
Snail That Snored, The	I	F	250+	Phonics Readers Plus	Steck-Vaughn
Snail Trail to 100	J	RF	212	PM Math Readers	Rigby
Snail Trail, The	I	F	243	Sunshine	Wright Group/McGraw Hill
Snail, The	B	I	75	Rigby Flying Colors	Rigby
Snails	A	I	40	First Stories	Pacific Learning
Snails	E	I	67	Foundations	Wright Group/McGraw Hill
Snails	O	I	250+	Holmes, Kevin J.	Red Brick Learning
Snails	K	I	170	Watch It Grow	Capstone Press
Snails and Slugs	E	I	54	Sun Sprouts	ETA/Cuisenaire
Snails in School	H	I	181	Discovery Links	Newbridge
Snake	H	I	67	Joy Starters	Pearson Learning Group
Snake	B	I	42	Zoozoo-Animal World	Cavallo Publishing
Snake Alarm	M	RF	250+	Krailing, Tessa	Barron's Educational
Snake and the Birds	J	F	420	Sails	Rigby
Snake at the Lake	J	F	250+	The Wright Skills	Wright Group/McGraw Hill
Snake Gets Lost	H	F	259	Springboard	Wright Group/McGraw Hill
Snake Goes Away	C	F	55	Literacy by Design	Rigby
Snake Goes Away	C	F	55	Rigby Literacy	Rigby
Snake Hunts for Lunch	E	RF	115	Hoenecke, Karen	Kaeden Books
Snake Is Going Away!	C	F	57	Rigby Star	Rigby
Snake Safari	Q	I	250+	Explorer Books-Pathfinder	National Geographic
Snake Safari	P	I	250+	Explorer Books-Pioneer	National Geographic
Snake Slithers, A	H	I	82	Reading Unlimited	Pearson Learning Group
Snake That Couldn't Hiss, The	I	F	250+	Storyworlds	Heinemann
Snake!	M	RF	641	Sunshine	Wright Group/McGraw Hill
Snake, The	O	I	250+	Crewe, Sabrina	Steck-Vaughn
Snake, The	A	F	30	Sails	Rigby
Snakebite	J	RF	271	Story Box	Wright Group/McGraw Hill
Snakes	E	I	37	All About Pets	Capstone Press
Snakes	Q	I	250+	Explorers	Wright Group/McGraw Hill
Snakes	O	I	250+	First Reports	Compass Point Books
Snakes	K	I	259	Foundations	Wright Group/McGraw Hill
Snakes	S	I	250+	Keeping Unusual Pets	Heinemann Library
Snakes	F	I	98	Life Cycles	Lerner Publishing Group
Snakes	I	I	208	Momentum Literacy Program	Troll Associates
Snakes	H	I	145	Nonfiction Set 5	Literacy Footprints
Snakes	I	I	242	Sails	Rigby
Snakes	R	I	250+	Simon, Seymour	Scholastic
Snakes	J	I	448	Sunshine	Wright Group/McGraw Hill

* Collection of short stories   # Graphic text
^ Mature content with lower level text demands

TITLE	LEVEL	GENRE	WORD COUNT	AUTHOR / SERIES	PUBLISHER / DISTRIBUTOR
Snakes	J	I	450	Time for Kids	Teacher Created Materials
Snakes	LB	I	25	Twig	Wright Group/McGraw Hill
Snakes	E	I	37	Visions	Wright Group/McGraw Hill
Snakes	L	I	252	Wonder World	Wright Group/McGraw Hill
Snakes and Lizards	I	I	205	Yellow Umbrella Books	Red Brick Learning
Snake's Big Mouth	H	F	199	Gear Up!	Wright Group/McGraw Hill
Snake's Dinner	E	F	156	Alphakids	Sundance
Snake's Sore Head	F	F	139	Storyteller-Moon Rising	Wright Group/McGraw Hill
Snakes That Rattle	I	I	374	Sails	Rigby
Snakes!	M	I	250+	National Geographic Kids	Scholastic
Snakes!	L	I	250+	Recht Penner, Lucille	Random House
Snakes!: Deadly Predators or Harmless Pets?	S	I	250+	High Five Reading	Red Brick Learning
Snakes: Cold-Blooded Crawlers	M	I	250+	The Wild World of Animals	Red Brick Learning
Snap Happy	E	RF	164	Rigby Rocket	Rigby
Snap Likes Ginger Cookies	E	F	63	Gosset, Rachel	Scholastic
Snap!	B	F	50	Leveled Literacy Intervention/ Green System	Heinemann
Snap!	B	F	31	Sunshine	Wright Group/McGraw Hill
Snap! Splash!	G	I	48	Pacific Literacy	Pacific Learning
Snap! Splat!	C	F	25	Sunshine	Wright Group/McGraw Hill
Snap!: A Book About Alligators and Crocodiles	L	I	250+	Berger, Melvin & Gilda	Scholastic
Snap, Crackle, and Flow	U	I	250+	Navigators Science Series	Benchmark Education
Snapshots	D	RF	20	Bebop Books	Lee & Low Books Inc.
Snapshots from the Wedding	O	RF	250+	Soto, Gary	PaperStar
Snarf Attack: Underfoodle and the Secret of Life: The Riot Brothers Tell All	O	RF	250+	Amato, Mary	Holiday House
Snarling Suspect, The	O	RF	250+	Klooz	Stone Arch Books
Sneakers	K	I	388	Sunshine	Wright Group/McGraw Hill
Sneakers	T	I	4478	Where's the Science Here?	Lerner Publishing Group
Sneakers! Sneakers!	F	F	49	Little Celebrations	Pearson Learning Group
Sneaky Salamanders	L	I	370	Pull Ahead Books	Lerner Publishing Group
Sneaky Snake, The	M	F	250+	Tristars	Richard C. Owen
Sneaky Spider	J	F	511	Red Rocket Readers	Flying Start Books
Sneaky, Spinning Baby Spiders	R	I	250+	Markle, Sandra	Walker & Company
Sneeze, The	C	F	85	Sails	Rigby
Sneezes	F	RF	36	Literacy 2000	Rigby
Sneezles, The	L	F	1262	Big Cat	Pacific Learning
Sneezy the Snowman	L	F	250+	Wright, Maureen	Marshall Cavendish
Snickers	I	RF	250+	Momentum Literacy Program	Troll Associates
Snick-Snack Sniffle-Nose	H	F	187	Supersonics	Rigby
Sniffer's Golden Nose	L	F	250+	I Am Reading	Kingfisher
Sniffy	F	RF	290	Rigby Rocket	Rigby
Snip, Snap	I	F	250+	Sunshine	Wright Group/McGraw Hill
Snip-Snap, Clickety-Click	C	F	54	Little Celebrations	Pearson Learning Group
^Snitch	T	RF	250+	Orca Soundings	Orca Books
Snog Log, The	Z+	RF	250+	Coleman, Michael	Marshall Cavendish
Snook Alone	R	F	250+	Nelson, Marilyn	Candlewick Press
Snore, Dinosaur, Snore	H	F	43	Bendal-Brunello, John	Marshall Cavendish
Snorkeling	I	RF	233	Leveled Readers Language Support	Houghton Mifflin Harcourt
Snorkeling For Fun!	S	I	250+	For Fun!	Compass Point Books
Snorp on the Slopes	J	F	397	Stone Arch Readers	Stone Arch Books
Snot Stew	P	F	250+	Wallace, Bill	Pocket Books

S

* Collection of short stories   # Graphic text
^ Mature content with lower level text demands

TITLE	LEVEL	GENRE	WORD COUNT	AUTHOR / SERIES	PUBLISHER / DISTRIBUTOR
Snotty Book of Snot, The	S	I	250+	The Amazingly Gross Human Body	Capstone Press
Snow	E	I	28	Book Bank	Wright Group/McGraw Hill
Snow	B	I	29	Discovery Links	Newbridge
Snow	B	I	33	Hoenecke, Karen	Kaeden Books
Snow	I	RF	237	Sails	Rigby
Snow	C	RF	47	Science	Outside the Box
Snow	D	I	21	Sunshine	Wright Group/McGraw Hill
Snow	E	RF	92	The King School Series	Townsend Press
Snow	A	I	11	Vocabulary Readers	Houghton Mifflin Harcourt
Snow	K	I	370	Yellow Umbrella Books	Red Brick Learning
Snow	H	RF	217	Young Writers' World	Nelson/Michaels Assoc.
Snow and Ice	G	I	340	Sails	Rigby
Snow Baby, The	F	RF	337	Easy Stories	Norwood House Press
Snow Baby: The Arctic Childhood of Admiral Robert E. Peary's Daring Daughter, The	X	B	250+	Kirkpatrick, Katherine	Holiday House
Snow Bright and the Seven Sumos	M	F	250+	Supa Doopers	Sundance
Snow Bright and the Tooth Magician	M	F	250+	Supa Doopers	Sundance
Snow Buddy!	G	F	134	McGougan, Kathy	Buddy Books Publishing
Snow Cover	C	RF	29	Little Celebrations	Pearson Learning Group
Snow Danny	E	F	57	Coulton, Mia	Maryruth Books
Snow Daughter, The	L	TL	505	Sunshine	Wright Group/McGraw Hill
Snow Day	I	RF	250+	Bliss, Corinne Demas	Random House
Snow Day!	K	RF	719	Laminack, Lester L.	Peachtree
Snow Dog	C	RF	32	Potato Chip Books	American Reading Company
Snow Falling in Spring	Z	B	250+	Li, Moying	Farrar, Straus, & Giroux
Snow Family	M	F	250+	Kirk, Daniel	Scholastic
Snow Fun	D	RF	96	Kaleidoscope Collection	Hameray Publishing Group
Snow Games: A Robot and Rico Story	G	F	283	Stone Arch Readers	Stone Arch Books
Snow Goes To Town	L	F	250+	Literacy 2000	Rigby
Snow in the Kitchen	L	RF	250+	Cambridge Reading	Pearson Learning Group
Snow Is Cold	C	I	47	Little Readers	Houghton Mifflin Harcourt
Snow Joe	D	RF	59	Rookie Readers	Children's Press
Snow Mouse	B	F	35	Brand New Readers	Candlewick Press
Snow on the Hill	H	RF	213	PM Extensions-Green	Rigby
Snow Queen, The	U	TL	250+	Lewis, Naomi	Candlewick Press
Snow Rescue	K	RF	250+	Reading Safari	Mondo Publishing
Snow Treasure	R	HF	250+	McSwigan, Marie	Scholastic
Snow Walk	LB	RF	32	Reading Corners	Pearson Learning Group
Snow Walker, The	L	HF	250+	Wetterer, Margaret K. & Charles M.	Carolrhoda Books
Snow White and Rose Red	K	TL	250+	Hunia, Fran	Ladybird Books
Snow White and the Seven Dwarfs	I	TL	250+	Enrichment	Wright Group/McGraw Hill
Snow White and the Seven Dwarfs	K	TL	250+	PM Tales and Plays-Gold	Rigby
Snow, The	G	RF	112	Burningham, John	Crowell
Snow, The	B	F	36	Sails	Rigby
Snow, The	D	RF	36	Sunshine	Wright Group/McGraw Hill
Snow? Let's Go!	F	RF	55	Nagel, Karen Berman	Scholastic
Snowball Attack	N	RF	250+	Girlz Rock!	Mondo Publishing
Snowball Fight	WB	RF	0	Rigby Literacy	Rigby
Snowball Fight!	D	RF	35	Wonder World	Wright Group/McGraw Hill
Snowball War, The	K	RF	250+	Chardiet, Bernice	Scholastic
Snowball, The	G	F	92	Armstrong, Jennifer	Random House
Snowball, the White Mouse	G	RF	223	PM Plus Story Books	Rigby

S

TITLE	LEVEL	GENRE	WORD COUNT	AUTHOR / SERIES	PUBLISHER / DISTRIBUTOR
Snowball: The Puppy Place	N	RF	250+	Miles, Ellen	Scholastic
Snowballs	J	RF	119	Ehlert, Lois	Harcourt
Snowbear's Christmas Countdown	K	F	250+	Smythe, Theresa	Square Fish
Snowboard Champ	T	RF	250+	Christopher, Matt	Little Brown and Company
Snowboard Duel	P	RF	250+	Maddox, Jake	Stone Arch Books
Snowboard Maverick	S	RF	250+	Christopher, Matt	Norwood House Press
Snowboard Showdown	R	RF	250+	Christopher, Matt	Norwood House Press
Snowboarding	S	I	250+	Download	Hameray Publishing Group
Snowboarding	A	I	37	Nonfiction Set 1	Literacy Footprints
Snowboarding	M	I	250+	To the Extreme	Capstone Press
Snowboarding	Q	I	250+	X-Sports	Capstone Press
Snowboarding Diary	O	I	250+	PM Nonfiction-Emerald	Rigby
Snowboarding for Fun!	S	I	250+	Sports for Fun	Compass Point Books
Snowbound!	T	RF	250+	Power Up!	Steck-Vaughn
Snowden	K	F	576	Carlson, Nancy	Carolrhoda Books
Snowdrops for Cousin Ruth	S	RF	250+	Katz, Susan	Simon & Schuster
Snowflake Bentley	Q	B	250+	Martin, Jacqueline Briggs	Houghton Mifflin Harcourt
Snowflake, The: A Watercycle Story	M	I	779	Waldman, Neil	Millbrook Press
Snowflakes	H	I	110	All About Winter	Capstone Press
Snowflakes	F	RF	80	Seedlings	Continental Press
Snowflakes	D	RF	49	Urmston, Kathleen; Evans, Karen	Kaeden Books
Snowman	LB	RF	14	Smart Start	Rigby
Snowman	A	RF	19	Story Box	Wright Group/McGraw Hill
Snowman	C	RF	21	Sunshine	Wright Group/McGraw Hill
Snowman Day	B	RF	72	First Stories	Pacific Learning
Snowman Mystery, The	I	RF	200	InfoTrek	ETA/Cuisenaire
Snowman, A	C	I	59	Foundations	Wright Group/McGraw Hill
Snowman, The	WB	F	0	Briggs, Raymond	Random House
Snowman, The	B	RF	76	Leveled Readers Emergent	Houghton Mifflin Harcourt
Snowman, The	E	RF	76	Oxford Reading Tree	Oxford University Press
Snowman, The	B	F	30	Sails	Rigby
Snowman, The	B	I	32	Story Steps	Rigby
Snowman,The	C	RF	33	Gear Up!	Wright Group/McGraw Hill
Snowmobile Racing	S	I	250+	Motor Sports	Red Brick Learning
Snowmobiles	M	I	250+	Horsepower	Capstone Press
Snowmobiles	Q	I	250+	Wild Rides!	Red Brick Learning
Snowmobiling	S	I	250+	The Great Outdoors	Red Brick Learning
Snowplows	I	I	127	Mighty Machines	Capstone Press
Snowplows	L	I	450	Pull Ahead Books	Lerner Publishing Group
Snowshoe Thompson	K	HF	250+	Levinson, N. Smiler	HarperTrophy
#Snowshowing Adventure of Milton Daub, Blizzard Trekker, The	O	HF	1101	History's Kid Heroes	Graphic Universe
Snowstorm, The	H	F	231	Arctic Stories	Pioneer Valley
Snowy	B	I	24	Weather	Lerner Publishing Group
Snowy Day, A	G	I	232	Leveled Readers	Houghton Mifflin Harcourt
Snowy Day, A	G	I	232	Leveled Readers/CA	Houghton Mifflin Harcourt
Snowy Day, A	G	I	232	Leveled Readers/TX	Houghton Mifflin Harcourt
Snowy Day, A	E	I	54	Pebble Books	Capstone Press
Snowy Day, A	E	I	112	Weather	Lerner Publishing Group
Snowy Day, The	J	RF	319	Keats, Ezra Jack	Scholastic
Snowy Days	I	I	163	Literacy by Design	Rigby
Snowy Gets a Wash	E	RF	181	PM Extensions-Yellow	Rigby
Snowy Owls	H	I	124	Polar Animals	Capstone Press
Snowy the Polar Teddy	B	F	28	Reading Safari	Mondo Publishing

S

* Collection of short stories   # Graphic text
^ Mature content with lower level text demands

| --- | --- | --- | --- | --- | --- |
Snug as a Bug	C	F	76	Literacy by Design	Rigby
Snuggle Up	F	RF	125	Harrison, P.; Worthington, Denise	Continental Press
So Big!	B	F	63	Leveled Literacy Intervention/ Orange System	Heinemann
So Do I	D	RF	49	Teacher's Choice Series	Pearson Learning Group
So Far From the Bamboo Grove	V	HF	250+	Watkins, Yoko Kawashima	William Morrow
So Far from the Sea	R	RF	250+	Bunting, Eve	Sandpiper Books
So Fast	B	I	52	Red Rocket Readers	Flying Start Books
So Long Stinky Queen	M	RF	250+	First Flight	Fitzhenry & Whiteside
So Many Birthdays	I	RF	250+	Momentum Literacy Program	Troll Associates
So Many Circles	C	I	36	Yellow Umbrella Books	Red Brick Learning
So Many Houses	D	I	79	Rookie Readers	Children's Press
So Many Legs	E	F	110	In Step Readers	Rigby
So Many Snakes	I	I	152	Rosen Real Readers	Rosen Publishing Group
So Many Sounds	F	I	153	Vocabulary Readers	Houghton Mifflin Harcourt
So Many Sounds	F	I	153	Vocabulary Readers/CA	Houghton Mifflin Harcourt
So Many Sounds	F	I	153	Vocabulary Readers/TX	Houghton Mifflin Harcourt
So Many Strawberries	E	RF	75	Books for Young Learners	Richard C. Owen
So Many Things to Do	A	RF	21	Home Connection Collection	Rigby
So Much	I	RF	250+	Cooke, Trish	Candlewick Press
So Much to Do	H	RF	250+	On Our Way to English	Rigby
So Much To Tell You	Z+	RF	250+	Marsden, John	Lothian Books
So Sleepy	D	RF	33	Books for Young Learners	Richard C. Owen
So That's What It Is!	F	I	133	Rigby Literacy	Rigby
So What?	I	RF	250+	Cohen, Miriam	Bantam Books
So You Want to Be a Teacher?	L	I	715	Springboard	Wright Group/McGraw Hill
So You Want to Be a Writer?	O	I	250+	Springboard	Wright Group/McGraw Hill
So You Want to Be an Inventor?	P	I	250+	St. George, Judith; Small, David	Philomel
So You Want to Be President?	S	I	250+	St. George, Judith	Philomel
So You Want to Move a Building?	M	I	380	Pacific Literacy	Pacific Learning
So You Want to Work in Publishing?	W	I	2842	Vocabulary Readers	Houghton Mifflin Harcourt
So You Want to Work in Publishing?	W	I	2842	Vocabulary Readers/CA	Houghton Mifflin Harcourt
So, So Sam	G	RF	107	TOTTS	Tott Publications
Soak It Up	J	I	458	InfoTrek	ETA/Cuisenaire
Soap Soup and Other Verses	K	TL	250+	Kuskin, Karla	HarperTrophy
Soap Story, A	H	RF	95	City Stories	Rigby
Soaring Bald Eagles	K	I	377	Pull Ahead Books	Lerner Publishing Group
Soaring without an Engine	Q	I	1154	Take Two Books	Wright Group/McGraw Hill
Soccer	S	I	250+	Boldprint	Steck-Vaughn
Soccer	M	I	250+	Little Celebrations	Pearson Learning Group
Soccer	K	I	250+	On Deck	Rigby
Soccer	C	I	40	Readlings	American Reading Company
Soccer	F	I	128	Readlings/Sports	American Reading Company
Soccer	K	I	440	Red Rocket Readers	Flying Start Books
Soccer	E	I	78	Sun Sprouts	ETA/Cuisenaire
Soccer	K	I	270	Take Two Books	Wright Group/McGraw Hill
Soccer	G	I	189	Vocabulary Readers	Houghton Mifflin Harcourt
Soccer	G	I	189	Vocabulary Readers/CA	Houghton Mifflin Harcourt
Soccer	G	I	189	Vocabulary Readers/TX	Houghton Mifflin Harcourt
Soccer at the Park	E	RF	131	PM Extensions-Yellow	Rigby
Soccer Chick Rules	Z	RF	250+	Fitzgerald, Dawn	Square Fish
Soccer Cousins	K	RF	250+	Marzollo, Jean	Scholastic
Soccer for Fun	S	I	250+	Sports for Fun	Compass Point Books
Soccer Fun!	N	RF	661	Leveled Readers	Houghton Mifflin Harcourt

S

TITLE	LEVEL	GENRE	WORD COUNT	AUTHOR / SERIES	PUBLISHER / DISTRIBUTOR
Soccer Game	B	F	21	Reading Street	Pearson
Soccer Game!	F	RF	63	Maccarone, Grace	Scholastic
Soccer Game, The	F	RF	278	Leveled Literacy Intervention/ Green System	Heinemann
Soccer Halfback	S	RF	250+	Christopher, Matt	Norwood House Press
Soccer Hero	Q	RF	250+	Christopher, Matt	Little Brown and Company
Soccer Mania!	M	RF	250+	Tamar, Erika	Random House
#Soccer Sabotage: A Graphic Guide Adventure	T	RF	250+	O'Donnell, Liam	Orca Books
Soccer Sam	C	RF	70	Handprints B	Educators Publishing Service
Soccer Sam	M	RF	250+	Marzollo, Jean	Random House
Soccer Scoop	S	RF	250+	Christopher, Matt	Norwood House Press
Soccer Shootout	P	RF	250+	Maddox, Jake	Stone Arch Books
Soccer Showdown	Q	F	1720	Zucker, Jonny	Stone Arch Books
Soccer Sisters	R	RF	1541	Leveled Readers	Houghton Mifflin Harcourt
Soccer Sisters	R	RF	1541	Leveled Readers/CA	Houghton Mifflin Harcourt
Soccer Sisters	R	RF	1541	Leveled Readers/TX	Houghton Mifflin Harcourt
Soccer Song	F	RF	157	Green Light Readers	Harcourt
Soccer Star, The	F	RF	190	Windows on Literacy	National Geographic
Soccer Stars, Best Friend Face-off	R	RF	250+	Costello, Emily	Dell
Soccer Superstar	M	F	250+	Too Cool	Pacific Learning
Soccer Team Upset	R	RF	250+	Bowen, Fred	Peachtree
Soccer with Dad	F	RF	127	The King School Series	Townsend Press
Soccer: Get in the Game!	S	I	250+	Explore More	Wright Group/McGraw Hill
Social Justice: How You Can Make a Difference	T	I	250+	Take Action	Capstone Press
Society of Dread, The: Candle Man, Book Two	U	F	250+	Dakin, Glenn	Egmont USA
Society of Unrelenting Vigilance, The: Candle Man, Book One	U	F	250+	Dakin, Glenn	Egmont USA
*Sock Gobbler and Other Stories, The	M	F	250+	Learning Media	Pacific Learning
Socks	C	RF	40	Bonnell, Kris	Reading Reading Books
Socks	O	RF	250+	Cleary, Beverly	Avon Books
Socks	E	RF	70	Dominie Readers	Pearson Learning Group
Socks	B	RF	21	Ready Readers	Pearson Learning Group
Socks	D	RF	250+	Rigby Literacy	Rigby
Socks	LB	RF	21	Smart Starts	Rigby
Socks for Supper	I	F	250+	Kent, Jack	Parent's Magazine Press
Socks Off	H	RF	177	Alphakids	Sundance
Socks!	B	RF	54	Windows on Literacy	National Geographic
Socrates: Greek Philosopher	X	B	250+	Primary Source Readers	Teacher Created Materials
Sod Houses on the Great Plains	N	I	250+	Rounds, Glen	Holiday House
Soda Pop	A	RF	26	Bonnell, Kris	Reading Reading Books
Soddies	M	I	250+	Twig	Wright Group/McGraw Hill
Soft and Hard	B	I	65	Early Explorers	Benchmark Education
Soft and Hard	B	I	40	Explorations	Okapi Educational Materials
Soft and Hard	B	I	40	Explorations	Eleanor Curtain Publishing
Soft and Hard: An Animal Opposites Book	J	I	250+	Animal Opposites	Capstone Press
Softwire, The: Betrayal on Orbis 2	X	SF	250+	Haarsma, PJ	Candlewick Press
Softwire, The: Virus on Orbis 1	X	SF	250+	Haarsma, PJ	Candlewick Press
Soil	R	I	2027	Early Bird Earth Systems	Lerner Publishing Group
Soil	Q	I	250+	Exploring the Earth	Capstone Press
Soil	S	I	250+	Let's Rock	Heinemann Library
Soil	N	I	250+	Simply Science	Compass Point Books
Soil	F	I	93	What Earth Is Made Of	Lerner Publishing Group
Soil	K	I	381	Windows on Literacy	National Geographic

* Collection of short stories   # Graphic text
^ Mature content with lower level text demands

TITLE	LEVEL	GENRE	WORD COUNT	AUTHOR / SERIES	PUBLISHER / DISTRIBUTOR
Soil - It Takes All Kinds	O	I	250+	InfoTrek	ETA/Cuisenaire
Soil Basics	J	I	140	Nature Basics	Capstone Press
Soil on the Move	O	I	250+	InfoTrek	ETA/Cuisenaire
Soil: A Resource Our World Depends On	V	I	250+	Managing Our Resources	Heinemann
Sojourner Truth	T	B	250+	Amazing Americans	Wright Group/McGraw Hill
Sojourner Truth	Q	B	250+	Early Biographies	Compass Point Books
Sojourner Truth	M	B	250+	Famous Americans	Red Brick Learning
Sojourner Truth	S	B	4018	History Maker Bios	Lerner Publishing Group
Sojourner Truth	U	B	250+	Let Freedom Ring	Red Brick Learning
Sojourner Truth	P	B	1367	Leveled Readers Language Support	Houghton Mifflin Harcourt
Sojourner Truth	P	B	1551	On My Own Biography	Lerner Publishing Group
Sojourner Truth	P	B	250+	Photo-Illustrated Biographies	Red Brick Learning
Sojourner Truth, Speaker for Equal Rights	O	B	374	Independent Readers Social Studies	Houghton Mifflin Harcourt
Sojourner Truth: Ain't I a Woman?	V	B	250+	McKissack, Fredrick & Patricia	Scholastic
^Sojourner Truth: Early Abolitionist	P	B	250+	On Deck	Rigby
Sojourner Truth: Freedom Fighter	P	B	250+	Great African Americans	Capstone Press
Solar Energy	K	I	167	Larkin, Bruce	Wilbooks
Solar Energy	V	I	2068	Leveled Readers Science	Houghton Mifflin Harcourt
Solar Energy	N	I	476	Nonfiction Indigo	Pioneer Valley
Solar Power	X	I	250+	Energy at Work	Capstone Press
Solar Storms	R	I	250+	Rosen Real Readers	Rosen Publishing Group
Solar System	T	I	250+	Mission: Science	Compass Point Books
Solar System and Beyond, The	V	I	2234	Reading Street	Pearson
Solar System Sights	R	I	250+	In Step Readers	Rigby
Solar System Sights	R	I	250+	Literacy by Design	Rigby
Solar System, The	Q	I	250+	A True Book	Children's Press
Solar System, The	Q	I	1769	Early Bird Astronomy	Lerner Publishing Group
Solar System, The	N	I	714	Our Universe	Lerner Publishing Group
Solar System, The	S	I	2061	Science Support Readers	Houghton Mifflin Harcourt
Solar System, The	N	I	250+	Simply Science	Compass Point Books
Solar System, The	Q	I	250+	The Galaxy	Capstone Press
Solar System, The	U	I	250+	The Heinle Reading Library	Thomson Learning
Solar System, The	O	I	607	Time for Kids	Teacher Created Materials
Solar-Powered Sam	J	F	148	Books for Young Learners	Richard C. Owen
Soldier and Founder: Alexander Hamilton	T	B	250+	We the People	Compass Point Books
Soldier Athletes	U	B	250+	Good Sports	Houghton Mifflin Harcourt
Soldier Boy	T	HF	250+	Burks, Brian	Harcourt Trade
Soldier's Heart	V	HF	250+	Paulsen, Gary	Random House
Soldiers of Halla, The: Pendragon	X	F	250+	MacHale, D.J.	Aladdin
^Soldiers of the U.S. Army	N	I	155	People of the U.S. Armed Forces	Capstone Press
Soldier's Secret: The Story of Deborah Sampson	Z+	HF	250+	Klass, Sheila Solomon	Henry Holt & Co.
Solid or Not?	G	I	113	Early Connections	Benchmark Education
Solid Shapes	K	I	372	Yellow Umbrella Books	Red Brick Learning
#Solid Truth About States of Matter with Max Axiom Super Scientist, The	W	I	250+	Graphic Library	Capstone Press
Solid, Liquid, Gas: What Is Matter?	R	I	250+	Rosen Real Readers	Rosen Publishing Group
Solids	R	I	250+	Navigators Science Series	Benchmark Education
Solids and Liquids: Who Messed Up My Sand?	O	I	947	iScience	Norwood House Press
Solids Are Interesting	K	I	189	Larkin, Bruce	Wilbooks
Solids, Liquids and Gases	K	I	361	Science Support Readers	Houghton Mifflin Harcourt
Solids, Liquids, and Gases	J	I	119	Nature Basics	Capstone Press
Solids, Liquids, Gases	N	I	250+	Simply Science	Compass Point Books

S

* Collection of short stories   # Graphic text
^ Mature content with lower level text demands

TITLE	LEVEL	GENRE	WORD COUNT	AUTHOR / SERIES	PUBLISHER / DISTRIBUTOR
Solitary Blue, A	W	RF	250+	Voigt, Cynthia	Scholastic
Solo Flyer	L	RF	605	PM Collection	Rigby
Solo Girl	M	RF	250+	Pinkey, Andrea Davis	Hyperion
Solve It!	K	RF	250+	Goldish, Meish	Scholastic
*Solve This!	M	F	250+	Storyteller-Lightning Bolts	Wright Group/McGraw Hill
Solving Math Problems	O	I	253	Windows on Literacy	National Geographic
Solving Problems	G	RF	246	InfoTrek	ETA/Cuisenaire
Somalia	O	I	250+	Countries of the World	Red Brick Learning
Some Birds Can Fly	B	I	48	Sails	Rigby
Some Birds Cannot Fly	B	I	48	Sails	Rigby
Some Days Are Like That	D	RF	69	Teacher's Choice Series	Pearson Learning Group
Some Dog!	O	RF	250+	PM Collection	Rigby
Some Dogs Do	J	F	250+	Alborough, Jez	Candlewick Press
Some Dogs Don't	B	F	29	Tiger Cub	Peguis
Some Friend	T	RF	250+	Bradby, Marie	Aladdin
Some Friend	R	RF	250+	Warner, Sally	Alfred A. Knopf
Some Kids Are Blind	J	I	134	Understanding Differences	Red Brick Learning
Some Kids Are Deaf	J	I	158	Understanding Differences	Red Brick Learning
Some Kids Have Autism	M	I	154	Understanding Differences	Capstone Press
Some Kids Use Wheelchairs	H	I	121	Understanding Differences	Capstone Press
Some Kids Wear Leg Braces	H	I	142	Understanding Differences	Capstone Press
Some Kind of Love: A Family Reunion in Poems	S	RF	250+	Dant, Traci	Marshall Cavendish
Some Like it Hot	Z+	RF	250+	Dean, Zoey	Little Brown and Company
Some Machines are Enormous	J	I	250+	Bookshop	Mondo Publishing
*Some of the Kinder Planets	U	SF	250+	Wynne-Jones, Tim	Penguin Group
Some People	D	I	50	Reading Corners	Pearson Learning Group
Some Snakes	J	I	118	Voyages	SRA/McGraw Hill
Some Things Float	C	I	41	Windows on Literacy	National Geographic
Some Things Go Together	C	RF	133	Twig	Wright Group/McGraw Hill
Some Things Keep Changing	M	I	250+	Explorations	Eleanor Curtain Publishing
Some Things Keep Changing	M	I	250+	Explorations	Okapi Educational Materials
Some Things Push and Some Things Pull	D	I	42	Dominie Factivity Series	Pearson Learning Group
Somebody Moved in Next Door	Q	RF	250+	PM Chapter Books	Rigby
Someday a Tree	P	RF	250+	Bunting, Eve	Clarion
Someday Cyril	N	RF	250+	Gershator, Phillis	Mondo Publishing
*Somehow Tenderness Survives: Stories of Southern Africa	Z	HF	250+	Rochman, Hazel	HarperTrophy
Someone Is Following Pip Ramsey	N	RF	250+	Roy, Ron	Random House
Someone Just Like Me	L	F	250+	Use Your Imagination	Steck-Vaughn
Someone to Count On	T	RF	250+	Hermes, Patricia	Language for Learning Assoc.
Someone to Love Me	Z+	RF	250+	Schraff, Anne	Townsend Press
Something Beautiful	L	RF	250+	Wyeth, Sharon Dennis	Random House
Something Else	L	F	250+	Cave, Kathryn	Mondo Publishing
Something Everyone Needs	J	RF	250+	Ready Readers	Pearson Learning Group
Something Evil	T	SF	250+	Orme, David	Stone Arch Books
Something Fishy	B	RF	36	Rigby Rocket	Rigby
Something for Everyone	R	RF	1371	Leveled Readers	Houghton Mifflin Harcourt
^Something Girl	Z	RF	250+	Orca Soundings	Orca Books
*Something Is There and Other Stories	J	F	250+	Story Steps	Rigby
Something Is Waiting	J	I	94	Literacy Tree	Rigby
Something Nasty	I	F	250+	Popcorn	Sundance
Something New	D	I	72	Little Celebrations	Pearson Learning Group

* Collection of short stories   # Graphic text
^ Mature content with lower level text demands

TITLE	LEVEL	GENRE	WORD COUNT	AUTHOR / SERIES	PUBLISHER / DISTRIBUTOR
Something New and Different	K	RF	250+	The Rowland Reading Program Library	Rowland Reading Foundation
Something Noise, The	J	RF	276	Windmill Books	Rigby
Something Queer at the Ball Park	N	RF	250+	Levy, Elizabeth	Bantam Books
Something Queer at the Haunted School	N	RF	250+	Levy, Elizabeth	Bantam Books
Something Queer at the Lemonade Stand	N	RF	250+	Levy, Elizabeth	Bantam Books
Something Queer at the Library	N	RF	250+	Levy, Elizabeth	Bantam Books
Something Queer at the Scary Movie	N	RF	250+	Levy, Elizabeth	Hyperion
Something Queer in Outer Space	N	RF	250+	Levy, Elizabeth	Hyperion
Something Queer in the Cafeteria	N	RF	250+	Levy, Elizabeth	Hyperion
Something Queer in the Wild West	N	RF	250+	Levy, Elizabeth	Hyperion
Something Queer Is Going On	N	RF	250+	Levy, Elizabeth	Bantam Books
Something Queer on Vacation	N	RF	250+	Levy, Elizabeth	Bantam Books
Something Rotten at Vilage Market	U	RF	250+	Power Up!	Steck-Vaughn
Something Slimy on Primrose Drive	Q	F	9739	Wallace, Karen	Stone Arch Books
Something Soft for Danny Bear	M	F	493	Literacy 2000	Rigby
Something Special	L	RF	250+	Moon, Nicola	Peachtree
Something Special	J	I	207	Vocabulary Readers	Houghton Mifflin Harcourt
Something Special	J	I	207	Vocabulary Readers/CA	Houghton Mifflin Harcourt
Something Special For Miss Margery	J	F	250+	Voyages	SRA/McGraw Hill
Something to Do	P	RF	1455	Reading Street	Pearson
Something to Hold	W	HF	250+	Noe, Katherine Schlick	Clarion Books
Something to Munch	E	RF	58	Ready Readers	Pearson Learning Group
Something to Share	D	RF	98	Carousel Readers	Pearson Learning Group
Something Upstairs	T	F	250+	Avi	Language for Learning Assoc.
Something Very Sorry	R	RF	250+	Bohlmeijer, Arno	G.P. Putnam's Sons Books for Young Readers
Something, The	N	F	250+	Babbitt, Natalie	Dell
Something's Different	N	I	294	Shelley Rotner's Early Childhood Library	Millbrook Press
Something's Hiding	G	F	89	Nayer, Judy	Willowisp Press
Sometimes	E	F	70	Green Light Readers	Harcourt
Sometimes	B	RF	18	Literacy 2000	Rigby
Sometimes	A	I	28	On Our Way to English	Rigby
Sometimes	C	RF	25	Wonder World	Wright Group/McGraw Hill
Sometimes . . .	F	RF	31	City Stories	Rigby
Sometimes . . .	B	RF	25	Home Connection Collection	Rigby
Sometimes Bad Things Happen	J	I	137	Shelley Rotner's Early Childhood Library	Millbrook Press
Sometimes I Feel Like a Storm Cloud	M	RF	250+	Bookshop	Mondo Publishing
Sometimes I Share	H	RF	108	Ziefert, Harriet	HarperCollins
Sometimes I'm Silly	C	RF	24	Visions	Wright Group/McGraw Hill
Sometimes Things Change	G	I	71	Rookie Readers	Children's Press
Somewhere	J	TL	93	Bookshop	Mondo Publishing
Somewhere in the Darkness	X	RF	250+	Myers, Walter Dean	Scholastic
Somewhere in the Universe	I	I	167	Literacy Tree	Rigby
Son of Liberty, A Novel of the American Revolution	V	HF	250+	Massie, Elizabeth	Tom Doherty
Son of the Mob	Z+	RF	250+	Korman, Gordon	Hyperion
Song and Dance Man	L	RF	250+	Ackerman, Karen	Scholastic
Song for Summer, A	Z+	HF	250+	Korman, Gordon	Hyperion
Song Heard 'Round the World, A	T	I	1331	Leveled Readers	Houghton Mifflin Harcourt
Song Heard 'Round the World, A	T	I	1331	Leveled Readers/CA	Houghton Mifflin Harcourt

S

* Collection of short stories   # Graphic text
^ Mature content with lower level text demands

TITLE	LEVEL	GENRE	WORD COUNT	AUTHOR / SERIES	PUBLISHER / DISTRIBUTOR
Song Heard 'Round the World, A	T	I	1331	Leveled Readers/TX	Houghton Mifflin Harcourt
Song Lee and the Hamster Hunt	L	RF	250+	Kline, Suzy	Penguin Group
Song Lee and the Leech Man	L	RF	250+	Kline, Suzy	Penguin Group
Song Lee in Room 2B	L	RF	250+	Kline, Suzy	Penguin Group
Song Makers Go to Salem, The	N	RF	2177	Reading Street	Pearson
Song of Middle C	M	RF	250+	McGhee, Alison	Candlewick Press
Song of the Giraffe	O	RF	250+	Jacobs, Shannon K.	Little Brown and Company
Song of the Mantis, The	S	I	250+	Literacy 2000	Rigby
Song of the Stranger	T	RF	250+	Tung, Angela	Lowell House
Song of the Trees	R	HF	250+	Taylor, Mildred	Bantam Books
Song of the Whales, The	U	F	250+	Orlev, Uri	Houghton Mifflin Harcourt
Song Quest	W	F	250+	Roberts, Katherine	Scholastic
Song to Sing, A	I	RF	249	Wright, Shannon	C Unique Creations Inc.
Songbird, The	B	F	39	Ray's Readers	Outside the Box
Songs for the People	P	B	871	Leveled Readers	Houghton Mifflin Harcourt
Songs for the People	P	B	871	Leveled Readers/CA	Houghton Mifflin Harcourt
Songs for the People	P	B	871	Leveled Readers/TX	Houghton Mifflin Harcourt
Sonic Moutain Bike	M	F	250+	Too Cool	Pacific Learning
Sonny Gets Lost	G	RF	197	Springboard	Wright Group/McGraw Hill
Sons of Destiny: The Saga of Darren Shan	Y	F	250+	Shan, Darren	Little Brown and Company
Sons of Liberty	Y	RF	250+	Griffin, Adele	Hyperion
Sonya's Guide Dog	H	I	134	Gear Up!	Wright Group/McGraw Hill
Sophie and Sadie Build a Sonnet	N	RF	1100	Poetry Builders	Norwood House Press
Sophie and the Wonderful Picture	K	F	250+	Umansky, Kate	Good Books
Sophie Hits Six	M	F	250+	King-Smith, Dick	Candlewick Press
Sophie in Charge	K	F	250+	Umansky, Kate	Good Books
Sophie in the Saddle	M	F	250+	King-Smith, Dick	Candlewick Press
Sophie Is Seven	M	F	250+	King-Smith, Dick	Candlewick Press
Sophie the Awesome	M	RF	250+	Bergen, Lara	Scholastic
Sophie the Chatterbox	M	RF	250+	Bergen, Lara	Scholastic
Sophie the Hero	M	RF	250+	Bergen, Lara	Scholastic
Sophie the Sapphire Fairy: Rainbow Magic	L	F	250+	Meadows, Daisy	Scholastic
Sophie's Box	G	F	174	Cambridge Reading	Pearson Learning Group
Sophie's Chicken	H	RF	107	Tadpoles	Rigby
Sophie's Lucky	M	F	250+	King-Smith, Dick	Candlewick Press
Sophie's Singing Mother	J	RF	313	Jellybeans	Rigby
Sophie's Snail	M	F	250+	King-Smith, Dick	Candlewick Press
Sophie's Tom	M	F	250+	King-Smith, Dick	Candlewick Press
Sophie's Wheels	H	RF	137	Pearson, Debora	Annick Press
Sor Juana Inez de la Cruz	O	B	693	Leveled Readers Social Studies	Houghton Mifflin Harcourt
Sorceress	Z	HF	250+	Rees, Celia	Candlewick Press
Sorceress, The: The Secrets of the Immortal Nicholas Flamel	X	F	250+	Scott, Michael	Delacorte Press
Sort it Out!	L	F	418	Mariconda, Barbara	Sylvan Dell Publishing
Sorta Sisters, The	U	RF	250+	Fogelin, Adrian	Peachtree
Sorting at the Market	F	I	124	Math Around Us	Heinemann Library
Sorting at the Nature Center	G	RF	175	Early Explorers	Benchmark Education
Sorting at the Park	E	I	123	Early Explorers	Benchmark Education
Sorting Color	J	I	327	Sorting	Capstone Press
Sorting it Out	R	I	250+	Ribgy Literacy	Rigby
Sorting Leaves	D	I	66	PM Math Readers	Rigby
Sorting Money	K	I	348	Sorting	Capstone Press
Sorting My Money	J	I	209	Early Connections	Benchmark Education
Sorting Size	K	I	337	Sorting	Capstone Press

S

* Collection of short stories # Graphic text
^ Mature content with lower level text demands

TITLE	LEVEL	GENRE	WORD COUNT	AUTHOR / SERIES	PUBLISHER / DISTRIBUTOR
Sorting Toys	J	I	357	Sorting	Capstone Press
Sort-of-Difficult Origami	R	I	250+	Origami	Capstone Press
SOS on the Inca Trail	P	RF	250+	WorldScapes	ETA/Cuisenaire
SOS Titanic	V	HF	250+	Bunting, Eve	Harcourt Trade
SOS!: Rescue Heroes	R	I	250+	Boldprint	Steck-Vaughn
Sosu's Call	P	RF	250+	Asare, Meshack	Kane/Miller Book Publishers
Sound	Q	I	2236	Early Bird Energy	Lerner Publishing Group
^Sound	P	I	250+	Our Physical World	Capstone Press
Sound	N	I	250+	Windows on Literacy	National Geographic
Sound of Colors, The: A Journey of the Imagination	R	F	250+	Liao, Jimmy	Little Brown and Company
Sound, Heat & Light: Energy at Work	L	I	250+	Berger, Melvin	Scholastic
Sound: Loud, Soft, High, and Low	M	I	250+	Amazing Science	Picture Window Books
Sound: Music to Our Ears	P	I	2404	iScience	Norwood House Press
Sounder	T	RF	250+	Armstrong, William	Scholastic
Sounds	F	I	109	Big Cat	Pacific Learning
Sounds	J	I	200	Early Connections	Benchmark Education
Sounds	N	I	250+	Lighthouse	Rigby
Sounds all Around	G	I	153	Discovery Links	Newbridge
Sounds All Around	A	I	28	Independent Readers Science	Houghton Mifflin Harcourt
Sounds All Around	L	I	411	Springboard	Wright Group/McGraw Hill
Sounds All Around Us	K	I	168	Phonics Readers	Compass Point Books
Sounds Around Us, The	C	I	22	Rosen Real Readers	Rosen Publishing Group
Sounds in the Night	F	RF	126	Visions	Wright Group/McGraw Hill
Sounds Like Music	R	I	250+	Orbit Chapter Books	Pacific Learning
Sounds of Music, The	G	I	140	Leveled Readers Science	Houghton Mifflin Harcourt
Soup	A	RF	24	Handprints A	Educators Publishing Service
Soup	A	I	17	Little Celebrations	Pearson Learning Group
Soup	Q	HF	250+	Peck, Robert Newton	Bantam Books
Soup	I	F	250+	Sunshine	Wright Group/McGraw Hill
Soup Can Telephone	I	I	190	Wonder World	Wright Group/McGraw Hill
Soup Fit for a King	J	RF	250+	Sunshine	Wright Group/McGraw Hill
Soup for Snail	E	F	61	Leveled Readers Language Support	Houghton Mifflin Harcourt
*Soup in a Group, New Blue Boot, A Moose Is Loose	K	F	431	Easy-for-Me Reading	Child 1st Publications
Sources of Forces: Science Fun with Forcefields	T	I	250+	Science Fun with Vicki Cobb	Millbrook Press
Sources of Light	W	HF	250+	McMullan, Margaret	Houghton Mifflin Harcourt
South	WB	F	0	McDonnell, Patrick	Little Brown and Company
South Africa	O	I	250+	Countries of the World	Red Brick Learning
South Africa	P	I	2059	Country Explorers	Lerner Publishing Group
South Africa	Q	I	250+	First Reports: Countries	Compass Point Books
South Africa	LB	I	14	Readlings	American Reading Company
South Africa: A Question and Answer Book	P	I	250+	Question and Answer Countries	Capstone Press
South America	N	I	250+	Continents	Capstone Press
South America	N	I	446	Pull Ahead Books	Lerner Publishing Group
South America: Geography and Environments	W	I	250+	Reading Expeditions	National Geographic
South America: People and Places	X	I	250+	Reading Expeditions	National Geographic
South Carolina	T	I	250+	Hello U.S.A.	Lerner Publishing Group
South Carolina	T	I	250+	Theme Sets	National Geographic
South Carolina	R	I	250+	This Land Is Your Land	Compass Point Books
South Carolina Colony, The	R	I	250+	The American Colonies	Capstone Press
South Carolina State Symbols	M	I	113	Larkin, Bruce	Wilbooks

TITLE	LEVEL	GENRE	WORD COUNT	AUTHOR / SERIES	PUBLISHER / DISTRIBUTOR
South Carolina: Facts and Symbols	O	I	250+	The States and Their Symbols	Capstone Press
South Dakota	T	I	250+	Hello U.S.A.	Lerner Publishing Group
South Dakota	R	I	250+	This Land Is Your Land	Compass Point Books
South Dakota: Facts and Symbols	O	I	250+	The States and Their Symbols	Capstone Press
South Korea	O	I	250+	Countries of the World	Red Brick Learning
South Korea	P	I	1709	Country Explorers	Lerner Publishing Group
South Pole Bound	O	RF	788	Leveled Readers	Houghton Mifflin Harcourt
South Shore Smugglers	U	RF	3385	Laurence, Sandy	January Books
Southeast Indians, The: Daily Life in the 1500s	O	I	250+	Native American Life	Capstone Press
Southeast Today, The	S	I	250+	Reading Expeditions	National Geographic
Southeast, The	R	I	250+	Navigators Social Studies Series	Benchmark Education
Southeast, The	T	I	250+	Reading Expeditions	National Geographic
Southeast, The: Its History and People	S	I	250+	Reading Expeditions	National Geographic
Southern Coast Missions in California	V	I	5115	Exploring California Missions	Lerner Publishing Group
Southern Sounds	S	I	2194	Independent Readers Social Studies	Houghton Mifflin Harcourt
Southwest Indians, The: Daily Life in the 1500s	O	I	250+	Native American Life	Capstone Press
Southwest Today, The	S	I	250+	Reading Expeditions	National Geographic
Southwest, The	R	I	250+	Navigators Social Studies Series	Benchmark Education
Southwest, The	T	I	250+	Reading Expeditions	National Geographic
Southwest, The: Its History and People	S	I	250+	Reading Expeditions	National Geographic
Southwest's History, The	Y	I	2847	Vocabulary Readers/CA	Houghton Mifflin Harcourt
Southwest's History, The	Y	I	2847	Vocabulary Readers	Houghton Mifflin Harcourt
Souvenirs	K	RF	179	Literacy 2000	Rigby
Sovay	Y	HF	250+	Rees, Celia	Bloomsbury Children's Books
Space	H	I	100	Sunshine	Wright Group/McGraw Hill
Space	I	I	80	Windows on Literacy	National Geographic
Space	R	I	250+	Worldwise	Franklin Watts
Space Age, The	K	I	400	Red Rocket Readers	Flying Start Books
Space Aliens in Our School	D	F	45	Joy Readers	Pearson Learning Group
Space and Time: Earth Matters	L	I	250+	Bookworms	Marshall Cavendish
Space Animals	P	I	474	Independent Readers Science	Houghton Mifflin Harcourt
Space Ant	F	F	194	Rigby Star	Rigby
Space Ant Goes Home	F	F	194	Rigby Literacy	Rigby
Space Ark, The	B	SF	20	Sunshine	Wright Group/McGraw Hill
Space Boots	L	SF	250+	Rigby Rocket	Rigby
Space Captain	M	F	250+	Too Cool	Pacific Learning
Space Cat	K	F	250+	Sails	Rigby
Space Commander: Eileen Collins	U	B	250+	Leveled Readers Language Support	Houghton Mifflin Harcourt
#Space Cops	P	F	250+	Bowkett, Steve	Stone Arch Books
Space Disasters	W	I	7416	Disasters Up Close	Lerner Publishing Group
Space Dog and Roy	L	F	250+	Standiford, Natalie	Random House
Space Dog and the Pet Show	L	F	250+	Standiford, Natalie	Random House
Space Dog in Trouble	L	F	250+	Standiford, Natalie	Random House
Space Dog the Hero	L	F	250+	Standiford, Natalie	Random House
Space Exploration	S	I	250+	Navigators Science Series	Benchmark Education
Space Exploration	S	I	250+	Our Solar System	Compass Point Books
Space Exploration	R	I	1133	Time for Kids	Teacher Created Materials
Space Explorers	O	I	724	Gear Up!	Wright Group/McGraw Hill
Space Fairy	H	F	182	Galaxy Girl	Literacy Footprints
Space Fort, The	D	F	108	Galaxy Girl	Literacy Footprints
^Space Games	O	SF	1939	Orme, David	Stone Arch Books

* Collection of short stories   # Graphic text
^ Mature content with lower level text demands

S

TITLE	LEVEL	GENRE	WORD COUNT	AUTHOR / SERIES	PUBLISHER / DISTRIBUTOR
Space Is an Amazing Place	G	RF	182	Windows on Literacy	National Geographic
Space Journey	A	F	19	Sunshine	Wright Group/McGraw Hill
Space Junk	Q	RF	250+	Sails	Rigby
Space Junk	M	I	250+	The Solar System	Capstone Press
Space Junk	O	RF	250+	Wildcats	Wright Group/McGraw Hill
Space Life	M	I	250+	Incredible Space	Capstone Press
Space Mail	R	RF	250+	On Our Way to English	Rigby
Space Math	R	I	250+	Rosen Real Readers	Rosen Publishing Group
^Space Missions	N	I	250+	Explore Space!	Red Brick Learning
Space Monster Saves the Day	J	F	871	Spaceboy	Literacy Footprints
Space Monster's Birthday Party	H	F	257	Galaxy Girl	Literacy Footprints
Space Odyssey	R	SF	250+	Take Two Books	Wright Group/McGraw Hill
^Space Pirates	O	SF	1967	Orme, David	Stone Arch Books
Space Play	V	F	250+	Power Up!	Steck-Vaughn
Space Probes	M	I	250+	The Solar System	Capstone Press
Space Program, The	V	F	250+	Bookshop	Mondo Publishing
Space Quest	O	I	250+	Discovery World	Rigby
Space Quest	O	F	250+	Infotrek Plus	ETA/Cuisenaire
Space Quiz	N	I	250+	Trackers	Pacific Learning
Space Race	F	RF	196	Rigby Rocket	Rigby
Space Race	J	F	213	Sunshine	Wright Group/McGraw Hill
Space Robots	N	I	250+	Explore Space!	Red Brick Learning
^Space Robots	M	I	250+	Incredible Space	Capstone Press
Space Rock	L	F	250+	Buller, Jon	Random House
Space Rocks: A Look at Asteroids and Comets	M	I	250+	Rosen Real Readers	Rosen Publishing Group
Space Sailors	I	I	181	On Our Way to English	Rigby
Space Shuttle, The	G	I	104	Nonfiction Set 5	Literacy Footprints
Space Shuttle, The	D	I	45	Sunshine	Wright Group/McGraw Hill
Space Shuttle, The	R	I	1308	Vocabulary Readers	Houghton Mifflin Harcourt
Space Shuttle, The	R	I	1308	Vocabulary Readers/CA	Houghton Mifflin Harcourt
Space Shuttle, The	R	I	1308	Vocabulary Readers/TX	Houghton Mifflin Harcourt
^Space Shuttles	N	I	250+	Explore Space!	Red Brick Learning
Space Shuttles	M	I	250+	The Solar System	Capstone Press
Space Station	Q	I	250+	Orbit Double Takes	Pacific Learning
Space Station Orion	L	F	250+	Rigby Literacy	Rigby
*Space Station Plot and Other Cases, The	O	RF	250+	Simon, Seymour	Avon Books
Space Station: Accident on Mir	T	I	250+	DK Readers	DK Publishing
Space Stations	Q	I	250+	A True Book	Children's Press
^Space Stations	N	I	250+	Explore Space!	Red Brick Learning
Space Stations	M	I	250+	Incredible Space	Capstone Press
Space Stations	O	I	250+	Take Two Books	Wright Group/McGraw Hill
Space Stations	M	I	250+	The Solar System	Capstone Press
^Space Suits	N	I	250+	Explore Space!	Red Brick Learning
Space Tourism	M	I	250+	Incredible Space	Capstone Press
Space Tourism	M	I	250+	The Solar System	Capstone Press
Space Trace, The	T	F	250+	Reading Safari	Mondo Publishing
Space Travel	U	I	250+	The Heinle Reading Library	Thomson Learning
Space Travelers	M	I	250+	Incredible Space	Capstone Press
Space Walk	J	I	281	Reading Street	Pearson
^Space Walks	N	I	250+	Explore Space!	Red Brick Learning
Space Wardrobe	W	I	1501	Independent Readers Science	Houghton Mifflin Harcourt
^Space Wreck	O	SF	250+	Orme, David	Stone Arch Books
Space Zoo, The	J	F	612	Spaceboy	Literacy Footprints
Space, Stars, and Planets	J	I	332	Sails	Rigby

* Collection of short stories   # Graphic text
^ Mature content with lower level text demands

TITLE	LEVEL	GENRE	WORD COUNT	AUTHOR / SERIES	PUBLISHER / DISTRIBUTOR
Spaceboy Finds a Friend	E	F	94	Spaceboy	Literacy Footprints
Spaceboy Plays Hide and Seek	D	F	80	Spaceboy	Literacy Footprints
Spacecraft	M	I	250+	Incredible Space	Capstone Press
Spaceheadz: Book # 2	Q	F	250+	Scieszka, Jon	Simon & Schuster
Spaceheadz: Book #1	Q	SF	250+	Scieszka, Jon	Simon & Schuster
Spacejacked!	Q	F	250+	Story Surfers	ETA/Cuisenaire
Spaceship	B	I	27	Hoenecke, Karen	Kaeden Books
Spaceship Earth	T	I	250+	Science Readers	Teacher Created Materials
Spaceship One: Making Dreams Come True	T	I	250+	High Five Reading	Red Brick Learning
Spaceships, Aliens, and Robots You Can Draw	R	I	1557	Ready, Set, Draw!	Millbrook Press
Spaghetti and Meatballs	K	RF	250+	HSP/Harcourt Trophies	Harcourt, Inc.
Spaghetti Party, The	K	RF	250+	Bank Street	Bantam Books
Spaghetti! Spaghetti!	G	RF	85	Book Bank	Wright Group/McGraw Hill
Spain	P	I	1743	Country Explorers	Lerner Publishing Group
Spain: A Question and Answer Book	P	I	250+	Question and Answer Countries	Capstone Press
Spanish and English	H	RF	171	The King School Series	Townsend Press
^Spanish Colonies in the Americas	S	I	250+	On Deck	Rigby
Spanish Conquests in the Americas	X	I	2534	Reading Street	Pearson
Spanish Mustang, The	R	I	250+	Horses	Capstone Press
Spanish Omelette	L	RF	250+	PM Story Books-Silver	Rigby
Spanish-American War, The	V	I	250+	America Goes to War	Red Brick Learning
Spanish-American War, The	W	I	250+	Cornerstones of Freedom	Children's Press
Sparky's Bone	F	F	273	Ready Readers	Pearson Learning Group
Sparrow Road	W	RF	250+	O'Connor, Sheila	G.P. Putnam's Sons
Sparrow's Gift, The	L	TL	250+	On Our Way to English	Rigby
Sparrows, The	F	I	60	Books for Young Learners	Richard C. Owen
Speak	Z	RF	250+	Anderson, Laurie Halse	Penguin Group
Speak	Z	RF	250+	Edge	Hampton Brown
Speak Up!	F	F	194	Sunshine	Wright Group/McGraw Hill
Speak Your Mind	U	I	250+	Sails	Rigby
Speaking in Sign	O	I	778	Vocabulary Readers	Houghton Mifflin Harcourt
Speaking in Sign	O	I	778	Vocabulary Readers/CA	Houghton Mifflin Harcourt
Speaking Out	T	I	250+	Power Up!	Steck-Vaughn
Special Beach Day	I	RF	215	Reading Street	Pearson
Special Buildings	M	I	555	Reading Street	Pearson
Special Cake, The	K	RF	250+	Cambridge Reading	Pearson Learning Group
Special Clothes	J	RF	411	Leveled Readers	Houghton Mifflin Harcourt
Special Day, A	E	RF	92	Windows on Literacy	National Geographic
Special Days, Special Food	J	I	306	Reading Street	Pearson
Special Delivery	B	F	54	Bookshop	Mondo Publishing
Special Effects	P	I	250+	Wildcats	Wright Group/McGraw Hill
Special Family Party, A	G	RF	140	The King School Series	Townsend Press
Special Festival, A	M	RF	1070	Reading Street	Pearson
Special Foods, Special Places	WB	I	0	Windows on Literacy	National Geographic
Special Friend, A	F	RF	80	Carousel Readers	Pearson Learning Group
Special Garden, A	G	I	183	PM Science Readers	Rigby
Special Gifts	M	RF	250+	Rylant, Cynthia	Aladdin
Special Guests	I	F	414	Springboard	Wright Group/McGraw Hill
Special Invitation for Sherman, A	H	RF	277	Seedlings	Continental Press
Special Night, A	U	HF	2340	Leveled Readers	Houghton Mifflin Harcourt
Special Night, A	U	HF	2340	Leveled Readers/CA	Houghton Mifflin Harcourt
Special Night, A	U	HF	2340	Leveled Readers/TX	Houghton Mifflin Harcourt
Special Places	E	RF	96	Rigby Literacy	Rigby
Special Places at School	J	I	250+	Explorations	Eleanor Curtain Publishing

* Collection of short stories   # Graphic text
^ Mature content with lower level text demands

TITLE	LEVEL	GENRE	WORD COUNT	AUTHOR / SERIES	PUBLISHER / DISTRIBUTOR
Special Places at School	J	I	250+	Explorations	Okapi Educational Materials
Special Present, The	L	F	250+	Take Two Books	Wright Group/McGraw Hill
Special Ride, The	K	RF	647	PM Collection	Rigby
Special Saris	N	RF	1677	Take Two Books	Wright Group/McGraw Hill
Special Stories	J	I	189	Vocabulary Readers	Houghton Mifflin Harcourt
Special Table, The	J	RF	450	Gear Up!	Wright Group/McGraw Hill
Special Talents: Extraordinary Lives	P	B	2021	Reading Street	Pearson
Special Things	G	RF	128	Literacy 2000	Rigby
Special Tools	J	I	266	Vocabulary Readers	Houghton Mifflin Harcourt
Special Tools	J	I	266	Vocabulary Readers/CA	Houghton Mifflin Harcourt
Special Tools	J	I	266	Vocabulary Readers/TX	Houghton Mifflin Harcourt
Special Trees	E	RF	124	The King School Series	Townsend Press
Special Tricks	L	I	320	Sails	Rigby
Special Trip, A	O	RF	910	Leveled Readers Science	Houghton Mifflin Harcourt
Specs	J	B	250+	Ready Set Read	Steck-Vaughn
Spectacular Spectacles (Fancy Nancy)	J	RF	250+	O'Connor, Jane	HarperCollins
Spectacular Spiders	L	I	369	Glaser, Linda	Millbrook Press
Spectacular Stone Soup	L	RF	250+	Giff, Patricia Reilly	Yearling Books
Speech, The	P	RF	250+	Leveled Readers Language Support	Houghton Mifflin Harcourt
Speeches on the Air	Z	I	2358	Leveled Readers	Houghton Mifflin Harcourt
Speed Boat, The	C	RF	170	Sunshine	Wright Group/McGraw Hill
Speed Machines and Other Record-Breaking Vehicles	W	I	250+	Kingfisher Knowledge	Kingfisher
Speed of Light	S	F	250+	Story Surfers	ETA/Cuisenaire
Speed Racer	F	RF	74	Leveled Readers Science	Houghton Mifflin Harcourt
^Speed Star	Q	F	1608	Zucker, Jonny	Stone Arch Books
Speedboats	M	I	250+	Horsepower	Capstone Press
*Speeding Sleigh and Other Cases, The	O	RF	250+	Simon, Seymour	Avon Books
Speedway Switch	Q	RF	5269	Maddox, Jake	Stone Arch Books
Speedway, The	B	RF	43	InfoTrek	ETA/Cuisenaire
Speedy Bee	D	F	106	PM Plus Story Books	Rigby
Speedy Bee's Dance	E	F	166	PM Stars	Rigby
Speedy Cheetah, The	G	I	84	Windows on Literacy	National Geographic
Speedy Cheetahs	K	I	379	Pull Ahead Books	Lerner Publishing Group
*Speedy Pasta and Other Cases, The	O	RF	250+	Simon, Seymour	Avon Books
*Speedy Snake and Other Cases, The	O	RF	250+	Simon, Seymour	Avon Books
*Speedy Soapbox Car and Other Cases, The	O	RF	250+	Simon, Seymour	Avon Books
Spell Casters, Phoebe's Fortune	R	F	250+	Warriner, Holly	Aladdin
Spellbinder	U	F	250+	Stringer, Helen	Feiwel and Friends
Spellbound	W	F	250+	Dale, Anna	Bloomsbury Children's Books
Spelldown	Y	RF	250+	Luddy, Karon	Aladdin
Spelling Bee, The	R	RF	1753	Reading Street	Pearson
Spelling Contest, The	M	RF	986	Leveled Readers	Houghton Mifflin Harcourt
Spelling Contest, The	M	RF	986	Leveled Readers/CA	Houghton Mifflin Harcourt
Spelling It Out	L	F	688	Rigby Gigglers	Rigby
Spencer School Sleepover, The	M	RF	250+	Sunshine	Wright Group/McGraw Hill
Spending Money	L	I	250+	Learning About Money	Capstone Press
Spending Money	O	I	250+	Let's See	Compass Point Books
Spending Money	E	I	102	Money	Lerner Publishing Group
Spending Money	E	I	127	Money Around the World	Heinemann Library
Sphere	D	I	32	Solid Shapes	Lerner Publishing Group
Spheres	K	I	260	3-D Shapes	Capstone Press

S

TITLE	LEVEL	GENRE	WORD COUNT	AUTHOR / SERIES	PUBLISHER / DISTRIBUTOR
Sphynx Are the Best!	Q	I	1135	The Best Cats Ever	Lerner Publishing Group
Sphynx Cats	R	I	250+	All About Cats	Capstone Press
Sphynx Cats	I	I	122	Cats	Capstone Press
Spices	U	I	250+	Theme Sets	National Geographic
Spicy-Herby Day, A	G	RF	117	Evangeline Nicholas Collection	Wright Group/McGraw Hill
Spider	D	F	43	Sunshine	Wright Group/McGraw Hill
Spider and Buffalo	N	I	250+	Storyteller	Wright Group/McGraw Hill
Spider and the King, The	L	TL	250+	Literacy 2000	Rigby
Spider Bank, The	L	I	250+	Story Steps	Rigby
Spider Boy	R	RF	250+	Fletcher, Ralph	Bantam Books
Spider Can't Fly	G	F	149	Book Bank	Wright Group/McGraw Hill
Spider Homes	D	I	97	Sails	Rigby
Spider in My Bedroom, A	K	RF	477	PM Plus Story Books	Rigby
^Spider Invasion	V	SF	250+	The Extraordinary Files	Hameray Publishing Group
Spider Kane and the Mystery at Jumbo Nightcrawler's	O	F	250+	Osborne, Mary Pope	Random House
Spider Kane and the Mystery Under the May-Apple	O	F	250+	Osborne, Mary Pope	Random House
Spider Legs	D	I	52	Twig	Wright Group/McGraw Hill
Spider Man	M	I	250+	Literacy 2000	Rigby
Spider Night	K	F	250+	Kunari, Anna	Hampton Brown
Spider Plant, The	I	I	222	Rigby Flying Colors	Rigby
Spider Power	O	I	947	Springboard	Wright Group/McGraw Hill
Spider Relatives	Q	I	250+	Literacy 2000	Rigby
Spider Sandwich	F	RF	148	Kaleidoscope Collection	Hameray Publishing Group
Spider Soup	J	F	556	Rigby Gigglers	Rigby
Spider Spins	D	F	36	Ray's Readers	Outside the Box
Spider, Spider	D	F	70	Sunshine	Wright Group/McGraw Hill
Spider, The	O	I	250+	Crewe, Sabrina	Steck-Vaughn
Spider, The	B	F	36	Sails	Rigby
Spiders	M	I	250+	Bookshop	Mondo Publishing
Spiders	G	I	99	Bugs, Bugs, Bugs	Red Brick Learning
Spiders	E	I	53	Discovery Links	Newbridge
Spiders	R	I	250+	Explorer Books-Pathfinder	National Geographic
Spiders	P	I	250+	Explorer Books-Pioneer	National Geographic
Spiders	O	I	250+	Holmes, Kevin J.	Red Brick Learning
Spiders	O	I	250+	I Can Read About	Troll Associates
Spiders	P	I	250+	Mini Pets	Steck-Vaughn
Spiders	N	I	250+	Minibeasts	Franklin Watts
Spiders	O	I	250+	Nature's Friends	Compass Point Books
Spiders	H	I	153	Nonfiction Set 6	Literacy Footprints
Spiders	C	I	98	Vocabulary Readers	Houghton Mifflin Harcourt
Spiders	C	I	98	Vocabulary Readers/CA	Houghton Mifflin Harcourt
Spiders	E	I	75	Wonder World	Wright Group/McGraw Hill
Spiders and the Web	K	I	187	Animal Homes	Capstone Press
Spiders and Their Webs	I	I	162	Sunshine	Wright Group/McGraw Hill
Spiders Are Special Animals	J	I	166	Sunshine	Wright Group/McGraw Hill
Spiders Everywhere	D	F	36	Books for Young Learners	Richard C. Owen
Spiders Everywhere!	Q	I	787	Red Rocket Readers	Flying Start Books
Spiders in Space	I	F	242	Sunshine	Wright Group/McGraw Hill
Spiders Spin Silk	J	I	183	Windows on Literacy	National Geographic
Spider's Web	N	I	250+	Back, Christine	Silver Burdett Press
Spider's Web	B	RF	31	Sails	Rigby
Spider's Web, A	L	I	323	Wonder World	Wright Group/McGraw Hill

S

* Collection of short stories   # Graphic text
^ Mature content with lower level text demands

TITLE	LEVEL	GENRE	WORD COUNT	AUTHOR / SERIES	PUBLISHER / DISTRIBUTOR
Spiders!	B	I	33	Bonnell, Kris	Reading Reading Books
Spiders!	J	I	185	Rosen Real Readers	Rosen Publishing Group
Spiders!	L	I	250+	Time for Kids	HarperCollins
Spiders, Spiders Everywhere!	D	RF	80	Learn to Read	Creative Teaching Press
Spiders, The	S	RF	250+	Sails	Rigby
Spiderweb for Two	V	RF	250+	Enright, Elizabeth	Henry Holt & Co.
Spiderwort and the Princess of Haiku: The Fairy Chronicles	Q	F	12500	Sweet, J. H.	Sourcebooks
Spies Go Shopping	I	RF	323	Sails	Rigby
Spies on the Devil's Belt	W	HF	250+	Haynes, Betsy	Scholastic
Spies! Real People, Real Stories	T	I	250+	High Five Reading	Red Brick Learning
Spies, The	A	RF	24	Sails	Rigby
Spike and the Concert	L	RF	250+	Cambridge Reading	Pearson Learning Group
Spike Lee: By Any Means Necessary	Z	B	250+	Edge	Hampton Brown
Spikes, Scales, and Armor	H	I	185	Sails	Rigby
Spiky, Slimy, Smooth: What is Texture?	M	I	500	Jane Brocket's Clever Concepts	Millbrook Press
Spilling Ink: A Young Writer's Handbook	T	I	250+	Mazer, Anne & Potter, Ellen	Roaring Brook Press
Spin Around: Verbs in Action	K	I	250+	Bookworms	Marshall Cavendish
^Spin Off	Q	F	1663	Zucker, Jonny	Stone Arch Books
Spin, Spider, Spin!	D	I	32	Bookworms	Marshall Cavendish
Spin, Weave, Knit, and Knot	P	I	250+	PM Extensions	Rigby
Spinach-Eating Machine, The	K	F	536	Springboard	Wright Group/McGraw Hill
Spines	I	I	165	Animal Spikes and Spines	Heinemann Library
Spines, Stingers, and Teeth	S	I	250+	Underwater Encounters	Hameray Publishing Group
Spines, Stings, and Teeth	K	I	274	Big Cat	Pacific Learning
Spinning Snake, A	F	RF	156	Sunshine	Wright Group/McGraw Hill
Spinning Spiders	L	I	320	Pull Ahead Books	Lerner Publishing Group
Spinning Top	I	I	182	Wonder World	Wright Group/McGraw Hill
Spinning Tops	G	RF	201	PM Photo Stories	Rigby
Spiny Sea Stars	L	I	452	Pull Ahead Books	Lerner Publishing Group
Spirit of a New Nation, The	W	I	250+	Reading Expeditions	National Geographic
Spirit of Christmas, The	R	F	250+	Tillman, Nancy	Feiwel and Friends
Spirit of Hope	N	F	250+	Bookshop	Mondo Publishing
Spirit of St. Louis, The	V	I	250+	Cornerstones of Freedom	Children's Press
Spirit Quest	S	RF	250+	Sharpe, Susan	Scholastic
Splash	C	F	34	Foundations	Wright Group/McGraw Hill
Splash!	A	I	35	Bebop Books	Lee & Low Books Inc.
Splash!	A	F	21	Bonnell, Kris	Reading Reading Books
Splash!	H	F	250+	Green Light Readers	Harcourt
Splash!	E	RF	85	Joy Readers	Pearson Learning Group
Splash!	A	RF	21	Leveled Readers	Houghton Mifflin Harcourt
Splash!	E	RF	85	Leveled Readers Language Support	Houghton Mifflin Harcourt
Splash!	A	RF	21	Leveled Readers/CA	Houghton Mifflin Harcourt
Splash!	D	I	31	Little Celebrations	Pearson Learning Group
Splash!	D	RF	63	New Way Red	Steck-Vaughn
Splash!	D	F	35	Sun Sprouts	ETA/Cuisenaire
Splash!: A Little Book About Bouncing Back	K	F	193	Van Lieshout, Maria	Feiwel and Friends
Splashdown	M	RF	250+	PM Plus Chapter Books	Rigby
Splashing Dad	C	RF	37	Early Emergent	Pioneer Valley
Splashy Fins, Flashy Skins: Deep-Sea Rhymes To Make You Grin	M	I	423	Silly Millies	Millbrook Press
Splatter	N	RF	250+	Orbit Chapter Books	Pacific Learning
Splendid Speller (Fancy Nancy)	J	RF	250+	O'Connor, Jane	HarperCollins

S

TITLE	LEVEL	GENRE	WORD COUNT	AUTHOR / SERIES	PUBLISHER / DISTRIBUTOR
Splinters	T	RF	250+	Sails	Rigby
Splish Splash!	B	RF	28	Windmill Books	Wright Group/McGraw Hill
Splish! Splash!	D	F	45	Little Celebrations	Pearson Learning Group
Splish! Splash!: A Book About Rain	M	I	250+	Amazing Science	Picture Window Books
Splishy-Sploshy	E	F	127	Story Basket	Wright Group/McGraw Hill
Split	Z	SF	250+	Petrucha, Stefan	Walker & Company
Split Second, The: The Seems	V	SF	250+	Hulme, John and Wexler, Michael	Bloomsbury Children's Books
Splitting the Herd: A Corral of Odds and Evens	L	RF	1050	Harris, Trudy	Millbrook Press
^Splitzaroni	P	SF	1743	White, K.I.	Stone Arch Books
Splosh	C	F	47	Story Box	Wright Group/McGraw Hill
Spoiled Rotten	L	RF	250+	DeClements, Barthe	Hyperion
^Spoiled Rotten	S	RF	250+	Orca Currents	Orca Books
Sponges	I	I	102	Under the Sea	Capstone Press
Spooky Halloween Party, The	J	RF	250+	Step into Reading	Random House
Spooky House	R	RF	250+	Sails	Rigby
Spooky Pet	B	RF	24	Smart Start	Rigby
Spooky Riddles	I	TL	182	Brown, Marc	Random House
*Spooky Spine Chillers	W	I	250+	DK Readers	DK Publishing
Spooky Swamp Sound, The	G	F	179	Sunshine	Wright Group/McGraw Hill
Spooky Tail of Prewitt Peacock, The	M	F	250+	Peet, Bill	Houghton Mifflin Harcourt
Spoon	K	F	250+	Rosenthal, Amy Krouse	Hyperion
Sport Rules	S	I	250+	The News	Richard C. Owen
Sports	B	I	43	Kaleidoscope Collection	Hameray Publishing Group
Sports and Motion	Q	I	1474	Vocabulary Readers	Houghton Mifflin Harcourt
Sports and Motion	Q	I	1474	Vocabulary Readers/CA	Houghton Mifflin Harcourt
Sports and Motion	Q	I	1474	Vocabulary Readers/TX	Houghton Mifflin Harcourt
Sports Are Fun	B	I	21	Pair-It Books	Steck-Vaughn
Sports Around the World	I	I	192	Early Connections	Benchmark Education
Sports Around the World	I	I	145	Shutterbug Books	Steck-Vaughn
Sports Bag	F	I	147	Sun Sprouts	ETA/Cuisenaire
Sports Bloopers	P	I	250+	Hollander, Phyllis & Zander	Scholastic
Sports Car Racing	W	I	4751	Motor Mania	Lerner Publishing Group
Sports Cars	M	I	250+	Horsepower	Capstone Press
Sports Cars	W	I	6306	Motor Mania	Lerner Publishing Group
^Sports Cars	N	I	171	Rev It Up!	Capstone Press
Sports Day	C	RF	24	Home Connection Collection	Rigby
Sports Day	B	RF	39	Rigby Rocket	Rigby
Sports for All	Q	I	250+	Explorers	Wright Group/McGraw Hill
Sports for You	S	I	250+	The News	Richard C. Owen
*Sports Hall of Fame	O	B	250+	Bookshop	Mondo Publishing
Sports Heroes	R	I	250+	PM Nonfiction-Ruby	Rigby
Sports Legends	O	B	250+	Navigators Biography Series	Benchmark Education
Sports Math	S	I	250+	Navigators Math Series	Benchmark Education
Sports Matters: A Magazine for Kids	L	I	250+	Rigby Literacy	Rigby
Sports Mysteries: Case of the Basketball Video	P	RF	250+	Edwards, T. J.	Scholastic
Sports Mysteries: Case Of The Missing Pitcher	P	RF	250+	Edwards, T. J.	Scholastic
Sports News	S	RF	250+	Sails	Rigby
Sports of the First Americans	T	I	1590	Leveled Readers Social Studies	Houghton Mifflin Harcourt
Sports on the Edge	P	I	250+	Literacy by Design	Rigby
Sports on Wheels	R	I	250+	PM Nonfiction-Ruby	Rigby
Sports Picture Puzzles	M	I	155	Look, Look Again	Capstone Press
Sports Planet: Sports Played Around the World	R	I	250+	Power Up!	Steck-Vaughn
Sports Skills	S	I	250+	Sunshine	Wright Group/McGraw Hill

* Collection of short stories   # Graphic text
^ Mature content with lower level text demands

TITLE	LEVEL	GENRE	WORD COUNT	AUTHOR / SERIES	PUBLISHER / DISTRIBUTOR
Sports Technology	Y	I	7338	Cool Science	Lerner Publishing Group
Sports Technology	R	I	250+	PM Nonfiction-Ruby	Rigby
Sports: From Ancient Olympics to the Super Bowl	U	I	250+	Timeline History	Heinemann Library
Sportsmanship	M	I	250+	Character Education	Red Brick Learning
Spot	B	RF	62	Springboard	Wright Group/McGraw Hill
Spot That Cat!	J	I	208	Story Box	Wright Group/McGraw Hill
Spot the Sporty Puppy	L	RF	250+	Dale, Jenny	Aladdin
Spotlight on Africa	N	I	250+	Spotlight on the Continents	Capstone Press
Spotlight on Antarctica	N	I	250+	Spotlight on the Continents	Capstone Press
Spotlight on Asia	N	I	250+	Spotlight on the Continents	Capstone Press
Spotlight on Australia	N	I	250+	Spotlight on the Continents	Capstone Press
Spotlight on Europe	N	I	250+	Spotlight on the Continents	Capstone Press
Spotlight on North America	N	I	250+	Spotlight on the Continents	Capstone Press
Spotlight on South America	N	I	250+	Spotlight on the Continents	Capstone Press
Spotlight on Stacey	M	RF	250+	Social Studies Connects	Kane Press
Spots	A	I	24	Gear Up!	Wright Group/McGraw Hill
Spots	E	RF	83	Joy Starters	Pearson Learning Group
Spots	A	I	32	Leveled Literacy Intervention/ Orange System	Heinemann
Spots	E	RF	48	Literacy 2000	Rigby
Spots	E	RF	116	Real Kids Readers	Millbrook Press
Spots	I	I	226	Sails	Rigby
Spots	LB	RF	27	Smart Start	Rigby
Spots	C	I	41	Sunshine	Wright Group/McGraw Hill
Spots	B	F	31	Visions	Wright Group/McGraw Hill
Spots	B	I	62	Vocabulary Readers	Houghton Mifflin Harcourt
Spots	B	I	62	Vocabulary Readers/CA	Houghton Mifflin Harcourt
Spots	B	I	62	Vocabulary Readers/TX	Houghton Mifflin Harcourt
Spots and Other Lumps and Bumps	S	I	250+	High-Fliers	Pacific Learning
Spots and Stripes	C	F	60	Red Rocket Readers	Flying Start Books
Spots and Stripes	A	I	24	Rosen Real Readers	Rosen Publishing Group
Spot's Birthday Party	I	F	97	Hill, Eric	G.P. Putnam's Sons Books for Young Readers
Spot's First Christmas	J	RF	102	Hill, Eric	G.P. Putnam's Sons Books for Young Readers
Spot's First Walk	G	F	63	Hill, Eric	G.P. Putnam's Sons Books for Young Readers
Spots or Stripes?	B	I	24	Shutterbug Books	Steck-Vaughn
Spots!	E	RF	55	Oxford Reading Tree	Oxford University Press
Spots, Feathers and Curly Tails	C	I	42	Tafuri, Nancy	Morrow
Spots: Counting Creatures from Sky to Sea	N	I	128	Regan, Laura	Harcourt Brace
Spotted Beetles: Ladybugs in Your Backyard	M	I	250+	Backyard Bugs	Picture Window Books
Spotted Owl, The	E	I	103	Bonnell, Kris/Animals in Danger	Reading Reading Books
*Spotted Pony, The: A Collection of Hanukkah Stories	U	TL	250+	Kimmel, Eric A.	Holiday House
Spotting for Nellie	Z+	RF	250+	Lowell, Pamela	Marshall Cavendish
Spraying Skunks	K	I	391	Pull Ahead Books	Lerner Publishing Group
Spray-Paint Mystery, The	O	RF	250+	Medearis, Angela Shelf	Scholastic
Spread the Word	N	I	693	Vocabulary Readers	Houghton Mifflin Harcourt
Spread the Word	N	I	693	Vocabulary Readers/CA	Houghton Mifflin Harcourt
Spreading the Word	Q	I	250+	Wildcats	Wright Group/McGraw Hill
Spring	C	I	47	Carousel Readers	Pearson Learning Group
Spring	C	I	34	Gear Up!	Wright Group/McGraw Hill
Spring	I	I	142	Pebble Books	Capstone Press

S

TITLE	LEVEL	GENRE	WORD COUNT	AUTHOR / SERIES	PUBLISHER / DISTRIBUTOR
Spring	E	I	49	Seasons	Lerner Publishing Group
Spring	E	I	58	Sunshine	Wright Group/McGraw Hill
Spring Festivals Around the World	P	I	250+	Literacy by Design	Rigby
Spring Fever!	T	F	250+	Lerangis, Peter	Language for Learning Assoc.
Spring Has Sprung	K	I	250+	Spyglass Books	Compass Point Books
Spring in the City	M	F	46	Leveled Readers	Houghton Mifflin Harcourt
Spring in the City	B	I	46	Leveled Readers Emergent	Houghton Mifflin Harcourt
Spring Is Coming	C	I	30	Bonnell, Kris	Reading Reading Books
Spring Is Here	C	RF	62	Gear Up!	Wright Group/McGraw Hill
Spring Out: Verbs in Action	K	I	250+	Bookworms	Marshall Cavendish
Spring Pops Up	C	I	26	Instant Readers	Harcourt School Publishers
Spring Rain	A	I	24	Vocabulary Readers	Houghton Mifflin Harcourt
Spring Rose, Winter Bear	H	I	218	Reading Street	Pearson
Spring Shower	D	RF	105	In Step Readers	Rigby
Spring Snow	D	RF	48	Little Books for Early Readers	University of Maine
Spring, Summer, Fall, Winter	G	I	64	Windows on Literacy	National Geographic
Springs	F	I	142	Alphakids	Sundance
Springs	M	I	245	Books for Young Learners	Richard C. Owen
Springtime Rock and Roll, The	H	F	249	Literacy Tree	Rigby
Sprint Cars	M	I	250+	Horsepower	Capstone Press
Sprint Cars	Q	I	250+	Wild Rides!	Capstone Press
Sprout	Z+	RF	250+	Peck, Dale	Bloomsbury Children's Books
Spunky Tells All	N	F	250+	Cameron, Ann	Farrar, Straus, & Giroux
Spy	X	I	250+	Eyewitness Books	DK Publishing
^Spy Basics	X	I	250+	Spies	Capstone Press
Spy Cat	S	F	250+	Kehret, Peg	Puffin Books
Spy Danny	I	F	230	Coulton, Mia	Maryruth Books
Spy Down the Street, The	M	F	250+	Woodland Mysteries	Wright Group/McGraw Hill
^Spy Gear	X	I	250+	Spies	Capstone Press
Spy in the Attic, The	M	RF	250+	Scheffler, Ursel	North-South Books
Spy in the White House, A	N	RF	250+	Roy, Ron	Scholastic
Spy Manual	M	I	250+	Sails	Rigby
Spy Maps	N	F	250+	Sails	Rigby
Spy on Third Base, The	M	RF	250+	Christopher, Matt	Little Brown and Company
Spy School	J	F	477	Sails	Rigby
^Spy Skills	X	I	250+	Spies	Capstone Press
Spy Technology	X	I	7165	Cool Science	Lerner Publishing Group
Spy Tools	L	I	335	Sails	Rigby
Spy!	Y	I	250+	Myers, Anna	Walker & Company
Spy, The	B	RF	30	Sails	Rigby
Spycatcher	N	RF	250+	Damian Drooth Supersleuth	Stone Arch Books
Spymail	T	RF	250+	Sails	Rigby
Spyology: The Complete Book of Spycraft	X	I	250+	Blake, Spencer	Candlewick Press
Squanto	S	B	250+	Amazing Americans	Wright Group/McGraw Hill
Squanto and the First Thanksgiving	L	HF	250+	Celsi, Teresa	Steck-Vaughn
Squanto and the First Thanksgiving	N	I	1371	On My Own Holidays	Lerner Publishing Group
Squanto: Friend of the Pilgrims	O	B	250+	Bulla, Clyde Robert	Scholastic
Square	B	I	32	Shapes	Lerner Publishing Group
Squares	D	I	31	Bookworms	Marshall Cavendish
Squares	B	I	27	Harry's Math Books	Outside the Box
Squares Around Town	J	I	292	Shapes Around Town	Capstone Press
Squares Everywhere	C	I	26	Discovery Links	Newbridge

* Collection of short stories   # Graphic text
^ Mature content with lower level text demands

TITLE	LEVEL	GENRE	WORD COUNT	AUTHOR / SERIES	PUBLISHER / DISTRIBUTOR
Squares: Seeing Squares All Around Us	K	I	183	Shapes	Capstone Press
Squash in the Schoolyard	N	I	1100	Vocabulary Readers/TX	Houghton Mifflin Harcourt
Squashed	U	RF	250+	Bauer, Joan	Speak
Squeaking Bats	K	I	319	Pull Ahead Books	Lerner Publishing Group
Squeaky Car, The	G	RF	200	New Way Green	Steck-Vaughn
Squeaky Clean	C	RF	29	Stewart, Josie	Continental Press
Squid Monster	T	RF	250+	Sails	Rigby
Squids	I	I	129	Under the Sea	Capstone Press
Squiggles and Strokes	U	I	250+	Bookweb	Rigby
Squire Takes a Wife, A	J	F	250+	Ready Set Read	Steck-Vaughn
Squirm, Earthworm, Squirm!	D	I	32	Bookworms	Marshall Cavendish
Squirrel Monkeys	I	I	402	Sails	Rigby
Squirrel School	A	F	28	Springboard	Wright Group/McGraw Hill
Squirrel Wife, The	P	TL	250+	Pearce, Philippa	Candlewick Press
Squirrels	I	I	250+	Pebble Books	Red Brick Learning
Squirrels	F	RF	109	Ready Readers	Pearson Learning Group
Squirrels	N	I	460	Storyteller Nonfiction	Wright Group/McGraw Hill
Squirrels and Their Nests	J	I	130	Animal Homes	Capstone Press
Squirrels in the School	Q	RF	250+	Baglio, Ben M.	Scholastic
Squirrel's World	K	F	250+	Moser, Lisa	Candlewick Press
Squirrels: Furry Scurriers	M	I	250+	The Wild World of Animals	Red Brick Learning
Squirts and Spurts: Science Fun with Water	T	I	250+	Science Fun with Vicki Cobb	Millbrook Press
Ssh, Don't Wake the Baby	F	RF	135	Voyages	SRA/McGraw Hill
Sss Snakes	C	I	48	Bonnell, Kris	Reading Reading Books
Sssh!	C	RF	49	Book Bank	Wright Group/McGraw Hill
St. Lawrence Seaway, The	O	I	371	Independent Readers Social Studies	Houghton Mifflin Harcourt
St. Louis Cardinals, The	S	I	250+	Team Spirit	Norwood House Press
St. Louis Cardinals, The (Revised Edition)	S	I	250+	Team Spirit	Norwood House Press
St. Louis Rams, The	S	I	250+	Team Spirit	Norwood House Press
St. Louis, Gateway to the West	W	I	2714	Vocabulary Readers	Houghton Mifflin Harcourt
St. Louis, Gateway to the West	W	I	2714	Vocabulary Readers/CA	Houghton Mifflin Harcourt
St. Louis, Gateway to the West	W	I	2714	Vocabulary Readers/TX	Houghton Mifflin Harcourt
St. Louis, Missouri	Q	I	250+	Theme Sets	National Geographic
St. Patrick's Day	Q	I	250+	Holiday Histories	Heinemann
St. Patrick's Day	M	I	250+	Holidays and Celebrations	Picture Window Books
St. Patrick's Day	J	I	136	Holidays and Celebrations	Capstone Press
St. Patrick's Day	P	I	250+	Let's See	Compass Point Books
St. Patrick's Day: Day of Irish Pride	M	I	250+	Holidays and Culture	Capstone Press
Stables Are for Horses	I	I	66	Windmill Books	Wright Group/McGraw Hill
Stacey and the Haunted Masquerade	O	RF	250+	Martin, Ann M.	Scholastic
Stacey and the Missing Ring	O	RF	250+	Martin, Ann M.	Scholastic
Stacey and the Mystery at the Mall	O	RF	250+	Martin, Ann M.	Scholastic
Stacey and the Mystery Money	O	RF	250+	Martin, Ann M.	Scholastic
Stacey the Soccer Fairy: Rainbow Magic	L	F	250+	Meadows, Daisy	Scholastic
Stacks of Trouble	L	RF	250+	Math Matters	Kane Press
Stacy Says Good-Bye	L	RF	250+	Giff, Patricia Reilly	Bantam Books
Stage Fright	O	RF	250+	Klooz	Stone Arch Books
Stage Fright	N	RF	250+	Martin, Ann M.	Scholastic
Stage Fright	O	RF	250+	Orbit Double Takes	Pacific Learning
Stagecoach Travel	Q	I	916	Vocabulary Readers	Houghton Mifflin Harcourt
Stagecoach Travel	Q	I	916	Vocabulary Readers/CA	Houghton Mifflin Harcourt
Stagecoach Travel	Q	I	916	Vocabulary Readers/TX	Houghton Mifflin Harcourt
Stagecoach Years, The	P	I	250+	Rigby Flying Colors	Rigby

S

TITLE	LEVEL	GENRE	WORD COUNT	AUTHOR / SERIES	PUBLISHER / DISTRIBUTOR
Stained Glass	L	I	190	Windows on Literacy	National Geographic
Staircase to the Sky	E	RF	133	Visions	Wright Group/McGraw Hill
Staircase, The	Y	HF	250+	Rinaldi, Ann	Harcourt, Inc.
Stallion in Spooky Hollow	Q	RF	250+	Baglio, Ben M.	Scholastic
Stallion's Call, The	E	F	77	Salem, Lynn; Stewart, Josie	Continental Press
Stampede of the Edmontosaurus: Dinosaur Cove	N	F	250+	Stone, Rex	Scholastic
Stamping Art: Imprint Your Designs	Q	I	250+	Crafts	Capstone Press
Stamping for Fun!	S	I	250+	For Fun! Crafts	Compass Point Books
Stamps	G	I	58	Wonder World	Wright Group/McGraw Hill
Stan Packs	E	RF	84	Ready Readers	Pearson Learning Group
Stan the Hot Dog Man	K	RF	250+	Kessler, Ethel & Leonard	HarperTrophy
Stand Tall	U	RF	250+	Bauer, Joan	Penguin Group
Stand Tall, Molly Lou Melon	L	RF	250+	Lovell, Patty	Scholastic
Standing Against the Wind	X	RF	250+	Jones, Traci L.	Farrar, Straus, & Giroux
Standing in the Light	U	HF	250+	Dear America	Scholastic
Standing Stones	X	I	250+	WorldScapes	ETA/Cuisenaire
*Standing Tall: The Stories of Ten Hispanic Americans	X	B	250+	Palacios, Argentina	Scholastic
Stanley	I	F	250+	Hoff, Syd	HarperTrophy
Stanley and the Class Pet	K	F	250+	Saltzberg, Barney	Candlewick Press
Stanley and the Magic Lamp	N	F	250+	Brown, Jeff	HarperTrophy
Stapler, The	H	RF	205	The King School Series	Townsend Press
Star	M	RF	250+	Simon, Jo Ann	Random House
Star and Patches	K	RF	440	PM Plus Story Books	Rigby
Star Boy's Surprise	K	F	647	Big Cat	Pacific Learning
Star Child	T	F	250+	Hopkins, Cathy	Kingfisher
Star Discovered, A: Lucky Foot Stable Series	R	RF	33427	Dawson, JoAnn S.	Sourcebooks
Star Fisher, The	S	RF	250+	Yep, Lawrence	Scholastic
Star Garden, The	L	I	862	Sun Sprouts	ETA/Cuisenaire
Star Gazing	L	I	573	Explorations	Eleanor Curtain Publishing
Star Gazing	L	I	573	Explorations	Okapi Educational Materials
Star Gazing in Our Solar System	J	I	202	Independent Readers Science	Houghton Mifflin Harcourt
Star Island	Z+	RF	250+	Hiaasen, Carl	Grand Central Publishing
Star of the Sea: A Day in the Life of a Starfish	N	I	250+	Halfmann, Janet	Henry Holt & Co.
Star of Wonder: Lucky Foot Stable Series	R	RF	32540	Dawson, JoAnn S.	Sourcebooks
Star Pictures	K	I	96	Books for Young Learners	Richard C. Owen
Star Pictures	D	I	43	iOpeners	Pearson Learning Group
Star Shard, The	V	F	250+	Durbin, Frederic S.	Houghton Mifflin Harcourt
Star Struck	O	F	250+	High-Fliers	Pacific Learning
Star Thief	P	RF	250+	Orbit Chapter Books	Pacific Learning
Star Tracks	R	I	2014	Reading Street	Pearson
Star Wars: Feel the Force!	R	SF	250+	DK Readers	DK Publishing
Star Zoo, The	W	SF	8915	Oxford Bookworms Library	Oxford University Press
Starclimber	Y	F	250+	Oppel, Kenneth	HarperCollins
Starcross: A Stirring Adventure of Spies, Time Travel and Curious Hats	Y	F	250+	Reeve, Philip	Bloomsbury Children's Books
Starfish	I	I	237	Sails	Rigby
Starfish & Urchins	L	I	322	Marine Life For Young Readers	Pearson Learning Group
Starfishers to the Rescue	M	SF	250+	Dreyer, Ellen	Pearson Learning Group
Stargazers	C	F	83	Galaxy Girl	Literacy Footprints
Stargazer's Club, The	O	RF	812	Leveled Readers	Houghton Mifflin Harcourt
Stargazer's Club, The	O	RF	812	Leveled Readers/CA	Houghton Mifflin Harcourt
Stargirl	V	RF	250+	Edge	Hampton Brown

* Collection of short stories   # Graphic text
^ Mature content with lower level text demands

TITLE	LEVEL	GENRE	WORD COUNT	AUTHOR / SERIES	PUBLISHER / DISTRIBUTOR
Stargirl	V	RF	250+	Spinelli, Jerry	Alfred A. Knopf
Starlight: Warriors, The New Prophecy	U	F	250+	Hunter, Erin	HarperCollins
Starring First Grade	J	RF	250+	Cohen, Miriam	Bantam Books
Starring Grace	O	RF	250+	Hoffman, Mary	Puffin Books
Starring Rosie	N	RF	250+	Giff, Patricia Reilly	Penguin Group
Stars	Q	I	250+	A True Book	Children's Press
Stars	H	I	181	Discovery Links	Newbridge
Stars	Q	I	1851	Early Bird Astronomy	Lerner Publishing Group
Stars	I	I	137	Exploring the Galaxy	Capstone Press
Stars	N	I	835	Our Universe	Lerner Publishing Group
Stars	P	I	250+	Reading Expeditions	National Geographic
Stars	H	I	99	Space	Lerner Publishing Group
Stars	G	I	105	Sunshine	Wright Group/McGraw Hill
Stars	Q	I	250+	The Galaxy	Red Brick Learning
Stars	I	I	181	Yellow Umbrella Books	Red Brick Learning
Stars & Planets	X	I	250+	Navigators	Kingfisher
Stars amd Galaxies	T	I	250+	Reading Expeditions	National Geographic
Stars and Planets	Z	I	250+	Stott, Carole	Scholastic
Stars Around Town	J	I	334	Shapes Around Town	Capstone Press
Stars in the Sky	F	I	161	In Step Readers	Rigby
Stars in the Sky	F	I	153	Literacy by Design	Rigby
Stars in the Sky	I	I	207	PM Science Readers	Rigby
Stars of the Show	L	RF	426	Rigby Flying Colors	Rigby
Stars! Stars! Stars!	O	F	250+	Wallace, Nancy Elizabeth	Marshall Cavendish
Stars, The	J	I	320	Dominie Factivity Series	Pearson Learning Group
Stars, The	K	I	102	Out In Space	Red Brick Learning
Stars: Seeing Stars All Around Us	J	I	193	Shapes	Capstone Press
Starshine	H	F	224	Sunshine	Wright Group/McGraw Hill
^Starship Rescue	Q	SF	3859	Breslin, T.	Stone Arch Books
Star-Spangled Banner in Translation, The: What It Really Means	V	I	250+	Kids' Translations	Capstone Press
Star-Spangled Banner, The	O	I	1575	On My Own History	Lerner Publishing Group
Star-Spangled Banner, The	T	I	250+	Symbols of America	Marshall Cavendish
Starstruck!	M	RF	250+	Bookweb	Rigby
Start and Stop	F	I	49	The Way Things Move	Red Brick Learning
Start of the American Revolutionary War, The: Paul Revere Rides at Midnight	S	I	250+	Headlines from History	Rosen Publishing Group
Starting a Business	S	I	596	Vocabulary Readers	Houghton Mifflin Harcourt
Starting a Rock Collection	T	I	250+	Independent Readers Science	Houghton Mifflin Harcourt
Starting Points	Y	I	250+	iOpeners	Pearson Learning Group
Starting School	E	RF	97	Voyages	SRA/McGraw Hill
State Plants of the United States	K	I	286	Springboard	Wright Group/McGraw Hill
State Quarters	N	I	632	Vocabulary Readers	Houghton Mifflin Harcourt
State Quarters	N	I	632	Vocabulary Readers/CA	Houghton Mifflin Harcourt
State Quarters	N	I	632	Vocabulary Readers/TX	Houghton Mifflin Harcourt
States of Matter	L	I	160	Windows on Literacy	National Geographic
Stateswoman to the World: A Story About Eleanor Roosevelt	R	B	8674	Creative Minds Biographies	Carolrhoda Books
Statue of Liberty, The	S	I	250+	A True Book	Children's Press
Statue of Liberty, The	N	I	250+	American Symbols	Capstone Press
Statue of Liberty, The	I	I	136	Early Explorers	Benchmark Education
Statue of Liberty, The	Q	I	250+	Let's See	Compass Point Books
Statue of Liberty, The	N	I	359	Lightning Bolt Books	Lerner Publishing Group
Statue of Liberty, The	Q	I	250+	National Landmarks	Red Brick Learning

S

TITLE	LEVEL	GENRE	WORD COUNT	AUTHOR / SERIES	PUBLISHER / DISTRIBUTOR
Statue of Liberty, The	N	I	250+	On Our Way to English	Rigby
Statue of Liberty, The	J	I	250+	Penner, Lucille	Random House
Statue of Liberty, The	P	I	580	Pull Ahead Books	Lerner Publishing Group
Statue of Liberty, The	T	I	250+	Symbols of America	Marshall Cavendish
Statue of Liberty, The	V	I	250+	The Heinle Reading Library	Thomson Learning
Statue of Liberty, The: From Paris to New York City	P	I	390	Reading Street	Pearson
Statues Across America	K	I	293	Vocabulary Readers	Houghton Mifflin Harcourt
Stay Away from Simon!	O	RF	250+	Carrick, Carol	Clarion
Stay Away!	E	I	71	Explorations	Eleanor Curtain Publishing
Stay Away!	E	I	71	Explorations	Okapi Educational Materials
Stay Clear!: What You Should Know about Skin Care	V	I	7457	Health Zone	Lerner Publishing Group
Stay Cool	E	F	134	Start to Read	School Zone
Stay Fit!: How You Can Get in Shape	U	I	6630	Health Zone	Lerner Publishing Group
Stay Safe!	E	I	122	Literacy by Design	Rigby
Stay Safe!: How You Can Keep Out of Harm's Way	Y	I	6926	Health Zone	Lerner Publishing Group
Stay Tuned	W	I	250+	Boldprint	Steck-Vaughn
Stay! Keeper's Story	U	F	250+	Lowry, Lois	Random House
Staying Clean	M	I	746	Pull Ahead Books	Lerner Publishing Group
Staying Cool in the Heat	Q	I	969	Leveled Readers	Houghton Mifflin Harcourt
Staying Cool in the Heat	Q	I	969	Leveled Readers/CA	Houghton Mifflin Harcourt
Staying Cool in the Heat	Q	I	969	Leveled Readers/TX	Houghton Mifflin Harcourt
Staying Fat for Sarah Byrnes	Z+	RF	250+	Crutcher, Chris	Greenwillow Books
Staying Happy	N	I	611	Pull Ahead Books	Lerner Publishing Group
Staying Healthy	W	I	250+	iOpeners	Pearson Learning Group
Staying Healthy	H	RF	199	The King School Series	Townsend Press
Staying Healthy	I	I	248	Time for Kids	Teacher Created Materials
Staying Healthy	LB	I	7	Windows on Literacy	National Geographic
Staying Healthy in Space	I	I	291	Leveled Readers/CA	Houghton Mifflin Harcourt
Staying Healthy in Space	I	I	291	Leveled Readers/TX	Houghton Mifflin Harcourt
Staying Healthy in Space	I	I	291	Leveled Readers	Houghton Mifflin Harcourt
Staying Healthy: Eating Right	O	I	250+	McGinty, Alice B.	Franklin Watts
Staying Nine	O	RF	250+	Conrad, Pam	HarperTrophy
Staying Power: Tales of Survival	S	I	250+	Kids Discover Reading	Wright Group/McGraw Hill
Staying Safe Around Fire	J	I	250+	Staying Safe	Capstone Press
Staying Safe Around Strangers	J	I	250+	Staying Safe	Capstone Press
Staying Safe in Emergencies	L	I	446	Pull Ahead Books	Lerner Publishing Group
Staying Safe in the Water	F	I	264	Rigby Flying Colors	Rigby
Staying Safe on the Playground	J	I	250+	Staying Safe	Capstone Press
Staying Safe on the School Bus	J	I	250+	Staying Safe	Capstone Press
Staying Well	F	I	154	Early Connections	Benchmark Education
Staying with Big Bill	F	F	207	Sails	Rigby
Staying with Grandma Norma	F	RF	168	Salem, Lynn; Stewart, Josie	Continental Press
Steal Away . . . to Freedom	Z	RF	250+	Armstrong, Jennifer	Scholastic
Steal Away Home	V	HF	250+	Ruby, Lois	Aladdin
Stealing Freedom	U	HF	250+	Carbone, Elisa	Random House
Stealing Home	R	RF	250+	Christopher, Matt	Little Brown and Company
Stealing Home: The Story of Jackie Robinson	V	B	250+	Denenberg, Barry	Scholastic
Stealth Attack Fighters: The F-117A Nighthawks	V	I	250+	War Planes	Capstone Press
Stealth Bombers: The B-2 Spirits	U	I	250+	War Planes	Capstone Press
^Steam Engine, The: Fueling the Industrial Revolution	R	I	250+	On Deck	Rigby

* Collection of short stories   # Graphic text
^ Mature content with lower level text demands

TITLE	LEVEL	GENRE	WORD COUNT	AUTHOR / SERIES	PUBLISHER / DISTRIBUTOR
Steam Power	L	I	308	Rigby Focus	Rigby
^Steel Eyes	S	F	250+	Zucker, Jonny	Stone Arch Books
Stegosaurus	I	I	126	Dinosaur and Prehistoric Animals	Capstone Press
Steinbeck's Ghost	W	F	250+	Buzbee, Lewis	Feiwel and Friends
Stella	E	RF	57	Storyteller-Moon Rising	Wright Group/McGraw Hill
Stella the Star Fairy: Rainbow Magic	L	F	250+	Meadows, Daisy	Scholastic
Stellaluna	N	F	250+	Cannon, Janell	Scholastic
Stellar Stargazer (Fancy Nancy)	J	RF	250+	O'Connor, Jane	HarperCollins
Stems	E	I	30	Parts of Plants	Lerner Publishing Group
Stems	K	I	231	Pebble Books	Capstone Press
Stems	I	I	122	Plant Parts	Capstone Press
Stencils, Prints, and Special Effects: How To Create Models, Cards, Decorations, and Pictures With a Difference	Q	I	250+	Bookshop	Mondo Publishing
Step Fourth, Mallory!	O	RF	17656	Friedman, Laurie	Carolrhoda Books
Step On It!	L	F	356	Gear Up!	Wright Group/McGraw Hill
Stephen Hawking	V	B	2515	Leveled Readers Science	Houghton Mifflin Harcourt
Stepping Back in Time	W	RF	2045	Leveled Readers	Houghton Mifflin Harcourt
Stepping on the Cracks	V	HF	250+	Hahn, Mary Downing	Avon Books
Stepping Stones	C	F	42	Sunshine	Wright Group/McGraw Hill
Stepping Through Time	N	I	250+	Rigby Literacy	Rigby
Steps	W	I	250+	Boldprint	Steck-Vaughn
Steps, The	T	RF	250+	Cohn, Rachel	Simon & Schuster
Sterkarm Handshake, The	Z	F	250+	Price, Susan	Scholastic
#Steve Jobs, Steve Wozniak, and the Personal Computer	T	B	250+	Inventions and Discovery	Capstone Press
^Steve Jobs: Apple and Beyond	S	B	250+	Hameray Biography Series	Hameray Publishing Group
Steve Nash	P	B	2062	Amazing Athletes	Lerner Publishing Group
Steve's Room	G	RF	171	Ready Readers	Pearson Learning Group
Stew for Egor's Mom, A	G	F	162	Ready Readers	Pearson Learning Group
Stick Insects	U	I	250+	Insect World: Masters of Defense	Lerner Publishing Group
Stick Kid	J	F	250+	Holwitz, Peter	Philomel
Stick Out Your Tongue!: Fantastic Facts, Features, and Functions of Animals and Human Tongues	O	I	250+	Bonsignore, Joan	Peachtree
Stick to It!: The Story of Wilma Rudolph	M	B	250+	Spyglass Books	Compass Point Books
Sticking to It!	L	F	1372	Auto-B-Good	Rising Star Studios
Sticks and Stones	W	I	250+	Boldprint	Steck-Vaughn
^Sticks and Stones	Z+	RF	250+	Orca Soundings	Orca Books
Sticks and Stones, Bobbie Bones	P	RF	250+	Roberts, Brenda C.	Scholastic
#Sticky Burr: Adventures in Burrwood Forest	Q	F	250+	Lechner, John	Candlewick Press
Sticky Problem, A	J	RF	488	In Step Readers	Rigby
Sticky Rice with Mango	H	I	191	In Step Readers	Rigby
Sticky Stanley	F	F	97	First Start	Troll Associates
Stickybeak the Parrot	B	RF	50	Red Rocket Readers	Flying Start Books
Still Around!	N	I	250+	Rigby Literacy	Rigby
Still Just Grace	O	RF	250+	Harper, Charise Mericle	Houghton Mifflin Harcourt
Still Standing	O	I	388	Independent Readers Science	Houghton Mifflin Harcourt
Stingers	A	I	24	Sails	Rigby
Stingrays	E	I	72	Bonnell, Kris/About	Reading Reading Books
Stingrays	I	I	126	Wonder World	Wright Group/McGraw Hill
Stink and the Great Guinea Pig Express	M	RF	250+	McDonald, Megan	Candlewick Press
Stink and the Incredible Super-Galactic Jawbreaker	M	RF	250+	McDonald, Megan	Candlewick Press
Stink and the Midnight Zombie Walk	M	RF	250+	McDonald, Megan	Candlewick Press

Organized Alphabetically by Title
Storable Database at www.fountasandpinnellleveledbooks.com

TITLE	LEVEL	GENRE	WORD COUNT	AUTHOR / SERIES	PUBLISHER / DISTRIBUTOR
Stink and the Ultimate Thumb-Wrestling Smackdown	M	RF	250+	McDonald, Megan	Candlewick Press
Stink and the World's Worst Super-Stinky Sneakers	M	RF	250+	McDonald, Megan	Candlewick Press
Stink: Solar System Superhero	M	RF	250+	McDonald, Megan	Candlewick Press
Stink: The Incredible Shrinking Kid	M	RF	250+	McDonald, Megan	Candlewick Press
Stinkers!	I	I	215	Sails	Rigby
Stinkiest Animals, The	L	I	250+	EXtreme Animals	Capstone Press
Stink-O-Pedia: Super Stinky Stuff From A -Z	O	RF	250+	McDonald, Megan	Candlewick Press
#Stinky	K	F	250+	Davis, Eleanor	Toon Books
Stinky and Successful: The Riot Brothers Never Stop	P	RF	250+	Amato, Mary	Holiday House
Stinky Skunk, The	L	F	556	Leveled Readers	Houghton Mifflin Harcourt
Stinky Skunk, The	L	F	556	Leveled Readers/CA	Houghton Mifflin Harcourt
Stinky Skunk, The	L	F	556	Leveled Readers/TX	Houghton Mifflin Harcourt
Stitches	G	RF	250+	Ziefert, Harriet	Puffin Books
Stock Car Kings	Q	I	250+	All Aboard Reading	Grosset & Dunlap
Stock Cars	M	I	250+	Horsepower	Capstone Press
Stock Cars	H	I	130	Mighty Machines	Capstone Press
Stock Cars	W	I	5618	Motor Mania	Lerner Publishing Group
Stock Cars	N	I	514	Pull Ahead Books	Lerner Publishing Group
^Stock Cars	N	I	156	Rev It Up!	Capstone Press
Stock Cars	T	I	250+	The World's Fastest	Red Brick Learning
Stock Market, The	W	I	250+	How Economics Works	Lerner Publishing Group
Stolen Car	Z+	RF	250+	Jones, Patrick	Walker & Company
Stolen Sun, The	N	TL	250+	WorldScapes	ETA/Cuisenaire
Stolen Words	Y	RF	3372	Leveled Readers	Houghton Mifflin Harcourt
Stolen Words	Y	RF	3372	Leveled Readers/CA	Houghton Mifflin Harcourt
Stolen Words	Y	RF	3372	Leveled Readers/TX	Houghton Mifflin Harcourt
Stomach Full of Stones, A	J	I	412	Sails	Rigby
Stomachs	N	I	250+	Sails	Rigby
Stomp It!: Board Sports and Riders Who Rip	V	I	250+	Boldprint	Steck-Vaughn
Stone Age Boy	M	F	250+	Kitamura, Satoshi	Candlewick Press
Stone Cutter, The	H	TL	276	Big Cat	Pacific Learning
Stone Dragon: The Great Wall of China	N	I	250+	In Step Readers	Rigby
Stone Fox	P	RF	250+	Gardiner, John Reynolds	HarperTrophy
Stone Goddess, The	X	HF	250+	Edge	Hampton Brown
Stone Hat, The	M	RF	849	Books for Young Learners	Richard C. Owen
Stone in My Hand, A	W	RF	250+	Clinton, Cathryn	Candlewick Press
Stone in the Road, A	L	TL	250+	Bookshop	Mondo Publishing
Stone is Strong	M	I	250+	Yellow Umbrella Books	Red Brick Learning
Stone Mouse, The	K	F	250+	Lighthouse	Rigby
Stone Soup	I	TL	555	Leveled Literacy Intervention/ Green System	Heinemann
Stone Soup	J	TL	932	McGovern, Ann	Scholastic
Stone Soup	M	TL	250+	Muth, John J.	Scholastic
Stone Soup	J	TL	250+	PM Tales and Plays-Turquoise	Rigby
Stone Soup	K	TL	555	Red Rocket Readers	Flying Start Books
Stone Soup	H	TL	250+	Rigby Literacy	Rigby
Stone Soup	J	F	250+	Ross, Tony	Dial/Penguin
*Stone Soup and Other Stories	L	TL	250+	New Way Literature	Steck-Vaughn
Stone Soup, A Traditional Tale	H	TL	250+	Rigby Star	Rigby
Stone Works	K	I	124	Wonder World	Wright Group/McGraw Hill
^Stonehenge	X	I	250+	The Unexplained	Capstone Press

* Collection of short stories   # Graphic text
^ Mature content with lower level text demands

S

TITLE	LEVEL	GENRE	WORD COUNT	AUTHOR / SERIES	PUBLISHER / DISTRIBUTOR
Stonehenge: Mystery Unsolved?	U	I	1754	Leveled Readers	Houghton Mifflin Harcourt
Stonehenge: Still a Mystery	T	I	250+	Leveled Readers Language Support	Houghton Mifflin Harcourt
Stones in Water	X	RF	250+	Napoli, Donna Jo	Puffin Books
Stones of the Sky	N	TL	250+	Windows on Literacy	National Geographic
Stonewall Jackson: Spirit of the South	Y	B	250+	The Civil War	Carus Publishing Company
Stop	C	F	54	Story Box	Wright Group/McGraw Hill
Stop and Go!	B	RF	18	Bonnell, Kris	Reading Reading Books
Stop and Go, Yes and No: What Is an Antonym?	O	I	303	Words Are CATegorical	Millbrook Press
Stop Going Cock-a-Doodle-Doo	E	F	146	Sails	Rigby
Stop Knitting, Nina!	I	F	250+	Home Connection Collection	Rigby
Stop Teasing Taylor!	I	RF	490	We Both Read	Treasure Bay
Stop That	C	F	41	Ready Readers	Pearson Learning Group
Stop That Noise!	A	F	21	KinderReaders	Rigby
Stop That Noise!	C	RF	41	Pacific Literacy	Pacific Learning
Stop That Noise!	K	RF	1183	Real Kids Readers	Millbrook Press
Stop That Rabbit	G	F	168	First Start	Troll Associates
Stop That Robot!	WB	F	0	Big Cat	Pacific Learning
Stop the Car!	G	RF	179	Lighthouse	Rigby
Stop Thief!	J	TL	250+	Lighthouse	Ginn & Co.
Stop!	C	F	68	Literacy by Design	Rigby
Stop!	B	RF	90	PM Starters	Rigby
Stop!	A	RF	12	Ready Readers	Pearson Learning Group
Stop!	C	RF	31	Wonder World	Wright Group/McGraw Hill
*Stop! And Other Stories	E	F	161	Story Steps	Rigby
Stop, Drop, and Flop in the Slop	J	F	173	Sounds Like Reading	Lerner Publishing Group
Stop, Look, and Listen	C	RF	71	Lighthouse	Rigby
Stop, Look, and Listen	G	RF	102	Literacy Tree	Rigby
Stop, Quinn, Stop	D	F	66	Reading Street	Pearson
Stop, Stop	M	F	250+	Hurd, Edith Thacher	HarperCollins
Store Clerks: Then and Now	M	I	250+	Primary Source Readers	Teacher Created Materials
Stores	C	RF	66	Carousel Readers	Pearson Learning Group
Stories	C	RF	43	Learn to Read	Creative Teaching Press
*Stories for Children	V	TL	250+	Singer, Isaac Bashevis	Farrar, Straus, & Giroux
*Stories From the Days of Christopher Columbus	U	HF	250+	Young, Richard; Young, Judy Dockery	August House Publishers
*Stories from the Five Towns	U	RF	5540	Oxford Bookworms Library	Oxford University Press
Stories From the Underground Railroad	R	I	250+	Explorer Books-Pathfinder	National Geographic
Stories From the Underground Railroad	Q	I	250+	Explorer Books-Pioneer	National Geographic
*Stories Huey Tells, The	O	RF	250+	Cameron, Ann	Alfred A. Knopf
Stories in Stone	M	I	250+	Pacific Literacy	Pacific Learning
Stories in Stone: The World of Animal Fossils	U	I	250+	A First Book	Franklin Watts
*Stories Julian Tells, The	O	RF	250+	Cameron, Ann	Alfred A. Knopf
Stories of Me	D	RF	80	Teacher's Choice Series	Pearson Learning Group
*Stories of Ponies	L	RF	250+	Dickins, Rosie	Usborne Publishing Ltd.
*Stories of Sherlock Holmes	V	RF	250+	High-Fliers	Pacific Learning
*Stories of the North	Y	RF	250+	London, Jack	Scholastic
*Stories of the Sky: Tales from Three Cultures	M	TL	250+	Windows on Literacy	National Geographic
Stories to Tell	Q	F	250+	Reading Safari	Mondo Publishing
Storm at Coldwater Creek	M	HF	250+	Sunshine	Wright Group/McGraw Hill
Storm at Sea, A	R	HF	1145	Leveled Readers	Houghton Mifflin Harcourt
Storm Book, The	P	I	250+	Zolotow, Charlotte	HarperCollins
Storm Called Katrina, A	R	RF	250+	Uhlberg, Myron	Peachtree
Storm Chaser	U	RF	250+	Platt, Chris	Peachtree

S

* Collection of short stories   # Graphic text

^ Mature content with lower level text demands

TITLE	LEVEL	GENRE	WORD COUNT	AUTHOR / SERIES	PUBLISHER / DISTRIBUTOR
Storm Chasers	R	I	1371	Leveled Readers	Houghton Mifflin Harcourt
Storm Chasers	R	I	1371	Leveled Readers/CA	Houghton Mifflin Harcourt
Storm Chasers	L	RF	250+	Navigators Fiction Series	Benchmark Education
Storm Chasers: On the Trail of Deadly Tornadoes	S	I	250+	High Five Reading	Red Brick Learning
Storm Danger!	S	I	1739	Reading Street	Pearson
#Storm in the Barn, The	U	F	250+	Phelan, Matt	Candlewick Press
Storm in the Night	N	RF	250+	Stolz, Mary	HarperCollins
Storm Is Coming!	K	F	250+	Tekavec, Heather	Dial/Penguin
Storm Is Coming, A	H	I	172	Explorations	Eleanor Curtain Publishing
Storm Is Coming, A	H	I	172	Explorations	Okapi Educational Materials
Storm on the Beach, A	I	RF	72	Book Bank	Wright Group/McGraw Hill
Storm Runners	U	RF	250+	Smith, Roland	Scholastic
Storm Surfer	P	RF	250+	Maddox, Jake	Stone Arch Books
Storm Surge: The Science of Hurricanes	X	I	250+	Headline Science	Compass Point Books
Storm the Lightning Fairy: Rainbow Magic	L	F	250+	Meadows, Daisy	Scholastic
Storm Thief	X	F	250+	Wooding, Chris	Scholastic
Storm Warning (The 39 Clues)	U	F	250+	Park, Linda Sue	Scholastic
Storm!	E	I	49	Wonder World	Wright Group/McGraw Hill
Storm!	N	RF	250+	Wonder World	Wright Group/McGraw Hill
Storm, The	G	RF	75	Books for Young Learners	Richard C. Owen
Storm, The	A	I	24	Davidson, Avelyn	Scholastic
Storm, The	E	RF	71	Foundations	Wright Group/McGraw Hill
Storm, The	D	RF	30	Gear Up!	Wright Group/McGraw Hill
Storm, The	E	F	154	Leveled Literacy Intervention/ Green System	Heinemann
Storm, The	D	I	71	Leveled Readers	Houghton Mifflin Harcourt
Storm, The	D	I	71	Leveled Readers/CA	Houghton Mifflin Harcourt
Storm, The	E	RF	33	Literacy 2000	Rigby
Storm, The	D	RF	40	Potato Chip Books	American Reading Company
Storm, The	O	F	250+	Rylant, Cynthia	Aladdin
Storm, The	C	RF	29	Story Box	Wright Group/McGraw Hill
Storm, The	B	I	19	Sunshine	Wright Group/McGraw Hill
Storm, The	C	I	28	Voyages	SRA/McGraw Hill
Stormbreaker	Z	SF	250+	Horowitz, Anthony	Scholastic
#Stormbreaker: The Graphic Novel	Z	SF	250+	Horowitz, Anthony	Philomel
Storms	E	I	49	Canizares, Susan & Chessen, Betsey	Scholastic
Storms	N	I	250+	PM Plus Story Books	Rigby
Storms	H	I	284	Sails	Rigby
Storms	O	I	250+	Simon, Seymour	Mulberry Books
Storms	N	I	250+	Windows on Literacy	National Geographic
Storms!	L	I	359	Pair-It Books	Steck-Vaughn
Stormy Seas: A Story from the Shetland Islands	R	RF	250+	Reading Expeditions	National Geographic
Stormy Weather	N	F	253	Gliori, Debi	Walker & Company
Stormy Weather	O	I	250+	Navigators Science Series	Benchmark Education
Stormy Weather	H	I	208	PM Science Readers	Rigby
Stormy Weather	S	I	1618	Reading Street	Pearson
Stormy Weather	G	I	88	Twig	Wright Group/McGraw Hill
Stormy, Misty's Foal	R	RF	250+	Henry, Marguerite	Aladdin
Story Blanket, The	L	F	250+	Wolff, Ferida & Savitz, Harriet May	Peachtree
Story Box, The	K	RF	592	Leveled Readers	Houghton Mifflin Harcourt
Story of a Book, The	L	I	250+	Take Two Books	Wright Group/McGraw Hill

TITLE	LEVEL	GENRE	WORD COUNT	AUTHOR / SERIES	PUBLISHER / DISTRIBUTOR
Story of a Dolphin	M	RF	250+	Orr, Katherine	Carolrhoda Books
Story of a Girl	Z+	RF	250+	Zarr, Sara	Little Brown and Company
Story of Alexander Graham Bell, Inventor of the Telephone	O	B	250+	Davidson, Margaret	Scholastic
Story of Amy Johnson, The: Pioneering Woman Navigator	R	B	250+	Literacy 2000	Rigby
Story of Anne and Maud, The	W	B	1926	Leveled Readers	Houghton Mifflin Harcourt
Story of Anne and Maud, The	W	B	1926	Leveled Readers/CA	Houghton Mifflin Harcourt
Story of Anne and Maud, The	W	B	1926	Leveled Readers/TX	Houghton Mifflin Harcourt
Story of Atlas, The	Q	TL	776	Sun Sprouts	ETA/Cuisenaire
Story of Benjamin Franklin, Amazing American	O	B	250+	Davidson, Margaret	Scholastic
Story of Big Bess Call, The	M	TL	250+	Sunshine	Wright Group/McGraw Hill
Story of Books, The	O	I	250+	Sunshine	Wright Group/McGraw Hill
Story of Britain, The: From the Norman Conquest to the European Union	Y	I	250+	Dillion, Patrick	Candlewick Press
Story of Bunker's Cove	R	HF	250+	Leveled Readers Language Support	Houghton Mifflin Harcourt
Story of Cars, The	M	I	250+	Pair-It Turn and Learn	Steck-Vaughn
Story of Cheese, The	K	I	221	Pair-It Turn and Learn	Steck-Vaughn
Story of Chicken Licken	I	TL	250+	Ormerod, Jan	Lothrop
Story of Communication, The	L	I	444	Reading Street	Pearson
Story of Corn, The	H	I	171	Ready Readers	Pearson Learning Group
Story of Doña Chila, The	P	B	250+	Moore, Eva	Scholastic
Story of Dorothea Lange, The	U	B	1954	Leveled Readers	Houghton Mifflin Harcourt
Story of Dorothea Lange, The	U	B	1954	Leveled Readers/CA	Houghton Mifflin Harcourt
Story of Dorothea Lange, The	U	B	1954	Leveled Readers/TX	Houghton Mifflin Harcourt
Story of Ferdinand, The	K	F	250+	Leaf, Munro	Viking/Penguin
Story of Flight, The	T	I	2357	Reading Street	Pearson
Story of Frog Belly Rat Bone, The	N	F	250+	Ering, Timothy Basil	Candlewick Press
Story of George Washington Carver, The	Q	B	250+	Moore, Eva	Bantam Books
Story of Geronimo, The	T	B	250+	Cornerstones of Freedom	Children's Press
Story of Harriet Tubman, The: Conductor of the Underground Railroad	S	B	250+	McMullan, Kate	Scholastic
Story of Harriet Tubman, The: Freedom Train	T	B	250+	Sterling, Dorothy	Bantam Books
Story of High Street, The	WB	RF	0	Goodall, John S.	Andre Deutsch
Story of Hoover Dam, The	P	I	250+	Literacy by Design	Rigby
Story of Hungbu and Nolbu, The	K	TL	250+	Bookshop	Mondo Publishing
Story of Ice Cream, The	O	I	250+	Windows on Literacy	National Geographic
Story of Jackie Robinson, The: Bravest Man in Baseball	O	B	250+	Davidson, Margaret	Scholastic
#Story of Jamestown, The	T	I	250+	Graphic Library	Capstone Press
Story of Jeans, The	M	I	250+	Discovery World	Rigby
Story of Johnny Appleseed, The	M	B	250+	Aliki	Aladdin
Story of Juan Bobo, The	D	TL	58	Leveled Readers Language Support	Houghton Mifflin Harcourt
Story of Jumping Mouse, The	P	TL	250+	Steptoe, John	HarperTrophy
Story of Laura Ingalls Wilder, Pioneer Girl, The	Q	B	250+	Stine, Megan	Bantam Books
Story of Libraries, The	V	I	2145	Reading Street	Pearson
Story of Money, The	J	I	250+	On Our Way to English	Rigby
Story of Muhammad Ali: Heavyweight Champion of the World, The	S	B	250+	Denenberg, Barry	Dell
Story of My Life, The	X	B	250+	Keller, Helen	Bantam Books
Story of My Life, The	P	B	250+	Leveled Readers Language Support	Houghton Mifflin Harcourt
Story of Orange Juice, The	M	I	250+	Yellow Umbrella Books	Red Brick Learning
Story of Oskar Schindler, The	Z	B	2470	Leveled Readers	Houghton Mifflin Harcourt

S

TITLE	LEVEL	GENRE	WORD COUNT	AUTHOR / SERIES	PUBLISHER / DISTRIBUTOR
Story of Pathos	S	HF	4191	Take Two Books	Wright Group/McGraw Hill
Story of Pluto, The	S	I	2306	Leveled Readers Science	Houghton Mifflin Harcourt
Story of Pocahontas, The	M	B	250+	DK Readers	DK Publishing
Story of Ruby Bridges, The	O	B	250+	Coles, Robert	Scholastic
Story of Running Water, The	J	TL	287	Cambridge Reading	Pearson Learning Group
Story of Sacagawea, The	O	B	250+	Rosen Real Readers	Rosen Publishing Group
Story of Small Fry, The	P	I	250+	Action Packs	Rigby
Story of Sue, The: T Rex	X	I	2391	Independent Readers Science	Houghton Mifflin Harcourt
Story of the Bicycle, The	K	I	257	Dominie Factivity Series	Pearson Learning Group
Story of the Blues, The	U	I	1357	Vocabulary Readers	Houghton Mifflin Harcourt
Story of the Blues, The	U	I	1357	Vocabulary Readers/CA	Houghton Mifflin Harcourt
Story of the Blues, The	U	I	1357	Vocabulary Readers/TX	Houghton Mifflin Harcourt
Story of the Lonely Tree, The	H	RF	207	Take Two Books	Wright Group/McGraw Hill
Story of the Mayflower Compact, The	T	I	250+	Cornerstones of Freedom	Children's Press
Story of the Mexican Jumping Bean, The	M	TL	250+	Story Vines	Wright Group/McGraw Hill
Story of The Persian Gulf War, The	W	I	250+	Cornerstones of Freedom	Children's Press
Story of the Pony Express, The	P	I	250+	Windows on Literacy	National Geographic
Story of The Sinking of the Battleship Maine, The	W	I	250+	Cornerstones of Freedom	Children's Press
Story of The Surrender at Yorktown, The	V	I	250+	Cornerstones of Freedom	Children's Press
Story of the Three Bears, The	G	TL	379	Traditional Tales	Pioneer Valley
Story of the Three Kingdoms, The	O	TL	250+	Myers, Walter Dean	HarperCollins
Story of the White House, The	S	I	250+	Waters, Kate	Scholastic
Story of The Women's Movement, The	V	I	250+	Cornerstones of Freedom	Children's Press
Story of Thomas Alva Edison, Inventor, The	R	B	250+	Davidson, Margaret	Scholastic
Story of Walt Disney, Maker of Magical Worlds, The	O	B	250+	Selden, Bernice	Bantam Books
Story of Waltzing Matilda, The	V	I	2872	Independent Readers Social Studies	Houghton Mifflin Harcourt
Story of Water, The: A Moving Adventure	R	I	250+	Literacy by Design	Rigby
Story of William Tell, The	M	TL	250+	PM Story Books-Silver	Rigby
Story of Writing, The	V	I	1880	Reading Street	Pearson
Story of You, The	M	I	482	Sunshine	Wright Group/McGraw Hill
Story Sticks	F	I	58	Instant Readers	Harcourt School Publishers
Story Teller's Story, A	O	B	250+	Meet The Author	Richard C. Owen
Story Time	X	F	250+	Bloor, Edward	Harcourt
Story Time	C	RF	32	Ready Readers	Pearson Learning Group
Story With Pictures, A	N	F	250+	Kanninen, Barbara	Holiday House
Story, a Story, A: An African Tale	M	TL	250+	Haley, Gail E.	Aladdin
*Storyteller Quilts	R	I	250+	Storyteller-Raging Rivers	Wright Group/McGraw Hill
Storyteller, The	L	RF	1071	Leveled Readers/TX	Houghton Mifflin Harcourt
Storytellers	L	I	506	Storyteller Nonfiction	Wright Group/McGraw Hill
Storyteller's Beads, The	Y	RF	250+	Kurtz, Jane	Harcourt Trade
Storyteller's Journey, A	Q	I	250+	Bookweb	Rigby
Storytelling	O	I	955	Gear Up!	Wright Group/McGraw Hill
Storytelling Around the World	Q	I	1269	Vocabulary Readers	Houghton Mifflin Harcourt
Storytelling Around the World	P	I	573	Vocabulary Readers	Houghton Mifflin Harcourt
Storytelling Around the World	Q	I	1269	Vocabulary Readers/CA	Houghton Mifflin Harcourt
Storytelling Through the Years	Q	I	930	Vocabulary Readers	Houghton Mifflin Harcourt
Storytelling Through the Years	Q	I	930	Vocabulary Readers/CA	Houghton Mifflin Harcourt
Storytelling Through the Years	Q	I	930	Vocabulary Readers/TX	Houghton Mifflin Harcourt
Stowaway	W	HF	250+	Hesse, Karen	Simon & Schuster
Straight and Curvy, Meek and Nervy: More About Antonyms	O	I	270	Cleary, Brian P.	Lerner Publishing Group

S

* Collection of short stories   # Graphic text
^ Mature content with lower level text demands

TITLE	LEVEL	GENRE	WORD COUNT	AUTHOR / SERIES	PUBLISHER / DISTRIBUTOR
Straight from the Horse's Mouth	P	I	250+	Sunshine	Wright Group/McGraw Hill
Straight Line Wonder, The	J	F	250+	Bookshop	Mondo Publishing
Stranded in Boringsville	T	RF	250+	Bateson, Catherine	Holiday House
Stranded in the Desert	R	RF	250+	Reading Safari	Mondo Publishing
Stranded in the Snow!: Eric LeMarque's Story of Survival	R	I	250+	True Tales of Survival	Capstone Press
Stranded!: Amy Racina's Story of Survival	S	I	250+	True Tales of Survival	Capstone Press
Strange Animals	N	I	250+	Windows on Literacy	National Geographic
Strange Bird, A	P	F	1024	Leveled Readers	Houghton Mifflin Harcourt
Strange Case of Dr. Jekyll and Mr. Hyde, The	Z+	F	250+	Stevenson, Robert Louis	Penguin Group
Strange Case of Origami Yoda, The	T	RF	250+	Angleberger, Tom	Amulet Books
*Strange Clues and Other Cases, The	O	RF	250+	Simon, Seymour	Avon Books
Strange Creatures	N	SF	250+	Orbit Chapter Books	Pacific Learning
Strange Day at the Zoo, A	M	F	1398	Take Two Books	Wright Group/McGraw Hill
Strange Day in Mayville, A	L	TL	250+	Leveled Readers Language Support	Houghton Mifflin Harcourt
*Strange Happenings	S	F	250+	Avi	Harcourt, Inc.
Strange Jobs	Q	I	250+	Sunshine	Wright Group/McGraw Hill
Strange Life of Undersea Vents, The	W	I	2522	Leveled Readers	Houghton Mifflin Harcourt
Strange Meetings	Q	F	250+	Literacy 2000	Rigby
*Strange Museum and Other Cases, The	O	RF	250+	Simon, Seymour	Avon Books
Strange Plants	E	I	30	Books for Young Learners	Richard C. Owen
Strange Plants	J	I	433	Leveled Readers Science	Houghton Mifflin Harcourt
Strange Plants	O	I	250+	Windows on Literacy	National Geographic
Strange Rocks	U	I	2135	Leveled Readers Science	Houghton Mifflin Harcourt
Strange Shoe, The	L	TL	250+	PM Tales and Plays-Silver	Rigby
Strange Sports with Weird Gear	S	I	1454	Reading Street	Pearson
Strange Suckers	P	I	250+	Infotrek Plus	ETA/Cuisenaire
Strange Things	L	RF	289	Books for Young Learners	Richard C. Owen
Stranger at Green Knowe, A	T	F	250+	Boston, L.M.	Harcourt, Inc.
Stranger at the Window	U	RF	250+	Alcock, Vivien	Houghton Mifflin Harcourt
Stranger Came Ashore, A	U	F	250+	Hunter, Mollie	HarperTrophy
Stranger in Right Field	M	RF	250+	Christopher, Matt	Norwood House Press
Stranger on the Silk Road: A Story of Ancient China	O	HF	250+	Historical Tales	Picture Window Books
Stranger With My Face	Y	RF	250+	Duncan, Lois	Laurel-Leaf Books
Stranger's Gift, The	L	TL	250+	Literacy 2000	Rigby
Strangest Rock on Earth, The	Q	RF	250+	Pair-It Books	Steck-Vaughn
Stravaganza: City of Flowers	Z+	F	250+	Hoffman, Mary	Bloomsbury Children's Books
Stravaganza: City of Masks	Z+	F	250+	Hoffman, Mary	Bloomsbury Children's Books
Stravaganza: City of Secrets	Z+	F	250+	Hoffman, Mary	Bloomsbury Children's Books
Stravaganza: City of Ships	Z+	F	250+	Hoffman, Mary	Bloomsbury Children's Books
Stravaganza: City of Stars	Z+	F	250+	Hoffman, Mary	Bloomsbury Children's Books
Straw House, The	E	TL	241	Storyworlds	Heinemann
Straw into Gold	V	F	250+	Schmidt, Gary D.	Clarion Books
Strawberries	C	I	37	Little Books for Early Readers	University of Maine
Strawberries	F	I	92	Plant Life Cycles	Lerner Publishing Group
Strawberry Hill	R	HF	250+	Hoberman, Mary Ann	Little Brown and Company
Strawberry Hill	Y	RF	250+	LaFaye, A.	Simon & Schuster
Strawberry Jam	E	RF	77	Oxford Reading Tree	Oxford University Press

S

TITLE	LEVEL	GENRE	WORD COUNT	AUTHOR / SERIES	PUBLISHER / DISTRIBUTOR
Strawberry Moon	O	RF	250+	Orca Young Readers	Orca Books
Strawberry Picking	J	RF	250+	Cambridge Reading	Pearson Learning Group
Strawberry Pie	E	RF	138	Windows on Literacy	National Geographic
Strawberry Pop And Soda Crackers	K	RF	396	Little Celebrations	Pearson Learning Group
Stray Dog, The	J	RF	205	Simont, Marc	Scholastic
Stray, The	R	RF	250+	King-Smith, Dick	Alfred A. Knopf
Streak, The	N	RF	250+	Kroll, Stephen	Avon Books
Stream, The	C	RF	24	Science	Outside the Box
Stream, The	F	F	43	Voyages	SRA/McGraw Hill
Streams to the River, River to the Sea	X	HF	250+	O'Dell, Scott	Houghton Mifflin Harcourt
Street Action	O	I	250+	Wildcats	Wright Group/McGraw Hill
Street Fair	E	RF	94	The King School Series	Townsend Press
Street Musicians	J	RF	283	Sunshine	Wright Group/McGraw Hill
Street Performers	I	I	270	Vocabulary Readers	Houghton Mifflin Harcourt
Street Performers	I	I	270	Vocabulary Readers/CA	Houghton Mifflin Harcourt
Street Skating: Grinds and Grabs	Q	I	250+	Skateboarding	Capstone Press
Street Sweepers	I	I	138	Mighty Machines	Capstone Press
Streets of Gold	U	HF	1933	Leveled Readers	Houghton Mifflin Harcourt
Streetsweeper, The	M	RF	250+	Bookweb	Rigby
Strega Nona	M	TL	250+	DePaola, Tomie	Scholastic
Strength and Stability	O	I	250+	InfoTrek	ETA/Cuisenaire
Strength in Numbers	O	I	250+	InfoQuest	Rigby
Strep Throat	K	I	250+	Health Matters	Capstone Press
Stressbusters	M	RF	250+	Social Studies Connects	Kane Press
Strider	R	RF	250+	Cleary, Beverly	HarperCollins
Strike	O	I	250+	Pacific Literacy	Pacific Learning
Strike Fighters: The F/A-18E/F Super Hornets	V	I	250+	War Planes	Capstone Press
Strike Four!	H	RF	250+	Ziefert, Harriet	Puffin Books
Strike Me Down with a Stringbean	L	F	404	Read Alongs	Rigby
Strike Now!	W	HF	250+	Reading Expeditions	National Geographic
Strike Out!	M	RF	250+	Howard, Tristan	Scholastic
Striking, Grappling, and Ground Fighting: The Skills Behind Mixed Martial Arts	T	I	250+	The World of Mixed Martial Arts	Capstone Press
String Food	K	I	250+	Home Connection Collection	Rigby
String Performers	J	I	250+	Home Connection Collection	Rigby
String Things	G	I	165	Springboard	Wright Group/McGraw Hill
Strings	C	I	53	Storyteller-First Snow	Wright Group/McGraw Hill
Strings, Ropes, and Cables	I	I	250+	Home Connection Collection	Rigby
Striped Ice Cream	N	RF	250+	Lexau, Joan M.	Scholastic
Stripes	WB	I	0	Big Cat	Pacific Learning
Stripes	B	I	24	Explorations	Eleanor Curtain Publishing
Stripes	B	I	24	Explorations	Okapi Educational Materials
Stripes	LB	I	28	Twig	Wright Group/McGraw Hill
Stripes and Spots	A	I	32	Sails	Rigby
Stripes and Stars	L	I	250+	Trackers	Pacific Learning
Stroll and Walk, Babble and Talk: More about Synonyms	O	I	238	Cleary, Brian P.	Millbrook Press
Strongest Animal, The	F	RF	58	Books for Young Learners	Richard C. Owen
Strongest Animals, The	L	I	250+	EXtreme Animals	Capstone Press
Strongest One of All, The	H	TL	222	Instant Readers	Harcourt School Publishers
Structures of Life: What Is This Fossil?	R	I	250+	iScience	Norwood House Press
Struggle for Equality, The	W	I	250+	Reading Expeditions	National Geographic
Struggle for Higher Education, The	Y	I	2321	Reading Street	Pearson
Strum Family Band, The	J	RF	250+	The Story Basket	Wright Group/McGraw Hill

* Collection of short stories   # Graphic text
^ Mature content with lower level text demands

S

TITLE	LEVEL	GENRE	WORD COUNT	AUTHOR / SERIES	PUBLISHER / DISTRIBUTOR
Strum! Hum! Play a Drum!	I	I	110	The Rowland Reading Program Library	Rowland Reading Foundation
Stuart Goes to School	M	F	250+	Pennypacker, Sara	Scholastic
Stuart Little	R	F	250+	White, E. B.	HarperTrophy
Stuart's Cape	M	F	250+	Pennypacker, Sara	Scholastic
Stuart's Moon Suit	R	RF	1075	Reading Street	Pearson
Stubborn Goat, The	I	F	212	Alphakids	Sundance
Stuck at Camp	S	RF	2198	Leveled Readers	Houghton Mifflin Harcourt
Stuck at Camp	S	RF	2198	Leveled Readers/CA	Houghton Mifflin Harcourt
Stuck at Camp	S	RF	2198	Leveled Readers/TX	Houghton Mifflin Harcourt
Stuck at the End of the Ice Age	Z	I	1877	Leveled Readers	Houghton Mifflin Harcourt
Stuck in Neutral	Z	RF	250+	Edge	Hampton Brown
Stuck in Neutral	Z	RF	250+	Trueman, Terry	HarperCollins
Stuck in the Ice	M	I	250+	Leveled Readers Language Support	Houghton Mifflin Harcourt
Stuck in the Muck	E	F	139	Spinelle, Nancy Louise	Kaeden Books
Stuck in the Mud	E	RF	120	Lighthouse	Rigby
Stuck in the Tar Pits	W	I	250+	Independent Readers Science	Houghton Mifflin Harcourt
Stuck on an Island	H	RF	181	Sunshine	Wright Group/McGraw Hill
Stuck on Earth	X	SF	250+	Klass, David	Farrar, Straus, & Giroux
Student of the Week	N	HF	250+	HSP/Harcourt Trophies	Harcourt, Inc.
Study Science at the Glacier Institute	K	I	182	Larkin, Bruce	Wilbooks
Studying a Glacier	M	I	501	Leveled Readers Science	Houghton Mifflin Harcourt
Studying the Past	T	I	512	Vocabulary Readers	Houghton Mifflin Harcourt
#Stuff of Life, The: A Graphic Guide to Genetics and DNA	Z	I	250+	Schultz, Mark	Farrar, Straus, & Giroux
^Stuff We All Get	V	RF	250+	Denman, K. L./Orca Currents	Orca Books
^Stuffed	T	RF	250+	Orca Soundings	Orca Books
Stuk's Village	S	HF	1553	Reading Street	Pearson
Stump Hill	K	RF	627	Early Connections	Benchmark Education
Stumptown Kid	W	HF	250+	Gorman, Carol & Findley, Ron J.	Peachtree
Stumpy's Secret	P	RF	250+	Hager, Mandy	Pacific Learning
Stunt Planes	Q	I	250+	Wild Rides!	Capstone Press
Sturdy Turtles	L	I	399	Pull Ahead Books	Lerner Publishing Group
Stuyvesant, Peter: New Amsterdam and the Origins of New York	W	B	250+	Power Plus	Rosen Publishing Group
Style	Z	I	250+	Boldprint	Steck-Vaughn
Style All Her Own, A	K	RF	737	Friedman, Laurie	Carolrhoda Books
Sub, The	P	RF	250+	Peterson, P. J.	Puffin Books
Submarine Pitch, The	Q	RF	250+	Christopher, Matt	Little Brown and Company
Submarine, The	T	I	250+	Tales of Invention	Heinemann Library
Submarines	T	I	250+	Land and Sea	Capstone Press
Submarines	J	I	118	Mighty Machines	Capstone Press
Submarines	V	I	4440	Military Hardware in Action	Lerner Publishing Group
Submarines	N	I	389	Pull Ahead Books	Lerner Publishing Group
Submarines	O	I	250+	Rigby Flying Colors	Rigby
Subtraction Action	L	F	250+	Leedy, Loreen	Holiday House
Sub-Saharan Africa	W	I	250+	Primary Source Readers	Teacher Created Materials
Substitute Groundhog	K	F	250+	Miller, Pat	Albert Whitman & Co.
Substitute Teacher Plans	L	F	250+	Johnson, Doug	Square Fish
Subtle Knife, The	Z	F	250+	Pullman, Philip	Ballantine Books
Subtraction	C	I	30	Early Math	Lerner Publishing Group
Subtraction Fun	K	I	250+	Yellow Umbrella Books	Capstone Press
Suburban Community of the 1950s, A	R	I	250+	Reading Expeditions	National Geographic

S

TITLE	LEVEL	GENRE	WORD COUNT	AUTHOR / SERIES	PUBLISHER / DISTRIBUTOR
Subway Mouse, The	L	F	250+	Reid, Barbara	Scholastic
^Sudden Impact	T	RF	250+	Orca Soundings	Orca Books
Sudden Secrets	N	RF	250+	Rigby Literacy	Rigby
Sudden Silence, A	Y	RF	250+	Bunting, Eve	Harcourt, Inc.
Sudden Storm, A	S	RF	250+	Power Up!	Steck-Vaughn
Sue and Drew	I	RF	440	Reading Street	Pearson
Sue Hendrickson	M	B	631	Leveled Readers	Houghton Mifflin Harcourt
Sue Hendrickson	M	B	631	Leveled Readers/CA	Houghton Mifflin Harcourt
Sue Hendrickson	M	B	631	Leveled Readers/TX	Houghton Mifflin Harcourt
Sue Hendrickson: Fossil Hunter	L	B	671	Leveled Readers	Houghton Mifflin Harcourt
Sue Hendrickson: Fossil Hunter	L	B	671	Leveled Readers/CA	Houghton Mifflin Harcourt
Sue Hendrickson: Fossil Hunter	L	B	671	Leveled Readers/TX	Houghton Mifflin Harcourt
Sue Hendrickson: Modern Adventurer	R	B	250+	Explore More	Wright Group/McGraw Hill
Sue Likes Blue	G	RF	131	Start to Read	School Zone
Sue's Hummingbird	M	RF	893	Reading Street	Pearson
Sugar and Ice	W	RF	250+	Messner, Kate	Walker & Company
Sugar and Spice and All Things Nice	L	I	250+	Storyteller Chapter Books	Wright Group/McGraw Hill
Sugar Bush, The	K	I	250+	Greetings	Rigby
Sugar Cakes Cyril	M	RF	4022	Gershator, Phillis	Mondo Publishing
Sugar Changed the World: A Story of Magic, Spice, Slavery, Freedom, and Science	Z	I	250+	Aronson, Marc & Budhos, Marina	Clarion Books
Sugar Gliders	O	I	2266	Early Bird Nature Books	Lerner Publishing Group
Sugar Snow	J	HF	250+	Wilder, Laura Ingalls	HarperCollins
Sugaring Season (Making Maple Syrup)	S	I	250+	Burns, Diane	Carolrhoda Books
Sugaring Time	S	I	250+	Lasky, Kathryn	Macmillan
Sugaring Weather	R	HF	1449	Leveled Readers	Houghton Mifflin Harcourt
Sugaring Weather	R	HF	1449	Leveled Readers/CA	Houghton Mifflin Harcourt
Sugaring Weather	R	HF	1449	Leveled Readers/TX	Houghton Mifflin Harcourt
Sugaring-Off Party, The	Q	RF	1683	London, Jonathan	Fitzhenry & Whiteside
Suitcase	N	RF	250+	Walter, Mildred Pitts	Scholastic
Suki and the Case of the Lost Bunnies	K	RF	250+	Ready Readers	Pearson Learning Group
Sulky Simon	J	RF	246	Windmill Books	Rigby
Sultan's Challenge, The	N	TL	250+	WorldScapes	ETA/Cuisenaire
Sultanta's Sandals	K	TL	250+	The Rowland Reading Program Library	Rowland Reading Foundation
Summer	B	RF	45	Leveled Readers Language Support	Houghton Mifflin Harcourt
Summer	I	I	178	Pebble Books	Capstone Press
Summer	E	I	53	Seasons	Lerner Publishing Group
Summer	E	I	73	Sunshine	Wright Group/McGraw Hill
Summer at Cove Lake	G	RF	288	Ready Readers	Pearson Learning Group
Summer Ball	V	RF	250+	Lupica, Mike	Philomel
Summer Camp	J	RF	182	City Kids	Rigby
Summer Camp	A	F	25	Leveled Readers	Houghton Mifflin Harcourt
Summer Camp	A	F	25	Leveled Readers/CA	Houghton Mifflin Harcourt
Summer Day Slushes	L	RF	250+	Windows on Literacy	National Geographic
Summer Day, A	C	I	74	Leveled Readers	Houghton Mifflin Harcourt
Summer Fun	A	I	24	Bonnell, Kris	Reading Reading Books
Summer Fun	E	RF	30	Literacy 2000	Rigby
Summer Fun	J	I	261	Spyglass Books	Compass Point Books
Summer I Shrank My Grandmother, The	Q	F	250+	Woodruff, Elvira	Bantam Books
Summer in Antarctica	M	I	250+	Explorations	Eleanor Curtain Publishing
Summer in Antarctica	M	I	250+	Explorations	Okapi Educational Materials
Summer in the South, A	Q	F	250+	Marshall, James	Houghton Mifflin Harcourt

Organized Alphabetically by Title
Storable Database at www.fountasandpinnellleveledbooks.com

* Collection of short stories   # Graphic text
^ Mature content with lower level text demands

S

TITLE	LEVEL	GENRE	WORD COUNT	AUTHOR / SERIES	PUBLISHER / DISTRIBUTOR
Summer Is Here!	D	RF	47	Windows on Literacy	National Geographic
*Summer Life, A	Z	RF	250+	Soto, Gary	Bantam Books
Summer Mail	W	RF	3361	Leveled Readers	Houghton Mifflin Harcourt
Summer of Baseball Parks, The	K	RF	690	Leveled Readers	Houghton Mifflin Harcourt
Summer of Baseball Parks, The	K	RF	690	Leveled Readers/CA	Houghton Mifflin Harcourt
Summer of Baseball Parks, The	K	RF	690	Leveled Readers/TX	Houghton Mifflin Harcourt
Summer of Fear	Z	RF	250+	Duncan, Lois	Little Brown and Company
Summer of Hurricane Andrew, The	O	RF	1259	Reading Street	Pearson
Summer of Kings, A	Z	HF	250+	Nolan, Han	Harcourt, Inc.
Summer of My German Soldier	Z	HF	250+	Greene, Bette	Dell
Summer of Secrets	Z+	RF	250+	Langan, Paul	Townsend Press
Summer of the Great-Grandmother, The	Z	B	250+	L'Engle, Madeleine	HarperCollins
Summer of the Swans, The	U	RF	250+	Byars, Betsy	Penguin Group
Summer Party, The	O	RF	250+	On Our Way to English	Rigby
Summer Rays	V	RF	3077	Leveled Readers	Houghton Mifflin Harcourt
Summer Reading is Killing Me!	P	F	250+	Scieszka, Jon	Penguin Group
Summer Sabotage	Q	RF	250+	Reading Safari	Mondo Publishing
Summer Sands	M	RF	839	Evangeline Nicholas Collection	Wright Group/McGraw Hill
Summer School! What Genius Thought That Up?	R	RF	250+	Winkler, Henry and Oliver, Lin	Grosset & Dunlap
Summer Sun Risin'	N	RF	355	Bebop Books	Lee & Low Books Inc.
Summer Switch	R	F	250+	Rodgers, Mary	HarperTrophy
Summer to Die, A	T	RF	250+	Lowry, Lois	Dell
Summer to Fall	H	I	204	Early Explorers	Benchmark Education
Summer Trips	I	I	272	Visions	Wright Group/McGraw Hill
^Summer Trouble	P	RF	1603	Zucker, Jonny	Stone Arch Books
Summer Wheels	N	B	250+	Bunting, Eve	Harcourt Trade
Summer with the Grandparents	S	RF	3324	Reading Street	Pearson
Summer with Uncle Vince	Q	F	1497	Leveled Readers	Houghton Mifflin Harcourt
Summer with Uncle Vince	Q	F	1497	Leveled Readers/CA	Houghton Mifflin Harcourt
Summer with Uncle Vince	Q	F	1497	Leveled Readers/TX	Houghton Mifflin Harcourt
Summertime in the Big Woods	J	HF	250+	Wilder, Laura Ingalls	HarperCollins
Summing up Sport	U	I	250+	News Extra	Richard C. Owen
Sun	S	I	250+	Our Solar System	Compass Point Books
Sun	H	I	131	Space	Lerner Publishing Group
Sun	Q	I	250+	The Galaxy	Red Brick Learning
Sun & Spoon	R	RF	250+	Henkes, Kevin	Penguin Group
*Sun Above and the River Below, The	P	TL	250+	Literacy by Design	Rigby
Sun and Moon, Ice and Snow	X	F	250+	George, Jessica Day	Bloomsbury Children's Books
Sun and the Moon, The	C	RF	41	PM Stars	Rigby
Sun and the Wind, The	E	TL	173	Storyworlds	Heinemann
Sun Chariot, The	N	TL	250+	Sun Sprouts	ETA/Cuisenaire
Sun Flower, A	B	RF	42	Foundations	Wright Group/McGraw Hill
Sun Power	P	I	250+	Rigby Focus	Rigby
Sun Power	G	I	79	Windows on Literacy	National Geographic
Sun Racers	M	I	749	Rigby Flying Colors	Rigby
Sun Shines on Me, The	B	I	34	Science	Outside the Box
*Sun Smile	I	F	250+	Story Box	Wright Group/McGraw Hill
Sun Up, Sun Down	H	I	148	Independent Readers Science	Houghton Mifflin Harcourt
Sun Up, Sun Down: The Story of Day and Night	Q	I	250+	Science Works	Picture Window Books
Sun, a Flower, A	LB	I	42	Foundations	Wright Group/McGraw Hill
Sun, Earth, and Moon	L	I	391	Vocabulary Readers	Houghton Mifflin Harcourt
Sun, Earth, and Moon	L	I	391	Vocabulary Readers/CA	Houghton Mifflin Harcourt

S

TITLE	LEVEL	GENRE	WORD COUNT	AUTHOR / SERIES	PUBLISHER / DISTRIBUTOR
Sun, Moon, and Stars: A Cosmic Case	Q	I	2414	iScience	Norwood House Press
Sun, Moon, Earth	E	I	53	Leveled Readers Science	Houghton Mifflin Harcourt
Sun, Rain, and Snow	B	I	72	Leveled Readers Emergent	Houghton Mifflin Harcourt
Sun, The	E	I	42	Discovery Links	Newbridge
Sun, The	Q	I	1648	Early Bird Astronomy	Lerner Publishing Group
Sun, The	R	I	250+	Explorer Books-Pathfinder	National Geographic
Sun, The	P	I	250+	Explorer Books-Pioneer	National Geographic
Sun, The	I	I	183	Exploring the Galaxy	Capstone Press
Sun, The	D	I	119	Leveled Readers	Houghton Mifflin Harcourt
Sun, The	N	I	573	Leveled Readers Science	Houghton Mifflin Harcourt
Sun, The	D	I	119	Leveled Readers/CA	Houghton Mifflin Harcourt
Sun, The	D	I	119	Leveled Readers/TX	Houghton Mifflin Harcourt
Sun, The	N	I	250+	Literacy 2000	Rigby
Sun, The	N	I	956	Our Universe	Lerner Publishing Group
Sun, The	K	I	135	Out In Space	Red Brick Learning
Sun, The	B	I	32	Rigby Focus	Rigby
Sun, The	M	I	250+	The Solar System	Capstone Press
Sun, The	N	I	250+	Windows on Literacy	National Geographic
Sun, The	J	I	219	Wonder World	Wright Group/McGraw Hill
Sun, The	E	I	66	Yellow Umbrella Books	Red Brick Learning
Sun, the Wind & Tashira, The	J	TL	371	Folk Tales	Mondo Publishing
Sun, the Wind, and the Rain, The	G	RF	170	PM Plus Nonfiction	Rigby
Sunburn	J	RF	176	City Kids	Rigby
Sunburn	B	I	48	Prokopchak, Ann	Kaeden Books
Sunday Best	I	RF	250+	Ford, Juwanda G.	Scholastic
Sunday Horse	N	RF	250+	Literacy Tree	Rigby
Sunday Potatoes, Monday Potatoes	G	RF	114	Avenues	Hampton Brown
Sunflower	G	RF	77	Ford, Miela	Hampton Brown
Sunflower	E	I	55	Joy Starters	Pearson Learning Group
Sunflower	N	I	250+	Life Cycles	Creative Teaching Press
Sunflower Seeds	D	I	48	Story Box	Wright Group/McGraw Hill
Sunflower That Went Flop, The	K	F	637	Story Box	Wright Group/McGraw Hill
Sunflower, The	C	I	27	Pacific Literacy	Pacific Learning
Sunflowers	E	I	69	Bonnell, Kris/About	Reading Reading Books
Sunflowers	E	I	33	Books for Young Learners	Richard C. Owen
Sunflowers	D	I	35	Pebble Books	Capstone Press
Sunflowers	F	I	110	Plant Life Cycles	Lerner Publishing Group
Sunflower's Life, A	F	I	163	Watch It Grow	Heinemann Library
Sunflowers, Magnolia Trees & Other Flowering Plants	Y	I	250+	Kingdom Classification	Compass Point Books
#Sunjata: Warrior King of Mali	U	TL	3046	Graphic Myths and Legends	Lerner Publishing Group
Sunken Treasure	P	I	250+	Gibbons, Gail	Houghton Mifflin Harcourt
Sunny	C	I	26	Weather	Lerner Publishing Group
Sunny Day, A	E	I	65	Pebble Books	Capstone Press
Sunny Day, A	E	I	90	Weather	Lerner Publishing Group
Sunny or Cloudy?	D	F	94	Bonnell, Kris	Reading Reading Books
Sunny the Yellow Fairy: Rainbow Magic	L	F	250+	Meadows, Daisy	Scholastic
Sunny-Side Up	M	RF	250+	Giff, Patricia Reilly	Bantam Books
Sunrise	C	F	46	Literacy 2000	Rigby
Sunrise Over Fallujah	Z+	RF	250+	Myers, Walter Dean	Scholastic
Sun's Family of Planets, The	L	I	250+	Read-About Science	Children's Press
Sun's Magic, The	B	I	28	Seedlings	Continental Press
Sun's Strength, The: An Ancient Chinese Myth	W	TL	1972	Leveled Readers	Houghton Mifflin Harcourt

* Collection of short stories   # Graphic text
^ Mature content with lower level text demands

TITLE	LEVEL	GENRE	WORD COUNT	AUTHOR / SERIES	PUBLISHER / DISTRIBUTOR
Sunscreen for Plants	U	I	4588	A Great Idea	Norwood House Press
Sunset of the Sabertooth	M	F	250+	Osborne, Mary Pope	Random House
Sunset Pond, The	J	RF	433	Appleton-Smith, Laura	Flyleaf Publishing
Sunset: Warriors, The New Prophecy	U	F	250+	Hunter, Erin	HarperCollins
Sunsets of Miss Olivia Wiggins, The	Q	RF	250+	Laminack, Lester L.	Peachtree
Sunshine	WB	RF	0	Ormerod, Jan	Lothrop, Lee & Shepard
Sunshine	L	I	307	Weather	Capstone Press
Sunshine Street	H	RF	110	Sunshine	Wright Group/McGraw Hill
Sunshine, Moonshine	E	RF	128	Armstrong, Jennifer	Random House
Sunshine, the Black Cat	G	RF	143	Carousel Readers	Pearson Learning Group
Sunshine: A Book About Sunlight	M	I	250+	Amazing Science	Picture Window Books
Super Amos	R	RF	250+	Paulsen, Gary	Bantam Books
Super Animals	F	I	149	Leveled Readers Science	Houghton Mifflin Harcourt
Super Ben	C	RF	33	Big Cat	Pacific Learning
Super Bob and the Birthday Surprise	K	F	525	Rigby Gigglers	Rigby
Super Bob and the Howling Bucket	K	F	250+	Rigby Gigglers	Rigby
Super Bowl, The: 40 Years of Amazing Games	U	I	250+	Christopher, Matt	Little Brown and Company
Super Brother	H	RF	245	The Rowland Reading Program Library	Rowland Reading Foundation
Super Car	B	F	21	Rigby Rocket	Rigby
Super Danny	C	F	35	Coulton, Mia	Maryruth Books
Super Dog	E	F	86	Jack and Daisy	Pioneer Valley
Super Fly Guy	H	F	296	Arnold, Tedd	Scholastic
Super Fox	G	F	265	Leveled Literacy Intervention/ Blue System	Heinemann
Super Hero	B	RF	33	Sunshine	Wright Group/McGraw Hill
Super Hero ABC	Q	F	250+	McLeod, Bob	HarperCollins
Super- Hungry Mice Eat Onions and Other Painless Tricks for Memorizing Geography Facts	T	I	2975	Adventures in Memory	Millbrook Press
Super Parrot	J	RF	250+	Real Reading	Steck-Vaughn
Super Pig's Adventures	E	F	133	New Way Blue	Steck-Vaughn
Super Safari	L	F	212	Amazing Animals	Kingfisher
Super Sandwich	E	I	72	Little Red Readers	Sundance
Super Science Book	U	I	250+	Time for Kids	Capstone Press
Super Sculptures	J	I	282	Big Cat	Pacific Learning
Super Shadows	K	I	250+	Science Rocks!	ABDO Publishing Company
Super Shake, The	M	F	250+	Reading Safari	Mondo Publishing
Super Shopping	D	RF	41	Rigby Literacy	Rigby
Super Shopping	D	RF	56	Rigby Star	Rigby
Super Smile Shop, The	H	F	254	Story Basket	Wright Group/McGraw Hill
Super Soccer Freak Show	Q	F	250+	Wiley & Grampa's Creature Features	Little Brown and Company
Super Soybean, The	S	I	250+	Bial, Raymond	Albert Whitman & Co.
Super Space Stations	M	I	250+	Rosen Real Readers	Rosen Publishing Group
Super Spiders	F	I	105	Red Rocket Readers	Flying Start Books
Super Stock Rookie	X	RF	250+	Weaver, Will	Farrar, Straus, & Giroux
Super Storms	M	I	250+	Simon, Seymour	Chronicle Books
Super Strawberries	I	I	344	Rigby Flying Colors	Rigby
Super Supermarket Plan, The	J	RF	250+	Home Connection Collection	Rigby
Super Suzy	J	RF	323	InfoTrek	ETA/Cuisenaire
Super Terrific Me!	D	RF	64	Early Learning Modules	Steck-Vaughn
Super Winter Survivors	U	I	250+	Literacy by Design	Rigby
Superbikes	M	I	250+	Horsepower	Capstone Press
Superbikes	T	I	250+	The World's Fastest	Red Brick Learning

S

* Collection of short stories   # Graphic text
^ Mature content with lower level text demands

TITLE	LEVEL	GENRE	WORD COUNT	AUTHOR / SERIES	PUBLISHER / DISTRIBUTOR
Supercharged Infield	P	RF	250+	Christopher, Matt	Little Brown and Company
Supercomputer Pizzas	M	F	250+	Bookweb	Rigby
SuperCroc	Q	I	250+	Explorer Books-Pathfinder	National Geographic
SuperCroc	P	I	250+	Explorer Books-Pioneer	National Geographic
SuperCroc	O	I	250+	Windows on Literacy	National Geographic
SuperCroc Found	N	I	1752	On My Own History	Lerner Publishing Group
Supercross	W	I	6107	Motor Mania	Lerner Publishing Group
Supercross Motorcylces	N	I	442	Pull Ahead Books	Lerner Publishing Group
Supercross Racing	Q	I	250+	Dirt Bikes	Capstone Press
Superdome	O	I	250+	Windows on Literacy	National Geographic
Super-Duper Sandwich, The	I	F	202	Books for Young Learners	Richard C. Owen
Super-Duper Shoes	H	RF	82	Rigby Star	Rigby
Super-Duper Sunflower Seeds, The	I	F	389	Book Bank	Wright Group/McGraw Hill
Superfudge	Q	RF	250+	Blume, Judy	Bantam Books
Superhero School	O	F	250+	Reynolds, Aaron	Bloomsbury Children's Books
Superheroes Save the Day	J	F	714	Leveled Readers	Houghton Mifflin Harcourt
Superheroes Save the Day	J	F	714	Leveled Readers/CA	Houghton Mifflin Harcourt
Superheroes Save the Day	J	F	714	Leveled Readers/TX	Houghton Mifflin Harcourt
Superheroes to the Rescue	J	F	735	Leveled Readers	Houghton Mifflin Harcourt
Superheroes to the Rescue	J	F	735	Leveled Readers/CA	Houghton Mifflin Harcourt
Superheroes to the Rescue	J	F	735	Leveled Readers/TX	Houghton Mifflin Harcourt
Superkids	H	F	165	Sunshine	Wright Group/McGraw Hill
Superkids' Album, The	F	RF	84	The Rowland Reading Program Library	Rowland Reading Foundation
Supermarket Chase, The	K	RF	438	Sunshine	Wright Group/McGraw Hill
Supermarket Managers	M	I	250+	Community Helpers	Red Brick Learning
Supermarket on Mars	B	F	38	Rigby Rocket	Rigby
Supermarket, The	K	I	263	Pebble Books	Capstone Press
Supernaturalist, The	W	SF	250+	Colfer, Eoin	Hyperion
Supernova	N	RF	250+	PM Collection	Rigby
Supersonic Fighters: The F-16 Fighting Falcons	V	I	250+	War Planes	Capstone Press
Superstars	I	F	252	Sunshine	Wright Group/McGraw Hill
Super-tuned!	N	RF	250+	PM Collection	Rigby
Supper for Cal	H	RF	189	Leveled Readers	Houghton Mifflin Harcourt
Supply and Demand	L	I	436	Early Explorers	Benchmark Education
Supreme Court of the United States, The	W	I	250+	American Civics	Red Brick Learning
Supreme Court, The	S	I	250+	A True Book	Children's Press
Supreme Court, The	Q	I	527	Vocabulary Readers	Houghton Mifflin Harcourt
Supreme Court, The	Q	I	527	Vocabulary Readers/CA	Houghton Mifflin Harcourt
Supreme Court, The	M	I	583	Vocabulary Readers/TX	Houghton Mifflin Harcourt
Supreme Sailor	M	F	250+	Too Cool	Pacific Learning
Surf Carnival, The	K	RF	434	PM Story Books	Rigby
Surf Girls	N	RF	250+	Girlz Rock!	Mondo Publishing
Surfer, The	D	RF	40	Wonder World	Wright Group/McGraw Hill
Surfing Pro	M	F	250+	Too Cool	Pacific Learning
Surfing the Information Highway	H	I	137	Wonder World	Wright Group/McGraw Hill
Surf's Up	P	RF	250+	Wildcats	Wright Group/McGraw Hill
Surf's Up!	L	RF	250+	Go Girl!	Feiwel and Friends
Surfs Up, Geronimo!	O	F	250+	Stilton, Geronimo	Scholastic
Surge, The: Storm Runners	U	RF	250+	Smith, Roland	Scholastic
Surprise Box, The	I	RF	250+	Voyages	SRA/McGraw Hill
Surprise Cake	C	F	32	Literacy 2000	Rigby
Surprise Dinner, The	L	RF	680	PM Collection	Rigby

Organized Alphabetically by Title
Storable Database at www.fountasandpinnellleveledbooks.com

* Collection of short stories   # Graphic text
^ Mature content with lower level text demands

S

TITLE	LEVEL	GENRE	WORD COUNT	AUTHOR / SERIES	PUBLISHER / DISTRIBUTOR
Surprise Feast, The	O	I	250+	Rigby Focus	Rigby
Surprise for Jake	D	RF	80	Windows on Literacy	National Geographic
Surprise for Mom	E	RF	101	Urmston, Kathleen; Evans, Karen	Kaeden Books
Surprise for Mom, A	E	I	177	Leveled Literacy Intervention/ Green System	Heinemann
Surprise for Ms. Green, A	J	RF	393	Leveled Readers	Houghton Mifflin Harcourt
Surprise for Ms. Green, A	J	RF	393	Leveled Readers/CA	Houghton Mifflin Harcourt
Surprise for Ms. Green, A	J	RF	393	Leveled Readers/TX	Houghton Mifflin Harcourt
Surprise for Roxy, A	D	F	107	Leveled Literacy Intervention/ Blue System	Heinemann
Surprise for the Bears, A	M	RF	966	Leveled Readers	Houghton Mifflin Harcourt
Surprise for the Bears, A	M	RF	966	Leveled Readers/CA	Houghton Mifflin Harcourt
Surprise for the Bears, A	M	RF	966	Leveled Readers/TX	Houghton Mifflin Harcourt
Surprise for the Big Bad Wolf, A	L	F	562	Leveled Literacy Intervention/ Blue System	Heinemann
Surprise for Zack, A	I	RF	250+	PM Plus Story Books	Rigby
Surprise from the Sky	H	RF	292	Red Rocket Readers	Flying Start Books
Surprise from the Sky	I	F	295	Windmill Books	Rigby
Surprise Invitation, The	J	RF	250+	PM Plus Story Books	Rigby
Surprise Moon	I	RF	206	Bebop Books	Lee & Low Books Inc.
Surprise Party	E	F	94	Bella and Rosie Series	Literacy Footprints
Surprise Party	K	I	333	Hutchins, Pat	Macmillan
Surprise Party	M	RF	250+	Tristars	Richard C. Owen
Surprise Party, The	I	F	192	New Way Green	Steck-Vaughn
Surprise Party, The	J	RF	250+	Prager, Annabelle	Random House
Surprise Pet, A	C	F	54	Leveled Readers Language Support	Houghton Mifflin Harcourt
Surprise Snow, The	K	RF	545	Leveled Readers	Houghton Mifflin Harcourt
*Surprise Visit, The	G	F	250+	New Way Blue	Steck-Vaughn
Surprise Visitor, The	K	RF	534	Red Rocket Readers	Flying Start Books
Surprise!	M	RF	882	Gear Up!	Wright Group/McGraw Hill
Surprise!	I	RF	168	Little Celebrations	Pearson Learning Group
Surprise!	D	RF	28	My First Reader	Grolier
Surprise!	H	RF	434	Real Kids Readers	Millbrook Press
Surprise!	D	F	28	Story Steps	Rigby
Surprise, A	B	RF	27	Kaleidoscope Collection	Hameray Publishing Group
Surprise, The	E	F	225	Leveled Literacy Intervention/ Green System	Heinemann
Surprise, The	H	F	124	Literacy 2000	Rigby
Surprise, The	G	RF	199	Rigby Flying Colors	Rigby
Surprise, The	D	RF	101	Springboard	Wright Group/McGraw Hill
Surprise, The	A	F	14	Story Box	Wright Group/McGraw Hill
Surprises According to Humphrey	Q	F	250+	Birney, Betty G.	Puffin Books
Surprising Myself	O	B	250+	Meet The Author	Richard C. Owen
Surprising Sharks	N	I	250+	Read and Wonder	Candlewick Press
Surprising Swimmers: Nature's Most Amazing Animals	R	I	250+	Fredericks, Anthony D.	NorthWord Press
Surprising World of Plants, The	T	I	250+	Pair-It Books	Steck-Vaughn
Surrender	Z+	RF	250+	Hartnett, Sonya	Candlewick Press
Surrender at Appomattox, The	U	I	1530	Leveled Readers Social Studies	Houghton Mifflin Harcourt
Surrender at Yorktown	P	I	250+	Leveled Readers	Houghton Mifflin Harcourt
Surrender at Yorktown	S	I	600	Leveled Readers Social Studies	Houghton Mifflin Harcourt
Surrender Tree, The	Z	HF	250+	Engle, Margarita	Henry Holt & Co.
Surrounded By Sea: Life on a New England Fishing Island	N	I	250+	Gibbons, Gail	Holiday House

S

TITLE	LEVEL	GENRE	WORD COUNT	AUTHOR / SERIES	PUBLISHER / DISTRIBUTOR
Survival Animal Adaptations	V	I	250+	iOpeners	Pearson Learning Group
Survival at Plymouth Colony	V	I	2316	Vocabulary Readers	Houghton Mifflin Harcourt
Survival at Plymouth Colony	V	I	2316	Vocabulary Readers/CA	Houghton Mifflin Harcourt
Survival at Plymouth Colony	V	I	2316	Vocabulary Readers/TX	Houghton Mifflin Harcourt
Survival Fun	T	I	250+	High-Fliers	Pacific Learning
Survival in Cyberspace	T	SF	250+	Storyteller-Whispering Pines	Wright Group/McGraw Hill
Survival in the Snow	N	HF	1766	On My Own History	Millbrook Press
Survival in the Storm	X	HF	250+	Janke, Katelan	Scholastic
Survival of Fish, The	M	I	946	Sunshine Science	Wright Group/McGraw Hill
^Survive	O	RF	250+	Buckton, Chris	Stone Arch Books
Survive!	Q	RF	250+	Wildcats	Wright Group/McGraw Hill
Surviving Brick Johnson	N	RF	250+	Myers, Laurie	Houghton Mifflin Harcourt
^Surviving Death Valley: Desert Adaptation	T	I	250+	Extreme Life	Capstone Press
Surviving Hitler: A Boy in the Nazi Death Camps	Y	B	250+	Warren, Andrea	HarperTrophy
Surviving in the Tundra	N	I	747	Springboard	Wright Group/McGraw Hill
Surviving in the Wild	N	I	250+	Rigby Literacy	Rigby
Surviving Jamestown: The Adventures of Young Sam Collier	W	HF	250+	Karwaski, Gail Langer	Peachtree
Surviving the Applewhites	T	RF	250+	Tolan, Stephanie S.	Scholastic
Surviving the Odds	P	I	250+	WorldScapes	ETA/Cuisenaire
Surviving the Weather: Animals in Their Environments	R	I	1905	Reading Street	Pearson
Surviving Volcanoes and Glaciers	T	I	250+	Reading Expeditions	National Geographic
Survivors	X	I	250+	Boldprint	Steck-Vaughn
Survivors	O	I	250+	InfoQuest	Rigby
Survivors in the Frozen North	L	RF	250+	PM Plus Story Books	Rigby
Survivors, The	U	F	250+	Book Blazers	ETA/Cuisenaire
Susan B. Anthony	Q	B	250+	Early Biographies	Compass Point Books
Susan B. Anthony	S	B	3840	History Maker Bios	Lerner Publishing Group
Susan B. Anthony	N	B	237	Pebble Books	Capstone Press
Susan B. Anthony	P	B	250+	Photo-Illustrated Biographies	Red Brick Learning
Susan B. Anthony	Q	B	796	Time for Kids	Teacher Created Materials
Susan B. Anthony and Elizabeth Cady Stanton	V	B	250+	Amazing Americans	Wright Group/McGraw Hill
Susan B. Anthony, Fighter for Women's Rights	N	B	381	Independent Readers Social Studies	Houghton Mifflin Harcourt
Susan B. Anthony: A Life of Fairness	O	B	532	Pull Ahead Books	Lerner Publishing Group
Susan B. Anthony: Champion of Women's Rights	R	B	250+	Monsell, Helen Albee	Simon & Schuster
Susanna of the Alamo	T	B	250+	Jakes, John	Language for Learning Assoc.
Susan's Missing Painting	L	RF	757	Reading Street	Pearson
Susie Goes Shopping	F	F	194	First Start	Troll Associates
Suspect	W	RF	250+	Nightez, Kristen Wolden	Peachtree
Suspense…	Y	I	250+	Boldprint	Steck-Vaughn
Suzi Clue: The Prom Queen Curse	Z+	RF	250+	Kehm, Michelle	Dutton Children's Books
Suzie Ridinghood	R	RF	250+	Reading Safari	Mondo Publishing
Suzy Mule	J	F	377	Let's Read Together	Kane Press
Swamp Explorer	R	I	250+	On Our Way to English	Rigby
Swamp Hen	F	I	59	Pacific Literacy	Pacific Learning
Swamp Monsters	K	F	250+	Christian, Mary Blount	Puffin Books
Swamp of the Hideous Zombies	M	F	250+	Hayes, Geoffrey	Random House
Swamp Song	L	F	250+	Ketteman, Helen	Marshall Cavendish
Swamp Stomp	T	RF	250+	Power Up!	Steck-Vaughn
Swampland	N	I	250+	Habitats	Children's Press

* Collection of short stories   # Graphic text
^ Mature content with lower level text demands

TITLE	LEVEL	GENRE	WORD COUNT	AUTHOR / SERIES	PUBLISHER / DISTRIBUTOR
Swan Family, The	F	RF	172	PM Plus Story Books	Rigby
Swan Kingdom, The	Z	F	250+	Marriott, Zoe	Candlewick Press
Swan Maiden, The	X	F	250+	Tomlinson, Heather	Square Fish
Swans	D	I	53	Joy Readers	Pearson Learning Group
Swan's Child, The	X	F	250+	Kuyper, Sjoerd	Holiday House
Swap Meet, The	M	RF	250+	HSP/Harcourt Trophies	Harcourt, Inc.
Swat it!	D	F	46	Bauer, Roger	Kaeden Books
SWAT Teams	S	I	250+	Law Enforcement	Capstone Press
^SWAT Teams	S	I	250+	Line of Duty	Capstone Press
Sweaty Book of Sweat, The	S	I	250+	The Amazingly Gross Human Body	Capstone Press
Sweeping Tsunamis	T	I	250+	Awesome Forces of Nature	Heinemann Library
Sweet 15	Z	RF	250+	Adler, Emily, & Echevarria, Alex	Marshall Cavendish
Sweet Bees	F	RF	96	Gear Up!	Wright Group/McGraw Hill
Sweet Clara and the Freedom Quilt	S	HF	250+	Hopkinson, Deborah	Scholastic
Sweet Dreams: How Animals Sleep	J	I	106	Kajikawa, Kimiko	Henry Holt & Co.
Sweet Face's Adventure	K	F	250+	Jasper the Cat	Pioneer Valley
Sweet Land of Liberty	Q	HF	250+	Hopkinson, Deborah	Peachtree
Sweet Mangoes: A Tale from India	M	TL	250+	In Step Readers	Rigby
Sweet Memories Still	Q	RF	250+	Kinsey-Warnock, Natalie	Bantam Books
Sweet or Sour?	I	I	177	Sunshine	Wright Group/McGraw Hill
Sweet Potato Pie	E	RF	72	Rockwell, Anne	Random House
Sweet to Eat	I	RF	105	Pacific Literacy	Pacific Learning
Sweetest Fig, The	P	F	250+	Van Allsburg, Chris	Houghton Mifflin Harcourt
Sweetest Present, The	E	F	80	Leveled Readers	Houghton Mifflin Harcourt
Sweethearts	Z+	RF	250+	Zarr, Sara	Little Brown and Company
Sweetness at the Bottom of the Pie, The	Z	RF	250+	Bradley, Alan	Delacorte Press
Swift Rivers	W	RF	250+	Meigs, Cornelia	Walker & Company
Swift Thief: The Adventure of Velociraptor	N	I	250+	Dinosaur World	Picture Window Books
Swiftly Tilting Planet, A	V	F	250+	L'Engle, Madeleine	Bantam Books
Swim Through the Sea, A	Q	I	170	Sharing Nature with Children	Dawn Publications
Swim!	A	I	31	Leveled Literacy Intervention/ Green System	Heinemann
Swim, Climb, and Fly	B	I	30	Sails	Rigby
Swimming	C	RF	65	Carousel Readers	Pearson Learning Group
Swimming	A	I	24	Leveled Readers	Houghton Mifflin Harcourt
Swimming	A	I	24	Leveled Readers/CA	Houghton Mifflin Harcourt
Swimming Across the Pool	J	RF	250+	PM Plus Story Books	Rigby
Swimming Around the World	M	I	250+	InfoTrek Plus	ETA/Cuisenaire
Swimming for Fun	S	I	250+	Sports for Fun	Compass Point Books
Swimming Lessons	H	RF	178	Handprints D	Educators Publishing Service
Swimming Lessons	W	RF	2005	Leveled Readers	Houghton Mifflin Harcourt
Swimming Lessons	J	RF	253	McAlpin, MaryAnn	Short Tales Press
Swimming Lessons	I	I	200	Storyteller Nonfiction	Wright Group/McGraw Hill
Swimming Pool, The	C	RF	29	Visions	Wright Group/McGraw Hill
Swimming Safely	T	I	2315	Reading Street	Pearson
Swimming Salmon	L	I	393	Pull Ahead Books	Lerner Publishing Group
Swimming Silently	T	SF	2811	Leveled Readers	Houghton Mifflin Harcourt
Swimming Silently	T	SF	2811	Leveled Readers/CA	Houghton Mifflin Harcourt
Swimming Silently	T	SF	2811	Leveled Readers/TX	Houghton Mifflin Harcourt
Swimming With a Dragon	H	RF	230	PM Plus Story Books	Rigby
Swimming with Dolphins	M	I	810	Big Cat	Pacific Learning
Swimming with Dolphins	R	I	1715	Reading Street	Pearson

S

TITLE	LEVEL	GENRE	WORD COUNT	AUTHOR / SERIES	PUBLISHER / DISTRIBUTOR
Swimming With Dolphins	I	RF	376	Red Rocket Readers	Flying Start Books
Swimming with Sharks	N	RF	250+	Hicks, Betty	Roaring Brook Press
Swimming with Sharks	N	B	250+	In Step Readers	Rigby
Swimming, Springing, Splashing, Singing, Humpbacks	L	I	250+	The Rowland Reading Program Library	Rowland Reading Foundation
Swimmy	M	F	250+	Lionni, Leo	Scholastic
Swing	A	RF	18	Story Box	Wright Group/McGraw Hill
Swing Dancing	S	I	250+	Dance	Capstone Press
Swing, Swing, Swing	C	F	93	Tuchman, G.; Dieterichs, S.	Scholastic
^Swiped	Q	RF	250+	Orca Currents	Orca Books
Swish: The Quest for Basketball's Perfect Shot	U	I	12024	Stewart, Mark & Kennedy, Mike	Millbrook Press
Switch It On	S	I	250+	InfoQuest	Rigby
Switcharound	P	RF	250+	Lowry, Lois	Random House
Switzerland	O	I	250+	Countries of the World	Red Brick Learning
Switzerland	P	I	1617	Country Explorers	Lerner Publishing Group
Switzerland	B	I	36	Nonfiction Set 2	Literacy Footprints
Swivelhead	P	F	250+	High-Fliers	Pacific Learning
Swoop!	I	RF	250+	PM Plus Story Books	Rigby
Sword in the Stone, The	J	TL	250+	Maccarone, Grace	Scholastic
*Sword of the Samurai: Adventure Stories From Japan	S	HF	250+	Kimmel, Eric A.	HarperCollins
Sword Thief, The (The 39 Clues)	U	F	250+	Lerangis, Peter	Scholastic
Swords	U	I	250+	Boos, Ben	Candlewick Press
Sybil Ludington's Midnight Ride	N	HF	1851	On My Own History	Lerner Publishing Group
Sydney - Where Biscuits Go Surfing	R	RF	250+	Coy, Michael	Scholastic
Sydney and the Kangaroo	J	F	250+	Rigby Rocket	Rigby
Sylvia Earle	W	B	250+	Just the Facts Biographies	Lerner Publishing Group
Sylvia Earle and the Deep Ocean	T	B	1370	Leveled Readers	Houghton Mifflin Harcourt
Sylvia Earle and the Deep Ocean	T	B	1370	Leveled Readers/CA	Houghton Mifflin Harcourt
Sylvia Earle and the Deep Ocean	T	B	1370	Leveled Readers/TX	Houghton Mifflin Harcourt
Sylvia Earle, First Lady of the Sea	G	B	98	Independent Readers Science	Houghton Mifflin Harcourt
Sylvia Earle: Protecting the Seas	T	I	250+	Reading Expeditions	National Geographic
Symbols of Freedom	O	I	250+	Windows on Literacy	National Geographic
Symbols of Our Country	P	I	250+	Navigators Social Studies Series	Benchmark Education
Symmetry in Our World	O	I	250+	Early Connections	Benchmark Education
Symphony of Whales, A	P	RF	250+	Schuch, Steve	Scholastic
^Symphony That Was Silent, The	Q	RF	250+	Brezenoff, Steve/Field Trip Mysteries	Stone Arch Books
Synchro Swans	T	I	250+	WorldScapes	ETA/Cuisenaire
Syria: A Question and Answer Book	P	I	250+	Question and Answer Countries	Capstone Press
#System Shock	S	F	3476	O'Donnell, Liam	Stone Arch Books

* Collection of short stories   # Graphic text
^ Mature content with lower level text demands

TITLE	LEVEL	GENRE	WORD COUNT	AUTHOR / SERIES	PUBLISHER / DISTRIBUTOR
T	LB	I	14	Readlings	American Reading Company
T Is for Terrible	L	F	122	McCarty, Peter	Square Fish
T Rex	G	I	145	Red Rocket Readers	Flying Start Books
T. J.'s Tree	G	RF	77	Literacy 2000	Rigby
T. Rex	M	I	250+	Read and Wonder	Candlewick Press
T. Rex Trek	L	F	594	Springboard	Wright Group/McGraw Hill
T. Rex Troy Tells the Tale	M	F	250+	Springboard	Wright Group/McGraw Hill
T. Rex: The Adventure of Tyrannosaurus Rex	N	I	250+	Dinosaur World	Picture Window Books
T.J.'s Secret Pitch	O	RF	250+	Bowen, Fred	Peachtree
Tabby	WB	RF	0	Aliki	HarperCollins
Tabby Cat at Night	B	RF	39	Brand New Readers	Candlewick Press
Tabby Cat's Scare	D	F	41	Brand New Readers	Candlewick Press
Tabby Cat's Scarf	D	RF	41	Brand New Readers	Candlewick Press
Tabby in the Tree	F	RF	200	PM Story Books	Rigby
Table for Two	L	TL	250+	Little Celebrations	Pearson Learning Group
Tac's Bunk Bed	F	RF	149	The Rowland Reading Program Library	Rowland Reading Foundation
Tactical Fighters: The F-15 Eagles	V	I	250+	War Planes	Capstone Press
Tadpole Diary	O	I	250+	Literacy Tree	Rigby
Tadpole Rescue	M	RF	250+	Windows on Literacy	National Geographic
Tag Along	C	RF	38	Potato Chip Books	American Reading Company
Tag, You're It!	C	F	32	Brand New Readers	Candlewick Press
Tag-Along Tim	J	RF	358	Leveled Readers	Houghton Mifflin Harcourt
Tag-Along Tim	J	RF	358	Leveled Readers/CA	Houghton Mifflin Harcourt
Tag-Along Tim	J	RF	358	Leveled Readers/TX	Houghton Mifflin Harcourt
Taiga	W	I	250+	Biomes Atlases	Raintree
Taiga Biome, The	U	I	3085	Reading Street	Pearson
Tail of Emily Windsnap, The	S	F	250+	Kessler, Liz	Candlewick Press
Tails	B	I	33	Animal Traits	Lerner Publishing Group
Tails	E	I	90	Bonnell, Kris/About	Reading Reading Books
Tails	B	I	42	Book Bank	Wright Group/McGraw Hill
Tails	E	I	59	Bookshop	Mondo Publishing
Tails	E	I	59	Discovery Links	Newbridge
Tails	C	I	69	Explorations	Eleanor Curtain Publishing
Tails	C	I	69	Explorations	Okapi Educational Materials
Tails	D	I	108	Leveled Literacy Intervention/ Blue System	Heinemann
Tails	F	I	47	Literacy 2000	Rigby
Tails	B	I	49	Sails	Rigby
Tails	I	I	170	Sunshine	Wright Group/McGraw Hill
Tails	D	I	115	Vocabulary Readers	Houghton Mifflin Harcourt
Tails	D	I	115	Vocabulary Readers/CA	Houghton Mifflin Harcourt
Tails	D	I	52	Wonder World	Wright Group/McGraw Hill
Tails and Claws	C	I	65	Wonder World	Wright Group/McGraw Hill
Tails Can Tell	I	I	346	Wonder World	Wright Group/McGraw Hill
Tails, Tails, Tails	E	I	131	Sails	Rigby
Take a Backyard Bird Walk	U	I	250+	Take a Walk Books	Stillwater Publishing
Take a Bite	C	F	19	Little Celebrations	Pearson Learning Group
Take a Bow, Jody	D	RF	78	Eaton, Audrey; Kennedy, Jane	Continental Press
Take a Chance	X	RF	2464	Leveled Readers	Houghton Mifflin Harcourt
Take a Chance on Me: Gossip Girl, the Carlyles	Z+	RF	250+	von Ziegesar, Cecily	Little Brown and Company
Take a City Nature Walk	U	I	250+	Take a Walk Books	Stillwater Publishing
Take a Guess	C	F	45	Little Celebrations	Pearson Learning Group
Take a Guess	G	I	202	Shutterbug Books	Steck-Vaughn

T

TITLE	LEVEL	GENRE	WORD COUNT	AUTHOR / SERIES	PUBLISHER / DISTRIBUTOR
Take a Guess: A Look at Estimation	K	I	164	Spyglass Books	Compass Point Books
Take a Look	N	I	250+	Wildcats	Wright Group/McGraw Hill
Take a Look at My Family	F	RF	155	Phonics and Friends	Hampton Brown
Take a Ride	F	I	105	Gear Up!	Wright Group/McGraw Hill
Take a Seat!	L	I	346	Gear Up!	Wright Group/McGraw Hill
Take a Stand! What You Can Do about Bullying	V	I	7438	Health Zone	Lerner Publishing Group
Take a Tree Walk	U	I	250+	Take a Walk Books	Stillwater Publishing
Take a Trip to China	L	I	301	Vocabulary Readers	Houghton Mifflin Harcourt
Take a Trip to China	L	I	301	Vocabulary Readers/CA	Houghton Mifflin Harcourt
Take a Trip to China	L	I	301	Vocabulary Readers/TX	Houghton Mifflin Harcourt
Take a Walk with Butterflies and Dragonflies	U	I	250+	Take a Walk Books	Stillwater Publishing
Take a Walk, Johnny	K	RF	250+	Easy Stories	Norwood House Press
Take a Walk, Johnny	K	RF	250+	Hillert, Margaret	Pearson Learning Group
Take Away	E	I	81	Yellow Umbrella Books	Red Brick Learning
Take Care of Our Earth	M	I	250+	Pair-It Books	Steck-Vaughn
Take Care Out There	Q	I	250+	Orbit Collections	Pacific Learning
Take Me Out to the Ballpark	K	RF	711	Leveled Readers	Houghton Mifflin Harcourt
Take Me Out to the Ballpark	K	RF	711	Leveled Readers/CA	Houghton Mifflin Harcourt
Take Me Out to the Ballpark	K	RF	711	Leveled Readers/TX	Houghton Mifflin Harcourt
Take Me to Your Leader!	L	SF	888	Rigby Gigglers	Rigby
Take Me with You	W	HF	250+	Marsden, Carolyn	Candlewick Press
Take One	Q	RF	250+	Sails	Rigby
Take the Subway	F	I	111	Vocabulary Readers	Houghton Mifflin Harcourt
Take Two	G	RF	228	PM Math Stories	Rigby
Take-away Puppy, The	G	RF	248	PM Math Stories	Rigby
Takeaway!	G	F	40	Book Bus	Creative Edge
Taken by the Wind	M	RF	250+	Wahman, Joe	Wright Group/McGraw Hill
Taking Care of a Hamster	D	I	65	Leveled Readers Science	Houghton Mifflin Harcourt
Taking Care of Animals	R	I	1343	Leveled Readers	Houghton Mifflin Harcourt
Taking Care of Animals	R	I	1343	Leveled Readers/CA	Houghton Mifflin Harcourt
Taking Care of Animals	R	I	1343	Leveled Readers/TX	Houghton Mifflin Harcourt
Taking Care of Babies	I	I	117	Sails	Rigby
Taking Care of Baby	G	I	159	Discovery Links	Newbridge
Taking Care of Farm Animals	WB	I	0	Windows on Literacy	National Geographic
Taking Care of Meli	F	I	205	Leveled Literacy Intervention/ Blue System	Heinemann
Taking Care of My Ears	G	I	137	Keeping Healthy	Capstone Press
Taking Care of My Eyes	G	I	131	Keeping Healthy	Capstone Press
Taking Care of My Hair	G	I	118	Keeping Healthy	Capstone Press
Taking Care of My Hands and Feet	G	I	102	Keeping Healthy	Capstone Press
Taking Care of My Skin	G	I	122	Keeping Healthy	Capstone Press
Taking Care of My Teeth	G	I	125	Keeping Healthy	Capstone Press
Taking Care of Our World	H	I	137	Rosen Real Readers	Rosen Publishing Group
Taking Care of Our World	E	I	137	Visions	Wright Group/McGraw Hill
Taking Care of Ourselves	J	I	250+	PM Plus Nonfiction	Rigby
Taking Care of Pets	B	I	55	Yellow Umbrella Books	Red Brick Learning
Taking Care of Rosie	E	RF	61	Salem, Lynn; Stewart, Josie	Continental Press
Taking Care of Terrific	S	RF	250+	Lowry, Lois	Dell
Taking Care of the Earth	N	I	1274	Reading Street	Pearson
Taking Care of Yoki	R	RF	250+	Campbell, Barbara	HarperTrophy
Taking Flight	O	I	250+	Scooters	ETA/Cuisenaire
Taking It to the Extreme	O	I	971	Leveled Readers	Houghton Mifflin Harcourt
Taking It to the Extreme	O	I	971	Leveled Readers/CA	Houghton Mifflin Harcourt
Taking Jason to Grandma's	F	RF	118	Book Bank	Wright Group/McGraw Hill

* Collection of short stories   # Graphic text
^ Mature content with lower level text demands

TITLE	LEVEL	GENRE	WORD COUNT	AUTHOR / SERIES	PUBLISHER / DISTRIBUTOR
Taking Liberty	X	HF	250+	Rinaldi, Ann	Simon & Schuster
Taking Off	Y	HF	250+	Moss, Jenny	Walker & Company
Taking Our Photo	E	RF	132	Voyages	SRA/McGraw Hill
Taking Photographs	M	I	788	Early Connections	Benchmark Education
Taking Pictures	E	RF	137	Alphakids	Sundance
Taking Pictures	A	F	20	Leveled Readers	Houghton Mifflin Harcourt
Taking Pictures	A	F	20	Leveled Readers/CA	Houghton Mifflin Harcourt
Taking Sides	S	RF	250+	Soto, Gary	Harcourt Trade
Taking to the Air	Q	I	250+	Literacy Tree	Rigby
Taking Turns	E	RF	177	Rigby Flying Colors	Rigby
Taking You Places: A Book About Bus Drivers	H	I	127	Community Workers	Picture Window Books
Tale of a Great White Fish: A Sturgeon Story	N	I	250+	de Vries, Maggie	Greystone Books
Tale of Antarctica, A	Q	F	250+	Glimmerveen, Ulco	Scholastic
Tale of Cowboy	A	RF	31	Reading Unlimited	Pearson Learning Group
Tale of Cowboy Roy, The	H	F	185	Ready Readers	Pearson Learning Group
#Tale of Despereaux	S	F	250+	Smith, Matt and Tilton, David (Retold)	Candlewick Press
Tale of Despereaux, The	U	F	250+	DiCamillo, Kate	Candlewick Press
Tale of Despereaux, The	S	F	250+	Michalak, Jamie (Retold)	Candlewick Press
Tale of Despereaux: A Hero's Quest	O	F	250+	Ross, Gary (Retold)	Candlewick Press
Tale of Despereaux: No Ordinary Mouse	N	F	250+	Ross, Gary (Retold)	Candlewick Press
Tale of Despereaux: The Mouse and the Princess	O	F	250+	Ross, Gary (Retold)	Candlewick Press
Tale of La Llorona, The	N	TL	1933	On My Own Folklore	Millbrook Press
Tale of Peter Rabbit, The	L	TL	250+	Potter, Beatrix	Scholastic
Tale of Sir Spiffing Biffing, The	M	F	250+	Rigby Rocket	Rigby
Tale of the Christmas Mouse	H	F	97	First Start	Troll Associates
Tale of the Golden Goose, The	L	TL	250+	Behr, Alexandra	Hampton Brown
Tale of the Swamp Rat	T	F	250+	Crocker, Carter	Philomel
Tale of the Turnip, The	I	TL	250+	PM Traditional Tales-Orange	Rigby
Tale of Toad and Badger, The (Willow Buds)	K	F	250+	Begin, Mary Jane	Little Brown and Company
Tale of Two Bad Mice, The	M	F	250+	Potter, Beatrix	Crown Publishers
Tale of Two Mice, The	K	F	250+	Brown, Ruth	Candlewick Press
Tale of Veruschka Babuschka, The	M	TL	250+	Literacy 2000	Rigby
Talent Contest, The	K	RF	250+	PM Story Books-Silver	Rigby
Talent Night at School	F	RF	102	Little Red Readers	Sundance
Talent Show	N	RF	250+	Girlz Rock!	Mondo Publishing
Talent Show	E	F	227	Leveled Literacy Intervention/ Green System	Heinemann
Talent Show from the Black Lagoon, The	N	F	250+	Black Lagoon Adventures	Scholastic
Talent Show, The	R	RF	250+	Gutman, Dan	Simon & Schuster
Talent Show, The	K	RF	828	PM Stars Bridge Books	Rigby
Talented Alex	O	RF	772	Leveled Readers	Houghton Mifflin Harcourt
Talented Clementine, The	O	RF	250+	Pennypacker, Sara	Hyperion
Tales for Hard Times: A Story About Charles Dickens	R	B	8559	Creative Minds Biographies	Carolrhoda Books
Tales from Gull Island	U	RF	250+	Power Up!	Steck-Vaughn
*Tales from Longpuddle	W	RF	6490	Oxford Bookworms Library	Oxford University Press
Tales from Moominvalley	S	F	250+	Jansson, Tove	Farrar, Straus, & Giroux
*Tales from Near and Far	P	TL	250+	Literacy by Design	Rigby
*Tales from Parc la Fontaine	J	F	311	Schwartz, Roslyn	Annick Press
*Tales from the Homeplace: Adventures of a Texas Farm Girl	S	RF	250+	Burandt, Harriet; Dale, Shelley	Bantam Books
Tales from the Hood: The Sisters Grimm	U	F	250+	Buckley, Michael	Amulet Books
Tales from the Odyssey	Z	TL	3197	Leveled Readers	Houghton Mifflin Harcourt

T

TITLE	LEVEL	GENRE	WORD COUNT	AUTHOR / SERIES	PUBLISHER / DISTRIBUTOR
Tales from the Odyssey	Z	TL	3197	Leveled Readers/CA	Houghton Mifflin Harcourt
Tales from the Odyssey	Z	TL	3197	Leveled Readers/TX	Houghton Mifflin Harcourt
Tales from the Secrets Closet (Billy Bones)	U	F	250+	Lincoln, Christopher	Little Brown and Company
*Tales from the Underground Railroad	S	HF	250+	Connell, Kate	Steck-Vaughn
*Tales from the Waterhole	L	F	250+	Candlewick Sparks	Candlewick Press
Tales Mummies Tell	W	I	250+	Lauber, Patricia	Scholastic
Tales of a Fourth Grade Nothing	Q	RF	250+	Blume, Judy	Bantam Books
*Tales of Amanda Pig	L	F	250+	Van Leeuwen, Jean	Puffin Books
*Tales of Beedle the Bard	U	F	250+	Rowling, J. K.	Scholastic
Tales of Hercules	U	TL	1315	Leveled Readers	Houghton Mifflin Harcourt
Tales of Hercules	U	TL	1315	Leveled Readers/CA	Houghton Mifflin Harcourt
Tales of Hercules	U	TL	1315	Leveled Readers/TX	Houghton Mifflin Harcourt
*Tales of Mystery and Imagination	Y	F	11960	Oxford Bookworms Library	Oxford University Press
Tales of Olga da Polga, The	P	F	250+	Bond, Michael	Houghton Mifflin Harcourt
*Tales of Oliver Pig	L	F	250+	Van Leeuwen, Jean	Puffin Books
Tales of Real Escape	X	B	250+	Dowswell, Paul	Scholastic
*Tales of Terror from the Black Ship	V	F	250+	Priestley, Chris	Bloomsbury Children's Books
*Tales of the Full Moon	R	TL	250+	Hart, Sue	Fulcrum Publishing
*Tales of Travelers	O	TL	250+	Literacy by Design	Rigby
Tales, Fables and Rhymes	N	I	250+	Tristars	Richard C. Owen
Talk	Z+	RF	250+	Koja, Kathe	Square Fish
Talk About a Family	O	RF	250+	Greenfield, Eloise	HarperTrophy
Talk Back	U	I	250+	The News	Richard C. Owen
Talk! Talk! Talk!	N	I	50	Little Celebrations	Pearson Learning Group
Talk, Talk, Talk	C	RF	56	Literacy 2000	Rigby
Talkin' About Bessie: The Story of Aviator Elizabeth Coleman	S	B	250+	Grimes, Nikki	Scholastic
Talking Earth, The	U	RF	250+	George, Jean Craighead	HarperTrophy
Talking Eggs, The	P	TL	250+	San Souci, Robert D.	Scholastic
Talking Teeth	M	I	250+	Brain Bank	Scholastic
Talking to Faith Ringgold	S	B	250+	Ringgold, Faith; Freeman, Linda; Roucher, Nancy	Crown Publishers
Talking to Our Friends	F	I	138	Rigby Focus	Rigby
Talking to the Animals	J	F	360	InfoTrek	ETA/Cuisenaire
Talking Yam, The	I	F	340	Little Readers	Houghton Mifflin Harcourt
Tall	I	I	249	Sails	Rigby
Tall Baby Giraffe, The	E	RF	92	Seedlings	Continental Press
Tall Cool One	Z+	RF	250+	Dean, Zoey	Little Brown and Company
Tall Giraffe	B	F	51	Zoozoo-Into the Wild	Cavallo Publishing
Tall Stories About Snakes	G	I	141	Voyages	SRA/McGraw Hill
Tall Tails: Cross-Country with Lewis and Clark	Q	F	250+	Smith, Donna	Scholastic
*Tall Tale and Other Cases, The	O	RF	250+	Simon, Seymour	Avon Books
Tall Tale of John Henry, The	N	TL	250+	Neufeld, David	Scholastic
#Tall Tale of Paul Bunyan, The	O	TL	250+	Graphic Spin	Stone Arch Books
Tall Tale to Tell, A	O	I	860	Independent Readers Social Studies	Houghton Mifflin Harcourt
Tall Tale Tuesday	M	RF	825	Leveled Readers	Houghton Mifflin Harcourt
Tall Tale Tuesday	M	RF	825	Leveled Readers/CA	Houghton Mifflin Harcourt
Tall Tale Tuesday	M	RF	825	Leveled Readers/TX	Houghton Mifflin Harcourt
Tall Tales	I	RF	139	Literacy Tree	Rigby
Tall Tales	O	RF	250+	PM Collection	Rigby
Tall Tales	O	TL	615	Vocabulary Readers	Houghton Mifflin Harcourt
Tall Things	D	I	83	PM Nonfiction-Red	Rigby

* Collection of short stories   # Graphic text
^ Mature content with lower level text demands

TITLE	LEVEL	GENRE	WORD COUNT	AUTHOR / SERIES	PUBLISHER / DISTRIBUTOR
Tall Tony	K	RF	383	Leveled Readers	Houghton Mifflin Harcourt
Tall, Tall Giant, A	E	F	66	Dominie Readers	Pearson Learning Group
Talladega Superspeedway	S	I	250+	NASCAR Racing	Capstone Press
Tallahassee Higgins	T	RF	250+	Hahn, Mary Downing	Clarion Books
Taller and Smaller	D	F	29	Sun Sprouts	ETA/Cuisenaire
Taller Than Molly	C	F	43	Harry's Math Books	Outside the Box
Tallest Boy in the Class, The	J	RF	396	Leveled Readers Language Support	Houghton Mifflin Harcourt
Tallest Sunflower, The	I	I	250+	Counters & Seekers	Steck-Vaughn
Tallest Tower, The	M	F	250+	Bookweb	Rigby
Tallest Tower, The	J	HF	304	Leveled Readers	Houghton Mifflin Harcourt
Tallest Tower, The	J	HF	304	Leveled Readers/CA	Houghton Mifflin Harcourt
Tallest Tower, The	J	HF	304	Leveled Readers/TX	Houghton Mifflin Harcourt
Tallgrass Prairie, The	P	I	873	Gear Up!	Wright Group/McGraw Hill
Tally Cat Keeps Track	L	F	503	Harris, Trudy	Millbrook Press
Tally Charts	K	I	250+	Making Graphs	Capstone Press
Tam and Sam Go to the Zoo	B	RF	32	Reading Street	Pearson
Tam and Sam in the Orange Grove	D	RF	36	Reading Street	Pearson
Tam at the Beach	B	RF	29	Reading Street	Pearson
Tame and Wild	I	I	180	Sails	Rigby
Tame and Wild	L	I	306	Spyglass Books	Compass Point Books
Tamika and the Wisdom Rings	O	RF	250+	Yarbrough, Camille	Random House
Taming of Lola, The: A Shrew Story	N	F	250+	Weiss, Ellen	Harry N. Abrams
Taming the Star Runner	Z	RF	250+	Hinton, S. E.	Laurel-Leaf Books
Tammy Toodlepepper Paints the Town	I	RF	250+	Reading Safari	Mondo Publishing
Tammy Toodlepepper Solves the Case	N	F	250+	Reading Safari	Mondo Publishing
Tammy Toodlepepper to the Rescue	T	F	250+	Reading Safari	Mondo Publishing
Tammy Toodlepepper, Collector	P	RF	250+	Reading Safari	Mondo Publishing
Tammy's Goal	N	RF	921	Leveled Readers	Houghton Mifflin Harcourt
Tammy's Goal	N	RF	921	Leveled Readers/CA	Houghton Mifflin Harcourt
Tammy's Goal	N	RF	921	Leveled Readers/TX	Houghton Mifflin Harcourt
Tammy's Toys	B	RF	47	Windows on Literacy	National Geographic
Tampa Bay Buccaneers, The	S	I	250+	Team Spirit	Norwood House Press
Tampa Bay Rays, The	S	I	250+	Team Spirit	Norwood House Press
Tampa Bay Rays, The (Revised Edition)	S	I	250+	Team Spirit	Norwood House Press
Tangerine	U	RF	250+	Bloor, Edward	Scholastic
Tangle Wreck	W	F	250+	Winterson, Jeanette	Bloomsbury Children's Books
Tangled Threads: A Hmong Girl's Story	Z	RF	250+	Shea, Pegi Deitz	Clarion
Tango	T	F	250+	Beha, Eileen	Bloomsbury Children's Books
Tania's Tooth	I	RF	131	Sunshine	Wright Group/McGraw Hill
Tanks	H	I	102	Mighty Machines	Capstone Press
Tanks	V	I	4716	Military Hardware in Action	Lerner Publishing Group
Tanks	N	I	386	Pull Ahead Books	Lerner Publishing Group
Tanya On Track	U	RF	1978	Leveled Readers	Houghton Mifflin Harcourt
Tanzania	P	I	1459	Country Explorers	Lerner Publishing Group
Tap Dancing	S	I	250+	Dance	Capstone Press
Tap into Sap	O	I	250+	InfoQuest	Rigby
Tap! Rap! Bam!	D	RF	63	Reading Street	Pearson Learning Group
Tape Measure	C	I	33	Simple Tools	Lerner Publishing Group
Tapenum's Day: A Wampanoag Indian Boy in Pilgrim Times	Q	I	250+	Waters, Kate	Scholastic
Tapping Tale, The	E	RF	93	Green Light Readers	Harcourt

TITLE	LEVEL	GENRE	WORD COUNT	AUTHOR / SERIES	PUBLISHER / DISTRIBUTOR
Tar Beach	P	HF	250+	Ringgold, Faith	Crown Publishers
Tara Pays Up!	L	RF	250+	Social Studies Connects	Kane Press
Tarantula	M	I	250+	A Day in the Life: Rain Forest Animals	Heinemann Library
Tarantula	K	I	144	Alphakids	Sundance
Tarantula in My Purse, The	S	B	250+	George, Jean Craighead	HarperCollins
Tarantula Power!	N	RF	250+	Nagda, Ann Whitehead	Holiday House
Tarantula Vs. Bird	L	I	250+	Predator Vs. Prey	Raintree
Tarantulas	O	I	1708	Early Bird Nature Books	Lerner Publishing Group
Tarantulas	K	I	97	Pebble Books	Red Brick Learning
Tarantulas	F	I	83	Readlings/ Bugs	American Reading Company
Tarantulas	N	I	250+	Spiders	Capstone Press
Tarantulas are Spiders	F	I	39	Bookshop	Mondo Publishing
Tarantulas!	K	I	250+	On Our Way to English	Rigby
Tardy Tim: Dependability	K	RF	1445	Salerno, Tony Character Classics	Character Building Company
Tarp Monster, The	E	RF	71	Kaleidoscope Collection	Hameray Publishing Group
Tasmanian Devils	P	I	2075	Animal Scavengers	Lerner Publishing Group
Tasmanian Devils	R	I	250+	Orbit Chapter Books	Pacific Learning
Tasmanian Devils	M	I	250+	PM Animal Facts: Gold	Rigby
^Tasmanian Tiger	N	I	250+	Extinct Monsters	Capstone Press
Taste Bud Travels	O	I	250+	Bookweb	Rigby
Taste of America	T	I	250+	iOpeners	Pearson Learning Group
Taste of Blackberries, A	S	RF	250+	Smith, Doris Buchanan	Scholastic
Taste of Salt: The Story of Modern Haiti	W	I	250+	Temple, Frances	HarperTrophy
Taste of the Domincan Republic, A	S	I	675	Vocabulary Readers	Houghton Mifflin Harcourt
Taste of the Dominican Republic, A	S	I	675	Vocabulary Readers/CA	Houghton Mifflin Harcourt
Taste Sensation	E	I	115	Visions	Wright Group/McGraw Hill
Taste Test, The	G	I	215	PM Science Readers	Rigby
Tasting	I	I	141	Pebble Books	Red Brick Learning
Tasting	E	I	79	Senses	Lerner Publishing Group
Tasting	M	I	250+	The Senses	Capstone Press
Tasty Bug, A	D	I	50	Little Celebrations	Pearson Learning Group
Tattercoat and the Magical Flute, A Cinderella Tale from England	M	TL	692	Leveled Readers Language Support	Houghton Mifflin Harcourt
Tattercoat, A Cinderella Tale from England	N	TL	250+	Leveled Readers	Houghton Mifflin Harcourt
Taxi, The	C	F	45	Joy Readers	Pearson Learning Group
Taylor's Job	E	RF	100	Larkin's Little Readers	Wilbooks
T-Ball	D	RF	35	Visions	Wright Group/McGraw Hill
Tchin the Storyteller	N	B	269	Vocabulary Readers	Houghton Mifflin Harcourt
Tea	K	I	267	Wonder World	Wright Group/McGraw Hill
Tea Leaves	O	RF	250+	Bookshop	Mondo Publishing
Tea Overboard! The Boston Tea Party	V	I	1753	Leveled Readers	Houghton Mifflin Harcourt
Tea Party	C	RF	38	Carousel Readers	Pearson Learning Group
Tea Party, The	C	F	76	Storyteller-First Snow	Wright Group/McGraw Hill
Tea Time	I	RF	78	Board Buddies	Marshall Cavendish
Teach Us, Amelia Bedelia	L	F	250+	Parish, Peggy	Scholastic
Teacher	C	I	22	Work People Do	Lerner Publishing Group
Teacher from the Black Lagoon, The	K	F	250+	Thaler, Mike	Scholastic
Teacher Named Confucius, A	W	B	2106	Leveled Readers	Houghton Mifflin Harcourt
Teacher Named Confucius, A	W	B	2106	Leveled Readers/CA	Houghton Mifflin Harcourt
Teacher Named Confucius, A	W	B	2106	Leveled Readers/TX	Houghton Mifflin Harcourt
Teacher Talk	H	RF	68	City Stories	Rigby
Teacher Ted and His Classroom	LB	I	16	Run to Reading	Discovery Peak

T

* Collection of short stories   # Graphic text
^ Mature content with lower level text demands

TITLE	LEVEL	GENRE	WORD COUNT	AUTHOR / SERIES	PUBLISHER / DISTRIBUTOR
Teacher, The	G	I	155	PM Nonfiction-Blue	Rigby
Teachers	C	I	57	Bonnell, Kris/About	Reading Reading Books
Teachers	M	I	250+	Community Helpers	Red Brick Learning
Teachers	L	I	250+	Community Workers	Compass Point Books
Teachers	J	I	547	Pull Ahead Books	Lerner Publishing Group
Teachers at Our School	I	RF	115	City Kids	Rigby
Teacher's Funeral, The	V	HF	250+	Peck, Richard	Puffin Books
Teacher's Pet	L	RF	250+	Dicks, Terrance	Scholastic
Teacher's Pet	O	RF	250+	Hurwitz, Johanna	Scholastic
Teacher's Pet	G	RF	156	The King School Series	Townsend Press
Teacher's Pets	K	RF	250+	Dodds, Dayle Ann	Candlewick Press
*Teacher's Secret and Other Folk Tales, The	S	TL	4100	Dominoes one	Oxford University Press
Teachers!: Sharing, Helping, Caring	J	RF	193	Hubbell, Patricia	Marshall Cavendish
Teachers: Then and Now	O	I	250+	Primary Source Readers	Teacher Created Materials
Team Like No Other, A	Z	RF	250+	Graham, Georgia	Red Deer Press
Team of Two, A	P	I	566	Vocabulary Readers	Houghton Mifflin Harcourt
Team Player, The	S	RF	1115	Leveled Readers	Houghton Mifflin Harcourt
Team Players	Q	I	555	Vocabulary Readers	Houghton Mifflin Harcourt
Team Sports	B	I	23	Twig	Wright Group/McGraw Hill
Team Supper, The	X	RF	3216	Leveled Readers	Houghton Mifflin Harcourt
Team Supper, The	X	RF	3216	Leveled Readers/CA	Houghton Mifflin Harcourt
Team Supper, The	X	RF	3216	Leveled Readers/TX	Houghton Mifflin Harcourt
Team Work	C	F	112	Leveled Readers	Houghton Mifflin Harcourt
Team Work	C	F	112	Leveled Readers/CA	Houghton Mifflin Harcourt
Teaming Up	R	I	250+	Power Up!	Steck-Vaughn
Teammates	S	B	250+	Golenbock, Peter	Harcourt Brace
Teamwork	L	RF	929	PM Plus Story Books	Rigby
Teamwork	F	I	148	Yellow Umbrella Books	Capstone Press
Teamwork Saves the Day	K	RF	250+	On Our Way to English	Rigby
Tear Collector, The	Z+	F	250+	Jones, Patrick	Walker & Company
Tearing Down the Kingdom	P	I	250+	Rigby Literacy	Rigby
Tears of a Tiger	Z	RF	250+	Draper, Sharon M.	Simon & Schuster
Teasing Dad	F	RF	158	PM Extensions-Blue	Rigby
Teasing Mom	H	RF	239	PM Plus Story Books	Rigby
Tec and the Hole	B	RF	28	Big Cat	Pacific Learning
Technology	Z	I	250+	Navigators	Kingfisher
Technology and the Civil War	V	I	250+	Navigators Social Studies Series	Benchmark Education
Technology Today	J	I	166	Early Connections	Benchmark Education
Technology: Past and Present	K	I	250+	Literacy by Design	Rigby
Technosports	P	I	250+	Bookweb	Rigby
Tecumseh	V	B	250+	Cornerstones of Freedom	Children's Press
Tecumseh	S	B	3702	History Maker Bios	Lerner Publishing Group
Tecumseh: Shawnee Leader	V	B	250+	Let Freedom Ring	Capstone Press
Ted Kennedy: A Remarkable Life in the Senate	T	B	5488	Gateway Biographies	Lerner Publishing Group
Tedd & Huggly	C	F	47	Canizares, Susan; Berger, Samantha	Scholastic
Teddy Bear for Sale	G	F	152	Herman, Gail	Scholastic
Teddy Bear, Teddy Bear	E	F	38	Tiger Cub	Peguis
Teddy Bear, The	B	I	56	Rigby Flying Colors	Rigby
Teddy Bears	I	I	180	Purkis, Sallie	Nelson/Michaels Assoc.
Teddy Bears at School!	I	RF	304	InfoTrek	ETA/Cuisenaire
Teddy Bears Cure a Cold	K	F	240	Gretz, Susanna	Scholastic
Teddy Bear's Picnic	D	F	66	PM Plus Story Books	Rigby
Teddy Roosevelt: The People's President	O	B	250+	Stories of Famous Americans	Aladdin

T

TITLE	LEVEL	GENRE	WORD COUNT	AUTHOR / SERIES	PUBLISHER / DISTRIBUTOR
Teddy's Sticky Mess	K	F	639	Sun Sprouts	ETA/Cuisenaire
Ted's Letter	E	RF	76	Dominie Phonics Reader	Pearson Learning Group
Ted's Red Ball	G	F	131	Supersonics	Rigby
Ted's Red Sled	D	RF	69	Ready Readers	Pearson Learning Group
Tee Off	U	I	250+	WorldScapes	ETA/Cuisenaire
Tee-Ball	C	RF	53	Little Celebrations	Pearson Learning Group
#Teen Agent	S	SF	250+	Recon Academy	Stone Arch Books
Teen Cuisine	T	I	250+	Locricchio, Matthew	Marshall Cavendish
Teen Guide to Breakfast on the Go, A	T	I	250+	Teen Cookbooks	Compass Point Books
Teen Guide to Creative, Delightful Dinners, A	T	I	250+	Teen Cookbooks	Compass Point Books
Teen Guide to Fast, Delicious Lunches, A	T	I	250+	Teen Cookbooks	Compass Point Books
Teen Guide to Quick, Healthy Snacks, A	T	I	250+	Teen Cookbooks	Compass Point Books
Teen's Guide to Working, A	X	I	250+	Power Up!	Steck-Vaughn
Teens in Argentina	U	I	250+	Global Connections	Compass Point Books
Teens in Greece	U	I	250+	Global Connections	Compass Point Books
Teens in Pakistan	Y	I	250+	Global Connections	Compass Point Books
Teens in South Africa	Z+	I	250+	Global Connections	Compass Point Books
Teens in Thailand	W	I	250+	Global Connections	Compass Point Books
Teeny Tiny	I	TL	250+	Bennett, Jill	G.P. Putnam's Sons Books for Young Readers
Teeny Tiny	H	TL	250+	Rigby Literacy	Rigby
Teeny Tiny Taste, A	H	RF	112	City Stories	Rigby
Teeny Tiny Tina	C	F	34	Literacy 2000	Rigby
Teeny Tiny Woman, The	F	TL	250+	O'Connor, Jane	Random House
Teeny Tiny Woman, The	J	TL	369	Seuling, Barbara	Scholastic
Teeny tiny Woman, The	I	TL	329	Traditional Tales	Pioneer Valley
Teeny Weeny Bop	L	F	250+	MacDonald, Margaret Read	Albert Whitman & Co.
Teeny-Tiny Woman, The	H	TL	231	Ziefert, Harriet	Puffin Books
Teeter-Totter, The	C	TL	35	Joy Readers	Pearson Learning Group
Teeth	I	I	160	Animal Spikes and Spines	Heinemann Library
Teeth	N	I	250+	Literacy By Design	Rigby
Teeth	F	I	150	Red Rocket Readers	Flying Start Books
Teeth	N	I	250+	Rigby Literacy	Rigby
Teeth	D	I	71	Story Box	Wright Group/McGraw Hill
Teeth	K	I	470	Sunshine	Wright Group/McGraw Hill
Teeth	J	I	188	Take Two Books	Wright Group/McGraw Hill
Teeth	C	I	26	Wonder World	Wright Group/McGraw Hill
Telephone	S	I	250+	Theme Sets	National Geographic
Telephone, The	P	I	250+	Great Inventions	Red Brick Learning
Telephone, The	J	I	167	Reading Street	Pearson
Telephone, The	T	I	250+	Tales of Invention	Heinemann Library
Telephone, The: A Great Invention	J	I	165	Leveled Readers Social Studies	Houghton Mifflin Harcourt
Telephones	O	I	250+	Let's See	Compass Point Books
Telephones	J	I	196	Leveled Readers Language Support	Houghton Mifflin Harcourt
Telephones Through Time	N	I	654	Reading Street	Pearson
^Telescope, The; Looking into Space	R	I	250+	On Deck	Rigby
Television	O	I	250+	Let's See	Compass Point Books
Television	S	I	250+	Theme Sets	National Geographic
Television Drama	Q	RF	250+	Literacy 2000	Rigby
Television, The	Q	I	250+	Great Inventions	Capstone Press
^Television, The: Window to the World	R	I	250+	On Deck	Rigby
^Tell	Y	RF	250+	Orca Soundings	Orca Books
Tell All About It	A	F	27	Leveled Readers	Houghton Mifflin Harcourt

* Collection of short stories   # Graphic text
^ Mature content with lower level text demands

T

TITLE	LEVEL	GENRE	WORD COUNT	AUTHOR / SERIES	PUBLISHER / DISTRIBUTOR
Tell All About It	A	F	27	Leveled Readers/CA	Houghton Mifflin Harcourt
Tell It in Code	I	I	166	Vocabulary Readers	Houghton Mifflin Harcourt
Tell It in Code	L	I	166	Vocabulary Readers/CA	Houghton Mifflin Harcourt
Tell It to a Friend	K	I	250+	Home Connection Collection	Rigby
Tell Me a Scary Story-But Not Too Scary!	N	RF	250+	Reiner, Carl	Little Brown and Company
Tell Me a Story	R	I	250+	InfoQuest	Rigby
Tell Me a Story	O	B	250+	Meet The Author	Richard C. Owen
Tell Me a Story	J	RF	236	Voyages	SRA/McGraw Hill
Tell Me a Story, Grandpa	L	RF	250+	Little Celebrations	Pearson Learning Group
Tell Me a Story, Mama	L	RF	250+	Johnson, Angela	Scholastic
Tell Me About Turtles	D	I	31	Rosen Real Readers	Rosen Publishing Group
Tell Me How!	M	I	250+	Trackers	Pacific Learning
Tell Me No Lies	Q	RF	250+	Ragged Island Mysteries	Wright Group/McGraw Hill
Tell Me Why Planes Have Wings	O	I	250+	Whiz Kids	Franklin Watts
Tell Me, Tree: All About Trees for Kids	O	I	250+	Gibbons, Gail	Little Brown and Company
Tell Them We Remember	Y	I	250+	Bachrach, Susan D.	Little Brown and Company
Tell Us a Tale, Hans!: The Life of Hans Christian Andersen	R	B	250+	Bookshop	Mondo Publishing
Telling Stories Through Art	N	I	250+	Take Two Books	Wright Group/McGraw Hill
Telling the Truth	H	RF	229	PM Stars	Rigby
Telling Time	E	I	88	Early Connectinos	Benchmark Education
Telling Time Through the Ages	Q	I	250+	Navigators Social Studies Series	Benchmark Education
Tell-Tale	H	RF	250+	Story Box	Wright Group/McGraw Hill
Temperate Climate	R	I	250+	Theme Sets	National Geographic
Temperate Forest Food Chain, A	U	I	7680	Follow That Food Chain	Lerner Publishing Group
Temperate Forests	W	I	250+	Biomes Atlases	Raintree
Temperate Forests	Q	I	250+	Ecosystems	Red Brick Learning
Temperate Forests	S	I	250+	Theme Sets	National Geographic
Temperate Grasslands	W	I	250+	Biomes Atlases	Raintree
^Temperature	P	I	250+	Our Physical World	Capstone Press
Temperature: Heating Up and Cooling Down	M	I	250+	Amazing Science	Picture Window Books
#Tempest, The	W	F	2565	Dominoes starter	Oxford University Press
#Tempest, The	Z	F	250+	Manga Shakespeare	Amulet Books
Temple of the Ruby Fire, The	O	F	250+	Stilton, Geronimo	Scholastic
Tempted: (House of Night)	Z+	F	250+	Cast, P. C. & Kristin	St. Martin's Griffin
Ten	LB	I	17	Count on It!	Marshall Cavendish
Ten Apples Up on Top	J	F	250+	LeSieg, Theo	Random House
Ten Bears in My Bed	G	F	252	Mack, Stan	Pantheon
Ten Black Dots	I	I	176	Crews, Donald	Greenwillow Books
Ten Blue Things	F	I	193	InfoTrek	ETA/Cuisenaire
Ten Bright Eyes	M	TL	256	Hindley, Judy	Peachtree
Ten Cats Have Hats: A Counting Book	E	F	89	Marzollo, Jean	Scholastic
Ten Crazy Caterpillars	C	F	40	Voyages	SRA/McGraw Hill
Ten Days and Nine Nights	J	RF	148	Heo, Yumi	Schwartz & Wade Books
Ten Easy Tips for Staying Safe	L	I	250+	Rosen Real Readers	Rosen Publishing Group
Ten for Me	K	RF	825	Mariconda, Barbara	Sylvan Dell Publishing
Ten Frogs for the Pond	F	I	193	PM Math Readers	Rigby
Ten Happy Elephants	I	F	201	Sunshine	Wright Group/McGraw Hill
Ten in the Bed	J	F	312	Cabrera, Jane	Holiday House
Ten in the Den	H	F	229	Butler, John	Peachtree
Ten in the Meadow	J	F	132	Butler, John	Peachtree
Ten Little Bears	G	F	211	Reading Unlimited	Pearson Learning Group
Ten Little Caterpillars	F	F	102	Literacy 2000	Rigby
Ten Little Chickens	F	RF	170	InfoTrek	ETA/Cuisenaire

TITLE	LEVEL	GENRE	WORD COUNT	AUTHOR / SERIES	PUBLISHER / DISTRIBUTOR
Ten Little Chickens	F	F	155	Joy Starters	Pearson Learning Group
Ten Little Garden Snails	H	F	101	PM Story Books	Rigby
Ten Little Ladybugs in My Jar	G	F	172	Rigby-Wilcox, Carey	C Unique Creations Inc.
Ten Little Men	E	F	38	Literacy 2000	Rigby
Ten Loopy Caterpillars	I	F	191	Jellybeans	Rigby
Ten Minutes Till Bedtime	LB	RF	16	Rathmann, Peggy	G.P. Putnam's Sons Books for Young Readers
Ten O'Clock Club, The	N	F	250+	York, Carol Beach	Scholastic
Ten Oni Drummers	M	F	157	Bebop Books	Lee & Low Books Inc.
Ten Red Sleds	D	RF	82	Reading Street	Pearson
Ten Sleepy Sheep	G	F	65	Keller, Holly	Greenwillow Books
Ten Terrific Authors for Teens	X	B	250+	Collective Biographies	Enslow Publishers, Inc.
Ten Thumb Sam	P	RF	250+	Orca Young Readers	Orca Books
Ten Traveling Tigers	H	F	165	Little Readers	Houghton Mifflin Harcourt
*Ten True Animal Rescues	O	I	250+	Betancourt, Jeanne	Scholastic
Ten Yellow Buses	H	RF	146	Twig	Wright Group/McGraw Hill
Ten, Nine, Eight	H	RF	59	Bang, Molly	Scholastic
Ten-Book Summer	T	RF	250+	Power Up!	Steck-Vaughn
Tenement Writer, The: An Immigrant's Story	T	B	250+	Sonder, Ben	Steck-Vaughn
Ten-Gallon Bart Beats the Heat	L	F	250+	Crummel, Susan Stevens	Marshall Cavendish
Ten-Gallon Hat, The	K	F	250+	Voyages	SRA/McGraw Hill
Tennessee	T	I	250+	Hello U.S.A.	Lerner Publishing Group
Tennessee	R	I	250+	This Land Is Your Land	Compass Point Books
Tennessee Is the Volunteer State	O	I	222	Larkin, Bruce	Wilbooks
Tennessee Summer	R	RF	2198	Leveled Readers	Houghton Mifflin Harcourt
Tennessee Titans, The	S	I	250+	Team Spirit	Norwood House Press
Tennessee Tornado, The: Wilma Rudolph	T	B	2097	Leveled Readers	Houghton Mifflin Harcourt
Tennessee: Facts and Symbols	O	I	250+	The States and Their Symbols	Capstone Press
Tennis	K	I	250+	On Deck	Rigby
Tennis Ace	N	RF	250+	Boyz Rule!	Mondo Publishing
Tennis Ace	M	F	250+	Too Cool	Pacific Learning
Tennis Lessons	M	RF	250+	Rigby Flying Colors	Rigby
Tennis Match, The	D	F	85	Springboard	Wright Group/McGraw Hill
Tennyson	W	HF	250+	Blume, Lesley M. M.	Yearling Books
Ten-Second Race, The	F	F	102	Learn to Read	Creative Teaching Press
Tension of Opposites, The	Z+	RF	250+	McBride, Kristina	Egmont USA
Tent, The	K	RF	283	Dominie Math Stories	Pearson Learning Group
Tent, The	Z	RF	250+	Paulsen, Gary	Bantam Books
Tentacles	Y	SF	250+	Smith, Roland	Scholastic
Tents	I	RF	175	Reading Unlimited	Pearson Learning Group
Tents	I	I	319	Sails	Rigby
Teotihuacan: Designing an Ancient Mexican City	T	I	250+	Math for the Real World	Rosen Publishing Group
Tepee	L	I	157	Bookworms	Marshall Cavendish
Termite Bites	B	F	35	Brand New Readers	Candlewick Press
Termite Bounces	D	F	21	Brand New Readers	Candlewick Press
Termite Eats	B	F	36	Brand New Readers	Candlewick Press
Termite Flies	D	F	26	Brand New Readers	Candlewick Press
Termite Helps	C	F	36	Brand New Readers	Candlewick Press
Termite in the Canoe	D	F	33	Brand New Readers	Candlewick Press
Termite Measures	D	F	36	Brand New Readers	Candlewick Press
Termite Taps	E	F	42	Brand New Readers	Candlewick Press
Termites	I	RF	130	Books for Young Learners	Richard C. Owen
Termites	I	I	72	Pebble Books	Red Brick Learning

T

* Collection of short stories   # Graphic text
^ Mature content with lower level text demands

TITLE	LEVEL	GENRE	WORD COUNT	AUTHOR / SERIES	PUBLISHER / DISTRIBUTOR
Termites	I	I	226	Sails	Rigby
Termites: Hardworking Insect Families	T	I	2520	Insect World	Lerner Publishing Group
Terra-Cotta Army	P	I	920	Vocabulary Readers	Houghton Mifflin Harcourt
Terra-Cotta Army	P	I	920	Vocabulary Readers/CA	Houghton Mifflin Harcourt
Terracotta Girl, The: A Story of Ancient China	O	HF	250+	Historical Tales	Picture Window Books
Terrible Armadillo	I	F	229	Jellybeans	Rigby
Terrible Fright, A	K	TL	291	Story Box	Wright Group/McGraw Hill
Terrible Plop, The	K	F	250+	Dubosarsky, Ursula	Farrar, Straus, & Giroux
Terrible Power of House Rabbit, The	O	F	250+	High-Fliers	Pacific Learning
*Terrible Test Mark and Other Cases, The	O	RF	250+	Simon, Seymour	Avon Books
Terrible Tiger	G	F	124	Rigby Literacy	Rigby
Terrible Tiger	G	F	133	Rigby Star	Rigby
*Terrible Tiger and Sleeping Beauty	L	TL	250+	New Way Literature	Steck-Vaughn
Terrible Tiger, The	G	F	140	Sunshine	Wright Group/McGraw Hill
Terrible Times	U	F	250+	Ardagh, Philip	Scholastic
Terrible Twos	E	RF	86	Tadpoles	Rigby
Terrible, Unbearable Giant, The	K	F	250+	Sun Sprouts	ETA/Cuisenaire
Terrific Shoes	C	RF	19	Ready Readers	Pearson Learning Group
Terrific Teeth	J	I	250+	InfoTrek	ETA/Cuisenaire
Terrific Trees	K	I	250+	Rigby Literacy	Rigby
Terrifying Tornadoes	T	I	250+	Awesome Forces of Nature	Heinemann Library
Terrifying, Bone-Chilling Rituals and Sacrifices	W	I	250+	Horrible Things	Capstone Press
Terror at Turtle Mountain	W	HF	250+	Draper, Penny	Fitzhenry & Whiteside
^Terror Bird	N	I	250+	Extinct Monsters	Capstone Press
#Terror in Ghost Mansion	U	F	11820	Twisted Journeys	Graphic Universe
Terror in the Towers	O	I	250+	Kerson, Adrian	Random House
Terror in Tights (Melvin Beederman, Superhero)	N	F	250+	Trine, Greg	Henry Holt & Co.
Terror of the Pink Dodo Balloons, The	O	F	250+	David, Lawrence	Puffin Books
^Terror World	S	F	1350	Norman, Tony	Stone Arch Books
Tess and Paddy	J	RF	242	Sunshine	Wright Group/McGraw Hill
Tess and the Cat	D	RF	81	Sun Sprouts	ETA/Cuisenaire
Tess Went to Work	D	RF	52	Windows on Literacy	National Geographic
Tessa Tiger's Temper Tantrums	K	F	742	Animal Antics A to Z	Kane Press
Test of Time, The	R	I	250+	InfoQuest	Rigby
Texas	T	I	250+	Hello U.S.A.	Lerner Publishing Group
Texas	S	I	250+	Land of Liberty	Red Brick Learning
Texas	Q	I	250+	One Nation	Capstone Press
Texas	R	I	250+	This Land Is Your Land	Compass Point Books
Texas Is the Lone Star State	O	I	221	Larkin, Bruce	Wilbooks
Texas Rangers, The	S	I	250+	Team Spirit	Norwood House Press
Texas Rangers, The (Revised Edition)	S	I	250+	Team Spirit	Norwood House Press
Texas Rangers: Legendary Lawmen	T	I	250+	Spradlin, Michael P.	Walker & Company
Texas State Symbols	M	I	98	Larkin, Bruce	Wilbooks
Texas: Facts and Symbols	O	I	250+	The States and Their Symbols	Capstone Press
Textiles	M	I	250+	Start with Art	Heinemann Library
Textiles from Around the World	Q	I	851	Leveled Readers	Houghton Mifflin Harcourt
Textiles from Around the World	Q	I	851	Leveled Readers/CA	Houghton Mifflin Harcourt
Textiles from Around the World	Q	I	851	Leveled Readers/TX	Houghton Mifflin Harcourt
Thailand	O	I	250+	Countries of the World	Red Brick Learning
Thailand	P	I	2041	Country Explorers	Lerner Publishing Group
Thank You	J	I	250+	Ready to Read	Pacific Learning
Thank You!	D	I	41	Chessen, Betsey; Chanko, Pamela	Scholastic
Thank You, Amelia Bedelia	L	F	250+	Little Readers	Houghton Mifflin Harcourt

TITLE	LEVEL	GENRE	WORD COUNT	AUTHOR / SERIES	PUBLISHER / DISTRIBUTOR
Thank You, Jackie Robinson	P	B	250+	Cohen, Barbara	Scholastic
Thank You, Nicky!	F	F	119	Ziefert, Harriet	Penguin Group
Thank You, Sandra Cisneros	N	RF	250+	Leveled Readers	Houghton Mifflin Harcourt
Thankful for My Family	V	HF	2609	Leveled Readers	Houghton Mifflin Harcourt
Thankful for My Family	V	HF	2609	Leveled Readers/CA	Houghton Mifflin Harcourt
Thankful for My Family	V	HF	2609	Leveled Readers/TX	Houghton Mifflin Harcourt
Thanks to Sandra Cisneros	O	RF	940	Leveled Readers Language Support	Houghton Mifflin Harcourt
Thanks to the Triangle!	I	I	91	Windows on Literacy	National Geographic
Thanksgiving	J	I	114	American Holidays	Lerner Publishing Group
Thanksgiving	Q	I	250+	Celebrate!	Capstone Press
Thanksgiving	E	I	95	Fiesta Holiday Series	Pearson Learning Group
Thanksgiving	B	F	40	First Stories	Pacific Learning
Thanksgiving	J	I	181	Holidays and Celebrations	Capstone Press
Thanksgiving	K	I	250+	Holidays and Celebrations	Picture Window Books
Thanksgiving	O	I	250+	Holidays and Festivals	Compass Point Books
Thanksgiving	L	I	205	Holidays and Festivals	Heinemann Library
Thanksgiving	P	I	250+	Let's See	Compass Point Books
Thanksgiving	F	F	75	Urmston, Kathleen; Evans, Karen	Kaeden Books
Thanksgiving Crafts	N	I	250+	Thanksgiving	Picture Window Books
Thanksgiving Day	M	I	250+	Holiday Histories	Heinemann
Thanksgiving Day	H	I	218	Literacy by Design	Rigby
Thanksgiving Day	L	I	132	National Holidays	Red Brick Learning
Thanksgiving Day	LB	I	12	Shutterbug Books	Steck-Vaughn
Thanksgiving Dinner	F	RF	148	Joy Starters	Pearson Learning Group
Thanksgiving Dinner	D	RF	61	Kaleidoscope Collection	Hameray Publishing Group
Thanksgiving Dinner	E	RF	84	McAlpin, MaryAnn	Short Tales Press
Thanksgiving Recipes	N	I	250+	Thanksgiving	Picture Window Books
Thanksgiving Rules	L	RF	250+	Friedman, Laurie	Carolrhoda Books
Thanksgiving Then and Now	C	I	43	Early Connections	Benchmark Education
Thanksgiving Then and Now	M	I	250+	Thanksgiving	Picture Window Books
Thanksgiving: A Day of Thanks	M	I	250+	Holidays and Culture	Capstone Press
Thanksgiving: Why We Celebrate It the Way We Do	P	I	250+	Hintz, Martin & Kate	Red Brick Learning
Thao Kham, the Pebble Shooter	M	TL	250+	Story Vines	Wright Group/McGraw Hill
That Bear is Back!	K	F	493	Rigby Gigglers	Rigby
That Cat	D	RF	52	Bonnell, Kris	Reading Reading Books
That Cat	B	RF	56	First Stories	Pacific Learning
That Cat!	G	RF	146	Ready Readers	Pearson Learning Group
That Cat!	I	RF	418	Real Kids Readers	Millbrook Press
That Dog!	G	RF	213	Foundations	Wright Group/McGraw Hill
That Fat Hat	K	F	250+	Barkan, Joanne	Scholastic
That Fly	C	F	26	Ready Readers	Pearson Learning Group
That Is Math!	E	I	84	On Our Way to English	Rigby
That Is Not My Hat!	K	RF	1418	Real Kids Readers	Millbrook Press
That Is Symmetry!	G	I	190	On Our Way to English	Rigby
That Looks Different!	K	I	227	Windows on Literacy	National Geographic
That Old House	K	F	250+	Rigby Literacy	Rigby
That Pig Can't Do a Thing	F	F	83	Ready Readers	Pearson Learning Group
That Summer	T	RF	250+	Johnston, Tony	Harcourt, Inc.
That Wild Berries Should Grow	U	HF	250+	Whelan, Gloria	Eerdman's Books for Young Readers
*That's a Laugh: Four Funny Fables	M	TL	250+	Literacy 2000	Rigby

T

* Collection of short stories   # Graphic text
^ Mature content with lower level text demands

TITLE	LEVEL	GENRE	WORD COUNT	AUTHOR / SERIES	PUBLISHER / DISTRIBUTOR
That's a Wacky Idea	R	I	1500	Vocabulary Readers	Houghton Mifflin Harcourt
That's a Wacky Idea	R	I	1500	Vocabulary Readers/CA	Houghton Mifflin Harcourt
That's a Wacky Idea	R	I	1500	Vocabulary Readers/TX	Houghton Mifflin Harcourt
That's About Right: A Book About Estimating	S	I	250+	On Our Way to English	Rigby
That's Dangerous	D	F	71	Voyages	SRA/McGraw Hill
That's Determination!	L	RF	250+	Rigby Literacy	Rigby
That's Disgusting!	Y	I	250+	Boldprint	Steck-Vaughn
That's Easy	F	F	205	Handprints D, Set 1	Educators Publishing Service
That's Entertainment!	W	I	250+	Boldprint	Steck-Vaughn
That's Exercise	D	RF	59	Gear Up!	Wright Group/McGraw Hill
That's Extreme!	O	I	250+	Trackers	Pacific Learning
That's Fair, Bear	H	F	250+	Sun Sprouts	ETA/Cuisenaire
That's Good! That's Bad! on Santa's Journey	K	F	250+	Cuyler, Margery	Henry Holt & Co.
That's Hard, That's Easy	H	RF	393	Real Kids Readers	Millbrook Press
That's HOT!	L	I	250+	Spyglass Books	Compass Point Books
That's It!	S	I	250+	Orbit Collections	Pacific Learning
That's Love	J	RF	201	Williams, Sam	Holiday House
That's Mine!	LB	RF	15	Rigby Literacy	Rigby
That's Mine!	LB	RF	15	Rigby Star	Rigby
That's Not All	G	F	105	Start to Read	School Zone
That's Not How You Play Soccer, Daddy!	L	RF	828	Shahan, Sherry	Peachtree
That's Not My Hobby!	J	RF	250+	Rigby Literacy	Rigby
That's Not My Hobby!	J	RF	250+	Rigby Star	Rigby
That's Not Our Dog	I	RF	250+	PM Plus Story Books	Rigby
That's One Dollar	K	RF	460	Dominie Math Stories	Pearson Learning Group
That's Our Custodian!	M	I	992	That's Our School	Millbrook Press
That's Our Librarian!	M	I	734	That's Our School	Millbrook Press
That's Our Nurse!	M	I	866	That's Our School	Millbrook Press
That's Our Principal!	M	I	593	That's Our School	Millbrook Press
That's Our Teacher!	M	I	608	That's Our School	Millbrook Press
That's Papa's Way	K	RF	250+	Banks, Kate	Farrar, Straus, & Giroux
That's Really Weird!	K	F	129	Read Alongs	Rigby
That's Some Sun!	O	I	250+	Literacy By Design	Rigby
That's the Life!	I	RF	216	Storyteller	Wright Group/McGraw Hill
That's Us	G	I	172	Sails	Rigby
That's Working Together!	G	I	235	Shutterbug Books	Steck-Vaughn
Thea Stilton and the Mountain of Fire	P	F	250+	Stilton, Geronimo	Scholastic
Theater Actors: Then and Now	Q	I	250+	Primary Source Readers	Teacher Created Materials
Theater, The	P	I	840	Leveled Readers	Houghton Mifflin Harcourt
Theater, The	P	I	840	Leveled Readers/CA	Houghton Mifflin Harcourt
Theft in Time, A: Timedetectors II	V	SF	250+	Action Packs	Rigby
Then & Now	C	I	60	Berger, Samantha; Moreton, Daniel	Scholastic
Then Again, Maybe I Won't	T	RF	250+	Blume, Judy	Language for Learning Assoc.
Then and Now	J	I	250+	Discovery World	Rigby
Then and Now	J	RF	250+	Early Connections	Benchmark Education
Then and Now	H	I	250+	iOpeners	Pearson Learning Group
Then and Now	J	I	245	Red Rocket Readers	Flying Start Books
Then and Now	H	I	241	Rigby Rocket	Rigby
Then and Now	H	RF	219	The King School Series	Townsend Press
Then and Now	K	I	115	Windows on Literacy	National Geographic

T

* Collection of short stories   # Graphic text
^ Mature content with lower level text demands

Organized Alphabetically by Title   **753**
Storable Database at www.fountasandpinnellleveledbooks.com

TITLE	LEVEL	GENRE	WORD COUNT	AUTHOR / SERIES	PUBLISHER / DISTRIBUTOR
Then There Were Five	V	RF	250+	Enright, Elizabeth	Square Fish
Theodore	D	F	35	Ray's Readers	Outside the Box
Theodore Boone: Kid Lawyer	T	RF	250+	Grisham, John	Puffin Books
Theodore Roosevelt	R	B	250+	Amazing Americans	Wright Group/McGraw Hill
Theodore Roosevelt	S	B	3356	History Maker Bios	Lerner Publishing Group
Theodore Roosevelt	N	B	208	Pebble Books	Capstone Press
Theodore Roosevelt	Q	B	250+	Photo-Illustrated Biographies	Red Brick Learning
Theodore Roosevelt	U	B	250+	Profiles of the Presidents	Compass Point Books
#Theodore Roosevelt: Bear of a President	R	B	250+	Graphic Library	Capstone Press
Theodore Roosevelt: Friend of Nature	P	B	756	Leveled Readers	Houghton Mifflin Harcourt
Theodore Roosevelt: Twenty-sixth President	R	B	250+	Getting to Know the U.S. Presidents	Children's Press
Theodosia and the Last Pharoah	V	F	250+	LaFevers, R. L.	Houghton Mifflin Harcourt
Theodosia and the Serpents of Chaos	V	F	250+	LaFeuers, R.L.	Houghton Mifflin Harcourt
Theory of Evolution, The: A History of Life on Earth	Y	I	250+	Exploring Science	Compass Point Books
Therapy Dogs to the Rescue	L	I	250+	Rigby Literacy	Rigby
There Are Cats in This Book	K	F	209	Schwarz, Viviane	Candlewick Press
There Are Mice in Our School	I	RF	95	City Kids	Rigby
There Are No Polar Bears Down There	G	I	48	Voyages	SRA/McGraw Hill
There Are Spots On . . .	LB	I	14	Little Books for Early Readers	University of Maine
There Are Things I Don't Know	P	RF	250+	On Our Way To English	Rigby
There Goes Peanut Butter!	C	RF	22	Ketch, Ann	Kaeden Books
There Goes Ted Williams: The Greatest Hitter Who Ever Lived	R	B	250+	Tavares, Matt	Candlewick Press
There Is a Carrot in My Ear and Other Noodle Tails	J	TL	250+	Schwartz, Alvin	HarperTrophy
There Is a Planet	C	I	52	Sunshine	Wright Group/McGraw Hill
There Is a Town	D	RF	116	Herman, Gail	Random House
There Is No Water	J	RF	250+	Home Connection Collection	Rigby
There She Blows!	T	I	250+	Orbit Chapter Books	Pacific Learning
There Stood Our Dog	I	F	250+	Voyages	SRA/McGraw Hill
There Was a Crooked Man	E	F	40	Sunshine	Wright Group/McGraw Hill
There Was a Mouse	D	RF	77	Books for Young Learners	Richard C. Owen
There Was an Old Man Who Painted the Sky	M	TL	250+	Sloat, Teri	Henry Holt & Co.
There Was an Old Monkey Who Swallowed a Frog	K	TL	250+	Ward, Jennifer	Marshall Cavendish
There's a Bear in My Chair	H	F	193	Magoun, James	Kaeden Books
There's A Boy In The Girls' Bathroom	Q	RF	250+	Sachar, Louis	Alfred A. Knopf
There's a Dinosaur!	L	I	250+	Stone, Evelyn	Hampton Brown
There's a Dog in the Yard	I	I	119	City Kids	Rigby
There's a Frog in My Oatmeal!	J	F	250+	Scooters	ETA/Cuisenaire
There's a Frog in My Sleeping Bag	R	RF	250+	Clymer, Susan	Scholastic
There's a Frog in My Throat: 440 Animal Sayings a Little Bird Told Me	N	I	250+	Leedy, Loreen & Street, Pat	Holiday House
There's a Hamster in My Lunchbox	R	RF	250+	Clymer, Susan	Scholastic
There's a Hippopotamus Under My Bed	J	F	250+	Thaler, Mike	Avon Books
There's a Monster in the Tree	E	F	250+	Learn to Read	Creative Teaching Press
There's a Mouse in the House	B	F	42	Bookshop	Mondo Publishing
There's a Nightmare in My Closet	I	F	153	Mayer, Mercer	Penguin Group
There's a Rainbow in the River	L	RF	250+	Home Connection Collection	Rigby
There's a Ship Outside My Window	O	RF	250+	PM Collection	Rigby
There's a Tarantula in My Homework	R	RF	250+	Clymer, Susan	Scholastic
There's an Alligator Under My Bed	J	RF	250+	Mayer, Mercer	Penguin Group
There's an Owl in the Shower	Q	RF	250+	George, Jean Craighead	HarperCollins

* Collection of short stories   # Graphic text
^ Mature content with lower level text demands

TITLE	LEVEL	GENRE	WORD COUNT	AUTHOR / SERIES	PUBLISHER / DISTRIBUTOR
There's No One Like Me!	D	I	80	Sunshine	Wright Group/McGraw Hill
There's No Place Like Home	I	I	205	Brown, Marc	Parent's Magazine Press
There's No Place Like Home	R	I	250+	Hill, David	Pacific Learning
There's No Place Like Home!	Q	I	250+	Rigby Literacy	Rigby
There's Something in My Attic	J	RF	258	Mayer, Mercer	Penguin Group
Thermometer	C	I	32	Simple Tools	Lerner Publishing Group
These Lands Are Ours: Tecumseh's Fight For the Old Northwest	T	B	250+	Connell, Kate	Steck-Vaughn
These Legs	C	I	42	Foundations	Wright Group/McGraw Hill
These Old Rags	M	RF	352	Evangeline Nicholas Collection	Wright Group/McGraw Hill
Theseus and the Minotaur	S	I	250+	High-Fliers	Pacific Learning
^Theseus and the Minotaur	W	I	250+	World Mythology	Capstone Press
#Theseus: Battling the Minotaur	V	TL	2955	Graphic Myths and Legends	Graphic Universe
They All Ran Away	C	F	82	Lighthouse	Rigby
They Are Sick	C	RF	39	Reading Street	Pearson
They Call Me . . .	D	I	31	The Candid Collection	Pearson Learning Group
They Came from Center Field	R	RF	250+	Gutman, Dan	Scholastic
They Changed the World	R	I	250+	iOpeners	Pearson Learning Group
They Changed the World	Q	I	250+	Orbit Chapter Books	Pacific Learning
They Help Animals	C	RF	33	Reading Street	Pearson
They Led the Way	N	B	551	Yellow Umbrella Books	Red Brick Learning
They Led the Way: 14 American Women	O	B	250+	Johnston, Johanna	Scholastic
They Shall Be Heard: Susan B. Anthony & Elizabeth Cady Stanton	T	B	250+	Connell, Kate	Steck-Vaughn
They Survived Mount St. Helens!	O	I	250+	Stine, Megan	Random House
They Worked Together	O	I	250+	iOpeners	Pearson Learning Group
Thief in the House of Memory, A	X	RF	250+	Wynne-Jones, Tim	Farrar, Straus, & Giroux
*Thief in the Village, A	V	RF	250+	Berry, James	Puffin Books
Thief Lord, The	V	F	250+	Funke, Cornelia	Scholastic
Thief of Hearts	K	F	250+	Martha Speaks	Houghton Mifflin Harcourt
Thief of Hearts	V	RF	250+	Yep, Laurence	HarperCollins
Thief Queen's Daughter, The	X	F	250+	Haydon, Elizabeth	Tom Doherty
Thimble Summer	U	RF	250+	Enright, Elizabeth	Square Fish
*Thimbleberry Stories	N	F	250+	Rylant, Cynthia	Harcourt
Thin Executioner, The	Y	F	250+	Shan, Darren	Little Brown and Company
Thin Wood Walls	V	HF	250+	Patneaude, David	Houghton Mifflin Harcourt
Thing about Georgie, The	T	RF	250+	Graff, Lisa	HarperTrophy
Thing in the Log, The	H	RF	81	Reading Unlimited	Pearson Learning Group
Thing on the Wing Can Swing, The	J	F	172	Sounds Like Reading	Lerner Publishing Group
Things Are Looking Grimm, Jill	N	F	250+	Orca Young Readers	Orca Books
Things Birds Eat, The	C	I	38	Chessen, Betsey	Scholastic
Things Can Change	B	I	27	Leveled Readers Science	Houghton Mifflin Harcourt
Things Change	M	I	569	Bourne, Phyllis Montenegro	Hampton Brown
Things Don't Change Much	L	RF	250+	Home Connection Collection	Rigby
Things Fall Apart	Z+	HF	250+	Edge	Hampton Brown
Things Hoped For	V	F	250+	Clements, Andrew	Puffin Books
Things I Can Do	B	F	47	Leveled Readers	Houghton Mifflin Harcourt
Things I Can Do	B	F	47	Leveled Readers/CA	Houghton Mifflin Harcourt
Things I Can Do	B	I	36	Little Readers	Houghton Mifflin Harcourt
Things I Can Do	B	I	30	Little Red Readers	Sundance
Things I Do for Fun	B	I	36	Little Red Readers	Sundance
Things I Do with My Friends	B	I	35	Little Red Readers	Sundance
Things I Like	D	F	42	Browne, Anthony	Random House
Things I Like	C	RF	42	Carousel Earlybirds	Pearson Learning Group

TITLE	LEVEL	GENRE	WORD COUNT	AUTHOR / SERIES	PUBLISHER / DISTRIBUTOR
Things I Like	C	I	39	Little Readers	Houghton Mifflin Harcourt
Things I Like	B	RF	25	Storyteller	Wright Group/McGraw Hill
Things I Like Doing	A	I	24	Early Connections	Benchmark Education
Things I Like to Do	C	RF	63	Carousel Earlybirds	Pearson Learning Group
Things I Like to Do	C	RF	58	Foundations	Wright Group/McGraw Hill
Things I Like to Do	B	F	56	Leveled Readers	Houghton Mifflin Harcourt
Things I Like to Do	B	F	56	Leveled Readers/CA	Houghton Mifflin Harcourt
Things I Need	A	I	21	On Our Way to English	Rigby
Things I See	A	I	28	Leveled Readers Emergent	Houghton Mifflin Harcourt
Things Not Seen	V	F	250+	Clements, Andrew	Scholastic
Things on Wheels	C	I	69	Little Red Readers	Sundance
Things People Do for Fun	H	I	124	Foundations	Wright Group/McGraw Hill
Things People Do, The	W	I	250+	Story Surfers	ETA/Cuisenaire
Things That Are	V	F	250+	Clements, Andrew	Philomel
Things That Are Most in the World	H	F	179	Barrett, Judi	Scholastic
Things That Drag Behind	D	I	42	Teacher's Choice Series	Pearson Learning Group
Things That Fly	B	I	72	Leveled Literacy Intervention/ Blue System	Heinemann
Things That Go Fast	A	I	39	Leveled Literacy Intervention/ Orange System	Heinemann
Things That Go: A Traveling Alphabet	L	I	250+	Reit, Seymour	Bantam Books
Things That Help Me	C	I	18	Pacific Literacy	Pacific Learning
Things That Melt	G	I	84	Leveled Readers Science	Houghton Mifflin Harcourt
Things That People Make	N	I	250+	Explorations	Okapi Educational Materials
Things That People Make	N	I	250+	Explorations	Eleanor Curtain Publishing
Things That Protect You	D	RF	51	Foundations	Wright Group/McGraw Hill
Things That Sting	G	I	84	Gear Up!	Wright Group/McGraw Hill
Things to Do	G	I	170	Time for Kids	Teacher Created Materials
Things to Make	H	I	198	Time for Kids	Teacher Created Materials
Things to Read	LB	I	18	Little Books for Early Readers	University of Maine
Things to See in Maine	LB	I	14	Little Books for Early Readers	University of Maine
Things Will Never Be the Same	P	B	250+	DePaola, Tomie	Puffin Books
Things with Wings	F	I	116	Red Rocket Readers	Flying Start Books
Things With Wings	J	I	267	Storyteller Nonfiction	Wright Group/McGraw Hill
Things You Either Hate or Love	Z+	RF	250+	Lowry, Brigid	Holiday House
Think Again!	M	TL	1207	Big Cat	Pacific Learning
Think and Be Safe	H	I	211	InfoTrek	ETA/Cuisenaire
Think Before You Speak	S	RF	1904	Leveled Readers	Houghton Mifflin Harcourt
Think Before You Speak	S	RF	1904	Leveled Readers/CA	Houghton Mifflin Harcourt
Think Before You Speak	S	RF	1904	Leveled Readers/TX	Houghton Mifflin Harcourt
Think Big!	J	F	411	Carlson, Nancy	Carolrhoda Books
Think Happy!	J	F	233	Carlson, Nancy	Carolrhoda Books
Think Like a Photographer! (and shoot better pictures)	W	I	250+	Bookshop	Mondo Publishing
Think Like a Scientist	Q	I	250+	Burke, Melissa Blackwell	Steck-Vaughn
Think of an Eel	N	I	250+	Read and Wonder	Candlewick Press
Think, Think, Think: Learning About Your Brain	M	I	250+	Amazing Body	Picture Window Books
Thinking About Ants	L	I	250+	Bookshop	Mondo Publishing
Thinking It Through	T	I	250+	Reading Expeditions	National Geographic
Third Gift, The	S	TL	250+	Park, Linda Sue	Clarion Books
Third Grade Bullies	N	RF	250+	Levy, Elizabeth	Hyperion
Third Grade Stars	P	RF	250+	Ransom, Candice	Troll Associates
Third Grade Wedding Bells?	N	RF	250+	McKenna, Colleen O'Shaughnessy	Holiday House

T

* Collection of short stories   # Graphic text
^ Mature content with lower level text demands

TITLE	LEVEL	GENRE	WORD COUNT	AUTHOR / SERIES	PUBLISHER / DISTRIBUTOR
Thirsty	Z+	F	250+	Anderson, M.T.	Candlewick Press
Thirsty Animals, The	E	RF	46	Windows on Literacy	National Geographic
Thirsty Cats, The	D	F	98	Springboard	Wright Group/McGraw Hill
Thirteen	X	RF	250+	Myracle, Lauren	Puffin Books
Thirteen	R	RF	250+	Ransom, Candice	Scholastic
Thirteen Colonies, The	T	I	250+	Reading Expeditions	National Geographic
Thirteen Days to Midnight	Y	F	250+	Carman, Patrick	Little Brown and Company
Thirteen Reasons Why	Z+	RF	250+	Asher, Jay	Penguin Group
Thirteen Ways to Sink a Sub	S	RF	250+	Gilson, Jamie	Marshall Cavendish
Thirteenth Tale, The	Z+	F	250+	Setterfield, Diane	Simon & Schuster
Thirty-Nine Steps, The	Z+	RF	250+	Buchan, John	Penguin Group
This and That	D	RF	22	Home Connection Collection	Rigby
This Baby	O	RF	269	Banks, Kate	Farrar, Straus, & Giroux
This Book Is Haunted	J	F	250+	Rocklin, Joanne	HarperTrophy
This Book Is Not Good for You	U	F	250+	Bosch, Pseudonymous	Little Brown and Company
This Can't Be Happening at Macdonald Hall	S	RF	250+	Korman, Gordon	Scholastic
This Desert	C	I	37	Little Celebrations	Pearson Learning Group
This Farm	C	I	39	Yellow Umbrella Books	Red Brick Learning
This Food Grows Here	A	I	16	Windows on Literacy	National Geographic
This Fox and That Fox	E	RF	78	Reading Street	Pearson
This Game	B	I	63	Carousel Earlybirds	Pearson Learning Group
This Gecko	E	I	57	Twig	Wright Group/McGraw Hill
This Gorgeous Game	Z	RF	250+	Freitas, Donna	Farrar, Straus, & Giroux
This Gum For Hire: A Chet Gecko Mystery	Q	F	250+	Hale, Bruce	Harcourt, Inc.
This Hat	D	RF	52	Little Celebrations	Pearson Learning Group
This Is a Desert	K	I	220	Readlings/Ecosytems	American Reading Company
This Is a Family	D	I	76	Bonnell, Kris	Reading Reading Books
This Is a Fish	B	I	49	Springboard	Wright Group/McGraw Hill
This Is a Forest	A	I	32	In Step Readers	Rigby
This Is a Forest	J	I	139	Readlings/Ecosytems	American Reading Company
This Is a Prairie	I	I	161	Readlings/Ecosytems	American Reading Company
This Is an Island	D	RF	46	Windows on Literacy	National Geographic
This Is an Ocean	I	I	127	Readlings/Ecosytems	American Reading Company
This Is for Me	B	F	42	Sails	Rigby
This Is George	I	I	86	Pair-It Turn and Learn	Steck-Vaughn
This Is Lobstering	A	I	27	Little Books for Early Readers	University of Maine
This Is Me	E	RF	70	Rigby Literacy	Rigby
This Is Me	D	RF	70	Rigby Star Quest	Rigby
This Is Me	B	I	70	Sun Sprouts	ETA/Cuisenaire
This Is Me	B	I	27	Time for Kids	Teacher Created Materials
This Is Me and Where I Am	G	RF	111	Fitzgerald, Joanne	Fitzhenry & Whiteside
This Is Me!	A	I	23	Gear Up!	Wright Group/McGraw Hill
This Is Me!	B	I	44	InfoTrek	ETA/Cuisenaire
This Is Me! Mel B.!	R	B	250+	High-Fliers	Pacific Learning
This Is My Family	A	I	21	Leveled Readers Social Studies	Houghton Mifflin Harcourt
This Is My Family	D	RF	77	On Our Way to English	Rigby
This Is My Family	D	I	36	Read-More Books	Pearson Learning Group
This Is My Friend	C	RF	77	Foundations	Wright Group/McGraw Hill
This Is My Home	C	F	51	Joy Readers	Pearson Learning Group
This Is My House	L	I	250+	Dorros, Arthur	Scholastic
This Is My Street	I	RF	229	Windows on Literacy	National Geographic
This Is New Jersey	O	I	229	Larkin, Bruce	Wilbooks
This Is Ohio	O	I	195	Larkin, Bruce	Wilbooks
This Is Our House	K	RF	250+	Rosen, Michael	Candlewick Press

TITLE	LEVEL	GENRE	WORD COUNT	AUTHOR / SERIES	PUBLISHER / DISTRIBUTOR
This Is the Bear	I	F	211	Hayes, Sarah & Craig	Harper & Row
This Is the House That Bjorn…	I	RF	172	Tiger Cub	Peguis
This Is the Oasis	O	I	250+	Moss, Miriam	Kane/Miller Book Publishers
This Is the Place for Me	I	F	250+	Cole, Joanna	Scholastic
This Is the Plate	D	RF	28	Little Celebrations	Pearson Learning Group
This Is the Rain	P	I	250+	Schaefer, Lola M.	Greenwillow Books
This Is the Register	F	RF	81	Cambridge Reading	Pearson Learning Group
This Is the Sea That Feeds Us	N	I	551	Sharing Nature with Children	Dawn Publications
This Is the Seed	I	F	171	Little Celebrations	Pearson Learning Group
This Is the Seed	D	RF	115	Seedlings	Continental Press
This Is the Tree: A Story of the Baobab	O	I	332	Moss, Miriam	Kane/Miller Book Publishers
This Is the Way	F	RF	200	Learn to Read	Creative Teaching Press
This Is the Way We Go to School	T	RF	2879	Reading Street	Pearson
This Is the Way We Go to School: A Book About Children Around the World	L	I	250+	Baer, Edith	Scholastic
This Is the Way We Make Our Cookies	E	I	196	Factivity Series	Pearson Learning Group
This Is Water	B	I	24	Bookshop	Mondo Publishing
This Is What I Did	Z+	RF	250+	Ellis, Ann Dee	Little Brown and Company
This Isn't What It Looks Like	U	F	250+	Bosch, Pseudonymous	Little Brown and Company
This Land Is Our Land	O	I	781	Reading Street	Pearson
This Land Is Your Land: America's National Parks	S	I	250+	Explore More	Wright Group/McGraw Hill
This Little Boy	J	I	308	Springboard	Wright Group/McGraw Hill
This Little Chick	F	F	207	Lawrence, John	Candlewick Press
This Little Critter	D	I	98	Springboard	Wright Group/McGraw Hill
This Little Pig	D	F	43	Seedlings	Continental Press
This Little Seed	E	I	58	Rigby Focus	Rigby
This Mouth	D	I	64	Wonder World	Wright Group/McGraw Hill
This Old Car	H	RF	79	Voyages	SRA/McGraw Hill
This One Can Run	B	I	34	Science	Outside the Box
This Piece or That Piece?	E	F	88	Leveled Readers	Houghton Mifflin Harcourt
This Place Is Dry	R	I	250+	Cobb, Vicki	Walker & Company
This Place Is Wet	R	I	250+	Cobb, Vicki	Walker & Company
This Room Is a Mess!	I	RF	250+	Ready Readers	Pearson Learning Group
This Tail Belongs to . . .	B	I	24	Science	Outside the Box
This Tall	B	RF	41	Foundations	Wright Group/McGraw Hill
This Way to School	H	I	170	Gear Up!	Wright Group/McGraw Hill
This Year's Play	N	F	250+	Springboard	Wright Group/McGraw Hill
Thistle and the Shell of Laughter: The Fairy Chronicles	Q	F	12190	Sweet, J.H.	Sourcebooks
Thomas Adams Invents Chewing Gum	N	B	417	Reading Street	Pearson
Thomas Alva Edison	T	B	2977	People to Remember Series	January Books
Thomas Alva Edison: Great Inventor	R	B	250+	Levinson, Nancy Smiler	Scholastic
Thomas Edison	P	B	250+	Early Biographies	Compass Point Books
Thomas Edison	N	B	196	First Biographies	Capstone Press
Thomas Edison	S	B	3651	History Maker Bios	Lerner Publishing Group
Thomas Edison	T	B	250+	In Their Own Words	Scholastic
Thomas Edison	P	B	250+	Photo-Illustrated Biographies	Red Brick Learning
Thomas Edison	K	B	145	Windows on Literacy	National Geographic
Thomas Edison and the Developers of Electromagnetism	U	B	250+	Mission Science	Compass Point Books
Thomas Edison and the Light Bulb	Q	B	619	Independent Readers Science	Houghton Mifflin Harcourt
#Thomas Edison and the Lightbulb	U	B	250+	Inventions and Discovery	Capstone Press
Thomas Edison and the Pioneers of Electromagnetism	U	B	250+	Science Readers	Teacher Created Materials

TITLE	LEVEL	GENRE	WORD COUNT	AUTHOR / SERIES	PUBLISHER / DISTRIBUTOR
Thomas Edison to the Rescue	K	B	250+	Childhood of Famous Americans	Aladdin
Thomas Edison: Inventor with a Lot of Bright Ideas	R	B	250+	Getting to Know the World's Greatest Inventors and Scientists	Children's Press
Thomas Had a Temper	F	RF	139	Alphakids	Sundance
Thomas Jefferson	T	B	250+	Amazing Americans	Wright Group/McGraw Hill
Thomas Jefferson	Q	B	250+	Early Biographies	Compass Point Books
Thomas Jefferson	N	B	198	First Biographies	Capstone Press
Thomas Jefferson	S	B	3374	History Maker Bios	Lerner Publishing Group
Thomas Jefferson	N	B	157	Independent Readers Social Studies	Houghton Mifflin Harcourt
Thomas Jefferson	X	B	250+	Just the Facts Biographies	Lerner Publishing Group
Thomas Jefferson	V	B	250+	Let Freedom Ring	Capstone Press
Thomas Jefferson	Q	B	250+	Photo-Illustrated Biographies	Red Brick Learning
Thomas Jefferson	T	B	3393	Presidential Series	January Books
Thomas Jefferson	U	B	250+	Primary Source Readers	Teacher Created Materials
Thomas Jefferson	U	B	250+	Profiles of the Presidents	Compass Point Books
^Thomas Jefferson and the Louisiana Purchase	Q	I	250+	On Deck	Rigby
Thomas Jefferson: A Life of Patriotism	O	B	557	Pull Ahead Books	Lerner Publishing Group
Thomas Jefferson: Author, Inventor, President	N	B	250+	Rookie Biographies	Children's Press
Thomas Jefferson: Man with a Vision	U	B	250+	Crisman, Ruth	Scholastic
Thomas Jefferson: Third President	R	B	250+	Getting to Know the U.S. Presidents	Children's Press
Thomas Peters A Remarkable Man	U	B	2255	Leveled Readers/CA	Houghton Mifflin Harcourt
Thomas Peters A Remarkable Man	U	B	2255	Leveled Readers/TX	Houghton Mifflin Harcourt
Thomas Peters, A Remarkable Man	U	B	2255	Leveled Readers	Houghton Mifflin Harcourt
Thomas Tries Something New	L	F	570	Springboard	Wright Group/McGraw Hill
#Thor & Loki: In the Land of Giants	W	TL	2731	Graphic Myths and Legends	Lerner Publishing Group
Thorn, The	I	F	386	Pawprints Teal	Pioneer Valley
Thoroughbred Horses	I	I	159	Horses	Capstone Press
Thor's Wedding Day	R	F	250+	Coville, Bruce	Harcourt, Inc.
Those Amazingly Useful Ears	O	I	250+	Frederick, Shirley	Hampton Brown
Those Birds!	K	RF	250+	Storyteller-Lightning Bolts	Wright Group/McGraw Hill
Those Shoes	L	RF	250+	Boelts, Maribeth	Candlewick Press
Those Tricky Animals	M	I	250+	Literacy Tree	Rigby
Those Yucky Meanies!	H	F	153	The Joy Cowley Collection	Hameray Publishing Group
Thoughts, Pictures, and Words	O	B	250+	Meet The Author	Richard C. Owen
Thousand Miles to Freedom, A: The Escape of Ellen and William Craft	Q	B	250+	Scott Foresman Reading	Pearson Learning Group
Thousand Words, A	O	RF	688	Leveled Readers	Houghton Mifflin Harcourt
Thousand Words, A	O	RF	688	Leveled Readers/CA	Houghton Mifflin Harcourt
Thousand Words, A	O	RF	688	Leveled Readers/TX	Houghton Mifflin Harcourt
Threads of Deceit	U	RF	250+	High-Fliers	Pacific Learning
Three	LB	I	17	Count on It!	Marshall Cavendish
Three Ancient Communities	Q	I	250+	Navigators Social Studies Series	Benchmark Education
Three Armadillies Tuff, The	N	TL	226	Hopkins, Jackie Mims	Peachtree
Three Bears' Christmas, The	J	F	250+	Duval, Kathy	Holiday House
Three Bears' Halloween, The	M	F	250+	Duval, Kathy	Holiday House
Three Bears, The	E	TL	201	Fairy Tales and Folklore	Norwood House Press
Three Bears, The	G	TL	344	Folk Tales	Pioneer Valley
Three Bears, The	K	TL	873	Galdone, Paul	Clarion
Three Bears, The	E	TL	116	Leveled Literacy Intervention/ Green System	Heinemann
Three Bears, The	D	TL	101	Lighthouse	Rigby
Three Bears, The	I	TL	250+	Tiger Cub	Peguis
Three Big Cities	N	I	535	Springboard	Wright Group/McGraw Hill

TITLE	LEVEL	GENRE	WORD COUNT	AUTHOR / SERIES	PUBLISHER / DISTRIBUTOR
Three Billy Goats Gruff	A	TL	33	Red Rocket Readers	Flying Start Books
Three Billy Goats Gruff	I	TL	250+	Sunshine	Wright Group/McGraw Hill
Three Billy Goats Gruff	I	TL	536	Traditional Tales	Pearson Learning Group
Three Billy Goats Gruff, The	K	TL	250+	Asbjornsen, P. C.; Moe, J. E.	Harcourt School Publishers
Three Billy Goats Gruff, The	I	TL	549	Brown, Marcia	Harcourt School Publishers
Three Billy Goats Gruff, The	F	TL	250+	Folk Tales	Pioneer Valley
Three Billy Goats Gruff, The	I	TL	250+	Literacy Tree	Rigby
Three Billy Goats Gruff, The	G	TL	140	Little Readers	Houghton Mifflin Harcourt
Three Billy Goats Gruff, The	H	TL	250+	New Way Green	Steck-Vaughn
Three Billy Goats Gruff, The	I	TL	450	PM Traditional Tales-Orange	Rigby
Three Billy Goats Gruff, The	G	TL	250+	Shapiro, Sara	Scholastic
Three Billy Goats Gruff, The	I	F	250+	Southgate, Vera	Ladybird Books
Three Billy Goats Gruff, The	K	TL	478	Stevens, Janet	Harcourt School Publishers
Three Billy Goats, The	J	TL	532	Leveled Literacy Intervention/ Green System	Heinemann
Three Billy Goats, The	E	TL	133	Storyworlds	Heinemann
Three Blind Mice Mystery, The	L	F	250+	Krensky, Stephen	Bantam Books
Three Brothers, The	M	TL	250+	Rigby Flying Colors	Rigby
*Three by the Sea	J	RF	250+	Marshall, Edward	Puffin Books
Three Cheers for Hippo	G	F	90	Stadler, John	HarperCollins
Three Cheers for Mallow!: Butterfly Meadow	M	F	250+	Moss, Olivia	Scholastic
Three Claws: The Mountain Monster	I	F	362	Stone Arch Readers	Stone Arch Books
Three Days on a River in a Red Canoe	K	I	250+	Williams, Vera B.	Scholastic
Three Ducks Went Wandering	K	F	250+	Roy, Ron	Clarion
Three Friends or Two?	S	RF	1940	Leveled Readers	Houghton Mifflin Harcourt
Three Friends or Two?	S	RF	1940	Leveled Readers/CA	Houghton Mifflin Harcourt
Three Friends or Two?	S	RF	1940	Leveled Readers/TX	Houghton Mifflin Harcourt
*Three Funny Tales	K	TL	900	Springboard	Wright Group/McGraw Hill
Three Goats, The	E	TL	220	Fairy Tales and Folklore	Norwood House Press
Three Goats, The	F	TL	128	Storyteller-Setting Sun	Wright Group/McGraw Hill
Three Hedgehogs, The	K	F	552	Rigby Gigglers	Rigby
Three Historical Communities of North America	P	I	250+	Navigators Social Studies Series	Benchmark Education
Three Horrid Little Pigs, The	O	TL	250+	Pichon, Liz	Tiger Tales
Three Immigrant Communities: New York City in 1900	P	I	250+	Navigators Social Studies Series	Benchmark Education
Three Investigators, The Mystery of the Fiery Eye	Y	RF	250+	Arthur, Robert	Random House
Three Jars Full	F	I	89	Rigby Focus	Rigby
Three Kinds of Bears	Q	I	3256	Leveled Readers Science	Houghton Mifflin Harcourt
Three Kinds of Water	F	I	116	Early Explorers	Benchmark Education
Three Kittens	G	F	116	Ginsburg, Mirra	Crown Publishers
Three Little Pigs	A	TL	26	Red Rocket Readers	Flying Start Books
Three Little Bears Build	C	F	57	Brand New Readers	Candlewick Press
Three Little Bears Eat	C	F	50	Brand New Readers	Candlewick Press
Three Little Bears Juggle	C	F	40	Brand New Readers	Candlewick Press
Three Little Bears Jump	C	F	30	Brand New Readers	Candlewick Press
Three Little Beavers	M	F	601	Diehl, Jean Heilprin	Sylvan Dell Publishing
Three Little Ducks	E	F	102	Story Box	Wright Group/McGraw Hill
Three Little Kittens	H	TL	164	Ready Readers	Pearson Learning Group
Three Little Monkeys	E	F	36	Sunshine	Wright Group/McGraw Hill
Three Little Pigs	L	TL	919	Galdone, Paul	Houghton Mifflin Harcourt
Three Little Pigs	H	TL	39	Hunia, Fran	Ladybird Books
Three Little Pigs	L	TL	250+	Once Upon a Time	Wright Group/McGraw Hill

Organized Alphabetically by Title
Storable Database at www.fountasandpinnellleveledbooks.com

* Collection of short stories   # Graphic text
^ Mature content with lower level text demands

T

TITLE	LEVEL	GENRE	WORD COUNT	AUTHOR / SERIES	PUBLISHER / DISTRIBUTOR
Three Little Pigs	C	TL	39	Sunshine	Wright Group/McGraw Hill
Three Little Pigs and a Big Bad Wolf	F	TL	267	Leveled Literacy Intervention/ Green System	Heinemann
Three Little Pigs and One Big Pig	E	TL	123	Ready Readers	Pearson Learning Group
Three Little Pigs Go into Town, The	J	TL	250+	InfoTrek	ETA/Cuisenaire
Three Little Pigs Wise Up and The Princess, the Prince, and the Vegetables, The	M	F	250+	Navigators Fiction Series	Benchmark Education
Three Little Pigs, The	F	TL	274	Alphakids	Sundance
Three Little Pigs, The	E	TL	189	Fairy Tales and Folklore	Norwood House Press
Three Little Pigs, The	C	TL	99	Folk Tales	Pioneer Valley
Three Little Pigs, The	M	TL	250+	Guarnaccia, Steven	Harry N. Abrams
Three Little Pigs, The	I	TL	250+	Literacy 2000	Rigby
Three Little Pigs, The	G	TL	250+	Little Readers	Houghton Mifflin Harcourt
Three Little Pigs, The	L	TL	250+	Marshall, James	Scholastic
Three Little Pigs, The	H	TL	392	New Way Blue	Steck-Vaughn
Three Little Pigs, The	I	TL	523	PM Traditional Tales-Orange	Rigby
Three Little Pigs, The	H	TL	346	Reading Corners	Pearson Learning Group
Three Little Pigs, The	H	TL	276	Reading Unlimited	Pearson Learning Group
Three Little Pigs, The	I	TL	568	Traditional Tales	Pearson Learning Group
Three Little Pigs, The	C	TL	114	Traditional Tales	Pioneer Valley
Three Little Pigs, The	G	TL	250+	We Both Read	Treasure Bay
Three Little Pigs, The	I	TL	250+	Ziefert, Harriet	Puffin Books
Three Little Witches	G	F	189	First Start	Troll Associates
Three Little Wolves and the Big Bad Pig, The	O	TL	250+	Trivizas, Eugene	Scholastic
Three Lives to Live	T	F	250+	Lindbergh, Anne	Little Brown and Company
Three Magicians, The	K	F	250+	Literacy 2000	Rigby
*Three More Stories You Can Read to Your Cat	L	F	250+	Miller, Sara Swan	Houghton Mifflin Harcourt
*Three More Stories You Can Read to Your Dog	L	F	250+	Miller, Sara Swan	Houghton Mifflin Harcourt
Three Muddy Monkeys	F	F	180	Foundations	Wright Group/McGraw Hill
Three Musketeers, The	Y	HF	10847	Dominoes two	Oxford University Press
Three Names	N	HF	250+	MacLachlan, Patricia	Scholastic
Three Names of Me	N	RF	250+	Cummings, Mary	Albert Whitman & Co.
Three Naughty Ostriches	J	F	369	Springboard	Wright Group/McGraw Hill
Three of the Greats	M	B	360	Reading Street	Pearson
Three on Three	S	RF	250+	Orca Young Readers	Orca Books
Three Pigs	G	F	126	Gear Up!	Wright Group/McGraw Hill
Three Pigs, The	D	TL	113	Leveled Literacy Intervention/ Green System	Heinemann
Three Rivers Rising: A Novel of the Johnstown Flood	Z	HF	250+	Richards, Jame	Random House
Three R's, The	U	RF	3211	Leveled Readers	Houghton Mifflin Harcourt
Three R's, The	U	RF	3211	Leveled Readers/CA	Houghton Mifflin Harcourt
Three R's, The	U	RF	3211	Leveled Readers/TX	Houghton Mifflin Harcourt
Three Scoops and a Fig	N	RF	250+	Akin, Sara Laux	Peachtree
Three Ships for Columbus	N	I	250+	Stories of America	Steck-Vaughn
Three Sillies, The	L	TL	250+	Literacy 2000	Rigby
Three Silly Cowboys, The	H	F	213	Ready Readers	Pearson Learning Group
Three Silly Monkeys	E	F	150	Foundations	Wright Group/McGraw Hill
Three Silly Monkeys Go Fishing	I	F	163	Foundations	Wright Group/McGraw Hill
Three Sisters, The	J	I	313	Vocabulary Readers	Houghton Mifflin Harcourt
Three Sisters, The	J	I	313	Vocabulary Readers/CA	Houghton Mifflin Harcourt
Three Sisters, The	J	I	313	Vocabulary Readers/TX	Houghton Mifflin Harcourt
Three Smart Pals	L	RF	250+	Rocklin, Joanne	Scholastic
*Three Stories You Can Read to Your Cat	K	F	250+	Miller, Sara Swan	Houghton Mifflin Harcourt

T

TITLE	LEVEL	GENRE	WORD COUNT	AUTHOR / SERIES	PUBLISHER / DISTRIBUTOR
*Three Stories You Can Read to Your Dog	K	F	250+	Miller, Sara Swan	Houghton Mifflin Harcourt
*Three Stories You Can Read to Your Teddy Bear	L	F	250+	Miller, Sara Swan	Houghton Mifflin Harcourt
Three Strangers, The	U	RF	11680	Oxford Bookworms Library	Oxford University Press
*Three Twentieth-Century Dictators	Y	B	250+	Navigators Biography Series	Benchmark Education
*Three Up a Tree	J	RF	250+	Marshall, James	Puffin Books
Three White Sheep	B	F	20	Ready Readers	Pearson Learning Group
Three Wishes	L	F	250+	Popcorn	Sundance
Three Wishes	H	TL	250+	Ready Readers	Pearson Learning Group
Three Wishes: Palestinian and Israeli Children Speak	Z	I	250+	Ellis, Deborah	Groundwood Books
Three Wishes, The	L	TL	250+	Bookshop	Mondo Publishing
*Three Wishes, The	O	TL	250+	Literacy 2000	Rigby
Three Wishes, The	I	TL	250+	Storyworlds	Heinemann
Three Wishes, The	K	TL	501	Sunshine	Wright Group/McGraw Hill
Three Women Reporters	X	I	2956	Vocabulary Readers	Houghton Mifflin Harcourt
Three Women Reporters	X	I	2956	Vocabulary Readers/CA	Houghton Mifflin Harcourt
Three Women Reporters	X	I	2956	Vocabulary Readers/TX	Houghton Mifflin Harcourt
Three-Horn: The Adventure of Triceratops	N	I	250+	Dinosaur World	Picture Window Books
Three-Legged Race, The	H	RF	202	Windmill Books	Rigby
Three-Minute Speech, A: Lincoln's Remarks at Gettysburg	S	I	250+	Armstrong, Jennifer	Aladdin
Three's A Crowd	N	RF	250+	Literacy by Design	Rigby
Three's a Crowd: Jane and the Dragon	O	F	250+	Baynton, Martin	Candlewick Press
Three-Toed Sloths	O	I	926	Springboard	Wright Group/McGraw Hill
Threw and Through	K	F	255	Sunshine	Wright Group/McGraw Hill
Thrill of the Ride, The	Q	I	250+	Power Up!	Steck-Vaughn
Thrill Rides!: All About Roller Coasters	V	I	250+	Bookshop	Mondo Publishing
Thrills at the Fair	J	RF	250+	The Wright Skills	Wright Group/McGraw Hill
Thrills on the Water	M	I	445	Sails	Rigby
Throne of Fire	W	F	250+	Riordan, Rick	Hyperion
Through Grandpa's Eyes	P	RF	250+	MacLachlan, Patricia	HarperTrophy
Through My Eyes	X	B	250+	Bridges, Ruby	Scholastic
Through the Cell Wall	Z	I	2080	Independent Readers Science	Houghton Mifflin Harcourt
Through the Day	C	I	76	Rigby Literacy	Rigby
Through the Eyes of Your Ancestors: A Step-by-Step Guide to Uncovering Your Family's History	V	I	250+	Taylor, Maureen	Houghton Mifflin Harcourt
Through the Fence	Q	F	1862	Take Two Books	Wright Group/McGraw Hill
Through the Garden Door	M	F	250+	Reeves, Barbara	Pearson Learning Group
Through the Looking-Glass	T	F	10605	Oxford Bookworms Library	Oxford University Press
Through the Medicine Cabinet	N	F	250+	The Zack Files	Grosset & Dunlap
Throw-Away Pets	N	RF	250+	Duffey, Betsy	Puffin Books
Throwing Heat	R	RF	250+	Bowen, Fred	Peachtree
Throwing Like a Girl	W	RF	250+	Mackie, Weezie Kerr	Marshall Cavendish
Throwing Parties	V	I	250+	10 Things You Need To Know About	Capstone Press
*Throwing Shadows	T	RF	250+	Konigsburg, E. L.	Language for Learning Assoc.
Thumb in the Box, The	S	RF	250+	Roberts, Ken	Groundwood Books
Thumb on a Diamond	S	RF	250+	Roberts, Ken	Groundwood Books
Thumbelina	K	TL	807	Tales from Hans Andersen	Wright Group/McGraw Hill
Thumbelina	K	TL	736	Traditional Tales	Pioneer Valley
Thumbprint Critters	D	I	27	Little Celebrations	Pearson Learning Group
Thumper's Sore Paw	F	RF	136	Springboard	Wright Group/McGraw Hill
Thumpety-Rah!	G	F	98	Sunshine	Wright Group/McGraw Hill
Thump-Thump: Learning About Your Heart	M	I	250+	Amazing Body	Picture Window Books

T

Organized Alphabetically by Title
Storable Database at www.fountasandpinnellleveledbooks.com

* Collection of short stories   # Graphic text
^ Mature content with lower level text demands

TITLE	LEVEL	GENRE	WORD COUNT	AUTHOR / SERIES	PUBLISHER / DISTRIBUTOR
Thunder and Lightning	K	I	250+	Pfeffer, Wendy	Scholastic
Thunder at Gettysburg	S	I	250+	Gauch, Patricia Lee	Bantam Books
Thunder Cave	W	RF	250+	Smith, Roland	Hyperion
Thunder Falls (Dinotopia)	T	F	250+	Ciencin, Scott	Random House
#Thunder Rolling Down the Mountain: The Story of Chief Joseph and the Nez Perce	V	B	250+	Graphic Library	Capstone Press
Thunder Rolling in the Mountains	U	HF	250+	O'Dell, Scott; Hall, Elizabeth	Bantam Books
Thunder Valley	T	RF	250+	Paulsen, Gary	Bantam Books
^Thunderbowl	Z+	RF	250+	Orca Soundings	Orca Books
Thunderstorm Is Coming!, A	I	I	130	Vocabulary Readers	Houghton Mifflin Harcourt
Thunderstorms	O	I	250+	A True Book	Children's Press
Thunderstorms	M	I	501	Pull Ahead Books	Lerner Publishing Group
Thunderstruck Stork, The	L	F	250+	Olson, David J.	Albert Whitman & Co.
Thura's Diary: My Life in Wartime Iraq	Y	B	250+	Edge	Hampton Brown
Thurgood Marshall	U	B	250+	Amazing Americans	Wright Group/McGraw Hill
Thurgood Marshall	S	B	1264	Leveled Readers	Houghton Mifflin Harcourt
Thurgood Marshall	S	B	1264	Leveled Readers/CA	Houghton Mifflin Harcourt
Thurgood Marshall	S	B	1264	Leveled Readers/TX	Houghton Mifflin Harcourt
Thurgood Marshall	L	B	250+	Pebble Books	Red Brick Learning
Thurgood Marshall	P	B	250+	Photo-Illustrated Biographies	Red Brick Learning
Thurgood Marshall and Civil Rights	V	B	2540	Independent Readers Social Studies	Houghton Mifflin Harcourt
Thurgood Marshall: Civil Rights Champion	P	B	250+	Great African Americans	Capstone Press
Thurgood Marshall: First Black Supreme Court Justice	N	B	250+	Rookie Biographies	Children's Press
Thurgood Marshall: Supreme Court Justice	N	B	250+	Beginning Biographies	Pearson Learning Group
THWONK	Y	F	250+	Bauer, Joan	Speak
Tia the Tulip Fairy: Rainbow Magic	L	F	250+	Meadows, Daisy	Scholastic
Tiananmen Square	Y	I	250+	Snapshots in History	Compass Point Books
Tiara Club Winter Wonderland, The	L	F	250+	French, Vivian	HarperCollins
Tick Tock World Clocks	F	I	43	iOpeners	Pearson Learning Group
Tick, Tock, Check the Clock!	C	F	64	Literacy by Design	Rigby
Ticket to Canada	U	RF	1904	Leveled Readers	Houghton Mifflin Harcourt
Tickle Monster Is Coming, The	J	F	266	Thach, James Otis	Bloomsbury Children's Books
Tickle, Tickle! Itch, Twitch!	J	F	216	Olson, Julie	Marshall Cavendish
Tickle-Bugs, The	J	F	250+	Literacy 2000	Rigby
Tick-Tock	C	RF	53	Story Box	Wright Group/McGraw Hill
Tic-Tac-Toe: Three in a Row	H	RF	132	Stamper, Judith Bauer	Scholastic
Tide of Terror: Vampirates	Z+	F	250+	Somper, Justin	Little Brown and Company
Tide Pool, The	B	I	57	Leveled Literacy Intervention/Blue System	Heinemann
Tide Pools	K	I	388	Leveled Readers	Houghton Mifflin Harcourt
Tide Pools	K	I	388	Leveled Readers/CA	Houghton Mifflin Harcourt
Tide Pools	K	I	388	Leveled Readers/TX	Houghton Mifflin Harcourt
Tide Pools: Life at the Edge of the Sea	U	I	3477	Nature Watch	Lerner Publishing Group
Tides	L	I	250+	Books for Young Learners	Richard C. Owen
Tides	M	I	596	Red Rocket Readers	Flying Start Books
Tides	I	I	210	Wonder World	Wright Group/McGraw Hill
Tides of Change	V	I	250+	InfoQuest	Rigby
Tidy the Clown	H	F	240	InfoTrek	ETA/Cuisenaire
Tidy Titch	I	RF	231	Hutchins, Pat	Morrow
Tidy Up!	J	I	127	Small World	Lerner Publishing Group
Tie, The	O	I	819	Vocabulary Readers	Houghton Mifflin Harcourt
Tie, The	O	I	819	Vocabulary Readers/CA	Houghton Mifflin Harcourt

T

TITLE	LEVEL	GENRE	WORD COUNT	AUTHOR / SERIES	PUBLISHER / DISTRIBUTOR
Ties That Bind, Ties That Break	Y	HF	250+	Edge	Hampton Brown
Ties That Bind, Ties That Break	Y	HF	250+	Namioka, Lensey	Delacorte Press
Tig in the Dumps	M	RF	1229	Big Cat	Pacific Learning
Tig the Talented Pig	B	F	50	Reading Street	Pearson
Tiger	C	I	38	Zoozoo-Into the Wild	Cavallo Publishing
Tiger & the Mad Millionaire, The	L	F	250+	Voyages	SRA/McGraw Hill
Tiger and Monkey	D	F	92	Sails	Rigby
Tiger and the Jackal, The	I	TL	250+	Storyworlds	Heinemann
Tiger Cub Grows Up, A	K	I	684	Baby Animals	Carolrhoda Books
Tiger Dave	G	F	33	Books for Young Learners	Richard C. Owen
Tiger Dreams	J	RF	193	Cambridge Reading	Pearson Learning Group
Tiger Eyes	W	RF	250+	Blume, Judy	Bantam Books
Tiger Hunt	J	RF	250+	Rigby Literacy	Rigby
Tiger Is a Scaredy Cat	F	F	220	Phillips, Joan	Random House
Tiger Math: Learning to Graph from a Baby Tiger	Q	I	250+	Nagda, Ann Whitehead & Bickel, Cindy	Henry Holt & Co.
Tiger Moon	Z+	F	250+	Michaelis, Antonia	Amulet Books
Tiger Rising, The	T	RF	250+	DiCamillo, Kate	Candlewick Press
Tiger Runs Away	G	RF	213	PM Extensions-Blue	Rigby
^Tiger Shark	N	I	250+	Shark Zone	Capstone Press
Tiger Shark	J	I	136	Sharks	Capstone Press
Tiger Sharks	I	I	142	Readlings/ Marine Life	American Reading Company
Tiger Tales	O	F	250+	Little Celebrations	Pearson Learning Group
Tiger Taming: The Pet Sitter	O	F	250+	Sykes, Julie	Kingfisher
^Tiger Threat	U	RF	250+	Orca Sports	Orca Books
Tiger Trek	P	I	250+	WorldScapes	ETA/Cuisenaire
Tiger Turcotte Takes on the Know-It-All	M	RF	4908	Flood, Pansie Hart	Carolrhoda Books
Tiger Woods	V	B	250+	A&E Biography	Lerner Publishing Group
Tiger Woods	P	B	1617	Amazing Athletes	Lerner Publishing Group
Tiger Woods	N	B	250+	Biography	Benchmark Education
Tiger Woods	Q	B	1081	Leveled Readers	Houghton Mifflin Harcourt
Tiger Woods	Q	B	1081	Leveled Readers/CA	Houghton Mifflin Harcourt
Tiger Woods	Q	B	1081	Leveled Readers/TX	Houghton Mifflin Harcourt
Tiger Woods	R	B	250+	Sports Heroes	Red Brick Learning
Tiger Woods	U	B	250+	Sports Heroes and Legends	Lerner Publishing Group
Tiger Woods: An American Master	R	B	250+	Edwards, Nicholas	Scholastic
Tiger Woods: Revised Edition	P	B	1617	Amazing Athletes	Lerner Publishing Group
Tiger Woods: Unbeatable!	X	B	2056	Leveled Readers	Houghton Mifflin Harcourt
Tiger, the Brahman, & the Jackal, The	M	TL	250+	Book Blazers	ETA/Cuisenaire
Tiger, the Man, and the Jackal, The	K	TL	520	Leveled Readers	Houghton Mifflin Harcourt
Tiger, Tiger	C	F	55	PM Story Books	Rigby
Tigers	O	I	1462	Early Bird Nature Books	Lerner Publishing Group
Tigers	I	I	324	Sails	Rigby
Tiger's Apprentice, The	T	F	250+	Yep, Laurence	HarperTrophy
Tigers at Twilight	M	F	250+	Osborne, Mary Pope	Random House
Tiger's Blood	T	F	250+	Yep, Laurence	HarperTrophy
Tiger's Clock	C	F	28	Learn to Read	Creative Teaching Press
Tigers of Asia	A	I	56	Readlings/Animals of Asia	American Reading Company
^Tigers on the Hunt	N	I	250+	Killer Animals	Capstone Press
Tiger's Promise, Based on a Folktale from India, The	J	TL	250+	Leveled Readers Language Support	Houghton Mifflin Harcourt
Tiger's Tale	L	F	1443	Big Cat	Pacific Learning
Tiger's Tummy Ache	I	TL	220	Ready Readers	Pearson Learning Group
Tigers, Elephants, and Giraffes	A	I	18	Vocabulary Readers	Houghton Mifflin Harcourt

* Collection of short stories   # Graphic text
^ Mature content with lower level text demands

TITLE	LEVEL	GENRE	WORD COUNT	AUTHOR / SERIES	PUBLISHER / DISTRIBUTOR
Tigers: Striped Stalkers	M	I	250+	The Wild World of Animals	Red Brick Learning
Tight End	T	RF	250+	Christopher, Matt	Little Brown and Company
Tightwad Tod	K	RF	250+	Math Matters	Kane Press
Tikki Tikki Tembo	N	TL	250+	Mosel, Arlene	Scholastic
Tiling with Shapes	L	I	371	Yellow Umbrella Books	Red Brick Learning
Till Death Do Us Bark: 43 Old Cemetery Road: Book Three	U	F	250+	Klise, Kate	Sandpiper Books
Till's Christmas	R	RF	250+	Thacker, Nola	Scholastic
Tilly the Trickster	M	RF	250+	Shannon, Molly	Harry N. Abrams
Tiltawhirl John	U	RF	250+	Paulsen, Gary	Penguin Group
Tim and the Tooth Fairy	I	RF	250+	Rigby Rocket	Rigby
Tim Berners-Lee: Spinning the World Wide Web	W	B	250+	Explore More	Wright Group/McGraw Hill
Tim Does It Again	K	RF	250+	Rigby Gigglers	Rigby
Tim Duncan	P	B	2203	Amazing Athletes	Lerner Publishing Group
Tim Duncan	U	B	250+	Sports Heroes and Legends	Lerner Publishing Group
Tim Lincecum	P	B	2114	Amazing Athletes	Lerner Publishing Group
Tim the Tortoise	D	F	89	Early Connections	Benchmark Education
Timber Box, The	M	TL	250+	Enrichment	Wright Group/McGraw Hill
Timberwolf Prey	R	RF	250+	Orca Echoes	Orca Books
Timberwolf Rivals	R	RF	250+	Orca Echoes	Orca Books
Time	A	RF	31	Davidson, Avelyn	Scholastic
Time	K	I	500	Red Rocket Readers	Flying Start Books
Time	Q	RF	1841	Take Two Books	Wright Group/McGraw Hill
^Time and Again	P	SF	10061	Childs, Rob	Stone Arch Books
Time and Routines	H	I	65	Windows on Literacy	National Geographic
Time Apart, A	T	RF	250+	Stanley, Diane	William Morrow
Time Benders	T	SF	250+	Paulsen, Gary	Bantam Books
Time by the Clock	P	I	250+	Windows on Literacy	National Geographic
Time Capsule	Q	F	250+	Bookweb	Rigby
Time Capsule, The	M	SF	257	Book Bank	Wright Group/McGraw Hill
Time Capsule, The	J	RF	250+	Reading Safari	Mondo Publishing
Time Flies	R	I	250+	Literacy 2000	Rigby
Time Flies	WB	F	0	Rohmann, Eric	Crown Publishers
Time for a Bath	D	RF	60	Mader, Jan	Kaeden Books
Time for a Bath	D	RF	36	Potato Chip Books	American Reading Company
Time for a Change	C	RF	31	Pacific Literacy	Pacific Learning
Time for a Family	K	I	108	Literacy Tree	Rigby
Time for a Party	F	I	111	Discovery World	Rigby
Time for a Swim	E	F	199	Red Rocket Readers	Flying Start Books
Time for Andrew	S	F	250+	Hahn, Mary	Avon Books
Time for Bed	C	RF	31	Rigby Rocket	Rigby
Time for Bed	C	RF	27	Rosen Real Readers	Rosen Publishing Group
Time for Bed	B	RF	28	Science	Outside the Box
Time for Bed	C	RF	28	Smart Start	Rigby
Time for Bed, Little Bear	I	F	303	Story Basket	Wright Group/McGraw Hill
Time for Bed?	H	RF	256	Real Kids Readers	Millbrook Press
Time for Breakfast	B	RF	25	Gear Up!	Wright Group/McGraw Hill
Time for Breakfast!	A	F	20	Leveled Readers	Houghton Mifflin Harcourt
Time for Breakfast!	A	F	20	Leveled Readers/CA	Houghton Mifflin Harcourt
Time for Carter to Barter	J	RF	494	Gear Up!	Wright Group/McGraw Hill
Time for Dancing, A	Z+	RF	250+	Hurwin, Davida Wills	Little Brown and Company
Time for Dinner	B	I	38	PM Starters	Rigby
Time for Dinner	LB	F	15	Smart Start	Rigby
Time for Kids Almanac 2010	V	I	250+	Time for Kids	Capstone Press

T

TITLE	LEVEL	GENRE	WORD COUNT	AUTHOR / SERIES	PUBLISHER / DISTRIBUTOR
Time for Lunch	D	F	122	Leveled Literacy Intervention/ Green System	Heinemann
Time for Lunch	B	RF	28	Ready Readers	Pearson Learning Group
Time for Lunch!	I	F	250+	Rigby Rocket	Rigby
Time for Pizza	F	RF	165	The King School Series	Townsend Press
Time for Play	D	RF	85	PM Plus Nonfiction	Rigby
Time for Sale	Q	F	250+	Literacy 2000	Rigby
Time for School	A	I	32	At School Series	Pioneer Valley
Time for Sleep!	D	F	62	Sunshine	Wright Group/McGraw Hill
Time for Soup!	LB	I	12	Vocabulary Readers	Houghton Mifflin Harcourt
Time for Tacos	B	RF	26	Bebop Books	Lee & Low Books Inc.
Time for Tea	B	RF	20	Phonics and Friends	Hampton Brown
Time Garden, The	T	F	250+	Eager, Edward	Harcourt
Time Keeper's Moon, The	Y	F	250+	Sensel, Joni	Bloomsbury Children's Books
Time Line of the American Revolution, A	R	I	250+	Rosen Real Readers	Rosen Publishing Group
Time Lines: 1900-2000	O	I	250+	Windows on Literacy	National Geographic
*Time Machine and Other Cases, The	O	RF	250+	Simon, Seymour	Avon Books
#Time Machine, The	T	F	250+	Davis, Terry (Retold)	Stone Arch Books
Time Machine, The	Z	SF	250+	Wells, H. G.	Scholastic
Time of Angels, A	W	F	250+	Hesse, Karen	Hyperion
Time of Change, A: Women in the Early Twentieth Century	S	I	1877	Reading Street	Pearson
Time of the Witches	Y	HF	250+	Myers, Anna	Walker & Company
Time Song, The	G	I	99	Learn to Read	Creative Teaching Press
Time Spinner	S	F	250+	Bookshop	Mondo Publishing
Time Thief, The	Y	SF	250+	Buckley-Archer, Linda	Aladdin
Time to Celebrate!	M	I	250+	iOpeners	Pearson Learning Group
Time to Eat	B	RF	27	Reading Street	Pearson
Time to Eat	LB	I	3	Windows on Literacy	National Geographic
Time to Estimate	L	I	250+	Yellow Umbrella Books	Capstone Press
Time to Go	D	F	89	Literacy by Design	Rigby
Time to Go	D	F	89	On Our Way to English	Rigby
Time to Play!	H	RF	161	Gray, Nigel	Candlewick Press
Time to Play!	C	RF	70	InfoTrek	ETA/Cuisenaire
Time to Sleep	C	I	52	Independent Readers Science	Houghton Mifflin Harcourt
Time to Sleep	B	I	44	Sails	Rigby
Time to Sleep, A	I	I	239	Sails	Rigby
Time to Swim	B	F	36	Tiny Treasures	Pioneer Valley
Time to Tell Time	L	I	116	Spyglass Books	Compass Point Books
Time to Unite, A	V	I	1327	Vocabulary Readers	Houghton Mifflin Harcourt
Time to Unite, A	V	I	1327	Vocabulary Readers/CA	Houghton Mifflin Harcourt
Time to Wake Up!	D	RF	54	Bonnell, Kris	Reading Reading Books
#Time Travel Trap, The	U	F	10548	Twisted Journeys	Graphic Universe
Time Travel: Pioneer Community	O	SF	250+	InfoTrek	ETA/Cuisenaire
Time Travel: Pioneer Tools	O	SF	250+	InfoTrek	ETA/Cuisenaire
*Time Travelers' Handbook, The	U	I	250+	Stride, Lottie	Feiwel and Friends
Time Travelers: Adventures in Archaeology	W	I	250+	PM Collection	Rigby
Time Warp, The	N	SF	1684	Take Two Books	Wright Group/McGraw Hill
Timedetectors	V	SF	250+	Literacy 2000	Rigby
Timedetectors	N	SF	250+	Supa Doopers	Sundance
Timekeepers, The	Y	I	3385	Leveled Readers	Houghton Mifflin Harcourt
Timekeepers, The	Y	I	3385	Leveled Readers/CA	Houghton Mifflin Harcourt
Timekeepers, The	Y	I	3385	Leveled Readers/TX	Houghton Mifflin Harcourt

* Collection of short stories   # Graphic text
^ Mature content with lower level text demands

TITLE	LEVEL	GENRE	WORD COUNT	AUTHOR / SERIES	PUBLISHER / DISTRIBUTOR
Timeline of Electricity	S	I	948	Leveled Readers Science	Houghton Mifflin Harcourt
Timelock	Y	F	250+	Klass, David	Farrar, Straus, & Giroux
Times of the Day	H	I	169	Measuring Time	Heinemann Library
Time's Up!	L	F	250+	Sunshine	Wright Group/McGraw Hill
Time-Travel: Pioneer Children	O	SF	250+	InfoTrek	ETA/Cuisenaire
Time-Travel: Pioneer Food	O	SF	250+	InfoTrek	ETA/Cuisenaire
Timid Boy and Mama Bear a Pueblo Legend	L	TL	543	Leveled Readers	Houghton Mifflin Harcourt
Timid Boy and Mama Bear, A Pueblo Legend	L	TL	543	Leveled Readers/CA	Houghton Mifflin Harcourt
Timid Boy and Mama Bear, A Pueblo Legend	L	TL	543	Leveled Readers/TX	Houghton Mifflin Harcourt
Timmy	E	RF	54	Literacy 2000	Rigby
Timmy Tries	C	RF	22	Little Celebrations	Pearson Learning Group
Timothy Turtle	G	F	146	Dominie Readers	Pearson Learning Group
Timothy Whuffenpuffen-Whippersnapper	S	F	250+	Literacy 2000	Rigby
Timothy's Five-City Tour	M	F	250+	Pair-It Books	Steck-Vaughn
Tim's Bedtime	J	F	250+	Supersonics	Rigby
Tim's Favorite Toy	F	RF	202	PM Extensions-Blue	Rigby
Tim's Garden	C	RF	31	Reading Street	Pearson
Tim's Ice Cream Store	I	I	143	Windows on Literacy	National Geographic
Tim's Paintings	A	RF	33	Smart Start	Rigby
Tim's Pig	B	F	41	Leveled Readers	Houghton Mifflin Harcourt
Tim's Pig Eats	B	F	39	Leveled Readers Language Support	Houghton Mifflin Harcourt
Tim's Pumpkin	I	RF	250+	Home Connection Collection	Rigby
Tin Can Man, The	E	RF	105	Real Kids Readers	Millbrook Press
Tin Lizzy	K	F	500	Red Rocket Readers	Flying Start Books
Tin Lizzy	M	RF	425	Windmill Books	Rigby
Tin Treasures	J	I	250+	Greetings	Rigby
Tina and The Statue of Liberty	M	F	965	In Step Readers	Rigby
Tina's Taxi	F	RF	83	Franco, Betsy	Scholastic
Tink	Z	RF	250+	Bredsdorff, Bodil	Farrar, Straus, & Giroux
*Tiny & Hercules	M	F	250+	Schwartz, Amy	Roaring Brook Press
Tiny and the Big Wave	F	RF	163	PM Extensions-Yellow	Rigby
Tiny Baby Kangaroos	L	I	296	Leveled Readers	Houghton Mifflin Harcourt
Tiny Baby Kangaroos	L	I	296	Leveled Readers/CA	Houghton Mifflin Harcourt
Tiny Baby Kangaroos	L	I	296	Leveled Readers/TX	Houghton Mifflin Harcourt
Tiny Christmas Elf, The	G	F	173	First Start	Troll Associates
Tiny Creatures	J	I	250+	Discovery World	Rigby
Tiny Dinosaurs	L	RF	250+	PM Story Books	Rigby
Tiny Family, A	I	F	250+	Bridwell, Norman	Scholastic
Tiny Island Fever	P	F	250+	Scooters	ETA/Cuisenaire
Tiny Little Woman, The	D	F	74	Joy Readers	Pearson Learning Group
Tiny Seed, The	L	F	250+	Carle, Eric	Aladdin
Tiny Teddies' Picnic, The	D	RF	103	PM Photo Stories	Rigby
Tiny Tiger	J	F	328	Let's Read Together	Kane Press
Tiny Woman's Coat, The	H	F	147	Sunshine	Wright Group/McGraw Hill
Tiny Workers: Ants in Your Backyard	M	I	250+	Backyard Bugs	Picture Window Books
Tiny's Big Adventure	J	F	234	Waddell, Martin	Candlewick Press
Tippu	K	F	250+	Soar To Success	Houghton Mifflin Harcourt
Tip-Tap Pop	N	RF	250+	Lynn, Sarah	Marshall Cavendish
Tiptoe Round the Corner	H	F	96	Voyages	SRA/McGraw Hill
Tires	F	RF	180	Foundations	Wright Group/McGraw Hill
Tisquantum and the Pilgrims	R	B	250+	Harcourt Trophies	Harcourt, Inc.
^Titan Clash	V	RF	250+	Orca Sports	Orca Books
Titanic	S	HF	250+	Duey, Kathleen; Bale, Karen A.	Simon & Schuster

T

TITLE	LEVEL	GENRE	WORD COUNT	AUTHOR / SERIES	PUBLISHER / DISTRIBUTOR
Titanic Crossing	R	HF	250+	Williams, Barbara	Scholastic
Titanic Disaster at Sea	U	I	250+	Jenkins, Martin	Candlewick Press
Titanic Disaster Inquiry, The	Y	I	2862	Vocabulary Readers	Houghton Mifflin Harcourt
Titanic Disaster Inquiry, The	Y	I	2862	Vocabulary Readers/CA	Houghton Mifflin Harcourt
Titanic Sinks!, The	T	I	250+	Conklin, Thomas	Random House
Titanic, The	V	I	250+	Cornerstones of Freedom	Children's Press
Titanic, The	O	I	727	Rigby Flying Colors	Rigby
^Titanic, The: An Interactive History Adventure	T	HF	250+	You Choose Books	Capstone Press
Titanic, The: Lost . . . and Found	N	I	250+	Donnelly, Judy	Random House
Titan's Curse, The	W	F	250+	Riordan, Rick	Hyperion
Titch	G	RF	121	Hutchins, Pat	Penguin Group
Title IX	Y	I	2959	Leveled Readers	Houghton Mifflin Harcourt
Title IX	Y	I	2959	Leveled Readers/CA	Houghton Mifflin Harcourt
Title IX	Y	I	2959	Leveled Readers/TX	Houghton Mifflin Harcourt
Title Run	W	RF	250+	Redline Racing Series	Fitzhenry & Whiteside
Tittle-Tattle Goose	E	F	117	Story Box	Wright Group/McGraw Hill
TJ and the Cats	O	RF	250+	Orca Young Readers	Orca Books
TJ and the Haunted House	O	RF	250+	Orca Young Readers	Orca Books
TJ and the Quiz Kids	O	RF	250+	Orca Young Readers	Orca Books
TJ and the Rockets	O	RF	250+	Orca Young Readers	Orca Books
TJ and the Sports Fanatic	O	RF	250+	Orca Young Readers	Orca Books
To Bathe a Boa	L	F	297	Kudrna, C. Imbior	Carolrhoda Books
To Be a Kid	I	I	124	Ajmera, Maya & Ivanko, John D.	Charlesbridge
To Be a King: Guardians of Ga'Hoole	V	F	250+	Lasky, Kathryn	Scholastic
To Be a Slave	Z	I	250+	Lester, Julius	Dial/Penguin
To Be Free	T	HF	250+	Power Up!	Steck-Vaughn
To Be Tall	D	RF	42	Dominie Math Stories	Pearson Learning Group
To Build or Not to Build?	X	RF	3029	Leveled Readers	Houghton Mifflin Harcourt
To Build or Not To Build?	X	RF	3029	Leveled Readers/CA	Houghton Mifflin Harcourt
To Build or Not To Build?	X	RF	3029	Leveled Readers/TX	Houghton Mifflin Harcourt
To Catch a Cold	I	RF	774	Spirn, Michele	January Books
To Catch a Mermaid	S	F	250+	Selfors, Suzanne	Little Brown and Company
To Fly with the Swallows: A Story of Old California	S	I	250+	deRuiz, Dana Catharine	Steck-Vaughn
To Grandma's House	D	RF	73	Math Stories	Pearson Learning Group
To JJ From CC	P	RF	250+	Literacy 2000	Rigby
To Kill a Mockingbird	Z	HF	250+	Lee, Harper	Warner Books
To Market, To Market	Q	I	1245	Reading Street	Pearson
*To Market, To Market	I	TL	393	Story Box	Wright Group/McGraw Hill
To New York	D	RF	32	Story Box	Wright Group/McGraw Hill
To Reach the Top	R	I	250+	Power Up!	Steck-Vaughn
To Root, to Toot, to Parachute: What is a Verb?	O	I	382	Words Are CATegorical	Millbrook Press
To School	A	F	22	Sunshine	Wright Group/McGraw Hill
To Space and Back	T	I	250+	Ride, Sally	Beech Tree Books
To Stand Forever	T	HF	250+	Literacy by Design	Rigby
To Tell the Truth, A Native American Cinderella Tale	L	TL	250+	Leveled Readers Language Support	Houghton Mifflin Harcourt
To the Beach	D	RF	43	Urmston, Kathleen; Evans, Karen	Kaeden Books
To the Moon and Beyond	S	I	250+	Sunshine	Wright Group/McGraw Hill
To the Moon!	S	SF	1767	Reading Street	Pearson
To the Ocean	C	I	26	Twig	Wright Group/McGraw Hill
To the Point: A Story About E.B. White	R	B	6638	Creative Minds Biographies	Carolrhoda Books
To the Rescue	P	I	250+	InfoQuest	Rigby
To the Rescue	T	I	250+	WorldScapes	ETA/Cuisenaire

* Collection of short stories   # Graphic text
^ Mature content with lower level text demands

TITLE	LEVEL	GENRE	WORD COUNT	AUTHOR / SERIES	PUBLISHER / DISTRIBUTOR
To the Space Station	D	F	89	Springboard	Wright Group/McGraw Hill
To the Top of Mount Everest	T	I	2432	Leveled Readers Science	Houghton Mifflin Harcourt
To the Top!: Climbing the World's Highest Mountain	N	B	250+	Kramer, Sydelle	Random House
To Town	F	F	148	Story Box	Wright Group/McGraw Hill
To Trade or Not To Trade	T	I	250+	On Our Way to English	Rigby
To Wake a King	L	F	250+	Sun Sprouts	ETA/Cuisenaire
To Work	C	RF	43	Sunshine	Wright Group/McGraw Hill
Toad for Tuesday, A	O	F	250+	Erickson, Russell E.	Beech Tree Books
Toad or Frog?	I	I	134	Seedlings	Continental Press
Toad Takes Off	I	F	216	Schade, Susan; Buller, John	Random House
Toads and Diamonds	V	F	250+	Tomlinson, Heather	Henry Holt & Co.
Toad's Birthday	E	F	135	Leveled Readers	Houghton Mifflin Harcourt
Toad's Birthday	E	F	135	Leveled Readers/CA	Houghton Mifflin Harcourt
Toad's Birthday	E	F	135	Leveled Readers/TX	Houghton Mifflin Harcourt
Toast	F	RF	240	Bonnell, Kris	Reading Reading Books
Toast	C	RF	82	First Stories	Pacific Learning
Toast for Mom	I	RF	250+	Ready Readers	Pearson Learning Group
Toby	C	F	40	McAlpin, MaryAnn	Short Tales Press
Toby Alone	Z	F	250+	de Fombelle, Tomothee	Candlewick Press
Toby and B. J.	I	F	307	PM Story Books-Orange	Rigby
Toby and the Accident	J	F	329	PM Story Books	Rigby
Toby and the Big Red Van	I	F	291	PM Story Books-Orange	Rigby
Toby and the Big Tree	I	F	298	PM Story Books-Orange	Rigby
Toby at Stony Bay	J	F	494	PM Story Books	Rigby
Toby Tomato	D	F	54	Little Celebrations	Pearson Learning Group
Toby's Great Day	I	RF	190	Reading Safari	Mondo Publishing
Toby's New Home	H	F	238	McAlpin, MaryAnn	Short Tales Press
Toby's Vacation	R	RF	1596	Reading Street	Pearson
Toc's Chicken Pox	I	RF	250+	The Rowland Reading Program Library	Rowland Reading Foundation
Today	I	RF	151	Early Connections	Benchmark Education
Today and Long Ago	F	I	125	Rigby Star Quest	Rigby
Today I Got Yelled At	J	RF	174	City Kids	Rigby
Today Is Monday	E	TL	103	Instant Readers	Harcourt School Publishers
Today: August 17, 1929	O	F	250+	Tristars	Richard C. Owen
Today's Weather Is . . . A Book of Experiments	O	I	250+	Bookshop	Mondo Publishing
Todd's Teacher	F	RF	200	Cherrington, Janelle	Scholastic
Todd's Tomatoes	J	RF	480	Leveled Readers	Houghton Mifflin Harcourt
Todd's Tomatoes	J	RF	480	Leveled Readers/CA	Houghton Mifflin Harcourt
Toenails	E	I	83	Voyages	SRA/McGraw Hill
Toes	L	I	250+	Sunshine	Wright Group/McGraw Hill
Together	C	RF	37	Sunshine	Wright Group/McGraw Hill
Together and Apart	D	I	33	Shutterbug Books	Steck-Vaughn
Together for Thanksgiving	I	I	154	Reading Street	Pearson
Toilet Paper Tigers, The	Q	RF	250+	Korman, Gordon	Bantam Books
Tokyo Japan's Capital	J	I	208	In Step Readers	Rigby
Tolerance	L	I	250+	Character Education	Red Brick Learning
Tolerance	M	I	250+	Everyday Character Education	Capstone Press
Toliver's Secret	T	HF	250+	Brady, Esther Wood	Alfred A. Knopf
Tom	A	RF	24	Leveled Literacy Intervention/ Orange System	Heinemann
Tom and His Tractor	C	RF	27	Cat on the Mat	Oxford University Press
Tom and Pam	E	RF	69	Reading Street	Pearson

TITLE	LEVEL	GENRE	WORD COUNT	AUTHOR / SERIES	PUBLISHER / DISTRIBUTOR
Tom Brady	P	B	1599	Amazing Athletes	Lerner Publishing Group
Tom Brady	U	B	21355	Sports Heroes and Legends	Lerner Publishing Group
Tom Edison's Bright Idea	N	B	250+	Keller, Jack	Steck-Vaughn
Tom Gets Fit	D	RF	150	New Way Red	Steck-Vaughn
Tom Is Brave	D	RF	57	PM Story Books	Rigby
Tom Sawyer	J	B	250+	Jumbled Tumbled Tales & Rhymes	Rigby
Tom the TV Cat	J	F	250+	Heilbroner, Joan	Random House
Tom Thumb	E	TL	296	Fairy Tales and Folklore	Norwood House Press
#Tom Thumb	N	TL	250+	Graphic Spin	Stone Arch Books
Tom Turkey and Erik Eagle	O	F	250+	Davidson, Sandra Calder	Arcade Publishing
Tom Turtle	D	F	87	Hill, Christopher	Ginn & Co.
*Tom, Babette & Simon	T	F	250+	Avi	Avon Books
Tom, the Dragon	M	F	522	New Way Orange	Steck-Vaughn
Tomahawk Beckwourth	T	B	250+	High-Fliers	Pacific Learning
Tomato Picking Day	L	I	250+	Take Two Books	Wright Group/McGraw Hill
Tomato Rose	I	RF	250+	Phonics Readers Plus	Steck-Vaughn
Tomato Soup	K	F	250+	Hurd, Thacher	Crown Publishers
Tomatoes	F	I	94	Plant Life Cycles	Lerner Publishing Group
Tomatoes	M	I	250+	Take Two Books	Wright Group/McGraw Hill
Tomatoes and Bricks	E	RF	126	Windmill Books	Wright Group/McGraw Hill
Tomatoes Everywhere	J	I	162	On Our Way to English	Rigby
Tomatoes Grow on a Vine	K	I	160	How Fruits and Vegetables Grow	Capstone Press
Tomb of Nebamun, The	S	I	250+	Cambridge Reading	Pearson Learning Group
Tomb Raiders	U	I	250+	High-Fliers	Pacific Learning
Tomie dePaola	L	B	196	First Biographies	Red Brick Learning
Tommy Douglas	X	B	250+	The Canadians	Fitzhenry & Whiteside
Tommy Snake's Problem	H	F	328	TOTTS	Tott Publications
Tommy Thompson's Ship of Gold	P	I	685	Leveled Readers	Houghton Mifflin Harcourt
Tommy's Treasure	I	RF	232	Literacy 2000	Rigby
Tommy's Tummy Ache	C	F	20	Literacy 2000	Rigby
Tomoko's Playhouse	D	RF	82	Reading Safari	Mondo Publishing
Tomorrow's Energy	Q	I	250+	Orbit Chapter Books	Pacific Learning
Tomorrow's Wizard	R	F	250+	MacLachlan, Patricia	Scholastic
Tom's Box	I	F	250+	Cambridge Reading	Pearson Learning Group
Tom's Friend	M	RF	250+	Voyages	SRA/McGraw Hill
Tom's Midnight Garden	V	F	250+	Pearce, Philippa	HarperTrophy
Tom's Ride	G	RF	185	PM Plus Story Books	Rigby
Tom's Rubber Band	E	RF	82	Sunshine	Wright Group/McGraw Hill
Tom's Trousers	G	RF	173	Storyteller-Night Crickets	Wright Group/McGraw Hill
Tom's Zoo	Q	I	250+	Trackers	Pacific Learning
Tomßs and the Library Lady	N	HF	1205	Avenues	Hampton Brown
Tom-Ti-Ra and the Mysterious Noise	B	F	26	Book Bus	Creative Edge
Tongue Twister Prize, The	J	RF	331	Little Books	Sadlier-Oxford
Tongues	H	I	223	Sails	Rigby
Tongues Are for Tasting, Licking, Tricking	L	I	250+	Literacy 2000	Rigby
Toni Morrison: Author	N	B	250+	Beginning Biographies	Pearson Learning Group
Tonight on the Titanic	M	F	250+	Osborne, Mary Pope	Random House
Toning the Sweep	Z	RF	250+	Johnson, Angela	Scholastic
Tony and the Butterfly	J	RF	250+	Literacy Tree	Rigby
Tony Blair	X	B	250+	A&E Biography	Lerner Publishing Group
Tony Dungy	U	B	20198	Sports Heroes and Legends	Lerner Publishing Group
Tony Hawk	P	B	1640	Amazing Athletes	Lerner Publishing Group
Tony Hawk	U	B	250+	The Heinle Reading Library	Thomson Learning

Organized Alphabetically by Title
Storable Database at www.fountasandpinnellleveledbooks.com

* Collection of short stories   # Graphic text
^ Mature content with lower level text demands

TITLE	LEVEL	GENRE	WORD COUNT	AUTHOR / SERIES	PUBLISHER / DISTRIBUTOR
Tony Hawk: Skateboarding Legend	Q	B	250+	Skateboarding	Capstone Press
Tony Romo	P	B	2045	Amazing Athletes	Lerner Publishing Group
Tony the Shoemaker	J	I	194	Dominie Factivity Series	Pearson Learning Group
Tony's Dad	J	RF	399	Sails	Rigby
Tony's Taxi	LB	I	7	Reading Street	Pearson
Tony's Trail	S	RF	2333	Leveled Readers	Houghton Mifflin Harcourt
Tony's Trail	S	RF	2333	Leveled Readers/CA	Houghton Mifflin Harcourt
Too Big and Heavy	I	F	405	Red Rocket Readers	Flying Start Books
Too Big for Me	D	F	70	Story Box	Wright Group/McGraw Hill
Too Big for Me!	C	RF	90	First Stories	Pacific Learning
Too Big to Play	E	RF	162	Bonnell, Kris	Reading Reading Books
Too Busy for Pets!	J	RF	472	Sunshine	Wright Group/McGraw Hill
Too Close to the Sun	P	TL	250+	Windows on Literacy	National Geographic
Too Fast	A	F	36	Reading Corners	Pearson Learning Group
Too High!	D	RF	66	Ready Readers	Pearson Learning Group
Too Hot to Handle	Q	RF	250+	Christopher, Matt	Little Brown and Company
Too Hot!	C	RF	39	Lighthouse	Rigby
Too Late!	G	F	226	Foundations	Wright Group/McGraw Hill
Too Little	E	RF	119	Foundations	Wright Group/McGraw Hill
Too Little	D	RF	83	Sun Sprouts	ETA/Cuisenaire
Too Many Animals	G	F	111	Alphakids	Sundance
Too Many Animals on a Raft	D	F	109	Larkin's Little Readers	Wilbooks
Too Many Babas	K	TL	250+	Croll, Carolyn	HarperTrophy
Too Many Babas	K	TL	250+	Little Readers	Houghton Mifflin Harcourt
Too Many Balloons	D	RF	182	Rookie Readers	Children's Press
*Too Many Bones	G	F	125	New Way Blue	Steck-Vaughn
Too Many Cars	LB	RF	15	Hartley, Susan; Armstrong, Shane	Scholastic
Too Many Clothes	C	RF	24	Literacy 2000	Rigby
Too Many Dogs	B	F	28	Dominie Math Stories	Pearson Learning Group
Too Many Fairies: A Celtic Tale	N	TL	250+	MacDonald, Margaret Read	Marshall Cavendish
Too Many Mice	J	F	250+	Bank Street	Bantam Books
Too Many Nuts	H	RF	132	Books for Young Learners	Richard C. Owen
Too Many Pets	D	RF	93	Rigby Rocket	Rigby
Too Many Puppies	J	RF	250+	Brewster, Patience	Scholastic
Too Many Rabbits	J	RF	250+	Parish, Peggy	Bantam Books
Too Many Seagulls	F	RF	150	Kaleidoscope Collection	Hameray Publishing Group
Too Many Signs!	L	RF	978	Leveled Readers	Houghton Mifflin Harcourt
Too Many Signs!	L	RF	978	Leveled Readers/CA	Houghton Mifflin Harcourt
Too Many Signs!	L	RF	978	Leveled Readers/TX	Houghton Mifflin Harcourt
Too Many Steps	J	RF	424	Foundations	Wright Group/McGraw Hill
Too Many Tamales	M	RF	250+	Soto, Gary	G.P. Putnam's Sons Books for Young Readers
Too Many Teeth	L	F	487	Leveled Literacy Intervention/Blue System	Heinemann
Too Many Tickets	N	RF	250+	On Our Way to English	Rigby
Too Much	B	RF	27	Teacher's Choice Series	Pearson Learning Group
Too Much Ketchup	D	F	30	Ready Readers	Pearson Learning Group
Too Much Magic	R	F	250+	Sterman, Betsy & Samuel	HarperTrophy
Too Much Noise	H	TL	340	Literacy 2000	Rigby
Too Much Noise	J	TL	250+	McGovern, Ann	Scholastic
Too Much Rain: Katie Woo	J	RF	250+	Manushkin, Fran	Picture Window Books
Too Much Stuff	B	F	75	Leveled Literacy Intervention/Green System	Heinemann
Too Much Stuff!	M	RF	250+	Literacy by Design	Rigby

TITLE	LEVEL	GENRE	WORD COUNT	AUTHOR / SERIES	PUBLISHER / DISTRIBUTOR
*Too Much Talk and Other Stories	J	TL	250+	New Way Literature	Steck-Vaughn
Too Much Talk!	I	TL	250+	Rigby Star	Rigby
Too Much Trouble for Grandpa	K	F	250+	Lewis, Rob	Mondo Publishing
Too Much Trouble for Grandpa	J	F	250+	Sokoloff, Myka-Lynne	Sadlier-Oxford
Too Much!	C	RF	73	The King School Series	Townsend Press
Too Pickley!	I	RF	47	Reidy, Jean	Bloomsbury Children's Books
Too Purpley!	I	RF	48	Reidy, Jean,	Bloomsbury Children's Books
Too Small Jill	J	RF	306	Little Books	Sadlier-Oxford
Too Small!	I	RF	245	InfoTrek	ETA/Cuisenaire
Too Soon to Say Goodbye	S	RF	250+	Kent, Deborah	Scholastic
Too Tall	J	F	423	Leveled Literacy Intervention/ Green System	Heinemann
Too Tall Tina	J	RF	250+	Math Matters	Kane Press
Too-Good-to-Be-True Shoes	O	F	250+	High-Fliers	Pacific Learning
Tool Box, The	H	RF	144	Rockwell, Anne	Macmillan
Tools and Gadgets	T	I	250+	Historic Communities	Crabtree
Tools Can Help Us See	G	I	107	Windows on Literacy	National Geographic
Tools Measure Weather	I	I	145	Windows on Literacy	National Geographic
Tools of Investigators, The	M	I	575	Vocabulary Readers	Houghton Mifflin Harcourt
Tools of Investigators, The	M	I	575	Vocabulary Readers/CA	Houghton Mifflin Harcourt
Tools Scientists Use	K	I	184	Windows on Literacy	National Geographic
Tools to Use	D	I	42	Little Red Readers	Sundance
#Toon Treasury of Classic Children's Comics, The	T	F	250+	Spiegelman, Art & Mouly, Francoise	Abrams Comicarts
Toot & Puddle: A Present for Toot	M	F	250+	Hobbie, Holly	Little Brown and Company
Toot & Puddle: Charming Opal	M	F	250+	Hobbie, Holly	Little Brown and Company
Toot & Puddle: I'll Be Home For Christmas	M	F	250+	Hobbie, Holly	Little Brown and Company
Toot & Puddle: Let It Snow	M	F	250+	Hobbie, Holly	Little Brown and Company
Toot & Puddle: Puddle's ABC	L	F	250+	Hobbie, Holly	Little Brown and Company
Toot & Puddle: The New Friend	M	F	250+	Hobbie, Holly	Little Brown and Company
Toot & Puddle: The One and Only	M	F	250+	Hobbie, Holly	Little Brown and Company
Toot & Puddle: Top of the World	M	F	250+	Hobbie, Holly	Little Brown and Company
Toot & Puddle: Wish You Were Here	M	F	250+	Hobbie, Holly	Little Brown and Company
Toot & Puddle: You Are My Sunshine	M	F	250+	Hobbie, Holly	Little Brown and Company
Toot and Puddle	M	F	250+	Hobbie, Holly	Little Brown and Company
Toot! Toot!	LB	F	21	Joy Readers	Pearson Learning Group
Toot, Toot	C	I	47	Wildsmith, Brian	Oxford University Press
Too-Tall Paul, Too-Small Paul	H	RF	325	Real Kids Readers	Millbrook Press
Tooter Pepperday	L	RF	250+	Spinelli, Jerry	Random House
*Tooth and Claw	W	F	8255	Oxford Bookworms Library	Oxford University Press
Tooth Fairy in Trouble	K	F	250+	I Am Reading	Kingfisher
Tooth Fairy Tells All, The	K	F	513	Silly Millies	Millbrook Press
Tooth Fairy, The	WB	F	0	Collington, Peter	Wright Group/McGraw Hill
Tooth Fairy, The	D	F	57	My First Reader	Grolier
Tooth Fairy's First Night	L	F	935	Bowen, Anne	Carolrhoda Books
Tooth on the Loose	H	RF	235	Literacy by Design	Rigby
Tooth Race, The	I	RF	250+	Little Readers	Houghton Mifflin Harcourt
Tooth Trouble	L	RF	250+	Klein, Abby	Scholastic
Toothbrush Tale	G	F	117	New Way Blue	Steck-Vaughn
Toothless!	M	F	250+	Rigby Gigglers	Rigby
Toothpaste Millionaire, The	T	RF	250+	Merrill, Jean	Houghton Mifflin Harcourt
Toothwalkers	N	I	250+	Sails	Rigby

T

* Collection of short stories   # Graphic text
^ Mature content with lower level text demands

TITLE	LEVEL	GENRE	WORD COUNT	AUTHOR / SERIES	PUBLISHER / DISTRIBUTOR
Too-Tight Shoes	I	RF	170	Evangeline Nicholas Collection	Wright Group/McGraw Hill
Top Cat	O	I	250+	Byars, Betsy	Penguin Group
Top Cat	K	F	250+	Story Steps	Rigby
Top Dinosaurs	I	I	176	Big Cat	Pacific Learning
Top Dog	H	F	250+	The Rowland Reading Program Library	Rowland Reading Foundation
Top Hat, the Detective	O	RF	1364	Reading Street	Pearson
Top Hats	K	I	250+	The Rowland Reading Program Libary	Rowland Reading Foundation
Top of the Order	U	RF	250+	Coy, John	Feiwel and Friends
Top of the World, The: Climbing Mount Everest	R	I	250+	Jenkins, Steve	Houghton Mifflin Harcourt
Top Secret: The World of Spies	Y	I	250+	Boldprint	Steck-Vaughn
*Top Ten Shakespeare Stories	Z	HF	250+	Terry, Deary	Scholastic
Top to Toe Counting	F	I	122	Red Rocket Readers	Flying Start Books
Tops & Bottoms	M	TL	250+	Stevens, Janet	Harcourt
Topsy-Turvy Bedtime	L	F	250+	Levine, Joan	Candlewick Press
Torn Thread	W	HF	250+	Isaacs, Anne	Scholastic
Tornado	O	I	250+	Byars, Betsy	HarperTrophy
Tornado	T	I	250+	Kramer, Stephen	Lerner Publishing Group
Tornado	E	I	37	Spinelle, Nancy Louise	Kaeden Books
Tornado Chasers	T	RF	1520	Independent Readers Science	Houghton Mifflin Harcourt
Tornado Tony	H	RF	182	Well-Being Series	Pearson Learning Group
Tornado Warning!	N	I	545	Gear Up!	Wright Group/McGraw Hill
Tornado Watch	O	I	250+	In Step Readers	Rigby
Tornado Watch	O	I	250+	Literacy by Design	Rigby
Tornado!	R	RF	1470	Leveled Readers Social Studies	Houghton Mifflin Harcourt
Tornado, The	L	RF	250+	PM Story Books	Rigby
Tornadoes	F	I	106	Bonnell, Kris/About	Reading Reading Books
Tornadoes	W	I	250+	Disasters Up Close	Lerner Publishing Group
Tornadoes	M	I	156	Earth in Action	Capstone Press
Tornadoes	S	I	250+	Natural Disasters	Capstone Press
Tornadoes	M	I	664	Pull Ahead Books	Lerner Publishing Group
Tornadoes	S	I	250+	Theme Sets	National Geographic
Tornadoes	O	I	250+	Weather Update	Capstone Press
Tornadoes and Hurricanes	L	I	393	Time for Kids	Teacher Created Materials
Tornadoes!	N	I	250+	Hopping, Lorraine Jean	Scholastic
Toronto Blue Jays, The	S	I	250+	Team Spirit	Norwood House Press
Toronto Blue Jays, The (Revised Edition)	S	I	250+	Team Spirit	Norwood House Press
Toronto Maple Leafs, The	S	I	5080	Team Spirit	Norwood House Press
Toronto Raptors, The	S	I	4091	Team Spirit	Norwood House Press
Tortilla Cat, The	P	F	250+	HSP/Harcourt Trophies	Harcourt, Inc.
Tortilla Factory, The	M	RF	1175	Reading Street	Pearson
Tortilla Sundays	E	RF	90	Kaleidoscope Collection	Hameray Publishing Group
Tortillas	E	RF	71	Gonzalez-Jensen, Margarita	Scholastic
Tortillas and Lullabies	I	RF	151	Reiser, Lynn	Greenwillow Books
Tortoise and the Hare Race Again, The	N	TL	250+	Bernstein, Dan	Holiday House
Tortoise and the Hare, The	L	TL	250+	Storybook Classics	Picture Window Books
Tortoise and the Hare,The	H	TL	148	Cambridge Reading	Pearson Learning Group
Tortoise and the Jackrabbit, The	M	TL	250+	Lowell, Susan	Rising Moon
*Tortoise Shell and Other African Stories, The	N	TL	250+	Smith, Geof	Scholastic
Tortoise Soup!	K	TL	753	PM Stars Bridge Books	Rigby
Tortoise's Trick	L	TL	607	Red Rocket Readers	Flying Start Books
Toss It	C	RF	37	The Rowland Reading Program Library	Rowland Reading Foundation

T

TITLE	LEVEL	GENRE	WORD COUNT	AUTHOR / SERIES	PUBLISHER / DISTRIBUTOR
Tossed Salad	C	I	28	Twig	Wright Group/McGraw Hill
Total Eclipse of the Sun	W	I	250+	Independent Readers Science	Houghton Mifflin Harcourt
Totally Extreme Sports : A Quiz	P	I	250+	Trackers	Pacific Learning
Totara Tree, The	M	RF	391	Book Bank	Wright Group/McGraw Hill
Totem Poles	D	I	46	Leveled Readers Social Studies	Houghton Mifflin Harcourt
Totem Poles	L	I	246	Twig	Wright Group/McGraw Hill
Totem Poles of North America	D	I	42	Leveled Readers Social Studies	Houghton Mifflin Harcourt
Touch	O	SF	250+	Sails	Rigby
Touch	C	I	39	Twig	Wright Group/McGraw Hill
Touch Blue	R	RF	250+	Lord, Cynthia	Scholastic
Touch It!	E	I	61	Shutterbug Books	Steck-Vaughn
*Touch of Gold and Other Stories, The	M	TL	250+	Lane, Sheila; Kemp, Marion	Wood Lock Educational
Touch of Sepia, A	M	RF	250+	Voyages	SRA/McGraw Hill
Touch the Earth	L	RF	250+	Bookshop	Mondo Publishing
Touch the Moon	H	F	238	Gear Up!	Wright Group/McGraw Hill
Touchdown for Tommy	Q	RF	250+	Christopher, Matt	Little Brown and Company
Touchdown Trouble	R	RF	250+	Bowen, Fred	Peachtree
Touchdown!	X	I	250+	Boldprint	Steck-Vaughn
Touchdown! Dear Dragon	E	F	188	Dear Dragon	Norwood House Press
Touchdown!: You Can Play Football	M	I	250+	Game Day	Picture Window Books
Touching	J	I	142	Pebble Books	Capstone Press
Touching	E	I	92	Senses	Lerner Publishing Group
Touching	M	I	250+	The Senses	Capstone Press
Touching Spirit Bear	Y	F	250+	Mikaelsen, Ben	HarperCollins
Tough Choices	W	RF	250+	Power Up!	Steck-Vaughn
Tough Nut to Crack, A	Q	RF	250+	Birdseye, Tom	Holiday House
Tough Times	S	I	970	Vocabulary Readers	Houghton Mifflin Harcourt
Tough Times	S	I	970	Vocabulary Readers/CA	Houghton Mifflin Harcourt
Tough Times	S	I	970	Vocabulary Readers/TX	Houghton Mifflin Harcourt
^Tough Trails	U	RF	250+	Orca Soundings	Orca Books
Toughboy & Sister	S	RF	250+	Hill, Kirkpatrick	Puffin Books
Touring the Cities of the World	U	I	250+	Explore More	Wright Group/McGraw Hill
Tourists	J	I	189	Larkin, Bruce	Wilbooks
Tournament Trouble	R	RF	250+	Costello, Emily	Dell
Tow Trucks	I	I	132	Mighty Machines	Capstone Press
Tow Trucks	L	I	493	Pull Ahead Books	Lerner Publishing Group
Tower, The	A	RF	40	InfoTrek	ETA/Cuisenaire
Tower, The	P	SF	250+	Orbit Double Takes	Pacific Learning
Towers	M	I	250+	Rigby Literacy	Rigby
Town Auction, The	M	RF	866	Leveled Readers	Houghton Mifflin Harcourt
Town Auction, The	M	RF	866	Leveled Readers/CA	Houghton Mifflin Harcourt
Town Auction, The	M	RF	866	Leveled Readers/TX	Houghton Mifflin Harcourt
Town in Trouble, A	P	F	1019	Leveled Readers	Houghton Mifflin Harcourt
Town Mouse and Country Mouse	E	TL	170	Folk Tales	Pioneer Valley
Town Mouse and Country Mouse	K	TL	250+	PM Tales and Plays-Purple	Rigby
Town Mouse and Country Mouse	I	TL	276	Sun Sprouts	ETA/Cuisenaire
Town Mouse and Country Mouse, The	I	TL	172	Aesop	Wright Group/McGraw Hill
Town Mouse and the Country Mouse, The	K	TL	250+	Aesop	Troll Associates
Town Mouse and the Country Mouse, The	F	TL	203	Storyworlds	Heinemann
^Toxic Waste: Chemical Spills in Our World	R	I	250+	On Deck	Rigby
Toy Box, A	LB	I	19	Literacy 2000	Rigby
Toy Box, The	B	I	49	PM Plus Starters	Rigby
Toy Box, The	LB	RF	14	Ready Readers	Pearson Learning Group
Toy Box, The	B	RF	49	Sun Sprouts	ETA/Cuisenaire

* Collection of short stories   # Graphic text
^ Mature content with lower level text demands

TITLE	LEVEL	GENRE	WORD COUNT	AUTHOR / SERIES	PUBLISHER / DISTRIBUTOR
Toy Farm, The	I	RF	311	PM Story Books-Orange	Rigby
Toy for Vik, A	C	RF	66	Rigby Rocket	Rigby
Toy Maker, The	B	RF	31	Ray's Readers	Outside the Box
Toy Models	A	I	40	Early Connections	Benchmark Education
Toy Shop, The	L	RF	250+	Book Project	Sundance
Toy Store	B	F	37	Reading Street	Pearson
Toy Store, The	B	RF	55	Leveled Readers Emergent	Houghton Mifflin Harcourt
Toy Tooth, The	I	RF	250+	Rigby Literacy	Rigby
Toy Town	C	I	36	Home Connection Collection	Rigby
Toy Trouble	H	F	250+	Bookshop	Mondo Publishing
Toy Trouble	K	F	250+	Martha Speaks	Houghton Mifflin Harcourt
Toymil and the Bear	I	RF	233	Story Box	Wright Group/McGraw Hill
Toys	B	RF	37	Foundations	Wright Group/McGraw Hill
Toys	A	RF	30	Leveled Literacy Intervention/ Orange System	Heinemann
Toys	E	I	76	Talk About Books	Pearson Learning Group
Toys	D	RF	106	Tiger Cub	Peguis
Toys	C	I	41	Windows on Literacy	National Geographic
Toys and Games Then and Now	H	I	111	Then and Now	Lerner Publishing Group
Toys and Play	F	RF	194	PM Plus Nonfiction	Rigby
Toys Can Move	LB	I	7	Windows on Literacy	National Geographic
Toys Go Out	N	F	250+	Jenkins, Emily	Yearling Books
Toys Long Ago	D	I	54	Yellow Umbrella Books	Red Brick Learning
Toys' Party, The	F	F	48	Oxford Reading Tree	Oxford University Press
Toys' Picnic, The	B	RF	67	First Stories	Pacific Learning
Toys That Can Go	B	I	44	Red Rocket Readers	Flying Start Books
Toys with Wheels	C	I	41	Home Connection Collection	Rigby
Toys, Then and Now	G	I	108	Take Two Books	Wright Group/McGraw Hill
Toytown Bus Helps Out, The	E	F	125	PM Stars	Rigby
Toytown Fire Engine, The	D	F	105	PM Plus Story Books	Rigby
Toytown Helicopter, The	D	F	97	PM Plus Story Books	Rigby
Toytown Race Car, The	F	F	188	PM Plus Story Books	Rigby
Toytown Rescue, The	D	F	100	PM Plus Story Books	Rigby
Tracey and the Sun	M	F	250+	Sails	Rigby
Tracing the Anasazi	P	I	830	Independent Readers Social Studies	Houghton Mifflin Harcourt
Tracing the Harlem Renaissance	W	I	1965	Vocabulary Readers	Houghton Mifflin Harcourt
Tracing the Harlem Renaissance	W	I	1965	Vocabulary Readers/CA	Houghton Mifflin Harcourt
Track	K	I	250+	On Deck	Rigby
Track and Field	M	I	788	Springboard	Wright Group/McGraw Hill
Track Attack	N	RF	250+	Hicks, Betty	Roaring Brook Press
Tracker	T	RF	250+	Paulsen, Gary	Scholastic
Trackers of Dynamic Earth	S	B	250+	Navigators Biography Series	Benchmark Education
Tracking Animal Migrators	T	I	250+	Reading Expeditions	National Geographic
#Tracking Bigfoot: An Isabel Soto Investigation Adventure	S	F	250+	Graphic Expeditions	Capstone Press
Tracking Our Class Garden	O	RF	2522	Reading Street	Pearson
Tracking the Caribou	O	I	250+	Lighthouse	Ginn & Co.
Tracking Trash: Flotsam, Jetsam, and the Science of Ocean Motions	W	I	250+	Burns, Loree Griffin	Houghton Mifflin Harcourt
Tracking Triple Seven	Z	RF	250+	Bastedo, Jamie	Fitzhenry & Whiteside
Tracking with Uncle Joe	K	RF	653	Appleton-Smith, Laura	Flyleaf Publishing
Tracks	C	I	25	Sunshine	Wright Group/McGraw Hill
Tracks	C	I	49	Twig	Wright Group/McGraw Hill

T

TITLE	LEVEL	GENRE	WORD COUNT	AUTHOR / SERIES	PUBLISHER / DISTRIBUTOR
Tracks	L	I	250+	Voyages	SRA/McGraw Hill
Tracks in the Sand	I	I	125	Levin, Amy	Scholastic
Tracks in the Sand	H	I	190	Sails	Rigby
Tracks in the Sand	L	I	250+	Sunshine	Wright Group/McGraw Hill
Tracks in the Snow	E	I	207	Sails	Rigby
Tracks in the Snow	G	RF	265	Yee, Wong Herbert	Square Fish
Tracks on the Ground	N	I	250+	Pacific Literacy	Pacific Learning
Tractor Trailers	N	I	250+	Transportation	Red Brick Learning
Tractors	M	I	250+	Transportation	Compass Point Books
Trading Places	L	RF	1063	Rigby Flying Colors	Rigby
Trading Talents	S	RF	1952	Leveled Readers	Houghton Mifflin Harcourt
Trading Talents	S	RF	1952	Leveled Readers/CA	Houghton Mifflin Harcourt
Trading Talents	S	RF	1952	Leveled Readers/TX	Houghton Mifflin Harcourt
Tradition of the Harvest, The	P	RF	250+	Leveled Readers Language Support	Houghton Mifflin Harcourt
Traditional Crafts of Mexico	Q	I	1053	Reading Street	Pearson
Traffic	A	I	28	Leveled Literacy Intervention/ Green System	Heinemann
Traffic	A	I	30	Lighthouse	Rigby
Traffic Jam	F	RF	55	City Stories	Rigby
Traffic Jam	C	RF	76	First Stories	Pacific Learning
Traffic Jam	E	RF	133	Harper, Leslie	Kaeden Books
Traffic Jam	D	RF	18	Little Red Readers	Sundance
Traffic Jam	LB	RF	18	Voyages	SRA/McGraw Hill
Traffic Jam, The	A	RF	33	Handprints B	Educators Publishing Service
Traffic Light Rap	I	RF	261	Sun Sprouts	ETA/Cuisenaire
Traffic Light Sandwich	H	I	87	Wonder World	Wright Group/McGraw Hill
Trail Home, The	S	RF	2004	Leveled Readers	Houghton Mifflin Harcourt
Trail of Bones	U	SF	250+	Williams, Mark London	Candlewick Press
Trail of Tears, 1838, The	V	I	250+	Let Freedom Ring	Capstone Press
Trail of Tears, The	R	I	250+	Bruchac, Joseph	Random House
Trailblazers!	O	RF	250+	Action Packs	Rigby
Train	V	I	250+	Eyewitness Books	DK Publishing
Train Ghost, The	G	RF	224	The Joy Cowley Collection	Hameray Publishing Group
Train Music	N	RF	250+	PM Extensions	Rigby
Train Ride	C	RF	15	Bebop Books	Lee & Low Books Inc.
Train Ride Story, The	I	F	189	Sunshine	Wright Group/McGraw Hill
Train Ride, The	D	RF	127	In Step Readers	Rigby
Train Ride, The	C	F	29	Literacy 2000	Rigby
Train that Ran Away	I	F	32	Jellybeans	Rigby
Train Time	L	I	250+	Baehr, Lisa	Hampton Brown
Train to the West?	O	I	279	Vocabulary Readers	Houghton Mifflin Harcourt
Train Trip, A	L	I	172	Vocabulary Readers	Houghton Mifflin Harcourt
Train Wreck	S	HF	250+	Duey, Kathleen; Bale, Karen A.	Simon & Schuster
Train Wreck!	T	I	2383	Reading Street	Pearson
Train, Car, Boat, Plane	E	RF	180	Leveled Readers	Houghton Mifflin Harcourt
Train, Car, Boat, Plane	E	RF	180	Leveled Readers/CA	Houghton Mifflin Harcourt
Train, The	C	I	38	Gear Up!	Wright Group/McGraw Hill
Train, The	C	RF	27	Visions	Wright Group/McGraw Hill
Training a Dog	M	I	591	Vocabulary Readers	Houghton Mifflin Harcourt
Training a Dog	M	I	591	Vocabulary Readers/CA	Houghton Mifflin Harcourt
Training a Guide Dog	N	I	250+	Literacy by Design	Rigby
Training a Police Dog	G	I	103	Vocabulary Readers	Houghton Mifflin Harcourt

* Collection of short stories   # Graphic text
^ Mature content with lower level text demands

TITLE	LEVEL	GENRE	WORD COUNT	AUTHOR / SERIES	PUBLISHER / DISTRIBUTOR
Training for Space	T	I	508	Vocabulary Readers	Houghton Mifflin Harcourt
Training for the Olympics	T	I	1381	Independent Readers Science	Houghton Mifflin Harcourt
Training My Dog	L	I	917	Leveled Readers Science	Houghton Mifflin Harcourt
Training Peanut	M	RF	1278	Reading Street	Pearson
Training Pickles	I	RF	350	PM Stars Bridge Books	Rigby
Trains	H	I	250+	Albanese, Rachel	Scholastic
Trains	N	I	461	Leveled Readers Language Support	Houghton Mifflin Harcourt
Trains	Q	I	250+	Literacy 2000	Rigby
Trains	H	I	122	Mighty Machines	Capstone Press
Trains	M	I	525	Nonfiction Crimson	Pioneer Valley
Trains	K	I	339	Pull Ahead Books	Lerner Publishing Group
Trains	E	I	137	Sails	Rigby
Trains	F	I	146	Springboard	Wright Group/McGraw Hill
Trains	T	I	250+	The World's Fastest	Red Brick Learning
Trains	A	I	36	Vocabulary Readers	Houghton Mifflin Harcourt
Trains	A	I	36	Vocabulary Readers/CA	Houghton Mifflin Harcourt
Trains	A	I	36	Vocabulary Readers/TX	Houghton Mifflin Harcourt
Trains and How They Work	Q	I	895	Time for Kids	Teacher Created Materials
^Trains of the Past	M	I	250+	On Deck	Rigby
Trains on the Move	K	I	339	Lightning Bolt Books	Lerner Publishing Group
Trains on the Rails	K	I	250+	PM Plus	Rigby
Trains!	M	I	250+	Step Into Reading	Random House
Trains: Steaming! Pulling! Huffing!	L	RF	224	Hubbell, Patricia	Marshall Cavendish
TrainTrip, A	L	I	172	Vocabulary Readers/CA	Houghton Mifflin Harcourt
Traitor Game, The	Z+	F	250+	Collins, B.R.	Bloomsbury Children's Books
Traitor: The Case of Benedict Arnold	X	B	250+	Fritz, Jean	G.P. Putnam's Sons Books for Young Readers
Tranportation: From Walking to High-Speed Rail	U	I	250+	Timeline History	Heinemann Library
Transcontinental Railroad, The	V	I	250+	Cornerstones of Freedom	Children's Press
Transcontinental Railroad, The	T	I	250+	Navigators Social Studies Series	Benchmark Education
Transcontinental Railroad, The	S	I	250+	The Library of the Westward Expansion	Rosen Publishing Group
Transcontinental Railroad, The: Connecting America	S	I	250+	Explore More	Wright Group/McGraw Hill
Transforming Trash	S	I	250+	Orbit Chapter Books	Pacific Learning
Transportation	Y	I	250+	From Fail to Win! Learning from Bad Ideas	Raintree
Transportation	C	I	17	We Are Alike and Different	Lerner Publishing Group
Transportation	F	I	24	Windows on Literacy	National Geographic
Transportation Firsts	T	I	250+	High-Fliers	Pacific Learning
Transportation in Many Cultures	I	I	89	Life Around the World	Capstone Press
#Transportation in the city	L	I	250+	First Grahics: My Community	Capstone Press
Transportation Museum, The	C	I	79	Little Red Readers	Sundance
Transportation Then and Now	I	I	123	Then and Now	Lerner Publishing Group
Transportation Through Time	Q	I	250+	Rigby Focus	Rigby
Transportation Time Line, A	P	I	250+	Discovery World	Rigby
Transportation Yesterday and Today	M	I	659	Relf, Coco	Harcourt School Publishers
Transportation: Going, Going, Gone	R	I	250+	Kids Discover Reading	Wright Group/McGraw Hill
Trap, The	U	RF	250+	Smelcer, John	Square Fish
Trapdoor Spiders	N	I	250+	Spiders	Capstone Press
Trapezoid	L	I	33	Shapes	Lerner Publishing Group
Trapp Family Singers, The	X	B	2962	Leveled Readers	Houghton Mifflin Harcourt

TITLE	LEVEL	GENRE	WORD COUNT	AUTHOR / SERIES	PUBLISHER / DISTRIBUTOR
Trapp Family Singers, The	X	B	2962	Leveled Readers/CA	Houghton Mifflin Harcourt
Trapp Family Singers, The	X	B	2962	Leveled Readers/TX	Houghton Mifflin Harcourt
Trapped	I	F	248	Fried, Mary	Keep Books
Trapped	S	F	250+	Moloney, James	Stone Arch Books
Trapped by a Teacher	Q	RF	250+	Action Packs	Rigby
Trapped by the Ice!: Shackleton's Amazing Antarctic Adventure	T	I	250+	McCurdy, Michael	Walker & Company
Trapped Genie, The	M	F	250+	Tristars	Richard C. Owen
Trapped in a Canyon!: Aron Ralston's Story of Survival	R	I	250+	True Tales of Survival	Capstone Press
^Trapped in Space	P	SF	250+	Johnson, David	Stone Arch Books
Trapped!	N	RF	250+	High-Fliers	Pacific Learning
Trapped!	L	RF	250+	New Way Literature	Steck-Vaughn
Trapped!	O	SF	250+	Sails	Rigby
Trapped!	O	RF	250+	Supa Doopers	Sundance
Trash	I	I	242	Springboard	Wright Group/McGraw Hill
Trash	H	I	154	Sun Sprouts	ETA/Cuisenaire
Trash	H	F	130	Sunshine	Wright Group/McGraw Hill
Trash and Treasure	M	RF	250+	PM Extensions	Rigby
Trash Art	LB	I	18	Shutterbug Books	Steck-Vaughn
Trash Can Band, The	J	RF	252	Little Books	Sadlier-Oxford
Trash Trucks!	N	F	250+	Kirk, Daniel	Troll Associates
Trash with Dash	T	I	250+	Power Up!	Steck-Vaughn
Trauma Shift: Have You Got What It Takes to Be an ER Nurse?	V	I	250+	On the Job	Compass Point Books
Travel	G	I	110	Then and Now	Heinemann Library
Travel in the U.S.A., Then & Now	P	I	739	Time for Kids	Teacher Created Materials
Travel Money, U.S.A.	I	I	245	Early Connections	Benchmark Education
Travel Smart	P	I	250+	iOpeners	Pearson Learning Group
Travel Team	X	RF	250+	Lupica, Mike	Puffin Books
Travelers and the Bear, The	M	TL	250+	Literacy by Design	Rigby
Travelers and Traders	Q	I	250+	Explorers	Wright Group/McGraw Hill
Traveling	C	F	86	Foundations	Wright Group/McGraw Hill
Traveling Across Australia	O	I	250+	Windows on Literacy	National Geographic
Traveling Animals	M	I	381	Sails	Rigby
Traveling Around the City	M	I	387	Rigby Flying Colors	Rigby
Traveling by Train	O	I	485	Leveled Readers Social Studies	Houghton Mifflin Harcourt
Traveling Guitar, The	O	RF	674	Leveled Readers	Houghton Mifflin Harcourt
Traveling in America	O	I	250+	On Our Way to English	Rigby
Traveling Ted's Postcards	C	F	161	Little Celebrations	Pearson Learning Group
Traveling the Freedom Road	W	I	250+	Osborne, Linda Barrett	Harry N. Abrams
Traveling Tom and the Leprechaun	O	F	250+	Bateman, Teresa	Holiday House
*Travels and Travails	U	B	250+	High-Fliers	Pacific Learning
Travels of Alvar Nunez Cebeza de Vaca, The	X	B	3751	Leveled Readers Social Studies	Houghton Mifflin Harcourt
Travels of Marco Polo, The	T	I	250+	Explorers & Exploration	Steck-Vaughn
Travels of Marco Polo, The	S	B	250+	WorldScapes	ETA/Cuisenaire
Travels to Distant Lands : 1000-1400	V	I	250+	Reading Expeditions	National Geographic
Travels with Rainie Marie	S	B	250+	Martin, Patricia	Hyperion
Travis Pastrana	P	B	1818	Amazing Athletes	Lerner Publishing Group
Travis Pastrana: Motocross Legend	Q	B	250+	Dirt Bikes	Capstone Press
Treacherous Tentacles	S	I	250+	Underwater Encounters	Hameray Publishing Group
Treasure Bath, The	WB	F	0	Andreasen, Dan	Henry Holt & Co.
Treasure Cave, The	L	F	250+	Cambridge Reading	Pearson Learning Group
Treasure Hunt	O	I	250+	Early Connections	Benchmark Education

* Collection of short stories   # Graphic text
^ Mature content with lower level text demands

TITLE	LEVEL	GENRE	WORD COUNT	AUTHOR / SERIES	PUBLISHER / DISTRIBUTOR
Treasure Hunt	LB	F	14	Smart Start	Rigby
Treasure Hunt, The	I	RF	350	InfoTrek	ETA/Cuisenaire
Treasure Hunt, The	K	RF	250+	Literacy by Design	Rigby
Treasure Hunt, The (Little Bill)	L	RF	250+	Cosby, Bill	Scholastic
Treasure Hunting	M	RF	250+	Literacy 2000	Rigby
Treasure Hunting: Looking for Lost Riches	S	I	250+	High Five Reading	Red Brick Learning
Treasure in the Attic	K	RF	568	PM Stars Bridge Books	Rigby
Treasure in the Attic	G	RF	153	Seedlings	Continental Press
#Treasure Island	U	HF	2256	Coleman, Wim & Perrin, Pat (Retold)	Stone Arch Books
Treasure Island	W	HF	250+	High-Fliers	Pacific Learning
Treasure Island	Z	HF	250+	Stevenson, Robert Lewis	Scholastic
Treasure Island, A	F	RF	177	PM Plus Story Books	Rigby
Treasure Lost at Sea: The Nuestra Senora de Atocha	T	I	250+	Rigby Literacy	Rigby
Treasure Map, The	B	F	32	Harry's Math Books	Outside the Box
Treasure Map, The	K	F	675	InfoTrek	ETA/Cuisenaire
Treasure Map, The	L	F	306	Leveled Readers	Houghton Mifflin Harcourt
Treasure Map, The	L	F	306	Leveled Readers/CA	Houghton Mifflin Harcourt
Treasure Map, The	L	F	306	Leveled Readers/TX	Houghton Mifflin Harcourt
Treasure Map, The	K	RF	250+	Windows on Literacy	National Geographic
Treasure of Alpheus Winterborn, The	S	F	250+	Bellairs, John	Penguin Group
*Treasure of Dead Man's Lane and Other Case Files, The: Saxby Smart, Private Detective	S	RF	250+	Cheshire, Simon	Roaring Brook Press
Treasure of El Patrón, The	T	RF	250+	Paulsen, Gary	Bantam Books
#Treasure of Mount Fate, The	U	F	11250	Twisted Journeys	Graphic Universe
Treasure of the Lost Lagoon, The	K	F	250+	Hayes, Geoffrey	Random House
Treasure on Fraser Street, The	K	RF	250+	Home Connection Collection	Rigby
Treasure!	J	RF	250+	Phonics Readers Plus	Steck-Vaughn
Treasure, The	B	RF	31	Sails	Rigby
Treasure, The	K	F	250+	Shulevitz, Uri	Farrar, Straus, & Giroux
Treasures	L	RF	263	Books for Young Learners	Richard C. Owen
Treasures	T	I	250+	Connectors	Pacific Learning
Treasures from the Sea	U	I	250+	Connectors	Pacific Learning
Treasures in the Dust	U	HF	250+	Porter, Tracey	HarperTrophy
*Treasury of Pirate Stories, A	S	F	250+	Bradman, Tony	Kingfisher
Treat Me Right!	Q	I	250+	Kids Talk	Picture Window Books
Treat, The	E	F	96	Leveled Readers Language Support	Houghton Mifflin Harcourt
Tree	W	I	250+	Eyewitness Books	DK Publishing
Tree Branch, The	WB	RF	0	Instant Readers	Harcourt School Publishers
Tree by Leaf	V	F	250+	Voigt, Cynthia	Simon & Schuster
Tree Can Be, A	E	I	74	Nayer, Judy	Scholastic
Tree Falls Down, A	M	F	250+	Orbit Double Takes	Pacific Learning
Tree Fell Over the River, A	C	RF	72	Little Red Readers	Sundance
Tree for All Seasons, A	L	I	250+	Bernard, Robin	National Geographic
Tree for all Seasons, A	B	I	24	Independent Readers Science	Houghton Mifflin Harcourt
Tree for All Seasons, A	B	I	24	Science Support Readers	Houghton Mifflin Harcourt
Tree for Emmy, A	L	RF	250+	Rodman, Mary Ann	Peachtree
Tree for Spring, A	G	RF	186	PM Collection	Rigby
Tree Fort Adventure	H	RF	219	Adams, Lorraine & Bruvold, Lynn	Eaglecrest Books
Tree Fort, The	G	RF	182	Adams, Lorraine & Bruvold, Lynn	Eaglecrest Books
Tree Fort, The	H	RF	160	Early Transitional, Set 2	Pioneer Valley
Tree Frogs	J	I	87	Pebble Books	Red Brick Learning

T

TITLE	LEVEL	GENRE	WORD COUNT	AUTHOR / SERIES	PUBLISHER / DISTRIBUTOR
Tree Horse, A	H	RF	220	PM Plus Story Books	Rigby
Tree House Fun	G	RF	165	First Start	Troll Associates
Tree House, The	N	RF	250+	Boyz Rule!	Mondo Publishing
Tree House, The	E	RF	25	Brown, Roberta; Carey, Sue	Scholastic
Tree House, The	I	RF	322	Explorations	Eleanor Curtain Publishing
Tree House, The	I	RF	322	Explorations	Okapi Educational Materials
Tree House, The	F	F	198	Leveled Literacy Intervention/ Green System	Heinemann
Tree House, The	A	F	20	Leveled Readers	Houghton Mifflin Harcourt
Tree House, The	A	F	20	Leveled Readers/CA	Houghton Mifflin Harcourt
Tree House, The	B	F	30	Story Box	Wright Group/McGraw Hill
Tree House, The	B	RF	32	Sunshine	Wright Group/McGraw Hill
Tree in the Ancient Forest, The	M	I	586	Sharing Nature with Children	Dawn Publications
Tree Is a Home, A	H	I	203	Learn to Read	Creative Teaching Press
Tree Is a Home, A	I	I	135	Pacific Literacy	Pacific Learning
Tree Is a Plant, A	K	I	250+	Lets-Read-and-Find-Out Science	HarperCollins
Tree Is My Home, A	G	RF	114	Leveled Readers Science	Houghton Mifflin Harcourt
Tree of Birds	J	F	250+	Leveled Readers Language Support	Houghton Mifflin Harcourt
Tree of Her Own, A	I	RF	248	Windows on Literacy	National Geographic
Tree of Life, The	M	I	502	Springboard	Wright Group/McGraw Hill
Tree Stump, The	B	TL	34	Little Celebrations	Pearson Learning Group
Tree Truck, The	A	I	78	Readlings	American Reading Company
Tree With Eyes, The	O	F	250+	The Adventures of Sam X	Stone Arch Books
Tree, The	G	I	94	Alphakids	Sundance
Tree, The	F	RF	101	Sunshine	Wright Group/McGraw Hill
Tree, the Trunk, and the Tuba, The	Q	RF	250+	Literacy 2000	Rigby
Treehouse	D	I	43	Hoenecke, Karen	Kaeden Books
Treehouse Club, The	F	RF	158	Home Connection Collection	Rigby
Treehouse Club, The	N	RF	250+	Navigators Fiction Series	Benchmark Education
Trees	L	I	158	Bookshop	Mondo Publishing
Trees	K	I	388	Early Connections	Benchmark Education
Trees	J	I	124	Literacy 2000	Rigby
Trees	H	I	194	Momentum Literacy Program	Troll Associates
Trees	G	I	351	Sails	Rigby
Trees	H	I	28	Sun Sprouts	ETA/Cuisenaire
Trees	A	I	28	Twig	Wright Group/McGraw Hill
Trees	G	I	149	Vocabulary Readers	Houghton Mifflin Harcourt
Trees	G	I	149	Vocabulary Readers/CA	Houghton Mifflin Harcourt
Trees	G	I	149	Vocabulary Readers/TX	Houghton Mifflin Harcourt
Trees and Leaves	F	I	33	iOpeners	Pearson Learning Group
Trees and Leaves	S	I	250+	Nature Club	Troll Associates
Trees and Plants in the Rain Forest	O	I	250+	Pirotta, Saviour	Steck-Vaughn
Trees Are Special	I	I	85	Sunshine	Wright Group/McGraw Hill
Trees Are Terrific!	G	I	123	Yellow Umbrella Books	Red Brick Learning
Trees Belong to Everyone	L	I	250+	Literacy 2000	Rigby
Trees for Life	L	I	768	Sun Sprouts	ETA/Cuisenaire
Tree's Life, A	J	I	102	Windows on Literacy	National Geographic
Trees Please!	L	I	250+	Storyteller Chapter Books	Wright Group/McGraw Hill
Trees:Worlds Within Leaves	O	I	1219	iScience	Norwood House Press
Trek to the Top	N	I	655	Reading Street	Pearson
Trek, The	I	RF	158	Jonas, Ann	Greenwillow Books
Trekking in Nepal	S	I	250+	WorldScapes	ETA/Cuisenaire
Trent and Grace Make a Home	D	F	100	Springboard	Wright Group/McGraw Hill

T

* Collection of short stories   # Graphic text
^ Mature content with lower level text demands

TITLE	LEVEL	GENRE	WORD COUNT	AUTHOR / SERIES	PUBLISHER / DISTRIBUTOR
Trevor from Trinidad	Q	RF	1685	Leveled Readers	Houghton Mifflin Harcourt
Trevor's New Home	O	RF	250+	Leveled Readers Language Support	Houghton Mifflin Harcourt
Trevor's Wiggly-Wobbly Tooth	J	RF	250+	Laminack, Lester L.	Peachtree
Trial by Jury	R	I	1357	Vocabulary Readers	Houghton Mifflin Harcourt
Trial by Jury	R	I	1357	Vocabulary Readers/CA	Houghton Mifflin Harcourt
Trial of the Amazons: Wonder Woman	Q	F	250+	DC Superheroes	Stone Arch Books
Trials in Salem	T	I	1334	Leveled Readers Social Studies	Houghton Mifflin Harcourt
Trials of Death: The Saga of Darren Shan	Y	F	250+	Shan, Darren	Little Brown and Company
Triangle	B	I	34	Shapes	Lerner Publishing Group
Triangle Fire, The: Hannah's Diary	Q	HF	250+	Orbit Chapter Books	Pacific Learning
Triangles	D	I	28	Bookworms	Marshall Cavendish
Triangles	I	I	178	Shapes	Red Brick Learning
Triangles Around Town	J	I	271	Shapes Around Town	Capstone Press
Triathlon	Q	I	250+	Extreme Sports	Red Brick Learning
Triathlon	N	I	423	Nonfiction Set 9	Literacy Footprints
Triathlon Team, The	H	RF	352	Rigby Flying Colors	Rigby
Tribes	Z+	RF	250+	Slade, Arthur	Random House
Triceratops	I	I	139	Dinosaur and Prehistoric Animals	Capstone Press
Triceratops	J	I	277	Red Rocket Readers	Flying Start Books
Triceratops and the Crocodiles, The	I	HF	250+	PM Plus Story Books	Rigby
Triceratops on the Farm	L	F	208	Wesley & the Dinosaurs	Wright Group/McGraw Hill
*Trick of the Tale	T	TL	250+	Matthews, John and Caitlin	Candlewick Press
Trick or Treat Halloween	F	RF	131	First Start	Troll Associates
Trick or Treat on Monster Street	M	F	250+	Schnitzlein, Danny	Peachtree
Trick, The	J	TL	550	Leveled Readers/TX	Houghton Mifflin Harcourt
Trick, The	F	RF	65	New Way Red	Steck-Vaughn
Tricking the Eye	U	I	2024	Reading Street	Pearson
Tricking the Tiger	J	TL	250+	PM Plus Story Books	Rigby
Tricking Tracy	F	RF	125	Tadpoles	Rigby
Tricks	I	I	218	Sun Sprouts	ETA/Cuisenaire
Tricks to Doing Magic	Q	I	2054	Reading Street	Pearson
Trickster Ghost, The	O	F	250+	Showell, E.	Scholastic
Tricksters	M	RF	250+	Supa Doopers	Sundance
Tricksters of Fringle, The	P	I	250+	Sails	Rigby
Tricksters, The	D	F	49	Ray's Readers	Outside the Box
Tricky Fox	M	TL	796	Red Rocket Readers	Flying Start Books
Tricky Insects and Other Fun Creatures	K	I	250+	Spyglass Books	Compass Point Books
Tricky Rabbit	I	TL	198	Books for Young Learners	Richard C. Owen
Tricky Sticky Problem, The	H	RF	71	Pacific Literacy	Pacific Learning
Tricky Tangrams	I	I	193	Red Rocket Readers	Flying Start Books
Tricky Tooth, The: Katie Woo	J	RF	250+	Manushkin, Fran	Picture Window Books
Tricky Twins, The	H	RF	248	Domine Readers	Pearson Publishing Group
Triffic the Extraordinary Pig	R	F	250+	King-Smith, Dick	Bantam Books
Trigger	Z+	RF	250+	Vaught, Susan	Bloomsbury Children's Books
Trilobites	K	I	141	Books for Young Learners	Richard C. Owen
Trino's Choice	Y	RF	250+	Bertrand, Diane Gonzales	Pinata Publishing
Trino's Time	Y	RF	250+	Bertrand, Diane Gonzales	Pinata Publishing
Trip Across the Country, A	C	RF	47	Independent Readers Social Studies	Houghton Mifflin Harcourt
Trip Around the Gulf of Mexico, A	M	I	250+	People, Spaces & Places	Rand McNally
Trip by Train, A	J	RF	298	InfoTrek	ETA/Cuisenaire
Trip into Space, A	I	I	129	Little Red Readers	Sundance

TITLE	LEVEL	GENRE	WORD COUNT	AUTHOR / SERIES	PUBLISHER / DISTRIBUTOR
Trip into Space, A	H	I	79	Story Steps	Rigby
Trip of a Lifetime, The	S	RF	250+	Reading Safari	Mondo Publishing
Trip on the Erie Canal, A	L	RF	260	Independent Readers Social Studies	Houghton Mifflin Harcourt
Trip Through Africa, A	O	I	971	Vocabulary Readers	Houghton Mifflin Harcourt
Trip Through Africa, A	O	I	971	Vocabulary Readers/CA	Houghton Mifflin Harcourt
Trip Through Our Solar System, A	L	I	250+	Rosen Real Readers	Rosen Publishing Group
Trip Through the Airport, A	L	I	250+	Rigby Literacy	Rigby
Trip Through Time, A	M	I	357	Gear Up!	Wright Group/McGraw Hill
Trip to a Pond	B	RF	33	Leveled Readers Science	Houghton Mifflin Harcourt
Trip to Freedom	M	B	250+	Greetings	Rigby
Trip to Japan, A	M	I	250+	Rosen Real Readers	Rosen Publishing Group
Trip to the Aquarium, A	LB	RF	18	Kloes, Carol	Kaeden Books
Trip to the Beach, A	F	F	258	Bella and Rosie Series	Literacy Footprints
Trip to the Beach, A	E	I	44	iOpeners	Pearson Learning Group
Trip to the Capitol, A	S	I	1043	Reading Street	Pearson
Trip to the City, A	E	F	119	Bookshop	Mondo Publishing
Trip to the Dentist, A	I	I	196	Rosen Real Readers	Rosen Publishing Group
Trip to the Doctor, A	B	I	36	Windows on Literacy	National Geographic
Trip to the Farm, A	G	RF	165	The King School Series	Townsend Press
Trip to the Fire Station	K	I	182	Rosen Real Readers	Rosen Publishing Group
Trip to the Fire Station	A	I	25	Vocabulary Readers	Houghton Mifflin Harcourt
Trip to the Fire Station	A	I	25	Vocabulary Readers/CA	Houghton Mifflin Harcourt
Trip to the Laundromutt, A	H	F	229	Leveled Literacy Intervention/ Green System	Heinemann
Trip to the Moon	H	F	332	Red Rocket Readers	Flying Start Books
Trip to the Park, The	H	RF	277	Foundations	Wright Group/McGraw Hill
Trip to the Past, A	Q	RF	250+	HSP/Harcourt Trophies	Harcourt, Inc.
Trip to the Post Office, A	I	I	191	Rosen Real Readers	Rosen Publishing Group
Trip to the Rock	B	F	90	Leveled Readers	Houghton Mifflin Harcourt
Trip to the Rock	B	F	90	Leveled Readers/CA	Houghton Mifflin Harcourt
Trip to the Rock	B	F	90	Leveled Readers/TX	Houghton Mifflin Harcourt
Trip to the Station, A	I	I	241	Rosen Real Readers	Rosen Publishing Group
Trip to the Video Store, A	H	RF	203	Foundations	Wright Group/McGraw Hill
Trip to the Zoo, A	C	RF	78	Carousel Readers	Pearson Learning Group
Trip to the Zoo, A	F	I	93	Independent Readers Science	Houghton Mifflin Harcourt
Trip to the Zoo, A	F	I	112	Rosen Real Readers	Rosen Publishing Group
Trip with Grandma, A	K	F	727	Ohi, Ruth	Annick Press
Trip, The	E	F	224	Leveled Literacy Intervention/ Blue System	Heinemann
Trip, The	E	F	108	Ready Readers	Pearson Learning Group
Trip, Trap!	I	TL	315	Red Rocket Readers	Flying Start Books
Triple Rotten Day, The	L	RF	250+	Seuling, Barbara	Scholastic
Triple Threat	S	RF	250+	Orca Young Readers	Orca Books
Triplet Trouble and the Bicycle Race	L	RF	250+	Dadey, Debbie; Jones, Marcia Thornton	Scholastic
Triplet Trouble and the Class Trip	L	RF	250+	Dadey, Debbie; Jones, Marcia Thornton	Scholastic
Triplet Trouble and the Cookie Contest	L	RF	250+	Dadey, Debbie; Jones, Marcia Thornton	Scholastic
Triplet Trouble and the Field Day Disaster	L	RF	250+	Dadey, Debbie; Jones, Marcia Thornton	Scholastic
Triplet Trouble and the Pizza Party	L	RF	250+	Dadey, Debbie; Jones, Marcia Thornton	Scholastic
Triplet Trouble and the Red Heart Race	L	RF	250+	Dadey, Debbie; Jones, Marcia Thornton	Scholastic

T

* Collection of short stories   # Graphic text
^ Mature content with lower level text demands

TITLE	LEVEL	GENRE	WORD COUNT	AUTHOR / SERIES	PUBLISHER / DISTRIBUTOR
Triplet Trouble and the Runaway Reindeer	L	RF	250+	Dadey, Debbie; Jones, Marcia Thornton	Scholastic
Triplet Trouble and the Talent Show Mess	L	RF	250+	Dadey, Debbie; Jones, Marcia Thornton	Scholastic
#Tristan & Isolde: The Warrior and the Princess	X	TL	3189	Graphic Myths and Legends	Lerner Publishing Group
Tri-State Tornado, The	V	HF	250+	Reading Expeditions	National Geographic
Triumph on Everest: A Photobiography of Sir Edmund Hillary	W	B	250+	Coburn, Broughton	National Geographic
Trixie	L	RF	250+	Voyages	SRA/McGraw Hill
Trixie and the Cyber Pet	M	F	250+	Krailing, Tessa	Barron's Educational
Trixie the Halloween Fairy: Rainbow Magic	L	F	250+	Meadows, Daisy	Scholastic
Trixie's Summer	J	RF	250+	PM Plus Story Books	Rigby
Trog	J	F	432	Sunshine	Wright Group/McGraw Hill
Trojan Horse, The	N	I	250+	Literacy 2000	Rigby
Trojan Horse, The: How the Greeks Won the War	Q	TL	250+	Little, Emily	Random House
#Trojan Horse, The: The Fall of Troy	W	TL	3155	Graphic Myths and Legends	Lerner Publishing Group
#Trojan Horse, The: The Fall of Troy	W	TL	250+	Edge	Hampton Brown
Trojan Horse: The World's Greatest Adventure	W	I	250+	DK Readers	DK Publishing
Troll from the Mill, The	C	F	35	Rigby Star	Rigby
Troll Tricks	H	TL	250+	Phonics Readers	Scholastic
Trollerella	O	F	250+	Stegman-Bourgeois, Karen	Holiday House
Trolley Ride	A	I	16	Vocabulary Readers	Houghton Mifflin Harcourt
Trolley Ride, The	C	F	87	Tadpoles	Rigby
Trolls	S	RF	250+	Horvath, Polly	Square Fish
Trolls Don't Ride Roller Coasters	M	F	250+	Dadey, Debbie; Jones, Marcia Thornton	Scholastic
Trolls on Vacation	N	F	250+	MacDonald, Alan	Bloomsbury Children's Books
Troll's Story, The	K	TL	250+	Reading Safari	Mondo Publishing
Trong's Hero	H	RF	282	In Step Readers	Rigby
Troop of Little Dinosaurs, A	J	HF	250+	PM Story Books	Rigby
Tropical Climate	R	I	250+	Theme Sets	National Geographic
Tropical Forests	W	I	250+	Biomes Atlases	Raintree
Tropical Grasslands	W	I	250+	Biomes Atlases	Raintree
Tropical Rain Forest and You	P	I	1192	Reading Street	Pearson
Tropical Rain Forests	O	I	250+	A True Book	Children's Press
Tropical Rain Forests	S	I	250+	Theme Sets	National Geographic
Tropical Rain Forests	O	I	250+	Trackers	Pacific Learning
Tropical Rainforests	N	I	250+	Habitats of the World	Pearson Learning Group
Troquois, The: Longhouse Builders	R	I	250+	America's First Peoples	Capstone Press
Troubadour	X	HF	250+	Hoffman, Mary	Bloomsbury Children's Books
Trouble	X	RF	250+	Schmidt, Gary D.	Houghton Mifflin Harcourt
Trouble	E	RF	113	Teacher's Choice Series	Pearson Learning Group
Trouble According to Humphrey	Q	F	250+	Birney, Betty G.	Puffin Books
Trouble Dolls	P	F	250+	Buffett, Jimmy; Savannah, Jane	Harcourt School Publishers
Trouble for Jasper	J	F	659	Jasper the Cat	Pioneer Valley
Trouble for Lucy	Q	HF	250+	Stevens, Carla	Clarion Books
Trouble Gum	M	F	250+	Cordell, Matthew	Feiwel and Friends
Trouble in a Tree	C	F	36	Bonnell, Kris	Reading Reading Books
Trouble in Space	M	I	723	Leveled Readers	Houghton Mifflin Harcourt
Trouble in Space	M	I	723	Leveled Readers/CA	Houghton Mifflin Harcourt
Trouble in Space	M	I	723	Leveled Readers/TX	Houghton Mifflin Harcourt
Trouble in the Ark	J	F	119	Rose, Gerald	Oxford University Press

T

TITLE	LEVEL	GENRE	WORD COUNT	AUTHOR / SERIES	PUBLISHER / DISTRIBUTOR
Trouble in the Sandbox	J	RF	318	Foundations	Wright Group/McGraw Hill
Trouble is My Beeswax: A Chet Gecko Mystery	Q	F	250+	Hale, Bruce	Harcourt, Inc.
Trouble on a Trip to the Moon	M	I	723	Leveled Readers	Houghton Mifflin Harcourt
Trouble on a Trip to the Moon	M	I	723	Leveled Readers/CA	Houghton Mifflin Harcourt
Trouble on a Trip to the Moon	M	I	723	Leveled Readers/TX	Houghton Mifflin Harcourt
Trouble on the Farm: How Farmers Meet the Challenges of Nature	U	I	250+	Literacy by Design	Rigby
Trouble on the Trail	M	RF	250+	On Our Way to English	Rigby
Trouble on the Walking Path	J	F	250+	Reading Safari	Mondo Publishing
Trouble River	S	HF	250+	Byars, Betsy	Scholastic
Trouble Under the Big Top	O	RF	250+	Klooz	Stone Arch Books
Trouble with Babies, The	Q	RF	250+	Freeman, Martha	Holiday House
Trouble with Buster, The	N	RF	250+	Lorimer, Janet	Scholastic
Trouble with Cats, The	Q	RF	250+	Freeman, Martha	Holiday House
Trouble with Dragons, The	L	F	250+	Gliori, Debi	Walker & Company
Trouble with Elephants, The	I	F	197	Riddell, Chris	HarperTrophy
Trouble with Gran, The	L	F	214	Cole, Babette	Collins Publishing Group
Trouble with Heathrow, The	I	RF	173	Sunshine	Wright Group/McGraw Hill
Trouble with Herbert, The	L	F	1830	Eyles, Heather	Mondo Publishing
^Trouble with Liberty, The	Z	RF	250+	Orca Soundings	Orca Books
Trouble with Mum, The	L	F	194	Cole, Babette	Collins Publishing Group
Trouble with Oatmeal, The	O	RF	250+	PM Collection	Rigby
Trouble with Parents, The	N	RF	250+	Supa Doopers	Sundance
Trouble with Patrick, The	O	RF	250+	Action Packs	Rigby
Trouble with Rules, The	S	RF	250+	Bulion, Leslie	Peachtree
Trouble with Squids, The (Splurch Academy)	Q	F	250+	Berry, Julie & Gardner, Sally	Grosset & Dunlap
Trouble with Triplets	M	RF	829	Leveled Readers	Houghton Mifflin Harcourt
Trouble with Triplets	M	RF	829	Leveled Readers/CA	Houghton Mifflin Harcourt
Trouble with Triplets	M	RF	829	Leveled Readers/TX	Houghton Mifflin Harcourt
Trouble with Tuck, The	R	RF	250+	Taylor, Theodore	Avon Books
Trouble with Twins, The	Q	RF	250+	Freeman, Martha	Holiday House
Troublemaker	M	RF	250+	Supa Doopers	Sundance
Trouble-Maker	T	RF	250+	Clements, Andrew	Atheneum Books
Troubles with Bubbles	E	F	89	New Reader Series	Bungalo Books
Troubling a Star	V	F	250+	L'Engle, Madeleine	Dell
Trout Are Made of Trees	M	I	178	Sayre, April Pulley	Charlesbridge
Trout Summer	T	RF	250+	Conly, Jane Leslie	Scholastic
Troy High	X	RF	250+	Norris, Shana	Amulet Books
Troy's Cake	I	F	289	Gear Up!	Wright Group/McGraw Hill
Troy's Cold	J	F	302	Gear Up!	Wright Group/McGraw Hill
Troy's Flying Machine	K	F	373	Gear Up!	Wright Group/McGraw Hill
Truck	LB	I	43	Crews, Donald	Scholastic
Truck Is Stuck, The	B	RF	23	Ready Readers	Pearson Learning Group
Truck Parade, The	K	RF	483	PM Plus Story Books	Rigby
Truck Stop, The	LB	RF	25	Kloes, Carol	Kaeden Books
Truck Stuck	K	RF	133	Wolf, Sallie	Charlesbridge
Truck, The	C	F	77	Sails	Rigby
Trucker	P	RF	250+	Beale, Fleur	Pacific Learning
Trucks	A	RF	56	Bookshop	Mondo Publishing
Trucks	E	I	196	Foundations	Wright Group/McGraw Hill
Trucks	B	I	75	Leveled Literacy Intervention/ Green System	Heinemann
Trucks	I	I	38	Literacy 2000	Rigby
Trucks	C	I	38	Literacy 2000	Rigby

* Collection of short stories   # Graphic text
^ Mature content with lower level text demands

TITLE	LEVEL	GENRE	WORD COUNT	AUTHOR / SERIES	PUBLISHER / DISTRIBUTOR
Trucks	A	I	35	Little Books for Early Readers	University of Maine
Trucks	C	I	27	Pebble Books	Capstone Press
Trucks	D	I	147	Sails	Rigby
Trucks	C	I	37	Stenger, Lisa	Kaeden Books
Trucks	T	I	250+	The World's Fastest	Red Brick Learning
Trucks	C	I	24	Twig	Wright Group/McGraw Hill
Trucks	C	I	81	Vocabulary Readers	Houghton Mifflin Harcourt
Trucks	C	I	81	Vocabulary Readers/CA	Houghton Mifflin Harcourt
Trucks and Other Big Machines	C	I	79	Springboard	Wright Group/McGraw Hill
Trucks on the Road	K	I	250+	PM Plus	Rigby
Trucks, The	B	F	36	Sails	Rigby
Trucks: The Ins and Outs of Monster Trucks, Semis, Pickups, and Other Trucks	V	I	250+	Velocity-RPM	Capstone Press
Truckster	F	F	194	Instant Readers	Harcourt School Publishers
True (...Sort of)	T	RF	250+	Hannigan, Katherine	Greenwillow Books
True Confessions	S	RF	250+	Tashjian, Janet	Scholastic
True Confessions of Charlotte Doyle, The	V	HF	250+	Avi	Avon Books
True Cortez, A	P	RF	685	Leveled Readers	Houghton Mifflin Harcourt
True Crime	Z	I	250+	Boldprint	Steck-Vaughn
*True Crimes and How They Were Solved	Z	I	250+	Larsen, Anita	Scholastic
True Meaning of Cleavage, The	Z+	RF	250+	Fredericks, Mariah	Simon & Schuster
True North	Y	F	3229	Leveled Readers	Houghton Mifflin Harcourt
True North	Y	F	3229	Leveled Readers/CA	Houghton Mifflin Harcourt
True North	Y	F	3229	Leveled Readers/TX	Houghton Mifflin Harcourt
True or False?	G	I	119	Ready Readers	Pearson Learning Group
True Stories about Abraham Lincoln	O	B	250+	Gross, Ruth Belov	Scholastic
True Story of Pocahontas, The	N	B	250+	Penner, Lucille Recht	Scholastic
True Story of the 3 Little Pigs!, The	Q	TL	250+	Scieszka, Jon	Puffin Books
True Story of the Three Little Pigs, The	Q	TL	250+	Scieszka, Jon	Scholastic
True Talents	Y	F	250+	Lubar, David	Tom Doherty
*True-Life Treasure Hunts	N	I	250+	Donnelly, Judy	Random House
Truman's Aunt Farm	K	F	250+	Soar To Success	Houghton Mifflin Harcourt
Trumpet of the Swan, The	R	F	250+	White, E. B.	Scholastic
Trumpeter of Krakow, The	Z	HF	250+	Kelly, Eric P.	Aladdin
Trunks, Humps, and Tails	I	I	298	Sails	Rigby
^Truth	Z+	RF	250+	Orca Soundings	Orca Books
Truth About Great White Sharks, The	U	I	250+	Cerullo, Mary	Scholastic
Truth About Ogres, The	N	I	250+	Fairy-Tale Superstars	Picture Window Books
Truth About Red Allen, The	S	RF	250+	Power Up!	Steck-Vaughn
Truth About Rodents, The	R	I	912	Vocabulary Readers	Houghton Mifflin Harcourt
Truth About Rodents, The	R	I	912	Vocabulary Readers/CA	Houghton Mifflin Harcourt
Truth About Rodents, The	R	I	912	Vocabulary Readers/TX	Houghton Mifflin Harcourt
Truth About Sparrows, The	U	HF	250+	Hale, Marian	Square Fish
Truth About the Moon, The	M	TL	250+	Bess, Clayton	Houghton Mifflin Harcourt
Truth About Truman School, The	X	RF	250+	Butler, Dori Hillestad	Albert Whitman & Co.
Truth About Witches, The	N	I	250+	Fairy-Tale Superstars	Picture Window Books
Truth and Salsa	W	RF	250+	Lowery, Linda	Peachtree
Truthful Toad, The: Truthfulness	K	F	1322	Salerno, Tony Character Classics	Character Building Company
Try Again, Emma	I	RF	250+	Lighthouse	Rigby
Try Again, Hannah	G	RF	228	PM Extensions-Green	Rigby
Try It	D	RF	49	Reading Corners	Pearson Learning Group
Try It!	T	I	250+	iOpeners	Pearson Learning Group

T

TITLE	LEVEL	GENRE	WORD COUNT	AUTHOR / SERIES	PUBLISHER / DISTRIBUTOR
Try This!	I	I	250+	Rigby Literacy	Rigby
Try to Be a Brave Girl, Sarah	F	RF	102	Windmill Books	Wright Group/McGraw Hill
Try Your Best	F	RF	190	Green Light Readers	Harcourt
T-Shirt Triplets, The	L	RF	344	Literacy 2000	Rigby
T-Shirts	F	RF	112	Pacific Literacy	Pacific Learning
Tsunami	Z	I	2393	Leveled Readers	Houghton Mifflin Harcourt
Tsunami Survival Stories	O	I	770	Springboard	Wright Group/McGraw Hill
Tsunami!	Q	I	784	Independent Readers Science	Houghton Mifflin Harcourt
Tsunami! Wave of Destruction	T	I	250+	Sails	Rigby
Tsunami!: Deadly Wall of Water	S	I	250+	High Five Reading	Red Brick Learning
Tsunamis	W	I	250+	Disasters Up Close	Lerner Publishing Group
Tsunamis	M	I	174	Earth in Action	Capstone Press
Tsunamis	R	I	250+	Navigators Science Series	Benchmark Education
Tsunamis	M	I	737	Pull Ahead Books	Lerner Publishing Group
ttfn	Z+	RF	250+	Myracle, Lauren	Amulet Books
ttyl	Z+	RF	250+	Myracle, Lauren	Amulet Books
Tub That Became a Boat, The	E	F	56	Dominie Readers	Pearson Learning Group
Tuba Lessons	WB	RF	0	Bartlett, T. C.; Monique, Felix	Harcourt School Publishers
Tubes in My Ears: My Trip to the Hospital	K	I	250+	Bookshop	Mondo Publishing
Tuck Everlasting	W	F	250+	Babbitt, Natalie	Farrar, Straus, & Giroux
Tucker Finds Adventure	J	F	250+	Fletcher, Rusty	Pearson Learning Group
Tuckerbean at Big Bone Bowl	I	F	250+	Read-it! Readers	Picture Window Books
Tuckerbean at the Movies	I	F	133	Read-it! Readers	Picture Window Books
Tuckerbean on the Moon	I	F	145	Read-it! Readers	Picture Window Books
Tucket's Gold	U	HF	250+	Paulsen, Gary	Bantam Books
Tucket's Ride	U	HF	250+	Paulsen, Gary	Bantam Books
Tudley Didn't Know	L	F	958	Himmelman, John	Sylvan Dell Publishing
Tuesday	WB	F	0	Wiesner, David	Clarion
Tuff Fluff: The Case of Duckie's Missing Brain	M	F	250+	Nash, Scott	Candlewick Press
Tug of War	I	TL	250+	Folk Tales	Wright Group/McGraw Hill
Tug of War, The	G	TL	194	Story Steps	Rigby
Tug of War, The	I	TL	250+	Storyworlds	Heinemann
Tugboats	I	I	116	Mighty Machines	Capstone Press
Tugboats	O	I	250+	Transportation	Red Brick Learning
Tug-of-War	C	F	68	Leveled Literacy Intervention/ Blue System	Heinemann
Tug-of-War	G	TL	215	Red Rocket Readers	Flying Start Books
Tug-of-War, The	L	TL	648	Rigby Flying Colors	Rigby
Tuk Becomes a Hunter	N	TL	838	Leveled Readers	Houghton Mifflin Harcourt
Tuk Becomes a Hunter	N	TL	838	Leveled Readers/CA	Houghton Mifflin Harcourt
Tuk Becomes a Hunter	N	TL	838	Leveled Readers/TX	Houghton Mifflin Harcourt
Tuk the Hunter	N	TL	1077	Leveled Readers	Houghton Mifflin Harcourt
Tuk the Hunter	N	TL	1077	Leveled Readers/CA	Houghton Mifflin Harcourt
Tuk the Hunter	N	TL	1077	Leveled Readers/TX	Houghton Mifflin Harcourt
Tulip Sees America	N	RF	250+	Rylant, Cynthia	Scholastic
Tulips	F	I	102	Life Cycles	Lerner Publishing Group
Tulips	M	RF	250+	O'Callahan, Jay	Peachtree
Tulips for Annie's Mother	O	HF	781	Reading Street	Pearson
Tulips for Dad	J	RF	250+	Cambridge Reading	Pearson Learning Group
Tulips for My Teacher	G	RF	209	PM Photo Stories	Rigby
Tullian Trouble	T	SF	250+	Sails	Rigby
Tullian Trouble	T	SF	250+	Sails	Rigby
Tumbleweed Stew	J	TL	250+	Crummel, Susan Stevens	Harcourt
Tumbleweed Stew	J	TL	250+	Green Light Readers	Harcourt

T

* Collection of short stories   # Graphic text
^ Mature content with lower level text demands

TITLE	LEVEL	GENRE	WORD COUNT	AUTHOR / SERIES	PUBLISHER / DISTRIBUTOR
Tummy Ache	J	RF	104	Sunshine	Wright Group/McGraw Hill
*Tumtum & Nutmeg: Adventures Beyond Nutmouse Hall	T	F	250+	Bearn, Emily	Little Brown and Company
Tundra	Q	I	250+	First Reports	Compass Point Books
Tundra Food Chain, A	U	I	7371	Follow That Food Chain	Lerner Publishing Group
Tundra Food Webs	Q	I	2538	Early Bird Food Webs	Lerner Publishing Group
Tundras: Frosty, Treeless Lands	N	I	250+	Amazing Science	Picture Window Books
Tuning Up	O	B	250+	Meet the Author	Richard C. Owen
Tunnel, The	B	F	30	Sails	Rigby
Tunneling Earthworms	L	I	457	Pull Ahead Books	Lerner Publishing Group
Tunnels	M	I	250+	Explorations	Okapi Educational Materials
Tunnels	M	I	250+	Explorations	Eleanor Curtain Publishing
Tunnels	W	F	250+	Gordon, Roderick & Williams, Brian	Scholastic
Tunnels	I	I	179	Sails	Rigby
Tunnels	L	I	262	Windows on Literacy	National Geographic
Tunnels of Blood: The Saga of Darren Shan	Y	F	250+	Shan, Darren	Little Brown and Company
Tupac Shakur	Z+	B	250+	Just the Facts Biographies	Lerner Publishing Group
^Tupac Shakur	Z	B	250+	Rock Music Library	Capstone Press
Turbulence Ahead	Q	I	250+	InfoQuest	Rigby
Turkey	Q	I	1636	Country Explorers	Lerner Publishing Group
Turkey	E	F	106	Sails	Rigby
Turkey That Ate My Father, The	Q	F	250+	Marney, Dean	Scholastic
Turkey Trouble	M	RF	250+	Giff, Patricia Reilly	Bantam Books
Turkey Trouble	K	F	250+	Silvano, Wendi	Marshall Cavendish
Turkey, The	B	F	30	Sails	Rigby
Turkey: Between Europe and Asia	Y	I	3597	Leveled Readers Social Studies	Houghton Mifflin Harcourt
Turkeys on the Farm	I	I	94	Pebble Books	Red Brick Learning
Turkeys' Side of It, The	N	RF	250+	Smith, Janice Lee	HarperTrophy
Turn Homeward, Hannalee	T	HF	250+	Beatty, Patricia	William Morrow
Turn Into: Verbs in Action	K	I	250+	Bookworms	Marshall Cavendish
Turn It Down!	U	I	250+	iOpeners	Pearson Learning Group
Turn of the Screw, The	Y	F	10750	Dominoes two	Oxford University Press
Turn on a Faucet	L	I	238	Windows on Literacy	National Geographic
Turn Up the Radio	R	I	795	Independent Readers Social Studies	Houghton Mifflin Harcourt
Turning the Tide for Turtles	P	I	250+	Literacy by Design	Rigby
Turnip, The	F	TL	250+	Ziefert, Harriet	Puffin Books
Turtle and Hare	D	TL	94	Leveled Readers	Houghton Mifflin Harcourt
Turtle and Hare	D	TL	94	Leveled Readers/CA	Houghton Mifflin Harcourt
Turtle and Hare	D	TL	94	Leveled Readers/TX	Houghton Mifflin Harcourt
Turtle and Snake	E	F	145	Sails	Rigby
Turtle Beach Mystery	L	RF	250+	Windows on Literacy	National Geographic
Turtle Flies South	K	F	250+	Literacy 2000	Rigby
Turtle in the Sun, A	C	F	38	Bonnell, Kris	Reading Reading Books
Turtle Nest	H	I	85	Books for Young Learners	Richard C. Owen
Turtle Summer	O	I	1067	Monroe, Mary Alice	Sylvan Dell Publishing
Turtle Tale	J	F	250+	Asch, Frank	Scholastic
Turtle Talk	I	I	217	Storyteller-Setting Sun	Wright Group/McGraw Hill
Turtle Trouble	E	RF	157	Seedlings	Continental Press
Turtle Trouble	S	I	250+	WorldScapes	ETA/Cuisenaire
Turtle Who Wanted to Fly, The	J	F	250+	The Rowland Reading Program Library	Rowland Reading Foundation
Turtle, The	D	I	68	Foundations	Wright Group/McGraw Hill

TITLE	LEVEL	GENRE	WORD COUNT	AUTHOR / SERIES	PUBLISHER / DISTRIBUTOR
Turtles	S	I	250+	A First Book	Franklin Watts
Turtles	E	I	41	All About Pets	Capstone Press
Turtles and Hatchlings	B	I	33	Animal Families	Lerner Publishing Group
Turtle's Big Race	J	TL	250+	Pair-It Books	Steck-Vaughn
Turtle's Boat	C	F	48	Gear Up!	Wright Group/McGraw Hill
Turtles in My Sandbox	M	RF	1578	Curtis, Jennifer Keats	Sylvan Dell Publishing
Turtle's Life, A	F	I	134	Watch It Grow	Heinemann Library
Turtle's Small Pond	J	TL	572	Leveled Readers	Houghton Mifflin Harcourt
Turtles Take Their Time	L	I	250+	Read-About Science	Children's Press
Turtle's Trouble	D	F	110	Sails	Rigby
Turtles, Tortoises, and Terrapins	N	I	250+	Storyteller Summer Skies	Wright Group/McGraw Hill
Tut, Tut	P	F	250+	Scieszka, Jon	Penguin Group
Tutankhamen's Gift	R	I	250+	Sabuda, Robert	Simon & Schuster
Tutankhamun	V	B	250+	Demi	Marshall Cavendish
Tuti's Play	H	RF	134	Bebop Books	Lee & Low Books Inc.
Tut's Mummy: Lost and Found	P	I	250+	Donnelly, Judy	Random House
Tuttle's Shell	K	F	250+	Bookshop	Mondo Publishing
TV Kid, The	R	RF	250+	Byars, Betsy	Puffin Books
TV Kid, The	R	B	1199	Leveled Readers	Houghton Mifflin Harcourt
TV Kid, The	R	B	1199	Leveled Readers/CA	Houghton Mifflin Harcourt
TV Kid, The	R	B	1199	Leveled Readers/TX	Houghton Mifflin Harcourt
TV Reporters	M	I	250+	Community Helpers	Red Brick Learning
TV Takeover: Questioning Television	S	I	250+	Media Literacy	Capstone Press
TV Time-Out	M	RF	250+	Sunshine	Wright Group/McGraw Hill
Twas the Night Before Thanksgiving	P	F	250+	Pilkey, Dav	Scholastic
Tweedle Dee Dee	G	TL	241	Voake, Charlotte	Candlewick Press
Tweedle-De-Dee Tumbleweed	G	F	103	Reese, Bob	Children's Press
Tweezers	C	I	33	Simple Tools	Lerner Publishing Group
Twelve	U	RF	250+	Myracle, Lauren	Puffin Books
Twelve Balloons for the Clown	J	RF	404	PM Math Readers	Rigby
Twelve Dancing Princesses	M	TL	250+	Enrichment	Wright Group/McGraw Hill
Twelve Dancing Princesses, The	P	TL	250+	Cech, John	Sterling Publishing
Twelve Days of Christmas, The	L	TL	250+	Spirin, Gennady	Marshall Cavendish
Twelve Days of Springtime, The: A School Counting Book	K	RF	250+	Rose, Deborah Lee	Harry N. Abrams
Twelve Days of Winter, The	K	RF	250+	Rose, Deborah Lee	Harry N. Abrams
Twelve Rounds to Glory: The Story of Muhammad Ali	V	B	250+	Smith, Charles R. Jr.	Candlewick Press
Twelve Travelers, Twenty Horses	U	HF	250+	Robinet, Harriette Gillem	Aladdin Paperbacks
Twenty Boy Summer	Z+	RF	250+	Ockler, Sarah	Little Brown and Company
Twenty Steps to the Treasure	H	RF	194	PM Math Readers	Rigby
Twenty-Four-Hour Challenge, The	M	RF	727	In Step Readers	Rigby
Twenty-One Balloons, The	V	SF	250+	DuBois, William	Scholastic
Twice as Nice	L	I	691	Sun Sprouts	ETA/Cuisenaire
Twiddle Twins' Haunted House, The	L	F	1141	Goldsmith, Howard	Mondo Publishing
Twiddle Twins' Music Box Mystery, The	L	F	250+	Goldsmith, Howard	Mondo Publishing
Twiddle Twins' Single Footprint Mystery, The	L	F	250+	Goldsmith, Howard	Mondo Publishing
Twiga and the Moon	I	F	250+	Storyworlds	Heinemann
Twilight	Z+	F	250+	Meyer, Stephanie	Little Brown and Company
Twilight in Grace Falls	W	RF	250+	Honeycutt, Natalie	Avon Books
Twilight of the Wolves	V	F	7348	Reading Street	Pearson
Twilight Prisoner, The	W	F	250+	Marsh, Katherine	Hyperion
#Twilight Zone, The: Deaths-Head Revisited	Z+	F	250+	Sterling, Rod	Walker & Company
#Twilight Zone, The: The After Hours	X	F	250+	Serling, Rod	Walker & Company
#Twilight Zone, The: The Midnight Sun	X	F	250+	Serling, Rod	Walker & Company

* Collection of short stories   # Graphic text
^ Mature content with lower level text demands

TITLE	LEVEL	GENRE	WORD COUNT	AUTHOR / SERIES	PUBLISHER / DISTRIBUTOR
#Twilight Zone, The: The Monsters Are Due on Maple Street	Z	F	250+	Serling, Rod	Walker & Company
#Twilight Zone, The: The Odyssey of Flight 33	X	F	250+	Serling, Rod	Walker & Company
#Twilight Zone, The: Walking Distance	X	F	250+	Serling, Rod	Walker & Company
Twilight: Warriors, The New Prophecy	U	F	250+	Hunter, Erin	HarperTrophy
Twin Competition, The	J	RF	410	PM Stars Bridge Books	Rigby
Twin Giants, The	M	F	250+	King-Smith, Dick	Candlewick Press
Twinkie Squad, The	S	RF	250+	Korman, Gordon	Scholastic
Twinkle and the Busy Bee: Butterfly Meadow	M	F	250+	Moss, Olivia	Scholastic
Twinkle Dives In: Butterfly Meadow	M	F	250+	Moss, Olivia	Scholastic
Twinkle, Twinkle, Little Star	L	TL	250+	Trapani, Iza	Charlesbridge
Twins	H	RF	149	The Rowland Reading Program Library	Rowland Reading Foundation
Twins	H	I	113	Vocabulary Readers	Houghton Mifflin Harcourt
Twin's Surprise, The	M	RF	720	Red Rocket Readers	Flying Start Books
Twins This and That, The	J	F	494	Appleton-Smith, Laura	Flyleaf Publishing
Twins, The	H	RF	250+	Early Transitional, Set 1	Pioneer Valley
Twisted	Z+	RF	250+	Anderson, Laurie Halse	Speak
Twisted Window, The	Z+	RF	250+	Duncan, Lois	Laurel-Leaf Books
^Twister Trap, The	T	F	250+	Dahl, Michael	Stone Arch Books
Twisters	M	I	250+	Early Connections	Benchmark Education
Twisters and Other Terrible Storms	R	I	250+	Osborne, Will; Osborne, Mary Pope	Random House
Twisters and Other Wind Storms	P	I	250+	Wildcats	Wright Group/McGraw Hill
Twisters!	M	I	250+	DK Readers	DK Publishing
Twisting Up a Storm	S	I	250+	Orbit Chapter Books	Pacific Learning
Twits, The	S	F	250+	Dahl, Roald	Penguin Group
Twitter and Tweet: Bringing Home a Bird	N	I	250+	Get a Pet	Picture Window Books
Two	E	RF	84	Carousel Readers	Pearson Learning Group
Two	LB	I	17	Count on It!	Marshall Cavendish
Two	A	I	17	Little Celebrations	Pearson Learning Group
Two African Countries	Q	I	250+	High-Fliers	Pacific Learning
Two Against the Mississippi	T	HF	2187	Leveled Readers	Houghton Mifflin Harcourt
Two Against the Mississippi	T	HF	2187	Leveled Readers/CA	Houghton Mifflin Harcourt
Two Against the Mississippi	T	HF	2187	Leveled Readers/TX	Houghton Mifflin Harcourt
Two and Three	B	RF	45	Reading Street	Pearson
Two Baby Elephants	I	F	240	Lighthouse	Rigby
Two Badges: The Lives of Mona Ruiz	Z+	B	250+	Edge	Hampton Brown
Two Baskets	E	RF	181	Bookshop	Mondo Publishing
Two Bear Cubs	H	F	89	Jonas, Ann	Morrow
Two Bobbies: A True Story of Hurricane Katrina, Friendship, and Survival	M	HF	250+	Larson, Kirby & Nethery, Mary	Walker & Company
Two by Two	G	TL	88	Cambridge Reading	Pearson Learning Group
Two Can Do It!	C	RF	32	Canizares, Susan; Chessen, Betsey	Scholastic
Two Cities: Traveling Through Place Value	S	I	250+	In Step Readers	Rigby
Two Class Trips	N	RF	250+	InfoTrek	ETA/Cuisenaire
Two Cold Ears	O	B	560	Leveled Readers	Houghton Mifflin Harcourt
Two Crazy Pigs	I	F	250+	Nagel, Karen Berman	Scholastic
Two Cultures Meet	U	I	250+	Reading Expeditions	National Geographic
Two Eyes, A Nose, and a Mouth	I	I	169	Grobel Intrater, Roberta	Scholastic
Two Eyes, Two Ears	D	I	83	PM Nonfiction-Red	Rigby
*Two Fables of Aesop to Read and Tell	J	TL	411	Books for Young Learners	Richard C. Owen
Two Feet	F	RF	129	Pescoe, Gwen	Educational Insights
Two Foolish Cats, The	K	F	250+	Literacy 2000	Rigby

T

TITLE	LEVEL	GENRE	WORD COUNT	AUTHOR / SERIES	PUBLISHER / DISTRIBUTOR
^Two Foot Punch	Y	RF	250+	Orca Sports	Orca Books
Two Giants, The	K	TL	250+	Storyworlds	Heinemann
Two Girls of Gettysburg	Z	HF	250+	Klein, Lisa	Bloomsbury Children's Books
Two Great Rivers	S	I	1893	Reading Street	Pearson
Two Halves and Four Quarters	I	RF	250+	PM Math Readers	Rigby
Two Heads Are Better Than One	Q	RF	250+	Mazer, Anne	Scholastic
Two Heroes	I	F	282	Leveled Readers	Houghton Mifflin Harcourt
Two Heroes	I	F	282	Leveled Readers/CA	Houghton Mifflin Harcourt
Two Heroes	I	F	282	Leveled Readers/TX	Houghton Mifflin Harcourt
Two Homes	G	RF	166	Masurel, Claire	Candlewick Press
Two Homes	F	RF	126	The King School Series	Townsend Press
Two Hungry Hippos	M	I	250+	Early Connections	Benchmark Education
Two Imporant Debates	X	I	2805	Vocabulary Readers/CA	Houghton Mifflin Harcourt
Two Imporant Debates	X	I	2805	Vocabulary Readers/TX	Houghton Mifflin Harcourt
Two Important Debates	X	I	2805	Vocabulary Readers	Houghton Mifflin Harcourt
Two Is a Pair	E	I	78	Teacher's Choice Series	Pearson Learning Group
Two Labors of Hercules	P	TL	956	Gear Up!	Wright Group/McGraw Hill
Two Languages	K	I	202	Vocabulary Readers	Houghton Mifflin Harcourt
*Two Little Birds and Other Stories	D	RF	60	Story Steps	Rigby
Two Little Boys from Toolittle Toys	M	F	250+	Kirsch, Vincent X.	Bloomsbury Children's Books
Two Little Chicks	C	F	32	KinderReaders	Rigby
Two Little Dogs	E	F	74	Story Box	Wright Group/McGraw Hill
Two Little Ducks Get Lost	F	F	178	PM Plus Story Books	Rigby
Two Little Goldfish	I	RF	344	PM Story Books-Orange	Rigby
Two Little Houses	H	RF	252	InfoTrek	ETA/Cuisenaire
Two Little Mice, The	I	F	163	Literacy 2000	Rigby
Two Loves of Will Shakespeare, The	Z+	RF	250+	Lawlor, Laurie	Holiday House
Two More	LB	F	16	Voyages	SRA/McGraw Hill
Two of Us, The	C	I	135	Vocabulary Readers	Houghton Mifflin Harcourt
Two of Us, The	C	I	135	Vocabulary Readers/CA	Houghton Mifflin Harcourt
Two Ogres, The	F	F	116	Joy Readers	Pearson Learning Group
Two Parties, One Tux and a Very Short Film About the Grapes of Wrath	Z+	RF	250+	Goldman, Steven	Bloomsbury Children's Books
Two Pirates	I	F	356	Red Rocket Readers	Flying Start Books
Two Plus One Goes A.P.E.	L	RF	250+	Springstubb, Tricia	Scholastic
Two Plus Two	E	RF	44	Teacher's Choice Series	Pearson Learning Group
Two Points	B	RF	40	Kennedy, Jane; Eaton, Audrey	Continental Press
Two Red Tugs	L	F	547	PM Story Books	Rigby
Two Runaways, The	M	RF	250+	Woodland Mysteries	Wright Group/McGraw Hill
Two Sides of Mining, The	X	I	1907	Reading Street	Pearson
*Two Silly Trolls	J	F	250+	Jewell, Nancy	HarperTrophy
Two Sisters Play Tennis	J	I	327	Leveled Readers	Houghton Mifflin Harcourt
Two Sisters Play Tennis	J	I	327	Leveled Readers/CA	Houghton Mifflin Harcourt
Two Sisters Play Tennis	J	I	327	Leveled Readers/TX	Houghton Mifflin Harcourt
Two Stupid Cats	G	F	140	Sunshine	Wright Group/McGraw Hill
Two Sweet Peas	M	RF	250+	Bebop Books	Lee & Low Books Inc.
Two Teams	H	I	146	Leveled Literacy Intervention/Green System	Heinemann
Two Tickets to Freedom: The True Story of Ellen and William Craft	S	B	250+	Freedman, Florence	Scholastic
Two Tooth Fairies	L	F	1043	InfoTrek	ETA/Cuisenaire
Two Traditions of Dance	P	I	382	Vocabulary Readers	Houghton Mifflin Harcourt
Two Travelers and Bear	L	TL	610	Rigby Flying Colors	Rigby

* Collection of short stories   # Graphic text
^ Mature content with lower level text demands

TITLE	LEVEL	GENRE	WORD COUNT	AUTHOR / SERIES	PUBLISHER / DISTRIBUTOR
*Two Tricky Tales	L	TL	250+	Pacific Literacy	Pacific Learning
Two Turtles	LB	RF	13	Ready Readers	Pearson Learning Group
Two Week Diary	H	RF	208	Sun Sprouts	ETA/Cuisenaire
Two Women Astronauts	S	B	1353	Reading Street	Pearson
Two Worlds Meet: The Travels of Francisco de Coronado	T	B	250+	On Our Way to English	Rigby
Two Yellow Eyes	F	F	211	Sun Sprouts	ETA/Cuisenaire
Two-Minute Drill	S	RF	250+	Lupica, Mike	Puffin Books
Two-Part Invention	Z	B	250+	L'Engle, Madeleine	HarperCollins
Two-Star Day	O	RF	446	Leveled Readers	Houghton Mifflin Harcourt
Two-Timer	I	RF	465	Rigby Flying Colors	Rigby
Tye May and the Magic Brush	M	TL	250+	Bang, Molly Garrett	Mulberry Books
Tygrine Cat, The	W	F	250+	Iserles, Inbali	Candlewick Press
Tyler Toad and Thunder	M	F	250+	Crowe, Robert	Dutton Children's Books
Tyler's Train	C	RF	42	Little Celebrations	Pearson Learning Group
Types of Communities	K	I	307	Early Explorers	Benchmark Education
Types of Trees	D	I	29	Vocabulary Readers	Houghton Mifflin Harcourt
Tyra Banks: From Supermodel to Role Model	T	B	6057	Gateway Biographies	Lerner Publishing Group
Tyrannosaurus Dad	K	F	250+	Rosenberg, Liz	Roaring Brook Press
Tyrannosaurus Drip	L	F	250+	Donaldson, Julia	Feiwel and Friends
Tyrannosaurus Game, The	L	F	250+	Kroll, Steven	Marshall Cavendish
Tyrannosaurus Rex	O	I	250+	A True Book	Children's Press
Tyrannosaurus Rex	I	I	117	Dinosaur and Prehistoric Animals	Capstone Press
Tyrannosaurus Rex	N	I	250+	Discovering Dinosaurs	Capstone Press
Tyrannosaurus Rex	M	I	250+	Prehistoric Creatures Then and Now	Steck-Vaughn
Tyrannosaurus the Terrible	L	F	182	Wesley & the Dinosaurs	Wright Group/McGraw Hill
Ty's One-man Band	L	RF	250+	Walter, Mildred Pitts	Scholastic
Ty's Triple Trouble	L	RF	250+	Social Studies Connects	Kane Press

T

TITLE	LEVEL	GENRE	WORD COUNT	AUTHOR / SERIES	PUBLISHER / DISTRIBUTOR
^U.S. Air Force Space Command, The	S	I	250+	The U.S. Armed Forces	Capstone Press
U.S. Air Force Special Forces: Pararescue	V	I	250+	Warfare and Weapons	Capstone Press
U.S. Air Force Special Operations	Y	I	8537	U.S. Armed Forces	Lerner Publishing Group
^U.S. Air Force Spy Planes	R	I	250+	Military Vehicles	Capstone Press
^U.S. Air Force Thunderbirds, The	S	I	250+	The U.S. Armed Forces	Capstone Press
U.S. Air Force, The	M	I	142	Military Branches	Capstone Press
U.S. Air Force, The	Q	I	7489	U.S. Armed Forces	Lerner Publishing Group
^U.S. Airforce, The	S	I	250+	The U.S. Armed Forces	Capstone Press
U.S. Army at War, The	V	I	250+	On the Front Lines	Capstone Press
^U.S. Army Golden Knights, The	S	I	250+	The U.S. Armed Forces	Capstone Press
^U.S. Army Humvees	R	I	250+	Military Vehicles	Capstone Press
^U.S. Army Infantry Fighting Vehicles	R	I	250+	Military Vehicles	Capstone Press
^U.S. Army National Guard, The	S	I	250+	The U.S. Armed Forces	Capstone Press
^U.S. Army Rangers, The	S	I	250+	The U.S. Armed Forces	Capstone Press
U.S. Army Special Operations Forces	Y	I	7169	U.S. Armed Forces	Lerner Publishing Group
U.S. Army, The	M	I	121	Military Branches	Capstone Press
^U.S. Army, The	S	I	250+	The U.S. Armed Forces	Capstone Press
U.S. Army, The	Y	I	7218	U.S. Armed Forces	Lerner Publishing Group
^U.S. Border Patrol, The: Guarding the Nation	S	I	250+	Line of Duty	Capstone Press
^U.S. Coast Guard Cutters	Q	I	250+	Military Vehicles	Capstone Press
U.S. Coast Guard, The	M	I	137	Military Branches	Capstone Press
U.S. Coast Guard, The	Y	I	6397	U.S. Armed Forces	Lerner Publishing Group
#U.S. Congress, The	V	I	250+	Cartoon Nation	Capstone Press
U.S. Congress, The	Q	I	250+	Let's See	Compass Point Books
U.S. Constitution, The	M	I	149	Allen, Kathy	Capstone Press
#U.S. Constitution, The	V	I	250+	Cartoon Nation	Capstone Press
U.S. Constitution, The	O	I	250+	Our Government	Capstone Press
U.S. Constitution, The	M	I	138	Pebble Plus	Capstone Press
U.S. Constitution, The	T	I	250+	We The People	Compass Point Books
#U.S. Immigration	T	I	250+	Cartoon Nation	Capstone Press
^U.S. Marine Corps Assault Vehicles	R	I	250+	Military Vehicles	Capstone Press
U.S. Marine Corps at War, The	V	I	250+	On the Front Lines	Capstone Press
U.S. Marine Corps Combat Jets	R	I	250+	Military Vehicles	Capstone Press
U.S. Marine Corps, The	M	I	143	Military Branches	Capstone Press
^U.S. Marine Corps, The	S	I	250+	The U.S. Armed Forces	Capstone Press
U.S. Marine Corps, The	Y	I	6650	U.S. Armed Forces	Lerner Publishing Group
^U.S. Marine Expeditionary Units	S	I	250+	The U.S. Armed Forces	Capstone Press
^U.S. Marshals Service, The: Catching Fugitives	S	I	250+	Line of Duty	Capstone Press
U.S. Naval Special Warfare Forces	Y	I	7871	U.S. Armed Forces	Lerner Publishing Group
^U.S. Navy Cruisers	R	I	250+	Military Vehicles	Capstone Press
^U.S. Navy Destroyers	R	I	250+	Military Vehicles	Capstone Press
U.S. Navy Special Forces: Seal Teams	V	I	250+	Warfare and Weapons	Capstone Press
U.S. Navy, The	M	I	131	Military Branches	Capstone Press
^U.S. Navy, The	S	I	250+	The U.S. Armed Forces	Capstone Press
U.S. Navy, The	Y	I	7664	U.S. Armed Forces	Lerner Publishing Group
^U.S. Secret Service, The: Protecting Our Leaders	S	I	250+	Line of Duty	Capstone Press
#U.S. Supreme Court, The	V	I	250+	Cartoon Nation	Capstone Press
U.S. Supreme Court, The	Q	I	250+	Let's See	Compass Point Books
U.S. Symbols	K	I	123	Government	Lerner Publishing Group
^UFOs	X	I	250+	The Unexplained	Capstone Press
UFOs	Z	I	7472	The Unexplained	Lerner Publishing Group
^UFOs and Aliens	S	I	250+	Download	Hameray Publishing Group
UFOs: Are They Real?	O	I	250+	Trail Blazers	Ransom Publishing

UV

* Collection of short stories   # Graphic text
^ Mature content with lower level text demands

TITLE	LEVEL	GENRE	WORD COUNT	AUTHOR / SERIES	PUBLISHER / DISTRIBUTOR
^UFOs: The Unsolved Mystery	R	I	250+	Mysteries of Science	Capstone Press
Ugh! A Bug!	F	I	108	Silly Millies	Millbrook Press
Uglies	Z	SF	250+	Westerfeld, Scott	Simon Pulse
Ugly Duckling, The	I	TL	359	Folk Tales	Pioneer Valley
Ugly Duckling, The	J	TL	563	Leveled Literacy Intervention/ Blue System	Heinemann
Ugly Duckling, The	I	TL	250+	Literacy 2000	Rigby
Ugly Duckling, The	J	TL	452	PM Tales and Plays-Turquoise	Rigby
Ugly Duckling, The	E	TL	148	Rigby Rocket	Rigby
Ugly Duckling, The	F	TL	246	Storyworlds	Heinemann
Ugly Duckling, The	J	TL	558	Tales from Hans Andersen	Wright Group/McGraw Hill
Ugly Duckling, The	I	TL	359	Traditional Tales	Pioneer Valley
Ugly Duckling, The	H	TL	340	Ziefert, Harriet	Puffin Books
Ugly Mug	P	RF	250+	Joseph, Vivienne	Pacific Learning
Ugly Pugsy	O	F	250+	Bookweb	Rigby
Ugly Vegetables, The	L	RF	250+	Lin, Grace	Charlesbridge
Uh-Oh!	D	RF	62	Literacy by Design	Rigby
Uh-Oh!	D	RF	62	Rigby Literacy	Rigby
Uh-Oh! Said the Crow	J	F	250+	Oppenheim, Joanna	Bantam Books
Ukraine	Q	I	250+	Theme Sets	National Geographic
Ultimate Field Trip 1: Adventures in the Amazon Rain Forest	T	I	250+	Goodman, Susan E.	Simon & Schuster
Ultimate Weapon: The Race to Develop the Atomic Bomb, The	Z	I	250+	Sullivan, Edward T.	Holiday House
Ultra-Organized Cell Systems	Z	I	250+	Microquests	Lerner Publishing Group
Ulysses S. Grant	S	B	3899	History Maker Bios	Lerner Publishing Group
Ulysses S. Grant	U	B	250+	Let Freedom Ring	Red Brick Learning
Ulysses S. Grant	S	B	250+	Primary Source Readers	Teacher Created Materials
Ulysses S. Grant	U	B	250+	Profiles of the Presidents	Compass Point Books
Ulysses S. Grant: Confident Leader and Hero	Y	B	250+	The Civil War	Carus Publishing Company
Ulysses S. Grant: Eighteenth President	R	B	250+	Getting to Know the U.S. Presidents	Children's Press
Umbrella	C	F	73	Story Box	Wright Group/McGraw Hill
Umbrella, The	N	TL	250+	Brett, Jan	Scholastic
Umbrellas	L	I	430	Sunshine	Wright Group/McGraw Hill
Umma Ungka's Unusual Umbrella	K	F	723	Animal Antics A to Z	Kane Press
Unbelievable Johnny Appleseed, The	N	B	250+	Leveled Readers Language Support	Houghton Mifflin Harcourt
Unbelievable!	T	I	250+	Boldprint	Steck-Vaughn
Unbelievable!	K	SF	250+	Shulman, Lisa	Hampton Brown
Uncertain Princess, The	J	F	479	InfoTrek	ETA/Cuisenaire
Uncharted Waters	T	RF	250+	Bulion, Leslie	Peachtree
Unclaimed Treasures	X	RF	250+	MacLachlan, Patricia	HarperTrophy
Uncle Buncle's House	C	RF	56	Sunshine	Wright Group/McGraw Hill
Uncle Carlos's Barbecue	H	RF	207	Foundations	Wright Group/McGraw Hill
Uncle Elephant	J	F	1784	Lobel, Arnold	HarperCollins
Uncle Elephant and Uncle Tiger	D	TL	77	Joy Readers	Pearson Learning Group
Uncle Jed's Barbershop	S	RF	250+	Mitchell, Margaree King	Scholastic
Uncle Jim	G	RF	127	Windmill Books	Rigby
Uncle Joe	H	F	149	Pacific Literacy	Pacific Learning
Uncle Rabbit	N	TL	890	Leveled Readers	Houghton Mifflin Harcourt
Uncle Rabbit	N	TL	890	Leveled Readers/CA	Houghton Mifflin Harcourt
Uncle Rabbit	N	TL	890	Leveled Readers/TX	Houghton Mifflin Harcourt
Uncle Sam	O	I	250+	American Symbols	Picture Window Books
Uncle Sam	S	I	250+	Symbols of America	Marshall Cavendish

UV

TITLE	LEVEL	GENRE	WORD COUNT	AUTHOR / SERIES	PUBLISHER / DISTRIBUTOR
Uncle Tease	N	RF	250+	Literacy Tree	Rigby
Uncle Ted and the Hiccups	I	RF	281	Sails	Rigby
Uncle Ted Is Tricky!	F	RF	224	Sails	Rigby
Uncle Ted's Big Jump	I	F	448	Sails	Rigby
Uncle Ted's Teeth	F	RF	211	Sails	Rigby
Uncle Terry's Glasses	L	RF	250+	Windows on Literacy	National Geographic
Uncle Timi's Sleep	G	RF	102	Pacific Literacy	Pacific Learning
Uncles	F	I	44	Families	Capstone Press
Uncles	D	I	36	Pebble Books	Capstone Press
Uncle's Bakery	H	RF	81	Early Readers	Compass Point Books
Uncle's Clever Tricks	D	RF	61	Joy Readers	Pearson Learning Group
Uncommon Reader, The	Z+	RF	250+	Bennett, Alan	Farrar, Straus, & Giroux
Uncommon Revolutionary: A Story About Thomas Paine	R	B	8127	Creative Minds Biographies	Carolrhoda Books
Uncovering Classical Athens	X	I	3004	Reading Street	Pearson
Uncovering Earth's History	T	I	250+	Reading Expeditions	National Geographic
#Uncovering Mummies: An Isabel Soto Archaeology Adventure	S	F	250+	Graphic Expeditions	Capstone Press
Uncovering the Past	M	I	478	Leveled Readers	Houghton Mifflin Harcourt
Uncovering the Past	M	I	478	Leveled Readers/CA	Houghton Mifflin Harcourt
Uncovering the Past	M	I	478	Leveled Readers/TX	Houghton Mifflin Harcourt
Uncovering the Secrets of Ancient Egypt	Y	I	2309	Reading Street	Pearson
Uncovering the Structure of DNA	V	I	250+	Reading Expeditions	National Geographic
Under a Full Moon	D	F	65	Leveled Readers	Houghton Mifflin Harcourt
Under a Living Sky	P	RF	250+	Orca Young Readers	Orca Books
Under a Microscope	H	I	254	Sunshine	Wright Group/McGraw Hill
Under a Red Sky: Memoirs of a Childhood in Communist Russia	Z+	B	250+	Molnar, Haya Leah	Farrar, Straus, & Giroux
Under Construction	S	I	250+	Kids Discover Reading	Wright Group/McGraw Hill
Under Lock and Key	N	RF	250+	Literacy by Design	Rigby
Under Lock and Key	N	RF	250+	On Our Way To English	Rigby
Under My Bed	C	F	42	Literacy 2000	Rigby
Under My Bed	C	F	49	Little Celebrations	Pearson Learning Group
Under My Nose	O	B	250+	Meet The Author	Richard C. Owen
Under My Sombrero	F	F	79	Books for Young Learners	Richard C. Owen
Under One Rock: Bugs, Slugs and other Ughs	O	I	950	Sharing Nature with Children	Dawn Publications
Under Siege!: Three Children at the Civil War Battle for Vicksburg	X	I	250+	Warren, Andrea	Farrar, Straus, & Giroux
Under the Banyan Tree	X	RF	250+	DePalma, Toni	Holiday House
Under the Bed	A	RF	28	Smart Start	Rigby
Under the Big Top	E	I	103	Twig	Wright Group/McGraw Hill
Under the Blood-Red Sun	W	HF	250+	Salisbury, Graham	Bantam Books
Under the Bright Lights	R	I	466	Vocabulary Readers	Houghton Mifflin Harcourt
Under the City	K	I	206	Sunshine	Wright Group/McGraw Hill
Under the Ground	LB	I	12	Animal Homes	Lerner Publishing Group
Under the Ground	C	I	42	Foundations	Wright Group/McGraw Hill
Under the Ground	B	I	28	Gear Up!	Wright Group/McGraw Hill
Under the Ground	P	I	250+	Literacy 2000	Rigby
Under the Ground	K	I	250+	Pluckrose, Henry	Franklin Watts
Under the Ground	B	I	44	Sails	Rigby
Under the Ground	Q	I	250+	Wildcats	Wright Group/McGraw Hill
Under the Hawthorn Tree	T	HF	250+	Conlon-McKenna, Marita	The O'Brien Press
Under the Hood	S	I	250+	NASCAR Racing	Capstone Press
Under the Ice	C	I	88	Sails	Rigby

UV

* Collection of short stories   # Graphic text
^ Mature content with lower level text demands

TITLE	LEVEL	GENRE	WORD COUNT	AUTHOR / SERIES	PUBLISHER / DISTRIBUTOR
Under the Leaf	D	F	100	Sails	Rigby
Under the Microscope	H	I	164	Sails	Rigby
Under the Moon	U	SF	5320	Oxford Bookworms Library	Oxford University Press
Under the Ocean	U	I	250+	The Natural World	Scholastic
Under the Ocean	T	I	614	Vocabulary Readers	Houghton Mifflin Harcourt
Under the Old Oak Tree	G	F	205	Seedlings	Continental Press
Under the Persimmon Tree	Y	RF	250+	Staples, Suzanne Fisher	Farrar, Straus, & Giroux
Under the Royal Palms	V	B	250+	Ada, Alma Flor	Scholastic
Under the Sea	N	I	250+	Quick Draw	Kingfisher
Under the Sea with Gogool and Googolplex	L	SF	250+	Orca Echoes	Orca Books
Under the Sky	C	I	44	Learn to Read	Creative Teaching Press
Under the Snow	M	I	250+	Stewart, Melissa	Peachtree
Under the Umbrella	C	RF	60	Phonics and Friends	Hampton Brown
Under Water	A	I	35	Twig	Wright Group/McGraw Hill
Under Wraps	U	I	250+	Goldish, Meish	Scholastic
Under, Over, By the Clover: What is a Preposition?	O	I	200	Words Are CATegorical	Millbrook Press
Undercover Tailback	Q	RF	250+	Christopher, Matt	Scholastic
Underdog	S	RF	250+	Orca Young Readers	Orca Books
Underfoot	N	I	250+	Look Once Look Again	Creative Teaching Press
Undergardeners, The	O	F	250+	Orca Young Readers	Orca Books
Underground	C	I	31	Twig	Wright Group/McGraw Hill
Underground Adventure	N	RF	250+	PM Plus Chapter Books	Rigby
Underground and All Around	N	I	250+	Rigby Literacy	Rigby
Underground Homes	L	I	693	Rigby Flying Colors	Rigby
Underground Homes	N	I	800	Vocabulary Readers	Houghton Mifflin Harcourt
Underground Homes	N	I	800	Vocabulary Readers/CA	Houghton Mifflin Harcourt
Underground Railroad, The	V	I	250+	Bial, Raymond	Houghton Mifflin Harcourt
Underground Railroad, The	V	I	250+	Cornerstones of Freedom	Children's Press
Underground Railroad, The	U	I	250+	Reading Expeditions	National Geographic
Underground Railroad, The	N	I	250+	Twig	Wright Group/McGraw Hill
^Underground Railroad, The: An Interactive History Adventure	T	HF	250+	You Choose Books	Capstone Press
Underground Railroad, The: Bringing Slaves North to Freedom	V	I	250+	Let Freedom Ring	Capstone Press
Underground Rescue	W	RF	2180	Leveled Readers	Houghton Mifflin Harcourt
Underneath, The	Y	F	250+	Appelt, Kathi	Atheneum Books
Undersea World	V	I	250+	Boldprint	Steck-Vaughn
Understanding Electricity	V	I	250+	Reading Expeditions	National Geographic
Understanding Global Warming	X	I	11190	Saving Our Living Earth	Lerner Publishing Group
#Understanding Global Warming with Max Axiom, Super Scientist	U	I	250+	Graphic Library	Capstone Press
Understanding Newton's Laws	Y	I	2888	Leveled Readers Science	Houghton Mifflin Harcourt
#Understanding Photosynthesis with Max Axiom, Super Scientist	U	I	250+	Graphic Library	Capstone Press
Understanding the Brain	X	I	250+	Reading Expeditions	National Geographic
#Understanding Viruses with Max Axiom Super Scientist	W	I	250+	Graphic Library	Capstone Press
Understood Betsy	S	RF	250+	Fisher, Dorothy Canfield	Henry Holt & Co.
Understudies	P	RF	250+	Bookweb	Rigby
^Undertaker	T	B	250+	Stars of Pro Wrestling	Capstone Press
Underwater	I	I	100	Start to Read	School Zone
Underwater	T	I	250+	The News	Richard C. Owen
Underwater Animals	Q	I	250+	Explorers	Wright Group/McGraw Hill
Underwater Journey	F	I	60	Sunshine	Wright Group/McGraw Hill

TITLE	LEVEL	GENRE	WORD COUNT	AUTHOR / SERIES	PUBLISHER / DISTRIBUTOR
Underwater Spiders	I	I	223	Sails	Rigby
Underwater with Jacques Cousteau	L	B	633	Leveled Readers Science	Houghton Mifflin Harcourt
Undone	Z+	RF	250+	Taylor, Brooke	Walker & Company
Undying Glory: The Story of the Massachusetts 54th Regiment	U	HF	250+	Cox, Clinton	Scholastic
Unexpected Hero, An	W	RF	2407	Leveled Readers	Houghton Mifflin Harcourt
Unexpected Music	V	I	2742	Reading Street	Pearson
Unexpected Treasure	Q	RF	250+	Ragged Island Mysteries	Wright Group/McGraw Hill
Unfinished Angel, The	U	F	250+	Creech, Sharon	HarperCollins
Unhappy Medium: Suddenly Supernatural	R	F	250+	Kimmel, Elizabeth Cody	Little Brown and Company
Unhappy Troll, The	D+	F	47	Ray's Readers	Outside the Box
*Unicorn Treasury, The	V	F	250+	Coville, Bruce	Harcourt, Inc.
Unicorns	Q	I	250+	Mythical Creatures	Raintree
Unicorns Don't Give Sleigh Rides	M	F	250+	Dadey, Debbie; Jones, Marcia Thornton	Scholastic
Unicorn's Tale, The (Nathaniel Fludd Beastologist Book Four)	R	F	250+	LaFevers, R. L.	Houghton Mifflin Harcourt
Uninvited Guests	S	I	250+	Sails	Rigby
Union General and 18th President: Ulysses S. Grant	T	B	250+	We the People	Compass Point Books
United Kingdom	P	I	2442	Country Explorers	Lerner Publishing Group
United Nations, The	R	I	250+	Rigby Focus	Rigby
United States ABCs, The: A Book About the People and Places of the United States	Q	I	250+	Country ABCs	Picture Window Books
United States and Russian Space Race, The	V	I	3331	Reading Street	Pearson
United States Constitution, The	V	I	250+	Let Freedom Ring	Red Brick Learning
United States Geography	M	I	169	Windows on Literacy	National Geographic
United States Goes West, The	T	I	1285	Reading Street	Pearson
United States Holocaust Memorial Museum, The	W	I	250+	Cornerstones of Freedom	Children's Press
United States Marshals Service	S	I	250+	Law Enforcement	Capstone Press
United States, The	Q	I	250+	First Reports: Countries	Compass Point Books
United States, The: A Question and Answer Book	P	I	250+	Questions & Answers: Countries	Capstone Press
United States, The: Region by Region	S	I	250+	Pair-It Books	Steck-Vaughn
*Universal Solvent and Other Cases, The	O	RF	250+	Simon, Seymour	Avon Books
Universe, The	Q	I	250+	Pair-It Books	Steck-Vaughn
Unknowns, The	Y	RF	250+	Carey, Benedict	Amulet Books
Unlocking the Secrets of Your Amazing Brain	W	I	250+	Explore More	Wright Group/McGraw Hill
Unmaking of Duncan Veerick, The	X	RF	250+	Levin, Betty	Front Street
Uno's Garden	M	F	250+	Base, Graeme	Harry N. Abrams
Unseen by the Eye	T	I	250+	Connectors	Pacific Learning
Unsinkable Madame C. J. Walker, The	Y	B	3573	Leveled Readers	Houghton Mifflin Harcourt
"Unsinkable" Titanic, The	S	I	1403	Reading Street	Pearson
Unsung American Hero, An	U	B	2605	Leveled Readers	Houghton Mifflin Harcourt
Unsung American Hero, An	U	B	2605	Leveled Readers/CA	Houghton Mifflin Harcourt
Unsung American Hero, An	U	B	2605	Leveled Readers/TX	Houghton Mifflin Harcourt
Untamed: (House of Night)	Z+	F	250+	Cast, P. C. & Kristin	St. Martin's Griffin
Until We Got Princess	E	RF	94	Bookshop	Mondo Publishing
Until We Meet Again	Z	RF	250+	Schraff, Anne	Townsend Press
Untold Story, The	W	I	250+	WorldScapes	ETA/Cuisenaire
Unusual Amphibians	L	I	197	Larkin's Little Readers	Wilbooks
Unusual Coin, The	O	F	951	Leveled Readers	Houghton Mifflin Harcourt
Unusual Creepy-Crawlies	N	I	801	Springboard	Wright Group/McGraw Hill
Unusual Machines	J	I	229	Little Red Readers	Sundance

UV

* Collection of short stories   # Graphic text
^ Mature content with lower level text demands

TITLE	LEVEL	GENRE	WORD COUNT	AUTHOR / SERIES	PUBLISHER / DISTRIBUTOR
Unusual Recipe Competition, The	N	RF	250+	Springboard	Wright Group/McGraw Hill
Unusual Show, An	H	F	63	Blonder, Ellen	Scholastic
Unusual Spiders	N	I	250+	Take Two Books	Wright Group/McGraw Hill
Unusual Suspects, The: The Sisters Grimm	U	F	250+	Buckley, Michael	Amulet Books
Unvisibles, The	T	F	250+	Whybrow, Ian	Holiday House
Up and Away	Q	I	250+	Explorers	Wright Group/McGraw Hill
Up and Away	S	RF	250+	Reading Safari	Mondo Publishing
Up and Away!: Taking a Flight	N	RF	250+	Bookshop	Mondo Publishing
Up and Away, Curious George	A	F	22	Leveled Readers/CA	Houghton Mifflin Harcourt
Up and Away, Curious George!	A	F	22	Leveled Readers	Houghton Mifflin Harcourt
Up and Down	C	RF	92	Handprints C, Set 1	Educators Publishing Service
Up and Down	B	I	25	Little Books for Early Readers	University of Maine
Up and Down	D	RF	99	New Way Red	Steck-Vaughn
Up and Down	C	I	81	PM Plus Nonfiction	Rigby
Up and Down	B	I	41	Red Rocket Readers	Flying Start Books
Up and Down	C	RF	68	Rigby Literacy	Rigby
Up and Down	D	I	102	Sails	Rigby
Up and Down	E	RF	79	Storyteller-Setting Sun	Wright Group/McGraw Hill
Up and Down	I	I	213	Where Words	Capstone Press
Up and Down and All Around	J	I	250+	InfoTrek	ETA/Cuisenaire
Up and Down on the Playground	B	RF	22	Bonnell, Kris	Reading Reading Books
Up and Down the Hill	D	F	78	Early Connections	Benchmark Education
Up and Under	D	I	97	Sails	Rigby
Up and Up	WB	RF	0	Hughes, Shirley	Lothrop, Lee & Shepard
Up Before Daybreak: Cotton and People in America	Y	I	250+	Hopkinson, Deborah	Scholastic
Up Close	G	I	123	Discovery Links	Newbridge
Up Cloudy Mountain	S	RF	250+	Sails	Rigby
Up Down	B	I	74	Bookworms	Marshall Cavendish
Up Here	E	F	36	Potato Chip Books	American Reading Company
Up High in the Mountains	N	RF	250+	Wildcats	Wright Group/McGraw Hill
Up in a Tree	D	RF	111	Leveled Literacy Intervention/ Green System	Heinemann
Up in a Tree	C	RF	47	Sunshine	Wright Group/McGraw Hill
Up in the Air	P	I	250+	Wildcats	Wright Group/McGraw Hill
Up in the Sky	B	I	56	PM Plus Starters	Rigby
Up in the Sky	B	I	23	Reach	National Geographic
Up North and Down South: Using Map Directions	N	I	250+	Map Mania	Capstone Press
Up the Amazon	Q	I	250+	Windows on Literacy	National Geographic
Up the Down Staircase	Z+	RF	250+	Kaufman, Bel	HarperCollins
Up the Haystack	H	RF	251	Bookshop	Mondo Publishing
Up the Hill	LB	RF	16	Handprints A	Educators Publishing Service
Up the Tree	B	RF	38	First Stories	Pacific Learning
Up the Tree	D	RF	41	New Way Red	Steck-Vaughn
Up the Tree	B	RF	41	Rigby Rocket	Rigby
Up They Go	B	RF	30	Ready Readers	Pearson Learning Group
Up to the Challenge	S	I	250+	Connectors	Pacific Learning
Up Went Edmond	D	F	26	Pacific Literacy	Pacific Learning
Up Went the Goat	C	F	38	Start to Read	School Zone
Up, Down, and All Around	D	I	44	Windows on Literacy	National Geographic
Up, Down, and Around	H	I	82	Ayres, Katherine	Candlewick Press
Up, Over, and Down	LB	F	24	Reading Safari	Mondo Publishing

* Collection of short stories   # Graphic text
^ Mature content with lower level text demands

TITLE	LEVEL	GENRE	WORD COUNT	AUTHOR / SERIES	PUBLISHER / DISTRIBUTOR
Up, Up and Away	M	I	250+	Yellow Umbrella Books	Red Brick Learning
Up, Up, and Away	F	F	250+	Easy Stories	Norwood House Press
Up, Up, and Away	B	I	40	Lighthouse	Rigby
Up, Up, and Away	T	I	1870	Reading Street	Pearson
Up, Up, and Away	M	I	250+	Twig	Wright Group/McGraw Hill
Up, Up, and Away!	Q	I	1113	Leveled Readers	Houghton Mifflin Harcourt
Up, Up, and Away!	Q	I	1113	Leveled Readers/CA	Houghton Mifflin Harcourt
Up, Up, and Away!	Q	I	1113	Leveled Readers/TX	Houghton Mifflin Harcourt
Up, Up, and Away: The Story of Amelia Earhart	F	B	42	Canizares, Susan; Chanko, Pamela	Scholastic
Updos: Cool Hairstyles for All Occasions	Q	I	250+	Crafts	Capstone Press
Uphill Race, The	D	F	77	Bonnell, Kris	Reading Reading Books
Ups and Downs of Carl Davis III, The	T	RF	250+	Guy, Rosa	Language for Learning Assoc.
Upside Down	B	I	36	Sails	Rigby
Upside Down Boy, The	N	RF	250+	Herrera, Juan Felipe	Children's Book Press
Upside-Down Elephant, The	K	RF	396	Leveled Readers	Houghton Mifflin Harcourt
Upside-Down Reader, The	L	F	250+	Gruber, Wolfram	North-South Books
Upside-Down Voyage, The	S	HF	250+	Bookshop	Mondo Publishing
Upstairs Mouse, Downstairs Mole	L	F	250+	Wong, Herbert Yee	Houghton Mifflin Harcourt
Upstate Autumn	R	RF	1676	Leveled Readers	Houghton Mifflin Harcourt
Uptown	N	RF	250+	Collier, Bryan	Henry Holt & Co.
Uranus	Q	I	250+	A True Book	Children's Press
Uranus	Q	I	1322	Early Bird Astronomy	Lerner Publishing Group
Uranus	J	I	136	Exploring the Galaxy	Capstone Press
Uranus	S	I	250+	Our Solar System	Compass Point Books
Uranus	N	I	792	Our Universe	Lerner Publishing Group
Uranus	Q	I	250+	The Galaxy	Red Brick Learning
Uranus	M	I	250+	The Solar System	Capstone Press
Urban Legends	Y	I	250+	Boldprint	Steck-Vaughn
Urban Wildlife	R	I	1212	Leveled Readers	Houghton Mifflin Harcourt
Urchin and the Heartstone: The Mistmantle Chronicles	X	F	250+	McAllister, M.I.	Hyperion
Urchin of the Riding Stars: The Mistmantle Chronicles	X	F	250+	McAllister, M.I.	Hyperion
Ursus Travels	N	F	1066	Leveled Readers	Houghton Mifflin Harcourt
Ursus Travels	N	F	1066	Leveled Readers/CA	Houghton Mifflin Harcourt
Ursus Travels	N	F	1066	Leveled Readers/TX	Houghton Mifflin Harcourt
Ursus, the Traveling Bear	N	F	1038	Leveled Readers	Houghton Mifflin Harcourt
Ursus, the Traveling Bear	N	F	1038	Leveled Readers/CA	Houghton Mifflin Harcourt
Ursus, the Traveling Bear	N	F	1038	Leveled Readers/TX	Houghton Mifflin Harcourt
US and A	R	I	3003	Take Two Books	Wright Group/McGraw Hill
Us and Uncle Fraud	S	RF	250+	Lowry, Lois	Houghton Mifflin Harcourt
USA, The	V	I	10188	Oxford Bookworms Library	Oxford University Press
Usborne Book of Inventors, The: From Davinci to Biro	X	B	250+	Reid, Struan; Fara, Patricia	Scholastic
Usborne Book of Scientists, The: From Archimedes to Einstein	X	B	250+	Reid, Struan; Fara, Patricia	Scholastic
Use Your Beak!	F	RF	106	Erickson, Betty	Continental Press
Used Any Numbers Lately?	J	I	70	Allen, Susan & Lindaman, Jane	Millbrook Press
Useful Nose, A	J	F	547	Red Rocket Readers	Flying Start Books
Using a Beak	M	I	250+	Sails	Rigby
Using a Microscope	H	I	182	Rigby Focus	Rigby
Using a Tail	M	I	250+	Sails	Rigby
Using Addition at Home	F	I	157	Math Around Us	Heinemann Library

UV

* Collection of short stories   # Graphic text
^ Mature content with lower level text demands

TITLE	LEVEL	GENRE	WORD COUNT	AUTHOR / SERIES	PUBLISHER / DISTRIBUTOR
Using Color	J	I	249	Explorations	Eleanor Curtain Publishing
Using Color	J	I	249	Explorations	Okapi Educational Materials
Using Energy	U	I	250+	Reading Expeditions	National Geographic
Using Force and Motion	W	I	250+	Reading Expeditions	National Geographic
Using Graphs	K	I	359	Red Rocket Readers	Flying Start Books
Using Leaves	H	I	176	Sails	Rigby
Using Magnets	F	I	160	Early Connections	Benchmark Education
Using Nature's Gifts	K	I	250+	People, Spaces & Places	Rand McNally
Using Numbers at Work	C	I	75	Early Connections	Benchmark Education
Using Resources	K	I	624	Science Support Readers	Houghton Mifflin Harcourt
Using Resources to Build	K	I	248	Early Explorers	Benchmark Education
Using Rocks	C	I	62	Explorations	Eleanor Curtain Publishing
Using Rocks	C	I	62	Explorations	Okapi Educational Materials
Using Rocks	K	I	167	Windows on Literacy	National Geographic
Using Special Talents	T	I	2350	Reading Street	Pearson
Using Subtraction at the Park	F	I	154	Math Around Us	Heinemann Library
Using the Library	L	I	291	Wonder World	Wright Group/McGraw Hill
Using the River	M	I	250+	Rigby Literacy	Rigby
Using the River	M	I	250+	Rigby Star Quest	Rigby
Using Tools	C	I	30	Discovery Links	Newbridge
Using Tools at Work	E	I	118	Early Connections	Benchmark Education
Using Wheels	G	I	115	Little Red Readers	Sundance
Using Your Five Senses	P	I	250+	Windows on Literacy	National Geographic
Using Your Safety Senses	K	I	413	Leveled Readers Science	Houghton Mifflin Harcourt
Using Your Senses at School	F	I	37	Windows on Literacy	National Geographic
Utah	T	I	250+	Hello U.S.A.	Lerner Publishing Group
Utah	R	I	250+	This Land Is Your Land	Compass Point Books
Utah Jazz, The	S	I	250+	Team Spirit	Norwood House Press
Utah: Facts and Symbols	O	I	250+	The States and Their Symbols	Capstone Press
Utes, The	P	I	250+	Native Peoples	Red Brick Learning
Utterly Me, Clarice Bean	O	RF	250+	Child, Lauren	Candlewick Press
V is for Vest	C	I	35	Learn to Read	Creative Teaching Press
Vacation at Lighthouse Rock	L	RF	897	PM Plus Story Books	Rigby
Vacation for MM Mouse, A	I	F	275	Sails	Rigby
Vacation Journal, A	M	B	250+	Discovery World	Rigby
Vacation on Earth	P	F	250+	Scooters	ETA/Cuisenaire
Vacation Under the Volcano	M	F	250+	Osborne, Mary Pope	Random House
Vacation with a Great Aunt	N	RF	250+	Sails	Rigby
Vacation, The	C	RF	94	Emergent	Pioneer Valley
Vacation, The	B	F	30	Sails	Rigby
Vacations	B	RF	22	Smart Start	Rigby
Vacation's Over!: Return of the Dinosaurs	L	F	305	Kulka, Joe	Carolrhoda Books
Vagabond Crabs	J	I	117	Literacy 2000	Rigby
Valentine Star, The	M	RF	250+	Giff, Patricia Reilly	Bantam Books
Valentine's Checkup	C	RF	45	Little Books	Sadlier-Oxford
Valentine's Day	E	I	132	Fiesta Holiday Series	Pearson Learning Group
Valentine's Day	Q	I	250+	Holiday Histories	Heinemann
Valentine's Day	J	I	109	Holidays and Celebrations	Capstone Press
Valentine's Day	M	I	250+	Holidays and Celebrations	Picture Window Books
Valentine's Day	O	I	250+	Holidays and Festivals	Compass Point Books
Valentine's Day	P	I	250+	Let's See	Compass Point Books
Valentine's Day	C	F	49	Story Box	Wright Group/McGraw Hill
Valentine's Day	E	RF	110	The King School Series	Townsend Press
Valentine's Day Disaster	O	F	250+	Stilton, Geronimo	Scholastic

UV

TITLE	LEVEL	GENRE	WORD COUNT	AUTHOR / SERIES	PUBLISHER / DISTRIBUTOR
Valentine's Day Is…	M	I	250+	Gibbons, Gail	Holiday House
Valentine's Day Mess	H	F	248	Craig, Janet	Troll Associates
Valentines for Little Fox	G	F	249	Handprints D	Educators Publishing Service
Valentines: Cards and Crafts from the Heart	Q	I	250+	Crafts	Capstone Press
Valley Forge	S	I	250+	Ammon, Richard	Scholastic
Valley Forge	X	I	3045	Vocabulary Readers	Houghton Mifflin Harcourt
Valley Forge	X	I	3045	Vocabulary Readers/CA	Houghton Mifflin Harcourt
Valley Forge	X	I	3045	Vocabulary Readers/TX	Houghton Mifflin Harcourt
Valley of Hope	T	RF	250+	Reading Safari	Mondo Publishing
Valley of the Giant Skeletons	O	F	250+	Stilton, Geronimo	Scholastic
Valleys	J	I	294	Landforms	Lerner Publishing Group
Vampire Bats, Bookworms, and Clothes Moths	M	I	778	Springboard	Wright Group/McGraw Hill
Vampire Bunny, The	L	F	250+	Howe, James	Scholastic
#Vampire Hunt	U	F	10378	Twisted Journeys	Graphic Universe
^Vampire Kiss	W	F	250+	The Extraordinary Files	Hameray Publishing Group
Vampire Mountain: The Saga of Darren Shan	Y	F	250+	Shan, Darren	Little Brown and Company
Vampire Prince, The: The Saga of Darren Shan	Y	F	250+	Shan, Darren	Little Brown and Company
Vampire Trouble	L	F	250+	Dadey, Debbie; Jones, Marcia Thornton	Scholastic
Vampire Who Came for Christmas, The	Q	F	250+	Regan, Dian Curtis	Bantam Books
Vampireology: The True History of the Fallen Ones	Y	F	250+	Brookes, Archer	Candlewick Press
Vampires	X	I	4943	Monster Chronicles	Lerner Publishing Group
Vampires	Q	I	250+	Mythical Creatures	Raintree
Vampire's Assistant, The: The Saga of Darren Shan	Y	F	250+	Shan, Darren	Little Brown and Company
Vampires Don't Wear Polka Dots	M	F	250+	Dadey, Debbie; Jones, Marcia Thornton	Scholastic
Van Gogh	Z	B	250+	Eyewitness Books	DK Publishing
Van Gogh	S	B	250+	Masterpieces: Artists and Their Works	Red Brick Learning
Van Gogh Cafe, The	S	RF	250+	Rylant, Cynthia	Harcourt School Publishers
Van, The	C	F	55	Georgie Giraffe	Literacy Footprints
Van, The	B	RF	48	Phonics and Friends	Hampton Brown
Vandal	Y	RF	250+	Simmons, Michael	Square Fish
Vanished	Z	I	6364	The Unexplained	Lerner Publishing Group
Vanished!	S	I	250+	Bookweb	Rigby
Vanished!: The Mysterious Disappearance of Amelia Earhart	P	B	250+	Kulling, Monica	Random House
Vanishing Chip, The: Misfits # 1	W	RF	250+	Delaney, Mark	Peachtree
Vanishing Cultures	R	I	250+	Explorer Books-Pathfinder	National Geographic
Vanishing Cultures	P	I	250+	Explorer Books-Pioneer	National Geographic
Vanishing Game, The	Z+	F	250+	Myers, Kate Kae	Bloomsbury Children's Books
Varmints	T	F	250+	Ward, Helen	Candlewick Press
Vegetable Garden, The	A	I	21	Leveled Readers	Houghton Mifflin Harcourt
Vegetable Garden, The	A	I	21	Leveled Readers/CA	Houghton Mifflin Harcourt
Vegetable Group, The	H	I	88	The Food Guide Pyramid	Capstone Press
Vegetable Soup	C	RF	60	Bonnell, Kris	Reading Reading Books
Vegetable Soup	E	F	67	Leveled Readers	Houghton Mifflin Harcourt
Vegetable Soup	G	RF	84	Morris, Ann	Scholastic
Vegetable Soup	A	I	24	Vocabulary Readers	Houghton Mifflin Harcourt
Vegetables	F	I	85	Food Groups	Lerner Publishing Group
Vegetables	I	I	154	Healthy Eating	Heinemann Library

UV

* Collection of short stories   # Graphic text
^ Mature content with lower level text demands

TITLE	LEVEL	GENRE	WORD COUNT	AUTHOR / SERIES	PUBLISHER / DISTRIBUTOR
Vegetables	H	I	180	Sun Sprouts	ETA/Cuisenaire
Vegetables	LB	I	7	Windows on Literacy	National Geographic
Vegetables and How They Grow	F	I	86	Rosen Real Readers	Rosen Publishing Group
Vegetables Around the World	O	I	709	Vocabulary Readers	Houghton Mifflin Harcourt
Vegetables Around the World	O	I	709	Vocabulary Readers/CA	Houghton Mifflin Harcourt
Vegetables We Eat	M	I	250+	Gibbons, Gail	Holiday House
Vegetarians	K	I	216	Take Two Books	Wright Group/McGraw Hill
Vehicles	B	I	60	Nonfiction Set 2	Literacy Footprints
Vehicles for Fun and Sports	K	I	439	PM Plus	Rigby
Vehicles in the Air	K	I	436	PM Plus	Rigby
Velveteen Rabbit, The	Q	F	250+	Williams, Margery	Hearst
Venezuela	O	I	1699	A Ticket to …	Carolrhoda Books
Venezuela	P	I	2300	Country Explorers	Lerner Publishing Group
Venezuela: A Question and Answer Book	P	I	250+	Question and Answer Countries	Capstone Press
Venus	Q	I	250+	A True Book	Children's Press
Venus	Q	I	1590	Early Bird Astronomy	Lerner Publishing Group
Venus	J	I	118	Exploring the Galaxy	Capstone Press
Venus	S	I	250+	Our Solar System	Compass Point Books
Venus	N	I	732	Our Universe	Lerner Publishing Group
Venus	Q	I	250+	The Galaxy	Capstone Press
Venus	M	I	250+	The Solar System	Capstone Press
Venus	Q	I	250+	Vogt, Gregory L.	Millbrook Press
^Venus	W	I	250+	World Mythology	Capstone Press
Venus & Serena Williams	P	B	1536	Amazing Athletes	Lerner Publishing Group
Venus & Serena Williams (Revised Edition)	P	B	250+	Amazing Athletes	Lerner Publishing Group
Venus and Serena Williams: The Smashing Sisters	R	B	250+	High Five Reading	Red Brick Learning
Venus and the Comets	O	RF	10650	Tamar, Erika	Darby Creek Publishing
Venus Flytraps	Q	I	1980	Early Bird Nature Books	Lerner Publishing Group
Venus: The Flytrap Who Wouldn't Eat Flies	M	F	601	Leveled Literacy Intervention/ Blue System	Heinemann
Vermeer Interviews, The: Conversations with Seven Works of Art	V	I	5381	Raczka, Bob	Millbrook Press
Vermont	T	I	250+	Hello U.S.A.	Lerner Publishing Group
Vermont	R	I	250+	This Land Is Your Land	Compass Point Books
Vert Skating: Mastering the Ramp	Q	I	250+	Skateboarding	Capstone Press
Very Best Fish, The	N	RF	250+	Leveled Readers Language Support	Houghton Mifflin Harcourt
Very Big	D	I	49	Ready Readers	Pearson Learning Group
Very Big Potato, The	H	RF	250+	Cherrington, Janelle	Scholastic
Very Boastful Kangaroo, The	I	F	232	Green Light Readers	Harcourt
Very Busy Hen, The	D	F	123	Leveled Literacy Intervention/ Green System	Heinemann
Very Busy Spider, The	I	F	263	Carle, Eric	Philomel
Very Clean Car, The	D	RF	65	Kaleidoscope Collection	Hameray Publishing Group
Very Fairy Princess, The	K	RF	250+	Andrews, Julie & Hamilton, Emma Walton	Little Brown and Company
Very Funny Act, A	H	RF	181	Home Connection Collection	Rigby
Very Good Idea, A	J	RF	448	Springboard	Wright Group/McGraw Hill
Very Greedy Bee, The	L	F	250+	Smallman, Steve	Tiger Tales
Very Greedy Dog, The	H	TL	228	Aesop's Fables	Pearson Learning Group
Very Happy Birthday, A	M	RF	1017	Jellybeans	Rigby
Very Hungry Caterpillar, The	J	F	237	Carle, Eric	Philomel
Very Improbable Story, A	P	F	250+	Einhorn, Edward	Charlesbridge
Very Long Night, The	I	RF	252	Dominie Math Stories	Pearson Learning Group

TITLE	LEVEL	GENRE	WORD COUNT	AUTHOR / SERIES	PUBLISHER / DISTRIBUTOR
Very Merry Christmas, A	O	F	250+	Stilton, Geronimo	Scholastic
Very Nice Lunch, A	D	F	115	Leveled Readers	Houghton Mifflin Harcourt
Very Nice Lunch, A	D	F	115	Leveled Readers/CA	Houghton Mifflin Harcourt
Very Noisy Night, The	J	F	250+	Hendry, Diana	Dutton Children's Books
Very Quiet Cricket, The	K	F	250+	Carle, Eric	Philomel
Very Silly School, A	G	F	200	Cherrington, Janelle	Scholastic
Very Special Birthdays	L	I	404	Reading Street	Pearson
Very Special Effects: Computers in Filmmaking	U	I	2087	Reading Street	Pearson
Very Special Gift, A	T	HF	3082	Reading Street	Pearson
Very Special Kwanzaa, A	O	I	250+	Chocolate, Deborah M. Newton	Scholastic
Very Strange Dollhouse, A	L	F	250+	Dussling, Jennifer	Grosset & Dunlap
Very Strong Baby, The	E	F	74	Joy Readers	Pearson Learning Group
Very Thin Cat of Alloway Road, The	L	RF	250+	Literacy 2000	Rigby
Vespers Rising (The 39 Clues)	U	F	250+	Riordan, Rick, Lerangis, Peter, Korman, Gordon & Watson, Jude	Scholastic
Veterans Day	J	I	101	American Holidays	Lerner Publishing Group
Veterans Day	K	I	250+	Cotton, Jaqueline S.	Scholastic
Veterans Day	Q	I	250+	Holiday Histories	Heinemann
Veterans Day	N	I	555	Leveled Readers Social Studies	Houghton Mifflin Harcourt
Veterans Day	L	I	96	National Holidays	Red Brick Learning
Veterans Day	N	I	1574	On My Own Holidays	Lerner Publishing Group
Veteran's Day	M	I	204	Holidays and Festivals	Heinemann Library
Veterinarian	D	I	32	Benchmark Rebus	Marshall Cavendish
Veterinarians	L	I	250+	Community Helpers	Red Brick Learning
Veterinarians	M	I	250+	Community Workers	Compass Point Books
Vibrations	H	I	38	The Way Things Move	Red Brick Learning
Vicar of Nibbleswick, The	O	RF	250+	Dahl, Roald	Puffin Books
Vicky the High Jumper	K	I	250+	Literacy 2000	Rigby
Vicky's Box	J	F	412	Cambridge Reading	Pearson Learning Group
Victor and the Computer Cat	F	RF	92	Oxford Reading Tree	Oxford University Press
Victor and the Kite	F	RF	84	Oxford Reading Tree	Oxford University Press
Victor and the Martian	H	RF	109	Oxford Reading Tree	Oxford University Press
Victor and the Sail-cart	H	RF	94	Oxford Reading Tree	Oxford University Press
Victor Makes a TV	H	F	85	Reading Unlimited	Pearson Learning Group
Victor Sews	P	RF	1323	Leveled Readers	Houghton Mifflin Harcourt
Victor Takes a Sewing Class	N	RF	250+	Leveled Readers Language Support	Houghton Mifflin Harcourt
Victor the Champion	G	RF	102	Oxford Reading Tree	Oxford University Press
Victor the Hero	H	RF	103	Oxford Reading Tree	Oxford University Press
Victoria Woodhull: Fearless Feminist	Z	B	250+	Trailblazer Biographies	Carolrhoda Books
Video Game	F	RF	109	Alphakids	Sundance
Video Game, The	C	RF	94	InfoTrek	ETA/Cuisenaire
Video Games	U	I	250+	Boldprint	Steck-Vaughn
Video Games: From Start to Finish	R	I	250+	Power Up!	Steck-Vaughn
Viet Nam	LB	I	14	Readlings	American Reading Company
Vietnam	O	I	2179	A Ticket to …	Carolrhoda Books
Vietnam	O	I	250+	Countries of the World	Red Brick Learning
Vietnam	P	I	2092	Country Explorers	Lerner Publishing Group
Vietnam	Q	I	250+	First Reports: Countries	Compass Point Books
Vietnam	Q	I	250+	Theme Sets	National Geographic
Vietnam Diary	N	I	250+	InfoTrek Plus	ETA/Cuisenaire
Vietnam Veterans Memorial, The	Q	I	250+	National Landmarks	Red Brick Learning
Vietnam Women's Memorial, The	W	I	250+	Cornerstones of Freedom	Children's Press
Vietnam: A Question and Answer Book	P	I	250+	Question and Answer Countries	Capstone Press

UV

Organized Alphabetically by Title
Storable Database at www.fountasandpinnellleveledbooks.com

* Collection of short stories   # Graphic text
^ Mature content with lower level text demands

TITLE	LEVEL	GENRE	WORD COUNT	AUTHOR / SERIES	PUBLISHER / DISTRIBUTOR
View from Above, A	M	I	250+	Rigby Literacy	Rigby
View from Saturday, The	U	RF	250+	Konigsburg, E. L.	Atheneum Books
Viking	X	I	250+	Eyewitness Books	DK Publishing
Viking It and Liking It	P	F	250+	Scieszka, Jon	Penguin Group
Viking Longship, The	U	I	1515	Vocabulary Readers	Houghton Mifflin Harcourt
Viking Longship, The	U	I	1515	Vocabulary Readers/CA	Houghton Mifflin Harcourt
Viking Longship, The	U	I	1515	Vocabulary Readers/TX	Houghton Mifflin Harcourt
Viking Ships at Sunrise	M	F	250+	Osborne, Mary Pope	Random House
Viking World, The: Civilizations Past to Present	S	I	250+	Reading Expeditions	National Geographic
Vikings	S	I	250+	Fierce Fighters	Raintree
Vikings	T	I	250+	Warriors of History	Capstone Press
Vikings in North America, The	Y	I	3212	Vocabulary Readers	Houghton Mifflin Harcourt
Vikings in North America, The	Y	I	3212	Vocabulary Readers/CA	Houghton Mifflin Harcourt
Vikings, The	Q	I	250+	High-Fliers	Pacific Learning
Vikings, The	S	I	250+	Journey Into Civilization	Chelsea House
Vile Village, The	V	F	250+	Snicket, Lemony	Scholastic
Village by the Sea, The	U	RF	250+	Fox, Paula	Bantam Books
Village of Round and Square Houses, The	P	TL	250+	Grifalconi, Ann	Little Brown and Company
Villains	S	I	250+	Boldprint	Steck-Vaughn
Violent Volcanoes	T	I	250+	Awesome Forces of Nature	Heinemann Library
Violet Raines Almost Got Struck by Lightning	T	RF	250+	Haworth, Danette	Walker & Company
VIP Pass to a Pro Baseball Game Day: From the Locker Room to the Press Box (and Everything in Between)	R	I	250+	Sports Illustrated Kids Game Day	Capstone Press
VIP Pass to a Pro Basketball Game Day: From the Locker Room to the Press Box (and Everything in Between)	R	I	250+	Sports Illustrated Kids Game Day	Capstone Press
VIP Pass to a Pro Football Game Day: From the Locker Room to the Press Box (and Everything in Between)	R	I	250+	Sports Illustrated Kids Game Day	Capstone Press
VIP Pass to a Pro Hockey Game Day: From the Locker Room to the Press Box (and Everything in Between)	R	I	250+	Sports Illustrated Kids Game Day	Capstone Press
Viper's Nest, The (The 39 Clues)	U	F	250+	Lerangis, Peter	Scholastic
Virginia	T	I	250+	Hello U.S.A.	Lerner Publishing Group
Virginia	T	I	250+	Theme Sets	National Geographic
Virginia	R	I	250+	This Land Is Your Land	Compass Point Books
Virginia Colony, The	R	I	250+	The American Colonies	Capstone Press
Virginia Is the Old Dominion State	O	I	204	Larkin, Bruce	Wilbooks
Virginia Opossums	K	I	418	Springboard	Wright Group/McGraw Hill
Virginia: Facts and Symbols	O	I	250+	The States and Their Symbols	Capstone Press
Virtual Danger	Z	I	250+	What's the Issue?	Compass Point Books
Virtual Fred	O	SF	250+	Courtney, Vincent	Random House
Virtually True: Questioning Online Media	S	I	250+	Media Literacy	Capstone Press
Visconti House	U	RF	250+	Edgar, Elsbeth	Candlewick Press
Vision of Beauty: The Story of Sarah Breedlove Walker	U	B	250+	Lasky, Kathryn	Candlewick Press
Visit from Aunt Bee, A	C	RF	58	Leveled Literacy Intervention/ Orange System	Heinemann
Visit to a Butterfly Greenhouse, A	J	I	170	Reading Street	Pearson
Visit to a Farm, A	I	I	322	Time for Kids	Teacher Created Materials
Visit to a Museum	N	I	306	Leveled Readers Social Studies	Houghton Mifflin Harcourt
Visit to a Publisher, A	K	I	325	Time for Kids	Teacher Created Materials
Visit to a Pueblo, A	K	I	129	Vocabulary Readers	Houghton Mifflin Harcourt
Visit to an Automobile Factory, A	J	I	325	Time for Kids	Teacher Created Materials
Visit to Antarctica, A	R	I	1162	Leveled Readers	Houghton Mifflin Harcourt

UV

* Collection of short stories   # Graphic text
^ Mature content with lower level text demands

Organized Alphabetically by Title   **803**
Storable Database at www.fountasandpinnellleveledbooks.com

TITLE	LEVEL	GENRE	WORD COUNT	AUTHOR / SERIES	PUBLISHER / DISTRIBUTOR
Visit to Antarctica, A	R	I	1162	Leveled Readers/CA	Houghton Mifflin Harcourt
Visit to Antarctica, A	R	I	1162	Leveled Readers/TX	Houghton Mifflin Harcourt
Visit to Cousin Boris	I	F	250+	Popcorn	Sundance
Visit to Dr. Jane, A	D	RF	116	Joy Starters	Pearson Learning Group
Visit to the Airport, A	H	I	105	A Visit to…	Red Brick Learning
Visit to the Andes, A	O	I	865	Vocabulary Readers	Houghton Mifflin Harcourt
Visit to the Andes, A	O	I	865	Vocabulary Readers/CA	Houghton Mifflin Harcourt
Visit to the Animal Shelter, The	J	I	367	InfoTrek	ETA/Cuisenaire
Visit to the Apple Orchards, A	H	I	114	A Visit to…	Red Brick Learning
Visit to the City, A	C	RF	64	Leveled Literacy Intervention/ Green System	Heinemann
Visit to the City, A	D	I	54	Vocabulary Readers	Houghton Mifflin Harcourt
Visit to the Coral Reef, A	L	I	291	The Rowland Reading Program Library	Rowland Reading Foundation
Visit to the Dentist's Office, A	H	I	116	A Visit to…	Red Brick Learning
Visit to the Doctor, A	A	I	28	Little Books for Early Readers	University of Maine
Visit to the Dominican Republic, A	N	I	601	Vocabulary Readers	Houghton Mifflin Harcourt
Visit to the Dominican Republic, A	N	I	601	Vocabulary Readers/CA	Houghton Mifflin Harcourt
Visit to the Dominican Republic, A	N	I	601	Vocabulary Readers/TX	Houghton Mifflin Harcourt
#Visit to the Library, A	L	I	250+	First Grahics: My Community	Capstone Press
Visit to the Library, A	E	I	109	Foundations	Wright Group/McGraw Hill
Visit to the Library, A	F	I	140	Springboard	Wright Group/McGraw Hill
Visit to the Planetarium, A	M	I	250+	Burke, Melissa Blackwell	Houghton Mifflin Harcourt
Visit to the Police Station, A	I	I	115	A Visit to…	Capstone Press
#Visit to the Police Station, A	L	I	250+	First Grahics: My Community	Capstone Press
Visit to the Statue of Liberty, A	G	I	77	Independent Readers Social Studies	Houghton Mifflin Harcourt
Visit to the United Nations, A	N	I	437	Early Explorers	Benchmark Education
Visit to Vancouver Island, A	O	RF	1261	Leveled Readers Social Studies	Houghton Mifflin Harcourt
Visiting a Park	A	I	20	Vocabulary Readers	Houghton Mifflin Harcourt
Visiting a Park	A	I	20	Vocabulary Readers/CA	Houghton Mifflin Harcourt
Visiting a Village	T	I	250+	Kalman, Bobbie	Scholastic
Visiting Grandma and Grandpa	G	RF	136	Carousel Readers	Pearson Learning Group
Visiting Grandma and Grandpa	A	I	24	Leveled Readers	Houghton Mifflin Harcourt
Visiting Grandma and Grandpa	A	I	24	Leveled Readers/CA	Houghton Mifflin Harcourt
Visiting the Dentist	J	I	250+	Growing Up	Heinemann Library
Visiting the Eagle Hotel	M	I	250+	Rigby Literacy	Rigby
Visiting the Police Station	I	I	200	Rosen Real Readers	Rosen Publishing Group
Visiting the Spirit Bear	K	I	166	Larkin, Bruce	Wilbooks
Visiting the Vet	H	I	259	Foundations	Wright Group/McGraw Hill
Visiting the Vet	H	I	140	Sun Sprouts	ETA/Cuisenaire
Visiting the Zoo	A	RF	26	Leveled Readers	Houghton Mifflin Harcourt
Visiting the Zoo	A	RF	26	Leveled Readers/CA	Houghton Mifflin Harcourt
Visiting Wahington, D.C.	O	I	188	Larkin, Bruce	Wilbooks
Visitor for Bear, A	K	F	250+	Becker, Bonny	Candlewick Press
Visitor, The	I	F	250+	Popcorn	Sundance
Visitors	E	RF	46	Literacy 2000	Rigby
Viva America	U	I	2222	Reading Street	Pearson
Viva Mexico	L	I	432	Leveled Readers Social Studies	Houghton Mifflin Harcourt
Viva México!: A Story of Benito Juárez and Cinco de Mayo	Q	B	250+	Stories of America	Steck-Vaughn
Vlad the Impaler: The Real Count Dracula	Y	B	250+	A Wicked History	Scholastic
Vladimir Putin	X	B	250+	A&E Biography	Lerner Publishing Group
Voice for Equality, A	S	B	1263	Leveled Readers	Houghton Mifflin Harcourt

Organized Alphabetically by Title
Storable Database at www.fountasandpinnellleveledbooks.com

* Collection of short stories   # Graphic text
^ Mature content with lower level text demands

TITLE	LEVEL	GENRE	WORD COUNT	AUTHOR / SERIES	PUBLISHER / DISTRIBUTOR
Voice for Equality, A	S	B	1263	Leveled Readers/CA	Houghton Mifflin Harcourt
Voice for Equality, A	S	B	1263	Leveled Readers/TX	Houghton Mifflin Harcourt
Voice for the Animals, A	S	I	250+	Navigators Social Studies Series	Benchmark Education
Voice of Freedom	X	I	2235	Leveled Readers	Houghton Mifflin Harcourt
Voice of Freedom	X	I	2235	Leveled Readers/CA	Houghton Mifflin Harcourt
Voice of Freedom	X	I	2235	Leveled Readers/TX	Houghton Mifflin Harcourt
Voice of Freedom: A Story About Frederick Douglass	R	B	8445	Creative Minds Biographies	Carolrhoda Books
Voice of Her Own, A: Becoming Emily Dickinson	Y	HF	250+	Dana, Barbara	HarperCollins
Voice of Her Own, A: The Story of Phillis Wheately, Slave Poet	S	B	250+	Lasky, Kathryn	Candlewick Press
Voice of the People, The: American Democracy in Action	V	I	250+	Maestro, Betsy & Giulio	William Morrow
Voice of the Pioneer: Carrie Chapman Catt	R	B	1916	Leveled Readers Social Studies	Houghton Mifflin Harcourt
Voice That Challenged a Nation, The: Marian Anderson and the Struggle for Equal Rights	Y	B	250+	Freedman, Russell	Sandpiper Books
Voices	S	RF	250+	Book Blazers	ETA/Cuisenaire
Voices From the Civil War	U	I	250+	Navigators Social Studies Series	Benchmark Education
*Voices from the Fields: Children of Migrant Farmworkers Tell Their Stories	Z	I	250+	Atkin, S. Beth	Little Brown and Company
Voices in St. Augustine	R	F	250+	Wood, Jane R.	Bluefish Bay Publishing
Volcanic Eruption!: Susan Ruff and Bruce Nelson's Story of Survival	R	I	250+	True Tales of Survival	Capstone Press
Volcano	U	I	250+	Lauber, Patricia	Scholastic
Volcano	C	I	44	Science	Outside the Box
Volcano Awakes!, The	S	I	250+	Sails	Rigby
Volcano Explorers	O	I	250+	Landform Adventurers	Raintree
Volcano Goddess Will See You Now, The	N	F	250+	The Zack Files	Grosset & Dunlap
Volcano Man	N	I	250+	On Our Way to English	Rigby
Volcano Project	M	I	677	Sun Sprouts	ETA/Cuisenaire
Volcano Woman	M	TL	250+	Cambridge Reading	Pearson Learning Group
Volcano!	R	I	250+	Explorer Books-Pathfinder	National Geographic
Volcano!	P	I	250+	Explorer Books-Pioneer	National Geographic
Volcano! Sleeping Giants Awake	U	I	250+	Explore More	Wright Group/McGraw Hill
Volcanoes	O	I	250+	A True Book	Children's Press
Volcanoes	W	I	250+	Disasters Up Close	Lerner Publishing Group
Volcanoes	R	I	250+	Early Bird Earth Science	Lerner Publishing Group
Volcanoes	N	I	250+	Early Connections	Benchmark Education
Volcanoes	M	I	159	Earth in Action	Capstone Press
Volcanoes	T	I	250+	Earth Science	Franklin Watts
Volcanoes	N	I	250+	Earthforms	Capstone Press
Volcanoes	Q	I	250+	Explorers	Wright Group/McGraw Hill
Volcanoes	N	I	679	Gear Up!	Wright Group/McGraw Hill
Volcanoes	V	I	250+	iOpeners	Pearson Learning Group
Volcanoes	M	I	626	Pull Ahead Books	Lerner Publishing Group
Volcanoes	P	I	250+	Reading Expeditions	National Geographic
Volcanoes	F	I	115	Red Rocket Readers	Flying Start Books
Volcanoes	L	I	250+	Sunshine	Wright Group/McGraw Hill
Volcanoes	R	I	250+	The Wonders of Our World	Crabtree
Volcanoes	M	I	387	Time for Kids	Teacher Created Materials
Volcanoes	Q	I	250+	Windows on Literacy	National Geographic
Volcanoes	Q	I	250+	Worldwise	Franklin Watts
Volcanoes and Earthquakes	T	I	250+	Lauber, Patricia	Language for Learning Assoc.

UV

TITLE	LEVEL	GENRE	WORD COUNT	AUTHOR / SERIES	PUBLISHER / DISTRIBUTOR
Volcanoes and Earthquakes	T	I	250+	Reading Expeditions	National Geographic
Volcanoes and Geysers	O	I	250+	PM Plus Story Books	Rigby
Volcanoes and Other Natural Disasters	R	I	250+	DK Readers	DK Publishing
Volcanoes Around the World	O	I	380	Vocabulary Readers	Houghton Mifflin Harcourt
Volcanoes Inside and Out	N	I	1784	On My Own Science	Lerner Publishing Group
Volcanoes National Park	S	I	1396	Leveled Readers Science	Houghton Mifflin Harcourt
Volcanoes: When a Mountain Explodes	S	I	250+	High Five Reading	Red Brick Learning
Volcanoes: Wonders of Nature	L	I	250+	Bookworms	Marshall Cavendish
Volleyball for Fun!	S	I	250+	Sports for Fun!	Compass Point Books
Volunteer Helps, A	J	I	233	Early Explorers	Benchmark Education
Voodoo Island	T	F	5910	Oxford Bookworms Library	Oxford University Press
Vote	E	I	110	Early Explorers	Benchmark Education
Vote for Larry	Z+	RF	250+	Tashjian, Janet	Henry Holt & Co.
Vote for Our Zoo	L	RF	250+	Read it! Readers	Picture Window Books
Vote!: The Complicated Life of Claudia Cristina Cortez	S	RF	250+	Gallagher, Diana G.	Stone Arch Books
Votes for Women	V	I	250+	Reading Expeditions	National Geographic
Voting and Elections	Q	I	250+	Let's See	Compass Point Books
Voyage Across the Pacific	S	I	1250	Leveled Readers	Houghton Mifflin Harcourt
Voyage into Space	J	F	250+	Storyworlds	Heinemann
Voyage of Mae Jemison, The	H	B	46	Canizares, Susan; Berger, Samantha	Scholastic
Voyage of Patience Goodspeed, The	U	HF	250+	Frederick, Heather Vogel	Simon & Schuster
Voyage of the Clowns, The	J	F	250+	The Wright Skills	Wright Group/McGraw Hill
Voyage of the Fram, The	R	I	611	Vocabulary Readers	Houghton Mifflin Harcourt
Voyage of the Frog, The	S	RF	250+	Paulsen, Gary	Bantam Books
#Voyage of the Mayflower, The	T	I	250+	Graphic Library	Capstone Press
Voyage to Antarctica	N	I	250+	InfoTrek Plus	ETA/Cuisenaire
Voyage to Antartica	T	I	2505	Leveled Readers Science	Houghton Mifflin Harcourt
Voyage to California	R	HF	1428	Leveled Readers	Houghton Mifflin Harcourt
Voyage to California	R	HF	1428	Leveled Readers/CA	Houghton Mifflin Harcourt
Voyage to California	R	HF	1428	Leveled Readers/TX	Houghton Mifflin Harcourt
Voyage, The	M	F	250+	Pair-It Books	Steck-Vaughn
Voyager: An Adventure Through Space	Q	I	250+	Gustafson, John	Scholastic
Voyages of Christopher Columbus, The	T	I	250+	Navigators Social Studies Series	Benchmark Education
Voyages to the Indies: 1400-1520s	V	I	250+	Reading Expeditions	National Geographic
Vroom!	G	F	167	Rigby Literacy	Rigby
Vroom!	G	F	169	Rigby Star	Rigby
Vulpes the Red Fox	T	F	250+	George, Jean Craighead	Puffin Books
Vultures	P	I	1513	Animal Scavengers	Lerner Publishing Group
Vultures	O	I	1509	Early Bird Nature Books	Lerner Publishing Group
Vultures	S	I	250+	Stone, Lynn M.	Carolrhoda Books
Vultures on Vacation	C	F	36	Ready Readers	Pearson Learning Group

UV

* Collection of short stories   # Graphic text
^ Mature content with lower level text demands

TITLE	LEVEL	GENRE	WORD COUNT	AUTHOR / SERIES	PUBLISHER / DISTRIBUTOR
W.E.B. DuBois and the Fight for a Just Society	R	B	904	Leveled Readers Social Studies	Houghton Mifflin Harcourt
W.K. Kellogg	R	B	3919	History Maker Bios	Lerner Publishing Group
Wabi Sabi	T	F	250+	Reibstein, Mark	Little Brown and Company
Wackiest White House Pets	R	RF	250+	Davis, Gibbs	Scholastic
Wacky Jacks	L	RF	250+	Adler, David A.	Random House
Wacky Museums and Roadside Sights	Q	I	250+	Power Up!	Steck-Vaughn
Wacky Plant Cycles	O	I	250+	Bookshop	Mondo Publishing
Wacky Trees	S	I	250+	Plants and Fungi	Franklin Watts
Wacky Wheels	N	I	250+	Pacific Literacy	Pacific Learning
Waddles	M	F	250+	McPhail, David	Harry N. Abrams
Waddling Duck	K	TL	599	Red Rocket Readers	Flying Start Books
Wading Birds	L	I	446	Pull Ahead Books	Lerner Publishing Group
Wager, The	Z+	F	250+	Napoli, Donna Jo	Henry Holt & Co.
Wagon Ride, The	E	RF	115	Teacher's Choice Series	Pearson Learning Group
Wagon Train	M	HF	250+	All Aboard Reading	Grosset & Dunlap
Wagon Wheels	K	HF	250+	Brenner, Barbara	HarperTrophy
Wagon, The	H	RF	78	Reading Unlimited	Pearson Learning Group
Wainscott Weasel, The	T	F	250+	Seidler, Tor	HarperCollins
Wait for Me	G	F	121	Jack and Daisy	Pioneer Valley
Wait for Me	C	RF	75	Little Books	Sadlier-Oxford
Wait for Me	D	RF	185	Visions	Wright Group/McGraw Hill
Wait for Your Turn!	H	RF	141	Teacher's Choice Series	Pearson Learning Group
Wait Skates	G	RF	58	Rookie Readers	Children's Press
Wait Till Helen Comes	U	F	250+	Hahn, Mary Downing	Houghton Mifflin Harcourt
Wait Until Next Year	V	RF	2226	Leveled Readers	Houghton Mifflin Harcourt
Waiting	G	RF	59	Literacy 2000	Rigby
Waiting	A	RF	28	Story Box	Wright Group/McGraw Hill
Waiting	E	RF	75	Voyages	SRA/McGraw Hill
Waiting Alligators	K	I	445	Pull Ahead Books	Lerner Publishing Group
Waiting for a Frog	G	RF	124	Coats, Glenn	Kaeden Books
Waiting for Aunt Ro	Q	RF	1267	Leveled Readers	Houghton Mifflin Harcourt
Waiting for Aunt Ro	Q	RF	1267	Leveled Readers/CA	Houghton Mifflin Harcourt
Waiting for Aunt Ro	Q	RF	1267	Leveled Readers/TX	Houghton Mifflin Harcourt
Waiting for Benjamin	O	RF	250+	Altman, Alexandra Jessup	Albert Whitman & Co.
Waiting for Granny	F	RF	179	Leveled Readers Language Support	Houghton Mifflin Harcourt
Waiting for the Magic	Q	F	250+	MacLachlan, Patricia	Atheneum Books
Waiting for the Rain	J	RF	307	Foundations	Wright Group/McGraw Hill
Waiting for Wings	J	I	147	Ehlert, Lois	Harcourt, Inc.
Waiting in Line	F	RF	74	City Stories	Rigby
Wake Me in Spring	J	F	301	Preller, James	Scholastic
Wake Up Ginger	C	F	70	Bookshop	Mondo Publishing
Wake Up Mom!	C	RF	94	Sunshine	Wright Group/McGraw Hill
Wake Up!	F	RF	104	Gear Up!	Wright Group/McGraw Hill
Wake Up!	C	F	62	Story Steps	Rigby
Wake Up, Dad	C	RF	67	PM Story Books	Rigby
Wake Up, Emily, It's Mother's Day	M	RF	250+	Giff, Patricia Reilly	Yearling Books
Wake Up, Jack	C	F	59	Tiny Treasures	Pioneer Valley
Wake Up, Scooterville	K	RF	250+	Stamper, Judith Bauer	Scholastic
Wake Up, Sleepyheads!	F	RF	35	Little Books	Sadlier-Oxford
Wake Up, Sun!	E	F	250+	Harrison, David	Random House
Wake Up, Wake Up!	D	F	110	Wildsmith, Brian & Rebecca	Scholastic
Wake Up, Young Soldier	R	I	864	Independent Readers Social Studies	Houghton Mifflin Harcourt

W

TITLE	LEVEL	GENRE	WORD COUNT	AUTHOR / SERIES	PUBLISHER / DISTRIBUTOR
Wakeboarding	M	I	250+	To the Extreme	Capstone Press
Wake-Up, Baby!	J	F	209	Oppenheim, Joanna	Bantam Books
Waking Up	A	F	50	Leveled Literacy Intervention/ Green System	Heinemann
Waking Up	H	RF	250+	Seese, Ellen	Kaeden Books
Wali Dad's Gift	P	TL	1003	Leveled Readers	Houghton Mifflin Harcourt
Wali Dad's Gifts	P	TL	1003	Leveled Readers/CA	Houghton Mifflin Harcourt
Wali Dad's Gifts	P	TL	1003	Leveled Readers/TX	Houghton Mifflin Harcourt
Walk Across America, A	T	I	250+	Literacy by Design	Rigby
Walk Around the City, A	L	I	435	Reading Street	Pearson
Walk at Night, A	G	RF	198	Leveled Literacy Intervention/ Green System	Heinemann
Walk at the Farm, A	J	F	618	Gilbert the Pig	Pioneer Valley
Walk for Jasper, A	D	RF	87	Jasper the Cat	Pioneer Valley
Walk for Pickles, A	D	RF	82	Pickles the Dog Series	Pioneer Valley
Walk in Antarctica, A	E	F	118	Reading Street	Pearson
Walk in My Woods, A	D	I	83	Independent Readers Science	Houghton Mifflin Harcourt
*Walk in My World, A	Y	RF	250+	Mazer, Anne	Persea Books
Walk in the Boreal Forest, A	T	I	2143	Biomes of North America	Lerner Publishing Group
Walk in the Deciduous Forest, A	T	I	1959	Biomes of North America	Lerner Publishing Group
Walk in the Desert, A	T	I	2115	Biomes of North America	Lerner Publishing Group
Walk in the Mountains, A	K	I	373	Reading Street	Pearson
Walk in the Park, A	C	I	57	Dominie Factivity Series	Pearson Learning Group
Walk in the Prairie, A	T	I	2207	Biomes of North America	Lerner Publishing Group
Walk in the Rain Forest, A	T	I	2124	Biomes of North America	Lerner Publishing Group
Walk in the Rain Forest, A	L	RF	1005	InfoTrek	ETA/Cuisenaire
Walk in the Rain, A	B	RF	28	Pair-It Books	Steck-Vaughn
Walk in the Tundra, A	T	I	2168	Biomes of North America	Lerner Publishing Group
Walk in the Woods, A	F	F	212	Leveled Readers	Houghton Mifflin Harcourt
Walk in the Woods, A	A	RF	20	Leveled Readers	Houghton Mifflin Harcourt
Walk in the Woods, A	A	RF	20	Leveled Readers/CA	Houghton Mifflin Harcourt
Walk On!: A Guide for Babies of All Ages	N	I	198	Frazee, Marla	Houghton Mifflin Harcourt
Walk Tall	N	I	250+	Pacific Literacy	Pacific Learning
Walk Through a Rainforest, A: Life in the Ituri Forest of Zaire	V	RF	250+	Jenike, David & Mark	HarperCollins
Walk Through History on the Freedom Trail	Q	I	828	Leveled Readers Social Studies	Houghton Mifflin Harcourt
Walk Two Moons	W	RF	250+	Creech, Sharon	HarperCollins
Walk with a Wolf	N	RF	250+	Read and Wonder	Candlewick Press
Walk with Dad, A	C	I	59	Bonnell, Kris	Reading Reading Books
Walk with Grandpa, A	L	RF	388	Read Alongs	Rigby
Walk with John Muir, A	U	B	2237	Independent Readers Social Studies	Houghton Mifflin Harcourt
Walk with Meli, A	E	RF	200	Leveled Literacy Intervention/ Green System	Heinemann
Walk, Ride, Run	D	RF	116	PM Plus Story Books	Rigby
Walk, The	B	RF	29	Early Emergent	Pioneer Valley
Walk, The	G	RF	129	Reading Unlimited	Pearson Learning Group
Walk-Around Tacos and Other Likeable Lunches	R	I	250+	Kids Dish	Picture Window Books
Walkathon, The	K	RF	250+	PM Story Books-Silver	Rigby
Walker's Crossing	X	RF	250+	Naylor, Phyllis Reynolds	Aladdin
Walking	M	I	250+	Literacy 2000	Rigby
Walking Backward	W	RF	250+	Austen, Catherine	Orca Books
Walking by the Rio	K	RF	118	Books for Young Learners	Richard C. Owen
Walking for Freedom: The Montgomery Bus Boycott	R	I	250+	Kelso, Richard	Steck-Vaughn

W

TITLE	LEVEL	GENRE	WORD COUNT	AUTHOR / SERIES	PUBLISHER / DISTRIBUTOR
Walking Home Alone	J	RF	327	Books for Young Learners	Richard C. Owen
Walking in the Autumn	H	I	206	PM Nonfiction-Green	Rigby
Walking in the Forest	E	RF	39	Reading Street	Pearson
Walking in the Jungle	E	RF	113	Little Red Readers	Sundance
Walking in the Spring	H	I	168	PM Nonfiction-Green	Rigby
Walking in the Summer	H	I	233	PM Nonfiction-Green	Rigby
Walking in the Winter	H	I	251	PM Nonfiction-Green	Rigby
Walking on Earth & Touching the Sky: Poetry and Prose by Lakota Youth at Red Cloud Indian School	W	I	250+	McLaughlin, Timothy P.	Harry N. Abrams
*Walking on the Moon	N	I	250+	Explore Space!	Red Brick Learning
*Walking Stars	Z	TL	250+	Edge	Hampton Brown
*Walking the Choctaw Road	Y	TL	250+	Tingle, Tim	Cinco Puntos Press
Walking the Dog	L	RF	250+	Scooters	ETA/Cuisenaire
Walking the Dog	D	RF	69	Sun Sprouts	ETA/Cuisenaire
Walking the Dogs	H	RF	80	City Stories	Rigby
Walking the Road to Freedom: A Story About Sojourner Truth	R	B	7713	Creative Minds Biographies	Carolrhoda Books
Walking the Road to Freedom: A Story About Sojourner Truth	Q	B	250+	Ferris, Jeri	Dell
Walking to School	C	RF	38	Voyages	SRA/McGraw Hill
Walking Up Walls	I	I	140	Windows on Literacy	National Geographic
Walking, Walking	C	I	32	Twig	Wright Group/McGraw Hill
Walkingsticks	I	I	89	Bugs, Bugs, Bugs	Capstone Press
Walkingsticks	I	I	83	Pebble Books	Red Brick Learning
Wall of Names, A: The Story of the Vietnam Veterans Memorial	P	I	250+	Donnelly, Judy	Random House
Wall, The	P	HF	250+	Bunting, Eve	Clarion
Wall: Growing Up Behind the Iron Curtain, The	Y	I	250+	Sis, Peter	Farrar, Straus, & Giroux
Walls of the World	X	I	250+	iOpeners	Pearson Learning Group
Wally Walrus	J	F	483	Let's Read Together	Kane Press
Walrus	B	I	38	Zoozoo-Animal World	Cavallo Publishing
Walruses	I	I	55	Pebble Books	Red Brick Learning
Walruses	H	I	117	Under the Sea	Capstone Press
Walruses	N	I	250+	World of Mammals	Capstone Press
Walt Disney	R	B	3555	History Maker Bios	Lerner Publishing Group
Walt Disney	P	B	250+	Photo-Illustrated Biographies	Red Brick Learning
^Walt Disney: Master of Movie Magic and Make-Believe	Q	B	250+	Hameray Biography Series	Hameray Publishing Group
Walt Disney's World	G	I	96	Leveled Readers Social Studies	Houghton Mifflin Harcourt
Walter and the Food Fair	O	RF	1046	Leveled Readers/TX	Houghton Mifflin Harcourt
Walter and the Inventor's Garden	L	F	250+	Pacific Literacy	Pacific Learning
Walter Hottle Bottle	L	RF	250+	Voyages	SRA/McGraw Hill
Walter the Baker	M	F	250+	Carle, Eric	Scholastic
Walter the Warlock	M	F	250+	Hautzig, Deborah	Random House
Walter Warthog's Wonderful Wagon	K	F	747	Animal Antics A to Z	Kane Press
Walter, the Water Taxi	F	F	140	Springboard	Wright Group/McGraw Hill
Walter's Worries	L	F	250+	Pacific Literacy	Pacific Learning
Waltur Buys a Pig in a Poke and Other Stories	K	F	250+	Gregorich, Barbara	Houghton Mifflin Harcourt
Wampanoag, The: The People of the First Light	S	I	250+	American Indian Nations	Capstone Press
Wampum Beads	P	I	526	Springboard	Wright Group/McGraw Hill
Wand in the Word, The: Conversations with Writers of Fantasy	X	I	250+	Marcus, Leonard S.	Candlewick Press
Wanderer, The	V	RF	250+	Creech, Sharon	HarperCollins
Wanna Buy an Alien?	O	SF	250+	Bunting, Eve	Houghton Mifflin Harcourt

W

* Collection of short stories   # Graphic text
^ Mature content with lower level text demands

Organized Alphabetically by Title   **809**
Storable Database at www.fountasandpinnellleveledbooks.com

TITLE	LEVEL	GENRE	WORD COUNT	AUTHOR / SERIES	PUBLISHER / DISTRIBUTOR
Want to Go Private?	Z+	RF	250+	Littman, Sarah Darer	Scholastic
Wanted . . . Mud Blossom	P	RF	250+	Byars, Betsy	Dell
Wanted Dead or Alive: The True Story of Harriet Tubman	P	B	250+	McGovern, Ann	Scholastic
Wanted: Fun & Fantastic Jobs	L	I	250+	The Rowland Reading Program Library	Rowland Reading Foundation
War and Peace	U	I	250+	Kids Discover Reading	Wright Group/McGraw Hill
War Comes to Willy Freeman	U	HF	250+	Collier, James & Christopher	Dell
*War Dog Heroes: True Stories of Dog Courage in Wartime	S	I	250+	Sanderson, Jeannette	Scholastic
War Heroes	X	I	250+	Boldprint	Steck-Vaughn
*War Heroes	V	B	250+	Storyteller-Mountain Peaks	Wright Group/McGraw Hill
War in the Middle East, A Reporter's Story: Black September and the Yom Kippur War	Z	I	250+	Hampton, Wilborn	Candlewick Press
*War Is: Soldiers, Surviors, and Storytellers Talk About War	Z+	I	250+	Aronson, Marc & Campbell, Patty	Candlewick Press
War Life	R	I	250+	Trackers	Pacific Learning
War of 1812, The	S	I	250+	A First Book	Franklin Watts
War of 1812, The	V	I	250+	America Goes to War	Red Brick Learning
War of 1812, The	V	I	250+	Let Freedom Ring	Capstone Press
War of 1812, The	U	I	250+	Primary Source Readers	Teacher Created Materials
War of the Ember, The: Guardians of Ga'Hoole	V	F	250+	Lasky, Kathryn	Scholastic
War of the Roses, The	U	HF	250+	Reading Expeditions	National Geographic
War of the Witches	Z+	F	250+	Carranza, Maite	Bloomsbury Children's Books
War of the Worlds, The	Z	SF	250+	Wells, H. G.	Tom Doherty
War Shirt, The	M	RF	250+	Greetings	Rigby
War Torn	U	RF	250+	Power Up!	Steck-Vaughn
War With Grandpa, The	S	RF	250+	Smith, Robert Kimmel	Bantam Books
Warlord's Alarm, The	Q	HF	250+	Pilegard, Virginia Walton	Pelican Publishing Company
Warlord's Beads, The	Q	HF	250+	Pilegard, Virginia Walton	Pelican Publishing Company
Warlord's Fish, The	Q	HF	250+	Pilegard, Virginia Walton	Pelican Publishing Company
Warlord's Kites, The	Q	HF	250+	Pilegard, Virginia Walton	Pelican Publishing Company
Warlord's Messengers, The	Q	HF	250+	Pilegard, Virginia Walton	Pelican Publishing Company
Warlord's Puppeteers, The	Q	HF	250+	Pilegard, Virginia Walton	Pelican Publishing Company
Warlord's Puzzle, The	Q	HF	250+	Pilegard, Virginia Walton	Pelican Publishing Company
Warm and Fuzzy	I	F	270	Reading Street	Pearson
Warm Clothes	C	I	51	Preparing for Winter	Capstone Press
Warming Up! Cooling Off!	I	I	553	Sunshine	Wright Group/McGraw Hill
Warning Lights in the Dark	L	I	393	Rigby Flying Colors	Rigby
Warning: Volcano!: The Story of Mount St. Helens	O	I	250+	Rosen Real Readers	Rosen Publishing Group
Warren G. Harding	U	B	250+	Profiles of the Presidents	Compass Point Books
Warren G. Harding: Twenty-ninth President	R	B	250+	Getting to Know the U.S. Presidents	Children's Press
Warrior Queens	V	I	250+	WorldScapes	ETA/Cuisenaire
Warriors	X	I	250+	Boldprint	Steck-Vaughn
Warriors	W	I	250+	Brereton, Catherine, Steele, Philip & Wilson, Hannah	Kingfisher
Warriors Don't Cry	Y	B	250+	Edge	Hampton Brown

W

* Collection of short stories   # Graphic text
^ Mature content with lower level text demands

TITLE	LEVEL	GENRE	WORD COUNT	AUTHOR / SERIES	PUBLISHER / DISTRIBUTOR
#Warrior's Refuge	P	F	250+	Hunter, Erin	HarperCollins
Warrior's Refuge: Warriors Manga	U	F	250+	Hunter, Erin	HarperCollins
Warrior's Return: Warriors Manga	U	F	250+	Hunter, Erin	HarperCollins
Warships	V	I	4310	Military Hardware in Action	Lerner Publishing Group
Warships	N	I	441	Pull Ahead Books	Lerner Publishing Group
Warthogs	O	I	250+	Holmes, Kevin J.	Red Brick Learning
Warton and the King of the Skies	O	F	250+	Erickson, Russell E.	Houghton Mifflin Harcourt
Was There Really a Gunfight at the O.K. Corral?: And Other Questions About the Wild West	U	I	5165	Is That a Fact?	Lerner Publishing Group
Wash Day	Q	HF	250+	Cole, Barbara H.	Star Bright Books
Wash Day	E	RF	94	Real Kids Readers	Millbrook Press
Wash Day	A	RF	35	Voyages	SRA/McGraw Hill
Wash Up!	J	I	114	Small World	Lerner Publishing Group
Wash Your Hands!	J	F	246	Ross, Tony	Kane/Miller Book Publishers
Washed Away!	M	RF	250+	PM Plus Chapter Books	Rigby
Washing	E	RF	150	Foundations	Wright Group/McGraw Hill
Washing Our Dog	H	RF	120	Alphakids	Sundance
Washing the Dishes	D	RF	111	Rigby Flying Colors	Rigby
Washing the Dog	G	I	84	Little Readers	Houghton Mifflin Harcourt
Washing the Dog	G	I	84	Little Red Readers	Sundance
Washing the Elephant	B	F	35	Lighthouse	Rigby
Washington	T	I	250+	Hello U.S.A.	Lerner Publishing Group
Washington	R	I	250+	This Land Is Your Land	Compass Point Books
Washington Is Burning	O	HF	1851	On My Own History	Lerner Publishing Group
Washington Monument, The	N	I	331	Lightning Bolt Books	Lerner Publishing Group
Washington Monument, The	Q	I	250+	National Landmarks	Red Brick Learning
Washington Monument, The	P	I	535	Pull Ahead Books	Lerner Publishing Group
Washington Nationals, The	S	I	250+	Team Spirit	Norwood House Press
Washington Nationals, The (Revised Edition)	S	I	250+	Team Spirit	Norwood House Press
Washington Redskins, The	S	I	250+	Team Spirit	Norwood House Press
Washington Wizards, The	S	I	4674	Team Spirit	Norwood House Press
Washington, D.C.	T	I	250+	Hello U.S.A.	Lerner Publishing Group
Washington, D.C.	F	I	113	Reading Street	Pearson
Washington, D.C.	L	I	163	Rosen Real Readers	Rosen Publishing Group
Washington, D.C.	R	I	250+	This Land Is Your Land	Compass Point Books
Washington, D.C.	K	I	187	Windows on Literacy	National Geographic
Washington, D.C.: A Scrapbook	Q	I	250+	Benson, Laura Lee	Charlesbridge
Washington, D.C.: Facts and Symbols	O	I	250+	The States and Their Symbols	Capstone Press
Washington: Facts and Symbols	O	I	250+	The States and Their Symbols	Capstone Press
Wasps	H	I	112	Bugs, Bugs, Bugs!	Capstone Press
Wasps	I	I	59	Pebble Books	Red Brick Learning
Wasps	H	I	158	Readlings/ Bugs	American Reading Company
Wasps	A	I	56	Readlings/ Predator Bugs	American Reading Company
Waste Not: Time to Recycle	K	I	250+	Spyglass Books	Compass Point Books
Waste of Space, A	M	RF	250+	Supa Doopers	Sundance
Waste Watchers	T	RF	250+	Reading Expeditions	National Geographic
Watch a Butterfly Grow	J	I	143	Early Explorers	Benchmark Education
Watch a Frog Grow	H	I	354	Early Explorers	Benchmark Education
Watch by the Sea, The	L	RF	250+	Cambridge Reading	Pearson Learning Group
Watch Girl, The	S	SF	2280	Leveled Readers	Houghton Mifflin Harcourt
Watch Girl, The	S	SF	2280	Leveled Readers/CA	Houghton Mifflin Harcourt
Watch Girl, The	S	SF	2280	Leveled Readers/TX	Houghton Mifflin Harcourt
Watch It Grow	K	I	243	Spyglass Books	Compass Point Books

W

TITLE	LEVEL	GENRE	WORD COUNT	AUTHOR / SERIES	PUBLISHER / DISTRIBUTOR
Watch Me	E	RF	151	Handprints C, Set 2	Educators Publishing Service
Watch Me Grow!	I	I	296	InfoTrek	ETA/Cuisenaire
Watch Me Swim	B	I	57	Red Rocket Readers	Flying Start Books
Watch Me Zoom	C	RF	45	Windmill Books	Rigby
Watch Out	B	F	44	Bookshop	Mondo Publishing
Watch Out for Trash Cans!	G	F	278	Sails	Rigby
Watch Out for Whales	I	RF	244	Red Rocket Readers	Flying Start Books
Watch Out!	C	F	27	Literacy 2000	Rigby
Watch Out!	M	I	504	Reading Street	Pearson
Watch Out! Polar Bears!	L	I	602	Leveled Readers	Houghton Mifflin Harcourt
Watch Out! Polar Bears!	L	I	602	Leveled Readers/CA	Houghton Mifflin Harcourt
Watch Out! Polar Bears!	L	I	602	Leveled Readers/TX	Houghton Mifflin Harcourt
Watch Out, Man-Eating Snake	L	RF	250+	Giff, Patricia Reilly	Bantam Books
Watch Out, William!	I	F	250+	I Am Reading	Kingfisher
Watch Out, World - Rosy Cole Is Going Green!	N	RF	250+	Greenwald, Sheila	Farrar, Straus, & Giroux
Watch the Ball	K	RF	501	Red Rocket Readers	Flying Start Books
Watch the Sky	D	I	41	Windows on Literacy	National Geographic
Watch Your Whiskers, Stilton!	O	F	250+	Stilton, Geronimo	Scholastic
Watcher, The	Z	RF	250+	Howe, James	Simon & Schuster
Watchers: I.D.	V	SF	250+	Lerangis, Peter	Scholastic
Watchers: Island	V	SF	250+	Lerangis, Peter	Scholastic
Watchers: Lab 6	V	SF	250+	Lerangis, Peter	Scholastic
Watchers: Last Stop	V	SF	250+	Lerangis, Peter	Scholastic
Watchers: Rewind	V	SF	250+	Lerangis, Peter	Scholastic
Watchers: War	V	SF	250+	Lerangis, Peter	Scholastic
Watchful Wolves	K	I	306	Pull Ahead Books	Lerner Publishing Group
Watching Chimps	Q	I	250+	Explorer Books-Pathfinder	National Geographic
Watching Chimps	P	I	250+	Explorer Books-Pioneer	National Geographic
Watching Clouds	H	I	201	PM Science Readers	Rigby
Watching Every Drop	M	I	250+	Home Connection Collection	Rigby
Watching Josh	Q	RF	250+	Ragged Island Mysteries	Wright Group/McGraw Hill
Watching the Game	G	RF	210	Momentum Literacy Program	Troll Associates
Watching the Weather	G	I	142	Discovery Links	Newbridge
Watching the Whales	L	RF	267	Foundations	Wright Group/McGraw Hill
Watching TV	E	RF	89	Foundations	Wright Group/McGraw Hill
Watching TV	B	RF	18	Sunshine	Wright Group/McGraw Hill
Water	H	I	74	Asch, Frank	Hampton Brown
Water	H	I	74	Avenues	Hampton Brown
Water	C	RF	20	Carousel Readers	Pearson Learning Group
Water	E	I	99	Early Connections	Benchmark Education
Water	C	I	12	Geography	Lerner Publishing Group
Water	F	I	55	Joy Starters	Pearson Learning Group
Water	B	I	28	Literacy 2000	Rigby
Water	B	I	24	Little Celebrations	Pearson Learning Group
Water	J	I	250+	Momentum Literacy Program	Troll Associates
Water	H	I	215	Neye, Emily	Penguin Group
Water	K	I	211	Nonfiction Set 8	Literacy Footprints
Water	G	I	126	On Our Way to English	Rigby
Water	T	I	250+	PM Plus Nonfiction	Rigby
Water	B	I	36	Science	Outside the Box
Water	C	I	48	Seedlings	Continental Press
Water	N	I	250+	Simply Science	Compass Point Books
Water	B	RF	33	Sunshine	Wright Group/McGraw Hill

Organized Alphabetically by Title
Storable Database at www.fountasandpinnellleveledbooks.com

W

* Collection of short stories   # Graphic text
^ Mature content with lower level text demands

TITLE	LEVEL	GENRE	WORD COUNT	AUTHOR / SERIES	PUBLISHER / DISTRIBUTOR
Water	Q	I	250+	Theme Sets	National Geographic
Water	D	I	54	Time for Kids	Teacher Created Materials
Water	H	I	89	What Earth Is Made Of	Lerner Publishing Group
Water	J	I	164	Windows on Literacy	National Geographic
Water	H	I	94	Wonder World	Wright Group/McGraw Hill
Water	A	HF	21	Yellow Umbrella Books	Red Brick Learning
Water All Around	C	I	26	Leveled Readers Science	Houghton Mifflin Harcourt
Water All Around the Earth	P	I	250+	On Our Way to English	Rigby
Water and Wind	N	I	250+	PM Plus Story Books	Rigby
Water Animals	P	I	250+	Animals Are Amazing	Carus Publishing Company
Water as a Gas	L	I	127	Pebble Books	Capstone Press
Water as a Liquid	I	I	141	Pebble Books	Red Brick Learning
Water as a Solid	J	I	113	Pebble Books	Red Brick Learning
Water at Work	K	I	159	Instant Readers	Harcourt School Publishers
Water Balloons	C	F	26	Brand New Readers	Candlewick Press
Water Basics	J	I	131	Nature Basics	Capstone Press
Water Beds: Sleeping in the Ocean	M	I	422	Karowski, Gail Langer	Sylvan Dell Publishing
Water Boatman, The	F	I	44	Pacific Literacy	Pacific Learning
Water Buffalo Days	P	B	250+	Huynh, Quong Nhuong	HarperTrophy
Water Bugs	I	I	76	Pebble Books	Red Brick Learning
Water Caller, The	T	SF	250+	Power Up!	Steck-Vaughn
Water Can Be . . .	B	I	17	Science	Outside the Box
Water Can Change	K	I	138	Windows on Literacy	National Geographic
Water Changes	C	I	36	Discovery Links	Newbridge
Water Changes	D	I	25	Instant Readers	Harcourt School Publishers
Water Cycle of Africa, The	U	I	1453	Reading Street	Pearson
Water Cycle, The	T	I	250+	Earth Science	Franklin Watts
Water Cycle, The	N	I	647	Gear Up!	Wright Group/McGraw Hill
Water Cycle, The	J	I	296	Instant Readers	Harcourt School Publishers
Water Cycle, The	L	I	146	Pebble Books	Capstone Press
Water Cycle, The	K	I	411	Red Rocket Readers	Flying Start Books
Water Cycle, The	S	I	1209	Science Support Readers	Houghton Mifflin Harcourt
Water Cycle, The	J	I	113	Water	Lerner Publishing Group
Water Cycle, The	J	I	250+	Yellow Umbrella Books	Capstone Press
Water Dance	Q	I	250+	Locker, Thomas	Harcourt
Water Falling	D	I	41	Literacy 2000	Rigby
Water Fight, The	E	RF	64	Oxford Reading Tree	Oxford University Press
Water for Life	T	I	250+	WorldScapes	ETA/Cuisenaire
Water for the World	M	I	250+	Home Connection Collection	Rigby
Water from Air: Water-Harvesting Machines	U	I	7610	A Great Idea	Norwood House Press
#Water Goes Round: The Water Cycle	M	I	250+	First Graphics	Capstone Press
Water Goes Up! Water Goes Down!	K	I	299	Early Connections	Benchmark Education
Water Hole, The	M	F	250+	Base, Graeme	Harry N. Abrams
Water Hole, The	B	I	48	Sails	Rigby
*Water Lilies and Other Stories	L	TL	250+	New Way Literature	Steck-Vaughn
Water Monsters	Z	I	250+	Unsolved Mysteries	Steck-Vaughn
Water Moves	C	I	39	Explorations	Eleanor Curtain Publishing
Water Moves	C	I	39	Explorations	Okapi Educational Materials
Water Park, The	D	F	123	Georgie Giraffe	Literacy Footprints
Water Park, The	A	RF	24	Sails	Rigby
Water Patrol, The: Saving Surfers' Lives in Big Waves	Q	I	250+	High Five Reading	Capstone Press
Water Police	N	I	250+	Sun Sprouts	ETA/Cuisenaire
Water Power	J	I	86	Windows on Literacy	National Geographic

W

* Collection of short stories   # Graphic text
^ Mature content with lower level text demands

Organized Alphabetically by Title   **813**

Storable Database at www.fountasandpinnellleveledbooks.com

TITLE	LEVEL	GENRE	WORD COUNT	AUTHOR / SERIES	PUBLISHER / DISTRIBUTOR
Water Resources	T	I	1862	Science Support Readers	Houghton Mifflin Harcourt
Water Scientists	T	B	250+	Science Readers	Teacher Created Materials
Water Slide Winner	M	F	250+	Too Cool	Pacific Learning
Water Slides, The	D	RF	82	Adams, Lorraine	Eaglecrest Books
Water Spiders	N	I	250+	Spiders	Capstone Press
Water Sports	O	I	250+	Extreme Sports	Raintree
Water to Ice	C	I	75	Red Rocket Readers	Flying Start Books
Water Toys, The	C	RF	58	Adams, Lorraine & Bruvold, Lynn	Eaglecrest Books
Water Wise	R	I	250+	InfoQuest	Rigby
Water Wise	N	I	250+	iOpeners	Pearson Learning Group
Water Wise	K	RF	250+	Read-it! Readers	Picture Window Books
Water Wonders of the World: From Killer Waves to Monsters of the Deep	W	I	250+	Bookshop	Mondo Publishing
Water Works	I	I	191	Early Explorers	Benchmark Education
Water! Water!	F	I	186	Story Basket	Wright Group/McGraw Hill
Water! Water!	C	I	33	Sunshine	Wright Group/McGraw Hill
Water, Ice, and Steam	I	I	143	Rosen Real Readers	Rosen Publishing Group
Water, Land, and Air	H	I	76	Windows on Literacy	National Geographic
Water, The	B	F	36	Sails	Rigby
Water, Water	B	I	48	Rigby Literacy	Rigby
Water, Water	C	F	112	Sails	Rigby
Water, Water Everywhere	F	RF	61	Books for Young Learners	Richard C. Owen
Water, Water Everywhere!	C	I	27	Leveled Readers Science	Houghton Mifflin Harcourt
Water: A Natural Resource	P	I	250+	Rigby Focus	Rigby
Water: A Resource Our World Depends On	V	I	250+	Managing Our Resources	Heinemann
Water: Liquid, Solid, Gas	M	I	240	Twig	Wright Group/McGraw Hill
Water: Up, Down, and All Around	M	I	250+	Amazing Science	Picture Window Books
Water: Watch It Change	Q	I	2161	iScience	Norwood House Press
Waterbirds	P	I	250+	InfoQuest	Rigby
Waterbirds	H	I	200	Rigby Flying Colors	Rigby
Watercolor	Z	I	250+	Eyewitness Books	DK Publishing
Watercolors	K	I	369	Vocabulary Readers	Houghton Mifflin Harcourt
Watercolors	K	I	369	Vocabulary Readers/CA	Houghton Mifflin Harcourt
Waterfall Watchers	P	I	250+	Landform Adventurers	Raintree
Waterfalls, Glaciers, and Avalanches	M	I	250+	PM Plus Nonfiction	Rigby
Waterfalls: Wonders of Nature	L	I	250+	Bookworms	Marshall Cavendish
Waterhole	K	I	149	Planet Earth	Rigby
Waterhole, The	L	F	250+	Sunshine	Wright Group/McGraw Hill
Watermelon	J	I	61	Books for Young Learners	Richard C. Owen
Watermelon	E	I	81	Rise & Shine	Hampton Brown
Watermelon for Lunch	G	F	196	Leveled Readers	Houghton Mifflin Harcourt
Watermelon, The	D	RF	80	Joy Readers	Pearson Learning Group
Watermelons	WB	I	0	Windows on Literacy	National Geographic
Water-Powered Mills	R	I	250+	Theme Sets	National Geographic
Water's Journey	G	I	114	Instant Readers	Harcourt School Publishers
Watership Down	Y	F	250+	Adams, Richard	Avon Books
Watersmeet	X	F	250+	Abbott, Ellen Jensen	Marshall Cavendish
Waterstone, The	X	F	250+	Rupp, Rebecca	Candlewick Press
Watsons Go to Birmingham - 1963, The	U	HF	250+	Curtis, Christopher Paul	Bantam Books
^Wave Warrior	W	RF	250+	Orca Soundings	Orca Books
Wave, The	Y	RF	250+	Edge	Hampton Brown
Waves	E	F	70	Voyages	SRA/McGraw Hill
Waves and Rays	Y	I	2452	Independent Readers Science	Houghton Mifflin Harcourt
Waves: The Changing Surface of the Sea	J	I	204	Wonder World	Wright Group/McGraw Hill

* Collection of short stories   # Graphic text
^ Mature content with lower level text demands

TITLE	LEVEL	GENRE	WORD COUNT	AUTHOR / SERIES	PUBLISHER / DISTRIBUTOR
Waving Goodbye	F	RF	122	The King School Series	Townsend Press
Waving Sheep, The	H	RF	252	PM Story Books	Rigby
Wax Man, The	I	TL	250+	Loya, Olga	Scholastic
Wax Museum	L	I	250+	Cook, Donald	Grosset & Dunlap
Way Down Deep	U	RF	250+	White, Ruth	Farrar, Straus, & Giroux
Way Down South	F	F	109	Learn to Read	Creative Teaching Press
Way Home, A	X	RF	3493	Leveled Readers	Houghton Mifflin Harcourt
Way Home, A	X	RF	3493	Leveled Readers/CA	Houghton Mifflin Harcourt
Way Home, A	X	RF	3493	Leveled Readers/TX	Houghton Mifflin Harcourt
Way Home, The	K	RF	250+	HSP/Harcourt Trophies	Harcourt, Inc.
Way I Go to School, The	B	I	53	PM Starters	Rigby
Way Things Were, The	D	I	39	iOpeners	Pearson Learning Group
Way to Go	E	RF	138	Bookshop	Mondo Publishing
Way West, The: Journal of a Pioneer Woman	R	B	250+	Knight, Amelia Stewart	Simon & Schuster
Way with Words, A	R	I	250+	InfoQuest	Rigby
Wayne Gretzky	U	B	250+	Sports Heroes and Legends	Lerner Publishing Group
Wayne's Box	E	F	114	Cambridge Reading	Pearson Learning Group
Wayra's Gift: A Story from Peru	S	RF	250+	Reading Expeditions	National Geographic
Ways Things Move	I	I	98	Forces and Motion	Lerner Publishing Group
Ways to Find Your Way: Types of Maps	N	I	250+	Map Mania	Capstone Press
Ways to Go	D	RF	37	Early Readers	Compass Point Books
Ways to Live Forever	U	RF	250+	Nicholls, Sally	Arthur A. Levine Books
Ways We Communicate	E	I	96	Yellow Umbrella Books	Red Brick Learning
*Wayside School Gets a Little Stranger	P	F	250+	Sachar, Louis	Avon Books
*Wayside School Is Falling Down	P	F	250+	Sachar, Louis	Avon Books
Wayward Satellite, The	T	SF	250+	Take Two Books	Wright Group/McGraw Hill
We All Help	C	RF	56	InfoTrek	ETA/Cuisenaire
We All Move	D	I	71	Disabilities and Differences	Heinemann Library
We All Need Goods	L	I	339	Larkin, Bruce	Wilbooks
We All Play Sports	C	I	26	Pacific Literacy	Pacific Learning
We All Scream For Ice Cream	I	I	219	Early Connections	Benchmark Education
We Are a Big Family	A	RF	28	Leveled Readers Emergent	Houghton Mifflin Harcourt
We Are a Team	D	I	63	Bookworms	Marshall Cavendish
We Are All Alike	M	I	250+	Early Connections	Benchmark Education
We Are All Alike We Are All Different	F	I	250+	The Cheltenham Elementary School Kindergartners	Scholastic
We Are Best Friends	H	RF	629	Aliki	Morrow
We Are Firefighters	I	I	67	Vocabulary Readers	Houghton Mifflin Harcourt
We Are Kind	D	I	52	Bookworms	Marshall Cavendish
We Are Monsters	E	F	56	Packard, Mary	Scholastic
We Are Painting	A	RF	38	Alexander, Francie	Scholastic
We Are Playing	B	RF	19	Rigby Literacy	Rigby
We Are Scientists	I	I	176	Dominie Factivity Series	Pearson Learning Group
We Are Singing	B	RF	26	Ready Readers	Pearson Learning Group
We Are the Weather Makers: The History of Climate Change	Z	I	250+	Flannery, Tim	Candlewick Press
We Are Twins	A	I	24	Little Books for Early Readers	University of Maine
We Are Up Here	B	I	74	Rigby Flying Colors	Rigby
We Are We Going?	F	RF	211	InfoTrek	ETA/Cuisenaire
*We Are Witnesses: Five Diaries of Teenagers Who Died in the Holocaust	Y	B	250+	Boas, Jacob	Square Fish
We Are Working	C	I	63	On Our Way to English	Rigby
We Belong Together: A Book About Adoption and Families	I	RF	190	Parr, Todd	Little Brown and Company

W

TITLE	LEVEL	GENRE	WORD COUNT	AUTHOR / SERIES	PUBLISHER / DISTRIBUTOR
We Can	A	F	21	KinderReaders	Rigby
We Can Be Helpers!	G	RF	231	On Our Way to English	Rigby
We Can Do It!	LB	RF	19	Rigby Focus	Rigby
We Can Eat the Plants	C	RF	38	Learn to Read	Creative Teaching Press
We Can Fan	C	RF	44	Reading Street	Pearson
We Can Help The Earth	K	I	212	Pair-It Turn and Learn	Steck-Vaughn
We Can Make Graphs	D	I	58	Learn to Read	Creative Teaching Press
We Can Make Pizza	A	I	30	Little Books for Early Readers	University of Maine
We Can Measure!	H	RF	180	On Our Way to English	Rigby
We Can Play	E	RF	58	TOTTS	Tott Publications
We Can Recycle	I	I	231	Independent Readers Science	Houghton Mifflin Harcourt
We Can Recycle	B	I	28	Leveled Readers Science	Houghton Mifflin Harcourt
We Can Run	C	RF	77	PM Starters	Rigby
We Can See Three	C	I	73	PM Math Readers	Rigby
We Can Share at School	B	RF	35	Learn to Read	Creative Teaching Press
We Can Share It	H	F	140	Little Celebrations	Pearson Learning Group
We Can Use Coins	G	I	104	Early Explorers	Benchmark Education
We Care	E	RF	144	InfoTrek	ETA/Cuisenaire
We Care for Our School	I	I	134	Wonder World	Wright Group/McGraw Hill
We Clean Up	B	I	38	InfoTrek	ETA/Cuisenaire
We Clean Up!	D	RF	35	Home Connection Collection	Rigby
We Dance	C	I	30	Pacific Literacy	Pacific Learning
We Dress Up	B	RF	56	PM Plus Starters	Rigby
We Eat Rice	C	RF	46	Bebop Books	Lee & Low Books Inc.
We Eat Together!	WB	I	0	Reach	National Geographic
We Fish	B	RF	33	Early Connections	Benchmark Education
We Follow the Rules	C	I	59	Bookworms	Marshall Cavendish
We Forgot	E	RF	11	Red Rocket Readers	Flying Start Books
We Get Squished!	B	F	31	First Stories	Pacific Learning
We Get the Cookies	E	I	60	Early Explorers	Benchmark Education
We Go Out	A	I	41	PM Starters	Rigby
We Go Shopping	B	I	35	Explorations	Eleanor Curtain Publishing
We Go Shopping	B	I	35	Explorations	Okapi Educational Materials
We Go to Grandma's House	C	I	63	Windows on Literacy	National Geographic
We Go to School	B	RF	27	Carousel Earlybirds	Pearson Learning Group
We Go to School	B	F	27	Tiny Treasures	Pioneer Valley
We Got An Idea!	T	I	250+	Rigby Literacy	Rigby
We Have Rules	I	I	174	Early Explorers	Benchmark Education
We Honor America	H	I	132	Rosen Real Readers	Rosen Publishing Group
We Just Moved!	I	F	250+	Krensky, Stephen	Scholastic
We Like	C	RF	42	Foundations	Wright Group/McGraw Hill
We Like Apples	A	I	30	InfoTrek	ETA/Cuisenaire
We Like Apples	A	RF	35	Leveled Readers	Houghton Mifflin Harcourt
We Like Apples	A	RF	35	Leveled Readers/CA	Houghton Mifflin Harcourt
We Like Balloons	A	RF	28	Tiny Treasures	Pioneer Valley
We Like Fish	D	I	109	PM Starters	Rigby
We Like Fruit	B	I	31	Big Cat	Pacific Learning
We Like Fruit	B	RF	33	Lee, Millen	Scholastic
We Like Fruit!	A	RF	24	In Step Readers	Rigby
We Like Hats	B	F	38	Bella and Rosie Series	Literacy Footprints
We Like Mud	I	I	249	The Rowland Reading Program Library	Rowland Reading Foundation
We Like Pie!	A	RF	28	Leveled Readers Emergent	Houghton Mifflin Harcourt
We Like Puddles	C	RF	51	Kolodny, Cynthia	Kaeden Books

* Collection of short stories   # Graphic text
^ Mature content with lower level text demands

TITLE	LEVEL	GENRE	WORD COUNT	AUTHOR / SERIES	PUBLISHER / DISTRIBUTOR
We Like School	A	I	23	Gear Up!	Wright Group/McGraw Hill
We Like Summer!	C	RF	41	Blevins, Wiley	Scholastic
We Like the Beach	B	I	34	Bonnell, Kris	Reading Reading Books
We Like the Sun	C	RF	30	Pair-It Books	Steck-Vaughn
We Like to Graph	C	I	48	Coulton, Mia	Kaeden Books
We Like to Play	C	RF	70	Tarlow, Ellen	Scholastic
We Like to Play!	A	I	28	Leveled Readers Emergent	Houghton Mifflin Harcourt
We Like to Read: A Picture Book for Pre-Readers and Their Parents	I	I	159	April, Elyse	Hohm Press
We Listen	D	I	48	Bookworms	Marshall Cavendish
We Live Here	B	RF	25	Salzman, Gabriel	Scholastic
We Live Here Too!	Q	I	250+	Kids Talk	Picture Window Books
We Live in North America	M	I	250+	Yellow Umbrella Books	Red Brick Learning
We Look at Dinosaurs	E	I	62	Reading Street	Pearson
We Love Pets	A	I	24	Bonnell, Kris	Reading Reading Books
We Love Recess	C	I	63	Fiesta Series	Pearson Learning Group
We Love the Dirt	H	F	250+	Johnston, Tony	Scholastic
We Love the Farm	C	RF	54	Lighthouse	Rigby
We Love You, Ms. Pinkerville	L	RF	808	Leveled Readers	Houghton Mifflin Harcourt
We Love You, Ms. Pinkerville	L	RF	808	Leveled Readers/CA	Houghton Mifflin Harcourt
We Love You, Ms. Pinkerville	L	RF	808	Leveled Readers/TX	Houghton Mifflin Harcourt
We Made a Dragon	K	I	628	Explorations	Okapi Educational Materials
We Made a Dragon	K	I	628	Explorations	Eleanor Curtain Publishing
We Made a Quilt Today	I	RF	237	InfoTrek	ETA/Cuisenaire
We Make Cookies	E	RF	48	Pair-It Books	Steck-Vaughn
We Make Music	D	F	44	Literacy 2000	Rigby
We Make Patterns	B	RF	30	Gear Up!	Wright Group/McGraw Hill
We Make Pizza	C	RF	37	Carousel Readers	Pearson Learning Group
We Need a New School	F	RF	151	Developing Books Set 4	Pioneer Valley
We Need Auto Mechanics	I	I	79	Pebble Books	Red Brick Learning
We Need Child Care Workers	E	I	58	Helpers in Our community	Red Brick Learning
We Need Construction Workers	I	I	59	Helpers in Our Community	Red Brick Learning
We Need Custodians	E	I	33	Pebble Books	Capstone Press
We Need Dentists	H	I	54	Pebble Books	Red Brick Learning
We Need Directions!	I	I	250+	Rookie Read-About Geography	Children's Press
We Need Doctors	H	I	42	Pebble Books	Red Brick Learning
We Need Farmers	H	I	45	Pebble Books	Red Brick Learning
We Need Fire Fighters	G	I	64	Pebble Books	Red Brick Learning
We Need Garbage Collectors	I	I	77	Helpers in Our Community	Red Brick Learning
We Need Insects	N	I	250+	iOpeners	Pearson Learning Group
We Need Librarians	I	I	78	Pebble Books	Red Brick Learning
We Need Mail Carriers	G	I	61	Pebble Books	Red Brick Learning
We Need Nurses	H	I	65	Pebble Books	Red Brick Learning
We Need Pharmacists	I	I	81	Pebble Books	Red Brick Learning
We Need Plumbers	I	I	107	Pebble Books	Red Brick Learning
We Need Police Officers	G	I	59	Pebble Books	Red Brick Learning
We Need Principals	E	I	53	Pebble Books	Capstone Press
We Need Rain	B	I	21	Shutterbug Books	Steck-Vaughn
We Need School Bus Drivers	G	I	112	Pebble Books	Capstone Press
We Need Teachers	E	I	38	Pebble Books	Capstone Press
We Need the Sun	G	I	202	PM Science Readers	Rigby
We Need Trees	C	I	33	Hoenecke, Karen	Kaeden Books
We Need Veterinarians	G	I	48	Pebble Books	Red Brick Learning
We Need Water	I	I	99	Pebble Books	Red Brick Learning

W

TITLE	LEVEL	GENRE	WORD COUNT	AUTHOR / SERIES	PUBLISHER / DISTRIBUTOR
We Need Water	D	I	26	Science	Outside the Box
We Need Zoo Keepers	H	I	72	Helpers in Our Community	Red Brick Learning
We Play Music	A	RF	20	Bebop Books	Lee & Low Books Inc.
We Play Together	A	RF	22	Blevins, Wiley	Scholastic
We Read	A	I	20	Blevins, Wiley	Scholastic
We Read	A	RF	35	The King School Series	Townsend Press
We Recycle	D	I	50	Kaleidoscope Collection	Hameray Publishing Group
We Remember the Holocaust	Y	I	250+	Adler, David A.	Henry Holt & Co.
We Ride	C	RF	55	Bonnell, Kris	Reading Reading Books
We Ride	B	I	40	Carousel Earlybirds	Pearson Learning Group
We Ride!	A	I	31	Vocabulary Readers	Houghton Mifflin Harcourt
We Scream for Ice Cream	K	RF	250+	Chardiet, Bernice; Maccarone, Grace	Scholastic
We See the City	A	I	21	Bonnell, Kris	Reading Reading Books
We See Them Grow	F	RF	73	Reading Street	Pearson
We Shall Not Be Moved	Z	I	250+	Dash, Joan	Scholastic
We Shall Overcome	Z	I	250+	Edge	Hampton Brown
We Shall Overcome	V	I	1593	Reading Street	Pearson
We Share	B	I	60	Bookworms	Marshall Cavendish
We Ski	B	I	35	Storyteller-First Snow	Wright Group/McGraw Hill
We Subtract	E	I	132	Early Explorers	Benchmark Education
We Tell the Truth	B	I	69	Bookworms	Marshall Cavendish
We the Children (Benjamin Pratt and the Keepers of the School)	S	RF	250+	Clements, Andrew	Simon & Schuster
We Trust Gabriella	S	RF	1503	Leveled Readers	Houghton Mifflin Harcourt
We Trust Gabriella	S	RF	1503	Leveled Readers/CA	Houghton Mifflin Harcourt
We Trust Gabriella	S	RF	1503	Leveled Readers/TX	Houghton Mifflin Harcourt
We Use Honey	H	I	120	Reading Street	Pearson
We Use Numbers	J	I	298	Early Connections	Benchmark Education
We Use Water	C	I	48	Early Connections	Benchmark Education
We Use Water	E	I	89	Water	Lerner Publishing Group
We Use Water	B	I	42	Windows on Literacy	National Geographic
We Want Jobs!: A Story of the Great Depression	R	I	250+	Norrell, Robert J.	Steck-Vaughn
We Want That	F	RF	158	Visions	Wright Group/McGraw Hill
We Want Watermelon	B	RF	49	Phonics and Friends	Hampton Brown
We Went Flying	C	RF	40	Carousel Earlybirds	Pearson Learning Group
We Went to the Zoo	B	I	32	Little Red Readers	Sundance
We Were There, Too!: Young People in U.S. History	Y	B	250+	Hoose, Phillip	Farrar, Straus, & Giroux
We Wrote to Grandma	H	RF	239	Momentum Literacy Program	Troll Associates
^Weapons of Ancient Times	T	I	250+	Weapons of War	Capstone Press
^Weapons of the American Indians	T	I	250+	Weapons of War	Capstone Press
^Weapons of the Civil War	T	I	250+	Weapons of War	Capstone Press
^Weapons of the Cold War	T	I	250+	Weapons of War	Capstone Press
^Weapons of the Middle Ages	T	I	250+	Weapons of War	Capstone Press
^Weapons of the Modern Day	T	I	250+	Weapons of War	Capstone Press
^Weapons of the Revolutionary War	T	I	250+	Weapons of War	Capstone Press
^Weapons of the Vikings	T	I	250+	Weapons of War	Capstone Press
^Weapons of World War I	T	I	250+	Weapons of War	Capstone Press
^Weapons of World War II	T	I	250+	Weapons of War	Capstone Press
Weather	C	I	54	Chanko, Pamela; Moreton, Daniel	Scholastic
Weather	E	I	138	Early Connections	Benchmark Education
Weather	M	I	250+	Explorations	Okapi Educational Materials
Weather	M	I	250+	Explorations	Eleanor Curtain Publishing

W

* Collection of short stories   # Graphic text
^ Mature content with lower level text demands

TITLE	LEVEL	GENRE	WORD COUNT	AUTHOR / SERIES	PUBLISHER / DISTRIBUTOR
Weather	O	I	250+	Fleisher, Julian	Scholastic
Weather	N	I	250+	Literacy 2000	Rigby
Weather	B	I	23	On Our Way to English	Rigby
Weather	P	I	250+	Science Kids	Kingfisher
Weather	T	I	2887	Science Support Readers	Houghton Mifflin Harcourt
Weather	I	I	347	Science Support Readers	Houghton Mifflin Harcourt
Weather	R	I	250+	Simon, Seymour	Smithsonian
Weather	N	I	250+	Simply Science	Compass Point Books
Weather	LB	I	14	Smart Start	Rigby
Weather	E	I	50	Time for Kids	Teacher Created Materials
Weather	E	I	39	Vocabulary Readers/TX	Houghton Mifflin Harcourt
Weather Alert!	N	I	314	Independent Readers Social Studies	Houghton Mifflin Harcourt
Weather Alert!	T	I	250+	Sails	Rigby
Weather and Climate	S	I	250+	Pair-It Books	Steck-Vaughn
Weather and Climate	T	I	250+	Reading Expeditions	National Geographic
Weather and Seasons	E	I	53	Windows on Literacy	National Geographic
Weather Box, The	N	F	250+	On Our Way to English	Rigby
Weather Chart, The	B	I	24	Sunshine	Wright Group/McGraw Hill
Weather Days	A	I	24	Vocabulary Readers	Houghton Mifflin Harcourt
Weather Drum, The	M	TL	250+	Cambridge Reading	Pearson Learning Group
Weather Engine, The	V	I	250+	InfoQuest	Rigby
Weather Every Day	K	I	291	Early Explorers	Benchmark Education
Weather Forecast, The	I	F	272	Story Box	Wright Group/McGraw Hill
Weather Forecasting	Q	I	250+	Wonder World	Wright Group/McGraw Hill
Weather in the City	B	I	64	Windows on Literacy	National Geographic
Weather in the USA	M	I	223	Windows on Literacy	National Geographic
Weather or Not	M	I	415	Reading Street	Pearson
Weather Report	B	I	32	Big Cat	Pacific Learning
Weather Report, The	E	F	106	Red Rocket Readers	Flying Start Books
Weather Report, The	E	I	119	Rosen Real Readers	Rosen Publishing Group
Weather Scientists	S	B	250+	Science Readers	Teacher Created Materials
Weather Today	H	RF	129	Windows on Literacy	National Geographic
Weather Tools	G	I	117	Early Explorers	Benchmark Education
Weather Watch	N	I	624	Wonders!	Hampton Brown
Weather Watcher, The	K	I	245	Spyglass Books	Compass Point Books
Weather Watchers	N	I	677	Leveled Readers	Houghton Mifflin Harcourt
Weather Watchers	N	I	677	Leveled Readers/CA	Houghton Mifflin Harcourt
Weather Watching	Q	I	250+	Explorers	Wright Group/McGraw Hill
Weather Watching	L	I	339	Rigby Focus	Rigby
Weather Wise	L	I	250+	Spyglass Books	Compass Point Books
Weather Words	F	I	174	In Step Readers	Rigby
Weather Words and What They Mean	R	I	926	Avenues	Hampton Brown
Weather Words and What They Mean	R	I	250+	Gibbons, Gail	Scholastic
Weather Works	T	I	250+	The News	Richard C. Owen
Weather, The	A	I	21	On Our Way to English	Rigby
Weathering the Storm	W	RF	2125	Leveled Readers	Houghton Mifflin Harcourt
Weatherworks	S	I	250+	Navigators How-to Series	Benchmark Education
Weaver's Gift, The	K	RF	269	Leveled Readers	Houghton Mifflin Harcourt
Weavers of the World	K	I	246	Gear Up!	Wright Group/McGraw Hill
Weaving	K	I	256	Vocabulary Readers	Houghton Mifflin Harcourt
Weaving	K	I	256	Vocabulary Readers/CA	Houghton Mifflin Harcourt
Weaving	K	I	256	Vocabulary Readers/TX	Houghton Mifflin Harcourt
*Weaving Contest, The	O	TL	250+	Literacy 2000	Rigby

W

TITLE	LEVEL	GENRE	WORD COUNT	AUTHOR / SERIES	PUBLISHER / DISTRIBUTOR
Web at Dragonfly Pond, The	P	RF	1970	Sharing Nature with Children	Dawn Publications
^Webcam Scam	P	RF	250+	Powell, J.	Stone Arch Books
Webster's Great Pond	N	I	250+	Rigby Literacy	Rigby
Wedding Crasher	O	F	250+	Stilton, Geronimo	Scholastic
Wedding Day Disaster	M	RF	250+	Supa Doopers	Sundance
Wedding, The	D	RF	52	Joy Starters	Pearson Learning Group
Wedding, The	F	RF	50	Literacy 2000	Rigby
Wedding, The	J	RF	250+	Sunshine	Wright Group/McGraw Hill
Wedges to the Rescue	O	I	250+	Simple Machine to the Rescue	Capstone Press
Wednesday Wars, The	X	HF	250+	Schmidt, Gary D.	Clarion Books
Wee Book of Pee, The	T	I	250+	The Amazingly Gross Human Body	Capstone Press
Wee Whopper	H	F	181	Windmill Books	Rigby
Wee Willie Winkie	D	RF	34	Seedlings	Continental Press
Weed Is a Flower, A: The Life of George Washington Carver	N	B	250+	Aliki	Aladdin
Weedflower	X	HF	250+	Kadohata, Cynthia	Aladdin
Weedy Sea Dragons	G	I	106	Seedlings	Continental Press
Week at Grandma Ruth's, A	K	F	1224	Coulton, Mia	Maryruth Books
Week in the Woods, A	T	RF	250+	Clements, Andrew	Simon & Schuster
Week of Surprises, A	F	RF	138	Leveled Readers Language Support	Houghton Mifflin Harcourt
Week of the Jellyhoppers, The	R	F	250+	Literacy 2000	Rigby
Week of Treats, A	E	RF	84	Bonnell, Kris	Reading Reading Books
Week of Weather, A	B	I	56	Early Explorers	Benchmark Education
Week with Aunt Bea, A	D	RF	62	Bookshop	Mondo Publishing
Week with My Aunt, A	G	RF	190	Red Rocket Readers	Flying Start Books
Week, A	F	I	111	Calendars	Lerner Publishing Group
Week, A	H	I	115	The Calendar	Capstone Press
Weekend Project, The	K	RF	722	InfoTrek	ETA/Cuisenaire
Weight Lifting	Q	I	250+	Extreme Sports	Red Brick Learning
Weimaraners	Q	I	250+	All About Dogs	Capstone Press
Weird and Wacky Inventions	O	I	250+	Tristars	Richard C. Owen
Weird Chemistry: Kitchen Creations	S	I	250+	Explore More	Wright Group/McGraw Hill
Weird Physics: Feel the Force	V	I	250+	Explore More	Wright Group/McGraw Hill
Weird Walkers	R	I	250+	Fredericks, Anthony D.	NorthWord Press
Weird Weather	N	I	250+	Rigby Rocket	Rigby
Weird, Wacky & Wonderful, Amazing World Records	Q	I	250+	Story Surfers	ETA/Cuisenaire
Welcome Home	L	I	250+	Early Connections	Benchmark Education
Welcome Home!	L	RF	1133	InfoTrek	ETA/Cuisenaire
Welcome to Brazil	M	I	250+	Spyglass Books	Compass Point Books
Welcome to California	O	I	196	Larkin, Bruce	Wilbooks
Welcome to Canada	M	I	250+	Spyglass Books	Compass Point Books
Welcome to Hong Kong!	J	I	174	Vocabulary Readers	Houghton Mifflin Harcourt
Welcome to Indiana	O	I	207	Larkin, Bruce	Wilbooks
Welcome to Japan	M	I	250+	Spyglass Books	Compass Point Books
Welcome to Japan	O	I	250+	Windows on Literacy	National Geographic
Welcome to Kenya	M	I	250+	Spyglass Books	Compass Point Books
Welcome to Mexico	M	I	250+	Spyglass Books	Compass Point Books
Welcome to Mississippi	O	I	202	Larkin, Bruce	Wilbooks
Welcome to Oregon	O	I	226	Larkin, Bruce	Wilbooks
Welcome to Our Home	J	I	191	Avenues	Hampton Brown
Welcome to Our School	G	RF	101	Leveled Readers Social Studies	Houghton Mifflin Harcourt

W

* Collection of short stories   # Graphic text
^ Mature content with lower level text demands

TITLE	LEVEL	GENRE	WORD COUNT	AUTHOR / SERIES	PUBLISHER / DISTRIBUTOR
Welcome to Our World	I	RF	412	Red Rocket Readers	Flying Start Books
Welcome to Russia	M	I	250+	Spyglass Books	Compass Point Books
Welcome to South Carolina	O	I	198	Larkin, Bruce	Wilbooks
Welcome to the Bakery	J	I	122	Vocabulary Readers	Houghton Mifflin Harcourt
Welcome to the Community	J	RF	525	InfoTrek	ETA/Cuisenaire
Welcome to the Globe: The Story of Shakespeare's Theater	V	I	250+	DK Readers	DK Publishing
Welcome to the Outback	T	RF	250+	Reading Safari	Mondo Publishing
Welcome to the White House	F	I	106	Independent Readers Social Studies	Houghton Mifflin Harcourt
Welcome to the Zigzag Zoo	B	F	42	Phonics and Friends	Hampton Brown
Welcome, Grandma!	C	RF	57	Windows on Literacy	National Geographic
Welcome, Wilma	O	F	667	Leveled Readers	Houghton Mifflin Harcourt
Welcoming New Neighbors	M	I	916	Vocabulary Readers	Houghton Mifflin Harcourt
Welcoming New Neighbors	M	I	916	Vocabulary Readers/CA	Houghton Mifflin Harcourt
Well Done, Oscar!	F	RF	201	The Joy Cowley Collection	Hameray Publishing Group
Well Done, Sam	I	RF	250+	Cambridge Reading	Pearson Learning Group
*Well I Never	K	F	2517	Story Box	Wright Group/McGraw Hill
We'll Never Forget You, Roberto Clemente	Q	B	250+	Engel, Trudie	Scholastic
We'll Race You, Henry: A Story About Henry Ford	R	B	5706	Creative Minds Biographies	Carolrhoda Books
Well, The	T	HF	250+	Taylor, Mildred D.	Puffin Books
Well-fed Bear, The	E	F	35	Literacy 2000	Rigby
Well-Trained Dog, A	M	RF	797	Leveled Readers	Houghton Mifflin Harcourt
Well-Trained Dog, A	M	RF	797	Leveled Readers/CA	Houghton Mifflin Harcourt
Well-Trained Dog, A	M	RF	797	Leveled Readers/TX	Houghton Mifflin Harcourt
Welly Dancing	F	RF	158	Rigby Rocket	Rigby
Welsh Lamb, A	L	RF	250+	Cambridge Reading	Pearson Learning Group
Wemberly Worried	L	F	250+	Henkes, Kevin	Scholastic
Wendy Worm's Adventure	I	F	286	Springboard	Wright Group/McGraw Hill
We're a Team!	H	RF	100	City Stories	Rigby
Were Early Computers Really the Size of a School Bus?: And Other Questions about Inventions	U	I	5258	Is That a Fact?	Lerner Publishing Group
We're Going Camping	J	I	111	Windows on Literacy	National Geographic
We're Going on a Bear Hunt	I	TL	363	Rosen, Michael	Macmillan
We're Going on a Nature Hunt	I	RF	250+	Metzger, Steve	Scholastic
We're Going on a Picnic	H	RF	250+	Cambridge Reading	Pearson Learning Group
We're in Big Trouble, Black Board Bear	I	F	250+	Alexander, Martha	Dial/Penguin
We're Just Looking	E	RF	115	Seedlings	Continental Press
We're Off to Look for Aliens	N	F	250+	McNaughton, Colin	Candlewick Press
We're Off to Thunder Mountain	L	RF	250+	Bookshop	Mondo Publishing
Were Potato Chips Really Invented by an Angry Chef?: And Other Questions About Food	U	I	5010	Is That a Fact?	Lerner Publishing Group
Werewolf Chronicles, The	T	F	250+	Philbrick, Rodman; Harnett, Lynn	Scholastic
^Werewolf Eclipse	U	F	250+	The Extraordinary Files	Hameray Publishing Group
Werewolf Moon	L	RF	250+	Science Solves It!	Kane Press
Werewolves	X	I	5026	Monster Chronicles	Lerner Publishing Group
Werewolves	Q	I	250+	Mythical Creatures	Raintree
Werewolves Don't Go To Summer Camp	M	F	250+	Dadey, Debbie; Jones, Marcia Thornton	Scholastic
Weslandia	P	F	250+	Fleischman, Paul	Candlewick Press
West Asia: Geography and Environments	W	I	250+	Reading Expeditions	National Geographic
West Asia: People and Places	X	I	250+	Reading Expeditions	National Geographic

W

TITLE	LEVEL	GENRE	WORD COUNT	AUTHOR / SERIES	PUBLISHER / DISTRIBUTOR
West Side Kids: Don't Call Me Slob-O	R	RF	250+	Orgel, Doris	Hyperion
West Side Kids: The Big Idea	R	RF	250+	Schecter, Ellen	Hyperion
West Side Kids: The Pet Sitters	R	RF	250+	Schecter, Ellen	Hyperion
West Today, The	S	I	250+	Reading Expeditions	National Geographic
West Virginia	T	I	250+	Hello U.S.A.	Lerner Publishing Group
West Virginia	R	I	250+	This Land Is Your Land	Compass Point Books
West Virginia: Facts and Symbols	O	I	250+	Feeney, Kathy	Red Brick Learning
West Virginia: Facts and Symbols	O	I	250+	The States and Their Symbols	Capstone Press
West, The	T	I	250+	Reading Expeditions	National Geographic
West, The: Its History and People	S	I	250+	Reading Expeditions	National Geographic
Western States, The	R	I	250+	Navigators Social Studies Series	Benchmark Education
Westing Game, The	V	RF	250+	Raskin, Ellen	Penguin Group
^Westward Expansion: An Interactive History Adventure	V	HF	250+	You Choose Books	Capstone Press
Westward Ho!	T	I	250+	Carlson, Laurie	Chicago Review Press
Westward Ho!	T	I	250+	Kids Discover Reading	Wright Group/McGraw Hill
Wet and Dry: An Animal Opposites Book	K	I	250+	Animal Opposites	Capstone Press
Wet Day at School, A	J	RF	130	Sunshine	Wright Group/McGraw Hill
Wet Dry	B	I	74	Bookworms	Marshall Cavendish
Wet Grass	H	RF	188	Story Box	Wright Group/McGraw Hill
Wet Paint	E	F	92	Storyteller-Setting Sun	Wright Group/McGraw Hill
Wet Weather Camping	J	RF	250+	PM Plus Story Books	Rigby
Wet World	N	RF	250+	Boyz Rule!	Mondo Publishing
Wet, Wet, Wet	C	RF	55	Kaleidoscope Collection	Hameray Publishing Group
Wetland	F	I	92	Habitats	Lerner Publishing Group
Wetland Adventure	R	RF	250+	Reading Expeditions	National Geographic
Wetland Animals	D	I	44	Benchmark Rebus	Marshall Cavendish
Wetland Birds	J	I	219	Sun Sprouts	ETA/Cuisenaire
Wetland Home, A	Q	I	250+	Sunshine	Wright Group/McGraw Hill
Wetland Plants	N	I	250+	Life in the World's Biomes	Capstone Press
Wetlanders	U	RF	250+	Reading Expeditions	National Geographic
Wetlands	W	I	250+	Biomes Atlases	Raintree
Wetlands	Q	I	250+	Ecosystems	Red Brick Learning
Wetlands	Q	I	250+	First Reports	Compass Point Books
Wetlands	K	I	175	Rigby Focus	Rigby
Wetlands	S	I	250+	Theme Sets	National Geographic
We've Got Mail! Sending Mail in the United States from Past to Present	Q	I	250+	Literacy by Design	Rigby
Whale	V	I	250+	Eyewitness Books	DK Publishing
Whale in the Water, The	G	I	89	Benchmark Rebus	Marshall Cavendish
Whale in the Well, The	H	F	163	Rigby Star	Rigby
Whale Is Not A Fish, A: And Other Animal Mix-ups	P	I	250+	Berger, Melvin	Scholastic
Whale Music	N	RF	771	Leveled Readers	Houghton Mifflin Harcourt
Whale Rescue	K	I	254	In Step Readers	Rigby
Whale Rescue	K	F	506	Red Rocket Readers	Flying Start Books
^Whale Shark	N	I	250+	Shark Zone	Capstone Press
Whale Shark	J	I	136	Sharks	Capstone Press
Whale Songs	K	I	173	Vocabulary Readers	Houghton Mifflin Harcourt
Whale Songs	K	I	173	Vocabulary Readers/CA	Houghton Mifflin Harcourt
Whale Tales	N	I	250+	Orbit Chapter Books	Pacific Learning
Whale Talk	Z+	RF	250+	Crutcher, Chris	Random House
Whale Watch	B	I	27	Ready Readers	Pearson Learning Group
Whale Watchers, The	E	F	63	Windmill Books	Rigby

W

* Collection of short stories   # Graphic text
^ Mature content with lower level text demands

TITLE	LEVEL	GENRE	WORD COUNT	AUTHOR / SERIES	PUBLISHER / DISTRIBUTOR
Whale Watching	J	I	250+	Pacific Literacy	Pacific Learning
Whale! Nantucket Whaling Days	S	I	2363	Independent Readers Social Studies	Houghton Mifflin Harcourt
Whale, The	O	I	250+	Crewe, Sabrina	Steck-Vaughn
Whales	O	I	250+	Bookshop	Mondo Publishing
Whales	O	I	1664	Early Bird Nature Books	Lerner Publishing Group
Whales	G	I	150	Foundations	Wright Group/McGraw Hill
Whales	O	I	250+	Holmes, Kevin J.	Red Brick Learning
Whales	I	I	45	Pebble Books	Red Brick Learning
Whales	N	I	250+	PM Animal Facts: Silver	Rigby
Whales	G	I	86	Readlings/ Marine Animals	American Reading Company
Whales	O	I	250+	Simon, Seymour	Houghton Mifflin Harcourt
Whales	O	I	250+	Soar To Success	Houghton Mifflin Harcourt
Whales	I	I	102	Under the Sea	Capstone Press
Whales	M	I	333	Wonder World	Wright Group/McGraw Hill
Whales - The Gentle Giants	L	I	250+	Milton, Joyce	Random House
Whales and Dolphins	L	I	250+	I Wonder Why	Kingfisher
Whales and Other Animal Wonders	P	I	1555	Reading Street	Pearson
Whales in the Ocean	D	I	35	Rosen Real Readers	Rosen Publishing Group
Whales of the World	U	I	1500	Leveled Readers/TX	Houghton Mifflin Harcourt
Whales on Stilts	S	SF	250+	Anderson, M. T.	Harcourt Achieve
Whales on the Move	N	I	250+	Little Celebrations	Pearson Learning Group
Whales Passing	L	RF	250+	Bunting, Eve	Scholastic
Whales' Song, The	N	I	250+	Sheldon, Dyan	Penguin Group
Whale's Year, The	J	I	212	Lighthouse	Rigby
Whales: Giants of the Deep	M	I	250+	The Wild World of Animals	Red Brick Learning
Whaling Community of the 1840s, A	S	I	250+	Reading Expeditions	National Geographic
Whaling Community, A: New Bedford, Massachusetts	O	I	250+	Navigators Social Studies Series	Benchmark Education
What a Bad Dog!	D	RF	52	Oxford Reading Tree	Oxford University Press
What a Birthday!	G	RF	138	Leveled Readers Language Support	Houghton Mifflin Harcourt
What a Cat Can Do	B	RF	63	Literacy by Design	Rigby
What a Catch!	G	RF	118	Instant Readers	Harcourt School Publishers
What a Catch!	E	RF	91	Rigby Rocket	Rigby
What a Century!	V	I	250+	InfoQuest	Rigby
What a Clown!	A	F	18	Rigby Rocket	Rigby
What a Day!	J	RF	621	Avenues	Hampton Brown
What a Day!	J	RF	621	Miranda, Anne	Hampton Brown
What a Dog!	F	RF	134	First Start	Troll Associates
What a Dog!	H	RF	223	Story Basket	Wright Group/McGraw Hill
What a Duck!	J	F	250+	Literacy by Design	Rigby
What a Funny Thing to Do	K	RF	236	Stepping Stones	Nelson/Michaels Assoc.
What a Great Idea!	L	RF	250+	Home Connection Collection	Rigby
What a Great Idea!	S	I	1390	Reading Street	Pearson
What A Great Idea! Inventions That Changed the World	V	I	250+	Tomecek, Stephen M.	Scholastic
What a Haircut!	J	RF	250+	Voyages	SRA/McGraw Hill
What a Hamster Needs	C	I	46	Leveled Readers Science	Houghton Mifflin Harcourt
What a Job!	R	I	250+	Discovery Links	Newbridge
What a Job!	M	I	250+	Rigby Literacy	Rigby
What a Load of Garbage	L	I	250+	Lighthouse	Rigby
What a Load of Rubbish	L	I	250+	Lighthouse	Ginn & Co.
What a Machine!	M	F	1028	Dominie MathStories	Pearson Learning Group

W

TITLE	LEVEL	GENRE	WORD COUNT	AUTHOR / SERIES	PUBLISHER / DISTRIBUTOR
What a Mess!	C	RF	79	Bookshop	Mondo Publishing
*What a Mess!	G	RF	124	New Way Blue	Steck-Vaughn
What a Mess!	LB	RF	14	Smart Start	Rigby
What a Mess!	C	RF	51	Story Box	Wright Group/McGraw Hill
What a Noise!	I	RF	165	Pacific Literacy	Pacific Learning
What a Nose!	H	I	154	Sails	Rigby
What a Plant!	S	I	250+	Sunshine	Wright Group/McGraw Hill
What a School	F	RF	100	Salem, Lynn; Stewart, Josie	Continental Press
What a Shower!	B	RF	23	Instant Readers	Harcourt School Publishers
What a Spelling Test!	I	F	123	City Stories	Rigby
What a Street!	B	RF	28	Bebop Books	Lee & Low Books Inc.
What a Tale!	C	RF	38	Wildsmith, Brian	Oxford University Press
#What a Team!	M	F	250+	Mr. Badger and Mrs. Fox	Graphic Universe
What a Treasure!	I	F	242	Hillenbrand, Jane & Will	Holiday House
What a Trip, Amber Brown	L	RF	250+	Danziger, Paula	Puffin Books
What a Waste	H	I	180	Sun Sprouts	ETA/Cuisenaire
What a Wedding!	N	I	250+	Sails	Rigby
What a Week!	I	RF	372	Avenues	Hampton Brown
What a Week!	C	RF	36	Home Connection Collection	Rigby
What a Week!	C	RF	64	Rigby Literacy	Rigby
What a Week!	C	RF	89	Rigby Star	Rigby
What a Wonderful Idea	O	RF	1059	Leveled Readers	Houghton Mifflin Harcourt
What a Year	N	B	250+	DePaola, Tomie	Penguin Group
What About Bennie?	H	RF	124	Literacy Tree	Rigby
What Am I Eating?	X	I	3086	Vocabulary Readers	Houghton Mifflin Harcourt
What Am I Eating?	X	I	3086	Vocabulary Readers/CA	Houghton Mifflin Harcourt
What Am I Going to Be?	H	RF	111	Storyteller-Moon Rising	Wright Group/McGraw Hill
What Am I Made Of?	N	I	250+	Bennett, David	Scholastic
What Am I?	I	I	100	Foundations	Wright Group/McGraw Hill
What Am I?	B	RF	50	Handprints B	Educators Publishing Service
What Am I?	LB	RF	16	Just Beginning	Pearson Learning Group
What Am I?	E	RF	250+	Let's Play	Norwood House Press
What Am I?	D	I	111	Leveled Literacy Intervention/ Green System	Heinemann
What Am I?	C	I	146	Rigby Flying Colors	Rigby
What Am I?	D	I	51	Story Steps	Rigby
What Am I?	F	I	100	Sun Sprouts	ETA/Cuisenaire
What Am I?	G	I	124	Sunshine	Wright Group/McGraw Hill
What Am I?	C	I	51	Williams, Deborah	Kaeden Books
What Am I? An Animal Guessing Game	L	F	250+	Trapani, Iza	Charlesbridge
What Am I? Weird and Wonderful Sea Animals	L	I	470	Explorations	Eleanor Curtain Publishing
What Am I? Weird and Wonderful Sea Animals	L	I	470	Explorations	Okapi Educational Materials
What an Adventure!	K	I	305	Reading Street	Pearson
What Ancient Astronomers Knew	U	I	2852	Leveled Readers Science	Houghton Mifflin Harcourt
What Angela Needs	K	RF	250+	Voyages	SRA/McGraw Hill
What Animal Lives Here?	H	I	250+	Woolley, M.; Pigdon, K.	Mondo Publishing
What Animals Do You See?	F	RF	100	Reading Street	Pearson
What Animals Do You See?	C	I	50	Read-More Books	Pearson Learning Group
What Animals Eat	D	I	112	Leveled Readers	Houghton Mifflin Harcourt
What Animals Eat	D	I	112	Leveled Readers/CA	Houghton Mifflin Harcourt
What Animals Eat	E	I	75	Little Red Readers	Sundance
What Animals Need	F	I	21	Windows on Literacy	National Geographic
What Animals Really Like	L	F	250+	Robinson, Fiona	Harry N. Abrams

W

* Collection of short stories   # Graphic text
^ Mature content with lower level text demands

What Animals Say	E	F	80	Dominie Readers	Pearson Learning Group
What Are Baby Koalas Called?	N	I	250+	Why In the World?	Capstone Press
What Are Caves?	K	I	108	Pebble Books	Red Brick Learning
What Are Deserts?	K	I	105	Pebble Books	Capstone Press
What Are Forests?	K	I	114	Pebble Books	Capstone Press
What Are Friends For?	C	I	32	Little Celebrations	Pearson Learning Group
What Are Friends For?	C	I	33	Rosen Real Readers	Rosen Publishing Group
What Are Goods?	J	I	171	Early Explorers	Benchmark Education
What are Inclined Planes?	M	I	70	Pebble Books	Red Brick Learning
What Are Lakes?	K	I	92	Pebble Books	Red Brick Learning
What Are Levers?	M	I	66	Pebble Books	Red Brick Learning
What Are Mountains?	K	I	70	Pebble Books	Capstone Press
What Are My Chances?	J	I	393	Early Connections	Benchmark Education
What Are Natural Resources?	K	I	175	Larkin, Bruce	Wilbooks
What Are Oceans?	K	I	97	Pebble Books	Capstone Press
What Are Pulleys?	M	I	88	Pebble Books	Red Brick Learning
What Are Purple Elephants Good For?	H	F	136	Reading Corners	Pearson Learning Group
What Are Rivers?	K	I	111	Pebble Books	Red Brick Learning
What Are Screws?	M	I	65	Pebble Books	Red Brick Learning
What Are the Parts of a Tree?	J	I	218	Early Explorers	Benchmark Education
What Are Volcanoes?	K	I	108	Pebble Books	Red Brick Learning
What Are We Doing?	A	F	21	KinderReaders	Rigby
What Are Wedges?	M	I	60	Pebble Books	Red Brick Learning
What Are Wheels and Axles?	M	I	70	Pebble Books	Red Brick Learning
*What Are You Afraid Of?: Stories About Phobias	Z+	RF	250+	Gallo, Donald	Candlewick Press
What Are You Called?	C	I	66	Voyages	SRA/McGraw Hill
What Are You Doing?	D	RF	101	Foundations	Wright Group/McGraw Hill
What Are You Figuring Now? A Story About Benjamin Banneker	R	B	250+	Ferris, Jeri	Scholastic
What Are You Figuring Now? A Story About Benjamin Banneker	R	B	7346	Creative Minds Biographies	Carolrhoda Books
What Are You Going to Buy?	F	F	180	Read Alongs	Rigby
What Are You Scared of?	P	I	250+	Trackers	Pacific Learning
What Are You Waiting For?	E	RF	48	Silly Millies	Millbrook Press
What Are You?	A	F	27	Literacy 2000	Rigby
What Bear Cubs Like to Do	I	I	83	Little Books	Sadlier-Oxford
What Bears Like	A	I	21	Cherrington, Janelle	Scholastic
What Bird Am I?	D	I	97	Bonnell, Kris	Reading Reading Books
What Birds Eat	B	I	60	Sails	Rigby
What Blows in the Wind?	A	RF	36	Science	Outside the Box
What Boo and I Do	G	I	171	Bebop Books	Lee & Low Books Inc.
What Came Out of My Bean?	H	RF	158	Book Bank	Wright Group/McGraw Hill
What Can a Diver See?	D	I	44	Windows on Literacy	National Geographic
What Can Buddy See?	C	RF	55	McGougan, Kathy	Buddy Books Publishing
What Can Bugs Do?	A	I	24	Bonnell, Kris	Reading Reading Books
What Can Change?	G	I	96	Discovery Links	Newbridge
What Can Float?	B	I	27	Ready Readers	Pearson Learning Group
What Can Float?	D	I	87	Red Rocket Readers	Flying Start Books
What Can Float?	B	I	32	Windmill Books	Rigby
What Can Fly?	B	I	29	Discovery Links	Newbridge
What Can Fly?	C	I	33	Joy Readers	Pearson Learning Group
What Can Fly?	B	I	28	Literacy 2000	Rigby
What Can Fly?	A	I	31	Nonfiction Set 1	Literacy Footprints
What Can Fly?	B	RF	33	Red Rocket Readers	Flying Start Books

TITLE	LEVEL	GENRE	WORD COUNT	AUTHOR / SERIES	PUBLISHER / DISTRIBUTOR
What Can Go Fast?	B	I	37	Little Red Readers	Sundance
What Can Hurt?	B	I	30	Windmill Books	Rigby
What Can I Buy?	E	RF	66	InfoTrek	ETA/Cuisenaire
What Can I Buy?	F	RF	156	Moriarty, Julie	Scholastic
What Can I Buy?	C	I	33	Rosen Real Readers	Rosen Publishing Group
What Can I Do Today?	A	I	20	Windows on Literacy	National Geographic
What Can I Do?	C	I	42	Foundations	Wright Group/McGraw Hill
What Can I Do?	C	RF	61	Gear Up!	Wright Group/McGraw Hill
What Can I Do?	H	I	250+	Greetings	Rigby
What Can I Do?	C	I	42	Read-More Books	Pearson Learning Group
What Can I Read?	A	RF	28	Carousel Earlybirds	Pearson Learning Group
What Can I See?	C	I	42	Foundations	Wright Group/McGraw Hill
What Can I See?	B	RF	36	Storyteller	Wright Group/McGraw Hill
What Can It Be?	N	I	250+	Early Connections	Benchmark Education
What Can It Be?	F	I	113	Storyteller-First Snow	Wright Group/McGraw Hill
What Can Jigarees Do?	A	F	22	Story Box	Wright Group/McGraw Hill
What Can Jump?	C	I	78	Sails	Rigby
What Can Jump?	B	I	28	Shutterbug Books	Steck-Vaughn
What Can Jump?	B	I	32	Windmill Books	Rigby
What Can Live in a Desert?	J	I	113	Animal Adaptations	Lerner Publishing Group
What Can Live in a Forest?	J	I	125	Animal Adaptations	Lerner Publishing Group
What Can Live in a Grassland?	J	I	115	Animal Adaptations	Lerner Publishing Group
What Can Live in a Lake?	J	I	113	Animal Adaptations	Lerner Publishing Group
What Can Live in the Mountains?	J	I	118	Animal Adaptations	Lerner Publishing Group
What Can Live in the Ocean?	J	I	92	Animal Adaptations	Lerner Publishing Group
What Can Rosa Paint?	J	RF	383	Leveled Readers	Houghton Mifflin Harcourt
What Can Rosa Paint?	J	RF	383	Leveled Readers/CA	Houghton Mifflin Harcourt
What Can Rosa Paint?	J	RF	383	Leveled Readers/TX	Houghton Mifflin Harcourt
What Can She Do?	A	I	21	Little Books for Early Readers	University of Maine
What Can Sing?	D	I	65	Sun Sprouts	ETA/Cuisenaire
What Can Swim?	B	I	30	Windmill Books	Rigby
What Can This Animal Do?	B	I	28	Foundations	Wright Group/McGraw Hill
What Can We Do Today?	G	RF	146	Carousel Readers	Pearson Learning Group
What Can We Do?	J	RF	439	Leveled Readers Social Studies	Houghton Mifflin Harcourt
What Can We Make?	E	I	115	InfoTrek	ETA/Cuisenaire
What Can We Make?	D	RF	64	Windows on Literacy	National Geographic
What Can We Smell?	C	I	44	Windmill Books	Rigby
What Can You Be?	C	I	166	Tiger Cub	Peguis
What Can You Do with a Ball of String?	G	RF	250+	Home Connection Collection	Rigby
What Can You Do with an Elephant House?	R	I	250+	Gaynor, Miriam; Goodwin, A.	Pacific Learning
What Can You Do with an Old Red Shoe?: A Green Activity Book About Reuse	O	I	250+	Alter, Anna	Henry Holt & Co.
What Can You Do with Money?: Earning, Spending, and Saving	L	I	446	Lightning Bolt Books	Lerner Publishing Group
What Can You Do?	A	F	21	Avenues	Hampton Brown
What Can You Do?	C	I	59	Tiger Cub	Peguis
What Can You Do?	A	I	18	Vocabulary Readers	Houghton Mifflin Harcourt
What Can You Do? A Book About Discovering What You Do Well	J	I	196	Shelley Rotner's Early Childhood Library	Millbrook Press
What Can You Hear?	D	I	80	Tiger Cub	Peguis
What Can You Make?	B	I	22	Ready Readers	Pearson Learning Group
What Can You Measure With a Lollipop?	H	I	159	Early Connections	Benchmark Education
What Can You Read?	G	RF	138	Red Rocket Readers	Flying Start Books
What Can You See in a Desert?	A	I	28	Early Explorers	Benchmark Education
What Can You See on Farms?	A	I	28	Gear Up!	Wright Group/McGraw Hill

* Collection of short stories   # Graphic text
^ Mature content with lower level text demands

W

TITLE	LEVEL	GENRE	WORD COUNT	AUTHOR / SERIES	PUBLISHER / DISTRIBUTOR
What Can You See?	C	I	25	Literacy 2000	Rigby
What Can You See?	B	I	41	Red Rocket Readers	Flying Start Books
What Can You See?	C	RF	31	Rigby Literacy	Rigby
What Can You See?	B	I	31	Tiger Cub	Peguis
What Can You See?	C	I	43	Vocabulary Readers	Houghton Mifflin Harcourt
What Can You Smell?	B	I	41	Red Rocket Readers	Flying Start Books
What Can You Taste?	B	I	45	Windmill Books	Rigby
What Cat Is That?	J	RF	250+	Real Reading	Steck-Vaughn
What Causes Forest Fires?	N	I	868	Leveled Readers Science	Houghton Mifflin Harcourt
What Changes Our Earth?	K	I	273	People, Spaces & Places	Rand McNally
What Children Play	M	I	250+	HSP/Harcourt Trophies	Harcourt, Inc.
What Color Is Caesar?	M	F	250+	Kumin, Maxine	Candlewick Press
What Color Is It?	B	I	29	Properties of Matter	Lerner Publishing Group
What Color Is the Sky?	F	I	74	Windows on Literacy	National Geographic
What Columbus Found	J	HF	195	Kurtz, Jane	Aladdin
What Comes First?	C	I	56	Bookshop	Mondo Publishing
What Comes from a Cow?	G	I	85	Sunshine	Wright Group/McGraw Hill
What Comes from Eggs?	B	I	74	Bookshop	Mondo Publishing
What Comes in Groups?	F	I	133	Shutterbug Books	Steck-Vaughn
What Comes in Threes?	C	F	41	Learn to Read	Creative Teaching Press
What Comes in Twos?	D	I	125	Early Connections	Benchmark Education
What Comes Next?	J	I	250+	Early Connections	Benchmark Education
What Comes Out at Night?	B	I	48	Little Red Readers	Sundance
What Computers Do	I	I	186	Yellow Umbrella Books	Red Brick Learning
What Could I Be?	C	RF	64	Foundations	Wright Group/McGraw Hill
What Could I Be?	F	I	132	Red Rocket Readers	Flying Start Books
What Could it Be?	B	RF	19	Instant Readers	Harcourt School Publishers
What Could You See?	E	F	107	Dominie Readers	Pearson Learning Group
What Daddies Do Best	F	F	113	Numeroff, Laura Joffe	Simon & Schuster
What Damian Didn't Know About Dinosaurs	J	RF	250+	Rigby Rocket	Rigby
What Day Is It?	D	F	79	Green Light Readers	Harcourt
What Did Abuela Say?	M	RF	439	Valentin, Karen; Allie's World	Marimba Books
What Did Ben Want?	A	RF	28	Smart Start	Rigby
What Did I Forget?	D	RF	43	Teacher's Choice Series	Pearson Learning Group
What Did I Use?	C	I	65	Discovery World	Rigby
What Did Kim Catch?	C	RF	48	Literacy 2000	Rigby
What Did People Use Long Ago?	I	I	250+	Shutterbug Books	Steck-Vaughn
What Did Robot Want?	E	F	166	Joy Starters	Pearson Learning Group
What Did the Ancient Chinese Do for Me?	W	I	250+	Linking the Past and Present	Heinemann Library
What Did the Ancient Egyptians Do for Me?	W	I	250+	Linking the Past and Present	Heinemann Library
What Did the Ancient Greeks Do for Me?	W	I	250+	Linking the Past and Present	Heinemann Library
What Did the Ancient Romans Do for Me?	W	I	250+	Linking the Past and Present	Heinemann Library
What Did the Aztecs Do for Me?	W	I	250+	Linking the Past and Present	Heinemann Library
What Did the Vikings Do for Me?	W	I	250+	Linking the Past and Present	Heinemann Library
What Did They Drive?	D	RF	73	Windows on Literacy	National Geographic
What Did They Want?	C	RF	28	Smart Start	Rigby
What Did You Bring?	B	I	23	Ready Readers	Pearson Learning Group
What Did You Eat Today?	L	F	250+	Literacy Tree	Rigby
What Did You Lose, Santa?	WB	F	0	Amoss, Berthe	Harper & Row
What Dinah Saw	M	F	250+	Lighthouse	Rigby
What Dinosaurs Ate	F	I	44	Planet Earth	Rigby
What Do Animals Do?	E	I	29	Little Red Readers	Sundance
What Do Archaeologists Do?	W	I	2557	Reading Street	Pearson

W

TITLE	LEVEL	GENRE	WORD COUNT	AUTHOR / SERIES	PUBLISHER / DISTRIBUTOR
What Do Artists Use?	F	I	31	Canizares, Susan; Berger, Samantha	Scholastic
What Do Blue Bears Eat?	C	F	90	Bonnell, Kris	Reading Reading Books
What Do Cats Like?	B	I	19	Bonnell, Kris	Reading Reading Books
What Do Communities Have?	A	I	27	Early Explorers	Benchmark Education
*What Do Fish Have To Do With Anything?	W	RF	250+	Avi	Candlewick Press
What Do I See in the Garden?	F	I	108	Wonder World	Wright Group/McGraw Hill
What Do I See?	A	I	18	Gear Up!	Wright Group/McGraw Hill
What Do I See?	A	I	32	Literacy by Design	Rigby
What Do I See?	B	I	28	Twig	Wright Group/McGraw Hill
What Do I Use?	D	I	57	Scooters	ETA/Cuisenaire
What Do I Wear?	J	I	40	Leveled Readers Social Studies	Houghton Mifflin Harcourt
What Do Insects Do?	A	I	24	Canizares, Susan; Chanko, Pamela	Scholastic
What Do Parents Do? (When You're Not Home)	L	F	250+	Ransom, Jeanie Franz	Peachtree
What Do Pets Need?	E	I	106	Early Connections	Benchmark Education
What Do Pets Need?	E	I	67	Windows on Literacy	National Geographic
What Do Scientists Do?	H	I	79	Discovery Links	Newbridge
What Do Scientists Do?	O	I	1576	Gear Up!	Wright Group/McGraw Hill
What Do Scientists Do?	B	I	24	Twig	Wright Group/McGraw Hill
What Do Sharks Eat for Dinner?: Questions & Answers About Sharks	R	I	250+	Berger, Melvin & Gilda	Scholastic
What Do Teachers Do (After You Leave School)	L	F	501	Bowen, Anne	Carolrhoda Books
What Do We Buy?: A Look at Goods and Services	M	I	414	Lightning Bolt Books	Lerner Publishing Group
What Do We Have to Get?	E	RF	117	Ready Readers	Pearson Learning Group
What Do We Have?	C	F	28	Step-By-Step Series	Pearson Learning Group
What Do We Like Best?	E	I	90	InfoTrek	ETA/Cuisenaire
What Do We Measure?	I	I	157	Gear Up!	Wright Group/McGraw Hill
What Do We Need?	C	I	51	Learn to Read Social Studies	Creative Teaching Press
What Do We Need?	F	I	147	On Our Way to English	Rigby
What Do You Do at the Zoo?	G	RF	182	Silly Millies	Millbrook Press
What Do You Do on an Farm?	F	F	188	Silly Millies	Millbrook Press
What Do You Do With a Tail Like This?	L	I	250+	Jenkins, Steve & Page, Robin	Houghton Mifflin Harcourt
What Do You Do?	G	F	125	Little Celebrations	Pearson Learning Group
What Do You Do?	E	I	162	Tiger Cub	Peguis
What Do You Have?	C	I	165	Tiger Cub	Peguis
What Do You Have?	C	I	88	Windmill Books	Rigby
What Do You Hear When Cows Sing?	J	F	250+	Maestro, Marco & Giulio	HarperTrophy
What Do You Hear?	C	I	60	Windmill Books	Rigby
What Do You Know About Dolphins?	J	I	137	Windows on Literacy	National Geographic
What Do You Like to Eat?	D	I	99	Foundations	Wright Group/McGraw Hill
What Do You Like to Wear?	D	I	50	Read-More Books	Pearson Learning Group
What Do You Like?	B	I	52	Little Books for Early Readers	University of Maine
What Do You Like?	B	RF	52	Storyteller	Wright Group/McGraw Hill
What Do You Like?	B	I	29	Tiny Treasures	Pioneer Valley
What Do You Play?	A	I	25	Science	Outside the Box
What Do You See at the Pet Store?	C	I	27	Read-More Books	Pearson Learning Group
What Do You See by the Sea?	A	I	14	Little Books	Sadlier-Oxford
What Do You See?	A	I	40	Animals	American Reading Company
What Do You See?	B	I	20	Carousel Readers	Pearson Learning Group
What Do You See?	F	F	89	Learn to Read	Creative Teaching Press
What Do You See?	B	I	67	On Our Way to English	Rigby
What Do You See?	A	RF	71	Phonics and Friends	Hampton Brown

W

* Collection of short stories # Graphic text
^ Mature content with lower level text demands

TITLE	LEVEL	GENRE	WORD COUNT	AUTHOR / SERIES	PUBLISHER / DISTRIBUTOR
What Do You See?	C	I	46	Reach	National Geographic
What Do You See?	E	I	71	Science	Harcourt School Publishers
What Do You See?	B	I	35	Windmill Books	Rigby
What Do You See?	D	I	78	Windows on Literacy	National Geographic
What Do You See? A Book About the Seasons	D	I	92	Shapiro, Sara	Scholastic
What Do You Think?	U	I	250+	Sails	Rigby
What Do You Think?	O	I	250+	Wildcats	Wright Group/McGraw Hill
What Do You Touch?	B	I	50	Windmill Books	Rigby
What Do You Want That For?	E	RF	149	Lighthouse	Rigby
What Does a Book Designer Do?	N	I	250+	Trackers	Pacific Learning
What Does a Detective Do?	H	RF	128	Reading Street	Pearson
What Does a Firefighter Do?	G	I	136	Yellow Umbrella Books	Red Brick Learning
What Does a Garden Need?	G	I	118	Discovery Links	Newbridge
What Does a Governor Do?	L	I	288	Independent Readers Social Studies	Houghton Mifflin Harcourt
What Does an Electrician Do?	T	I	1322	Independent Readers Science	Houghton Mifflin Harcourt
What Does Greedy Cat Like?	C	RF	35	Pacific Literacy	Pacific Learning
What Does It Do?	J	I	198	Ready Set Read	Steck-Vaughn
What Does Light Do?	G	I	82	Dominie Factivity Series	Pearson Publishing Group
What Does Lucy Like?	A	RF	11	Little Books	Sadlier-Oxford
What Does the President Do?	J	I	201	Miller, Amanda/Scholastic News	Children's Press
What Else?	I	RF	154	Sunshine	Wright Group/McGraw Hill
What Every Girl (except me) Knows	V	RF	250+	Baskin, Nora Raleigh	Little Brown and Company
What Feels Cold?	B	I	33	Red Rocket Readers	Flying Start Books
What Feels Cold?	B	I	30	Windmill Books	Rigby
What Feels Hot?	A	I	28	Windmill Books	Rigby
What Feels Sticky?	B	I	36	Red Rocket Readers	Flying Start Books
What Feels Sticky?	A	I	26	Windmill Books	Rigby
What Fell Out?	D	RF	32	Carousel Readers	Pearson Learning Group
What Floats?	D	I	46	Sun Sprouts	ETA/Cuisenaire
What Floats?	C	I	16	Twig	Wright Group/McGraw Hill
What Floats? What Sinks?	J	I	185	Early Connections	Benchmark Education
What Floats? What Sinks?: A Look at Density	M	I	407	Lightning Bolt Books	Lerner Publishing Group
What Fun!	F	F	250+	Sun Sprouts	ETA/Cuisenaire
What Game Shall We Play?	H	F	306	Hutchins, Pat	Sundance
What Gives You Goose Bumps?	H	RF	140	Home Connection Collection	Rigby
What Goes Around and Around?	B	I	46	Windmill Books	Rigby
What Goes Fast?	B	I	42	InfoTrek	ETA/Cuisenaire
What Goes Fast?	B	I	66	Red Rocket Readers	Flying Start Books
What Goes in the Bathtub?	C	RF	31	Literacy 2000	Rigby
What Goes into a Salad?	C	RF	22	Home Connection Collection	Rigby
What Goes Together?	A	I	28	Leveled Readers Science	Houghton Mifflin Harcourt
What Goes Up and Down?	B	I	40	Windmill Books	Rigby
What Goes Up High?	B	I	75	Red Rocket Readers	Flying Start Books
What Goes Up High?	A	I	38	Windmill Books	Rigby
What Goes Up?	B	I	42	Rigby Literacy	Rigby
What Grows from a Tree?	I	I	250+	Yellow Umbrella Books	Red Brick Learning
What Grows Here?	C	I	37	Windows on Literacy	National Geographic
What Grows in the Garden?	C	I	42	Reach	National Geographic
What Grows on Trees?	E	I	49	Start to Read	School Zone
What Grows There	P	I	448	Independent Readers Social Studies	Houghton Mifflin Harcourt
What Grows?	B	I	21	Rigby Focus	Rigby
What Grows?	A	I	15	Shutterbug Books	Steck-Vaughn

W

TITLE	LEVEL	GENRE	WORD COUNT	AUTHOR / SERIES	PUBLISHER / DISTRIBUTOR
What Hangs from the Tree?	C	I	42	Questions & Answers	Pearson Learning Group
What Happened at the Boston Tea Party?	Q	I	250+	Rosen Real Readers	Rosen Publishing Group
What Happened on Maple Street?	Q	RF	1252	Leveled Readers	Houghton Mifflin Harcourt
What Happened on Maple Street?	Q	RF	1252	Leveled Readers/CA	Houghton Mifflin Harcourt
What Happened on Maple Street?	Q	RF	1252	Leveled Readers/TX	Houghton Mifflin Harcourt
What Happened to Aunt Cordelia?	J	RF	250+	Voyages	SRA/McGraw Hill
What Happened to Bodie?	T	I	250+	Rigby Literacy	Rigby
What Happened to Cass McBride?	Z+	RF	250+	Giles, Gail	Little Brown and Company
What Happened to Humpty Dumpty?	D	F	74	Reading Safari	Mondo Publishing
What Happened to Lani Garver	Z+	RF	250+	Plum-Ucci, Carol	Harcourt Trade
What Happened to the Dinosaurs?: A Book About Extinction	N	I	250+	Why in the World?	Capstone Press
What Happened?	G	I	60	Learn to Read	Creative Teaching Press
What Happens at the Bank?	K	I	388	Leveled Readers Social Studies	Houghton Mifflin Harcourt
What Happens to Trash?	J	I	181	Little Green Readers	Sundance
What Happens When You Recycle?	K	I	215	Discovery World	Rigby
What Has Changed?	A	I	18	Windows on Literacy	National Geographic
What Has Changed?	K	I	250+	Yellow Umbrella Books	Red Brick Learning
What Has Mom Lost?	E	RF	120	The King School Series	Townsend Press
What Has Spots?	B	I	29	Literacy 2000	Rigby
What Has Stripes?	C	I	25	Ballinger, Margaret	Scholastic
What Has Three Branches?	N	I	323	Leveled Readers	Houghton Mifflin Harcourt
What Has Three Branches?	N	I	323	Leveled Readers/CA	Houghton Mifflin Harcourt
What Has Wheels?	A	I	28	Hoenecke, Karen	Kaeden Books
What Has Wings?	H	RF	250+	Momentum Literacy Program	Troll Associates
What Hatches?	J	I	250+	Yellow Umbrella Books	Capstone Press
What Have You Got?	D	RF	155	Red Rocket Readers	Flying Start Books
What Hearts	S	RF	250+	Brooks, Bruce	Language for Learning Assoc.
What Helps a Bird to Fly?	F	I	95	Birds Series	Pearson Learning Group
What Holds Us to Earth?: A Look at Gravity	M	I	440	Lightning Bolt Books	Lerner Publishing Group
What Homework?	K	RF	892	Science Solves It!	Kane Press
What I Had Was Singing: The Story of Marian Anderson	V	B	250+	Trailblazer Biographies	Carolrhoda Books
What I Left on My Plate	C	RF	54	Teacher's Choice Series	Pearson Learning Group
What I Like at School	C	I	64	Little Red Readers	Sundance
What I Like to Wear	D	I	93	Home Connection Collection	Rigby
What I See	A	RF	46	Green Light Readers	Harcourt
What I Want to Be	J	RF	377	Leveled Readers	Houghton Mifflin Harcourt
What I Want to Be	J	RF	377	Leveled Readers/CA	Houghton Mifflin Harcourt
What I Want to Be	J	RF	377	Leveled Readers/TX	Houghton Mifflin Harcourt
What I Wear	B	I	28	Leveled Readers Language Support	Houghton Mifflin Harcourt
What I Wear	D	RF	76	Sun Sprouts	ETA/Cuisenaire
What I Would Do	I	RF	173	Read Alongs	Rigby
What I'd Like to Be	F	I	112	Little Red Readers	Sundance
What If . . .	E	RF	57	Teacher's Choice Series	Pearson Learning Group
What If a Stranger Approaches You?	J	I	250+	Danger Zone	Picture Window Books
What If Everybody Did That?	K	RF	250+	Javernick, Ellen	Marshall Cavendish
What If There Is a Fire?	J	I	250+	Danger Zone	Picture Window Books
What If You Get Lost?	J	I	250+	Danger Zone	Picture Window Books
What if You Get Lost?	D	I	40	Rosen Real Readers	Rosen Publishing Group
What If...?	F	RF	118	InfoTrek	ETA/Cuisenaire
What If?	C	F	41	Little Celebrations	Pearson Learning Group

W

* Collection of short stories   # Graphic text
^ Mature content with lower level text demands

TITLE	LEVEL	GENRE	WORD COUNT	AUTHOR / SERIES	PUBLISHER / DISTRIBUTOR
What If . . . ?	E	F	66	Dominie Readers	Pearson Learning Group
What in the World is the World Wide Web?	S	I	250+	Orbit Chapter Books	Pacific Learning
What Is a Bird?	H	I	71	Pebble Books	Red Brick Learning
What Is a Desert?	O	I	250+	Harcourt Trophies	Harcourt, Inc.
What Is a Family?	J	I	250+	Spyglass Books	Compass Point Books
What Is a Fish?	H	I	77	Pebble Books	Red Brick Learning
What Is a Fly?	M	I	561	Sunshine	Wright Group/McGraw Hill
What Is a Food Chain?	G	I	71	Instant Readers	Harcourt School Publishers
What Is a Fossil?	M	I	460	The Rowland Reading Program Library	Rowland Reading Foundation
What Is a Frog?	K	I	333	Springboard	Wright Group/McGraw Hill
What Is a Gas?	K	I	126	States of Matter	Lerner Publishing Group
What Is a Good Citizen?	H	I	232	Early Explorers	Benchmark Education
What Is a Government?	W	I	250+	iOpeners	Pearson Learning Group
What Is a Huggles?	B	F	41	Sunshine	Wright Group/McGraw Hill
What Is a Hundred?	L	I	409	Yellow Umbrella Books	Red Brick Learning
What Is a Liquid?	K	I	104	States of Matter	Lerner Publishing Group
What Is a Mammal?	I	I	70	Pebble Books	Red Brick Learning
What Is a Mammal?	F	I	102	Rosen Real Readers	Rosen Publishing Group
What Is a Map?	H	I	250+	Yellow Umbrella Books	Red Brick Learning
What Is a Mountain?	I	I	231	Rosen Real Readers	Rosen Publishing Group
What Is a Park?	H	I	138	Discovery World	Rigby
What Is a Park?	J	I	230	People, Spaces & Places	Rand McNally
What Is a Poem?	G	I	69	Vocabulary Readers	Houghton Mifflin Harcourt
What Is a Rainbow?	H	I	115	Rosen Real Readers	Rosen Publishing Group
What Is a Reptile?	M	I	183	Now I Know	Troll Associates
What Is a Reptile?	I	I	67	Pebble Books	Red Brick Learning
What Is a Solid?	K	I	116	States of Matter	Lerner Publishing Group
What Is an Amphibian?	K	I	85	Pebble Books	Red Brick Learning
What Is an Elephant?	H	TL	165	Story Box	Wright Group/McGraw Hill
What Is an Insect?	H	I	57	Pebble Books	Red Brick Learning
What Is an Insect?	A	I	36	Yellow Umbrella Books	Red Brick Learning
What Is at the Top?	E	F	197	Ready Readers	Pearson Learning Group
What Is Bat?	G	F	136	Literacy 2000	Rigby
What Is Being Moved?	WB	RF	0	Windows on Literacy	National Geographic
What Is Big?	D	RF	72	Armstrong, Shane; Hartley, Susan	Scholastic
What Is Blue?	C	I	31	Carousel Earlybirds	Pearson Learning Group
What Is CGI?	L	I	285	Big Cat	Pacific Learning
What Is Congress?	P	I	628	Leveled Readers Social Studies	Houghton Mifflin Harcourt
What Is Delicious?	B	I	25	Windmill Books	Rigby
What Is Democracy?	Q	I	250+	Rigby Focus	Rigby
What Is Elephant's Present?	C	F	43	Reading Safari	Mondo Publishing
What Is Enormous?	B	I	33	Windmill Books	Rigby
What Is Fast?	A	I	30	Windmill Books	Rigby
What Is Fierce?	B	I	32	Windmill Books	Rigby
What Is Fun?	A	I	34	Red Rocket Readers	Flying Start Books
What Is Fun?	B	I	34	Windmill Books	Rigby
What Is Government?	K	I	94	Government	Lerner Publishing Group
What Is Gravity?	L	I	250+	On Our Way to English	Rigby
What Is Green Technology?	W	I	2318	Leveled Readers	Houghton Mifflin Harcourt
What Is Green Technology?	W	I	2318	Leveled Readers/CA	Houghton Mifflin Harcourt
What Is Green Technology?	W	I	2318	Leveled Readers/TX	Houghton Mifflin Harcourt
What Is Green?	B	I	30	Carousel Earlybirds	Pearson Learning Group
What Is He Looking For?	A	F	42	KinderReaders	Rigby

W

TITLE	LEVEL	GENRE	WORD COUNT	AUTHOR / SERIES	PUBLISHER / DISTRIBUTOR
What Is He?	B	F	35	Rigby Star	Rigby
What Is Hearing?	J	I	230	Lightning Bolt Books	Lerner Publishing Group
What Is Hidden?	B	I	27	Little Celebrations	Pearson Learning Group
What Is Hiding?	C	I	116	Rigby Flying Colors	Rigby
What Is in a Forest?	E	I	85	Early Explorers	Benchmark Education
What Is in Space?	C	I	41	Sunshine Science	Wright Group/McGraw Hill
What Is in Space?	B	I	35	Yellow Umbrella Books	Red Brick Learning
What Is in the Box?	D	RF	51	Instant Readers	Harcourt School Publishers
What Is in the Box?	B	RF	30	Rigby Rocket	Rigby
What Is in the Closet?	E	F	107	Story Box	Wright Group/McGraw Hill
What Is in the Garden?	C	I	70	Red Rocket Readers	Flying Start Books
What Is in the Sky?	J	I	174	Phonics Readers	Compass Point Books
What Is in the Sky?	C	I	71	Red Rocket Readers	Flying Start Books
What Is in the Sky?	B	I	32	Rosen Real Readers	Rosen Publishing Group
What Is in the Wind?	L	I	472	Leveled Readers	Houghton Mifflin Harcourt
What Is in the Wind?	L	I	472	Leveled Readers/CA	Houghton Mifflin Harcourt
What Is in the Wind?	L	I	472	Leveled Readers/TX	Houghton Mifflin Harcourt
What Is Inside?	B	I	49	Red Rocket Readers	Flying Start Books
What Is It Called?	D	RF	48	Reading Unlimited	Pearson Learning Group
What Is It Like Today?	D	I	102	On Our Way to English	Rigby
What Is It Made Of?	J	I	250+	Independent Readers Science	Houghton Mifflin Harcourt
What Is It Made Of?	D	I	107	InfoTrek	ETA/Cuisenaire
What Is It Made Of?	D	I	119	PM Science Readers	Rigby
What Is It Made Of?	G	I	156	Red Rocket Readers	Flying Start Books
What Is It Worth?	J	RF	300	Avenues	Hampton Brown
What Is It?	J	F	53	Avenues	Hampton Brown
What Is It?	B	I	25	Avenues	Hampton Brown
What Is It?	E	F	232	Easy Stories	Norwood House Press
What Is It?	F	I	135	Foundations	Wright Group/McGraw Hill
What Is It?	G	I	69	iOpeners	Pearson Learning Group
What Is It?	B	F	35	Rigby Literacy	Rigby
What Is It?	B	RF	16	Rigby Rocket	Rigby
What Is It?	E	I	69	Storyteller-First Snow	Wright Group/McGraw Hill
What Is It? Said the Dog	H	F	256	Allen, Margaret Buell	Ginn & Co.
What Is Little?	LB	I	22	Rise & Shine	Hampton Brown
What Is Matter?	L	I	250+	Early Connections	Benchmark Education
What Is Matter?	S	I	250+	Reading Expeditions	National Geographic
What Is Money Anyway?: Why Dollars and Coins Have Value	M	I	449	Lightning Bolt Books	Lerner Publishing Group
What Is Money?	M	I	250+	Learning About Money	Capstone Press
What Is Motion?	I	I	159	Early Explorers	Benchmark Education
What Is Mount Rushmore?	K	I	186	Falk, Laine/Scholastic News	Children's Press
What Is Noisy?	B	I	34	Red Rocket Readers	Flying Start Books
What Is Noisy?	B	I	31	Windmill Books	Rigby
What Is Old?	B	I	32	Windmill Books	Rigby
What Is Pollution?	K	I	154	Larkin, Bruce	Wilbooks
What Is Quiet?	A	I	33	Red Rocket Readers	Flying Start Books
What Is Rain?	H	I	142	Dominie Factivity Series	Pearson Learning Group
What Is Red?	B	I	27	Carousel Earlybirds	Pearson Learning Group
What Is Red?	B	I	30	Literacy 2000	Rigby
What Is Round?	I	I	155	Early Explorers	Benchmark Education
What Is Round?	B	I	57	Red Rocket Readers	Flying Start Books
What Is Scary?	B	I	31	Windmill Books	Rigby
What Is Sight?	J	I	285	Lightning Bolt Books	Lerner Publishing Group

W

* Collection of short stories   # Graphic text
^ Mature content with lower level text demands

TITLE	LEVEL	GENRE	WORD COUNT	AUTHOR / SERIES	PUBLISHER / DISTRIBUTOR
What Is Slippery?	B	I	26	Windmill Books	Rigby
What Is Slow?	C	I	29	Windmill Books	Rigby
What Is Slow? What Is Fast?	E	I	101	Early Connections	Benchmark Education
What Is Smell?	J	I	296	Lightning Bolt Books	Lerner Publishing Group
What Is Soft?	B	I	30	Windmill Books	Rigby
What Is Tall?	A	I	30	Windmill Books	Rigby
What Is Taste?	J	I	286	Lightning Bolt Books	Lerner Publishing Group
What Is That Ball Made From?	J	I	259	Take Two Books	Wright Group/McGraw Hill
What Is That?	F	RF	54	Pair-It Turn and Learn	Steck-Vaughn
What Is That?	C	I	61	Ready Readers	Pearson Learning Group
What Is That? Said the Cat	F	F	118	Maccarone, Grace	Scholastic
What Is the Media?	T	I	2493	Independent Readers Social Studies	Houghton Mifflin Harcourt
What Is the Moon Made Of?: And Other Questions Kids Have About Space	O	I	250+	Kids' Questions	Picture Window Books
What Is the Pattern?	B	I	16	Windows on Literacy	National Geographic
What Is the Season?	D	I	100	Early Explorers	Benchmark Education
What Is the Story of Our Flag?	K	I	230	Behrens, Janice/Scholastic News	Children's Press
What Is the Teacher Doing?	C	RF	78	Kaleidoscope Collection	Hameray Publishing Group
What Is the U.S. Constitution?	R	I	250+	Rosen Real Readers	Rosen Publishing Group
What Is the Weather Today?	B	I	49	Leveled Readers Science	Houghton Mifflin Harcourt
What Is the Weather Today?	H	I	250+	Momentum Literacy Program	Troll Associates
What Is This Skeleton?	C	I	48	Sunshine Science	Wright Group/McGraw Hill
What Is This?	A	I	29	KinderReaders	Rigby
What Is This?	A	I	25	Little Books for Early Readers	University of Maine
What Is This?	C	I	28	Ready Readers	Pearson Learning Group
What Is This?	A	I	25	Tiger Cub	Peguis
What Is Touch?	J	I	247	Lightning Bolt Books	Lerner Publishing Group
What Is Under the Hat?	B	F	29	Ready Readers	Pearson Learning Group
What Is Up When You Are Down?	E	I	65	Rookie Readers	Children's Press
What Is Very Long?	C	I	85	Leveled Literacy Intervention/Orange System	Heinemann
What Is Water?	E	I	71	Water	Lerner Publishing Group
What Is Wet?	A	I	32	Literacy by Design	Rigby
What Is White?	B	I	26	Carousel Earlybirds	Pearson Learning Group
What Is Wind?	H	I	142	Dominie Factivity Series	Pearson Publishing Group
What Is Yellow?	B	I	26	Carousel Earlybirds	Pearson Learning Group
What Is Young?	B	I	31	Windmill Books	Rigby
What Jamie Saw	T	RF	250+	Coman, Carolyn	Penguin Group
What Jessie Really Likes	C	RF	59	Lighthouse	Rigby
What Joe Hamster Finds	J	F	250+	Sunshine	Wright Group/McGraw Hill
What Joy Found	L	RF	250+	Ready Readers	Pearson Learning Group
What Keeps Them Warm?	L	I	156	Pacific Literacy	Pacific Learning
What Kind of Animals?	D	I	37	Leveled Readers Science	Houghton Mifflin Harcourt
What Kind of Babysitter Is This?	L	RF	250+	Johnson, Dolores	Scholastic
What Kind of Day?	D	I	67	Pair-It Turn and Learn	Steck-Vaughn
What Kind of Dog Am I?	C	I	21	Twig	Wright Group/McGraw Hill
What Kind of Sound?	G	I	110	Pair-It Turn and Learn	Steck-Vaughn
What Kind of Sound?	B	I	25	Yellow Umbrella Books	Red Brick Learning
What Lays Eggs?	I	I	216	Momentum Literacy Program	Troll Associates
What Lays Eggs?	D	I	56	Storyteller Nonfiction	Wright Group/McGraw Hill
What Lived in That Shell?	N	I	575	Springboard	Wright Group/McGraw Hill
What Lives in a Rotting Log?	L	I	465	Springboard	Wright Group/McGraw Hill
What Lives in a Swamp?	B	I	36	Windows on Literacy	National Geographic

W

TITLE	LEVEL	GENRE	WORD COUNT	AUTHOR / SERIES	PUBLISHER / DISTRIBUTOR
What Lives in a Tide Pool?	J	I	187	Windows on Literacy	National Geographic
What Lives on a Prairie?	N	I	250+	Rosen Real Readers	Rosen Publishing Group
What Made Teddalik Laugh	M	TL	250+	Folk Tales	Wright Group/McGraw Hill
What Made This?	B	I	21	Science	Outside the Box
What Magnets Can Do	K	I	250+	Fowler, Allan	Scholastic
What Makes a Bird a Bird?	O	I	250+	Garelick, May	Mondo Publishing
What Makes a Community?	P	I	250+	Reading Expeditions	National Geographic
What Makes a Garden Grow?	E	I	83	Independent Readers Science	Houghton Mifflin Harcourt
What Makes a Human a Human?	W	I	250+	Navigators Science Series	Benchmark Education
What Makes a Plant a Plant?	S	I	250+	Navigators Science Series	Benchmark Education
What Makes a Shadow?	B	I	27	Leveled Readers Science	Houghton Mifflin Harcourt
What Makes a Tiger Hard to See?	I	I	253	Windows on Literacy	National Geographic
What Makes an Animal an Animal?	S	I	250+	Navigators Science Series	Benchmark Education
What Makes Great Athletes	T	I	2156	Reading Street	Pearson
What Makes It Go?	C	I	29	iOpeners	Pearson Learning Group
What Makes It Go?	E	I	143	Red Rocket Readers	Flying Start Books
What Makes It Work?	U	I	3412	Take Two Books	Wright Group/McGraw Hill
What Makes Light?	F	I	119	Sunshine	Wright Group/McGraw Hill
What Makes Me Healthy?	H	I	132	Windows on Literacy	National Geographic
What Makes Ten?	D	I	34	Yellow Umbrella Books	Red Brick Learning
What Makes This Sound?	E	I	72	Factivity Series	Pearson Learning Group
What Makes You Cough, Sneeze, Burp, Hiccup, Blink, Yawn, Sweat, and Shiver?	P	I	250+	My Health	Franklin Watts
What Momma Left Me	Z	RF	250+	Watson, Renee	Bloomsbury Children's Books
What Mommies Do Best	F	F	113	Numeroff, Laura Joffe	Simon & Schuster
What My Dog Knows	L	RF	866	Leveled Readers Science	Houghton Mifflin Harcourt
What My Mother Doesn't Know	Z	RF	250+	Sones, Sonya	Simon & Schuster
What Mynah Bird Saw	F	TL	90	Sunshine	Wright Group/McGraw Hill
What Needs the Sun	B	I	65	Literacy by Design	Rigby
What Next, Baby Bear?	L	F	313	Murphy, Jill	Dial/Penguin
What Next?	F	F	277	Story Basket	Wright Group/McGraw Hill
What on Earth?	I	F	133	Sunshine	Wright Group/McGraw Hill
What People Do	E	I	113	Early Connections	Benchmark Education
What People Do	H	I	148	Little Red Readers	Sundance
What People Wore During the American Revolution	T	I	250+	Clothing, Costumes and Uniforms Throughout American History	Rosen Publishing Group
What People Wore During the Westward Expansion	T	TL	250+	Clothing, Costumes and Uniforms Throughout American History	Rosen Publishing Group
What People Wore in Colonial America	T	I	250+	Clothing, Costumes and Uniforms Throughout American History	Rosen Publishing Group
What People Wore in Early America	T	I	250+	Clothing, Costumes and Uniforms Throughout American History	Rosen Publishing Group
What Plant Is This?	B	I	22	Windows on Literacy	National Geographic
What Plants and Animals Need	K	I	200	Phonics Readers	Compass Point Books
What Plays Music?	C	I	36	Questions & Answers	Pearson Learning Group
What Pushes? What Pulls?	I	I	141	Early Connections	Benchmark Education
What Rhymes With . . .	A	I	9	Ready Readers	Pearson Learning Group
What Rhymes With Cat?	LB	F	4	Ready Readers	Pearson Learning Group
What Road to Follow?	T	HF	1365	Leveled Readers	Houghton Mifflin Harcourt
What Road to Follow?	T	HF	1365	Leveled Readers/CA	Houghton Mifflin Harcourt
What Road to Follow?	T	HF	1365	Leveled Readers/TX	Houghton Mifflin Harcourt
What Rots?	M	I	250+	Trackers	Pacific Learning
What School Was Like Long Ago	K	I	499	Leveled Readers/TX	Houghton Mifflin Harcourt
What Season Is it?	F	I	79	Leveled Readers Social Studies	Houghton Mifflin Harcourt

W

* Collection of short stories   # Graphic text
^ Mature content with lower level text demands

TITLE	LEVEL	GENRE	WORD COUNT	AUTHOR / SERIES	PUBLISHER / DISTRIBUTOR
What Season Is This?	C	I	24	Wonder World	Wright Group/McGraw Hill
What Shall I Do?	M	RF	584	Sunshine	Wright Group/McGraw Hill
What Shall I Wear?	E	I	58	Book Bank	Wright Group/McGraw Hill
What Shall Workers Do?	W	I	2287	Independent Readers Social Studies	Houghton Mifflin Harcourt
What Shape Is It?	B	I	35	Properties of Matter	Lerner Publishing Group
What Shape Is This?	B	I	35	Red Rocket Readers	Flying Start Books
What Shape Is Water?	G	I	188	Sun Sprouts	ETA/Cuisenaire
What Shapes Do You See?	B	I	38	Windows on Literacy	National Geographic
What Should I Wear?	C	RF	70	Lighthouse	Rigby
What Should We Wear?	F	I	50	iOpeners	Pearson Learning Group
What Smells Good?	B	I	26	Windmill Books	Rigby
What Smells?	N	I	250+	Infotrek Plus	ETA/Cuisenaire
What Some People Will Do	T	RF	250+	Power Up!	Steck-Vaughn
What Tastes Good?	C	I	66	Red Rocket Readers	Flying Start Books
What the Dickens	W	F	250+	Maguire, Gregory	Candlewick Press
What the Dinosaurs Saw	I	I	123	Schlein, Miriam	Scholastic
What the Dog Saw	G	F	131	Reading Street	Pearson
What the Grizzly Knows	L	F	234	Elliot, David	Candlewick Press
What the King Likes	B	F	32	Sun Sprouts	ETA/Cuisenaire
What the President Did Today	O	I	785	Leveled Readers	Houghton Mifflin Harcourt
What the President Did Today	O	I	785	Leveled Readers/CA	Houghton Mifflin Harcourt
What the President Does	O	I	817	Leveled Readers	Houghton Mifflin Harcourt
What the President Does	O	I	817	Leveled Readers/CA	Houghton Mifflin Harcourt
What the Sea Saw	P	I	250+	St. Pierre, Stephanie	Peachtree
*What They Found: Love on 145th Street	Z+	RF	250+	Myers, Walter Dean	Wendy Lamb Books
What Things Go Together	LB	RF	26	Literacy 2000	Rigby
What Tigers Do	A	I	18	Bonnell, Kris	Reading Reading Books
What Time Is It?	B	RF	48	Instant Readers	Harcourt School Publishers
What Time Is It?	W	I	35	iOpeners	Pearson Learning Group
What Time Is It?	D	I	43	Learn to Read	Creative Teaching Press
What Time is It?	D	I	53	Little Celebrations	Pearson Learning Group
What Time Is It?	D	RF	65	Moriarty, Julie	Scholastic
What Time Is It?	B	I	48	Rosen Real Readers	Rosen Publishing Group
What Time Is It?	I	I	189	Shutterbug Books	Steck-Vaughn
What Time Is It?	H	I	207	Springboard	Wright Group/McGraw Hill
What Time Is It?	E	RF	136	Teacher's Choice Series	Pearson Learning Group
What Time Is It?	J	I	269	Windows on Literacy	National Geographic
What To Do About Alice?	R	B	250+	Kerley, Barbara	Scholastic
What to Do About Woolsey?	I	RF	250+	Literacy by Design	Rigby
What to Do in an Emergency	J	I	391	Reading Street	Pearson
What to Wear?	D	RF	42	Harry's Math Books	Outside the Box
What Tommy Did	E	RF	125	Literacy 2000	Rigby
What Was That?	E	RF	66	Leveled Readers	Houghton Mifflin Harcourt
What Was That?	H	RF	250+	Scooters	ETA/Cuisenaire
What Was the Continental Congress?: And Other Questions about the Declaration of Independence	T	I	5159	Six Questions of American History	Lerner Publishing Group
What Was This?	F	I	53	Wonder World	Wright Group/McGraw Hill
What We Do at School	A	F	31	Bookshop	Mondo Publishing
What We Like	B	RF	43	Early Connections	Benchmark Education
What We Like	D	RF	71	Little Red Readers	Sundance
What Were Castles For?	R	I	250+	Usborne Starting Point History	EDC Publishing
What Will Alex Do?	C	F	75	Abbatiello, Toya	Kaeden Books

TITLE	LEVEL	GENRE	WORD COUNT	AUTHOR / SERIES	PUBLISHER / DISTRIBUTOR
What Will Float?	G	I	224	Sunshine	Wright Group/McGraw Hill
What Will Happen Today?	E	I	115	Windows on Literacy	National Geographic
What Will He Wear?	C	I	28	Reach	National Geographic
What Will I Be?	D	I	104	Early Connections	Benchmark Education
What Will I Be?	C	I	41	Reach	National Geographic
What Will the Weather Be?	O	I	250+	DeWitt, Lynda	HarperTrophy
What Will the Weather Be?	H	I	207	Rigby Literacy	Rigby
What Will You Pack?	B	RF	35	Ready Readers	Pearson Learning Group
What Would Joey Do?	T	RF	250+	Gantos, Jack	Farrar, Straus, & Giroux
What Would the Zoo Do?	D	F	59	Salem, Lynn	Continental Press
What Would You Do?	G	RF	160	Sunshine	Wright Group/McGraw Hill
What Would You Do?	M	I	392	Vocabulary Readers	Houghton Mifflin Harcourt
What Would You Like?	D	F	52	Sunshine	Wright Group/McGraw Hill
What Would You Rather Be?	K	I	381	The Rowland Reading Program Library	Rowland Reading Foundation
What You See Is What You Get	I	F	192	McLenighan, Valjean	Pearson Learning Group
What's in the Trunk?	J	RF	886	Spirn, Michele	January Books
Whatcha Got?	M	RF	250+	Social Studies Connects	Kane Press
Whatever Am I Going to Do Now?	M	RF	250+	Little Celebrations	Pearson Learning Group
Whatever Happened to Janie?	Y	RF	250+	Cooney, Caroline B.	Laurel-Leaf Books
#Whatever Happened to the World of Tomorrow?	Y	HF	250+	Fies, Brian	Abrams Comicarts
Whatever the Weather	K	I	250+	DK Readers	DK Publishing
Whatever Will These Become?	E	I	47	Literacy 2000	Rigby
Whatever!: The Complicated Life of Claudia Cristina Cortez	S	RF	250+	Gallagher, Diana G.	Stone Arch Books
What's Alike?	WB	I	0	Windows on Literacy	National Geographic
What's Alive?	D	I	53	Discovery Links	Newbridge
What's Alive?	M	I	250+	Let's-Read-and-Find-Out Science	HarperCollins
What's Around the Corner?	H	RF	90	Literacy Tree	Rigby
What's Behind This Door?	B	I	43	Twig	Wright Group/McGraw Hill
What's Best for Red?	K	RF	444	Avenues	Hampton Brown
What's Best for Red?	K	RF	444	Eggers, Casey	Hampton Brown
What's Black and White and Moos?	E	I	78	Twig	Wright Group/McGraw Hill
What's Coming for Christmas?	O	F	250+	Banks, Kate	Farrar, Straus, & Giroux
What's Cooking, Jenny Archer?	M	RF	250+	Conford, Ellen	Little Brown and Company
What's Cooking?	H	RF	287	Bookshop	Mondo Publishing
What's Cooking?	Q	I	250+	Orbit Chapter Books	Pacific Learning
What's Eating You?: Parasites - The Inside Story	T	I	250+	Davies, Nicola	Candlewick Press
What's for Breakfast?	C	F	36	Big Cat	Pacific Learning
What's for Dinner, Dad?	K	RF	459	Sunshine	Wright Group/McGraw Hill
What's for Dinner?	B	I	35	Hoenecke, Karen	Kaeden Books
What's for Dinner?	B	I	38	Sails	Rigby
What's for Dinner?	E	RF	112	Seedlings	Continental Press
What's for Dinner?	Q	I	250+	Sunshine	Wright Group/McGraw Hill
What's for Lunch	E	F	91	New Way Red	Steck-Vaughn
What's for Lunch?	C	F	48	Carle, Eric	Scholastic
What's for Lunch?	H	F	169	Ready Readers	Pearson Learning Group
What's for Lunch?	D	I	49	Rise & Shine	Hampton Brown
What's for Lunch?	B	F	36	Story Box	Wright Group/McGraw Hill
What's For Lunch?	A	I	30	Vocabulary Readers	Houghton Mifflin Harcourt
What's Going On?	C	RF	21	Learn to Read	Creative Teaching Press
What's Going On?	H	RF	377	Real Kids Readers	Millbrook Press

Organized Alphabetically by Title
Storable Database at www.fountasandpinnellleveledbooks.com

             * Collection of short stories   # Graphic text
             ^ Mature content with lower level text demands

W

TITLE	LEVEL	GENRE	WORD COUNT	AUTHOR / SERIES	PUBLISHER / DISTRIBUTOR
What's Happening?: A Book of Explanations	Q	I	250+	Bookshop	Mondo Publishing
What's in a Name?	P	I	1151	Reading Street	Pearson
What's in a Name?: A Story about George Eliot	T	B	250+	PM Chapter Books	Rigby
What's in a Park?	G	I	46	Chessen, Betsey; Chanko, Pamela	Scholastic
What's in Here?	E	I	122	Sun Sprouts	ETA/Cuisenaire
What's in My Pocket	F	I	72	Learn to Read	Creative Teaching Press
What's in Orbit?	S	I	250+	Take Two Books	Wright Group/McGraw Hill
What's in the Bag?	E	HF	98	Visions	Wright Group/McGraw Hill
What's in the Box?	B	I	24	Rigby Literacy	Rigby
What's in the Witch's Kitchen?	K	F	250+	Sharratt, Nick	Candlewick Press
What's in the Woods?	J	RF	250+	The Wright Skills	Wright Group/McGraw Hill
What's in This Egg?	A	F	16	Sunshine	Wright Group/McGraw Hill
What's in Washington, D.C.?	J	I	199	Falk, Laine/Scholastic News	Children's Press
What's Inside a Fire Truck?	L	I	250+	Bookworms	Marshall Cavendish
What's Inside a Firehouse?	L	I	250+	Bookworms	Marshall Cavendish
What's Inside a Hospital?	L	I	250+	Bookworms	Marshall Cavendish
What's Inside a Police Car?	L	I	250+	Bookworms	Marshall Cavendish
What's Inside a Police Station?	L	I	250+	Bookworms	Marshall Cavendish
What's Inside a Rattlesnake's Rattle?: And Other Questions Kids Have About Snakes	N	I	250+	Kids' Questions	Picture Window Books
What's Inside an Ambulance?	L	I	250+	Bookworms	Marshall Cavendish
What's Inside?	C	I	35	Big Cat	Pacific Learning
What's Inside?	G	I	50	Foundations	Wright Group/McGraw Hill
What's Inside?	LB	RF	47	Hoenecke, Karen	Kaeden Books
What's Inside?	E	I	37	Sunshine	Wright Group/McGraw Hill
What's Inside?	H	I	138	Windows on Literacy	National Geographic
What's Inside?	K	I	238	Wonder World	Wright Group/McGraw Hill
What's It For?	D	I	47	Visions	Wright Group/McGraw Hill
What's It Like to Be a Fish?	L	I	250+	Little Readers	Houghton Mifflin Harcourt
What's It Made Of?	E	I	131	Rigby Star Quest	Rigby
What's Living at Your Place?	Q	I	250+	Orbit Chapter Books	Pacific Learning
What's Missing?	K	I	252	Book Bank	Wright Group/McGraw Hill
What's Missing?	D	RF	102	Spinelle, Nancy Louise	Kaeden Books
What's Money All About?	R	I	1344	Reading Street	Pearson
What's My Job?	B	I	25	Windows on Literacy	National Geographic
What's New at the Zoo?	H	F	151	Instant Readers	Harcourt School Publishers
What's New at the Zoo?: An Animal Adding Adventure	M	I	1027	Slade, Suzanne	Sylvan Dell Publishing
What's New with Dinosaur Fossils?	V	I	2566	Reading Street	Pearson
What's New?	T	I	250+	Sails	Rigby
What's Next, Nina?	J	RF	250+	Math Matters	Kane Press
What's on My Farm?	B	RF	38	Rise & Shine	Hampton Brown
What's on the Road?	B	I	34	Windows on Literacy	National Geographic
What's on the Ships?	G	I	170	Windows on Literacy	National Geographic
What's on the Truck?	I	I	137	Windows on Literacy	National Geographic
What's on Your T-Shirt?	C	RF	64	Carousel Readers	Pearson Learning Group
What's Poisoning the Garden?	U	RF	250+	Reading Expeditions	National Geographic
What's Round?	LB	I	14	Discovery Links	Newbridge
What's So Funny?	R	I	250+	Boldprint	Steck-Vaughn
What's That Noise?	I	RF	250+	Rigby Rocket	Rigby
What's That Noise?	B	RF	23	Science	Outside the Box
What's That Smell?	H	RF	56	Pacific Literacy	Pacific Learning
What's That Sound?	K	RF	1268	Science Solves It!	Kane Press
What's That, Mittens?	G	RF	147	Schaefer, Lola M.	HarperTrophy

W

TITLE	LEVEL	GENRE	WORD COUNT	AUTHOR / SERIES	PUBLISHER / DISTRIBUTOR
What's That?	C	RF	27	Carousel Earlybirds	Pearson Learning Group
What's That?	I	F	250+	Popcorn	Sundance
What's That?	B	RF	33	Sunshine	Wright Group/McGraw Hill
What's That?	C	F	28	The Book Project	Sundance
What's the Address?	L	I	186	iOpeners	Pearson Learning Group
What's the Big Idea, Ben Franklin?	O	B	250+	Fritz, Jean	Scholastic
What's the Chance?	T	I	250+	Reading Expeditions	National Geographic
What's the Difference Between a Butterfly and a Moth?	N	I	250+	What's the Difference?	Picture Window Books
What's the Difference Between a Frog and a Toad?	N	I	250+	What's the Difference?	Picture Window Books
What's the Difference Between a Leopard and a Cheetah?	N	I	250+	What's the Difference?	Picture Window Books
What's the Difference Between an Alligator and a Crocodile?	N	I	250+	What's the Difference?	Picture Window Books
What's the Difference?	P	I	250+	Literacy by Design	Rigby
What's the Difference?	Q	I	250+	Orbit Collections	Pacific Learning
What's the Difference? : An Endangered Animal Subtraction Story	M	I	1039	Slade, Suzanne	Sylvan Dell Publishing
What's the Matter in Mr. Whiskers Room?	N	RF	250+	Ross, Michael Elsohn	Candlewick Press
What's the Matter with Herbie Jones?	N	RF	250+	Kline, Suzy	Penguin Group
What's the Matter, Kelly Beans?	N	RF	250+	Enderle, Judith R.; Tessler, S. G.	Candlewick Press
What's the Problem?	Q	I	250+	Orbit Collections	Pacific Learning
What's the Time	F	RF	74	Cambridge Reading	Pearson Learning Group
What's the Time Mr. Wolf?	C	F	49	Windmill Books	Wright Group/McGraw Hill
What's the Time, Grandma Wolf?	L	F	250+	Brown, Ken	Peachtree
What's the Time, Little Wolf?: Another Little Wolf and Smellybreff Adventure	K	F	603	Whybrow, Ian	Carolrhoda Books
What's the Time?	H	I	217	Sun Sprouts	ETA/Cuisenaire
What's the Weather Like Today?	D	I	119	Learn to Read	Creative Teaching Press
What's the Weather?	B	RF	21	Cali, Jennifer	Scholastic
What's This Matter?	F	I	88	Independent Readers Science	Houghton Mifflin Harcourt
What's This Spider Doing?	E	I	89	Story Steps	Rigby
What's This?	N	I	250+	Literacy 2000	Rigby
What's This?	L	I	462	Sun Sprouts	ETA/Cuisenaire
What's Under My Bed?	C	RF	18	Visions	Wright Group/McGraw Hill
What's Under the Ocean	H	I	108	Now I Know	Troll Associates
What's Underground?	I	I	207	Big Cat	Pacific Learning
What's Underneath?	K	I	200	Discovery World	Rigby
What's Up?	E	RF	26	Instant Readers	Harcourt School Publishers
What's Up?	B	I	26	Pacific Literacy	Pacific Learning
What's Up?: Watching the Night Sky	L	I	250+	Rigby Literacy	Rigby
What's With Wulf?	Q	F	250+	Extreme Monsters	Penny Candy Press
What's Wrong With Gilbert?	J	F	664	Gilbert the Pig	Pioneer Valley
What's Your Angle, Pythagoras?	S	HF	250+	Ellis, Julie	Scholastic
What's Your Opinion?	Q	I	250+	Sails	Rigby
What's Your Source? Questioning the News	T	I	250+	Media Literacy	Capstone Press
What's Your Story?	WB	RF	0	Voyages	SRA/McGraw Hill
What's Zero?	I	I	250+	Yellow Umbrella Books	Red Brick Learning
Wheat	D	I	52	Canizares, Susan; Chanko, Pamela	Scholastic
Wheat Doll, The	O	HF	250+	Randall, Alison L.	Peachtree
Wheat We Eat, The	K	I	250+	Rookie Read About Science	Children's Press
Wheel Sports	O	I	250+	Extreme Sports	Raintree

W

* Collection of short stories   # Graphic text
^ Mature content with lower level text demands

TITLE	LEVEL	GENRE	WORD COUNT	AUTHOR / SERIES	PUBLISHER / DISTRIBUTOR
Wheel, The	C	RF	102	Joy Readers	Pearson Learning Group
Wheelbarrow Garden, The	H	RF	231	PM Plus Story Books	Rigby
#Wheelies of Justice: Bike Rider	S	F	250+	Lemke, Donnie	Stone Arch Books
Wheels	B	I	39	Big Cat	Pacific Learning
Wheels	D	I	69	Cobb, Annie	Random House
Wheels	C	I	29	Discovery Links	Newbridge
Wheels	E	I	93	Explorations	Okapi Educational Materials
Wheels	E	I	93	Explorations	Eleanor Curtain Publishing
Wheels	H	I	129	Gear Up!	Wright Group/McGraw Hill
Wheels	A	I	32	Leveled Literacy Intervention/ Orange System	Heinemann
Wheels	C	I	27	Literacy 2000	Rigby
Wheels	E	RF	62	Nayer, Judy	Scholastic
Wheels	D	I	49	Rise & Shine	Hampton Brown
Wheels	B	F	25	Sails	Rigby
Wheels	D	I	33	Sun Sprouts	ETA/Cuisenaire
Wheels	C	I	39	Sunshine	Wright Group/McGraw Hill
Wheels	D	RF	27	Voyages	SRA/McGraw Hill
Wheels	D	I	33	Windows on Literacy	National Geographic
Wheels and Axles	Q	I	1689	Early Bird Energy Physics Books	Lerner Publishing Group
Wheels and Axles to the Rescue	O	I	250+	Simple Machine to the Rescue	Capstone Press
Wheels Around	T	I	250+	The News	Richard C. Owen
Wheels Around Us	P	I	250+	Windows on Literacy	National Geographic
Wheels on the Bike Go Round and Round, The	T	I	2241	Reading Street	Pearson
Wheels on the Bus, The	I	TL	362	Kovalski, Mary Ann	Little Brown and Company
Wheels on the Bus, The	J	TL	250+	Traditional Songs	Picture Window Books
Wheels on the Racecar, The	I	F	250+	Zane, Alexander	Scholastic
When a Storm Comes	J	I	172	Windows on Literacy	National Geographic
When Arthur Wouldn't Sleep	I	F	280	Big Cat	Pacific Learning
When Baby Is Happy	D	RF	52	Joy Starters	Pearson Learning Group
When Beep-Beep Came to Earth	L	F	250+	InfoTrek	ETA/Cuisenaire
When Birds Get Flu and Cows Go Mad!	W	I	250+	24/7 Science Behind the Scenes	Scholastic
When Bob Woke Up Late	G	RF	139	Ready Readers	Pearson Learning Group
When Calick Was a Puppy	D	RF	71	McAlpin, MaryAnn	Short Tales Press
When Children Worked	N	I	292	Independent Readers Social Studies	Houghton Mifflin Harcourt
When Cultures Meet	R	I	250+	Reading Expeditions	National Geographic
When Dad Came Home	F	RF	46	Literacy 2000	Rigby
When Dad Got Lost	F	RF	113	City Stories	Rigby
When Dad Went Fishing	H	RF	250+	Cambridge Reading	Pearson Learning Group
When Dad Went to Daycare	H	RF	211	Sunshine	Wright Group/McGraw Hill
When Daddy's Truck Picks Me Up	K	RF	250+	Hunter, Jana Novothy	Albert Whitman & Co.
When Day Turned to Night: April 14, 1935	T	I	250+	Rigby Literacy	Rigby
When Did George Washington Fight His First Military Battle?: And Other Questions about the French and Indian War	T	I	250+	Six Questions of American History	Lerner Publishing Group
When Do Cars Stop?	C	I	62	Questions & Answers	Pearson Learning Group
When Do You Feel . . .	F	I	132	Twig	Wright Group/McGraw Hill
When Enviornments Change	R	I	1093	Science Support Readers	Houghton Mifflin Harcourt
When Everybody Wore a Hat	N	B	250+	Steig, William	HarperCollins
When Goldilocks Went to the House of the Bears	F	TL	156	Bookshop	Mondo Publishing
When Goldilocks Went to the House of the Bears	E	TL	165	Tiger Cub	Peguis
When Grandma Visits Me	D	F	113	Dominie Readers	Pearson Learning Group

W

TITLE	LEVEL	GENRE	WORD COUNT	AUTHOR / SERIES	PUBLISHER / DISTRIBUTOR
When Grandpa Was a Boy	C	RF	93	Leveled Readers	Houghton Mifflin Harcourt
When Grandpa Was a Boy	C	RF	93	Leveled Readers/CA	Houghton Mifflin Harcourt
When Grandpa Was a Boy	C	RF	93	Leveled Readers/TX	Houghton Mifflin Harcourt
When Grandpa Was Young	L	I	250+	Rigby Focus	Rigby
When Hitler Stole Pink Rabbit	X	HF	250+	Kerr, Judith	Scholastic
When I Broke the Office Window	L	RF	257	City Kids	Rigby
When I Crossed No-Bob	W	HF	250+	McMullan, Margaret	Houghton Mifflin Harcourt
When I First Came to This Land	K	TL	250+	Ziefert, Harriet	Scholastic
When I Forgot	N	RF	250+	Orbit Chapter Books	Pacific Learning
When I Get Bigger	K	RF	205	Mayer, Mercer	Donovan
When I Go See Gram	G	RF	123	Ready Readers	Pearson Learning Group
When I Go to Grandma's House	K	RF	199	Cleary, Brian	Kaeden Books
When I Grow Up	B	RF	58	Lighthouse	Rigby
When I Grow Up	A	I	35	Red Rocket Readers	Flying Start Books
When I Grow Up	F	RF	63	Rhythm 'N' Rhyme Readers	Pearson Learning Group
When I Grow Up	D	RF	112	Rigby Rocket	Rigby
When I Grow Up	C	RF	38	Rise & Shine	Hampton Brown
When I Grow Up	H	RF	176	The King School Series	Townsend Press
When I Look Up	B	RF	55	Foundations	Wright Group/McGraw Hill
When I Looked Out My Window	H	RF	215	Springboard	Wright Group/McGraw Hill
When I Play	C	RF	31	Literacy 2000	Rigby
When I Pretend	C	RF	40	Literacy 2000	Rigby
When I Turned Six	I	HF	150	Voyages	SRA/McGraw Hill
When I Visit My Cousin	E	I	67	Independent Readers Social Studies	Houghton Mifflin Harcourt
When I Was a Baby	C	I	101	Gear Up!	Wright Group/McGraw Hill
When I Was a Baby	D	I	64	Rigby Rocket	Rigby
When I Was Little	B	I	79	Leveled Readers	Houghton Mifflin Harcourt
When I Was Little	B	I	79	Leveled Readers/CA	Houghton Mifflin Harcourt
When I Was Little: A Four-Year-Old's Memoir of Her Youth	I	RF	250+	Curtis, Jamie Lee	Scholastic
When I Was Seven	K	RF	704	InfoTrek	ETA/Cuisenaire
When I was Sick	D	RF	62	Explorations	Eleanor Curtain Publishing
When I was Sick	D	I	62	Explorations	Okapi Educational Materials
When I Was Sick	F	RF	53	Literacy 2000	Rigby
*When I Was Young and Wild Bill's Secret Wish	P	RF	250+	Orbit Chapter Books	Pacific Learning
*When I Was Your Age: Original Stories About Growing Up (Vol. 1)	W	B	250+	Ehrlich, Amy (Ed.)	Candlewick Press
When I Wore My Sailor Suit	M	F	250+	Shulevitz, Uri	Farrar, Straus, & Giroux
When I'm Older	F	RF	156	Literacy 2000	Rigby
When It Rains	C	RF	39	Foundations	Wright Group/McGraw Hill
When It Rains	F	I	106	Frankford, Marilyn	Kaeden Books
When It Rains	E	RF	36	Voyages	SRA/McGraw Hill
When It Rains . . .	C	I	37	Teacher's Choice Series	Pearson Learning Group
When It Rains, It Pours	S	I	250+	WorldScapes	ETA/Cuisenaire
When It Snowed	C	RF	33	Home Connection Collection	Rigby
When Itchy Witchy Sneezes	C	F	39	Sunshine	Wright Group/McGraw Hill
When Jackie and Hank Met	R	I	250+	Fishman, Cathy Goldberg	Marshall Cavendish
When Jessie Came Across the Sea	S	HF	250+	Hest, Amy	Candlewick Press
When Johnny Went Marching: Young Americans Fight the Civil War	Y	I	250+	Wisler, B. Clifton	HarperCollins
When Jose Hits That Ball	G	RF	45	Pacific Literacy	Pacific Learning
When Justice Failed: The Fred Korematsu Story	U	B	250+	Chin, Steven A.	Steck-Vaughn
When Lana Was Absent	F	RF	78	Tadpoles	Rigby

W

* Collection of short stories   # Graphic text
^ Mature content with lower level text demands

TITLE	LEVEL	GENRE	WORD COUNT	AUTHOR / SERIES	PUBLISHER / DISTRIBUTOR
When Lincoln Was a Boy	E	I	132	Twig	Wright Group/McGraw Hill
When Lucy Goes Out Walking: A Puppy's First Year	K	RF	250+	Wolff, Ashley	Henry Holt & Co.
When Lulu Went to the Zoo	K	F	392	Ellis, Andy	Andersen Press USA
When Marian Sang	R	B	250+	Ryan, Pam Munoz	Scholastic
When Mr. Quinn Snored	C	F	31	Little Books	Sadlier-Oxford
When My Dad Came to School	M	RF	230	City Kids	Rigby
When My Name Was Keoko	Y	HF	250+	Park, Linda Sue	Dell
When Plague Strikes	Z	I	250+	Giblin, James Cross	HarperCollins
When Rain Falls	L	I	250+	Stewart, Melissa	Peachtree
When Robins Sing	H	I	238	Twig	Wright Group/McGraw Hill
When She Was Good	Z	RF	250+	Mazer, Norma Fox	Scholastic
When Someone Dies	N	RF	250+	Greenlee, Sharon	Peachtree
When Sophie Gets Angry - Really, Really Angry . . .	K	RF	166	Bang, Molly	Scholastic
When Spring Comes	D	I	23	Windows on Literacy	National Geographic
*When the Beginning Began: Stories About God, the Creatures, and Us	U	TL	250+	Lester, Julius	Harcourt Brace
When the Circus Came to Town	R	RF	250+	Horvath, Polly	Sunburst
When the Circus Comes to Town	A	I	40	Little Red Readers	Sundance
When the Cookernup Store Burned Down	K	F	250+	Sunshine	Wright Group/McGraw Hill
When the Disaster's Over	U	I	2566	Reading Street	Pearson
When the Earth Was Bare	P	TL	250+	Voyages	SRA/McGraw Hill
*When the Giants Came to Town	L	F	250+	Leonard, Marcia	Scholastic
When the King Rides By	J	F	247	Bookshop	Mondo Publishing
When the Moon Forgot	L	F	250+	Liao, Jimmy	Little Brown and Company
When the Moon Was Blue	I	F	174	Literacy 2000	Rigby
When the Rain Comes	C	I	54	Windows on Literacy	National Geographic
When the Sun Goes Down	G	I	109	Wonder World	Wright Group/McGraw Hill
When the Tide Goes Out	D	I	74	Story Steps	Rigby
When the Toy Shop Shuts	WB	F	0	The Book Project	Sundance
When the Tripods Came	V	F	250+	Christopher, John	Aladdin
When the Truck Got Stuck!	M	RF	250+	Cowley, Joy	Pacific Learning
When the TV Broke	H	RF	209	Ziefert, Harriet	Puffin Books
When the Volcano Erupted	J	F	262	PM Collection	Rigby
When the Water Closes Over My Head	R	RF	250+	Napoli, Donna	Puffin Books
When the Wind Blows	G	I	107	Rigby Focus	Rigby
When the Wolves Returned: Restoring Nature's Balance in Yellowstone	S	I	250+	Patent, Dorothy Hinshaw	Walker & Company
When the World Is Ready for Bed	J	F	146	Shields, Gillian	Bloomsbury Children's Books
When They Were Little Like Me	E	I	70	Leveled Readers Social Studies	Houghton Mifflin Harcourt
When This World Was New	M	RF	1275	Avenues	Hampton Brown
When Toady Met Ratty (Willow Buds)	K	F	250+	Begin, Mary Jane	Little Brown and Company
When Tony Got Lost at the Zoo	L	RF	122	City Kids	Rigby
When Tsunamis Strike	T	I	1836	Vocabulary Readers	Houghton Mifflin Harcourt
When Tsunamis Strike	T	I	1836	Vocabulary Readers/CA	Houghton Mifflin Harcourt
When We Are Big	E	RF	123	Ready Readers	Pearson Learning Group
When Will I Read?	I	RF	250+	Cohen, Miriam	Bantam Books
When Will We Be Sisters?	K	RF	250+	Kroll, Virginia	Scholastic
When Willard Met Babe Ruth	R	HF	250+	Hall, Donald	Voyager Books
When You Meet a Bear on Broadway	L	F	250+	Hest, Amy	Farrar, Straus, & Giroux
When You Reach Me	W	F	250+	Stead, Rebecca	Wendy Lamb Books
When You Visit Grandma & Grandpa	K	RF	552	Bowen, Anne	Carolrhoda Books
When You Were a Baby	G	RF	104	Jonas, Ann	Morrow

W

TITLE	LEVEL	GENRE	WORD COUNT	AUTHOR / SERIES	PUBLISHER / DISTRIBUTOR
When Young Melissa Sweeps	M	RF	105	Turner, Nancy Byrd	Peachtree
When Zachary Beaver Came to Town	Y	RF	250+	Holt, Kimberly Willis	Dell
Where Am I?	C	RF	34	Pair-It Turn and Learn	Steck-Vaughn
Where and Why?	C	RF	28	Learn to Read	Creative Teaching Press
Where Are All the Bats?	F	RF	105	Reading Street	Pearson
Where Are My Glasses?	E	RF	62	Dominie Readers	Pearson Learning Group
Where Are My Socks?	D	RF	42	Pacific Literacy	Pacific Learning
Where Are the Babies?	B	I	8	PM Starters	Rigby
Where Are the Baby Chicks?	D	F	64	Gilbert the Pig	Pioneer Valley
Where Are the Bears?	K	F	250+	Winters, Kay	Bantam Books
Where Are the Car Keys?	B	RF	36	Windmill Books	Wright Group/McGraw Hill
Where Are the Dinosaurs?	B	I	60	Bookshop	Mondo Publishing
Where Are the Eggs?	F	I	152	Discovery Links	Newbridge
Where Are the Monkeys?	G	RF	217	On Our Way to English	Rigby
Where Are the Seeds?	D	I	67	Wonder World	Wright Group/McGraw Hill
Where Are the Sunhats?	D	RF	130	PM Story Books	Rigby
Where Are the Wolves?	R	I	250+	Motil, Rebecca	Scholastic
Where Are They Going?	C	F	42	Story Box	Wright Group/McGraw Hill
Where Are They Going?	C	I	38	Windows on Literacy	National Geographic
Where Are They?	C	RF	24	Humphrey, Kiesha	Scholastic
Where Are They?	D	RF	98	Rigby Literacy	Rigby
Where Are They?	B	I	98	Rosen Real Readers	Rosen Publishing Group
Where Are We Going?	C	RF	70	In Step Readers	Rigby
Where Are We?	B	RF	72	Early Emergent	Pioneer Valley
Where Are We?	J	I	234	Early Explorers	Benchmark Education
Where Are You Going, Aja Rose?	D	RF	100	Sunshine	Wright Group/McGraw Hill
Where Are You Going, Little Mouse?	H	F	148	Kraus, Robert	Greenwillow Books
Where Are You Going?	B	F	42	KinderReaders	Rigby
Where Are You Going?	D	RF	66	Learn to Read	Creative Teaching Press
Where Are You, Mouse?	E	RF	170	Sails	Rigby
Where Babies Play	C	F	36	Instant Readers	Harcourt School Publishers
Where Can a Hippo Hide?	D	F	41	Ready Readers	Pearson Learning Group
Where Can I Play?	C	RF	45	Windows on Literacy	National Geographic
Where Can I Write?	C	RF	42	Early Emergent	Pioneer Valley
Where Can It Be?	E	RF	83	Jonas, Ann	Morrow
Where Can Kitty Sleep?	B	RF	15	Windmill Books	Wright Group/McGraw Hill
Where Can Louis Sleep?	D	RF	75	Bonnell, Kris	Reading Reading Books
Where Can Pussy Sleep?	B	RF	15	Windmill Books	Wright Group/McGraw Hill
Where Can Teddy Go?	E	RF	141	Foundations	Wright Group/McGraw Hill
Where Can We Go from Here?	F	I	54	Spinelle, Nancy Louise	Kaeden Books
Where Can We Put an Elephant?	B	F	48	Windmill Books	Wright Group/McGraw Hill
Where Can You Shop?	C	I	82	Windows on Literacy	National Geographic
Where Did All the Water Go?	F	I	139	PM Plus Nonfiction	Rigby
Where Did It Go?	F	F	216	Learn to Read	Creative Teaching Press
Where Did Sacagawea Join the Corps of Discovery?: And Other Questions about the Lewis and Clark Expedition	T	I	5698	Six Questions of American History	Lerner Publishing Group
Where Did the Maya Go?	P	F	250+	Action Packs	Rigby
Where Did the Maya Go?	T	F	250+	WorldScapes	ETA/Cuisenaire
Where Did They Go?	D	RF	102	Teacher's Choice Series	Pearson Learning Group
Where Dinosaurs Walked	K	I	189	Phonics Readers	Compass Point Books
Where Do All the Birds Go?	M	RF	250+	Wonder World	Wright Group/McGraw Hill
Where Do Animals Live?	F	I	187	Bookshop	Mondo Publishing
Where Do Birds Live?	C	I	57	Chessen, Betsey	Scholastic

W

* Collection of short stories   # Graphic text
^ Mature content with lower level text demands

TITLE	LEVEL	GENRE	WORD COUNT	AUTHOR / SERIES	PUBLISHER / DISTRIBUTOR
Where Do Bugs Live?	D	I	33	Pair-It Books	Steck-Vaughn
Where Do Frogs Come From?	H	I	144	Green Light Readers	Harcourt
Where Do I Live?	C	I	29	Visions	Wright Group/McGraw Hill
Where Do I Sleep?	M	RF	250+	Wonder World	Wright Group/McGraw Hill
Where Do Monsters Live?	C	F	56	Learn to Read	Creative Teaching Press
Where Do Plants Grow?	D	I	28	iOpeners	Pearson Learning Group
Where Do Polar Bears Live?	O	I	250+	Let's-Read-and-Find-Out Science	HarperCollins
Where Do Puddles Go?	J	I	250+	Rookie Read-About Science	Children's Press
Where Do Snakes Live?	G	I	251	Sails	Rigby
Where Do the Puddles Go?	L	I	170	Windows on Literacy	National Geographic
Where Do They Go?	B	I	43	InfoTrek	ETA/Cuisenaire
Where Do They Go?	D	RF	66	Rigby Literacy	Rigby
Where Do They Live?	Q	I	250+	Orbit Collections	Pacific Learning
Where Do They Live?	C	I	45	Ready Readers	Pearson Learning Group
Where Do We Go?	B	RF	22	Ready Readers	Pearson Learning Group
Where Do We Keep Money?: How Banks Work	N	I	526	Lightning Bolt Books	Lerner Publishing Group
Where Do You Live?	N	I	250+	People, Spaces & Places	Rand McNally
Where Do You Live?	C	I	68	Tiger Cub	Peguis
Where Do You Live?	L	I	250+	Twig	Wright Group/McGraw Hill
Where Do You Live?	I	I	68	Windows on Literacy	National Geographic
Where Do You Play?	D	I	131	Twig	Wright Group/McGraw Hill
Where Do You Think You're Going, Christopher Columbus?	S	B	250+	Fritz, Jean	G.P. Putnam's Sons Books for Young Readers
Where Does a Leopard Hide?	C	I	108	Foundations	Wright Group/McGraw Hill
Where Does All the Garbage Go?	K	I	250+	Twig	Wright Group/McGraw Hill
Where Does Breakfast Come From?	H	I	170	Discovery World	Rigby
Where Does Breakfast Come From?	E	I	56	iOpeners	Pearson Learning Group
Where Does Energy Come From?	J	I	245	Leveled Readers Social Studies	Houghton Mifflin Harcourt
Where Does Food Come From?	H	RF	298	InfoTrek	ETA/Cuisenaire
Where Does Food Come From?	I	I	169	PM Plus Nonfiction	Rigby
Where Does Food Come From?	G	I	361	Shelley Rotner's Early Childhood Library	Millbrook Press
Where Does Food Grow?	D	I	43	Blevins, Wiley	Scholastic
Where Does Garbage Go?	K	I	250+	Soar To Success	Houghton Mifflin Harcourt
Where Does It Go?	C	I	61	Questions & Answers	Pearson Learning Group
Where Does It Park?	C	I	51	Canizares, Susan	Scholastic
Where Does Lightning Come From?	N	I	250+	Why In the World?	Capstone Press
Where Does Mrs. Brown Live?	J	I	159	Springboard	Wright Group/McGraw Hill
Where Does Rain Come From?	N	I	250+	Rosen Real Readers	Rosen Publishing Group
Where Does the Butterfly Go When It Rains?	K	RF	250+	Bookshop	Mondo Publishing
Where Does the Garbage Go?	M	I	250+	Soar To Success	Houghton Mifflin Harcourt
Where Does the Mail Go?	F	I	115	Yellow Umbrella Books	Red Brick Learning
Where Does the Rabbit Hop?	E	I	71	Ready Readers	Pearson Learning Group
Where Does the Teacher Sleep?	C	F	50	Gibson, Kathleen	Continental Press
Where Does the Water Go?	L	I	189	Windows on Literacy	National Geographic
Where Does the Wind Go?	M	I	95	Bookshop	Mondo Publishing
Where Have All the Pandas Gone?	R	I	250+	Berger, Melvin & Gilda	Scholastic
Where I Live	B	RF	36	Carousel Earlybirds	Pearson Learning Group
Where I Live	C	RF	35	Pacific Literacy	Pacific Learning
Where I'd Like to Be	S	RF	250+	Dowell, Frances O'Roark	Aladdin
Where in the World	X	RF	250+	French, Simon	Peachtree
Where in the World Is the Perfect Family?	P	RF	250+	Hest, Amy	Penguin Group
Where in the World?	D	I	41	Nelson, May	Scholastic
Where Is a Bear?	A	I	36	Bonnell, Kris	Reading Reading Books

W

TITLE	LEVEL	GENRE	WORD COUNT	AUTHOR / SERIES	PUBLISHER / DISTRIBUTOR
Where Is Baby Lamb?	C	I	42	Bonnell, Kris	Reading Reading Books
Where Is Benny Button?	B	RF	16	Reading Safari	Mondo Publishing
Where Is Ben's Red Car?	D	RF	58	Bonnell, Kris	Reading Reading Books
Where Is Blackbeard's Ship?	O	I	286	Vocabulary Readers	Houghton Mifflin Harcourt
Where Is Buddy Going?	C	F	97	McGougan, Kathy	Buddy Books Publishing
Where Is Catkin?	K	RF	250+	Lord, Janet	Peachtree
Where Is Cow's Lunch?	H	RF	321	Leveled Readers	Houghton Mifflin Harcourt
Where Is Cow's Lunch?	H	RF	321	Leveled Readers/CA	Houghton Mifflin Harcourt
Where Is Cow's Lunch?	H	RF	321	Leveled Readers/TX	Houghton Mifflin Harcourt
Where Is Curly?	D	F	69	Rigby Literacy	Rigby
Where Is Curly?	D	F	88	Rigby Star	Rigby
Where Is Custodian Kate?	D	RF	127	Run to Reading	Discovery Peak
Where Is Daniel?	E	RF	135	Carousel Readers	Pearson Learning Group
Where Is Eric?	I	F	193	Munoz, Isabel	Scholastic
Where Is Eric?	C	RF	29	Rigby Literacy	Rigby
Where Is Fluffy?	E	RF	98	Adams, Lorraine & Bruvold, Lynn	Eaglecrest Books
Where Is Gabby?	B	RF	21	Early Emergent	Pioneer Valley
Where Is Gus-Gus?	L	RF	861	Leveled Readers	Houghton Mifflin Harcourt
Where Is Gus-Gus?	L	RF	861	Leveled Readers/CA	Houghton Mifflin Harcourt
Where Is Gus-Gus?	L	RF	861	Leveled Readers/TX	Houghton Mifflin Harcourt
Where Is Hannah?	D	RF	141	PM Extensions-Red	Rigby
Where Is Happy Monkey?	C	F	46	Joy Readers	Pearson Learning Group
Where Is He?	C	I	48	Reach	National Geographic
Where Is Hoppy?	K	RF	250+	Literacy by Design	Rigby
Where Is It Going?	A	I	20	Windows on Literacy	National Geographic
Where Is It Safe to Play?	D	I	103	PM Plus Nonfiction	Rigby
Where Is it?	D	RF	32	Book Bus	Creative Edge
Where Is It?	LB	I	8	Reading Street	Pearson
Where Is It?	B	RF	21	Ready Readers	Pearson Learning Group
Where Is It?	D	RF	32	Rookie Readers	Children's Press
Where Is It?	F	I	250+	Tiger Cub	Peguis
Where Is Jake?	E	RF	35	My First Reader	Grolier
Where Is Jodi?	I	RF	315	Springboard	Wright Group/McGraw Hill
Where Is Joe?	K	I	146	Rigby Star Quest	Rigby
Where Is Kate's Skate?	D	RF	46	KinderReaders	Rigby
Where Is Kazam?	D	F	31	Brand New Readers	Candlewick Press
Where Is Liam's Frog?	G	F	92	Larkin's Little Readers	Wilbooks
Where Is Little Bo Peep?	E	TL	127	Rigby Rocket	Rigby
Where Is Lunch?	B	F	25	Pacific Literacy	Pacific Learning
Where Is Marco?	C	F	75	Bookshop	Mondo Publishing
Where Is Matt's Cap?	F	RF	107	Plass, Beverly	Kaeden Books
Where Is Max?	D	RF	62	Rookie Readers	Children's Press
Where Is Max?	C	F	54	Sun Sprouts	ETA/Cuisenaire
Where Is Miss Pool?	D	RF	55	Pacific Literacy	Pacific Learning
Where Is Mittens?	G	RF	30	Schaefer, Lola M./Rookie Readers	Children's Press
Where Is Muffin?	F	RF	298	Haight, Angela	Kaeden Books
Where Is My Ball?	B	F	24	The Book Project	Sundance
Where Is My Bear?	C	RF	73	Springboard	Wright Group/McGraw Hill
Where Is My Bone?	C	F	42	Sunshine	Wright Group/McGraw Hill
Where Is My Book?	B	RF	81	InfoTrek	ETA/Cuisenaire
Where Is My Boy?	D	F	46	Potato Chip Books	American Reading Company
Where Is My Cat?	D	RF	102	Handprints C, Set 1	Educators Publishing Service
Where Is My Caterpillar?	H	F	277	Wonder World	Wright Group/McGraw Hill

W

* Collection of short stories   # Graphic text
^ Mature content with lower level text demands

TITLE	LEVEL	GENRE	WORD COUNT	AUTHOR / SERIES	PUBLISHER / DISTRIBUTOR
Where Is My Continent?	J	I	131	Where Am I?	Lerner Publishing Group
Where Is My Country?	I	I	122	Where Am I?	Lerner Publishing Group
Where Is My Dinosaur?	D	RF	119	Rigby Flying Colors	Rigby
Where Is My Glove?	E	RF	99	The King School Series	Townsend Press
Where Is My Grandma?	C	RF	74	Foundations	Wright Group/McGraw Hill
Where Is My Home?	E	I	118	Where Am I?	Lerner Publishing Group
Where Is My Pencil?	C	RF	34	Little Celebrations	Pearson Learning Group
Where Is My Pet?	A	RF	34	Smart Starts	Rigby
Where Is My Puppy?	B	RF	33	Bebop Books	Lee & Low Books Inc.
Where Is My Spider?	H	RF	225	Story Box	Wright Group/McGraw Hill
Where Is My State?	H	I	136	Where Am I?	Lerner Publishing Group
Where Is My Teacher?	B	I	43	Little Books for Early Readers	University of Maine
Where Is My Town?	G	I	109	Where Am I?	Lerner Publishing Group
Where Is Nancy?	E	RF	56	Literacy 2000	Rigby
Where Is Papa?	I	F	201	McCarrier, Andrea	Keep Books
Where Is Patch?	B	RF	31	Rigby Star	Rigby
Where Is Patch?	C	RF	73	Springboard	Wright Group/McGraw Hill
Where Is Peanut?	D	RF	71	Emergent Set 4	Pioneer Valley
Where Is Sam?	B	RF	40	Springboard	Wright Group/McGraw Hill
Where Is Santa?	E	F	158	Little Elf	Literacy Footprints
Where Is She?	A	I	35	Little Books for Early Readers	University of Maine
Where Is Skunk?	D	F	65	Story Box	Wright Group/McGraw Hill
Where Is Tabby Cat?	C	RF	37	Brand New Readers	Candlewick Press
Where Is Teddy's Head?	A	RF	27	Windmill Books	Wright Group/McGraw Hill
Where Is That Dog?	D	RF	29	Potato Chip Books	American Reading Company
Where Is the Barn Owl Going?	D	I	57	Bonnell, Kris	Reading Reading Books
Where Is the Bear?	K	F	250+	Nims, Bonnie	Whitman
Where Is the Big Cat?	E	RF	90	Bonnell, Kris	Reading Reading Books
Where Is the Cake Now?	WB	F	0	Khing, T.T.	Harry N. Abrams
Where Is the Cake?	WB	F	0	Khing, T.T.	Harry N. Abrams
Where Is the Cat?	A	RF	55	On Our Way to English	Rigby
Where Is the Cat?	C	I	28	Read-More Books	Pearson Learning Group
Where Is the Crab?	C	I	30	Vocabulary Readers	Houghton Mifflin Harcourt
Where Is the Dog Collar?	S	F	1449	Leveled Readers	Houghton Mifflin Harcourt
Where Is the Dog Collar?	S	F	1449	Leveled Readers/CA	Houghton Mifflin Harcourt
Where Is the Dog?	A	I	18	Vocabulary Readers	Houghton Mifflin Harcourt
Where Is the Ladybug Going?	D	I	53	Bonnell, Kris	Reading Reading Books
Where Is the Milk?	D	RF	87	Foundations	Wright Group/McGraw Hill
Where Is the Party?	E	F	121	Sails	Rigby
Where Is the Queen?	H	F	109	Ready Readers	Pearson Learning Group
Where Is the School Bus?	D	RF	40	Carousel Readers	Pearson Learning Group
Where Is the Snake?	C	F	60	The Book Project	Sundance
Where Is the Spy?	D	F	138	Sails	Rigby
Where Is the Sun?	D	I	70	Leveled Readers Science	Houghton Mifflin Harcourt
Where Is the Wind?	C	F	69	Big Cat	Pacific Learning
Where Is Water?	C	I	36	Twig	Wright Group/McGraw Hill
Where Is Water?	E	I	79	Water	Lerner Publishing Group
Where Is White Rabbit?	K	RF	250+	Pacific Literacy	Pacific Learning
Where Is Your Home?	I	I	126	Phonics Readers	Compass Point Books
Where Is Zig?	D	F	63	Leveled Readers	Houghton Mifflin Harcourt
Where Jeans Come From	K	I	250+	Ready Readers	Pearson Learning Group
Where on Earth Is My Bagel?	L	F	250+	Park, Frances & Park, Ginger	Lee & Low Books Inc.
Where on Earth?	P	I	1581	Big Cat	Pacific Learning
Where People Live	J	RF	259	Early Connections	Benchmark Education

W

* Collection of short stories   # Graphic text
^ Mature content with lower level text demands

TITLE	LEVEL	GENRE	WORD COUNT	AUTHOR / SERIES	PUBLISHER / DISTRIBUTOR
Where People Live	F	I	68	Windows on Literacy	National Geographic
Where Should Turtle Be?	M	F	632	Ring, Susan	Sylvan Dell Publishing
Where Teddy Bears Come From	L	F	250+	Burgess, Mark	Peachtree
Where the Black Bug Sat	C	F	40	Dominie Readers	Pearson Learning Group
*Where the Flame Trees Bloom	U	B	250+	Ada, Alma Flor	Simon & Schuster
Where the Great Hawk Flies	U	HF	250+	Ketchum, Liza	Scholastic
Where the Ground Meets the Sky	Y	HF	250+	Davies, Jacqueline	Marshall Cavendish
Where the Lilies Bloom	Y	RF	250+	Cleavers, Vera & Bill	HarperTrophy
Where the Money Is	S	I	250+	WorldScapes	ETA/Cuisenaire
Where the Mountain Meets the Moon	T	F	250+	Lin, Grace	Little Brown and Company
Where the Red Fern Grows	X	RF	250+	Rawls, Wilson	Bantam Books
Where the River Runs: A Portrait of a Refugee Family	W	B	250+	Graff, Nancy Price	Scholastic
Where the Wild Things Are	J	F	339	Sendak, Maurice	Harper & Row
Where There Was Smoke	M	I	250+	Martinucci, Suzanne	Scholastic
Where Things Grow	C	I	81	Leveled Literacy Intervention/ Green System	Heinemann
Where to Buy It	B	I	45	Rosen Real Readers	Rosen Publishing Group
Where to Look for a Dinosaur	O	F	250+	Most, Bernard	Harcourt Brace
Where Was Atlantis?	Z	I	250+	Unsolved Mysteries	Steck-Vaughn
Where Was Patrick Henry on the 29th of May?	R	B	250+	Fritz, Jean	Scholastic
Where We Live	J	I	250+	The Rowland Reading Program Libary	Rowland Reading Foundation
Where We Live	C	I	34	Vocabulary Readers	Houghton Mifflin Harcourt
Where Will I Sit?	F	RF	78	Teacher's Choice Series	Pearson Learning Group
Where Will You Sleep Tonight?	C	I	77	Foundations	Wright Group/McGraw Hill
Where?	D	I	119	Yellow Umbrella Books	Red Brick Learning
Where's Al?	D	F	49	Barton, Byron	Houghton Mifflin Harcourt
Where's Baby Tom?	D	RF	91	Book Bank	Wright Group/McGraw Hill
Where's Bear?	C	F	41	Windmill Books	Wright Group/McGraw Hill
Where's Boo Boo?	I	RF	361	McAlpin, MaryAnn	Short Tales Press
Where's Cupcake?	D	RF	71	Little Readers	Houghton Mifflin Harcourt
Where's Grandma?	M	F	250+	Literacy by Design	Rigby
Where's Harley?	J	RF	250+	Math Matters	Kane Press
Where's Henry?	F	RF	112	Home Connection Collection	Rigby
Where's Little Mole?	C	F	43	Little Celebrations	Pearson Learning Group
Where's Lulu?	I	RF	250+	Hooks, William H.	Bantam Books
Where's My Backpack?	C	RF	27	Little Celebrations	Pearson Learning Group
Where's My Daddy?	F	F	87	Watanabe, Shigeo	G.P. Putnam's Sons Books for Young Readers
Where's My Mummy?	K	F	250+	Crimi, Carolyn	Candlewick Press
Where's My Snack?	I	RF	250+	Sunshine	Wright Group/McGraw Hill
Where's My Teddy?	I	F	221	Alborough, Jez	Candlewick Press
Where's My Yellow Yo-Yo?	B	RF	36	Phonics and Friends	Hampton Brown
Where's Our Car?	D	RF	69	Rigby Star	Rigby
Where's Spot?	E	F	65	Hill, Eric	G.P. Putnam's Sons Books for Young Readers
Where's Sylvester's Bed?	F	RF	78	Wonder World	Wright Group/McGraw Hill
Where's That Bone?	J	RF	250+	Math Matters	Kane Press
Where's the Baby?	E	RF	139	Alphakids	Sundance
Where's the Bus?	L	F	250+	Sunshine	Wright Group/McGraw Hill
Where's the Dog?	B	RF	36	Windmill Books	Rigby
Where's the Egg Cup?	B	RF	25	Windmill Books	Wright Group/McGraw Hill
Where's the Fish?	B	F	39	Gomi, Taro	Morrow
Where's the Frog?	D	I	46	Discovery Links	Newbridge

W

Organized Alphabetically by Title
Storable Database at www.fountasandpinnellleveledbooks.com

* Collection of short stories   # Graphic text
^ Mature content with lower level text demands

TITLE	LEVEL	GENRE	WORD COUNT	AUTHOR / SERIES	PUBLISHER / DISTRIBUTOR
Where's the Halloween Treat?	C	RF	102	Ziefert, Harriet	Penguin Group
Where's the Puppy?	D	RF	70	Dwight, Laura	Checkerboard
Where's the Snow?	G	RF	142	Seedlings	Continental Press
Where's Tim?	C	F	38	Sunshine	Wright Group/McGraw Hill
Where's Tony?	J	RF	114	City Kids	Rigby
Where's Tumpty?: A Tilly and Friends Book	I	F	264	Dunbar, Polly	Candlewick Press
Where's Your Lunch?	G	RF	243	InfoTrek	ETA/Cuisenaire
Where's Your Smile, Crocodile?	K	F	250+	Freedman, Claire	Peachtree
Where's Your Tooth?	C	RF	53	Learn to Read	Creative Teaching Press
Wherever the Wind Takes Us	O	RF	1934	Take Two Books	Wright Group/McGraw Hill
Which Animal Is That?	I	I	250+	Momentum Literacy Program	Troll Associates
Which Animal Is Which?	M	I	250+	The Rowland Reading Program Library	Rowland Reading Foundation
Which Animal?	B	I	14	Foundations	Wright Group/McGraw Hill
Which Baby Animal?	I	I	250+	Scooters	ETA/Cuisenaire
Which Clothes Do You Wear?	C	I	49	Foundations	Wright Group/McGraw Hill
Which Comes First?	J	I	250+	Voyages	SRA/McGraw Hill
Which Does Not Belong?	A	I	35	Shutterbug Books	Steck-Vaughn
Which Egg Is Mine?	D	F	65	Avenues	Hampton Brown
Which Egg Is Mine?	D	F	65	Rise & Shine	Hampton Brown
Which Hat Today?	E	RF	94	Gosset, Rachel; Ballinger, Margaret	Scholastic
Which Holiday Is It?	I	I	110	Phonics Readers	Compass Point Books
Which House?	I	I	231	Scooters	ETA/Cuisenaire
Which Insects Live Here?	J	I	129	Rigby Literacy	Rigby
Which Is Better?	G	I	104	Pair-It Turn and Learn	Steck-Vaughn
Which Is Different?	B	I	28	Rigby Star Quest	Rigby
Which Is Heavier?	D	I	51	Questions & Answers	Pearson Learning Group
Which Is the tallest?	G	I	95	Windows on Literacy	National Geographic
Which Juice Would You Like?	C	F	28	Step-By-Step Series	Pearson Learning Group
Which One Does Not Belong?	B	I	20	Windows on Literacy	National Geographic
Which One is Different?	A	I	28	Windows on Literacy	National Geographic
Which One Is It?	D	I	48	InfoTrek	ETA/Cuisenaire
Which One Is It?	D	RF	99	Red Rocket Readers	Flying Start Books
Which One Is Which?	G	I	187	Sunshine	Wright Group/McGraw Hill
Which Toys?	D	I	40	Home Connection Collection	Rigby
Which Way Home?	C	RF	26	Little Celebrations	Pearson Learning Group
Which Way Next?	L	I	465	Red Rocket Readers	Flying Start Books
Which Way, Jack?	O	F	250+	Action Packs	Rigby
Which Way, Wendy	M	RF	250+	Social Studies Connects	Kane Press
Which Wheels Are Best?	M	I	250+	Scooters	ETA/Cuisenaire
Which Witch?	S	F	250+	Ibbotson, Eva	Puffin Books
While We Sleep	J	I	387	Gear Up!	Wright Group/McGraw Hill
While We Were Out	J	F	250+	Lee, Ho Baek	Kane/Miller Book Publishers
While You Were Sleeping	J	RF	250+	Butler, John	Peachtree
Whipping Boy, The	R	F	250+	Fleischman, Sid	Troll Associates
Whirlers and Twirlers: Science Fun with Spinning	T	I	250+	Science Fun with Vicki Cobb	Millbrook Press
Whirligig	Y	RF	250+	Fleischman, Paul	Laurel-Leaf Books
Whirlwind	Z+	F	250+	Klass, David	Square Fish
Whiskers	B	RF	24	Gear Up!	Wright Group/McGraw Hill
Whiskers	C	I	32	Wonder World	Wright Group/McGraw Hill
Whisker's Excuses	L	F	540	Springboard	Wright Group/McGraw Hill

W

TITLE	LEVEL	GENRE	WORD COUNT	AUTHOR / SERIES	PUBLISHER / DISTRIBUTOR
Whisper	R	TL	1000	Leveled Readers/TX	Houghton Mifflin Harcourt
Whisper and Shout	C	I	92	Twig	Wright Group/McGraw Hill
Whisper of the Stars, The	R	I	250+	WorldScapes	ETA/Cuisenaire
Whispering Mountain, The	Y	F	250+	Aiken, Joan	Tom Doherty
Whistle for Willie	L	RF	380	Keats, Ezra Jack	Penguin Group
Whistle Like a Bird	D	RF	53	Pair-It Books	Steck-Vaughn
Whistle Tooth, The	H	RF	188	Storyteller-Night Crickets	Wright Group/McGraw Hill
Whistler's Hollow	T	HF	250+	Dadey, Debbie	Bloomsbury Children's Books
Whistling Wings	N	F	1002	Goering, Laura	Sylvan Dell Publishing
White Bird	N	RF	250+	Bulla, Clyde Robert	Random House
White Cat	Z+	RF	250+	Black, Holly	Margaret K. McElderry Books
White Death	Z+	RF	6600	Oxford Bookworms Library	Oxford University Press
White Dragon: Anna Allen in the Face of Danger	R	I	1253	Leveled Readers	Houghton Mifflin Harcourt
White Elephants	L	RF	250+	Sunshine	Wright Group/McGraw Hill
White Elephants and Yellow Jackets	O	I	250+	Action Packs	Rigby
White Everywhere	J	I	314	Lightning Bolt Books	Lerner Publishing Group
White Fang	W	RF	10840	Dominoes two	Oxford University Press
White Fang	Y	RF	250+	London, Jack	Scholastic
White Horse, The	K	F	250+	Literacy 2000	Rigby
White House Autumn	Z+	RF	250+	White, Ellen Emerson	Feiwel and Friends
White House Dog	N	F	250+	Martha Speaks	Houghton Mifflin Harcourt
White House, The	N	I	250+	American Symbols	Capstone Press
White House, The	V	I	250+	Cornerstones of Freedom	Children's Press
White House, The	E	I	89	Early Explorers	Benchmark Education
White House, The	Q	I	250+	Let's See	Compass Point Books
White house, The	N	I	462	Lightning Bolt Books	Lerner Publishing Group
White House, The	P	I	619	Pull Ahead Books	Lerner Publishing Group
White House, The	S	I	250+	Symbols of America	Marshall Cavendish
White Jaguar, The	U	RF	250+	WorldScapes	ETA/Cuisenaire
White Mountain, The	Q	I	1079	Leveled Readers	Houghton Mifflin Harcourt
White Mountain, The	Q	I	1079	Leveled Readers/CA	Houghton Mifflin Harcourt
White Mountains, The	V	F	250+	Christopher, John	Aladdin
White Paw, Black Paw	C	F	41	KinderReaders	Rigby
White Rhino, The	E	I	78	Bonnell, Kris/Animals in Danger	Reading Reading Books
White Sands, Red Menace	W	HF	250+	Klages, Ellen	Puffin Books
White Wednesday	H	RF	321	Literacy 2000	Rigby
White White Snow, The	C	I	60	Bonnell, Kris	Reading Reading Books
White Witch, The	X	HF	250+	Graber, Janet	Roaring Brook Press
White Wolf	S	F	250+	Branford, Henrietta	Candlewick Press
White Wolf, The	N	RF	250+	A to Z Mysteries	Random House
White: Seeing White All Around Us	L	I	250+	Colors	Capstone Press
Whitemen	W	HF	250+	High-Fliers	Pacific Learning
Whiteout	N	RF	1029	Leveled Readers	Houghton Mifflin Harcourt
Whiteout	P	RF	250+	Orca Young Readers	Orca Books
White-Tailed Deer	O	I	1849	Early Bird Nature Books	Lerner Publishing Group
White-Tailed Deer, The	R	I	250+	Wildlife of North America	Red Brick Learning
Whitewater Rafting	G	I	66	Nonfiction Set 4	Literacy Footprints
Whitewater Scrubs	O	RF	4067	McEwan, Jamie	Darby Creek Publishing
Whizz! Click!	L	RF	285	Pacific Literacy	Pacific Learning
Who Am I ?	D	I	81	Rise & Shine	Hampton Brown
Who Am I?	E	I	64	Christensen, Nancy	Scholastic

W

* Collection of short stories   # Graphic text
^ Mature content with lower level text demands

TITLE	LEVEL	GENRE	WORD COUNT	AUTHOR / SERIES	PUBLISHER / DISTRIBUTOR
Who Am I?	S	I	250+	Orbit Collections	Pacific Learning
Who Am I?	B	F	32	The Book Project	Sundance
Who Are the Three Musketeers?	V	I	1710	Vocabulary Readers	Houghton Mifflin Harcourt
Who Are the Three Musketeers?	V	I	1710	Vocabulary Readers/CA	Houghton Mifflin Harcourt
Who Are the Three Musketeers?	V	I	1710	Vocabulary Readers/TX	Houghton Mifflin Harcourt
Who Are We?	C	RF	30	Home Connection Collection	Rigby
Who Are You?	C	RF	55	Book Bank	Wright Group/McGraw Hill
Who Ate the Broccoli?	E	F	42	Little Readers	Houghton Mifflin Harcourt
Who Ate the Pizza?	C	RF	59	Foundations	Wright Group/McGraw Hill
Who Broke Lincoln's Thumb?	N	RF	250+	Roy, Ron	Random House
Who Builds?	I	I	97	Yellow Umbrella Books	Red Brick Learning
Who Came By Here?	C	RF	31	Rise & Shine	Hampton Brown
Who Came Out?	F	F	45	Ready Readers	Pearson Learning Group
Who Can Be a Hero?	A	I	41	Leveled Readers Social Studies	Houghton Mifflin Harcourt
Who Can Be an Astronaut?	U	I	1484	Vocabulary Readers	Houghton Mifflin Harcourt
Who Can Be an Astronaut?	U	I	1484	Vocabulary Readers/CA	Houghton Mifflin Harcourt
Who Can Be an Astronaut?	U	I	1484	Vocabulary Readers/TX	Houghton Mifflin Harcourt
Who Can Be President?	R	I	1310	Leveled Readers	Houghton Mifflin Harcourt
Who Can Be President?	R	I	1310	Leveled Readers/CA	Houghton Mifflin Harcourt
Who Can Curly See?	LB	F	16	Rigby Star	Rigby
Who Can Fix the Computer?	G	RF	178	Handprints D, Set 1	Educators Publishing Service
Who Can Help?	F	I	93	Gear Up!	Wright Group/McGraw Hill
Who Can Help?	L	I	588	Reading Street	Pearson
Who Can Hop?	C	I	35	Questions & Answers	Pearson Learning Group
Who Can Play?	B	RF	26	Sun Sprouts	ETA/Cuisenaire
Who Can Read?	C	RF	72	Handprints C, Set 1	Educators Publishing Service
Who Can See the Camel?	C	RF	70	Story Box	Wright Group/McGraw Hill
Who Can Swim?	B	I	47	Tiny Treasures	Pioneer Valley
Who Can Wiggle?	A	I	33	Bonnell, Kris	Reading Reading Books
Who Can?	B	RF	35	Bookshop	Mondo Publishing
Who Cleans the Museum?	I	RF	85	Books for Young Learners	Richard C. Owen
Who Cloned the President?	N	RF	250+	Roy, Ron	Random House
Who Cracked the Liberty Bell? And Other Questions About the American Revolution	R	I	250+	Roop, Peter & Connie	Scholastic
Who Cried for Pie?	D	F	86	First Start	Troll Associates
Who Did it?	O	RF	250+	Sails	Rigby
Who Did It?	H	RF	206	Storyworlds	Heinemann
Who Do I Look Like?	G	RF	143	Rookie Readers	Children's Press
*Who Do You Think You Are?: Stories of Friends and Enemies	Z	RF	250+	Rochman, Hazel & McCampbell, Darlene	Little Brown and Company
Who Eats What?	N	I	697	Leveled Readers Science	Houghton Mifflin Harcourt
Who Eats What?	T	I	250+	The News	Richard C. Owen
Who Eats What?: Food Chains and Food Webs	M	I	250+	Lauber, Patricia	Scholastic
Who Fed the Chickens?	C	F	14	Little Celebrations	Pearson Learning Group
Who Goes in the Water?	D	I	77	Bonnell, Kris	Reading Reading Books
Who Goes Out on Halloween?	G	RF	163	Alexander, Sue	Bantam Books
Who Goes to School?	E	RF	298	Easy Stories	Norwood House Press
Who Grows Up in the Desert?: A Book About Desert Animals and Their Offspring	L	I	250+	Who Grows Up Here?	Picture Window Books
Who Grows Up in the Forest?: A Book About Forest Animals and Their Offspring	L	I	250+	Who Grows Up Here?	Picture Window Books
Who Grows Up in the Ocean?: A Book About Ocean Animals and Their Offspring	L	I	250+	Who Grows Up Here?	Picture Window Books

W

* Collection of short stories   # Graphic text
^ Mature content with lower level text demands

Organized Alphabetically by Title   **849**
Storable Database at www.fountasandpinnellleveledbooks.com

TITLE	LEVEL	GENRE	WORD COUNT	AUTHOR / SERIES	PUBLISHER / DISTRIBUTOR
Who Grows Up in the Rain Forest?: A Book About Rain Forest Animals and Their Offspring	L	I	250+	Who Grows Up Here?	Picture Window Books
Who Grows Up in the Snow?: A Book About Polar Animals and Their Offspring	L	I	250+	Who Grows Up Here?	Picture Window Books
Who Grows Up on the Farm?: A Book About Farm Animals and Their Offspring	L	I	250+	Who Grows Up Here?	Picture Window Books
Who Has a Belly Button?	R	I	250+	Batten, Mary	Peachtree
Who Has a Hump?	B	F	24	Bonnell, Kris	Reading Reading Books
Who Has a Tail?	G	I	186	Ready Readers	Pearson Learning Group
Who Has Claws?	A	I	37	Red Rocket Readers	Flying Start Books
Who Has More?	B	I	55	Shutterbug Books	Steck-Vaughn
Who Has Stripes?	A	I	37	Red Rocket Readers	Flying Start Books
Who Has Wings?	C	I	30	Questions & Answers	Pearson Learning Group
Who Helps Me?	C	I	57	Red Rocket Readers	Flying Start Books
Who Hid?	B	RF	25	Leber, Nancy	Scholastic
Who Hops?	J	I	170	Davis, Katie	Scholastic
Who Is a Friend?	F	I	191	Yellow Umbrella Books	Capstone Press
Who Is Asleep?	A	I	32	Springboard	Wright Group/McGraw Hill
Who Is Carrie?	W	HF	250+	Collier, James & Christopher	Bantam Books
Who Is Coming?	E	RF	28	Rookie Readers	Children's Press
Who Is Hungry?	D	I	134	Rigby Flying Colors	Rigby
Who Is in Your Family?	F	I	229	Vocabulary Readers	Houghton Mifflin Harcourt
Who Is in Your Family?	F	I	229	Vocabulary Readers/CA	Houghton Mifflin Harcourt
Who Is in Your Family?	F	I	229	Vocabulary Readers/TX	Houghton Mifflin Harcourt
Who Is It?	I	F	163	Grindley, Sally	Peachtree
Who Is Maria Tallchief?	R	B	250+	Who Was...?	Grosset & Dunlap
Who Is Ready?	C	RF	36	Ready Readers	Pearson Learning Group
Who Is Taller?	C	RF	26	Learn to Read	Creative Teaching Press
Who Is Taller?	F	I	163	Sun Sprouts	ETA/Cuisenaire
Who Is the Robot?	C	RF	67	Pacific Literacy	Pacific Learning
Who Is the Tallest?	F	I	91	Alphakids	Sundance
Who Is the Tallest?	D	RF	46	Sunshine	Wright Group/McGraw Hill
Who Is Who?	D	RF	115	Rookie Readers	Children's Press
Who Keeps Us Safe?	B	I	28	Yellow Umbrella Books	Red Brick Learning
Who Killed Mr. Boddy?	P	RF	250+	Parker, A. E.	Scholastic
Who Laid These Eggs?	C	I	62	Little Celebrations	Pearson Learning Group
Who Lays Eggs?	G	I	132	Twig	Wright Group/McGraw Hill
Who Likes Grass?	D	I	74	Bonnell, Kris	Reading Reading Books
Who Likes Ice Cream?	A	F	15	Literacy 2000	Rigby
Who Likes It Hot?	K	F	250+	Bookshop	Mondo Publishing
Who Likes the Cold?	A	I	29	Twig	Wright Group/McGraw Hill
Who Likes the Night?	G	RF	250+	Phonics and Friends	Hampton Brown
Who Likes to Swim?	D	I	100	Teacher's Choice Series	Pearson Learning Group
Who Likes Water?	B	F	35	KinderReaders	Rigby
Who Lives at the Zoo?	LB	I	11	Windows on Literacy	National Geographic
Who Lives Here?	C	I	62	Learn to Read	Creative Teaching Press
Who Lives Here?	F	I	100	Leveled Readers Science	Houghton Mifflin Harcourt
Who Lives Here?	I	I	230	Little Readers	Houghton Mifflin Harcourt
Who Lives Here?	C	I	42	Questions & Answers	Pearson Learning Group
Who Lives Here?	D	RF	102	Reed, Janet	Scholastic
Who Lives Here?	C	I	28	Story Box	Wright Group/McGraw Hill
Who Lives Here?	F	I	185	Storyteller Nonfiction	Wright Group/McGraw Hill
Who Lives Here?	B	I	43	Windows on Literacy	National Geographic

* Collection of short stories   # Graphic text
^ Mature content with lower level text demands

W

TITLE	LEVEL	GENRE	WORD COUNT	AUTHOR / SERIES	PUBLISHER / DISTRIBUTOR
Who Lives in a Tree?	B	I	46	Canizares, Susan; Moreton, Daniel	Scholastic
Who Lives in a Tree?	C	I	43	Discovery Links	Newbridge
Who Lives in the Arctic?	B	I	48	Canizares, Susan; Chanko, Pamela	Scholastic
Who Lives in the Sea?	B	I	69	Bookshop	Mondo Publishing
Who Lives in the Woods?	F	I	110	Pair-It Books	Steck-Vaughn
Who Lives in this Hole?	C	I	25	Twig	Wright Group/McGraw Hill
Who Lives on a Farm?	B	I	48	Red Rocket Readers	Flying Start Books
Who Lives on a Farm?	B	I	36	Story Steps	Rigby
Who Looks After Me?	M	I	250+	Literacy 2000	Rigby
Who Looks After Me?	B	I	20	Windows on Literacy	National Geographic
Who Looks After Our World?	E	I	45	Home Connection Collection	Rigby
Who Loves Buddy?	E	F	99	McGougan, Kathy	Buddy Books Publishing
Who Loves Getting Wet?	I	F	204	Sunshine	Wright Group/McGraw Hill
Who Loves Me Best?	E	RF	91	Hall, Kirsten	Reader's Digest Children's Books
Who Loves the Fall?	K	RF	49	Raczka, Bob	Albert Whitman & Co.
Who Made That?	C	RF	31	Ready Readers	Pearson Learning Group
Who Made These Tracks?	B	I	24	Literacy 2000	Rigby
Who Made These Tracks?	D	I	45	Teacher's Choice Series	Pearson Learning Group
Who Makes the Rules?	M	I	250+	Schafer, Lola M.	Benchmark Education
Who Needs It?	L	RF	250+	Social Studies Connects	Kane Press
Who Needs Math?	K	RF	349	Story Box	Wright Group/McGraw Hill
Who Needs Plants?	F	I	97	Yellow Umbrella Books	Red Brick Learning
Who Needs Rooster?	G	F	223	Literacy by Design	Rigby
Who Needs Teeth?	I	I	116	Phonics Readers	Compass Point Books
Who Needs Two Wings?	K	TL	2501	Deedy, Carmen Agra	Hampton Brown
^Who Owns Kelly Paddik?	Y	RF	250+	Orca Soundings	Orca Books
Who Passed Through?	K	RF	380	Leveled Readers	Houghton Mifflin Harcourt
Who Provides Services?	M	I	297	Larkin, Bruce	Wilbooks
Who Pushed Humpty?	K	TL	250+	Literacy 2000	Rigby
Who Put That Hair in My Toothbrush?	V	RF	250+	Spinelli, Jerry	Little Brown and Company
Who Put the Butter in Butterfly?	Y	I	250+	Feldman, David	HarperCollins
Who Reads?	B	I	25	Teacher's Choice Series	Pearson Learning Group
Who Really Killed Cock Robin?	U	RF	250+	George, Jean Craighead	HarperTrophy
Who Rides the Bus?	C	RF	19	Little Celebrations	Pearson Learning Group
Who Sank the Boat?	K	F	219	Allen, Pamela	Coward
Who Says?	D	F	36	My First Reader	Grolier
Who Says?	C	I	49	Twig	Wright Group/McGraw Hill
Who Shares Your Home?	N	I	250+	Tristars	Richard C. Owen
Who Shot the Movies?	T	I	250+	The News	Richard C. Owen
Who Shot the President?: The Death of John F. Kennedy	P	I	250+	Donnelly, Judy	Random House
Who Should...?	F	RF	149	InfoTrek	ETA/Cuisenaire
Who Spilled the Beans?	E	F	87	Story Basket	Wright Group/McGraw Hill
Who Stole the Cookies?	F	F	153	All Aboard Reading	Grosset & Dunlap
Who Stole the Fish?	H	F	250+	Cambridge Reading	Pearson Learning Group
Who Stole the Tiger's Eye?	Q	F	250+	Sunshine	Wright Group/McGraw Hill
Who Stole the Wizard of Oz?	P	RF	250+	Avi	Alfred A. Knopf
Who the Man	X	RF	250+	Lynch, Chris	HarperCollins
Who Took Our Cake?	E	RF	98	Rigby Focus	Rigby
Who Took the Cake?	C	RF	32	First Stories	Pacific Learning
Who Took the Cookies from the Cookie Jar?	D	F	81	Learn to Read	Creative Teaching Press

W

TITLE	LEVEL	GENRE	WORD COUNT	AUTHOR / SERIES	PUBLISHER / DISTRIBUTOR
Who Took the Farmer's Hat?	I	F	340	Nodset, Joan	Scholastic
Who Took the Teacher's Scissors?	F	F	175	Springboard	Wright Group/McGraw Hill
Who Uses These Tools?	B	I	23	Twig	Wright Group/McGraw Hill
Who Wants a Ride?	I	RF	214	Bernard, Robin	Scholastic
Who Wants Arthur?	J	F	250+	Leveled Readers Language Support	Houghton Mifflin Harcourt
Who Wants One?	I	F	212	Serfozo, Mary	Macmillan
Who Wants to Live in My House?	D	RF	60	Book Bank	Wright Group/McGraw Hill
Who Wants to See the Doctor?	F	I	116	Adventures in Reading	Pearson Learning Group
Who Was Albert Einstein?	R	B	250+	Who Was...?	Grosset & Dunlap
Who Was Ben Franklin?	S	B	250+	Fradin, Dennis Brindell	Grosset & Dunlap
Who Was Ben Franklin?	P	B	250+	Windows on Literacy	National Geographic
Who Was Betsy Ross?	M	B	250+	Rosen Real Readers	Rosen Publishing Group
Who Was Harriet Tubman?	R	B	250+	Who Was...?	Grosset & Dunlap
Who Was Harry Houdini?	R	B	250+	Who Was...?	Grosset & Dunlap
Who Was Helen Keller?	Q	B	250+	Who Was...?	Grosset & Dunlap
Who Was Johnny Appleseed?	Q	B	250+	Who Was...?	Grosset & Dunlap
Who Was Marco Polo?	R	B	250+	Who Was...?	Grosset & Dunlap
Who Was Marjorie Harris Carr?	O	B	597	Leveled Readers Science	Houghton Mifflin Harcourt
Who Was Martin Luther King, Jr.?	M	B	237	Avenues	Hampton Brown
Who Was Paul Revere?	M	B	250+	Rosen Real Readers	Rosen Publishing Group
Who Was Poor Richard? Colonials to Remember	V	B	2615	Independent Readers Social Studies	Houghton Mifflin Harcourt
Who Was Sitting Bull?: And Other Questions about the Battle of Little Bighorn	T	I	5144	Six Questions of American History	Lerner Publishing Group
Who Wears This Hat?	B	I	42	Windmill Books	Wright Group/McGraw Hill
Who Wears This Hat?	H	I	139	Windows on Literacy	National Geographic
Who Were the Beatles?	R	B	250+	Who Was...?	Grosset & Dunlap
Who Were the First People?	R	I	250+	Usborne Starting Point History	EDC Publishing
Who Were the Romans?	R	I	250+	Usborne Starting Point History	EDC Publishing
Who Were the Vikings?	R	I	250+	Usborne Starting Point History	EDC Publishing
Who Were the Wright Brothers?	W	B	3260	Vocabulary Readers	Houghton Mifflin Harcourt
Who Were the Wright Brothers?	W	B	3260	Vocabulary Readers/CA	Houghton Mifflin Harcourt
Who Will Be My Friends?	F	RF	205	Hoff, Syd	HarperTrophy
Who Will Be My Mother?	E	F	156	Story Box	Wright Group/McGraw Hill
Who Will Help Me?	C	RF	53	Home Connection Collection	Rigby
Who Will Help?	B	RF	20	Carousel Readers	Pearson Learning Group
Who Will Help?	D	TL	93	Learn to Read	Creative Teaching Press
Who Will Help?	F	RF	74	New Way Red	Steck-Vaughn
Who Will Look Out for Danny?	S	RF	250+	Action Packs	Rigby
Who Will Marry Maisie?	G	F	250+	Rigby Rocket	Rigby
Who Will Use This?	H	I	154	Rigby Literacy	Rigby
Who Will Win the Race?	D	RF	53	Sunshine	Wright Group/McGraw Hill
Who Will Win?	H	RF	234	In Step Readers	Rigby
Who Works at the Beach?	G	I	102	Windows on Literacy	National Geographic
Who Works at the Supermarket?	K	I	325	Springboard	Wright Group/McGraw Hill
Who Works at the Zoo?	D	I	31	Windows on Literacy	National Geographic
Who Works Here?	D	I	57	Questions & Answers	Pearson Learning Group
Who Works in Government?	J	I	187	Early Explorers	Benchmark Education
Who Works with Tools?	K	I	197	Larkin's Little Readers	Wilbooks
Who You Are on the Inside	G	I	126	Shutterbug Books	Steck-Vaughn
Who?	E	F	46	Storyteller-Setting Sun	Wright Group/McGraw Hill
Whoa! UFO!	K	RF	1490	Science Solves It!	Kane Press

W

* Collection of short stories   # Graphic text
^ Mature content with lower level text demands

TITLE	LEVEL	GENRE	WORD COUNT	AUTHOR / SERIES	PUBLISHER / DISTRIBUTOR
Whoever You Are	I	I	90	Fox, Mem	Harcourt
Whole Days Outdoors	O	B	250+	Meet the Author	Richard C. Owen
Whole Nother Story, A	V	F	250+	Soup, Dr. Cuthbert	Bloomsbury Children's Books
Whole World in One City, A	O	RF	1185	Reading Street	Pearson
Who'll Hold the Baby?	F	RF	181	Voyages	SRA/McGraw Hill
Whoo Goes There?	K	F	250+	Ericsson, Jennifer A.	Roaring Brook Press
Whoops	I	F	250+	Supersonics	Rigby
Whoops!	E	RF	49	Little Celebrations	Pearson Learning Group
Whoops!	E	RF	147	Rigby Rocket	Rigby
Whoops! It Works!	O	I	250+	Lopez, Orlando	Pearson Learning Group
Whoosh! The Story of Snowboarding	M	I	250+	Literacy by Design	Rigby
Who's a Pest?	J	F	250+	Bonsall, Crosby	HarperTrophy
Who's Afraid of Shadows?	I	RF	219	Talking Point Series	Pearson Learning Group
Who's Afraid of the Big, Bad Bully?	K	RF	250+	Slater, Teddy	Scholastic
Who's Afraid of the Dark?	I	RF	250+	Bonsall, Crosby	HarperTrophy
Who's Afraid?	I	RF	165	Reading Unlimited	Pearson Learning Group
Who's at School?	A	I	36	Rosen Real Readers	Rosen Publishing Group
Who's Behind the Door at My House?	G	RF	184	Salmon, Michael	Steck-Vaughn
Who's Behind the Door at My School?	G	RF	187	Salmon, Michael	Steck-Vaughn
Who's Buying? Who's Selling?: Understanding Consumers and Producers	M	I	494	Lightning Bolt Books	Lerner Publishing Group
Who's Coming for a Ride?	B	F	25	Literacy 2000	Rigby
Who's Going to Lick the Bowl?	C	RF	18	Story Box	Wright Group/McGraw Hill
Who's Got Spots?	K	RF	250+	Math Matters	Kane Press
Who's Hiding There?	I	RF	242	Pair-It Books	Steck-Vaughn
Who's Hiding?	D	I	51	Learn to Read	Creative Teaching Press
Who's Hiding?	F	F	26	Onishi, Satoru	Kane/Miller Book Publishers
Who's in Love with Arthur?	M	F	250+	Brown, Marc	Little Brown and Company
Who's in the Jungle?	F	I	116	Ready Readers	Pearson Learning Group
Who's in the Nest?	E	F	75	Start to Read	School Zone
Who's in the Shed?	I	F	202	Literacy Tree	Rigby
Who's Looking After the Baby?	H	RF	127	Foundations	Wright Group/McGraw Hill
Who's That Stepping on Plymouth Rock?	R	I	250+	Fritz, Jean	G.P. Putnam's Sons Books for Young Readers
Who's the Alien?	M	SF	250+	Rigby Gigglers	Rigby
Who's the Boss?	J	F	647	Jasper the Cat	Pioneer Valley
Who's There?	B	F	49	Bookshop	Mondo Publishing
Who's There?	E	F	92	Story Box	Wright Group/McGraw Hill
Whose Birthday Is It Today?	C	RF	50	Book Bank	Wright Group/McGraw Hill
Whose Bones?	B	I	28	Fernandez, Queta	Scholastic
Whose Ears Are These?: A Look at Animal Ears- Short, Flat, and Floppy	M	I	250+	Whose Is It? Science	Picture Window Books
Whose Egg Is This?	E	F	99	Story Steps	Rigby
Whose Eggs Are These?	E	RF	125	Sunshine	Wright Group/McGraw Hill
Whose Equipment Is This?	I	I	196	Community Helper Mysteries	Capstone Press
Whose Eyes Are These?: A Look at Animal Eyes- Big, Round, and Narrow	M	I	250+	Whose Is It? Science	Picture Window Books
Whose Feet Are These? A Look at Hooves, Paws, and Claws	M	I	250+	Whose Is It? Science	Picture Window Books
Whose Footprints?	D	I	125	Lighthouse	Rigby
Whose Forest Is It?	C	RF	45	Learn to Read	Creative Teaching Press
Whose Hooves?	I	I	132	Gear Up!	Wright Group/McGraw Hill
Whose Legs Are These?: A Look at Animal Legs- Kicking, Running, and Hopping	M	I	250+	Whose Is It? Science	Picture Window Books

W

TITLE	LEVEL	GENRE	WORD COUNT	AUTHOR / SERIES	PUBLISHER / DISTRIBUTOR
Whose List Is This?	C	F	14	Little Celebrations	Pearson Learning Group
Whose Mouse Are You?	H	F	98	Kraus, Robert	Macmillan
Whose Mouth Is This?: A Look at Bills, Suckers, and Tubes	M	I	250+	Whose Is It? Science	Picture Window Books
Whose Nose Is This?: A Look at Beaks, Snouts, and Trunks	M	I	250+	Whose Is It? Science	Picture Window Books
Whose Shoes Would You Choose?	J	F	165	Sounds Like Reading	Lerner Publishing Group
Whose Shoes?	K	RF	250+	Sunshine	Wright Group/McGraw Hill
Whose Shoes?	D	I	84	Twig	Wright Group/McGraw Hill
Whose Side Are You On?	K	TL	250+	Cisco, Cheyenne	Sadlier-Oxford
Whose Side Are You On?	Q	RF	250+	Moore, Emily	Bantam Books
Whose Skin Is This?: A Look at Animal Skin - Scaly, Furry, and Prickly	M	I	250+	Whose Is It? Science	Picture Window Books
Whose Tail Is This?	B	I	65	Red Rocket Readers	Flying Start Books
Whose Tail Is This?: A Look at Tails - Swishing, Wiggling, and Rattling	M	I	250+	Whose Is It? Science	Picture Window Books
Whose Tools Are These?	I	I	174	Community Helper Mysteries	Capstone Press
Whose Tracks?	B	I	14	Little Celebrations	Pearson Learning Group
Whose Way Today?	M	RF	683	Leveled Readers	Houghton Mifflin Harcourt
Why Animals Never Got Fire: A Story of the Coeur d'Alene Indians	J	TL	237	Books for Young Learners	Richard C. Owen
Why Bananas Are Yellow and Bent	Q	F	4391	Take Two Books	Wright Group/McGraw Hill
Why Bear Sleeps All Winter	L	TL	647	Leveled Readers	Houghton Mifflin Harcourt
Why Bears Have Short Tails	I	TL	250+	Rigby Rocket	Rigby
Why Bears Have Short Tails, A Norwegian Tale	Q	TL	1093	Leveled Readers	Houghton Mifflin Harcourt
Why Can't I Fly?	G	F	449	Gelman, Rita	Scholastic
Why Caterpillars Become Butterflies	H	F	198	Gear Up!	Wright Group/McGraw Hill
Why Cats Hunt at Night	H	TL	288	Rigby Rocket	Rigby
Why Cats Wash After Dinner	I	TL	128	Pacific Literacy	Pacific Learning
Why Clouds Have Shapes	J	F	165	Dominie Readers	Pearson Learning Group
Why Coyote Howls at Night	K	TL	274	Little Books	Sadlier-Oxford
Why Coyote Howls at Night	Q	TL	250+	Moore, Emily	Farrar, Straus, & Giroux
Why Coyote Howls at the Moon	K	TL	250+	Literacy by Design	Rigby
Why Crocodiles Live in Rivers	J	TL	415	Sunshine	Wright Group/McGraw Hill
Why Cry?	I	I	121	Sunshine	Wright Group/McGraw Hill
Why Did English Settlers Come to Virginia?: And Other Questions about the Jamestown Settlement	T	I	5167	Six Questions of American History	Lerner Publishing Group
Why Did the Chicken Cross the Road?	H	F	200	Reed, Janet	Scholastic
Why Did They Come?	N	I	157	Windows on Literacy	National Geographic
Why Do Bears Sleep All Winter?: A Book About Hibernation	N	I	250+	Why in the World?	Capstone Press
Why Do Birds Sing?	N	I	250+	Why In the World?	Capstone Press
Why Do Elephants Wear Hats?	J	F	115	O'Toole, Mary	Pearson Learning Group
Why Do Geese Fly South in Winter?: A Book About Migration	N	I	250+	Why in the World?	Capstone Press
Why Do I Feel Safe?	D	I	61	Questions & Answers	Pearson Learning Group
Why Do I Need to Know When?	G	RF	198	Visions	Wright Group/McGraw Hill
Why Do Leaves Change Color?	N	I	250+	Let's-Read-and-Find-Out Science	HarperTrophy
Why Do Moving Objects Slow Down?: A Look at Friction	M	I	475	Lightning Bolt Books	Lerner Publishing Group
Why Do My Teeth Fall Out?: And Other Questions Kids Have About the Human Body.	O	I	250+	Kids' Questions	Picture Window Books
Why Do the Seasons Change?	S	I	250+	Tell Me Why, Tell Me How	Marshall Cavendish
Why Do Tigers Have Stripes?: A Book About Camouflage	N	I	250+	Why in the World?	Capstone Press

W

Organized Alphabetically by Title
Storable Database at www.fountasandpinnellleveledbooks.com

* Collection of short stories   # Graphic text
^ Mature content with lower level text demands

TITLE	LEVEL	GENRE	WORD COUNT	AUTHOR / SERIES	PUBLISHER / DISTRIBUTOR
Why Do We Work?	J	I	215	Early Explorers	Benchmark Education
Why Do Worms Come Up When It Rains?	I	I	202	Seedlings	Continental Press
Why Does It Rain?	N	I	1571	On My Own Science	Lerner Publishing Group
Why Does It Work?	Y	I	2160	Independent Readers Science	Houghton Mifflin Harcourt
Why Don't You Get a Horse, Sam Adams?	R	B	250+	Fritz, Jean	G.P. Putnam's Sons
Why Elephants Have Long Noses	G	TL	175	Literacy 2000	Rigby
^Why German Immigrants Came to America	S	I	250+	On Deck	Rigby
Why I Like Laura	G	RF	193	Phonics and Friends	Hampton Brown
^Why Irish Immigrants Came to America	S	I	250+	On Deck	Rigby
Why Is a Bird a Bird?	H	I	164	Red Rocket Readers	Flying Start Books
Why Is the Sahara So Dry?: A Book About Deserts	N	I	250+	Why in the World?	Capstone Press
Why Is the Sky Blue?	T	I	250+	Tell Me Why, Tell Me How	Marshall Cavendish
Why Is the South Pole So Cold?: A Book About Antarctica	N	I	250+	Why in the World?	Capstone Press
Why Islands Don't Swim	J	F	250+	Rigby Rocket	Rigby
Why Isn't Pluto a Planet?	N	I	250+	Why In the World?	Capstone Press
^Why Italian Immigrants Came to America	S	I	250+	On Deck	Rigby
^Why Japanese Immigrants Came to America	S	I	250+	On Deck	Rigby
Why Me?	U	RF	250+	Power Up!	Steck-Vaughn
^Why Mexican Immigrants Came to America	S	I	250+	On Deck	Rigby
Why Mosquitoes Buzz in People's Ears	N	TL	250+	Aardema, Verna	Scholastic
Why Night Follows Day	I	TL	169	Gear Up!	Wright Group/McGraw Hill
Why Not?	G	RF	167	Voyages	SRA/McGraw Hill
Why People Move	K	I	250+	People, Spaces & Places	Rand McNally
Why Polar Bears Like Snow . . . and Flamingos Don't	O	I	250+	Navigators Science Series	Benchmark Education
Why Quincy Couldn't Quack	J	F	522	Pair-It Turn and Learn	Steck-Vaughn
Why Rabbit's Ears Are Long	I	TL	239	Dominie Readers	Pearson Learning Group
Why Rabbits Have Long Ears	L	TL	250+	Literacy 2000	Rigby
Why Rabbit's Tail Is Short	G	TL	296	Leveled Readers	Houghton Mifflin Harcourt
Why Recycle?	M	I	501	Red Rocket Readers	Flying Start Books
Why Should I Protect Nature?.	J	RF	250+	Why Should I?	Barron's Educational
Why the Bear's Tail Is Short	J	TL	431	Sunshine	Wright Group/McGraw Hill
Why the Crab Has No Head	L	TL	250+	Knutson, Barbara	Carolrhoda Books
Why the Frog Has Big Eyes	G	TL	132	Green Light Readers	Harcourt
Why the Kangaroo Hops	K	TL	391	Sunshine	Wright Group/McGraw Hill
Why the Leopard Has Spots	L	TL	250+	Pair-It Books	Steck-Vaughn
Why the Moon Is Ivory	N	TL	250+	On Our Way to English	Rigby
Why the Ocean Is Salty	Q	I	250+	Leonhardt, Alice	Steck-Vaughn
Why the Rooster Crows at Sunrise	K	TL	250+	Sunshine	Wright Group/McGraw Hill
Why the Sea Is Salty	L	TL	250+	Literacy 2000	Rigby
Why the Turtle Does Not Fly: A South Pacific Folktale	K	TL	571	Springboard	Wright Group/McGraw Hill
Why There Are Shooting Stars	K	TL	362	Pacific Literacy	Pacific Learning
Why Turtles Have Shells	J	TL	283	Dominie Readers	Pearson Learning Group
^Why Vietnamese Immigrants Came to America	S	I	250+	On Deck	Rigby
Why We Have Thanksgiving	F	HF	470	Easy Stories	Norwood House Press
Why We Measure	K	I	178	Spyglass Books	Compass Point Books
Why We Measure	D	I	88	Yellow Umbrella Books	Red Brick Learning
Why We Need Trees	T	I	2072	Vocabulary Readers	Houghton Mifflin Harcourt
Why We Need Trees	T	I	2072	Vocabulary Readers/CA	Houghton Mifflin Harcourt
Why Write?	D	I	47	Moreton, Daniel; Berger, Samantha	Scholastic
Why?	P	B	250+	DePaola, Tomie	Puffin Books

W

TITLE	LEVEL	GENRE	WORD COUNT	AUTHOR / SERIES	PUBLISHER / DISTRIBUTOR
Why?	P	I	250+	Prap, Lila	Kane/Miller Book Publishers
Why?	D	I	68	Twig	Wright Group/McGraw Hill
Wibble Wobble, Albatross!	H	I	101	Pacific Literacy	Pacific Learning
Wibble-Wobble	H	RF	263	Storyteller-Night Crickets	Wright Group/McGraw Hill
Wicked Girls	Z+	HF	250+	Hemphill, Stephanie	HarperCollins
Wicked Pirates, The	I	F	226	Sunshine	Wright Group/McGraw Hill
Wicked Weather	R	I	250+	Explorer Books-Pathfinder	National Geographic
Wicked Weather	Q	I	250+	Explorer Books-Pioneer	National Geographic
Widdermaker	O	F	1067	Schnetzler, Pattie	Carolrhoda Books
Wide Awake!	H	F	289	Leveled Literacy Intervention/Blue System	Heinemann
Wide Window, The	V	F	250+	Snicket, Lemony	Scholastic
Wide-Mouthed Frog	J	F	443	PM Stars Bridge Books	Rigby
Wide-mouthed Frog, The	E	F	121	Literacy 2000	Rigby
Widget	J	F	346	McFarland, Lyn, Rossiter, and James	Farrar, Straus, & Giroux
Widow's Broom, The	Q	F	250+	Van Allsburg, Chris	Houghton Mifflin Harcourt
Wig for Pig, A	D	F	52	Leveled Readers	Houghton Mifflin Harcourt
Wiggle and Giggle	H	RF	163	Cambridge Reading	Pearson Learning Group
*Wiggle and Waggle	J	F	250+	Arnold, Caroline	Charlesbridge
Wigglebottom	G	RF	134	Cambridge Reading	Pearson Learning Group
Wiggling Worms at Work	O	I	250+	Pfeffer, Wendy	Scholastic
Wiggly Tooth	F	RF	166	Red Rocket Readers	Flying Start Books
Wiggly Tooth, The	G	RF	148	Gear Up!	Wright Group/McGraw Hill
Wiggly Worm	G	F	115	Literacy 2000	Rigby
Wiggly, Jiggly, Joggly, Tooth, A	E	RF	61	Little Celebrations	Pearson Learning Group
Wiggly-Jiggly Line, The	I	F	128	Book Bank	Wright Group/McGraw Hill
Wilamina and the Weather Conditions	M	F	250+	Take Two Books	Wright Group/McGraw Hill
Wilbert Took a Walk	H	F	216	Ready Readers	Pearson Learning Group
Wilbur & Orville Wright: Taking Flight	W	B	250+	Trailblazer Biographies	Carolrhoda Books
*Wilbur's Wild Ride and Other Stories	E	RF	164	Story Steps	Rigby
Wild Adaptations	N	I	250+	Bridger, Maggie	Houghton Mifflin Harcourt
Wild Adaptations	P	I	924	Independent Readers Science	Houghton Mifflin Harcourt
Wild and Wooly Mammoths	P	I	250+	Aliki	HarperCollins
Wild Animal, A	J	RF	809	The Fawn	Pioneer Valley
Wild Animals	P	I	250+	Animals Are Amazing	Carus Publishing Company
Wild Animals	LB	I	10	Beginning Word Books	American Reading Company
Wild Animals	A	I	28	Belle River Readers	Belle River Readers, Inc.
Wild Animals	L	I	250+	Trackers	Pacific Learning
Wild Babies	O	I	250+	Simon, Seymour	HarperCollins
Wild Baby Animals	N	I	250+	Little Celebrations	Pearson Learning Group
Wild Bear	A	I	21	Pacific Literacy	Pacific Learning
*Wild Bird and Other Stories of Adventure	O	RF	250+	Belcher, Angie	Pacific Learning
Wild Cat Guide, The	M	I	250+	Lighthouse	Rigby
Wild Cats	Q	I	250+	Leonhardt, Alice	Steck-Vaughn
Wild Cats	N	I	250+	Wonder World	Wright Group/McGraw Hill
Wild Crayons	J	F	270	Story Box	Wright Group/McGraw Hill
Wild Culpepper Cruise, The	O	RF	250+	Paulsen, Gary	Bantam Books
*Wild Easts and the Wild West, The	K	RF	250+	Storyteller-Shooting Stars	Wright Group/McGraw Hill
Wild Girl & Gran	Q	RF	1560	Gregory, Nan	Northern Lights Books for Children
Wild Horses	R	I	250+	Action Packs	Rigby
Wild Horses	M	I	485	Gear Up!	Wright Group/McGraw Hill
Wild Magic	V	F	250+	Weatherill, Cat	Walker & Company

* Collection of short stories   # Graphic text
^ Mature content with lower level text demands

W

TITLE	LEVEL	GENRE	WORD COUNT	AUTHOR / SERIES	PUBLISHER / DISTRIBUTOR
Wild Nature	M	I	340	Gear Up!	Wright Group/McGraw Hill
Wild Parrots of San Francisco, The	M	I	250+	Books for Young Learners	Richard C. Owen
Wild Party, A	L	RF	638	Red Rocket Readers	Flying Start Books
Wild Planet	T	I	250+	InfoQuest	Rigby
Wild Ponies	R	I	250+	Explorer Books-Pathfinder	National Geographic
Wild Ponies	P	I	250+	Explorer Books-Pioneer	National Geographic
Wild Rabbits	J	I	405	Sails	Rigby
Wild Race in the Sun, A	S	RF	250+	Sails	Rigby
Wild Ride	N	RF	250+	Girlz Rock!	Mondo Publishing
Wild Ride, The	E	RF	159	The Joy Cowley Collection	Hameray Publishing Group
#Wild Ride: A Graphic Guide Adventure	T	RF	250+	O'Donnell, Liam	Orca Books
Wild Rides: Amusement Parks Around the World	S	I	250+	Explore More	Wright Group/McGraw Hill
Wild Swans, The	L	TL	754	Tales from Hans Andersen	Wright Group/McGraw Hill
Wild Turkeys	O	I	1435	Early Bird Nature Books	Lerner Publishing Group
Wild Washerwomen, The	L	F	826	Yeoman, John	Andersen Press USA
Wild Weather	F	I	174	Extreme Readers	School Specialty Publishing
Wild Weather	V	I	2411	Leveled Readers Science	Houghton Mifflin Harcourt
Wild Weather	T	I	2277	Reading Street	Pearson
Wild Weather	J	I	355	Red Rocket Readers	Flying Start Books
Wild Weather	K	I	187	Rigby Focus	Rigby
Wild Weather, Tall Tales	M	F	321	Vocabulary Readers	Houghton Mifflin Harcourt
Wild West Women	X	B	250+	Just the Facts Biographies	Lerner Publishing Group
Wild West, The	T	I	250+	Boldprint	Steck-Vaughn
Wild West, The	T	I	6300	Dominoes one	Oxford University Press
^Wild West, The: An Interactive History Adventure	W	HF	250+	You Choose Books	Capstone Press
Wild Wet Wellington Wind	I	RF	104	Pacific Literacy	Pacific Learning
Wild Wicked Winifred and Horrible Hank	L	F	250+	Popcorn	Sundance
Wild Wicked Winifred and the Pirates	L	F	250+	Popcorn	Sundance
Wild Wicked Winifred and the Sea Serpent	L	F	250+	Popcorn	Sundance
Wild Wicked Winifred and the Treasure Map	L	F	250+	Popcorn	Sundance
Wild Willie and King Kyle, Detectives	N	F	250+	Joosse, Barbara M.	Bantam Books
Wild Wind, The	H	F	246	Story Box	Wright Group/McGraw Hill
Wild Winds and Thunderclouds	R	I	250+	Explore More	Wright Group/McGraw Hill
Wild Wings	U	RF	250+	Lewis, Gill	Atheneum Books
Wild World of Sports	S	I	250+	Boldprint	Steck-Vaughn
Wild, Wet and Windy	S	I	250+	WorldScapes	ETA/Cuisenaire
Wild, Wild West, The	O	F	250+	Stilton, Geronimo	Scholastic
Wild, Wild Wolves	M	I	250+	Milton, Joyce	Random House
Wild, Wooly Child, The	J	F	315	Read Alongs	Rigby
Wilde Street Club and Molly, The	M	RF	965	Sunshine	Wright Group/McGraw Hill
Wilde Street Club and the Duck Man, The	M	RF	1057	Sunshine	Wright Group/McGraw Hill
Wildebeest	L	I	250+	A Day in the Life: Grassland Animals	Heinemann Library
Wilderness Challenge	U	I	250+	WorldScapes	ETA/Cuisenaire
Wilderness Road, 1775, The	V	I	250+	Let Freedom Ring	Capstone Press
^Wilderness Road, The	Q	I	250+	On Deck	Rigby
Wilderness Talk	Q	RF	250+	Pair-It Books	Steck-Vaughn
Wildfire!	R	I	1323	Vocabulary Readers	Houghton Mifflin Harcourt
Wildfire!	R	I	1323	Vocabulary Readers/CA	Houghton Mifflin Harcourt
Wildfires	O	I	250+	A True Book	Children's Press

W

TITLE	LEVEL	GENRE	WORD COUNT	AUTHOR / SERIES	PUBLISHER / DISTRIBUTOR
Wildfires	M	I	174	Earth in Action	Capstone Press
Wildflower Girl	T	HF	250+	Conlon-McKenna, Marita	The O'Brien Press
Wildlife	T	RF	250+	DeFelice, Cynthia	Farrar, Straus, & Giroux
Wildlife	J	I	250+	Independent Readers Science	Houghton Mifflin Harcourt
Wildlife	J	I	145	Independent Readers Social Studies	Houghton Mifflin Harcourt
Wildlife Buffet, A	J	RF	373	Reading Street	Pearson
Wildlife Detectives	T	I	250+	Connectors	Pacific Learning
Wildlife Helpers	G	I	132	Twig	Wright Group/McGraw Hill
Wildlife in the City	S	I	250+	PM Plus Nonfiction	Rigby
Wildlife on Film - Telling a Story	T	I	250+	Connectors	Pacific Learning
Wildlife Photographer Frank Greenway	T	I	250+	iOpeners	Pearson Learning Group
Wildlife Visit	N	I	806	Red Rocket Readers	Flying Start Books
Wildlife Watching	O	I	250+	Wonder World	Wright Group/McGraw Hill
Wilfrid Gordon McDonald Partridge	N	RF	250+	Fox, Mem	Kane/Miller Book Publishers
Wilfrid Laurier	X	B	250+	The Canadians	Fitzhenry & Whiteside
Will and Orv	N	B	1505	On My Own History	Lerner Publishing Group
Will and Squill	K	F	501	Clark, Emma Chichester	Carolrhoda Books
Will It Float?	C	I	43	Gear Up!	Wright Group/McGraw Hill
Will It Rain on the Parade?	H	RF	102	Wonder World	Wright Group/McGraw Hill
Will on a Jet	E	RF	53	Reading Street	Pearson
Will Power	I	RF	250+	Rigby Literacy	Rigby
Will Rogers	O	B	250+	Schott, Jane A.	Carolrhoda Books
Will Smith	V	B	250+	Just the Facts Biographies	Lerner Publishing Group
Will Smith: The Funny, Funky, and Confident Fresh Prince	R	B	250+	High Five Reading	Red Brick Learning
Will to Survive, The	U	I	250+	Power Up!	Steck-Vaughn
Will We Miss Them? Endangered Species	N	I	250+	Wright, Alexandra	Charlesbridge
Will We See Animals?	E	I	86	Reading Street	Pearson
Will You Play With Me?	D	RF	84	Book Bus	Creative Edge
Will You Play With Me?	E	RF	149	On Our Way to English	Rigby
Will You Play with Us?	D	RF	62	Bookshop	Mondo Publishing
Will You Play?	D	F	96	Sun Sprouts	ETA/Cuisenaire
Will You Show Me How?	H	RF	263	The Rowland Reading Program Library	Rowland Reading Foundation
Will You Sign Here, John Hancock?	T	B	250+	Fritz, Jean	Scholastic
William Bradford and Plymouth: A Colony Grows	R	B	250+	The Library of the Pilgrims	Rosen Publishing Group
William Henry Harrison	U	B	250+	Profiles of the Presidents	Compass Point Books
William Henry Harrison: Ninth President	R	B	250+	Getting to Know the U.S. Presidents	Children's Press
William Howard Taft	U	B	250+	Profiles of the Presidents	Compass Point Books
William Howard Taft: Twenty-seventh President	R	B	250+	Getting to Know the U.S. Presidents	Children's Press
William Jefferson Clinton	U	B	250+	Profiles of the Presidents	Compass Point Books
William McKinley	U	B	250+	Profiles of the Presidents	Compass Point Books
William McKinley: Twenty-fifth President	R	B	250+	Getting to Know the U.S. Presidents	Children's Press
William Penn	T	B	250+	Amazing Americans	Wright Group/McGraw Hill
William Penn	V	B	2200	Independent Readers Social Studies	Houghton Mifflin Harcourt
William Penn: A Life of Tolerance	O	B	584	Pull Ahead Books	Lerner Publishing Group
#William Penn: Founder of Pennsylvania	S	B	250+	Graphic Library	Capstone Press
William Penn: Founder of the Pennsylvania Colony	V	B	250+	Let Freedom Ring	Capstone Press
William Problem, The	S	RF	250+	Baker, Barbara	Puffin Books

* Collection of short stories   # Graphic text
^ Mature content with lower level text demands

W

TITLE	LEVEL	GENRE	WORD COUNT	AUTHOR / SERIES	PUBLISHER / DISTRIBUTOR
William Shakespeare	Z	B	9135	Oxford Bookworms Library	Oxford University Press
William Shakespeare: His Life and Times	Y	B	250+	McDermott, Kristen & Berk, Ari	Candlewick Press
William Tell	I	TL	127	Jumbled Tumbled Tales & Rhymes	Rigby
*#William Tell and Other Stories	R	TL	2088	Dominoes starter	Oxford University Press
#William Tell: One Against an Empire	W	TL	4212	Graphic Myths and Legends	Lerner Publishing Group
William, Where Are You?	F	F	239	Gerstein, Mordicai	Crown Publishers
William's Journal	N	HF	250+	Early Connections	Benchmark Education
Williams Sisters, The	J	I	318	Leveled Readers	Houghton Mifflin Harcourt
Williams Sisters, The	J	I	318	Leveled Readers/CA	Houghton Mifflin Harcourt
Williams Sisters, The	J	I	318	Leveled Readers/TX	Houghton Mifflin Harcourt
William's Skateboard	G	RF	100	Windmill Books	Wright Group/McGraw Hill
William's Wet Week	F	RF	188	Haley, Patty	Kaeden Books
William's Wheelchair Race	J	RF	279	Sunshine	Wright Group/McGraw Hill
Williamsburg	V	I	250+	Cornerstones of Freedom	Children's Press
Williamsburg	U	I	250+	We The People	Compass Point Books
Willie Covan Loved to Dance!	T	B	250+	Bookshop	Mondo Publishing
Willie Mays	J	B	380	Leveled Readers	Houghton Mifflin Harcourt
Willie Mays	J	B	380	Leveled Readers/CA	Houghton Mifflin Harcourt
Willie Mays	J	B	380	Leveled Readers/TX	Houghton Mifflin Harcourt
Willie McLean and the Civil War Surrender	P	HF	1997	On My Own History	Lerner Publishing Group
Willie the Slowpoke	G	F	125	First Start	Troll Associates
Willie's Wonderful Pet	I	RF	315	Cebulash, Mel	Scholastic
Williwaw!	V	RF	250+	Bodett, Tom	Alfred A. Knopf
Willoughbys, The	U	F	250+	Lowry, Lois	Yearling Books
Willow Pattern, The	P	TL	250+	Action Packs	Rigby
Willows and Whirligigs	V	I	250+	Rigby Literacy	Rigby
Willy the Helper	D	RF	79	Little Readers	Houghton Mifflin Harcourt
Willy the Scrub	O	RF	4190	McEwan, Jamie	Darby Creek Publishing
Willy the Wizard	C	F	42	Learn to Read	Creative Teaching Press
Willy's Hats	E	RF	65	Stewart, Josie.; Salem, Lynn	Continental Press
Wilma Mankiller	P	B	250+	Lowery, Linda	Carolrhoda Books
Wilma Rudolph	N	B	204	First Biographies	Capstone Press
Wilma Rudolph	N	B	250+	On My Own Biography	Lerner Publishing Group
Wilma Rudolph	U	B	250+	Sports Heroes and Legends	Lerner Publishing Group
Wilma Unlimited: How Wilma Rudolph Became the World's Fastest Woman	Q	B	250+	Krull, Kathleen	Scholastic
Wilma's Wagon	D	RF	48	Ready Readers	Pearson Learning Group
Wimpy Kid Movie Diary, The: How Greg Heffley Went Hollywood	T	I	250+	Kinney, Jeff	Amulet Books
Win a Prize!	F	RF	235	PM Math Readers	Rigby
Wind	E	RF	89	Ready to Read	Pearson Learning Group
Wind	G	I	154	Red Rocket Readers	Flying Start Books
Wind	Q	I	250+	Theme Sets	National Geographic
Wind	L	I	430	Vocabulary Readers	Houghton Mifflin Harcourt
Wind	L	I	430	Vocabulary Readers/CA	Houghton Mifflin Harcourt
Wind and Rain	F	I	84	Factivity Series	Pearson Learning Group
Wind and Storms	K	I	868	Sunshine	Wright Group/McGraw Hill
Wind and Sun	G	TL	170	Literacy 2000	Rigby
Wind and Sun	I	TL	238	Sunshine	Wright Group/McGraw Hill
*Wind and the Sun and Other Stories, The	J	F	250+	New Way Orange	Steck-Vaughn
Wind and the Sun, The	I	TL	350	Leveled Literacy Intervention/ Blue System	Heinemann
Wind and the Sun, The	K	TL	399	Leveled Readers	Houghton Mifflin Harcourt

W

TITLE	LEVEL	GENRE	WORD COUNT	AUTHOR / SERIES	PUBLISHER / DISTRIBUTOR
Wind and the Sun, The	I	TL	189	Pair-It Turn and Learn	Steck-Vaughn
Wind and the Sun, The: An Aesop Fable	G	TL	234	Rigby Literacy	Rigby
Wind and Water: Two Great Powers	U	I	2567	Independent Readers Social Studies	Houghton Mifflin Harcourt
Wind at Work, The	Q	I	250+	Literacy by Design	Rigby
Wind Blew, The	J	RF	169	Hutchins, Pat	Puffin Books
Wind Blows Strong, The	E	RF	114	Sunshine	Wright Group/McGraw Hill
Wind Blows, The	B	RF	90	First Stories	Pacific Learning
Wind Blows, The	C	RF	38	Learn to Read	Creative Teaching Press
Wind Eagle, The	K	TL	375	Avenues	Hampton Brown
Wind Eagle, The	K	TL	375	Wonders	Hampton Brown
Wind in the Door, A	V	F	250+	L'Engle, Madeleine	Bantam Books
Wind in the Pines	O	I	919	Leveled Readers/TX	Houghton Mifflin Harcourt
Wind in the Willows	S	F	11540	Oxford Bookworms Library	Oxford University Press
Wind Instruments	M	I	391	Vocabulary Readers	Houghton Mifflin Harcourt
Wind Instruments	M	I	391	Vocabulary Readers/CA	Houghton Mifflin Harcourt
Wind Power	V	I	250+	Energy at Work	Capstone Press
Wind Power	J	I	103	Pacific Literacy	Pacific Learning
Wind Power	I	I	116	Windows on Literacy	National Geographic
Wind Surfing	D	RF	224	Sunshine	Wright Group/McGraw Hill
Wind That Would Not Blow, The	M	TL	250+	Kunari, Anna	Hampton Brown
Wind, The	D	I	82	Big Cat	Pacific Learning
Wind, The	E	I	36	Discovery Links	Newbridge
Wind, The	C	I	46	Gear Up!	Wright Group/McGraw Hill
Wind, The	L	I	445	Leveled Readers	Houghton Mifflin Harcourt
Wind, The	L	I	445	Leveled Readers/CA	Houghton Mifflin Harcourt
Wind, The	L	I	445	Leveled Readers/TX	Houghton Mifflin Harcourt
Wind, The	E	I	64	Pacific Literacy	Pacific Learning
Wind, The	K	I	179	Spyglass Books	Compass Point Books
Wind, The	F	I	84	Voyages	SRA/McGraw Hill
Wind, The	D	RF	34	Wonder World	Wright Group/McGraw Hill
Wind, Water and Ice	R	I	1829	Independent Readers Science	Houghton Mifflin Harcourt
Wind, Water, and Sunlight	K	I	113	Windows on Literacy	National Geographic
Windchaser (Dinotopia)	T	F	250+	Ciencin, Scott	Random House
Windmill, The	T	F	250+	Book Blazers	ETA/Cuisenaire
Windmills	S	I	783	Independent Readers Science	Houghton Mifflin Harcourt
Window to the Past	O	F	990	Springboard	Wright Group/McGraw Hill
Window, The	V	RF	250+	Ingold, Jeanette	Harcourt Trade
Windows to the Past	N	F	749	Gear Up!	Wright Group/McGraw Hill
Windows to the Past	R	I	943	Reading Street	Pearson
Windows, Rings and Grapes - a Look at Different Shapes	N	I	505	Math Is CATegorical	Millbrook Press
Windy	B	I	27	Weather	Lerner Publishing Group
Windy Day, A	E	I	53	Pebble Books	Capstone Press
Windy Day, A	E	I	85	Weather	Lerner Publishing Group
Windy Ways	G	I	97	Independent Readers Science	Houghton Mifflin Harcourt
Winesburg, Ohio	Z+	RF	250+	Anderson, Sherwood	Random House
Wing High, Goofah	Q	RF	250+	Literacy 2000	Rigby
Wing Nut	T	RF	250+	Auch, MJ	Square Fish
Wing Nuts: Screwy Haiku	N	F	244	Janeczko, Paul & Lewis, J. Patrick	Little Brown and Company
Winged and Toothless: The Adventure of Pteranodon	N	I	250+	Dinosaur World	Picture Window Books
Winged Cat, The: A Tale of Ancient Egypt	U	TL	250+	Lattimore, Deborah Nourse	HarperCollins

W

* Collection of short stories   # Graphic text
^ Mature content with lower level text demands

TITLE	LEVEL	GENRE	WORD COUNT	AUTHOR / SERIES	PUBLISHER / DISTRIBUTOR
Winging It	U	I	250+	iOpeners	Pearson Learning Group
Wingman	O	F	250+	Pinkwater, Daniel	Bantam Books
Wingman on Ice	Q	RF	250+	Christopher, Matt	Little Brown and Company
Wings	B	I	22	Animal Traits	Lerner Publishing Group
Wings	W	I	250+	Boldprint	Steck-Vaughn
Wings	Q	F	250+	Brittain, Bill	HarperTrophy
Wings	F	I	109	Explorations	Okapi Educational Materials
Wings	F	I	109	Explorations	Eleanor Curtain Publishing
Wings	LB	I	14	KinderReaders	Rigby
Wings	M	F	250+	Myers, Christopher	Scholastic
Wings	A	I	24	Rigby Literacy	Rigby
Wings	A	I	20	Rigby StarQuest	Rigby
Wings	C	I	85	Sails	Rigby
Wings	G	I	152	Spot the Difference	Heinemann Library
Wings	W	TL	250+	Yolen, Jane; Nolan, Dennis	Harcourt Brace
^Wings Above the Waves	T	F	250+	Dragonblood	Stone Arch Books
Wings and Things	C	I	41	Reach	National Geographic
Wings for a Day	T	F	1842	Leveled Readers	Houghton Mifflin Harcourt
Wings!	D	I	95	Vocabulary Readers	Houghton Mifflin Harcourt
Wings!	D	I	95	Vocabulary Readers/CA	Houghton Mifflin Harcourt
Wings: A Fairy Tale	X	F	250+	Baker, E.D.	Bloomsbury Children's Books
Winking, Blinking, Wiggling, and Waggling	M	I	250+	DK Readers	DK Publishing
Winklepoo the Wicked	M	F	1614	Sunshine	Wright Group/McGraw Hill
Winner, The	J	RF	585	Gear Up!	Wright Group/McGraw Hill
Winners	E	RF	114	Joy Starters	Pearson Learning Group
Winner's Guide to Staying Fit, A	S	I	250+	Power Up!	Steck-Vaughn
Winners Take All	Q	RF	250+	Bowen, Fred	Peachtree
Winnie Dancing on Her Own	M	RF	250+	Jacobson, Jennifer Richard	Houghton Mifflin Harcourt
Winnie Finn, Worm Farmer	L	RF	250+	Brendler, Carol	Farrar, Straus, & Giroux
Winnie Wakes Up	D	RF	24	Brand New Readers	Candlewick Press
Winnie's Bedtime	C	RF	38	Brand New Readers	Candlewick Press
Winnie's Walk	C	RF	23	Brand New Readers	Candlewick Press
Winnie's War	V	HF	250+	Moss, Jenny	Walker & Company
Winning Combination, A	X	RF	2436	Leveled Readers	Houghton Mifflin Harcourt
Winning Combination, A	X	RF	2436	Leveled Readers/CA	Houghton Mifflin Harcourt
Winning Combination, A	X	RF	2436	Leveled Readers/TX	Houghton Mifflin Harcourt
Winning Edge	U	I	250+	The News	Richard C. Owen
Winning Hit, The	G	RF	274	Leveled Readers	Houghton Mifflin Harcourt
Winning Hit, The	G	RF	274	Leveled Readers/CA	Houghton Mifflin Harcourt
Winning Hit, The	G	RF	274	Leveled Readers/TX	Houghton Mifflin Harcourt
Winning Team, A	X	RF	2418	Leveled Readers	Houghton Mifflin Harcourt
Winning Team, A	X	RF	2418	Leveled Readers/CA	Houghton Mifflin Harcourt
Winning Team, A	X	RF	2418	Leveled Readers/TX	Houghton Mifflin Harcourt
*Winning Words: Sports Stories and Photographs	T	RF	250+	Smith, Charles R. Jr.	Candlewick Press
Winslow Homer, American Painter	N	I	348	Independent Readers Social Studies	Houghton Mifflin Harcourt
Winston Churchill	V	B	250+	Primary Source Readers	Teacher Created Materials
^Winston Churchill: Saving England in Its Darkest Hour	U	B	250+	Hameray Biography Series	Hameray Publishing Group
Winter	C	I	49	Carousel Readers	Pearson Learning Group
Winter	E	I	56	Discovery Links	Newbridge
Winter	C	I	54	Foundations	Wright Group/McGraw Hill

W

TITLE	LEVEL	GENRE	WORD COUNT	AUTHOR / SERIES	PUBLISHER / DISTRIBUTOR
Winter	B	I	79	Leveled Readers	Houghton Mifflin Harcourt
Winter	B	I	79	Leveled Readers/CA	Houghton Mifflin Harcourt
Winter	B	I	79	Leveled Readers/TX	Houghton Mifflin Harcourt
Winter	I	I	240	Pebble Books	Capstone Press
Winter	D	RF	33	Reading Street	Pearson
Winter	E	I	58	Seasons	Lerner Publishing Group
Winter	H	I	172	Storyteller-Setting Sun	Wright Group/McGraw Hill
Winter	C	RF	48	Tiny Treasures	Pioneer Valley
#Winter at Valley Forge	T	I	250+	Graphic Library	Capstone Press
Winter Bed, A	E	RF	91	Reading Street	Pearson
Winter Camping	M	I	250+	The Rowland Reading Program Library	Rowland Reading Foundation
Winter Days in the Big Woods	J	HF	250+	Wilder, Laura Ingalls	HarperCollins
Winter Fun	LB	RF	13	Teacher's Choice Series	Pearson Learning Group
^Winter Hawk Star	W	RF	250+	Orca Sports	Orca Books
Winter Holidays	O	RF	1706	Reading Street	Pearson
Winter in Alaska	O	I	347	Vocabulary Readers	Houghton Mifflin Harcourt
Winter Is Here	D	I	55	Weinberger, Kimberly	Scholastic
Winter Is Here	E	I	24	Windows on Literacy	National Geographic
Winter King, Summer Queen	L	F	250+	Lister, Mary	Barefoot Books
Winter on the Farm	J	HF	250+	Wilder, Laura Ingalls	HarperCollins
Winter on the Ice	L	F	506	PM Plus Story Books	Rigby
Winter Recess	D	RF	87	Emergent Books	Pioneer Valley
Winter Room, The	U	RF	250+	Paulsen, Gary	Bantam Books
Winter Sleep	C	F	92	Leveled Readers	Houghton Mifflin Harcourt
Winter Sleep	C	F	92	Leveled Readers/CA	Houghton Mifflin Harcourt
Winter Sleeps	F	RF	158	Reading Corners	Pearson Learning Group
Winter Solstice, The	Q	I	250+	Jackson, Ellen	Millbrook Press
Winter Sports: Fun on Ice and Snow	R	I	250+	Explore More	Wright Group/McGraw Hill
Winter Sunshine	N	I	250+	Wonder World	Wright Group/McGraw Hill
Winter Survival	O	I	250+	Literacy Tree	Rigby
Winter to Spring	I	I	231	Early Explorers	Benchmark Education
Winter Trees	N	RF	250+	Gerber, Carole	Charlesbridge
Winter Vacation	A	RF	24	Leveled Readers	Houghton Mifflin Harcourt
Winter Vacation	A	F	24	Leveled Readers/CA	Houghton Mifflin Harcourt
Winter Weather Fun	C	I	71	Early Connections	Benchmark Education
Winter Wind, The	H	F	250+	Momentum Literacy Program	Troll Associates
Winter Wind, The	F	F	234	Springboard	Wright Group/McGraw Hill
Winter Wonderland, A	H	RF	230	Literacy by Design	Rigby
Winter Woollies	K	I	289	Storyteller Nonfiction	Wright Group/McGraw Hill
Winter, Spring, Summer, Fall	F	RF	102	Appleton-Smith, Laura	Flyleaf Publishing
Winterdance: The Fine Madness of Running the Iditarod	W	B	250+	Paulsen, Gary	Harcourt Trade
Wintergirls	Z+	RF	250+	Anderson, Laurie Halse	Speak
Winter's Song	H	RF	233	Ready Readers	Pearson Learning Group
^Wipeout	Q	RF	250+	West, J.	Stone Arch Books
^Wired	U	RF	250+	Orca Currents	Orca Books
Wired World: A Short History of the Internet	U	I	1527	Leveled Readers Social Studies	Houghton Mifflin Harcourt
Wireless Technology	Z	I	6323	Cool Science	Lerner Publishing Group
Wisconsin	T	I	250+	Hello U.S.A.	Lerner Publishing Group
Wisconsin	R	I	250+	This Land Is Your Land	Compass Point Books
Wisconsin: Facts and Symbols	O	I	250+	The States and Their Symbols	Capstone Press
Wise Blackbird, The	I	F	507	Leveled Literacy Intervention/ Blue System	Heinemann

* Collection of short stories   # Graphic text
^ Mature content with lower level text demands

W

TITLE	LEVEL	GENRE	WORD COUNT	AUTHOR / SERIES	PUBLISHER / DISTRIBUTOR
Wise Eyes Club, The	K	RF	537	Springboard	Wright Group/McGraw Hill
Wise Old Turtle, The	K	TL	250+	World Quest Adventures	World Quest Learning
Wise Queen Catherine	P	TL	250+	HSP/Harcourt Trophies	Harcourt, Inc.
*Wish Fish, The	P	TL	250+	Action Packs	Rigby
Wish Giver, The	T	F	250+	Brittain, Bill	HarperTrophy
Wish House, The	Z+	RF	250+	Rees, Celia	Candlewick Press
Wish on a Unicorn	T	RF	250+	Hesse, Karen	Penguin Group
Wishes Don't Come True	M	RF	250+	Bookshop	Mondo Publishing
Wishing	O	RF	251	Tiller, Ruth	Peachtree
Wishing for a Horse	D	RF	105	Carousel Readers	Pearson Learning Group
Wishing for Fishing	H	RF	250+	Phonics Readers Plus	Steck-Vaughn
Wishing Shell, The	S	TL	250+	WorldScapes	ETA/Cuisenaire
Wishing with Pennies	B	F	61	Early Explorers	Benchmark Education
Wishy-Washy Day	E	F	65	Story Basket	Wright Group/McGraw Hill
Witch Catcher	U	F	250+	Hahn, Mary Downing	Sandpiper Books
Witch Child	Z	HF	250+	Rees, Celia	Candlewick Press
Witch Hunt: It Happened in Salem Village	Q	I	250+	Krensky, Stephen	Random House
Witch of Blackbird Pond, The	W	HF	250+	Speare, Elizabeth George	Bantam Books
Witch of Clattering Shaws, The	X	F	250+	Aiken, Joan	Yearling Books
*Witch of Fourth Street, The	S	HF	250+	Levoy, Myron	Language for Learning Assoc.
Witch Who Was Afraid of Witches, The	K	F	250+	Low, Alice	HarperTrophy
Witch Who Went for a Walk, The	E	F	250+	Easy Stories	Norwood House Press
Witch, Witch Come to My Party	G	F	148	Druce, Arden	Child's Play Ltd
Witchcraft of Salem Village, The	U	I	250+	Jackson, Shirley	Random House
Witches Don't Do Backflips	M	F	250+	Dadey, Debbie; Jones, Marcia Thornton	Scholastic
Witches' Kitchen, The	X	F	250+	Williams, Allen	Little Brown and Company
Witches of Pendle, The	Y	HF	5730	Oxford Bookworms Library	Oxford University Press
Witches of Worm, The	V	F	250+	Snyder, Zilpha K.	Random House
Witches, The	R	F	250+	Dahl, Roald	Penguin Group
Witch's Cat	P	F	250+	Chew, Ruth	Scholastic
Witch's Guide to Cooking with Children, The	T	F	250+	McGowan, Keith	Henry Holt & Co.
Witch's Haircut, The	G	F	135	Windmill Books	Wright Group/McGraw Hill
With a Dance and a Roar	P	I	663	Leveled Readers	Houghton Mifflin Harcourt
*With Courage: Seven Women Who Changed America	T	B	250+	Bookshop	Mondo Publishing
With Every Drop of Blood	Y	HF	250+	Collier, James Lincoln and Collier, Christopher	Laurel-Leaf Books
With Help From Abuelo	O	RF	2576	In Step Readers	Rigby
With Love, J: Letters from the Past	S	RF	250+	Harcourt Trophies	Harcourt, Inc.
With My Mom and Dad	C	I	63	Early Connections	Benchmark Education
With Open Hands: A Story about Biddy Mason	R	B	8691	Creative Minds Biographies	Carolrhoda Books
Withered Arm, The	W	F	5735	Oxford Bookworms Library	Oxford University Press
Within Reach: My Everest Story	X	B	250+	Pfetzer, Mark & Galvin, Jack	Scholastic
Witness	Z	HF	250+	Hesse, Karen	Scholastic
Wiz	D	F	76	Voyages	SRA/McGraw Hill
Wizard and the Rainbow, The	K	F	250+	Sunshine	Wright Group/McGraw Hill
Wizard and Wart at Sea	J	F	250+	Smith, Janice Lee	HarperTrophy
Wizard Came to Visit, A	K	F	250+	Sunshine	Wright Group/McGraw Hill
Wizard Heir, The	Z	F	250+	Chima, Cinda Williams	Hyperion
Wizard of Dark Street, The	V	F	250+	Odyssey, Shawn Thomas	Egmont USA
Wizard of Earthsea, A	Z	F	250+	Le Guin, Ursula K.	Bantam Books
Wizard of Oz, The	U	F	250+	Baum, L. Frank	Scholastic

W

TITLE	LEVEL	GENRE	WORD COUNT	AUTHOR / SERIES	PUBLISHER / DISTRIBUTOR
Wizard of Oz, The	L	TL	903	Hunia, Fran	Ladybird Books
Wizard of Oz, The	T	F	5440	Oxford Bookworms Library	Oxford University Press
Wizard of Sound: A Story About Thomas Edison, The	R	B	8084	Creative Minds Biographies	Carolrhoda Books
Wizards and Witches	U	I	250+	Fantasy Chronicles	Lerner Publishing Group
Wizards Don't Need Computers	M	F	250+	Dadey, Debbie; Jones, Marcia Thornton	Scholastic
Wobbly Tooth, The	D	RF	102	Literacy 2000	Rigby
Wobbly Tooth, The	F	RF	74	Oxford Reading Tree	Oxford University Press
Wole Soyinka	X	B	1951	Leveled Readers Social Studies	Houghton Mifflin Harcourt
Wolf and the Kids, The	G	TL	241	Storyworlds	Heinemann
Wolf and the Old Woman, The	I	TL	250+	Voyages	SRA/McGraw Hill
Wolf and the Seven Little Kids	L	TL	250+	Hunia, Fran	Ladybird Books
Wolf and the Seven Little Kids, The	J	TL	254	Literacy Tree	Rigby
Wolf Island (The Demonata Series)	Z+	F	250+	Shan, Darren	Little Brown and Company
Wolf Master	S	RF	250+	Storyteller-Whispering Pines	Wright Group/McGraw Hill
Wolf Pie	M	F	250+	Seabrooke, Brenda	Clarion Books
Wolf Song	J	RF	130	Books for Young Learners	Richard C. Owen
Wolf Spiders	N	I	250+	Spiders	Capstone Press
Wolf Stalker	T	RF	250+	Mysteries in Our National Parks	National Geographic
Wolf Talk	H	I	159	Instant Readers	Harcourt School Publishers
Wolf Vs. Elk	L	I	250+	Predator Vs. Prey	Raintree
Wolf Who Cried Boy, The	M	F	250+	Hartman, Bob	Scholastic
Wolf, The	S	I	250+	Dahl, Michael	Red Brick Learning
Wolf, The	Z+	RF	250+	Herrick, Steven	Front Street
Wolfgang Amadeus Mozart: Musical Genius	N	B	250+	Rookie Biographies	Children's Press
Wolfman Sam	O	RF	250+	Levy, Elizabeth	HarperTrophy
Wolfmen Don't Hula Dance	M	RF	250+	Dadey, Debbie; Jones, Marcia Thornton	Scholastic
Wolf's Cake	I	F	250+	Sunshine	Wright Group/McGraw Hill
Wolf's Chicken Stew, The	J	F	250+	Leveled Readers Language Support	Houghton Mifflin Harcourt
Wolf's First Deer	M	RF	434	Book Bank	Wright Group/McGraw Hill
Wolverines	P	I	2089	Animal Scavengers	Lerner Publishing Group
Wolves	P	I	1805	Animal Predators	Lerner Publishing Group
Wolves	L	F	116	Gravett, Emily	Simon & Schuster
Wolves	Q	I	250+	Literacy 2000	Rigby
Wolves	I	I	188	Pair-It Books	Steck-Vaughn
Wolves	N	I	250+	PM Animal Facts: Silver	Rigby
Wolves	N	RF	250+	PM Plus Chapter Books	Rigby
Wolves	A	I	70	Readlings/ Predator Animals	American Reading Company
Wolves	I	I	233	Sails	Rigby
Wolves	E	I	68	Seedlings	Continental Press
Wolves	U	I	250+	The Untamed World	Steck-Vaughn
Wolves	F	I	132	Twig	Wright Group/McGraw Hill
Wolves	Q	RF	250+	Voyages	SRA/McGraw Hill
Wolves	H	I	95	Woodland Animals	Capstone Press
Wolves Have Pups	M	I	250+	Animals and Their Young	Compass Point Books
Wolves of Willoughby Chase, The	V	HF	250+	Aiken, Joan	Bantam Books
Woman and the Tiny Bird, The	G	TL	198	PM Stars	Rigby
*Woman Hollering Creek and Other Stories	Z	RF	250+	Cisneros, Sandra	Random House
Woman Who Flummoxed the Fairies, The	O	TL	250+	Forest, Heather	Harcourt Trade
Woman Who Fooled the Fairies, The	K	TL	794	Big Cat	Pacific Learning
Woman Who Outshone the Sun, The	M	TL	250+	Martinez, Alejandro Cruz	Children's Press

* Collection of short stories   # Graphic text
^ Mature content with lower level text demands

TITLE	LEVEL	GENRE	WORD COUNT	AUTHOR / SERIES	PUBLISHER / DISTRIBUTOR
Wombats	J	I	166	Australian Animals	Capstone Press
Women at Work	G	I	112	Foundations	Wright Group/McGraw Hill
Women at Work in the West	Q	I	1428	Leveled Readers	Houghton Mifflin Harcourt
Women at Work in the West	Q	I	1428	Leveled Readers/CA	Houghton Mifflin Harcourt
Women in the Renaissance	W	I	250+	Navigators Social Studies Series	Benchmark Education
Women in the Vietnam War	U	I	848	Independent Readers Social Studies	Houghton Mifflin Harcourt
*Women Inventors	O	B	250+	Blashfield, Jean	Red Brick Learning
Women Inventors	P	I	996	Leveled Readers Science	Houghton Mifflin Harcourt
Women of Courage	U	I	250+	Boldprint	Steck-Vaughn
Women of the American Revolution	U	B	250+	Bookshop	Mondo Publishing
Women of Valor	U	B	250+	Real Lives	Troll Associates
Women Pioneers in Medicine	T	I	2664	Independent Readers Science	Houghton Mifflin Harcourt
Women Pioneers of Medicine	R	B	2018	Leveled Readers Science	Houghton Mifflin Harcourt
Women Space Pioneers	X	B	250+	Just the Facts Biographies	Lerner Publishing Group
Women Suffrage Movement, 1848-1920, The	V	I	250+	Let Freedom Ring	Capstone Press
Women Who Dared	U	B	250+	Navigators Biography Series	Benchmark Education
*Women Who Made a Difference	O	B	830	Reading Street	Pearson
Women Who Shaped the West	V	B	250+	Cornerstones of Freedom	Children's Press
Women Work for Change	Q	I	250+	Reading Expeditions	National Geographic
Women Writers: Voices from the 1800s	T	I	2535	Independent Readers Social Studies	Houghton Mifflin Harcourt
Women's Baseball League	W	I	2641	Vocabulary Readers	Houghton Mifflin Harcourt
Women's Baseball League	W	I	2641	Vocabulary Readers/CA	Houghton Mifflin Harcourt
Women's Baseball League	W	I	2641	Vocabulary Readers/TX	Houghton Mifflin Harcourt
Women's Movement, The	W	I	2439	Reading Street	Pearson
#Women's Right to Vote	V	I	250+	Cartoon Nation	Capstone Press
Women's Right to Vote	V	I	250+	Cornerstones of Freedom	Children's Press
Women's Voting Rights	V	I	250+	Cornerstones of Freedom	Children's Press
Wonder Horse: The True Story of the World's Smartest Horse	P	HF	250+	McCully, Emily Arnold	Henry Holt & Co.
Wonder Kid Meets the Evil Lunch Snatcher	M	RF	250+	Duncan, Lois	Little Brown and Company
Wonder of Bald Eagles, The	M	I	250+	Soar To Success	Houghton Mifflin Harcourt
Wonder of Our Solar System, The	S	I	250+	Science Readers	Teacher Created Materials
Wonder of Outer Space, The	S	I	250+	Science Readers	Teacher Created Materials
Wonder of the Winds, The	T	I	250+	Connectors	Pacific Learning
Wonder of Whales, The	N	I	250+	Book Treks	Pearson Learning Group
Wonder of Wolves, The	M	I	250+	Soar To Success	Houghton Mifflin Harcourt
Wonderer, The	M	RF	250+	Rigby Flying Colors	Rigby
Wonderful Alexander and the Catwings	N	F	250+	Le Guin, Ursula	Scholastic
Wonderful Ears	I	I	1017	Sunshine Science	Wright Group/McGraw Hill
Wonderful Eyes	M	I	1070	Sunshine Science	Wright Group/McGraw Hill
*Wonderful Sky Boat, The: And Other Native American Tales of the Southeast	S	TL	250+	Curry, Jane Louise	Simon & Schuster
*Wonderful Story of Henry Sugar, The: And Six More	U	F	250+	Dahl, Roald	Penguin Group
Wonderful Things	F	RF	98	Early Readers	Compass Point Books
Wonderful Water	C	I	33	Gear Up!	Wright Group/McGraw Hill
Wonderful Water Cycle, The	L	I	250+	On Our Way to English	Rigby
*Wonderful Women of Science, The	T	B	2616	Reading Street	Pearson
Wonderful World of Birds, The	M	I	1180	Reading Street	Pearson
Wonderful World of Camouflage, The	U	I	1792	Vocabulary Readers	Houghton Mifflin Harcourt
Wonderful World of Camouflage, The	U	I	1792	Vocabulary Readers/CA	Houghton Mifflin Harcourt
Wonderful Worms	J	I	190	Glaser, Linda	Millbrook Press

W

TITLE	LEVEL	GENRE	WORD COUNT	AUTHOR / SERIES	PUBLISHER / DISTRIBUTOR
Wonderful Worms	K	I	343	Rigby Flying Colors	Rigby
Wonderland	Z+	RF	250+	Nadin, Joanna	Candlewick Press
Wonders of the World	N	I	250+	Sunshine	Wright Group/McGraw Hill
Wonders of the World	P	I	250+	Trackers	Pacific Learning
Wonders of the World - Megastructures	T	I	250+	Connectors	Pacific Learning
Wonders of Water	T	I	250+	Reading Expeditions	National Geographic
Won't Take No for an Answer!	U	B	250+	Bookshop	Mondo Publishing
Wood	G	I	106	Materials	Lerner Publishing Group
Wood	B	I	26	Twig	Wright Group/McGraw Hill
Wood	E	I	48	Windows on Literacy	National Geographic
Wood and Other Materials	G	I	97	Discovery World	Rigby
Wood Frog	O	I	250+	Life Cycles	Creative Teaching Press
Wood Stork Swamp	N	RF	250+	Orbit Double Takes	Pacific Learning
Woodcutter and the Bear, The: A Play	M	TL	250+	Rigby Literacy	Rigby
Wooden Mile, The: Something Wickedly Weird	R	F	250+	Mould, Chris	Roaring Brook Press
Wood-Hoopoe Willie	N	RF	250+	Kroll, Virginia	Charlesbridge
Woodland Desert People	O	I	250+	Literacy by Design	Rigby
Woodlanders Begin, The	M	F	250+	Woodland Mysteries	Wright Group/McGraw Hill
Woodpeckers	I	I	85	Pebble Books	Red Brick Learning
Woodrow Wilson	S	B	250+	Amazing Americans	Wright Group/McGraw Hill
Woodrow Wilson	S	B	3524	History Maker Bios	Lerner Publishing Group
Woodrow Wilson	U	B	250+	Primary Source Readers	Teacher Created Materials
Woodrow Wilson	U	B	250+	Profiles of the Presidents	Compass Point Books
Woodrow Wilson: Twenty-eighth President	R	B	250+	Getting to Know the U.S. Presidents	Children's Press
Woods, Irons, and Greens	R	I	250+	Wildcats	Wright Group/McGraw Hill
Woodsong	T	B	250+	Paulsen, Gary	Dell
Woody Guthrie	I	B	199	Leveled Readers Social Studies	Houghton Mifflin Harcourt
Woody Guthrie: America's Folksinger	W	B	250+	Trailblazer Biographies	Carolrhoda Books
Woof!	A	F	42	Leveled Literacy Intervention/ Green System	Heinemann
Woof!	C	F	40	Literacy 2000	Rigby
Wool	M	I	660	Leveled Readers	Houghton Mifflin Harcourt
Wool	M	I	660	Leveled Readers/CA	Houghton Mifflin Harcourt
Wool	M	I	660	Leveled Readers/TX	Houghton Mifflin Harcourt
Wool	F	I	91	Sunshine	Wright Group/McGraw Hill
Wool from Sheep	K	I	531	Rigby Flying Colors	Rigby
Wool Keeps Me Warm	K	I	214	Windows on Literacy	National Geographic
Woolly Mammoth	I	I	132	Dinosaur and Prehistoric Animals	Capstone Press
Woolly Mammoths	N	I	1410	On My Own Science	Lerner Publishing Group
Woolly Sally	I	RF	147	Pacific Literacy	Pacific Learning
Woolly the Caterpillar	D	F	126	Bonnell, Kris	Reading Reading Books
Woolly, Woolly	E	F	136	Literacy 2000	Rigby
Woosh!	E	RF	124	Story Box	Wright Group/McGraw Hill
Word After Word After Word	Q	RF	250+	MacLachlan, Patricia	HarperCollins
Word Building With Teacher Ted	E	I	149	Run to Reading	Discovery Peak
Word Eater, The	T	F	250+	Amato, Mary	Holiday House
^Word Eater, The	T	F	250+	Dahl, Michael	Stone Arch Books
^Word Evidence	W	I	250+	Forensic Crime Solvers	Capstone Press
Word Machine, The	D	F	33	Sunshine	Wright Group/McGraw Hill
Wordful Child, A	O	B	250+	Meet The Author	Richard C. Owen
Words	E	RF	82	Happy Baby	Priddy Books
Words	M	I	578	Pacific Literacy	Pacific Learning

* Collection of short stories   # Graphic text
^ Mature content with lower level text demands

W

TITLE	LEVEL	GENRE	WORD COUNT	AUTHOR / SERIES	PUBLISHER / DISTRIBUTOR
Words	U	RF	250+	Paulsen, Gary	Penguin Group
Words Are Everywhere	E	I	46	Literacy 2000	Rigby
Words By Heart	U	HF	250+	Sebestyen, Ouida	Bantam Books
Words in the Dust	W	RF	250+	Reedy, Trent	Scholastic
Words of (Questionable) Wisdom from Lydia Goldblatt & Julie Graham-Chan	T	RF	250+	Ignatow, Amy	Amulet Books
Words of Promise: A Story about James Weldon Johnson	S	B	8127	Creative Minds Biographies	Lerner Publishing Group
Words of Stone	V	RF	250+	Henkes, Kevin	Penguin Group
Words: A Computer Lesson	F	F	45	Silly Millies	Millbrook Press
Wordsong	K	RF	192	DLM Literature Library	Wright Group/McGraw Hill
Work	Q	I	1746	Early Bird Energy Physics Books	Lerner Publishing Group
Work	A	I	17	On Our Way to English	Rigby
Work	C	RF	65	TOTTS	Tott Publications
Work for Play	O	RF	250+	Windows on Literacy	National Geographic
Work Helicopter, The	I	F	250+	PM Plus Story Books	Rigby
Work It Out	Q	I	250+	Orbit Collections	Pacific Learning
Work of Leonardo Da Vinci, The	T	I	1810	Leveled Readers Science	Houghton Mifflin Harcourt
Work Together	A	F	21	Reading Street	Pearson
Work Trucks	A	I	80	Readlings	American Reading Company
Work Vehicles	J	I	245	Windows on Literacy	National Geographic
Work We Do, The	K	I	250+	Spyglass Books	Compass Point Books
Work: From Plows to Robots	U	I	250+	Timeline History	Heinemann Library
Worker Bees	E	I	65	Reading Street	Pearson
Workers	LB	F	16	KinderReaders	Rigby
Workers	C	I	41	Time for Kids	Teacher Created Materials
Worker's Tools, A	F	I	93	Discovery World	Rigby
Working	C	I	174	Instant Readers	Harcourt School Publishers
Working	G	I	174	Yellow Umbrella Books	Red Brick Learning
Working Animals	H	I	132	Red Rocket Readers	Flying Start Books
Working at a TV Station	O	I	250+	Working Here	Children's Press
Working at Home	B	I	28	Little Red Readers	Sundance
Working at the Airport	K	I	374	HSP/Harcourt Trophies	Harcourt, Inc.
Working Cotton	N	RF	250+	Williams, Sherley Anne	Harcourt Trade
Working Dogs	L	I	266	Gear Up!	Wright Group/McGraw Hill
Working for Dad	D	RF	31	Visions	Wright Group/McGraw Hill
Working in Space	L	I	250+	The Solar System	Capstone Press
Working in the Park	E	RF	118	Leveled Readers	Houghton Mifflin Harcourt
Working in the Park	E	RF	118	Leveled Readers/CA	Houghton Mifflin Harcourt
Working in the Park	E	RF	118	Leveled Readers/TX	Houghton Mifflin Harcourt
Working on Water	L	I	250+	Home Connection Collection	Rigby
Working Then and Now	I	I	207	Then and Now	Lerner Publishing Group
Working Together	C	I	50	Early Connections	Benchmark Education
Working Together	I	I	222	Rigby Focus	Rigby
Working Together	G	I	205	Yellow Umbrella Books	Red Brick Learning
Working with Animals	I	I	250+	Home Connection Collection	Rigby
Working with Electricity and Magnetism	V	I	250+	Navigators Science Series	Benchmark Education
Working with Estimation	K	I	250+	Early Explorers	Benchmark Education
Working with Metal	L	I	299	Rigby Focus	Rigby
Working with Others	M	I	314	Pull Ahead Books	Lerner Publishing Group
Working With Plants	I	I	308	Rigby Flying Colors	Rigby
Working with Wood	P	I	250+	PM Extensions	Rigby
World According to Humphrey, The	Q	F	250+	Birney, Betty G.	Puffin Books

TITLE	LEVEL	GENRE	WORD COUNT	AUTHOR / SERIES	PUBLISHER / DISTRIBUTOR
World According to Kaley, The	S	RF	8551	Regan, Dian Curtis	Darby Creek Publishing
World Around Us, The	C	I	29	Little Red Readers	Sundance
World at His Fingertips: A Story About Louis Braille, The	R	B	8248	Creative Minds Biographies	Carolrhoda Books
World Beneath the Waves	T	I	250+	Navigators Math Series	Benchmark Education
World Beyond Earth, The -Unmanned Explorers and Orbiters	T	I	250+	Connectors	Pacific Learning
^World Collides, The: The Battle of Gallipoli	X	I	250+	Bloodiest Battles	Capstone Press
World Cultures	Q	I	250+	Trackers	Pacific Learning
World Cup	U	I	250+	Christopher, Matt	Little Brown and Company
World in a Supermarket, The	LB	I	24	Learn to Read	Creative Teaching Press
World in Grandfather's Hands, The	V	RF	250+	Strete, Craig Kee	Clarion
World in Your Kitchen, The	L	I	347	Independent Readers Social Studies	Houghton Mifflin Harcourt
World of Animals, The	U	I	250+	Science Readers	Teacher Created Materials
World of Ants	M	I	582	Vocabulary Readers	Houghton Mifflin Harcourt
World of Ants	M	I	582	Vocabulary Readers/CA	Houghton Mifflin Harcourt
World of Ants	M	I	582	Vocabulary Readers/TX	Houghton Mifflin Harcourt
World of Birds, A	B	I	49	Bookshop	Mondo Publishing
World of Birthdays, A	L	I	579	Gear Up!	Wright Group/McGraw Hill
World of Bread!, The	M	I	357	Reading Street	Pearson
World of Clouds	O	I	901	Vocabulary Readers	Houghton Mifflin Harcourt
World of Clouds	O	I	901	Vocabulary Readers/CA	Houghton Mifflin Harcourt
World of Computers, A	K	I	271	Gear Up!	Wright Group/McGraw Hill
World of Dogs, The	Q	I	250+	Pair-It Books	Steck-Vaughn
World of Dummies, The	N	I	250+	Pacific Literacy	Pacific Learning
World of Elements and Their Properties, The	Y	I	250+	Science Readers	Teacher Created Materials
World of Fish, A	N	I	974	Rigby Flying Colors	Rigby
#World of Food Chains with Max Axiom, Super Scientist; The	T	I	250+	Graphic Library	Capstone Press
World of Food, A	K	I	340	Leveled Readers	Houghton Mifflin Harcourt
World of Food, A	K	I	340	Leveled Readers/CA	Houghton Mifflin Harcourt
World of Food, A	K	I	340	Leveled Readers/TX	Houghton Mifflin Harcourt
World of Fun, A	G	I	176	Instant Readers	Harcourt School Publishers
World of Games, A	P	RF	676	Leveled Readers	Houghton Mifflin Harcourt
World of Genetics, The	Y	I	250+	Science Readers	Teacher Created Materials
World of Homes, A	M	I	732	Rigby Flying Colors	Rigby
World of Imagination, A	R	I	250+	Literacy 2000	Rigby
World of Kites, A	M	I	272	Vocabulary Readers	Houghton Mifflin Harcourt
World of Knowing: A Story About Thomas Hopkins Gallaudet, A	R	B	7226	Creative Minds Biographies	Carolrhoda Books
World of Masks, A	L	I	404	Rigby Flying Colors	Rigby
World of Patterns, A	J	I	250+	On Our Way to English	Rigby
World of Plants, A	Q	I	250+	Reading Expeditions	National Geographic
World of Plants, The	R	I	250+	Science Readers	Teacher Created Materials
World of Robots	T	I	1500	Vocabulary Readers	Houghton Mifflin Harcourt
World of Robots	T	I	1500	Vocabulary Readers/CA	Houghton Mifflin Harcourt
World of Robots	T	I	1500	Vocabulary Readers/TX	Houghton Mifflin Harcourt
World of Rocks & Minerals, The	U	I	250+	Science Readers	Teacher Created Materials
World of Silence, The	S	I	3382	Take Two Books	Wright Group/McGraw Hill
World of Snow, A	M	RF	250+	Livorse, Kay	Houghton Mifflin Harcourt
World of Sport, A	M	I	250+	Rigby Star Quest	Rigby
World of Treats, A	N	I	250+	InfoQuest	Rigby
World of Trees, The	P	I	1185	Vocabulary Readers	Houghton Mifflin Harcourt

W

* Collection of short stories   # Graphic text
^ Mature content with lower level text demands

TITLE	LEVEL	GENRE	WORD COUNT	AUTHOR / SERIES	PUBLISHER / DISTRIBUTOR
World of Trees, The	P	I	1185	Vocabulary Readers/CA	Houghton Mifflin Harcourt
World of Water, The	O	I	250+	Orbit Chapter Books	Pacific Learning
World of Wonders: The Most Mesmerizing Natural Phenomena on Earth	T	I	250+	Roman, Elisabeth	Harry N. Abrams
World Safari	R	I	250+	In Step Readers	Rigby
World Safari	R	I	250+	Literacy by Design	Rigby
World Series, The: The Greatest Moments of the Most Exciting Games	T	I	250+	Christopher, Matt	Little Brown and Company
World Solar Challenge, The	N	I	250+	Windows on Literacy	National Geographic
World Tour of Cultures, A	O	I	814	Reading Street	Pearson
World War I	W	I	250+	Primary Source Readers	Teacher Created Materials
World War II	W	I	250+	Primary Source Readers	Teacher Created Materials
^World War II Spies	X	I	250+	Spies	Capstone Press
^World War II: An Interactive History Adventure	W	HF	250+	You Choose Books	Capstone Press
World Worth Keeping, A	V	I	250+	Sunshine	Wright Group/McGraw Hill
World's Best Dog-Walker, The	Q	RF	250+	Zollman, Pam	Steck-Vaughn
World's Biggest Baby, The	H	I	239	Ready Readers	Pearson Learning Group
World's Biggest Machines, The	N	I	250+	Extreme Machines	Raintree
World's Deadliest Poisons, The	X	I	250+	The World's Top 10s	Capstone Press
World's Dirtiest Machines, The	M	I	250+	Extreme Machines	Raintree
World's Fastest Animals, The	Q	I	250+	The World's Top 10s	Capstone Press
World's Fastest Boats, The	W	I	250+	Built for Speed	Capstone Press
World's Fastest Cars, The	W	I	250+	Built for Speed	Capstone Press
World's Fastest Machines, The	N	I	250+	Extreme Machines	Raintree
World's Fastest Military Airplanes, The	W	I	250+	Built for Speed	Capstone Press
World's Greatest Juggler, The	E	F	105	Little Readers	Houghton Mifflin Harcourt
World's Greatest Showman, The	Q	B	250+	Power Up!	Steck-Vaughn
World's Greatest Toe Show, The	M	RF	250+	Lamb, Nancy; Singer, Muff	Troll Associates
World's Largest Plants, The: A Book About Trees	M	I	250+	Growing Things	Picture Window Books
World's Longest Toenail, The	L	F	862	Rigby Gigglers	Rigby
World's Most Amazing Survival Stories, The	V	I	250+	The World's Top 10s	Capstone Press
World's Most Dangerous Jobs, The	V	I	250+	The World's Top 10s	Capstone Press
World's Most Dangerous Machines, The	U	I	250+	The World's Top 10s	Capstone Press
World's Most Notorious Crooks, The	W	I	250+	The World's Top 10s	Capstone Press
World's Most Unusal Machines, The	N	I	250+	Extreme Machines	Raintree
World's Smartest Machines, The	N	I	250+	Extreme Machines	Raintree
World's Toughest Machines, The	N	I	250+	Extreme Machines	Raintree
World's Wildest Roller Coasters, The	W	I	250+	Built for Speed	Capstone Press
Worm Book, The	A	F	36	Bonnell, Kris	Reading Reading Books
Worm Builds	C	F	31	Brand New Readers	Candlewick Press
Worm Farm, The	G	RF	205	Take Two Books	Wright Group/McGraw Hill
Worm Is Hot	D	F	30	Brand New Readers	Candlewick Press
Worm Is Stuck	B	F	32	Brand New Readers	Candlewick Press
Worm Looks for Lunch	I	F	364	Big Cat	Pacific Learning
Worm Paints	C	F	40	Brand New Readers	Candlewick Press
Worm Rap	H	F	251	Alphakids	Sundance
Worm Smells	B	F	33	Brand New Readers	Candlewick Press
Worm Watches	D	F	33	Brand New Readers	Candlewick Press
Worm Work	P	I	250+	Sails	Rigby
Worm, The	C	F	38	Sun Sprouts	ETA/Cuisenaire
Worms	F	I	91	Animal Life Cycles	Lerner Publishing Group
Worms	D	F	39	Literacy 2000	Rigby

W

TITLE	LEVEL	GENRE	WORD COUNT	AUTHOR / SERIES	PUBLISHER / DISTRIBUTOR
Worms	P	I	250+	Mini Pets	Steck-Vaughn
Worms	N	I	250+	Nature's Friends	Compass Point Books
Worms Eat Our Garbage	G	RF	227	On Our Way to English	Rigby
Worms for Breakfast	I	TL	250+	Little Readers	Houghton Mifflin Harcourt
Worm's Home, A	K	I	281	Independent Readers Science	Houghton Mifflin Harcourt
Worms, Wonderful Worms	L	I	250+	Voyages	SRA/McGraw Hill
Worrisome Wombat, The	M	F	250+	Voyages	SRA/McGraw Hill
Worry Tree, The	Q	RF	250+	Musgrove, Marianne	Henry Holt & Co.
Worrywart, The	J	RF	412	InfoTrek	ETA/Cuisenaire
Worst Day of My Life, The	L	RF	250+	Cosby, Bill	Scholastic
Worst Enemies/ Best Friends: Beacon Street Girls	U	RF	250+	Bryant, Annie	Simon & Schuster
Worst Gymnast, The	L	RF	250+	Go Girl!	Feiwel and Friends
Worst House, The	L	RF	250+	Bookweb	Rigby
Worst of the Vikings, The	P	F	250+	High-Fliers	Pacific Learning
Worst Show-and-Tell Ever, The	J	SF	250+	Walsh, Rita	Troll Associates
Worst Team in the World, The	P	RF	250+	High-Fliers	Pacific Learning
Worst Witch at Sea, The	P	F	250+	Murphy, Jill	Candlewick Press
Worst Witch Saves the Day, The	P	F	250+	Murphy, Jill	Candlewick Press
Worst Witch Strikes Again, The	P	F	250+	Murphy, Jill	Candlewick Press
Worst Witch, The	P	F	250+	Murphy, Jill	Puffin Books
Worzzle, The	N	RF	250+	Reading Safari	Mondo Publishing
Would I Lie to You	Z+	RF	250+	von Ziegesar, Cecily	Little Brown and Company
Would I Trade My Parents?	K	RF	250+	Numeroff, Laura	Harry N. Abrams
Would They Love a Lion?	I	RF	242	Denton, Kady MacDonald	Kingfisher
Would You Like to Fly?	C	F	52	Twig	Wright Group/McGraw Hill
Would You Snitch?	T	RF	1454	Leveled Readers	Houghton Mifflin Harcourt
Would You Snitch?	T	RF	1454	Leveled Readers/CA	Houghton Mifflin Harcourt
Would You Snitch?	T	RF	1454	Leveled Readers/TX	Houghton Mifflin Harcourt
Wounded Brains: True Survival Stories	Z	I	3280	Powerful Medicine	Lerner Publishing Group
Wow!	D	F	145	Bookshop	Mondo Publishing
Wow! Look at This!	B	I	34	Science	Outside the Box
Wow! Said the Owl	J	F	250+	Hopgood, Tim	Farrar, Straus, & Giroux
Wow! What a Week!	J	RF	364	Wonders	Hampton Brown
Wrap-n-Bake Egg Rolls and Other Chinese Dishes	R	I	250+	Kids Dish	Picture Window Books
Wreck Trek	S	I	250+	Belcher, Angie	Pacific Learning
Wrecked! Shipping Disasters	T	I	250+	Story Surfers	ETA/Cuisenaire
Wrestling Sturbridge	Z	RF	250+	Wallace, Rich	Random House
Wright 3, The	T	RF	250+	Balliett, Blue	Scholastic
Wright Brothers	L	B	461	Leveled Readers/TX	Houghton Mifflin Harcourt
#Wright Brothers and the Airplane, The	S	B	250+	Graphic Library	Capstone Press
Wright Brothers, First Flyers, The	V	B	2700	Independent Readers Science	Houghton Mifflin Harcourt
Wright Brothers, The	M	B	250+	Biography	Benchmark Education
Wright Brothers, The	P	B	250+	Early Biographies	Compass Point Books
Wright Brothers, The	K	B	250+	Famous People in Transportation	Red Brick Learning
Wright Brothers, The	L	B	236	Famous People in Transportation	Red Brick Learning
Wright Brothers, The	Y	B	250+	Freedman, Russell	Holiday House
Wright Brothers, The	S	B	3396	History Maker Bios	Lerner Publishing Group
Wright Brothers, The	L	B	461	Leveled Readers	Houghton Mifflin Harcourt
Wright Brothers, The	L	B	461	Leveled Readers/CA	Houghton Mifflin Harcourt
Wright Brothers, The	U	B	250+	Sobol, Donald J.	Scholastic
Wright Brothers, The	P	B	250+	Windows on Literacy	National Geographic

W

* Collection of short stories   # Graphic text
^ Mature content with lower level text demands

TITLE	LEVEL	GENRE	WORD COUNT	AUTHOR / SERIES	PUBLISHER / DISTRIBUTOR
Wringer	U	RF	250+	Spinelli, Jerry	HarperTrophy
Wrinkle in Time, A	W	F	250+	L'Engle, Madeleine	Bantam Books
Wrinkles	C	I	32	Literacy 2000	Rigby
Wrinkly Socks Make Me Giggle	H	RF	146	Wake, Shelley	Kaeden Books
Write It Down!	U	I	250+	iOpeners	Pearson Learning Group
Write Up a Storm with the Polk Street School	M	RF	250+	Giff, Patricia Reilly	Bantam Books
Write Your Own Adventure Story	U	I	250+	Write Your Own	Compass Point Books
Write Your Own Article	U	I	250+	Write Your Own	Compass Point Books
Write Your Own Autobiography	U	I	250+	Write Your Own	Compass Point Books
Write Your Own Biography	U	I	250+	Write Your Own	Compass Point Books
Write Your Own Fable	U	I	250+	Write Your Own	Compass Point Books
Write Your Own Fairy Tale	U	I	250+	Write Your Own	Compass Point Books
Write Your Own Fantasy Story	U	I	250+	Write Your Own	Compass Point Books
Write Your Own Folktale	U	I	250+	Write Your Own	Compass Point Books
Write Your Own Graphic Novel	U	I	250+	Write Your Own	Compass Point Books
Write Your Own Historical Fiction	U	I	250+	Write Your Own	Compass Point Books
Write Your Own Legend	U	I	250+	Write Your Own	Compass Point Books
Write Your Own Mystery Story	U	I	250+	Write Your Own	Compass Point Books
Write Your Own Myth	U	I	250+	Write Your Own	Compass Point Books
Write Your Own Nonfiction	U	I	250+	Write Your Own	Compass Point Books
Write Your Own Poetry	U	I	250+	Write Your Own	Compass Point Books
Write Your Own Realistic Fiction Story	U	I	250+	Write Your Own	Compass Point Books
Write Your Own Science Fiction Story	U	I	250+	Write Your Own	Compass Point Books
Write Your Own Tall Tale	U	I	250+	Write Your Own	Compass Point Books
Writer from the Prairie	R	B	1434	Leveled Readers	Houghton Mifflin Harcourt
Writer from the Prairie	R	B	1434	Leveled Readers/CA	Houghton Mifflin Harcourt
Writer from the Prairie	R	B	1434	Leveled Readers/TX	Houghton Mifflin Harcourt
Writer of the Plains: A Story about Willa Cather	Q	B	250+	Streissguth, Tom	Carolrhoda Books
Writer Who Changed America, The	U	B	1976	Leveled Readers	Houghton Mifflin Harcourt
Writer Who Changed America, The	U	B	1976	Leveled Readers/CA	Houghton Mifflin Harcourt
Writer Who Changed America, The	U	B	1976	Leveled Readers/TX	Houghton Mifflin Harcourt
Writers	J	I	264	Vocabulary Readers	Houghton Mifflin Harcourt
Writers	J	I	264	Vocabulary Readers/CA	Houghton Mifflin Harcourt
Writer's Work, A	N	I	481	Wonder World	Wright Group/McGraw Hill
Writers: Then and Now	O	I	250+	Primary Source Readers	Teacher Created Materials
Writing a Biography: Henry Ford	M	I	374	Rigby Flying Colors	Rigby
Writing Bug, The	O	B	250+	Meet The Author	Richard C. Owen
Writing for Freedom: A Story About Lydia Maria Child	R	B	8090	Creative Minds Biographies	Carolrhoda Books
^Writing in Ancient China	U	I	250+	On Deck	Rigby
^Writing in Ancient Egypt	U	I	250+	On Deck	Rigby
^Writing in Ancient India	U	I	250+	On Deck	Rigby
^Writing in Ancient Mesopotamia	U	I	250+	On Deck	Rigby
^Writing in Ancient Phonecia	U	I	250+	On Deck	Rigby
Writing Places	E	I	30	Chanko, Pamela	Scholastic
Writing the U.S. Constitution	N	I	250+	Our American Story	Picture Window Books
Written Anything Good Lately?	M	RF	218	Allen, Susan & Lindaman, Jane	Millbrook Press
Written in Bone: Buried Lives of Jamestown and Colonial Maryland	X	I	28803	Walker, Sally M.	Carolrhoda Books
Wrong Trousers, The	S	F	4023	Dominoes one	Oxford University Press
Wrong Way Around Magic	N	F	250+	Chew, Ruth	Scholastic
Wrong Way Reggie	J	RF	304	Little Celebrations	Pearson Learning Group
Wrong-Way Rabbit, The	J	F	304	Slater, Teddy	Scholastic

W

TITLE	LEVEL	GENRE	WORD COUNT	AUTHOR / SERIES	PUBLISHER / DISTRIBUTOR
Wuthering Heights	Z	RF	250+	High-Fliers	Pacific Learning
WWW	W	I	250+	Boldprint	Steck-Vaughn
Wyoming	T	I	250+	Hello U.S.A.	Lerner Publishing Group
Wyoming	R	I	250+	This Land Is Your Land	Compass Point Books
Wyoming: Facts and Symbols	O	I	250+	The States and Their Symbols	Red Brick Learning
Wyverns' Treasure, The (Nathaniel Fludd Beastologist Book Three)	R	F	250+	LaFevers, R. L.	Houghton Mifflin Harcourt

W

* Collection of short stories # Graphic text
^ Mature content with lower level text demands

TITLE	LEVEL	GENRE	WORD COUNT	AUTHOR / SERIES	PUBLISHER / DISTRIBUTOR
X Games: Action Sports Grab the Spotlight	S	I	250+	High Five Reading	Red Brick Learning
X Marks the Spot	N	I	250+	Home Connection Collection	Rigby
X Marks the Spot	K	RF	250+	Math Matters	Kane Press
X Marks the Spot	I	RF	309	Pair-It Turn and Learn	Steck-Vaughn
X Ray, The	C	RF	48	Learn to Read	Creative Teaching Press
#X: A Biography of Malcolm X	W	B	250+	Graphic Library	Capstone Press
Xavier Ox's Xylophone Experiment	K	F	752	Animal Antics A to Z	Kane Press
X-Games, The: Skateboarding's Greatest Event	Q	I	250+	Skateboarding	Capstone Press
Xiaosaurus and Other Dinosaurs of the Dashanpu Digs in China	N	I	250+	Dinosaur Find	Picture Window Books
X-rays	X	I	3158	Leveled Readers Science	Houghton Mifflin Harcourt
X-Rays	A	I	32	Red Rocket Readers	Flying Start Books
X-Rays	O	I	250+	Voyages	SRA/McGraw Hill
Xuanzang, Chinese Hero	W	B	3100	Leveled Readers Social Studies	Houghton Mifflin Harcourt
^Y Is for Yowl!: A Scary Alphabet	N	I	250+	Alphabet Fun	Capstone Press
Yabby Tale, A	N	RF	250+	Sunshine	Wright Group/McGraw Hill
Yahoo for You	E	RF	137	Early Readers	Compass Point Books
Yakkity-Yak	C	F	49	Learn to Read	Creative Teaching Press
Yaks	I	I	221	Sails	Rigby
Yang the Eldest and His Odd Jobs	P	RF	250+	Namioka, Lensey	Bantam Books
Yang the Second and Her Secret Admirer	P	RF	250+	Namioka, Lensey	Bantam Books
Yang the Third and Her Impossible Family	P	RF	250+	Namioka, Lensey	Bantam Books
Yang the Youngest and His Terrible Ear	P	RF	250+	Namioka, Lensey	Bantam Books
Yankee Girl	Y	HF	250+	Rodman, Mary Ann	Farrar, Straus, & Giroux
Yao Ming	P	B	1945	Amazing Athletes	Lerner Publishing Group
Yao Ming	U	B	19632	Sports Heroes and Legends	Lerner Publishing Group
Yao's Wild Ride	Q	HF	250+	Leveled Readers Language Support	Houghton Mifflin Harcourt
Yard for All, A	B	F	55	Reading Street	Pearson
Yard Sale	H	RF	167	Pair-It Turn and Learn	Steck-Vaughn
Yard Sale, The	E	RF	200	Cherrington, Janelle	Scholastic
Yard Sale, The	F	RF	136	Early Explorers	Benchmark Education
Yard Sale, The	I	RF	250+	Little Readers	Houghton Mifflin Harcourt
Yard Sale, The	K	RF	250+	Windows on Literacy	National Geographic
Yasmin and the Flood	F	RF	81	Oxford Reading Tree	Oxford University Press
Yasmin's Box	G	F	170	Cambridge Reading	Pearson Learning Group
Yazhi Laughs	K	RF	320	Gear Up!	Wright Group/McGraw Hill
Year at a Construction Site, A	M	I	250+	Time Goes By	Millbrook Press
Year at a Farm, A	M	I	250+	Time Goes By	Millbrook Press
Year Down Yonder, A	V	HF	250+	Peck, Richard	Penguin Group
Year in a Castle, A	M	I	250+	Time Goes By	Millbrook Press
Year in Antartica, A	R	I	250+	iOpeners	Pearson Learning Group
Year in the Desert, A	M	I	250+	Yellow Umbrella Books	Red Brick Learning
Year in the World of Dinosaurs, A	M	I	250+	Time Goes By	Millbrook Press
Year Mom Won the Pennant, The	P	RF	250+	Christopher, Matt	Little Brown and Company
Year of Fun, A	A	I	32	Leveled Readers	Houghton Mifflin Harcourt
Year of Fun, A	A	I	32	Leveled Readers/CA	Houghton Mifflin Harcourt
Year of Impossible Goodbyes	W	HF	250+	Choi, Sook Nyui	Yearling Books
Year of Sharing, The	W	SF	6390	Oxford Bookworms Library	Oxford University Press
Year of the Dog, The	Q	RF	250+	Lin, Grace	Little Brown and Company
Year of the Hangman, The	Y	HF	250+	Blackwood, Gary	Scholastic
Year of the Panda, The	N	RF	250+	Soar To Success	Houghton Mifflin Harcourt
Year of the Rat, The	Q	RF	250+	Lin, Grace	Little Brown and Company
Year of the Sawdust Man, The	Y	RF	250+	LaFaye, A.	Simon & Schuster

TITLE	LEVEL	GENRE	WORD COUNT	AUTHOR / SERIES	PUBLISHER / DISTRIBUTOR
Year on a Pirate Ship, A	M	I	250+	Time Goes By	Millbrook Press
Year We Disappeared, The	Z	I	250+	Busby, Cylin and John	Bloomsbury Children's Books
Year with Mother Bear, A	I	I	164	Storyteller Nonfiction	Wright Group/McGraw Hill
Year Without a Santa Claus, The	M	F	250+	McGinley, Phyllis	Marshall Cavendish
Year Without Rain, A	J	HF	137	Avenues	Hampton Brown
Year, A	H	I	137	The Calendar	Capstone Press
Yearling, The	X	RF	250+	Rawlings, Marjorie Kinnan	Simon & Schuster
Yellow	B	I	53	Bookworms	Marshall Cavendish
Yellow	B	I	26	Colors	Lerner Publishing Group
Yellow	B	I	32	Literacy 2000	Rigby
Yellow Ball	LB	RF	18	Bang, Molly	Morrow
Yellow Bird	F	F	229	Sails	Rigby
Yellow Boat, The	E	RF	208	Easy Stories	Norwood House Press
Yellow Elephants	N	F	250+	Larios, Julie	Harcourt, Inc.
Yellow Everywhere	J	I	325	Lightning Bolt Books	Lerner Publishing Group
Yellow Flowers	C	RF	49	Bonnell, Kris	Reading Reading Books
^Yellow Line	Z+	RF	250+	Orca Soundings	Orca Books
Yellow Overalls	L	F	250+	Literacy 2000	Rigby
Yellow Raft in Blue Water, The	Z+	RF	250+	Dorris, Michael	Henry Holt & Co.
Yellow Star, The: The Legend of King Christian X of Denmark	S	HF	250+	Deedy, Carmen Agra	Peachtree
Yellow Yarn Mystery, The	B	F	61	Little Books	Sadlier-Oxford
Yellow: Seeing Yellow All Around Us	K	I	250+	Colors	Capstone Press
Yellowstone 1988: Summer of Fire	W	I	250+	Lauber, Patricia	Scholastic
Yellowstone National Park	O	I	250+	A True Book	Children's Press
Yellowstone National Park	N	I	522	Lightning Bolt Books	Lerner Publishing Group
Yellowstone, Our First National Park	R	I	1288	Leveled Readers Social Studies	Houghton Mifflin Harcourt
Yellowstone: Our First National Park	N	I	250+	Rosen Real Readers	Rosen Publishing Group
Yemi's Beads	L	RF	250+	Literacy by Design	Rigby
Yen's Story: From China to California	T	HF	250+	Reading Expeditions	National Geographic
Yes Ma'am	H	RF	125	Story Box	Wright Group/McGraw Hill
Yes We Can! A Salute to Children From President Obama's Victory Speech	I	I	85	Obama, Barack	Scholastic
Yes We Can: A Biography of President Barack Obama	W	B	250+	Thomas, Garen	Feiwel and Friends
Yes, I Can	C	RF	30	Teacher's Choice Series	Pearson Learning Group
Yes, I Can!	D	F	45	Ready Readers	Pearson Learning Group
Yes, I Know the Monkey Man	Y	RF	250+	Butler, Dori Hillestad	Peachtree
Yes, It Does	D	I	91	Teacher's Choice Series	Pearson Learning Group
Yes, Please!	B	RF	48	Red Rocket Readers	Flying Start Books
Yes, She Can!	U	B	250+	Good Sports	Sandpiper Books
Yes, We Can!	B	I	56	On Our Way to English	Rigby
Yesterday and Today: Going to School	G	I	189	Factivity Series	Pearson Learning Group
Yesterday and Today: Having Fun	H	I	239	Dominie Factivity Series	Pearson Learning Group
Yikes! Grandma's a Teenager	N	F	250+	The Zack Files	Grosset & Dunlap
#Yikes, It's a Yeti!	O	F	250+	Wallace, Karen	Stone Arch Books
Yin's Special Thanksgiving	K	RF	524	Dolgin, Phyllis	January Books
Yippy-Day-Yippy-Doo!	E	RF	117	Sunshine	Wright Group/McGraw Hill
Yo Ho! Yo Ho!	I	F	164	Voyages	SRA/McGraw Hill
Yo! Yes?	LB	RF	34	Raschka, Chris	Scholastic
Yoga Class	B	RF	28	Bebop Books	Lee & Low Books Inc.
Yoga Stretches	D	I	65	Gear Up!	Wright Group/McGraw Hill
Yogurt and Cheeses and Ice Cream That Pleases: What Is in the Milk Group?	N	I	350	Food is CATegorical	Millbrook Press

* Collection of short stories   # Graphic text
^ Mature content with lower level text demands

TITLE	LEVEL	GENRE	WORD COUNT	AUTHOR / SERIES	PUBLISHER / DISTRIBUTOR
Yoko Yak's Yakety Yakking	L	F	748	Animal Antics A to Z	Kane Press
Yolonda's Genius	V	RF	250+	Fenner, Carol	Aladdin
Yoma Helps a Friend	I	RF	354	InfoTrek	ETA/Cuisenaire
Yonder	M	RF	250+	Johnston, Tony	Penguin Group
Yonderfel's Castle: A Medieval Fable	L	TL	250+	Gralley, Jean	Henry Holt & Co.
Yoo Hoo, Moon!	I	F	250+	Blocksma, Mary	Bantam Books
Yorkshire Terriers	R	I	250+	All About Dogs	Capstone Press
Yorkshire Terriers	I	I	150	Dogs	Capstone Press
Yorkshire Terriers Are the Best!	Q	I	1722	The Best Dogs Ever	Lerner Publishing Group
Yoshiko's Surprise	E	RF	81	Seedlings	Continental Press
Yoshi's Feast	N	RF	250+	Kajikawa, Kimiko	DK Publishing
Yossi's Goal	O	RF	250+	Orca Young Readers	Orca Books
You	C	I	20	Carousel Earlybirds	Pearson Learning Group
You and Me Together: Moms, Dads, and Kids Around the World	G	RF	85	Kerley, Barbara	National Geographic
You and Your Genes	X	I	250+	Reading Expeditions	National Geographic
You and Your Teeth	I	I	1009	Sunshine	Wright Group/McGraw Hill
You Are Much Too Small	J	F	250+	Bank Street	Bantam Books
You Are Special	K	I	250+	Sunshine	Wright Group/McGraw Hill
You Are Unique!	L	I	340	Pair-It Turn and Learn	Steck-Vaughn
*You Be The Detective	Q	RF	250+	Miller, Marvin	Scholastic
*You Be The Detective II	Q	RF	250+	Miller, Marvin	Scholastic
*You Be The Jury	Q	I	250+	Miller, Marvin	Scholastic
*You Be The Jury: Courtroom V	Q	I	250+	Miller, Marvin	Bantam Books
You Can Always Tell Cathy from Caitlin	K	RF	583	Sunshine	Wright Group/McGraw Hill
You Can Canoe!: A Book of Sporting Activities	O	I	250+	Literacy Tree	Rigby
You Can Cook	M	I	250+	Woo, Lornette	Steck-Vaughn
You Can Do It	F	F	176	Sun Sprouts	ETA/Cuisenaire
You Can Do It!	Q	I	250+	Orbit Collections	Pacific Learning
You Can Do It!: Perserverance	K	RF	1550	Salerno, Tony Character Classics	Character Building Company
You Can Do It, Sam	K	F	250+	Hest, Amy	Candlewick Press
You Can Draw Construction Vehicles	LB	I	99	Cerato, Mattia/You Can Draw	Picture Window Books
You Can Draw Dinosaurs	LB	I	86	You Can Draw	Picture Window Books
You Can Draw Dragons, Unicorns, and Other Magical Creatures	LB	I	64	Cerato, Mattia/You Can Draw	Picture Window Books
You Can Draw Fairies and Princesses	LB	I	80	Sexton, Brenda/You Can Draw	Picture Window Books
You Can Draw Flowers	LB	I	63	You Can Draw	Picture Window Books
You Can Draw Monsters and Other Scary Things	LB	I	74	You Can Draw	Picture Window Books
You Can Draw Pets	LB	I	86	You Can Draw	Picture Window Books
You Can Draw Planes, Trains, and Other Vehicles	LB	I	76	You Can Draw	Picture Window Books
You Can Draw Zoo Animals	LB	I	61	You Can Draw	Picture Window Books
You Can Have a Party Anywhere	J	RF	371	Sails	Rigby
You Can Make a Difference!	M	I	686	Reading Street	Pearson
You Can Make a Memory Scrapbook	J	I	179	How-To Series	Benchmark Education
You Can Make a Pom-pom	G	I	39	Windows on Literacy	National Geographic
You Can Make a Timer	F	I	124	How-To Series	Benchmark Education
You Can Make Skittles	G	I	128	Sunshine	Wright Group/McGraw Hill
You Can Recycle!	K	I	219	Rigby Focus	Rigby
You Can Sort Boats	I	I	174	Early Explorers	Benchmark Education
You Can, Tucan, Math: Word Problem-Solving Fun	N	I	250+	Adler, David A.	Holiday House
You Can't Catch Me	J	F	250+	Oppenheim, Joanne	Houghton Mifflin Harcourt

* Collection of short stories   # Graphic text
^ Mature content with lower level text demands

TITLE	LEVEL	GENRE	WORD COUNT	AUTHOR / SERIES	PUBLISHER / DISTRIBUTOR
You Can't Catch Me!	I	F	244	Cambridge Reading	Pearson Learning Group
You Can't Catch Me!	D	RF	89	Lighthouse	Rigby
You Can't Eat Your Chicken Pox, Amber Brown	N	RF	250+	Danziger, Paula	Scholastic
You Can't Have It!	C	RF	28	Potato Chip Books	American Reading Company
You Can't See Your Bones with Binoculars	P	I	250+	Ziefert, Harriet	Scholastic
You Can't Taste a Pickle With Your Ear	O	I	250+	Ziefert, Harriet	Scholastic
You Couldn't Pay Me Enough To Do This Job!	S	I	250+	Rigby Literacy	Rigby
You Did It!	G	RF	246	Sunshine	Wright Group/McGraw Hill
You Do Ride Well	H	RF	165	Windmill Books	Rigby
*You Don't Even Know Me: Stories and Poems About Boys	Z	RF	250+	Flake, Sharon G.	Disney Book Group
You Don't Know Me	X	RF	250+	Klass, David	HarperCollins
You Don't Look Like Your Mother	L	F	250+	Bookshop	Mondo Publishing
You Have Mail: True Stories of Cybercrime	W	I	250+	24/7 Science Behind the Scenes	Scholastic
You Just Can't Get Enough: Gossip Girl, the Carlyles	Z+	RF	250+	von Ziegesar, Cecily	Little Brown and Company
You Know You Love Me	Z+	RF	250+	Dean, Zoey	Little Brown and Company
You Look Funny	G	RF	180	First Start	Troll Associates
You Might Fall	H	RF	180	Stepping Stones	Nelson/Michaels Assoc.
*You Read to Me, I'll Read to You: Very Short Fables to Read Together	M	TL	250+	Hoberman, Mary Ann	Little Brown and Company
*You Read to Me, I'll Read to You: Very Short Fairy Tales to Read Together	M	TL	250+	Hoberman, Mary Ann	Little Brown and Company
*You Read to Me, I'll Read to You: Very Short Mother Goose Tales to Read Together	M	TL	250+	Hoberman, Mary Ann	Little Brown and Company
*You Read to Me, I'll Read to You: Very Short Scary Tales to Read Together	M	F	250+	Hoberman, Mary Ann	Little Brown and Company
*You Read to Me, I'll Read to You: Very Short Stories to Read Together	M	F	250+	Hoberman, Mary Ann	Little Brown and Company
You See a Circus I See…	J	RF	250+	Downs, Mike	Charlesbridge
You See with Your Eyes	G	I	218	PM Science Readers	Rigby
You Should Try That with a Rhino	E	F	123	Home Connection Collection	Rigby
You Shouldn't Have to Say Good-bye	T	RF	250+	Hermes, Patricia	Scholastic
You Think You Know Giraffes	A	I	36	Readlings/Animals of Africa	American Reading Company
You Think You Know Hippos	A	I	39	Readlings/Animals of Africa	American Reading Company
You Think You Know Zebras	A	I	30	Readlings/Animals of Africa	American Reading Company
You Want Women to Vote, Lizzie Stanton?	W	B	250+	Fritz, Jean	Penguin Group
You'll Roar	H	F	73	Instant Readers	Harcourt School Publishers
You'll Soon Grow into Them Titch	H	RF	191	Hutchins, Pat	Morrow
Young Arthur Ashe: Brave Champion	L	B	250+	First-Start Biography	Troll Associates
Young Cam Jansen and the Baseball Mystery	J	RF	250+	Adler, David A.	Puffin Books
Young Cam Jansen and the Dinosaur Game	J	RF	250+	Adler, David A.	Puffin Books
Young Cam Jansen and the Double Beach Mystery	J	RF	250+	Adler, David A.	Puffin Books
Young Cam Jansen and the Ice Skate Mystery	J	RF	250+	Adler, David A.	Puffin Books
Young Cam Jansen and the Library Mystery	J	RF	250+	Adler, David A.	Puffin Books
Young Cam Jansen and the Lost Tooth	J	RF	250+	Adler, David A.	Puffin Books
Young Cam Jansen and the Missing Cookie	J	RF	250+	Adler, David A.	Puffin Books
Young Cam Jansen and the Pizza Shop Mystery	J	RF	250+	Adler, David A.	Puffin Books
Young Cam Jansen and the Spotted Cat Mystery	J	RF	250+	Adler, David A.	Scholastic
Young Champions: It's All About Attitude	Q	I	250+	High Five Reading	Capstone Press
Young Charles Darwin and the Voyage of the Beagle	W	B	250+	Ashby, Ruth	Peachtree
Young Clara Barton: Battlefield Nurse	L	B	250+	First-Start Biography	Troll Associates
Young Dancer, A: The Life of an Ailey Student	N	I	250+	Gladstone, Valerie	Henry Holt & Co.
Young Davy Crockett: Frontier Fighter	L	B	250+	First-Start Biography	Troll Associates

* Collection of short stories   # Graphic text
^ Mature content with lower level text demands

XYZ

TITLE	LEVEL	GENRE	WORD COUNT	AUTHOR / SERIES	PUBLISHER / DISTRIBUTOR
Young Eagle and His Horse	Q	HF	1267	Leveled Readers	Houghton Mifflin Harcourt
Young Eagle and His Horse	Q	HF	1267	Leveled Readers/CA	Houghton Mifflin Harcourt
Young Eagle and His Horse	Q	HF	1267	Leveled Readers/TX	Houghton Mifflin Harcourt
Young Frederick Douglass	N	B	250+	First-Start Biography	Scholastic
Young Fredle	R	F	250+	Voight, Cynthia	Alfred A. Knopf
Young Fu of the Upper Yangtze	W	HF	250+	Lewis, Elizabeth Foreman	Square Fish
Young Geographers	O	I	250+	People, Spaces & Places	Rand McNally
Young George Washington: America's First President	L	B	250+	Woods, Andrew	Troll Associates
Young Helen Keller: Woman of Courage	L	B	250+	First-Start Biography	Troll Associates
Young Heroes of the North and South	Y	I	250+	The Civil War	Carus Publishing Company
Young Jackie Robinson: Baseball Hero	L	B	250+	First-Start Biography	Troll Associates
Young Jim Thorpe: All-American Athlete	L	B	250+	First-Start Biography	Troll Associates
Young Joan	X	HF	250+	Dana, Barbara	HarperTrophy
Young Land Lords, The	X	RF	250+	Myers, Walter Dean	Penguin Group
Young Man and the Sea, The	S	RF	250+	Philbrick, Rodman	Scholastic
Young Martin Luther King, Jr.	M	B	250+	First-Start Biography	Scholastic
Young Martin's Promise	N	B	250+	Stories of America	Steck-Vaughn
Young Mozart	O	B	250+	Isadora, Rachel	Penguin Group
Young Orville and Wilbur Wright: First to Fly	L	B	250+	First-Start Biography	Troll Associates
Young Reggie Jackson: Hall of Fame Champion	L	B	250+	First-Start Biography	Troll Associates
Young Robin's Hood	R	TL	250+	Bookshop	Mondo Publishing
Young Rosa Parks: Civil Rights Heroine	L	B	250+	First-Start Biography	Troll Associates
Young Squanto: The First Thanksgiving	L	B	250+	First-Start Biography	Troll Associates
Young Thurgood Marshall: Fighter for Equality	L	B	250+	First-Start Biography	Troll Associates
Young Tom Edison: Great Inventor	L	B	250+	First-Start Biography	Troll Associates
Young Unicorns, The	Y	F	250+	L'Engle, Madeleine	Farrar, Straus, & Giroux
Young Wolf's First Hunt	M	RF	250+	Shefelman, Janice	Random House
Youngest Giraffe, The	I	RF	250+	PM Plus Story Books	Rigby
Youngest in the Family	F	RF	144	Visions	Wright Group/McGraw Hill
Youngest Templar, The: Trail of Fate	X	HF	250+	Spradlin, Michael P.	G.P. Putnam's Sons
Your Amazing Body!	K	I	293	Reading Street	Pearson
Your Body	J	I	208	Early Connections	Benchmark Education
Your Body Battles a Broken Bone	S	I	1909	Body Battles	Lerner Publishing Group
Your Body Battles a Cavity	S	I	1945	Body Battles	Lerner Publishing Group
Your Body Battles a Cold	S	I	1483	Body Battles	Lerner Publishing Group
Your Body Battles a Skinned Knee	S	I	1147	Body Battles	Lerner Publishing Group
Your Body Battles a Stomachache	S	I	1530	Body Battles	Lerner Publishing Group
Your Body Battles an Earache	S	I	1400	Body Battles	Lerner Publishing Group
Your Body in Balance	O	I	250+	Orbit Chapter Books	Pacific Learning
Your Body Up Close	M	I	250+	Rigby Rocket	Rigby
Your Bones	P	I	250+	Your Body	Red Brick Learning
Your Brain	P	I	250+	Your Body	Red Brick Learning
Your Great State	K	I	786	Avenues	Hampton Brown
Your Guide to Pet Care	P	I	1552	Vocabulary Readers	Houghton Mifflin Harcourt
Your Guide to Pet Care	P	I	1552	Vocabulary Readers/CA	Houghton Mifflin Harcourt
Your Guide to Pet Care	P	I	1552	Vocabulary Readers/TX	Houghton Mifflin Harcourt
Your Heart	L	I	250+	Early Connections	Benchmark Education
Your Heart	P	I	250+	Your Body	Red Brick Learning
Your Heart and Blood	M	I	250+	Rigby Focus	Rigby
Your Heart, Your Blood: The Human Circulatory System	U	I	250+	Explore More	Wright Group/McGraw Hill
Your Lungs	P	I	250+	Your Body	Red Brick Learning
Your Mother Was a Neanderthal	P	F	250+	Scieszka, Jon	Penguin Group

XYZ

TITLE	LEVEL	GENRE	WORD COUNT	AUTHOR / SERIES	PUBLISHER / DISTRIBUTOR
Your Move, J. P.!	R	RF	250+	Lowry, Lois	Random House
Your Muscles	P	I	250+	Your Body	Red Brick Learning
Your Muscles on the Move	T	I	250+	Explore More	Wright Group/McGraw Hill
Your Nervous System	M	I	366	Early Connections	Benchmark Education
Your Nervous System	S	I	250+	Reading Expeditions	National Geographic
Your Senses	H	I	138	Pebble Books	Red Brick Learning
Your Senses Tell You So!	D	I	36	Pair-It Turn and Learn	Steck-Vaughn
Your Stomach	P	I	250+	Your Body	Red Brick Learning
Your Super Computer	P	I	250+	Rigby Focus	Rigby
Your Teeth	J	I	131	Dental Health	Capstone Press
Your Terrific Teeth	I	I	156	Gear Up!	Wright Group/McGraw Hill
You're in Big Trouble, Brad!	K	RF	1345	Real Kids Readers	Millbrook Press
You're My Nikki	M	RF	250+	Eisenberg, Phyllis Rose	Penguin Group
You're Never Too Young to Save the Planet	L	I	250+	Literacy by Design	Rigby
You're on Camera!	T	I	1759	Vocabulary Readers	Houghton Mifflin Harcourt
You're on Camera!	T	I	1759	Vocabulary Readers/CA	Houghton Mifflin Harcourt
You're Out	N	RF	250+	Kroll, Stephen	Avon Books
You're So Clever	H	RF	188	Voyages	SRA/McGraw Hill
You're Special: Contentment	K	RF	1254	Salerno, Tony Character Classics	Character Building Company
You're the One That I Want: Gossip Girl	Z+	RF	250+	von Ziegesar, Cecily	Little Brown and Company
Yours Truly, Goldilocks	Q	F	250+	Ada, Alma Flor	Aladdin
Yourspace: Questioning New Media	V	I	250+	Media Literacy	Capstone Press
YouTube	T	I	5137	A Great Idea	Norwood House Press
You've Got Cheetah-Mail	M	I	250+	World Quest Adventures	World Quest Learning
You've Got Dragons	L	F	250+	Cave, Kathryn	Peachtree
Yo-Yo a Go-Go	F	RF	177	Rigby Literacy	Rigby
Yo-Yo Ma: Musical Superstar	Q	B	250+	Leveled Readers Language Support	Houghton Mifflin Harcourt
Yo-Yo Tricks	P	I	250+	Games Around the World	Compass Point Books
Yo-yos	G	RF	62	City Kids	Rigby
Yo-Yo's	O	I	250+	PM Nonfiction-Emerald	Rigby
#Yu The Great: Conquering the Flood	V	TL	3078	Graphic Myths and Legends	Graphic Universe
Yuck Soup	B	F	25	Sunshine	Wright Group/McGraw Hill
Yuck!	K	F	250+	Leveled Readers Language Support	Houghton Mifflin Harcourt
Yucky Reptile Alphabet Book, The	N	I	250+	Pallotta, Jerry	Charlesbridge
Yucky Worms	M	RF	250+	French, Vivian	Candlewick Press
Yucky, Mucky Mud	H	F	271	Sun Sprouts	ETA/Cuisenaire
Yukadoos	I	F	121	Jellybeans	Rigby
Yum and Yuk	I	F	125	Story Box	Wright Group/McGraw Hill
Yum!	A	I	40	On Our Way to English	Rigby
Yum! Yum!	D	F	84	Bookshop	Mondo Publishing
Yum! Yum!	C	F	36	Storyworlds	Heinemann
Yummy Lunch, A	B	RF	22	Early Emergent	Pioneer Valley
Yummy Snack, A	E	I	114	On Our Way to English	Rigby
Yummy Yummy! Food for My Tummy!	L	F	250+	Lloyd, Sam	Tiger Tales
Yummy, Tum, Tee	C	F	51	Little Celebrations	Pearson Learning Group
Yummy, Yummy	F	F	115	Grey, Judith	Troll Associates
Yum-Yum House, The	L	RF	250+	Math Matters	Kane Press
Yun's Visit	J	RF	250+	On Our Way to English	Rigby
^Z Is for Zoom!: A Race Car Alphabet	N	I	250+	Alphabet Fun	Capstone Press
Zac and Chirpy	C	RF	61	PM Photo Stories	Rigby
Zac and Puffing Billy	C	RF	66	PM Photo Stories	Rigby

* Collection of short stories   # Graphic text
^ Mature content with lower level text demands

TITLE	LEVEL	GENRE	WORD COUNT	AUTHOR / SERIES	PUBLISHER / DISTRIBUTOR
Zac and the Ducks	C	RF	77	PM Photo Stories	Rigby
Zac Efron	S	B	250+	Star Biographies	Capstone Press
Zachary and the Pony Express	P	HF	250+	Leveled Readers Language Support	Houghton Mifflin Harcourt
Zachary Taylor	U	B	250+	Profiles of the Presidents	Compass Point Books
Zachary Taylor: Twelfth President	R	B	250+	Getting to Know the U.S. Presidents	Children's Press
Zachary Zebra's Zippity Zooming	L	F	747	Animal Antics A to Z	Kane Press
Zachary Zormer: Shape Transformer	O	RF	250+	Reisberg, Joanne	Charlesbridge
Zachary's Ball	N	F	250+	Tavares, Matt	Candlewick Press
Zacharys' Plans, The	O	F	250+	Sails	Rigby
Zachary's Ride	R	HF	1780	Leveled Readers	Houghton Mifflin Harcourt
Zach's Lie	X	RF	250+	Smith, Roland	Hyperion
Zack and Nate	H	RF	250+	Early Emergent, Set 2	Pioneer Valley
Zack's Alligator	K	F	250+	Little Readers	Houghton Mifflin Harcourt
Zack's Alligator	K	F	250+	Mozelle, Shirley	HarperTrophy
Zack's Alligator Goes to School	K	F	250+	Mozelle, Shirley	HarperTrophy
Zack's Halloween Costume	D	RF	103	Early Emergent, Set 3	Pioneer Valley
Zack's House	D	RF	114	Early Emergent, Set 2	Pioneer Valley
Zack's Moving Day Surprise	F	RF	122	Developing Books, Set 3	Pioneer Valley
Zack's Spots	I	F	327	Sails	Rigby
Zac's Train Ride	E	RF	126	PM Photo Stories	Rigby
Zac's Train Set	B	RF	46	PM Photo Stories	Rigby
Zala Runs for Her Life	J	F	250+	PM Story Books-Purple	Rigby
Zamboni's Bath	L	RF	1000	Burns, Vicki Scott	Kaeden Books
Zane's Trace	Z+	RF	250+	Wolf, Allan	Candlewick Press
Zap!	G	F	83	Seedlings	Continental Press
Zap! I'm a Mind Reader	N	SF	250+	The Zack Files	Grosset & Dunlap
Zathura	R	F	250+	Van Allsburg, Chris	Houghton Mifflin Harcourt
#Z-Boys and Skateboarding, The	S	I	250+	Inventions and Discovery	Capstone Press
Zebra	C	I	38	Zoozoo-Into the Wild	Cavallo Publishing
^Zebra Shark	N	I	250+	Shark Zone	Capstone Press
Zebra Shark	J	I	141	Sharks	Capstone Press
Zebras	I	I	122	African Animals	Capstone Press
Zebras	S	I	250+	Animal Prey	Lerner Publishing Group
Zebras	O	I	2484	Early Bird Nature Books	Lerner Publishing Group
Zebras	O	I	250+	Holmes, Kevin J.	Red Brick Learning
Zebras	N	I	250+	Meadows, Graham; Vial, Claire	Pearson Learning Group
Zebras	U	I	5802	Nature Watch Books	Lerner Publishing Group
Zebras	H	I	78	Seedlings	Continental Press
Zebras and Oxpeckers Work Together	K	I	250+	Animals Working Together	Capstone Press
Zebras Don't Brush Their Teeth!	B	I	54	Evans, Lynette	Scholastic
Zebra's Yellow Van	C	F	31	Ready Readers	Pearson Learning Group
Zebulon Pike: Soldier and Explorer	V	B	250+	Let Freedom Ring	Capstone Press
Zeely	R	RF	250+	Hamilton, Virginia	Macmillan
Zeely Zebra	J	F	325	Let's Read Together	Kane Press
Zeep's Safety Scare	K	F	250+	InfoTrek	ETA/Cuisenaire
^Zee's Way	T	RF	250+	Orca Soundings	Orca Books
*Zeke and Emily, Green Grapes for Zeke, Monkey Pete	J	F	366	Easy-for-Me Reading	Child 1st Publications
Zeke Takes a Bath	J	F	532	Leveled Readers	Houghton Mifflin Harcourt
*Zelda and Ivy: The Big Picture	K	F	250+	Kvasnosky, Laura McGee	Candlewick Press
*Zelda and Ivy and the Boy Next Door	K	F	250+	Kvasnosky, Laura McGee	Candlewick Press
Zelda and Ivy One Christmas	K	F	250+	Kvasnosky, Laura McGee	Candlewick Press

XYZ

TITLE	LEVEL	GENRE	WORD COUNT	AUTHOR / SERIES	PUBLISHER / DISTRIBUTOR
Zelda and Ivy the Runaways	J	F	250+	Kvasnosky, Laura McGee	Candlewick Press
*Zelda and Ivy: Keeping Secrets	K	F	250+	Kvasnosky, Laura McGee	Candlewick Press
Zemti	L	TL	250+	Books for Young Learners	Richard C. Owen
*Zen Shorts	N	F	250+	Muth, Jon J.	Scholastic
Zenith	Y	SF	250+	Bertagna, Julie	Walker & Company
Zero	Z+	RF	250+	Tullson, Diane	Fitzhenry & Whiteside
Zero Gravity	M	I	250+	Trackers	Pacific Learning
Zeros and Ones	S	I	250+	Wildcats	Wright Group/McGraw Hill
Zero's Slider	M	RF	250+	Christopher, Matt	Little Brown and Company
^Zeus	W	I	250+	World Mythology	Capstone Press
Zia	W	HF	250+	O'Dell, Scott	Laurel-Leaf Books
Ziba Came on a Boat	Q	RF	250+	Lofthouse, Liz	Kane/Miller Book Publishers
#Zig and Wikki in Something Ate My Homework	M	SF	250+	Spiegelman, Nadja & Loeffler, Trade	Toon Books
#Zig and Wikki in the Cow	M	F	250+	Spiegelman, Nadja & Loeffler, Trade	Toon Books
Ziggy and the Cat	E	RF	72	Windmill Books	Rigby
Zigzag Kayak Trip, The	K	F	467	Springboard	Wright Group/McGraw Hill
Zigzag Movement	F	I	50	The Way Things Move	Red Brick Learning
#Zinc Alloy	P	SF	250+	Lemke, Donald	Stone Arch Books
Zinnia, The	B	RF	34	Ray's Readers	Outside the Box
Zinnia's Zaniness: The Sisters 8	Q	F	250+	Baratz-Logsted, Lauren	Sandpiper Books
Zip Me Up	E	RF	171	Handprints C, Set 2	Educators Publishing Service
Zip the Squirrel	A	RF	30	Kaleidoscope Collection	Hameray Publishing Group
Zippers	C	RF	21	Books for Young Learners	Richard C. Owen
Zipping, Zapping, Zooming Bats	N	I	250+	Soar To Success	Houghton Mifflin Harcourt
Zippity Zinger, The	R	RF	250+	Winkler, Henry and Oliver, Lin	Grosset & Dunlap
Zippy Zebra Finds a Friend	F	F	140	Springboard	Wright Group/McGraw Hill
Zippy's Lost Stripes	I	F	327	In Step Readers	Rigby
Zippy's Tall Tale: Butterfly Meadow	M	F	250+	Moss, Olivia	Scholastic
Zip-Zip, Rattle-Bang!	E	F	141	Story Basket	Wright Group/McGraw Hill
Zithers	G	RF	55	Little Celebrations	Pearson Learning Group
Zlata's Diary	X	B	250+	Filipovic, Zlata	Puffin Books
Zoe and the Lights	I	RF	416	Leveled Readers	Houghton Mifflin Harcourt
Zoe and the Lights	I	RF	416	Leveled Readers/CA	Houghton Mifflin Harcourt
Zoe at the Fancy Dress Ball	J	RF	250+	Literacy 2000	Rigby
Zoe the Skating Fairy: Rainbow Magic	L	F	250+	Meadows, Daisy	Scholastic
Zoe's Birthday Presents	D	RF	83	Emergent	Pioneer Valley
Zombie Blondes	Z	RF	250+	James, Brian	Feiwel and Friends
Zombie Nite CafT, The	M	F	250+	Kutner, Merrily	Holiday House
^Zombie Who visited New Orleans, The	Q	RF	250+	Brezenoff, Steve/Field Trip Mysteries	Stone Arch Books
Zombies Don't Play Soccer	M	F	250+	Dadey, Debbie; Jones, Marcia Thornton	Scholastic
Zomo the Rabbit: A Trickster Tale from West Africa	M	TL	250+	McDermott, Gerald	Harcourt Trade
Zoo Animals 1 2 3	I	I	208	Counting Books	Capstone Press
Zoo Babies	F	I	51	Little Celebrations	Pearson Learning Group
Zoo Crew, The	I	I	154	Gear Up!	Wright Group/McGraw Hill
Zoo Dinners	B	RF	30	Sails	Rigby
Zoo Food	C	I	58	Reading Corners	Pearson Learning Group
Zoo in Willy's Bed, The	E	RF	81	Gorman, Kate Sturnman	Continental Press
Zoo Keepers	M	I	250+	Community Helpers	Red Brick Learning
Zoo Map	G	I	96	Windows on Literacy	National Geographic

XYZ

* Collection of short stories   # Graphic text
^ Mature content with lower level text demands

TITLE	LEVEL	GENRE	WORD COUNT	AUTHOR / SERIES	PUBLISHER / DISTRIBUTOR
Zoo Overnight	L	RF	250+	Pacific Literacy	Pacific Learning
Zoo Party	H	RF	271	Leveled Readers	Houghton Mifflin Harcourt
Zoo Party	H	RF	271	Leveled Readers/CA	Houghton Mifflin Harcourt
Zoo Party	H	RF	271	Leveled Readers/TX	Houghton Mifflin Harcourt
Zoo Party, A	H	RF	134	Book Bank	Wright Group/McGraw Hill
Zoo Picture Puzzles	M	I	148	Look, Look Again	Capstone Press
Zoo Trip!	O	F	250+	Tristars	Richard C. Owen
Zoo Trip, The	E	I	115	Springboard	Wright Group/McGraw Hill
Zoo Vet	L	I	250+	Windows on Literacy	National Geographic
Zoo, A	LB	I	14	Literacy 2000	Rigby
Zoo, The	C	RF	33	Carousel Readers	Pearson Learning Group
Zoo, The	B	I	32	Handprints B	Educators Publishing Service
Zoo, The	C	I	52	Tiny Treasures	Pioneer Valley
Zoo, The	B	I	31	Wonder World	Wright Group/McGraw Hill
Zookeepers Sleepers, The	E	F	76	New Reader Series	Bungalo Books
Zoola Palooza: A Book of Homographs	P	F	250+	Barretta, Gene	Henry Holt & Co.
Zoo-Looking	G	RF	149	Bookshop	Mondo Publishing
Zoom In!	M	I	250+	Storyteller-Lightning Bolts	Wright Group/McGraw Hill
Zoom!	L	RF	111	Adams, Diane	Peachtree
Zoom!	A	I	24	Leveled Readers	Houghton Mifflin Harcourt
Zoom!	A	I	24	Leveled Readers/CA	Houghton Mifflin Harcourt
Zoom! Boom! Bully (Jon Scieszka's Trucktown)	H	F	100	Scieszka, Jon	Aladdin
Zoom! Zoom!	C	F	43	Joy Readers	Pearson Learning Group
Zoom! Zoom!	B	RF	68	Red Rocket Readers	Flying Start Books
Zooman Sam	P	RF	250+	Lowry, Lois	Houghton Mifflin Harcourt
Zoomers, The	A	F	28	Kinderstarters	Rigby
Zoos	N	I	1550	Take Two Books	Wright Group/McGraw Hill
Zoos Back to Nature?	W	I	250+	iOpeners	Pearson Learning Group
Zora and Me	U	HF	250+	Bond, Victoria & Simon, T. R.	Candlewick Press
Zounds! Sounds!	O	I	250+	Trackers	Pacific Learning
Zulu Dog	V	RF	250+	Ferreira, Anton	Farrar, Straus, & Giroux
Zulu Warriors	T	I	250+	Warriors of History	Capstone Press
Zuni, The	R	I	250+	First Reports	Compass Point Books
Zunid	J	RF	250+	Stepping Stones	Nelson/Michaels Assoc.
Zvuvi's Israel	R	I	2492	Lehman-Wilzig, Tami	Kar-Ben Publishing

XY

BOOK PUBLISHERS AND DISTRIBUTORS

ABDO Publishing Company
P.O. Box 398166
Minneapolis, MN 55439
1-800-800-1312
www.abdopub.com

Abrams & Company/Abrams Learning Trends
16310 Bratton Lane Suite 250
Austin, TX 78728
1-800-227-9120
www.abramslearningtrends.com

Abrams Comicarts
115 West 18th Street 6th Floor
New York, NY 10011
(212) 206-7715
www.abramsbooks.com/comicarts

Ace Books
375 Hudson Street
New York, NY 10014
212-366-2000
www.us.penguingroup.com/pages
/publishers/adult/ace.html

Aladdin Paperbacks
1230 Avenue of the Americas
New York, NY 10020
(212) 698-7000
http://imprints.simonandschuster.biz
/aladdin

Albert Whitman & Co.
250 South Northwest Highway, Suite 320
Park Ridge, IL 60068
800-255-7675
http://www.albertwhitman.com/

Alfred A. Knopf
1745 Broadway
New York, NY 10019
212-782-9000
http://knopfdoubleday.com/imprint
/knopf/

American Reading Company
201 South Gulph Rd.
King of Prussia, PA 19406
1-866-810-2665
http://www.americanreading.com/

Amulet Books
115 West 18th Street 6th Floor
New York, NY 10011
(212) 206-7715
www.abramsbooks.com/comicarts

Andersen Press USA
241 First Ave N
Minneapolis, MN 55401
1-800-328-4929
https://www.lernerbooks.com/about
-lerner/Pages/Andersen-Press-USA.aspx

Andre Deutsch
387 Park Avenue South
New York, NY 10016
(800) 367 9692
http://www.carltonbooks.co.uk/imprints
/andredeutsch

Annick Press
15 Patricia Avenue
Toronto, ON M2M 1H9
Canada
416-221-4802
http://www.annickpress.com/

Arcade Publishing
307 West 36th Street, 11th Floor
New York, NY 10018
(212) 643-6816
http://www.arcadepub.com/

Arte Publico
University of Houson, 4902 Gulf Fwy, Bldg
19, Rm 100
Houston, TX 77204
1-800-633-ARTE
http://www.latinoteca.com/arte-publico
-press/

Arthur A. Levine Books
557 Broadway
New York, NY 10012
http://www.arthuralevinebooks.com/

Atheneum Books
1230 Avenue of the Americas
New York, NY 10020
(212) 698-7000
http://imprints.simonandschuster.biz
/atheneum

Atman Press
2104 Cherokee Avenue
Columbus, GA 31906
706-323-6377
http://www.atmanpress.com/

Atria Books
1230 Avenue of the Americas
New York, NY 10020
(212) 698-7000
http://imprints.simonandschuster.biz/atria

August House Publishers
3500 Piedmont Road, ste. 310
Atlanta, GA 30305
800.284.8784
http://www.augusthouse.com/

Avon Books
10 East 53rd Street
New York, NY 10022
212-207-7000
http://www.avonromance.com/

Ballantine Books
1745 Broadway
New York, NY 10019
212-782-9000
http://ballantine.atrandom.com/

Bantam Books
1745 Broadway
New York, NY 10019
212-782-9000
http://bantam-dell.atrandom.com/

Barefoot Books
2067 Massachusetts Avenue
Cambridge, MA 02140
866.215.1756
www.barefootbooks.com

Barron's Educational
250 Wireless Blvd
Hauppauge, NY 11788
1-800-645-3476
http://www.barronseduc.com/

Beech Tree Books
4 Redwood Rd
Sag Harbor, NY 11963
(631) 725-7722
http://beechtreebooks.com/

Belle River Readers, Inc.
P.o. Box 1224
Lapeer, MI 48446

Bellwether Media
5357 Penn Ave S
Minneapolis, MN 55419
(800) 679-8068
http://www.bellwethermedia.com/

Benchmark Education
629 FIFTH AVENUE
Pelham, NY 10803
1-877-236-2465
http://www.benchmarkeducation.com/

Berkley Books
375 Hudson Street
New York, NY 10014
212-366-2000
www.us.penguingroup.com/static/pages
/publishers/adult/berkley.html

Beyond Words
20827 NW Cornell Rd, Suite 500
Hillsboro, OR 97124
(503) 531.8700
http://www.beyondword.com/

Blackbirch Press
27500 Drake Rd
Farmington Hills, MI 48331
1-800-877-4253
http://www.gale.cengage.com/greenhaven
/blackbirch.htm

Bloomsbury Children's Books
1385 Broadway, Fifth Floor
New York, NY 10018
(212) 419 5300
http://www.bloomsbury.com/us/childrens/

Blue Sky Press
557 Broadway Avenue
New York, NY 10012
1-800-724-6527
http://www.scholastic.com/home/

Blueberry Hill Books
11 Donna Place
East St. Paul, MB R2E 0H6
Canada
780-489-1736
http://www.blueberryhillbooks.com/

Bluefish Bay Publishing
1093 A1A BEACH BLVD
St. Augustine, FL 32080
904-471-3142

Books for a Cause, Inc.
1334 W Chester Pike
West Chester, PA 19382

Boyds Mills Press
815 Church Street
Honesdale, PA 18431
1-800-490-5111
http://www.boydsmillspress.com/

Buddy Books Publishing
PO Box 3354
Pinehurst, NC 28374
910-295-2876
http://www.buddybookspublishing.com/

Bungalo Books
829 Norwest Rd, Ste. 337
Kingston, ON K7P 2N3
Canada
613-374-1243
http://bungalobooks.com/

C Unique Creations Inc.
Site 707, Box 71, RR7
Saskatoon, SK S7K 1N2
306-241-1638
http://www.seeabook.com/index.htm

Candlewick Press
99 Dover St.
Somerville, MA 02144
http://www.candlewick.com/

Capstone Press
1710 Roe Crest Drive
North Mankato, MN 56003
800-747-4992
http://www.capstonepub.com/

Carolrhoda Books
241 First Ave N
Minneapolis, MN 55401
1-800-328-4929
https://www.lernerbooks.com/About
-Lerner/pages/carolrhoda-books.aspx

Carus Publishing Company
30 Grove Street, Suite C
Peterborough, NH 03458
800-821-0115
http://www.cricketmag.com/

Cavallo Publishing
2633 Lincoln Blvd., #617
Santa Monica, CA 90405
866-311-0111
http://www.cavallopublishing.com/

Cengage/National Geographic
10650 Toebben Drive
Independence, KY 41051
1-800-487-8488
http://www.cengage.com/us/

Chariot Victor Publishing
4050 Lee Vance View
Colorado Springs, CO 80918
719-536-0100

Charlesbridge
85 Main St.
Watertown, MA 02472
800-225-3214
http://www.charlesbridge.com/

Checkerboard
P.O. Box 398166
Minneapolis, MN 55439
1-800-800-1312
http://www.abdopub.com/shop/pc
/viewCategories.asp?idCategory=203

Chelsea House
132 West 31st Street, 17th Floor
New York, NY 10001
1-800-322-8755
http://www.infobasepublishing.com/
Default.aspx

Chicago Review Press
814 N. Franklin St
Chicago, IL 60610
312.337.0747
http://www.chicagoreviewpress.com/

Child 1st Publications
3907 Fraser ST. NE
Rockford, MI 49341
800.881.0912
http://www.child-1st.com/new_site/index
.html

Child's Play Ltd
250 Minot Avenue
Auburn, ME 04210
207-784-7252
http://www.childs-play.com/usa/home
-page.html

Children's Book Press
95 MADISON AVENUE, SUITE # 1205
New York, NY 10016
212-779-4400
http://www.leeandlow.com/p/overview
_cbp.mhtml

Children's Press
557 Broadway Avenue
New York, NY 10012
1-800-724-6527
http://www.scholastic.com/
internationalschools/childrenspress.htm

Chronicle Books
680 Second Street
San Fransisco, CA 94107
415-537-4200
http://www.chroniclebooks.com/

Cinco Puntos Press
701 Texas Ave
El Paso, TX 79901
1-800-566-9072
http://www.cincopuntos.com/

Clarion
222 Berkeley Street
Boston, MA 02116
800.225.5425
http://www.houghtonmifflinbooks.com
/hmh/site/hmhbooks/home/kids

Clarion Books
222 Berkeley Street
Boston, MA 02116
800.225.5425
http://www.houghtonmifflinbooks.com
/hmh/site/hmhbooks/home/kids

Collins Publishing Group (see HarperColins)

Compass Point Books
1710 Roe Crest Drive
North Mankato, MN 56003
800-747-4992
http://www.capstonepub.com/category
/LIB_PUBLISHER_CPB

Continental Press
520 East Bainbridge Street
Elizabethtown, PA 17022
800.233.0759
https://www.continentalpress.com/

Crabtree
PMB 59051, 350 Fifth Avenue, 59th Floor
New York, NY 10118
1-800-387-7650
http://www.crabtreebooks.com/

Creative Education
PO Box 1066
Falls Church, VA 22041
703-856-7005
http://www.
creativeeducationandpublishing.com
/store/

Creative Teaching Press
PO Box 2723
Huntington Beach, CA 92647
800-287-8879
http://www.creativeteaching.com/

Cricket Books
30 Grove Street, Suite C
Peterborough, NH 03458
800-821-0115
http://www.cricketmag.com/

Crown Publishers
1745 Broadway
New York, NY 10019
212-782-9000
http://crownpublishing.com/

Curriculum Press
PO Box 177
Carlton South, VIC 3053
Australia
+61 3 9207 9600
http://www.curriculumpress.edu.au/

Cypress
P.O. Box 2636
Tallahassee, FL 32316
(850) 576-8820
http://www.cypresspublications.com/

Darby Creek Publishing
241 First Ave N
Minneapolis, MN 55401
1-800-328-4929
https://www.lernerbooks.com/About
-Lerner/pages/darby-creek.aspx

David Fickling Books
31 Beaumont Street
Oxford, OX1 2NP
Canada
http://www.davidficklingbooks.com/

David R. Godine
PO Box 450
Jaffrey, NH 03452
800-344-4771
http://www.godine.com/

Dawn Publications
12402 Bitney Springs Rd
Nevada City, CA 95959
1-800-545-7475
http://www.dawnpub.com/

Delacorte Press
1745 Broadway
New York, NY 10019
212-782-9000
http://bantam-dell.atrandom.com/

Dell
1745 Broadway
New York, NY 10019
212-782-9000
http://bantam-dell.atrandom.com/

Dial/Penguin
375 Hudson Street
New York, NY 10014
212-366-2000
www.us.penguingroup.com/static/pages
/publishers/yr/dial.html

Disney Book Group
44 S Broadway
White Plains, NY 10601
(212) 807-5875

DK Publishing
375 Hudson St
New York, NY 10014
(646) 674-4000
http://us.dk.com/

Dog Ear Publishing
4010 West 86th Street, Suite H
Indianapolis, IN 46268
888-568-8411
http://dogearpublishing.net/

Donovan
28 South Street, Suite 4
Hingham, MA 02043
781.741.8182
http://donovanpublishing.net/

Doubleday Books
1745 Broadway
New York, NY 10019
212-782-9000
http://knopfdoubleday.com/imprint
/doubleday/

Douglas & McIntyre
4437 Rondeview Road
Madeira Park, BC V0N 2H0
Canada
1-800-667-2988
http://www.dmpibooks.com/home

Dover Publications
31 East 2nd Street
Mineola, NY 11501
http://store.doverpublications.com/

Dragonfly Books
112 W Water Street
Decorah, IA 52101
563.382.4275
http://www.dragonflybooks.com/

Dutton Children's Books
375 Hudson Street
New York, NY 10014
212-366-2000
www.us.penguingroup.com/static/pages
/publishers/yr/dutton.html

Eaglecrest Books
#209B-5462 Trans Canada Hwy
Duncan, BC V9L 6W4
Canada
250.748.3744
http://www.eaglecrestbooks.com/home
.htm

EDC Publishing
P.O. Box 470663
Tulsa, OK 74147
800-475-4522
http://www.edcpub.com/

Educational Insights
18730 S. Wilmington Avenue
Rancho Dominguez, CA 90220
(800) 995 4436
http://www.educationalinsights.com

Educators Publishing Service
625 Mt. Auburn Street, 3rd Floor
Cambridge, MA 02138
800-225-5750
http://eps.schoolspecialty.com/

Eerdman's Books for Young Readers
2140 Oak Industrial Dr. NE
Grand Rapids, MI 49505
800-253-7521
http://www.eerdmans.com/youngreaders/

Egmont USA
443 Park Avenue South, Suite 806
New York, NY 10016
212-685-0102
http://www.egmontusa.com/blog/books/

Eleanor Curtain Publishing
Level 1, Suite 3, 102 Toorak Road
South Yarra, VIC 3141
Australia
+613 9867 4880
http://ecpublishing.com.au/

Enslow Publishers, Inc.
Box 398, 40 Industrial Road, F61
Berkeley Heights, NJ 07922
1-800-398-2504
www.enslow.com/

ETA/Cuisenaire
500 Greenview Court
Vernon Hills, IL 60061
800-445-5985
http://www.hand2mind.com/

FaithWords
3 CENTER PLAZA
BOSTON, MA 02108
(800) 759-0190
http://www.faithwords.com/

Farrar, Straus, & Giroux
18 West 18th Street
New York, NY 10011
212-741-6900
http://us.macmillan.com/FSG.aspx

Feiwel and Friends
175 Fifth Avenue
New York, NY 10010
888.330.8477
http://us.macmillan.com/MacKids.aspx

Firefly Books
c/o Frontier Distributing, 1000 Young
Street, Suite 160
Tonawanda, NY 14150
800-387-5085
http://www.fireflybooks.com/

Fitzhenry & Whiteside
195 Allstate Parkway
Markham, ON L3R 4T8
Canada
1-800-387-9776
http://www.fitzhenry.ca/

Flying Start Books
8345 NW 66th St. #6695
Miami, FL 33166
1-888-269-4059
http://www.flyingstartbooks.com/

Flyleaf Publishing
400 Bedford Street, 1st floor SW-03
Manchester, NH 03101
800-449-7006
http://www.flyleafpublishing.com/

Follett
2233 West Street
River Grove, IL 60171
800.621.4345
http://www.follett.com/

Four Winds
PO Box 21597
Charleston, SC 29413
(843) 323-6822
http://fourwindsbooks.org/

Frances Lincoln
74-77 White Lion Street, Islington
London, N1 9PF
UK
020 7284 9300
http://www.franceslincoln.com/

Franklin Watts
557 Broadway Avenue
New York, NY 10012
1-800-724-6527
http://www.hachettechildrens.co.uk
/homepage_franklinwatts.page

Free Spirit Publishing
217 Fifth Avenue North, Suite 200
Minneapolis, MN 55401
1.800.735.7323
http://www.freespirit.com/

Front Street Press
815 Church Street
Honesdale, PA 18431
1-800-490-5111
http://www.boydsmillspress.com/reviews
/front-street

Fulcrum Publishing
4690 Table Mountain Drive, Suite 100
Golden, CO 80403
800-992-2908
http://www.fulcrum-books.com/

G.P. Putnam's Sons
375 Hudson Street
New York, NY 10014
212-366-2000
www.us.penguingroup.com/static/pages
/publishers/adult/putnam.html

G.P. Putnam's Sons Books for Young Readers
375 Hudson Street
New York, NY 10014
212-366-2000
www.us.penguingroup.com/static/pages
/publishers/yr/putnam.html

Gallopade International
PO Box 2779
Peachtree City, GA 30269
800.536.2438
http://www.gallopade.com/

Gecko Press
PO Box 9335, Marion Square
Wellington, 6141
New Zealand
+64 (0)4 801 9333
http://www.geckopress.co.nz/

Ginn & Co. (see also Silver Burdett or Pearson
Education)
Halley Court Jordan Hill
Oxford, OX2 8EJ
UK
(01865) 888044

Golden
1745 Broadway
New York, NY 10019
212-782-9000
http://www.randomhouse.com/golden/

Good Books
PO Box 419
Intercourse, PA 17534
(800) 762-7171
http://www.goodbooks.com/

Grand Central Publishing
3 CENTER PLAZA
BOSTON, MA 02108
(800) 759-0190
http://www.hachettebookgroup.com
/publishers/grand-central-publishing/

Graphia
222 Berkeley Street
Boston, MA 02116
800.225.5425
http://www.houghtonmifflinbooks.com
/graphia/

Graphic Universe
241 First Ave N
Minneapolis, MN 55401
1-800-328-4929
https://www.lernerbooks.com/About
-Lerner/pages/graphic-universe.aspx

Green Tiger Press
3645 Interlake N
Seattle, WA 98103
(800) 354-0400
http://greentigerpress.com/

Greenwillow Books
10 East 53rd Street
New York, NY 10022
212-207-7000
http://harpercollins.com/imprints/index
.aspx?imprintid=517996

Greystone Books
Suite 201, 343 Railway Street
Vancouver, BC V6A 1A4
Canada
(604) 875-1550
http://www.greystonebooks.com/

Grolier
90 Sherman Turnpike
Danbury, CT 06816
800-621-1115
http://teacher.scholastic.com/products
/grolier/index.htm

Grosset & Dunlap
375 Hudson Street
New York, NY 10014
212-366-2000
www.us.penguingroup.com/static/pages
/publishers/yr/grosset.html

Grosset & Dunlap
375 Hudson Street
New York, NY 10014
212-366-2000
http://www.us.penguingroup.com/static
/pages/publishers/yr/grosset.html

Groundwood Books
110 Spadina Ave., Suite 801
Toronto, ON M5V 2K4
Canada
41-363-4343
http://www.houseofanansi.com/

Gulf
P.O. Box 2608
Houston, TX 77252
(713) 529-4301
http://www.gulfpub.com/

Hameray Publishing Group
11545 Sorrento Valley Road, Suite 310
San Diego, CA 92121
1-866-918-6173
http://www.hameraypublishing.com/

Hampton Brown
1 Lower Ragsdale, Building 1, Suite 200
Monterey, CA 93940
888-915-3276
http://www.hbedge.net/

Harcourt School Publishers
5513 North Cumberland Avenue
Chicago, IL 60656
(773) 594- 5110
http://www.harcourtschool.com/

Harper & Row (see HarperCollins)
10 East 53rd Street
New York, NY 10022
212-207-7000
http://www.harpercollins.com/

Harper Tempest
10 East 53rd Street
New York, NY 10022
212-207-7000
http://www.harpercollins.com/imprints
/index.aspx?imprintid=518004

HarperCollins Publishers
10 East 53rd Street
New York, NY 10022
212-207-7000
http://www.harpercollins.com/

HarperPerennial
10 East 53rd Street
New York, NY 10022
212-207-7000
http://www.harpercollins.com/imprints
/index.aspx?imprintid=517986

HarperTrophy
10 East 53rd Street
New York, NY 10022
212-207-7000
http://harpercollins.com/imprints/index
.aspx?imprintid=517987

Harry N. Abrams
115 West 18th Street, 6th Floor
New York, NY 10011
(212) 206-7715
http://www.abramsbooks.com/

Health Communications
3201 S.W. 15th Street
Deerfield Beach, FL 33442
1.800.441.5569
http://www.hcibooks.com/

Heinemann
P. O. Box 6926
Portsmouth, NH 03802
800.225.5800
http://www.heinemann.com/

Henry Holt & Co.
175 Fifth Avenue
New York, NY 10010
646-307-5095
http://us.macmillan.com/HenryHolt.aspx

Herald Press
490 Dutton Drive, Unit C8
Waterloo, ON N2L 6H7
Canada
1-800-245-7894
http://www.heraldpress.com/

Heritage House
#340 - 1105 Pandora Ave.
Victoria, BC V8V 3P9
250.360.0829
http://www.heritagehouse.ca/

High Noon Books
20 Commercial Boulevard
Novato, CA 94949
(800) 422-7249
http://www.highnoonbooks.com/index
-hnb.tpl

Hohm Press
PO BOX 4410
CHINO VALLEY, AZ 86323
1-800-381-2700
http://www.hohmpress.com/

Holiday House
425 Madison Avenue
New York, NY 10017
212-421-6134
http://www.holidayhouse.com/

Houghton Mifflin Harcourt
222 Berkeley Street
Boston, MA 02116
(617) 351-5000
http://www.hmhco.com/

Hyperion
1500 Broadway, 3rd Floor
New York, NY 10036
http://www.hyperionbooks.com/

Hyperion Books for Children
44 S Broadway
White Plains, NY 10601
(212) 807-5875

Hyperion/Madison Press
18321 SE McLoughlin Blvd
Portland, OR 97267
http://www.exodusbooks.com/publisher
.aspx?id=214

Ideals Children's Books
39 Old Ridgebury Road, Ste. 2AB
Danbury, CT 06810
800-586-2572
http://www.idealsbooks.com/

Ideals Publications Inc.
39 Old Ridgebury Road, Ste. 2AB
Danbury, CT 06810
800-586-2572
http://www.idealsbooks.com/

Imagination Stage
4908 Auburn Avenue
Bethesda, MD 20814
301-961-6060
http://www.imaginationstage.org/

Intercultural Center for Research in
Education
366 Massachusetts Avenue, 2nd flr.
Arlington, MA 02474
(781) 643-2142
http://www.incre.org/

Jamestown Publishers
PO Box 182605
Columbus, OH 43218
877-833-5524
http://www.glencoe.com/gln/jamestown/

Jumping Cow Press
P.O. Box 8982
Scarborough, NY 10510
914-373-9816
http://www.jumpingcowpress.com/

Just Us Books
356 Glenwood Ave.
East Orange, NJ 07017
(973) 672-7701
http://justusbooks.blogspot.com/

Kaeden Books
P.O. Box 16190
Rocky River, OH 44116
1-800-890-7323
http://www.kaeden.com/

Kane Press
350 Fifth Avenue, Suite 7206
New York, NY 10118
212-268-1435
http://www.kanepress.com/

Kane/Miller Book Publishers
4901 Morena Blvd Ste 213
San Diego, CA 92117
1-800-611-1655
http://www.kanemiller.com/

Kar-Ben Publishing
241 First Ave N
Minneapolis, MN 55401
1-800-328-4929
https://www.lernerbooks.com/About
-Lerner/pages/kar-ben-publishing.aspx

Katherine Tegan Books
10 East 53rd Street
New York, NY 10022
212-207-7000
http://www.harpercollinschildrens.com
/Home/ImprintBooks.aspx?TCId=
100&SIId=9452&ST=7

Keep Books
1100 Kinnear Rd.
Columbus, OH 43212
800-678-6484
http://www.keepbooks.org/

Kids Can Press
2250 Military Road
Tonawanda, NY 14150
416-479-7000
http://www.kidscanpress.com/

Kim.FIG.Fern
P.O. Box 415
Oakmont, PA 15139
412-828-0394
http://www.kimfigfern.com/

Kingfisher
175 Fifth Avenue
New York, NY 10010
646-307-5151
http://us.macmillan.com/kingfisher.aspx

Kiva Publishing
21731 E. Buckskin Dr.
Walnut, CA 91789
1-800-634-5482
http://www.kivapub.com/

Ladybird Books
80 Strand
London, WC2R 0RL
UK
0845 313 4444
http://www.ladybird.co.uk/

Language for Learning Assoc.
Shoppenhangers Road, Maidenhead
Berkshire, SL6 2QL
UK
http://mcgraw-hill.co.uk/sra
/languageforlearning.htm

Laurel-Leaf Books
18321 SE McLoughlin Blvd
Portland, OR 97267
http://www.exodusbooks.com/publisher
.aspx?id=71

Lee & Low Books Inc.
95 MADISON AVENUE, SUITE # 1205
New York, NY 10016
212-779-4400
http://www.leeandlow.com/

Lerner Publishing Group
241 First Ave N
Minneapolis, MN 55401
1-800-328-4929
https://www.lernerbooks.com/Pages
/Home.aspx

Linnet Books
2 Linsley Street
North Haven, CT 06473
203-239-2702
http://www.shoestringpress.com/linnet
.html

Little Brown and Company
237 Park Avenue
New York, NY 10017
(800) 759-0190
http://www.littlebrown.com/

Llumina Press
7580 NW 5th Street, #16535
Fort Lauderdale, FL 33318
866-229-9244
http://www.llumina.com/

London Town Press
P.O. Box 585
Montrose, CA 91011
(818) 248-4000
http://www.londontownpress.com/

Longman
Edinburgh Gate, Harlow
Essex, CM20 2JE
UK
+44(0) 1279 623925
http://www.pearsonelt.com/

Longman Group UK
Edinburgh Gate, Harlow
Essex, CM20 2JE
UK
+44(0) 1279 623925
http://www.pearsonelt.com/

Longman/Bow
Edinburgh Gate, Harlow
Essex, CM20 2JE
UK
+44(0) 1279 623925
http://www.pearsonelt.com/

Lost Coast Press
155 Cypress St
Fort Bragg, CA 95437
707-964-9520

Lothian Books
Level 2, 437 St Kilda Rd
Melbourne, VIC 3004
Australia
03 9694 4900
http://www.lothian.com.au/

Lothrop, Lee & Shepard
1350 Avenue of the Americas
New York, NY 10019
212-261-6641

MacAdam/Cage Publishing
155 Sansome Street
San Fransisco, CA 94104
415-986-7503
http://macadamcage.com/

Macmillan
175 Fifth Avenue
New York, NY 10010
888.330.8477
http://us.macmillan.com/

Macmillan/McGraw Hill
PO Box 182605
Columbus, OH 43218
800-334-7344
https://www.mheonline.com/

Margaret K. McElderry Books
1230 Avenue of the Americas
New York, NY 10020
(212) 698-7000
http://imprints.simonandschuster.biz
/margaret-k-mcelderry-books

Marimba Books
356 Glenwood Ave.
East Orange, NJ 07017
(973) 672-7701
http://www.justusbooksonlinestore.com
/categories/Marimba-Books/

Marshall Cavendish
99 White Plains Road
Tarrytown, NJ 10591
(914) 332 8888
www.marshallcavendish.us

Maryruth Books
18660 Ravenna Road, Building 2
Chagrin Falls, OH 44023
877-834-1105
http://www.maryruthbooks.com/

McElderry
1230 Avenue of the Americas
New York, NY 10020
(212) 698-7000
http://imprints.simonandschuster.biz
/margaret-k-mcelderry-books

Meadowbrook Press
6110 Blue Circle Drive, Suite 237
Minnetonka, MN 55343
800-338-2232
http://www.meadowbrookpress.com/

Milkweed Editions
1011 Washington Avenue South, Open
Book Building, Suite 300
Minneapolis, MN 55415
(800) 520-6455
http://milkweed.org/

Millbrook Press
241 First Ave N
Minneapolis, MN 55401
1-800-328-4929
https://www.lernerbooks.com/About
-Lerner/pages/millbrook-press.aspx

Millmark Education
7101 Wisconsin Avenue, Suite 1204
Bethesda, MD 20814
1-877-322-8020
http://www.millmarkeducation.com/

Modern Curriculum
1550 Oak Industrial Lane, Suite F
Cumming, GA 30041
800-401-9931
http://www.learningthings.com/articles
/mcp-modern-curriculum-press.aspx

Mondo Publishing
980 Avenue of the Americas
New York, NY 10018
888-886-6636
http://www.mondopub.com/

Montana Magazine
317 Cruse
Helena, MT 59604
1-888-666-8624
http://www.montanamagazine.com/

Morning Glory Press
6595 San Haroldo Way
Buena Park, CA 90620
1-888-612-8254
http://www.morningglorypress.com/

National Geographic (see Cengage)
10650 Toebben Drive
Independence, KY 41051
1-800-487-8488
http://www.cengage.com/us/

New Directions
80 Eighth Avenue
New York, NY 10011
http://ndbooks.com/

Newbridge
33 Boston Post Road West, Suite 440
Marlborough, MA 01752
800-867-0307
http://www.newbridgeonline.com/

Newmark Learning
629 Fifth Ave
Pelham, NY 10803
1-855-232-1960
http://www.newmarklearning.com/

North-South Books
350 7th Avenue Room 1400
New York, NY 10001
212-706-4545
http://www.northsouth.com/

NorthWord Press
18705 Lake Dr. E
Chanhassen, MN 55317
(952)936-4700

Norwood House Press
P.O. Box 316598
Chicago, IL 60631
1-866-565-2900
http://www.norwoodhousepress.com/

Okapi Educational Materials
42381 Rio Nedo
Temecula, CA 92590
(866) 652-7436
http://myokapi.com/

Options Publishing Inc.
PO Box 1749
Merrimack, NH 03054
603-424-1176
http://www.triumphlearning.com/

Orca Book Publishers
PO Box 468
Custer, WA 98240
800.210.5277
http://www.orcabook.com

Orca Books
PO Box 468
Custer, WA 98240
1.800.210.5277

Orchard Books
557 Broadway Avenue
New York, NY 10012
1-800-724-6527
http://www.hachettechildrens.co.uk
/homepage_orchardbooks.page

Oxford University Press
198 Madison Avenue
New York, NY 10016
800-445-9714
http://www.oup.com/us/

Pacific Learning
PO Box 2723
Huntington Beach, CA 92647
800-276-0737
http://www.pacificlearning.com/

Pantheon
1745 Broadway
New York, NY 10019
212-782-9000
http://knopfdoubleday.com/imprint/
pantheon/

Peachtree
1700 Chattahoochee Avenue
Atlanta, GA 30318
1-800-241-0113
http://peachtree-online.com/

Pearson
One Lake Street
Upper Saddle River, NJ 07458
http://www.pearson.com/

Pearson Learning Group
One Lake Street
Upper Saddle River, NJ 07459
http://www.k12pearson.com/teach_learn
_cycle/PLG/plg.html

Pearson Publishing Group
One Lake Street
Upper Saddle River, NJ 07460
http://www.k12pearson.com/teach_learn
_cycle/PLG/plg.html

Pelican Publishing Company
1000 Burmaster Street
Gretna, LA 70053
1-800-843-1724
http://www.pelicanpub.com/

Penguin Group
375 Hudson Street
New York, NY 10014
212-366-2000
www.us.penguingroup.com/

Persea Books
277 Broadway, Suite 708
New York, NY 10007
(212) 260-9256
http://www.perseabooks.com/index.php

Peter Smith Publications
5 Lexington Ave.
Glouchester, MA 01930
(978)525-3562

Philomel
375 Hudson Street
New York, NY 10014
212-366-2000
www.us.penguingroup.com/static/pages
/publishers/yr/philomel.html

Picture Window Books
1710 Roe Crest Drive
North Mankato, MN 56003
800-747-4992
http://www.capstonepub.com/category
/LIB_PUBLISHER_PWB

Pinata Publishing
University of Houson, 4902 Gulf Fwy, Bldg
19, Rm 100
Houston, TX 77204
1-800-633-ARTE
http://www.latinoteca.com/arte-publico
-press/

Pioneer Valley
155A Industrial Drive
Northampton, MA 01060
888-482-3906
http://www.pioneervalleybooks.com/

Play In A Book
P.O. Box 25629
Chicago, IL 60625
(773) 329-0920
www.playinabook.com/

Pleasant Company Publications
P.O. Box 620991
Middleton, WI 53562
1-800-233-0264
http://www.americangirlpublishing.com/

Pocket Books
1230 Avenue of the Americas
New York, NY 10020
(212) 698-7000
http://imprints.simonandschuster.biz
/gallery-books

Portage and Main
100-318 McDermot Avenue
Winnipeg, MB R3A 0A2
Canada
1-800-667-9673
http://www.portageandmainpress.com
/index.cfm

Prentice-Hall
375 Hudson Street
New York, NY 10014
212-366-2000
http://www.phschool.com/

Priddy Books
175 Fifth Avenue
New York, NY 10010
888.330.8477
http://us.macmillan.com/MacKids.aspx

Puffin Books
375 Hudson Street
New York, NY 10014
212-366-2000
www.us.penguingroup.com/static/pages
/publishers/yr/puffin.html

Raincoast Books
2440 Viking Way
Richmond, BC V6V 1N2
Canada
604-448-7100
http://www.raincoast.com/

Raintree
Brunel Road, Houndmills
Basingstoke Hants, RG21 6XS
UK
+44 (0) 1865 312262
http://www.raintreepublishers.co.uk/

Rand McNally
9855 Woods Drive
Skokie, IL 60077
http://www.randmcnally.com/

Random House
1745 Broadway
New York, NY 10019
212-782-9000
http://www.randomhouse.com/

Ransom Publishing
8 St. Cross Road, Winchester
Hampshire, SO23 9HX
UK
+44 (0) 1962 862307
http://www.ransom.co.uk/

Reader's Digest Children's Books
44 S Broadway
White Plains, NY 10601
(914) 238-1000
http://www.rdtradepublishing.com/

Reading Matters
806 Main Street
Akron, PA 17501
(888) 255-6665
http://readingmatters.net/

Reading Reading Books
PO Box 6654
Reading, PA 19610

Red Brick Learning
P.O. Box 669
Mankato, MN 56002
888-262-6135
http://www.capstoneclassroom.com
/content/RedBrick

Red Cygnet Press
2245 Enterprise St. Suite 110
Escondido, CA 92029
http://www.redcygnet.com/

Red Deer Press
195 Allstate Parkway
Markham, ON L3R 4T8
UK
1-800-387-9776 Ext. 225
http://www.reddeerpress.com/

Reflections Publishing
5395 Foxhound Way
San Diego, CA 92130
http://www.reflectionspublishing.com/

Richard C. Owen
PO Box 585
Katonah, NY 10536
800/262-0787
http://www.rcowen.com/

Rigby
Specialized Curriculum Group, 9205
Southpark Center Loop
Orlando, FL 32819
800-225-5425
www.rigby.com

Rising Moon
4501 Forbes Blvd.
Lanham, MD 20706
928-774-5251
http://www.nbnbooks.com/

Rising Star Studios
5251 W 73rd St, Suite C
Edina, MN 55439
952-831-8532
http://www.risingstarstudios.com/

Roaring Brook Press
Edinburgh Gate, Harlow
New York, NY 10010
888.330.8477
http://us.macmillan.com/MacKids.aspx

Roberts Rinehart
4501 Forbes Boulevard Suite 200
Lanham, MD 20706
303-543-7835 x 318
http://www.rowmanlittlefield.com/

Rosen Publishing Group
29 East 21st St.
New York, NY 10010
800-237-9932
https://www.rosenpublishing.com/

Rourke Classroom Resources
P.O. Box 643328
Vero Beach, FL 32964
800-380-2289
http://rourkeclassroom.com/

Rowland Reading Foundation
6120 University Avenue
Middleton, WI 53562
888-378-9258
http://www.rowlandreading.org/

Sadlier-Oxford
9 Pine Street
New York, NY 10005
800-221-5175
http://www.sadlier-oxford.com/

Sandpiper Books
222 Berkeley Street
Boston, MA 02116
800.225.5425
http://www.houghtonmifflinbooks.com
/hmh/site/hmhbooks/home/kids

Scholastic
557 Broadway Avenue
New York, NY 10012
1-800-724-6527
http://www.scholastic.com/home/

School Specialty Publishing
PO Box 35665
Greensboro, NC 27425
800-321-0943
http://www.carsondellosa.com/cd2/default
.aspx

School Zone
1819 Industrial Drive, PO Box 777
Grand Haven, MI 49417
616-846-5030
http://www.schoolzone.com/

Schwartz & Wade Books
1745 Broadway
New York, NY 10019
(212) 782-9000
https://www.facebook.com
/schwartzandwadebooks

Scribner
1230 Avenue of the Americas
New York, NY 10020
(212) 698-7000
http://imprints.simonandschuster.biz
/scribner

Sea-to-Sea Publications
P.O. Box 3263
North Mankato, MN 56002
507-388-1607
http://www.blackrabbitbooks.com/

Seal Press
1700 4th Street
Berkeley, CA 94710
(510) 595-3664
http://www.sealpress.com/home.php

SeaScape Press
5717 TANNER RIDGE AVE
WESTLAKE VILLAGE, CA 91362
805-963-7878

SeaStar Books
875 Sixth Avenue
New York, NY 10001

Secret Passage Press
814 N. Franklin Street
Chicago, IL 60610
(800) 888-4741
http://www.ipgbook.com/secret-passage
-press-publisher-SEC.php

Seven Footer Press
247 West 30th Street, 11th Floor
New York, NY 10001
(212) 710-9340
http://www.sevenfooterpress.com/

Seven Stories Press
140 Watts Street
New York, NY 10013

Short Tales Press
75 Barret Drive, PO Box 1524
Webster, NY 14580
585-509-1600
http://shorttalespress.com/

Shortland Publications
PO Box 11-904
Auckland, 5
New Zealand
(09) 687-0128

Signet Classics
375 Hudson Street
New York, NY 10014
212-366-2000
http://www.us.penguingroup.com/static
/pages/signetclassics/

Silver Burdett Press
One Lake Street
Upper Saddle River, NJ 07459
http://www.k12pearson.com/teach_learn
_cycle/PLG/plg.html

Simon & Schuster
1230 Avenue of the Americas
New York, NY 10020
(212) 698-7000
http://www.simonandschuster.com/

Simon Pulse
1230 Avenue of the Americas
New York, NY 10020
(212) 698-7000
http://imprints.simonandschuster.biz
/simon-pulse